Editor-in-Chief
Asa S. Knowles

Chancellor, Northeastern University

THE
INTERNATIONAL
ENCYCLOPEDIA
OF HIGHER
EDUCATION

Volume 3
B-C

Jossey-Bass Publishers
San Francisco • Washington • London • 1978

THE INTERNATIONAL ENCYCLOPEDIA OF HIGHER EDUCATION
Volume 3
Asa S. Knowles, Editor-in-Chief

Copyright © 1977 by: Jossey-Bass, Inc., Publishers
433 California Street
San Francisco, California 94104
&
Jossey-Bass Limited
28 Banner Street
London EC1Y 8QE

Library of Congress Cataloging in Publication Data

Main entry under title:

The international encyclopedia of higher education.

Includes index.
1. Education, Higher—Dictionaries. I. Knowles,
Asa Smallidge, 1909–
LB15.157   378'.003   77-73647
ISBN 0-87589-323-6 (set)
ISBN 0-87589-326-0 (v. 3)

Manufactured in the United States of America
Composition by Chapman's Phototypesetting
Printing by Hamilton Printing Company
Binding by Payne Edition Bindery

COVER DESIGN BY WILLI BAUM
FIRST EDITION
First printing: December 1977
Second printing: November 1978

Code 7725

THE INTERNATIONAL ENCYCLOPEDIA OF HIGHER EDUCATION

B

BACCALAUREATE SERVICE
See Ceremonies.

BAHAMAS, COMMONWEALTH OF THE

Population: 198,000 (mid 1974 estimate). Student enrollment in primary and secondary education: 45,000 (1975); higher education: 2971, plus 128 abroad on government scholarship (1975). Language of instruction: English. Academic calendar: September to June. Percentage of national budget expended on education: 22% (1973).

Very little research has been done and very little has been published on the history of education in the Bahamas. Most of the existing material is concerned with the evolution of public primary and secondary schooling. However, this material indicates that the roots of formal higher education lay largely in the need to supply teachers for the islands' schools.

As in most territories that were ruled by Great Britain, much of the early work in education was connected with English missionary societies—principally the Society for the Promotion of Christian Knowledge, the Society for the Propagation of the Gospel in Foreign Parts, and the Associates of Dr. Bray. These societies operated at least as early as the second decade of the eighteenth century, while government concern for education dates from the first Education Act of 1746. This act and subsequent legislation in the next seventy years dealt with the provision of monies for the erection of school buildings, the payment of teachers' salaries, and the management of schools.

The development of higher education in the Bahamas can be traced from the introduction of the Madras System in 1816. Known also as the Monitorial System, it sought to solve some of the major personnel and financial problems of teacher training. It provided already available teachers with untrained assistants or monitors, who relayed, largely by rote, such learning as they had. The legislature also provided public funds for traveling expenses and salaries to attract foreign teachers who would introduce and implement the system in the Bahamas. The Madras System became firmly entrenched and was the method by which almost all teachers were trained until the middle of the twentieth century.

During the 1930s the Madras System received strong criticism, but severe financial difficulties did not permit the creation of a more effective teacher training method. Between 1930 and 1940, however, some attempts were made to rectify the situation: the head teacher of a school for senior pupils in Nassau operated a night school to prepare pupil-teachers for the academic overseas junior-level examinations of the University of Cambridge Schools Examination Board; annual teachers' conferences concerned with improving the professional efficiency of teachers were held during the summers for most of the 1930s; and summer schools were organized for the benefit of the islands' teachers who had been taking correspondence courses. Between 1936 and 1941 a number of teachers were trained at the Booker T. Washington Institute in Tuskegee, Alabama, in the United States. Eight pursued a one-year course, while thirty-two attended summer programs which included courses in agriculture, domestic science, and woodwork. The 1930s also witnessed the establishment of the successful Dundas Civic Centre. Financed by an annual government grant and augmented by a small weekly fee, the center provided training in hotel and domestic service.

It was not until after World War II, however, that the basic features of higher education in the Bahamas began to emerge. A scholarship program was introduced, enabling teachers to improve their academic and professional skills by periods of study abroad; and courses leading to basic teacher certification were institutionalized in teachers' colleges. At the same time, technical and vocational education and training were emphasized. More recently, on several of the islands, evening institutes have provided instruction in various academic areas.

The scholarship program began in the latter part of the 1940s; when it started, just over thirty Bahamians were studying in colleges and universities abroad. Most of them were teachers with some experience who were taking short certificate courses; financed by the British government, these teachers usually studied in the United Kingdom. In 1967, when the Progressive Liberal Party came to power, there was an increase in the number and value of government-financed awards, and the majority of the recipients began to study in

the United States; the single foreign institution attracting most Bahamians was the regional University of the West Indies, in Jamaica, which the Bahamian government has supported financially since 1964. Although most of the awards are for teachers, the government has also sponsored students in a number of other fields.

The institutionalization of teacher training certification had its roots in the late 1940s. In 1950 a teachers training college opened in Nassau, closed in 1957, and reopened in 1961; in 1968 a second teachers college was established.

Technical and vocational training dates from the opening of the Nassau Technical School in 1949. In 1966 it was renamed Nassau Technical College. Course offerings were extended to include hotel-related skills and commercial and secretarial studies. Part-time day-release courses for employees of some government technical departments were initiated in 1962.

The second half of the 1960s witnessed a phenomenal economic expansion in the Bahamas and a resultant increase in manpower requirements, which technical and vocational education and training were required to meet. In 1968 a technical center was built and equipped; in 1970–71 this center was amalgamated with the college to form the Claudius Roland Walker Technical Institute.

Another significant feature of further education emerging in the middle 1960s was the evening institute. The evening institutes, located throughout the islands, are centers for citizens who have completed high school and who wish or need opportunities to obtain the national or British certificates that are a normal part of high school education. In general, these institutes are conducted in high school facilities and are administered by high school principals. They are classified as "further" or "higher" education because the students have completed regular attendance at high school. The Minister of Education and Culture subsidizes as many of them as his resources permit; however, fees are charged, and some of the institutes are totally self-supporting.

An extramural unit of the University of the West Indies until recently also provided evening programs of recreational and general interest for the public. Occasionally this unit sponsors short seminars, which are conducted by visiting lecturers from the regional university on aspects of business management and political and social science. It also sponsored structured programs for law students who were already employed by law firms.

The bill to establish the College of the Bahamas, which passed the legislature in October and November 1974, has initiated a new phase in the development of higher education in the Bahamas. This community college permits integration, economy, and expansion at the higher educational level.

Legal Basis of Educational System

The principal legislation governing the function of the Ministry of Education and Culture is the Education Act. Passed in 1962, this act provides for the appointment of a minister who has responsibility for the promotion, supervision, direction, and control of all commonwealth primary, secondary, and further education maintained by government funds, and for the supervision of all other education in the nation. The act also provides for the establishment of a central administration and for the appointment of a permanent secretary who is responsible for the organization and administration of the Department and the appointment of a director who will advise and serve as technical executive officer to the minister. The Education Act further establishes a Central Advisory Council, which will render advice on educational matters to the minister from outside the statutory system of education.

The Education Act describes the three stages of this statutory system and gives the minister the duty to provide for compulsory education for all pupils of primary age (roughly ages six to eleven) and sec-

ondary age (up to fourteen). The minister is permitted, within his resources, to provide education for pupils beyond the compulsory attendance limit of fourteen years.

Amendments to the basic Education Act in 1968 and 1970 provide for ministerial control over institutions of further education; the 1968 amendment provides for control over the term *university* and the granting of degrees and other academic distinctions within the Bahamas. All private institutions of higher education must first register with the Minister of Education and Culture before beginning operation. Subsidiary legislation to the Education Act and its amendments includes rules and regulations for effecting the provisions of this act.

The act passed in late October 1974 eventually will lead to the incorporation of all types and levels of postsecondary education and training provided by government under the auspices of the College of the Bahamas.

Types of Institutions

Under the October 1974 College of the Bahamas Act, provision is made for all public postsecondary education and training to be conducted in a single community college type of institution, the College of the Bahamas. To permit the developments envisaged by the College of the Bahamas Act, existing structures may be reshaped. Moreover, the administration, organization, and control of almost all public institutions, institutes, and training courses—which were previously responsible to the Ministry of Education and Culture—will be transferred gradually to the College of the Bahamas administration. Training programs operated by other government ministries, departments, and agencies will also come under the college's jurisdiction.

Initially, however, the College of the Bahamas will be concerned with the "further education" that has been sponsored by the Bahamas government through the Ministry of Education and Culture. It is in the process of taking responsibility for teacher and technical education, access to which is determined by attainment in high school, entrance tests, and the applicant's overall school record. Technical education within the college will include instruction for which successful attainment at high school is prerequisite, as well as lower-level technician, craft, and job training programs.

Several government ministries, departments, and government-affiliated public utility corporations have their own training units for their employees; notable among these units is the School of Nursing in the Ministry of Health, which trains nurses and other paramedical personnel for the health services. The government also sponsors a training center for administrative officers and clerical personnel. The courses span the entire range of clerical and administrative skills. Some of them require applicants to have attained stipulated successes in the national and external examinations taken in high schools; others require possession of a first degree. Mention must be made of a highly successful venture in cooperative financial sponsorship between government, the Hotel Employers Association, and the Hotel Employees Association, to train personnel for the whole range of hotel work. International oil companies operating on Grand Bahama Island conduct ongoing training programs for their employees; personnel of the College of the Bahamas help to plan and evaluate these programs and to relate them to courses offered at the college.

Relationship with Secondary Education and Admission Requirements

Although the compulsory school attendance period ends at age fourteen, the Education Act permits students to continue to attend secondary school to age nineteen. Since provision is made for five or six years of secondary education, most pupils in fact remain at school at least to age sixteen or seventeen. Students then have the opportunity for further studies at the College of the Bahamas.

Most secondary schools, whether the usual graduating age is fourteen, sixteen, or eighteen, give diplomas to students who complete the course of instruction. Some of these diplomas record student attainments and are equal to graduation certificates. For the most part, secondary school graduation certificates are external to the school, granted by outside examining bodies. Among the certificates given are the National Bahamas Junior Certificate, normally achieved between the ages of fourteen and sixteen; the General Certificate of Education (GCE) of the University of London, ordinary level, normally awarded at age sixteen, when the student completes senior high school; and the General Certificate of Education of the University of London, advanced level, achieved about two years after the ordinary-level certificate. A number of secondary schools also enter pupils for the Britain-based examinations conducted by the Pitman Examinations Institute and the Royal Society of Arts; these examinations cover various academic and commercial subjects.

Administration and Control

According to the 1974 act, the government, control, and administration of the college is vested in a nine-member college council, which includes the principal; a Ministry of Education officer, as well as six other persons appointed by the minister; a student; and a secretary (the registrar). The act permits the minister to give the council directions on the exercise of its functions and to establish fees and other charges for courses of study. The council will determine terms and conditions of employment and salaries and wield overall authority, particularly in financial matters. The act also provides for the establishment of an academic board, consisting of the principal (chairman), the registrar (secretary), the heads of the main academic divisions, the college librarian, a student, and three members to be selected by the principal and appointed by the council. The board is responsible for all academic matters.

It is anticipated that the council, the academic board, and teaching departments of the College of the Bahamas will establish a variety of ongoing and ad hoc committees, both internal and external to the college, and that, where appropriate, membership will include nonacademic persons.

Programs and Degrees

The following academic programs and fields of study are available in postsecondary education: two-year courses leading to the advanced-level certificate of the University of London in basic academic pre-university subjects; two- and three-year basic teacher education courses for primary and secondary school teachers, leading to an examination and certificate monitored and approved by the University of the West Indies; a Bachelor of Education course, being offered as of 1976, and in 1977 the faculty of Hotel Management and Tourism of the University of the West Indies will be located on the campus of the College of the Bahamas. The College is also cooperating with other foreign universities to provide higher level qualifications that include degree courses for Bachelor of Business Administration, Master of Education, and Master of Business Administration; and thirty- to thirty-six-week courses leading to College of the Bahamas certificates in various vocational subjects and to examinations and certificates of examining authorities in Britain. There are twelve-week courses leading to College of the Bahamas certificates in management, masonry, diesel mechanics, painting and decorating, and welding. Two- and three-year banking courses leading to a College of the Bahamas certificate or a variety of external British certificates also are available. Many of the above courses are available in stages and certified by stages of twelve- or thirty-six-week units.

Financing

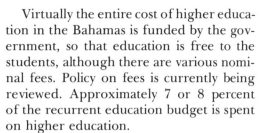

Virtually the entire cost of higher education in the Bahamas is funded by the government, so that education is free to the students, although there are various nominal fees. Policy on fees is currently being reviewed. Approximately 7 or 8 percent of the recurrent education budget is spent on higher education.

The College of the Bahamas Act vests considerable financial control of education in the government's minister of finance. When the college is firmly established, however, and not overwhelmingly dependent upon government funding, administrative arrangements will be made that will satisfy the law and still permit development toward financial autonomy. Other than what the act provides, there is little financial autonomy for educational institutions in the Bahamas. They are invited to submit budgets to their parent ministries, who review and submit them to the Ministry of Finance as a part of the parent ministry's annual budget proposal. Ministries make special internal accounting arrangements to allow for more freedom of expenditure in higher education institutions than in programs at lower levels.

Student Financial Aid

The most significant feature of student financial aid is seen in the two teacher education institutions, where almost all students are government officers and receive the usual full salaries. There are no tuition fees in teacher education. Generally, government officers and some private employers permit students who attend courses in technical and commercial services during working hours to retain their salaries.

Student Social Background and Access to Higher Education

Access to higher education in the Bahamas is determined by the academic prerequisites and by the availability of staff and facilities. There are no formal or apparent limitations of access that relate to the social background, race, or sex of the students. For entry into technical or vocational training, students must be sixteen. Seventeen is the entry age for teacher education programs.

Teaching Staff

Instructional staff are generally categorized as lecturers, assistant lecturers, instructors, assistant instructors, and trainee lecturers and/or instructors. Higher ranks are heads of departments, vice-principals, and principals of institutions. The main selection procedures are the advertising of vacancies and an interview. Staff in higher education are appointed by the governor general on recommendation of the Ministry of Education and the government's Public Service Commission. In the College of the Bahamas, lecturers and assistant lecturers will be selected by the college's appointments board, composed of ex officio and elected members. Appointments are to be approved by the council. Chairmen of divisions are to be elected by members of a division. There will be no formal tenure procedures, and salaries will be determined by the council.

Salary scales are based on academic and professional qualifications and relevant experience. Promotion to posts of responsibility (department head or senior lecturer) depends on the recommendation of the principals of institutions. Tenure for full-time staff in higher education is as secure as it is for all government officers and is generally dependent on an annual confidential report made to the Public Service Commission. The provision for dismissal of government officers includes generous protection for officers. Many non-Bahamian officers in higher education are employed on two- or three-year contracts which provide the same conditions of service as apply to permanent government officers.

Research Activities

Except for unpublished student dissertations on aspects of Bahamian life, there has been little in the way of formal research conducted in or by institutions of higher education in the Bahamas. The College of the Bahamas intends, at an early date, to establish a department of Bahamian studies, which will have research, mostly of the socioeconomic type, as a prime function. Work is under way on plans for funding such research and on the development of research policies. Several government ministries and departments conduct ongoing research.

Current Problems and Trends

The integration of higher education under the College of the Bahamas is a major step of much promise—and must be followed by researching, planning, and executing new models of education to improve and radically alter the organization of postsecondary education and training and to ensure continued acceptance of and support for these activities. Although economy and increased efficiency can be expected to result from certain innovations, costs are bound to increase as the numbers of students and the necessary expanded variety of courses become a reality. Funding for this expansion, as well as for the development of a central campus for the fields of science and technology, is a major problem.

Apart from the problems of capital development and the provision for instruction, there will have to be an extensive program for development of the Bahamian instructional staff—particularly in the areas of science, technology, and crafts at the high school and higher education levels. Many of the Bahamians who had the opportunity for higher education abroad still need experience and opportunities to develop lecturing and research skills as quickly as possible, if all that is promised by the College of the Bahamas development is to be effectively realized. The research and teaching functions of the colleges will have to relate to the manpower needs of all areas of the Bahamas, which is geographically an archipelago. In addition, they will have to contribute to the solution of the wide range of challenges that is a consequence of its geography. The college will inevitably have a profound influence on all the schools, and the national problems of teacher supply and curriculum development will be an important concern.

The major innovation in higher education in the Bahamas is the College of the Bahamas, which has a special mandate to provide for the manpower needs of the Bahamas as well as the continuing education of all citizens. Plans are at hand to expand and revamp the academic postsecondary education programs so that students can obtain at least the first two years of college in the Bahamas and can negotiate for transfer of credits. There are also plans to minimize the duplication of intramural courses by integrating as much of the instruction as possible. It is anticipated that in many areas there will be a shift of emphasis away from the inherited strong intramural base for education and training. Innovative arrangements will relate the activities of the College of the Bahamas to the needs of pupils and the needs of the nation, as directly and as profitably as possible.

Relationship with Industry

In technical and vocational training programs, students work in and are sponsored by industry. Representatives from industry serve as a moderation panel, and the curriculum in technical-vocational institutions is partly determined by industrial needs. A successful tripartite arrangement exists whereby government cooperates with the hotel industry for training purposes. Cooperation also exists between the oil companies on Grand Bahama and the College of the Bahamas on the design of syllabi, conduct of examinations, and award of certificates for employees. Similar arrangements are made on an ad hoc and a contin-

uing basis for government agencies which operate in technical and service fields, banks, and large business houses. There is little in the way of direct financial aid to public higher education for funding these ventures, although there is a willingness to assist in the provision of some material and in locating instructional staff. As a general principle, higher education courses are not offered in fields where employment opportunities are poor.

International Cooperation

Efforts in the area of international cooperation are still new. Contracts are being made with various foreign colleges and universities to negotiate credit transfer and cooperative programs for faculty exchange. This kind of exchange already exists with the University of the West Indies in Jamaica, and links are now being forged with many United States institutions, particularly in Florida. Financial assistance is also being negotiated with various Commonwealth and Caribbean regional organizations.

LIVINGSTONE N. COAKLEY

Educational Association

Bahamas Union of Teachers
P.O. Box N3482
Nassau, Bahamas

Bibliography

Educational Development in an Archipelagic Nation. Report of a Review Team Invited by the Government of the Commonwealth of the Bahamas. Nassau: Government of the Commonwealth of the Bahamas, 1974. (Mimeographed.)

Figueroa, J. J. *Society, Schools and Progress in the West Indies.* Oxford, England: Pergamon Press, 1971.

Focus on the Future. Nassau: Ministry of Education and Culture, n.d.

Sherlock, P. M. *The Land and People of the West Indies.* Philadelphia: Lippincott, 1967.

Williams, E. *Education in the British West Indies.* New York: University Place Book Shop, 1968.

Williams, E. *From Columbus to Castro: The History of the Caribbean 1492–1969.* London: André Deutsch, 1970.

BAHRAIN, STATE OF

Population: 250,000 (1974 estimate). Student enrollment in primary school: 41,818; secondary school (academic, vocational, technical): 17,400; higher education: 603 in Bahrain, 2199 abroad. Student enrollment in higher education as percentage of age group (18–22): 1.2%. Language of instruction: English, Arabic. Academic calendar: October to June. Percentage of gross national product (GNP) expended on education: 2.6%. Percentage of national budget expended on education: 8.2%. [Unless otherwise noted, figures are for 1975–76. Source: Ministry of Education.]

The State of Bahrain, a British protectorate from 1820 to independence in 1971, is located off the west coast of the Arabian Gulf. The general system of education in Bahrain consists of six years of primary school, two years of intermediate school, and three years of secondary school. At the completion of secondary education, students sit for one of several examinations; general secondary education students take the *al-thanawiya al'ammah* (general secondary education examination), while students in the technical, religious, and commercial secondary schools take appropriate examinations leading to a diploma.

Higher education in Bahrain is available at the Gulf Technical College and at two teacher training colleges. The majority of secondary school graduates, however, continue their studies abroad, primarily in higher education institutions in Egypt, Iraq, Kuwait, Lebanon, Saudi Arabia, and Syria.

The Gulf Technical College was founded in 1968 and has received financial assistance from the governments of Abu Dhabi, Bahrain, Oman, Qatar, and the United Kingdom. The college offers full-time, evening, sandwich (programs alternating a period of study with a period of work), and part-time day-release courses in engineering and business. The engineering specialties include automatic, civil, electrical, and mechanical engineering, fabrication and welding, and draftsmanship. The business program includes accounting, administration, commerce, commercial arithmetic, economics, office practice, shorthand, statistics, storekeeping, and supervision.

Admission to a full-time program is normally determined by the appropriate secondary school-leaving certificate. Full-time students generally enroll in either a two-year secretarial course sanctioned by British certificates of the Royal Society of Arts and the Pitman Examinations Institute or enter a College Orientation Year in preparation for a two-year program in business or engineering, which leads to a college diploma. Part-time day-release students are usually sponsored by the government or by local firms. Courses are either especially designed for these students or correspond to those offered by the City and Guilds of London Institute. Evening courses are open to all and generally lead to either a United Kingdom qualification or entry to the full-time or part-time college program. In 1975 a technical teacher training unit was established to train in-service teachers and new teachers. Gulf Technical College is coeducational, and the medium of instruction is English. During the 1975–76 academic year 332 students were enrolled at the college.

In 1966 a teacher training college for men was opened, followed in 1967 by a teacher training college for women. The colleges offer a two-year program of theoretical and practical courses designed to prepare teachers for primary and intermediate schools. Enrollment at the two colleges in 1975–76 totaled 281 students. The Bahrain government finances education at all levels and also provides scholarships for university study abroad. Host countries, private companies, and local voluntary organizations also offer several scholarships.

[Information provided by Jalil E. Arrayed, Under-Secretary, Ministry of Education, Manama, Bahrain.]

Bibliography

Clark, D. O., and Mertz, R. A. *The Coastal Countries of the Arabian Peninsula: A Guide to the Academic Placement of Students from Kuwait, Bahrain, Qatar, United Arab Emirates, Sultanate of Oman, People's Democratic Republic of Yemen and Yemen Arab Republic in Educational Institutions in the U.S.A.* World Education Series. Washington, D.C.: American Association of Collegiate Registrars and Admissions Officers (AACRAO), 1974.

Mertz, R. A. *Education and Manpower in the Arabian Gulf.* Washington, D.C.: American Friends of the Middle East, 1972.

Who's Who in the Arab World 1974–1975. (4th ed.) Beirut, Lebanon: Publitec Publications, 1974.

See also: Science Policies: Less Developed Countries: Arab World.

BANGLADESH, PEOPLE'S REPUBLIC OF

Population: 71,316,000. Student enrollment in primary school: 6,000,000 (1972 estimate); secondary school (academic, vocational, technical): 1,030,000 (1972 estimate); higher education (universities and colleges): 105,000. Language of instruction: Bengali and English. Academic calendar: July to June, three terms. Percentage of national budget expended on all education: 18%. [Unless otherwise indicated, figures are 1974 estimates.]

Bangladesh declared its independence in 1971. Between 1947 and 1971 the area constituted the eastern segment of Pakistan, whose western and eastern sectors were separated by India. During the period from the mid eighteenth century to 1947, when the Indian subcontinent was under British control, the area was part of the province of East Bengal, India.

Education in what is today Bangladesh dates back many thousand years. Early education centered on the Vedas, sacred hymns, poems, and ballads composed before 1000 B.C. The period from 1000 to 200 B.C. was a period of intellectual flourishing, and mathematics and science were developed on the Indian subcontinent.

Education was originally secular and available also to women. After 200 B.C. a slow decline started; after 500 A.D. the caste system became more established, and education became restricted to the Brahman class—that is, to the religious teachers. Education for women also declined as child marriages and early childbearing became common. In addition, the area experienced an intellectual impoverishment as a result of warfare and foreign attacks. As the Muslim cultural influence increased after the Muslim annexation in the early thirteenth century, Buddhist art and education slowly declined; and, although Hinduism survived through private patronage, Muslim education, available in Koranic schools and *madrassas,* dominated until the arrival of Europeans—at first the Portuguese and then the Dutch and the French. The British arrived in the mid eighteenth century and soon dominated the subcontinent.

The British East India Company established a Committee of Public Instruction for Bengal in the early 1820s, but its work had little effect because the content of the educational system on the subcontinent—Western learning or Oriental learning—could not be agreed upon. In 1835 a ruling was made that the medium of instruction should be English and the system Western oriented. After the British government assumed the administration of India from the British East India Company in 1859, the responsibility of education was transferred to provincial authorities, under whose jurisdiction private schools were founded. The government itself neglected education. In 1904 the lack of education was deplored in an official survey, which found that four of five villages had no schools. The system as conceived became a colonial system; that is, it was concerned mainly with training public servants for the colonial bureaucracy. Indigenous education was rejected, and Western culture was implanted in the schools. As early as 1937 an All-India National Educational Conference had suggested use of national tongues for education. However, English remained the language of instruction until the independence of Bangladesh in 1971, when Bengali became the medium of instruction in the new republic.

The University of Dacca, in what is today Bangladesh, was established in 1921 by an act of the imperial legislature. It became an affiliating (examining rather than teaching) university after East Bengal became the eastern section of Pakistan in 1947. By 1960 the number of universities in both parts of Pakistan had risen to six. The literacy rate was 21.5 percent for East Pakistan, and modernization of education was attempted within financial restrictions. In East Pakistan, Rajshahi University had been established (1953) to relieve the enrollment pressures in Dacca. By the time East Pakistan became the independent sovereign state of Bangladesh in 1971, four more universities, including specialized and agricultural institutions, had been created in the area: Bangladesh Agricultural University (1961), Bangladesh University of Engineering and Technology (1961), the University of Chittagong (1966), and Jahangirnagar University (1970).

During the war that separated the eastern section of Pakistan into the independent nation of Bangladesh, destruction of educational resources was considerable, and a great number of students and professors died in the struggle for independence. Despite political instability and financial problems since 1971, the government has worked to formulate a cohesive national educational system.

National Educational Policy

In 1972 the government appointed a National Education Commision to formulate a suitable national educational policy. The commission recommended that the length of primary education be extended from five to eight years. The improvement of basic education; the adaptation of higher education to manpower needs in science, health, industry, and agriculture; and a deemphasis on humanities and related studies are all issues under consideration.

Legal Basis of Educational System

The universities in Bangladesh were originally established under acts and ordinances of the colonial government of India and the government of Pakistan. In 1921 the University of Dacca was established under Act 18 of the imperial legislature. In 1947 the university became an affiliating institution under the East Bengal Educational Ordinance; each of the subsequent universities was established under its own ordinance.

After 1971 criticism by students and teachers in Bangladesh of what they perceived to be undemocratic provisions for the administration of the universities led to demands for new legislation to replace the existing so-called "black book" ordinances and bring the legal basis of the institutions into line with the principles of the new government. The university orders passed in 1973 supported an autonomous structure of the universities and a democratization of their activities by limiting the power of university officers and by increasing faculty and student participation in administration.

Types of Institutions

The system of education in Bangladesh resembles the Indian system established during British rule. It consists of six universities. Three are affiliating institutions— that is, they are largely examining institutions, although they may have some teaching functions. Three universities are unitary— university teaching and research takes place on a single campus. Two of the unitary institutions are specialized universities for agriculture and engineering. The three affiliating institutions—the Universities of Dacca, Rajshahi, and Chittagong—are responsible for establishing the standard for physical facilities and teaching staff, determining curricula, and administering the common examination of their affiliated colleges, which are managed and maintained by the government or by private bodies. The affiliated colleges, most of which are private, offer general and professional undergraduate programs; some also offer honors studies and postgraduate training. University departments (or combinations of departments organized as constituent colleges) and university institutes conduct undergraduate and most of the postgraduate programs.

The principal institution of higher education in Bangladesh is the University of Dacca, with more than one hundred affiliated and fifteen constituent colleges, as well as four institutes for business administration, education and research, nutrition, and statistical research and training. The University of Rajshahi, located in northern Bangladesh, has eighty-one affiliated colleges. This institution, established in 1953, became the second affiliating university in the country and was founded to relieve the concentration of educational activity in Dacca. The University of Chittagong, located near the southern seaport of Chittagong, has forty-four affiliated colleges. Jahangirnagar University, located eighteen miles from Dacca, is a unitary teaching and residential university. Bangladesh Agricultural University, at Mymensingh in the jute-growing country of northeastern Bangladesh, includes the Radiation Genetics Institute, started by the Bangladesh Atomic Energy Commission in 1975. The Bangladesh University of Engineering and Technology, situated in Dacca, provides facilities in agriculture and allied fields.

Nonuniversity higher education takes place in some learned societies and research organizations, which train those with master's degrees in techniques of research.

Relationship with Secondary Education

Higher education is based on twelve years of preuniversity education. Primary education in Bangladesh is designed to provide basic skills. The student generally enters at age five and continues for five years; however, the National Education Commission has recommended extension of this program to eight years.

Secondary education in Bangladesh is under the control of four boards of intermediate and secondary education, one for each zone of the country. Most of the secondary programs are privately sponsored but are managed by public officials elected according to regulations set by the Education Department. Some of the secondary programs are public and under the direct control of the department.

General secondary schools provide education in grades 6 through 10. Eleventh- and twelfth-grade education is given at two-year higher secondary colleges and in the first half of four-year colleges. Many of the four-year colleges offer both higher secondary programs and first-degree university programs. They are affiliated to an intermediate and secondary education board for secondary studies and to a university for higher studies. In addition to the general secondary institution, there are separate institutions for religious instruction, which function within the established system and receive some government funding; there are also technical institutes which offer three-year programs leading to a diploma for graduates of the tenth grade.

The general secondary schools can be divided into junior high school (grades 6–8) and high school (grades 9–10). At the end of grade 8, students take an examination for entry into high school programs, the best students receiving scholarships to continue their education. After grade 10, students who successfully pass another examination are awarded the Secondary School Certificate (SSC); those with the highest grades again are eligible for scholarships for higher secondary colleges. Students who pass the Higher Secondary Certificate (HSC) examination are eligible for tertiary programs.

Admission Requirements

Entry into two-year programs for the first degree at universities in Bangladesh is based on possession of the HSC, although successful completion does not automatically assure entry into higher study. Candidates for admission must also take departmental examinations, and rejection at this stage is often high, as high as 75 percent for engineering and medical programs. Those who are rejected may reapply to less crowded programs.

An admission committee—the deans of the faculties in each institution, selected department heads, and the registrar—establishes criteria for submission of applications to honors programs and master's degree programs. Applicants are required to take oral and written examinations conducted by the departments. A minimum requirement for applicants to master's degree study is the appropriate two-year first degree.

Administration and Control

The two major agencies concerned with higher education are the University Grants Commission (UGC) and the Education Commission, both of which were formed after Bangladesh became a sovereign state. The UGC is responsible for planning higher education within the framework of economic development and for determining financial needs and allocating grants to universities. It consists of a chairman, two permanent members, and two vice-chancellors replaced biannually by vote of the combined university vice-chancellors. The Education Commission was constituted in 1972 to advise the government on policies and general guidelines for the development of all levels of education; it will probably recommend revision of the administration of higher education. At present the Ministry of Education has no direct role in the administration of higher education other than allocation of the annual government grants to the universities.

The Association of Universities of Bang-ladesh, with its standing committee of vice-chancellors, facilitates communication among the institutions, coordinates their activities, and acts as a liaison between the universities and the top level of administration. The association is composed of three representatives from each university: the vice-chancellor and two members nominated by the academic council to serve one year. Meetings of the association are open to the educational adviser of the government, but he has no vote. The standing committee is the executive branch of the association.

Each of the universities is a corporate, autonomous body that maintains academic and administrative control of constituent departments and colleges. The affiliating universities, however, only set academic standards for their affiliated institutions. The president of Bangladesh is the chancellor of all universities in the country.

Among the governing bodies of each university are the syndicate, senate, academic council, faculties, and a variety of committees and boards. The syndicate is the executive body of the university while the senate ratifies proposals of the syndicate and approves its annual report, the annual accounts, and financial estimates. The university vice-chancellor, as principal executive officer, is the chairman of the syndicate, senate, and academic council. The vice-chancellor is appointed for a four-year term by the chancellors from among three nominees for the position selected by the university senate. According to the new statute for the University of Rajshahi, the authority of the vice-chancellor is curtailed in favor of a more equitable distribution of internal administrative power. Five student representatives are now part of the university senate, and the deans of the faculties are elected by teaching staff rather than appointed by the vice-chancellor. Since 1973 students have been members of certain committees of all universities, such as the committees dealing with regulations and examinations.

The direct administrative control of

the affiliated government colleges is the responsibility of the appropriate government department; administrative control of the private colleges is exercised by private interests who interact with government only for grants-in-aid, requests for affiliation, and other matters that require government sanction. The public and private affiliated colleges are managed by their heads in accordance with government policy under the guidance of their governing bodies, which consist of elected and nominated members and the chief executive of the college as a member ex officio. Since the University of Dacca was originally a unitary institution and later became affiliating, some of its institutes have separate boards of governors with some autonomous powers.

Programs and Degrees

The institutions of higher education in Bangladesh provide programs in agriculture, commerce and business administration, communications (journalism), education science and teacher training, engineering and technology, fine and applied arts, home economics, humanities, law, mathematics, medicine and allied health fields, military science, natural sciences, and social and behavioral sciences. The undergraduate degrees are the Bachelor of Arts (B.A.), the Bachelor of Science (B.Sc.), and the Bachelor of Commerce (B.Com.), awarded after two years of study. Three years are required for a degree with honors.

Graduate degrees consist of the Master of Arts (M.A.), the Master of Science (M.Sc.), and the Master of Commerce (M.Com.), awarded after two years of study beyond the regular bachelor's degree and one additional year after the bachelor's with honors. Master's degree candidates are evaluated at the end of the academic year by essay examination. Candidates for the doctorate do not pursue regular course work but must study independently with a professor. The doctorate is awarded on submission of a dissertation which is approved by a committee of professors.

In general, the two-year undergraduate first-degree program is followed at affiliated colleges, but the undergraduate honors programs and the graduate programs are taken at constituent university colleges or in university departments. Some of the older affiliated colleges, however, which have accredited faculty and facilities, offer the three-year honors programs; the high demand for admission to graduate studies has caused the government to allow a limited number of colleges to conduct graduate work under the egis of their affiliating universities.

Financing

Two thirds of the income of the universities is supplied by annual grants made by the Ministry of Education, through the UGC; the remainder is generated by fees for tuition, examinations, and registration. The public affiliated colleges receive funds which have been designated for their particular departments by the government. The private colleges rely on tuition, donations, and subsidies received from the government. The accounts of the universities are subject to strict audit by the auditor general of the country; approved government auditors examine accounts of the affiliated institutions.

Teaching Staff

The ranks of teaching staff at the universities in Bangladesh are professor, associate professor, assistant professor, and lecturer. The majority of the universities also employ demonstrators for laboratory work. The teaching staff with professorial status are required to have research experience. Some universities require applicants to a lectureship to show evidence of a research degree or publication of research. The professorial staff are eligible for study leave of up to four years; the University of Dacca has designed a plan to grant leave to senior professors for postdoctoral study.

A selection committee comprised of

nominees of the syndicate, the academic council, and the chancellor chooses candidates for appointment.

Current Problems and Trends

Bangladesh is the eighth most populous nation—and one of the most densely populated nations—in the world. Added to the normal burden of increasing educational opportunity for great numbers of people in a newly independent nation is the task of reconstructing the economic and social systems damaged by war. The difficulty of the task is compounded by an administrative system inherited from the British colonial government and not always well suited to the needs of a developing nation.

While the government examines the overall problems of reconstruction, the specific problems of education proliferate. The quality of education is of prime concern. Results of degree examinations published in 1975 show that students have been inadequately prepared for college study. Many who passed the "duplicate examination" (introduced after independence as a substitute for earlier examinations) never received proper basic and secondary education. Further, the many new, private, largely proprietary colleges, which have been established since 1971, are not up to standard and have served to increase rather than alleviate the problem. Exacerbating the issue is the shortage of inexpensive quality textbooks published in the country.

International Cooperation

Since 1974 Bangladesh has had close alliances with the Soviet Union and several Eastern European countries, including the German Democratic Republic and Yugoslavia. These governments provide full scholarships, including living and travel expenses, to Bangladesh students. A number of students from Bangladesh also study in the United States and Western European countries; they generally provide their own financing or receive private scholarships. Few foreign students study in Bangladesh because of the difficulty of mastering Bengali, the language of instruction.

Under a credit agreement with the government of Bangladesh, the Netherlands has extended material aid to the University of Dacca.

Bangladesh is a member of the Colombo Plan for Co-operative Economic Development in South and Southeast Asia. Under the plan, equipment for domestic technical training and research is made available, as are opportunities for study abroad in higher technology programs.

Bibliography

Ashby, E. *Universities: British, Indian, African.* London: Weidenfeld and Nicolson, 1966.
Latif, A. H. "Educational Administration in Bangladesh." *Bulletin of the UNESCO Regional Office for Education in Asia,* June 1974, *15,* 20–34.
Nyrop, R. F., and others. *Area Handbook for Pakistan.* Washington, D.C.: U.S. Government Printing Office, 1971.

See also: Agriculture in Higher Education: Agricultural Research, Extension Services, and Field Stations; Archives: Africa and Asia, National Archives of; Financing of Higher Education: University Grants Committees; Health Services, Worldwide University; South Asia: Regional Analysis.

BARBADOS

Population: 247,506 (1973). Student enrollment in primary school: 37,500; secondary school (academic, vocational, technical): 24,000; university: 995 (1974–75). Language of instruction: English. Academic calendar: October to June, three terms. Percentage of national budget expended on all education: 20%; higher education: 2%.

Barbados, the easternmost island of the West Indies, was settled by the English in 1627 and remained a British crown colony until it achieved independent dominion status in 1966. The history of its education until independence reflected its colonial status. Focus was on educating the ruling class in relation to European standards at the expense of national development.

During the colonial period probably the most significant educational event was the founding in 1711 of Codrington College. In 1703 Christopher Codrington, a wealthy sugar planter, had made a will bequeathing his two plantations in the Island of the Barbados to the Society for the Propagation of the Gospel in Foreign Parts. He stipulated that "three hundred negroes, at least, [should] always [be] kept thereon; and a convenient number of professors and scholars maintained there who shall be obliged to study and practice physic and chirurgery, as well as Divinity." In 1711 the Society for the Propagation of the Gospel in Foreign Parts sent a catechist to the plantations; six years later the building of a college began; and in 1745 a grammar school, now known as the Lodge School, was opened. That Codrington College began as a grammar school, when Codrington had requested a theological institution, might seem strange. However, there was at that time no organized education on the island which could provide the foundation for a theological college. For the next seventy-five years the college floundered as the authorities argued about the very concept of educating blacks, and about the function of the institution; but in 1825, with the arrival from England of the first Episcopal Bishop of Barbados, William Hart Coleridge, an effort was made to effect Codrington's wishes. Coleridge recruited staff and improved the quality of instruction; and in 1875 Codrington College became affiliated with Durham University in England, and its students read for Durham degrees in the classics and theology. This is the earliest example of the provision of university education in the West Indies.

In 1955 the Mirfield Fathers, a British monastic order, took over the running of the college. They emphasized theological training, organized religious retreats in Barbados and other islands, and engaged in pastoral work among the population and in the schools. In 1965 Codrington College renewed its university links, this time through affiliation with the regional University of the West Indies. Throughout its history Codrington College has made a significant contribution to local education; it prompted the beginning of a long involvement of the Anglican church in Barbados in all levels of education, and it was instrumental in stimulating the growth of new institutions—including the Rawle Institute, the earliest attempt locally at teacher training; the Lodge School, a grammar school of high repute; Society Mixed, a primary school serving the area; Codrington High School, currently a private grammar school; and Society Chapel, an Anglican church catering to the pastoral needs of the area.

In 1963 the University of the West Indies opened a campus, the College of Arts and Sciences, at Cave Hill in Barbados. In addition to the main campus in Mona, Jamaica, another campus had been opened in 1960 at St. Augustine, Trinidad; Cave Hill thus was the third campus of the regional university. Teaching began in temporary quarters in 1963. The permanent buildings were opened in 1968 with British aid for capital expenditure. The lands were provided by the government of Barbados.

Since 1950 education in the Barbados has become less elitist and more oriented to the needs of the local community. In 1952 nonselective secondary schools were established with a view to mitigating the harshly selective entry requirements of the older secondary schools and making higher education accessible to more Barbadians. Students who received minimal ordinary-level passes from the new schools might go on to Barbados Community College or Erdiston Teachers' College and hence to university-level studies.

In 1953 the Technical Institute, later superseded by the Samuel Jackman Prescod Polytechnic, began to train skilled craftsmen to work on the island, and since the mid 1960s there has been a significant increase in professional and paraprofessional training facilities. These are designed to meet specific local needs, especially in the production sectors of the economy. Under the exclusive system academic excellence was idolized, and tertiary education tended to be viewed in terms of university education. Under the present system tertiary education is conceived in more comprehensive and pragmatic terms. As a result of the demands of economic development and a more open society, the wastage of human resources inherent in the exclusive system has come under strong attack. Emphasis is now being placed on developing the academic *and* nonacademic abilities of the population. Perhaps the best example of this shift toward more broad-based tertiary education is the Barbados Community College, which was established in 1968.

National Educational Policy

The philosophy underlying the Barbadian education system is that the potential of every citizen should be developed to the fullest extent, so as to enable him or her to live harmoniously in the environment and make a useful contribution to the economic society. To this end a wide and varied range of educational experience is made available to the student at every stage, from nursery to university level.

Types of Institutions

All postsecondary education in Barbados is officially styled tertiary education. The 1975 Education Act stipulates that students in tertiary programs should be older than seventeen years and defines tertiary education as "university education and instruction normally available at institutions for teacher training, vocational training, and technical training." Tertiary-level programs are thus offered at two levels: postsecondary and university. The former level is concerned with broad-based training to meet local needs for a variety of middle-level skills in the paraprofessional, business, and technical fields. Some of these postsecondary programs are terminal, but others lead to university study.

The following institutions provide non-

university tertiary education: Erdiston Teachers' College offers a two-year nongraduate teacher training course for teachers of government primary and nonselective schools. Barbados Community College offers two-year courses in the divisions of liberal arts, science, commerce, health services, and technology (from which students may go on to the university); its community services division serves community needs outside certificate programs. Samuel Jackman Prescod Polytechnic, established in 1970, develops trade skills and occupational competence up to the level of skilled craftsman and prepares students either for entry into employment or for further education in the division of technology at Barbados Community College. The Housecraft Center provides training in home economics for teachers, homemakers, and persons wishing to take up domestic service, as well as a one-year course for domestic science teachers in primary and secondary schools and for other persons who have had a secondary education. The Hotel School trains persons in crafts, supervisory, and middle-management skills for the hotel industry.

The institutions providing tertiary education at the university level are the University of the West Indies (Cave Hill campus) and Codrington College (affiliated with the University of the West Indies). In addition, since the University of the West Indies has three campuses (Jamaica, Trinidad, Barbados), the facilities at any campus are fully available to Barbadian students who meet the various requirements.

Special postsecondary classes are offered for adult students in a variety of subjects at other institutions in Barbados. Barbados Evening Institute conducts classes in commercial and academic subjects at six centers in nineteen rural areas. Barbados Technical Institute provides day and evening classes for students from the technical streams in the secondary schools and also offers training courses for teachers of woodworking and metalwork. The Ministry of Agriculture runs training courses for peasant agricultural instructors, and the Department of Medical Services trains nurses, sanitary inspectors, and public health visitors. Workers' education is provided at the Barbados Workers' Union Labor College at Mangrove, St. Philip. This college, which was opened in 1974, marks the culmination of efforts by the Barbados Workers' Union to provide organized relevant training for its membership. The main aims of the college are to create educational opportunities for workers at all levels of leadership in the trade union movement and to contribute toward the preservation of harmonious industrial relations by providing appropriate workers' education programs. The college is residential and is equipped with a wide range of educational technology necessary to support teaching methods suited to mature adults.

Relationship with Secondary Education

The majority of primary and secondary schools in Barbados are run by the government, but there are also a number of private institutions, particularly at the secondary level. Education at government infant, primary, and secondary schools is free.

The government primary school system is composed of infant schools, (for children five to seven), junior schools (for ages seven to eleven), and in some areas all-age schools (for students five to fourteen).

There are two types of secondary schools in Barbados. The first is comprised of ten older or selective secondary schools equivalent to the British grammar school. Here entry is based on a competitive Common Entrance Examination, the program extends for five years, and the students are prepared to write the ordinary-level examinations of various United Kingdom examining boards. In four of the ten selective schools students passing these examinations study another two years to prepare for the advanced-level examinations required for entrance to British and Commonwealth universities. The newer schools established in 1952 are nonselective. Their most able students prepare for the Gen-

eral Certificate of Education Examination at the ordinary level; other pupils write the locally accredited Barbados Secondary Certificate Examination.

For persons who have left school, the adult education program provides evening courses in academic, commercial, and technical subjects.

Admission Requirements

The shift toward a more broad-based conception of tertiary education has led to more flexible entry requirements for the various programs. In general, irrespective of the type of secondary school attended, students who have the minimal ordinary-level entrance qualifications can be admitted to Barbados Community College, although there is some variation in requirements contingent on the program to be followed. The qualifications for admission to the college in the division of technology include passes in elementary mathematics and passes in two other subjects. A person who (a) holds the City and Guilds of London Institute Advanced Craft Certificate, (b) has successfully completed an advanced craft course at the Samuel Jackman Prescod Polytechnic, or (c) has passed such examination as the board considers equivalent to these qualifications may also be admitted as a student of the college in the division of technology.

Entrance to Erdiston Teachers' College is the same as that for the community college. Trained teachers who wish to become specialist home economics teachers take a one-year full-time course at the Housecraft Center after graduation from Erdiston.

At Samuel Jackman Prescod admission is based primarily on performance in the entrance examination in mathematics and English. All persons who have completed at least six years of primary education are eligible to write the entrance examination.

Entry requirements at the Barbados Hotel School depend on the course being taken. Thus, for the two-year middle-management course students are required to have passed

English, mathematics, and two other subjects in any of the overseas examinations. Students in the nine-month receptionist course are required to have passes in two subjects (English and one other subject) at ordinary level or equivalent. For the other courses the entry requirement is the Barbados Secondary School Certificate.

The entry requirements for the University of the West Indies and the affiliated Codrington College are those for admission to the degree programs of the University of the West Indies. These requirements include passing advanced-level examinations of the various overseas examining boards given at four of the ten selective secondary schools. Also, entry into Erdiston Teachers' College and/or Barbados Community College enables students to enter the university if they meet the minimal university entry requirements. Thus, students in the nonselective secondary schools can in effect enter the university, although by a longer route than their counterparts in the selective schools. In addition to these minimal requirements, there are usually specific faculty requirements. Thus, because the Erdiston teachers' certificate is endorsed by the University of the West Indies School of Education, graduates of Erdiston Teachers' College who reach a prescribed level in their course are admitted to the University of the West Indies, even though they may not hold advanced-level qualifications.

Administration and Control

The Ministry of Education, through its tertiary section, is legally and administratively responsible for all postsecondary education. In actual practice, however, agencies such as the University of the West Indies Extra-Mural Department and various professional bodies collaborate with the Ministry of Education in providing programs at the tertiary level.

The chief administrator of the Cave Hill campus of the University of the West Indies is the principal, assisted by senior administrative staff. Decision making in regard to academic matters and research is generally the responsibility of the faculty, subject to the approval of the academic board and, in some cases, other university committees. The academic board consists of the principal, deans, heads of departments, a representative of the academic staff of each faculty, the resident tutor of the Extra-Mural Department, one representative of the senate of the university, the president of the guild of undergraduates, and one student representative from each faculty.

Programs and Degrees

Courses available at the University of the West Indies (Cave Hill campus) include economics, English, French, Spanish, history, mathematics, sociology, government, law, physics, chemistry, biology, and meteorology. First-year courses in linguistics and Latin are also available. The course structure makes available a number of options. Cross-faculty registration is possible in many instances.

The full-time program for the bachelor's degree generally requires three years of study. Evening students complete four years and are expected to attend full time during their last two years of study. Law students who have successfully completed three years of their program at Cave Hill continue their professional training at the law schools in Mona, Jamaica, or St. Augustine, Trinidad. The university also offers a one-year in-service program for the Diploma in Education (Dip.Ed.). Students in this program attend classes during holidays, on Saturdays, and in the evening. The master's degree in arts and general studies usually requires two years of study, although the actual time required is set by the faculty concerned, taking into account the program of study and whether the candidate is employed full time.

In addition to the teaching facilities outlined above, branches of the following units, concerned primarily with applied research, are situated at Cave Hill: (1) University of the West Indies School of Education (Northeastern Area); (2) Institute of Social and Economic Research (ISER); (3) East Caribbean Farm Institute. Where practicable, the staff of these research units participate in the teaching program. The School of Education at Cave Hill has three sections: research and evaluation, curriculum and teachers college development, and teaching.

Codrington College, which became affiliated in 1965 with the University of the West Indies, initially offered only the Licentiate in Theology (L.Th.). Currently, however, students can also read for the B.A. (Theology) of the faculty of arts and general studies of the University of the West Indies (Cave Hill).

The tertiary programs for students over seventeen but not on the university level are made up of four types: academic, technical-vocational, community oriented, and adult education.

The academic programs are designed primarily to enable students to satisfy university entrance requirements. As a result, the content of these programs is determined primarily by the requirements of the United Kingdom examining boards for advanced-level examinations. In addition to persons wishing to pursue university education, the advanced-level programs are pursued by persons wishing to enhance their employment possibilities or even to obtain incremental credit and/or greater security of tenure.

Technical programs are offered at three levels: skilled craftsman, technician level, and full professional level. Skilled craftsmen obtain their education at the Samuel Jackman Prescod Polytechnic, where courses are offered in construction, electrical, and engineering trades, and in commercial skills. By arrangement with employers, a limited number of students in employment attend the polytechnic on specified days to pursue studies related to their employment—for example, motor mechanics. Students in the craft courses write the appropriate examination(s) of the City and Guilds of London Institute and/or As-

sociated Examining Board. Students in the commercial courses write the examinations of the Pitman's Examinations Institute. Students at the technician level acquire their education through the division of technology of Barbados Community College. The division was opened in January 1973 to provide two-year technician-level courses in a number of technical studies. Courses in mechanical engineering, electrical engineering, and construction and civil engineering lead to the Ordinary Technician Diploma of the City and Guilds of London Institute. Courses in drafting lead to an Associated Examining Board examination at the advanced level. Land-surveying courses are accredited according to the requirements of the local Land Surveyor's License and monitored by the local professional land surveyors—thereby ensuring maintenance of standards throughout the Caribbean region.

A major feature of the development of tertiary-level education in Barbados since 1965 has been the significant increase in professional and paraprofessional training facilities designed to meet specific local needs, especially in the productive sectors of the economy. Most of the courses currently available are offered by, or in collaboration with, Barbados Community College. Divisions in the college include commerce, health services, and technology. Teacher training for primary schools and for nonselective secondary schools is available at Erdiston Teachers' College and at Barbados Community College; teacher training for graduate teachers in selective secondary schools is offered at the University of the West Indies; and training for nurses is available at the Tercentenary School of Nursing, Queen Elizabeth Hospital. Other professionally oriented courses are available at the Barbados Hotel School.

A major innovation in community-based education was the establishment of the community services division of Barbados Community College. Geared to respond to community needs for particular types of training related to improving the quality of community life, course offerings include communications, community recreation, and the history of the Caribbean. The emphasis is on the applied aspects, with fieldwork assignments providing central focus.

The tertiary section of the Ministry of Education—assisted by the Extra-Mural Department of the University of the West Indies, through the local resident tutor—is responsible for adult education programs.

Financing and Student Financial Aid

According to the statistics of revenue and expenditure for the period 1969–1975, 20 percent of the total revenue was spent on education and ancillary services. Further analysis indicates that approximately 10 percent of monies voted for education was allocated to tertiary education.

In 1962 tuition fees were abolished in all government educational institutions. Education is thus free from the primary level to university study at the Cave Hill campus of the University of the West Indies. At the University of the West Indies the main cost components are (1) tuition and examination fees, (2) caution money (refundable deposits), (3) accommodations in a residence hall or off campus, (4) membership in the Guild of Undergraduates, and (5) economic cost of the particular course. The contributing governments meet the costs under (5) for their nationals; a special scale of fees exists for students from territories that do not contribute to the university.

The Barbados Ministry of Education, through its tertiary section, administers a wide range of scholarships, bursaries, enabling grants, and loans. Recipients are usually bonded to work in Barbados on graduation for a period equivalent to the duration of the course of study. The various forms of aid administered by the Ministry of Education are available for study at any approved university.

Teaching Staff

Members of the teaching staff at Barbados Community College are classified as tutors, senior and assistant tutors, and in-structors. The number of staff is determined by the board of management with prior approval by the minister of education. After a one-year probationary period, academic staff members may be appointed by the board to a permanent post. At the University of the West Indies, the ranks of the full-time academic staff are professor, reader, senior lecturer, lecturer, associate and assistant lecturer, and tutor. There are also part-time lecturers and teachers. Academic and administrative staff below the rank of senior lecturer are recommended by the campus selection board, subject to ratification by the appropriate university committee. Staff of the rank of senior lecturer and above are recommended for appointment by the appropriate university selection board. A university committee, the Assessment and Promotions Committee, is responsible for promotion, tenure, and contract renewals of staff at all campuses. This committee is composed of a representative cross section of the university academic staff. The criteria are publicly stated in the university regulations.

The West Indies Group of University Teachers (WIGUT) at Cave Hill is the accredited bargaining agent for academic staff at Cave Hill. Salary claims are discussed by WIGUT and a committee of the University Grants Committee (UGC). Any agreements are subject to ratification by the full UGC, on which all contributing governments are represented.

Research Activities

Research projects are carried out at the University of the West Indies, Cave Hill campus. Funds for publication and research are provided from the following sources: the University of the West Indies budget; external agencies such as foundations and government aid agencies; and private enterprise or individual governments (for specific projects).

Current Problems and Trends

The main features of the development of education in Barbados since the 1950s have been the rapid progress toward the democratization of education at all levels, including tertiary; the diversification of educational programs, partly as a result of the democratization process and partly in response to the emergence of a more open society as well as the demands of economic development; and the pivotal role played by politics in influencing the nature, direction, and emphases of educational expansion.

The shift toward an inclusive system of education has led to an increasing emphasis, at the tertiary level, on programs that are clearly career oriented and linked to the manpower needs of the country. This trend has shown itself in various ways. In the first place, the major expansion at the community college, the key tertiary-level institution, has been in commerce, health services, and technology, rather than in the traditional liberal arts and sciences. In addition, government scholarships for study at the tertiary level have increasingly been tied to developmental needs; indeed, even the styling "National Development Scholarships" is indicative of their purpose. Finally, various educational institutions designed to give intensive training in the knowledge and skills demanded by the productive sectors of the economy have mushroomed; an example is the Barbados Institute for Management and Productivity, established to improve managerial and entrepreneurial knowledge and skills.

At all levels of education there has been a move toward local or regional accreditation. In addition, at the tertiary level accreditation procedures are tending to become more flexible, with the traditional written examination being replaced or complemented by practical fieldwork assignments.

An important feature of all tertiary education in Barbados is that there are no age limits. In addition, the organization of the tertiary-level programs permits students to enter at one time and then, at some later time, to reenter and retrain if they so desire. This reentry possibility is particularly true of the community college. Thus, education becomes a lifelong process linked to individual motivation rather than to specific chronological age.

DESMOND C. CLARKE

Bibliography

Bennett, H. J. *Bondsmen and Bishops: Slavery and Apprenticeship on the Codrington Plantations of Barbados 1710–1838.* Berkeley: University of California Press, 1958.

Figueroa, J. J. *Society, Schools and Progress in the West Indies.* Oxford, England: Pergamon Press, 1971.

Gordon, S. C. *Century of West Indian Education: A Source Book.* Essex, England: Longman Group, 1963.

Hoyos, F. A. "Two-Hundred Years: History of the Lodge School." *Barbados Advocate,* 1945.

Irvine, J. C. *Report of the West Indies Committee of the Commission on Higher Education in the Colonies.* London: H. M. Stationery Office, 1945.

Langley, N. *Christopher Codrington and His College.* London: Society for Promoting Christian Knowledge, 1964.

Schomburgk, R. H. *History of Barbados.* Essex, England: Longman Group, 1848.

See also: Caribbean: Regional Analysis.

BARGAINING, FACULTY

See Faculty Unionism: The United States and Great Britain; Legal Status of Faculty Unionization in the United States.

BAVARIAN STATE INSTITUTE OF HIGHER EDUCATIONAL RESEARCH AND PLANNING (Bayerisches Staatsinstitut für Hochschulforschung und Hochschulplanung), Federal Republic of Germany

The Bavarian State Institute of Higher Educational Research and Planning was founded in Munich, Federal Republic of Germany, in January 1973, to support the work of the Bavarian State Ministry of Education in the area of higher education. Directly responsible to the ministry, the institute conducts research in higher education within the framework of a program established annually by the two bodies. Research topics of major concern at the institute include the following: costs and capacity models in higher education, manpower planning, curricula and instruction, student counseling, regionalization in higher education, and reform in higher education. In addition to research activities, the institute conducts seminars and offers a documentation service.

Financed by the ministry, the institute also receives support from research contracting services. The staff includes eleven research professionals, one administrator, two secretaries, and two librarians. Located in the *Zentrum für Bildungsforschung* (Bavarian Center for Educational Research), the institute has a computer terminal and a library containing documents on higher education with particular emphasis on Bavaria.

Most of the results of the institute's work are published in the series *Bayerische Hochschulforschung-Materialien*. Distributed free of charge to a number of government agencies and universities, the publications are in German with summaries in English. The institute's research results are also published by planning bodies in the Federal Republic of Germany and the Organisation of Economic Co-operation and Development. The institute edits an informal journal, *ad acta,* which is distributed to a limited number of subscribers and contains reports of work in progress as well as short articles on university financing, statistics, capacity models, and law.

Arabellastrasse 1
D-8000 Munich 81
Federal Republic of Germany

BAVARIAN STATE LIBRARY
See Libraries: Bavarian State Library, Federal Republic of Germany.

BEHAVIORAL SCIENCES
See Social and Behavioral Sciences (field of study).

BELGIUM, CENTRAL ARCHIVES OF
See Archives: Northern Europe, National Archives of.

BELGIUM, KINGDOM OF

Population: 9,756,600 (1974). Student enrollment in primary school: 987,186; secondary school (academic, vocational, technical): 784,624; higher education (university): 79,477. Student enrollment in higher education as percentage of age group (18–22): 9.4%. Language of instruction: Dutch, French. Academic calendar: October to July. Percentage of gross national product (GNP) expended on all education: 5.07%; on higher education: .72%. [Unless otherwise noted, figures are for 1973–74.]

Until 1965 university education in Belgium was centralized in four towns: Louvain, with the *Université catholique de Louvain* (Catholic University of Louvain), founded in 1425; Ghent, with *Rijksuniversiteit te Gent* (State University of Ghent), founded in 1816; Liège with the *Université de l'état à Liège* (State University of Liège), founded in 1816; and Brussels, with the *Université libre de Bruxelles* (Free University of Brussels), founded in 1834. Until 1830, when French replaced it, Latin was the medium of instruction in the universities. At the end of the nineteenth century, the Dutch-speaking part of the population demanded a Dutch-language university, a demand that was not met until 1930, when programs at the University of Ghent were given completely in Dutch. Subsequently, the universities at Louvain and Brussels also began to organize courses in Dutch.

The four universities maintained an ideological equilibrium until 1965. Neutral state education was provided at Ghent and Liège, Catholic education at Louvain, and liberal education at Brussels. After 1965 this equilibrium was disturbed by the establishment of new university centers and by the division of the universities at Brussels and Louvain into Dutch-language and French-language institutions. These expansion measures were taken not only to accommodate the increasing number of students but also to augment Dutch-language education and promote greater cultural equality between the French- and Dutch-speaking populations.

Alongside the universities, a number of postsecondary schools and institutes, especially in technical education and commercial sciences, have been established over the years. A legislative act of July 7, 1970, elevated these schools and institutes to the level of higher education.

National Educational Policy

Higher educational policy in Belgium is reflected in a series of laws passed since 1960. Prior to that period, a distinction existed between state universities, those operated and financed by the state, and free universities, those independent of the central government and largely financed by private interests. The new laws provided for increased state financial support to the free universities, and, thus, in effect, the state/free distinction became a nominal one. The new laws also promoted the decentralization of the traditional university concentration in four towns by establishing university centers or new sites for university-level study. They increased autonomy in the management of state universities; increased participation in administration of universities by students, researchers, and faculty; and provided for elevation of higher schools and institutes into the higher education sector.

Legal Basis of Educational System

Among the recent significant laws and acts establishing the legal basis of higher education are the law of August 2, 1960, which sanctioned greater state financial support for the free universities; the act of June 8, 1964, which increased opportunities for admission to the universities; the act of April 9, 1965, on the first phase of university expansion, which made possible the creation of university centers and new universities; the act of May 28, 1970,

on the division of the universities at Brussels and Louvain; the act of July 7, 1970, on the general structure of higher education; the act of July 16, 1970, concerning the financing of university buildings; the act of March 24, 1971, which provided for wider participation in the administration of the state universities by faculty and students; the act of April 7, 1971, on the organization of university education at Antwerp; the act of May 28, 1971, on the second phase of university expansion, which included granting increased administrative autonomy to state universities; the act of July 17, 1971, on the conferment of educational grants and loans; and the act of July 27, 1971, on the financing and control of universities.

Types of Institutions

University-level education in Belgium is available at seven universities, at various faculties, at university centers, and at those institutes and schools elevated to higher education level by the act of July 7, 1970. The seven universities are the four founded in the nineteenth century; the Dutch-language universities at Louvain and Brussels; and the State University at Mons, founded in 1965. The faculties include the *Faculté polytechnique de Mons, Faculté universitaire catholique de Mons, Facultés universitaires Notre-Dame de la Paix, Facultés universitaires Saint-Louis, Universitaire faculteiten Sint-Aloysius, Universitaire faculteiten Sint-Ignatius,* and *Faculté des sciences agronomiques de l'etat à Gambloux.* There are three university centers, two in Antwerp and one in Limburg. These centers and the faculties differ from full universities in that they offer only a limited number of disciplines. The institutes and schools elevated to university level include *Institut de médicine tropicale Prince Léopold, Ecole des hautes études commerciales et consulaires, Handelshogeschool, Institut catholique des hautes études commerciales de Bruxelles, Institut supérieur de commerce Saint-Louis,* and *Economische hogeschool Limburg,* among others.

In principle these latter institutions can

offer two- and three-cycle programs requiring three to four years of study and
culminating in a licentiate or higher degrees. Most of them, however, provide only
one- or two-cycle programs.

Nonuniversity-level higher education is
also available at a number of schools and
institutes which offer career-oriented
courses in technical, economic, agricultural, paramedical, social science, and
pedagogical education.

Relationship with Secondary Education

Two types of secondary education—
traditional and "renovated"—are offered
in Belgium. Traditional secondary education comprises general and technical education, each subdivided into two cycles of
three years' duration. The lower cycle is
attended by students twelve to fifteen years
old and the upper cycle by students fifteen
to eighteen. Students may choose from
among several areas of study, including
Latin-Greek, Latin-mathematics, Latin-
sciences, industrial-sciences, and economics.

Based on the principle of comprehensive
education, "renovated" secondary schooling has been developing gradually since
1969 in the French-language part of Belgium and since 1970 in the Dutch-language
part. It is composed of three cycles of two
years each: the observation cycle, the
orientation cycle, and the determination
cycle, in that order; and it distinguishes
between *fundamental* and *complementary*
study options in that the number of subjects taken in common by all students diminishes rapidly throughout the six years.
The "renovated" program has been introduced mainly in the state secondary schools,
although similar programs have been
initiated in the free (Catholic) secondary
programs.

Primary education for children six to
twelve years of age is divided into three
stages of two years' duration. The six-year
program is conducted at independent
schools or is attached to teacher training,
technical, or secondary schools.

Since 1914 education in Belgium has
been compulsory to age fourteen. There is
a movement to extend the minimum age to
fifteen or sixteen, and, in practice, most
pupils remain in school until sixteen.

Admission Requirements

To be admitted to university education,
a student must have an ability certificate
and an approved diploma of completed
upper secondary education. The certificate
is omnivalent; that is, students holding it
are admitted to all fields of study taught at
the universities, except civil engineering
programs, for which a separate entrance
examination is conducted. To obtain the
certificate (instituted in 1964), the student
must pass a maturity examination, taken
either at the secondary school or before a
central examining board. The examination
consists of a written essay in the language
of the appropriate cultural group, a con-
versation on the subject of the essay, and
an oral examination on one main subject or
two subsidiary subjects.

To be admitted to other forms of higher
education, the student needs only the approved diploma of completed general or
technical upper secondary education.

Since 1970 several changes in the conditions of access to higher education, especially university education, have been
announced; but all proposals put forward
have been subject to discussion, and new
regulations are not expected until the late
1970s. The following changes have been
proposed: abolition of the maturity examination, the institution of an entrance examination for all students, the introduction
of a *numerus clausus* (closed-number) system.

Administration and Control

On behalf of the Ministry of National
Education, a government commissioner
supervises the day-to-day working of the
state universities; at the free (independent)
universities this function is fulfilled by a
government representative. State control
is also exercised by an inspector of finance.

Since the 1969–70 academic year, the free universities have acceded to the wish, expressed particularly in 1968, that all sections of the university community should be represented on the governing board of the university. The new administrative structures which have evolved vary among the free institutions. In 1971 the governing boards of the state universities assumed a more democratic form; they are composed of the rector of the university, who acts as president of the board; the vice-rector of the university, who acts as vice-president of the board; ten representatives of the teaching staff; four representatives of the scientific personnel; two representatives of the administrative and technical personnel; four representatives of the students; three representatives of the social sector; three representatives of the economic sector; and three representatives of the public authorities. In addition, in order to implement the administrative, budgetary, and financial management of the university, a new position—administrator of the university—was created.

Through the new form of administration, the state universities also are able to make changes in their internal structure; for example, they may make changes in faculty councils or create new departments and sections. Nevertheless, most of the decisions taken by the governing boards of the state universities must also be submitted for approval to the Ministry of National Education. This requirement does not, however, apply to the free universities.

There are several organizations for interuniversity cooperation and promotion of teaching and research activities. The Conference of Belgian University Rectors provides a forum for interuniversity consultation on questions affecting the institutions, including those pertaining to issues arising from membership in international bodies. When discussions concern not only the universities but also the other institutions classified at the university level, their rectors may join the deliberations.

Programs and Degrees

University education falls into three cycles, each ending with conferral of a degree. The first cycle culminates in the *candidate,* awarded after two years of study, each followed by an examination. The *candidate* in medicine, however, is awarded after three years of study. The next degree (second cycle) is usually the *licentiate,* which also requires two years of study and annual examination. An additional requirement for the *licentiate* is a thesis written under the supervision of a professor. In some branches of study the second cycle takes longer to complete. The degree of *licentiate* in law, in dentistry, and sometimes in psychology and in education takes three years and as many examinations to obtain. Three years are also required for prospective pharmacists, civil engineers, agronomic engineers, chemical engineers, and engineers specializing in agricultural industry; and four years are necessary for prospective doctors of medicine. Concurrent with the *licentiate* the degree of *agrégé* of upper secondary education, which grants qualification to teach, may be obtained after a separate examination.

The third cycle consists of specialization, or work toward a doctoral degree, which may be obtained after submitting, and defending in public, a written thesis. The highest degree, the *agrégé* of higher education, may be obtained after the doctoral degree; it requires submitting and defending a written thesis, as well as delivering a lecture before a university audience.

Degrees awarded by the universities are categorized as either legal or scientific. Legal degrees are granted after a candidate successfully pursues a program in which the curriculum, the length of studies, and the conditions of admission have been set by law; scientific degrees are granted by universities in accordance with their own standards. The academic programs offered by the universities and university-level faculties are in five subject areas: philosophy and letters, law, science, medicine, and applied science; other programs offered include social-political-economic sciences, psychology and education, and agriculture.

Most nonuniversity programs are a single cycle of education, generally lasting two to three years but sometimes extending up to five years in duration and leading to a certificate. The training of nursery and kindergarten teachers, primary school teachers, and lower secondary school teachers takes place at higher pedagogical institutes (normal schools). The program is two years in length. Prospective technical engineers receive their professional training—which takes three or sometimes four years—in higher technical institutes, where they may choose among several specialties. Students preparing for commercial or administrative careers receive their professional training (two to four years of study) in institutes of higher economic education. Higher agricultural education is offered in schools of agriculture. The training program is generally three years in length. Specialties such as nursing, dietetics, ergotherapy, logopedics, and clinical chemistry are taught at institutes of higher paramedical education. The program requires two or three years. The training of social workers and of assistant psychologists takes place at institutes of higher social education in a program lasting three years. Finally, there are institutes of higher artistic education, where, for instance, architects are offered five years of training.

Financing

Capital as well as recurrent expenditures for university education are almost totally financed by the government. Funds for capital expenditures are allocated through the Department for the Financing and Control of University Investments, and state control is exercised over their use. For state institutions this allocation is direct, by way of annual credits; for the free universities the allocation is indirect, by provision of low-interest loans. All allotments are made according to objective and uniform norms, officially established in 1975: a fixed number of square meters are allotted per student at a fixed cost per square meter. A distinction in allotment is made according to the field of study.

Allocations to the universities for recurrent expenditures cover costs for management, teaching, and research. The act of July 27, 1971, provided for a complete equalization of these allocations per student for both the free and the state university establishments; the law also provided that the state exercise the same control over the use of allocations by state and free universities. As an objective norm for the allocations, a contractual cost price is computed per student; the number of students times the cost price determines the allocations. A basic minimum and maximum number of pupils is also taken into consideration in determining funding. This means that for a student number in excess of the maximum figure—to be fixed annually per field of study—the cost price is lowered. For university institutions offering undergraduate and postgraduate programs (all three cycles), the minimum basic figure is five thousand; in institutions offering only one or two cycles of education, the minimum figure depends on the study group and the cycle of studies concerned.

Since 1960 subsidies for student services have been allocated to universities. The subsidies are determined per fraction of one thousand students. For the establishments offering only one or two cycles, this figure has been reduced proportionally.

The only private contribution to meeting the university teaching expenditure is the matriculation fee, which was fixed in 1972 at 5000 Belgian francs per student and per registration; however, this amount is subject to changes in the general economy.

In addition to the above sources of income for the universities, three public foundations administer grants to promote higher educational activities. The University Foundation subsidizes efforts to develop Belgian higher education and culture.

For example, it aids in administering academic prizes, gives scholarships for study abroad, and provides grants for publication of books and reviews. The National Science Research Fund supplies grants for the promotion of scientific research. The Francqui Foundation awards an annual prize of 500,000 francs to a Belgian scholar under fifty years of age for a significant contribution to the growth of knowledge, and, at its discretion, finances undertakings for the advancement of higher education and research.

Student Financial Aid

Grants and loans are awarded by the Ministry of National Education to students of Belgian nationality studying at Belgian higher education establishments. Study grants and loans are allowed to all students of limited means meeting certain requirements: the income of the students in question or of the persons upon whom they depend should not exceed a certain amount; these students must also have succeeded in their examinations during the previous school or academic year or should eventually meet the conditions of admission for certain fields of study.

Study grants do not ordinarily have to be paid back. In contrast, study loans must be reimbursed, although they are granted without any interest requirements. Study loans either supplement study grants or are allotted to students receiving no study grants. If a student who receives a study grant or loan fails to attend lectures and practicals, or fails without good reason to take part in the examinations, the student must immediately return the grant or loan money.

In all Belgian provinces, there are private foundations for the support of students. Under certain conditions, they grant scholarships to students who undertake higher studies. Moreover, a number of private organizations grant scholarships to students who opt for certain specific fields of study. War orphans and children of war invalids and war victims may receive support from the national agency of these private organizations.

Student Social Background and Access to Education

In spite of a number of measures taken by the government, the democratization of university education in Belgium has not yet become a fact. The Omnivalence Act of June 8, 1964, which was designed to increase access to the universities, has not accomplished the result expected, as may be determined by studying the ratio of first-year students to the number of certificates and diplomas awarded for completion of upper secondary education. During the 1963–64 academic year, before the Omnivalence Act came into effect, 9002 first-year students were studying at Belgian universities, while during the 1962–63 school year, 17,795 school-leaving certificates were awarded at the upper secondary level. At the end of the 1973–74 school year, 52,086 students from upper secondary and technical schools received their school-leaving certificates; during the academic year 1974–75, however, only 16,659 first-year students matriculated at the Belgian universities. Although it cannot be assumed that all entering students actually completed their secondary studies during the immediately preceding school year, the above ratio seems to indicate diminishing participation in university education.

Moreover, several studies show that the participation of children of working-class families has barely increased. Students with a working-class background constitute about 10 percent of the total student population, although they constitute a far greater part of the population of the country. In view of the existing system of study grants and study loans, financial problems clearly cannot be regarded as the most important reason for this low attendance rate. Differences in value systems and in aspirations seem to be more important factors. Consequently, the idea that raising the educational level of children of the lower social classes should begin at kindergarten and primary school is gaining support; in other words, the democratization of higher education should begin at the bottom. So far, the democratization of higher education seems to have benefited mainly the middle classes.

The number of women attending Belgian universities tripled during the period 1965–1975: in 1975, 24,279 matriculated, against 8920 in 1965. The ratio of men to women thus was reduced from 3:1 in 1965 to 2:1 in 1975. Although the opportunity of women for graduation from upper secondary school is close to that of men, is still not equal: 47 percent of all students who completed their secondary education during the school year 1973–74 were female.

Teaching Staff

A distinction is made between the scientific personnel and the teaching staff of the universities. The former category is composed of assistants, those with temporary appointments; first-class assistants, those who obtain permanent appointment after receipt of a doctoral degree; *chefs de travaux* (Dutch: *werkleiders*), an academic level reached after ten years of service; and faculty *agrégés* (Dutch: *geaggregeerden*), the highest rank. These personnel assist the professors in the supervision of practical work, in teaching, and in pursuit of scientific research. To the second category belong the associate professors, *chargés de cours* (Dutch: *docenten*), the extraordinary professors, and the ordinary professors. Professors whose main activity lies outside the university exercise the same functions under the same titles on a part-time basis. An ordinary or extraordinary professor who holds a chair may be assisted by an associate *chargé de cours*, who in time can be promoted to the rank of associate professor.

Appointments of scientific personnel and teaching staff at the state universities are made by royal decree, at the recommendation of the university concerned; the free

universities, on the other hand, enjoy complete autonomy in choice of staff in the two categories. The state and free institutions, however, are subject to the same regulations on salary grades; uniformity of grades among the institutions is prescribed by the act of July 27, 1971, on the financing and control of the universities.

Research Activities

The universities in Belgium maintain among themselves over 130 institutes and centers for research in general studies, natural sciences, medicine, technology, economic and social sciences, law, human sciences, and religion. In addition, there are about one hundred research academies, centers, stations, and institutes in the above broad subject categories (including thirty agricultural stations and two interuniversity research organizations for law and history).

Most of the funding for scientific research at the universities is provided by outside organizations, such as the National Foundation of Scientific Research, the Foundation of Collective Fundamental Research, the Foundation of Scientific Medical Research, the Interuniversity Institute of Nuclear Science *(Faculté polytechnique de Mons),* and the Institute for the Promotion of Scientific Industrial and Agricultural Research.

Current Problems and Trends

Since 1960 a number of laws concerned with education in Belgium have underscored attempts at change in the system, but educational innovations in individual institutions have occurred only slowly. The traditional universities especially seem to have difficulty in relinquishing long-standing teaching methods and examination systems. Efforts to make teaching more student-oriented are, however, evident in the new establishments, where student numbers are smaller, members of the academic staff are younger, and possibilities of practice teaching for students are greater.

Other innovations include the new, specialized, university town and campus for the French-language Catholic University of Louvain, which became operational in the early 1970s. Named Louvain-la-Neuve, it is expected to have a population of 50,000 by 1990 and includes a science research park plus business and commercial facilities set in an environmentally designed layout. Another new feature is the cooperation of the two universities at Brussels with the Interuniversity Institute of Nuclear Sciences. They have created an Interuniversity Institute of High Energy Physics for research into the properties and interactions of the elementary particles.

A major problem concerns the large percentage of first-year university students who fail their examinations (50-60 percent at the older universities). Although this figure is somewhat lower in the newly established, smaller universities, public authorities considering the problem from a financial point of view have raised the question of finding an adequate technique for distinguishing between qualified and unqualified students. This question in turn has raised the problem of preselection. However, preselection seems unjustified as long as the teaching process has not reached its optimum degree of perfection. The idea that the present student failure rate is largely caused by deficiencies in teaching is becoming more prevalent. Traditional teaching methods, especially *ex cathedra* lecturing and subjective evaluation techniques, have come to be considered unfit for offering every possible chance to the mass of students. Those interested in new teaching methods are striving for a form of teaching oriented more to the individual student or groups of students with different abilities, as well as for more objective and reliable evaluations which conform to previously defined standards of judgment.

University training of prospective secondary school teachers also constitutes a problem. Pedagogical training, which is offered concurrently with scientific train-ing proper, is often rather neglected and scattered. A definitive solution to this problem would become possible only after a change in the legal provisions for pedagogical training.

Relationship with Industry

Relationships between higher education and industry are established either through personal contacts or through activities of professional and other associations where industrialists and university graduates may meet at regular or irregular intervals. A number of contacts also take place within the framework of facilities specially created for the purpose, such as specialized courses for leading cadre personnel. Such programs are organized mainly at university centers. In addition to the contact in the classroom during these programs, cooperation between higher education and industry is also promoted at the centers through systematic studies, case studies, and projects carried out by the program participants. The Industry-University Foundation promotes and coordinates programs of lectures, seminars, and research, to bring about improvement in the administration of business.

International Cooperation

International cooperation between universities manifests itself particularly through participation in collective research and through the exchange of teaching staff and scientific personnel. This cooperation may occur through the universities themselves or through organizations outside the universities, such as the Council of Europe, the North Atlantic Treaty Organization (NATO), and UNESCO. In addition, Belgium has concluded cultural agreements with thirty-two countries.

KAREL DE CLERCK

Educational Associations

Universitas Belgica
(Association of Belgian University Teachers)
43 rue des Champs-Elysées
B-1050 Brussels

Fédération belge des femmes diplômées des
  universités
(Belgian Federation of University Women)
45 avenue Legrand
B-1050 Brussels

Mouvement des étudiants universitaires belges
  d'expression française
(Movement of French-Speaking Belgian
  Students)
61 rue Belliard
B-1040 Brussels

Vereniging der vlaamse studenten (VVS)
(Association of Flemish Students)
Koopliedenstraat 20
B-1000 Brussels

Bibliography

Albright, A. D. *Management des universités en
  Belgique.* Brussels: Institut administration-
  université, 1970. (Also in Dutch.)
*Classification of Educational Systems in OECD
  Member Countries: Belgium, Denmark, United
  States.* Paris: Organisation for Economic
  Co-operation and Development, 1972.
*Conférence de la renovation de l'enseignement
  supérieur.* Brussels: Ministère de l'éducation
  nationale, 1968. (Also in Dutch.)
Craeybeckx, L. *Universiteit van deze tijd.* Ant-
  werp, Netherlands: De Nederlandsche
  boekhandel, 1969.
Dejean, C., and Binnemans, C. *L'université
  belge. Du pari au défi.* Brussels: Institut de
  sociologie, Université libre de Bruxelles,
  1971.
L'expansion universitaire. (2 vols.) Brussels:
  Conseil national de la politique scientifique,
  1968–1969. (Also in Dutch.)
Janne, H. *Les principes généraux de la planification
  universitaire.* Brussels: Institut de sociologie,
  Université libre de Bruxelles, 1971.
Mallinson, V. "Education in Belgium." *Comparative Education Review,* October 1967,
  11, 275–287.
*Reform and Expansion of Higher Education in
  Europe: National Reports 1962–1967.* Stras-
  bourg, France: Council of Europe, Council
  for Cultural Co-operation, 1965.
Swing, E. S. "Separate but Equal: An Inquiry
  into the Impact of the Language Contro-
  versy on Education in Belgium." *Western
  European Education,* Winter 1973–74, *5,*
  6–33.
Université 1980. Brussels: Fondation industrie-
  université, 1970. (Also in Dutch.)
Vanbergen, P. "Educational Reform—The
  State of the Question." *Western European
  Education,* Fall 1972, *3,* 180–195.
Wieers, J. L. *Universiteit als opgave.* Hasselt:
  Economische hogeschool Limburg, 1971.

See also: Academic Dress and Insignia; Ar-
chives: Northern Europe, National Archives
of; Cooperative Education and Off-Campus
Experience: Cooperative Education World-
wide; Health Services, Worldwide University;
Research: Financing and Control of Research;
Science Policies: Highly Industrialized Nations:
Western Europe; Towns, University.

BELIZE

*Population: 130,000. Student enrollment
in primary school: 32,378; secondary school:
5025; postsecondary education: 297; university (abroad): 180. Language of instruction:
English. [Figures are for 1974.]*

Belize, a British territory with internal
self-government, is located in Central America, on the Caribbean coast, with Mexico to the north and Guatemala to the
southwest.

Education is compulsory between ages
six and fourteen. The system of education
follows the British model. Belize is one of
the territories contributing to the University of the West Indies, whose main campus is located in Mona, Jamaica, with branch
campuses located in Cave Hill, Barbados,
and St. Augustine, Trinidad. The university maintains a resident tutor in Belize.

Among postsecondary institutions in Belize are Belize Technical College, which
awards certificates and diplomas in programs of one to three years; and Belize
Teachers' College, which awards a diploma
after two years of study. All other higher
education takes place abroad.

In addition to the University of the West
Indies, Canada and the United Kingdom
are the principal countries attracting students from Belize.

[Information supplied by Ministry of Education and Housing, Belmopan, Belize.]

See also: Caribbean: Regional Analysis.

BENELUX COUNTRIES, ARCHIVE INSTITUTE OF

See Archives: Northern Europe, National
Archives of.

BENIN, PEOPLE'S REPUBLIC OF

*Population: 2,941,000 (1974 estimate).
Student enrollment in primary school: 186,000;
secondary school (academic, professional, technical, teacher training): 31,553 (1972); university: 1135 (1973). Language of instruction:
French. Academic calendar: October to July,
three semesters. Percentage of national budget
expended on education: 31.2% (1972).*

The People's Republic of Benin (prior
to October 1975 the Republic of Dahomey)
gained independence from France in 1960,
after nearly seventy years of colonial rule.
France had established a fort in Benin in
the seventeenth century; however, accelerated colonialization of the area did not
begin until the middle 1800s, when several
French trading posts were established on
the coast. By 1893 French troops had conquered most of the southern portion of
the country despite the fierce resistance
of the indigenous population. In the middle 1890s the French gained control of the
northern hinterland and in 1898 of the
western part of Borgu. When the French
conquest of Benin was completed in 1899,
the area was incorporated as a colony into
the federation of French West Africa.

Western education in Benin was introduced by missionaries in the middle of
the nineteenth century and was formalized
by the colonial administration in the late
1800s. Before 1899 Benin was administered separately from the rest of French
West Africa, and a fairly extensive school
system was developed there, comparable
to the system developed in Senegal. The
French colonial schools were designed
mainly to prepare supportive personnel—
such as clerks, inspectors, and foremen—to
supplement the insufficient number of
Europeans available for the colonial administration. Because of their relatively well-
developed school systems, Benin and Senegal supplied many of the trained civil
servants for the colonial administration in
other areas of French West Africa.

In 1956 the French passed the *loi
cadre* (enabling law), which granted self-

determination to the African territories.
Four years later, conceding to the demands
of African leaders, France granted independence to the countries in French West
Africa. With independence came the desire
to fill civil service positions with nationals;
thus, Benin civil servants, who were functionaries in other West African countries,
were often expelled and forced to return
to Benin. Many of the returning civil servants could not be absorbed into the limited
employment sector and faced unemployment or underemployment. The excess of
highly qualified personnel contributed to
the political instability of Benin, which has
experienced no less than six bloodless *coups
d'états* since independence.

At independence Benin had more than
550 primary schools—31 percent of which
were operated by missions—and twenty
secondary schools. In 1961, approximately
22 percent of the school-age population
was enrolled in school. Considerable expansion occurred after independence, and
by 1970 Benin had increased to 28.4 percent the school-age population actually
attending school. One out of every three
children between the ages of six and thirteen was attending school in 1970, as opposed to one out of five in 1960.

In 1962 the *Institut d'enseignement supérieur
du Bénin* (Higher Education Institute of
Benin) was established to serve students
from Benin and Togo. With the assistance
of France and Canada, the institute's science
section, which was located in Cotonou, became the nucleus for the University of
Dahomey in 1970, renamed the National
University of Benin on January 30, 1976.

Despite the impressive gains made in
education since independence, a major
portion of the school-age population did
not yet have access to education by the early
1970s. The nation's educational system was
a reflection of the system of education in
France and had little applicability to the
realities of Benin. Thus, in 1973 the *Commission nationale de la réforme de l'enseignement
et de l'éducation* (National Commission for
the Reform of Teaching and Education)

was formed under the auspices of the Ministry of National Education, Culture, Youth and Sports. The commission recommended a new system of education designed to meet the development needs of Benin. In 1974 Dahomey formally adopted Marxism-Leninism as official policy (*Africa Contemporary Record*, 1975, p. B624). Under the leadership of Lieutenant Colonel Mathieu Kerekou, the National Revolutionary Council began implementing a new educational system during the 1974–75 academic year, and implementation is expected to continue gradually throughout the 1970s in accordance with financial means.

National Educational Policy

According to the findings of the 1973 reform commission, the educational system of Benin had changed little since independence and thus did not reflect the needs of Benin but rather those of a colonized country. As a result, the commission determined that the entire system—its structures, programs, teaching methods, and financing—should be revised. The system should be free from foreign domination and the cultural alienation of students, created by focusing on French culture and values rather than on indigenous culture. Thus, it will enable citizens to become aware of the problems in Benin and to participate in its economic and social development. Above all, the new system should eliminate the elitism which characterized the French system and replace it with free, public, and secular education, designed to serve all the people.

Legal Basis of Educational System

In January 1976 several ordinances were passed by the central committee of the People's Revolutionary Party of Benin concerning the restructuring of the government. Among the offices created by Ordinance 1.075 were those of the *Ministère de l'enseignement du premier degré* (Ministry of Education of the First Level) and the *Ministère des enseignements technique et su-*

périeur (Ministry of Technical and Higher Education.) Under the same ordinance, the University of Dahomey, established by Presidential Decree 70.217/CP in August 1970, became the National University of Benin.

Types of Institutions

University education is provided by the National University of Benin. The university is divided into a school of education and departments of scientific and technical studies, medical and paramedical studies, literary and linguistic studies, economics and law, and agricultural and agrotechnical studies.

In addition to the training facilities at the university's school of education, teachers for the nation's schools are trained in several postsecondary teacher training institutes. Students with the certificate *brevet d'études du premier cycle*, who pass an entrance examination, may enroll in a teacher training school, where they first earn a *baccalauréat* and then a *certificat d'études pédagogiques*.

Adult education is a major concern of the revolutionary government of Benin, and plans call for the establishment of a *Centre populaire d'éducation, de perfectionnement et d'initiation à la production* (CPEPIP: People's Center for Education, Further Training, and Introduction to Practical Work) to oversee all adult activities, including literacy training, correspondence, further training, and practical training courses. Of primary importance to the government is an increase in the educational opportunities for some 90 percent of the population, who live in rural areas and are engaged in agricultural production—the mainstay of the national economy. With financial assistance from the United Nations Development Programme (UNDP) and technical assistance from the Food and Agriculture Organization (FAO) of the United Nations, the government has operated a program of agricultural education by radio. Since 1968 various topics concerning agricultural development, general health, and community development are prepared in French, translated into the country's ten principal spoken languages, and then broadcast each week in half-hour segments throughout the country.

Relationship with Secondary Education

Until the proposed reform of the educational system can be implemented, the schools of Benin will continue to resemble those in France. Primary education, which extends six years, is free and technically compulsory. Upon completion of the primary school program, successful students receive the *certificat d'études primaires élémentaires*. Secondary education is divided into two cycles of general or technical and vocational studies, which lead to either higher education or employment. The first cycle ends after four years with the award of the *brevet d'études du premier cycle*. Upon completion of the second cycle, students in the programs leading to higher education sit for the *baccalauréat*, a prerequisite for university admission. General secondary education is provided in *lycées* and *collèges d'enseignement général*. Technical and vocational secondary education is offered at technical *lycées*, apprenticeship centers, and a school of domestic science *(école ménagère)* for women.

Under the proposed reform the educational system will include education at two levels, *premier degré* and *second degré*. The first level will include a two-year nursery school *(enseignement maternel)*, a five-year basic school *(enseignement de base)*, and either a comprehensive polytechnic school *(complexe polytechnique)*, consisting of two three-year cycles, or a middle school *(enseignement moyen)* of two three-year cycles. The second level is higher education.

Parallel to the formal educational system will be the adult education program coordinated by the CPEPIP. Under the new system examinations will be deemphasized or eliminated and replaced by a continuing evaluation of the student's progress. Existing diplomas are expected to be replaced with aptitude certificates, which indicate that the student has mastered a specific area of study.

Admission Requirements

The general requirement for admission to the university is the *baccalauréat* or an equivalent diploma, although students may be admitted to the university on the basis of a special entrance examination. Certain faculties may have additional requirements, such as mathematical proficiency in the faculty of science.

Under the new system, students who have completed the second cycle of the middle school or the comprehensive polytechnic school, or employed persons who have received training through the CPEPIP may be admitted to one of the specialized institutes of the university, based on the decision of a guidance council *(conseil d'orientation)*.

Administration and Control

The National University of Benin operates under the auspices of the Ministry of Technical and Higher Education. The university's rector and administrative staff are appointed by the minister of technical and higher education. The rector is the chief administrative officer at the university. He is assisted by a director general and a secretary general. Academic affairs are the responsibility of the director general; the secretary general oversees administrative detail. The university is divided into one school and five departments, each headed by a director.

Programs and Degrees

The school and the departments at the University of Benin have a unified degree structure that follows the French model. The program of study is divided into three cycles, each lasting two years. The first cycle leads to the *diplôme universitaire d'études littéraires* (DUEL) in humanities or the *diplôme universitaire d'études scientifiques* (DUES) in sciences or agronomy. One year of study in the second cycle leads to the first degree, the *licence,* in humanities, sciences, or law. The second year leads to the award of the *maîtrise* in the humanities or sciences. In education a teacher certification, *certificat d'aptitude au professorat de l'enseignement secondaire* (CAPES), is awarded after a one-year program of professional training to students with a *licence.* In agronomy, the second cycle is completed upon receipt of a *diplôme d'agronomie générale.* Medical study lasts three years in the second cycle and, depending upon specialization, leads to the *diplôme de docteur en médecine* (diploma of medical doctor), *diplôme de technicien supérieur de la santé* (diploma of higher health technician), or *diplôme de specialité en médecine.* In the third cycle, a higher qualification is available in agronomy, the *diplôme d'ingénieur agronome* (diploma of agricultural engineer).

As envisioned in the proposed reform, the programs offered at the university will become more closely adapted to national development needs. Students will immediately begin training in a specialty upon entering the university and will concentrate on the course work and research activities of one department. There is to be a close liaison between theory and practice in the degree programs, so that students will participate in practical work while studying. Each degree program is expected to include 70 percent theoretical and practical work, 20 percent political training and civil education, and 10 percent military preparation, physical education, and sports.

Financing

The National University of Benin is financed mainly by the government with French assistance. Since 1960 the nation's educational budget has steadily increased. In 1960, 21.7 percent of the total national budget was allotted to education, as compared to 31.2 percent in 1972.

The contribution of France to the university in 1972 totaled 538,000,000 CFA francs: 70,000,000 francs for operating costs, 5,000,000 francs for library materials, 61,000,000 for stipends and travel expenses for personnel, 155,000,000 for salaries of technical assistants and nationals, and 247,000,000 for university construction *(Rapport de la Commission,* 1973*).*

The university also raises funds through tuition and examination fees and has been a recipient of assistance from international organizations such as the World Health Organization. As part of the reform of education, the government of Benin plans to assume greater control over the distribution of external aid.

Student Financial Aid

The government of Benin provides scholarships for higher studies at home and abroad for those in financial need. In 1972 the government awarded scholarships to three hundred of six hundred students who applied.

Scholarships are also provided to students from Benin by the governments of France and Belgium. For instance, in 1973–74, 1218 students from Benin attended higher education institutions in France, and Belgium provided a number of one-year scholarships for study at Belgian institutions.

Student Social Background and Access to Education

Benin inherited an elitist educational system from France. As proposed by the National Commission for the Reform of Teaching and Education, the new system of education will eliminate this elitism and substitute education for the masses. The new system is designed to eliminate the geographical and social barriers that have limited access to education. School fees are to be eliminated, and equal opportunities are to be extended to the female population, which has so far been underrepresented in the educational system. To ensure easier promotion through the educational system, existing examinations and diplomas are to be reevaluated and either replaced or eliminated.

The planned People's Center for Education, Further Training and Introduction to Practical Work for the first time will give equal access to students who were excluded from the educational system that existed prior to 1973, to students who left the system, and to students enrolled in the formal system of education.

Teaching Staff and Research Activities

In 1974 the university teaching staff numbered 139, including 91 full-time and 48 part-time members. Teachers are civil servants. France contributes a large number of the teaching staff. One of the goals of the government is to replace the remaining expatriate teachers with nationals.

According to the proposed reform of education, research activities will center in the university and will be carried out under the auspices of the *Commission nationale de la recherche* (National Research Commission), a specialized commission of the *Conseil national de l'éducation, de l'enseignement de la formation permanente et de la recherche* (National Council of Education, Recurrent Education, and Research). Although the university will serve as the center of research activities, specialized research units will also operate throughout the country. Emphasis will be placed on national and African research studies, and plans call for an in-depth study of traditional medicine and pharmacy.

Since independence most research in Benin has been carried out with assistance from international organizations, which have provided both the funds and the staff. The major portion of the external funds has supplied the salaries of the foreign staff. Thus, in 1972 the total expenditure for research in Benin included 55 percent for salaries for foreign personnel, 25 percent for personnel from Benin, and 20 percent for actual operating costs. Under the reform, the government of Benin plans to exercise greater control over external aid designated for research, in an effort to ensure that the research undertaken will contribute to national development and will involve a majority of local staff.

Current Problems and Trends

As a result of limited financial resources, implementation of the proposed reform of education will be gradual. By 1975 the government had taken several steps to implement the educational reform program. Subsidies to private schools were abolished; primary schools operated by the Roman Catholic church were nationalized; and a twelve-month national civil service was made mandatory for all students completing their studies on the secondary or higher levels.

The national civil service, which involves military and ideological training, is a prerequisite to employment.

International Cooperation

Benin has been the recipient of substantial foreign educational assistance, especially from France and agencies of the United Nations. More than a thousand students from Benin study in France, most of them on French government scholarships.

The National University of Benin is a member of the International Association of Universities, the Association of African Universities, and the *Association des universités partiellement ou entièrement de langue française* (Association of Partially or Wholly French-Language Universities).

Bibliography

Africa Contemporary Record: Annual Survey and Documents, 1974–75. London: Rex Collings, 1975.

Annuaire statistique du Dahomey. Cotonou: Institut national de la statistique et de l'analyse économique, 1973.

Bulletin hebdomadaire d'information et de documentation. Cotonou: Chambre de commerce et d'industrie de la République populaire de Bénin, January 30, 1976, and February 13, 1976.

Discours programme. Cotonou: Gouvernement militaire révolutionnaire, November 30, 1972.

Rapport de la commission nationale de la réforme de l'enseignement et de l'éducation au Dahomey. Porto-Novo: Ministère de l'éducation nationale, de la culture, de la jeunesse et des sports, 1973.

See also: Africa, Sub-Saharan: Regional Analysis; Archives: Africa and Asia, National Archives.

BERDAHL REPORT
See University Government in Canada (Higher Education Report).

BERMUDA, COLONY OF

Population: 53,000. Student enrollment in primary and secondary schools: 13,000; higher education: 520 full time, 1500 part time. Language of instruction: English. Academic calendar: September to June, three terms. Expenditure on higher education as percentage of educational budget: 2.17%. [Figures are for 1974.]

Since the islands of Bermuda occupy only 22 square miles and include a population of only 53,000, the government has been reluctant to establish any formal higher education. The policy has been to provide generous scholarships and loans to enable students to go abroad to study in the United Kingdom. In 1972, however, the government, although aware that the establishment of a university or any form of degree-granting institution on the islands would not necessarily be in Bermuda's best interest, decided to establish a postsecondary facility that would be similar to a North American junior college. The three educational institutions that had provided some form of further education—an academic sixth form, a hotel school, and a technical institute—were combined under one central administrative unit into Bermuda College, the only institution of higher education in Bermuda. After a one-year trial period the concept of a Bermuda College was accepted by the minister of education, and in July 1974 the Bermuda College Act was formally passed by the Bermuda legislature.

Legal Basis of Educational System

The legal authority for the conduct of higher education in Bermuda is specifically set out in the Bermuda College Act. Previously the general authority had rested in the Education Act of 1954. The new act clearly spells out provisions for full- and part-time education of persons over the age of sixteen.

Types of Institutions

Bermuda College, which is basically a junior or community college, provides education in three areas: (1) preuniversity work, which is undertaken through the department of academic studies, essentially a sixth form or grade 13; (2) hotel and catering, studied in the department of hotel technology, which trains students to go into hotel and catering industries; and (3) commerce and technology, undertaken in the department of commerce and technology, which trains the student for entry into business.

Relationship with Secondary Education

The compulsory school age in Bermuda, as set by the Education Act of 1954, is from five to sixteen. A close relationship exists between Bermuda College and the nine government and four private secondary schools (two of which are denominational). These schools are modeled on the pattern of education in the United Kingdom, and students take the external examinations for the British General Certificate of Education (at the ordinary level) and similar examinations. In 1974 the Ministry of Education introduced into the first year of secondary schooling a course of studies which leads to the development of Bermuda's own formal secondary school certificate. By 1979 the first students will graduate with the uniform Bermuda Secondary School Certificate.

Secondary school students complete their education with either an academic emphasis, which generally leads to postsecondary education, or a technical commercial emphasis, which prepares a student to go directly into the business world or into further studies overseas.

Admission Requirements

Admission requirements vary slightly, but in every instance the applicant must have the equivalent of five years of secondary school, which is the equivalent of twelve years of education. By 1980, following the successful introduction of the Bermuda

Secondary School Certificate, all students who wish to enter the college will need to have a full certificate.

Administration and Control

The administration and control of Bermuda College rest with the board of governors, who, according to the act of incorporation, shall be responsible for the general management and control of the college. The board is appointed directly by the minister of education and consists of a chairman, a deputy chairman, and not more than seven other persons appointed by the minister. Each member of the board holds office for such time as may be specified in his appointment, but which does not generally exceed one year. The permanent secretary of education is, in addition, an ex officio member of the board and is responsible for giving the views of the minister on policy and planning.

The board of governors has "the custody, control and disposition of all property, fees, and investments of the college." It is responsible for making all appointments of instructional staff and other employees and may conduct examinations; award diplomas, certificates and other academic distinctions; and "award and administer bursaries and scholarships, whether tenable at the college or elsewhere." The board is subject to limited control by the minister of education, who must be consulted and whose approval must be given whenever the board wishes to make any changes within the administrative structure of the college. Thus, for example, the minister is consulted on the creation of new departments; the setting of fees; and any plans, agreements, and arrangements that might be made with other institutions of further education "for the provision of instruction on the granting of degrees, diplomas, certificates and other academic distinctions."

The college is administered by a central administrative office under a senior officer called the chief executive officer.

Because of the recent incorporation, there are as yet no faculty or student councils and no formal input by faculty and students into the policymaking machinery. Nonetheless, faculty opinion is channeled through the central office directly to the board of governors.

Programs and Degrees

The academic programs offered at Bermuda College are (1) a two-year course in the department of academic sciences, leading to the advanced level; (2) a two-year certificate course in the department of commerce and technology, which in addition to internally determined standards uses external examinations such as the City and Guilds of London examinations; and (3) one- and two-year courses (plus a three-year course in administration) in the department of hotel technology, which follow a program internally set but which may also include such external examinations as the City and Guilds of London and the United States American Hotel and Motel Association examinations. Graduates are awarded a Diploma of Bermuda College in commerce, hotel technology, or academic studies.

Individuals who wish to study for a degree may avail themselves of the off-campus courses provided by Queen's University of Ontario, Canada, which offers summer courses in Bermuda; they may also attend classes organized by the University of Maryland in the United States and offered at the local United States base.

Financing and Student Financial Aid

The financing of higher education is provided entirely through government aid. In 1974–75 the government spent 2.17 percent of its total educational budget on higher education. The tuition fee for full-time study at Bermuda College is nominal.

No financial assistance is given students studying at Bermuda College, because the tuition fees are exceedingly low. However, the government provided B$428,000 for study abroad in 1974: B$100,000 for interest-free loans and B$328,000 in scholarships.

The students studying at the Bermuda

College represent a cross section of the population.

Teaching Staff

All staff are classified as tutors and are paid according to experience and teaching qualifications. Selection and appointment of staff are done through a procedure involving the board of governors, its technical officers, and an officer of the Ministry of Education. Salary is set in accordance with academic qualifications and the budgetary guidelines provided by the government in its agreement with the Amalgamated Bermuda Union of Teachers, which represents the teaching staff. There is no tenure at the college.

Research Activities

No research is carried out at the college because of the limitations of size and budget. The major research organization on the island is the Bermuda Biological Station, which is independent but has close links to the college.

Current Problems and Trends

The main problem facing the board of governors is to provide space for increasing enrollments. Future plans call for the development of a unified campus; at present the three buildings are geographically separated. This plan can be seen as a clear commitment of the government to formalized higher education on the islands.

The new department of hotel technology with a small training hotel will be a unique facility; it is expected to become one of the major institutions of its type in the Western Hemisphere.

Relationship with Industry

For each of the three departments within the college, there is an advisory committee made up of individuals from the business community who offer their expertise toward a relevant and up-to-date curriculum. Industry also participates through the provision of some scholarships, especially in the department of hotel technology.

DAVID J. SAUL

Bibliography

National Association for Foreign Student Affairs. *The Admission and Academic Placement of Students from the Caribbean.* San Juan, Puerto Rico: North South Center, 1973.

Parker, P. "Change and Challenge in Caribbean Higher Education." Unpublished doctoral dissertation, Florida State University, Tallahassee, 1971.

Williams, E. *From Columbus to Castro: The History of the Caribbean 1492–1969.* London: André Deutsch, 1970.

BHUTAN, KINGDOM OF

Population: 1,145,000 (1974 estimate). Students enrolled in primary and secondary school: approximately 16,000; higher education (abroad): 500 (1974).

The Kingdom of Bhutan—a landlocked country in the Himalayas, bounded by Tibet in the north and India in the south—offers eleven years of free education in some 105 government-maintained primary and middle schools and in four secondary schools. One teacher training institution is available. There is presently no provision for higher education in the country. Some 500 students attend higher education institutions in India on scholarships sponsored by their government or the Indian government.

See also: South Asia: Regional Analysis.

BIBLIOTHÈQUE DE L'ARSENAL
See Libraries: National Library of France (Bibliothèque nationale), France.

BIBLIOTHÈQUE NATIONALE
See Libraries: National Library of France (Bibliothèque nationale), France.

BIOENGINEERING
(Field of Study)

Bioengineering is the application of engineering technology and methodology to problems in biology and medicine. Activity in the field of bioengineering includes (1) the uncovering of new knowledge in areas of biological science and medical practice by engineering methods (for example, the application of communication engineering to studies of the electrical communication between nerve cells); (2) the study and solution of medical and biological problems through engineering analysis techniques (for example, the application of modeling, computer simulation, control theory, and irreversible thermodynamics to the study of bodily processes); (3) the design and development of patient-related instrumentation, prostheses, biocompatible materials, and diagnostic and therapeutic devices (for example, an artificial heart prosthesis must solve the following problems: development of tissue-compatible materials, design of an implantable power source, design of systems for removing waste heat, design of transducers to monitor the heart's performance, development of electronic control circuitry, bench and field testing of the device in animals, and ultimate application to patients); and (4) the analysis, design, and implementation of improved health care delivery systems and apparatus to improve patient care and reduce health care costs (for example, the clinical engineer writes procurement specifications in consultation with medical and hospital staff, inspects equipment for safe operation and conformity with specifications, trains medical personnel in proper use of equipment, tests a hospital for electrical safety, and adapts instruments to specific applications). Normally the field of bioengineering is considered to cover the whole spectrum of engineering applications in biology and medicine; biomedical engineering is a smaller subset concerned with the area of medical and clinical problems.

The diverse nature of bioengineering is illustrated by some typical examples: artificial internal organs (application of transport and membrane phenomena and compatibility of materials); bioinstrumentation (telemetry and the design and development of transducers, signal processors, and recording or display devices for detecting a physiological event); biological signal analysis (analysis of bioelectrical phenomena, such as EKGs and EEGs, and other biomedical data by means of communication engineering and optical techniques; pattern recognition systems); biological systems and models (development of basic mathematical relationships for living systems; computer simulation); biomaterials (properties and compatibility of implant materials used in orthopedics, dental and other internal body systems; cosmesis; and clinical materials, such as surgical sutures, adhesives, and drainage tubes); biomechanics (mechanical properties and functions of living tissue in physiology, surgery, and trauma); biomedical applications of computers (patient monitoring and information systems, computer-aided instruction, simulation, feedback control of patient management, and biomedical statistics); bionics (study of living systems in search for useful models and concepts for engineering and communications applications); and radiation physics (diagnostic and therapeutic applications of ionizing radiation, radioisotopes, nonionizing electromagnetic radiation, and ultrasound).

A number of other fields also are concerned with the interactions of technology and living systems and therefore are directly related to bioengineering: (1) agricultural engineering, the applications of engineering techniques and principles to the area of living systems involving plants and animals; (2) biochemical engineering, concerned with fermentation processes, drug production, and the use of bacteria to consume spilled crude oil; (3) biophysics, the study of the basic physics of biological processes; and (4) environmental health and safety engineering, concerned with public health and safety in particular environments (air, water, and soil pollution) and the problems of occupational and radiation health, sewage disposal, and sanitary systems; (5) genetic engineering, dealing with technology for synthesizing hereditary transmission and organismal characteristics; and (6) human factor engineering, concerned with the anatomical, physiological, and psychological response and limitations of the human operator in the performance of various tasks.

The history of bioengineering can be traced back to the earliest beginnings of medicine, when the physician often was also an engineer. In 1791 Luigi Galvani demonstrated the contraction of muscles by connecting the nerve and muscle of a frog to a couple of dissimilar metals. One year later Alessandro Volta, trying to refute Galvani's theory of animal electricity, showed that a continuous current could originate from dissimilar metals placed in an electrolyte. The work of these two individuals, who were physicists as well as physicians, led to the discovery by Volta in 1800 of the voltaic or galvanic cell, the first device to produce a steady electric current flow. As time progressed, individuals tended to work mainly in either the life sciences or the physical sciences. Many medical discoveries were the result of improvements in the technology and instrumentation of the physical sciences. For example, Wilhelm Röntgen's discovery of X rays from a Crookes tube in 1895 opened up the field of radiology. X rays were used medically for the first time in Boston in 1896 and in 1897 during the Greco-Turkish War. In numerous other instances as well, engineering and technology have significantly advanced the state of medicine.

Formal education in bioengineering began in the 1950s, when a few schools offered graduate programs. In 1975, approximately 120 schools in the United States offered bioengineering degrees or programs. Some of these schools have full-fledged bioengineering departments offering the Bachelor of Science, Master of Science, and Doctor of Philosophy degrees; some offer bioengineering option programs through one of the classical engineering departments, such as electrical engineering. Approximately 4000 students were enrolled in these programs in 1975, and over 3000 have graduated since 1965. Many schools admit students with backgrounds in engineering, physical sciences, mathematics, and life sciences. The curriculum normally includes courses in engineering (electronics, mechanics, computer science, thermodynamics, fluid dynamics, physics) and in life sciences (anatomy, biochemistry, physiology). In addition, certain specialized courses (for instance, biomechanics and biological signal analysis) combine engineering with specific areas in life science. Thesis projects involving the application of engineering techniques or principles to the solution of problems in biology or medicine are normally required for the degree programs.

Because the general level of health of the population is a prime consideration for any country, the field of bioengineering is international in scope. Technological innovations in the medical field eventually permeate to all corners of the earth, but the rate of this transfer depends on the state of national development and the affluence of the individual country. A number of international organizations—among them the International Federation for Medical and Biological Engineering, the International Institute for Medical Electronics and Biological Engineering, and the International Organization for Medical Physics—focus primarily on bioengineering. These organizations disseminate knowledge in the field of bioengineering through scientific papers presented and discussed at international congresses. Bioengineering technology transfer between countries has been enhanced through a series of six international biomedical engineering workshops held in Yugoslavia during 1972–73. These workshops brought together individuals of diverse national and geographical backgrounds to examine methods and technology that could be used to solve current medical problems. The Alliance for Engineering in Medicine and Biology, an affiliation of eighteen United States medical and engineering societies, is sponsoring a technology transfer project with Egypt in the area of diagnostic ultrasound.

The bioengineering needs of developing countries are different from the needs of industrialized countries. Specifically, developing countries mainly need engineers trained at the Bachelor of Science level to do hospital work involving the calibration, maintenance, and repair of equipment; in industrialized countries a relatively higher proportion of bioengineering activity takes place in research areas requiring advanced postgraduate training. The emphasis is shifting in the developed countries, however, toward training more engineers to work directly in hospitals and the health care delivery system.

In general, most bioengineering training programs around the world are offered at the graduate level, with formal bioengineering degree programs or with bioengineering options in electrical, mechanical, chemical, or civil engineering degree programs. In the United States, however, undergraduate bioengineering programs have recently been introduced. In 1975 twenty-five universities offered formal bachelor's degree programs; at the graduate level there were thirty-seven master's degree and thirty-eight Ph.D. degree programs. Also in 1975 sixteen Canadian universities offered graduate-level degrees (M.S. and Ph.D.) through formal bioengineering programs or options in other departments. Though the United Kingdom (like Canada) had no undergraduate bioengineering programs, it had thirteen graduate degree programs in bioengineering. Each school in the United Kingdom has its own specialty, such as biomechanics or medical physics. Three of the five technical engineering colleges of the German-speaking countries (the Federal Republic of Germany, Austria, and Switzerland) offered a diploma program with a specialization in biomedical engineering; the other two colleges offered technical electives in biomedical engineering. The ten universities of these countries offered no formal curriculum leading to a bioengineering degree but, instead, offered students in physical and natural sciences and engineering the opportunity to pursue Ph.D. thesis topics in the area of biomedical engineering. In some cases electives were also offered to engineering students in electrical, mechan-

ical, and chemical engineering. Most other European countries had a limited number of formal bioengineering degree postgraduate programs in 1975 and made use of an option through a classical engineering department.

The Middle Eastern countries are just beginning to develop bioengineering programs. Egypt has announced a new undergraduate bioengineering program, and Israel has had graduate students enrolled in the area of bioengineering for a number of years. The Soviet Union and Eastern European countries have had formal graduate training since the early 1950s.

Few Asian countries have formal bioengineering curricula. In countries outside of the United States and Canada, most bioengineers receive on-the-job training. Little information is available concerning the formal bioengineering training programs in Latin America or Africa.

Levels and Programs of Study

Programs in bioengineering generally require as a prerequisite a secondary education, usually with emphasis on science subjects, and lead to the following awards: certificate or diploma, Bachelor of Science or Engineering, Master of Science or Engineering, the doctorate, or their equivalents. Programs deal with the principles and practices of bioengineering and consist of classroom and laboratory instruction and, on advanced levels, study, seminar or group discussion, research projects, and hospital internship programs. The field of activity associated with bioengineering includes basic and applied research in the biomedical sciences by the application of engineering methods; the design and development of instrumentation, biocompatible materials, prosthetic, and diagnostic and therapeutic devices; and the design and implementation of improved health care delivery systems.

Programs that lead to a certification not equivalent to a first university degree deal with the principles and practices of biomedical electronics technology.

These programs are concerned with maintenance, calibration, procurement, repair, and safety of hospital instrumentation and equipment. Principal course content usually includes some of the following: physics, chemistry, mathematics, applied mechanics, computer programing, electrical measurements, circuit analysis, electronics, electrical machines, medical instrumentation, human physiology, medical terminology, and hospital operations.

Programs that lead to a first university degree deal with the principles and practices of bioengineering. Principal course content usually includes electric and electronic circuits, control systems, signal analysis, mass and heat transfer, material science, computer technology, continuum and fluid mechanics, thermodynamics, anatomy and physiology, biochemistry, physical chemistry, biological systems, bioinstrumentation, medical and clinical engineering, biomechanics, and biomaterials. Usual background courses include mathematics, physics, chemistry, and biology.

On the graduate level students concentrate on a specialized area of bioengineering (for example, bioinstrumentation, biomaterials, biomechanics, or clinical engineering). Advanced course work in the engineering related field is normally taken along with basic and advanced courses in the biological and medical sciences (for example, physiology, neurophysiology, pathology, pharmacology, and psychology). Emphasis is placed on project and research work as substantiated by the presentation of a scholarly thesis or dissertation. In some cases internship experience may be preliminary or concurrent with the thesis.

ROBERT A. PEURA

Major International and National Organizations

INTERNATIONAL

International Federation for Medical and
  Biological Engineering (IFMBE)
Institute of Medical Physics
45 Da Costakade
Utrecht, Netherlands

International Institute for Medical Electronics
  and Biological Engineering
47 boulevard de l'Hôpital
Paris 13, France

International Organization for Medical
  Physics (IOMP)
Department of Radiology
University Hospitals
Madison, Wisconsin 53706 USA

NATIONAL

Federal Republic of Germany:
  Deutsche Gesellschaft für
    biomedizinische Technik e.V.
  Markgrafenstrasse 11
  1000 Berlin 61

France:
  Association nationale française
    d'électronique médicale et biologique
  Paris

Japan:
  Japanese Society of Medical Electronics
    and Biomedical Engineering
  Kikai-Shinko Building, 3-5-8 Shiba Park
  Minato-ku, Tokyo

United States:
  Alliance for Engineering in Medicine
    and Biology
  4405 East West Highway
  Bethesda, Maryland 20014

  Association for the Advancement of
    Medical Instrumentation
  1901 North Fort Meyer Drive
  Arlington, Virginia 22209

  Biomedical Engineering Society
  P.O. Box 2399
  Culver City, California 90230

  Institute of Electrical and Electronic
    Engineers (IEEE)
  345 East 47th Street
  New York, New York 10017

For a more complete listing of national organizations see:

World Guide to Scientific Associations. New York: Bowker, 1974.

Principal Information Sources

GENERAL

Guides to the literature in the field include:

Allen, R. *An Annotated Bibliography of Biomedical Computer Applications.* Bethesda, Maryland: National Library of Medicine, 1969.
Cobbold, R. S. C. *A Selective Bibliography and Guide to the Literature in Bioengineering.* Win-

nipeg, Manitoba: Canadian Biological and Medical Engineering Society, 1971.

Force, R. *Guide to Literature on Biomedical Engineering*. Washington, D.C.: American Society for Engineering Education, 1972.

Kerker, A. E., and Murphy, H. T. *Biological and Biomedical Resource Literature*. Lafayette, Indiana: Purdue University, Engineering Experimental Station, 1968. Includes a bibliographical section of bioengineering, medical electronics, and cybernetics.

Kettlewell, P. J. "Biomedical Engineering—An Annotated Guide to Sources of Information." *Biomedical Engineering*, May 1974, *9*(5), 209–213; June 1974, *9*(6), 252–255.

Introductions to the field include:

Brown, J. H. U., and others. *Biomedical Engineering*. Philadelphia: F. A. Davis, 1970.

Engineering and Medicine. Washington, D.C.: National Academy of Engineering, 1970. A symposium discussing the relationship between engineering and technology and medicine, with a discussion of biomedical engineering and the role of the university.

Kenedi, R. M. (Ed.) *Perspectives in Biomedical Engineering*. (3 vols.) New York: Academic Press, 1973.

Rutstein, D. D., and Eden, M. *Engineering and Living Systems: Interfaces and Opportunities*. Cambridge, Massachusetts: MIT Press, 1970.

Wolff, H. S. *Biomedical Engineering*. New York: McGraw-Hill, 1970. Includes bibliographies; a good introductory work.

For a discussion of bio and biomedical engineering education see:

Britannica Review of Developments in Engineering Education. Chicago: Encyclopaedia Britannica, 1970. See chapter on "Bioengineering," by R. D. Nevins, pp. 251–272.

IEEE Transactions on Biomedical Engineering. March 1975, *22* (2), entire issue. A collection of thirteen papers on biomedical engineering education and employment.

Murphy, T. W. *Education in Bioengineering*. Santa Monica, California: Rand, 1965. A brief discussion of educational requirements in the development of bioengineering programs.

Prototype University Plans for the Development of Biomedical Engineering. Washington, D.C.: National Academy of Engineering, Committee on the Interplay of Engineering with Biology and Medicine, 1969.

CURRENT BIBLIOGRAPHIES

Current abstracting and indexing services contain useful information in the field:

Bioengineering Abstracts. New York: Engineering Index, Inc., 1974–.

Biomedical Engineering. London: Key Papers (formerly Abstracts Section), 1966–.

Biophysics, Bioengineering and Medical Instrumentation (formerly *Medical Instrumentation*). Section 27 of *Excerpta Medica: The International Abstracting Service*. Amsterdam: Excerpta Medica Foundation, 1967–.

Bulletin signalétique 310: Génie biomédical; Informatique médicale. Paris: Centre national de la recherche scientifique, 1972–.

Computers in Medicine Abstracts. New York: Council for Interdisciplinary Communication in Medicine, 1968–.

Engineering Index. New York: Engineering Index, Inc., 1884–. Includes sources on bioengineering.

Index Medicus. Washington, D. C.: United States National Library of Medicine, New Series, 1960–. Extensive coverage of fields of medicine; international in scope.

Medical Electronics and Communication Abstracts. Brentwood, Essex, England: Multi-Science Publishing Company, 1966–.

For progress reports covering recent developments in the field see:

Advances in Bioengineering and Instrumentation. New York: Plenum Press, 1966–.

Advances in Biomedical Engineering. New York: Academic Press, 1971–.

PERIODICALS

Annals of Biomedical Engineering (US), *Biomaterials, Medical Devices and Artificial Organs* (US), *Biomedical Engineering* (UK), *Biomedical Engineering* (US; English translation of USSR publication *Meditsinskaya tekhnika*), *Biomedical News* (US), *Biomédicine* (France), *Biomedizinische Technik/Biomedical Engineering* (FRG), *Biophysics* (US; English translation of USSR publication *Biofizika*), *Biotechnology and Bioengineering* (US), *Computers in Biology and Medicine* (US), *Computers and Biomedical Research* (US), *CRC Critical Reviews in Bioengineering* (US), *Electronique médicale* (France), *Engineering in Medicine* (UK), *IEEE Transactions on Biomedical Engineering* (US), *Journal of Biomechanics* (US), *Journal of Biomedical Materials Research* (US), *Medical and Biological Engineering* (UK), *Medical Instrumentation* (US), *Medical Research Engineering* (US), *Medizinische Technik* (FRG), *Physics in Medicine and Biology* (UK).

For additional journals see:

Force, R. *Guide to Literature on Biomedical Engineering*. Washington, D.C.: American Society for Engineering Education, 1972.

Ulrich's International Periodicals Directory. New York: Bowker, biennial.

ENCYCLOPEDIAS, DICTIONARIES, HANDBOOKS

Computers in Biomedical Research. New York: Academic Press, 1965.

Glossary of Terms Frequently Used in Biophysics. New York: American Institute of Physics, 1973.

Graf, R. F. *Modern Dictionary of Electronics.* Indianapolis, Indiana: H. W. Sams, 1972.

IEEE Standard Dictionary of Electrical and Electronic Terms. New York: Wiley-Interscience, 1972.

Markus, J. *Electronics and Nucleonics Dictionary.* (3rd ed.) New York: McGraw-Hill, 1966.

Ray, C. D. (Ed.) *Medical Engineering.* Chicago: Year Book Medical Publishers, Inc., 1974.

Thomas, H. E. *Handbook of Biomedical Instrumentation and Measurement.* Reston, Virginia: Reston Publishing Company, 1974.

DIRECTORIES

Biomedical Engineering Education Summary Directory. Washington, D.C.: American Institute of Biological Sciences, 1971.

Engineering College Research and Graduate Study. Washington, D.C.: American Society for Engineering Education, annual. Supplement to *Engineering Education.* Lists colleges and universities in the United States, Canada, and Puerto Rico.

Medical and Biological Engineering in Denmark, Finland, Norway, Sweden. Copenhagen: Danish Biomedical Engineering Committee, 1969. Covers institutions and firms in Scandinavia concerned with biomedical engineering.

BIOLOGICAL SCIENCES
(Field of Study)

The biological sciences concern the structure, development, function, distribution, and reproduction of living plants, animals, and protists (organisms, such as the microorganisms, which originated before typical plant or animal forms had evolved). Included in modern biology are studies ranging from the molecular and chemical phenomena of living matter to the environmental and behavioral interrelationships that have evolved.

Biology began as a part of the study of natural history, the attempt to observe and describe man's physical universe. Early man accumulated knowledge of animals and plants—knowledge that served him in hunting and food gathering and in selecting medicinal plants. Much later, food plants were cultivated and animals domesticated. The ancient Chinese cultivated rice, tea, oranges, and medicinal spices. Archeological evidence reveals similar advances among the Egyptians and Assyrians (4000 B.C.), who also cultivated such staples as wheat and barley. Early Egyptians possessed domesticated cattle, sheep, pigs, ducks, geese, and cats. Pre-Inca peoples of Peru (3000 B.C.) originated the cultivation of maize (corn), which by 1492 had become a major crop from the St. Lawrence River to Argentina. Early Americans also domesticated, cultivated, and improved potatoes, squash, cacao trees, avocados, and others.

Systems of medicine also were in use more than 5000 years ago. Many of these systems were based on plant ingredients supplied to the early Greeks by guilds of root cutters, who also named the source plants. Ancient Greek natural history, particularly of animals, culminated with Aristotle (384–322 B.C.), who compiled excellent descriptions of the animals known in his day. However, with few exceptions, the ancients were unable to develop naturalistic methods of interpreting their observations of the world.

During the Renaissance scientific attitudes and methods began to emerge in the newly founded universities. Taxonomies (classifications of plants and animals) were published, and educated observers were sometimes attached to expeditions whose main purpose was the conquest of new lands and the acquisition of riches. Gradually herbals and bestiaries, the early taxonomic works, gave way to huge works of natural history by Konrad von Gesner (1516–1565) and Leonhard Fuchs (1501–1566) and the first serious classification of the plant kingdom by Andrea Cesalpino (1519–1603). In addition to these studies, Andreas Vesalius (1514–1564) described the anatomy of the human body in greater detail than had ever been done before; Ulisse Aldrovandi (1522–1605) published three large books on birds and a treatise on insects; William Harvey (1578–1657) discovered the circulation of the blood; Marcello Malpighi (1628–1694) extended Harvey's work and made major strides in the study of embryology; Robert Hooke (1635–1703) first detected cellular structure in biological material; Anton van Leeuwenhoek (1632–1723), often considered the father of mcrobiology, built simple microscopes and described many microorganisms. Scientific societies and the publication of scientific journals also began in the seventeenth century.

Along with these discoveries, efforts were made to establish a modern classification of plants and animals, based on a natural system. The classification systems of John Ray (1627–1705) and Carolus Linnaeus (1707–1778) are still employed in modern form. That is, the classic methods for the study of form and structure have been greatly enhanced by advanced techniques of optical and electron microscopy; by immunological studies of fluids and tissues; and by numerical taxonomy, in which computers are used to determine the similarities and differences among organisms.

John Ray had also correctly explained fossils as remains of organisms that lived in past ages. However, the basic principles of paleontology, the study of fossils, were not generally accepted until the beginning of the nineteenth century, after William Smith (1769–1839) and the French zoologist Georges Cuvier (1769–1832) helped to establish it as a biological science. Various specialized fields subsequently emerged: paleobotany, the study of fossil plants; micropaleontology, the study of microscopic fossils, mostly protists; invertebrate animal paleontology; and vertebrate animal paleontology. Notable contributions also were made by the Russian Aleksandr Kovalcvski (1840–1901) and the United States scientists, Edward D. Cope (1840–1897) and Henry F. Osborn (1857–1935).

Since new fossils are continually being discovered, systematic paleontology is an active field. For example, a synthesis of paleontology with other biological sciences is emerging as a new field, historical biology. Paleontology is also given a different emphasis as a geological tool.

Although advances in taxonomy and paleontology represent important stages in the history of biology, 1859 is often considered the beginning of the modern era of biology, because in that year the British naturalist Charles Darwin (1809–1882) published *On the Origin of Species by Means of Natural Selection*. Darwin's watershed contributions grew out of the practice of exploration for obtaining scientific data. His voyage on the *Beagle* had its counterpart in that of Thomas Henry Huxley (1825–1895), the biologist who championed Darwin, and the oceanographic expedition of the British *Challenger* (1872–1876). Out of these explorations—as well as earlier studies by the German naturalist Alexander von Humboldt (1769–1859)—grew two additional biological specialties: biogeography, the study of the distribution of plants and animals; and ecology, the study of a region's plant and animal life, considered as a dynamic interrelated system. Alfred Russel Wallace (1823–1913)—an English naturalist who had independently arrived at the theory of natural selection—published a book on the biogeography of animals, *The Geographical Distribution of Animals*, in 1876. In 1915 a paper by W. D. Matthew (1871–1930), a United States paleontologist, stimulated progress in historical biogeography based on information from fossils and living organisms. With the works of the Danish botanist Johannes E. B. Warming (1841–1924) in 1895 and the German botanist Andreas F. W. Schimper (1856–1901) in 1898, plant ecology emerged as a distinct science. Today ecology is one of biology's most active fields. Environmental studies developing out of ecological concepts now draw upon engineering, physics, biochemistry, toxicology, economics, sociology, and medicine. The study of human ecology also draws upon basic biological knowledge, including ecology, physiology, and genetics.

Concomitant with the expansion of field biology was the development of the laboratory-based fields, many of which have blended with fields such as medicine. Modern anatomy can be traced to Andreas Vesalius's book on human anatomy in 1543, written from his unique experience with actual dissections. Also influential were the French zoologist Pierre Belon's (1517–1564) observations of correspondence between the bones of a bird and of a man, the first attempt at comparative anatomy. Later, a theoretically based comparative anatomy was founded in the typological approaches of Johann W. von Goethe (1749–1832), Lorenz Oken (1779–1851), and Richard Owen (1804–1892). Taught descriptively, comparative and human anatomy are valuable preparatory studies for careers in the medical and paramedical fields. Evolutionary comparative anatomy, moreover, is now an active research area in paleontology. Functional anatomy, a field much enlivened by new tools such as the electron microscope, is an interpretive modern amalgam of anatomy with physiology.

Physiology began to emerge as a science in 1628, with William Harvey's work on the circulation of the blood. His contributions and those of later investigators, however, continued to contain theological concepts until the work of the French physiologist Claude Bernard (1813–1878). Bernard's experimentation revealed most of the basic features of animal metabolism. Since Bernard, numerous specialized fields have emerged: cellular physiology, the study of phenomena within single cells; biophysics; biochemistry; medical physiology, which includes the study of endocrine systems and drugs; and sensory and nerve physiology, which extends into the mechanisms of behavior and into psychology.

Following discoveries in physiology, Johannes Peter Muller (1801–1858), a generalist whose interests ranged over almost all of biology, laid the foundations for neurophysiology in his studies of sensory and motor nerves in animals. Later contributions were made by Emil DuBois-Reymond (1818–1896), a student of Muller's, who made modern approaches to electrical phenomena in nerves and muscles; John Henri Fabre (1823–1915), who made observations of insect behavior; and Conway Lloyd Morgan (1852–1936) and Jacques Loeb (1859–1924), who influenced the study of animal behavior as a distinct branch of biology. Their work and that of Ivan P. Pavlov (1849–1936) significantly influenced ethology, the study of an animal's behavior in its normal environment.

The modern sciences of biochemistry and biophysics also have origins in biology. The basis of their divergence today is that modern physiology has a more directly biological approach. On the other hand, the biochemist and the biophysicist study specific chemical and physical processes, rather than their direct implications for the organism and its function.

An additional development in biology, the study of microorganisms, has depended on advances in methods for visualizing their form and structure and for detecting their functions and activities. Consequently, microbiology has advanced with optical and electron microscopy; physical and chemical analytical techniques such as chromatography, electrophoresis, and the use of tracer isotopes; and immunological and immunochemical methods. Applying simple lenses of great magnifying power, the Dutch naturalists Jan Swammerdam (1637–1680) and Anton van Leeuwenhoek (1632–1723) were able to observe red corpuscles, bacteria, other protists, and sperms and to make anatomical studies of small insects. Their observations and those of their colleagues were so wide ranging that most of what can be seen under moderate magnification had been described well before the nineteenth century. Louis Pasteur (1822–1895), a chemist, established much of the methodology of microbiology in his pioneering work on fermentation and rabies. Pasteur demonstrated the activities of microorganisms and their practical significance long before the intricacies of their morphology and structure could be established by modern techniques of optical and electron microscopy. Thus, the interdisciplinary ties were established quite early between microbiology, biochemistry, biophysics, and other fields. Pasteur's work also set the foundations for the emergence of several new fields, such as immunology and microbial fermentations, which opened the way to industrial microbiology and microbial physiology. Microbial physiology, coupled with genetics, has produced molecular biology. Medical bacteriology—a science basic to medical, public health, and paramedical curricula—emerged from Robert Koch's (1843–1910) studies of infectious diseases and bacterial cultures. Milestones in the treatment of infectious diseases have been Paul Ehrlich's (1909) development of Salvarsan, an organic arsenical, for treatment of syphilis; the discovery of the antibacterial action of sulfonamides by Gerhard Domagk in 1935; and the discovery of penicillin by Alexander Fleming in 1929, later developed by Howard W. Florey and his colleagues in 1939.

Biology became even more sophisticated as microscopy extended anatomical studies to the cellular level. Marie F. X. Bichat (1771–1802) and Theodor Schwann (1810–1882) first recognized that tissues develop from and are composed of cells and cellular secretions. In the 1860s Max J. S. Schultze (1825–1874) defined protoplasm as the essential medium of life and the cell as the structural unit of life. By 1858 Rudolf Virchow recognized that all cells are offspring of other cells, thus opening the way to the coupling of cell theory with evolutionary concepts. Histology (the study of tissues) and cytology (the study of cells) developed from these early beginnings.

Embryology, still another specialization of biology, studies the development of the individual organism and the mechanism by which a fertilized egg, consisting of two cells, grows, divides, and develops into different-functioning tissues, organs, and structures. This science assumed modern form with the work of Karl E. von Baer (1792–1876), who discovered the mammalian egg and traced it through fertilization to final form via a gradual process of cellular division and differentiation. Modern embryology, or developmental biology, is almost entirely experimental; it seeks biochemical and biophysical explanations for phenomena observed in the developing embryo.

Unlike most of the other biological sciences, genetics, the study of the mechanisms of inheritance, took many unproductive turns until about 1900, when the work of the Austrian monk Gregor Mendel (1822–1884) was rediscovered by Hugo De Vries (1848–1935) and elaborated by Thomas Hunt Morgan (1866–1945) and his students. "Mendelian genetics"—dealing with the heredity of single, separable gene mutations, their recombinations, and their association and sequence in the chromosomes—is still basic for geneticists, although it has expanded into a vast and increasingly intricate science. Study areas include gene interactions, the effects of the whole genetic apparatus, the physiological expressions of genes, extranuclear inheritance, and the relationship between the genetic apparatus and differentiation in the embryo. Often considered the youngest of the main biological sciences, genetics has become the parent of the subsciences of cytogenetics and population genetics. Cytogenetics is the study of inherited diseases and disorders and the effects of the physical and chemical environment upon the genetic mechanism. Mutagenesis, the study of induced mutations, has become an active environmental science. Population genetics is concerned with breeding patterns, random and selective changes in the genetic composition of populations, and other population phenomena studied in the field and the laboratory and by mathematical modeling.

Another turning point in the history of biology with profound implications for genetics and the molecular basis of life was reached in 1928, when Frederick Griffith demonstrated the transfer of the trait of pathogenicity from heat-killed cells of the pneumococcus bacterium to living nonpathogenic strains. In 1944 Oswald T. Avery, Colin MacLeod, and Maclyn McCarty showed the unknown transforming agent to be deoxyribonucleic acid (DNA). In 1953 James Watson and Francis Crick, using data from X-ray crystallography and other sources, proposed that DNA is arranged in the form of a double helix. This finding opened the way to new knowledge, such as DNA replication, protein and enzyme synthesis, various mechanisms of immunity and disease processes, and countless other phenomena of living matter. This new science draws heavily upon and contributes to advanced knowledge of biochemistry, biophysics, genetics, and many advances in technological fields. Although much of the knowledge of molecular biology has arisen from the study of microbes, molecular biologists and microbiologists approach their work differently. The former select the simplest microorganisms as models for the study of molecular phenomena. Microbiologists are interested in microbes in themselves and for the things they do in natural environments and laboratory cultures.

FRANCIS D. CRISLEY

Levels and Programs of Study

Programs in the biological sciences generally require as a minimum educational prerequisite a secondary education and lead to the following awards: certificate or diploma, bachelor's degree (B.Sc., B.A.), master's degree (M.Sc.), the doctorate (Ph.D.), or their equivalents. Programs deal with the principles and practices of biology and consist of classroom, seminar, and laboratory instruction.

Programs that lead to an award not equivalent to a first university degree deal with biological technology. Principal course content usually includes some of the following: general botany, general zoology, microbiology, plant physiology, taxonomic botany, mammalian anatomy, ecology, limnology, animal physiology, entomology, radiation biology, wildlife biology, biochemistry, breeding, and reproductive physiology. Background courses often included are animal and plant pathology, organic chemistry, inorganic chemistry, analytical chemistry, electronics, electronic measurements instruments, instrumental analysis, graphics, and photography.

Programs that lead to a first university degree treat the fundamental principles of biology. At this level, the theoretical and general principles of the subjects studied are emphasized, although practical application is not ignored. Principal course content usually includes some of the following: principles of general biology, history of biology, diversity of organisms, inheritance and evolution, environment of man, molecular biology, cellular biology, genetics, cytology, general physiology, comparative invertebrate physiology, comparative vertebrate anatomy, biology of lower plants, morphology of vascular plants, plant and animal taxonomy, biochemistry, ecology, histology, embryology, and microbiology. Background courses often included are general chemistry, general physics, mathematics, ethology, humanities, and social sciences.

Programs that lead to a postgraduate university degree deal with advanced topics in the field of biology. Emphasis is placed on original research work as substantiated by the presentation of a scholarly thesis or dissertation. Principal subject matter areas within which courses and research projects tend to fall include biometrics, ethology, human physiology, biological effects of radiation, cytogenetics, population genetics, molecular genetics, developmental genetics, theoretical and experimental embryology, microbial ecology, mycology, advanced algology, ichthyology, advanced vertebrate and invertebrate physiology, experimental endocrinology, advanced plant physiology and morphology of angiosperms and gymnosperms, limnology, cytology, histology, evolution and genetics, botanical techniques, animal and plant parasitology, pharmacogenetics, pharmacology of endocrine organs, pharmacology of psychoactive drugs, pharmacology of biologically active monamines, development of therapeutic agents, autonomic nervous system pharmacology, and advanced pharmacology methodology. Subject areas within which background studies tend to fall include biology, chemistry, physics, mathematics, and statistical analysis.

[This section was based on UNESCO's *International Standard Classification of Education (ISCED)* (Paris: UNESCO, 1976).]

Major International and National Organizations

INTERNATIONAL

Biometric Society
Laboratorium für Biometrie und
  Populationsgenetik
Eidgenössische technische Hochschule
8006 Zurich, Switzerland

Commission on Higher Education in Biology
% Professor Sladecek
Karlova University, Vinina 7
Prague, Czechoslovakia

European Cell Biology Organization (ECBO)
Laboratory for Electron Microscopy
10 Rijnsburgerweg
Leiden, Netherlands

European Molecular Biology Organization
  (EMBO)
University of Brussels
67 Paardestraat
1640 Rhode-St. Genèse, Belgium

International Academy of Cytology
Department of Pathology
Ohio State University
410 West 10th Avenue
Columbus, Ohio 43210 USA

International Association for Plant Taxonomy
Bureau for Plant Taxonomy and Nomenclature
Room 1904, Tweede Transitorium
Uithof, Utrecht, Netherlands

International Association of Microbiological
  Societies (IAMS)
64 Fuller Street
Ottawa, Ontario, Canada K1Y 3R8

International Association of Theoretical and
  Applied Limnology
W. K. Kellogg Biological Station

Michigan State University
Hickory Corners, Michigan 49060 USA

International Cell Research Organization
UNESCO
7 place de Fontenoy
75700 Paris, France

International Centre for Biological Research
  (CIRB)
121 rue de Lausanne
1202 Geneva, Switzerland

International Committee for Standardization
  in Human Biology (ICSHB)
Ecole de santé publique
100 rue Belliard
1040 Brussels, Belgium

International Committee of Photobiology
Chester Beatty Research Institute
Royal Cancer Hospital
Fulham Road
London SW3, England

International Federation of Cell Biology (IFCB)
Imperial Cancer Research Fund
Lincoln's Inn Fields
London WC2, England

International Society of Biometeorology
Hofbrouckerlaan 54
Oegstgeest (Leiden), Netherlands

International Society of Cytology
University of Tokyo
Tokyo, Japan

International Society of Development
  Biologists
% Dr. Robert L. DeHaan
Department of Anatomy
Emory University Medical School
Atlanta, Georgia 30322 USA

International Society of Mathematical Biology
11 bis avenue de la Providence
92 Antony, France

International Union of Biological Sciences
  (IUBS)
51 boulevard Montmorency
75016 Paris, France
  The major organization in the field.

Society for Experimental Biology
Department of Botany, University College
Gower Street
London WC1, England

Special Committee for the International
  Biological Programme (SCIBP)
7 Marylebone Road
London NW1 5HB, England

For lists of international organizations in the biological sciences, especially those in particular branches of the field, see:

Yearbook of International Organizations. Brussels: Union of International Associations, 1948–. Published biennially.

NATIONAL

For listings of the many national organizations in the field see:

Guide to World Science: A New Reference Guide to Sources of World Scientific Information. (2nd ed., 25 vols.) Guernsey, Channel Islands: Francis Hodgson, 1974–1975.
Minerva, Wissenschaftliche Gesellschaften. Berlin, Federal Republic of Germany: de Gruyter, 1972. Lists national organizations in the biological sciences.
World Guide to Scientific Associations. New York: Bowker; Pullach/Munich, Federal Republic of Germany: Verlag Dokumentation, 1974.
The World of Learning. London: Europa, 1947–. Published annually.

Principal Information Sources

GENERAL

Bibliographical guides to the literature in the field are:

Asimov, I. *Intelligent Man's Guide to Biological Sciences.* New York: Washington Square Press, 1968.
Bottle, R. T., and Wyatt, H. V. *The Use of Biological Literature.* London: Butterworth, 1967.
Kerker, A. E., and Murphy, H. T. *Biological and Biomedical Resource Literature.* Lafayette, Indiana: Purdue University, 1968.
Smith, R. C., and Reed, W. M. *Guide to the Literature of the Life Sciences.* (8th ed.) Minneapolis: Burgess, 1972.
Walford, A. J. *Guide to Reference Material.* Vol 1: *Science and Technology.* London: Library Association, 1973.
Winchell, C. M. *Guide to Reference Books.* (8th ed.) Chicago: American Library Association, 1967. Provides a general guide to literature in the field.

Guides to special branches of the biological sciences include:

Jackson, B. D. *Guide to the Literature of Botany.* New York: Hafner, 1964.
Smith, R. C., and Painter, R. H. *Zoology: Guide to the Literature of the Zoological Sciences.* Minneapolis: Burgess, 1967.
Swift, L. H. *Botanical Bibliographies: A Guide to Bibliographic Materials Applicable to Botany.* Minneapolis: Burgess, 1970.

Among the numerous introductions to the field are:

Beaver, W. C., and Nolan, G. B. *General Biology.* (8th ed.) St. Louis, Missouri: Mosby, 1970.
Curtis, H. *Biology.* New York: Worth, 1975.
Keeton, W. T. *Biological Science.* New York: Norton, 1967. A basic text.
Villee, C. A. *Biology.* (6th ed.) Philadelphia: Saunders, 1972.

Histories of the field include:

Dawes, B. *A Hundred Years of Biology.* London: Duckworth, 1952.
Gardner, E. J. *A History of Biology.* (3rd ed.) Minneapolis: Burgess, 1972.
Locy, W. A. *Biology and Its Makers.* (3rd ed.) New York: Holt, Rinehart and Winston, 1935.
Nordenskiold, E. *A History of Biology: A Survey.* (Trans. by L. B. Eyre.) New York: Tudor, 1935.
Singer, C. J. *A History of Biology* (Rev. ed.) New York: Abelard-Schuman, 1959. A standard history first published in 1931.

Abstracts and indexing services are offered by:

Berichte über die wissenschaftliche Biologie. Berlin, Federal Republic of Germany: Springer-Verlag, 1926–.
Biological Abstracts. Philadelphia: Biosciences Information Service of Biological Abstracts, 1927–.
BioResearch Index, Reporting the World's Literature in the Life Sciences. Philadelphia: Biosciences Information Service of Biological Abstracts, 1965.
Bulletin signalétique. Section 370: *Biologie et physiologie végétale.* Paris: Centre national de la recherche scientifique, 1961–.
CC-LS (Current Contents, Life Sciences). Philadelphia: Institute for Scientific Information, 1958–.
International Abstracts of Biological Sciences. Oxford, England: Pergamon Press for Biological and Medical Abstracts, 1956–.
Referativnyĭ zhurnal. Biologiya. Moscow: Akademiia nauk, SSSR, Institut nauchnoĭ informatsii, 1953–.

For additional sources see:

Owen, D. B., and Hanchey, M. M. *Abstracts and Indexes in Science and Technology: A Descriptive Guide.* Metuchen, New Jersey: Scarecrow Press, 1974.

PERIODICALS

General journals in biological sciences include *Annales de biologie animale, biochémie, biophysique* (France), *Annals of Applied Biology* (UK), *Année biologique* (France), *American Naturalist, Archives de biologie* (France), *Archives italiennes de biologie* (Italy), *Australian Journal of Biological Sciences, Biologia* (Czechoslovakia), *Biological Bulletin* (US), *Biological Review of the Cambridge Philosophical Society* (UK), *Biological Science* (Japan), *Biológico* (Brazil), *Biologische Abhandlungen* (FRG), *Biologisches Zentralblatt* (GDR), *Biologist* (US), *Bioscience* (US); *Doklady Akademiia nauk SSSR, Seriya Biologiya* (USSR), *Journal of Biological Education* (US), *Journal of Cell Biology* (US), *Life Sciences* (US), *Linnean Society Biological Journal* (UK), *Proceedings of the Royal Society. Series B. Biological Sciences* (UK), *Quarterly Review of Biology* (US).

For more complete listings of journals in the various branches of the biological sciences see:

BIOSIS List of Serials. Philadelphia: Biosciences Information Service of Biological Abstracts, 1971.

Ulrich's International Periodicals Directory. New York: Bowker, biennial.

United States Library of Congress, Science and Technology Division. *Biological Sciences Serial Publications: A World List 1950–54.* Philadelphia: Biological Abstracts, 1955.

Williams, P. C. (Comp.) *Abbreviated Titles of Biological Journals: A List Culled with Permission from the World List of Scientific Periodicals.* (3rd ed.) London: Biological Council, 1968.

ENCYCLOPEDIAS, DICTIONARIES, HANDBOOKS

Abercrombie, M., Hickman, C. J., and Johnson, M. L. *A Dictionary of Biology.* (6th ed.) Baltimore: Penguin, 1973.

Altman, P. L., and Dittmer, D. S. *Biology Data Book.* Washington, D.C.: Federation of American Societies for Experimental Biology, 1964. Revised version of Spector's *Handbook on Biological Data* (see below).

Crow, W. B. *A Synopsis of Biology.* (2nd ed.) Baltimore: Williams & Wilkins, 1964.

Delauney, A., and Erni, H. (Eds.) *Encyclopedia of Life Sciences.* (8 vols.) Garden City, New York: Doubleday, 1965.

Ghaleb, E. *Dictionnaire des sciences de la nature.* Beirut, Lebanon: Imprimerie catholique, 1966. A polyglot dictionary for the field.

Gray, P. (Ed.) *Encyclopedia of the Biological Sciences.* (2nd ed.) New York: Van Nostrand Reinhold, 1970.

Henderson, I. F., and Henderson, W. D. *A Dictionary of Biological Terms.* New York: Van Nostrand, 1963.

Spector, W. S. *Handbook of Biological Data.* Philadelphia: Saunders, 1956. Well-known compilation of biological information.

DIRECTORIES

Directories to scientific establishments and educational facilities in the biological sciences include:

American Universities and Colleges. Washington, D.C.: American Council on Education, 1928–. Published quadrennially.

Cass, J., and Birnbaum, M. *Comparative Guide to Programs in the Biological Sciences and Chemistry.* New York: Harper and Row, 1971. A United States directory.

Commonwealth Universities Yearbook. London: Association of Commonwealth Universities, 1914–. Published annually.

Gray, P. (Ed.) *AIBS (American Institute of Biological Sciences) Directory of Bioscience Departments and Facilities in the United States and Canada.* (2nd ed.) Stroudsburg, Pennsylvania: Dowden, Hutchinson and Ross, 1975.

Guide to World Science: A New Reference Guide to Sources of World Scientific Information. (2nd ed., 25 vols.) Guernsey, Channel Islands: Francis Hodgson, 1974–75. Includes descriptions of science policies and structures in various countries as well as a directory of scientific establishments worldwide.

Harvey, A. (Comp.) *Directory of Scientific Directories.* (2nd ed.) New York: International Publications Service, 1972. A world guide to national and international directories in the biological sciences.

Peterson's Annual Guides to Graduate Study, 1976. Book 3: Biological and Health Sciences. Princeton, New Jersey: Peterson's Guides, 1975.

World List of Universities. Paris: International Association of Universities, 1971–. Published biennially.

The World of Learning. London: Europa, 1947–. Published annually. Includes universities, colleges, learned societies, and research institutions worldwide.

RESEARCH CENTERS, INSTITUTES, INFORMATION CENTERS

The following are directories to information and/or research centers in the biological sciences:

Bottle, R. T., and Wyatt, H. V. *The Use of Biological Literature.* London: Butterworth, 1967. Pages 133–137 list national guides to research centers in the biological sciences.

Minerva, Forschungsinstitute. Berlin, Federal Republic of Germany: de Gruyter, 1972.

Research Centers Directory. (4th ed.) Detroit:

Gale Research, 1972. Updated three times a year by *New Research Centers*. Lists research centers throughout the world.

World Guide to Science Information and Documentation Services. Paris: UNESCO, 1965.

World Guide to Technical Information and Documentation Services. Paris: UNESCO, 1969. Companion volume to *World Guide to Scientific Information and Documentation Services*. Lists principal centers offering scientific and technical information and documentation services.

BIOMEDICAL ENGINEERING

See Bioengineering (field of study).

BLACKS, AMERICAN

See Access of Minorities: Blacks in the United States.

BLADEN COMMISSION REPORT

See Financing of Higher Education in Canada (Higher Education Report).

BLIND, HIGHER EDUCATION FOR THE

No definition of blindness is internationally accepted. Each country defines blindness in relation to its own social and economic conditions and uses its definitions to determine eligibility for assistance benefits and special services, including special educational services. Thus, any discussion of higher education for the blind internationally must take into account these national definitions.

For example, in the United States a person is considered eligible for special services and assistance if central visual acuity does not exceed 20/200 in the better eye with corrective lenses or if the visual field is less than an angle of 20 degrees. Even here, however, a trend is developing toward a functional definition of blindness and broadening the category of persons eligible for services to include those who have a severe visual impairment. This means that the primary concern in determining eligibility for services is how well a person with limited vision can function—in other words, how much visual impairment inhibits a person from leading a natural, normal life. Under this definition, anyone whose loss of vision affects normal functioning and performance would be eligible for materials, services, and training.

Generally, the more economically advanced nations use sophisticated ophthalmological and medical measurements as standards for blindness, while most developing nations restrict the definition of blindness to people who are either totally sightless or who have little more than light perception. Obviously, countries that have more money to spend on educating their citizenry as a whole can afford to broaden their definitions of blindness and countries whose educational resources are limited must keep their definitions narrow.

In 1954 UNESCO held a conference to arrive at a uniform worldwide definition of blindness, but no decision was reached. Since that time the only point of agreement at periodic international conferences on the subject has been that the definition of blindness in countries such as the United States and Canada is too generous and that of countries such as Iran (where a person is considered blind if deprived of sight from both eyes) is too strict.

The lack of a uniform standard to measure blindness makes it difficult to determine the number of blind students enrolled in higher education around the world. In the mid 1960s, about 600 blind students attended higher education institutions in the Soviet Union (Davis, 1965); in the mid 1970s, there were approximately 4600 blind college and university students in the United States (American Foundation for the Blind, 1975)—reflecting among other factors the large number of American college students in general. But, with the exception of Great Britain and the Federal Republic of Germany, the number of blind college students in other developed countries is insignificant. Denmark, for example, had only one blind university student in 1976.

In most developing countries the number of blind students in institutions of higher education and the information about these students is minimal. As of 1972, for example, Tunisia had only about forty such students at the university level, Peru about twenty-six, and Nigeria seven. And in Bolivia colleges and universities did not allow candidates with physical or mental deficiencies to enroll (*Rehabilitation Services for the Blind,* n.d.).

Regardless of differences of definition and enrollment from country to country, blind students in all countries face similar problems in attending college or university. No special institutions of higher education exist for the blind anywhere; blind students at the college and university level universally attend integrated classes with their sighted peers. Free college-level correspondence courses are available worldwide on an individual request basis from the Hadley School for the Blind in Winnetka, Illinois, in cooperation with the University of Wisconsin and other affiliates of the National University Extension Association, but these courses do not lead to a degree nor are they accepted for credit in universities outside the United States. The only other correspondence courses in higher education for blind persons are available from England through its Open University.

For on-campus students, three common problems worldwide are insufficient preparatory services, funding, and access to special services and appliances.

Preparatory Services

For blind students, especially those who have attended a residential school for the blind, the transition from secondary school to university represents more than just a simple transfer from one educational institution to another. Within a usually large and complex collegiate community without special living arrangements, they now must obtain services and locate facilities that were previously provided by their school and, at the same time, meet new social and academic demands without the benefit of family or trained teachers.

Admissions. One of the first hurdles facing most prospective students is meeting the admission requirements through demonstrated competency on entrance examinations. In the United States the Educational Testing Service provides for blind students both braille and large-type forms of the Scholastic Aptitude Test, which is required for admission by many colleges. In Japan the standard university entrance exams are transcribed into braille for blind students. In most other countries, however, blind applicants must make their own arrangements, such as having a reader present when the entrance examination is taken.

Precollege programs. In Düren, Federal Republic of Germany, a rehabilitation center that trains blind people for jobs in industry has been experimenting with developing a preuniversity center to help blind students overcome some of the difficulties of adjusting to university life, but as of 1976 this program was only in the beginning stages. Comprehensive precollege programs for the blind have been developed largely in the United States, where as of 1976, thirty-nine programs in thirty-four states were designed to prepare blind students for integration into the college community. Their curricula differ according to the goals and role perception of the teachers, rehabilitation counselors, and college administrators involved, but the three most common types involve either (1) a session in residence at a rehabilitation center with a college course included as part of the curriculum; (2) a workshop consisting of a few days of lectures and group discussions about adjustments to college life; or (3) a session in residence at a college campus with the students taking courses off campus in mobility, study skills, and personal management. Blind students are often advised to visit their chosen campus early to sign up for courses and arrange for textbooks to be brailled and for readers. (The Delta Gamma sorority has made free reading for blind college students a national volunteer project.)

Career counseling. Traditionally, the careers for which blind people have been trained have been limited to crafts or trades involving manual dexterity or keen sense of hearing, such as piano tuning, music, teaching the blind, massage, caning, and wicker work. These occupations are still widely practiced among the blind in developing countries. There has been a worldwide trend, however, toward counseling more blind people to enter the mainstream of a country's industrial life and therefore to attend vocational training and higher education programs in general.

In highly industrialized countries, such as the United States, the Federal Republic of Germany, the German Democratic Republic, and Great Britain, blind persons are studying to be computer programers, lawyers, mathematicians, social workers, civil servants, and other professionals. In 1976, in the United States, the first blind doctor in this century graduated from medical school with the intention of becoming a psychiatrist. In Japan special training facilities for the blind are attached to the Tokyo University of Education. In the Soviet Union blind people enrolled in institutions of higher education most often prepare for careers in mathematics; programing; economics; cybernetics; philosophy; psychology; Russian, Slavic, Romance, and Germanic language and literature; history; political economy; pedagogy; education; and music (*Education of Blind Youth,* n.d.). The All-Russia Society of the Blind influences students' choices of vocation in the Soviet Union. Elsewhere, accurate career and employment counseling remains a persistent problem.

Funding

The financial needs of blind students encompass not only tuition and living expenses, but also purchases of special equipment and services. Some of the industrialized countries provide funds for all of those needs and some for part of them.

In the developing countries, special financial aid for blind students is minimal or nonexistent.

The United States. In the United States during the late 1800s several states passed legislation providing college scholarships for tuition and reader services for blind college students. The first organized movement for federal funding of higher education for the blind occurred in 1902, when the American People's Higher Education and General Improvement Association (later to become the American Association of Workers for the Blind) attempted to secure an act of Congress that would support a national scholarship plan for blind students. Not until 1943, however, did the Barden-LaFollette Act (part of the Vocational Rehabilitation Act Amendments of that year) include the blind in the federal program of vocational rehabilitation through academic and vocational higher education. This act provided that any state with a legally constituted commission or agency for the blind could assign to it the administration of the federal-state vocational rehabilitation program for visually disabled persons. More recently, the Education of the Handicapped Act granted funds to institutions of higher education, including junior and community colleges, vocational and technical institutions, and other appropriate nonprofit educational agencies serving the blind. As of 1976, students seeking higher education receive federal and state funds through the vocational rehabilitation service in the Department of Health, Education and Welfare. These funds can be used for tuition, maintenance, transportation to and from college, reader service, books, supplies, and special equipment, such as tape recorders. Private assistance is also available either through regular institutional scholarships or through scholarships from private foundations.

Soviet Union. In the Soviet Union the All-Russia Society of the Blind supervises the labor training of older youth. According to the society's president, the state provides blind students in higher education with scholarships 50 percent larger than those for sighted students, while the society gives them a subsidy for secretarial assistance during examination periods and the preparation of diploma papers. After the first year of study, blind students receive a state pension in addition to their scholarship. The society has set favorable terms for students who buy equipment such as typewriters and tape recorders, and it provides postgraduate students, applicants for master's and doctoral degrees, and correspondence and evening students with funds for hiring secretary-readers to aid them in mastering their professions.

Other countries. In Sweden, England, the German Democratic Republic, and the Federal Republic of Germany, reader services are provided without cost. In the Federal Republic of Germany, the Association of Blind Intellectual Workers in Marburg provides funds for students, graduates, and all association members to purchase books and have them transcribed, besides giving scholarships to blind students. In other countries, government money is often channeled through organizations for or of the blind. In Spain the National Organization for the Blind provides some scholarship money. In Canada the Canadian National Institute for the Blind administers a local-federal funding program similar to the vocational rehabilitation program in the United States. In India the federal Department of Social Welfare, several state governments, and the Indian National Association for the Blind provide scholarships to a few blind students for academic higher education. In Australia the National Department of Social Service provides guidance and financial assistance for blind university students.

Special Resources and Services

Twentieth-century advances in technology have been reflected in special services for the blind. In addition to traditional braille books and the talking books introduced in the 1930s, smaller, more convenient tape cassettes are now available in many countries, and students have access to such resources as textbooks, printed music, and scientific and other specialized periodicals in one or another of those forms.

Services in the United States. In the United States a national library service for blind and physically handicapped persons who cannot hold a book was established in 1931 and provides talking books either on tape or microgroove discs, talking book machines, books in braille, and braille music. These materials are distributed postage-free by the Library of Congress Division for the Blind and Physically Handicapped in Washington to regional libraries that function as circulating centers, using the mails to serve readers. Most of these materials are of a general nature, however, and are not specifically aimed at students in colleges and universities.

Recording for the Blind, Inc. (RFB), New York, is the largest national voluntary organization in the United States that provides tape-recorded textbooks to blind high school and college students and other persons who require specialized reading materials to acquire, maintain, or improve professional and vocational skills. RFB not only records new books on request but also stores master tapes of all the titles it has recorded in its central Master Tape Library. There are currently 23,000 titles in its *Catalog of Recorded Books,* with an average of 350 newly recorded titles added each month. RFB employs over four thousand certified volunteer transcribers who record at twenty-three locations around the United States (Field, 1974). Many other smaller voluntary agencies across the country also record books on request, and the Library of Congress publishes a free listing of these groups in its "Volunteers Who Produce Books."

The main source of braille college and graduate texts in the United States is the Braille Book Bank (BBB) of the National Braille Association (NBA) in Midland Park, New Jersey. BBB maintains a collection of over 1100 titles of volunteer-produced braille books at the college and graduate level and also publishes the *BBB Catalog,* available in print or braille (Field, 1974). It sells thermoform copies of these books at approximately the cost of the print edition, with the balance being subsidized by the organization. NBA encourages volunteers who braille college material to deposit the braille masters with BBB so that their work may be duplicated on order. In addition, blind students who have used a master braille copy made especially for them will frequently send it to BBB after they have used it.

BBB also maintains the Braille Technical Tables Bank (BTTB), which contains approximately two hundred tables for the benefit of students or teachers of mathematics, chemistry, and other sciences (Field, 1974). Science for the Blind, in Bala-Cynwyd, Pennsylvania, publishes scientific and technical periodicals on tape and also distributes instruments and aids for use in scientific and technical work. The American Printing House for the Blind (APH), in Louisville, Kentucky, through its Instructional Materials Center, maintains a card file of hand-transcribed elementary and secondary books in braille that have been registered with the organization by volunteer transcribers. Various other private American organizations, such as the John Milton Society for the Blind and the American Bible Society, both in New York City, provide religious books worldwide in braille and recorded form.

Services elsewhere. In France the Valentin Haüy Association maintains that country's most extensive braille library and employs people who transcribe books into braille manually. Other specialized organizations, such as the Group of Blind and Visually Handicapped Intellectuals, which publishes computer-produced numerical tables in braille, also transcribe materials for blind persons.

In the Soviet Union the state publishing house, *Prosveshenie* (education), publishes braille textbooks for universities. Special libraries throughout the Soviet Union provide braille and talking books on open-reel tapes, offer study rooms specially equipped with tape recorders, and have voluntary readers available to record books on request.

In the Federal Republic of Germany, the Marburg Institute for the Intellectual Blind maintains a library of approximately 53,150 braille textbooks, handbooks, printed music, maps, and standard library books, as well as a tape library and a braille press that publishes school books, scientific works, laws and supplements to existing law texts, standard literary works, and special periodicals (Scholler, 1974). The institute trains blind academics for their university studies and professions and offers blind students professional and career counseling. Other facilities in the Federal Republic of Germany include a printing office in Hanover that publishes braille school books, braille libraries elsewhere in the country, and special reading rooms for blind students at some universities.

Great Britain has a talking book program that was initiated in 1935 with disc recordings but has now been switched to taped cassettes. Talking books on tape are also available throughout Europe, in Canada, the Soviet Union, Australia, New Zealand, South Africa, Japan, and several Latin American countries. Sweden publishes braille books for college students, and there are braille presses in many other countries, such as Argentina, Mexico, Japan, the Republic of China, and Brazil, that do not specifically transcribe textbooks but stock some books included in university courses. In Sri Lanka the government-sponsored National Center for the Deaf and Blind prints and tapes books for university students; in the state of Maharashtra in India some university textbooks are available on tape; in Korea a few private braille libraries transcribe college and university textbooks; and in Grahamstown, South Africa, the National Library of Embossed and Recorded Literature for the Visually Handicapped provides readers throughout South Africa and Namibia with books that are either in embossed type or on tape.

Specialized Aids and Appliances

Besides university-level textbooks and reader services, blind higher education students often need specially adapted aids and appliances to get to class, write their papers, take notes, and generally live independently within the campus environment.

In the United States the American Foundation for the Blind in New York City, the American Printing House for the Blind, the Perkins School for the Blind in Watertown, Massachusetts, and Science for the Blind in Pennsylvania all sell aids and appliances worldwide. Their catalogs, such as the AFB *International Catalog of Aids and Appliances for Blind and Visually Impaired Persons*, include braille writers, tools, tape recorders, electronic braille and audio calculators, mobility aids, and mathematical instruments.

Outside the United States the major worldwide distributors of aids and appliances that publish catalogs include the Royal National Institute for the Blind, London; the Valentin Haüy Association, Paris; the Institute for the Intellectual Blind, Marburg, Federal Republic of Germany; the Japan Braille Library, Tokyo; and the Institute of Defectology, Moscow. The Institute of Defectology also runs several laboratories in which technological and scientific advances are applied to solving the problems of handicapped people and in which specific devices are manufactured.

Other countries, such as New Zealand, Australia, and Yugoslavia, also publish listings of aids and appliances but generally do not distribute these appliances outside of their respective countries.

Bibliography

American Foundation for the Blind. *Facts About Blindness.* New York: American Foundation for the Blind, 1975.

Braley, A. E. "The Problem of Definition of Blindness." *AFB Research Bulletin Number 3,* August 1963, pp. 119–122.

Brown, H. R. "Orienting Blind College Students." *New Outlook for the Blind,* 1965, *59* (5), 180–181.

Davis, P. A. "The Adult Blind in the Soviet Union." *Education of the Visually Handicapped,* 1965, *7*(2), 60–62.

Education of Blind Youth. New York: American Foundation for Overseas Blind, n.d.

Education of the Visually Handicapped. London: H. M. Stationery Office, 1972.

Field, G. *Recorded and Braille Textbooks.* New York: American Foundation for the Blind, 1974.

Graham, M. D. "Toward a Functional Definition of Blindness." *AFB Research Bulletin Number 3,* August 1963, pp. 130–133.

Jones, J. W. "Problems in Defining and Classifying Blindness." *AFB Research Bulletin Number 3,* August 1963, pp. 123–129.

Kumpe, R. "Preparation of Blind Prospective College Students." *International Journal for the Education of the Blind,* 1968, *18*(3), 79–81.

McGill, W., and Frish, E. "Helping Blind Students Prepare for College." *The New Outlook for the Blind,* 1960, *54*(6), 219–221.

Proceedings of the World Assembly of the World Council for the Welfare of the Blind. (New York, July 31–August 11, 1964.) Paris: World Council for the Welfare of the Blind, 1964.

Proceedings of the World Assembly of the World Council for the Welfare of the Blind. (Rome, July 21–31, 1959.) Shrewsbury, England: Wilding and Son, n.d.

Rehabilitation Services for the Blind in Developing Countries. New York: Unit for the Disabled, Social Development Division, United Nations, n.d.

Russell, D. C. "College Preparation for Blind Students." *International Journal for the Education of the Blind,* 1964, *13*(3), 79–84.

Schloss, I. P. "Implications of Altering the Definition of Blindness." *AFB Research Bulletin Number 3,* August 1963, pp. 111–116.

Scholler, H. *The Purpose of an Association of Blind Intellectuals and Students—A German Experience.* Marburg, Federal Republic of Germany: Deutsche Blindenstudienanstalt, 1974.

Spungin, S. J. (Ed.) *Pre-College Programs for Blind and Visually Handicapped Students.* New York: American Foundation for the Blind, 1975.

Third Quinquennial Conference. Proceedings of the International Conference of Educators of Blind Youth, Hanover, Federal Republic of Germany, August 6–18, 1962. Watertown,

Massachusetts: Perkins School for the Blind, 1964.

Trosch, C. "First National Survey of Blind Students Enrolled in Colleges and Universities." *Higher Education,* 1958, *14*(8), 121–136.

SUSAN G. ISLAM

See also: Deaf, Higher Education for the; Handicapped, Higher Education for the; Special Education.

BOARD OF RECTORS OF DUTCH UNIVERSITIES (Rektoren college)

The *Rektoren college* (Board of Rectors of Dutch Universities), a nongovernmental organization of no official status, gives the rectors of universities an opportunity to consult with each other on university matters in general and on affairs of higher education and research in particular. The board of twelve members (and their substitutes, mostly members of the boards of faculty deans) is composed of rectors of universities, technical universities, and colleges of university standing in the Netherlands. Meetings are held five to six times a year, and the chairmanship rotates yearly among members. There is no formal funding of the board.

Activities of the board consist of establishing regular contacts with corresponding organizations in other countries and with the Standing Conference of Rectors and Vice-Chancellors of the European Universities. The minister of education is advised by the board on equivalences of foreign university diplomas.

Thorbeckelaan 360
The Hague, Netherlands

A. E. COHEN

BOARDS OF CONTROL
See Governance and Control of Higher Education.

BOARDS OF DIRECTORS
See Governance and Control of Higher Education.

BOARDS OF MANAGERS
See Governance and Control of Higher Education.

BODLEIAN LAW LIBRARIES
See Libraries: Bodleian Library, England.

BOLIVIA, REPUBLIC OF

Population: 5,470,000 (1974). Student enrollment in primary school: 769,923; secondary school: 107,327; university: 31,113 (1974); nonuniversity: 17,364. Student enrollment in higher education as percentage of age group (20–24): 7.12% (1971). Language of instruction: Spanish. Academic calendar: March to January, two semesters. Percentage of national budget expended on all education: 16.8% (1971); higher education: 5.0% (1971). [Figures are for 1973 unless otherwise indicated. Source: Ministry of Education].

The history of higher education in Bolivia began with the founding of the Royal and Pontifical University of San Francisco Xavier on March 27, 1624, in the city of La Plata (Sucre), which was at the time under the viceroyalty of Peru. The legal bases for the university had been articulated in the papal bull of Gregory XV in August 1621 and in the certificate of Philip III of February 2, 1622. During the Spanish colonial period, higher education was under the influence of St. Thomas Aquinas, whose work *Summa Theologica* was studied in depth. Studies at the university consisted of canon law and law, with degrees awarded only in theology and law. In 1776 the university established the Caroline Academy, which became a famous institute for the study of forensics. It drew students from a large part of South America, from the present-day republics of Argentina, Chile, Ecuador, and Peru, as well as from the area that is today the Republic of Bolivia. It received subsequent renown for training many of the men who later became leaders of the revolution against Spain, which started in the city of La Plata, or Chuquisaca, on May 25, 1809. Among these leaders can be named the brothers James and Manuel de Zudañez, Bernard Monteagudo, Mariano Moreno, and Rodríguez de Quiroqa.

On August 6, 1825, Bolivia became a republic, and shortly afterward two more universities were founded. The Bolivian University of "San Andrés" was started as a college in 1830 but, by the law of August 13, 1831, became the University of "San Andrés" in La Paz with the same privileges as the University of San Francisco Xavier. In 1832 the Bolivian University of "San Simón" in Cochabamba was founded by decree. The universities continued to specialize in theology and law, but in 1863 the Bolivian University of "San Simón" added a faculty of medicine. At this time the Bolivian universities were greatly influenced by the professional training and centralized system of the Napoleonic university, while the positivist ideas of Auguste Comte and later the evolutionary theories of Herbert Spencer also had an effect that was especially noticeable up to World War I.

In the late 1800s several other universities were founded. A decree of December 15, 1879, created the University of St. Thomas Aquinas, which was inaugurated in January 1880. In September of 1911 its name was changed to University of "Gabriel René Moreno." By a decree of September 1938 it became the Autonomous University of Santa Cruz. It is now known as the Bolivian University of "Gabriel René Moreno" in Santa Cruz. In 1892 the University of St. Augustine was founded. It became the University of Oruro in 1893; in 1937 it was granted autonomy and is now known as the Bolivian Technical University of Oruro. Also in 1892 the University of Potosí was founded and opened its doors on February 3, 1893. It is now known as the Bolivian University of "Tomás Frías." In 1886 a university district was created in Tarija. In June 1946 the district received its first university, the Bolivian University of "Juan Misael Saracho." The only public university developed in the twentieth century was the Bolivian University of "Gen-

eral José Ballivián," founded on November 18, 1967. In March 1966 the only private university, the Catholic University of Bolivia, was founded in La Paz by the Archbishop of La Plata. In August of the same year, it was recognized by the Bolivian government in Decree 07745 as the new Catholic University of Bolivia.

In 1930 a profound structural change took place in the Bolivian universities when the military junta instituted university autonomy by a statute of public education promulgated on July 25. Until 1930 the government had appointed all administrators and teaching staff at the universities. The new university autonomy allowed the university council, which was composed of teachers and student representatives, to appoint the rector and all the academic and administrative authorities of the university. Together with the authority to appoint their own staff, the universities were granted autonomy in academic matters and could then set their own study programs and teaching methods. In 1936 the universities also achieved economic autonomy.

Almost thirty years passed before further changes took place in the Bolivian universities. By Decree-Law 09873 of September 4, 1971, the government of General Hugo Banzer Suárez closed the universities and created a National Commission for University Reform. Its aim was to evaluate the programs of the Bolivian universities and restructure them to respond to the technical, economic, and social necessities of the country. As a result of the commission's work, a new Fundamental Law of the Bolivian University was promulgated in June of 1972, and by Decree-Law 10298 the National Council of Higher Education of the Bolivian University was founded and all universities in the country brought under its jurisdiction. The council directs, coordinates, plans, and supervises all institutions of higher education in Bolivia, which have now been included into one entity, the University of Bolivia. The 1972 law was modified by the New Fundamental

Law of the Bolivian University of October 17 and 20, 1975.

The new unified system of education—with a uniform program, calendar, evaluation, and teaching methods—permits free transfer of teachers and students from one university to another. This uniform structure has resulted in the following administrative changes: greater efficiency in the administrative structure; a common budgetary system; a new concept of the faculty as a group of related fields of study; a rational distribution of faculties in all parts of the country to avoid unnecessary duplication; a departmentalization of the faculties, with the departments constituting units of service and research; and a rational assessment of the fields of study in accordance with national needs.

National Educational Policy and Legal Basis of Educational System

The declared purpose of higher education in Bolivia is to develop graduates who will participate in the nation's growth. To this end the fundamental objective of the Bolivian university is to provide solid, modern career preparation through studies that are humanistic yet have a scientific/technological orientation. It is also the policy of the government to foster cooperation between all public and private institutions to achieve solutions to problems of national development.

The Bolivian system of higher education is regulated by the Fundamental Law of the Bolivian University as decreed in Law 12972 of October 17, 1975, and Law 12977 of October 20, 1975.

Types of Institutions

Only the University of Bolivia, consisting of eight state universities and one private university, is authorized to impart higher education to degree level. In addition to the universities, a number of private and state institutions under the authority of the Ministry of Education and Culture offer higher education below degree level. Among these institutions are teacher train-

ing schools (normal schools), commercial institutes, schools of fine arts, and the Higher National School of Industrial Study "Pedro Domingo Murillo," which provides a four-year technical training program at the intermediate level and a seven-year technical training program at the higher level. The duration of programs and the curricula at these institutions are varied and have not been standardized.

Relationship with Secondary Education and Admission Requirements

Primary education, *nivel básico* (basic level), lasts five years and is compulsory. It is followed by an intermediate level, which lasts three years, after which students enter a four-year secondary school. The school-leaving certificate is called the *bachillerato* and is issued by the Bolivian University after authorization by the Ministry of Education and Culture through its provincial and national authorities.

The basic requirements for entry to the University of Bolivia are the diploma *bachillerato*, a pass in an entrance examination, and a health certificate. Higher education below university level has various entrance requirements. Some institutions admit students on application, and some demand only the ability to pay. Most of these institutions are private and require much higher tuition than the nominal tuition at the university.

Administration and Control

In accordance with the constitution, the Bolivian University is under the authority of the National Council of Higher Education. The council—which is divided into a department of university education and scientific research, a department of general university administration, a department of planning and university statistics, and a department of educational coordination—plans, coordinates, and supervises all university education in the country. It is composed of five full members and two supplementary members who are designated by the president of the republic and who may not represent any particular university. The National Council of Higher Education is directly under the authority of the president of the republic. Its members are appointed for a period of four years and cannot be reelected until one period has passed. The president of the council is elected by secret ballot among its members. Appointment to the council requires that the person be Bolivian and at least thirty-five years of age, have the academic degree of doctor or *licenciado* or equivalent, have held the position of full professor in teaching or research for a minimum of five years, and be morally qualified.

The highest administrative structure of a public university consists of the university council, the rector's office, the vice-rector's office, and the general administrative department. Other bodies in charge of planning within the university are the academic and administrative commissions and various commissions established by the university council for study of special university problems. Members of the university council with the right to vote are the rector, who presides; the vice-rector; the general administrative director; the deans of the faculties; one teacher representative for each faculty; one representative of the teachers association; one student representative for each faculty; and the secretary general of the local university federation. Additional members without the right to vote are the secretary general of the university, the secretary general of the administrative personnel union, and the head of the Division of Planning of Scientific and Technological Research.

The duties of the university council are to implement the resolutions of the National Council of Higher Education and to enforce the rules of the Fundamental Law of the Bolivian University; to coordinate, plan, and evaluate the activities of the university; to propose to the National Council of Higher Education necessary changes in the statutes of the university; to propose to the National Council of Higher Educa-

tion the creation of new faculties, fields of study, and institutes and the modification of teaching plans; to contract for extraordinary professors, on the authorization of the rector of the university; to authorize the rector of the university to accept donations and endowments; and to submit the budget of the university to the National Council of Higher Education for approval.

The rector, the administrative head of the university, is assisted by the vice-rector and by the administrative director general and the secretary general. The rector is a full-time staff member and may not undertake other activities. His duties include enforcing the Fundamental Law of the Bolivian University, convening the university council and the faculty councils, representing the university in all outside relations, and conducting all other administrative duties of the university. He is appointed for four years and can be reelected for an additional four-year term. The requirements for his appointment are the same as those for appointment to the National Council of Higher Education. The vice-rector is also appointed for four years with the right to reelection for one consecutive term. However, he may not be elected rector until one term has expired after his mandate. The rector and the vice-rector are elected by the university assembly *(claustro universitario)*, which consists of all the full professors of the university and all the full-time students. The assembly convenes ninety days before the rector's or the vice-rector's period of service expires. It elects the new rector or vice-rector by a two-thirds vote.

The university is divided into faculties and is further subdivided into departments for administrative purposes. The faculties are governed by their dean and by the faculty council *(consejo facultativo)*. The departments are headed by heads of department *(jefes de departamento)*. The faculty councils consist of the dean, who presides; the study director; the heads of departments; and one student representative per field at the licentiate level. The faculty council is in charge of the academic, administrative, and disciplinary functions of the faculty. It presents proposals for faculty regulations to the academic commission for approval before submitting them to the university council. In addition, the council suggests a faculty budget to the administrative commission and vice-rector. The faculty also has a faculty assembly *(claustro facultativo),* which consists of the vice-rector, who presides, and all the full professors of the faculty. Its main duty is to elect the dean. The deans are elected for four years and may not be reelected for another term until one term has passed. To become a dean, an applicant must be a citizen, must be at least thirty years old, and must have taught at the university as a full professor.

Programs and Degrees

The authority charged with establishing and maintaining the standards of education under the fundamental law of the university is the National Council of Higher Education.

The Bolivian University, in its eight public universities and one private university, offers ninety-three fields of study. The university has nine faculties: architecture and arts, health sciences, social sciences, pure and natural sciences, humanities and sciences of education, technology, agriculture and animal husbandry, physical education and sports, and postgraduate study. The distribution, creation, continuation, or suspension of any of the faculties in the different universities are undertaken in accordance with national and regional needs. The program of study starts with a basic cycle, a general introductory program leading to the *licenciado* or other professional titles. The second stage is professional development, and the third stage is specialization at the postgraduate level.

Bolivia is one of the countries that have two different classes of titles: an academic título, which is awarded by the institution at the completion of study and which is rec-

ognized in other institutions of higher education for continuation of higher studies; and a professional title, which is awarded by the national government and which is necessary to work in a corresponding field. The professional title is awarded by the Bolivian University through the National Council of Higher Education and is the national authorization for practicing a given profession.

According to Article 88 of the fundamental law, the universities offer the following academic degrees: higher technician *(técnico superior), licenciado,* and *doctor.* Higher technician requires from six to eight semesters of study. In the mid 1970s consideration is being given to changing the title of advanced technician to an academic title, *bachiller académico,* and recent innovations have also made it possible for students to earn the title of intermediate technician after four or more semesters of studies.

Study at the professional level leads to two titles: the *licenciado* in the field of specialty and the professional title designating the professional function of the title holder. For example, in the field of economics the student may earn the academic title of licenciate in economics *(licenciado en economía)* and the professional title of economist *(economista).* To receive the professional title the applicant must have the academic degree, must have succeeded in the tests established by the regulations of the National Council of Higher Education, must have provided services to the community in accordance with the university regulations, and, if applicable, must have completed military service.

To obtain the academic degree of doctor an applicant must have the *licenciado* and the corresponding professional title; must have completed required programs, which extend through at least two academic years; and must have presented and received approval of a thesis.

The institutions of higher education below university level award academic titles in a number of fields of study, from a simple certificate of ability to an academic title of higher technician. In general, the academic titles are awarded after final examinations.

Financing

University education is principally financed from three sources. The national treasury provides funds up to some 44 percent of the total university budget. Assigned income from other sources amounts to about 50 percent, and the university's own resources contribute about 6 percent. Over the years, government laws have been passed that have created university resources which are paid directly into the universities' treasuries through collection agencies. The universities' own resources include business undertakings, research activities, and other income-producing ventures.

Nonuniversity higher education institutions are generally privately funded. Only a few state institutions, such as the Higher Institute of Public Administration *(Instituto superior de administración pública),* depend completely on the national budget. The universities charge a nominal tuition, while the private institutions generally rely on student tuition and contributions for their income.

Student Financial Aid and
Access to Education

The Bolivian University offers two kinds of scholarships: housing scholarships, which provide lodging in dormitories; and food scholarships, which provide meals in the university cafeterias. There are also other kinds of financial assistance offered by other sources—for instance, work scholarships, tuition waivers, and local, provincial, and international scholarship funds. Social services in the form of medical or pharmaceutical assistance are also available; however, in the mid 1970s services are restricted as a result of disproportionate cost increases in previous years, when there was a lack of control and government attention to the increases in these areas. Students

participate in the scholarship committees which select students for these awards.

In accordance with the university law, higher education throughout Bolivia is completely open to all candidates regardless of their social, political, or religious origin. However, since a *bachillerato* diploma is required for university entrance, access is limited to the 5 percent of the population that successfully completes secondary studies. In addition, students must pass an entrance examination; the success rate is generally from 60 to 70 percent of applicants, although in some instances it is 70 to 80 percent.

Students who enter the university are generally from higher economic classes. The number of students from the lower social groups, from the countryside, and from the centers remote from the cities is very small. There is a large percentage of women in higher education. Certain fields of study, such as social service, nursing, and health-related sciences, are almost exclusively reserved for women. Career programs in the social sciences, such as in economics and business administration, also have appreciable numbers of women students.

Student activities are conducted at three levels. The faculties have student centers, each focused on a particular field of study. There are also organizations called local university federations, which group together all the students in one university. Finally, there is a student organization that is national in scope, the Bolivian University Confederation *(Confederación universitaria boliviana:* CUB), which unites all the regional and local university federations. These three types of organizations coordinate all student activities and play a great role in social service programs for the university student and in programs of a social-cultural nature. The organizations also participate in university extension, a service that the university provides to the community. The university extension service offers local or regional programs and may give credit to those students who participate.

Teaching Staff

According to Article 107 of the Fundamental Law of the Bolivian University, there are three categories of teaching staff: ordinary professors, extraordinary professors, and teaching assistants. Ordinary professors are promoted according to their years of service and in accordance with requirements established by the Regulation on Teaching Staff. According to Article 108, ordinary professors are ranked as *catedráticos* (full professors), *profesores adjuntos* (associate professors), and *profesores asistentes* (assistant professors). The assistant professor, who is beginning his career as a teacher, must possess a university title and submit to a competition of merit. The assistant professor holds his position for two consecutive years. At the end of this period, he has a chance to become an associate professor if he fulfills the requirements for that post as established by the fundamental law. The associate professor must possess a university title; he must have been an assistant professor for at least two years and have successfully passed an examination of competency; and he must have conducted research in a specialty. The associate professor remains in his position for three years, after which he takes a new competitive examination. The full professor *(catedrático)* is the highest-ranking faculty member and has the responsibility for teaching and research within a department. A full professor must possess an academic degree and title; he must have been an associate professor for three years and have succeeded in the competitive merit examination; and he must have presented a general plan for research study, which includes an analytic examination of a problem relevant to his field. The *catedrático* remains five years in his position and may be reappointed for an equal period by the university council after an evaluation by the academic commission of his university.

The universities also may incorporate into their teaching staff professors from other universities or foreign countries at a level comparable to their previous rank. The university council of each university may also employ qualified persons who do not have an academic title but who have the requisite cultural or scientific knowledge.

According to Article 109 of the fundamental law, extraordinary professors are classified as contracted professors, visiting professors, professors emeritus, temporary professors, substitute professors, and assigned professors. A contracted professor is one who gives temporary services authorized by a resolution of the university council. A visiting professor is generally a foreign professor invited or contracted by the university council for a determined period. Professors emeritus are retired full-time professors who have given their time to teaching and research for at least twenty years. The final three categories are employed to teach specific courses, generally part time.

The university also has teaching assistants, graduates or students who have distinguished themselves in their studies and who wish to begin careers as university teachers. In all cases, these assistants are appointed through a competitive examination of the faculty to which they wish to become affiliated. Their appointment may not exceed two years but may be renewed.

According to Article 113 of the fundamental law, the professorial ranks can also be defined according to the time spent in the teaching positions. Appointments may be for *dedicación exclusiva* (exclusive dedication) or *tiempo completo* (full time), *tiempo medio* (half time), or *tiempo horario* (by the hour). Professors of exclusive dedication are those who teach and undertake research at the university and have no other outside paid employment. Full-time professors are those who teach and conduct research at the university for at least forty hours per week. They are allowed to have other paid employment. Half-time professors work twenty hours per week in teaching or research, while the part-time teachers are employed by the hour.

The Bolivian University offers teachers and students an atmosphere conducive to research and creation. Freedom of expression *(libertad de cátedra)* is guaranteed except for political partisanship. Retirement generally is at age sixty-five.

Research Activities

Research projects concerned with higher education are conducted at the Bolivian University. Such research is financed mainly from within the university; little funding comes from the central government or private sources. Some research relative to higher education but also associated with private enterprise may receive state funding. At the moment the government provides a portion of the research undertaken by the Bolivian University into the utilization of higher education and its practical application.

Current Problems and Trends

Bolivia's educational problems may be divided into academic problems and administrative or financial problems. Among academic problems is the lack of coordination between secondary and higher education, which manifests itself in the high incidence of failure and dropping out during the first semester of study at the university. This situation is complicated by the increases in student numbers. Another academic problem is the lack of qualified professionals to teach the almost one hundred programs offered at the university. There is also a need to strengthen library services in order that research activities may be increased.

Among administrative and financial problems is the lack of an adequate infrastructure to coordinate the growth of each individual university, to project the need for new fields of study, to establish the necessary laboratories and programs, and to decide on needed investments. The dependence on the national treasury for university funding limits expansion and has led to salaries that are lower at the university than in comparable levels of outside employment; as a consequence, there is the problem of acquiring an adequate and qualified teaching staff.

These problems are being addressed by the government; however, the success in overcoming them will depend on appropriation of the needed financing and cooperation between the internal university administration and the government.

Among new programs designed to integrate the university more closely into national development is short-cycle education for the training of intermediate technicians at the university. For this purpose the universities have established university polytechnics, which have set up two- and three-year programs leading to the titles of intermediate and advanced technician. In addition, the government is planning to establish a National Service for Technical Education *(Servicio nacional de educación técnica)*, dedicated to improving short-cycle education. The new service will cope with two problems: that of an increasing number of secondary school graduates who will not find places in the university and that of training needed manpower for intermediate positions which are now understaffed.

The educational problems in Bolivia are closely interwoven with those of the labor market: often some fields are saturated, with consequent underemployment of graduates, while other fields lack sufficient manpower. Attempts are being made to better guide the students toward needed careers. The overall coordination of education by the National Council of Higher Education is expected to allow for a more rational development of the whole sector of higher education.

Relationship with Industry

State and private industry are actively participating in the training of professionals, especially in technical fields. So far this training has been provided mainly by state enterprises; however, private industry is now extending greater cooperation in this area. The new *Centros de promoción de la investigación científica y tecnológica*

(CEPICT: Centers for the Promotion of Scientific and Technological Research) are designed to create closer cooperation between higher education and industry by joint cooperation and research into industrial problems.

International Cooperation

The Bolivian University is interested in international cooperation. It has formed many agreements with both European and American universities for technical and administrative cooperation and has actively cooperated in programs that are concerned with worldwide questions of a social, scientific, or technical nature.

Bolivia also participates in regional organizations and is a member of organizations such as the *Unión de universidades de América latina* (Union of Universities of Latin America) and the *Organización de universidades católicas de América latina* (Organization of Catholic Universities of Latin America).

PEDRO MORENO QUEVEDO

Bibliography

América en cifras, 1972. Situación cultural: Educación y otros aspectos culturales. Washington, D.C.: Secretaría del Instituto interamericano de estadística, 1974.
Censo universitario latinoamericano, 1971. Mexico City: Unión de universidades de América latina, 1974.
Current and Future. New York: International Council for Educational Development, 1973.
La educación superior en América latina. Washington, D.C.: Banco interamericano de desarrollo, 1973.
García Laguardia, J. M. *Legislación universitaria de América latina.* Mexico City: Universidad nacional autónoma de México, 1973.
Ley fundamental de la Universidad boliviana. La Paz: Consejo nacional de educación superior, 1973.
Monge Alfaro, C. *La universidad y la integración de América latina.* San José, Costa Rica: Universidad de Costa Rica, 1968.
Nueva ley fundamental de la Universidad boliviana. As published by *El diario*, November 16, 1975.
Ocampo Londoño, A. *Higher Education in Latin America: Current and Future.* New York: International Council for Educational Development, 1973.
Universidad boliviana catálogo general. La Paz: Consejo nacional de educación superior, 1973.

See also: Archives: Mediterranean, the Vatican, and Latin America, National Archives of; Science Policies: Advanced Developing Countries: Andean Common Market Countries; South America: Regional Analysis.

BOOKSTORES
See Business Management of Higher Education: Bookstores.

BOSTON PUBLIC LIBRARY
See Libraries: Boston Public Library, United States.

BOTSWANA, REPUBLIC OF

Population: 661,000 (1974 estimate). Student enrollment in primary school: 95,000; secondary school (academic, vocational, teacher training): 10,700; higher education (university): 413 (1975–76). Language of instruction: English. Academic calendar: July to April, three semesters. Percentage of national budget expended on education: 6.2% (1974 estimate). [Figures are for 1973–74 unless otherwise indicated.]

Botswana, which achieved independence in 1966, had been known as the British protectorate of Bechuanaland since 1885. During the colonial period education was largely provided by missionaries and was confined to the primary and secondary levels. In 1945 Pius XII College was founded in Roma, Lesotho, by the Oblates of Mary Immaculate. The college also provided undergraduate training for Botswana students who were preparing for the external degrees of the University of South Africa. In 1964 the British government and the Ford Foundation of the United States provided funds to purchase the college, which was incorporated as the University of Basutoland, Bechuanaland Protectorate and Swaziland. In 1966, shortly before the protectorate territories of Basutoland, Bechuanaland, and Swaziland gained their political independence, the name was changed to the University of Botswana, Lesotho and Swaziland. The university conferred its first degrees in April 1967.

Until the end of the 1970–71 academic year, the university was located only at Roma in Lesotho. Following the recommendations of an Academic Planning Mission, under the leadership of Sir Norman Alexander, the three nations agreed to develop university campuses in Botswana and Swaziland in addition to the original campus in Lesotho. A primary motive in setting up a joint university was the need to establish an economically viable institution. It therefore was essential to avoid the duplication of teaching facilities as much as possible. The university colleges were designed to meet the following criteria: (1) minimum duplication of teaching facilities and programs; (2) balanced development of the colleges in terms of student numbers, distribution of faculties, and physical facilities; and (3) cost efficiency and effectiveness. A three-stage development program was also agreed on by the trinational university council and the participating governments, and it provided for the following development pattern: Stage I—the establishment of Part I teaching in Botswana and Swaziland (the first two years of a four-year degree program); Stage II—the establishment of Part II teaching in Botswana and Swaziland (the last two years of a four-year degree program); and Stage III—the development of new programs in the university, which would be development oriented and help fulfill the manpower needs of the participating countries. Citizens of Botswana seeking higher education thus had the choice of enrolling at one of the three campuses or attending other universities in Africa or outside the continent.

In the fall of 1975, however, a challenge to the authority and autonomy of the university council by the government of Lesotho resulted in a court case. Lesotho lost the case and on October 20, 1975, passed a bill in its national assembly cutting ties from the University of Lesotho, Botswana and Swaziland and establishing a National University of Lesotho on the Roma campus. Botswana students were subsequently withdrawn from Lesotho. The two remaining constituent campuses will stay united under the name University of Botswana and Swaziland.

Legal Basis of Educational System

Until 1976 the chief ordinance directing higher education was the Education Law of 1966, which determined the administration and control of the institutions. The University of Botswana, Lesotho and Swaziland was regulated under the royal charter of 1964, which established it as the University of Basutoland, Bechuanaland Protectorate and Swaziland. It achieved its present name in 1966. After the withdrawal of Lesotho in 1975, the university was reconstituted as the University of Botswana and Swaziland under a government order which took effect on September 1, 1976.

Types of Institutions

Higher education for Botswana is provided by the University of Botswana and Swaziland, which consists of the University College of Botswana in Gaborone and the University College of Swaziland in Kwaluseni. Both the campuses in Botswana and Swaziland offer Part I programs (the first two years of a four-year program) in humanities, education, and science. Botswana students must go to Swaziland for Part I programs in agriculture and commerce and accounting. Part II programs in the humanities are to be offered at both campuses. Part II programs in economic and social studies and science are offered in Botswana; Part II programs in agriculture, agricultural education, commerce and accounting, and legal studies are provided in Swaziland. Part I science includes preparation for engineering and agriculture degrees and other science-oriented programs.

A school of education was established in Botswana in 1971 to offer programs below degree level and Part I degree programs for teachers, as well as in-service training and professional training for persons involved in the administration and professional supervision of education at all levels. The school allows input into the curriculum by the two Ministries of Education.

Primary teacher training colleges are institutions affiliated to the university. They offer two- and three-year programs and may accept students with a Junior Certificate.

In addition to the facilities mentioned above, there is a Division of Extra-Mural Services, which was an integral part of the university in Botswana for several years before the establishment of a university campus in the country. The Division of Extra-Mural Services offers adult education programs and thus enables the university to reach out to as many people as possible within the community. The division attempts to carry the university presence, its standards, and its disciplines from Gaborone into the towns and villages throughout the country. It is, in many ways, the instrument through which the university meets some of its obligations to the community outside its walls.

Relationship with Secondary Education

Primary education lasts seven years and is compulsory, although a lack of schools in certain rural areas has made the law difficult, if not impossible to enforce. Secondary education is not compulsory. It is divided into two cycles: a three-year junior secondary cycle leading to a Junior Certificate of Education and a two-year senior secondary cycle leading to the Cambridge Overseas School Certificate at ordinary level. Technical, vocational, and teacher training are also available at the secondary level. The Botswana Training Centre offers three-year programs to train carpenters, electricians, and mechanics. Agricul-

tural education is offered at specific schools and centers.

Admission Requirements

A first- or second-class pass in the Cambridge Overseas School Certificate at the ordinary level with credit in the English language admits students to the four-year degree B.A. programs of the university. For B.Sc. courses a pass in mathematics is also required. Lower achievements in the examination entitle students to enter diploma and certificate courses. Entrance requirements are determined by the university senate. The recognized equivalent qualifications for university entrance include (1) a General Certificate of Education (GCE), provided that the candidate has taken examinations in at least six subjects; (2) a pass at ordinary level in at least four subjects, including the English language; and (3) a matriculation certificate or a matriculation exemption from the Joint Matriculation Board of the Republic of South Africa, provided that the student has passed English with a stipulated grade.

There is no age limit for admission to the university, and all students who qualify academically are accepted.

Administration and Control

By an order which took effect on September 1, 1976, the charter of the University of Botswana, Lesotho and Swaziland was repealed and the University of Botswana and Swaziland constituted. The university consists of two autonomous colleges, the University College of Botswana in Gaborone and the University College of Swaziland in Kwaluseni. Each college is headed by a rector, and most of the financial and academic decisions are made at the college level. The university, however, has one governing body and one senate, which handle university-wide questions.

King Sobhuza II of Swaziland is chancellor of the university and will retain this title until June 1978, when the president of

Botswana becomes chancellor for a two-year period.

Programs and Degrees

In accordance with the agreed policy guidelines for development, there are three first degrees available in four-year programs at the Botswana campus: a Bachelor of Arts in the faculty of humanities and in the faculty of economic and social studies; and a Bachelor of Science in the faculty of science. Four-year degree programs in agriculture, commerce and accounting, and law are available only in Swaziland. There are also five diplomas and certificates available after two years of study: the Diploma in Statistics, the Diploma in Education, the Certificate in Primary Education, the Teachers Certificate, and the Certificate in Statistics.

Admission to any master's degree program is restricted and is dependent upon available staffing and research facilities for the particular research project contemplated for the degree. Four postgraduate degrees are currently available: Master of Arts, Master of Education, Master of Science, and Bachelor of Education (which requires a previous B.A. and is thus regarded as postgraduate).

Financing

The university obtains its funds from external aid agencies and also from the participating governments. The governments provide funds for the recurrent budget, which is determined by an external University Grants Committee. Capital requirements are the responsibility of each country.

Teaching Staff

The teaching staff of the university is international in character. Staff members are appointed by a senate council committee. The minimum qualification for a lectureship is a master's degree in the particular subject. All vacancies are advertised abroad and locally. The head of the department then sets up a selection committee, which includes the dean of the faculty and another member from a cognate subject. The selection committee makes its nominations to the senate council committee known as the Academic Staff Committee. Preference is given to local candidates, nationals of the two countries. Before any position is filled, the head of department has to satisfy the Academic Staff Committee that there are no nationals who could be considered for the position. The vast majority of posts, especially in the sciences, are filled by expatriates from a variety of nations. An increase in local staff is expected upon the return of a number of nationals, who are still undergoing training abroad.

Expatriates are employed on a four- or six-year contract, renewable by mutual consent. In addition to basic salary, they receive an inducement allowance in lieu of pension. Local members of staff are appointed on permanent and pensionable terms but have to serve a probationary period of two years before confirmation.

Depending on their qualifications, experience, and publications, staff members may be appointed to the ranks of professor, reader, senior lecturer, lecturer, or junior lecturer. Promotions are also given within these ranks, and an academic review takes place annually. For this review all staff members update their personal data and list academic honors and achievements acquired within the year. Promotion to a chair or to the position of reader is subject to external assessment. Contribution to the general life and well-being of the university, teaching effectiveness, and evidence of sound scholarship are taken into account for promotions from lecturer to senior lecturer.

Research Activities

The Botswana campus of the university is developing a National Institute for Research. The institute, founded in July 1975, will focus its research in the areas of economic development, agricultural development, scientific and industrial development, manpower needs and development, and African studies. The institute will identify, in consultation with the relevant university departments and government agencies, research areas which call for immediate attention and will design research programs to achieve these ends; it will also collaborate with government agencies in carrying out research needed by the government; in addition, the institute will organize conferences, seminars, symposia, and public lectures on development or research on southern Africa in general and Botswana in particular.

Current Problems and Trends

Government and educational authorities in Botswana are considering a revised strategy of higher education, which will necessarily depart from the traditional pattern of a four-year degree-granting university. The kind of institution or combination of institutions required will incorporate two levels of two years, each of which differs from the present Parts I and II pattern of the University of Botswana and Swaziland. The first level will offer degree studies in accordance with the UBLS outline, which provides a fairly wide range of terminal occupational or diploma courses, based upon manpower needs; it will also offer opportunities for the most able students from the diploma courses to proceed to degree-level studies, either in Botswana or Swaziland or elsewhere in Africa or overseas, and any feasible and needed adult education opportunities. The second level will consist of two additional years of studies leading to a university degree in fields of study relevant to the needs of Botswana.

Such a system of what might be called a polytechnic education will enroll relatively large numbers of students at the first level, broadening the base of postsecondary education and achieving a measure of cost efficiency. A key element in the system will be flexibility for students to complete a diploma level course at their own pace. Thus, they may enroll for a time, leave, and then return for completion of the program or degree-level studies.

It is anticipated that a number of postsecondary institutions in Botswana and Swaziland will be affiliated with such a system, including both the university and such other institutions as the Botswana Agricultural College, the Swaziland College of Technology, and the teacher training colleges. While maintaining an affiliation arrangement with the national system, the constituent colleges would continue to operate independently under their respective ministries.

Thus, the objective will be to develop and plan a university institution that will offer degree studies and will also provide a number of two-year terminal occupational programs at the first level of higher education.

International Cooperation

During 1974 an Institute of Development Management was established on the Botswana campus of the university. The physical facilities for the institute were provided through funds from the Ford Foundation in the United States and the Norwegian government. The Canadian Agency for International Development has provided the teaching staff.

The objectives of the Institute of Development Management are (1) to assist the localization programs in Botswana, Lesotho, and Swaziland by providing middle- and senior-management training and other educational activities in the public service, parastatal agencies, and private sectors of the three countries; (2) to assist with the improvement of job performance in the countries; (3) to undertake consultancy and research services related to the institute's training program and development policies in the countries; and (4) to undertake the publication of materials produced in connection with the work of the institute.

N. O. H. SETIDISHO

Bibliography

Loken, R. D. *Education in Transition: The Report of the Polytechnic Mission.* Washington, D.C.: American Council on Education, 1973.

Raum, O. F. "The Imbalances of Educational Development in Southern Africa (Botswana, Lesotho, Swaziland and South Africa)." *South African Journal of African Affairs,* 1971, *1*, 8–30.

Rose, B. "Education in the Former High Commission Territories of Bechuanaland (Botswana), Basutoland (Lesotho), and Swaziland." In B. Rose (Ed.), *Education in Southern Africa.* Johannesburg, South Africa: Macmillan, 1970.

Sasnett, M., and Sepmeyer, I. *Educational Systems of Africa: Interpretations for Use in the Evaluation of Academic Credentials.* Berkeley: University of California Press, 1966.

Stevens, R. P. *Lesotho, Botswana and Swaziland: The Former High Commission Territories in Southern Africa.* New York: Praeger, 1967.

See also: Africa, Southern: Regional Analysis; Africa, Sub-Saharan: Regional Analysis; Archives: Africa and Asia, National Archives of; Health Services, Worldwide University.

BOWLES REPORT

See Access to Higher Education (Higher Education Report), Multinational.

BRAILLE BOOKS

See Blind, Higher Education for the.

BRAIN DRAIN

See Manpower Planning: Migration of Talent.

BRANCH CAMPUSES

A multicampus college or university is an institution having more than one campus, either domestic or foreign. Although the multicampus institution is not restricted to the United States, it is found most often in that country; therefore, this essay focuses on the United States.

In a few multicampus institutions, the campuses are coequal, although not identical. Usually, however, the original campus is the main campus and the location of the most comprehensive program, and newer campuses are smaller, more limited satellite systems or simply special schools. It sometimes happens, however, that a branch campus becomes the larger campus as at Fairleigh Dickinson University in Rutherford, New Jersey. As a general rule, the branch campus is beyond a reasonable commuting distance from its parent institution. However, some universities have more than one campus in the same city, where separate specialty schools in law, medicine, fine arts, or social work, for example, may occupy separate facilities— sometimes an estate or a building contributed to establish that particular school.

In the 1970s, as a result of declining enrollments and increasing deficits, some formerly independent, small private institutions have been absorbed by state universities and have thus become branch campuses. In other instances, the original campus may disappear altogether as when New York University sold its old Washington Heights campus to New York City.

The multicampus college in the United States has developed largely since World War II. Romesburg, in his study of all public branch colleges within the United States (1972, p. 93), found that the most marked decline in growth of branch colleges occurred from 1951 to 1955, a decline which Romesburg says was reflected in the establishment of both two- and four-year branches. Between 1955 and 1969, two-year branches sharply increased, however, although four-year branches did not. From 1965 to 1970 the two-year branches again showed a decline.

Similarly, Lee and Bowen, in a 1971 study of nine multicampus systems in public four-year colleges and universities in North Carolina, Texas, California, New York, Illinois, Wisconsin, and Missouri, found them to be prospering but were surprised five years later to find these systems in "an unsteady state" (Lee and Bowen, 1975, p. 2). In view of shrinking college admissions, the contemporary trend is a diminution in multicampus private institutions and anxiety about the financial future of public multicampuses.

Development of Domestic Branch Campuses

Although multicampus systems in the United States developed for a variety of reasons, according to a study of multicampus systems by Romesburg, only "29.0 percent of the branch colleges were established on the basis of a feasibility study which investigated not only the need for an institution, but also the type of institution which should have been established" (p. 100). Among the reasons for the development of branch campuses are the parent institution's desire to expand its services or to expand its physical plant. Campuses also arise because of a desire for prestige, a wish to be innovative, the desire to stave off competition, a need to ensure the main campus of a supply of students for the junior and senior years, and a desire to fulfill the ideals and ambitions of the institution's founder.

Expansion of services. The decision to start a branch campus—usually with a two-year program—is made on the state level in most cases, although sometimes the community itself will prevail upon an existing university to set up a campus in its midst. One example is the Harlem branch of the City University of New York (CUNY), a four-year liberal arts college founded to train students from minority groups for health-related careers. Initially using the facilities of Hunter College and the Mount Sinai Hospital School of Medicine, the college was designed to correct the low ratio of minority group students in the senior units of CUNY and to alleviate the growing shortage of community health workers. Another example of response to community demands are the courses presented by community schools in cooperation with local public institutions of higher education. In Medford, Massachusetts, for example, courses are given in the community schools by faculty from Boston State Col-

lege. This off-campus satellite program is designed to meet the professional and personal needs of residents of Medford and surrounding areas. Courses are offered for both undergraduate and graduate credit. They range from courses with a decided professional emphasis, such as those in tests and measurement and secondary school administration, to those of more general interest, such as arts and crafts. Community colleges and state universities frequently offer such programs, utilizing community facilities. Such facilities are not, strictly speaking, branch campuses. However, the existence of these programs is a response to the same needs that have often led to the full-scale branch campus. A striking example of the trend toward bringing the campus to the student is the Burlington, Massachusetts, campus of Boston's Northeastern University, a private institution. This campus offers both full- and part-time day and evening study toward a variety of degrees, as well as a daytime continuing education program designed mainly for women in the suburban area near Burlington.

Expansion of physical plant. A branch campus may originate when an old campus is too small and offers little possibility for expansion. In some instances campuses become obsolete, either because of disrepair of old buildings or because of changes in the educational direction of the institution. A college may want a campus where it can have dormitories, for example, or more up-to-date laboratory facilities. In some instances, the entire college simply moves, as did Adelphi College to Garden City, New York, in 1929. But it is feasible to move the entire college only when it is a small institution, such as Colby College in Waterville, Maine, and Skidmore College in Saratoga Springs, New York.

If an overall move is impossible for financial reasons, a satellite campus may be established instead, especially since state educational building funds and loans from federal agencies have made new public campuses possible. However, these satellite campuses are often small, to counteract potential disadvantages of the move. Institutions, especially those in urban locations, are sometimes reluctant to dislocate faculty and to forfeit some of the income generated by the old campuses. Among private institutions, which rely on tuition income, the decision to establish a branch campus is sometimes hindered by anxiety about giving up an ensured source of income.

Institutional goals. Occasionally, an institution may want the prestige of multiple campuses; in the early years of higher education this happened with church-related schools, although such new campuses were independent. Another factor is the parent institution's desire to innovate. An interest in new forms of education motivated Antioch College in Ohio, for example, to establish twenty-five campuses throughout the world in the early 1970s. Another motive is that of staving off competition from other institutions. In such cases, the parent college hopes to colonize a growing area first, especially if the new area represents an improvement over the old campus. The parent institution may also desire to ensure upper level students for itself. In such cases, an institution may establish two-year freshman/sophomore extensions. The usual result is that either the two-year extension is very limited, or, if it develops, it becomes a four-year college which desires autonomy. Many four-year colleges in the United States evolved from two-year branches.

Individual goals. A fairly unusual motive for the establishment of branch campuses is the enthusiasm or ambition of an individual who wants to start a college and realizes he cannot do so on his own. He then arouses public sentiment and sells his idea to an existing institution. Typically, however, if the branch becomes financially self-sufficient, it seeks independence. Hofstra University, in Hempstead, Long Island, originally a branch of New York University, started in this way.

Administrative patterns and problems. There are nearly as many administrative patterns as there are reasons for the development of multicampuses in the United States. Furthermore, these patterns and the titles that accompany them change according to the strengths or weaknesses of the chief officer or the head of the branch campus. Romesburg (1972, p. 96) found that the chief official was called the director in 67.3 percent of the institutions studied. In the four-year branches, however, as many chief officials were given the weightier title of chancellor as were called director. Contrary to other investigators, however, Romesburg found little variation in administrative patterns.

Degree of autonomy. The history of multicampus institutions indicates that newer campuses very often want complete independence after a few years. The major interest of the branch campus is in financial subsidy, whereas that of the main campus is often in drawing additional income from the branch. The result inevitably is an uneasy federation between the parent campus and its branch campus. The distance from the parent campus influences the independence of a satellite campus. Romesburg's study showed that most of the branch campus chief administrators reported directly to the president or a vice-president of the main campus. This discovery "indicated that the branches did not have a large degree of autonomy in terms of decision making. Nearly all branches had to seek approval from the parent institution for curriculum, budget, and faculty appointments" (p. 97).

The Burlington, Massachusetts, campus of Northeastern University, for example, has its own dean, who is in charge of the operation of the physical plant and of student services. He is also responsible for the registration of students, for the general outline of the academic program, and for the operation of the library. Curriculum and course content are determined, however, by faculty and administration at the parent institution in Boston. The dean of liberal arts on the Boston campus is the dean for liberal arts academic affairs on all campuses, and staff of the University College in Boston (the division of the university responsible for all evening and part-time programs) serve as chairmen of academic departments for the branch campus. As on the main campus, course content is essentially defined by individual faculty members, but courses are overseen by faculty and administration from the parent campus, to ensure quality and comparability and recognition of these courses by the regular university faculty. Most courses at the branch campus are taught by part-time faculty. An attitude of superiority sometimes exists among full-time faculty when judging their part-time colleagues; the administrative pattern established for academic matters at Northeastern-Burlington is designed to overcome this attitude.

Faculty issues. Multicampuses face unique challenges in the role of the faculty. Crucial issues include questions of appointment standards, promotion, and sharing of outstanding members or instructors for whom full programs cannot be worked out on one campus. The growing trend toward faculty unionization further complicates these issues. The impetus toward unionization sometimes comes from the branch campus, as an indication of its independence. With the growth of unionization, issues such as sharing of faculty have become increasingly important, especially as a basis for seniority. Furthermore, given the unsteady state of higher education in the mid 1970s, tenure, whether systemwide or limited to one campus, and faculty retrenchment are crucial and painful issues. In some public institutions, the founding of a new campus led to faculty flight from the old. Anxious about tenure and rumors of faculty retrenchment, faculty members may feel there is more chance of a permanent position on a newer campus.

Some students of branch campuses see faculty on newer campuses as favoring independent curricula, independent courses, and independent administrative regula-

tions. Romesburg's discovery, however, that "nearly all branches had to seek approval from the parent institution for curriculum, budget, and faculty appointments" indicates that suggestion of innovation by faculty does not inevitably lead to its implementation. Romesburg further found that branch curricula often stressed service courses, offering "course work which included remedial work, general education, technical and vocational work, [and] adult education, as well as a number of highly specialized classes" (p. 102).

Communication between parent and branch campuses. According to some researchers, communication between a parent institution and its branches is the greatest single problem of branch campuses. Among the issues and facts to be communicated to the faculty and students are the overall philosophy, long-range planning, and major decisions of the board of trustees; the deliberations and decisions of the faculty as a whole; the catalog and all major publications; administrative regulations; student opinions and reactions; community movements and reactions that impinge upon the institution, including regional industrial developments; relevant state and national trends; and major movements, specific decisions, and special events of individual campuses, schools, and departments. The number and complexity of these matters underlines the need for establishing clear lines of communication and command.

A special problem of authority and autonomy is the question of the branch campus library, one of its most important and most expensive elements. Among the problems that must be solved are whether to purchase books centrally and how to meet the branch's need for rarely used and very expensive volumes. Inadequate library facilities, Romesburg found, were a frequent problem for branch campus officials. These officials also considered as crucial the problems of financial limitations and budgetary needs, inadequate classroom facilities, and limited campus life for students (p. 100).

Admission standards. Generally, the same academic standards are understood to apply throughout an institution. Some people argue, however, that good reasons may exist for lower standards at a subsidiary campus, both for admission and for continuing work. This argument usually applies in the case of a two-year branch set up to provide an education for less qualified students and supplying special guidance, skills development, flexible study arrangements, and evening programs. Romesburg's research, on the other hand, suggests that most institutions do not admit such a variance in standards (p. 98). He found, as did Becker (1964) and Medsker (1960, p. 309), that branch admission practices were determined by the main campus in 74.8 percent of the cases, and requirements were the same as those of the parent institution in 77.6 percent of the cases.

Administrative services. At a satellite campus, administrative services fall into two general categories: educational and noneducational or less educational. The first involves library service and guidance, both priority items at a well-run new campus. Guidance services may sometimes be better at a smaller campus than at a large one with a discrete guidance staff because at the new campus each faculty member might act as an adviser. Because of the greater camaraderie of the smaller campus, instructors know a student's problems better and thus may be more interested in his academic success and his future.

On the other hand, noneducational or less educational services, such as physical training and sports, generally tend to be less available on branch campuses because of the increase in per capita costs. On a new campus, therefore, the money is usually not available for the team sports found in older schools. Romesburg, moreover, found that students at a branch college, particularly at two-year branches, forfeited many of the conventional aspects

of campus student life, such as an auditorium, a gymnasium, a health center, dormitories, an orchestra, and a band (p. 95).

Financial Issues

In the establishment of a new campus, budgeting and accounting assume major importance. In a public institution, the money comes from the state, and; once the capital expenses have been decided on, the amount allocated for operational expenses is usually based on the number of students. In a private institution, on the other hand, capital expenses generally have to be lent from the general or endowment funds of the main campus or borrowed from a bank, and operating funds must also be ensured.

Phases of financing. A long-established college usually has its capital costs hidden in antiquity; a new subsidiary campus requires a more exact accounting. Its financing typically undergoes the initial capital expense for buildings and land; the pump-priming period, actually part of the initial capital expense phase; and the operational period. The first phase may be eliminated by renting quarters in public schools or in commercial buildings. Brooklyn College developed in this way when the then College of the City of New York rented commercial space for its branch in Brooklyn in the late 1920s. Sometimes it is possible to rent an estate, but usually as a transitional arrangement for later purchase. On the other hand, it may be possible to purchase land and construct one or more buildings.

Allocation of costs. According to good accounting practice, certain expenses are allocated to the new unit. Among these are, first, the cost of land. Also to be allocated to the new campus are the cost of new buildings or alterations to old buildings. Many specific items have to be investigated to determine actual operating costs of any new campus which involves existing buildings: water supply, sewerage, roads, parking, electrical circuits and lighting, toilet facilities, roofing, heating, ventilation, classrooms, auditorium, library, office space, laboratories, dining facilities, vending machines, and recreational facilities.

Equipment and supplies sent from the main campus become part of the branch's expenses; these items are usually to be paid for within a month or, at most, within the year. The time of any administrators, teachers, secretaries, or custodians from the main campus is also charged to the branch. In some cases, this cost is combined into one administrative overhead, which includes the salaries and expenses of all administrators whose responsibilities cover the two or more campuses.

Other items to be allocated to the new unit are accreditation expense (Romesburg found that 68.2 percent of the branch colleges had to undergo their own accreditation); printing of all university reports; radio and television programs benefiting all campuses; autos and trucks leaving the main campus; institutional advertising; trips of main campus personnel to the other campuses; fund raising done at the central office; loans of books or equipment; cost of auditing; and cost of data processing.

One way in which the complexity of budgetary problems may be handled is by putting all the nonallocable expenses involving all campuses into one category, and then allocating the expense on an established formula—for example, on the basis of enrollment. A later section of this essay will discuss the impact of declining enrollments today on the future of multicampuses.

No set way has been established to allocate money when a satellite campus becomes independent. In some cases loans have been made locally, and the newly independent campus assumes them. In cases where an estate or building has been contributed to the branch campus, the new institution acquires title. If the state acquires title, it may make some payment to the main institution. With the advent of bond issues by either the federal government or the state, this transition becomes more complex.

Advantages of the Multicampus Institution

Multicampus colleges have many advantages; however, financial considerations more than educational advantages may determine their future in the 1980s. Among the advantages of multicampuses are the educational superiority coming from having two or three smaller colleges rather than one large unit. The relationship with students becomes more personal, and communication and unity of purpose become easier. Another advantage of branch campuses, according to some supporters, is the atmosphere of exuberance that results from starting a new campus. Consequently, greater attention may be paid to students.

There are several financial advantages to branch campuses. The cost per student, at least in the first two years, is less, as was shown when Edward Williams College was established at Fairleigh Dickinson University. There is less administrative expense in many cases, and other costs such as those occasioned by computers, athletic teams, and overbuilding tend to be less. However, as already noted, Romesburg found the consequence of this reduction in expense was that conventional campus student life was greatly reduced. He also found that students at public branch institutions were charged student fees generally lower than those at the main campus. Large institutions with large enrollments are expensive, and increased layers of bureaucracy usually pay for themselves by adding to the expense per student. In private institutions this extra expense is borne by the student, and it accounts for a large portion of the rapidly increasing costs in such institutions.

Lee and Bowen also note lower costs and additional students as among the advantage of branch campus systems. In addition, the multicampus system can provide financial and technical support for campuses, while limiting risk to one campus; it can objectively evaluate experimental success or failure; and it has internal channels of communication to transfer successful innovations to a wider audience. Finally, because of its widely scattered physical and educational resources, a multicampus system can reach a statewide nonresident student body and draw on the resources of more than one campus in developing programs (Lee and Bowen, 1975, p. 7).

Goddard College has several external degree programs conducted in part at off-campus centers. Goddard's Adult Basic Degree Program, leading toward a bachelor of arts degree in liberal arts, is a program of independent study off-campus that has a two-week resident period on the Vermont campus in each of its six-month semesters. Another off-campus external degree program offered by Goddard is its Experimental Program in Further Education, a four-year program for adults leading toward a bachelor of arts degree. Most of the students hold full-time jobs while carrying on this program of independent study. The program is divided into two semesters of six months each, and students spend eight weekends per semester in residence on the Vermont campus or at one of the other two learning centers.

Overseas Branch Campuses

The discussion of branch campuses has been concerned thus far with branches in the United States; a number of United States universities have branch campuses overseas. For example, Ball State University, Muncie, Indiana, has offered the master of arts degree in counseling and executive development in public service at eight branch campuses in the Federal Republic of Germany. At various times, Ball State has also had two branches in Greece, two in the Netherlands, one in Italy, two in Spain, and six in the United Kingdom. Big Bend Community College, Moses Lake, Washington, has had an associate degree/vocational program at branches in the Azores, the Federal Republic of Germany, Greece, Italy, Turkey, and the United Kingdom. Boston University has offered three master's degree programs at its over-

seas branch campuses in Belgium, the Federal Republic of Germany, and Italy. Tufts University in Medford, Massachusetts also has a fairly extensive overseas program with branches in England, France, and the Federal Republic of Germany. All programs are under the administrative supervision of the dean of special studies on the Medford campus.

Tufts conducts two programs in England. Tufts-in-London is a one-year program of study conceived primarily (though not exclusively) for junior-year students of drama, English, and related subjects. Although one faculty member from the United States is assigned to the program each year, most faculty and administrative duties are carried out by the staff in London. The faculty is largely composed of British scholars and artists, especially from the theater. Tufts-in-England is a one-semester program designed for junior or senior students in child study and education from Tufts (and some from other institutions). The program is based at Crewe and Alsager College, a teacher training college in Cheshire, and focuses on the curriculum and methods of the "integrated-day" program of English infant and junior schools. As with Tufts-in-London, there is a resident British director of the program who functions as the responsible Tufts official.

Tufts-in-Tübingen, in cooperation with the Eberhard-Karls University, offers work toward a master of arts degree in German. The degree requires two years of study, the first on the campus of the Eberhard-Karls University, the second on the Tufts campus in Medford. At Tübingen, a Tufts resident director both teaches and assists students in planning a program of study at the university and offers a required weekly seminar on traditional and contemporary aspects of German culture. During the Medford year, each student must enroll in at least one graduate-level course each semester and in a graduate seminar. He is also expected to serve as a teaching assistant in the graduate department and to pass written and oral examinations.

Tufts-in-Paris is a more flexible program, designed for undergraduates. Each student must take a French language course; a course in contemporary European theater is also strongly recommended. Beyond that, students may enroll in courses of their choice at the University of Paris. Again, the program has a resident director with full authority. The students generally live with French families and the program staff includes a person specifically concerned with that aspect of the program.

Although the many army-inspired programs in various parts of the world tended to be temporary adjustments to our international activity, there developed a more permanent type of oversea campus, as, for example, the English campus of Fairleigh Dickinson University.

Three miles from Banbury, Wroxton College in Wroxton Abbey in Wroxton, England is a fifty-eight-acre campus completely owned and operated by Fairleigh Dickinson University. Wroxton Abbey was the ancestral home of Lord North. There are three sessions in English literature and institutions: fall and spring sessions for undergraduates, a summer session for graduate work.

History of overseas campuses. The expansion of United States higher education institutions offering programs at locations abroad has been a relatively recent phenomenon. Prior to World War II, United States students who studied abroad were affiliated with a foreign university, and they generally completed their studies with that institution or through a cooperative arrangement with their home institution. The concept of extending a campus away from its home environs received impetus during the war, when the United States Office of Education contracted with individual institutions to offer programs to service personnel in fields ranging from defense training and engineering to management and science. Some of these institutions offered their courses with "residence credit" at military bases, in government offices, in high schools, and at industrial sites. Most of these courses were provided through the extension or continuing education components of the university.

Between 1900 and 1950, United States colleges and universities reported a total of seventy-two programs of one year or longer at overseas locations. Most of these programs were initiated through faculty interest, including the Junior Year Abroad program first established in 1923 in Paris. In 1930 the Junior Year Abroad program was extended to Spain and Italy, but these programs were terminated by the Spanish Civil War and World War II. After the war, junior-year students resumed study first in Switzerland, then in France, and by 1950 six Junior Year Abroad programs were in existence. In 1965, 396 United States institutions reported 1314 diverse programs. By 1972 the number of institutions offering study programs abroad had increased to 450 colleges and universities. All of these were not branch campuses, however. In many cases, agreements were made between universities in other nations, under which American students from only one particular university (or from a limited number of universities) would be admitted as a regular student of the host university.

By the 1960s and the 1970s, many of the overseas programs sponsored by United States institutions had developed interdisciplinary area studies that allowed the student to experience a foreign culture by studying a combination of social sciences, languages, and the humanities. Of the total overseas programs requiring at least one year of study, operating between 1958 and 1965, 24.7 percent were in area studies; 17.7 percent were in the humanities; and 15.3 percent were in the social sciences (UNESCO, 1971).

In addition to these longer programs, short-term exposure of United States students to other cultures includes summer study abroad. The Institute of International Education listed 600 programs in 1974. In 1971–1972, a total of 34,218 students enrolled full-time in foreign institutions, 52 percent of which were in Europe. A study done by the University of Indiana in 1974 reported 397 summer programs, 154 semester-length programs, 126 semester-summer combinations, and 451 year-length study programs for United States students in seventy-nine different countries. Also, in 1972–1973, nearly 6,600 United States faculty members were reported abroad.

Programs for military personnel. One motivation behind the development of overseas branch campus was the education of United States military personnel abroad. The content of these programs has varied according to domestic and worldwide military requirements and the social and economic needs of the United States. Basically, however, their goal is to enable individuals to realize their potential, both as members of the armed forces and as citizens of the United States. For example, at the conclusion of World War I, when United States troops in Europe were awaiting shipment home, more than a million and a half course enrollments were amassed at post schools; educational centers; the American University of Beaune, France; mechanical schools; art training centers; and French and British universities.

Furthermore, at the beginning of World War II, the National University Extension Association and the American Council on Education joined with the federal government to mobilize United States education for the war effort. Toward the end of the war, the need for an education program for military personnel awaiting redeployment became apparent. In addition to enrolling military students in European universities, the War Department opened three United States university centers and one technical school in England, France, and Italy.

Then, at the request of the Department of Defense, the first complete college-level program was transplanted to six United States military bases in Europe in October 1949. Shortly thereafter, a United States university began offering courses at United States military installations in the Far East, and another institution inaugurated a program in the Caribbean. There have been as many as twenty-nine United States institutions offering undergraduate, graduate, and vocational courses to United States military personnel stationed in twenty-one countries on four continents. The program offered by the University of Maryland is one of the best known and most highly developed.

Financial arrangements and problems. In the unsteady financial climate of the mid 1970s, the future of overseas branch campuses was as problematic as that of domestic multicampus systems. Financial arrangements between a United States institution and its overseas branch are complicated. Illustrative of the financial problems faced by United States universities with branch campuses was Stanford University's decision in the mid 1970s to close down one of its overseas studies centers in Beutelsbach, Federal Republic of Germany, and to drastically review its program in West Berlin for non-German-speaking students. Stanford regarded these measures, expected to save about $250,000 annually, as a first step in reducing its overseas studies program, which operated at nine centers in five countries. Stanford also runs three small programs that are integrated with courses at the universities of Paris, Salamanca, and Bonn.

The largest program of its kind run by a United States university, Stanford's overseas branches provide six months of study for about 600 students per year; about 40 percent of Stanford's undergraduates take part in the program. The cuts in Stanford's overseas programs are part of a three-year program aimed at reducing the university's operating costs by ten million dollars. The university has appealed to Stanford alumni living in Europe, to United States businessmen in Europe, and to all students who have participated to help save the centers. Stanford has opened talks with the state-run University of California system, which also operates an extensive overseas program; but the possibility of merging the programs was thought to be slight.

Changes and Trends in Multicampus Systems

As a private university, Stanford is particularly susceptible to the "unsteady state" that Lee and Bowen studied in nine multicampus systems in seven states. Their study focuses on particular strategies for the future in the following crucial areas: academic program review, academic budgeting, program development, faculty retrenchment and renewal, and strategies for admission and transfer of students (Lee and Bowen, 1975).

In all nine multicampus systems, Lee and Bowen found growth-inhibiting factors that had emerged in the five years since their previous study and were expected to continue over the next five years. Primary among these were the uneven and unpredictable distribution of students across campuses, with a corresponding uncertainty in state and federal support.

Academic planning. Among the major changes Lee and Bowen found across the nine multicampus systems was a "dramatically increased emphasis on academic plans and planning procedures" (p. 134). In 1971 academic plans were "public relations statements rather than operational guidelines"; in 1975, however, they were "the direct concern of system chief executives and senior administrators. Planning statements explicitly recognize that times are difficult and expected to be more so. While projections of enrollment and physical facilities must still reach ten or fifteen years into the future, operational details of academic program planning rarely extend beyond the first five. Current reality has tempered earlier enthusiasm for long range—in retrospect, ivory tower—plans. General goals and missions remain an essential part of plans but are now supplemented by academic program projections that are sufficiently specific to be operational. Frequent review of operational

objectives—often coordinated with the annual or biennial budget cycle—is also required by the planning process" (p. 134).

Academic budgeting. Fiscal flexibility has always been a characteristic of multicampus systems because funds can be transferred among campuses, at least within major programs. In the 1970s, however, academic budgeting assumed a critical role because of declining enrollments. In easier financial times, continuing expansion of multicampus systems provided flexibility because the average cost of an additional student generally exceeded the actual marginal cost, and growth in enrollment in the following year caught up with errors in the budget period. As enrollments declined, however, adherence to the same financial formulas could reduce funding below cost savings.

Lee and Bowen found all multicampus systems in their study aware that adjustments were required to meet inflation. Although they state that "the authority of the multicampus system must permit it to encourage one campus to fund and staff programs differently from other campuses in a system," they found that the "uncertainty of federal and extramural funds further reduces the necessary guarantee of fiscal flexibility" (p. 138). A possible consequence of the "unsteady state" is the excessive intervention into the internal management of university academic affairs by state government. For this reason Lee and Bowen stress that procedures must be found to separate educational policy from fiscal decisions whenever possible.

New programs. In 1971 new programs—nontraditional, multicampus, innovative, and experimental—flourished. However, the following five years slowed this trend. Enrollment and resource constraints were prime factors in reduced development of multicampus programs, including regional coordination.

Experimentation can be healthy for a multicampus system. Lee and Bowen feel that nontraditional, off-campus, degree-credit programs for part-time students "hold the promise of permitting low-cost experimentation with new programs and new students without major and permanent resource commitments." Thus, nontraditional programs allow the system to continue its research and development function through testing specific student demands. Lee and Bowen concluded that multicampus programs are cost-effective because they give students and faculty new options. For this reason they should be encouraged by the central administration and by reform of systemwide and campus procedures.

Off-campus centers are another nontraditional institutional form that will likely share the problems facing multicampuses in the 1980s. Off-campus centers are "operations separated geographically from the main university campus where college-level programs are offered on a relatively permanent basis. They employ full-time administrative personnel, have permanent status in the community in which they are located, and duplicate or adapt portions of the programs of their parent institutions that lend themselves to off-campus operations" (Romesburg, 1972, p. 21). Empire State College, the external degree program of the State University of New York, has off-campus learning centers in each of the four major regions of the state. Goddard College, in Plainfield, Vermont, has learning centers in New Haven, Connecticut; Cambridge, Massachusetts; and Washington, D. C.

Lee and Bowen advise the central university administration to serve as a catalyst to stimulate innovative instructional programs, to disseminate experimental results throughout the system, to provide funding for new approaches to undergraduate education, and to provide effective evaluation of such experiments (p. 141).

Faculty retrenchment. Another consequence of the "unsteady state" is the decline in expansion and recruitment and a resultant concern with faculty retrenchment. The rights of both tenured and nontenured faculty in the face of these changes is an important issue, as is the growing role of faculty unions. Academic personnel policies and procedures in the late 1970s reflected fewer new faculty members and, in some cases, faculty layoffs. Also, internal programs reflected deliberate curricular changes and changing student demands. Inflation also created a demand for further university expenditure on faculty salaries.

Retrenchment and an overcrowded academic marketplace were real problems everywhere in higher education in the 1970s. However, the multicampus system was often less affected by these difficulties than were other educational institutions because such a system could temporarily transfer positions among campuses and utilize a systemwide pool of temporary positions as it made program adjustments. Nonetheless, a general conservatism among administrators prevented any widespread development of new campus centers or new programs.

Lee and Bowen recommend that tenure should be campus-based, not systemwide, largely because they do not think that mandatory mobility can be practically implemented. To help multicampuses survive the unsteady economy, Lee and Bowen also recommend that tenure quotas should not be set at either the system or the campus level. They suggest the creation of a campus pool of temporary positions, from which a position can be assigned to a department facing a renewal problem.

Student admissions and transfers. Unlike budgeting, academic planning, and program review, systemwide activity in student admissions and transfers was relatively untouched by curtailments in growth. "Programs of enrollment plateaus and declines are largely campus- and program-specific, and there appears little that multicampus systems, as systems, can do about these internal imbalances. Students, unlike budgets, are not readily transferable from one campus to another, and—as with the faculty—forced mobility is simply not an effective strategy" (Lee and Bowen, p. 144). Nevertheless, planning strategies for students in the 1980s focus on a shrinking applicant pool and the ripple effect of unilateral campus action on the system as a whole. Lee and Bowen suggest systemwide monitoring and approval of campus undergraduate admission requirements to counteract the danger of unwarranted competition among campuses for students. The inevitable competition for students and programs between senior and community colleges also suggests the need for continual systemwide review.

In determining its enrollment future, the multicampus system is advised to "increase the quality of campus programs in the face of tight resources, attract students by promoting the qualities of diversity, specialization, and cooperation—the defining characteristics of the multicampus system" (Lee and Bowen, p. 145).

Conclusion. Lee and Bowen's overall conclusion is that "multicampus systems have made a difference for students, for faculty, and for the educational enterprise of their states." As they see it, it has been a positive difference. The decisions made and changes established are better than if policies and decisions had been the responsibility of single campuses, dealing autonomously with each other or with federal and state officials and coordinating agencies (p. 146).

Rather precariously situated between the expansion of the 1960s and the unknown of the 1980s, multicampus systems are aware of a need to strive for a balance between centralization and campus authority. The task is difficult because state agencies will be under pressure to intervene in educational decisions. A further pressure will come from staff instability and collective bargaining. If they can reach a balance between campus and system, the multicampus systems will survive the "unsteady state" of the 1980s.

Bibliography

Becker, I. K. "The Case for Community Junior College." *Junior College Journal,* April 1964, *34*(28).

Berry, D. C. "Higher Education in the United States Army." Unpublished doctoral dissertation, University of Maryland, College Park, Maryland, 1974.

Bittner, W. S., and Mallory, H. F. *University Teaching by Mail.* New York: Macmillan, 1933.

Clark, H. F. and Sloan, H. S. *Classroom in the Military.* New York: Bureau of Publications, Teachers' College, Columbia University, 1963.

Coyne, J., and Hebert, T. *This Way Out.* New York: Dutton, 1972.

Drazek, S. J., and others. (Eds.) *Expanding Horizons . . . Continuing Education.* Minneapolis: National University Extension Association, 1965.

Garraty, J. A., and Adams, W. *From Main Street to the Left Bank.* East Lansing: Michigan State University Press, 1959.

Garraty, J. A., Adams, W., and Taylor, C. J. H. *The New Guide to Study Abroad.* New York: Harper & Row, 1969.

Institute of Advanced Projects. *The International Programs of American Universities.* Honolulu: Institute of Advanced Projects, 1966.

Institute of International Education. *Handbook on International Study for U. S. Nationals.* New York: Institute of International Education, 1970.

Institute of International Education. *U. S. College-Sponsored Programs Abroad: Academic Year.* New York: Institute of International Education, 1973.

Institute of International Education. *Summer Study Abroad.* New York: Institute of International Education, 1974.

Knowles, A. S., and others. *Handbook of Cooperative Education.* San Francisco: Jossey-Bass, 1971.

Lee, E. C., and Bowen, F. M. *Managing Multicampus Systems: Effective Administration in an Unsteady State.* San Francisco: Jossey-Bass, 1975.

Mathies, L., and Thomas, W. G. *Overseas Opportunities for American Educators.* New York: CCM Information Corporation, 1971.

Medsker, L. L. *The Junior College: Progress and Prospect.* New York: McGraw-Hill, 1960.

Parker, F. *American Dissertations on Foreign Education.* Troy, New York: Whitston, 1971.

Pitchell, R. J. *A Directory of U. S. College and University Degrees for Part-Time Students.* Washington, D. C.: NUEA, 1973.

Romesburg, K. D. *Characteristics of Branch Colleges in the United States.* Ann Arbor, Michigan: University Microfilms, 1972.

Sammartino, P. *Multiple Campuses.* Rutherford, New Jersey: Fairleigh Dickinson University Press, 1964.

Sanders, I. T., and Ward, J. C. *Bridges to Under-standing.* New York: McGraw-Hill, 1970.

UNESCO. *Students as Links Between Cultures.* Paris: UNESCO, 1970.

UNESCO. *Statistics of Students Abroad, 1962–1968.* Paris: UNESCO, 1971.

University of Illinois, Urbana. *The Future—International Programs at the University of Illinois.* Urbana, Illinois: University of Illinois, 1968.

PETER SAMMARTINO

BRAZIL, FEDERATIVE REPUBLIC OF

Population: 107,145,000 (July 1975 estimate). Student enrollment in primary school: 19,286,611; secondary school: 1,681,728; higher education 938,649. Percentage of age group (18–22) enrolled in higher education: 7%. Language of instruction: Portuguese. Academic calendar: March to December, two semesters. Percentage of national budget expended on all education: 4.7%; higher education: 2%. [Unless otherwise indicated, figures are for 1974. Budget figures include federal expenditures only. Source of enrollment statistics: Department of University Affairs and Service of Statistics, Ministry of Education, Brasília.]

The first Portuguese settlers arrived in Brazil in the sixteenth century, and the area remained a Portuguese colony until independence in 1822. The ties between Brazil and Portugal were strong; the Portuguese language was a unifying factor during the development of the colony and Portuguese social structures were established.

The first education in Brazil was imparted by missionaries; however, higher education did not exist until the idea of a university in Brazil, to be patterned on the University of Coimbra in Portugal, arose with a revolutionary group in the state of Minas Gerais. However, the rebellion of this group in 1789, led by José Joaquim da Silva Xavier, was crushed immediately. In 1808 the prince regent of Portugal, Dom John, moved the seat of the Portuguese empire to Brazil. During his tenure a mili-

tary academy and medical and law schools were founded in Brazil. Contrary to custom in Portugal, where higher education was imparted in universities, the first institutions of higher education in Brazil were professional schools, specializing in one field of study. They came to be known as isolated or single institutions *(instituições isoladas)*. These professional institutions provided the training in medicine, law, and engineering which was needed by a colonial society. In addition, there were centers of education maintained by religious orders. In these Catholic seminaries, education was offered in the humanities and theology; however, few of the institutions could be considered of higher education status.

Brazil became independent from Portugal in 1822. Higher education developed slowly in the new empire. By 1875 there were six professional schools and a population of ten million. When the first university, the University of Brazil (since 1965 called the Federal University of Rio de Janeiro), opened in 1920, there were sixty-one isolated institutions and a population of thirty-one million.

In 1976 Brazil had 852 institutions of higher education; the majority (786) were isolated schools, while the universities had increased to 63. The student enrollment at the tertiary level had grown to almost 1,000,000—up from 155,000 ten years earlier. This quantitative growth has caused great challenges in terms of physical facilities, curricula, staff, and financial resources. Following periods of student unrest, a major university reform movement started in 1966, and a profound revision of the higher education system was initiated by Law 5.540 on November 28, 1968. The 1968 law and subsequent legislation aimed to minimize duplication of teaching and research functions; utilize human and material resources more effectively; simplify the basic administrative structure by creating departments which can easily be grouped into larger entities, such as institutes or centers; create flexibility in individual programs and in regional offerings; and combine the physical plant of a university in one location, a campus, after the United States pattern.

In addition to internal administrative changes, Brazilian higher education institutions also have had to adjust to new manpower demands created by the rapid industrialization and development process which has taken place in Brazil since 1960. Table 1 shows enrollment trends in various fields of study between 1960 and 1974. The traditional fields of law, engineering, and medicine have been greatly affected. For instance, law accounted for 25 percent of enrollments in 1960 but only 10.7 percent in 1974. Although enrollments in medical studies dropped to 5.8, there is still a national average ratio of eight applicants per available place. As a result of the admissions between 1968 and 1973, it is expected that 50,000 new doctors will enter the job market between 1974 and 1979, which means a doubling of the number of doctors that were available in 1973. The market shifts, however, have not fully reflected the needs

for manpower. Although agriculture is a priority sector in the economy, enrollments in agriculture constituted only 1.6 percent of the total enrollments in 1974.

Brazil has also had a substantial growth in graduate programs during the period since 1960, and in 1976 over 50 institutions offered graduate studies in 150 specialties at the master's degree level and in 90 specialties at the doctoral level. The graduate programs, however, have been hampered by a need for staff and expanded facilities for research. To guide the continued growth of graduate education, a National Graduate Studies Council was created in 1975, and a first National Plan for Graduate Education was approved by the legislature.

National Educational Policy

The population in Brazil grows at 2.9 percent per year, and over 50 percent of the citizens are under twenty years of age. The illiteracy rate was 39 percent in 1960. Despite the efforts of MOBRAL, the Brazilian Movement for Literacy, some 21 percent of the population were still illiterate

Table 1. Enrollment Trends per Fields of Study in Brazil 1960–1974

	1960		1974	
	Enrollment	%	*Enrollment*	%
Administration and economics	8,838	9.5	148,816	16.6
Agriculture	1,936	2.1	14,494	1.6
Architecture and urban studies	1,589	1.7	12,006	1.3
Arts	2,813	3.0	14,272	1.5
Law	23,293	25.0	95,850	10.7
Nursing	1,624	1.7	6,446	0.7
Engineering	10,821	11.6	80,007	8.9
Pharmacy	1,841	2.0	7,610	0.8
Philosophy, humanities, and literature	20,418	21.9	231,244	25.9
Sciences (mathematics, physics, chemistry, biology)			85,053	9.5
Medicine	10,316	11.7	52,051	5.8
Veterinary medicine	802	0.9	6,258	0.7
Dentistry	5,591	6.0	16,400	1.8
Social services	1,289	1.4	11,862	1.3
Others (including general studies)	2,031	2.2	114,831	12.9
TOTAL	93,202	100.0	897,200	100.0

Source: Department of University Affairs.

in 1974. National priorities call for increased literacy, quantitative and qualitative improvements of the teaching staff, and expanded educational facilities at all levels, guided by the government in accordance with manpower demands.

Legal Basis of Educational System

Article 176 of the 1967 Brazilian constitution states: "Education, inspired by the principle of national unity and the ideals of liberty and human solidarity, is a right of all and a duty of the State." Article 8 empowers the federal government to legislate the basis and policies of education, while allowing the individual states to enact complementary legislation. Under the constitution, elementary education is free and compulsory while public secondary and higher education should be free for those unable to pay.

Major legal texts relating to the constitutional guidelines for education include Law 4024/1961 on "Directives and Basis of National Education," which was of basic importance for the decentralization of the Brazilian educational system from the elementary to the university level. The law also recognized and imparted new functions to the Federal Council of Education and to the State Councils of Education. Decree-Law 53/1966 provided for a reorganization of the federal university system, whereby teaching and research in the basic sciences were integrated into separate institutes. The basic sciences previously had been taught concurrently in different faculties of the university, duplicating facilities, laboratories, and libraries. Additional basic directives for the reform of all universities and other institutions of higher education of the country were provided in Law 5540/1968 and Decree-Law 464/1969. The Basic Education Law 5692/1971, which provided for a major educational reform, is still in the process of implementation. It introduced an eight-year program in the elementary schools, now called *education of the first degree*, and a three- or four-

year program in secondary schools, now called *education of the second degree.*

Types of Institutions

There are three types of higher education institutions: universities, isolated or single institutions *(instituições isoladas),* and university federations *(federações).* The 63 universities can be divided into 30 federal universities, 3 municipal universities, 8 state universities, and 22 private universities. The 786 single institutions (those generally specializing in one field of study) also can be divided, in accordance with administrative authority, into 608 private, 17 federal, 76 state, and 85 municipal institutions. The single institutions are referred to as schools, institutes, or faculties. There are also 3 university federations—that is, university consortia.

The organization and functioning of the universities are defined in statutes and bylaws, which must be approved by the Federal Council of Education and confirmed by the Ministry of Education and Culture. The statutes and bylaws of state universities, in states that had maintained universities for more than five years prior to 1968, may be approved by the State Council of Education.

The Federal Council of Education authorizes and recognizes new programs of study in public and private institutions and, after a federal investigation, may suspend the autonomy of any university if federal legal provisions or institutional bylaws have been violated.

Relationship with Secondary Education and Admission Requirements

The 1971 Basic Education Law introduced an eight-year compulsory primary school called *education of the first degree.* It encompasses four years of basic general studies, followed by a period of introduction to vocational studies in grades 5 to 8. This first stage includes the former programs known as *primário* and *ginasial* and ends with a certificate, which allows entry to the secondary stage of education. Students generally start school at age seven.

At the second level, called *education of the second degree,* students receive three or four years of education, which prepare for middle-level positions or for higher education.

Brazil has *numerus clausus* (restricted entry) in its higher education institutions in accordance with enrollment capacity and manpower demands. By law, however, completion of a secondary program of study or equivalent (an equivalency examination) and success in an entrance examination *(concurso vestibular)* are requisites for access to higher education institutions. There is no age limitation. The entrance examination is very competitive; the average national ratio of applicants to available openings is approximately 2.2:1, with variations according to fields of study.

Administration and Control

Under the constitution education is the responsibility of the states, while the federal government has a fundamental role in rectifying local deficiencies due to regional financial disparities. (Brazil is a federative republic consisting of twenty-two states, four territories, and one federal district.) Some states provide and fund virtually all education at all levels, from elementary school to graduate training; in the state of São Paulo, for instance, the education budget is practically equal to the federal education budget for the whole country. On the other hand, less economically developed states and the federal territories depend on supplementary funding from the federal government.

The Ministry of Education and Culture determines educational policy and is responsible for its implementation at the federal level. The ministry is assisted by a Federal Council of Education *(Conselho federal de educação:* CFE). The Department of University Affairs within the ministry is the chief administrative agency, charged with implementing the decisions of the Federal Council of Education in matters of higher education. The council is responsible for (1) providing guidelines for educational policy and planning; (2) giving opinions on educational questions submitted to it by the president of the country or by the minister of education; (3) adopting or proposing changes in the federal system of education; (4) accrediting universities and other institutions of higher education; (5) authorizing new universities and private isolated schools; (6) setting minimal standards for national undergraduate programs; (7) establishing norms and standards for graduate education; (8) coordinating its efforts with those of the State Councils of Education; (9) promoting educational research.

The council is composed of twenty-four members appointed from the public and private sectors by the president of the republic for a six-year term (staggered so that one third of the members retire every two years) and selected on the basis of merit and educational experience. The council is divided into three chambers, one for the first and second levels of education, another for higher education, and a third for legislative matters. Membership in the council takes precedence over all other activities of its members. The decisions of the council, including those affecting higher education, are subject to approval by the minister of education.

Each state has a State Council of Education, whose functions, powers, and composition are organized and defined by state law. The State Councils of Education are the decision-making bodies within the states, working in conjunction with the State Secretariats of Education, the Federal Council of Education, and the Ministry of Education and Culture.

The Department of University Affairs within the Ministry of Education is responsible not only for the supervision and provision of technical assistance to the federal universities and public isolated institutions but also for the inspection of all private institutions and for administering government subsidies to them.

Although not an official body, the Council of Rectors of the Brazilian Universities

(Conselho de reitores das universidades brasileiras), founded in 1966, has representation from all public and private universities and thus can exercise much leadership. The council advocated a number of educational changes in the 1960s and 1970s.

The rector *(reitor)* is the executive head of a university. In federal universities he is selected by the president of the republic for a period of four years from a list of six names elected by the university council and proposed to the president by the minister of education. The rector cannot be appointed for two consecutive terms. In state universities the rector is selected by the state governor from a list of three names elected by the university council. In private institutions the rector is selected in accordance with the charter of the particular university. The chief executive of an isolated institution is the director *(diretor),* who in federal institutions also is appointed by the president of the republic from a list of three names recommended by the congregation, a selected assembly of teachers and student representatives; the procedure is the same in state institutions, where the appointment is made by the state governor. In private isolated schools the director is appointed according to the charter of the respective institution.

According to legislation, the administrative structure of the universities consists of a general assembly, chaired by the rector, and of two central bodies, generally termed the university council and the council of teaching and research. Membership in the councils is drawn from the different ranks of the teaching staff as well as from alumni and the community. The universities are divided into departments, which, in turn, are grouped by subject matter and scientific areas into institutes, schools, faculties, or centers as intermediate administrative structures between the departments and the rector's office.

Programs and Degrees

The Federal Council of Education establishes the duration and content of the programs of study. The public universities may introduce programs within the limitations of the law; private institutions require approval for new programs from the Federal Council of Education. Programs in municipal and state institutions are approved by the State Council of Education.

Short-cycle technological programs, which lead to middle-level positions and last two to three years, are offered. The degree-level title *bacharel* is awarded in fields such as law (five years), administration (four years), and economics (four years). The title *licenciado,* awarded in fields such as teacher training, humanities, and sciences, also requires four years of study. Additional titles such as agronomist, dentist, engineer, medical doctor, and nurse are awarded after four to five years of study (six for medical doctors). The universities award the doctoral degrees; only in exceptional circumstances may doctoral degrees be awarded by isolated institutions.

Financing

Higher education financing in Brazil is provided by federal, state, municipal, and private sources. The extent of the private contribution is not easily identified. Data on financing are mainly available from the federal government; however, some of the states, such as São Paulo, expend almost as much on education as the federal government. Approximately 4.7 percent of the federal budget is allotted to education, 48.7 percent of this total was for higher education in 1974.

Student Financial Aid and Access to Education

The majority of the public universities charge no tuition fees. Limited housing facilities exist at some institutions that have established campuses. Most students, however, have to find housing outside the university. Costs for meals at the public universities are subsidized by the government or by the universities themselves. The *Instituto tecnológico de aeronáutica* (ITA), a prestigious federal institute in São Paulo, is the only federal institution where students receive free housing, food, medical services, and a monthly allowance. In the private sector tuition is charged, ranging from a low of US$400 yearly for a humanities program to US$1000–2500 in medical programs (1976).

In 1976 a national plan of educational credits was introduced to provide loans to students in private institutions and supply partial living expenses for students in private and public institutions. By June 1976 more than 100,000 students had applied for such loans. Since the 1960s the number of students from middle- and working-class backgrounds has increased steadily. In the mid 1970s some 10 percent of the student enrollment were from the working class. It is expected that the program of educational credits will assist in increasing this percentage.

Student organizations and activities are regulated by Decree-Laws 228 of 1967 and 477 of 1969. Student political activity is undertaken only within the formal political parties outside the university. Students are allowed on all university councils and commissions but may not exceed 20 percent of total membership on such bodies.

Teaching Staff

In the federal system and in some of the private institutions the ranks of the teaching staff are full professor, associate professor, and assistant professor. Professors may be appointed in accordance with the rules of the federal Statutes of Higher Education Staff or according to Brazilian labor laws. The professors and assistant professors have to undergo a public examination of titles and merits, while associate professors are appointed on the basis of an examination of their titles. The appointments are made, after approval by the respective departments, by the rector at the universities or by the director at the isolated schools.

Professors are appointed full time (that is, either with exclusive dedication, which precludes outside employment, or for forty hours per week) or part time, for twelve to twenty hours per week. By far the largest

number of teaching staff are employed part time. Table 2 lists the qualifications and teaching loads of teaching staff in 1973 and compares data for public and private institutions.

The salary structures differ between the public institutions, which employ larger numbers of teaching staff full time, and the private institutions, which overwhelmingly employ teaching staff by the hour.

Research Activities

Graduate education in Brazil encompasses those programs that lead to a master's or doctoral degree. Research is considered an essential part of the graduate programs.

Due to the large numbers of part-time teaching staff, Brazil has encountered difficulties in achieving "unity of teaching and research," which has been encouraged in recent educational reforms. It is estimated, however, that 80 percent of research in Brazil takes place in universities and other higher education institutions. An important element in the amount of research has been the Plan for Scientific

Table 2. Teaching Staff in Brazilian Institutions of Higher Education by Qualification and Teaching Load 1973

Qualification	Teaching staff in public institutions	Teaching staff in private institutions	Total	%
Ph.D. level	4,563	1,480	6,043	8.9
Masters'	3,106	2,565	5,671	8.3
Special courses	6,990	7,673	14,663	21.6
Bachelor's level	22,441	19,106	41,547	61.2
TOTAL	37,100	30,824	67,924	100.0
Part time[a]	28,553	28,384	56,937	83.8
Full time[b]	8,547	2,440	10,987	16.2
TOTAL	37,100	30,824	67,924	100.0

[a]Work load of 12 to 20 hours per week.
[b]Work load of 40 hours per week or exclusive dedicated to research and teaching.

and Technological Development, a three-year program to provide support for research in priority fields of study, such as the natural and exact sciences, biology, engineering, agriculture, health sciences, technology, and information sciences. A manpower training program is also being implemented under the National Plan for Graduate Education. The plan identified a need for upgrading of the qualifications of university staff and anticipated a need for an additional 16,800 master's degree and 1400 doctoral degree holders between 1975 and 1979. Fellowships which involve research projects are provided for study in Brazil or abroad by the Ministry of Education and the National Council for Scientific and Technological Development.

Minimal funding for research is provided by the universities themselves; additional funds are received from government agencies. The National Council for Scientific and Technological Development, created in 1951, has played a major role in the support of basic research and manpower training.

Current Problems and Trends

The Brazilian Movement for Literacy *(Movimento brasileiro de alfabetização:* MOBRAL*)* enrolls about five million adult illiterates in its programs. Brazil has been able to lower the percentage of illiteracy in the country from 39 percent in 1960 to 21 percent in 1974. Coupled with the effort to achieve a higher level of literacy is the effort toward qualitative improvements of teaching staff at all levels. The Teaching Expansion Program and other in-service programs attempt to improve teacher proficiency at the first two levels of education; expanded graduate programs aim to increase qualifications at the higher education level. Thus, programs such as the Full-Time Professorial Program, which provides funding for greater numbers of full-time teaching staff, and the National Plan for Graduate Education, which expands study opportunities at the graduate level, are being funded by the government.

The National Plan for Graduate Education is administered by the National Graduate Studies Council, which was established in 1975 to plan and analyze the national needs for teacher training for higher education institutions. The membership of this council reflects the seriousness of the government's efforts in this area. Agencies that are among the members of the council are the Ministry of Education, the Secretariat of Planning, the National Council for Scientific and Technological Development, the Department of University Affairs, and the National Economic Development Bank; in addition, there are representatives of public and private universities.

The Federal Council of Education is also engaged in a major revision of curricula in different fields of study. Curricula in engineering, geology, sciences (mathematics, physics, chemistry, and biology), and education were revised and approved during 1975 and 1976.

Among other trends evident in Brazilian higher education also can be mentioned the growth of short-cycle education (126 programs of study in 1976) in priority manpower areas; the introduction of experimental cooperative education in the engineering programs of three public universities; and the increased tendency to defer the selection of a major. Contrary to the history of higher education as professional specialization, greater numbers of students now enroll in a general studies program for a year or two. This deferment of professional selection has been made possible by the educational reforms, which consolidated basic studies into departmental groupings instead of providing them separately in each faculty. The new structural unity of the university also is evident in the trend in a number of the federal and private universities to establish physical facilities at a central campus.

HEITOR GURGULINO DE SOUZA

Bibliography

Amado, G. *Educação média e fundamental.* Rio de Janeiro: José Olympio, 1973.

Catálogo geral das instituições de ensino superior 1974. Brasília: Ministério da educação e cultura, 1975.

Estatísticas da educação nacional 1960–71. Rio de Janeiro: Serviço de estatística da educação e cultura, 1972.

Harrell, W. A. *Educational Reform in Brazil. The Law of 1961.* Washington, D.C.: U.S. Department of Health, Education and Welfare, 1968.

Harrell, W. A. *The Brazilian Education System: A Summary.* Washington, D.C.: U.S. Department of Health, Education and Welfare, 1970.

Havighurst, R. J., and Moreira, J. R. *Society and Education in Brazil.* Pittsburgh: University of Pittsburgh Press, 1964.

Heimer, F.-W. "Education and Politics in Brazil." *Comparative Education Review,* February 1975, *19*(1), 51–67.

See also: Academic Dress and Insignia; Academic Standards and Accreditation: International; Adult Education: Adult Education in Developing Countries, Government Programs; Archives: Mediterranean, the Vatican, and Latin America, National Archives of; Cooperative Education and Off-Campus Experience: Cooperative Education Worldwide; Instruction, Individualized; Military Training and Higher Education; Science Policies: Less Developed Countries: Argentina, Brazil, and Mexico; South America: Regional Analysis.

BRAZIL, SCIENCE POLICIES OF

See Science Policies: Less Developed Countries: Argentina, Brazil, and Mexico.

BRAZILIAN CENTER
OF EDUCATIONAL RESEARCH
(Centro brasileiro de
pesquisas educacionais)

The Brazilian Center of Educational Research of the *Instituto nacional de estudos pedagógicos* (INEP: National Institute of Pedagogical Studies) was founded in 1955 to promote and conduct research in education. Research studies are made in primary, secondary, higher, adult, and vocational education. Higher education research, with a national focus, is concerned with studies of university students and of medical education. In addition to research activities, the center supplies technical assistance for educational research, aids in the in-service training of teachers and administrators, and provides a documentation service on all aspects of Brazilian education.

The center is funded by the government and through publication sales. Its staff includes a director, 5 research professionals, 73 technicians, and 83 administrative personnel. The staff has access to a library, microfilm equipment, and photocopying equipment. The center has regional centers in São Paulo, Belo Horizonte, Salvador, Pôrto Alegre, and Recife.

Publications of the center include the *Revista brasileira de estudos pedagógicos, Bibliografie brasileira de educação,* and *Boletim informativo.*

Rua Voluntários de Pátria 107, ZC-02
20000 Rio de Janeiro, Brazil

BRITISH ACADEMY

The British Academy owes its origin to a meeting of academies in October 1899 at Wiesbaden, Germany, where it was resolved to set up an International Association of Scientific and Literary Academies throughout the world. In this new association the Royal Society represented the United Kingdom in the natural science section, but no existing institution of the humanities was deemed competent to represent the United Kingdom. Accordingly, on the initiative of the Royal Society, the British Academy was created in 1901 for the purpose of representing historical, philosophical, and philological studies under conditions which would satisfy the requirements of the international association. In the following year it was granted a Royal Charter by King Edward VII on the eve of his coronation.

The membership of the academy was originally restricted to one hundred fellows; in 1974 the total permitted number was raised to 350. Fellows become senior fellows at the age of seventy-two, and as such are not included in the total. Officers of the academy include a president, foreign secretary, secretary, and treasurer.

At first the academy was organized into four sections but subsequently encompassed fourteen sections, covering the fields of ancient history; medieval history; Biblical, theological, and religious studies; Oriental and African studies; classical literature and philology; medieval and modern literature and philology; philosophy; jurisprudence; economics and economic history; archeology; the history of art; social and political studies; modern history; and modern history from 1800.

Initially the work of the academy was funded, through the enterprise of the first secretary, by a number of benefactions; and in 1924 an annual grant was added by His Majesty's Treasury. Except for a short interruption, the academy has assumed increasing responsibilities as the recognized intermediary between the government and humanistic research beyond the routine operation of the universities.

In summary, the academy undertakes the following main functions: the support and development of British institutes and schools overseas; the provision of grants for research projects and publication, whether undertaken by individuals and institutions outside the academy or by the academy itself and its fellows; the organization and publication of lectures in the appropriate fields; the publication of monographs or serial publications relating to the humanities; and the maintenance of contacts with scholars abroad through the *Union académique internationale* (International Union of Academies), foreign academies, and participation in international congresses.

Publications include *Proceedings* (annual), *Schweich Lectures on Biblical Archaeology,* and monographs.

Burlington House, Piccadilly
London W1V 0NS, England

BRITISH COUNCIL

The British Council, granted a Royal Charter in 1940, was set up to represent British life and institutions abroad and to bring about a better understanding between the United Kingdom and other countries. Privately established in 1934 as the British Committee for Relations with Other Countries, with the support of the Foreign Office, the British Council assumed its present name in 1935. In its early days the council was concerned with projecting Britain in Europe, Latin America, and the Middle East, but since the 1950s the council has had a dual purpose: the fostering of cultural relations and the administration of educational aid.

The affairs of the council are directed by an executive committee of thirty members. Eight of these are nominated by ministers and include representatives of the Foreign and Commonwealth Office and Overseas Development Administration (ODA), the Department of Education and Science, and the Department of Trade and Industry. The remaining members are elected by the committee itself and include representatives of the universities, publishing, the arts, sciences, industry, the trade unions, and members of both houses of Parliament. Assistance is also given by advisory committees composed of leading figures in education, the sciences, the arts, and the professions as well as committees that advise on the special contributions made by Scotland and Wales to the culture of the United Kingdom and the council's work.

With a headquarters in London and a United Kingdom–based staff of more than two thousand, some 460 of whom are overseas, the council is active in seventy-six countries on five continents. Its annual income of more than nineteen million pounds is provided almost entirely from public funds. Although the treasury exercises close financial control, the council maintains a degree of autonomy in its undertakings. Over one third of the budget is allocated to educational activities; and, of this fraction, over two million pounds are spent on specific projects administered on behalf of the Overseas Development Administration.

The council is recognized as a leading authority in the teaching of English overseas, and this has always been one of its main activities. As the demand for the teaching of English overseas increased, the council no longer wished to assume the responsibility for direct teaching but preferred, whenever possible, to cooperate directly with Ministries of Education overseas in the training of teachers of English. Only when this is not possible is direct teaching relied upon and then principally for its value as a model. In general, and especially in developing countries, the council operates by providing staff to help train and organize in-service courses for teachers of English. The council advises on syllabi, textbooks, visual aids, and the use of mass media and is also active in a number of countries in the field of educational television. These activities call for close collaboration with the ODA, the Center for Educational Development Overseas, the Inter-University Council, and the Council for Technical Education and Training for Overseas Countries. An English-Teaching Information Centre is maintained in London to serve as a study center and clearinghouse for information on all aspects of teaching English as a second or foreign language.

The council is an important source of information and advice to educationists in all fields. In most developing countries it acts as adviser in educational matters to the British diplomatic missions, and in a number of countries it is charged with the responsibility for the administration of educational aid. British examinations abroad are conducted on behalf of such bodies as the Cambridge Board and on behalf of professional agencies such as members of the Council of Engineering Institutions. In addition, the council recruits several

hundred British teachers each year for service in overseas universities, teacher training colleges, and schools, and in advisory posts in ministries and departments of education. On behalf of the three or four societies associated with the British volunteer program, the council provides the administrative framework overseas for well over one thousand young volunteers, who serve for a year or more—mainly as teachers—in developing countries. The aims of the voluntary organizations and the council are closely allied.

The council maintains a high level of activity in the fields of science and medicine. Overseas science staff develop professional and scientific collaboration between British and other countries by fostering personal contacts and providing specific information about British science in all fields. They are supported by a specialist staff and by resources which include not only the council's own medical and scientific libraries at its London headquarters but also access to many British scientific, medical, and documentation sources.

An important part of the council's work is the fostering of personal contacts between specialists in the United Kingdom and overseas specialists. The council arranges for leading British representatives of education, science, the professions, and the arts to make short tours or advisory visits to meet overseas specialists, to discuss common problems, to advise or conduct courses, and to lecture.

On a much larger scale the council provides services to visitors coming to Britain for the purposes of study, research, observation, or training. These services include finance, accommodation, travel, and arrangement of programs and are provided particularly for students who have come to Britain for one year of postgraduate study in British Council–financed programs. Students financed at their own or their government's expense and those assisted by the council acting as agent for other organizations—for example, fellows financed by the United Nations and its specialized agencies—are also eligible for these services. The council offers many of the same facilities to tens of thousands of overseas students coming to Britain each year. Short courses, study tours, and recreational visits are arranged for them; and a large, council-run students' center offers a varied program of activities.

The council administers an official grant for accommodations for overseas students in Britain—in cooperation with centers of education, local authorities, and voluntary bodies and individuals. In addition, it administers funds officially provided for the promotion of international youth exchanges; in carrying out this function, it is advised by committees concerned with plans of individuals and by a consultative committee representing youth organizations throughout the United Kingdom.

To help meet the need for British books and periodicals overseas, the council maintains 126 libraries of its own and supplies books and periodicals to 100 associated libraries. These libraries—ranging from small reference collections to more comprehensive collections of up to 70,000 volumes—provide information in the education field, keep specialists in touch with recent British developments in their own fields, and support the council's work in education, the teaching of English, and science. The council organizes overseas every year over 150 exhibitions, both general and specialized, to publicize British books and periodicals, and its libraries supply specially compiled bibliographies. In addition, since 1959 the council has helped create and develop public library services in a number of countries, mainly in Africa; and since 1971 it has administered a program of book and periodical presentations in developing countries, financed by the ODA.

To ensure overseas access to British drama, music, and the visual arts, the council promotes or assists tours by British drama, ballet, and opera companies and by orchestras and soloists. In cooperation with local museums and art galleries over-

seas, it supplies British paintings and sculpture for exhibition. It also runs film-lending libraries. which contain films on English-language teaching and other specialized films in the arts, education, medicine, and science. Through an information and reference section for overseas specialists in the arts, the council sends copies of plays, records, music, and photographic displays to many of its libraries overseas.

Where there are bilateral cultural agreements between Britain and other countries, the council normally acts as the British government's agent. Whether or not such an agreement exists, the council's overseas staff take an interest in the cultural life of the country in which they work. In some of the newer countries, council centers are widely used for meetings, exhibitions, and performances by local dramatic, artistic, and other societies. Staff overseas foster appreciation of the cultural achievements of the country to which they have been assigned and bring together people of different races and nationalities for the enjoyment of common pursuits. The council recognizes that cultural relations are a two-way affair and aims at the promotion of understanding in both directions.

The council's role in providing bibliographical aid is evidenced by its special bibliographical publications, such as *New Approaches to the Teaching of Mathematics*, *British Books on Agriculture*, and *British Books on Educational Innovation*. It also publishes *British Book News*, a monthly publication giving a brief account of 240 new books of special interest to overseas readers; and *Writers and Their Work*, a series of critical essays on leading British writers.

In addition to publishing an annual report, the council publishes a number of scientific and medical journals, including *British Medicine* (monthly), *British Medical Bulletin* (three times a year), and *Science Education Newsletter* (three times a year). It also publishes a number of periodicals on the teaching of English as a second or foreign language. Every two years the council publishes jointly, with the Association of Commonwealth Universities, *Higher Education in the United Kingdom*, a handbook for students overseas; and also issues *How to Live in Britain*, a booklet of practical advice for students and others.

Lonsdale Chambers
27 Chancery Lane
London WC2A 1 PJ, England

BRITISH LIBRARY
See Libraries: British Library, England.

BRITISH MUSEUM
See Libraries: Bodleian Library.

BRITISH VIRGIN ISLANDS

Population: 12,000. Student enrollment in primary school: 2181 (1090 females); secondary school: 796 (430 females); postsecondary education, teacher training: 36 (32 females); abroad: approximately 146. Language of instruction: English. [Figures are for 1974.]

The British Virgin Islands, located in the eastern Caribbean, are a British crown colony. Education, which is patterned on the British model, is free and compulsory. Secondary education is the highest level of formal education provided on the islands, although there are some in-service training courses for teachers and extramural classes for youth and adults who wish to prepare for the London and Cambridge General Certificate of Education, ordinary level.

In 1974, approximately 150 students studied abroad—47 on government scholarships. The total included some 100 students attending institutions in the United States. Since all but two of those students were privately sponsored, exact enrollment figures are not available.

The British Virgin Islands is one of the areas contributing to the University of the West Indies, whose main campus is located in Mona, Jamaica, with branch campuses located in Cave Hill, Barbados, and St. Augustine, Trinidad. In 1974 fifteen students attended the university under government scholarships. Government scholarships were also available for technical study in the Caribbean and for study in Canada and Great Britain.

[Information supplied by the Education Department, Tortola, British Virgin Islands.]

BROWN REPORT
See UNISIST: Study Report on the Feasibility of a World Science Information System (Higher Education Report), Multinational.

BRUNEI, SULTANATE OF

Population: 150,000 (1975 estimate). Student enrollment in primary school: 30,700; secondary school (academic, vocational, technical) 13,000; higher education (abroad), 380 approximately. [Unless otherwise indicated, figures are for 1973].

The Sultanate of Brunei is located on the north coast of Borneo. Although Brunei is related to Britain in matters of foreign affairs and defense, it has been internally self-governing since 1971.

There are three systems of education in Brunei classified in accordance with the language of instruction: Malay, Chinese, or English. There are government-supported primary and secondary schools as well as denominational and private schools. Primary education, offered by 137 schools, lasts six years. The secondary program, offered in 26 general schools, leads to examinations for the Malaysian Examinations Syndicate or to the General Certificate of Education (GCE) of Cambridge, at ordinary or advanced level. Brunei has five technical/vocational schools at the secondary level offering specializations such as agriculture, engineering, or teacher training.

Students go abroad for higher education, generally to the United Kingdom or other Commonwealth countries.

BUDDHISM
See Religious Influences in Higher Education: Buddhism.

BUDGETING
See Financial Affairs: Budgeting.

BUILDING AND CONSTRUCTION ADMINISTRATION

The variables in institutions of higher education are too many and too great to offer more than a discussion of general principles of building and construction administration. The principles cited here are drawn mainly from experience in the United States; however, with adjustment for national and institutional variables, they can be of universal applicability.

Among the many variables that must be considered before making decisions about building and construction administration are the size of the student body, purposes and goals of curricula, the source of control, and the patterns of organization in the institution. The sources and amounts of both operating and capital funds are also very important, as are the size and setting of the physical plant, the numbers of buildings, and the ways in which they are used.

Because of the many differing factors, programs in building construction and administration have to be patterned to individual problems. The only universal rules are simplicity, economy, and flexibility.

Building and Construction Department Personnel

The director of building and construction administration is responsible for 10 percent or more of the operating costs of the institution and for the judgments involved in making major capital invest-

ments. He is responsible for distribution and functioning of utilities, such as light, heat, and power, without which operations can be paralyzed. It is advisable, therefore, for the director to be in the higher echelons of management, reporting directly to the president or other senior administrative officer. Generally, it is not desirable for him to report through academic channels, since he needs to be able to make objective evaluations of the demands of the academic staff for facilities and amenities. Fiscal channels may be as constrictive as the academic channels are expansive. The director should be the balance wheel between these two segments of the institution.

Qualifications of a director. The ideal director of building and construction administration need not be a specialist but should be able to evaluate the work of specialists. He needs a sense of good and bad design and familiarity with the design process and with the problems of an architectural office. An understanding of the various fields of engineering, in themselves and in their relationship to the architect and to operating costs, is also necessary, as is experience with the processes of construction from bidding procedures through inspection, approval, and acceptance of finished work.

The director also needs to understand the principles of a good maintenance program and to be ready to argue for a good program in order to minimize the high cost of deferred maintenance. Good management experience and capability are also important, since the director generally has to lead and evaluate a sizable staff. In addition, since the director will be presenting his programs to officers and trustees, he will need to be articulate and informed, ready to defend unpopular decisions.

Perhaps most important, the director should have a good sense of economy— that is, a sense of value and an awareness of good fiscal practice.

Experience rather than education will produce these ideal characteristics. The best directors most often have a background in construction or construction management. However, some of the most successful directors have had no technical training at all but have come from a background of general management that has taught them to use technicians to provide the expertise they may lack.

The director's staff. The size of the director's staff will vary with the size and complexity of the institution. A frequent mistake is the creation of large staffs, a result of the demand by academics and administrators that building and construction problems be handled expeditiously. The department wants to be ready for the maximum demand, if only to protect itself from criticism. Building departments also tend to keep excessive records, again for self-protection. That practice, too, leads to excessive staffing, as does the desire to have a wide spread of in-house capability. The belief that a large in-house staff will get work done faster and cheaper has generally proven false.

Excessive staffs are also the result of the complexity of the procedures used for requisitioning, record keeping, purchasing, and drawing contracts. It is much easier to prevent the establishment of complicated procedures than it is to get rid of them once they have been established.

In most institutions planning and design are best handled by outside architects, both for new buildings and for major remodeling or conversion to new use of old buildings. In large institutions there may be a sufficient quantity of small alteration or revised layout work to justify having one or two draftsmen on the staff. However, a fully qualified and registered architect is seldom, if ever, needed as a full-time staff member. There is a risk that an in-house architect might pass critical judgment on the work of outside architects employed by the institution, even though they may have greater expertise and experience. The outside architect might be inclined to accept these judgments to ensure his future employment by the institution.

If the director does not feel able to provide a stable architectural policy in matters of overall design and detail, then it would be desirable to employ a consulting architect from the outside on a continuing basis. The consultant might be precluded from handling individual projects in his office in order to ensure objectivity in his critique.

There are four primary functions of a building and construction department: planning and design, construction, maintenance, and mechanical services and utilities.

Planning and Design

Direction of long-range planning must come from within the institution, although outside help may be needed for special skills or expertise. Demographers, traffic engineers, and utility experts may be brought in, as may be those skilled in estimating construction costs, in establishing and controlling construction budgets, and in determining space utilization. Architects, landscape architects, and city planners are also hired as consultants. However, the institution must have first established its own objectives and requirements as an educational facility. These objectives must be clearly defined for all outside consultants, and the consultants' results in carrying out these objectives must be evaluated and coordinated from within. This task belongs logically to the building and construction administration.

In a long-range plan, the functional parts are arranged in a general skeletal pattern that includes the movement of people and vehicular traffic, the movement of material and supplies, and especially parking. In addition, many utilities are involved—water supply, heating, cooling, electricity, communications, and sewage. The design, procurement, operation, and maintenance of these functions are best handled by the building and construction administration.

Furthermore, it is generally conceded that long-range planning is not a one-time job. It is a continuing process because the criteria in which plans are developed are constantly changing. Thus, all aspects of a plan must be constantly updated and reviewed in the light of their possible effect on the long-range plan. Such a review is most effectively done by a permanent staff member, who can best interpret the effect of such decisions on physical plant needs and uses.

The building and construction administration carries the heavy responsibility for implementing the long-range plan through the design and construction of new buildings or the remodeling or conversion of old buildings. This task is part of the shorter-range planning process, covering five years or less. It requires (1) precise definition of occupancy requirements at the start of the architectural design process (bearing in mind that as much as two years may elapse for design and construction before the building is occupied); (2) evaluation of current space utilization; (3) availability of funds; (4) faculty and staff requirements (including their cost); and (5) cost of operating and maintaining the addition to the overall physical plant.

There is generally a resistance to the remodeling, renovation, and conversion to new uses of old buildings. The true reasons for this resistance are other than economic, though that fact is seldom admitted.

From the future occupant's point of view, the new building is always more desirable. It carries more prestige and has more glamor. A new building may eliminate the inconvenience of occupying a building that is being rejuvenated and will always provide greater freedom in arrangement. There is no limitation on its size other than the cost, and there is a choice of location.

Most architects will favor the new building because of the added detail work involved in renovation. Old buildings require a detailed survey of dimensional characteristics and, in rare cases, a check of structural suitability. Usually, in any major project all the mechanical facilities are newly provided; however, if any are to be reused, careful study and evaluation are needed. Fitting the program requirements to existing areas and shapes requires more time,

patience, and ingenuity. Finally, rebuilt structures are seldom discussed in the professional journals; they lack publicity value.

On the economic side, there are some arguments against the use of certain old buildings. An old building may be wasteful of valuable land area and could be replaced by a structure with more floor levels. Occasionally an old building will require excessive expenditures to make it structurally sound and adequately fire resistant, so that it conforms to local or state building codes. However, there are many more reasons of economy favoring rehabilitation or conversion. About one third to one half of the original value of a building will not deteriorate with time and hence will not require change at the time of rehabilitation. The excavation, footings and foundations, structural frame, exterior walls and glass, and the landscaping may all be reused, thus eliminating the contractors' overhead and profit on these items.

The components that do deteriorate, become obsolete, or require replacement include roofing, interior partitions, finished floors, wall finishes, painting, ceilings, plumbing and fixtures, heating, ventilating, air conditioning, and the electrical system, including the fixtures. Replacement of these items creates, in effect, a completely new building interior that will require no more maintenance than that of a new building.

Among the many other advantages to rehabilitation or conversion is the fact that planning and execution can usually be accomplished in less than half the time required for the new building. Also, old structures generally cost less to heat or air condition than new buildings, because of their heavy masonry walls and because of the more extensive use of glass in newer structures.

It is usual to find that less space is demanded by the occupant of the old building. The outside envelope is fixed, which necessitates screening the program to be located there. With new buildings, space needs beyond those originally planned often develop during the design period.

The location of an old building is usually better, having been selected when the campus was less crowded. Ceiling heights are more generous than can be afforded in modern buildings, while exterior facades may be more compatible and more comfortable with neighboring buildings. Finally, nostalgic values may be inherent in the old building.

The principles outlined below for selecting the architects, engineers, and consultants are generally the same for rehabilitation or conversion projects and new buildings. In addition, it is very important that applicants for rehabilitation or conversion assignments be sympathetic and enthusiastic about the remodeling possibilities. Many remodeling projects are made difficult by unsympathetic designers, who magnify the problems in an effort to get the project changed to a new building.

In remodeling it is especially desirable to employ a construction manager at the beginning of the project. He can establish a realistic budget, monitor the cost of program changes, and provide factual cost data relating to specific architectural and engineering problems that require decisions. A further reason for using the construction management process is that realistic bids or tenders are most difficult to obtain for remodeling.

Construction

During the actual construction, a building department protects the interests of the institution by making sure that the work is properly done and that payments for it do not exceed the degree of its completion. This is more than the supervision provided by the architect. Most architectural contracts stipulate that a clerk of the works is to be employed for day-to-day supervision; he is paid by the owner but reports to the architect. However, it is preferable to hire a capable individual who reports to the owner and is the owner's supervisor and not the clerk. He would thus report to the director deficiencies in both contract performance and architect's performance that might influence the quality or progress of the work.

In sizable institutions with a continuing construction program, this supervisor might be a permanent staff member who could also supervise the minimal design and planning work done in-house. Where there is no construction work other than small alteration jobs or partition moves, a good carpenter foreman is adequate as a supervisor.

Selection of an architect. The choice of an architect is an important decision and should be made only on the basis of skill. The lines of command should also be clear. Although the architect must work closely with the academic department head involved in determining the requirements of the structure, it is important that both parties understand that all final decisions will come from the building and construction director. Without this understanding, costs frequently get out of control and a time-consuming redesign is needed.

If possible the architect chosen will have had experience with the particular type of building under consideration. While an architect without that experience might be more innovative in his approach, the experienced architect will be able to profit by past mistakes.

The architect's office should ideally be near the proposed project and have a large enough staff to handle the work efficiently and to put extra manpower on the project if needed. Very small architectural firms are not suited for institutional work; even if they can subcontract out part of the drafting load, it is not a desirable working arrangement. On the other hand, very large offices usually give each project very little of the time of the well-known principals on their staffs.

The amount of work an architectural office has pending at the time of a new project requires active attention by the building department. In addition, the department needs to know who will be the active director of the proposed project and what his experience has been in a similar capacity on other projects. An actual visit to the architect's office is most desirable. Recent clients of the architect should also be contacted for their appraisal.

Selection of engineers. The normal engineering services needed in the design of an institutional building are supplied under the architect's contract, and their cost is included as part of his fee. It is therefore the architect's prerogative to select the engineers; however, the owner generally has, and should exercise, the right of approval. The elements considered in the selection of the architect are relevant here as well: experience with the planned structure, size of office, work on hand, experience and reputation of the director of the project. The choice of a very reputable firm will eliminate the chance of having architects make engineering decisions that might be contrary to the engineers' judgment. Engineers also should have access to the director of the hiring institution.

Selection of consultants. In many cases special consultants will be needed in areas outside the architect's expertise, such as traffic, communications, cost control during design, library planning, laboratory planning and equipment, food service, and construction management. These specialists are paid by the institution and thus should be selected by, and be responsible to, its administration. Obviously, consultants must be able to work cooperatively with architects and engineers.

Architectural style. It has been the dream of many campus planners to have all the buildings of one architectural style or design, especially when an entirely new institution is being developed. However, there are many obstacles to such an achievement. Original materials may later become unavailable or prohibitively expensive. Styles in buildings also change with time, and what was once thought to be modern and attractive becomes outdated or outmoded.

As different architects become involved, they will bring to the campus their own ideas based on new materials, their own architectural training, or the influence of their contemporaries. Furthermore, buildings come to have new uses very different from those envisioned in the original planning.

While it is not necessary to have uniformity in design in order to have a pleasing and attractive campus, it is desirable that the materials used and the general feeling of the new designs be compatible with the old. Extreme novelty in design can be disruptive.

The exterior facades of a building can have a substantial influence on the cost, because exterior walls are expensive components. Any design that unnecessarily increases the ratio of exterior wall to the area enclosed will increase the cost, as will the addition of corners. On the other hand, a round building is most expensive, because of the cost of building round walls and the special framing required for the unusually shaped interior. In addition, there is usually more wasted interior space in round buildings. Most of the building's furnishings, such as tables, desks, and beds, are rectangular and fit better in rectangular areas.

Financing for new construction. The most elementary, the most important, and the most often neglected factor in financing is the determination, as accurately as possible, of the complete cost of the project to be financed. Unless this determination is made at the outset, many problems may result. Inadequate financing can cause delays, costly renegotiations, the need for supplementary financing, and possibly even for a new method of financing.

Having determined the outside cost limit as accurately as possible, various methods of financing are available, depending on whether the institution is privately or state owned.

In government-owned institutions, the financing of physical plant construction is generally done through legislative appropriation of funds provided from tax revenues. The kind of financing available to private institutions may also be used by public institutions, providing that it has legislative approval.

Both private and public institutions may have state-backed bonds available as a source of building funds. Such bonds carry a lower interest rate than a privately issued bond. Funds for private bond issues are provided through regular bond channels. The interest rate is usually high, because interest is paid out of the more precarious operating revenues of an educational institution.

Some institutions have funds made available to them through outright gifts from affluent donors. Whatever the reason for the gift, it is important to have a firm commitment from the donor before the cost of design is undertaken. Some gifts may provide for only part of the cost, with the provision that the funds will be given only when the institution has raised the balance from some other source. Gifts are also available from foundations that have a particular interest in the institution or in the use of the proposed building and from government agencies that will sometimes provide funds for a specialized research building.

In addition, most institutions of higher education have an endowment fund, its magnitude dependent on the age, size, and prestige of the institution. Some endowment funds are restricted to specific uses, while others are free for general use or for the use of the income they produce. Free funds may be used as a source of capital borrowing for building purposes. If free funds are used in this way, the institution may use its operating revenues to pay back the original fund with or without interest over a period of years. In some instances, the money for building may be taken from the fund with no thought of returning it.

A modern method of financing, leasebacks, was pioneered by the retail chain-store field. In a leaseback, the property for the proposed structure is deeded to a financing agency that provides the funds for building purposes. The agency is then paid a rental for the use of the building under a long-term lease. The rental, drawn from operating revenues or from interest on the endowment, covers the amortization of the funds provided as well as providing a profitable interest on those funds. Usually, both real estate and building become the property of the institution when the term of the lease is completed.

When a new building is contemplated, a written financial projection is a necessary first step. This projection shows the source of the capital funds; the cost of interest and amortization, if any; the cost of building maintenance, custodial care (housekeeping), light, heat, water, power, and air conditioning; and the cost of the academic and clerical staff required for its operation.

Construction contracts. Contracting for the construction of a building is done differently throughout the world. The method used depends on local custom, the economic situation, the extent of inflation, the availability of material, the extent of government participation, and the time pressure for the completion of the work.

Since most projects of any size involve a number of the building trades, it is customary for architectural plans and specifications to be so prepared that the work of each trade is clearly identified. Prices are obtained from several contractors in each trade, and contracts are awarded to those who submit the best (usually lowest) bids or tenders. However, it is necessary to have one individual who is responsible for the construction of the entire building. Variations in construction practice depend on who has that responsibility, although a general contractor is usually in charge. In some cases (but not all) he provides labor and material for completing the work of certain trades and subcontracts for others.

Under the competitive-bidding method, selected general contractors submit bids or tenders for the entire project. Their price will include the cost of those trades they propose to handle themselves plus the cost of all other trades involved for which they will seek competitive bids. The cost of their own overhead expenses and a profit are also included in the bid. The owner thus has a known fixed cost for the entire building before he commits himself to proceed. Under this plan, the general contractor assumes the risk of rising prices or the cost of strikes or job delays that may add to his cost. Only contractors who are fully qualified to complete the project should be allowed to bid.

An alternate contract method, the cost-plus method, is designed to eliminate the risks to the contractor of the competitive-bidding method. In the cost-plus method, a single general contractor is selected and given an open-ended contract based on his actual costs and the cost to him of the subcontractors, plus a fixed or percentage fee for his overall services. Under this plan, the institution takes all the risks for rising prices and contingencies, and the final cost of the project is not known in advance.

A modification of this plan is "cost plus with a guaranteed total." In this instance, the general contractor prepares a generous estimate of the total cost to protect himself in case the cost exceeds the guarantee. The owner or the institution then has a final figure to rely on, even if it is substantially inflated. A further provision may be added, under which the contractor and the owner share (in varying percentages) any savings that may result from the total cost being less than the guaranteed figure. The general objection to all types of cost-plus contracts is that they remove from the contractor the pressure to economize.

Because of inflation, rapidly rising costs, and material shortages, a new technique, known as construction management, has been developed for the construction process. Under this process, a construction manager coordinates the owner's needs, the architectural and engineering designs, and the construction process. Working directly for the owner, he provides preliminary advice on the probable cost of a structure, based on the space requirements by category. For example, in a typical educational facility, office space, classrooms, lec-ture rooms, and laboratory areas have different costs on a square-foot basis. The mix determines the total cost. The construction manager is experienced in detecting wasteful arrangements of space and is a valued consultant to the owner in interpreting the architects' schematic plans and their effect on cost.

The construction manager has a staff of estimators experienced in all the trades, especially the mechanical trades. In addition, he has expertise in "value engineering"—that is, in advising on the use of materials or designs based not only on their original cost but also on their life expectancy and their influence on maintenance and operating costs. For all these reasons, the construction manager is in a position to help determine the best method of contracting for the work. His incentive is the enhancement of his own reputation by getting the best value in a structure; he receives no percentage of the cost, but works for either a fixed fee or a fee based on time spent on the work.

The method of contracting for the work should be thoroughly discussed with the architect prior to his employment. The architect's role in the construction process and the question and amount of extra compensation for a greater than normal work schedule should be settled in advance.

In many countries the costs of materials required by each trade are taken off the plans and specifications by the trade contractors, who are responsible for their own accuracy. However, both duplication of effort and excess cost result from this process.

In Britain and many of its former colonies, the quantity-survey method is used. The architect employs a quantity surveyor (a skill in its own right) to take off the quantities, which are then supplied to all the contractors who have been asked to submit tenders or bids. In theory this method reduces the cost of bidding; however, it makes the owner responsible for the accuracy of the figures. Quantity surveyors also prepare estimates, analyze bids, and check quantities during construction to prepare interim valuations for partial payments due the contractor.

In another variation, found in Britain and elsewhere, the mechanical engineer does not prepare designs for bidding. Instead, the architect defines the results that each mechanical system must produce. The architect's conclusions are then given to mechanical contractors (chosen by selection or by competition), who are expected both to design and to build the system to produce a specified result.

In some countries where bids or tenders are submitted, it is customary to select the median rather than the low bidder. The assumption is that the price paid to the median bidder will be more fair and that there will be less incentive to skimp on the job.

Contracts with the Japanese government and local governments in Japan follow a similar practice; the contract is awarded to the bidder who is closest to the government's or the architect's estimate. The particular estimate is kept secret. Bids that are too low are assumed to be irresponsible, which could cause failure in performance.

Project costs. The complete project cost in the United States includes the bid of the main or principal contractor, bids of all subcontractors, architect and engineering fees, fees of consultants (such as interior decorators), costs of connecting utilities and mechanical services, furnishings, carpeting, objects of art, and the salaries of the clerk of the works and his staff (the owner's representatives in dealing with architects, engineers, and contractors). Another cost sometimes added to complete project cost is total overhead and salaries of the institution's full-time maintenance, buildings, and grounds staff, who may assist in the construction project. Similarly, the time of top officials of the university devoted to working with contractors, architects, and engineers while construction is in progress may be calculated and added to the project.

The so-called upset price of management contracts, which is in reality a maximum price, usually includes prices to be paid by the owner of the building for contractor, architect, and engineering fees, as well as the costs of connecting utilities.

A complete project cost may also include interest on money borrowed during construction, legal fees for right of way, and other title complications. Such legal issues are rare, however, when the building is to be located on a property owned by the university or college.

Maintenance

It is advisable for plant maintenance to be a responsibility of the building and construction administration department. Such an arrangement facilitates the coordination of design and maintenance and cuts initial costs, while also preventing later higher maintenance costs. In addition, a separately directed maintenance department frequently demands excessive initial costs in order to minimize maintenance costs. The proper balance between design and maintenance can be realized only when the two functions are under the same authority. Centralization of these functions also avoids control of maintenance by academic departments or building occupants.

The degree of competence needed to supervise a maintenance program depends on the size and complexity of the physical plant, especially of the mechanical equipment. In smaller institutions a top-grade mechanic with supervisory ability will frequently be adequate. In larger plants it may be desirable to have a full-time mechanical engineer on the staff. In addition to directing the maintenance program, the mechanical engineer can also serve to provide guidance in the interpretation of the utility requirements and in their design and operation. If no one on the staff can serve these multiple purposes, it would then be desirable to employ a consulting mechanical engineer from outside.

Other functions are frequently assigned to the director of buildings and construction. These may include custodial care (housekeeping), security (campus police), communications (telephone and telegraph), postal service (mail distribution), and purchasing. Such an arrangement is highly questionable, especially if the institution is of any size. The ability of the director of building and construction to do his complex job could be lessened by adding these extra responsibilities. Custodial care, security, communications, and the postal service might be grouped and placed under a separate supervisor, who reports to the same institutional officer. The independence of purchasing in any organization is so essential that the person in charge of purchasing should also report directly to top authority.

In institutions large enough to have general purchasing departments, the question arises of the proper relationship among building and construction, maintenance, and general purchasing. The most satisfactory solution to likely conflicts among the departments is that general purchasing should procure "materials only" for the other two functions. The construction and maintenance organization would specify the quality of these materials. Where contracts covering both labor and material are involved, construction and maintenance departments should procure materials directly. These departments are better qualified to judge the performance of contractors and to make or withhold payments as may be required. Furthermore, they can conduct any negotiations more knowledgeably.

In order to have meaningful figures, it is important that maintenance costs be carefully separated from such costs as custodial care or housekeeping; grounds maintenance; building changes and additions; capital expenditures; maintenance of furniture, fixtures, and movable equipment; and the cost of utilities. Building maintenance includes the cost of maintaining building equipment, such as fans, pumps, and motors, which are involved in operating the heating, ventilating, plumbing, electrical, and elevating systems. Movable equipment includes such items as portable fans, window air conditioners, autoclaves, and walk-in refrigerators.

Obviously, budgets must be prepared in the same categories of expense that are used for cost keeping. Three major identifications are needed for a building maintenance cost item: the nature or type of work, location of work, and source of payment. (Information on the source of payment is necessary only when there are buildings within the institution that have separate fiscal responsibility or sources of income.)

Within each of these budget categories, it is desirable that there be a further distinction between routine maintenance and major maintenance. Routine maintenance includes the necessary daily, weekly, or monthly items that remain fairly constant over the years. The only way to evaluate maintenance costs and performance meaningfully is to compare these items yearly by trade or category within the same building. Maintenance can thus be budgeted accordingly.

Major maintenance occurs irregularly at generally unpredictable intervals from five to twenty-five years. It cannot be budgeted statistically by averages or by experience, but must be budgeted by periodic (at least annual) examination of existing conditions and by an educated guess as to the likely date and cost of a major expenditure.

The segregation of routine and major maintenance items facilitates the establishment of an efficient budgeting method, the five-year progressive major maintenance program. This method uses a simple columnar spread sheet, with such lateral column heads as the following: brief description of item, budget category, location (building), source of funds (when necessary). At least five vertical columns are needed, one for each of the succeeding five calendar years, with extra blank columns for later years. The items are listed at the time of the annual budget inspection or whenever they are discovered, with the estimated cost entered in its column. When the annual budget is prepared, the list for all five years is carefully reviewed. It may be found that some items scheduled for the following year can be deferred or that later-year items should be moved forward. All the estimates of cost are updated. The major maintenance budget for the following year is the total of the items listed for that year.

There are many advantages to a five-year progressive major maintenance program. Major maintenance items, once discovered, cannot be ignored, and the timing and cost of each item are reviewed annually. In addition, the estimated total cost for each of the five future years is always at hand and reasonably up to date. With this program, the chance of a number of major items coming in any one year can be reduced, since there is usually enough flexibility in the timing. Finally, if the maintenance budget is cut by the fiscal authorities, the major maintenance work that must be deferred is seen immediately and becomes a future liability.

Many institutions have found it helpful in maintenance budgeting and accounting to have record keeping of costs done by the accounting office and not duplicated in the maintenance department. However, these costs should be kept in the manner that will make them most useful to the maintenance department and must always be available and up to date. Building changes and the maintenance of furniture and fixtures can be better controlled and evaluated if records are kept by academic or other departments rather than by the building department.

When the budget is being prepared, it is helpful to involve the foreman in each trade, who should also accept a responsibility for meeting the budget. In addition, a rate per hour should be established for in-house mechanics' time; this rate should include the various overhead items and be reviewed annually and adjusted when necessary. Only in this way can the cost of inside work be compared with that of outside contractors.

Major maintenance items, building changes, and even minor construction work should be handled by outside contractors whenever possible. In this way the maintenance crew can be maintained efficiently at the minimum, uniform level of performance.

Mechanical Services and Utilities

Mechanical services and utilities—the fourth major function of a building and construction department—are a consideration in each of the other major functions. The provision and management of these services and utilities are the responsibility of the buildings and grounds or maintenance department. Included in the mechanical services and utilities that may be provided are: electricity, gas, steam, chilled water for air conditioning, hot water for heating, compressed air, and natural gases. (For a detailed discussion of these considerations, see Knowles, 1970.)

The mechanical plant that provides these services and utilities is a subdivision of the physical plant, which includes classroom buildings, laboratories, libraries, museums, student centers, dormitories, president's home, faculty clubs, athletic facilities, grounds, walks, playing fields, and other facilities. The mechanical plant may provide all mechanical service and utilities to the physical plant from its own sources of energy; it may act as an intermediary between outside sources; or it may provide only some of the services, purchasing the other service needs from outside sources.

Many factors influence the decisions and policies on provision of services and utilities. Some of these factors are location of the campus; topography of the ground of the campus area; size of the campus; availability of conduits, pipe lines, and transmission lines; and availability of funds if an investment must be made to bring the services and utilities to the campus and to distribute them to various buildings and facilities on campus. A final decision may be based on the reliability of the source of the services as well as on cost considerations. Decisions about mechanical services and utilities will, of course, be different for a college with an existing facility and plant than for an entirely new campus or branch campus under development.

Bibliography

Knowles, A. S. (Ed.) *Handbook of College and University Administration.* Vol. 1: *General.* New York: McGraw-Hill, 1970.

Metcalf, K. D. *Planning Academic and Research Library Buildings.* New York: McGraw-Hill, 1965.

Sievert, W. A. "Renovating Old Buildings Called Often Wiser Than Building New Ones." *Chronicle of Higher Education,* 1971, 5, 6.

Wood, F. C. "Utilization and Maintenance of Essential Physical Facilities for Higher Education." *Educational Record,* 1962, *43*(1), 168–171.

Wood, F. C. "Sound Area Analysis Is Crucial to Controlling Costs of Buildings." *Engineering News-Record,* 1967, *179*(12), 90–92.

Wood, F. C. "Financial Considerations in Facilities Planning and Construction." In A. S. Knowles (Ed.), *Handbook of College and University Administration.* Vol. 1: *General.* New York: McGraw-Hill, 1970.

Wood, F. C. "Rehabilitating Campus Buildings—Is It Worth the Effort?" *American School and University,* 1971, *43*(11), 30–34.

FREDERIC C. WOOD

See also: Financial Affairs: Budgeting.

BUILDING TECHNOLOGY

See Construction and Building Technology (field of study).

BUILDINGS AND GROUNDS SUPERVISION

See Business Management of Higher Education: Facilities, Physical Plant.

BULGARIA, PEOPLE'S REPUBLIC OF

Population: 8,679,000 (1974 estimate). Student enrollment in primary and secondary school: 1,258,764 (1973–74); higher education (universities): 103,800 (1973–74). Language of instruction: Bulgarian. Academic calendar: September 15 to June 30. Percentage of national budget expended on education: 8.99% (1973).

Since World War II the People's Republic of Bulgaria has energetically engaged in efforts to develop its entire educational system. The government has continually experimented with, analyzed, and evaluated various programs and approaches to education. The basis for this activity is the belief that education plays a central role in the molding of the individual and, subsequently, his society, and that research and technical progress are essential for economic development and continual growth.

As a result of the initial postwar reorganization of the educational system, completed in 1949, the concept of compulsory education originally introduced in Bulgaria in 1879 was reiterated and a socialist orientation was adopted for the entire system. The most visible effect of this reorganization at the tertiary level was the introduction of such compulsory subjects in the curricula as the principles of Marxism-Leninism and dialectical materialism.

With the passage of the Law on Closer Ties Between the Schools and Life and on the Further Development of Education in 1959, compulsory education was increased from seven to eight years, and mandatory vocational education was introduced in the academic secondary schools (*gimnazia*). The vocational training program in the *gimnazia*, however, appeared to have a negative effect on the preparation of students applying for admission to institutions of higher education. Studies of applicants taking the university entrance examination in 1965 revealed that 46 percent of those taking the history examination failed, as did 55 percent of those taking the chemistry examination and 40 percent of those taking the Bulgarian language and literature examination. Most of these examinees had received excellent or good ratings in those same fields on the secondary level. Review of the 1967 examination scores revealed similar results, indicating that the secondary schools—perhaps because of the substitution of vocational programs for general education courses—were not adequately preparing students for higher education. Initial modification of the vocational training program in the *gimnazia* occurred in 1968 with the experimental establishment, in about twenty secondary schools, of a curriculum which included no vocational training. The problem of successfully coordinating general education with practical training and experience is constantly being reviewed at deliberations on educational planning in Bulgaria. A significant educational innovation during this same period was the creation of the two-year teacher training institutes for persons who would be teaching the first four years of elementary school.

In July 1969 the Central Committee plenum of the Bulgarian Communist party adopted a resolution that was to provide the general thrust for educational reform over the next fifteen to twenty years. As a result of these party directives and subsequent resolutions, the government embarked on a number of new programs in education. The most significant of these programs is the current effort to integrate scientific research institutes, institutions of higher education, and the various units engaged in production. The rationale for this reform is to create professional cooperation. Students will learn from research specialists and will be directly involved in solving actual production problems. The time lapse between recognition of production needs and determination of their solutions will be reduced. While a number of enterprises and research institutes have been integrated, the Academy of Agricultural Sciences "Georgi Dimitrov" is the ideal product of this reform, uniting agricultural research, education, and production activities in one scientific-educational complex.

National Educational Policy

The primary aims of education in Bulgaria are to instill in the citizenry a commitment to Marxism-Leninism and the social-ist development of the state and to produce the production workers, the skilled technicians, and the highly trained specialists necessary for economic development. Since the adoption of the Resolution of the Central Committee Plenum on Reform in Education in Bulgaria, in July of 1969, emphasis has been placed on the scientific basis of progress and the need to educate people to work creatively and independently while retaining their socialist spirit.

Legal Basis of Educational System

Higher education is regulated by several laws and decrees as well as by the constitution. The Law of Higher Education, Bulletin 12 of the Praesidium of the National Assembly, February 11, 1958, deals with aims, educational programs, and organization of higher education. Five major educational provisions are presented in Article 45 of the Constitution of the People's Republic of Bulgaria, adopted May 16, 1971: (1) Primary education is compulsory for eight years. (2) The right to education is guaranteed free of charge at all levels upon satisfaction of legal requirements. (3) The foundations of education are contemporary science and Marxist-Leninist ideology. (4) Citizens who are not of Bulgarian origin have a right to learn their national language in addition to compulsory study of Bulgarian. (5) The state actively encourages education, provides scholarships, and has responsibility for improving the educational institutions and establishments.

Other laws pertaining to higher education include the law for Scientific Degrees and Titles, confirmed by Decree 907 of May 9, 1972; Decree 1843 of March 18, 1972, which creates new governing bodies for higher education institutions, known as general assemblies; the regulations for the application of the Law for Higher Education of September 21, 1973; and Decree 2 of the Council of Ministers of February 7, 1973, which deals with the creation of a system for postgraduate qualification for specialists.

Types of Institutions

University-level education in Bulgaria takes place in twenty-six institutions. There are three universities: *Sofiiski universitet "Kliment Ohridski"* (University of Sofia, chartered in 1904), *Plovdivski universitet "Paissii Hilendarski"* (Plovdiv University, 1971), and *Velikotirnovski universitet "Kiril i Metodi"* (Cyril and Methodius University of Veliko Tirnovo, 1971). There are three scientific academies: the Academy for Social Sciences and Social Management, the Academy of Agricultural Sciences "Georgi Dimitrov," and the Academy of Medical Sciences. The latter two are the result of the integration, in 1971 and 1972 respectively, of the agricultural and medical research academies and higher institutes. Ten higher technical institutes include institutes of mining, building engineering, forestry, chemical technology, mechanical electrotechnology, and an institute for food industry. Four higher institutes for arts are devoted to music, dramatic arts, and fine arts. In addition, there are three higher economic institutes, a higher pedagogical institute, a higher institute for sports, and an institute for foreign students.

Postsecondary education below university level is available in the technical schools, in technical colleges, and in postsecondary institutes. In addition to accepting students who have completed only the eight years of compulsory education, the technical schools provide two- to three-year programs for persons who have already completed their secondary studies. In January of 1972 the Council of Ministers approved the development of new technical colleges which will offer two-year programs for secondary school graduates. The programs will train persons in technical production skills beyond the degree of expertise provided by secondary-level institutions. The three-stage development of the technical college system and programs is to be completed by 1980.

Teachers for the first four grades of compulsory education receive their training in two- or three-year programs offered by postsecondary teacher training institutes. Other postsecondary institutes include the Library Institute, the International Tourism Institute, a communications institute, and a sanitary inspection training institute. Total student enrollment in postsecondary institutes increased from 6187 in 1960–61 to 10,031 in 1969–70.

Relationship with Secondary Education

Education in Bulgaria is compulsory for eight years, starting at age seven. Secondary-level education is provided in four types of schools: the secondary general education and labor polytechnical school, the technical school, the secondary vocational school, and the vocational technical school. The government intends to make secondary education compulsory in the near future.

The concept of the secondary general education and labor polytechnic school is one of a continuous educational program from grade 1 through 11. This is a new approach to primary and secondary education, which has been implemented since the party resolution of 1969. To receive the secondary school-leaving certificate, students receive a general education and, after completion of the eleventh year, must pass the baccalaureate examination given in five basic subjects. After completing the first eight years of studies, students may enter the technical schools, which provide a four-year program to train persons as intermediate-level technicians and management personnel. Secondary vocational schools accept students after completion of the seventh grade and provide a four-year program which trains persons in various production skills. Graduates of both the technical schools and the secondary vocational schools must pass a written and oral examination in Bulgarian and mathematics and a practical examination in a specialty field to receive a secondary school-leaving certificate. Recipients of secondary school-leaving certificates from any of these three schools may apply for admission to institutions of higher education.

In addition to the above, vocational-technical schools affiliated with factories, plants, and agricultural enterprises provide one- to three-year programs to train skilled workers for industry.

Admission Requirements

Persons who have received a secondary school-leaving certificate may apply for admission to an institution of higher education. All applicants must be under age thirty-five and must take an entrance examination; the substance of the examination is determined by the secondary program completed by the applicant and by the proposed field of study. The Committee on Planning and the Committee for Science, Technical Progress and Higher Education determine admission based on the applicant's score on the entrance examination and the quota established for the particular field of specialization. The Committee on Planning is a ministry-level committee responsible for determining the overall state plan for the People's Republic of Bulgaria. The Committee for Science, Technical Progress and Higher Education, also a ministry-level committee, has administrative jurisdiction over all of the institutions of higher education. Determination of the quota for each field is based on national economic needs.

Administration and Control

In the People's Republic of Bulgaria, higher education is the responsibility of the Committee for Science, Technical Progress and Higher Education. The committee ensures that the higher education matches the requirements of the country's social, cultural, and scientific development; it controls the number of people with higher education. It also sets regulations governing all institutions of education; ensures pedagogical, methodological, and ideological control; and determines the contents of education (that is, it exercises control over

the textbooks and the teaching material). Other than this, external control of the institutions of higher learning comes under the jurisdiction of particular ministries and committees. The Academy of Medical Sciences with its branches is the administrative and economic responsibility of the Ministry of Health. The Academy of Agricultural Sciences "Georgi Dimitrov" and its branches are under the jurisdiction of the Ministry of Agriculture and Food Industry. The Committee for Culture and Art administers the higher institutes for fine arts, and the Committee for Youth and Sports assumes responsibility for the higher institute for sports. The Academy for Social Sciences and Social Management is the direct responsibility of the Central Committee of the Bulgarian Communist Party. The other higher institutions are under control of the Committee for Science, Technical Progress and Higher Education.

The structures for internal control of the higher education institutions are similar. The chief authority rests with the general assemblies, which are bodies charged with responsibility for management. Each institution also has an academic council, which is elected by the general assembly for a four-year term and is comprised of members of the various faculties at the particular institution. The third level is the faculty council, also elected for a four-year term by the general assembly. Decisions of the faculty council must be approved by the academic council of the institution.

Higher education institutions are headed by rectors, who, along with the vice-rectors, are elected from among the members of the academic council for a term of four years. Rectors are responsible to the Committee for Science, Technical Progress and Higher Education for the activities of their institutions; vice-rectors are answerable directly to the rector. One vice-rector is assigned responsibility for the scientific research activities conducted at the particular institution and is designated the head of the Scientific Research Section of the institution. Each faculty is headed by a dean, who is elected by the faculty council for a period of four years.

The basic educational and scientific research unit within higher education institutions is the department. The number of departments is determined by the Committee for Science, Technical Progress and Higher Education. Each department is headed by a person who has earned a scientific degree.

Programs and Degrees

The higher education institutions offer programs ranging from four to six years in length and leading to a *diplom za zavarcheni viche obrazovanie* (diploma of higher education) in the field of specialization after completion of diploma work or an appropriate state examination. The universities generally offer four-and-a-half-year programs in the sciences and four-year programs in education and teaching, while the academies offer six-year programs in medicine and four-and-a-half-year programs in agriculture. The higher institutes generally offer five-year programs in engineering and four-year programs in economics, fine arts, music, and physical culture. After an additional two years, the advanced degree of *kandidat* is awarded. The *doktor* usually requires approximately three years of postgraduate study.

Under the implementation of new programs formulated in 1972, students enrolled in higher education institutions are directed into one of two groups, block A or block B. Designed to enhance scientific research and guide the most gifted students into specialized scientific studies, the block system aims at producing persons who have achieved different levels of specialization in their respective fields. Thus, it attempts to satisfy the needs of the economy at all levels of production and research. Students in block A receive a more general education in their field of specialization, while students in block B receive in-depth specialized training, presumably to prepare them for advanced research and/or highly specialized employment. As this reorganization is further developed, it appears that each block will provide certain fields of study not available in the other, the differentiation being based primarily on the student's ability and the education necessary to master a field.

The most talented students may continue their education in a postgraduate studies program, which provides opportunities for individual research and creativity. Students not admitted to block-B or postgraduate studies may—every five years—attend refresher courses, known as postgraduate specialization programs, to study technical and scientific achievements in their respective fields.

In the postsecondary institutes the students are prepared to work as teachers in kindergartens, primary schools, and vocational schools and as specialists for service and management in transport and communications. The duration of the study program is from two up to three years and ends with a state examination. Successful completion of the examination, in addition to preparing the student for a career, also gives access to university-level institutes.

Extramural and evening studies programs requiring five or six years for completion are also available. Potential students must have completed a secondary education, be under the age of forty, have worked at least one year in an enterprise or industry related to the proposed field of study, and be recommended by their employer. Almost all Bulgarian universities offer extramural studies programs, but only three institutions of higher education, all located in Sofia, offer evening studies programs (the University of Sofia, the Karl Marx Higher Economic Institute, and the V. I. Lenin Higher Mechanical-Electrotechnical Institute). A variety of programs is offered in extramural studies, but the most popular ones include the technical, economic, mathematical, and natural sciences fields, and the humanities. The most popular evening studies programs are those in the field of economics. In 1971–72, 1.1 percent (1002) of the students enrolled in higher education (93,072) were enrolled in evening studies programs, while 25.5 percent (23,773) were enrolled in extramural studies programs (Tymowski and Januszkiewicz, 1975).

Financing and Student Financial Aid

The higher education system in Bulgaria is completely financed by the state. There are no tuition or registration fees for students enrolled in institutions of higher education. Students may receive support for living expenses in the form of scholarships granted by the state. Scholarships are awarded on the basis of the income of the student's family; students who receive excellent or very good grades, however, may receive increases in the amount of their grant. Students with children receive an additional family allowance.

Teaching Staff

The ranks of teaching staff at higher education institutions are professors, docents, major assistants, senior assistants, junior assistants, and lecturers. Applicants for positions must take a competitive examination; actual appointment is made by the faculty council.

Research Activities

Considerable emphasis is placed on research at institutions of higher education. All research must be approved by the Committee on Planning and the Committee for Science, Technical Progress and Higher Education. Teaching personnel are encouraged to retain their professional credibility by engaging in research in their respective fields of specialization. Students also are actively encouraged to participate in research conducted at their respective institutions. As a result of the integration of research and education, a lecture program, in which persons previously engaged only in research will lecture to students on a regular basis about the research projects in which they are involved, has been developed. The total state expenditure on research, including that conducted at institutions of higher education, has risen from .75 percent of the national income in 1963 to approximately 2.66 percent in 1975 (Atanassov, 1974, p. 39).

Relationship with Industry

The People's Republic of Bulgaria has developed a cooperative relationship between industry and education. Working people participating in evening and correspondence courses offered by institutions of higher education may receive special paid leave and/or reduced working schedules at the same salary to allow them more time for their studies. Graduates of higher education institutions must work on a state assignment for two years after completion of their studies (this is not a degree requirement).

International Cooperation

The higher education institutions of Bulgaria have been steadily increasing their contacts with higher education institutions of other countries, particularly through state cultural exchange agreements. The Institute for Foreign Students in Sofia provides a one-year course for non-Bulgarian citizens who will be attending Bulgarian institutions of higher education. Students learn the Bulgarian language and receive a basic introduction to their prospective field of study before enrolling in their respective institutions. Two years after these students receive their higher education diploma, they are invited back to Bulgaria for advanced studies. During the 1974–75 academic year there were approximately four thousand foreign students studying in Bulgaria.

[Information received from Ministry of Education.]

Educational Associations

Union of Bulgarian Teachers
"Lenin Square" #1
Sofia, Bulgaria

National Student Council of Bulgaria
11 Boulevard Stamboliiski
Sofia, Bulgaria

Bibliography

Apanasewicz, N., and Rosen, S. *Education in Bulgaria*. Washington, D.C.: United States Department of Health, Education and Welfare, 1965.

Apostolova, R. *University Youth in Bulgaria*. Sofia: Sofia Press, 1979.

Atanassov, Z. *Istoria na bŭlgarskoto obrazovanie*. Sofia: Sofiiski universitet "Kliment Ohridski," 1973.

Atanassov, Z. *Education and Science in the People's Republic of Bulgaria*. Sofia: Sofia Press, 1974.

Braĭnov, M. *Strukturni problemi na nauchnata organizatsiia na vissheto obrazovanie*. Sofia: Technika, 1971.

Education in People's Republic of Bulgaria, 1971–1973 School Year. Sofia: Sofia Press, 1973.

Grant, N. *Society, Schools and Progress in Eastern Europe*. Oxford, England: Pergamon Press, 1969.

Statisticheski godishnik na narodna Republika Bulgaria 1973. Sofia: Sofia Press, 1973.

Tymowski, J., and Januszkiewicz, F. *Postsecondary Education of Persons Already Gainfully Employed in European Socialist Countries*. Warsaw: Study prepared for UNESCO, 1975. (Mimeographed.)

Under the Banner of Internationalism, X Congress of the B.C.P. April 20–25, 1971. Sofia: Sofia Press, 1971.

See also: Eastern European Socialist Countries: Regional Analysis; Library Administration Outside the United States; Science Policies: Industrialized Planned Economics: Eastern European Socialist Countries.

BURMA EDUCATIONAL RESEARCH BUREAU
(Myanma nainggan pyinnya ye thutaythana a phwe)

Founded by the Burmese government in October 1965, the Burma Educational Research Bureau conducts research in education at all levels to prepare for major educational reforms in the country. Topics of research in higher education include the following: general administration, economics of higher education, manpower in higher education, educational planning, university students and faculty, educational technology, history of higher education, curricula and instruction, methodology of research in higher education, and reform in higher education. In addition to research activities, the bureau designs curricula, conducts undergraduate and postgraduate courses, develops evaluation tools such as tests and measurements, holds conferences, and provides a documentation service.

The bureau is funded by the Burmese government but also receives aid for research projects from UNICEF and UNESCO. In addition, since it is located in the Institute of Education at the Rangoon Arts and Science University, the bureau has access to the libraries of the university and the institute. The bureau's own library is equipped with microfiche equipment, installed with UNESCO funds. Staff members also may use the university's computer center.

Institute of Education Compound
University Estate
426 Prome Road
Rangoon, Burma

BURMA, SOCIALIST REPUBLIC OF THE UNION OF

Population: 28,885,867. Student enrollment in primary school: 3,358,700; secondary school (academic, vocational, technical): 883,793; higher education (university): 54,009; higher education (nonuniversity): 3690; higher education (total): 57,699. Language of instruction: Burmese. Academic calendar: September–December, January–April, May–August (three academic terms). Percentage of gross national product (GNP) expended on education: 1.9% (1972–73). [Except where otherwise indicated, figures are for 1973–74.]

The idea of a separate university for Burma originated in the year 1872, when the Government High School in Rangoon was opened as an affiliated branch of Calcutta University to enable scholars to take the Intermediate Entrance Examinations in the First Arts. This idea, however, did not find favor with the British colonial government of India until 1907, when the Indian Decentralization Committee visited Burma and recorded its formal opinion that the province required a university. Between 1909 and 1911 a draft university bill, similar to the newly passed Benares University Bill, was drawn up and revised. The draft bill underwent several additional revisions until passage in 1917. It then successfully combined the requirements of customary British university study with an emphasis on the Burmese language and literature.

The University of Rangoon was finally established in 1920. Its two constituent colleges, University College and Judson College, had grown out of the Government High School and the Cushing High School. The latter school, which had been founded by the Baptist Mission in Burma, was upgraded in 1894 to become Baptist College. Renamed Judson College in 1918, it continued as an integral part of the University of Rangoon until the Japanese invasion in 1942. From 1920 to 1941, student enrollment had increased from 829 to 2728. In 1942 the governor of Burma took over the assets and liabilities of the university. When Burma became independent of the British in 1948, the government decided to create a unitary university and appropriated most Judson College buildings, so that Judson College ceased to function.

After independence, the road to national unity and prosperity proved difficult, because Burma was the most severely damaged Asian country in World War II, and insurgent activities were rampant. Thus, in 1958 the prime minister called on the army to restore public order and prepare for a general election. The election, which was held in 1960, proved insufficient to bring unity to the nation; as a result, a Revolutionary Council assumed power in March of 1962. A month later, in its "Program of the Burmese Way to Socialism," the council stated its educational policy.

The policy called for a transformation of the existing educational system to make it more responsive to the needs of the people as they are understood in relation to socialistic moral values. Science was to be given precedence in education. During the period 1946–1962 enrollments again increased: from 2006 in 1946 to 16,514 in 1961–62.

In April of 1964 a national seminar on higher education—attended by rectors, principals, senior teaching staff and administrators, representatives of government departments and industries, prominent educators, and journalists—was convened to implement the stated policy. Its recommendations, with minor modifications, were incorporated into the 1964 University Education Law, which created new universities and institutes. For the first time in the history of university education in Burma, the aims of university education were prescribed by law.

With the advent of the new constitution of the Socialist Republic of the Union of Burma and the People's Congress, four significant laws—pertaining to university education, basic education, educational research, and the examination board—were enacted in 1973. In February of the following year, a fifth law—relating to technical, agricultural, and vocational education—was passed. The laws specify objectives, definitions, powers of institutions, functions, supervision, and management mechanisms designed to promote the building of a socialist society. These laws ended a decade of major educational reforms in the country.

Since the reorganization of the university system in 1964, there has been a marked increase in the number of students in university education: from 20,036 in 1964–65 to 53,602 in 1973–74. The increase has become stabilized at some 10,000 new entrants a year.

National Educational Policy

Burmese education is designed to bring basic education to all the people, but only citizens who show promise, potentiality, and industriousness are encouraged to pursue higher education. The broad aim of university education, according to the 1964 University Education Law, is to construct a Burmese socialist society through the creation of an intelligentsia devoted to the development of such a society. More specifically, university education is designed to provide instruction and training in science and technology for employment, to promote research, to inculcate a sense of pride in the dignity of labor, and to build character in keeping with socialist values and thought.

Legal Basis of Educational System

The system of higher education in Burma is based on the University of Rangoon Act of 1920, with amendments in 1924, 1939, 1949, and 1951; the University Education Law of 1964, which prescribed the aims of university education; and the five laws enacted in 1973–74 (in connection with the new constitution), concerning university education, basic education, educational research, the examination board, and technical, agricultural, and vocational education.

Types of Institutions

In the new system implemented in 1964, the number of universities was raised from two to ten, with eight affiliated colleges: (1) Rangoon Arts and Science University, with four affiliated colleges—Workers' College, Moulmein College, Bassein College, and Akyab College (open since 1974); (2) Mandalay Arts and Science University, with three affiliated colleges—Magwe College, Taunggyi College, and Myitkyina College; (3) the Institute of Medicine I, Rangoon, with one affiliated college—the College of Dental Medicine (which was raised to the Institute of Dental Medicine in 1974); (4) the Institute of Medicine II, Mingaladon; (5) the Institute of Medicine, Mandalay; (6) Rangoon Institute of Technology; (7) the Institute of Economics, Rangoon; (8) the Institute of Education, Rangoon; (9) the Institute of Agriculture,

Yezin; and (10) the Institute of Animal Husbandry and Veterinary Science, Insein. A Defense Services Academy under the authority of the Ministry of Defense also belongs to the university system.

The policy of the Revolutionary Council is to uphold the principle of freedom of worship in respect to all religions, and grants are made to institutions of the various religions professed in Burma. Among the outstanding institutions of religious study is the International Institute of Advanced Buddhistic Studies, opened in 1955, which aims at creating a World Buddhistic University. Other institutions are the Tipitakadara Selection Board, which holds annual scriptural examinations for the monks; and the Pali University and Dhammacariya Department, which hold annual Pali University Examinations for which degrees, certificates, and prizes are awarded.

Nonuniversity higher education is provided at the technician level in industrial technology at four government technical institutes and in agriculture at government agricultural institutes. At a similar level, teachers for primary and middle schools are being trained in teacher training institutes (also referred to as schools) and teacher training colleges, respectively. Teachers of the upper secondary school receive their education at university-level institutions.

Relationship with Secondary Education

As of the 1970s, there is no compulsory school attendance. School begins at the age of five. One year of kindergarten is followed by the primary cycle, called Standards I to IV. The six-year secondary school is divided into a four-year lower secondary school, also referred to as middle school (Standards V to VIII), and a two-year upper secondary school (Standards IX and X). There are three types of upper secondary schools: basic education high school, technical high school, and agricultural high school. The basic education high school corresponds to general education in other countries and is completed at about the age of sixteen, after eleven years of study. After passing the Basic Education High School Examination, a student receives the Basic Education High School Certificate. Eventually, the primary and middle school cycles will form the compulsory education component while the three types of high schools will lead to postsecondary education.

Admission Requirements

The Basic Education High School Examination is conducted by the Examination Board of the Ministry of Education and is taken by students at the end of the last year of high school. To be eligible for university study, students have to place on the "A" list; passes are required at this level in five compulsory subjects and one optional subject. This examination plays an important role for access to higher education and the different disciplines within the university: students with the highest scores on the "A" list are admitted to medical training and dentistry and, in descending order of scores, to engineering, economics, and education; the remaining students are listed for majors in the different disciplines of the arts and science universities. Students on the "B" list, with lower scores, are admitted to the teacher training schools or to agricultural or technical training.

Graduates from the eleven agricultural high schools are admitted to the government agricultural institutes, while the ablest students from the six technical high schools are admitted to government technical institutes.

Administration and Control

All universities and colleges are controlled by the state and are under the direction of the Department of Higher Education of the Ministry of Education. The ministry consists of the Department of Higher Education; the Department of Basic Education; the Department of Technical, Agricultural, and Vocational Education; the Educational Research Bureau; and the Examination Board.

As prescribed in the educational law,

university-level education is controlled and guided by two policymaking councils— the Universities' Central Council and the Council of University Academic Bodies— under the chairmanship of the minister of education, with the deputy minister of education as vice-chairman. Similarly, the Department of Technical, Agricultural, and Vocational Education, which is in charge of technical and vocational education, is directed by the Technical Education Council and the Vocational Education Council.

The Universities' Central Council is responsible for general policy and coordination of the work of the universities and colleges. The council has thirty-seven members, including deputy ministers; directors of departments concerned; university rectors and principals of colleges; representatives of the Burma Socialist Program Party, the People's Workers Council, and the People's Peasants Council; prominent educators; and journalists.

The Council of University Academic Bodies is charged with the framing of all academic regulations and coordination of all academic work. Members are directors of departments and corporations concerned, university rectors and college principals, representatives of the various university academic bodies, educators, and journalists. The council is broadly based and has over forty members.

Each university has an administrative and an academic body, while colleges have only the administrative body. Although all these institutions form independent units under direct control of the Department of Higher Education, close coordination exists among them, either through the two government councils or in meetings of heads of institutes. Statutes and regulations are uniform for all institutions offering the same courses.

The chief administrator of the universities is the rector. He is assisted by the registrar and the teaching staff, who are members of the academic body (senate). The senate forms boards of study—composed of representatives of the university, industry, and other interests—which are responsible for curriculum development and examinations. Studies are offered in departments headed by a professor, except at the Rangoon Institute of Technology, where the departments are headed by deans. The chief administrative officer of the colleges is the principal.

The independent Defense Services Academy, under the authority of the Ministry of Defense, which offers university-level courses to cadets in the army, navy, and air force, is administered by a director.

Programs and Degrees

The university curricula are constantly reviewed by the boards of study. In order to meet the changing needs of the country, applied sciences which will support and increase production are encouraged without neglecting the pure sciences.

All courses offered are specialized, requiring a major subject with appropriate minor courses. The duration of the first degree varies, according to field of study, from four years for a bachelor's degree in arts, natural sciences, or economics to five years for a bachelor's degree in education and agriculture. Architecture, engineering, and forestry require a six-year program, while the first degree in dentistry, medicine, and veterinary science is achieved in six and a half years of study. Short-cycle diploma courses, such as the diploma in statistics and a two-year correspondence course for a diploma in education, are also offered.

Some of the programs require practical training. For instance, in their third, fourth, and fifth years of study, engineering students contribute three summer vacations of practical work, and in their last year they do factory work for a six-month period. The students' course work is taught on site by university staff as well as factory managers and engineers serving as part-time lecturers. Thus, the idea of the students' contributing to society while receiving their education is woven into the educational

system. It is hoped that a practical work requirement can be introduced into all university-level studies.

Postgraduate degrees and diplomas are offered in almost all fields. Master's degrees are generally achieved in three years, while doctorates require an additional three to four years of study.

The government technical institutes offer diploma courses in various specializations of engineering: civil engineering (tools and power), electrical engineering (power and communication), and mining engineering. Courses generally last three years.

The government agricultural institutes have three-year diploma courses in agriculture, which include training in rural education. Graduates are eligible for employment by the Agriculture Corporation as extension agents at the level of deputy township managers.

The International Institute of Advanced Buddhistic Studies offers courses of a postgraduate nature in Theravada Buddhism. Seminars center on Pali Language, Abhidhamma Studies, and Buddha's Basic Teaching and Kammathana Practices, enriched by subjects such as philosophy, psychology, and literature. The degrees conferred on the venerable monks are the *patamaguy* (higher), the *patamalat* (middle), and the *patamagne* (elementary), according to the grades received. Titles offered are *agga maha pandita* and *maha pandita,* among others.

Financing and Student Financial Aid

Except for nominal tuition fees, all institutions of higher education are financed by the state. Five percent of the student body are exempt from even these nominal fees.

Government stipends to cover tuition costs are given to some 20 percent of the students according to need, parental status, and ability to meet expenses. One hundred new scholarships are offered annually to the best entrants in medicine, technology, other professions, and the arts and sciences. Other scholarships are available for study of economics, mathematics, chemistry, and physics, and a special scholarship is offered by the minister of education.

Student Social Background and Access to Education

A noteworthy aspect of student life in Burma is the role of students in national development. Many participate in field projects, workshops, and factories as part of their studies. During the government literacy campaign, about 25 percent of the student population served as volunteer teachers. The effort was so successful that Burma was awarded the Shah Reza Mohammed Pahlavi Prize by UNESCO in 1971 for outstanding achievement in pursuit of the eradication of adult illiteracy.

Access to higher education in Burma meets with no sex discrimination. Burmese women have always enjoyed a high measure of independence and have retained their social status as well as economic and legal rights (Article 154 of the constitution). In the post–World War II years especially, women have responded to educational openings on an equal basis with men. Fields such as administration, government service, law, health and social welfare, medicine, dentistry, economics, and business are open to any qualified woman. An appreciable number of women attend the Rangoon Institute of Technology, for studies in chemical and textile engineering, as well as the Institute of Agriculture, the Institute of Animal Husbandry and Veterinary Science, and the geology department of the Rangoon Arts and Science University.

Teaching Staff

At the universities the ranks of teaching staff are four: professor, lecturer, assistant lecturer, and tutor or demonstrator. At the colleges the highest rank is lecturer. The teaching staff are recruited locally. Selection and appointment are made by the Public Services Section and Training Board except for a few international appointees of the United Nations and its specialized agencies, the Colombo Plan (a plan for cooperative economic development in South and Southeast Asia), and other foreign organizations. Generally, senior staff have received their training abroad, in the United Kingdom, the United States, and other countries.

The requirements for appointment and promotion to professor are a Ph.D. degree as well as research and teaching experience. For a lectureship the requirements can be fulfilled by a Ph.D. degree or an M.A. or M.Sc. degree together with appropriate research and teaching experience. Assistant lecturers generally hold an M.Sc. or M.A. degree and have research and teaching experience. The B.A. or B.Sc. degree suffices for a post as tutor or demonstrator.

Staff members have tenure until age sixty. Reappointments are made beyond this age in special cases, such as special education officers, but need annual extensions from the Ministry of Education.

Research Activities

In accordance with the educational research law, guidelines for research are set by the Educational Research Policy Direction Board and the Educational Research Bureau, which is a department of the Ministry of Education. The policy board is empowered to form executive and ad hoc committees and delegate them appropriate responsibilities. The board has twelve research divisions, including agriculture, medical and social sciences, and language and culture.

Since research is an integral part of national development in Burma, the universities are closely linked to industry and government departments in joint research efforts. In addition, under the sponsorship of the United Nations and its specialized agencies, research has been undertaken in a number of fields—including agriculture, health services, technology, social welfare, forestry, and veterinary sciences.

In addition to providing teaching facilities, the new agricultural complex at Yezin will become the main research center for all agricultural research in the country.

Current Problems and Trends

Among the more serious educational problems is the discrepancy between employment prospects for graduates from professional programs, who generally find positions, and from the arts and sciences, an area in which graduates have experienced unemployment. This situation might be alleviated as a result of attempts to regulate university admissions in accordance with the nation's manpower needs and the availability of staff and facilities.

Since the university reform in 1964, much attention has been given to modernization of curricula, planned growth of the universities, and cooperation between the universities and development needs. Adoption of Burmese as the main medium of instruction at the university level, except in some graduate studies, is considered to be of great importance, since effective teaching can be done only in the student's mother tongue. Translation and standardization of technical terms, as well as production of suitable text materials, have been undertaken.

Among practical innovations are the student cooperative farms managed by students of the Institute of Agriculture at Yezin in cooperation with students of the agricultural high schools. Much attention is also given to literacy training, as is evident from the international acclaim that Burma has received for its efforts in this area.

Relationship with Industry

Cooperation between the universities and industry is close in order to achieve the needed economic and social development of the country. University professors and senior lecturers now serve on executive boards of various industries and have headed joint research projects, while industry representatives are members of boards of study at the universities. A close relationship between theory and practice is fostered in order to make university training utilitarian.

International Cooperation

International cooperation in fields such as education, health services, medicine, social welfare, and technology is usually carried out under the sponsorship of the United Nations and its specialized agencies. The National Vocational Training, Program, a research program, is being developed jointly with the United Nations Development Programme.

The International Institute of Advanced Buddhistic Studies in Rangoon is a center of postgraduate studies in Theravada Buddhism; it extends invitations to foreign scholars and plans to develop into a World Buddhistic University.

DAW HNIN MYA KYI

Bibliography

Daw Hnin Mya Kyi. *The Development of Higher Education in Burma*. Rangoon: Burma Educational Research Bureau, 1975.

Hayden, H., and others. *Higher Education and Development in Southeast Asia*. Vol. 1: *Director's Report*. Volume 2: *Country Profiles*. Paris: UNESCO, 1967.

U Kaung. "A Survey of the History of Education in Burma Before the British Conquest and After." *Journal of the Burma Research Society,* June 1963, *46,* Part 2.

U Khin Aung. *The Birth of Rangoon University. A Fiftieth Anniversary Publication*. Rangoon: Rangoon University Press, 1970.

Nyi Nyi. "The Development of University Education in Burma." *Journal of the Burma Research Society,* June 1964, *47,* 11-76

Nyi Nyi. *Higher Education in Burma*. Rangoon: Sarpay Beikman Press, 1972.

See also: Library Administration Outside the United States; Religious Influences in Higher Education: Buddhism; South Asia: Regional Analysis.

BURUNDI, REPUBLIC OF

Population: 3,680,000 (1974 estimate). Student enrollment in primary school: 127,176; secondary school (general, vocational, teacher training): 10,622; higher education (university): 774. Language of instruction: French. Academic calendar: October to July, two semesters. Percentage of national budget expended on education: 22%. [Figures are for 1974.]

Before declaring independence in 1962, the Republic of Burundi was part of the Belgian trust territory of Ruanda-Urundi, located in East Central Africa on the northern border of Lake Tanganyika. In 1890 Urundi (now Burundi) and the neighboring Ruanda (now Rwanda) became part of German East Africa; German control, however, was limited to a single military post, and there was no occupation of the area.

During World War I, Belgian forces from the Belgian Congo (now Zaire) defeated the Germans and gained control over Ruanda-Urundi. In 1919 the League of Nations mandated the area to Belgium; however, the mandate was not accepted by the Belgian government until 1924. A year later, in 1925, Ruanda-Urundi was administratively united to the Belgian Congo, although it retained its separate identity and budget.

After World War II Ruanda-Urundi remained in Belgian hands under a United Nations mandate. In 1962 the territory attained full independence as two separate states: the Republic of Rwanda and the Kingdom of Burundi. In 1966 the monarchy was abolished, and Burundi was declared a republic.

Western education began in Burundi in the 1890s, when the White Fathers, a Roman Catholic mission order, opened several schools to provide religious instruction and some elementary general studies. Starting in 1907 Lutheran missionaries from Germany also opened a few schools, but the outbreak of World War I forced both Catholic and Protestant mission schools to close. By 1916 Belgian missionaries began to found their own schools, and starting in 1919 the Belgian government initiated still others. Soon after the administrative union with the Belgian Congo, however, educational policy changed, and the mission

institutions were allowed to implement all primary education (McDonald and others, 1969, p. 93). Government subsidies were granted to approved schools—Catholic mission schools run by Belgians. These included lower primary schools, which provided two years of study, and upper primary schools, which offered an additional three years of schooling. Although the majority of students completed only the lower level of primary education, a sixth year of primary education was added in the early 1940s. In addition to the subsidized schools, nonsubsidized private chapel and reading schools, which provided religious instruction and basic reading skills, attracted many students.

During the mandate period, technical/vocational training in Ruanda-Urundi was limited to two institutions established by the Brothers of Charity, a Roman Catholic order: an educational center in Astrida (now Butare, Rwanda), established in 1929 to provide postprimary education for teachers and expanded in 1932 to provide training for civil service positions; and an institution at Gitega, opened in 1940 to prepare primary school teachers. It was not until 1954, however, when the Belgian government began to establish its own schools and decrease subsidies to mission schools that the first state secondary institution, the *Athénée royal de Bujumbura,* an interracial, coeducational school, was established to provide academic secondary programs. During the same period, the Belgian government also opened ten primary schools, a normal school in Bujumbura, and another secondary school in Gitega (McDonald and others, 1969, p. 94).

In 1956 the territory's first postsecondary institution was established in Astrida, Rwanda, to serve students from Rwanda, Burundi, and the then Belgian Congo. Burundi students also had access to Lovanium University at Léopoldville (now Kinshasa) and the Official University of the Belgian Congo and Ruanda-Urundi at Elisabethville (now Lubumbashi), both in present-day Zaire. A few students also studied in Belgium. In 1958 the Official University of the Belgian Congo and Ruanda-Urundi opened a faculty of agronomy, which—upon independence of the Belgian Congo in 1960—was transferred to Bujumbura and became the *Institut agronomique du Ruanda-Urundi*. In October 1960 several university-level faculties, including those of philosophy and letters and of social and economic sciences, were established in Bujumbura. That same year the *Collège de Saint-Esprit* was established by the Society of Jesus in Bujumbura.

In 1964—two years after Ruanda-Urundi attained full independence—all the higher educational facilities merged to form the *Université officielle de Bujumbura* (Official University of Bujumbura). In 1965 a second institution of higher education, the *Ecole normale supérieure* (Higher Normal School), was opened in Bujumbura to train teachers for the nation's secondary schools.

In 1968 the government launched the first five-year development plan (1968–1972). Among the objectives of the educational sector of the plan was the expansion of primary education to include 215,000 students by the 1972–73 academic year and to increase secondary enrollments to 6000. An adult education program was to be initiated to combat illiteracy in the country—approximately 95 percent of the population was still illiterate. The plan also emphasized expansion of teacher training to train 15,000 new teachers for the primary schools during the plan period.

After formulation of the republic, university expansion also received priority; and, with Belgian cooperation, programs leading to the first university degree were established in the faculty of law in 1968. French and Swiss assistance also was received for the development of the other faculties. In 1974 the government of Burundi introduced several educational reforms designed to align the educational system with the needs of the country. Among

them was the reorganization of the existing higher education facilities to form the new *Université du Burundi* (University of Burundi), at Bujumbura.

National Educational Policy

The government of Burundi is committed to expand all educational facilities throughout the country to the limit of its financial ability. Primary education has been restructured to better meet the needs of the more than 90 percent of the population active in the agricultural sector. The function of primary education is to offer useful skills; it will no longer serve only as a preparation for secondary education. Kirundi will replace French as the language of instruction in primary school. At the secondary level, programs are being adapted to the employment realities of Burundi. The new University of Burundi was created in an effort to eliminate the duplication of programs at the higher education level and to increase the efficiency of higher education.

Legal Basis of Educational System

The general system of education in Burundi is organized according to Decree-Law 1/84 of August 29, 1967. The law sets forth the structure and programs of the primary and secondary educational systems, the conditions for the opening of schools, and diploma and certificate requirements.

The Official University of Bujumbura was established on January 10, 1964, by royal decree. Its name was legally changed to the University of Burundi in 1974. The Higher Normal School was established by Royal Decree 001/777 of September 22, 1965.

Types of Institutions

Higher education in Burundi is provided by the faculties and institutes of the University of Burundi. In 1964 the university consisted of faculties of philosophy and letters, economic and social sciences, and sciences. Enrollments during the 1965–66 academic year totaled 162 students, of whom 81 were Burundi nationals (McDonald and others, 1969, p. 99). By 1974 the university had added a faculty of law and a faculty of medicine and dental sciences. In addition, the Higher Normal School was incorporated into the university as the *Institut universitaire des sciences pour éducation* (University Institute for Education Sciences); and the *Ecole nationale d'administration* (National School of Administration), formerly a secondary-level institution, was also made part of the university.

Teachers for the nation's primary schools are prepared in four-year and seven-year institutions on the secondary level. Plans call for the expansion of several of the four-year institutions *(enseignement moyen pédagogique)* to seven-year institutions *(enseignement normal).*

In addition to literacy training, adult education courses are provided for public administration personnel in English, bookkeeping, stenography, Kirundi, and typing.

Relationship with Secondary Education and Admission Requirements

The general system of education consists of a six-year primary cycle, followed by one of the several secondary school programs leading to either employment or higher education. Primary and secondary education is provided in both public and private institutions. Primary education is divided into three two-year cycles. Upon completion of the third cycle, successful students receive the *certificat de fin d'études* (leaving certificate), which entitles them to pursue secondary education.

Secondary education is provided in schools offering general secondary programs, teacher training, technical/vocational training, and domestic science. *L'enseignement secondaire général* (general secondary education) is offered in two three-year cycles and leads to the *diplôme d'humanités complètes,* a prerequisite for university admission. The general secondary program and the seven-year program offered by

the normal schools are the only secondary programs leading to higher education.

Students are admitted to the university on the basis of the *diplôme d'humanités complètes* or to the new *Institut universitaire des sciences pour éducation* by the appropriate normal school-leaving certificate. Some faculties may also require special entrance examinations. Students who do not fulfill the entrance requirements may, on the recommendation of the faculty involved, enter the university as free students *(élèves libres)* and attend classes and sit for examinations.

Administration and Control

The University of Burundi is a state institution and operates under the auspices of the Ministry of Education and Culture. The chief administrative officer of the university is the rector, who is assisted by an administrative director. The main university governing bodies are the *conseil d'administration* (administrative council), which is composed of ten members appointed by the president of the republic; and the *conseil académique* (academic council), composed of the rector, administrative director, and the deans of faculties. The dean is the head of a faculty and is responsible for internal administration.

Programs and Degrees

The University of Burundi has five faculties: the faculty of sciences, the faculty of philosophy and letters, the faculty of economic and social sciences, the faculty of law, and the faculty of medicine and dental sciences. The University Institute for Education Sciences prepares teachers for the lower and upper levels of secondary education and provides refresher courses for in-service teachers. The National School of Administration provides training for administrative and development personnel.

After two or three years of study beyond the secondary level, students in the above programs receive the *candidature,* a prerequisite for study toward the *licence.* The *licence* is awarded after two years of study beyond the *candidature* but it is not yet available in all faculties. Students in medicine who receive the *candidature* must go abroad for five years of study to receive the degree Doctor of Medicine.

Financing and Student Financial Aid

The University of Burundi is financed by the state, with assistance from foreign governments and international organizations. The Belgian government, which was largely responsible for the establishment of the university, has provided the greatest amount of financial assistance.

Scholarships are provided to Burundi students for higher studies at home or abroad by the governments of Burundi, Belgium, and the United States as well as by international organizations and private concerns.

Student Social Background and Access to Education

Despite the gains made in education since the formation of the republic, the majority of school-age children do not have access to education. Male enrollments are double those of females, and educational facilities are more easily accessible in cities such as Bujumbura than in rural areas. The majority of students in the educational system are concentrated at the primary level, and enrollments sharply decrease at each level of education.

Teaching Staff

The university teaching staff consists of *professeurs ordinaires* (ordinary professors), *professeurs extraordinaires* (special professors), *professeurs chargés de cours extraordinaires* (special assistant lecturers), *professeurs chargés d'enseignement* (instructors), and *assistants* (assistants). In 1974 the university employed a teaching staff of seventy, mostly foreigners. Burundi teachers are civil servants, and their salaries are paid by the government; foreign staff are reimbursed by their respective governments.

Current Problems and Trends

Among the problems that have disrupted the implementation of a unified system of education is the political rivalry between the majority tribe, the Hutu, and the minority tribe, the Tutsi. The limited financial resources available for educational development also cause constraints. The government, therefore, relies heavily on international assistance to carry out development plans. The economic situation might be improved by the planned reorientation of the educational system, which is designed to bring about modernization in the agricultural sector and thereby increase agricultural production, the mainstay of the Burundi economy. As part of the educational development process, unqualified teachers are being replaced. The government is also focusing on reducing student wastage on the primary level—which totals 13 percent annually—and on decreasing the incidence of repetition in order to preserve educational resources.

International Cooperation

Burundi is the recipient of a substantial amount of international aid for education. Many of the country's primary and secondary schools are operated by Catholic and Protestant missions, although they receive some government subsidy. These schools are largely staffed by foreign personnel. At the higher education level, external financial aid has largely accounted for the establishment and further development of the university and the Higher Normal School (now the University Institute for Education Sciences). Foreign aid has also been provided in the form of technical expertise, materials, and teaching personnel. Burundi students study abroad, principally in Belgium, France, and Zaire but also in other countries, on scholarships provided by sources such as the government of Burundi, other governments, international agencies, or private sponsors.

[Assistance received from Gabriel Barakana, Recteur, Université de Burundi.]

Bibliography

Africa Contemporary Record. Annual Survey and Documents. 1974–1975. London: Rex Collings, 1975.

Boyayo, A. "Coup d'oeil sur l'évolution de l'enseignement secondaire au Burundi de 1890 à 1956." *Revue nationale d'éducation du Burundi, Année scolaire 1968/1969,* no. 1, pp. 1–4.

Boyayo, A. "Réalités et perspectives de l'éducation au Burundi." *Revue nationale d'éducation du Burundi, Année scolaire 1968/1969,* no. 4, pp. 1–4.

Cinq ans de la révolution burundaise. Bujumbura: Ministère de l'information, 1971.

"Discours prononcé le 3 novembre 1972 par le Révérend Père G. Barakana, recteur de l'Université officielle de Bujumbura à l'occasion de l'ouverture de l'année académique 1972–1973. (Extraits.)" *Revue nationale d'éducation du Burundi, Année scolaire 1972/1973,* no. 2, pp. 1–8.

Economic Commission for Africa. *Summaries of Economic Data: Burundi.* March 1975, *15,* 11, 15.

McDonald, G. C., and others. *Area Handbook for Burundi.* Washington, D.C.: U.S. Government Printing Office, 1969.

Nbabahagamye, B. "Discours d'ouverture des travaux du secrétariat général de la réforme de l'enseignement primaire." *Revue nationale d'éducation du Burundi, Année scolaire 1969/1970,* no. 6, pp. 1–4.

Plan quinquennal de développement économique et social du Burundi (1968–72). Bujumbura: Government Printing Office, 1968.

Répertoire des établissements d'enseignement primaire, secondaire et supérieur. Année scolaire 1970–1971. Bujumbura: Ministère de l'éducation nationale et de la culture, Direction générale de l'enseignement, Service des statistiques, 1971.

Sindigebura, A. "L'éducation au Burundi." *Revue nationale d'éducation du Burundi, Année scolaire 1971/1972,* no. 4, pp. 1–8.

Statistique scolaires 1969–1972. Bujumbura: Ministère de l'éducation nationale et de la culture, Direction générale de l'enseignement, Service des statistiques, 1970.

Varlet, H. "Le décret-loi No. 1/84 du 29 août 1967 portant organisation de l'enseignement au Burundi." *Revue nationale d'éducation du Burundi, Année scolaire 1967/1968,* no. 4, pp. 1–9.

See also: Africa, Sub-Saharan: Regional Analysis; Archives: Africa and Asia, National Archives of.

BUSINESS ADMINISTRATION

See Commerce and Business Administration (field of study); Management Education (field of study).

BUSINESS AND OFFICE TECHNOLOGIES (Field of Study)

The field of business and office technologies includes a wide variety of business-related curricula below the baccalaureate level. The curricula are designed to provide vocational training for semiprofessional positions in the business occupations. Consequently, programs emphasize learning skills to meet the immediate needs of potential employers, particularly local companies and other organizations, which often help design the necessary academic programs.

The branches of the field of business and office technologies covered here include secretarial science, data processing, and office auxiliary services. Other related areas, such as accounting, distribution, sales, financial management, and general business programs, are not included.

A secretary is an executive assistant who possesses a mastery of office skills, demonstrates an ability to assume responsibility, and makes decisions within the scope of assigned authority. Most academic programs in the secretarial area include courses in shorthand, typing, office machines operation, business communication, accounting, office simulation, records management, office systems and procedures, and human relations.

The branch of data processing encompasses three major areas: operations, programing, and applications (systems) analysis. The operator is the "technician" who is responsible for the actual running of the computer and its peripheral equipment. The programer is the "linguist" who translates a process or an algorithm into an executable computer program in one of the several computer languages. The systems analyst interacts with the user, analyzes his business problem, and structures it for application to an electronic data-processing system. In general, information systems technology is concerned with the management of data, including organization, storage, and manipulation.

Programs in office auxiliary services are concerned with the operation of commonly used business machines, such as the calculator, billing machine, cash register, keypunch machine, mimeograph machine, photocopy machine, and typewriter.

The secretarial science field is closely related to bookkeeping, lower-level accounting functions, specialized clerical functions, and office management. A secretary may be personally engaged in one or more of the above functions; if not personally engaged, he or she at least needs to interact with other individuals performing those tasks. In addition, a knowledge of the functional areas of business administration is necessary in many senior secretarial positions. Data processing is also very intimately tied in with other business areas, because a systems analyst, if he is to be of use as a problem solver, must have a keen appreciation of business problems. Engineering is another related field, because data-processing/information systems specialists work closely with engineers to understand and sometimes to initiate developments in computer technology. Since most computing and calculating machines are used in one or more of the accounting operations, the relation of business machines to accounting is obvious.

Although secretarial science is constantly influenced by changes in technology, its origins are in ancient Greece, where stenographers were used as early as 100 B.C. and perhaps before that. Secretarial skills have always been in demand, and in the English language alone, more than one thousand shorthand systems have been developed. Other secretarial and clerical skills—for instance, letter writing and bookkeeping—helped merchants and traders in local, regional, and international commerce. Formal training in the secretarial area, however, was practically nonexistent until the opening of "business colleges" between 1834 and 1860 in the United States; previously, training was on an apprenticeship basis. Private business colleges were largely responsible for secretarial programs in the 1880s and the following two decades, and the establishment of junior colleges in the early 1900s gave such programs further impetus. Education in the secretarial sciences has had its greatest growth at the community or junior college level.

In contrast to secretarial skills, data processing is a product of modern times, although its birth can be traced to the British mathematician Charles Babbage, who in 1822 demonstrated a small working model of a "difference machine," which could calculate mathematical tables. The growth of data processing as an academic discipline is closely related to the development of the computer. The computer industry's modern business birth began with the delivery of Univac I to the United States Bureau of the Census in 1951. In the early 1950s manufacturers offered short courses designed to help the user of a particular machine derive maximum benefit from the computer. Soon universities began offering short courses of a more general nature. Finally, in the late 1950s a comprehensive, occupation-oriented curriculum was offered.

The history of office auxiliary services begins with the invention of the first practical typewriter in 1860. Expanding business and industrial operations demanded a better and more efficient method of communication by letter. Although books on typewriting instruction were published by 1880, and the need for a touch system was recognized by the late 1880s, little was known about skill learning. Consequently, most of the early typewriter users were self-taught, and rote practice was emphasized in private colleges. The same approach was also used for the operation of other office machines. However, extensive research and experimentation in typewriting during the first half of the twentieth century led to the improvement of technique, speed, and accuracy. Improvements in typewriting skills went hand in hand with improvements in other office machines. The junior colleges in the United States are leading the way in developing office auxiliary services personnel. Internationally, instruction in this field was and is typically given by private institutions.

Because of technological advances, all three branches of business and office technologies have undergone vast changes. The invention of the Dictaphone, for instance, minimizes the importance of learning shorthand. Machines, already available commercially, which can understand voice patterns and execute commands will alter the field of secretarial sciences and business machines training. Many believe that only the surface of computer technology has been uncovered. Further developments, including laser technology and miniaturization, will continue to influence information systems, an area that requires constant reeducation.

Most programs in the field of business and commerce technologies are frequently offered at a level below the baccalaureate. In the field of data processing, however, many universities offer baccalaureate-level and even master's degree programs that emphasize systems analysis; programs in operations and programing, on the other hand, are still basically nondegree programs. Many courses in the secretarial and business machines area are also offered at the high school level. While universities do offer programs in these areas, they have done so reluctantly. In the United States the National Secretaries Association (International) has been instrumental in upgrading secretarial practice; largely as a result of its efforts, the Certified Professional Secretary's (CPS) program, which goes far beyond the basic secretarial skills, was established. Candidates for this certificate are tested in human relations, business law,

economics, management, financial analysis, mathematics, communication, decision making, and office procedures. While most secretarial programs in other parts of the world are less formalized, the emphasis on human relations, psychology, and personality development is increasing. In a similar but more specialized vein, the Data Processing Management Association of the United States awards a Certificate in Data Processing (CDP) to qualified individuals.

On successful completion of a program in business and commerce technology, the student is awarded a diploma or a certificate for a one-year course, an associate degree or a diploma for a two-year course, or a bachelor's degree for a four-year course. Most often, credit is also granted for relevant experience and demonstrated competency. It is likely that transferability of credit to degree programs will increase in the future.

The United States is perhaps the only major country in the world where universities are actively involved in offering certificate and associate and baccalaureate degree programs in secretarial science and office auxiliary services. In most other countries such programs are, by and large, offered by public technical colleges or private colleges and institutes. Standards vary significantly from one college to another. The larger colleges maintain close links with local businessmen to serve the potential employers' needs better and to find jobs for their students. Courses vary in length from six months to four years, and many programs are offered in the evenings to accommodate working people. In the United Kingdom public technical colleges and colleges of further education offer programs in business and office technology. This pattern is also emerging in other European countries, since the more elitist universities seem very reluctant to enter this field. Many universities in the Commonwealth countries, however, offer diploma programs in secretarial work and practice, with courses in business correspondence, office management, common law and procedures relating to meetings, bookkeeping, economics, and general commercial knowledge.

Formalized instruction in typing and business machines is practically unavailable at the university level in the Soviet Union and other Eastern European countries, where skills in these areas are learned primarily on the job. However, some universities and trade schools do offer limited courses in shorthand. Programs in data processing are offered by *tekhnikums,* or technical institutes, which admit students who have completed the eighth, ninth, or tenth grade in school.

Programs in information systems/data processing and office auxiliary services are, understandably, more numerous in the industrialized countries of the world. Outside of the United States, Canada, the United Kingdom, other developed European countries, Australia, Japan, and the Soviet Union, the large multinational computer firms are often the major providers of user-oriented education in information systems. In the future, however, universities probably will assume the major responsibility for regular programs.

ZOHER E. SHIPCHANDLER

Levels and Programs of Study

Although secretarial programs are concerned mainly with the practical aspects of secretarial work—including typing, shorthand, and general office procedures—they are increasingly spending more time on the general principles of office management. They usually require as a minimum prerequisite a secondary education, though applicants having relevant experience and aptitude are sometimes admitted with lower educational qualifications. The programs are given in community colleges, colleges of technology, and business colleges and are sponsored by a wide variety of agencies, including governments, business firms, and the armed services. The usual award for successful completion is a certificate, diploma, or degree. Principal course content usually includes typing and shorthand, business correspondence, records management, office systems, office simulation, office management procedures, and accounting. In general, this part of the program is designed to provide the secretarial skills required to support an executive. Some programs include other business subjects such as law, the operation of specialized office machines, and general subjects such as human relations, mathematics, literature, foreign languages, and human relations.

Information systems/data-processing programs are concerned mainly with the applications of computers. They usually require as a minimum prerequisite a secondary education, though for short courses, where employees need simply to be familiar with the role of the computer in their work setting, this requirement may be less stringently enforced. Programs of this kind are given by a wide variety of agencies, including schools and colleges of technology, manufacturers and sellers of computers, government agencies, and other large users of computers. A complete program often takes one year or more, but many organizations that use computers arrange short programs for a relatively high proportion of their employees to acquaint them with basic computer functioning. Between these extremes are programs and courses of intermediate length and intensity. The usual award for successful completion is a certificate, diploma, or bachelor's degree. Principal course content usually includes computer programming, storage devices, access methods, software systems, systems design, and developments in computer types. Background courses usually include mathematics, statistics, accounting, systems analysis, and human relations.

Office auxiliary service programs consist of study and practice in the operation of business machines (for example, electronic calculating machines, mailing machines, reprographic machines, electronic typewriting systems, and dictation playback systems), except electronic computers and their ancillary equipment. They usually require as a minimum prerequisite a secondary education, though applicants with relevant work experience and aptitude may be admitted with lower educational qualifications, particularly to the shorter programs. Programs of this type are usually given in a college of technology, community college, business college, or similar institution. They may be full time or part time and vary in duration from one month or two to more than a year. The usual award for successful completion is a certificate, diploma, or Associate in Arts degree. Principal course content depends on the particular kind of machine involved but generally includes the study of the operating principles of the machine and the procedures required to maintain it in good operating condition such as cleaning, lubricating, and normal maintenance. In addition, other related business subjects such as accountancy, business correspondence, typing, and records management are included. Some programs of this kind may include general subjects such as mathematics or literature.

[This section was based on UNESCO's *International Standard Classification of Education (ISCED)* (Paris: UNESCO, 1976), and was reviewed and modified by the National Secretaries Association, Kansas City, Missouri, USA.]

Major International and National Organizations

INTERNATIONAL

Committee of Commercial Clerical and
    Technical Employees in the EEC
37–41 rue Montagne-aux-Herbes-Potagères
1000 Brussels, Belgium

European Institute for Vocational Training
48 avenue de Villiers
75017 Paris, France
    European research and information exchange center for vocational training.

International Association for Educational and
    Vocational Information
20 rue de l'Estrapade
75005 Paris, France
    Supplies information for the guidance of college and university students.

International Association of Personnel Women
358 Fifth Avenue
New York, New York 10007 USA

International Federation for Information
    Processing
3 rue du Marché
1204 Geneva, Switzerland
    Stimulates research, development, and application of information science; encourages education and vocational training.

International Federation of Business and
    Professional Women
54 Bloomsbury Street
London WC1B 3QU, England

International Federation of Commercial
    Clerical and Technical Employees
15 avenue de Balexert
1211 Geneva 28, Switzerland

International Federation of Shorthand and
    Typewriting
Bernstrasse 98
CH-3072 Ostermundigen-Bern, Switzerland
    Collects, exchanges, and disseminates information of professional interest; organizes research work in the field.

International Personnel Management
    Association
1313 East 60th Street
Chicago, Illinois 60637 USA

International Society for Business Education
Chemin de la Croix
1052 Le Mont sur Lausanne, Switzerland
    Provides international courses on economic development and business education.

NATIONAL

A selection from the many organizations in the field includes:

Australia:
    Chartered Institute of Secretaries
    145 Macquarie
    SA Sydney, New South Wales 2000

Austria:
    Österreichischer Sekretärinnen-Verband
    Wahringer Gürtel 97
    A-1180 Vienna

Canada:
    Association of Administrative Assistants
        or Private Secretaries
    2408 SW Fifth Street
    Calgary, Alberta

    Chartered Institute of Secretaries
    3535 Trans Canada Highway
    Pointe Claire, Quebec

Institute of Chartered Secretaries and
Administrators in Canada
34 King Street West
Toronto, Ontario M5H 1R7

Denmark:
Dansk stenografisk forening
Sjaellandsgade 24
8900 Randers

Federal Republic of Germany:
Bund deutscher Sekretärinnen
Brehmstrasse 11
D-4000 Düsseldorf 1

Deutscher Sekretärinnen-Verband
Ritterstrasse 53
D–6700 Ludwigshafen/Rhein 14

India:
Institute of Secretaries
Lentin Chambers, Dalal Street
Fort Bombay 1

Ireland:
Irish Institute of Secretaries
112 Marlborough Street
Dublin 1

Italy:
Academia italiana di stenografia
via Soncin 17
35100 Padua

Netherlands:
Genootschap voor automatisering
% Studiecentrum informatica
Stadhouderskade
6 Amsterdam 1013
Education and training in data processing.

Spain:
Federación taquigráfica española
Cruz Num. 5
Madrid

Sweden:
Svenska dataföreningen
Skänstavägen 24
18400 Åkersberga
Promotes education and training in data processing

United Kingdom:
Chartered Institute of Secretaries
16 Park Crescent
London W1, England

Data Processing Management Association
5 Stewart Close
Fifield, Maidenhead, Banks, England

Institute of Bookkeepers and Related
Data Processing
139 Stoke Newington High Street
London N16, England

Institute of Qualified Private Secretaries
27 Hemberton Road
London SW9, England

United States:
American Personnel and Guidance
Association
1607 New Hampshire Avenue NW
Washington, D.C. 20009

American Society of Corporate
Secretaries
One Rockefeller Plaza
New York, New York 10020

Association of Independent Colleges and
Schools
1730 M Street NW, Suite 401
Washington, D.C. 20036

Data Processing Management Association
505 Busse Highway
Park Ridge, Illinois 60068

National Association of Legal Secretaries
3005 East Shelly Drive, Suite 120
Tulsa, Oklahoma 74104

National Business Education Association
1906 Association Drive
Reston, Virginia 22091

National Secretaries Association
(International)
Research and Education Foundation
Branch
2440 Pershing Road, Crown Center
Suite G-10
Kansas City, Missouri 64108
Sponsors research and educational
projects of benefit to secretaries, management personnel, and educators.

National Shorthand Reporters
Association
2361 South Jefferson Davis Highway
Arlington, Virginia 22202
Includes departments of professional
education, training, and vocational guidance; maintains a collection at the New
York Public Library.

Office Education Association
20 Leland Avenue
Columbus, Ohio 43214

Society for the Advancement of Business
Data Processing Education
1515 West Sixth Avenue
Stillwater, Oklahoma 74074

Society for Personnel Administrators
National Press Building
529 14th Street NW
Washington, D.C. 20004

Directories to national organizations throughout the world include:

Carter, C. *Guide to Reference Sources in Computer Sciences.* New York: Macmillan, 1974. Includes professional organizations.
Directory of European Associations. Part 1: *National Industrial, Trade and Professional Associations.* Part 2: *National Learned Scientific and Technical Societies.* Beckenham, Kent, England: CBD Research; Detroit: Gale Research, 1971, 1975.
Fisk, M. (Ed.) *Encyclopedia of Associations.* (9th ed.) Detroit: Gale Research, 1975.
Mallard, P. (Comp.) *Trade Associations and Professional Bodies of the United Kingdom.* (5th ed.) London and Elmsford, New York: Pergamon Press, 1971.
Zils, M. (Ed.) *World Guide to Trade Associations.* (2 vols.) New York: Bowker, 1974.

Principal Information Sources

GENERAL

Guides to the literature include:

Books for Occupational Educational Programs: A List for Community Colleges, Technical Institutes and Vocational Schools. New York: Bowker, 1971. Unannotated but comprehensive list of books covering all phases of business and commerce technologies.
Burgess, N. *How to Find Out About Secretarial and Office Practice.* Oxford, England: Pergamon Press, 1967.
Business Books in Print. New York: Bowker, annual. Includes vocational literature section and other listings for business and related fields.
Carter, C. *Guide to Reference Sources in Computer Sciences.* New York: Macmillan, 1974. Includes professional organizations, research centers, bibliographies, conference literature, encyclopedias, periodicals, directories, and dictionaries.
Forrester, G. *Occupational Literature: An Annotated Bibliography.* New York: Wilson, 1971. See specifically: Bookkeepers, Accountants, Data Processing Machine Operators, File Clerks, Office Machine Operators, Receptionists, Secretaries, Stenographers, Typists, Medical Secretaries.
International Computer Bibliography: A Guide to Books on the Use, Application and Effect of Computers in Scientific, Commercial, Industrial, and Social Environments. Manchester, England: National Computing Center, 1968. Supplemented monthly by *Literature on Automation.* Amsterdam: Studiecentrum voor administratieve automatisering.

Johnson, H. W. *How to Use the Business Library.* (3rd ed.) Cincinnati, Ohio: South-Western, 1964. Contains an annotated and extensive listing of books in general business.
Morrell, C. *Systems and Procedures Including Office Management Information Sources.* Detroit: Gale Research 1967.
Schuman, P. *Materials for Occupational Education: An Annotated Source Guide.* London and New York: Bowker, 1971. Also lists associations in the United States publishing occupational literature.

Overviews and broad introductions to the field include:

Anderson, R. I. *Secretarial Careers.* New York: Walck, 1961.
Cook, F. S., and Lenore, S. T. *The Dartnell Professional Secretaries Handbook.* Chicago: Dartnell, 1971. Describes the different positions available in business and commerce technologies: executive and private secretaries, office machine operators, stenographers, and typists.
Crozier, M. *World of the Office Worker.* Chicago: University of Chicago Press, 1971.
Logsdon, T. *An Introduction to Computer Science and Technology.* Palisades, New Jersey: Franklin, 1974. Gives a basic understanding of the history and technology of computers and the data-processing profession.
Maniotes, J., and Quasney, J. S. *Computer Careers: Planning, Prerequisites, Potential.* Rochelle Park, New Jersey: Hayden, 1974. An overview of the field as a career; includes information on educational training.
Mayo, L. G. *You Can Be an Executive Secretary.* New York: Macmillan, 1969.
Morrison, P., and others. *Opportunities in Today's Office.* New York: McGraw-Hill, 1969.
Noyes, N. B. *Your Future as a Secretary.* New York: Arco, 1970.
Office Machines Operator. (3rd ed.) New York: Arco, 1967.

Sources dealing with education in the field include:

"Business Education in Developing Countries." *Journal of Business Education,* May 1974, *49* (8), 326–328.
Garrison, C. "The Legal Secretary—Past, Present, and Future." *Balance Sheet,* February 1975, *56* (5), 207–208, 230.
Kallus, N. F. *An Office Employment Profile: Job Entry Requirements, Behavior Patterns, Career Opportunities.* Iowa City: Iowa Business Education Association, 1973.
Levin, H. A. "Education of Clerical Employees." *Journal of Business Education,* December 1974, *50* (3), 105–106.

"Training for Today's Office." *Balance Sheet,* March 1974, 55 (6), 257–260.

Wilkins, C., and others. "Computer Training and Education." Supplement to *Computer Weekly,* July 11, 1974.

Histories of the field include:

Archer, F. C. *The Origin and Extent of Standards in Clerical Work.* St. Cloud, Minnesota: State Teachers College, 1952. Includes bibliographies.

Benet, M. K. *The Secretarial Ghetto.* New York: Macmillan, 1973. Includes bibliographies.

Buller, E. H. *The Story of British Shorthand.* London: Pitman, 1957.

Gregg, J. R. *The Story of Shorthand.* New York: Gregg Publishing, 1913.

CURRENT BIBLIOGRAPHIES

For listings of articles and books dealing with business and office technology, particularly education in the field, consult:

Business Periodicals Index. New York: Wilson, 1958–. See secretaries, office workers.

Current Index to Journals in Education. New York: Macmillan, 1969–. See data processing occupations, business education, clerical occupations, clerical workers, business skills, office occupations (education), office practice, secretaries, stenography, typists.

Education Index. New York: Wilson, 1929–. See clerical work, office practice, secretaries.

PERIODICALS

Administrative Management (US), *Automation* (US), *BACIE Journal* (UK), *Balance Sheet* (US), *Bayerische Blätter für Stenografie* (FRG), *Bürotechnische Sammlung* (FRG), *Business Education Forum* (US), *Chartered Secretary* (Australia), *Chartered Secretary* (India), *Computer* (US), *Computers and Automation* (US), *Computerworld* (US), *Computing Newsletter for Schools of Business* (US), *Corriere stenografico* (Italy), *Data Processing* (UK), *DSTZ—Deutsche Stenografenzeitung* (FRG), *From Nine to Five or Thereabouts* (US), *Gabriele* (FRG), *International Review for Business Education* (Switzerland; text in English, French, German, Italian, Spanish), *Irish Accountant and Secretary* (Ireland), *Journal of Business Education* (US), *Journal of Data Education* (US), *Lettura stenografica* (Italy), *Management in Action* (UK), *Management Informatics* (Netherlands), *Memo International* (US), *Modern Office Administration* (Australia), *Modern Office Procedures* (US), *Mundo taquigráfico* (Spain), *National Shorthand Reporter* (US), *Neue stenografische Praxis* (FRG), *Office* (US), *Office Guide for Working Women* (US; formerly *Just Between Office Girls*), *Office Skills* (US), *Office Supervisors*

Bulletin (US), *Personal Report for the Professional Secretary* (US), *P. S. for Private Secretaries* (US), *Secretaries and Managers Journal of Australia, Secretary* (US), *Schoevers koerier* (Netherlands; summaries in English), *Sekretarska praxe* (Czechoslovakia; text in Czech, summaries in English, French, German, Russian), *Stenografisk tidskrift* (Denmark), *Studi grafici* (Italy), *Today's Secretary* (US).

For a more comprehensive listing of periodicals consult:

Current Periodicals Publications in Baker Library. Cambridge, Massachusetts: Harvard University, Graduate School of Business Administration, Baker Library, annual.

Ulrich's International Periodicals Directory. New York: Bowker, biennial. See "Office Management."

DICTIONARIES, ENCYCLOPEDIAS, HANDBOOKS

The following is a sampling of the numerous handbooks in the field:

Doris, L., and Miller, B. M. *Complete Secretary's Handbook.* (3rd ed.) Englewood Cliffs, New Jersey: Prentice-Hall, 1970.

Encyclopedia of Business Letters in Four Languages. (3 vols.) New York: Arco, 1972. Handbook giving examples of routine correspondence in English, French, Spanish, and German.

Fasnacht, H. D., and Bauernfeing, H. B. *How to Use Business Machines: A Brief Introductory Course.* (3rd ed.) New York: McGraw-Hill, 1969. A handbook for business schools, junior colleges, on-the-job training programs, or self-instruction.

Freedman, G. *Handbook for the Technical and Scientific Secretary.* New York: Dover, 1974.

Friedman, S., and Grossman, J. *Modern Clerical Practice.* (4th ed.) New York: Pitman, 1975.

Hanna, J. M., and others. *Secretarial Procedures and Administration.* (6th ed.) Cincinnati, Ohio: South-Western, 1973.

Heyel, C. (Ed.) *Handbook of Modern Office Management and Administrative Services.* New York: McGraw-Hill, 1972.

House, C. R., and Koebele, A. M. *Reference Manual for Office Personnel.* (5th ed.) Cincinnati, Ohio: South-Western, 1970.

Hutchinson, L. *Standard Handbook for Secretaries.* (8th ed.) New York: McGraw-Hill, 1969.

Janis, J. H., and Thompson, M. H. *New Standard Reference for Secretaries and Administrative Assistants.* New York: Macmillan, 1972. Covers letter writing, postal regulations, report preparation, and business terms.

Laird, E. S. *Data Processing Secretary's Complete Handbook.* Englewood Cliffs, New Jersey: Parker Publishing, 1973.

Leslie, L. A., and Coffin, K. B. *Handbook for the Legal Secretary.* New York: McGraw-Hill, 1968.

Taintor, S. A., and Monro, K. M. *The Secretary's Handbook: A Manual of Correct Usage.* (9th ed.) Fully revised by K. M. Monro and M. D. Shertzer. New York: Macmillan, 1969.

Terry, G. R. *Office Management and Control.* (7th ed.) Homewood, Illinois: Irwin, 1975.

Dictionaries and encyclopedias in the field include:

Burger, E. *Technical Dictionary of Data Processing, Computers, and Office Machines. English, German, French, Russian.* Elmsford, New York: Pergamon Press, 1970.

Clason, W. Z. (Comp.) *Elsevier's Dictionary of Computers, Automatic Control and Data Processing. In Six Languages, English/American, French, Spanish, Italian, Dutch, and German.* (2nd rev. ed.) Amsterdam: Elsevier, 1971. A classic work.

Duttweiler, G. *Les 20,000 phrases et expressions de la correspondance commerciale et privée.* Geneva: Editions générales, 1960. French phrases with English and German equivalents.

Harvard, J., and Miletto, M. M. *Bilingual Guide to Business and Professional Correspondence (Italian-English)/Guida bilingue alla corrispondenza commerciale e professionale (inglese-italiano).* Elmsford, New York: Pergamon Press, 1973.

Hegel, C. (Ed.) *The Encyclopedia of Management.* (2nd ed.) New York: Van Nostrand Reinhold, 1973.

Munniksma, F. *International Business Dictionary in Nine Languages.* Deventer, Netherlands: Kluwer B. V., 1975.

College Blue Book. (14th ed.) New York: CCM Information Corporation, 1972. Lists United States colleges and universities offering degrees in secretarial science, office management, office administration, and data-processing technologies.

Commonwealth Universities Yearbook. London: Association of Commonwealth Universities, 1914–. Published annually; lists degree programs under "Secretarial Studies," "Education: Business/Commercial," "Education: Industrial."

Directory of Accredited Institutions. Washington, D.C.: Association of Independent Colleges and Schools, annual.

Priestly, B. (Ed.) *British Qualifications.* (5th ed.) New York: International Publications Service, 1974. Lists colleges, universities, and other institutions in the United Kingdom which offer diplomas and degrees in commerce, business subjects, and secretarial work and shorthand and typing.

Russell, M. M. *The Blue Book of Occupational Education.* New York: CCM Information Corporation, 1971. Lists occupational schools in the United States offering programs of instruction in clerical skills, office management, and secretarial work.

Wiggs, G. D. (Ed.) *Career Opportunities: Marketing, Business and Office Specialists.* Chicago: Ferguson, 1970. Lists United States schools offering marketing, business, and office specialists programs.

[Bibliography prepared by Susan Johnson.]

BUSINESS, INTERNATIONAL

See International Business (field of study).

BUSINESS MACHINES TRAINING

See Business and Office Technology (field of study).

BUSINESS MANAGEMENT OF HIGHER EDUCATION

1. BOOKSTORES

2. FACILITIES, PHYSICAL PLANT

3. STUDENT HOUSING

4. STUDENT HOUSING: NORWEGIAN CASE STUDY

5. INSURANCE AND RISK MANAGEMENT

6. PURCHASING

1. BOOKSTORES

The college or university bookstore is primarily a retail outlet of books and supplies for students and faculty; as a commercial operation within an intellectual community, the bookstore can make a significant contribution to the university's educational processes.

Modern bookstores provide much more than textbooks and at some institutions are in effect small department stores. The paperback revolution stimulated stores' sales of trade books and professional books; the development of electronics for the classroom has introduced such divergent products as tapes, cassettes, and calculators; and other merchandise of interest to the academic community, from art supplies to athletic clothing, permits profits that can help subsidize the sale of textbooks and offset operational expenses, such as payroll and overhead.

College and university policymakers should choose a type of bookstore ownership that will serve the institution's purpose and meet the needs of the university community. If they choose institutional ownership, they should select professional bookstore management; advise management about store purposes and philosophy; plan for the proper disbursement of any profits; and ensure that the store uses accepted retail practice and reporting to determine profitability while meeting the educational supply needs of the campus.

Store Ownership

Institutions use several different methods of establishing bookstores, depending on which type of ownership will provide it with the most effective operation.

Institutional ownership. The institutional store is organized within the framework of the university administration and is generally controlled by the head of the student union; by the vice-president for business, the business manager, or the director of auxiliary enterprises; or by the purchasing agent of the university. Whatever the form of control, a store manager, or director, should be employed to run the operation of the store with the assistance of department heads, managing assistants, and clerks as required by the size of the operation. Profits can be returned to the university's general fund or used for various projects, such as the improvement and expansion of the store itself.

Because an institutional store comes under the direct control of the administration, store policies can be made to conform with the general principles of the university. A possible source of conflict in this kind of store, however, is between academic needs and business considerations. In most cases academic needs must take priority; for example, the store will be required to carry lines of merchandise that may not be profitable. Another source of conflict can arise from the tax-exempt status of these stores, which may earn the university disfavor with local merchants and other taxpayers.

Poor management or extenuating circumstances can cause these stores to run at a deficit, which the university must make up. University-managed stores must also handle any problems between professors and students in regard to deliveries, prices, and general handling of textbooks. Some colleges and universities feel that the problems inherent in operating a retail store are better left to people expert in the field and are more than willing to turn over the operation of the bookstore to lease operators or to private stores operating nearby. In fact, most European schools have left the matter to private enterprise, whereas most college stores in the United States and Canada are institutionally owned.

Private ownership. The private college store is not a new phenomenon. It is a store run by a merchant within or near the area of a college or university and can be owner operated, a corporation, or a partnership. Private stores in the United States and Canada often operate in direct competition with university-owned bookstores. The competition created by this situation tends to increase the efficiency of both the college store and the private store.

When a private store operates on a campus, the college or university should inform the private operator of the needs of its students and faculty and make every attempt to ensure that service is not ignored for the sake of profit. Further, both the institutional store and the private store, according to the National Association of College Stores (NACS), should be provided information on class requirements. A private store otherwise often has to search out book information from faculty.

A privately owned operation on campus frees the university or college from the responsibilities of a retail operation, but the university loses any profits that might have been generated by a store and loses control over store policies and practices.

Lease operation. Many small schools often find it unprofitable to run a bookstore and will lease operations to a firm that specializes in the operation of college bookstores. A lease operator (who is usually selected by bidding) will use university-owned space— often a vacated store. Usually the operator pays rent and provides the university with certain controls over the calculation of gross sales. At the end of the year the university receives a percentage of the gross. The lease owner provides personnel for the store and puts up operating capital.

One advantage of a lease operation, particularly for smaller schools, is that the administration has at least some assurance of a return without its bearing payroll and fringe benefit costs. The university can also expect to have a professional staff operating the store, but it still faces financial risks and may itself be unfavorably criticized if the store is poorly operated.

Corporate ownership with institutional support. The State University of New York system has partially adopted this type of operation, which they refer to as Faculty, Student, Administration stores (FSA). This type of store is separately incorporated within the corporate laws of each state. A board of directors is formed by students, faculty, and administrators, who determine the basic policies of the store and hire a manager with the authority to employ staff. Financing is generally provided by the school itself.

Because this store is a separate corporation, the university delegates its responsibility for the store's operation to a group of people within the institution who are primarily concerned with the proper operation of the store. However, should the individuals chosen to be on the board of directors lose interest or disagree on policy, the effectiveness of the operation may suffer.

Cooperative ownership. The basic premise behind this operation is the refund for patronage given to members of the cooperative. The number of cooperative college bookstores is small compared with the total number of college stores throughout the United States. The patronage rebate is usually not large, and the most successful cooperative bookstores are those that enjoy a large volume of nonmember traffic. The Harvard Cooperative, in Cambridge, Massachusetts, and the Yale Co-op, in New Haven, Connecticut, are examples of successful cooperatives; both are actually department stores, catering to the general population of the area.

The cooperative bookstore at the University of Connecticut in Storrs was formed in 1974 to replace an institutionally owned store. The cooperative, which signed a two-year contract with the university, has a provisional board made up of students, faculty, and administrators. Each student at the University of Connecticut is required to pay a thirty-five-dollar fee, which is part of the enrollment fee to be returned upon graduation. The cooperative was established with guidance and assistance from the Yale and Harvard cooperatives. Although at the end of its first year no rebates were available for members, it was expected that at the end of the second year rebates would be possible.

Because cooperative bookstores are independently owned, they must pay taxes on retained income, whereas institutional stores, within the framework of a nonprofit organization, would not have to pay these taxes. Also, because cooperatives must rebate, their employee pay scales are generally minimal, and thus their staff is usually nonprofessional. Without well-trained and well-paid employees, the efficiency of a store suffers and there is a lowering of gross profits and the rebate.

Student exchange. A student exchange is often simply an informal organization of students who get together for the purpose of exchanging books. Frequently, a bulletin board for listing such exchanges is placed in the student union. In most cases, all dealings are among the individuals themselves, and used rather than new books are exchanged.

The effective existence of an informal exchange may depend upon how long its organizers remain at the school. When a student exchange uses unpaid volunteers and expands business beyond simple exchanges, it must then consider sources of funding for space, staff, investment in books and other merchandise, and general operations.

Store Operations

College and university stores have two particular methods of operation: "clerk-manned" and "self-service." In the clerk-manned store the customer requests the desired merchandise, and it is retrieved by a clerk, who then records the sale on a cash register. This is generally an adequate method where volume is low. As a store grows and its operational volume gets larger, its variety of merchandise expands, and its stock of books grows, it is generally advantageous to institute self-service, whereby customers find the merchandise they want and take it to a cash register for payment. Self-service requires that books and supplies be displayed in some type of logical order for customer convenience. The most logical way of arranging textbooks is by course name or number, although some stores arrange them alphabetically by authors within each discipline. A "totally integrated" store is arranged so that all merchandise relating to a particular discipline is situated within the same area. For example, both engineering texts and supplies are situated in one section, art texts and supplies in another, and so on, with general supplies such as paper, pens, and pencils displayed in a central location.

Self-service operation tends to cut down on staff but also increases the probability of pilferage. Such devices as one-way entrances and exits, free lockers or check stands where customers are required to leave belongings upon entering the store, and cash registers at the exits help prevent pilferage.

College store policies may differ slightly from those of other retail operations because of their special clientele and merchandise. Some college stores offer discounts, either to all customers, to students, or only to institutional employees, and sometimes only on certain items. Charge accounts are often provided with the same variation as discounts. Sometimes students are allowed to purchase books and supplies from the store as part of scholarship provisions. Special services often provided by college stores include special orders on books; sale of class rings and fraternity and sorority insignia; food, laundry, barber, mail, and bank services; watch repair; film developing; engraving; magazine subscriptions; institutional stationery; and even a general supply department.

Textbook adoptions and orders. The textbook department is the prime reason for the existence of the college store. Generally 50 to 75 percent of all business transacted by American college bookstores is through the sale of textbooks. The most important, and often the most difficult textbook operation is obtaining adoption information from the faculty and registration figures from the administration in time to order books and have them on the shelves at the opening of each term. Although methods of obtaining order information, called adoptions or requisitions, vary, the best method is to have them processed by the administrative offices of the university, so that student registration figures can be put on the adoption sheets. In some stores, particularly private or lease-operated ones, faculty requests for information are handled directly by the bookstore; thus, a mutually cooperative relationship between the bookstore and the faculty must be established.

In all cases, a standard form should be used to provide a uniform procedure and convenient format for ordering textbooks.

This form should include course name, number, and section, and it should provide space for noting whether all students will be required to purchase the book. Provisions should also be made for listing author, title, publisher, edition, copyright date, and any other information that will simplify the ordering of books. Each completed form should show the number of students enrolled in the course and the number of books left over at the end of the term, in order to predict future orders and to avoid waste. These records can be stored on small cards, adoption forms themselves, or electronic data-processing materials.

The use of a standard purchase order by the bookstore is necessary not only to the store but also to the publisher. The purchase order's heading should include the name, address, phone number, and telex number (if any) of the store. Purchase orders must be consecutively numbered and differentiated by year. They should include the shipping address, the date, and a space for terms, such as deferring billing until the school term opens. Spaces for quantity, description of the item, and the buyer's signature should be provided. The original order should go to the vendor or publisher, and carbon copies should be made for the office and the receiver, if necessary. A fourth and fifth copy can be used for returning unsold books to the publisher at the end of the term.

Normally, purchase orders are sent through the mail, but if they are placed by telephone, a confirming purchase order should follow by mail. Many stores and publishers are using Western Union Telex or TWX (computerized teletype) machines, which allow for immediate transmittal of messages, such as purchase orders for used textbooks or for shipping schedules. Another method of rapidly transmitting purchase orders is the telecopier, which transmits a printed copy of the purchase order over telephone lines to the publisher.

Textbook costs. Publishers usually extend a 20 percent discount on the retail price to bookstores, but the bookstore pays the freight charges on shipments. For books not classified as textbooks but that are assigned for courses, the discount can be as high as 40 percent. Paperback books can be ordered from wholesalers, who often extend higher discounts than do publishers. Textbooks that are initially printed in paperback form are priced higher and in most cases carry a 20 percent discount. Depending upon the type and volume of paperbacks, trade books, and textbooks handled by a particular store, discounts can range from 20 to 25 percent. To compute the net cost of textbooks, the store manager must include freight charges, which in the United States average about 5 percent of the net price of the textbooks. Some allowance must also be made for the cost of returning unsold books to the publisher. The NACS operational survey shows that for bookstores the total cost of selling books averages around 23 percent of gross profit, which clearly indicates that textbook sales are not very profitable (NACS, 1965).

Textbook returns. One reason textbook publishers resist increasing textbook discounts is that they often extend return privileges to the bookstores for overstocked books. Every publisher has a return policy, and the NACS and the American Booksellers Association publish a listing of publishers' names, addresses, return addresses, and return policies. Most bookstores will have a return rate between 10 to 15 percent; a figure lower than 10 percent indicates that the store is not ordering enough books, whereas a return rate in excess of 15 percent indicates overstocking. Most publishers issue credit memos on the return of textbooks; thus, when returns are high, money is tied up and is not available for purchasing stock.

A store should use an accepted form for requesting permission to return books to a publisher. The NACS prints such a form for use by its member stores. A request for permission to return should include the publisher's name, a sequential return number, date of the request, the quantity ordered and the quantity returned, the facts of publication, the invoice number on which the books were billed originally, the invoice date, the list price and net price, and extensions. Some publishers may limit returns to a percentage of books purchased during a particular year; many larger publishers allow unlimited returns; and some publishers allow returns without prior permission (automatic return privileges).

When permission to return is granted, the publisher should send the bookstore a return authorization number and, in some cases, packaging labels for the returned books. Returned books should be cleaned, packed properly, and shipped. If credit or payment is not received from the publisher within five to six weeks, a letter of inquiry is in order. Transportation charges as well as employee wages for handling and accounting must be included in the cost of returning textbooks to a publisher, and thus returns should be kept to a minimum.

Used textbooks. Because of the high price of new textbooks, the used book market has increased dramatically in the 1970s. Bookstores can purchase used books from a wholesaler at 50 percent of the retail price of a new textbook and sell them at 75 percent of the retail price of new books, thus making a 33⅓ percent profit.

One drawback in handling used books is that they cannot be returned. This risk is not minimal, but used books tend to be the first books to sell out in a textbook department. The store buyer should be familiar with the used book market, so that the store does not purchase outdated editions.

The primary method of obtaining used books is through a used book wholesaler, and because turnover is rapid, most used book companies rely heavily on the telex for handling orders. Unlike a publisher, a used book company may not have a particular title in stock, and thus orders must be placed in advance. Used books for resale may also be purchased from students, usually at 50 percent of the retail price of a new book. The store then sells the book

for 75 percent of its retail price when new. When buying from students, the store should request identification from the seller to discourage the sale of stolen books. Books that are not to be used in future terms are generally purchased at a used book wholesaler's buying price, which is listed in the wholesaler's buying guide. Buying guide prices are ordinarily 20 to 25 percent of the price of a new book.

Some stores will purchase used books only at a specific time each term, usually during the final examination period. Often, because a used book company can offer more expertise, a store will arrange for a company to come in with its own buyers and its own money to purchase books from students during final examination periods. The company is given a list of books that the bookstore feels it will be using in upcoming terms, and these books are purchased by the company buyer at half price from the students. All other books are purchased at wholesale buying guide prices. Books purchased at half price are turned over to the bookstore, and the buyer is reimbursed. The used book company pays a commission on the books that it purchases for itself.

Used books can also be purchased from other college bookstores. The NACS publishes a weekly bulletin that lists the books member stores would like to sell or buy. In addition, many regional organizations of college stores in the United States and Canada exchange information regarding used and new books.

Shipping and receiving. The receiving department should list merchandise received on a copy of the purchase order. The quantities and price of the merchandise should be checked against the receiving or packing slip. A receiving room should keep a log of deliveries, which records purchase order number, vendor, shipper, receiving slip number, bill of lading number, number of cartons received, and date. Such information is useful in documenting discrepancies. The receiving copy of the purchase order should note the number of cartons received, date, and shipping company, so that the invoice clerk can later check in case the transportation charges have been prepaid by the publisher.

When the shipper delivers merchandise to the store, a bill of lading must be signed by the receiver, who should carefully check the number and condition of the cartons. In turn, when the store ships merchandise to vendors or customers, it should maintain a written record of all items shipped. When merchandise and books are returned to vendors, this record can be kept on the return form by listing the number of cartons, their weight, and the method of shipping. Records of shipment are needed for verifying shipment to the publisher and for filing insurance claims on lost or damaged shipments. Information regarding shipment of mail order merchandise can often be recorded on the customer's order form for future reference.

When processing invoices for payment, the invoice clerk must verify that the merchandise has actually been received and that prices and extensions are correct. Records of invoices for payment should include invoice number, amount of payment, invoice data, and the date that the invoice was passed for payment. In a private store or an institutional store that prepares and sends out its own checks, the invoice, or a copy of it, can be kept in the store itself. In an institutional store where payment is made by another department of the university, a copy of the invoice can be attached to the receiving copy.

Daily reports. At the end of the day, if not more often, a cashier will "cash out" a register by removing the cash that was advanced to the register at the start of the day. The remaining money is the receipts of the register. The receipts are matched against a reading from the daily cash register tape.

Only one cashier should operate and assume responsibility for a particular register or a single drawer of a multidrawer register. The cashier should fill out a cashier's daily report at the end of each particular period of operation. This will list the date, the cash register number, and the drawer number or letter and should also list the bills, coins, checks, petty cash vouchers, book vouchers, and voids from the register. The sum of these items indicates the total monies in the register, which, when compared against the register reading, will give the balance against the day's receipts. The report should then be signed by the cashier.

All sales, cash and charge, must go through a register, which should be cleared at least daily. A form for a daily total cash report, which should indicate the amount of money each department and register brought into the store that day, goes to the accounting department, and copies of these forms should always be kept at the store to enable management to keep track of daily receipts and long-term operations. Incorrect rings on a register or voids are removed from register totals, and the final totals indicate an overall overage or shortage for the day's receipts.

Transfers are records of merchandise shipped from the bookstore to another location, usually a branch store. Merchandise leaving a store should be recorded on a transfer sheet, which will debit the merchandise to one store and credit it to the other store. If the retail system of accounting is used, a transfer form should be made out each time merchandise is transferred from one department to another. Completed transfer forms should be dated, consecutively numbered, list the kind and quantity of merchandise and price, and be initialed by the sender and the receiver.

From the previous account of the daily reporting procedures, the importance of the cash register becomes evident. Although cash registers have recently been improved by technical developments, many stores still use the mechanical register, an electric-powered machine that keeps track of sales by listing each item as the cashier rings in the price. The register totals the prices and opens the drawer, allowing the cashier to deposit the customer's money and to return any change. The mechanical register can have up to ten cash drawers and usually has a receipt tape that can be presented to the customer as proof of purchase. It also has a detail tape that lists each sale and is sometimes broken down by department. Other features of the cash register include a key allowing the register to be locked; two types of reading positions that permit the cashier or the manager to compute subtotal receipts; and a position for reading drawer totals and department totals, which can be reset to zero to begin another day of business. Quite often this reset position has a nonresettable group total.

Mechanical registers are rapidly being superseded by the electronic register, which operates in the same manner as the mechanical cash register but allows more flexibility and has increased record-keeping capabilities. The electronic register uses the same receipt and detail tape as mechanical registers but operates more rapidly and can carry more departments. Although the possibilities of the electronic register have not been completely realized, it can be used to record the sale at the point of sale, subtract the item that is purchased from a perpetual inventory, credit a salesperson with a commission, record the sales on the customer's charge account, and alert a buyer when the inventory of a particular item has reached a low level. The electronic cash register can also be used in conjunction with a computer and the universal product code (UPC)—a merchandise code that makes possible the constant updating of cost and retail price on each item in the store. The code can also be used to ring in the retail price of each item on the cash register by the use of further electronic equipment that reads the code placed on each item by the manufacturer. The UPC approach has a level of sophistication not always needed or required by the smaller store.

Large-sized college stores have installed computer systems that have been able to reduce much of the staff work. In many stores computers are used to increase purchasing and inventory control, and computer printouts are replacing inventory sheets. Computer printouts can also be utilized to simplify and speed up the process of returning books to publishers. Computerization will be of greater utility to stores of almost all sizes, particularly since it can often be adapted to the needs of small stores.

Inventory. One of the most important aspects of the accounting system of any store is the total inventory. The cost of the total inventory is needed to determine the store's profitability because the inventory or stock of merchandise of the retail operation is one of the largest assets on its balance sheet. There are two methods of inventory accounting used by retail bookstores. One is the cost method of accounting, under which all inventory is tabulated at the cost of the merchandise. Under the cost method of accounting, the inventory must be counted item by item and listed under the vendor's name along with an accurate description of the item. The actual invoice cost of each item must be checked and totaled to arrive at the total inventory cost. The cost method is satisfactory only when there are few merchandise items and is suitable for extremely high turnover departments, such as a meat or produce department in a grocery store. In larger and more complex operations, the cost method becomes extremely burdensome.

Larger stores usually adopt the retail inventory method, under which the store utilizes its current retail prices and then applies a percent discount to estimate cost. The retail inventory method is considered superior to the cost method because it is more accurate, less expensive to operate, more flexible, and more effective as a device for making management decisions on the basis of the flow of merchandise and the level of the inventory as established by the retail purchase journal. A drawback of the retail method is that the merchandise cost is not exact. In fact, the cost under the retail method will often yield a 3 to 7 percent higher valuation than will the cost method of accounting. The retail method also requires extremely accurate and detailed record keeping of merchandise purchased.

Under the retail method, when an item is purchased and the invoice passed, the cost and retail price of the item is recorded in a purchase journal. The cost must include transportation charges. The departmental starting inventory is taken, and, at the end of a reasonable period (generally a month), the purchase journal figures are added to the starting inventory to obtain the total inventory for the month. The total sales of each department are then calculated by using the daily cash reports for the month, which list the retail value of the merchandise sold. The retail value of the merchandise sold is subtracted from the inventory to determine the remaining inventory. The purchase journal, which has been kept throughout the month, is totaled and then the average percentage of discount is calculated. The discount is applied to the total retail inventory to obtain the total inventory cost. This figure can be checked at the end of a period by running a physical retail inventory of all the merchandise within the store by departments. The value of this inventory should coincide with the figure that the purchase journal and the sales figures (or book inventory) established for the same period. The difference between the book inventory and the physical inventory is referred to as shrinkage and reflects stolen merchandise and errors in calculations. Necessarily, this system of accounting requires a number of forms to record the nature of all these transactions.

Whether the retail or cost method is used, every store should take an inventory at least once a year. This inventory should be either supervised or audited by an accredited firm of public accountants.

Facilities. The size of the bookstore should be sufficient to meet the needs of the student body. The NACS estimates that a school with an enrollment of under 2000

students needs a bookstore equal in area to four square feet (.4 square meters) per student; for 2000 to 3000 students, three and a half square feet (.3 square meters) per student; 5000 to 10,000 students, three square feet (.28 square meters) per student; and for more than 10,000 students, two square feet (.2 square meters) per student. In addition, office and storage area should equal approximately 20 percent of the selling space.

Other factors also bear on the determined size of the college store. In the presence of strong competition by local, privately operated stores, space needs would be reduced. A college store without competition would naturally need increased space. The type of school that the store serves is also a factor that regulates size: community colleges and junior colleges require less store space per student than do universities with strong upper divisions and graduate schools. If the emphasis is on technical and engineering disciplines, less store space is required than in schools that emphasize the social sciences and humanities (where more books are needed per student). Should the store service people other than the university community, a larger space would be required. Further, dormitory students require more services of a college store than do commuting students.

A college store should be placed near the student union building and in a centralized location attracting heavy traffic. An outside display should be set up to entice students into the store. The site should also provide convenient receiving and shipping facilities.

The layout of the store should be confined to one floor rather than to several levels. Less labor is needed, and in this way one type of merchandise will be able to complement the other. To discourage pilferage, the exit should be laid out as the only means of egress from the store. To encourage impulse buying, textbooks should be near the rear of the store, so that customers will have to pass through the miscellaneous areas. Paperbacks should be in a convenient and well-lighted area to allow for adequate browsing.

Bookstore fixtures should be lower than eye level, so that customers throughout the store can be observed. The store should be arranged so that there are no "blind areas"—places where theft cannot be observed. The openly designed store is also helpful when business slows down, because fewer people are needed to handle general operations. At the entrance of the store there should be book drops and free lockers, and service stands should be set up for servicing special orders and handling returns. The store should contain a controlled area with lockable glass showcases to display the smaller and more expensive merchandise; this area must be manned full time by a clerk who is knowledgeable of the merchandise. At the beginning of school terms and other peak periods, the store must allow space for additional cash registers. All entrance and exit aisles should be wide enough to accommodate wheelchairs. A store directory should be placed near the entrance and should include a written explanation of store policies.

Bibliography

American Council on Education. *College and University Business Administration.* Washington, D.C.: American Council on Education, 1968.

Controller Congress National Retail Merchants Association. *Retail Accounting Manual.* New York: CCNRMA, 1962.

National Association of College and University Business Officers. *College and University Business Administration.* Washington, D.C.: NACUBO, 1974.

National Association of College Stores. "Planning the College Store." *College Store Journal,* 1965, *32*, 141–145.

National Association of College Stores. "Store Planning Manual." *College Store Journal,* 1975, *62*, 1–11.

Powers, J. T. *The Inventory Method Made Practical.* New York: Controller Congress National Retail Merchants Association, 1971.

Reynolds, R. "Bookstore." In A. S. Knowles (Ed.), *Handbook of College and University Administration.* New York: McGraw-Hill, 1970.

RICHARD A. MALONEY

2. FACILITIES, PHYSICAL PLANT

In medieval Europe universities generally evolved from associations of scholars who delivered their lectures in cathedrals, monasteries, or public squares. Students banded together and took up common residence to avoid exploitation by local merchants. They lived where they pleased and acted as they pleased—undisciplined, irresponsible, and sometimes rowdy and troublesome to local authority. Wealthy patrons began to endow hostels, which subsequently became colleges for poor and deserving scholars. These colleges possessed no buildings of their own, and they rented or otherwise utilized churches or other buildings for their public functions. Toward the end of the fifteenth century, the colleges began to group their faculties together within a single building, and thus began the university physical plant. The University of Toulouse, established in 1229, is reputed to have been the first "planned" university; and Charles University, founded in Prague in 1348, was the first university to have a planned physical plant with a building for each of its faculties, a college for twelve masters, and student residences under the jurisdiction of a master. The precedents set by the deliberate creation of a university with a planned physical plant were destined to continue with only slight changes for the next six hundred years.

Styles of Facilities

Most educational institutions, to fulfill their mission, must have the shelter and services of a physical plant. The physical plants of most universities have many elements in common, such as a library, classrooms, and laboratories; however, each campus presents a unique combination of these elements. There can be no standard campus built to a predetermined formula because the architectural requirements of each university are usually determined by the requirements of the academic program, the terrain and land values, the climate, the local economic conditions, and the pedagogical philosophy of the institution. In most instances, these factors also preclude the use of only one architectural style on a campus.

Traditional. Although there is no special style that is characteristic of all higher education facilities, there are some styles that tend to be symbolic. The medieval Gothic architecture of the thirteenth, fourteenth, and fifteenth centuries in Europe has heavily influenced the design of many campuses throughout the temperate zones of the world. The Gothic style was contemporary when the first European university structures were erected and is an esthetically pleasing style of architecture consisting of balanced thrusts in stone masonry, a structure of visible sinews, curtain walls of pointed arches, and stone tracery.

Historically, the style has been expensive to construct and also presents some difficulties in climates having extremes of weather. The current need to develop centers for higher education in all zones of the world coupled with the increasing variety of available building materials, developing construction techniques, rapidly increasing demand for sophistication of university facilities, and severe economic pressures have greatly diminished the continuation of Gothic designs in the twentieth century. As late as the mid nineteenth century, the ecclesiastic effect was still a major influence, as evidenced by the continued cathedral styles. By 1950, university physical plant requirements became incompatible with the medieval designs, particularly in supplying the closely controlled environment required by the computer, the germfree areas required by some biological research, the acoustical controls required for the education of the handicapped, and the electronic, audio, and video retrieval systems used in the libraries.

Functional. A quotation from *Facts About Finland* (Benz, 1974, p. 21) expresses a worldwide new approach to university facility construction: "The prejudices of tradition discarded, the modern architecture of Finland—Finnish functionalism— is a creative art that exploits the opportunities offered by industrialization and standardization." In the developed and developing nations, functionalism is predominating over tradition in campus architecture.

The technological growth in higher education has spawned a new sense of campus architectural values. The Bishop at Oxford in 1214 and Cardinal Newman, again at Oxford in 1856, are almost certain to have envisioned a different academic environment than did architect Nils Koppel in 1959 at the Technical University of Denmark, in Lyngby, or architect Marcello Vivaqua in 1966 at the Federal University of Espírito Santo in Vitória, Brazil.

The Technical University of Denmark, the University of Tromsø in Norway, Scarborough College at the University of Toronto in Canada, Gujarat University at Ahmadabad in India, the Federal University of Espírito Santo in Brazil, and the University of South Florida in Tampa are examples of the functional approach to campus design. These campuses have been designed in response to the need for a changing student/teacher relationship and also in answer to the need for conservation of economic resources.

In each of these institutions, the overall plan has set tradition aside. Historically, schools maintained a large student/teacher ratio as a means of contending with the scarcity of teachers. This necessitated the cathedral style of building, where one individual could instruct a large number simultaneously. The style appeared adequate in a lecture-listen situation; however, the complexity and intensity of communicating, for instance, in the modern physical sciences, dictated a smaller student/teacher ratio. The building space required per capita in 1976 for science education is more than five times that of 1925 and more than twenty times that of three hundred years ago.

Modular. Modular designs for university buildings have been developed for economy and ease of future expansion. The modular style borrows techniques of mass production from the manufacturing industry and dramatically reduces the construction cost and time required for the building.

This style, when all under one roof, has been successfully utilized at Scarborough College at the University of Toronto, where teaching methods could not be properly served by the traditional designs. The cold climate also made it desirable to digress from the prior concept of scattered buildings to the erection of interconnected ones. The initial campus of Espírito Santo in Brazil used a single module, one level, in multiple configuration to compose compatible buildings on a multibuilding campus. Although diametrically opposite in outward appearance, the two universities still maximize functionalism, industrialization, and economy, and they provide an ease of changeability required to meet the yet undefined needs of the future.

Multinational. The nearly explosive growth of the science and technology fields in higher education since World War II has forced most institutions to adopt innovative campus structures. With the arrival of the jet age, the exchange of ideas through consultations and comparisons of international architectural styles has been expedited. Presently, there is a new crop of multinational design organizations.

One such jet-age partnership is the firm of McMillan, Griffis, Mileto (with offices in Rome, New York, and Lagos), which was commissioned to design the University of Lagos in Nigeria. The main portion of the campus, which was completed in 1966, consists of low, broad-brimmed, concrete buildings situated to look out over Lagos Lagoon. The broad, poured-in-place overhangs and precast grilles, designed to offer protection from the tropical sun, are a typical culmination of multinational talent and technology.

A conscious effort is made in campus planning and design to plan facilities that can be adapted to meet the needs of the times. Advances in science and technology require changes in study methods during the normal life expectancy of a building. An almost explosive growth rate in the worldwide campus community with its attendant economic pressures has directed new designs toward functionalism and away from traditionalism. The twentieth century campus atmosphere is one of change, and this atmosphere is being reflected in university landscape and architecture.

Management of Facilities

The activity in a physical plant organization can be classified in seven major accounts or functions. The Association of Physical Plant Administrators has amassed the experiences of many institutions and from these has established the following as a common basis of communication: physical plant administration, building maintenance, custodial services, utilities, landscape and grounds maintenance, major repairs and renovations, and other services.

Physical plant administration. The physical plant of a university represents the largest permanent investment of an institution. Between 10 and 20 percent of the total university annual operating budget is assigned to physical plant administration.

Physical plant administration has as its purpose the creation, operation, and maintenance of the physical facilities indigenous to a learning environment as well as the provision of those supportive services that enhance the use of the educational facilities.

Prior to 1910, the simplicity of facilities required no more administrative effort than was necessary to maintain basic structures and campus landscaping and to provide nominal custodial service. The Association of Physical Plant Administrators (APPA), formally organized in 1914, was the first recognition in the United States of a need for greater expertise in the effective and efficient management of facilities in higher education.

The need for administrative and management expertise came partially from the growth in the size of physical plants and partially from their increased complexity and sophistication. The advent of central heating and domestic water systems, electric lighting, and sanitary plumbing has created the need, within each institution, for a technical and functional organization which can manage and maintain facilities that were formerly handled by the teaching staff or students.

The organizational structure for physical plant administration varies from one country to another. In Latin America it is quite common for each college, through a secretary general, to direct the maintenance and operations of the facilities occupied by the college. Planning and new construction may be directed by the president's office. In the United Kingdom and many of its former colonies of Africa and the Far East, the structures and utilities are under the supervision of a university architect, who is also responsible for campus planning and new construction. In many institutions in these countries, the plant services are directed by college headmasters. In Canada and the United States, the maintenance of services usually is centralized under the guidance of a superintendent of buildings and grounds or a director of physical plant.

The small liberal arts schools, with a minimum of laboratories and residences, may require a maintenance staff of no more than six or eight persons under the part-time direction of a faculty member or business officer. More complex and extensive campuses may have a maintenance staff of more than a thousand craftsmen and, in addition, numerous professional engineers, architects, and technicians under administrative direction of a vice-president.

Regardless of the size of a university or its organizational structure, the admin-istration of the facilities involves the same fundamental functions. On a small campus one individual may assume responsibility for a variety of these functions. As the size and complexity of the campus increase, there is a need for greater individual specialization.

Figure 1 shows a physical plant organization typical of a small university. Figure 2 indicates the organization of the physical plant department characteristic of a large university.

By the middle 1970s the university campus had become a complex, sophisticated, highly perishable, and expensive asset. The maintenance of the university's largest outlay, if done properly, must be professionally planned and executed. The management expertise required of a physical plant director has been previously described. The expertise required of the submanagers is equally great but requires more specialization. In each area of expertise, the technical requirements are different but the general organizational effort is the same.

The proper administration of each subsection of a physical plant must be based on factual knowledge of the facilities and services to be provided by that unit. This type of information is best made available from an orderly and objective on-site survey and analysis. Professional management can evaluate buildings, utilities, landscape improvements, and services from a proper survey. The evaluation determines the precise needs and the effort to be applied for a judiciously chosen maintenance level, in addition to providing the lead time required for planning, financing, and implementation.

The best management techniques and plans will produce little useful effort unless their implementation is properly funded. Historically, all educational institutions have aspired to more financial resources than were available. Therefore, the budget processes developed are a means of setting priorities for financing. A budget request,

Figure 1. Typical plant organization for a small university.

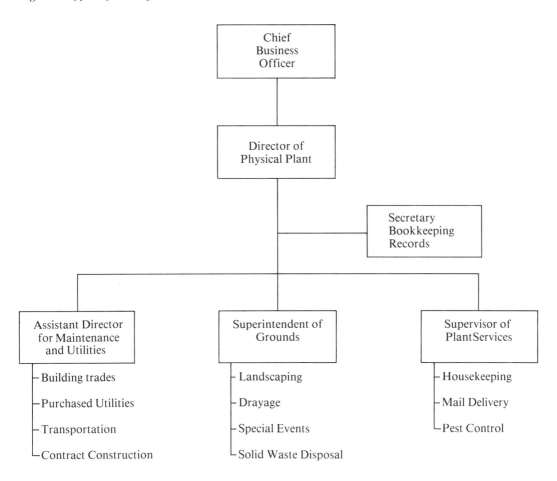

supported by a thoroughly documented facility evaluation, is a necessity in obtaining maintenance financial support.

The expenses of past operations are a substantial influence on future budgetary allocations. If there is to be effective fund management, it must have the support of a cost accounting system, which not only ensures appropriate use of available funds but also provides a basis for predicting future needs.

The supervision of a physical plant department requires a cooperative effort by several people—a management team, directed by a key person whose primary qualifications must be those of an administrator. The preferred title for this person is director of physical plant or physical plant administrator. This person's level of authority and relative position within the academic hierarchy is equivalent to that of the academic dean.

In smaller schools, the director also may carry one or more parallel secondary functions, such as stores manager, purchasing agent, student housing manager, professor, or manager of capital property inventory. Where there are nine or ten university functions to be conducted by four or five persons, the usual procedure is to assign one basic task to each individual and then distribute the others according to individual capabilities.

The campus maintenance force consists

Figure 2. Typical physical plant organization for a large university.

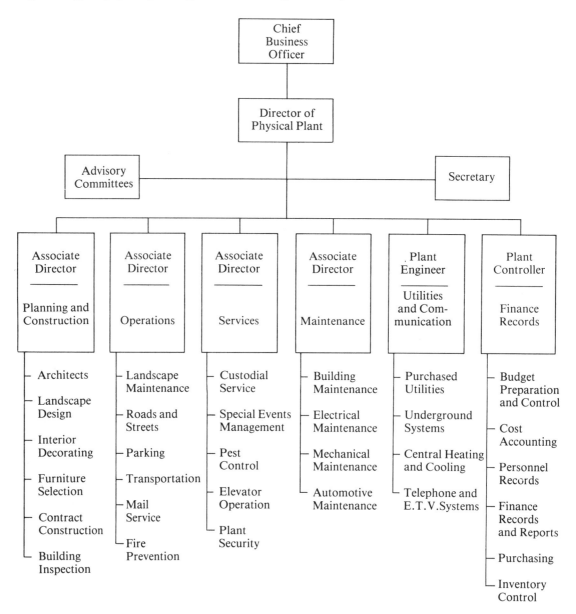

primarily of university employees; however, it may be supplemented by contract labor when such labor is available in the local community. A rural campus may have no alternative but to retain a large internal staff if there are no contract services locally available, whereas a campus in an urban community may find contract services more economical than in-house employees.

Astute management seeks the most economical and effective combination of these two sources. Routine maintenance is generally performed by campus employees, and seasonal tasks are frequently contracted out.

In the United States, where labor costs constitute the single greatest expense in physical plant operation, the size of the maintenance work force has a major budgetary impact on the entire campus community. The variety of labor skills required is affected by many factors, such as building styles, climate, and amount of facility usage. Table 1 shows some typical staffing requirements in a university. In countries having less complex facilities, the staffing levels are substantially less.

Building maintenance. In a university physical plant, maintenance may be defined as a controlled rate of deterioration. By this definition, building maintenance implies an activity that will extend the structural, architectural, functional, and economical life of a facility to some administratively determined age. A high degree of maintenance can prolong building life for an extended period. Low-level or poor maintenance may cause a facility to deteriorate rapidly.

Building maintenance is generally of two types: preventive and corrective. Preventive maintenance is performed while the element of the building is still serving its intended purpose and the maintenance is prior to but in anticipation of a structural failure. Corrective maintenance is commonly referred to as a repair, which is required after the element has failed.

For budgetary control purposes and for work planning, the activities of the building maintenance staff are generally classified as follows:

General and routine maintenance involves labor such as the repair of locks and door closers; replacement of leaking faucet washers; replacement of broken window glass; and replacement of defective light switches, light bulbs, and other minor unpredictable items. The needs are either discovered by a maintenance worker during a building inspection, or they are brought to the attention of the physical plant department by building occupants.

Scheduled maintenance is preventive in nature since it is usually planned to be accomplished before a failure occurs. The work includes those items that are anticipated on some periodic basis, such as off-season cleaning, lubrication, and minor parts replacements of cooling and heating equipment; periodic refinishing of classroom furniture; repainting on a five- to

Table 1. Approximate University Maintenance Staffing Requirements
United States Universities (1968–1973)

Craft	*Requirements*[a]
Automotive mechanic (autos and trucks)	1 per 35 pieces equipment
Automotive mechanic (heavy machinery)	1 per 20 pieces
Automotive service attendant	1 per 2000 services
Cabinetmaker (furniture repair)	1 per 10,000 pieces
Carpenter	1 per 200,000 GSF[b]
Electrician (includes relamping)	1 per 380,000 GSF
Locksmith (door hardware, door closers, keys, latches)	1 per 4000 doors
Maintenanceman (brick, roofing, sheet metal, and concrete)	1 per 500,000 GSF
Painters (7-year cycle)	1 per 200,000 square feet
Plumbers	1 per 390,000 GSF
for lavatories, urinals, and sinks	1 per 600 pieces
for commodes and showers	1 per 450 pieces
Refrigeration and air conditioning mechanics	1 per 450,000 GSF
for refrigerators and window units	1 per 300 pieces
for 2- to 25-ton package units	1 per 45 pieces
for 25- to 40-ton building systems	1 per 8 buildings
Total physical plant staff average	1 per 8000 GSF

[a]These are typical valu s and are partially dependent upon local job descriptions.
[b]Gross building floor area, in square feet.

seven-year room refinish schedule; and monthly cleaning, lubrication, and adjustment of elevator equipment.

A good building maintenance program requires the technical knowledge to identify needs and to define their scope, financial commitment to maintenance needs, and the management skills to use manpower and material economically, according to a logical system of priorities. Usually the building maintenance manager is an engineer, an architect, or someone who has had a technical education in the field plus experience in contract construction work.

Effective maintenance programs are implemented by work-order forms, used both as documented statements of need and as written instructions to a workman. The need may be a request for a departmental service or it may be an instruction from the maintenance supervisor for routine maintenance. Normally the work order describes the work to be done, the location, the time required, and anticipated job conditions. When completed, the work order becomes the basic record for performance evaluation and cost distribution. As such, it can be one of the most informational records in the physical plant department.

Custodial services. One of the largest items of expense in the physical plant department is the cleaning service. There is a direct correlation between the maintenance level of buildings and the respect and appreciation shown these facilities by the faculty and students. Unkept and disorderly surroundings usually impose a similar influence on student life, whereas an appropriate, clean, and well-maintained physical environment greatly contributes to the total learning environment. Cleanliness is one of the more visible signs of an effective physical plant department.

Each custodial service or housekeeping program must be based upon a detailed inventory of the area to be serviced. The inventory should determine the size of the areas to be cleaned, architectural features

that affect the cleaning effort, furnishings, space usage, and the times most appropriate for the cleaners to work. After all the data are collected, the standard times for each cleaning operation can be applied to determine man-hour requirements for the individual spaces and the entire facility. Every program must be periodically reviewed and updated if it is to remain efficient and effective. Since wages constitute 90 percent or more of the average cleaning service costs, high standards relative to manpower are essential.

There are two basic methods of organizing the custodial service program. One method arranges groups or squads of workers into a team moving from one work area to another, where each worker in the group is a specialist performing one kind of task. Another method assigns a single worker to one area and makes him responsible for all tasks within that area. Some universities use a combination of both methods.

Utilities. Utilities refer to services external to buildings. It is common practice in new construction contracting, under American Institute of Architecture guidelines, to set a dividing line five feet outside the perimeter of the building. Inside that line all services are considered part of the building. Outside of that line the services are classed as utilities. In the early phases of a new campus, when only one or two buildings are erected, financial limitations usually dictate that each building be self-sufficient and only minimum service capacity be provided. Normally, a one- or two-building campus cannot justify a sewage disposal plant, a domestic water-treating plant, or a central heating and cooling station. Conversely, large campuses, with more than 150 major structures that accommodate in excess of 30,000 students, may economically operate and manage their own utility systems. The size at which the university can change from total dependence to independence is determined by two things: need and economics.

If a university is located in a large urban area that has adequate public utilities available, the decision of whether to operate its own facility will be determined strictly by economics—whether the school can purchase services more cheaply than it can provide its own. When a school is located in a remote area or in an urban area where public facilities are not available, it has no choice but to provide its own facilities.

Utility plans should be part of a comprehensive campus plan. Long-range planning can anticipate the proper locations and sizes of future utility service needs and thereby avoid the expense of having to relocate utility lines that might subsequently interfere with future building sites and having to replace underground installations with larger-sized equipment.

Generally, electric power, if available at all from some outside source, can be purchased more cheaply than it can be generated on campus. The larger the generating station, the cheaper the unit cost of power. Therefore, a public utility that serves many consumers can almost always generate electric power more economically and reliably than can any single consumer.

Electricity is most economical and produces a more uniform voltage at the point of consumption if it is transmitted at high voltage and then transformed to lower voltage at the point of use. For this reason, the voltage at which power is received on campus is almost always at a high lethal level, usually above 2000 volts. Normally, the power used inside the buildings is at 115 or 230 volts. The transmission wiring, switches, transformers, and techniques for high voltage are quite different from those required at 230 volts or less. The skills of electricians capable of maintaining low-voltage systems are quite different from the skills of those who maintain high-voltage systems. On campuses where electric power is purchased as a utility, it is advisable to have the electric power company, using its trained personnel, maintain

the high-voltage portion of the system. The university will then need only the less specialized staff for on-campus electrical work.

In the past, there have been many adequate sources of germfree potable water. As world populations have increased, the quality of water available in many locations has decreased. Many cities and universities within those cities have in the past used water directly from wells, lakes, and rivers, without any purification treatment. This is no longer possible in a large number of the more populated regions. Rivers and lakes are being contaminated at a rate greater than natural purification can rectify. In addition, some well water is now contaminated by infiltration of contaminants from the surface.

As in the case of electricity, the unit cost of water is less if the water is treated in large quantities. For this reason, a public utility that serves a whole city can normally purify domestic water and decontaminate sanitary sewage more cheaply than can the university. There are some exceptions where, for example, a large university is located in a small city. But, in general, most universities are dependent upon local municipal water supplies and sanitary sewage systems.

The installation of every utility system involves a large first cost. Usually, a centralized installation requires a larger capital investment than does the same capacity if obtained in localized equipment. However, the long-term operating cost of centralized systems is far less and the services provided are generally more reliable. Heating and cooling systems must be included in these generalizations.

Campus utility distribution systems have been placed in underground tunnels on many campuses. Ease of access for maintenance and the advantage of having several services available at any intermediate point in the tunnels have made them most attractive. However, construction cost escalations of tunnels and the development of initial low-cost, direct-burial systems have made tunnels less economically attractive since 1960. The use of direct burial for utilities can provide satisfactory installation at cost savings of as much as 75 percent of tunnel construction.

Landscape and grounds maintenance. People respond to their environment. A person's mental attitude, expectations, and respect for the environment in an ornate, magnificent, formal garden will be quite different from the sensations produced by an unkept area. The attitude of the entire campus community is a direct function of its physical surroundings.

In the eyes of many people, landscape is only that portion of the area surrounding buildings that contains vegetation. On a university campus, landscape cannot be so limited. Landscaping is an integration of all of the outdoor features with which the campus community is in contact. The landscape features must be the unifying and cohesive forces between the natural and architectural elements on the campus.

The requirements for a continuing landscaping program are affected by such matters as terrain, soil conditions, climatic conditions, native plant life, transplantable vegetation, native building materials, cost and availability of local labor, cost of water and plant foods, and pest and insect control. Good landscaping begins with a practical plan designed on-site for the campus. Once such a plan is in hand, each university must have on its staff or consult a professionally experienced person who is capable of implementing the plan.

Like other labor costs, landscaping labor costs are increasing; as a result, many manual labor tasks are now being mechanized. There are some tasks that cannot be performed manually with the same expertise as they can be executed by a machine. The mowing of an athletic field is an example. There are other tasks where mechanization cannot be justified at all. The transplanting of annual flowering border plants remains a manual chore because it cannot be done economically by machine.

Repairs, rehabilitation, and services. Repair work is usually planned and budgeted as individual projects. Frequently, universities fail to budget sufficient funds necessary to accomplish all the repair work needed. As a result, some maintenance work is delayed until it incapacitates a vital facility. When the facility is inoperable, the administration must decide whether to abandon the facility or perform the major restoration task.

Alterations and remodeling are usually accomplished by building maintenance personnel or by a contractor directed by the physical plant staff. The cost of such work is not normally charged to the physical plant budget.

Most campuses have some kind of university-owned automotive transportation. A small institution may have but one minor vehicle, whereas a large university may have a centralized motor pool consisting of executive limousines, a fleet of buses, and several hundred special-purpose vehicles. Usually, it is not economical to maintain an automotive shop for fewer than fifty vehicles if local commercial services are available. The two controlling factors in the consideration of in-house versus commercial service are availability and economy.

In most universities construction planning and supervision is not a physical plant responsibility. It is common practice in most governmentally sponsored institutions for the function to be managed by a centralized system office that plans for many institutions. In privately sponsored institutions and some governmentally sponsored ones, the function is managed on campus but not always by the physical plant department. Decisions regarding new construction invariably involve large sums of money and commitments to land use. Unless a long-term program is anticipated, the architectural and engineering planning functions are costly and best obtained from project consultants.

Mail and messenger service is provided to some extent on every campus. In smaller institutions this activity is usually assigned to a person on the clerical staff. Larger institutions require a separate staff for on-campus deliveries because federally operated mail service usually will not deliver to more than one campus station. The campus mail and messenger service staff is usually an auxiliary unit of some major service component, often the physical plant department.

All campus departments purchase and store their own supplies and equipment to some degree. On campuses where this is a highly centralized activity, there may be a material support department with its own director, who reports to the campus business officer. It is also common practice for materials management to be assigned as part of a physical plant responsibility if a full-time officer is not needed. However, whichever department manages the purchasing and stores activity, the objective is the same: to provide the correct items at the proper place and time for the least cost.

A maintenance work force that is to produce timely and efficient service must have an appropriate shop facility. The shops should be in one location on the perimeter of the academic core of the campus. Unfortunately, a large number of campuses have not made such provisions, and frequently the shops have been placed in low-priority space without proper regard to the subsequent operational handicaps. Maintenance shops assigned to dispersed academic building basements make efficient operation virtually impossible. Every campus needs the benefits of a well-planned and centrally located physical plant or general services building.

Bibliography

Ahlberg, H. *Swedish Architecture of the Twentieth Century.* London: Benn, 1925.

Benz, A. *Facts About Finland.* River Edge, New Jersey: Arthur Vanouf, 1974.

Comparative Unit Cost and Wage Rate Report on Maintenance and Operation of Physical Plants of Universities and Colleges. Washington, D.C.: Association of Physical Plant Administrators, 1971.

Dober, R. P. *The New Campus in Britain: Ideas of Consequence for the United States.* New York: Educational Facilities Laboratories, 1965.

Ebert, H. F. *As instalações físicas da universidade.* Rio de Janeiro: Ministério da educação e cultura, 1974.

Feldman, E. B. *Industrial Housekeeping.* New York: Frederick Fell, 1963.

Fundamentals of Physical Plant Management, Planning, and Construction. Washington, D.C.: Association of Physical Plant Administrators, 1966.

George, N. L. *Effective School Maintenance.* West Nyack, New York: Parker Publishing, 1969.

Gross, R., and Murphy, J. *Educational Change and Architectural Consequences.* New York: Educational Facilities Laboratories, 1971.

Higher Education and Research in Finland. Helsinki: Ministry of Education, Government Printing Center, 1973.

Knowles, A. S. and Associates. *Handbook of College and University Administration.* New York: McGraw-Hill, 1970.

Newman, O. "The New Campus." *Architectural Forum,* 1966, *124*(4), 30–55.

An Official Handbook. Copenhagen: Ministry of Foreign Affairs, Press and Cultural Relations Department, 1974.

Sack, T. F. *Building and Plant Maintenance.* Englewood Cliffs, New Jersey: Prentice-Hall, 1963.

Sarra, J. W. *Trends, National Survey—Universities and Colleges Gross Square Feet per Journeyman Tradesmen.* Buffalo: State University of New York at Buffalo, 1968.

Smith, J. McCree. "Definition of Work Loads + Establishment of Units of Work = A Program of Personnel Requirements." *APPA Newsletter,* December 1971.

Weber, G. O. *A Basic Manual for Physical Plant Administrators.* Washington, D.C.: Association of Physical Plant Administrators, 1974.

Wheeler, R. *Splendors of the East (Asia Architecture).* New York: Putnam's, 1965.

HARRY F. EBERT

3. STUDENT HOUSING

Student housing programs vary tremendously. Many institutions offer no housing program at all. Others, including many of the most highly respected institutions in the United States and England, operate significant student housing programs that are carefully and systematically integrated into the overall educational objectives of the institutions. Some housing is generally provided at all levels of higher education, from initial postsecondary education through doctoral study, but the provisions of housing are by no means equally divided among the constituent groups. Although housing does exist for graduate students and for married students—indeed, some of the housing for these students is quite well developed—the overwhelming bulk of student housing around the world has been designed for single students in their late teens and early twenties. It is the very narrowness of the range of persons served by most student housing programs that has made student housing so distinctive. Societal attitudes toward youth and the particular developmental needs of a population in the transition period from late adolescence to adulthood have been significant factors in the development and operation of student housing.

Because of the extraordinary variation in student housing programs, generalizations are difficult. No systematic collection of information on international student housing exists, and information on national patterns is sparse and spotty at best. To provide an introduction to student housing issues, this article will review the development of student housing and current trends in the United States, and it will close with some comments on housing in other countries.

Development of Student Housing in the United States

Colleges in the colonies incorporated many of the concepts of English higher education, including the notion that institutions were responsible for the conduct of students both inside and outside the classroom. Fundamental to this "collegiate way of life" was the principle that the colleges stood *in loco parentis* to the student—they took the place of the parent while the student was in college and thus were responsible for the student's moral development as well as intellectual growth. Indeed, since a primary purpose of colonial colleges was to train clergymen, the education of the whole person was an unquestioned fundamental assumption of the colonial educational system. Even when students in the colonial colleges were permitted to live off campus and to board either with relatives or in private rooming houses, the colleges continued in their strong parental role. In his comprehensive history of Harvard University, Samuel Eliot Morison points out that nonresident students were subject to the same rules as on-campus residents. A 1660 rule passed by the Board of Overseers of Harvard required presidential approval of off-campus residence and stipulated that approved students would "be under college order and discipline, as others ought to do and be, that are resident in the college" (Morison, 1936, Vol. 2, p. 329).

In America, the distances between students' homes and the colleges necessitated special living arrangements. As a result, dormitories were built at the colonial colleges to house students and some of their teachers. These dormitories were owned and operated by the colleges, and they provided both a room for the student and his board or meals. However, student housing was not merely a convenient bed and board arrangement. It was part of the all-encompassing educational activity of the colleges.

Changing Residential Patterns

During the last half of the nineteenth century, important changes in American society and in the perceived mission of colleges and universities resulted in the initiation of new forms of housing.

First, the period following the United States Civil War was marked by a broadening of interests among the new clientele who came to colleges and universities. College or university attendance was seen more and more as preprofessional training and maturation prior to taking up work in an increasingly industrialized society. And as American society was becoming more industrialized, American higher education was undergoing tremendous expansion both in numbers and purpose. The expansion in numbers resulted partly from the federally sponsored establishment of land-grant colleges, which added technical and agricultural components to more traditional curricula. The expansion in purpose resulted not only from the added curricula designed to serve the needs of an expanding technological society but also from the fast-emerging movement to establish concerted European-style universities on American soil.

Whereas higher education in the United States before the civil war was marked by adherence to a modified English collegiate system, after the Civil War there were concerted efforts to establish the European, especially German, type of university in the United States. Such efforts were most often led by men who had themselves studied at German institutions. Even before the Civil War the groundwork had been laid by scholars and educators like George Ticknor, Edward Everett, and George Bancroft, who had studied at German university centers and brought back favorable impressions of them. The interest in the university "idea," as it was called, began to grow (Cowley, 1961).

The two phenomena of new clientele and the university movement, although seeming to have little in common, led to a modification of the strict monitoring of students' lives at many colleges and universities. The new students who came to the colleges had interests beyond the more pious ones of their predecessors, and hence the "extracurriculum" began to play an important role in students' lives. Moreover, the model European universities played no significant role in supervising students' out-of-class lives. While United States institutions still required their students and faculty to maintain fundamental, socially acceptable standards of behavior, many colleges and universities were increasingly unwilling to try to supervise students' out-of-class lives, and as a result a division grew up between the curriculum and the extracurriculum. More importantly, the educational function of residency decreased in importance.

Fraternities and other off-campus residences. As a result of such changes, the dormitory system went into decline, and it was replaced at many institutions by new living arrangements. An important development was the spread of social fraternities and the residential fraternity house. Of all the forms of housing and student life, the Greek-letter social fraternity is one that is unique to the United States.

Although the first Greek-letter society, Phi Beta Kappa, traces its birth to the year of United States independence, 1776, today's social fraternities trace their direct descent from organizations that began more than fifty years later. Three of the strongest and earliest fraternities, Kappa Alpha, Sigma Phi, and Delta Phi, were founded between 1825 and 1827 at Union College in Schenectady, New York (Brubacher and Rudy, 1968).

The American fraternity combines elements of the German dueling and drinking society, elements of the American Freemason movement, and elements of the English residential college. Although fraternity houses tend to be relatively small when contrasted with dormitories, they are often impressive structures, with their own cooks and servants, and they are very much the center of out-of-class activity for their members. Fraternities began as secret societies whose membership was by invitation only; although much of the secrecy is gone now, membership is still generally granted on an invitation basis. Prospective members attend screening parties given by the fraternities, and those persons selected are given "bids" (invited to join). Once they are members, most people in fraternities remain members for life, although they live in the fraternity house only during their education, most often at the undergraduate level.

Today in the United States there are approximately 150 national fraternities and about sixty-five national sororities (the female counterpart to the male fraternity), including nonresidential social and professional organizations. National social fraternities maintain chapters on approximately five hundred campuses; local fraternities also exist on some campuses *(Encyclopedia Americana,* 1976, Vol. 7, p. 253).

Another result of the congruence of the university movement and changing student bodies was the development, by a number of entrepreneurs in and around college and university towns, of boarding houses for students. The boarding house featured rooms for students and very often meals. For those who received no meals with their rooms, restaurants would fill the void. For the very wealthy, elegant residences were created. At Harvard University, for example, a "Gold Coast" of lavish student residences catering to upper-class students developed.

The movement to off-campus living was often a success. For example, Henry P. Tappan, the self-styled "chancellor" of the University of Michigan, persuaded that institution to abandon its only dormitory, and Amherst College tore down its largest and newest dormitory (Cowley, 1961).

The quadrangle system and the student personnel movement. Off-campus living arrangements for students fostered the separation of formal education and the student's life outside the classroom. So thoroughly was the extracurriculum emphasized that scholarship declined, and the so-called gentlemen's C (a grade that reflects mediocre work) came to be desired by some.

The still powerful notion of colleges standing *in loco parentis* and the dissatisfaction with off-campus living, including the excesses of fraternities, led to a sweeping new concern for educating the "whole student." A new force, the student personnel movement, gradually became a strong and influential factor in the development of student housing in the period following World War I.

The student personnel movement sought to bring back a personal quality into stu-

dents' lives in-college and stressed the responsibility of institutions for the extracurricular as well as the curricular aspects of student life. This movement did not suggest that the faculty return to the roles they had played under the colonial and federal systems; rather, it substituted professional counselors to deal with students' emotional needs.

The effort to reestablish on-campus housing for students reflected the desire for a more personal approach. The new kind of housing that was proposed was more closely patterned after the original English model than the dormitories had been. Among the earliest proposals was Woodrow Wilson's efforts to establish a quadrangle plan when he was president of Princeton University in New Jersey. Although he failed, others took up his plan. In the period between the world wars, Harvard and Yale Universities established quadrangle plans (called college plan at Yale and house plan at Harvard). Others took up the plan, and modified quadrangle plans were established at many institutions around the country.

The quadrangle type of housing differs from dormitories both in its physical configuration and in its programmatic aspects. Physically, quadrangle plans frequently congregate relatively small groups of students into suites of rooms, which are in turn a part of a larger quadrangle of rooms. Thus students benefit both from the intimacy and privacy of the smaller suite units and from the interaction with the large number of students in the quad. The quadrangle plan had as an aspect the more important notion of "programing" a student residence to further the education of the residents. Faculty masters and faculty tutors guided the educational development of the students residing in the quadrangle. This aspect of the quadrangle was by far the most significant, and many colleges and universities began to apply the quadrangle philosophy to traditional dormitories.

Apartments: the development of married

student housing. Just after World War II, American colleges and universities began erecting large numbers of apartments for students. This change, again, reflected a new clientele being served by higher education. For the large number of married veterans and their spouses and children, the dormitory or the quadrangle were not realistic options. Temporary apartment-style housing was put up at institutions across the country, and in time these temporary facilities were replaced by permanent married student and family housing. Today there are significant married student housing complexes at colleges and universities throughout the United States, but these units seldom command the educational resources or the attention that is focused on single-student housing.

Contemporary Student Housing in the United States

The 1960s and early 1970s in the United States were marked by considerable discord and social protest, most of it focused on two overriding issues: United States involvement in Vietnam and the disadvantaged status of certain groups in American society, especially racial minorities and women. College and university campuses were early rallying points for expressions of social discontent in the 1960s; in the process of debate and demonstration on these issues, the fundamental relationship of students to universities and colleges underwent a dramatic and, it now appears, permanent shift. By the mid 1970s the concept of *in loco parentis* was disavowed as an operative principle at most institutions in the country, especially the most highly regarded and prestigious.

The old paternalism of institutions was replaced by the recognition of certain student rights, including procedural requirements of due process in disciplinary cases and student self-determination in matters of personal behavior. Student governments and newspapers asserted increased independence and frequently clashed with institutional administrations. Curriculum reforms were common across the country, resulting in new course offerings and in the modification of degree requirements.

The full weight of these basic changes came to bear on student housing systems. For example, the sharp divergence of the student culture from behavioral norms of the established culture made enforcement of parietal regulations at many institutions difficult, if not impossible. Rapidly, and with little resistance, comprehensive sets of personal conduct regulations within dormitories—especially those dealing with relations between the sexes, students' whereabouts, and rigid personal appearance and behavior standards—were relaxed or abolished. More and more, students were allowed to set standards they thought most appropriate.

Coeducational housing. Coeducational housing, a phrase referring to the housing of men and women in the same living unit, had long been discussed, and in the mid and late 1960s cautious experiments in coeducational housing began at some leading institutions. Soon coeducational housing was the dominant form at many institutions. The phrase is used to cover a variety of arrangements—men and women in separate buildings but with some common lounge and dining areas; men and women on separate floors of the same building but sharing common lounge and dining areas; men and women on the same floor with adjacent rooms plus full sharing of all facilities except plumbing. Many schools began with the first type and quickly moved to the third type. For example, Stanford University, a major private university in California, experimented with its first coeducational house in 1967. After a satisfactory experiment the university rapidly converted most of its housing to coeducational units, the bulk of which had men and women living in adjacent rooms. So rapid was the transition that by 1976 all entering freshmen at Stanford lived in coeducational housing.

The changes in the basic nature of student housing from highly regulated, single-sex units to coeducational units where students are accorded adult liberties and responsibilities has not occurred at the same rate across the country. At many schools coeducational housing does not exist, and parietal regulations of some variety are maintained. There are significant variations from institution to institution, but those institutions that have traditionally set the standards for innovation and are acknowledged for academic excellence have been the first to move to coeducational housing without parietal hours.

Residential educational activities. The change to coeducational housing and the collapse of *in loco parentis* caused many institutions to emphasize a residence staff, whose primary responsibility is to counsel and advise students, thus extending the quadrangle approach of utilizing student residences as important environments to support and complement formal classroom education. Experiments in residential education programs, including formal classes in dormitories, special performing arts programs (dramatic productions in the Harvard houses and Yale colleges have long been a popular activity, and the University of Michigan has an impressive little theater in the basement of one of its dormitories), and residentially based academic advising, are common. Separate housing units based on themes—foreign language and culture, writing and literature, American studies—also exist, usually with faculty direction and with course credits available for some types of participation. Such educationally oriented housing is not a dominant pattern, but this use of student housing is being carefully looked at by educators and appears to set the direction for future developments.

Most common patterns. At colleges and universities in the United States in the mid 1970s, student housing provided by institutions or by private sources with institutional approval can be divided into three broad categories:

1. Large dormitories or dormitory complexes designed to house from one hundred to one thousand students. Rooms are for two persons, although single rooms and small suites for six to eight students do exist. These buildings usually include their own dining halls and common areas for recreation and study. Buildings of this type are most often run by the institution, but self-governing councils are common.

2. Small-group houses. Most fraternity and sorority houses are in this category, and many former fraternity and sorority houses are now run by colleges or universities as part of the institutional housing program. The cooperative is a very popular type of housing that usually has a high degree of student self-management of all aspects of the house; in many cases students and alumni corporations own and operate the houses. These units usually house from twenty-five to fifty students, and they are sometimes used quite successfully for residential education programs. A common characteristic of small-group houses is the high degree of community spirit among the residents.

3. Apartments or self-contained units. Apartments are common on many campuses, and virtually all married student and family housing is of the apartment variety. Residential education programs are not usually tried in apartment units. There is sometimes a community council or government, but for the most part apartment areas differ little from apartment areas away from campus.

Many schools have all types of housing on their campuses, and students may move from one type to another. The types of institutions and the housing they provide fit into four categories:

1. Institutions that house all or a significant proportion of their students and provide a residential education and counseling component in addition to the traditional management of the facilities.

2. Institutions that are capable of housing significant proportions of their student

bodies but do not use the facilities for more than lodging. There is little or no residential education and counseling.

3. Institutions that house a minor proportion of their student bodies but most often do not engage in residential education and counseling.

4. Institutions that house none of their students.

Knowledgeable observers of student housing programs in the United States see the trend toward coeducational housing continuing to spread throughout the country. In the late 1960s there was a brief concern over occupancy rates in student housing, but in the mid 1970s occupancy rates at all schools were very high. At many schools with traditionally strong residential education programs, new student housing was being planned or was under construction. Experiments in residential education continued to develop at many institutions, and these programs were being looked at carefully to see if they would set the tone for future developments in student housing.

Housing Patterns in Other Countries

Facts and statistical data pertaining to the nations cited herein are based on research of contributing authors and other research conducted under the auspices of the *International Encyclopedia of Higher Education*. These materials are now on file at the Center for International Higher Education Documentation at Northeastern University, Boston, Massachusetts.

Unlike institutions in the United States, Great Britain, and British-influenced countries, universities in most of the other countries of the world did not vigorously pursue student housing programs until after World War II. An increased willingness on the part of governments to involve themselves in providing student housing has become especially apparent since the war. This willingness results principally from three factors.

First, there has been a general concern with increasing the opportunities for post-secondary education. As nations have sought to democratize their societies, efforts to make higher education available to the masses have increased. Such efforts have manifested themselves not only in breaking down old barriers, such as the tracking systems within secondary schools, but also in providing additional spaces in higher education.

Second, there have been widespread efforts to improve general conditions in most countries, especially in housing. The increase in the number of students searching for low-income housing, especially in inner cities, immediately places a strain on housing available for nonstudents. Thus the university-sponsored housing serves the twin purposes of providing more housing in general and more housing for students.

Third, nations which previously sought to avoid any parental responsibility for students have come to recognize, as an economic reality, that the conditions under which students live can have profound influences on the effectiveness of their studies. Once a cost-benefit analysis is undertaken, nations frequently find that it is less costly to provide low-cost, desirable housing for students than to worry about students who prove ineffective in their education because of living factors.

The involvement of governments in providing for housing takes many forms. It can range from the incorporation of special bodies with responsibility for organizing and financing student housing to direct subsidies. Examples of the former are the Norwegian parliament's establishment of the Oslo Student Welfare Organization and similar regional student organizations at all higher education institutions in the country. In the United States, the New Jersey and New York state governments established dormitory authorities that finance construction on local campuses. Subsidies to housing are provided by the University Grants Committee in

England and by United States government low interest loans.

Some brief observations about student housing in selected countries around the world illustrate the diversity of student housing programs.

Federal Republic of Germany. The expansion of higher education and student housing in West Germany since World War II has not affected the traditional German view that higher education should deal exclusively with the students' intellect. The extension of housing to nearly 10 percent of Germany's 800,000 students resulted more from necessity than educational design (Kloss, 1975). Traditionally, the German student housing that existed was run by students through the *Deutsche Studentenwerk* (DSW), but increasingly it is administered by the universities. Nevertheless, the DSW continues to operate significant housing and must raise twenty-five million marks annually to repay the federal government. The construction of new housing is today borne equally by the federal and state governments, which actually control the universities. The federal government sets the standards for construction and design of housing.

England. England's attitude toward student housing has long differed from that of continental Europe. Not only do most English institutions view housing as a significant educational opportunity, but many provide extensive opportunities for housing. At Loughborough University, for example, 94 percent of the students live in student housing. At Oxford and Cambridge the residential colleges have long set the tone of education there. Unlike those European countries where the control of housing is the responsibility of student groups, England has long relied on the direction of residential life by the warden, a college official. As in the United States, the trend toward coeducational dormitories in England has begun in recent years.

The funding for new student housing is currently provided partly by loans from financial institutions and partly by grants and subsidies by the University Grants Committee.

Finland. One report suggests that nearly 27 percent of Finland's 63,000 university-level students live in student housing. Student-directed cooperatives operate the housing. One significant aspect of Finnish housing is that the housing fees are subvented by the government to keep them low.

Japan. As in most Asian nations, very little student housing is provided in Japan. At the University of Tokyo, for example, where 1700 students out of 14,000 are housed, there is no residency requirement. The housing that is available reflects, to some extent, American influences, tending to be nonprogramed, university run, and traditional dormitory in style.

Hong Kong. At both the University of Hong Kong and the Chinese University of Hong Kong, limited coeducational housing is available. Residency is not required at the University of Hong Kong, but the warden who controls a "hall" can admit students to membership in the hall either as residents or nonresidents. As at other British-influenced institutions, the warden has control of the hall and makes and enforces rules. He is aided by a student welfare committee, which may make recommendations to the university senate for alteration of the rules. In addition, the Committee of the Hall Association can request that the warden explain grounds for terminating a student's membership in the hall.

Thailand. Limited student housing is available in Thailand. At Chulalongkorn University, for example, housing is not coeducational; the men's housing has no dining facilities, but the women's does, and residents are required to take their morning and evening meals there.

Iraq. Reflecting the resources for higher education made increasingly possible by petroleum production in the country, the University of Mosul has recently constructed extensive student housing facilities of a dormitory nature and has adopted an American-style student personnel program. More than half of the university's students are housed in facilities that are provided without cost. Priority for housing is given to students whose academic performance is high (University of Mosul Catalogue, 1975, p. 31).

Uganda. Typical of British-influenced countries in Africa, the dormitories at Makerere University (Kampala) are single-sex. Each residence is under the control of a warden, who is responsible for the discipline and welfare of student members of the hall and who is helped by students who serve as resident tutors. If allowed to be nonresident, students must live in university-approved housing. Nonresident students, including married students, for whom accommodations are not provided, must take out membership in one of the halls.

South Africa. At the University of Natal, where almost all housing is single-sex and presided over by a warden, residence is not required but is available for 1,900 students. All residents have single bedrooms. The university gives preference for on-campus housing to students who live some distance from the university's two campuses and assists other students in finding off-campus housing.

Venezuela. Very little student housing is provided at the Central University of Venezuela (in Caracas), where most students live in private homes. In general, the South Americans tend to follow the patterns of Western Europe, where little student housing is provided.

The West Indies. The University of the West Indies (with campuses in Mona, Jamaica; St. Augustine, Trinidad; and Cave Hill, Barbados) follows the British pattern and is heavily residential, with a residency requirement at most of the campuses. The *in loco parentis* relationship between students and the university is much in evidence. At the Mona campus, for example, residency on campus is required for at least one year, and off-campus residence is permitted only in lodgings

approved by the vice-chancellor. Parietal rules are still strictly enforced. In addition, "a student who wishes to get married and remain a member of the university must obtain permission from the university authorities" (*University of the West Indies Calendar,* 1973, p. 156).

Bibliography

Angell, R. C. *The Campus: A Study of Contemporary Undergraduate Life in the American University.* New York: Appleton-Century-Crofts, 1928.

Astin, A. W. "The Impact of Dormitory Living on Students." *Educational Record,* Summer 1973.

Ben-David, J. *American Higher Education: Directions Old and New.* New York: McGraw-Hill, 1972.

Brubacher, J. S. *The Courts and Higher Education.* San Francisco: Jossey-Bass, 1971.

Brubacher, J. S., and Rudy, W. *Higher Education in Transition: A History of American Colleges and Universities, 1636–1968.* (Rev. ed.) New York: Harper & Row, 1968.

Chickering, A. W. *Commuting Versus Resident Students.* San Francisco: Jossey-Bass, 1974.

Committee on the Student in Higher Education. *The Student in Higher Education.* New Haven, Connecticut: Hazen Foundation, 1968.

Cowley, W. H. "The History of Student Residential Housing." *School and Society,* 1934, *40,* 1040–1041.

Cowley, W. H. *A Short History of American Higher Education.* Stanford, California: Published by the author and available at the Stanford University Library, 1961.

"Dorm Residency Upheld." *Chronicle of Higher Education,* December 23, 1975, p. 1.

Ebbers, L. H., and others. *Residence Halls in U.S. Higher Education: A Selective Bibliography.* Ames: Iowa State University Library, 1973.

Educational Facilities Laboratories. *Student Housing: A Report from Educational Facilities Laboratories.* New York: Educational Facilities Laboratories, 1972.

Encyclopedia Americana. Vol. 7. New York: Americana Corporation, 1976.

Feldman, K. A., and Newcomb, T. M. *The Impact of College on Students.* (2 vols.) San Francisco: Jossey-Bass, 1970.

Handlin, O., and Handlin, M. F. *The American College and American Culture: Socialization as a Function of Higher Education.* New York: McGraw-Hill, 1970.

Harms, H. E. *The Concept of In Loco Parentis in Higher Education.* Gainesville: University of

Florida Institute of Higher Education, 1970.

Hofstadter, R. *Academic Freedom in the Age of the College.* New York: Columbia University Press, 1955.

Horowitz, I. L., and Friedland, W. H. *The Knowledge Factory: Student Power and Academic Politics in America.* Carbondale: Southern Illinois University Press, 1970.

Horton, L. N., and others. *Undergraduate Student Housing Needs at Stanford, 1974–1984.* Stanford, California: Stanford University, 1974. Available through ERIC.

Jencks, C., and Riesman, D. *The Academic Revolution.* Garden City, New York: Doubleday, 1968.

Katz, J., and others. *No Time for Youth: Growth and Constraint in College Students.* A Publication of the Institute for the Study of Human Problems, Stanford University. San Francisco: Jossey-Bass, 1969.

Kloss, G. "Modest Rise in Residential Accommodations Despite Cuts." *Times (London) Higher Education Supplement,* November 21, 1975.

Korff, M. "Student Control and University Government at Stanford: The Evolving Student-University Relationship." Unpublished doctoral dissertation, Stanford University, 1975.

Lee, C. B. T. *The Campus Scene, 1900–1970: Changing Styles in Undergraduate Life.* New York: McKay, 1970.

Leonard, E. A. *Origin of Personnel Services in American Higher Education.* Minneapolis: University of Minnesota Press, 1956.

Mayhew, L. B. *Colleges Today and Tomorrow.* San Francisco: Jossey-Bass, 1969.

Metzger, W. P. *Academic Freedom in the Age of the University.* New York: Columbia University Press, 1955.

Morison, S. E. *Harvard College in the Seventeenth Century.* (2 vols.) Cambridge, Massachusetts: Harvard University Press, 1936.

Patton, C. H., and Field, W. T. *Eight O'Clock Chapel: A Study of New England College Life in the Eighties.* Boston: Houghton Mifflin, 1927.

President's Commission on Campus Unrest. *Report.* New York: Avon Books, 1971.

Riker, H. C., and Lopez, F. G. *College Students Live Here: A Study of College Housing.* New York: Educational Facilities Laboratories, 1961.

Rudolph, F. *The American College and University: A History.* New York: Vintage Books, 1962.

Sanford, N. (Ed.) *The American College: A Psychological and Social Interpretation of the Higher Learning.* New York: Wiley, 1962.

Sanford, N. *Where Colleges Fail: A Study of the Student as a Person.* San Francisco: Jossey-Bass, 1969.

Sheldon, H. D. *Student Life and Customs.* New York: Arno Press, 1969. (Originally published 1901.)

Spectorsky, A. C. (Ed.) *The College Years.* New York: Hawthorn, 1958.

University of Mosul Catalogue 1975–76. Mosul, Iraq: University of Mosul, 1975.

The University of the West Indies Calendar. Vol. 2: *Academic Year 1973–74.* Mona, Jamaica: University of the West Indies, 1973.

Veysey, L. R. *The Emergence of the American University.* Chicago: University of Chicago Press, 1965.

Yamamoto, K. (Ed.) *The College Student and His Culture: An Analysis.* Boston: Houghton Mifflin, 1968.

MICHAEL KORFF

LARRY N. HORTON

4. STUDENT HOUSING: NORWEGIAN CASE STUDY

The last twenty-five years have brought about a considerable change in the educational pattern of Norway, as in that of many other European countries. Between 1959 and 1969 the length of basic compulsory education was increased from seven to nine years. Furthermore, there is an increasing tendency among young people to continue their education after having completed the basic education at the age of sixteen. Of all seventeen-year-olds, 75 percent are engaged in some kind of education. Some are qualifying for the university entrance examination, which normally takes three years in addition to the basic education. Some are qualifying for a future job by vocational education. The percentage of all nineteen-year-olds who qualify for higher education increased from 9 percent in 1945 to 29 percent in 1975 and is projected to increase to 40 percent by 1985.

The student population in universities or other institutions of higher (tertiary) education is at present approximately sixty thousand and is expected to reach eighty to ninety thousand before 1985. Norway has four universities, eight university colleges, six district colleges, and well over fifty minor educational institutions, most of them teachers colleges. The number of students in higher education in 1975 was four times higher than in 1945. The role of education in Norwegian society can be illustrated by the following figures. Of a population of four million, close to 21 percent are involved in education, either as students or as teachers. These figures do not include children in kindergarten or state and municipal administrative and organizational staff in the educational system. These changes in the educational pattern brought about considerable changes in student housing.

Postwar Housing Problems

Up to 1945 most students who had to leave their homes to go to universities or colleges found themselves a room with a private family. The total number of rooms in student dormitories was negligible— only about five hundred before World War II, all situated in Oslo, the capital. During the war years, from 1940 to 1945, practically no new houses were built in Norway. Many houses were destroyed or damaged during the war, mainly in the cities, which also housed most of the educational facilities.

When the University of Oslo, for example, after having been closed during the latter part of the war, reopened its doors to teachers and students in 1945, most students had serious housing problems. In spite of the good will lavished upon them by the local population, many of whom had lost their own homes during the war, more than four thousand students had to accept improvised housing in bombed houses, military barracks, and other facilities that would have been unacceptable under normal conditions.

Similar conditions were in Bergen, Trondheim, and other towns. However, this appalling situation launched a discussion of how to solve the problems of student housing in a war-ruined society that was badly in need of houses for a great part of the population and with a climate

that did not allow for light construction. Solving the problems meant finding answers to organizational, financial, legal, and construction problems.

Student welfare organizations. The question of organization was the easiest to solve. Even before the outbreak of World War II representatives from the Ministry of Education, the authorities of the University of Oslo, and student representatives had agreed to establish a special organization to take care of all areas of student welfare. This organization, called the Oslo Student Welfare Organization, was established by a special act of the Norwegian parliament in 1939. This act was amended in 1948 to make provisions for similar regional student welfare organizations in all centers of higher education in Norway (Oslo, Bergen, Aas, Trondheim, Tromsø, and Stavanger).

These organizations are significant in two respects: First, the law as such provides for a wide scope of operations, including planning, constructing, and operating student and university houses. Second, each organization is governed by a board, consisting of representatives from the Ministry of Education, the local university or college administration, the employees, and the students.

It was the responsibility of these local student welfare organizations to find a solution to the housing problems as well as to many other student problems.

Financing student housing. The financial problems connected with student housing were one side of a much bigger problem. Because priority had already been given to rebuilding the country's industry and shipping after the war, these were the first industries to be allotted monies that could be channeled through the banking system. Consequently, new means had to be found to provide money for housing purposes. This was done by setting up a special banking system. The Norwegian Housing Bank was established by act of parliament in 1946 to provide long-term, cheap capital for housing only, provided that the house builders accepted certain regulations. This new bank would also provide loans for student housing projects.

But to build a house, a site was necessary. When the first student housing scheme was launched by the Student Welfare Organization in Oslo, where the need was by far the greatest, ground for a one-thousand-room plant was provided by the municipal authorities. The site was situated not far from the new university area. However, according to the regulations, loan capital would cover only part of the cost, the rest had to be provided by the builder. And the builder in this case was a local student welfare organization that had no money. This problem of capital was resolved by an arrangement worked out between the local student welfare organization and the municipal communities. (The Kingdom of Norway is divided into 20 counties and 440 municipal communities.) A survey was conducted to find out where students lived, and a plan was then suggested whereby the student welfare organization would provide the housing scheme, building ground, and so forth if the community would pay a stipulated sum per student room and so provide the minimum required capital. This plan received a very positive response. Less than five years after World War II ended, the first permanent student dormitories started. Students have now lived in these buildings for more than twenty-five years.

However, it soon became obvious that providing cash capital by mobilizing local authorities had its drawbacks. In Norway, as in other parts of the world, there are local communities that are well off and some that are not as well off. It was thought unjust that the wealth or good will of a student's home town should be the criterion for acquiring a home in Oslo, Bergen, or Trondheim. A more equitable way of providing the necessary financing had to be found.

By tradition and political agreement,

education has, since the beginning of the nineteenth century, been a public concern in Norway. Building and operating schools, providing necessary equipment, paying teachers, and so forth are the responsibilities of local or central authorities. The responsibility for financing student housing should be equally a public concern.

These problems were for some years discussed with the government, and finally an agreement was reached. Money to build student homes was channeled to the builders—the student welfare organization—half through the Housing Bank as a long-term loan and half through the Ministry of Education as an outright cash grant. Thus the cost of living was reduced for the individual student, who, in addition, was entitled to loans and scholarships from the Educational Loan and Scholarship Bank.

This Education Loan and Scholarship Bank is also a postwar phenomenon, put into operation in 1947. Any student registered at public or private institutions of tertiary education is entitled to a yearly supply of cash money. The money is given partly as a loan, free of interest during the period of education, and partly as a scholarship. This provision makes it possible for any student, regardless of social, financial, or parental background, to obtain a higher education.

Norwegian students are generally between nineteen and twenty-seven years old, and more than 30 percent of all students are married. No fees are paid for the education itself, and anyone beyond the age of twenty, with no independent resources, is entitled to an annual allotment from the state in the form of grants and interest-free loans sufficient to cover the basic cost of living until graduation.

Within the framework of this combined loan-scholarship system an annual amount is reserved for financing 50 percent of the cost of student housing. This provides again for a continuity in the building process. The overall goal is to solve the housing problems on a supply-demand basis. The organization responsible for building and operating student housing will have to accept and comply with certain regulations concerning size, equipment, and financing.

New Housing Projects

The philosophy behind planning, building, and operating student housing is pragmatic. In some places in Norway there is an imbalance between required and available housing. This imbalance is found largely in centers of higher education where the need for student housing must be dealt with in addition to the housing shortage for the local population. As a result, the distribution of student housing throughout the country varies from town to town.

Since 1950, 9850 student housing units have been completed. Another 2900 units are either planned or under construction.

In 1960 the government accepted a plan for building ten thousand new student units (1 unit = 1 room for one single student; a family flat is $2^1/_2$ units). This plan was fulfilled some years ago, and at present building goes on according to a new plan, with the overall goals of solving the student housing problem. Student houses have been or are under construction in Tromsø (the world's northernmost university), Bodø (teachers college), Trondheim (technical university), Bergen (university and school of business administration), Molde (regional college), Stavanger (regional college), Kristiansand (regional college), Oslo, Telemark, Aas, and Lillehammer. Other Norwegian cities providing student housing are Alta, Blaker, Bö, Gjovik, Grimstad, Halden, Hamar, Levanger, Narvik, Nesna, Risor, Sogndal, Stord, and Volda.

Norway, like the rest of the world, has experienced considerable inflation recently. The effect of this inflation as regards building cost in student housing can be illustrated by the figures shown in Table 1.

If one compares student population

Table 1

Year	Construction cost per furnished unit (1 room—1 person) in N.kr.*	Percent rise in building cost from 1967
1967	30,000	
1968	32,280	7.6
1969	33,840	12.9
1970	36,600	22.0
1971	38,790	29.3
1972	41,670	38.9
1973	45,000	50.0
1974	51,210	70.7
1975	57,960	93.2

*These figures in Norwegian kroner cannot automatically be transferred to United States dollars because in the same period there has been a fall in dollar value on the world market compared with N.kr. Roughly, 1 U.S. dollar = N.kr. 5.20.

with the actual number of student houses in four of Norway's oldest educational centers—Oslo, Bergen, Trondheim, and Aas (an agricultural college outside Oslo)—the result is as shown in Table 2.

Concentration of student rooms differs from area to area. The number of rooms on any one site is more a result of the size of the site than of any farsighted planning. Greatest concentration of rooms in one area is 2400 in Oslo; the smallest concentration is 150.

Style and operation of student housing. Norwegian universities and colleges do not undertake responsibility *in loco parentis.* The behavior of students is not the concern of the housing administration, although there is a standard "rule of the house," with which everyone is made familiar when being allotted a room or a flat. Over the

Table 2

Center	Students	Housing Units	Percent of Students Housed
Oslo	22,000	4600	23
Trondheim	7740	2047	26
Bergen	8349	2320	28
Aas	845	650	77

years there have been few disciplinary cases.

For financial reasons, a high degree of standardization in layout, choice of materials, and so forth has been necessary in construction. However, the architects have been given a free hand in the design and arrangement of rooms.

Average gross space of one single room, part of kitchen, hall, and so forth varies from 250 to 300 square feet, whereas average net space of the single room itself varies from 140 to 150 square feet. Average net space for a family flat varies from 500 to 700 square feet.

Norwegian student housing has no built-in systems of counseling, catering, or other supplementary services, as often exists in the United States. Students who want meals at home will have to prepare them themselves. The local restaurants or catering are sometimes, but not always, avail-

able. Each unit of rooms for single students has a common kitchen. Supplies must be purchased in local stores, and all preparation and cleaning up is the responsibility of the students in the unit. A telephone is provided in each flat, the basic cost of which is included in the rent. Also included in the monthly rent are furniture, electricity, linen and laundry, and cleaning of all common areas. Each student is responsible for keeping his own room in order.

Inflation has of course had an influence on the operating costs of student housing. However, this has been balanced by a rise in scholarships and interest-free loans. An experiment in reducing operating costs in spite of rising construction and maintenance costs has been conducted at Bjerke, a housing site of 330 units that opened in 1972. This relatively small site, with no expenses for local administration

Table 3. Monthly Operating Costs For Student Housing Per Student

	Søgn		Bjerke	
	N.kr.	Percent of monthly cost	N.kr.	Percent of monthly cost
Room Expenses				
1. Loan interests	52,46	14.1	82,68	24.3
2. Loan installments	29,50	7.9	16,12	4.7
3. Maintenance	42,06	11.3	22,81	6.7
4. Dues (water, tax, and so forth)	25,36	6.8	33,07	9.7
5. Insurance	3,53	1.0	2,58	0.8
6. Caretaker expenses	25,03	6.7	16,38	4.8
7. Housekeeper expenses	7,81	2.1	4,13	1.2
8. Local administration	10,87	2.9		
9. Reception	4,40	1.2	8,28	2.4
10. Post distribution	7,02	1.9		
Total	208,04	55.9	186,05	54.6
Other Expenses				
1. Electricity, heating, and so on	40,70	11.0	37,46	11.0
2. Furniture, fittings, and so forth	27,93	7.5	31,55	9.3
3. Laundry (bed clothes)	11,62	3.1	14,21	4.2
4. Cleaning of stairs and lounges	34,38	9.3	11,24	3.3
5. Welfare (newspapers, magazines, television, radio, and so forth)	1,17	0.3	1,29	0.4
6. Telephone expenses	25,07	6.7		
Total	140,87	37.9	95,75	28.2
TOTAL	348,91		281,80	
OVERHEAD	23,09	6.2	58,73	17.3
TOTAL	372,00	100.0	340,53	100.0

and only local telephone service included, has been successful so far in holding down operating expenses. Its lower costs are illustrated in Table 3, which compares monthly operating costs per student per room in 1976 at Søgn, a housing site with 1700 units built between 1950 and 1962, to the costs at Bjerke.

In some areas of Norway student housing also serves another purpose. During the summer months, when students generally are away, some units are converted into summer hotels. This is done in agreement with the local authorities, the tourist administration, and the local hotels. For example, in the summer of 1976, 17 percent of the room capacity will, for a period of sixty to ninety days, be converted into summer hotels. The responsibility of the hotel operation itself lies with the Student Welfare Organization, and the hotel staff are mostly students. Over the years, more than two million tourists from 135 nations have been guests in these summer hotels. Any surplus from the hotel operation is put back into the housing budget, thus reducing the rents. As a consequence of this combined operation, students can be offered housing contracts of nine, ten, or twelve months' duration.

In conclusion, it can be said that even if the student housing situation in Norway so far has not been solved, there is reason to believe that within a few years supply and demand will be balanced.

Bibliography

Norwegian Acts, 1685–1971. Oslo: Grondahl, 1972.
Norwegian Ministry of Education. *Stortingsproposisjon No. 1.* Oslo: Government Printing Office, 1960–1976.
Social Problems of Students. Report on the Council of Europe Seminar, Oslo, Norway, 25–31 July 1965. Oslo: Universitetsforlaget, 1966.

KRISTIAN OTTOSEN

5. INSURANCE AND RISK MANAGEMENT

Risk may be defined as the probability of financial loss, through damage to property or other assets or through liability resulting from personal injury. The function of risk management encompasses a broad spectrum of factors: identifying risk; analyzing it; preventing, neutralizing, or reducing it; and protecting oneself against all or part of the possible financial consequences of its occurrence. Laws, insurance concepts, and requirements in policy language and coverages differ considerably around the world, and there does not exist a worldwide compilation of risk control practices as promulgated by either governmental sources or insurance companies. This article therefore discusses risk management procedures and insurance coverages as they exist in one country—the United States.

Developing a Risk Management Program

The beginning—and, on a continuing basis, the heart—of a risk management program is the definition and the statement in writing of policy objectives. Such a statement may be framed by administrative personnel, but it also requires the complete understanding and written approval of those with ultimate management responsibility. The espousal of a risk management philosophy must be accompanied by a clear expression of who is responsible for its implementation and performance, his degree of authority, and his reporting channels and responsibilities. Depending on the size of the institution, responsibility may be personally vested in the chief business officer of a college or university or assigned to another specific person or function in the administrative organization. The important considerations are that the statement of responsibility be precise and that it include a sufficient degree of authority.

In addition to the statement of policy, a cumulative functional manual is needed to articulate the risk management conditions and philosophy. This functional manual should be subject to periodic updating, and copies should be provided for all whose activities may initiate, broaden, or reduce risk in any of its varied forms. The manual will serve many purposes, prominent among which are (1) to emphasize the necessity of informing the risk manager, during the planning stage, of property additions or alterations, increases in staff or student body activities, or the many other items that could add new risks or affect existing ones; (2) to define whether, how, and to what extent the various risks are to be insured; (3) to specify risk-reducing, loss-prevention, and safety practices to be followed, with necessary delineations between departments or activities.

With such an established pattern of information flow, the risk manager will be in a fair position to identify risks or potential risks. In order to evaluate their extent, he will need to be in constant communication with those basically responsible for the property, facilities, or activities that initiate the potential hazards. In addition, to assess and measure potential hazards the risk manager may need to contact outside experts, who may also be able to suggest ways and means of preventing or reducing the risk. For example, in the field of property conservation and fire prevention, such groups as the Factory Mutuals and Factory Insurance Association are staffed and equipped to recommend needed physical improvements and to design fairly priced insurance coverage in accordance with a professional assessment of exposures and hazards. In such areas as protecting the safety of employees, students, and the public, companies that carry workmen's compensation and public liability insurance can recommend hazard-reducing practices and can provide insurance with built-in premium incentives for good loss experience. Independent brokers, appraisers, assessors, and inspection organizations are also available on a purely consulting basis. The employee safety practices of private institutions are monitored by the Occupational Safety and Health Administration (OSHA); knowledge of the OSHA codes serves the dual purpose of promoting safe operating practices and avoiding fines and penalties imposed for code violations.

When risks have been identified, evaluated, and controlled to the extent possible, there needs to be a conscious (and preferably recorded) decision (1) not to insure at all, (2) to self-insure, or (3) to insure with a conventional insurance carrier. Once this decision has been articulated, the risk manager's responsibility to protect the university's properties and assets from damage or liability potential takes on the related function of monitoring the outgo of the institution's funds for insurance premiums. Noninsurance means the deliberate assumption of the possibility of loss in circumstances in which the risk manager feels that the potential loss can be borne as a part of current maintenance costs; common examples are glass breakage and damage to or theft of movable equipment, such as lawn or snow removal apparatus. (At all times, but particularly when noninsurance is chosen, care should be exercised in framing contractual language to avoid assumption of risk whenever possible.) The next alternative, self-insurance, also means that conventional insurance will not be purchased from an outside source; but it differs from noninsurance in that the self-insurer establishes a specific fund (either initial or continuing) for payment of claims and keeps formal records of the cost of claims and administration, so that the current and continuing success of the procedure can be measured. This method has various features to recommend it, such as the ability to accrue interest on the investment of the fund reserve. Another advantage of self-insurance funding is the possibility of joining with other institutions in a self-funded reserve pool, thus possibly requiring a smaller investment by each member and facilitating lower-cost or more expert administration of the fund. The traditional practice of insuring with a conventional insurance carrier should almost always be chosen when the enormity of the exposure, or predictable frequency of loss, would be too great for the institution to prudently assume. It may also be a wise choice if the corollary services of the insurer or broker are of demonstrable value and possibly of almost equal weight with the risk-assumption feature. Even when wisdom dictates the need for insurance, however, it does not obviate consideration of partial noninsurance or self-insurance. In some circumstances, assumption of a "deductible" (standard initial sum to be paid by the insured on each claim regardless of the total amount of loss) in the insurance policy will result in a substantial premium savings. The measurement of such savings against single-loss or loss-frequency potential is not an exact art, but existence of previous loss records will be a valuable guide in this decision. The combination of outside insurance with a self-insurance reserve fund (to absorb losses less than the deductible) may be ideal in some risk categories.

No one insurance carrier is widely acknowledged to provide specific skills in handling the insurance needs of colleges and universities. When choosing an insurer, an institution should consider not only the cost of coverage but the value of the total insurance package. A good insurance company will offer proven financial capacity and stability, broad and up-to-date coverage concepts, the ability to design an appropriate policy, loss-prevention services, prompt and adequate claims adjustment, and a competitive (but not necessarily the lowest) price.

Risks Particular to Colleges and Universities

Among the more prominent high-value property exposures (assets vulnerable to loss) commonly found at colleges and universities are libraries, data-processing centers, and museums. Theft, vandalism, and fire are the obvious risks; and although there would be little argument as to the advisability of preventive measures and safeguards against the first two, there is some argument about what is the best system of protection against fire. In libraries and data-processing centers particularly, there is opposition to the use of automatic sprinklers because of the potential for water damage. However, acceptable techniques have been developed for drying water-soaked books, and many fire protection consultants also consider sprinklers a necessary protection in data-processing centers.

Another consideration, perhaps less conspicuous but possibly even more costly, is that of liability for personal injuries. Traditionally, there has been common law and statutory protection in many jurisdictions for institutions such as colleges and universities. Public institutions are sometimes protected under the doctrine of sovereign immunity; private institutions have sometimes been granted immunity from tort liability because they are eleemosynary (nonprofit) enterprises. However, the increasing application of consumerism in personal injury situations is replacing these traditions with the simplistic conclusion that "someone has to pay"; as a result, laws have been subject to revised interpretations or to actual change. In addition to institutions themselves, trustees, faculty, and staff members also are increasingly subjects of litigation, and such individuals look to the institution for insurance protection.

Schools with sports programs are becoming increasingly vulnerable to personal injury liability. One injured college football player, alleging inadequate coaching supervision and training and ill-fitting equipment, initiated a ten-million dollar suit in which the trustees of the college were codefendants with the school. Even if a formalized sporting event was not involved, any injury incurred while the student was in pursuit of an individual conditioning program in a gymnasium has been construed as somehow being "the school's fault."

Injury to spectators at a sporting event may also have a significant loss potential.

Insurance Coverages

There are three broad categories of insurance: (1) property; (2) liability (sometimes referred to as *casualty* or included in that term; (3) life and health. The risk manager of a college or university is almost always concerned with the first two of these coverages. Life and health coverage is generally considered an employee benefit and may be administered separately by a personnel officer.

Property insurance. This includes all coverage for direct loss of property (particularly, but not exclusively, the policyholder's property). It may also cover indirect or consequential losses resulting from direct loss. Educational institutions are most often concerned with the following property insurance coverages:

Fire insurance coverage is usually written to conform to a standard policy, which includes insurance against lightning. Extended coverage can be purchased to insure against loss from windstorm, hail, explosion, riot, civil commotion, damage by nonowned aircraft and vehicles, smoke, vandalism and malicious mischief, debris removal, demolition required by law, and sprinkler leakage. Damaged property is usually compensated on an actual cash value (that is, depreciated value) basis, although coverage on a repair or replacement (that is, undepreciated value) basis is available. Specified perils to buildings under construction may be covered on a fire policy by the addition of a builder's risk clause, which may provide compensation based either on the anticipated value of the completed building or on its actual cash value at the time of the loss.

Glass insurance covers replacement of all types of glass and may include compensation for damaged supporting frames, bars, lettering, and ornamentation.

Water-damage insurance covers against direct loss or damage caused by accidental discharge, leakage, or precipitation of water or steam, but does not cover flood damage. Flood may be covered in a separate policy or as part of an all-risk package.

Earthquake insurance is provided by an earthquake-damage-assumption endorsement, which can either be added to a fire policy or included in an all-risk package.

Tuition fees insurance covers actual loss of revenue, including tuition, room, board, and other fees resulting from damage to or destruction of college or university property by fire or other hazards. Although the damage or destruction must occur during the policy period, the resulting loss of fees that the policy covers may be sustained at any time prior to the opening day of the next academic year following restoration of the property. If the property cannot be restored by at least thirty days before opening day, the policy will indemnify for loss of fees during the ensuing academic year as well. Ordinary insurance for a business interruption would also cover net profit and continuing expenses while college or university operations were actually suspended; but it would not continue to cover once the property had been restored to operating condition.

Extra-expense coverage is available to indemnify colleges and universities against extra expense for temporary quarters necessitated by fire or other insured damage to office or classroom buildings and their contents.

Rental-value insurance protects a college or university against interruption of income from owned dormitories or other owned income-producing buildings while they are being repaired or rebuilt as a consequence of fire or other insured hazard.

Leasehold-interest insurance indemnifies a college or university that leases premises for the extra cost of renting substitute premises in case the original lease must be canceled because of fire or other insured hazard.

Boiler and machinery insurance, although generally classified as casualty insurance, protects the policyholder for damage to his own property and for damage to property of others to whom he may be liable; such damage is caused by breakdown of specified boilers, pressure vessels, and mechanical and electrical objects. Like fire insurance, boiler and machinery insurance can be written on a replacement value basis rather than according to the standard actual cash concept. It can also be extended to provide indemnity for indirect losses, such as loss of tuition or rental income.

Inland marine insurance, known as "all-risk" insurance, protects colleges or universities against all risks of loss of certain kinds of valuable property or, alternatively, against its loss from specified or "named" perils. The term *all risks* is not to be taken too literally: all policies exclude coverage for certain hazards, such as normal wear and tear, deliberate acts of the insured, and natural spoilage. In practice, all-risk coverage is limited to reasonably measurable hazards without a high catastrophe potential. Inland marine insurance is designed to apply primarily to portable property or to property in transit. A college or university might be interested in the following inland marine policies or "floaters": fine arts policy, musical instruments floater, neon sign insurance, outboard motor and boat floater, scientific instruments floater, sporting equipment floater, transportation floater, and yacht policy. In addition to the policies listed above, an inland marine policy or floater can be written to cover just about any kind of valuable, portable property.

Crime insurance is just as important for a college or university as it is for a business concern that handles comparable amounts of money. Crime hazard may arise from employee dishonesty or from burglary, theft, larceny, or robbery.

Fidelity bonds cover the policyholder (in this case, called the *obligee*) for loss of money, securities, and property (including property for which the insured is legally responsible) through larceny, theft, embezzlement, forgery, misappropriation, willful misapplication, or any other dishonest or fraudulent act committed by an employee. Inventory shortage is not covered unless it can be proven to have been caused by employee dishonesty. Bonds may be written to cover certain named employees (schedule name form bonds), employees in certain positions (schedule position form bonds), or all employees (blanket bonds). A schedule bond has two disadvantages: since it does not cover all employees, the employer must risk deciding which employees are most likely to be dishonest; and the employer must continually update the list of employees or positions covered. There are two types of blanket bonds: commercial blanket bonds, under which the limit of liability, or "penalty" of the bond, applies per loss regardless of the number of employees involved; and blanket position bonds, under which the penalty limit applies to each employee. A bond only covers losses occurring while the bond is in force or discovered within an agreed-upon time after cancellation.

The comprehensive dishonesty, disappearance, and destruction (3-D) policy and the blanket crime policy give the same protection against employee dishonesty as does a blanket bond. These policies also provide broad-form coverage for money and securities on and away from the college or university premises to insure against such events as safe burglary or robbery, either on the premises or in transit, and against loss due to acceptance of counterfeit paper money or money orders or due to forgery of checks or drafts. These coverages are optional with the insured under a 3-D policy but mandatory under the blanket crime policy. Separate limits per coverage apply to the 3-D policy: the blanket crime policy is subject to a single limit per loss or occurrence. Colleges and universities that do not need the broad coverages provided by the 3-D or blanket crime policies may purchase narrower forms limited to safe burglary, robbery, or holdup.

Liability insurance. Liability insurance protects the policyholder against loss resulting from financial responsibility for injury or damage to the persons or property of others. Two types of liability may be distinguished: liability to employees, which may be imposed either by statute (workmen's compensation) or by common law (employers' liability); and liability to third parties, against which there are various kinds of insurance, including general liability, automobile liability, aircraft liability, and malpractice or professional liability. Policies and coverages of interest to colleges or universities include the following:

Workmen's compensation insurance is necessary because most countries have laws requiring employers to provide for the payment of specified benefits to their employees who sustain injury in the course of, and arising out of, their employment. Workmen's compensation laws may be either compulsory or elective. A compulsory law applies to all employers; under an elective law, an employer who chooses not to be subject to it loses certain of his common-law rights. Most workmen's compensation laws provide penalties for employers who fail to comply with the insurance requirements; the insurance may be purchased from a private carrier unless— as in some states in the United States and in some countries—there is a monopolistic government fund within which employers are required to insure. Although workmen's compensation laws in different states or countries vary substantially in their particulars—many, for example, do not apply to domestic servants, agricultural workers, or casual labor—all cover accidental bodily injury, and most also cover occupational disease (disease arising solely out of employment independently of any accident), providing benefits to reimburse the injured employee's loss of income; his hospital, medical, and surgical charges; the cost of rehabilitation; and, if the employee should die as a result of the injury, the resultant loss of income to his family and the family's burial expenses. Workmen's compensation insurance policies cover liability under the workmen's compensation law within the limits of specified conditions and also cover liability at common law for negligence resulting in work-related injury or death of an employee.

General liability insurance protects an institution against legal liability for third-party bodily injury and/or property damage arising from the ownership, maintenance, or use of its premises (including elevators), or from the performance of all operations necessary or incidental thereto. It automatically covers liability assumed by the college or university under specified kinds of contracts, such as leases of premises, indemnification agreements required by municipal ordinance, and sidetrack and elevator maintenance agreements, and may be extended to cover other specified written contracts or, alternatively, to cover all written contracts. If a college or university maintains a hospital, an infirmary, or a clinic, it will also need professional liability (malpractice) insurance, which is a branch of general liability. General liability insurance may also be written to protect the university, as the owner, against liability: as a result of operations being performed for it by independent contractors; because of completed operations; arising from the consumption of food or beverages away from its premises; or as a result of the use of any product that it processes or sells. General liability insurance does not cover liability for automobiles (except for parking on the insured's premises), for watercraft away from the premises, or for aircraft anywhere; these may be covered under other forms of liability insurance. General liability does, however, usually cover liability for such self-propelled vehicles as power mowers and snow-removal equipment, as long as they do not have to be registered or are used exclusively on the premises. It may also cover liability assumed by contract for employee injuries. A comprehensive general liability policy can be endorsed to cover all liability hazards except nuclear energy liability, war risks, workmen's compensation and employers' liability, and the exceptions mentioned above. General liability policies may be extended to cover not only the liability of the college or university and its officers but the liability of trustees, faculty members, and teaching staff as well.

Medical-payments insurance, although not really a liability coverage, is often included in or endorsed on liability policies. It covers medical expenses resulting from accident whether or not the policyholder is legally responsible for the accident.

Automobile liability insurance protects the policyholder and certain others (such as persons using an insured automobile with the policyholder's permission) against legal liability for bodily injury or property damage resulting from the ownership, maintenance, or use of an insured automobile.

Automobile physical damage insurance is classified according to cause of loss by the following nondiscrete coverages: fire, including lightning and certain transportation perils; theft, robbery, or pilferage of the automobile but not of personal effects in the automobile, including resulting damage; collision or upset; windstorm, earthquake, hail, or explosion, including tornado, cyclone, and water damage; flood; riot and civil commotion, with or without malicious mischief and vandalism; comprehensive, including both fire and theft, as well as any other damage to the automobile (including damage from missiles and falling objects and glass breakage from any cause) except loss caused primarily by collision or upset; combined additional coverage (with or without insurance against malicious mischief and vandalism); and coverage comprising the miscellaneous perils of windstorm, earthquake, explosion, hail, external discharge or leakage of water, flood or rising waters, riot or civil commotion, or the forced landing or falling of any aircraft or of its parts or equipment. Coverage may also be written to cover loss of personal effects caused by fire and towing and labor costs resulting from accident or disablement of the automobile.

Automobile medical-payments insurance is an optional coverage under most automobile policies. Like the medical payments that can be provided as an option under most general liability policies, it is neither a liability coverage (since it is payable irrespective of liability) nor a physical damage coverage (since it pays in the event of injury to people, not damage to animals or to inanimate properties). There are a number of different automobile insurance policies adapted to the needs of colleges or universities.

Aircraft insurance may be written to cover physical damage to aircraft and liability to passengers and other third parties who are not employees in a manner similar to automobile insurance coverages.

Life and health insurance. On the whole, a college or university will not be concerned with purchasing life or health insurance. An institution might, however, wish to insure the life of a key officer whose death or disability would be costly to the college—such as a college president whose plans inspire the confidence of benefactors, or a distinguished scientist heading up an important, long-range research project from which the college ultimately expects substantial financial returns. "Key man" insurance covers this type of loss by making the institution the beneficiary of a policy on the lives of key individuals; this insurance will enable the institution to survive during the period of time necessary to find and train a capable successor.

An institution might also pay full or partial premiums on life or health insurance policies offered to faculty, staff, or students as fringe benefits. Faculty members may be able to obtain group insurance and pension plans through professional organizations; other employees are usually protected under plans negotiated by the college or university, which may also offer certain forms of group insurance to its students. The types of insurance plans to which educational institutions commonly contribute include the following:

Group life insurance plans may cover

employees and their dependents or employees alone. They may be contributory premiums (partially paid by the employee) or noncontributory (entire cost borne by the employer). The amount of insurance is usually a multiple of the employee's salary, but in some instances he may buy an additional amount at his own expense.

Accident and sickness disability plans replace income lost by an employee because he has been disabled by accident or sickness. Most employers offer some sort of accident and sickness benefit plan, usually in the form of insurance; some employers, in lieu of insurance, carry sick employees at full or partial pay during prolonged periods of disability. Some disability insurance plans also cover employees' dependents. Most are contributory, basing benefits on the employee's salary or hourly wage.

Accidental death and dismemberment plans are often set up to supplement disability insurance benefits. They are commonly offered as part of a disability income policy and are payable in addition to such life insurance as may have been provided for the deceased. The amount of the accidental death benefit is ordinarily equal to one or two annual salaries. A few plans cover the employee's dependents as well as the employee himself. The same benefit is also often payable for certain disabilities that, because of their severity (the loss of both hands or feet, for example), are presumed to be total and permanent.

Hospitalization, surgical, medical, and major-medical benefits may be provided either under separate plans or by a single comprehensive medical insurance policy and are often covered on a deductible basis. Some plans apply to employees only, others to their dependents as well.

Pension plans supplement the basic old-age benefits provided by social security. Most pension plans cover all but part-time and seasonal employees; coverage is contingent upon a minimum period of service and/or attainment of a specified age. Benefits are generally related to preretirement

earnings. In addition to providing pensions, many colleges and universities also continue all or some of their retired employees' basic insurance coverage, such as life insurance, hospitalization, or major medical. Many pension plans do not cease to cover upon the death of the retiree, but continue to protect the surviving spouse either with lifetime benefits or by transfer of the balance of benefits due the deceased employee. Some plans also cover dependent children until they attain a given age or while they are being educated.

Student accident insurance provides coverage against medical expenses because of accident or sickness. A policy may be written for the academic year or the full calendar year. It normally covers sports other than organized team activities; if it does cover organized sports, the insurer may require an additional premium for participants in those sports or, alternatively, require that the policy cover (and that premium be paid for) every member of the student body, athlete or not.

Student sports insurance reimburses students for medical expenses due to accidental injuries sustained while the students are engaged in supervised sports or while they are being transported to or from sports events. It may cover one or more designated sports or the entire athletic program of the college or university.

Combined coverage. Some insurance policies cover all risks except those specifically excluded. A "difference in conditions" property insurance policy covers all hazards except "wear and tear" (maintenance), nuclear reaction, and war. An "umbrella" liability policy extends the limits of coverage and also insures exposures such as intangible personal injuries, contractual liability, and worldwide liability above a stated deductible. A "special multiperil" policy combines basic property and liability coverage for buildings and operations and may be written to cover all property risks and comprehensive general liability. The "public and institutional property" policy is an insurance package specifically designed for facilities such as those of schools and colleges.

Insurance Carriers

Insurance carriers (companies) are often classified, according to their ownership, into stock companies, mutuals, reciprocal exchanges, Lloyd's (London and American), and state funds.

Stock companies. These companies are profit-making ventures. The capital subscribed by their stockholders, together with the premiums collected from their policyholders and such investment income as the company earns, provides the funds from which losses are paid. Investors are induced to buy the stock of insurance companies because profits are distributed to stockholders in the form of dividends. The stockholders elect the board of directors, which in turn manages the company. Most stock insurance companies are "nonparticipating," meaning that policyholders derive no direct financial benefit from successful operation of the company because the distributed profits go to the stockholders. Some stock companies, however, issue "participating" policies that provide for the return of at least part of the profits to the policyholders. Stock insurance companies usually operate through independent local agents appointed by the company.

Mutual companies. However widely they may differ one from another in their practices, mutual companies have one thing in common: they are owned by their policyholders. Each policyholder is a member of the company and entitled to vote in the election of its directors; and each policyholder is entitled to a share of any dividends resulting from efficient, successful operating of the company.

Otherwise, mutual companies (except some "farm mutuals" operating in limited local areas) do business in much the same way as their stock competition. Both operate on the "advance premium" basis, which means that, as a consideration for the carrier assuming his risk, the policyholder agrees to pay a specified premium in advance. Premiums of stock and mutual companies are usually based on the same rate schedules. The principal difference between the companies, then, is that most mutual companies return to policyholders rather than to stockholders the excess of premiums over losses, expenses, necessary reserves, and a reasonable contribution to surplus and dividends. A few mutuals, called "deviating" mutuals, charge a lower initial premium instead of paying a dividend. Some mutuals use both methods. Mutual companies may operate through independent local agents or as direct writers through their own salaried representatives.

Reciprocal exchanges. These companies, also known as "interinsurance exchanges," have many of the characteristics of mutuals. The underlying principle is shared risk: each subscriber is insured by all the other subscribers, while he in turn insures them, ordinarily for a stipulated amount. A reciprocal company has no capital but the assets of its subscribers. A separate account is maintained for each subscriber; into this account his annual premiums are paid, and out of this his share of the losses is taken. Premiums are allowed to accumulate for several years (usually two to three) before underwriting profits are returned to subscribers in the form of cash. The liability of each subscriber is limited to a specified number of annual premiums, usually five to ten. Reciprocals have little in the way of organization. Their chief officer is an attorney-in-fact, whose authority is derived from a power of attorney subscribed to by all who join the group. The applicant to a reciprocal exchange becomes an insurer on every contract of insurance that the attorney-in-fact issues; each member of the exchange is thus insurer and insured. The attorney-in-fact retains a percentage of the premiums as his compensation. A reciprocal exchange also usually has an advisory committee to represent the subscribers and control the custody and investment of all funds above those needed for operation of the company. The attorney-in-fact may be replaced by majority vote of the advisory committee.

Lloyd's of London. Lloyd's actually insures no one. It is not an insurance company, but an insurance center, which provides facilities for its members, who are called underwriters, to carry on their own individual businesses. Hence, insurance is placed "at Lloyd's" rather than "with Lloyd's." A "Lloyd's policy" is so called not because the Corporation of Lloyd's itself insures the risk but because the corporation physically prepared the policies underwritten by its members. As a matter of convenience in transacting business, underwriters at Lloyd's are grouped into syndicates. The participation of several syndicates may be required to provide the capacity to insure a particularly large risk. Nevertheless, every individual underwriting member of Lloyd's is liable by law, up to the last penny of his entire personal fortune, for the proper fulfillment of his underwriting obligations. Any large risk is so widely spread among Lloyd's syndicates, however, that the actual liability of an individual member under a single policy is not likely to be large.

American Lloyd's. These corporations are imitations of Lloyd's of London, with which they have absolutely no connection. American Lloyd's are groups of individuals and voluntary partnerships that underwrite risks through an attorney-in-fact; members of the group are committed to given percentages of a risk, subject to a specific maximum liability for each member.

Government insurance funds. Governments sometimes perform the functions of insurance carriers—by providing, for example, a monopolistic fund from which workmen's compensation insurance must be purchased.

Sources of international insurance. When adequate coverages and services are not available in a particular country, it is sometimes possible to insure with an international company. Not all international companies, however, are admitted (licensed or registered to do business) to insure property in every country. Insurance should be purchased from a foreign source only if it is an admitted carrier. The major American international insurers include Aetna Casualty and Surety Company, American Foreign Insurance Association, American International Group, Chubb and Son, CNA Insurance Group, Commercial Union/Employers Group of the United Kingdom, Continental (New York) Group, the Factory Mutual System, Insurance Company of North America, the Kemper Group, Royal Group of the United Kingdom, Switzerland General, and Travelers Insurance Companies. Summaries of insurance requirements and availability in selected countries may be found in the *AFIA World Guide* (American Foreign Insurance Association, 1972).

Bibliography

American Foreign Insurance Association. *AFIA World Guide.* Wayne, New Jersey: AFIA, 1972.

American Management Association. *Sourcebook of International Insurance and Employee Benefit Management.* Research Study 80. New York: AMA, 1968.

A. B. Best Company. *Best's Underwriting News Letters.* Oldwick, New Jersey: A. B. Best, published intermittently.

Business Insurance. *Risk Management Reports.* Chicago: Business Insurance, published intermittently.

Knowles, A. S. (Ed.) *Handbook of College and University Administration.* New York: McGraw-Hill, 1970.

Long, J. D., and Gregg, D. W. *Property and Liability Insurance Handbook.* Homewood, Illinois: Irwin, 1965.

Mehr, R. I., and Cammack, E. *Principles of Insurance.* Homewood, Illinois: Irwin, 1972.

Riegel, R., and Miller, J. S. *Insurance Principles and Practices.* Englewood Cliffs, New Jersey: Prentice-Hall, 1966.

JAMES J. McCORMICK

See also: Art Collections, College and University; Legal Aspects of Higher Education; Museum Administration, College and University; Remuneration: Faculty, Staff, and Chief Executive Officers.

6. PURCHASING

Modern universities and colleges buy an enormous volume of supplies, equipment, and services. Purchases by even small and medium-sized institutions include thousands of items, ranging from cleaning materials to exotic substances and complex medical and engineering equipment. As a higher education system continues to expand, the amount spent for these products and services grows accordingly. As faculty and students demand more sophisticated teaching materials and equipment as well as additional services, purchases will probably take an increasingly higher proportion of the educational budget. It follows that inefficient or wasteful purchasing is something institutions can ill afford. Late deliveries or the purchase of defective or inadequate supplies can affect the quality of instruction and research. Careless expenditure of funds, duplication of buying effort, and failure to combine like requirements to obtain favorable prices are particularly intolerable in view of the rising costs and severe financial problems many colleges and universities are facing.

Conversely, skillful management of purchasing and related activities, as detailed below, can have positive effects. Teachers and researchers will have confidence in an institutional supply system that meets their requirements and assists them in their professional pursuits. As Lee and Dobler observe (1971, p. 631), the savings that are the hallmark of any good purchasing operation can have the same effect as a gift to an institution's endowment fund. They cite as an example the savings of approximately $640,000 in one year made by the purchasing department of a large American university. With the university's income generated at roughly a 5 percent earning rate, the $640,000 recurring savings is equivalent to an endowment gift of $12,800,000. Stated differently, each dollar saved by effective purchasing has the same budgetary result

as a twenty-dollar gift to the institution's endowment fund.

Until the 1920s procurement of goods and services was usually one of the many official responsibilities of the university business officer. In actuality, many other people—from maintenance personnel to research scientists—were obtaining their requirements (if not committing funds) by dealing directly with suppliers. Requisitioning by brand name, rather than by specification, was common. In view of the ineffectiveness of these operations, over the past half century administrators have begun to realize the need for better control of the procurement function.

In general, that control has been obtained by (1) establishment of purchasing organizations as separate administrative departments headed by designated purchasing officers; (2) clear definition of purchasing authority and responsibility; (3) promulgation of specific procurement policies and procedures in regard to such matters as inventory control, requisitioning and ordering, relations with other departments, relations with suppliers, and ethics.

The advantages in centralization of purchasing activities in higher education institutions are perhaps best summarized by Ritterskamp, Abbott, and Ahrens (1961, pp. 6 and 7).

Centralized purchasing agencies can make significant contributions in the effective operation of educational institutions. Among these contributions are definite economies and better planning of the total purchase requirements through pooling of the common needs of various departments within an institution. Through the development of standard specifications for commodities, the agency obtains more uniform quality and less variety of materials, supplies, and equipment.

Definite economies are also obtained through the reduction of administrative and operational costs by eliminating multiple purchasing staffs, gaining more consistent acceptance of cash discounts by prompt handling of vendors' invoices, better budgetary and financial control of departmental expenditures, and reduction in inventories through closer supervision and better judgment.

As consumers, the departments and staff members benefit directly from the availability of qualified personnel with special expertise in the purchasing function. Prompt delivery and better service from suppliers are more readily obtainable through the careful selection and follow-up procedures a purchasing agency can provide. A purchasing agency can also make provision for adequate testing and inspection of purchased materials and bring to bear relevant market research and the benefits of competition in the selection of goods and services.

Overall, the centralizing of authority and responsibility for the purchasing function provides continuity of effort and greater cost and quality control that benefit educational institutions and vendors alike.

Among the foremost objectives of the purchasing agency is the procurement of the institution's requirements in materials, equipment, food, supplies, and services at the lowest cost consistent with the desired quality, service, and delivery. In line with this objective the agency reviews overall prices and makes recommendations for consolidation and standardization of the necessary goods and services as well as negotiating short- and long-term contracts and agreements as necessary. This price information also serves in developing budgets and requisition estimates.

In addition, the agency may serve resource functions by maintaining a current purchasing library with price and product information available to the personnel of the institution and by keeping abreast of the changing market conditions affecting the goods and services used by the institution. In conjunction with these research capacities, the agency continues to search for and evaluate satisfactory and continuous sources of supply and vendors.

Forms of organization and titles vary widely in college and university purchasing. The basic unit is a separate department staffed by purchasing specialists—a purchasing agent, purchasing director, or purchasing manager. (The terms are interchangeable in the United States. The term *purchasing officer* is widely used elsewhere, particularly in the United Kingdom.) The staff generally includes one or more buyers and clerical employees. The size of the buying staff and the degree to which buyers specialize in buying certain types of commodities—laboratory supplies, for example—will vary according to the size and nature of the institution. Administration policy on centralization or decentralization of purchasing and on delegation of authority to choose suppliers and negotiate prices affects the size and structure of the official purchasing organization. The purchasing department in many small and medium-sized colleges often consists of one purchasing agent or buyer and a clerk. The buying unit often comes under the jurisdiction of the business office. To overcome the limitations of a small staff, the purchasing officer allots blocks of purchase orders to various departments. Within certain monetary limits, department heads are authorized to issue orders directly to vendors of their own choice.

Larger institutions generally maintain closer control over all purchases. The usual approach to decentralization is to locate satellite purchasing operations in the larger units of the university—the medical center or a separate campus in the same geographical area, for example. Although the physical organization, including the buying staffs and storage and warehouse facilities, is decentralized, there is a central unit that enforces uniform purchasing policies and procedures and is responsible for buying and warehousing items commonly used throughout the university.

Some multicampus systems remain centralized, however. For example, the St. Louis junior college district, with an enrollment of approximately 30,000 in three locations in St. Louis County, Missouri, does all purchasing centrally. What little inventory is carried is stored at the same location. There are no warehouses at the other locations, and the purchasing, receiving, and distribution operations are designed to bring orders directly from the supplier to the using department or person.

Bacon (1971) makes a strong case for a combined centralized-decentralized type of purchasing, whether the institution has a single campus or several campuses, whereby the purchasing department is organized on a commodity-team basis with teams specializing in specific products or services. In addition, a purchasing representative is located at each faculty division or school to act as liaison between the purchasing department and the academic area. This type of organization, he says, provides a greater opportunity for purchasing to be of service to the academic community while taking advantage of the superior management techniques of a strong central purchasing organization.

In a logical progression, the purchasing department's responsibility has often been extended to other material functions besides buying, among them receipt, handling, storage, and distribution of materials and equipment. The combining of purchasing and related activities in a unified department is generally described as *materials management,* a concept that has been widely adopted in industry. The term is used rather loosely in institutional procurement to identify a wide range of departments, from those that have responsibility for only purchasing and stores to those that handle a variety of activities that may include printing facilities, bookstores, and food service. Here again, the organization will often be shaped to the special needs and requirements of the institution, and, it must be added, by the availability of personnel capable of handling a broad range of responsibilities.

Professionals of many types—engineers, doctors, researchers, teachers—often resent having their opinions and decisions

on products and vendors questioned or even reviewed by nonprofessionals. Questioning specifications or brand names, seeking alternative materials, developing new qualified suppliers, checking commercial aspects of major purchases—all these normal activities of a buyer intent on getting the best value for the institution— are frequently misinterpreted as price-cutting efforts that will endanger quality. The administrative controls in purchasing and the resulting paperwork are seen as unnecessary and the cause of delays in delivery of vital supplies.

Persuading professionals and other university personnel that good purchasing by experienced buyers is a help to them and to the institution rather than a hindrance requires tact, diplomacy, and consistently good performance by the purchasing department—and occasionally confrontation. Out of pride, personal bias, or caution, professionals may commit their institutions to the purchase of expensive equipment exclusively from one supplier. Because of a professional's superior technical knowledge or standing in the institution, the purchasing agent may hesitate to challenge such selections. But purchasing can and should question other vital aspects of such intended transactions, neglect of which can prove very costly to the using department and to the institution. These include delivery terms, payment terms, warranties, maintenance agreements, compatibility with electrical system, and service.

Standardization through increased efficiency and the elimination of waste are efforts that the purchasing department is in the best position to coordinate. These efforts are often misunderstood and resisted by professionals. In a notable example, the chief pediatrician of a major medical center flatly refused to consider a suggestion by the purchasing department that the hospital standardize on one brand and one supplier for all infant formula requirements (except in the case of special problems). Despite the fact that all four of the formulas being bought were made to the same exact specifications, he insisted standardization would "endanger the lives" of children under his care. The matter was decided by administration in favor of the purchasing officer. The center saved $40,000 a year on that one item.

Sound organization and the development of good relationships through education and performance notwithstanding, a well-defined purchasing policy with strong administrative support is essential. Equally important is the establishment of efficient procedures. Both policies and procedures are often disseminated in a purchasing manual that is distributed to all personnel in the institution and to suppliers as well.

A typical manual opens usually with a statement of the policy and objectives of the institution. This statement serves to establish the responsibility of the purchasing agency or department for obtaining maximum value in the procurement of supplies, equipment, and services rendered by outside agencies. Generally it limits the commitment of the institution to purchases made exclusively on purchase orders issued by the established purchasing unit. Selection of sources and vendors would also come under the agency's responsibility, though suggested vendors would be used when they proved competitive.

Along with outlining the objectives of the agency, the manual may also cover policies and procedures concerning requisitioning, bidding and ordering, capital expenditures, emergency orders, servicing and return of equipment and damaged goods, and the operations of stores. The impact of these policies and procedures is often well served by the endorsement of the institution's top administrators.

College and university purchasing departments have successfully adapted most of the techniques and methods from their counterparts in industry. These include such methods as blanket orders, which are single orders for a certain item or family of items, which usually provide price and delivery protection for a specified period of time and maintenance of given inventory by the supplier. Various streamlined methods of handling small orders can eliminate most of the paperwork inherent in an order—for example, the check-with-order system, which provides the supplier with immediate payment and eliminates invoicing. Computerized inventory control, cost-price analysis, and vendor evaluation are other techniques borrowed from industry that have improved the effectiveness of institutional purchasing. Yet there is one particularly effective technique that has not been widely adapted by many educational institutions.

Educational institutions that are wholly or partially governmentally funded are restricted in one of the most fundamental and effective industrial purchasing techniques—negotiation. Negotiation is a sophisticated form of bargaining between buyer and seller to achieve a mutually satisfactory agreement on prices and terms. Institutions operating under regulations established by political units, such as states, counties, provinces, and municipalities, are generally required to use formal requests for quotation or tender within certain monetary limits. In some provinces of Canada, for example, purchasing departments in governmentally funded universities require that purchasing obtain two or three quotations on orders for more than five hundred dollars and invite formal tenders on orders of two thousand dollars or more.

Yet there are signs that institutional managers and governmental authorities are aware that there is more to good purchasing than merely comparing bids and accepting the lowest. In a typical example of the more analytical type of procurement now being practiced in many institutions, the purchasing department of the University of Ottawa analyzed several tenders for supplying a large number of expensive microscopes. By projecting the costs of shipping, servicing, and maintenance of the instruments and adding them to the prices bid by various suppliers, purchasing determined that the lowest bidder did not offer the lowest total cost. On purchasing's recommendation, the business was placed with other than the lowest bidder without objection from the using department.

Some states—Florida, for example—have strong laws requiring that certain purchasing for state supported institutions be made through a central state purchasing agency. However, a group of university purchasing officers representing the Florida state university system—the Interinstitutional Committee on Purchasing—has been active in efforts to amend the regulations to give them greater flexibility in meeting the needs of their academic departments.

Bibliography

Bacon, P. A. "Centralized-Decentralized Purchasing in the Academic Institution." *Journal of Purchasing and Materials Management,* 1971, 7(3), 56–69.

Call, R. V. "Purchasing in the Academic Institution." *Journal of Purchasing and Materials Management,* 1968, 4(2), 70–77.

Heinritz, S. F., and Farrell, P. V. *Purchasing: Principles and Applications.* (5th ed.) Englewood Cliffs, New Jersey: Prentice-Hall, 1971.

Lee, L., Jr., and Dobler, D. W. *Purchasing and Materials Management.* (2nd ed.) New York: McGraw-Hill, 1971.

National Association of Educational Buyers. *Proceedings of Annual Meeting.* Westbury, New York: National Association of Educational Buyers, 1970–; published annually.

Ritterskamp, J. J., Jr., Abbott, F. L., and Ahrens, B. C. (Eds.) *Purchasing for Educational Institutions.* New York: Teachers College Press, Columbia University, 1961.

PAUL V. FARRELL

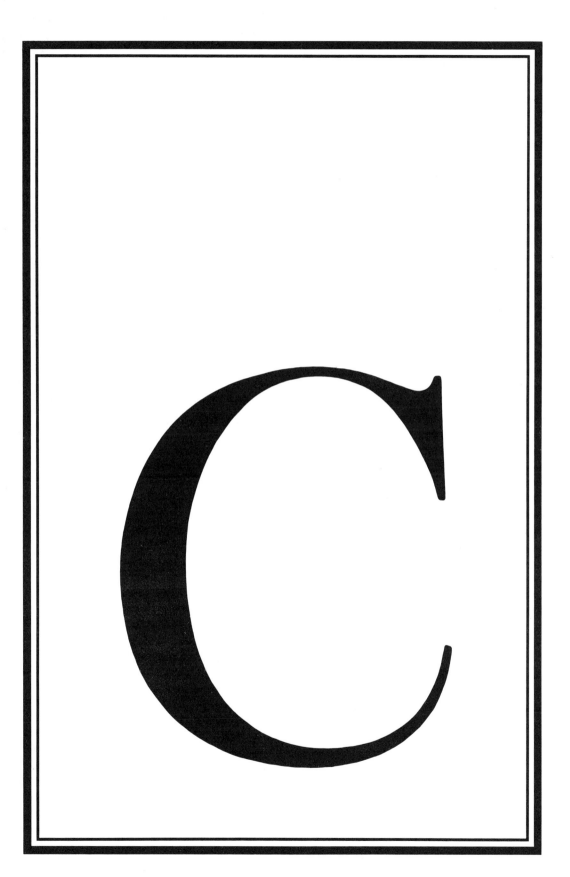

CALENDARS, ACADEMIC

The word *calendar* has more than one meaning in the world of academia: it may be used to refer to (1) the official catalogue or bulletin that describes an institution, its requirements for admission, the curriculum offered, or degree requirements; or (2) the period of time that an institution of higher learning is in operation each year, and, more specifically, the organization of that time period. In this article the second definition will be used. (Some nations, which use the first definition of calendar, use the word *schedule* to refer to the annual period of time that the institution is in operation.)

The civil calendar now used by many nations is the Gregorian Calendar, named after Pope Gregory who made it the official calendar of the Roman Catholic church in 1582. This calendar superseded the Julian Calendar, initiated in Rome by Julius Caesar. The year for the Julian Calendar system was assumed to contain exactly 365.25 days. The tropical calendar is about .008 of a day shorter. Thus, in the course of a thousand years the Julian Calendar was in error by nearly eight days. Although by 1582 the error was about thirteen days, Pope Gregory dropped only ten days from the calendar when instituting his Gregorian

system. The day following October 4, 1582, became October 15, 1582.

England and her colonies did not change to the new style until 1752. To correct the old calendar required that eleven days be dropped. Thus, the day following September 2, 1752, became September 14, 1752. In colonial Connecticut, Yale University was fifty-one years old in 1752. A change in date of the Yale commencement in 1752 is the only documentation marking Yale's adoption of the Gregorian Calendar. The Yale commencement, usually held on the second Wednesday of September, was held on the twentieth of the month due to the loss of days. The recorded notice of the change appears in the minutes of the Yale corporation meeting held during that commencement. While other minutes merely record the date of the meeting, these minutes begin as follows: "At a meeting of the President & Fellows of Yale College in New Haven in the College Library on the 2d Wednesday in Sept 1752 being the 20th Day of the Month." Apparently this historical calendar change had no other effect on the Yale academic calendar.

In colonial Massachusetts, the change to the "New Stile" calendar occurred when Harvard College was 116 years old. The president and fellows of Harvard College (the Corporation), in a meeting on August 27, 1752, voted "that the first quarter this year shall not end till the second Fryday in September next" and "all the after dates are according to the Kalendar as it hath been corrected by Act of Parliament." On May 21, 1753, the Corporation changed the date of Commencement from the first Wednesday to the third Wednesday in July.

The University of Cambridge in England, founded in the thirteenth century, had been in operation for five hundred years in 1752. In 1975, a "most thorough search," by the Keeper of the Archives, revealed "nothing in the official records which gives any indication at all, of what effect, if any, the calendar change in 1752 had on the University of Cambridge academic calendar."

Henceforth, all references to the calendar year or the civil calendar in this article are to the Gregorian Calendar unless specifically noted.

While most countries employ only one or two types of academic calendar in their systems of higher education, a few use many more. The United States provides perhaps the best illustration of the diversity that can exist in the educational system of one country.

The first institution of higher learning in the United States, Harvard College, founded in colonial Massachusetts in 1636, adopted the year-round calendar of four terms used by Oxford and Cambridge in England. The terms were of religious origin—Hilary, Easter, Trinity, and Michelmas—and varied in their starting dates; the academic year began, usually in the middle of August, with the Trinity quarter. The present quarter system, used by about one fourth of the institutions in the United States evolved from the Harvard College system, which it followed for 165 years.

Other colleges in colonial America apparently were not influenced by Harvard College with respect to their academic calendars. Records show that the College of William and Mary, founded in colonial Virginia in 1693, was using a three-term academic calendar in 1736. The academic year consisted of approximately ten months, starting in late September or early October with the Trinity term, followed by the Hilary term, and culminating with the Easter term in late June or early July.

The three-term plan was the dominant academic calendar for institutions of higher learning in the United States during the eighteenth and nineteenth centuries. The semester system, whereby the academic year is divided into two terms, first appeared in the middle of the nineteenth century, probably originating at Princeton University in New Jersey in 1823.

Under the auspices of the American Association of Collegiate Registrars and Admissions Officers (AACRAO), data on academic calendars in the United States have been obtained each year since the 1970–71 academic year. Six types of academic calendars have been defined.

In the traditional semester system the nine-month academic year is divided into two equal semesters. The first semester starts about September 10 and ends about January 25; the second semester starts about January 30 and ends early in June. Semester hours are used for credits.

In the early semester system the academic year is also divided into two semesters, but the first semester is slightly shorter than the second. The first semester starts about August 30 and ends about December 21; the second semester starts about January 15 and ends about May 20. Semester hours are used for credits.

In the quarter system the nine-month academic year is divided into three equal terms of about eleven or twelve weeks each, with a great variation in the starting and ending times. Quarter hours (three quarter hours equal two semester hours) are used for credits.

In the trimester system the twelve-month academic year is divided into three equal parts of about sixteen weeks each. The first trimester ends just before Christmas, the second trimester ends about April 15, and the third trimester ends about August 20. Semester hours are used for credits.

In the 4-1-4 system the nine-month year is divided into two equal terms of about sixteen weeks each plus a four-week term between the two. The first term ends just before Christmas and the second term starts February 1. The month of January is used for the four-week session, called either the interterm, interim, or winter session. The 4-1-4 title means four months, one month, four months; 4-1-4 also means four courses, one course, four courses. All courses are the same credit value (one unit), although some institutions use semester hours for credits.

The final category includes all academic calendars not defined by any of the five types listed above. Included in this group are variations of the old three-term quarter or trimester plan and the new modular calendar. The modular calendar consists of short terms of three and a half to seven weeks each, during which the student concentrates on one or two courses. In addition, many institutions operate on a year-round basis and offer programs on the cooperative plan of education, whereby students alternate periods of on-campus study with periods of off-campus learning experiences. Such institutions make use of a variety of calendars, including some that are unique to cooperative education programs. Many colleges and universities on the cooperative plan follow an alternating schedule of one period (quarter, semester, or other specific time period) on campus followed by a similar time period off-campus, but individual calendar arrangements are numerous. A complete discussion of the numerous cooperative calendar variations may be found in the *Handbook of Cooperative Education* (Knowles, 1971). Finally, most American institutions of higher learning also conduct summer sessions, which range in length from one- and two-week workshops to terms of eight weeks. Many institutions arrange their summer sessions in two five-week terms.

In the United States the early 1970s will be remembered by some as the period of the academic calendar revolution. During the first half of this century, some institutions experimented with the year-round trimester plan and other calendar innovations, but during the six-year period between 1969 and 1974, calendar changes were extensive. Curricular changes requiring a new calendar format resulted in the invention of the 4-1-4 and the modular calendars. The early semester became popular as a result of attempts to reduce budget increases by rearranging the academic calendar to permit more efficient use of facilities by enabling the university to offer longer summer sessions and to close down some university buildings during the cold winter months.

The most notable fact to emerge from the AACRAO survey is the decrease in the percentage of institutions using the traditional semester plan—from 76 percent prior to the 1967–68 academic year to 9 percent in the 1974–75 academic year—and the increase in the number of institutions adopting the early semester plan—from 3 percent prior to the 1967–68 academic year to 45 percent in 1974–75. The 4-1-4 calendar type, first used by Florida Presbyterian College (now Eckert College) in 1960–61, rapidly gained popularity, rising to 14 percent in 1974–75. The 4-1-4 calendar is most popular with the smaller liberal arts colleges, but it is also used by a few large universities, such as Case Western Reserve University, Southern Methodist University, and the Massachusetts Institute of Technology. A total of 483 institutions have used the 4-1-4 calendar for one or more years since 1966–67. The number of institutions using the quarter system has stabilized at 25 percent. The trimester has remained constant at 3 percent, having proven to be economically unsound.

In the six years that records have been kept, 1747 calendar changes have been made. An unknown repeat factor (one institution making more than one calendar change in the six-year period) precludes a definite statement, but it is probable that more than half of the 2400 to 2800 colleges and universities in the United States participating in the AACRAO survey have changed calendars since 1969.

Unlike the United States, the academic calendars of most countries have not changed much over the years. In the Federal Republic of Germany there are two types of academic calendars: the traditional semester and the trimester. The *Gesamthochschulen* (comprehensive universities), and *Fachhochschulen* (higher technical colleges) follow the traditional semester plan, and the *Hochschulen* (universities) of the federal army use the trimester calendar. Some newly founded universities in the Federal Republic, who use a year-round calendar, divided the year into two six-month periods.

In Turkey universities are organized on the traditional semester plan, but some variation in starting and stopping dates occurs.

In the Republic of South Africa there are eighteen universities and colleges plus six teacher training colleges. With the exception of the University of Port Elizabeth, which uses the traditional two-semester plan, the twelve-month academic year of all other institutions is divided into four quarters. Three of the universities are considering changing to the semester system in the near future.

In the Republic of Korea there are seventy-two colleges and universities. All academic calendars consist of two semesters. The first semester begins in late February or early March; the second semester ends just before Christmas. The summer vacation runs from late June or early July to late August.

In Canada most of the universities and colleges use an academic year, called the Winter Session, of approximately thirty weeks in length, starting early in September and ending late in April or early in May. A review of the academic calendars of forty-six Canadian universities shows that thirty-nine use the Winter Session calendar; of these, thirty divide the session into two semesters (with the students writing mid-

year as well as end-of-year examinations) and four do not divide the academic year at all. The full-time student normally studies five year-long (two-semester) courses of six credits each, although some one-semester courses are offered. Sixteen of the thirty-nine institutions also conduct a Spring Session of six weeks, from the middle of May to the end of June. One institution operates on a quarter system and six use the trimester. At least one of the colleges uses the 4-1-4 calendar.

In Australia the three-trimester and the two-semester calendars are used by approximately equal numbers of institutions. In some of the universities the first trimester begins on the "ninth Monday" and ends on the "Saturday before the eighteenth Monday" of the calendar year; the second trimester begins on the twenty-second Monday and ends on the Saturday before the thirty-first Monday; the third trimester begins on the thirty-fifth Monday and ends on the Saturday before the forty-fourth Monday. A 1975 report from one university indicates that, while there have been discussions about changing this calendar, no change is likely within the foreseeable future.

Examination of the academic calendars of fifty universities in the United Kingdom shows that the three-term plan, similar to the American quarter system, is used almost entirely. In many universities the three terms are Michaelmas, from early October to mid December; Hilary, from early or mid January to mid March; and Trinity, from mid April to mid June. Terms average ten to eleven weeks, but in a few cases Trinity term is only six weeks long. In some universities the terms are denominated Martinmas, Candlemas, and Whitsunday; in the newer universities they are called autumn, spring, and summer terms. Only one institution, the University of Sterling, divides the academic year into two semesters. City University, in London, uses both semesters and quarters.

Higher education institutions in Brazil

use either the two-semester plan or the one-year term. The first semester starts in early March and ends in late June; the second semester starts in early August and continues to the end of November. The one-year term begins the first of March and ends in November, with the month of July off for vacation.

Most other countries use only one type of academic calendar nationwide.

The following nations use a *three term system:* United Kingdom of Great Britain and Northern Ireland, Republic of Malta, Barbados, Jamaica, and Republic of Ghana (October-June); Trinidad and Tobago, United Republic of Cameroon, Republic of Sierra Leone, and Republic of Zambia (October-July); Federal Republic of Nigeria and Co-operative Republic of Guyana (September-June); Democratic Republic of the Sudan (July-April); Socialist Republic of the Union of Burma (September-August); Republic of Sri Lanka (January-October); the Federation of Malaysia (May-February); and New Zealand (February/March to October/November).

The following nations use a *two-semester system:* Kingdom of Denmark, Kingdom of Sweden, Empire of Iran, Kingdom of Norway, Republic of Iraq, and the Arab Republic of Egypt (September-June); Czechoslovak Socialist Republic, Hashemite Kingdom of Jordan, Republic of Tunisia, Socialist Federal Republic of Yugoslavia, and the Socialist Republic of Romania (October-June); the Republic of Turkey and the Swiss Confederation (October-July); the Republic of Finland (September-May); the Dominican Republic (August/September-June/July); the Republic of Liberia (March-December); Kingdom of Thailand (June-April); the Hungarian People's Republic (September-July); and the Polish People's Republic (October-September).

The State of Israel (October-September) and Japan (April-March) both use either the *two-semester* or the *three-term system.* The Kingdom of Saudi Arabia (October-June),

and the Kingdom of the Netherlands (September-July) each use the *one-term system,* while the Republic of Upper Volta (October-June) uses the *trimester system.*

Bibliography

Cowley, W. H. *A Study of the Relative Merits of the Quarter and Semester Systems.* Columbus: Ohio State University, Associate Provost for Special Programs, 1932.

Knowles, A. S., and Associates. *Handbook of Cooperative Education.* San Francisco: Jossey-Bass, 1971.

Oleson, L. C. *A Report on Academic Calendars.* Washington, D.C.: American Association of Collegiate Registrars and Admissions Officers, 1971.

Oleson, L. C. "Calendar Changes, Effective 1974–75." *American Association of Collegiate Registrars and Admissions Officers Newsletter,* Summer 1975.

Walz, O. C. "A Study of Major Calendar Changes in Selected Institutions of Higher Education in the United States, 1969–1972." Unpublished doctoral dissertation, University of Nebraska, 1972.

LOYD C. OLESON

CAMBODIA
See Democratic Cambodia.

CAMBRIDGE UNIVERSITY LIBRARY
See Libraries: Cambridge University Library, England.

CAMEROON, UNITED REPUBLIC OF

Population: 7,500,000 (1976 census). Student enrollment in primary school: 1,014,135; secondary school (academic, teacher training, technical): 108,009; higher education: 10,000 (1975). Language of instruction: French and English. Academic calendar: October 1 to July 31 (starting 1976–77). Percentage of national budget expended on all education: 22%; university education: 3.3% (1975–76).[Except where otherwise noted, figures are for 1973–74. Source: Ministry of Education.]

Western education was introduced to Cameroon in 1844, when Joseph Merrick of the London Baptist Missionary Society opened a school at Bimbia in what is now Fako, South West Province. For the next forty years, the society expanded and developed educational facilities but only for primary education. On July 12, 1884, Germany annexed Cameroon and set up a colonial regime. Educational facilities of the country were further developed during the thirty years of German rule; however, no secondary institutions were established. After World War I, Germany lost Cameroon, which was partitioned by France and Great Britain in accordance with a mandate from the League of Nations. After the end of World War II, the area continued to be administered by France and Great Britain as United Nations trust territories until independence in 1960 (French sector) and 1961 (British sector). Educational facilities developed both quantitatively and qualitatively during this period; however, neither the French, who had occupied 80 percent of the territory (what is now the United Republic of Cameroon), nor the British, whose 20 percent was administered as an integral part of its territory of Nigeria, provided any local facilities for higher education.

In 1946 the French Commission for Modernization of Overseas Territories recommended the establishment of a medical school in Cameroon, but no action was taken. In their 1947 annual reports to the United Nations on their respective sectors of Cameroon, France and Great Britain indicated the absence of higher education facilities but made no provisions for their establishment. Beginning in 1948, the various specialized agencies of the United Nations recommended that the administering authorities not only increase higher education scholarships but also establish higher education facilities. The United Nations Trusteeship Council, at its fifth session on July 19, 1949, unanimously adopted Resolution 110(v), which called on France to pay particular attention to Cameroon's higher education needs and consider the establishment of university institutes or colleges

there by 1952. France's response was negative. Despite continued pressure by United Nations specialized agencies, France was unwilling to change its position, maintaining that lack of finances, equipment, and an adequate number of qualified students made the establishment of a university in Cameroon at that time premature, inadvisable, and even unnecessary.

France granted Cameroon the status of self-governing state by Decree 57-501 of April 16, 1957. Education, with the exception of the curricula and examination regulations of secondary and higher education institutions, became the responsibility of the newly formed Cameroon government. Since the localization of the public service became the exclusive responsibility of the Cameroon government, the establishment of higher education facilities to train qualified personnel became imperative. Soon after setting up the Ministry of National Education, the Cameroon government undertook the necessary arrangements to establish a university preparatory class (at the Yaoundé *lycée*), a law school, and a national professional school, all of which would form the nucleus of a future Cameroon university. On December 30, 1958, a cultural convention signed with France stipulated that France would assist in the eventual establishment and development of a Cameroon university.

Cameroon (under French administration) gained full independence on January 1, 1960, and in April 1960 the Cameroon National School of Administration was opened, having been created by a decree in 1959. A magistracy section was added in 1964 to train administrative staff and magistrates for the public service. By Presidential Decree 61/55 of April 25, 1961 (all decrees are presidential), the National Institute of University Studies was established to offer preuniversity courses in arts (*lettres*), science, and law. After the conference of African states on the development of education in Africa, held in Addis Ababa in May 1961, the Cameroon government signed an agreement with the United

Nations Special Fund on June 13, 1961, to establish an advanced teacher training college to train secondary school teachers and primary school inspectors. By Decree 61/186, issued on September 30, 1961, the Cameroon Advanced Teacher Training College was created and opened in November 1961, under the supervision of UNESCO.

As plans were under way for the reunification of the Cameroon Republic (former French Cameroons) and the southern sector of the British Cameroons (which had voted in the February 11, 1961 plebiscite for reunification with the Cameroon Republic) to form the Federal Republic of Cameroon, the government of the Cameroon Republic, on August 18, 1961, sought the advice of UNESCO to plan for the future development of higher education and particularly for the establishment of a Cameroon university.

In December 1961 UNESCO set up an Advisory Commission for the Development of Higher Education in the Federal Republic of Cameroon, made up of five international experts and three Cameroonians, appointed by the Cameroon government. On the basis of its studies and recommendations, the Federal University of Cameroon was created on July 26, 1962, by Decree 62/DF/289 to provide higher education within the fundamental objectives of the nation's plan for economic and social development. Decree 62/DF/372, issued on October 8, 1962, listed all higher education institutions comprising the Federal University of Cameroon. All higher education establishments in existence or still to be created in Cameroon, except the Cameroon National School of Administration and the all-services Military School (which existed in Yaoundé on the eve of independence to train cadet officers), became part of the Federal University of Cameroon. Professional or specialized schools providing higher education were accorded a certain autonomy under the umbrella of the university.

Establishments comprising the Federal University of Cameroon at the beginning of the 1962–63 academic year included the faculty of law and economics, the faculty of arts and social sciences, and the faculty of science, all of which had developed from the National Institute of University Studies. The Advanced Teacher Training College became an integral part of the university in 1963. The National School of Agriculture—founded on May 8, 1960 (Decree 60/121), but effectively put into operation only in January 1962—became the Advanced School of Agriculture and was integrated into the Federal University of Cameroon on May 16, 1963, by Decree 63/DF/157. This move brought the total number of university establishments in 1963 to five: three faculties and two specialized schools.

The period 1962–1967 was one of transition for the Federal University of Cameroon. On December 28, 1967, Decree 67/DF/566 terminated the transitional period. Steps were taken to improve the physical plant of the university and to consolidate and bring the university programs more in line with the national development plan. By Decree 69/DF/207 of June 4, 1969, the Institute of Business Administration (IBA) was added to the university; however, it was placed under the umbrella of the faculty of law and economics. On June 14, 1969, the University Center for Health Sciences (UCHS) was created by Decree 69/DF/256 as another addition to the university, to train medical doctors, nurses, and senior health technicians and to carry out research on African health problems.

On April 17, 1970, representatives of the governments of Cameroon, Central African Republic, Gabon, Rwanda, and Chad signed a convention in Yaoundé to establish an International School of Journalism as part of the Federal University of Cameroon, with the specific objective of training African journalists and communications specialists and researchers. Consequently, the Yaoundé Advanced International School of Journalism was created by Decree 70/DF/21 on May 15, 1970; and the school opened six months later, on November 16, 1970. The Centre for Research in African Studies—founded in 1970 for the purpose of promoting, organizing, and carrying out specialized research in social, economic, and natural sciences and in technology—was brought under the egis of the university by Decree 71/DF/284 of June 15, 1971. Another addition to the university came on April 24, 1971, when a decree created the Cameroon Institute of International Relations (CIIR) to provide training in international relations and diplomacy. It is an international institute with only ten places allotted to Cameroon each year. On June 4, 1971, the Federal Advanced Polytechnic School was founded by Decree 71/DF/260 as part of the university. By Decree 73/326 of June 23, 1973, the Federal University of Cameroon became the University of Yaoundé; the Federal Advanced School of Agriculture became the National Advanced School of Agronomy; and the Federal Advanced Polytechnic School became the National Advanced Polytechnic School.

Types of Institutions

The University of Yaoundé is at present the only university in Cameroon. University-level courses are also offered by the National School of Administration and Magistracy (cycle A); the National Institute of Youth and Sports (teachers' section); the National Higher School of Posts and Telecommunications (inspectors' section); the National Advanced Police School, Yaoundé (as of 1968); the Demographic Institute (established in 1972); the Yaoundé International Insurance Institute (opened in 1973); the Protestant Faculty of Theology in Yaoundé (opened in 1963); the Roman Catholic Major Seminary in Nkolbisson; and the Regional Major Seminary, Bambui (founded in 1973). The Cameroon Military School, Yaoundé; the Institute for Statistical Training, Yaoundé (founded in 1961); the Pan-African Institute for Development; and some sections of the above-mentioned institutions also offer specialized postsecondary education of a nonuniversity type.

Relationship with Secondary Education

The primary and secondary programs have been restructured to provide seven years of primary education in both the French- and English-language sectors, followed by seven years of secondary education, divided into two cycles of five and two years, respectively. The school-leaving certificate is the Cameroon General Certificate of Education, at the ordinary and advanced levels. The first of the new examinations were held in June 1977.

Admission Requirements

Admission to the university requires one of the following qualifications: (1) possession of a *baccalauréat* diploma; (2) a General Certificate of Education with passes in at least four subjects at the ordinary level obtained in one sitting and two subjects at the advanced level obtained in one sitting (or more than two subjects at the advanced level obtained in more than one sitting); (3) qualifications equivalent to 1 or 2; or (4) a pass in the special entrance examinations given by the university lishment concerned. Only holders of the *baccalauréat*, GCE, or similar qualifications are eligible to take the special entrance examination given by some of the establishments. There are also age requirements, which vary from one establishment to another.

Admission requirements for nonuniversity institutions offering programs at the university level are similar to those at the university. Applicants are admitted with secondary school qualifications or, for more advanced programs, with a completed first degree. The National Advanced Police School and the National School of Administration and Magistracy also require success in competitive entrance examinations.

Administration and Control

The University of Yaoundé is a public institution. It was founded and received its administrative structure by Decree 62/ DF/289 of July 26, 1962. The university is governed by two councils: (1) the Council of Higher Education and Scientific and Technical Research; (2) the administrative council of the university.

The Council for Higher Education and Scientific and Technical Research is a government body, presided over by the president of the republic, consisting of sixteen ex officio members: thirteen ministers and two members of parliament in addition to the president. It also contains seven consultants such as the director of higher education, the director general and deputy director general of the National Office of Scientific and Technical Research, and the chancellor and vice-chancellor of the university. In accordance with Decree 74/358 of April 17, 1974, the Council for Higher Education and Scientific and Technical Research establishes policy and draws up plans for the development and operation of higher education. It also coordinates higher education training programs and scientific and technical research to align them with government policy, the nation's development plan, and international cooperation agreements. The council meets annually but may be convened by the chairman at other times to handle urgent matters.

The administrative council of the university is comprised of (1) ex officio members: the chancellor (chairman), the vice-chancellor (vice-chairman), representatives of four government departments, heads of university establishments and their deputies, the director and deputy director of higher education, the director of scientific and technical research, and the president of the recognized student union; (2) elected members: one representative from each category of permanent staff and two students representing each university establishment; (3) consultants: directors of foreign foundations, the central treasurer (*receveur*) of the university and his representative, the controller of finance, and, when necessary, persons competent in the matters discussed. The administrative council meets every three months or more frequently in cases of emergency. Meetings are convened by the chairman or vice-chairman, with the secretary general of the university acting as secretary. The council implements policies and plans laid down by the Council for Higher Education. It handles staff appointments, promotions, and discipline and is the final authority with regard to student discipline. It organizes and coordinates educational programs of the various university establishments and advises on all academic affairs relating to the university.

All administrative officers of the university are appointed by the president of Cameroon. Among them is the minister of national education, who is the head of the university. He ensures that the educational programs are in accord with the country's development plan, confers degrees, awards diplomas and certificates, safeguards academic freedom, and authorizes the implementation of programs approved by the administrative council. The director of higher education coordinates higher education activities at the ministerial level and applies government policies on higher education. Directly under the minister of national education is the chancellor of the university, who is the delegate of the government responsible for ensuring that the activities of the university, in their totality, embody the objectives of the national development plan and conform to the decisions of the Council for Higher Education. He is the chief executive officer responsible for the daily functioning of the university. He submits his annual report to the chairman of the Council for Higher Education through the minister of national education. The vice-chancellor is the academic head of the university, with supreme authority in academic affairs. He countersigns university degrees, diplomas, and certificates and promotes research, teaching, and student exchange programs. In addition to making comprehensive academic reports to the chancellor and the administrative council, he also presents an annual report to the minister of national education for processing to the chairman of the Council for Higher Education. The secretary general of the university is in charge of the central services of the university, including financial affairs, teaching and research, liaison and cultural activities, and central library services.

Each faculty of the university is headed by a dean assisted by a vice-dean, while each professional establishment is administered by a director assisted by a director of studies. The central services of each establishment are handled by a secretary general, and the finances are handled by a bursar. Schools are subdivided into departments, each under a department head. Each university establishment also has set up organizations that are academic, administrative, consultative, or deliberative in nature. Each faculty has a faculty council and a faculty assembly. The faculty council is comprised of the dean as chairman, the vice-dean, department heads, and professors. It handles student discipline, prepares the draft of the budget, and makes recommendations to the administrative council of the university regarding matters such as recruitment, appointments, and promotions of academic staff and creation of new departments. The faculty assembly—which consists of the dean as chairman, all permanent academic staff, and two student representatives—makes recommendations on matters of interest to the faculty, students, or the university.

The specialized establishments have managing boards, academic councils (which are the counterparts of the faculty councils), and school assemblies (which are the counterparts of faculty assemblies). Managing boards consist of representatives from the academic staff, students, government ministries or departments directly concerned with specialized training, and the directors of associated institutes. Their functions are similar to those of the faculty council. A Council for Guidance and Further Training is set up in every establishment by the minister of national education and consists

of the minister as chairman; members of the faculty council or managing board; a representative of the minister of public service; and the heads of university schools, government services concerned with higher education, and representatives of national activities with special interest in the establishments concerned. Its functions are general and advisory in nature.

Programs and Degrees

The faculty of law and economics offers a two-year program leading to the Certificate of Proficiency in Law and Economics (*capacité en droit et économie*). The four-year Bachelor of Law and Economics degree programs consist of a lower level of two years, leading to the Certificate of General Studies in Law and Economics; and an upper level consisting of two years, ending with the bachelor's degree.

The Institute of Business Administration comprises two sections, one offering a two-year certificate course and the other a one-year advanced diploma course.

The faculty of arts and social sciences offers a three-year bachelor's degree (*licence*) program and a one-year postgraduate diploma. The first two years of the degree program lead to the Diploma (or Certificate) of General Literary Studies. An additional year of study leads to the Certificate of Higher Studies, while the Diploma of Higher Studies is awarded after two more years of study.

The two-year first level of studies in the faculty of science leads to the Diploma of General Scientific Studies; the second level leads to the bachelor's degree after an additional year; and the third level leads to the Diploma of Higher Studies (postgraduate) after two further years of study. Bachelor's degrees are awarded in mathematics; physics and chemistry; natural sciences I, with biological sciences as a major; natural sciences II, with earth sciences as a major; physics; chemistry; and biological chemistry.

The structural organization of programs in the Advanced Teacher Training College (ATTC) were reconstructed according to Decree 75/221 of March 24, 1975, into three sections to provide training for teachers at three levels: (1) lower and upper general secondary teachers, (2) teachers of lower and upper technical secondary schools, and (3) teachers for grade 1 and grade 2 in primary teacher training institutions. The first section offers a three-year program in the arts and science divisions, leading to the Advanced Proficiency Certificate (*diplôme supérieur d'aptitude*), which entitles holders to teach in lower secondary schools. Two additional years in the same section and program are required for the postgraduate diploma (*concours national d'habilitation*), which qualifies the recipients either to teach in upper secondary schools or to apply for admission into the doctoral program. The second section offers a three-year program in industrial and commercial techniques, leading to the Advanced Certificate of Proficiency in Lower Technical Secondary School Teaching. A further two-year program ends with the postgraduate diploma, which is required for teachers in upper technical secondary schools. The third section offers a Diploma in the Science of Education, which qualifies graduates for teaching at a primary teacher training institution.

Students of the National Advanced School of Agronomy follow a special two-year program at the faculty of science, which ends with the Diploma of General Scientific Studies, with specialization in agronomy. Two further years at the school completes the four-year course leading to the *diplôme d'ingénieur agronome* (Diploma of Agricultural Engineering), which is equivalent to a Bachelor of Science degree in agronomy.

The University Centre for Health Sciences consists of (1) a medical section with a six-year Doctor of Medicine (M.D.) degree program; (2) an Advanced Nursing Training Centre, offering a two-year program leading to a Diploma in Advanced Nursing (plans are under way for a degree program in nursing); and (3) a section for training health technicians, which offers a three-year program.

The Cameroon Institute of International Relations offers (1) a two-year postgraduate program, for either a diploma or a doctoral degree in international relations; (2) one-year diplomatic and consular training courses, which lead to an "A" certificate for degree holders and a "B" certificate for nondegree holders; and (3) a four-month consular certificate course.

The Yaoundé Advanced International School of Journalism prepares its students for an Advanced Diploma in Journalism, which takes three years. The students spend the first two years in Yaoundé and the last year in France, under the auspices of the *Institut français de presse* of Paris II University. They return to Yaoundé at the end of the third trimester for their diploma.

The National Advanced Polytechnic School provides a three-year course for the training of foremen (*ingénieurs de travaux*) in various technical fields and a five-year course for the training of high-level technicians. During their first two years, students in the five-year program prepare for the Diploma of General Scientific Studies in Mathematics-Physics-Technology. Successful candidates of the last three years earn the *mâtrise des sciences de l'ingénieur* (Master of Science [Engineering]).

Financing and Student Financial Aid

The University of Yaoundé as a public institution is the financial responsibility of the Cameroon government All bilateral, multilateral, and private aid to the university is channeled through the government.

Cameroonians enrolled at the University of Yaoundé pay no tuition fees. Full-time students pay a registration fee, which is refunded if they get a scholarship. External and part-time students pay a nonrefundable registration fee. Eligible students receive scholarships (allowances), which range from 12,000 to 45,000 francs CFA (US$ 1 = 223 CFA); the highest amount goes to those in the specialized establishments, who are bonded for ten years and regarded as civil servants.

Student Social Background and Access to Education

Most of the students in higher education institutions in Cameroon are the children of farmers (cultivators), artisans, and unskilled workers. The university is open to everyone who fulfills the conditions and requirements for admission, regardless of race, sex, religion, or social background. Students of both sexes are actively engaged in club, extracurricular, union, cultural, and other activities.

Teaching Staff and Research Activities

Members of the teaching staff of the University of Yaoundé fall into two main categories: (1) those permanently employed to carry out teaching and research and (2) those employed on a temporary or part-time basis to carry out these same functions or to assist in the academic work of the university. The permanent staff are ranked as professor, assistant professor, lecturer, and assistant lecturer.

An application for a teaching position at the university is transmitted by the vice-chancellor to the head of the establishment concerned. The council or academic board makes its recommendation to the administrative council of the university. Temporary appointments as professor or assistant professor are made by the minister of national education; final appointments are made by the president of the republic; both temporary and final appointments as lecturer or assistant lecturer are made by the chancellor.

To qualify for appointment as a professor, the candidate must be at least thirty years of age and present at least one of the following qualifications: (1) have passed the French *agrégation* competitive examinations; (2) be a lecturer (*maître de conférences*); (3) hold an English Ph.D. degree with at least six years of teaching experience in an institution of higher learning and with evidence of research carried out at the highest

level; (4) have at least six years of experience as a senior lecturer in a British university; (5) be an assistant professor for at least six years and fulfill the first five conditions for appointment as lecturer at the University of Yaoundé; and (6) be an academician of international repute who has discharged or is discharging the highest functions at an internationally recognized higher education institution.

To be appointed to the rank of assistant professor, a candidate must either (1) have passed the French *agrégation* examinations; (2) be listed as one of those qualified to teach in French institutions of higher learning; (3) hold an English Doctor of Laws or Ph.D. degree and present a written evaluation of his dissertation by the chairman of his dissertation committee; (4) hold a University of Yaoundé diploma with at least six years of experience in his field of specialization following the receipt of his diploma and with evidence of scholarly research, originality, and innovation; (5) have been a lecturer in a British university for at least six years; or (6) have been a permanent university lecturer for a least six years.

Appointment as lecturer is based on the fulfillment of at least one of the following conditions and/or requirements: (1) hold a French *doctorat d'état* or *doctorat de troisième cycle;* (2) be listed among qualified French university assistant lecturers (*maître-assistant*); (3) hold a master's degree from an English university; (4) be a lecturer in a British university; (5) present a pass in the French *agrégation* of secondary education; (6) be a graduate of the National Advanced School of Agronomy of the University of Yaoundé, holding the Diploma of Agronomy with two additional years of study or research; (7) have qualifications declared by the administrative council as equivalent of the preceding; or (8) have been an established (tenured) assistant lecturer for at least six full academic years.

Holders of the following qualifications are eligible for appointment as assistant lecturers: (1) hold a Cameroonian or French bachelor's degree (*licence*) plus a postgraduate diploma; (2) hold a Cameroonian or French professional degree; (3) hold an English bachelor's degree (honors); (4) hold a Diploma of Agronomic Studies from the University of Yaoundé; or (5) present qualifications considered by the administrative council as equivalent of those previously mentioned.

The conditions and qualifications for appointment to the academic staff are being reviewed in accordance with the recommendations of the Council for Higher Education and Scientific and Technical Research of December 18–22, 1974. Foreign qualifications, such as the French *agrégation* (competitive examinations), and the applicant's appearance on foreign lists of qualified teachers are to be canceled. By early 1976 the changes had not yet been implemented.

All teaching staff of the university are expected and encouraged to carry out research. If facilities are not available in Cameroon, they are permitted to go abroad. All research is funded by the government through the university.

Current Problems and Trends

Most of Cameroon's higher education problems stem from the bilingual nature of the nation and the university. The fact that the university is bilingual is, in itself, an innovation in African higher education. Students of the higher education institutions are products of the British and French educational systems. Since English and French are the media of instruction at the university, students who do not know both languages may encounter difficulties.

Cameroon is also attempting to integrate the best in the British and French educational systems with the Cameroon system and is forging a system of higher education that is Cameroonian in nature and character. Like most, if not all, developing countries, Cameroon is constantly striving to make its educational system relevant to its needs and environment. To achieve a more balanced educational development, the government in June 1976 announced

a plan to develop four new university campuses: at Douala (business administration and commerce), Buea (languages and letters), Ngaoundere (sciences, animal husbandry), and Dschang (agriculture). Other important reforms are taking place at the university. The bachelor's degree program will no longer be three years but will require four years for all faculties and will be followed by a doctoral degree program. Details of the programs are presently being worked out. The combined law and economics degree program will be a separate entity to itself.

International Cooperation

The government of Cameroon has signed bilateral and multilateral cooperation agreements in the area of higher education. Technical assistance personnel in Cameroon higher education institutions work under the terms of the cooperation agreements. The departments of French and English of the faculty of arts and social sciences and the Advanced Teacher Training College cooperate with universities in France and Britain. After their first year, successful students in the bilingual series spend a year either in France (English-speaking students) or in Britain (French-speaking students) for intensive language courses. Students of the Yaoundé Advanced International School of Journalism spend their third year in France. Some students of the National School of Administration and Magistracy spend a few months to one year in France for practical training. The School of Journalism and the Cameroon Institute of International Relations are cooperative ventures between African nations and foreign foundations.

The Demographic Institute and the Institute for Statistical Training, established jointly by the United Nations and the Cameroon government, serve all francophone Africa and Madagascar. The International Insurance Institute was established by African countries, France, and Madagascar, all of which are members of the International Conference of Insurance

Control. The Protestant Faculty of Theology is an inter-African, international, and interdenominational establishment. The Roman Catholic Major Seminary, in Nkolbisson, which serves francophone Africa, is affiliated to the *Institut de sciences religieuses de Paris*, while the Regional Major Seminary, in Bambui, is seeking affiliation with the *Pontificia Universitas Urbaniana* in Rome.

SOLOMON NFOR GWEI

Bibliography

Gwei, S. N. "Education in Cameroon: Western Pre-Colonial and Colonial Antecedents and the Development of Higher Education." Unpublished doctoral dissertation, University of Michigan, Ann Arbor, 1975.

Moumouni, A. *Education in Africa.* New York: Praeger, 1968.

Note d'information rapide sur les missions de formation de l'Institut international des assurances de Yaoundé (IIA). Yaoundé: Institut international des assurances de Yaoundé, 1975.

Statistical Yearbook 1973–1974. Vol. 1: *Primary Education;* Vol. 2: *Secondary Schools, Teacher Training College and Higher Education.* Yaoundé: Ministry of National Education, 1975.

See also: Africa, Sub-Saharan: Regional Analysis; Archives: Africa and Asia, National Archives of; Health Services, Worldwide University.

CAMPUS AND THE CITY, THE (Higher Education Report), United States

The Campus and the City: Maximizing Assets and Reducing Liabilities (New York: McGraw-Hill, December 1972), a report of the Carnegie Commission on Higher Education, examines the relationship between higher education and the city in the United States. The report considers the three major functions of higher education institutions—teaching, research, and public service—as they relate to the urban setting. The following findings and recommendations are reported.

Urban universities have an environmental, economic, cultural, and political impact on the cities. Consequently, larger universities should create an office for urban affairs and an advisory council to provide information on urban activities to members of the campus and community. Colleges and universities should also develop policies to regulate institutional urban-related activities. In addition, metropolitan higher education councils should be formed to serve as coordinating agencies, and metropolitan educational opportunity counseling centers should be established.

Certain metropolitan areas should improve access to higher education, with particular emphasis on open admissions or flexible admissions. In addition, colleges and universities should provide individualized educational programs and increased counseling services and should devote a greater part of their resources to entry-level students. The commission supports efforts to disperse educational programs throughout metropolitan areas in off-campus facilities and recommends that learning pavilions be established at community colleges and comprehensive colleges as home bases for adult learners.

Community colleges are particularly well suited to meet the needs of the urban student and should expand their vocational and occupational programs; comprehensive colleges, on the other hand, should provide services, undertake needed applied research, and expand access to upper-division undergraduate studies; finally, universities in urban areas should focus on basic research and professional training.

Research is higher education's traditional response to urban problems, but the absence of basic social science research methodology has restricted its actual impact on urban affairs. Colleges and universities have also responded to the problems of the city by developing urban study programs that have become highly specialized but have not significantly influenced general curricula.

Recognizing the difficulties of increased university involvement with the cities, the commission cautions that knowledge is insufficient to solve the problems of the city, and institutions of higher education may better serve as creators of ideas than as vehicles for action. Nevertheless, it supports a renewed emphasis on public service with student, faculty, and institutional participation. Each institution should select service activities that are an integral part of its educational program and that do not duplicate the activities of other institutions.

The commission recommends increased state and federal spending for higher education programs in urban areas; it also recommends that the federal government provide urban grants to ten selected universities for the purpose of increasing their urban commitment. Finally, it warns that time for solving urban problems is short and stresses that colleges and universities, cities, counties, states, and the federal government must renew their commitment to enhancing the quality of urban life through the development of the urban campus.

CAMPUS CRUSADE FOR CHRIST INTERNATIONAL

Campus Crusade for Christ International, an interdenominational Christian movement of students and laymen, was founded in 1951. The organization operates with a staff of more than 4600 and active volunteer groups in sixty-eight countries of the world. Campus Crusade field ministries include campus, high school, lay, athletic, military, music, and international student groups. The Agape Movement is a ministry that provides men and women with an opportunity to use their vocational training to help reach many areas of the world with the message of Christ. The Mass Media Ministry works through literature, radio and television, audiovisual materials, and film.

At Campus Crusade's international headquarters in San Bernardino, California, and in other facilities around the world, Campus Crusade for Christ offers training in evangelism. Institutes of Biblical Studies are held to teach college and high school students more about the Bible and

how to live the Christian life. The organization has also sponsored two international congresses on evangelism. Some 80,000 Christians gathered in Dallas, Texas, for Explo '72; and in August 1974 more than 320,000 people from eighty countries met in Seoul, Korea, for Explo '74. Campus Crusade is supported entirely by contributions.

Publications include *Worldwide Challenge,* monthly; *Collegiate Challenge* and *Athletes in Action,* annuals; and *Student Action,* quarterly college and high school newspaper. *Revolution Now!* and *Come Help Change the World* (books by Dr. Bill Bright) and other manuals and booklets designed to help Christians grow in their faith are also available.

Arrowhead Springs
San Bernardino, California 92414 USA

CAMPUS INTERNATIONAL OFFICES
See Exchange, International: Campus International Offices.

CAMPUS SECURITY
See Security, Campus.

CAMPUS TENSIONS (Higher Education Report), United States

Campus Tensions: Analysis and Recommendations (Washington, D.C.: American Council on Education, 1970)—the report of a special committee established by the American Council on Education, under the chairmanship of S. Linowitz—examines tensions on United States college and university campuses and suggests constructive institutional responses.

Noting that only a minority of colleges have experienced disruptive protest but that student support for university reform is widespread, the report proposes areas for reform based on issues raised by students, faculty, administrators, and trustees. It recommends increased student autonomy and self-government in nonacademic areas, along with opportunities for participation in other university decisions. Tenure policies should be reappraised, and the balance between the faculty's research and teaching responsibilities should be redressed. New approaches to teaching and faculty involvement in institutional change should be encouraged. Administrative responsibility and accountability should be clearly defined, and open channels of communication and agreed-upon procedures for handling campus disruption should be established. The role of the trustees must also be clearly defined; reform of the board of trustees should include measures to promote public accountability and communication with students and faculty.

While characterizations of tensions and recommendations for reform are not uniformly applicable, the committee urges institutions of higher education to initiate self-examination and self-reform to resolve the problems revealed in its study of campus tensions.

CAMPUS UNREST
See Unrest, Campus.

CAMPUS UNREST
(Higher Education Report), United States

Campus Unrest (New York: Arno Press, 1970)—a report of the President's Commission on Campus Unrest, under the chairmanship of William Scranton—examines dissent, disorder, and violence in United States institutions of higher education. It reviews the history of campus unrest; examines the role and influence of the civil rights movement, the peace movement, the growing drive for university reform, and the new youth culture; and recommends means of dealing with grievances and minimizing violence. The following findings and recommendations are reported.

Contemporary protest has focused on the war in Vietnam, racial injustice, and the university. The causes of unrest are complex and are rooted in worldwide social and philosophical movements. Most protest is peaceful and fully protected under the first amendment to the United States Constitution. Responsibility for the violence that has occurred rests with politically extreme students and faculty, unwarranted force employed by law enforcement officers, universities inadequately prepared to respond to disruption, government actions and inactions, and the national failure to resolve the issues of race and war.

Only the moral leadership of the president of the United States can bring the country together again. The president is admonished that an end to the war is of primary importance. He is urged to renew the nation's commitment to social justice and to become fully informed of student and minority viewpoints. Government officials and organizations are urged to realize the impact of their public statements, review all policies affecting universities, increase financial aid to higher education, and institute strict controls over public access to firearms. Law enforcement agencies must be fully trained to deal legally and humanely with campus disorders.

The commission recommends that universities develop the capacity to deal internally with campus dissent, remove disruptive faculty, and reform governance procedures. It urges the universities to reaffirm the proper traditions of teaching and learning by maintaining political neutrality, decentralizing large campuses, and reducing outside commitments. In addition, students should exercise restraint in their demands and should respect the rule of the majority.

The commission upholds the full protection of all legal dissent and charges that the obligation for ending violence rests with all segments of society.

CAMPUSES, BRANCH
See Branch Campuses.

CAMPUSES, OVERSEAS

See Branch Campuses.

CANADA COUNCIL

The Canada Council is a corporation created by an Act of Parliament in 1957 to foster and promote the study and enjoyment of, and the production of works in, the arts, humanities, and social sciences. Setting its own policies within the terms of the Canada Council Act, the council reports to Parliament through the secretary of state and appears before the Standing Committee on Broadcasting, Films and Assistance to the Arts.

The Canada Council consists of a chairperson, a vice-chairperson, and nineteen other members, all appointed by the Canadian government. The council meets four or five times a year, usually in Ottawa, where the council offices are located. The council is assisted by a permanent staff and numerous outside advisers. The Advisory Arts Panel and the Advisory Academic Panel, for example, play a major role in the development of council policies and programs.

Annual grants from Parliament are the council's main source of income. The council is also supported by a fifty-million-dollar endowment fund established by Parliament in 1957. The council has received substantial amounts of private donations and bequests, usually for specific purposes.

Supporting music, opera, dance, theater, visual arts, film, video, photography, and writing, the council offers senior arts, arts, short-term, travel, and project-cost grants in these fields to professional artists and persons whose work is essential to the professional arts. The council makes operating and special-project grants available to professional arts organizations and arts support services; sponsors a limited number of artists-in-residence within universities, cultural organizations, and municipalities; and assists museums, libraries, and postsecondary institutions wishing to invite Canadian writers to give public readings of their works. In addition, the council offers production and postproduction grants to individuals and organizations for the creation of film and video works of an experimental and artistic nature.

The council offers grants to Canadian majority-owned publishing firms for the publication or translation of a wide range of books; supports literary and arts periodicals; and purchases Canadian books for free distribution to Canadian groups and foreign users through the Department of External Affairs. Through its Art Bank, the council purchases works by professional Canadian artists and rents them to government departments and agencies for display in public areas. Through its Touring Office, the council provides subsidies, technical assistance, and support services to encourage and coordinate touring by Canadian performing artists and companies and make their performances accessible to a wider audience. The council organizes regional training workshops for local sponsors; publishes the *Touring Directory of the Performing Arts* and the *Sponsors' Handbook for Touring;* and coordinates Canadian performing arts tours abroad on behalf of the Department of External Affairs.

The council's program in the humanities and social sciences includes assistance in some twenty-nine disciplines. In these disciplines and related interdisciplinary studies, the council offers special M.A., doctoral, and leave fellowships; research grants for individual research projects; program grants to university teams of researchers; major editorial grants for long-term publishing projects involving research; and general research grants to universities to cover small research expenses of their faculty.

The council assists Canadian learned journals and occasional scholarly conferences held in Canada and provides administrative support to a number of Canadian learned societies, the Humanities Research Council, and the Social Science Research

Council. The latter two organizations also receive block grants from the Canada Council to support publication of scholarly books and encourage attendance at annual meetings of Canadian learned societies.

Under its Explorations Program, the council supports projects dealing with Canada's cultural and historical heritage and projects that explore new forms of expression and creativity in the arts, humanities, and social sciences. Projects must deal directly with a Canadian situation or have strong implications for Canadians. Unlike other council programs, which are directed toward professional artists and scholars, the Explorations Program provides grants to any Canadian individual or organization whose project is judged to be deserving of assistance.

On behalf of the Canadian government, the council administers several programs of academic and cultural exchanges with foreign countries. Under these programs, the council supports visits to Canadian universities and cultural organizations by foreign researchers, lecturers, graduate students, and distinguished artists in all disciplines; it also supports visits abroad by Canadian researchers and lecturers in the humanities and social sciences.

The council administers the funds of the Canadian Cultural Institute in Rome. The institute's annual income has been used to offer fellowships to one or two prominent Canadian artists or scholars wishing to work or study in Italy.

Under the Killam Program, the council offers senior and postdoctoral research scholarships and I. W. Killam Memorial Awards to assist scholars of exceptional ability engaged in research projects of far-reaching significance in the humanities, social sciences, interdisciplinary studies, or studies embracing the natural sciences, medicine, or engineering.

Three prizes, worth twenty thousand dollars each, are given annually. Ranked among Canada's highest tokens of recognition for cultural achievement in the arts, humanities, or social sciences, they are fi-

nanced from a gift to the council by the Molson Foundation. The Governor General's Literary Awards are given each year for three English and three French books written by Canadians. Each winner receives twenty-five hundred dollars from the Canada Council. Translation prizes are offered by the council for the year's best translations of Canadian books. The two annual prizes, worth twenty-five hundred dollars each, are for the best English-to-French translation and the best French-to-English translation.

The Canada-Belgium Literary Prize is cosponsored by the Canadian and Belgian governments. Worth twenty-five hundred dollars, this prize is awarded in alternate years to a French-language Belgian or Canadian writer on the basis of the writer's complete works. The Vincent Massey Awards for Excellence in the Urban Environment—cosponsored by the Canada Council, the Massey Foundation, and the Central Mortgage and Housing Corporation—are given every two to four years. They are for Canadian projects that have made a significant contribution to the amenity of urban life.

The Canada Council provides the budget and secretariat for the Canadian Commission for UNESCO. The principal function of the commission is to serve as a nonpolitical liaison agency between UNESCO and Canadian public and private bodies concerned with education, science, culture, and communications. The commission operates the Canadian Communications Research Information Centre, a national clearinghouse of information on communications policy, research, resources, and activities.

The council has a number of publications that describe its programs and services. These publications are available at Information Canada Enquiry Centres, at regional offices of the Secretary of State Citizenship Branch, and at the council office.

P.O. Box 1047
Ottawa, Ontario, Canada K1P 5V8

CANADA, DOMINION OF

Population: 22,779,000. Student enrollment in primary school: 3,775,710; secondary school (academic, vocational, technical): 1,770,000; higher education (university): 314,650; higher education (nonuniversity): 238,560; higher education (total): 553,210. Student enrollment in higher education as percentage of age group (18–21) 33% (1975). Language of instruction: English, French. Academic calendar: September to May, two or three terms. Percentage of gross national product (GNP) expended on higher education (recurrent expenditures): 2.2% (1974). [Source: Statistics Canada; except where otherwise indicated, figures are 1975–76 estimates.]

Until the mid 1960s the term *higher education* was usually applied in Canada to all educational activity beyond secondary school, but by the mid 1970s its use had become more restrictive. With the establishment of a large number of nonuniversity colleges and the expansion of facilities for continuing education, the term *postsecondary education* has gained wide acceptance because it is more inclusive. The term *higher education* is now used to denote the sector within which undergraduate and professional programs, together with graduate studies and research, are centered in the universities. It is in this sense that the term is used in this article.

The roots of Canadian education reach deep into the colonial period. The four provinces that formed the Canadian confederation in 1867—Nova Scotia, New Brunswick, Quebec, and Ontario—had already well-established educational traditions. These were confirmed by the British North America Act (1867), which gave each provincial legislature control over education. The principle was reaffirmed when each of the six other provinces were admitted to confederation, three during the 1870s, two in 1905, and the latest in 1949.

Although there was no specific reference to higher education in the British North America Act, there were seventeen universities in Canada at the time of its enact-ment. This was a surprisingly large number of institutions for a population estimated at only 3,500,000. Only five of these enrolled over one hundred students. All held royal charters at the time of confederation; and, although there is no legal restriction preventing the federal government from granting university charters, all the existing institutions have obtained new or amended charters from the authorities of the province in which they are located.

Most of the colonial universities were under religious control. The oldest, *Université Laval*, traces its origin to a Jesuit college established in 1635 and to the *Séminaire de Québec*, which was opened in 1663. It was granted its charters as a university by Queen Victoria in 1852 and by the Pope in 1876. A provincial charter in 1970 replaced the earlier ones and made it a secular institution. In the maritime provinces of New Brunswick and Nova Scotia, which were colonies of British origin, King's Colleges were established, and over these the Anglican authorities usually claimed control. Such claims were strongly protested by the other denominational groups. As a result, in the maritime provinces of New Brunswick and Nova Scotia separate institutions were established for Baptists, Methodists, and Roman Catholics; and in Ontario a separate institution was established for Presbyterians as well. Only Dalhousie University in Halifax and McGill University in Montreal were nonsectarian.

During the preconfederation period, regional patterns of higher education became clearly established. In the maritime provinces the universities were small, residential, and denominational in character. In Ontario the University of Toronto became a secular institution within which a number of denominational universities were federated. Only the Presbyterian Queen's University and the Roman Catholic University of Ottawa remained private. In Quebec a system of classical colleges, eight-year institutions operated by various religious orders, developed around *Université Laval*. These colleges offered a combined secondary and undergraduate program that led to a B.A. degree awarded by the parent university. Eventually this system was expanded; and *Université de Montréal,* which itself had been an affiliate of Laval, was granted a separate charter in 1921 and developed a similar system of satellite colleges. In a modified form even McGill University adopted the same practice with a few colleges both within and outside the province.

Another element was introduced when the western provinces joined the confederation (Manitoba in 1870, British Columbia in 1871, Alberta and Saskatchewan in 1905). Provincial universities were established and supported directly by the provincial governments. These institutions were closely articulated with the other levels of the educational systems and were encouraged to provide extension services for the benefit of the general public.

It was only after the outbreak of World War II that the national importance of the universities became generally recognized. Until then—with the exceptions of McGill University and the University of Toronto, which had attained international reputations for scientific research and scholarship—Canadian universities were normally regarded as significant only in the region or province in which they were located. The war effort produced an abrupt change in attitude. Suddenly faced with the problems of securing highly qualified manpower for research, mass production, technical innovation, organization, and management, the federal government placed heavy and continuing demands on the universities. University leaders responded quickly to the challenge. New programs were introduced to support the armed services and to intensify scientific research, while committees were formed to advise the government on matters such as selective service and veterans' rehabilitation.

Out of this collaboration came the Veterans' Rehabilitation Program, by which the federal government paid tuition and cost-of-living grants to about 50,000 veterans in the five years after 1945. As a result, university enrollments more than doubled; although the increase was largest in several of the city institutions, almost all the universities participated in the program and benefited from it. Moreover, by increasing their capacity to accommodate the veterans, the universities were better prepared for the rising wave of graduates from the secondary schools who demanded entry in the early 1950s.

Growing national awareness of the importance of higher education led to the appointment of a Royal Commission on National Development in the Arts, Letters and Sciences, which showed its concern by stating in its report in 1951: "Universities have become essential institutions of Higher Education, of general culture, of specialized and professional training and of advanced scientific research. . . . if financial stringency prevents these great institutions from being, as they have said, 'nurseries of a truly Canadian civilization and culture,' we are convinced that this is a matter of national concern" (Royal Commission on National Development, 1951).

Since 1960 the action of the federal and provincial levels of government has altered the structure of higher education. Ten new university charters were granted in the 1950s and a dozen more since then. The total number in 1973 was sixty-six, of which a number held their degree-granting power in abeyance while in federation or affiliation with other universities. About twenty-five are multifaculty institutions with a full range of professional and graduate programs. All charge tuition fees, although political parties in some provinces have officially adopted a policy of free instruction. Furthermore, an alternative to university programs is now offered in more than a hundred nonuniversity colleges where tuition is low and, in one province (Quebec), even free. The number of part-time students in both the colleges and the universities is increasing rapidly.

Over the past century the institutions of higher education in Canada have moved step by step toward maturity. They have found a reasonable compromise between the traditions of Europe and the realities of an open society in North America. They have reconciled denominational origins with the liberalism of Canada's open society. Regional patterns of higher education have evolved which encourage interchange and cooperative planning among sister institutions. During and after World War II the universities provided leadership in all walks of public life, and they intensified and diversified their research programs to support the war effort and reconstruction. When hostilities were over, they opened their doors to men and women from the armed services, helping them to reestablish themselves in civilian life. In the 1960s they rose to the challenge of vastly increased enrollments, working closely with governments and other public agencies and, at the same time, reorganizing their own internal structures. Canadian universities have drawn from the examples of others; yet they have now developed an individuality of their own.

Admission Requirements

Admission to Canadian universities usually follows twelve years of schooling, although in the central provinces of Ontario and Quebec the requirement is thirteen years. Ontario requires an extended course in high school, while Quebec requires the completion of a two-year course in the colleges of general and vocational education. Each university, and in some instances each faculty, exercises control over its own admissions standards and policies. Until a few years ago applicants were judged on their record in the departmental examinations at the end of the high school course and on their general school record as reported by the principal. Since 1965, however, departmental examinations have been discontinued in most provinces, and the school record is now the basis for judgment, together with special tests such as those of the Educational Testing Service or the Service for Admission to College

and University. Almost all universities now make provision for "mature matriculation," which permits them to accept students whose qualifications do not meet normal admissions standards.

Administration and Control

The traditional form of university government in Canada is the "two-tier" system: a board of governors and an academic senate or council, with a president or principal acting as chief executive officer. By statute, the corporate power usually resides in the board of governors, which makes the final decisions on all matters of policy. The board is usually composed primarily of laymen but often includes faculty and students; the size and composition vary with the kind of control under which the university operates. In church-related universities the majority may be clerics; in provincial universities the power of nomination usually rests with the lieutenant-governor, and some members may represent the government directly; in other institutions the board is a self-perpetuating body, perhaps with representation from graduates and faculty.

The duties of the board include the appointment of the president or principal, the exercise of financial control, and approval of recommendations from the senate on academic matters. In practice, the board gives its attention to matters that are not strictly academic, although, because of its responsibilities in fund raising and the financial operations of the institution, it naturally exercises a good deal of influence on many academic decisions.

The senate is generally responsible for academic policy. Its membership is drawn from the administrative and academic staff, and the president or principal usually acts as the presiding officer. In some instances, particularly in the provincial universities, the senate may include members chosen by community groups with a special interest in the university. The charter usually specifies the powers to be exercised by the senate; normally these powers include admissions, approval of academic courses and programs, appointment of academic staff, student discipline, and the granting of degrees, both in-course and honorary.

As a rule, both the board and the senate deal with the recommendations from subsidiary bodies, such as statutory or ad hoc committees, faculties, and departments. In this way it is possible to draw on the advice of a much broader representation from the university than would be included in the membership of either body.

A third element in the internal government of the university is represented by the chancellor and vice-chancellor. The duties of the chancellor are usually performed by a person of distinction, who acts as the honorary or ceremonial head of the institution. In Roman Catholic universities, this is usually the bishop in whose diocese the institution is located. In some instances, the chancellor may preside at board meetings, but it is more usual for the board of governors to elect its own chairman.

The chief executive officer is titled, variously, president, principal, rector, or vice-chancellor. The title depends on the traditions of the institution: president is borrowed from the practice of the United States, vice-chancellor is copied from English universities, principal is borrowed from Scotland, and rector is the nomenclature used in France. As the senior administrative official, the president acts as a link between the lay board of governors and the academic senate. Although his appointment is made by the board, the senate and other representatives of the faculty and students are frequently consulted in making the nomination. As a rule, the candidate has been a university professor and is a person with a scholarly background.

Since 1965, with the growing complexity of university operations, most of the institutions have provided for the appointment of vice-presidents or vice-principals with responsibilities in such areas as academic policy, administration, research, finance, and planning. The number and duties of these senior officials vary from one institution to another, as does the manner in which they discharge their duties. Frequently they act through statutory bodies such as an academic or planning committee, reporting through the senate to the president and board of governors.

After conducting a survey of university government in Canada, Sir James Duff and Dr. R. O. Berdahl recommended a number of reforms in 1966. They suggested that the two-tier pattern of university government be retained but that the powers of the board of governors and senate be more clearly defined and the two bodies brought into closer contact at many stages in the legislative process. They also proposed that administrative officers—including the president, vice-presidents, and deans—be chosen by special committees on which staff and students are represented. As a result, at most universities students are now included on most committees, and faculty members and students are elected to the board of governors and the senate.

One of the more controversial experiments is the adoption of a one-tier system of government, sometimes with representation from all interested groups, including administrators, teachers, students, and graduates. Laval adopted a one-tier structure under its first charter in 1852; the University of Toronto has done so more recently. There is some evidence that other universities may move in the same direction.

Most Canadian universities are organized through faculties which are responsible for various aspects of internal administration: determining admission requirements, approving courses, recommending candidates for degrees, and establishing the calendar, timetables, and examination procedures. The traditional structure of European universities included four faculties: theology, law, medicine, and letters. This structure has been most closely followed in the French-language institutions, where faculties of philosophy and social sciences have also been added. In the English-language universities the central faculty is that of arts and science, which offers instruction in the humanities and the social, physical, and biological sciences. In a few universities the arts and science sections have now been separated into faculties, while in some of the smaller institutions there is a single faculty, as in the liberal arts colleges of the United States. New professional faculties have been added in most of the larger universities, where agriculture, commerce, dentistry, education, engineering, and music now enjoy separate status.

Within each faculty there is a departmental structure based on the individual discipline or subject. Specialization in recent years has led to a demand for the subdivision of many of the older departments. Where research has led to the introduction of graduate degrees, a faculty of graduate studies and research has usually been established, with undergraduate and graduate instruction provided by the same department.

The senior officer of each faculty is the dean, who is appointed—usually for a limited period of three to five years—by the board of governors on the recommendation of the president or principal after consultation with representatives of the staff and students. He is a member of the senate and is the official spokesman of the faculty. His duties include the preparation of the annual budget in consultation with each departmental chairman. Practices vary a good deal, both in the method of appointing chairmen and in the responsibilities confided to them. In the larger institutions they, or a certain number of their representatives, form a "faculty council" under the chairmanship of the dean.

Variations are found in internal structures at some universities, where departments are organized as colleges or schools. These may focus on particular areas of study, such as commerce or business administration, education, engineering, journalism, library science, pharmacy, or social work. Usually these units report through one of the faculties. With the demand for

interdisciplinary studies, even these innovations have not proved sufficiently flexible; consequently, in an experiment introduced at *Université du Québec*, the faculty structure has been abandoned and a modular pattern adopted in its place. Under this plan, the basic unit is the department to which each professor is attached. The student is related to a module, which is a course or program of study that may cut across departmental lines. The modules vary in size and are composed of professors and students, who have parity in the membership on the module council.

The demand for interdepartmental cooperation has been particularly strong in the areas of graduate studies and research. This demand has resulted in the establishment of various institutes and centers through which the resources of a number of departments may be directed toward problems considered of special character or urgency. Examples of these are the Islamic Institute at McGill University, the Centre for Culture and Technology at the University of Toronto, the Institute of Environmental Studies at the University of Waterloo (Ontario), the Center for Northern Studies at *Université Laval*, the Institute of Criminology at *Université de Montréal*, the Boreal Institute for Northern Studies at the University of Alberta, and the Institute of Oceanography at the University of British Columbia.

Programs and Degrees

Most universities offer the first or bachelor's degree after three or four years of full-time study, usually in the faculty of arts and science. In some institutions, however, a first degree is also granted in engineering and education. Admission to faculties of law, medicine, dentistry, business administration, and theology is frequently conditional upon the completion of part or all of the requirements for the first degree. A distinction is often made between general and honors degrees at the bachelor's level, the difference being that the honors degree is more specialized and usually requires an additional year of study.

The master's degree is awarded in the same fields as the bachelor's degree and requires from one to two years of full-time study. The doctoral degree, Ph.D., generally requires an additional three years beyond the master's degree and is awarded after completion of a comprehensive examination (usually in education) or a doctoral thesis.

Provision is made for part-time students, and a number of universities also conduct off-campus courses in various centers. For these part-time and off-campus students a "credit system" has been adopted, whereby one or more credits are granted upon successful completion of each course and the candidate is expected to accumulate a specific number of credits within a certain period of time. The usual requirement is twenty credits for the first degree.

Experiments have been initiated with both year-round operation and work-study programs. While most of the universities operate summer schools, only one has actually adopted a twelve-month calendar. This is Simon Fraser University, in Burnaby, British Columbia, where the academic year is divided into three terms and students may enter in the autumn, winter, or spring. They may choose to continue their studies without interruption and thereby speed up their courses if they wish to do so. Wellington College at the University of Guelph, in Ontario, has also adopted modified programs. The work-study pattern, whereby the student alternates between supervised regular employment and classroom study, has been adopted in the faculties of engineering, mathematics, and science at the University of Waterloo. It is also in operation in certain faculties of *Université de Sherbrooke* (Quebec), the University of Regina (Saskatchewan); the University of Lethbridge (Alberta), and Memorial University of Newfoundland.

There has been a steady trend toward greater flexibility in curriculum requirements. The practice of adopting a fixed pattern of course sequences has been modified, and students are permitted to choose from a number of options. Experiments have also been conducted in cooperative planning of courses, with students and faculty participating in the process of course design, and in the determination of requirements and methods of examination. Perhaps the most advanced of these programs is one offered by the University of Waterloo, where the student may set his own goals and proceed toward them through independent research, course work, seminars, tutorials, special projects, and fieldwork. Upon completion of the curriculum the candidate qualifies for the degree of Bachelor of Independent Studies.

The typical method of instruction in Canadian universities is still the formal lecture, usually given twice weekly and supplemented by a conference or laboratory period in smaller groups in the professional faculties. This is varied by clinical teaching in medicine, shopwork in engineering, and fieldwork in areas as different as surveying and social work. In recent years expanding enrollments have created problems which the authorities have attempted to meet by giving parallel instruction to several divisions, by the use of television, and, in a few instances, by computer-aided instruction. To meet the criticism of impersonal relations between professors and students, counseling services have been introduced for new students, and, whenever possible, seminars, conferences, and tutorial programs are used.

At most of the universities the language of instruction is English. French is used at *Université de Moncton* in New Brunswick; and two of the universities in Ontario, the University of Ottawa and Laurentian University of Sudbury, are bilingual. Of the seven universities in Quebec, four offer instruction in French, three in English. Since both English and French are official languages in Canada, the federal government has made special funds available for instruction and scholarships to encourage bilingualism.

Financing

As a result of the pressure built up during the operation of the Veterans' Rehabilitation Program in 1945 and the opinions expressed before the Royal Commission, the federal government took action in 1952 to support higher education directly. Parliament approved a vote of C$7,000,000 (50 cents per capita of the Canadian population) to be distributed to the provinces according to their population and divided among the universities on the basis of their full-time enrollment. The amount was subsequently increased: in 1957 to $1 per capita; in 1958 to $1.50 per capita; in 1962 to $2 per capita; and in 1965 to $5 per capita. Throughout this period the payments were made directly to the institutions. Following objections by some of the provinces that this practice was unconstitutional, the procedure was changed in 1966, and payments since then have been made directly to the provincial authorities instead of to the universities. Moreover, the payments are now based on the operating costs for all types of postsecondary education, the provinces being free to choose between a per capita grant or 50 percent of the admissible expenditures. The federal contribution has more than doubled since the program began in 1967 and in 1974 amounted to about one billion dollars.

Provincial governments also responded by increasing their financial support to universities which became integrated within the provincial system. This meant little adjustment in the western provinces, although each found it necessary to break the monopoly of a single provincial university, and one or more new charters were granted. In the central provinces and the maritime provinces (New Brunswick, Nova Scotia, and Prince Edward Island), however, most of the institutions were private, and, although none held large endowments, they were accustomed to draw some support from private and church sources. Virtually all have now accepted the restrictions imposed by the govern-

ments and are supported mainly from public funds. The restrictions include cooperation among themselves in planning new development, limitation of tuition fees, elimination of sectarian restrictions on staff and students, and, in some instances, the acceptance of guidelines for determining salaries. Public support has resulted in a decline in revenue from other sources. In order to protect the universities from excessive political interference, most provinces have created statutory councils or commissions with representation from the government, the universities, and the public. These bodies have authority to examine budgets and plans for development and to make recommendations to the government. In three provinces postsecondary institutions have been placed under a special minister and department of government to ensure that the problems of higher education are given special consideration. Thus, it may be said that virtually all Canadian universities are public institutions; and, because of the power of the provincial authorities, the fear has even been expressed that they are in danger of becoming provincial, rather than national or international, in outlook.

Student Social Background and Access to Education

Until the 1960s students were usually considered as minors. Although they were permitted to engage in a wide range of extracurricular activities, including athletics, drama, and publications, they had no voice in matters of academic policy or student discipline. Since then they have gained representation on departmental and faculty committees and even on the senate or board of governors. In some instances they have been included on committees for the appointment or promotion of members of staff, although this practice is by no means general. One factor in this change has been the action of the federal and provincial governments in lowering the voting age to eighteen—about the normal age for entry to the university and, although legal anomalies still exist, generally considered the age of majority.

Full-time attendance at universities in 1974 represented some 12 percent of the eighteen-year to twenty-four-year age group. This proportion is twice what it was in 1960. In addition, there are over 100,000 students registered in part-time programs. Men outnumber women by nearly two to one, but the proportion of women has been rising steadily in the 1970s and is expected to continue to do so. Participation rates vary from province to province and are naturally affected by the structure and retentiveness of the school system. Participation is highest in the western provinces, where the universities have always been articulated with the educational system and lowest in the maritime provinces, where most of the institutions are private and denominational.

The introduction of alternative institutions—the colleges of applied arts and technology in Ontario, the colleges of general and vocational education in Quebec, and community colleges elsewhere—has undoubtedly altered the composition of the student body in the universities. It may be expected that the universities will remain selective but that the criteria for selection will be raised to a higher level and the period of study may be reduced. The colleges will probably become responsible for providing general education to graduates of the high schools, while the universities will continue as centers of advanced, specialized, and professional studies and research.

Teaching Staff

For appointment to the staff of most Canadian universities, a doctoral degree is normally required. During the 1960s, however, when the number of professors more than tripled, it was not possible to maintain this standard; and, in practice, it is applied only in the pure sciences. In the social sciences and humanities many candidates are accepted who hold a master's degree, with the understanding that they will continue their studies toward higher qualifications. It is estimated that about half of the full-time university professors hold the doctoral degree.

The lowest rank is that of lecturer. This is usually a one-year appointment, and the Canadian candidate is expected to have completed his undergraduate studies with honors or distinction and to have obtained a master's degree. If he has continued in a doctoral program, it is frequently at a university in the United States, Britain, or France. After a year or more of satisfactory service and upon proof of suitable scholarship or experience, the candidate may be appointed to the rank of assistant professor on a two- or three-year contract. From this point he becomes eligible for promotion to associate professor and professor or, in the French-language institutions, *professeur agrégé* and *professeur titulaire*. The rules for promotion and tenure vary from one university to another, with the chairman of the department and dean of the faculty exercising a good deal of discretionary power, although most universities now require consideration by a promotion and tenure committee.

Current Problems and Trends

The process of change in recent years has been shaped in Canada by studies conducted either by provincial governments or by national organizations supported by the universities themselves. In 1961 Quebec took the initiative in appointing a Royal Commission to examine all aspects and types of education in the province, and the five-volume report devotes several chapters to reform in the universities (Royal Commission of Enquiry, 1963–1965). Other provinces have conducted similar studies, although usually concentrating their attention on one sector or problem at a time. In addition, the Association of Universities and Colleges of Canada, sometimes in cooperation with the Canadian Association of University

Teachers, has sponsored a number of studies in areas such as the financing of higher education, university government, and accessibility to higher education.

International Cooperation

University leaders in Canada have not been satisfied with introspection. Since the 1960s they have been deeply involved in programs to assist developing nations. Large numbers of foreign students have been admitted to Canadian universities on Commonwealth Scholarships and other similar projects. Institutes have been established on many campuses to encourage the study of special areas. Some universities have established and maintained service or instructional units in various parts of the world. The Canadian International Development Agency is responsible for educational and technical assistance, much of which is related to the universities. In 1970–71 the expenditure on foreign educational programs was C\$36,623,000. In that year nearly 1500 students and another 1200 trainees were studying in Canadian institutions, and 700 Canadian teachers were assigned to posts overseas.

DAVID C. MUNROE

Educational Association

Canadian Association of University Teachers
66 Lisgar Street
Ottawa, Ontario, Canada K2P 0C1

Bibliography

Adell, B. L., and Carter, D. C. *Collective Bargaining for University Faculty in Canada.* Kingston, Ontario: Industrial Relations Centre, Queen's University, 1972.

Campbell, G. *Community Colleges in Canada.* Scarborough, Ontario: McGraw-Hill Ryerson, 1971.

Canadian Universities and Colleges. Ottawa, Ontario: Department of External Affairs, Information Division, 1974. (Also available in French.)

Daust, G., and Bélanger, P. *L'université dans une société éducative, de l'éducation des adultes à l'éducation permanente.* Montreal, Quebec: Les presses de l'Université de Montréal, 1974.

Harris, R. S., and Tremblay, A. *A Bibliography of Higher Education in Canada.* Toronto, Ontario: University of Toronto Press, 1960. (Also available in French.) Supplements in 1965 and 1971.

Harvey, E. B., and Lennards, J. L. *Key Issues in Higher Education.* Toronto, Ontario: Ontario Institute for Studies in Education, 1973.

Houwing, J. F., and Michaud, L. F. *Changes in the Composition of Governing Bodies of Canadian Universities and Colleges 1965–70.* Ottawa, Ontario: Association of Universities and Colleges of Canada, Research Division, 1972. (Also available in French.)

Munroe, D. *The Organization and Administration of Education in Canada.* Ottawa, Ontario: Information Canada, 1974.

Ostry, S. (Ed.) *Canadian Higher Education in the Seventies: A Collection of Abridged Papers Presented by the Economic Council of Canada at Montebello, Quebec, October 29–31, 1971.* Ottawa, Ontario: Information Canada, 1972.

Pike, R. M. *Who Doesn't Get to University—and Why: A Study on Accessibility to Higher Education in Canada.* Ottawa, Ontario: Association of Universities and Colleges of Canada, 1970. (Also available in French.)

Royal Commission of Enquiry on Education. *Report.* (5 vols.) Montreal, Quebec: Government of Quebec, 1963–1965. See especially vol. 2, chap. 7; vol. 5, chap. 10.

Royal Commission on National Development in the Arts, Letters and Sciences. *Report.* Ottawa, Ontario: Queen's Printer, 1951.

Statistics Canada. Education, Science and Culture Division. *University Education Growth 1960–61 to 1971–72.* Ottawa, Ontario: Information Canada, 1974. (Also available in French.)

Statistics Canada. Higher Education Section. *Degrees, Diplomas and Certificates Awarded by Canadian Degree-Granting Institutions.* Ottawa, Ontario: Information Canada, 1972. (Also available in French.)

See also: Academic Standards and Accreditation: International; Adult Education: Elderly, Programs for the; Agriculture in Higher Education: History of Agricultural Education; Aid to Other Nations: Bilateral Participation in Higher Education; Archives: Canada, Public Archives of; Cooperative Education and Off-Campus Experience: Cooperative Education Worldwide, Sandwich Plan in Commonwealth Nations; Courts and Higher Education; Graduate and Professional Education: General History and Contemporary Survey; Library Administration Outside the United States; North

America: Regional Analysis; Planning, Development, and Coordination: Regional Planning of Higher Education; Prisoners, Higher Education Programs for; Research: Financing and Control of Research; Science Policies: Highly Industrialized Nations (Free Market Economies): Canada; Short-Cycle Education.

CANADA, PUBLIC ARCHIVES OF

See Archives: Canada, Public Archives of.

CANADA, SCIENCE POLICIES OF

See Science Policies: Highly Industrialized Nations: Canada.

CANADIAN ASSOCIATION OF UNIVERSITY TEACHERS

Founded in 1951, the Canadian Association of University Teachers (CAUT) is active in promoting the interests of teachers and researchers in Canadian universities and colleges, advancing the standards of their profession, and improving the quality of higher education in Canada. The association is involved in the areas of economic benefits, academic freedom, professional relationships, university government, and relations with the federal and provincial governments.

Since its founding, CAUT has handled each year scores of faculty grievances concerning renewal of contract, promotion, tenure, and dismissal. The CAUT also lobbies individual universities to ensure that proper procedures exist and that they are used. The CAUT and its local associations favor constitutional rule rather than personal whim as the norm for university contracts. CAUT acts to protect the rights of its members, especially the right to privacy.

In 1974 CAUT lobbied at the federal and provincial levels against proposed changes in the structure of such federal granting agencies as the National Research Council, the Medical Research Council, and the Canada Council; CAUT believes that the proposed changes might deleteriously affect the research potential of

Canadian universities. The association supports the federal fiscal transfer arrangement by which the federal government pays 50 percent of the operating costs of universities.

CAUT made representations, along with the Confederation of University Faculty Associations of British Columbia, to the government of British Columbia concerning the creation of a grants commission; lobbied, along with the Manitoba Organization of Faculty Associations, to the government of Manitoba concerning the implementation of the Oliver Report on postsecondary education; protested, along with the Ontario Confederation of University Faculty Associations, certain sections of proposed legislation in Ontario concerning grants commissions and also made representations to the Ontario Ministry of Colleges and Universities concerning educational ombudsmen; and protested to the government of Quebec concerning classification procedures.

Committed to faculty collective bargaining as a means of securing the goals of the association, CAUT works closely with associations that seek certification, providing them with qualified personnel and financial assistance. The association supports collective bargaining adapted to the circumstances of each university and opposes the attempts of traditional unions to intervene.

Involved in securing better working conditions for women academics, CAUT pursues questions of equal pay, equitable hiring, fairness in granting fringe benefits, and day care for children. Through its Committee on the Status of Women Academics, CAUT has created norms in such areas as maternity leave and nepotism regulations to ensure fair treatment for women.

The CAUT locals are bargaining agents under labor legislation for librarians at the University of Manitoba and Saint Mary's University in Halifax, Nova Scotia. Librarians are members of CAUT in most local chapters.

The CAUT central office prepares material concerning fringe benefits for local salary and fringe benefit committees. The association has lobbied Statistics Canada to ensure that local associations get adequate comparative statistics for salary negotiations. The CAUT executive gives top priority to the review and improvement of pension arrangements in Canadian universities. The association plans to issue a register of retired professors.

Many provinces have set up or are considering educational television production. CAUT has joined with the Association of Canadian Television and Radio Artists (ACTRA) in a national consortium to inform members of their rights and to ensure reasonable financial returns. CAUT has worked with provincial affiliates in various parts of the country to negotiate collective bargaining agreements with such authorities. The association has also established norms for university copyright and patent policies. The CAUT Copyright Committee, in conjunction with ACTRA, is making representations to the federal government concerning proposed changes in the copyright law.

The CAUT Income Tax Committee each year drafts a tax guide which reviews income tax legislation, cases, and rulings. The guide is published in a special column in the *CAUT Bulletin*. The *CAUT Bulletin* also includes news and feature articles, book reviews, and academic advertising. Through a cooperative agreement with Clarke, Irwin & Company, a Toronto book-publishing firm, CAUT is sponsoring a series of monographs dealing with teacher evaluation in Canadian universities.

66 Lisgar Street
Ottawa, Ontario, Canada K2P 0C1

CANADIAN COUNCIL FOR INTERNATIONAL COOPERATION
(Conseil canadien pour la coopération internationale)

The Canadian Council for International Cooperation (CCIC), incorporated under

Canadian Government Charter in 1968, aims to mobilize the interest and participation of Canadians in actions and issues related to the developing world. Membership includes more than eighty major nongovernmental agencies, including some universities, involved in international development. Nearly four hundred individuals who have a particular interest or expertise in international development are also members.

Maintaining a small library of material relevant to its objectives, CCIC keeps members and a wide network of agencies and individuals around the world up to date on matters dealing with international cooperation. The council is a standing forum for the discussion of common problems and concerns for the nongovernmental sector in Canada. It does not operate projects overseas or raise funds from the general public; it is funded by contributions from members, corporate donations, and Canadian government grants.

Members are informed about events in the Third World through the council's publications, including an occasional newsletter and the *Directory of Canadian NGOs*.

75 Sparks Street
Ottawa, Ontario, Canada K1P 5A5

CANADIAN SOCIETY FOR THE STUDY OF HIGHER EDUCATION
(Société canadienne pour l'étude de l'enseignement supérieur)

The Canadian Society for the Study of Higher Education was established during the annual sessions of the learned societies at the University of Manitoba in May 1970. The society encourages independent and critical study of issues and problems in postsecondary education in Canada and collects and disseminates information about these activities. Membership in the society is individual, although some institutional or group arrangements are possible. It is open to all scholars, researchers, administrators, and others interested in the broad field of higher education, particularly as it relates to Canada.

The interests of the society's members cover a broad range, including history and philosophy of higher education, comparative higher education, institutional research, structure and government, finance and economics, educational psychology, curriculum development, and structural methods. The purview of the society includes universities, postsecondary colleges of all forms, and continuing education. Membership in 1975 was approximately 450.

English and French are the working languages of the society, and either language may be used in its publications and at its meetings. The annual meeting of the society, held in conjunction with other learned societies of Canada, provides a forum for exchange of information, debates on various issues concerning higher education, and reading of scholarly communications.

Business of the society is directed by five officers and an executive council of nine persons elected at the annual meetings. The society does not have a permanent secretariat, but such services are provided on a voluntary basis.

The society publishes a newsletter, prepared principally by the members of the executive council, and *Canadian Journal of Higher Education/Révue canadienne d'enseignement supérieur.* Also known as STOA, the journal contains scholarly articles, book reviews, a select bibliography, and an inventory of research relevant to higher education in Canada. The editorial board of the journal is appointed by the executive council on recommendation of the editor.

Suite 8039
130 St. George Street
Toronto, Ontario, Canada M5S 2T4

CAPE VERDE ISLANDS

The Cape Verde Islands—ten large and a number of small islands located off the African coast in the Atlantic Ocean to the northeast of Senegal—became independent on July 5, 1975, after having been under Portuguese dominance for some five hundred years. At independence the islands had been ravaged by seven years of drought and suffered through ten years of liberation struggle. Large numbers of the population have emigrated, especially to the United States. In 1974 the islands had a population of approximately 291,000.

The Portuguese established the first secondary school, *liceu nacional,* on the islands in 1860. Seven years later a seminary was established, which in 1892 was transformed into a seminary-lyceum. A thorough reorganization of education took place in 1917, when several new schools were opened, including two higher primary schools, to take the place of the seminary, and vocational schools with programs in agriculture, industrial subjects, and fisheries. After another educational reorganization in 1950, the educational system consisted of primary education, elementary education, vocational education, general secondary education in *liceus,* and training in public service, art, and theology. Primary education was free and obligatory for children between six and twelve. In 1971, 17 percent of the population was literate (dos Santos, 1971, p. 83).

In 1973 there were over 500 primary schools, which enrolled 63,700 students, and eleven secondary and technical schools, which enrolled 3700 students. The language of instruction is Portuguese.

There is no higher education available on the islands. Students go abroad for further study, primarily to Portugal.

Bibliography

Cabo Verde. Pequena monografia. Lisbon: Agência-geral do ultramar, 1966.

da Silva Cunha, J. M. *Progresso de Cabo Verde.* Lisbon: Agência-geral do ultramar, 1969.

dos Santos, A. L. *Problemas de Cabo Verde. A situação mantém—se controlada.* Lisbon: Agência-geral do ultramar, 1971.

CAPITOL AND THE CAMPUS, THE (Higher Education Report), United States

The Capitol and the Campus: State Responsibility for Postsecondary Education (New York: McGraw-Hill, April 1971), a report of the Carnegie Commission on Higher Education, examines the role of state governments (specifically, the governor, the legislature, and recently created agencies that act as intermediaries between the state and higher education institutions) in the development of higher education in the United States. The commission commends the states' past achievements but urges continued efforts to ensure the development and maintenance of a diversified and accessible system of postsecondary education. The report sets forth guidelines that will enable each state to evaluate its success in providing effective educational opportunity and to determine its future obligations.

Although it opposes executive involvement in higher education and cautions against statewide regulatory boards, the commission favors statewide coordinating bodies that function as planning and consultative agencies. Some parameters for governing processes, protective of both public accountability and institutional freedom, are offered. States are encouraged to provide support to private institutions of higher education in such forms as student scholarships and service contracts. Moreover, states should abolish restrictive residency requirements and increase interinstitutional and interstate cooperation.

The primary governmental responsibility for higher education, the commission believes, should continue to rest with the states. Each state should provide a minimum of thirty places in both public and private higher education institutions for every hundred residents in the eighteen to twenty-one age group and should allocate at least .6 percent of per capita personal income spent through state and local taxes for higher education. Only with such provisions will the states be providing their fair share of resources needed to meet the increasing enrollment demands of the 1970s.

CAPS AND GOWNS

See Academic Dress and Insignia; Academic Dress, History of.

CAREER, VOCATIONAL, AND TECHNICAL EDUCATION

Career education's goals, objectives, and strategies for implementation are probably more easy to describe than the phrase *career education* is to define. Career education, notably labeled by proponents and opponents alike as a "reform movement" in American education, has had many definitions.

In early 1971, Sidney P. Marland, Jr., then serving as United States commissioner of education, announced that "career education" was a priority of the administration for the 1970s. From the beginning, the United States Office of Education (USOE) was reluctant to define the term precisely, and the number of definitions proliferated.

In his recent book on career education, Marland supports the approach of leaving definitions of career education to the individual practitioner: "Career education is a very large and complex proposition, carrying various levels of abstraction according to the setting. It has a definition for, say, a state department of education, a different level of detail for a fourth grade teacher or a dean of faculty at a university. It is not important, furthermore, that any one individual, whether a government official or not, declare a definition intended to serve all situations" (1974, p. 91).

In this section we shall attempt to define career education, recognizing that any definition of career education, as it is evolving today, should be considered a working definition.

Principles of Career Education

1. *Career educators emphasize the need for increasing both the quality and quantity of vocational education and career guidance for everyone.* Yet career education should not be viewed as synonymous with vocational education or with career guidance. Both these disciplines are considered to be *important components* of career education.

2. *Career education is a cradle-to-grave approach* to education. Most often described as a Kindergarten to Life educational model, career education emphasizes that educating for careers is a legitimate and important concern of education that has been overlooked often by professional educators in the past, or if recognized, relegated to a low priority status. Moreover, since career education should properly be considered a lifelong process, then career education must begin in the early grades and follow throughout a person's life.

3. The major emphasis of career education is one of *curriculum infusion.* Career education is not viewed as a "new course" or a "new program" (at whatever level); rather, it is a philosophy of education that permeates all instruction. It is based on the principle that every teacher of every course (whether that teacher be a college professor or a first-grade teacher) should place emphasis on the relationship between the subject matter being taught and its possible relationship to the career development of each student.

4. A related principle is concerned with strategies for teaching academics. This principle is based on the assumption that if academic instructors use *"hands-on" occupationally focused experiences* as methods for taching their academic content, then students will be more motivated to learn. This principle, as with all the basic foundation concepts of career education, is not a new one. At the public school level, the *Technology for Children* program has long offered the children of New Jersey activities in elementary school. Northeastern University's Cooperative Education for students in professional programs is a notable extension of this concept at the university

level. In American education, this concept traces its lineage to Benjamin Franklin, John Dewey, and David Snedden.

5. Another principle of career education is concerned with learning environments. This principle recognizes that different students learn better in some environments than others and is related to the above principle. Career educators view the classroom as only one of many optional learning environments. This principle extends the curriculum (the educational experiences programed for students) *into the community, into the home,* and *on the job.* There is, therefore, increased emphasis on work-study, work observation, cooperative education, and internship programs. Concurrently, educational systems are encouraged to bring the school-business-labor-community into the educational system and policy-making processes. Business people, for instance, not only will provide cooperative work sites outside the school's walls, but increasingly they are found to be participating in school activities on the campus as guest lecturers, personnel in industry-education exchange programs, experts offering technical assistance in curriculum development, and policymakers serving on advisory boards.

Related to this principle is the concept of *open entry/exit* provisions for public schools. This provision allows young persons and adults alike to leave the system for real-life experience and to return, at any time, for further education or upgrading of job skills.

6. A major concept is one which insists that schools must be held *responsible,* in terms of careers, for their students who leave, diploma or not. Career education mandates that each school provide placement services and follow-up for all its students, both on immediate exit and in the future, should the person require further assistance or training.

7. Career education is specific in its stated goal of providing every American with either an *entry-level, marketable skill* or preparation for further advanced career training beyond grade 12. The concept of

career training is a *comprehensive* one that distinguishes it from vocational education. Not only do students in a comprehensive career education system acquire mastery of actual job skills, they are expected to receive instruction that will help them achieve appropriate work attitudes, human relations skills, and familiarity with the world of work and alternate career choices. Figure 1 illustrates how the comprehensive Kindergarten to Life model works. This figure summarizes succinctly some of the more popular career education models.

Definitions of Career Education

The definitions presented are not detailed enough to specify all the principles, concepts, goals, and strategies of the total career education reform movement. These definitions, however, are broad enough to encompass the spectrum of ideas of the movement even though they may be somewhat vague on specifics. That is the nature and status of the movement as of this writing. The definitions should be considered as tentative ones and should be read only in the context of the principles (and the illustrative four-stage model) presented herein.

1. *A popular definition.* This definition appears in the first and second editions of a best-selling book on career education, *Career Education: What It Is and How to Do It,* coauthored by Kenneth B. Hoyt (currently U.S. associate commissioner of education and director of the U.S. Office of Career Education) and others. It is the more frequently quoted definition: "Career education is the total effort of public education and the community to help all individuals become familiar with the values of a work-oriented society, to integrate these values into their personal value system, and to implement these values in their lives in such a way that work becomes possible, meaningful, and satisfying to each individual" (1974, p. 15).

2. *The official definition.* In a recently published policy paper, *An Introduction to Career Education: A Policy Paper of the U.S. Office of Education,* the federal government defines, for the first time, the phrase *career education.* Concurrent with this definition are related definitions of the key terms *work, career,* and *education.* Work is defined as "conscious effort, other than that involved in activities whose primary purpose is either coping or relaxation, aimed at producing benefits for one's self and/or for one's self and others" (Hoyt, 1975, p. 3).

The USOE describes a "career" as the "totality of work one does in his or her lifetime" and "education" as the "totality of experiences through which one learns" (Hoyt, 1975, p. 3).

In the context of these definitions, career education is defined as "the totality of experiences through which one learns about and prepares to engage in work as part of her or his way of living" (Hoyt, 1975, p. 4).

3. *A tentative definition of postsecondary career education.* There has been no concentrated effort to date to define or develop the proposed model of career education illustrated in Figure 1 at Stage IV, higher education. Therefore, there is no preferred or official definition. The author offers this definition as a tentative or working definition: Postsecondary career education encompasses all the planned educational experiences of the public and private higher education system, in concert with the community, that are designed to ensure that all persons served are prepared to work each according to his or her own chosen life-style.

Postsecondary Career Education in Practice

Presently there is no one postsecondary institution in the United States that has systematically redesigned its entire curriculum for career education, as described in the preceding section. There are, of course, numerous examples of two- and four-year public and private institutions that offer programs consonant with the goals, principles, and strategies of career education. Consequently, we shall briefly delineate below some of the principles of career education that are being applied successfully at various institutions. (Note that the selection of examples in this and forthcoming sections of this article is an arbitrary one.)

Figure 1. Illustrative stages of school-based models.*

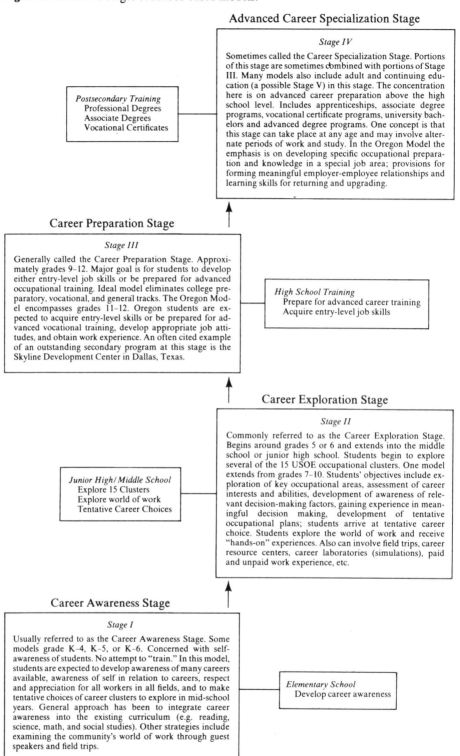

Advanced Career Specialization Stage

Stage IV

Sometimes called the Career Specialization Stage. Portions of this stage are sometimes combined with portions of Stage III. Many models also include adult and continuing education (a possible Stage V) in this stage. The concentration here is on advanced career preparation above the high school level. Includes apprenticeships, associate degree programs, vocational certificate programs, university bachelors and advanced degree programs. One concept is that this stage can take place at any age and may involve alternate periods of work and study. In the Oregon Model the emphasis is on developing specific occupational preparation and knowledge in a special job area; provisions for forming meaningful employer-employee relationships and learning skills for returning and upgrading.

Postsecondary Training
Professional Degrees
Associate Degrees
Vocational Certificates

Career Preparation Stage

Stage III

Generally called the Career Preparation Stage. Approximately grades 9–12. Major goal is for students to develop either entry-level job skills or be prepared for advanced occupational training. Ideal model eliminates college preparatory, vocational, and general tracks. The Oregon Model encompasses grades 11–12. Oregon students are expected to acquire entry-level skills or be prepared for advanced vocational training, develop appropriate job attitudes, and obtain work experience. An often cited example of an outstanding secondary program at this stage is the Skyline Development Center in Dallas, Texas.

High School Training
Prepare for advanced career training
Acquire entry-level job skills

Career Exploration Stage

Stage II

Commonly referred to as the Career Exploration Stage. Begins around grades 5 or 6 and extends into the middle school or junior high school. Students begin to explore several of the 15 USOE occupational clusters. One model extends from grades 7–10. Students' objectives include exploration of key occupational areas, assessment of career interests and abilities, development of awareness of relevant decision-making factors, gaining experience in meaningful decision making, development of tentative occupational plans; students arrive at tentative career choice. Students explore the world of work and receive "hands-on" experiences. Also can involve field trips, career resource centers, career laboratories (simulations), paid and unpaid work experience, etc.

Junior High/Middle School
Explore 15 Clusters
Explore world of work
Tentative Career Choices

Career Awareness Stage

Stage I

Usually referred to as the Career Awareness Stage. Some models grade K–4, K–5, or K–6. Concerned with self-awareness of students. No attempt to "train." In this model, students are expected to develop awareness of many careers available, awareness of self in relation to careers, respect and appreciation for all workers in all fields, and to make tentative choices of career clusters to explore in mid-school years. General approach has been to integrate career awareness into the existing curriculum (e.g. reading, science, math, and social studies). Other strategies include examining the community's world of work through guest speakers and field trips.

Elementary School
Develop career awareness

*Adapted with permission of author and publisher from D. C. Gardner, "Career Education," in M. B. Scott (Ed.), *The Essential Profession,* Stamford, Connecticut: Graylock Publishers, Inc., 1976, p. 76.

1. *The principle of integrating the world of work and academics as part of the instructional program.* This most often takes the form of cooperative education, work-study, and internships. Northeastern University, Boston, the international leader in this field, is the largest private university in the United States and the largest cooperative education university in the world, extending its experience and expertise beyond its own institutional goals through the Center for Cooperative Education. The center offers training programs and consulting services for other institutions that desire to develop their own programs of cooperative education. At the community college level, Bunker Hill Community College, Charlestown, Massachusetts, offers its office occupations students an outstanding internship program that successfully combines experiential learning with job placement and exploration. Mohawk Valley Community College, Utica, New York, has successfully applied the principles of cooperative education to its programing.

2. *The principle of providing more extensive career guidance, including more effective delivery of career information for students.* Boston University's recently established Advisory Resource Center exemplifies this principle. The center brings together career guidance and counseling services, a resource center for career information, and the placement office and services. The center, itself, also serves as an internship site for graduate students in counselor education. A series of workshops covering various aspects of career development, including decision-making and job hunting skills, is offered to students through the various divisions of the university under the auspices of the Advisory Resource Center. Under development is a computerized guidance and job placement system.

3. *The principle of curriculum modification to emphasize the career relevance of specific academic courses.* To date, career educators have, by and large, focused on developing curriculum infusion models in elementary and secondary schools. In addition to curriculum development and redesign, this principle also includes the upgrading and retraining of instructors. Alma College, a four-year liberal arts college in Alma, Michigan, is currently developing a totally integrated career preparation program for its liberal arts students. Alma has recently received financial support from both federal and private foundation sources for this program. The program is designed to maintain and strengthen the traditional liberal arts program while preparing students for the job market after graduation. At this writing, 330 students are directly involved, and 100 additional students are scheduled to begin in January 1977. Thirty liberal arts faculty members have been trained to serve as Career Preparation Coordinators. Specific activities are planned for each of the four-year programs which are designed to ensure that students develop an awareness of the world of work, develop career planning skills, and establish skills which will assist them in obtaining satisfactory employment after graduation.

Postsecondary Vocational/Technical Education

In the section on definitions of *career education*, it became evident that this term represents a philosophy (system of postulates, principles, concepts) of education for all persons of all ages. Career education, then, can be described as an umbrella term incorporating such areas as technical education, vocational education, occupational education, vocational guidance, and placement.

Historically, vocational education has been conceptualized as secondary education, focused on training persons for gainful employment in recognized occupations in skilled or semiskilled positions.

Technical education originally was established to train technicians in the engineering technologies. More recently, it has been defined more broadly to include all occupational education for the higher levels of subprofessionals in any occupational field. It is often thought of as a "level of education," that is, postsecondary, subbaccalaureate training. This definition excludes the "less sophisticated" vocational training typically taught in secondary schools. In recent years, however, *all* vocational education has been growing rapidly and has expanded to many postsecondary schools. This expansion allows for young adults to enroll in a vocational program after leaving high school without returning to a secondary school. For instance, distributive education programs are offered both in public secondary schools and in two-year, postsecondary schools. Distributive education is not, however, considered to be "technical education."

Another term, often used synonymously with vocational/technical education, is *occupational education.* In a federal directory of postsecondary schools with occupational programs (Kay, 1975, p. VII), occupational education is defined as "educational instruction designed to: (1) prepare individuals for gainful employment in recognized occupations and/or new and emerging occupations; (2) assist individuals in making informed and meaningful occupational choices; and (3) upgrade or update the skills of individuals already in an occupational field." This definition of occupational education is clearly synonymous with the definition of vocational education offered by a similar federal directory, which lists public and private secondary schools with occupational curriculums in 1971 (Osso, 1973, p. VIII): "Vocational education—educational instruction below the baccalaureate level designed: (a) to prepare individuals for gainful employment in recognized occupations and/or new and emerging occupations; (b) to assist individuals in making informed and meaningful occupational choices; and (c) to upgrade or update those individuals already in an occupational field."

Official definition: vocational education. The 1968 *Amendments to the Vocational Education Act of 1963* (p. 7) broadened the definition of vocational education to include both secondary and postsecondary programs, public and private:

The term "vocational education" means vocational or technical training or retraining which is given in schools or classes (including field or laboratory work and remedial or related academic and technical instruction incident thereto) under public supervision and control or under contract with a State board or local education agency and is conducted as part of a program designed to prepare individuals for gainful employment as semiskilled or skilled workers or technicians or subprofessionals in recognized occupations and in new and emerging occupations or to prepare individuals for enrollment in advanced technical education programs, but excluding any program to prepare individuals for employment in occupations which the Commissioner determines, and specifies by regulation, to be generally considered professional or which requires a baccalaureate or higher degree.

The definition also includes vocational guidance, job placement, instruction that facilitates occupational choice, and training of teachers to work with handicapped students. Vocational schools are broadly defined to include specialized vocational high schools, vocational departments of comprehensive high schools, post–high school technical or vocational schools, departments or divisions of community, junior colleges and universities providing vocational education in at least five occupational fields.

Official definition: postsecondary occupational education. The *Educational Amendments of 1972* (p. 87) specified the use of the phrase *postsecondary occupational education* to mean

education, training, or retraining (and including guidance, counseling, and placement services) for persons sixteen years of age or older who have graduated from or left elementary or secondary school, conducted by an institution legally authorized to provide postsecondary education within a State, which is designed to prepare individuals for gainful employment as semi-skilled or skilled workers or technicians or sub-professionals in recognized occupations (including new and emerging occupations), or to prepare individuals for enrollment in advanced technical education programs, but excluding any program to prepare individuals for employment in occupations which the Commissioner determines, and specifies by regulation, to be generally considered professional or which require a baccalaureate or advanced degree.

It is obvious from these two definitions, acted into law, that the definition of vocational education is the more comprehensive definition, including both secondary and postsecondary programs under its auspices. The definition of postsecondary occupational education, therefore, can be used synonymously with the term *postsecondary vocational/technical education*. Technical education in use may refer to a type of trained worker (for example, the person between the professional person and the craftsman); others see it referring to a specific class of occupations (for example, dental technicians and optical technicians). No matter which definition is chosen, technical education can be subsumed under the definition of postsecondary occupational education. All these terms logically may be considered major components of the broader approach to educational reform, "career education."

There has been and probably will continue to be considerable confusion over the use of such terms as *occupational* and *vocational* education in the United States. In this article the phrases *postsecondary occupational education* and *postsecondary vocational/technical education* shall be considered synonymous terms, as suggested by Gilli (1973, p. 3).

Postsecondary Vocational/Technical Education in Practice

Even a cursory review of the literature on vocational or occupational education at the postsecondary level would yield data on the tremendous growth of enrollments in postsecondary vocational/technical education as well as the diversity of the programs available for youth and adults. The impetus for this growth may be largely attributed to the Vocational Education Act of 1963, with its subsequent amendments. The USOE *Directory of Postsecondary Schools with Occupational Programs, 1973–74* (Kay, 1975)

cites some 10,266 schools (some 8065 are accredited): public schools (1938); private, profit-making, proprietary schools (6686); private, independent, nonprofit schools (1189); and private religious schools (453).

A study published in 1975 by Market Data Retrieval, Inc., *The Guide to Vocational Education in America: Trends to 1978* (1975), estimates that by 1978 vocational education enrollments at the postsecondary level will account for one out of five enrollments in all colleges and universities in the United States, while representing some 58 percent of enrollments in two-year programs and colleges. Moreover, projected 1978 vocational education enrollments for adult members of the work force are estimated to be approximately five million, or 8.6 percent of the estimated work force in 1978.

There is a great diversity of programs and institutions that are designed to meet the vocational/technical educational needs of Americans at the postsecondary, subprofessional (prebaccalaureate) level in the United States. Amid this diversity is a plethora of definitions of programs and types of schools. In this and the following section, no attempt will be made to resolve the confusion of sometimes conflicting and sometimes overlapping "terminology" associated with many of the programs described. Suffice it to say that there is no "typical" program which represents "all programs" in a specific category or definition. For instance, one can study "electromechanical technology" in a four-year university that offers two-year programs or in a community-funded, regional vocational/technical school that offers programs from grade 9 to 14. The outcomes may be relatively the same, for example, an associate degree. The range of postsecondary offerings stretches from cosmetology to secretarial, from police science to dental assistant, from landscaping to data processing.

The selection of programs, described below, therefore is an arbitrary one. By and large, these selections are probably representative of the majority of vocational instructional opportunities open to Americans at the postsecondary, prebaccalaureate level.

Types of programs:

1. Regional schools. The language used to describe this type of school is often overlapping and conflicting. It is particularly confusing when one compares the interpretation of federal legislation in the fifty states, the federal government's terminology, and common (layman) usage. The schools known as "area vocational schools," under the Vocational Education Act of 1963, with amendments, can range from specialized vocational high schools to departments in comprehensive high schools or community colleges to specialized programs within four-year universities. Most community colleges and universities, however, choose not to be so labeled.

From the layman's point of view, the most accepted "regional" or "area" vocational school is the public regional vocational/technical school. This type of school is physically, and academically, separate from other educational programs in the area. Most of these schools offer trade programs at the secondary level as well as postsecondary adult programs. Some public regional vocational/technical schools are classified in the USOE *Directory of Postsecondary Occupational Programs* (Kay, 1975) as vocational/technical schools, others as technical institutes. The basic distinction between these classifications is probably the level of program and whether or not an associate degree is granted.

It is difficult to determine the exact number of these institutions because of the overlapping of definitions. The USOE *Directory* (Kay, 1975) reports 585 public technical/vocational schools. However, some of these are not "regional schools," and others that are regional schools are categorized under "technical institutes."

Programs offered at the postsecondary level may include but are not limited to practical nursing, auto repair, secretarial and office studies, cosmetology, carpentry, commercial fishing, masonry, diesel mechanics, electronics, electricity, metalworking, metal fabrication, dental assistant, nurse assistant, auto mechanics, drafting, graphic arts, commercial foods, business data processing, business machine repair, X-ray technician, appliance repair, medical lab technicians.

2. Technical institutes. A technical institute is defined in the USOE *Directory of Postsecondary Occupational Programs* (Kay, 1975, p. XIV) as "an institution (usually 2-year) offering instruction in one or more of the technologies at a level above the skilled trades and below the professional level." Although this definition would probably be acceptable to most professionals and laymen, there is no typical "technical institute." For instance, in Massachusetts one "regional" school is classified as a "technical institute." It grants an associate degree in some postsecondary programs but not in others. Among its listed offerings is a dental assistant's program (nondegree). In the same state, a student can enroll in competing dental assistant programs in a four-year private university, a vocational/technical school's postsecondary program, a public junior college, and a proprietary vocational/technical school.

The USOE *Directory* lists 334 technical institutes in the United States, of which 158 are categorized as "public." Figures should be used with caution, however, since many institutions that could be categorized as "technical institutes" by virtue of program offerings which fit the definition of "technical institute" usually label themselves as "junior college," "community college," or "college" (four-year). The basic distinction between a technical institute and a postsecondary vocational/technical education school is probably one of level of sophistication. Moreover, the technical institute, although granting certificates, is probably more likely to grant an associate degree in applied science.

Wentworth Institute in Boston, for instance, grants a Certificate of Graduation to students who enroll in its industrial technology program (two-year) because of a lack of basic technical background. Depending on degree of competency, more advanced students elect associate degree programs that lead either to an Associate in Engineering degree (highest degree of competency) or an Associate in Applied Science degree (standard level). In addition to the usual engineering-based technical occupations, technical institutes offer a wide variety of certificate and/or associate degree programs in many other occupational clusters, including the health-related fields (for example, dental hygiene) and business and office occupations (for example, data processing, computer programing).

3. *Community and junior colleges.* The *Directory of Postsecondary Occupational Programs* (Kay, 1975, p. XIV) defines a junior/community college as an institution "offering the first 2 or 3 years of college instruction in occupational programs. It frequently grants a certificate or an associate degree but not a bachelor's degree." While in some instances it may be difficult to distinguish between a degree-granting technical institute and a junior/community college that offers a wide variety of technically oriented programs, the primary emphasis of the technical school is more likely to be "vocational," whereas the community or junior college is more likely to be "college-oriented."

As in all phases of postsecondary vocational/technical education, there is some overlapping of terminology and usage. "Junior college" is more likely to be used nationally to refer to a private, two-year, independent institution, whereas "community college" is more likely to mean a public, community-oriented, two-year institution.

Most community colleges were originally presented to the taxpayers as transfer programs for the children of local residents who could not initially meet the entrance requirements to four-year institutions. Occupational programs were added later, but many of the faculty members of these institutions continue to focus, at least attitudinally, on the "liberal arts" portion of the curriculum. By and large, however, most community colleges have been successful in broadening their community services and programs, adding both full-time and part-time occupational education programs for youth and adults in the surrounding community.

Most community colleges have open admissions policies, while exercising control over standards of retention, graduation, and placement. Almost without exception, all community colleges offer transfer programs to four-year colleges and universities.

The basic distinction between junior colleges and community colleges is that junior colleges generally maintain admissions standards. Moreover, junior colleges are more expensive. The student body may, therefore, tend to be drawn from more affluent groups. Also, there tends to be less emphasis on remedial programs and more on liberal arts.

The *Directory of Postsecondary Occupational Education Programs* (Kay, 1975) reports that in 1974 there were 750 public junior/community colleges, 59 private independent, 41 religious-sponsored, and 10 proprietary junior/community colleges in the United States. The following offerings are a compilation of the offerings listed in the USOE *Directory,* cited above, of three public community colleges, selected at random from the directory from the California, Illinois, and New York state listings: data processing, chemical technology, automotive technology, diesel mechanics, welding technology, construction, agriculture, forest technology, food service, ocean technology, business, accounting, hotel management, police science, education technology, fire technology, recreation/social technology, data processing, dental assistant, medical lab, nurse (RN), physical therapy, engineering graphics, electronic technology, marketing, transportation, library assistant, secretary. (Note: These listings may represent both full-time and/or part-time evening programs, with or without degrees or certificates.)

4. *Proprietary schools.* Proprietary schools are profit-making institutions that offer the flexibility (which many other institutions do not have) to meet some of the immediate employment needs of our rapidly changing technological society. A profit-making institution, whether it be in education, food processing, or engineering products, must be responsive to its markets; it must develop relationships that are mutually beneficial for both the customer (the student) and the organization. Proprietary schools, by and large, successfully develop these relationships with their students by providing practical, job-oriented training, designed to be immediately transferable into a specific occupation upon program completion.

Proprietary schools have also successfully filled the gap between the occupational training programs offered by nonprofit, public institutions and the training required by the labor market. For instance, 96 percent of the accredited business/ commercial schools at the postsecondary, nonbaccalaureate level are proprietary, and only one is public. Similarly, there are only 4 public cosmetology/barber schools out of the 1782 accredited schools.

Postsecondary proprietary schools with occupational programs represent 65 percent of all the schools listed in the USOE *Directory,* and the ratio of proprietary to all others (public and private) is almost two to one (2:1). Table 1 delineates the diversity of options from which American youth and adults may choose when selecting a proprietary school for initial, entry-level job training or for subprofessional, degree, and certificate education.

Proprietary schools include (1) those devoted to a specific occupation (such as secretary, barber, hairdresser, or commercial pilot; (2) those offering training in

Table 1. Proprietary Postsecondary Schools with Occupational Programs in the United States in 1974, Accredited, Nonaccredited[a]

Type of School	Accredited	Not Accredited	Percent Accredited
Tech/voc.	341	180	65
Tech inst.	137	17	88
Business/ commercial	814	421	66
Flight school	1227	242	84
Trade school	312	258	55
Home study	84	42	67
Cosmetology/ barber school	1776	619	74
Hospital school	21	3	88
Junior/comm. college	10	0	100
College	7	1	88
Other	16	158	9
TOTALS	4745	1941	71

[a]All figures from the tables on pages xxii and xxiii of the USOE *Directory of Postsecondary Schools with Occupational Programs, 1973–74* (1975).

one occupational cluster (for example, business and office occupation cluster); (3) corporate-owned and -operated schools (for example, Sylvania Technical Institute); and (4) those offering college-level instruction (for example, Burdett School, Boston).

Accreditation of private trade and technical schools (proprietary) is not mandatory. However, voluntary accreditation review and approval is provided by the National Association of Trade and Technical Schools.

5. *Industry programs.* Closely allied to the concept of proprietary schools are those training programs offered exclusively to employees of a specific company (or industry) but that are not open to the public. In most cases, these training programs are related to a specific job, are of short duration, and can be made readily available to the company's employees within their own time and geographical limitations. Many companies prefer to train their own sales-

people, and such training programs can range in duration from one day to six months.

Since these programs are not open to the public, the USOE *Directory* does not list them. Needless to say, there is a great deal of flux involved at this level of vocational/ technical education. For instance, a corporation may establish a training program to meet an immediate corporate need, such as training rolling mill supervisors to handle new alloy ingot. Sometimes corporations may establish a proprietary school in response to an increasing, industrywide need for trained personnel.

6. *Continuing education.* Definitions of continuing education (and adult education) are multitudinous. Grabowski (1976, p. 41) defines continuing education as "an unfolding process whereby an individual develops a learning program when basic formal education ends, and carries it on throughout a lifetime. It is a means of updating knowledge and skills in one's career, or can add new knowledge and skills in a different field. Continuing education embodies all forms of education, including vocational, remedial, recreational, liberal, technical, professional, religious and family life."

In this article the following definitions are used: first, from the point of view of the individual adult learner, *postsecondary, continuing occupational education* is defined as an individual adult's lifelong learning plan for his or her own continued career development beyond her or his own basic formal education. This plan may be a conscious or unconscious one, since career development is seen as a lifelong, unfolding process.

From the point of view of program delivery to meet the lifelong career development needs of adults, *continuing occupational education* is defined as all those learning activities designed to prepare individuals for gainful employment in a new occupation, upgrade or update skills in his present occupation or help him become more in-

formed in terms of making meaningful occupational choices.

Logically, then, almost any program that meets the needs of an adult's continuing occupational education plan could fit this definition. Most professionals, however, use the term to refer to formalized adult programs that are offered by technical institutes, regional technical schools, junior/ community colleges, and universities. For instance, Bunker Hill Community College, in Charlestown, Massachusetts, offers thirteen certificate programs in its Division of Continuing Education designed to introduce students to specific skills in a relatively short time. The USOE Directory lists over one million persons enrolled full time in postsecondary, prebaccalaureate occupational programs and nearly one million persons enrolled part time in 1973. Enrollment figures exclude all forms of study other than programs offered by established formal institutions. One can estimate that most of these part-time enrollments represent some form of adult continuing occupational education and that many of the full-time students are adults. These figures are also exclusive of professional-level offerings. Projected 1978 adult work force enrollments in vocational/technical education are five million persons.

7. *Military occupational education.* Paralleling the civilian public and private school system is a great segment of the educational system of the United States, the military system. Rupert Evans (1971) points out that if all the military schools were placed on one campus, that campus area would probably exceed the acreage occupied by our three largest cities: New York, Los Angeles, and Chicago.

Although many of the military schools train persons for occupations that are not transferable to civilian life, the military does provide technical/vocational training for servicemen, which, according to Evans, makes the United States military system the largest vocational/technical program anywhere in the world. Most military courses are less than a year in duration. The Department of Defense has recently published an occupational source book *(Occupations), 1975)* that describes most military occupation specialties, and, where appropriate, their civilian DOT code.

Trends and Issues in Career, Vocational, and Technical Education

Funding of programs. In this era of high unemployment, inflation, and high taxes, the impact of increasing costs of both public and private higher education has become a prime concern for many Americans. Business and labor leaders' problems are confounded by an increase of "overeducated" employees who are "underemployed" and by an acute shortage of technical employees.

Parents who want to send their children to specific university programs cannot afford to do so. The socioeconomic status of students entering private higher education is rising (with the exception of minority groups funded from special federal and state monies).

There are a number of advocates of free tuition for all citizens at public-sponsored institutions. Opponents of such legislation point to the possibility of its severe impact on the already financially squeezed private institutions. Private institutions are quick to point out that they are "more efficient" and their cost per pupil is lower. Many educational leaders in the private sector advocate a system where the state will pay a specified amount related to financial need per pupil and the pupil can choose to enter either a private or a public institution.

Teacher training and certification. A major issue in teacher training is that there is no vocational teacher. Each field is distinct from one another; each field is usually based on federal and state funding categories, such as "distributive education teacher," "business education teacher," and so on. If vocational education is to be broadly defined, to incorporate the concept of career education, then teacher training programs need to recognize and promote a "common core."

Another issue concerns the way vocational education programs are established, developed, improved, and, when necessary, abolished. The "task analysis" approach of most vocational educators, which is (1) to define the tasks and (2) to train for them, tends to promote a rigid system (Dolce, 1974). For whatever reason, vocational education has been criticized as representing the past, as not being flexible enough to alter or adjust curricula in response to society's rapidly changing needs.

The issue of certification as a requirement for teaching vocational/technical education at the secondary level has generally been resolved. At the postsecondary level, there have been increasingly more advocates of establishing certification requirements for vocational educators. The issue about what should be the requirements continues both in states with requirements and those without them. Most certification requirements are linked to a series of semester hour course work and actual years of work experience. Some educators favor giving the final authority to the state department of education (traditional method). Others see the responsibility for certification resting in the hands of university teacher training programs. Others would link certification to "competency examinations." Many postsecondary educators are opposed to certification because it would lower their programs to the status of secondary schools and limit flexibility in hiring policies.

Minority programs. The Vocational Education Act of 1963 and its subsequent amendments have given impetus to a strong movement to supply special programs of admissions, training, remedial options, and alternative programs for persons who have been previously discriminated against in vocational/technical education at the postsecondary level. These include minority groups, handicapped persons, and culturally disadvantaged groups.

In addition, increasing attention has been given to eliminating sex stereotyping in occupational training. Although professional educators accept these priorities, debate focuses on how such programs will be implemented. Moreover, there has been some resistance by minority groups to accept such programing because they feel that vocational/technical programs at the prebaccalaureate level will ensure their exclusion from professional education and occupations.

Competency-based education. The movement in American education toward competency-based education has also made inroads in vocational education at the postsecondary level. This approach to education would eliminate the traditional Carnegie unit that is used as a basis for awarding a credential in a given field. Instead, students would demonstrate a level of competency required for a particular occupation by examinations. In this series of examinations the student would meet certain behaviorally stated criteria. When he or she has demonstrated these criteria satisfactorily, the credential is awarded.

Competency-based education is not fully acceptable to all educators. In some occupations its principles are relatively easy to apply, but in other occupations the task of defining the criteria, and how they will be measured, is exceedingly complex and time consuming. Thus, many educators feel that "competency-based" instruction is not worth the effort.

Accountability and evaluation. Enrollments in vocational/technical education at all levels are increasing, and the budgets for such programing, from local, state, and federal sources, are skyrocketing. Vocational education is expensive, and taxpayers and professional groups are increasingly demanding that vocational educators account for their expenditures. This usually takes two forms: (1) There is an increased emphasis on cost effectiveness. Increasingly, vocational educators are being asked to be accountable, frugal, and more objective in their budgeting. As a result, many schools have adopted program, planning, and budgeting systems (PPBS), where budgets for programs are linked directly and precisely to program objectives. (2) There is an increased interest in cost-benefit analysis. More and more vocational/technical schools are being asked to demonstrate their program benefit to the community. Although this procedure is exceedingly complex to implement, many public institutions have studied their programs in depth and have publicized their findings. Undoubtedly, this trend will continue.

Summary

Vocational/technical education represents an enormously vital and growing sector of the American educational system. Over the past twenty years, it has experienced unprecedented growth, both in the number and in the variety of occupational education options and programs open to Americans. As a result of the phenomenal growth of the career education reform movement, the outlook for continued development of occupational education programs at the postsecondary, prebaccalaureate level seems assured.

Bibliography

Amendments to the Vocational Education Act of 1963. Public Law 90-576, October 16, 1968.

Course Descriptions and Programs: 1976–1977. Charlestown, Massachusetts: Bunker Hill Community College, 1976.

Dolce, C. J. "Decisions Ahead in Teacher Education." In A. G. Porreca (Ed.), *Decisions Ahead for Vocational-Technical Education.* Knoxville: University of Tennessee, 1974.

Educational Amendments of 1972. Public Law 92-318, June 23, 1972.

Evans, R. N. *Foundations of Vocational Education.* Columbus, Ohio: Merrill, 1971.

Gardner, D. C. "Career Education." In M. B. Scott (Ed.), *The Essential Profession.* Stamford, Connecticut: Greylock Publishers, 1976.

Gardner, D. C., and Warren, S. A. *Careers and Disabilities.* Stamford, Connecticut: Greylock Publishers, 1977.

Gilli, A. C., Sr. *Principles of Post-Secondary*

Vocational Education. Columbus, Ohio: Merrill, 1973.

Grabowski, S. M. "Continuing Education and How It Relates to a Life Long Process." In M. B. Scott (Ed.), *The Essential Profession.* Stamford, Connecticut: Greylock Publishers, 1976.

The Guide to Vocational Education in America: Trends to 1978. Westport, Connecticut: Market Data Retrieval, Inc., 1975.

Hoyt, K. B. *An Introduction to Career Education: A Policy Paper of the U.S. Office of Education.* Washington, D.C.: U.S. Government Printing Office, 1975.

Hoyt, K. B., Evans, R. N., and Mackin, E. F. *Career Education: What It Is and How to Do It.* Salt Lake City, Utah: Olympus Publishing, 1972, 1974.

Kay, E. R. *Directory of Postsecondary Schools with Occupational Programs, 1973–74.* Washington, D.C.: U.S. Office of Education, Department of Health, Education and Welfare, 1975.

Marland, S. P., Jr. *Career Education: A Proposal for Reform.* New York: McGraw-Hill, 1974.

Occupations: Military-Civilian Occupational Source Book. Washington, D.C.: U.S. Department of Defense, 1975.

Osso, N. A. *Directory of Secondary Schools with Occupational Curriculums, Public and Nonpublic, 1971.* Washington, D.C.: U.S. Office of Education, Department of Health, Education and Welfare, 1973.

The Wentworth Way (Bulletin). Boston: Wentworth Institute, 1975.

Wilms, W. W. *Public and Proprietary Vocational Training: A Study of Effectiveness.* Berkeley: University of California, 1974.

DAVID C. GARDNER

[The author would like to acknowledge the invaluable assistance of Prof. Marilyn Zwicker, Bunker Hill Community College, in researching the materials for this article.]

CARIBBEAN COMMUNITY

The Seventh Conference of Heads of Government of Commonwealth Caribbean Countries, meeting at Chaguaramas in Trinidad and Tobago, transformed the Caribbean Free Trade Association (CARIFTA) into the Caribbean Community (CARICOM). The treaty establishing the Caribbean Community was signed by Barbados, Guyana, Jamaica, and Trinidad and Tobago in Chaguaramas in July 1973. Belize, Dominica, Grenada, Montserrat, Saint Lucia, and Saint Vincent became members of the Caribbean Community in May 1974 and Antigua in July 1974.

The Caribbean Community has three areas of activity: economic integration (the Caribbean Common Market, which replaces and extends CARIFTA); cooperation in noneconomic areas and the operation of certain common services; and coordination of foreign policies of member states.

The Caribbean Common Market provides for the establishment of a common external tariff and common protective policy; adoption of a scheme for the harmonization of fiscal incentives to industry; double taxation arrangements among member countries; coordination of economic policies and development planning; and a special regime for the less developed countries of the community.

The community's two principal organs are the Heads of Government Conference, consisting of heads of government of member states, and the Common Market Council, consisting of a minister of government designated by each member state. The Heads of Government Conference is the final authority of the Caribbean Community and Common Market, and its primary responsibility is to determine the community's policy. The conference is responsible for the conclusion of treaties on behalf of the community and for relationships between the community and international organizations and states. The conference also has responsibility to meet financial expenses of the community.

The Common Market Council is the primary organ of the Caribbean Common Market. The council ensures the efficient operation and development of the Common Market, including the settlement of problems arising out of its functioning. The Heads of Government Conference, however, may issue policy directives. Decisions and recommendations in both organs are in the main taken on the basis of unanimity.

Publications include *CARIFTA and the New Caribbean; From CARIFTA to Caribbean Community; Economics of Devaluation Under West Indian Conditions; Caribbean Examinations Council Comes into Being; Guide for the Use of Exporters and Importers; Brussels Tariff Nomenclature; Caribbean Community: A Guide;* and *Treaty Establishing the Caribbean Community* (July 1973).

Bank of Guyana Building
P.O. Box 607
Georgetown, Guyana

CARIBBEAN: REGIONAL ANALYSIS

Increasingly, the Caribbean region is defined as the area bordering on the Caribbean Sea, but the term is not used here in that larger sense. Instead, it denotes the Caribbean archipelago, which extends for 2500 miles from Cuba to Trinidad and consists of two groups of islands: the Greater Antilles (Cuba, HVI PANIOLA, Jamaica, and Puerto Rico) and the Lesser Antilles (the Netherlands Antilles, the Virgin Islands, Saint Christopher–Nevis–Anguilla, Antigua, Montserrat, Dominica, Martinique, Guadeloupe, Saint Lucia, Barbados, Saint Vincent, Grenada, and Trinidad and Tobago). French Guiana, Surinam, and Guyana, which lie south of the Orinoco River on the South American mainland, and Belize (formerly British Honduras) in Central America, are considered part of the Caribbean and are all linked with the other islands socially and culturally.

Nine of the Caribbean countries are independent: Haiti (1804); the Dominican Republic (1844); Cuba (1902); Jamaica, and Trinidad and Tobago (1962); Barbados and Guyana (1966); Grenada (1974); and Surinam (1975). Linked with Britain as internally self-governing associated states are Antigua, Montserrat, Saint Christopher–Nevis–Anguilla, Dominica, Saint Lucia, and Saint Vincent. The main-land country of Belize is an internally self-governing British colony. The Virgin Islands are divided into two groups: the British Virgin Islands of Tortola, Virgin Gorda, Anegada, Jost Van Dyke, Peter, and Norman, and other small islands; and the Virgin Islands of the United States, consisting of St. Thomas, St. Croix, and St. John, and other islets. Martinique, Guadeloupe, and French Guiana are overseas departments of France. The Netherlands Antilles (Aruba, Bonaire, Curaçao, Saint Martin, Saba, and Saint Eustatius) are self-governing and part of the Kingdom of the Netherlands. Puerto Rico is a commonwealth in free association with the United States, with a considerable measure of control over its own affairs.

Language and culture are a better guide than politics to the history and nature of Caribbean societies. For example, French is spoken not only in the French departments but also in Haiti. English is the formal language and French patois the language of the home in Dominica, Saint Vincent, and independent Grenada. Dutch is the formal language of Surinam and the Netherlands Antilles, but Papiamento is the language of daily life in Curaçao and Aruba. Elements of French speech and of Spanish law survive in Trinidad. Dutch law still influences life in Guyana. English is the language of business in Puerto Rico; but Spanish is the language of many homes, and its continuing use is an assertion of Puerto Rican identity.

History of Caribbean Education

Educational systems everywhere reflect the history and values of their particular societies. When Spain began to settle the Caribbean, both the religion and the higher education system of that country were transplanted to the colonies. The city of Santo Domingo, for many years the capital of the Spanish Indies, was founded in 1496, and in 1538 a university was established there. The Autonomous University of Santo Domingo, in the Dominican Republic, is the oldest university in the Americas.

In 1728 Dominican fathers founded the University of Havana. These acts were significant not necessarily because of the quality of the institutions but because they demonstrated the concern of the Spanish crown and the church for higher education.

Colonial developments in the eastern Caribbean contrasted sharply with Spanish progress. Between 1625 and 1670 the Dutch, French, and English breached the Spanish monopoly of the Caribbean and founded colonies to cultivate such crops as cotton and tobacco for metropolitan markets. After the middle of the seventeenth century, sugar became the chief agricultural product of the area, and the increasing demand for labor led to vast expansion of the African slave trade. Profit became the priority. In the degraded slave-and-sugar-plantation society of the period there were no universities, no centers of intellectual life, and little interest in learning. Education reflected the racist nature of the society. Affluent white children were sent to school in the "home" country. Only small provision was made locally for poor white children. In 1703 Christopher Codrington, a wealthy sugar planter in Barbados, bequeathed his two plantations and the income from them to found an institution to instruct the three hundred blacks on the Codrington estates in medicine and theology, but it was not until the early nineteenth century that the first theological students were admitted to Codrington College. In 1729 John Wolmer, a Kingston jeweler, left money for founding a school for nonslave children, and in 1730 Harrison Free Grammar School (now Harrison College) in Barbados was begun for twenty-four indigent white boys. In general, these colonial societies were grossly materialistic, as Charles Leslie noted when he visited Jamaica in the 1740s. He found that Jamaica's white planter society held teachers in low esteem and despised scholarship.

After the abolition of slavery in the English colonies (1833) and in the French colonies (1848), education improved. By that time many European governments had accepted the responsibility for supporting primary education and this provision was extended to their colonies. However, because the educational system of each colony was closely modeled on that of the "home" country, much of the content of education was irrelevant to colonial students. In Trinidad, for instance, this irrelevancy appears to have been uncorrected for an entire century. In 1869, when the chief of inspection of the Board of National 'Education in Ireland was sent by the British government to advise on education in Trinidad, he perceived the need for a set of reading books oriented at least in half to the local history, resources, and culture of the colony. In 1968, the curriculum of British West Indian schools was not yet adapted to the needs of the community. Criticizing the curriculum that had been decreed by law for Jamaican schools, Eric Williams wrote: "The most obvious omission is the reference to anything West Indian." He also pointed out that the artificiality of the British West Indian school was largely due to the British colonial practice of using external examinations from Oxford and Cambridge (Williams, 1968, pp. 29–41).

Even more revealing and significant is the fact that the metropolitan model of education was embraced and defended by the local elite. As Albert Memmi points out, "The first ambition of the colonised is to become equal to that splendid model and to resemble him to the point of disappearing in him" (1967, p. 120). It is not simple, however, for a country built on racism to resemble one built on class distinctions. The metropolitan country had class distinctions, but it was a white country; it had never been a slave-and-sugar plantation. The educational system was elitist but the elite and the rest of the population belonged to one country, knew its history, were proud of its achievements, and could find within it their models of excellence. The reverse was the case in the

Caribbean countries. The system was elitist, but almost without exception the elite were white; the masses were black or brown. For three centuries, to be black meant to be a slave; to be white meant to be a master. The system of education perpetuated the prejudices and inculcated the prevailing value systems.

Growth of Higher Education

With a few exceptions, such as Autonomous University of Santo Domingo and the University of Havana, higher education in the Caribbean has been basically a twentieth-century phenomenon. Between 1900 and World War II four institutions of higher education were founded in Puerto Rico, but it was not until the late 1930s that the expansion of educational facilities at all levels was seen as necessary to national development. The 1940s and 1950s saw many advances in Caribbean higher education, bringing it for the first time within the reach of the West Indian masses.

Cuba. Cuba radically changed its traditional educational system toward the end of the 1950s, when the Cuban revolution moved out of its first phase of attempting to establish heavy industry into a second phase in which national effort centered on production. Because education was considered an indispensable instrument for national development, a new educational system was created. A massive and remarkably successful literacy campaign was organized to integrate the Cuban peasant into the new society, and scientific and technological studies were improved. The following figures indicate the change of direction in Cuban higher education: In 1959 just over 37 percent of the students in the University of Havana were in the humanities; in 1969 the proportion was 6 percent. In the same period the proportion of students in science rose from 7 percent to 16 percent; in technology, from 5 percent to 26 percent; in agriculture and veterinary science, from 3 percent to 7 percent; and in economics, from .6 percent to 6 percent. A visiting scientist found that

there was freedom in career choice but that the policy of the government and the general orientation of the schools had profoundly modified the motivation of students. He found also that the increase in total university enrollment in Cuba was not as great as increases in most Latin American countries. The indications are that the growth in university enrollment in science and technology is paralleled by a growth in scientific research in the university and in specialized institutions such as the National Scientific Research Centre and the Victoria de Girón Institute.

Dominican Republic. The changes in Cuba were brought about as part of the revolution. In other Caribbean countries, traditional patterns have been modified, new models adopted, and educational opportunity widened as a result of pressure for social and economic development and, in some cases, as a result of growing nationalism. In the Dominican Republic four new private universities have been established, the two largest being the University of Pedro Henríquez Ureña in Santo Domingo (1966) and the University of Madre y Maestra in Santiago (1962).

Puerto Rico. In Puerto Rico nearly 2 percent of the population is in institutions of higher education, compared with about 1 percent in most Western European countries. No other Caribbean country offers as wide an opportunity for university education. Although Puerto Rico was originally a Spanish colony, its system of higher education is modeled on that of the United States, which took control of the island in 1898 at the close of the Spanish-American War. In his 1901 report on education in Puerto Rico, the United States commissioner of education emphasized that the spirit of American institutions and the ideals of the American people should be the only ones incorporated into the school system of the island; and the University of Puerto Rico, established in 1903, was designed to fit that policy. In 1942 legislation opened the way for reforms, and the university was reorganized for the purpose of contributing effectively to fundamental changes in the social and economic structure of Puerto Rican society. After Puerto Rico became a commonwealth in free association with the United States, the educational system was brought into closer relationship with Puerto Rican goals and values by the Puerto Rican politician and statesman Muñoz Marin. The University of Puerto Rico developed into a university system with several campuses and regional colleges. In addition to the state university, there are various private universities, including the Inter-American University of Puerto Rico, the Catholic University of Puerto Rico at Ponce, Bayamón Central University, and the Mendez Foundation.

The West Indies region. The University of the West Indies is of special interest because it is the area's only regional university. It is a private corporation whose control and ownership are vested in a council whose members are representatives from each of the twelve supporting governments: Antigua, Bahamas, Barbados, Belize, Dominica, Grenada, Jamaica, Montserrat, Saint Lucia, Saint Christopher–Nevis–Anguilla, Saint Vincent, and the British Virgin Islands. The university started in 1946 as a small residential college in Mona, Jamaica, associated with the University of London. Residence was stressed because at the time there was no common meeting ground for West Indian students. Gradually, ties with London loosened, and in 1962 the university became an independent degree-granting institution. By then, it had developed curricula and courses more relevant to the region, had abandoned the requirement for residence, and had adopted a policy of decentralizing university facilities. A second campus was established in St. Augustine, Trinidad, in 1960 and a third at Cave Hill, Barbados, in 1963.

The outreach programs of the university provide an interesting example of the way in which a regional university can increase its impact on a widely dispersed community, for the programs serve people separated by the Caribbean Sea by as much as two thousand miles. The Institutes of Education and of Economic and Social Research and the Extension Department (Department of Extra-Mural Studies) are active in the countries that support the university.

The recently founded University of Guyana (1963) and the University of the West Indies have cooperated with the British Commonwealth governments in setting up, in January 1973, a Caribbean Examinations Council. This represents a far-reaching decision to increase the independence of the West Indies educational system.

Netherlands Antilles. The Netherlands Antilles and Surinam present a contrast to the French Antilles on the one hand and to the British associated states on the other. In their search for economic viability and autonomy, the associated states accepted a relationship with Britain that secured a measure of financial aid and full internal self-government but that left foreign affairs and defense in the hands of Britain. The French Antilles and French Guiana chose assimilation with France; as a result, they are parts of France, and their system of education is French. Surinam and the Netherlands Antilles had a different relationship with the Kingdom of the Netherlands, being partners in a tripartite kingdom. In 1975 Surinam gained complete political independence, and it established a university with assistance from the University of Leiden and other Dutch universities. As of 1976, Curaçao and Aruba share a school of law, and each is developing a higher education system of its own.

Association of Caribbean Universities and Research Institutes. Caribbean institutions have begun to work together for the development of the region. The Association of Caribbean Universities and Research Institutes was established in 1968 to secure cooperation and coordination among various branches of higher education. The association has grown from the original sixteen member institutions to fifty. It represents a rejection of the separateness and separatism that characterized the past and a further movement toward relating Caribbean education to Caribbean life and culture.

Bibliography

Cespedes, S. "Public Elementary Education in the Caribbean." In A. C. Wilgus (Ed.), *The Caribbean Contemporary Education.* Gainesville: University of Florida Press, 1960.

Comitas, L., and Lowenthal, D. (Eds.) *The Aftermath of Sovereignty: West Indian Perspective.* Garden City, New York: Doubleday, 1973.

Comitas, L., and Lowenthal, D. (Eds.) *Consequences of Class and Color: West Indian Perspective.* Garden City, New York: Doubleday, 1973.

Comitas, L., and Lowenthal, D. (Eds.) *Slaves, Free Men and Citizens: West Indian Perspective.* Garden City, New York: Doubleday, 1973.

Comitas, L., and Lowenthal, D. (Eds.) *Work and Family Life: West Indian Perspective.* Garden City, New York: Doubleday, 1973.

Demas, W. G. *The Political Economy of the English-Speaking Caribbean.* Study Paper 4. Port of Spain, Trinidad: Caribbean Ecumenical Consultation for Development, 1972.

Gordon, S. *Reports and Repercussions in West Indian Education: 1835–1933.* London: Ginn, 1968.

Leslie, C. *A New History of Jamaica.* London: Printed for J. Hodges at the Looking Glass on London Bridge, 1740.

Lewis, G. *Growth of the Modern West Indies.* London: McGibbon & Kee, 1968.

Marshall, R. "Direction and Management of the University." *Times* (London) *Higher Education Supplement,* August 24, 1973.

Memmi, A. *The Coloniser and the Colonised.* Boston: Beacon Press, 1967.

Parker, P. "Change and Challenge in Caribbean Higher Education." Unpublished doctoral dissertation, Florida State University, 1971.

Parry, J., and Sherlock, P. *Short History of the West Indies.* London: Macmillan, 1957.

Proudfoot, R. *Britain and the United States in the Caribbean.* London: Faber & Faber, 1954.

Sherlock, M. *The Land and People of the West Indies.* Philadelphia: Lippincott, 1967.

Sherlock, M. "Universities: Doldrums or Trade Winds." Commencement address, University of Miami, June 1971.

Sherlock, P. *West Indian Nations.* London: Macmillan, 1973.

Taylor, T. W. J. "The University College of the West Indies." *Caribbean Quarterly,* 1950, 2(1).

Thomas, H. *Cuba.* New York: Harper & Row, 1971.

Williams, E. *Education in the British West Indies.* New York: University Place Book Shop, 1968.

Williams, E. "The University in the Caribbean in the Late 20th Century." In M. D. Stephens and G. W. Roderick (Eds.), *Universities for a Changing World.* Devon, England: David & Charles, 1975.

PHILIP SHERLOCK

See also: Antigua; Barbados; Belize; Cuba, Republic of; French Guiana; Dominica; Grenada; Jamaica; Montserrat; Puerto Rico, Commonwealth of; Saint Christopher (St. Kitts) Nevis-Anguilla; Saint Lucia; Saint Vincent; Surinam; Trinidad and Tobago; Virgin Islands of the United States, The.

CARNEGIE COMMISSION ON HIGHER EDUCATION,
United States

The Carnegie Commission on Higher Education was founded in 1967 by the Carnegie Foundation for the Advancement of Teaching to study and make recommendations concerning higher education for the 1970s and ahead to the year 2000. Studying and reporting on such major aspects of higher education as governance, function, structure, demand and access, and effective use of resources, the commission has contributed enormously to existing literature on higher education. Although its investigations were carried out during a time of turmoil in higher education, the commission conducted its work in a fair-minded and realistic manner, disbanding after six and a half years of work in late 1973.

The members of the commission were men who had shown a continuing interest in higher education and had displayed ability and judgment in their handling of complex problems. When the committee was formed, six members were college or university presidents; one, the head of a junior college district; one, a professor; one, the head of a research institute; one, a publisher; one, a governor of a state; and three industrialists who were also university or college trustees. Some time later, five other persons were added to make the committee's membership more diverse: the deans of two law schools, the president of a four-year state college, a professor of psychology on a medical school faculty, and a British authority on international higher education—a total membership of nineteen, including the chairman. Members of the commission were:

Eric Ashby
The Master
Clare College
Cambridge, England

Ralph M. Besse
Partner
Squire, Sanders & Dempsey
Counsellors at Law

Joseph P. Cosand
Professor of Education and Director
Center for Higher Education
University of Michigan

William Friday
President
University of North Carolina

The Honorable Patricia Roberts Harris
Partner
Fried, Frank, Harris, Shriver & Kampelman,
Attorneys

David D. Henry
President Emeritus
Distinguished Professor of Higher Education
University of Illinois

Theodore M. Hesburgh, C.S.C.
President
University of Notre Dame

Stanley J. Heywood
President
Eastern Montana College

Carl Kaysen
Director
Institute for Advanced Study at Princeton

Kenneth Keniston
Professor of Psychology
School of Medicine
Yale University

Katharine E. McBride
President Emeritus
Bryn Mawr College

James A. Perkins
Chairman of the Board
International Council for Educational
Development

Clifton W. Phalen
Chairman of the Executive Committee
Marine Midland Banks, Inc.

Nathan M. Pusey
Former President, Harvard University
Former President, Andrew W. Mellon
Foundation

David Riesman
Henry Ford II Professor of Social Sciences
Harvard University

The Honorable William W. Scranton

Norton Simon

Kenneth Tollett
Distinguished Professor of Higher Education
Howard University

Clark Kerr
Chairman

The Carnegie Foundation for the Advancement of Teaching, with the financial assistance of the Carnegie Corporation of New York, provided five and two-thirds millions of dollars to fund the commission's work from 1967 to 1973. The commission's headquarters was in Berkeley, California. The Ford Foundation cooperated on several projects, and the Commonwealth Fund cooperated on one major project in the health field. A major survey project, conducted with the cooperation of the American Council on Education, was financed, to some extent, by the United States Office of Education.

The commission was privately controlled and financed. Officers of the foundation or trustees of the corporation were not asked to clear or approve the findings of the commission—thus ensuring its independence. The commission did not consider that it was beholden or answerable to any part of the higher education community—except for the accuracy of its material—or to the federal or state governments. On the flyleaf of each commission policy report, the following inscription is found: "The views and conclusions expressed in this report are solely those of the Carnegie Commission on Higher Education and do not necessarily reflect the views or opinion of the Carnegie Corporation of New York, the Carnegie Foundation for the Advancement of Teaching, or their trustees, directors, or employees."

The commission met on thirty-three occasions in twenty-six different cities for a total of seventy-seven days. Each commission report was discussed at three meetings and some at many more, each committee member participating in the discussion of each report. Twenty-one special reports issued by the commission, are listed below chronologically.

Carnegie Commission Reports

1. *Quality and Equality: New Levels of Federal Reponsibility for Higher Education*, December 1968; *Revised Recommendations*, June 1970
2. *A Chance to Learn: An Action Agenda for Equal Opportunity in Higher Education*, March 1970
3. *The Open-Door Colleges: Policies for Community Colleges*, June 1971
4. *Higher Education and the Nation's Health: Policies for Medical and Dental Education*, October 1971
5. *Less Time, More Options: Education Beyond the High School*, January 1970
6. *From Isolation to Mainstream: Problems of the Colleges Founded for Negroes*, February 1971
7. *The Capitol and the Campus: State Responsibility for Postsecondary Education*, April 1971
8. *Dissent and Disruption: Proposals for Consideration by the Campus*, June 1971
9. *New Students and New Places: Policies for the Future Growth and Development of American Higher Education*, October 1971
10. *Institutional Aid: Federal Support to Colleges and Universities*, February 1972
11. *The Fourth Revolution: Instructional Technology in Higher Education*, June 1972
12. *The More Effective Use of Resources: An Imperative for Higher Education*, June 1972
13. *Reform on Campus: Changing Students, Changing Academic Programs*, June 1972
14. *The Campus and the City: Maximizing Assets and Reducing Liabilities*, December 1972
15. *College Graduates and Jobs: Adjusting to a New Labor Market Situation*, April 1973
16. *Governance of Higher Education: Six Priority Problems*, April 1973
17. *The Purposes and the Performance of Higher Education in the United States: Approaching the Year 2000*, June 1973
18. *Higher Education: Who Pays? Who Benefits? Who Should Pay?* July 1973
19. *Continuity and Discontinuity: Higher Education and the Schools*, August 1973
20. *Opportunities for Women in Higher Education: Their Current Participation, Prospects for the Future, and Recommendations for Action*, September 1973
21. *Toward a Learning Society: Alternative Channels to Life, Work, and Service*, October 1973

Reports of the commission are infiltrating the literature of higher education read by administrators, educators, and laymen in the 1970s. They contain some 300 recommendations for consideration of the higher education community. The information in the listed reports is proving invaluable to policymakers in the field of higher education—colleges and universities and government agencies and organizations that have some interface with higher education.

Help was sought from countless authorities at home and abroad during the course of the commission's investigation—from such diverse fields as sociology, economics, history, education, and political science. Sixty-four reports sponsored by the commission, nineteen special studies, and thirty-one reprints are listed below (those preceded by an asterisk are not available for distribution):

Sponsored Studies

* 1. Howard R. Bowen, *The Finance of Higher Education*, August 1968
* 2. William G. Bowen, *The Economics of the Major Private Universities*, August 1968
* 3. Ronald A. Wolk, *Alternative Methods of Federal Funding for Higher Education*, December 1968
* 4. Dale M. Heckman and Warren Bryan Martin, *Inventory of Current Research on Higher Education, 1968*, December 1968
5. E. Alden Dunham, *Colleges of the Forgotten Americans: A Profile of State Colleges and Regional Universities*, November 1969
6. Andrew M. Greeley, *From Backwater to Mainstream: A Profile of Catholic Higher Education*, November 1969
* 7. Heinz Eulau and Harold Quinley, *State Officials and Higher Education: A Survey of the Opinions and Expectations of Policy Makers in Nine States*, May 1970
8. Stephen H. Spurr, *Academic Degree Structures: Innovative Approaches—Principles of Reform in Degree Structures in the United States*, May 1970
9. Dwight R. Ladd, *Change in Educational*

Policy: Self-Studies in Selected Colleges and Universities, July 1970

*10. Lewis B. Mayhew, *Graduate and Professional Education, 1980: A Survey of Institutional Plans*, August 1970

11. Oscar Handlin and Mary F. Handlin, *The American College and American Culture: Socialization as a Function of Higher Education*, September 1970

*12. Joe L. Spaeth and Andrew M. Greeley, *Recent Alumni and Higher Education: A Survey of College Graduates*, September 1970

13. Irwin T. Sanders and Jennifer C. Ward, *Bridges to Understanding: International Programs of American Colleges and Universities*, December 1970

14. Barbara B. Burn, with chapters by Clark Kerr, Philip Altbach, and James A. Perkins, *Higher Education in Nine Countries: A Comparative Study of Colleges and Universities Abroad*, February 1971

*15. Rashi Fein and Gerald Weber, *Financing Medical Education: An Analysis of Alternative Policies and Mechanisms*, February 1971

16. Earl Cheit, *The New Depression in Higher Education: A Study of Financial Conditions at 41 Colleges and Universities*, February 1971

17. Leland L. Medsker and Dale Tillery, *Breaking the Access Barriers: A Profile of Two-Year Colleges*, March 1971

18. Frank Bowles and Frank A. DeCosta, *Between Two Worlds: A Profile of Negro Higher Education*, April 1971

19. Eric Ashby, *Any Person, Any Study: An Essay on American Higher Education*, April 1971

20. Morris Keeton, *Models and Mavericks: A Profile of the Private Liberal Arts Colleges*, May 1971

21. Robert Hartman, *Credit for College: Public Policy for Student Loans*, June 1971

22. Howard R. Bowen and Gordon K. Douglass, *Efficiency in Liberal Education: A Study of Comparative Instructional Costs for Different Ways of Organizing Teaching-Learning in a Liberal Arts College*, September 1971

23. Eugene C. Lee and Frank M. Bowen, *The Multicampus University: A Study of Academic Governance*, September 1971

24. Harold L. Hodgkinson, *Institutions in Transition: A Profile of Change in Higher Education* (incorporating the 1970 statistical report), September 1971

25. Stephen B. Whithey and others, *A Degree and What Else? Correlates and Consequences of a College Education*, October 1971

26. Joseph Ben-David, *American Higher Education: Directions Old and New*, December 1971

27. Alexander W. Astin and Calvin B. T. Lee, *The Invisible Colleges: A Profile of Small, Private Colleges with Limited Resources*, January 1972

28. Harold Orlans, *The Nonprofit Research Institute: Its Origin, Operation, Problems, and Prospects*, March 1972

29. Edgar H. Schein, *Professional Education; Some New Directions*, March 1972

30. C. Robert Pace, *Education and Evangelism: A Profile of Protestant Colleges*, June 1972

31. Dael Wolfle, *The Home of Science: The Role of the University*, June 1972

32. Seymour E. Harris, *A Statistical Portrait of Higher Education*, June 1972

33. Roger E. Levien, *The Emerging Technology: Instructional Uses of the Computer in Higher Education*, November 1972

34. C. Arnold Anderson, Mary Jean Bowman, and Vincent Tinto, *Where Colleges Are and Who Attends: Effects of Accessibility on College Attendance*, November 1972

35. Herbert L. Packer and Thomas Ehrlich, *New Directions in Legal Education*, November 1972 (abridged paperback edition, April 1973)

36. James A. Perkins, *The University as an Organization*, February 1973

37. Richard Storr, *The Beginning of the Future: A Historical Approach to Graduate Education in the Arts and Sciences*, June 1973

38. David Riesman and Verne Stadtman (Eds.), *Academic Transformation: Seventeen Institutions Under Pressure*, June 1973

39. George Nash, *The University and the City: Eight Cases of Involvement*, June 1973

40. Jack Morrison, *The Rise of the Arts on the American Campus*, July 1973

41. Alexander Mood, *The Future of Higher Education: Some Speculations and Suggestions*, September 1973

42. Carl Kaysen (Ed.), *Content and Context: Essays on College Education*, October 1973

43. Everett C. Hughes, Barrie Thorne, Agostino M. DeBaggis, Arnold Gurin, and David Williams, *Education for the Professions of Medicine, Law, Theology, and Social Welfare*, October 1973

44. Michael Cohen and James March, *Leadership and Ambiguity: The American College President*, January 1974

45. Stephen Steinberg, *The Academic Melting Pot: Catholics and Jews in Higher Education*, January 1974

46. Alain Touraine, *The Academic System in American Society*, February 1974

47. Margaret S. Gordon (Ed.), *Higher Education and the Labor Market*, February 1974

48. Saul Feldman, *Escape from the Doll's House: Women in Graduate and Professional School Education*, April 1974

49. Edward Gross and Paul Grambsch, *Change in University Organization: 1964–1971*, May 1974

50. Richard A. Lester, *Antibias Regulation of Universities: Faculty Problems and Their Solutions*, July 1974

51. Harland G. Bloland and Sue M. Bloland, *American Learned Societies in Transition; The Impact of Dissent and Recession*, September 1974

52. Paul Taubman and Terence Wales, *Higher Education and Earnings: College as an Investment and a Screening Device*, November 1974

53. Thomas Juster and others, *Education, Income and Human Behavior*, December 1974

54. S. M. Lipset and David Riesman, *Education and Politics at Harvard*, May 1975

55. Everett Ladd and S. M. Lipset, *The Divided Academy: Professors and Politics*, May 1975

56. Earl Cheit, *The Useful Arts and the Liberal Tradition*, June 1975

57. Joseph Garbarino in association with Bill Aussieker, *Faculty Bargaining: Change and Conflict*, June 1975

58. Florence Howe and others, *Women and the Power to Change*, July 1975

59. Martin Trow and others, *Teachers and Students: Aspects of American Higher Education*, July 1975

60. John Fralick Rockart and Michael S. Scott Morton, *Computers and the Learning Process in Higher Education*, July 1975

61. Roy Radner and Leonard S. Miller with collaboration of Douglas L. Adkins and Frederick E. Balderston, *Demand and Supply in U.S. Higher Education*, November 1975

62. Allan Cartter, *The Ph.D. and the Labor Market*, March 1976

63. Richard Freeman, *Black Elite: The New Market for Highly Qualified Black Americans*, forthcoming

64. Joseph Ben-David, *Effectiveness of American Higher Education*, forthcoming

Technical Reports

* 1. Harold Hodgkinson, *Institutions in Transition: A Study of Change in Higher Education*, June 1970

* 2. June O'Neill, *Resource Use in Higher Education: Trends in Output and Input of American Colleges and Universities, 1930–1967*, July 1971

* 3. Mark S. Blumberg, *Trends and Projections of Physicians in the United States, 1967–2002*, July 1971

4. Richard E. Peterson and John A. Bilorusky, *May 1970: The Campus Aftermath of Cambodia and Kent State*, October 1971

* 5. Paul Taubman and Terence Wales, *Mental Ability and Higher Educational Attainment in the 20th Century*, June 1972

* 6. Richard E. Peterson, *American College and University Enrollment Trends in 1971*, June 1972

* 7. Alexander Mood and others, *Papers on Efficiency in the Management of Higher Education*, August 1972

* 8. Ann Heiss, *An Inventory of Academic Innovation and Reform*, March 1973

9. Earl Cheit, *The New Depression in Higher Education—Two Years Later*, May 1973

*10. Richard Eckaus, *Estimating the Returns to Education: A Disaggregated Approach*, May 1973

11. June O'Neill, *Sources of Funds to Colleges and Universities*, May 1973

12. Everett Ladd and S. M. Lipset, *Professors, Unions, and American Higher Education*, August 1973

13. Carnegie Commission on Higher Education, *A Classification of Institutions of Higher Education*, November 1973

*14. Margaret Fay and Jeff Weintraub, *Political Ideologies of Graduate Students: Crystallization, Consistency, and Contextual Effects*, February 1974

15 Thomas J. Karwin, *Flying a Learning Center: Design and Costs of an Off-Campus Space for Learning*, February 1974

16. C Robert Pace, *The Demise of Diversity? A Comparative Profile of Eight Types of Institutions*, March 1974

17. Carnegie Commission on Higher Education, *Tuition: A Supplemental Statement on the Report of the Carnegie Commission on Higher Education on Who Pays? Who Benefits? Who Should Pay?* April 1974

18. Michio Nagai, *An Owl Before Dusk*, October 1975

19. Douglas Adkins, *The Great American Degree Machine, An Economic Analysis of the Human Resource Output of Higher Education*, November 1975

20. Leonard S. Miller and Roy Radner, *Demand and Supply in the United States Higher Education: A Technical Supplement*, November 1975

Reprints

* 1. Theodore W. Schultz, "Resources for Higher Education: An Economist's View," reprinted from *The Journal of Political Economy*, vol. 76, no. 3, May/June 1968

* 2. Clark Kerr, "Industrial Relations and University Relations," reprinted from *Proceedings of the 21st Annual Winter Meeting of the Industrial Relations Research Association*, pp. 15–25

* 3. Clark Kerr, "New Challenges to the College and University," reprinted from *Agenda for the Nation*, Kermit Gordon (Ed.), Brookings Institution, Washington, D.C., 1968

* 4. Clark Kerr, "Presidential Discontent," reprinted from *Perspectives on Campus Tensions: Papers Prepared for the Special Committee on Campus Tensions*, David C. Nichols (Ed.), American Council on Education, Washington, D.C., September 1970

* 5. Harold Hodgkinson, "Student Protest— An Institutional and National Profile," reprinted from *The Record*, vol. 71, no. 4, May 1970

* 6. Kenneth Keniston, "What's Bugging the Students?" reprinted from *The Educational Record*, vol. 51, no. 2, Spring 1970

* 7. Seymour M. Lipset, "The Politics of Academia," reprinted from *Perspectives on Campus Tensions: Papers Prepared for the Special Committee on Campus Tensions*, David C. Nichols (Ed.), American Council on Education, Washington, D.C., September 1970

* 8. Seymour M. Lipset and Everett C. Ladd, Jr., ". . . And What Professors Think," reprinted from *Psychology Today*, vol. 4, no. 6, November 1970

* 9. Roy Radner and Leonard S. Miller, "Demand and Supply in U.S. Higher Education: A Progress Report," reprinted from *The American Economic Review*, vol. 60, no. 2, May 1970

*10. Kenneth Keniston and Michael Lerner, "The Unholy Alliance Against the Campus," reprinted from *The New York Times Magazine*, November 8, 1970

*11. Joseph W. Garbarino, "Precarious Professors: New Patterns of Representation," reprinted from *Industrial Relations*, vol. 10, no. 1, February 1971

*12. Earl F. Cheit, "Regent Watching," reprinted from *AGB Reports*, vol. 13, no. 6, March 1971

*13. Neil Timm, "A New Method of Measuring States' Higher Education Burden," reprinted from *The Journal of Higher Education*, vol. 42, no. 1, January 1971

*14. Seymour M. Lipset and Everett C. Ladd, Jr., "Jewish Academics in the United States: Their Achievements, Culture and Politics, reprinted from *American Jewish Year Book*, 1971.

*15. Seymour M. Lipset and Everett C. Ladd, Jr., "The Divided Professoriate," reprinted from *Change*, vol. 3, no. 3, May 1971

*16. Seymour M. Lipset and Everett C. Ladd, Jr., "The Politics of American Political Scientists," reprinted from *PS*, vol. 4, no. 2, Spring 1971

*17. Allan M. Cartter, "Scientific Manpower for 1970–1985," reprinted from *Science*, vol. 172, no. 3979, April 9, 1971

 18. Seymour M. Lipset and Everett C. Ladd, Jr., "American Social Scientists and the Growth of Campus Political Activism in the 1960s," reprinted from *Social Sciences Information*, vol. 10, no. 2, April 1971

*19. Mark S. Blumberg, "Accelerated Programs of Medical Education," reprinted from *Journal of Medical Education*, vol. 46, no. 8, August 1971

*20. Seymour M. Lipset and Everett C. Ladd, Jr., "College Generations—From the 1930s to the 1960s," reprinted from *The Public Interest*, no. 25, Summer 1971

*21. James A. Perkins, "International Programs of U.S. Colleges and Universities: Priorities for the Seventies," reprinted from *Occasional Paper No. 1*, International Council for Educational Development, July 1971

*22. Joseph W. Garbarino, "Faculty Unionism: From Theory to Practice," reprinted from *Industrial Relations*, vol. 11, no. 1, February 1972

*23. Virginia B. Smith, "More for Less: Higher Education's New Priority," reprinted from *Universal Higher Education: Costs and Benefits*, American Council on Education, Washington, D.C., 1971

*24. Seymour M. Lipset, "Academia and Politics in America," reprinted from *Imagination and Precision in the Social Sciences*, Thomas J. Nossiter (Ed.), Faber and Faber, London, 1972

 25. Everett C. Ladd, Jr., and Seymour M. Lipset, "Politics of Academic Natural Scientists and Engineers," reprinted from *Science*, vol. 176, no. 4039, June 9, 1972

 26. Seymour M. Lipset and Richard B. Dobson, "The Intellectual as Critic and Rebel: With Special Reference to the United States and the Soviet Union," reprinted from *Daedalus*, vol. 101, no. 3, Summer 1972

*27. Seymour M. Lipset and Everett C. Ladd, Jr., "The Politics of American Sociolo-

gists," reprinted from *The American Journal of Sociology,* vol. 78, no. 1, July 1972
28. Martin Trow, "The Distribution of Academic Tenure in American Higher Education," reprinted from *The Tenure Debate,* Bardwell Smith (Ed.), Jossey-Bass, San Francisco, 1972
29. Alan Pifer, "The Nature and Origins of the Carnegie Commission on Higher Education," based on a speech delivered to the Pennsylvania Association of Colleges and Universities on October 16, 1972, and reprinted by permission of the Carnegie Foundation for the Advancement of Teaching
30. Earl F. Cheit, "Coming of Middle Age in Higher Education," based on an address to the Joint Session of the American Association of State Colleges and Universities and the National Association of State Universities and Land-Grant Colleges in Washington, D.C., on November 13, 1972, and reprinted by permission of the National Association of State Universities and Land-Grant Colleges
31. Bill Aussieker and J. W. Garbarino, "Measuring Faculty Unionism: Quantity and Quality," reprinted from *Industrial Relations,* vol. 12, no. 2, May 1973
32. Martin Trow, *Problems in the Transition from Elite to Mass Higher Education.* Paper prepared for a conference on mass higher education held by the Organisation for Economic Co-operation and Development in Paris, June 1973

The Technical Advisory Committee assisted the commission by discussing each of the reports in draft form. Listed below are the members of this committee with the dates of their service:

Frederick Balderston
Chairman, Center for Research in Management Sciences
University of California, Berkeley, 1969–1973

David Blackwell
Professor of Statistics
University of California, Berkeley, 1969–1973

Lewis Butler
Planning Coordinator, Health Policy Program; and Adjunct Professor, School of Medicine
University of California, San Francisco, 1971–1973

Earl Cheit
Professor of Business Administration
University of California, Berkeley, 1970–1973

Charles Hitch
President of the University of California, 1967–1969

Eugene Lee
Director, Institute of Governmental Studies
University of California, Berkeley, 1970–1973

Seymour Martin Lipset
Fellow, Center for Advanced Studies in the Behavioral Sciences
Stanford, California, 1972–1973

Thomas R. McConnell
Professor of Education, Emeritus
University of California, Berkeley, 1967–1973

Joseph Pechman
then Visiting Professor, Department of Economics
University of California, Berkeley, 1970–1971

Roy Radner
Professor of Economics and Statistics
University of California, Berkeley, 1967–1973

David Riesman
then Fellow, Center for Advanced Studies in the Behavioral Sciences
Stanford, California, 1968–1969

George Shultz
then Fellow, Center for Advanced Studies in the Behavioral Sciences
Stanford, California, 1968–1969

Neil Smelser
University Professor of Sociology
University of California, Berkeley 1967–1973

Martin Trow
Professor of Sociology
University of California, Berkeley, 1967–1973

Lloyd Ulman
Director, Institute of Industrial Relations
University of California, Berkeley, 1968–1973

Three volumes comprise the summary report of the Carnegie Commission on Higher Education. *Priorities for Action: Final Report of the Carnegie Commission on Higher Education* reviews the objectives of the commission and presents final recommendations and findings. The second volume, *A Digest of Reports of the Carnegie Commission on Higher Education,* includes condensations of the twenty-one policy reports issued by the commission, an index to the commission's recommendations, and suggested assignments of responsibility for action on the recommendations.

The third volume, *Sponsored Research of the Carnegie Commission on Higher Education,* summarizes reports based on the more than eighty research projects sponsored in whole or in part by the commission.

2150 Shattuck Avenue
Berkeley, California 94704 USA

CARNEGIE CORPORATION AND FOUNDATION FOR THE ADVANCEMENT OF TEACHING

See Research: Role of Foundations in Academic Research.

CARNEGIE COUNCIL ON POLICY STUDIES IN HIGHER EDUCATION, United States

In 1973 the Carnegie Council on Policy Studies in Higher Education was created by the Carnegie Foundation for the Advancement of Teaching to make continuous, independent studies of higher education. Unlike the Carnegie Commission on Higher Education, a body of finite life span which concluded its work in December 1973, the council is a permanent study and research unit of the Carnegie Foundation for the Advancement of Teaching. Clark Kerr, who had served as chairman of the commission, was elected as chairman and staff director of the new council. The new council began its operations at its headquarters in Berkeley, California, in January 1974.

The Carnegie Council on Policy Studies in Higher Education has broad interests in developments and issues in higher education. Initially, however, its attention and resources will be focused on a relatively few specific concerns. Emphasis is currently being given to the impact of the "steady state" on higher education, the federal government and higher education, medical and dental education, the undergraduate curriculum at colleges and universities, and federal-state relations in higher education.

Other specific topics of present or future interest to the council are continuing enrollment projections for institutions of higher education, the private sector of higher education and private support for higher education, youth in American society, vocational training in postsecondary education, the financing of recurrent education, and benefits of higher education. Additional concerns are the states and collective bargaining in higher education, higher education and the problem-solving capacity of society, international aspects of higher education, and efficiency and diversity in higher education.

Members of the Carnegie Council on Policy Studies are elected by the board of trustees of the Carnegie Foundation for the Advancement of Teaching for three-year terms. A majority of the council's members are members of the Carnegie Foundation board. Current members of the council are:

Clark Kerr
Chairman

William G. Bowen
President, Princeton University

Ernest L. Boyer
Chancellor, State University of New York

Nolen Ellison
President, Cuyahoga Community College
Cleveland, Ohio

Elbert K. Fretwell, Jr.
President, State University of New York
College at Buffalo

Margaret L. A. MacVicar
Associate Professor of Physics
Massachusetts Institute of Technology
Cambridge, Massachusetts

Rosemary Park
Professor Emeritus, School of Education
University of California, Los Angeles

James A. Perkins
Chairman of the Board
International Council for Educational
Development

Alan Pifer
President
Carnegie Foundation for the Advancement
of Teaching

Joseph B. Platt
President, Harvey Mudd College
Claremont, California

Lois Rice
Vice-President, College Entrance Examination
Board

William M. Roth
Regent of the University of California

Pauline Tompkins
President, Cedar Crest College
Allentown, Pennsylvania

William Van Alstyne
Professor of Law, Duke University
Durham, North Carolina

Published results of the council are expected to take several forms. Some will be prepared by the council itself and by members of its staff. Others will be prepared by persons engaged in research sponsored by the council. In addition, each year the board of trustees of the Carnegie Foundation for the Advancement of Teaching, with the assistance of the council, produces a commentary on some significant problem or issue in higher education.

Studies of the council that have been published include the following:

The Federal Role in Postsecondary Education: Unfinished Business, 1975–1980
Carnegie Council on Policy Studies in Higher Education

More Than Survival: Prospects for Higher Education in a Period of Uncertainty
Carnegie Foundation for the Advancement of Teaching

Making Affirmative Action Work in Higher Education: An Analysis of Institutional and Federal Policies with Recommendations
Carnegie Council on Policy Studies in Higher Education

Low or No Tuition: The Feasibility of a National Policy for the First Two Years of College
Carnegie Council on Policy Studies in Higher Education

Managing Multicampus Systems: Effective Administration in an Unsteady State
Eugene C. Lee, Frank M. Bowen

Challenges Past, Challenges Present: An Analysis of American Higher Education Since 1930
David D. Henry

Presidents Confront Reality: From Edifice Complex to University Without Walls
Lyman A. Glenny, John R. Shea, Janet H. Ruyle, Kathryn H. Freschi

The States and Higher Education: A Proud Past and a Vital Future
Carnegie Foundation for the Advancement of Teaching

2150 Shattuck Avenue
Berkeley, California 94704 USA

CARR-SAUNDERS REPORT
See University Education in Malaya, Report of the Commission on (Higher Education Report), United States

CATHOLIC EDUCATIONAL ASSOCIATION OF THE PHILIPPINES

The Catholic Educational Association of the Philippines (CEAP) was founded in Manila in February of 1941 and incorporated with the Securities and Exchange Commission under the laws of the Philippines as a nonstock, nonprofit, religious educational corporation in February 1965. The association's general objectives are to advance and promote the educational work of the Catholic Church in the Philippines and to contribute to the development of responsible citizenship among the youth of the land. More specifically, CEAP seeks to update the Catholic educational system according to the directive of Vatican II; to assist Catholic schools, including those in established and mission areas, in realizing their common objectives as well as their specific aims; to represent the interests of Catholic educational institutions in the Philippines before the Department of Education and Culture, and to represent other government offices and agencies before the general public and international bodies; to uphold religious instruction as an essential element of education, character development, and morality in public and private life; to foster unity of action among Catholic schools in matters involving their common welfare; and—in collaboration with other educational groups, public and private—to undertake feasible projects for the advancement of education in the Philippines.

As of the school year 1975–76 CEAP's membership numbered 12 universities, 38 graduate schools, 180 colleges, 937 high schools, 466 elementary schools, and 73 seminaries, with a combined enrollment of about 1,000,000 students. Membership in the association is by application, either probationary or regular, in accordance with its bylaws. Diocesan and religious superintendents of Catholic schools are affiliated with CEAP as a body.

CEAP is governed by a board of directors, whose members are elected annually; national officers—including a president, a vice-president, a treasurer, an assistant treasurer, and a corporate secretary—are elected by the board from among its members. A representative of the Episcopal Commission on Education and Religious Instruction (ECERI) also sits on the board. The board meets once a month; its executive committee acts on urgent and important matters until the board meets.

The board of directors consults with an advisory council, composed of all past presidents, department chairmen, and representatives of ECERI and other religious congregations that conduct educational institutions. The advisory council meets four times a year. The day-to-day affairs of the association are handled by the national secretariat, which is headed by a permanent full-time executive vice-president and made up of three divisions: management services, operations, and educational planning.

CEAP is organized into five departments (seminaries, graduate schools, colleges, high schools, and elementary schools) and a commission of diocesan and religious superintendents. Each group is represented on the board of directors. Fifteen committees serviced by the national secretariat are formed to undertake special projects.

Some dioceses have their own association of Catholic schools. Of these a number are formally affiliated with CEAP as regional divisions which operate semiindependently. The other diocesan associations are indirectly linked with CEAP through individual schools which are also CEAP members. These regional units serve as clearinghouses on problems of a local nature: Northern Luzon Educational Association, Association of Private Schools in Isabela, Diocesan Association of Catholic Schools of Pampanga & Bataan, Zambales Private Schools Association, Malolos Diocese Catholic Schools Association, Manila Archdiocesan, Parochial Schools Association, Lipa Diocesan Catholic Schools Association, Caceres Educational Conference, Bicol Association of Catholic Schools, Catholic Educational Association of Sorsogon, Association of Private Schools in Albay, Catholic Educational Association of Legaspi, Masbate Catholic Educational Association, Negros Occidental Association of Catholic Schools, Antique Diocesan Association of Catholic Schools, Eastern Visayas Private Schools Association, Northern Mindanao Association of Colleges and Schools, Zamboanga & Basilan Association of Catholic Schools, Agusan Catholic Educational Association, Surigao Association of Catholic Schools, Northwestern Mindanao Educational Association, Notre Dame Educational Association, Mindanao Educational Conference, and Davao Association of Colleges and Schools.

The secretariat maintains a liaison staff to represent Catholic schools before the Department of Education and Culture, its staff bureaus (Bureau of Elementary Education, Bureau of Secondary Education, Bureau of Higher Education), and its twelve regional offices. CEAP also acts as liaison for Catholic schools with other government offices such as the Securities and Exchange Commission, Social Security System, Department of Labor, Bureau of Internal Revenue, and Philippine Veterans Administration. On the higher level, CEAP also makes representation for Catholic schools with Department of National Defense, National Board of Education, Department of Education and Culture, Fund for Assistance to Private Education, and other national policymaking bodies. Through its legislative committee the association keeps track of pending legislations and decrees affecting schools.

The secretariat also serves as a clearinghouse for teachers seeking positions in Catholic schools and schools looking for suitable teachers; distributes books coming in from abroad for schools in the Philippines through the Asia Foundation Book Program; and administers the scholarship founded by His Eminence, the late Francis Cardinal Spellman, Archbishop of New York, for the benefit of deserving Filipino students. The committee also administers the Jesus Paredes Memorial Scholarship.

CEAP is permanently represented in the National Board of Education and the UNESCO National Commission of the Philippines. The other associations in which it is represented are the Philippine Youth Welfare Coordinating Council, Children's Museum and Library, Foundation for Private Education in the Philippines, Family Life Workshop of the Philippines, World University Service, Coordinating Council of Private Educational Association, and the Private Education Assistance Committee. It is affiliated with the International Office of Catholic Education in Brussels and the International Association of Universities. The International Office of Catholic Education in Brussels transferred the Asia Regional Secretariat from Tokyo to Manila in 1964.

CEAP keeps member schools posted on all matters of interest to them through a regular bulletin service and press releases and through *The Catholic Teacher,* a quarterly magazine published jointly with the Catholic Teacher's Guild of the Philippines, and the monthly *CEAP News.*

Third Floor, Administration Building
Pius XII Catholic Center
1175 United Nations Avenue
Manila, Philippines
GERARDO R. ROSARIO

CATHOLICISM
See Religious Influences in Higher Education: Catholicism.

CAYMAN ISLANDS

Population: 11,300. Student enrollment in state primary schools: 1200; private primary and secondary schools: 900; comprehensive school: 1300. Language of instruction: English. [*Figures are for 1974.*]

The Cayman Islands, a British colony, consist of three islands—Grand Cayman, Little Cayman, and Cayman Brac—located to the west of Cuba in the Caribbean.

Education on the islands is free and compulsory between the ages of five and fifteen. There are nine government primary schools and one intermediate school. There is also a government-run comprehensive school, whose pupils sit for the overseas General Certificate of Education (GCE) at ordinary and advanced levels. In addition, there are five private schools. The two private secondary schools follow a United States curriculum, and are staffed by teachers from the United States. Another private school, the International College of the Cayman Islands on Grand Cayman, offers education to university level.

The government contributes to the University of the West Indies (located in Mona, Jamaica, with campuses in Cave Hill, Barbados, and St. Augustine, Trinidad), whose Department of Extra-Mural Studies provides extension services on the islands. The government makes available scholarships for higher study at the University of the West Indies or at institutions in Canada, the United Kingdom, and the United States.

CENTER FOR COMPARATIVE STUDIES ON HIGHER EDUCATIONAL SYSTEMS IN ENGLISH-SPEAKING COUNTRIES
(Centre d'études comparatives des systèmes d'enseignement supérieur des pays anglo-saxons), France

Founded in January 1974, the Center for Comparative Studies on Higher Educational Systems in English-Speaking Countries is located in the *Institut d'anglais Charles V* at the *Université Paris VII*. Focusing on comparative studies of national systems, the center undertakes research on the historical development and recent transformations of systems of higher education in English-speaking countries, in particular the United States. In addition, under the sponsorship of the *Centre national de la recherche scientifique* (National Center of Scientific Research), the center is engaged in a research project concerning the evolution of higher education in France.

In addition to research activities, the center acts as a clearinghouse for information on the higher education systems of English-speaking countries. Providing a documentation service for students on the master's and doctoral levels and for teachers, the center encourages the exchange of information with institutes throughout the world. The center conducts undergraduate and postgraduate courses and organizes meetings devoted to specific topics and problems in higher education.

The center is funded through the university as well as by special grants. The staff includes three research professionals and seven research assistants and/or graduate students. Library facilities are available to staff members.

The center has published brochures for teachers and students on the higher education systems of various countries.

Institut d'anglais Charles V
Université Paris VII
8 et 10 rue Charles V
75004 Paris, France

CENTER FOR CULTURAL AND TECHNICAL EXCHANGE BETWEEN EAST AND WEST
See East-West Center.

CENTER FOR EDUCATIONAL RESEARCH (Zentrum I Bildungsforschung), Federal Republic of Germany

Founded in 1966 at the University of Constance, Federal Republic of Germany,

the Center for Educational Research conducts research on primary, secondary, tertiary, and vocational education at the national, regional, and international levels. It concentrates on the following areas of higher education research: academic policies, university students and teachers, methodology of research in higher education, reform in higher education, and socialization in higher education.

The center is financed by university, government, and foundation grants. The staff—including thirty research professionals, five research assistants and/or graduate students, and twelve secretarial and clerical personnel—has access to a library and computer.

Universität Konstanz
Postfach 7733
D-775 Constance
Federal Republic of Germany

CENTER FOR EDUCATIONAL RESEARCH (Centar za isučavanja obrazovanja), Yugoslavia

The Center for Educational Research, located in the Institute for Social Research at the University of Zagreb, in Yugoslavia, was founded in 1965 to study education from a sociological and economic point of view. The center is concerned with local, national, and regional problems in secondary, higher, and vocational education. Research projects have included studies of general education and educational reforms, the efficiency of two-year postsecondary schools, students, the master's degree level, academic choices after secondary school, socioeconomic and educational aspects of part-time study, and scientific manpower. The center has also completed an analysis of the development of secondary and postsecondary education in Yugoslavia from 1966 to 1974 and has published a study of future development from 1976 to 1980.

In addition to research activities, the center holds professional meetings, conferences, and seminars for scholars interested in educational research. It has close ties with the Organisation of Economic Cooperation and Development and UNESCO.

The center publishes the results of research projects. A list is available on request.

Institut za društvena istraživanja
Sveučilište u Zagrebu, Illica 44
41000 Zagreb, Yugoslavia

CENTER FOR
EDUCATIONAL STUDIES
(Pusat pengajian ilmu pendikan), Malaysia

The Center for Educational Studies was founded in 1969 as a teaching unit at the University of Science, Penang, Malaysia. In 1973 a research program was initiated to study educational problems at all levels in Southeast Asia. Research in higher education at the center focuses on the following areas: administration, educational planning, educational technology, history of higher education, and methodology of research in higher education. The language unit of the center conducts research in bilingualism in tertiary education in Malaysia and neighboring countries.

Teaching activities at the center include teacher training to undergraduate students of physics, mathematics, chemical sciences, biological sciences, and humanities; inservice training at the graduate level for teachers, especially those in science, mathematics, and languages; and extension courses for university and college lecturers who wish to improve their teaching. The center also has courses in major Southeast Asian and selected European languages and in educational technology. In addition to research and teaching activities, the center designs and evaluates curricula; develops evaluation tools such as tests and measurements; and holds workshops, symposia, and seminars.

Funded by the government, the center has a staff consisting of three administrators, seventeen lecturers, three foreign advisers, one administrative assistant, and a visiting senior lecturer. The staff has access to libraries, microfiche and microfilm equipment, and computers.

Universiti sains Malaysia
Minden, Penang, Malaysia

CENTER FOR
EDUCATIONAL STUDIES
(Centro de estudios educativos), Mexico

The Center for Educational Studies was founded in 1963 in Mexico City as an independent research institution dedicated to the study of the educational problems of Mexico and Latin America. Conducting educational research on the primary, secondary, higher, and adult levels, the center encourages economic, social, political, and cultural changes that promote liberty and justice in Latin American societies. Higher education research is carried out in the following areas: economics of higher education, manpower in higher education, and reform in higher education. A research project, for example, has been conducted on the effects of higher education on the labor market and income distribution.

In addition to research activities, the center evaluates curricula, conducts postgraduate courses, and holds conferences. The center has a library of 15,000 volumes and 180 periodicals, a microcomputer, and a microfilm file of education news.

The research staff consists of six research professionals, four research assistants and/or graduate students, five technicians, one paid consultant, two administrative personnel, and four secretaries. The center is funded by individual private contributions, foundation grants, endowments, contractual research and consulting services, and publication sales.

A quarterly journal, *Revista del Centro de estudios educativos,* is published by the center. The journal contains articles on educational research, including higher education; reports of ongoing research projects in education; and abstracts in English and French. Each year, the statistical section of the journal is dedicated to a quantitative analysis of higher education, including enrollment, dropout and repetition rates, and financing.

avenida Revolución 1291
Mexico 20, D.F., Mexico

CENTER FOR HIGHER AND ADULT EDUCATION, United States

The Center for Higher and Adult Education, formerly the Center for the Study of Higher Education, was founded by Arizona State University in 1964. The title was changed in 1975 when the university's adult education program was incorporated into the center. Projects in higher education at the center include a study of the impact of student financial aid on access and choice and a statewide survey of the postsecondary plans of Arizona high school seniors. Other topics of higher education research include the following: administration, especially governance and academic policies; university students; and curricula and instruction.

In addition to research activities, the center offers an academic program leading to a doctoral degree for administrators and faculty of colleges and universities, including community colleges. The center also evaluates curricula, provides consultative services to institutions and agencies of higher education, and holds conferences and seminars.

The center is funded by the university. Its staff includes six research professionals, three research assistants and/or graduate students, and one secretary. Faculty and students have access to the university's computer system. The center has a resource library on higher education.

Arizona State University
Farmer Building 106
Tempe, Arizona 85281 USA

CENTER FOR HIGHER EDUCATION, Virginia, United States

The Center for Higher Education was founded at the University of Virginia's school of education as a research, service,

and instructional unit. The center conducts research in higher education, with a local, national, or regional focus, in the following areas: administration, in particular governance, academic policies, and legal issues; economics of higher education; university students and faculty; history of higher education; and curricula and instruction. In addition to research activities, the center conducts postgraduate courses leading to advanced degrees in higher education administration, student personnel work, community college instruction/administration, and adult education. It also sponsors conferences and seminars on higher education topics.

Funded primarily by the University of Virginia, the center also receives grants from foundations for special studies or projects. The staff includes three full-time and five part-time research professionals, three research assistants and/or graduate students, one administrative assistant, and one secretary. The center has complete access to the University of Virginia's facilities, including libraries, microfiche equipment, and computers.

The center publishes the Center for Higher Education Monograph Series—special reports issued once or twice a year, covering such topics as *Management by Objectives: An Analysis and Recommendation for Implementation* (1973), *The Community College Faculty Member as Researcher* (1974), and *Nonresident Student Enrollment in State Institutions of Higher Education* (1975).

University of Virginia
Charlottesville, Virginia 22903 USA

CENTER FOR RESEARCH AND DEVELOPMENT IN HIGHER EDUCATION, United States

The Center for Research and Development in Higher Education was established as a research unit at the University of California, Berkeley, in 1957. Seeking to improve the understanding, quality, effectiveness, and availability of higher education in the United States, the center conducts interdisciplinary research on such topics as governance; educational planning; economics of higher education; university students, especially women and minorities; and methodology of research in higher education. It develops models, materials, and guidelines for educational institutions, state agencies, and policymakers to improve the structures, practices, and curricula in higher education. Coordinating its research with such agencies as the American Council on Education and the Education Commission of the States, it maintains close contact with other major centers of higher education research and development.

Members of the center's staff act as advisers for research projects of other organizations throughout the United States, including the National Science Foundation, the National Institute of Education, the Fund for the Improvement of Postsecondary Education, the National Center for Educational Statistics, and various foundations. Cooperating with other national and regional organizations as well as state and federal agencies, the center holds workshops and conferences on problems in higher education.

Originally established with a grant from the Carnegie Corporation, the center receives support from the University of California, the United States government, and various foundations. It is primarily self-governing, although subject to the policies of the university's academic senate. The director reports to the chancellor of the Berkeley campus through the dean of the graduate division. A faculty advisory committee from the Berkeley academic senate, providing a liaison with the university, acts as a consultative body for the center. In addition, the National Advisory Panel, composed of educators throughout the United States, helps the center establish priorities and identify emerging higher education policy issues.

The center's staff is composed of twenty-three research professionals, including ten graduate students from schools or departments of business, economics, sociology, higher education, and political science on the Berkeley campus. The supporting staff

includes an administrative assistant and eleven secretarial and clerical personnel.

The center publishes the *Research Reporter,* sent to 15,000 researchers and policymakers in the United States and abroad. It also publishes research reports and monographs. A publications list is available on request.

University of California, Berkeley
2150 Shattuck Avenue
Berkeley, California 94704 USA

CENTER FOR RESEARCH INTO HIGHER EDUCATION (Instituut voor onderzoek van het wetenschappelijk onderwijs), Netherlands

The Center for Research into Higher Education was founded in 1967 at the Catholic University of Nijmegen, in the Netherlands, to conduct research to improve education at the higher education level. Focusing on local and national problems in higher education, research at the center is concerned with the following topics: university students, educational technology, and curricula and instruction. In addition to research activities, the center designs curricula; develops evaluation tools such as tests and measurement; trains university teachers, administrators, and researchers; and provides a documentation service.

The center is funded by the university. Its staff includes eight research professionals, two secretaries, and three temporary project assistants. The staff has access to a library, microfiche equipment, computers, and audiovisual centers.

Katholieke universiteit te Nijmegen
Oranjesingel 41
Nijmegen, Netherlands

CENTER FOR RESEARCH ON LEARNING AND TEACHING, United States

The Center for Research on Learning and Teaching was founded in 1962 to improve instruction at the University of

Michigan, Ann Arbor, through research and services. Research topics in higher education, focusing on local, national, and regional problems, include the following: university students and faculty, educational technology, curricula and instruction, and methodology of research in higher education. In addition to research activities, the center develops evaluation tools such as tests and measurement; trains university teachers, administrators, and researchers; holds seminars and conferences; and provides a documentation service.

Funded by the university as well as by government and foundation grants, the center has a staff consisting of ten research professionals, eight research assistants and/or graduate students, two technicians, three administrative personnel, four secretaries, and one assistant editor. The staff has access to the university's libraries, television studio, audiovisual education unit, and computer. The center's own facilities include a small specialized library of books, pamphlets, and journals on topics in higher education; seven computer terminals; and audiovisual equipment.

The center publishes *Memo to the Faculty,* quarterly; *Development and Experiment in College Teaching,* abstracts of innovations in college teaching at eleven universities in the United States, annually; *On-Line Newsletter,* reports on projects in instructional computing, six times a year; and *CRLT Reports,* descriptions of project reports by the center's staff members, irregularly.

University of Michigan
109 E. Madison Street
Ann Arbor, Michigan 48104 USA

CENTER FOR STUDIES IN HIGHER EDUCATION, United States

The Center for Studies in Higher Education was founded in 1966 at the University of Oklahoma, in Norman. The center offers an advanced graduate program in higher education and conducts

research in higher and adult education. Research, directed primarily toward the role and function of higher education and its administration, is also conducted in the following areas: educational planning, university students and faculty, history of higher education, and curricula and instruction. In addition to teaching and research activities, the center evaluates curricula, holds workshops on a regular basis, and offers public service programs aimed at the dissemination of research and development information to institutions in the area.

Financed by the University of Oklahoma, individual private contributions, and contractual research and consulting services, the center is composed of five research professionals, five research assistants, sixty-three graduate students, one technician, and three secretaries.

The center has published the results of special training programs held in 1972–73, 1973–74, and 1974–75: *A Study of Educational Administration: Papers from the Special Training Program,* edited by H. Hengst; and *Problems in Educational Administration: A Collection of Analyses,* edited by H. Hengst and associates.

University of Oklahoma
601 Elm Street
Norman, Oklahoma 73069 USA

CENTER FOR THE STUDY OF EDUCATION, United States

Established in 1957 within the Institute for Social Research at Florida State University, Tallahassee, the Center for the Study of Education conducts multidisciplinary research on all levels and offers graduate-level training in the application of sociology and economics to education. Concerned with institutional, national, regional, and international problems, research projects in higher education include the following topics: economics of higher education; manpower in higher education; university students; methodology of research in higher education; reform in higher education; and performance, scholarship, and professional activities of academic personnel. In addition to research and teaching activities, the center provides educational consulting services to local, state, national, and professional agencies.

The center is funded by the government, the university, and contractual research services. Members of the staff include three research professionals, four research assistants and/or graduate students, one technician, one administrative assistant, and one secretary.

Institute for Social Research
Florida State University
Tallahassee, Florida 32306 USA

CENTER FOR THE STUDY OF EDUCATION IN CHANGING SOCIETIES
(Centrum voor de studie van het onderwijs in veranderende maatschappijen), Netherlands

The Center for the Study of Education in Changing Societies was established in April 1963 as part of the Netherlands Universities Foundation for International Cooperation (NUFFIC) to study education at all levels in developing countries and to further international cooperation in the field of education. Until 1970 the center was concerned primarily with empirical field research in Tanzania, Surinam, and the Netherlands Antilles. After 1970 the center began to conduct basic research designed to evaluate the effectiveness of Dutch aid to developing countries, especially aid aimed at the modernization of educational systems in these countries. As a result of this latter emphasis, the center has become interested in tertiary education, since Dutch development aid is often directed to the university and vocational levels. The center has evaluated, for example, the projects of the Netherlands Programme for University Projects of Development Cooperation.

In addition to research activities, the center conducts undergraduate courses, holds symposia and seminars, organizes lectures, and provides a documentation service. It advises universities and NUFFIC on interuniversity cooperation, offers consultancy services to Dutch institutes of international education, and advises government and private organizations on educational development assistance. The center maintains close contact with agencies, institutes, and individuals working in the same and related fields in the Netherlands and abroad.

Administratively part of NUFFIC, which receives 100 percent government subsidy, the center has a staff of eight research professionals, two administrative personnel, and one secretary. The center has a specialized library and documentation center on subjects concerning educational problems in developing countries, including comparative education, institutional and sociological aspects of education, educational statistics, educational planning, home education, vocational and technical education, formal and out-of-school education on all levels, educational innovation, adult education, teacher training, and international education.

The center publishes a report series containing research results of staff members.

Molenstraat 27
The Hague, Netherlands

CENTER FOR THE STUDY OF HIGHER EDUCATION,
Ohio, United States

The Center for the Study of Higher Education, a research unit at the University of Toledo, in Ohio, conducts research in higher education with a national or regional focus. The center is concerned with studies of administration and educational planning, especially with respect to small-college survival. For example, it is studying the role of governing boards in small-college failure. In addition to research activities, the center holds conferences and seminars on problems of higher education.

Funded by the university as well as by publication sales, foundation grants, and contractual research services, the center has a staff consisting of four research professionals, one research assistant and/or graduate student, two administrative personnel, and one secretary. The center has a small library, but otherwise relies on university facilities.

The center publishes *Critique,* a triannual newsletter. It also publishes a monograph series periodically during the academic year.

University of Toledo
2801 W. Bancroft Street
Toledo, Ohio 43606 USA

CENTER FOR THE STUDY OF HIGHER EDUCATION, Pennsylvania, United States

Established in 1969, the Center for the Study of Higher Education at Pennsylvania State University, University Park, Pennsylvania, is a research unit responsible to the university's Office of the Provost. Conducting research in higher and adult education that focuses on institutional, state, and national problems, the center gives special attention to matters of governance and organization, such as statewide coordination, faculty senates, institutes and centers, collective bargaining, and the role of administrative offices. Other topics of concern include financing in higher education, management information systems, manpower and educational policy, legal foundations of policy, and instructional design.

In addition to research activities, the center organizes conferences and workshops, disseminates research findings, and encourages development activities. Members of the center support an instructional program at the doctoral level in higher education through consultation services and teaching.

Funds are received from Pennsylvania State University and contractual research services. Foundation grants are used to support special projects. The staff includes six research professionals, six graduate assistants, three technicians, one administrative assistant, and four secretaries. A research library in higher education, consisting of one thousand bound volumes and approximately fifty periodicals, is available at the center. Staff members also have access to the University Computing Center, which offers a wide range of library programs and specialized programming services.

The center has published bibliographies on community college staff development, university and the arts, student unrest on the American university campus, and higher education in general. It also publishes monographs, numbered reports, conference reports, and occasional papers.

Pennsylvania State University
119 Rackley Building
University Park
Pennsylvania 16802 USA

CENTER FOR THE STUDY OF HIGHER EDUCATION, University of Michigan, United States

The concept for the Center for the Study of Higher Education at the University of Michigan originated in 1950. By 1956 a Department of Higher Education had been designated within the School of Education. Two years later, with a grant of $400,000 from the Carnegie Corporation of New York, the center was established.

Funded by foundations, the government, contractual research, and consulting, the center conducts its educational research on the secondary and higher education levels with a staff of four research professionals, ten research assistants, three secretarial/clerical staff, and a part-time administrative assistant. The center's research on higher education administration emphasizes academic policies and governance, educational planning, college and university students, curricula and instruction, and reform. Research is conducted on a local, national, and regional level.

The academic program of the center exposes current and prospective administrators to relevant theoretical and practical knowledge about higher education as a complex human organization. The center serves higher education through the research efforts of its faculty and students, who bring various disciplinary perspectives to bear on issues in higher education. In addition to research and course offerings, the center sponsors topical institutes for practicing administrators and others. Although the majority of the center's programs lead to a doctoral degree, there are master's degree programs in community college teaching and administration.

Courses include organization and administration, financial administration, technical education, manpower development, institutional research and planning, the community college, the college professor, the college student, and history and philosophy. Seminar topics have included state planning and coordination, legal issues in higher education, the urban student, college curriculum, sociology of innovation, urban community colleges, national issues, and planning and development. A core of courses in higher education is required, but individual programs vary considerably with the career aspirations and the background and experience of individual students. A master's degree or course work in a cognate field is required and plays a central role in the student's doctoral research. An approved elective program in educational foundations courses is also required.

Programs at the center are administered in conjunction with the School of Education and the Horace H. Rackham School of Graduate Studies. Applicants generally have had solid experience in teaching, research, or administration in colleges and universities. The University of Michigan is strongly committed to increasing educational opportunities for minorities and

women and is especially concerned with the shortage of women and minority administrators in higher education and strongly encourages applications from these groups.

Publications of the center include *Projecting College and University Enrollments: Analyzing the Past and Focusing the Future; Affirmative Action: Its Legal Mandate and Organizational Implications; And Pleasantly Ignore My Sex: Academic Woman, 1974; At the Crossroads: A Report on the Financial Condition of the Forty-eight Liberal Arts Colleges Previously Studied in the Golden Years, The Turning Point; The Proprietary School: Assessing Its Impact on the Collegiate Sector; Aid to Higher Education: A Continuing Federal Dilemma;* and *Limited Growth in Higher Education: Indicators, Impacts, and Implications.*

School of Education
University of Michigan
Ann Arbor, Michigan 48109 USA

CENTER OF INTERDISCIPLINARY RESEARCH FOR THE DEVELOPMENT OF EDUCATION
(Centre de recherches interdisciplinaires pour le développement de l'éducation), Zaire

The Center of Interdisciplinary Research for the Development of Education is a research unit in primary, secondary, higher, and adult education at the National University of Zaire, Kisangani campus. Research in higher education focuses on local, national, and regional problems. Topics of concern include the following: academic policies, economics of higher education, educational planning, university students, history of higher education, curricula and instruction, methodology of research in higher education, and reform in higher education.

In addition to research activities, the center conducts undergraduate courses; trains university teachers, administrators, and researchers; organizes seminars and conferences; and provides a documentation service. Funded by the university, foundations, and publication sales, the center has a staff of two research professionals, six research assistants and/or graduate students, five administrative personnel, and four secretaries. Members of the staff have access to a library and a microfiche reader.

The center publishes *Revue zaïroise de psychologie et pédagogie* and *Cahiers du CRIDE*.

Université nationale du Zaïre
Boîte Postale 2012
Kisangani, Zaire

CENTRAL AFRICAN EMPIRE

Population: 1,720,000 (mid 1974 estimate). Student enrollment in primary school: 200,000; secondary school (academic, vocational, technical): 20,000; higher education: 500. Language of instruction: French. Academic calendar: September to June, two semesters. Percentage of national budget expended on education: 16.6% (1972). [Except where otherwise indicated, figures are for 1973–74.]

The Central African Republic achieved its independence from France on August 13, 1960. (The country's name was changed to Central African Empire in December 1976.) The French had entered the Gabon estuary about 1839 and by the early 1900s had conquered the surrounding area, consisting of the present states of Chad, Gabon, the People's Republic of the Congo, and the Central African Empire (originally called Ubangi-Shari). At first they named the area French Congo (1897–1910); but in 1910, when the four territories were joined together, the name was changed to French Equatorial Africa (1910–1960).

The French administrative and educational policies in this area followed the pattern established in French West Africa. The initial schools were started by missionaries. In 1905, after the separation of church and state in France, some public schools were opened; however, the government continued to support the mission schools throughout the colonial period. After 1911 mission schools were required to follow an official local curriculum, which offered basic education with a stress on the French language and culture.

The importance of the mission schools in French Equatorial Africa, and at the same time the low priority accorded education by the government, can be seen in the fact that in 1934–35 the mission schools enrolled 9300 students in their primary schools, compared to 6600 in government schools. The bulk of enrollments were in Gabon and the present People's Republic of the Congo.

Educational development throughout the area was slow. In 1957, when the French enabling act, the *loi-cadre*, went into effect and the African territories of France became self-determining, the four states combined enrolled 7.55 percent of the eligible age group in primary education, .46 percent in secondary education, and .057 percent in postsecondary education (Moumouni, 1968, p. 90).

During the first school year after independence, 1961–62, the Central African Empire enrolled some 90,000 students in primary education (about 41 percent of the eligible age group, six to fourteen). Some 2500 students attended secondary schools. In 1962 the mission schools were incorporated into one unified state education system. By the school year 1973–74 some 200,000 students (about 75 percent of those eligible) attended primary school while secondary enrollments had risen to 10 percent of primary enrollment, or some 20,000.

During the period of French rule, no institutions of higher education existed in the Central African Empire; but, especially after World War II, a small number of scholarships for both the secondary and postsecondary levels were made available for study in France. In 1959 France started regional university-level courses in Brazzaville (People's Republic of the Congo), which in 1961 developed into a higher education center, *Fondation de l'enseignement supérieur en Afrique centrale* (FESAC). Several of the specialized institutes of this center were located in the other three countries in the region. The Institute of Agronomy opened in M'Baiki in then Central African Republic in 1963. Later in the 1960s, however, the regional cooperation ceased, since each nation preferred to establish its own higher education institutions.

In the Central African Empire the *Ecole normale supérieure* (Higher Normal School) was founded in 1970, followed by the University Jean-Bedel Bokassa in Bangui in 1971. The university has since expanded to include three faculties, two institutes, and two research institutes. It has received assistance from France, Romania, and the Soviet Union in the form of teaching personnel.

Since 1974 the Ministry of National Education has been working on a reform of the total education system of the nation to better reflect the African reality and to this end has formed the National Pedagogical Institute to take charge of the planned changes. The importance of educational reform is recognized in the new name of the ministry, the Ministry of National Education and Educational Reform.

National Educational Policy

The importance of educational planning for the training of qualified personnel at all levels is recognized by the government of the Central African Empire. Special emphasis is given to technical training at the secondary level and professional training for agriculture and mining.

Legal Basis of Educational System

Significant for the higher education system is the agreement of cooperation between France and then Central African Republic of 1960. The University Jean-Bedel Bokassa was established by Ordinance 69/063 of November 12, 1969, and its statutes were approved by Decrèe 71/434 of October 15, 1971.

Types of Institutions

Higher education in the Central African Empire is available at the University Jean-Bedel Bokassa, which consists of faculties of law and economic sciences (1971), sciences (1972), and letters and human sciences (1972); two institutes, the *Institut universitaire de technologie agronomique* (University Institute of Agronomy at M'Baiki) and the *Institut universitaire de technologie des mines et de géologie* (University Institute of Mining and Geology); and two research institutes for research in mathematics instruction and archeology.

Education at the tertiary level for teachers of the *collèges d'enseignement général* (CEGs: schools of general education) is offered at the *Ecole normale supérieure* (1970). All other education is at the secondary level.

Relationship with Secondary Education

The educational system consists of two years of preschool, six years of primary, seven years of secondary education, and higher education. The six years of primary school lead to a certificate of primary education, *certificat d'études primaires élementaires* (CEPE). Secondary school requires an entrance examination and is divided into two cycles: a lower cycle of four years, available either in *collèges d'enseignement générale* or *collèges d'enseignement technique* (schools of general or technical education) or in *lycées*, leads to the diploma *brevet d'études du premier cycle* (BEPC) or the *brevet élémentaire*, which is becoming less common; a second cycle of three years, available in *lycées*, leads to the *baccalauréat* diploma in one of three specialties: sciences, technical study, or letters.

Admission Requirements

Admission to the university is based upon the *baccalauréat* diploma in the appropriate specialty or a special entrance examination to the faculty. Candidates are allowed to take the special examination (1) if they are over twenty-three years of age and have not received the *baccalauréat* during the previous year (and do not plan to take the *baccalauréat* in the coming year) or (2) if they are over twenty-five years of age. Two separate examinations are given:

one for fields such as letters, law, and economics; another for the sciences and technology.

For its preuniversity course, *capacité en droit*, the faculty of law accepts students with the BEPC certificate or candidates who have passed a special examination. The University Institute of Mining and Geology admits students with the appropriate *baccalauréat* diploma. Others, as well as students without the *baccalauréat*, will sit for a competitive examination to determine acceptance into a preparatory year. The University Institute of Agronomy also requires the appropriate *baccalauréat* diploma or success in an entrance examination. The *Ecole normale supérieure* will accept students with the *baccalauréat* or those who have passed examinations at the level of the final year in the *lycées*.

Administration and Control

Educational responsibility is centered in the Ministry of National Education and Educational Reform, assisted by five departments: the departments of primary education, secondary and technical education, educational statistics, budget and accounting, and higher education and scientific research. Close cooperation exists between the ministry and the university due to the minister's role as chancellor of the university. He also signs the diplomas awarded by the university.

Internally, the university is administered by a vice-chancellor, who is chairman of the university council. He is assisted by a secretary general. The university council deals with all specific problems of the university, while the faculty councils, chaired by the *chef d'établissement* (head of faculty), concern themselves with internal matters. Students have their own organization, the National Association of Central African Students, which attends to their problems.

Programs and Degrees

Founded in 1971–72, the university does not yet have complete cycles leading to

degrees. The faculty of letters and human sciences awards the *diplôme universitaire d'études littéraires* (DUEL) in modern literature, history/geography, and English after two years of study, while the faculty of sciences awards the equivalent diploma, *diplôme universitaire d'études scientifiques* (DUES), in mathematics/physics, physics/chemistry, and chemistry/biology/geology, also in a course of two years. The faculty of law and economic sciences has a two-year preuniversity program for the certificate *capacité en droit* and offers a three-year program in law and a two-year program in economic sciences, after which the students go to France to complete their study for a degree.

The University Institute of Agronomy prepares students for the *diplôme d'ingénieur agricole* in a course of two years or three years for animal husbandry, involving fifteen days of practical work during the first two years and thirty days in the third year. The University Institute of Mining and Geology also has a fifteen- to twenty-day practical work requirement in its program in the first two years of study. The *diplôme d'ingénieur de travaux*, with a specialty in mining or geology, is achieved in three years of study.

Financing and Student Financial Aid

All higher education is financed by the state, which is a recipient of financial assistance from France and other friendly nations. All students in higher education receive scholarships, either national or foreign. Precise statistics concerning financial aid for students have not yet been established.

Student Social Background and Access to Education

As in several of its neighboring countries, the population density in the Central African Empire varies between the more densely settled south and the more sparsely settled northern areas. In 1960 it was estimated that only some 15 percent of eligible students in the northern areas had access to education, against 45 percent of students enrolled in Bangui.

Teaching Staff

The teaching staff at the university have the ranks of *maître de conférences* (senior lecturer), *chargé de cours* (lecturer), *maître-assistant* (assistant lecturer), and assistant. If the teaching staff is contributed by the French government, the names of candidates are submitted by the French minister of cooperation, and the appointments are made by the government in the person of the minister of national education and educational reform, assisted by the director general of higher education and scientific research and the vice-chancellor of the university. Other foreign personnel recommended by their governments as well as candidates for local contracts are considered by the minister, assisted by the director general.

National teachers as well as other locally recruited personnel are paid through the national budget. Technical assistance personnel, paid by their own governments, receive a money subsidy from the Central African government in addition to free housing.

Of the total personnel of ninety-four at the university in 1974–75, twenty-four persons were employed part time. Fifty-eight were of French nationality, sixteen were from the Soviet Union, six were from Romania, ten were nationals, and the rest were foreigners on local contracts.

Current Problems and Trends

One of the major problems of education in the Central African Empire is to create a system of education truly reflective of the nation's needs, to build the higher education system in accordance with the stated goals of providing the needed manpower. As in most of the other former French colonies in Africa, the population in the Central African Empire is largely rural and consists of a number of different tribes. Although Sangho is the official language, many other languages are spoken. Because French, the language of instruction, consumes a large portion of instructional time at the lower levels, the students have less time for other subjects and therefore experience higher failure rates and repetition of classes.

In 1974, only about 10 percent of the staff at the university were nationals, and large numbers of teachers at the secondary level were French. A great educational expansion will be required to fulfill the stated policy of an educational system related to the needs of the nation.

International Cooperation

The University Jean-Bedel Bokassa does not yet exchange students with other universities but is a recipient of a large number of foreign teachers, especially from France. Projects are under way to arrange exchanges of both students and professors with French universities. The university is a member of the *Association des universités partiellement out entièrement de langue française* (AUPELF: Association of Partially or Wholly French-Language Universities). Its faculties and institutes participate in international seminars and conferences related to their specialities.

[Questionnaire answered by J. L. Psimhis, Ministre, Ministère de l'éducation nationale et de la réforme éducative, Bangui, CAR; and G. Canu, Recteur, Université Jean-Bedel Bokassa, Bangui.

Educational Association

Association nationale des étudiants
  centrafricains
(National Association of Central African
  Students)
Université Jean-Bedel Bokassa
Bangui, Central African Empire

Bibliography

Bolibaugh, J. B., and Hanna, P. R. *French Educational Strategies for Sub-Saharan Africa: Their Intent, Derivation and Development*. Stanford, California: Comparative Education Center, Stanford University, 1974.

*Etude sur l'enseignement et de la formation pro-
fessionnelle agricole dans les pays francophones
d'Afrique tropicale et à Madagascar. République
centrafricaine.* Paris: Ministère de coopéra-
tion, 1963.

Gardinier, D. E. "Education in the States of
Equatorial Africa: A Bibliographical Essay."
Africana Library Journal, 1972, *3*(3), 7–20.

Gardinier, D. E. "Schooling in the States of
Equatorial Africa." *Canadian Journal of African Studies,* 1974, *3*(3), 517–538.

Labrousse, A. *La France et l'aide à l'éducation dans
14 états africains et Malgache.* Paris: International Institute for Educational Planning,
1971.

Moumouni, A. *Education in Africa.* New York:
Praeger, 1968.

Scanlon, D. G. (Ed.) *Traditions of African Education.* New York: Teachers College Press,
Columbia University, 1964.

Scanlon, D. G. (Ed.) *Church, State and Education
in Africa.* New York: Teachers College Press,
Columbia University, 1966.

See also: Africa, Sub-Saharan: Regional Analysis; Archives: Africa and Asia, National Archives of.

CENTRAL AMERICA:
REGIONAL ANALYSIS

The independent countries of Central
America—Costa Rica, El Salvador, Guatemala, Honduras, Nicaragua, and Panama—
are bound by a common Spanish colonial
heritage: Panama was part of the viceroyalty
of New Granada established by Spain in
1538; the others constituted the captaincy
general of Guatemala, established in 1543
as part of the viceroyalty of *Nueva España,*
or New Spain. Central America remained
under Spanish control until 1821. Between
1838 and 1841, each of the five countries
under the former captaincy general became independent republics. Panama,
which became part of Colombia in 1821,
did not gain its independence until 1903.
Although geographically a part of Central
America, Belize (formerly British Honduras) is generally considered a Caribbean
country. Given its British colonial heritage
and social institutions and its close ties to
the Caribbean region, Belize is not included

in the following analysis of higher education in Central America.

University life in Central America began
very early in the Spanish colonial period.
According to the chronicler Fra Francisco
Vásquez, the dust had not yet settled and
they were still cleaning their arms and
shoeing the horses when Central Americans first petitioned the Spanish crown
for a university (Mata Gavidia, 1954). It was
not until 1676, however, that King Carlos
II authorized the first Central American
university, the University of San Carlos
in Guatemala. The second was the University of León, established in 1812 in Nicaragua and the last to appear in Central
America during the Spanish colonial period. Twenty-five years after the captaincy
general of Guatemala declared its independence, Central America had three new
universities: the University of El Salvador
(1841), the University of Santo Tomas,
Costa Rica (1843), and the University of
Honduras (1847). (The University of Panama was not established until 1935.) Like
their colonial predecessors, the new republican universities were essentially Spanish
in organization and philosophy. As in much
of Latin America, however, the advent of
the republics had the effect of profes-
sionalizing the university, with French or
Napoleonic ideals gradually superseding
the colonial system of education.

Under Spanish influence the university
had been a well-unified institution—a totality rather than an aggregate—with one
well-defined vision of the world, man, and
society. The movement for independence
in the early nineteenth century was directly
inspired by the French Enlightenment.
Independence opened the door to French
culture, which at the time represented the
vanguard of humanistic thought, culminating in the positivist philosophy of Auguste
Comte. It is not surprising, therefore, that
the newly constituted republics so willingly
embraced the Napoleonic model in attempting to reform the colonial universities,
which had fallen into a state of decay during the last years of the colonial period.

Instead of restructuring the university through original and authentic reforms, the republics preferred the far easier task of imitation, adopting an imported system—in this case that of the French university, which emphasized professionalism, deemphasized teaching, divided the university into an aggregate of professional schools, and relegated scientific investigation to separate academies, dissociated from the university. The latter half of the nineteenth century marked the appearance of the national university—a collection of professional schools under the authority of the respective ministers of education. Their objective was to train professionals for leadership roles in public administration and social reform. Higher education became the means of imparting professional and cultural skills to the ruling class, enabling them to better guide the newly constituted republics.

Reform of the National Universities

The *Reforma de Córdoba* (Reform of Córdoba), named because it originated at the University of Córdoba in Argentina, started in 1918 and eventually spread throughout Latin America. Independence had not substantially modified the university as a reflection of colonial society; it continued well into the twentieth century as an essentially elitist institution. Not even the professional orientation of the university in the early republics succeeded in altering this fact. The Córdoba reform movement was responsible for the first important comparison between a society that had begun to experience internal change and a university system that had become dangerously obsolete. It represented the first serious questioning of the Latin American university and symbolized the entry of Latin America into the twentieth century. The protagonist of this movement was the emerging middle class, which viewed the university as the most effective instrument by which to gain social and political power.

From the Córdoba manifesto stem all the attempts to reform the Latin American university system. Now, more than half a century after its first formulation, the principal accomplishments of the reform program can be enumerated: (1) university autonomy in all its political, instructional, administrative and economic aspects; (2) free election of all principal authorities of the university by the university community itself and participation of all its members—professors, students, and graduates—in its governing bodies; (3) competitive selection of professors and a limited tenure of chairs; (4) instructional freedom; (5) open attendance; (6) gratuity of instruction; (7) academic reorganization—creation of new faculties and modernization of teaching methods, active instruction, and amplification of the cultural background of future professionals; (8) democratization of university admissions, including financial assistance for students; (9) university extension—strengthening of the social function of the university, projection of university culture to the people, and a greater concern for national problems; and (10) Latin American unity—opposition to dictatorship and denunciation of imperialism.

Since 1918 university autonomy and the democratization of university government have been the reforms most vehemently called for by the Latin American university community. The Reform of Córdoba, with its successes and failures, has contributed more than any other event to the emergence of a singularly Latin American university. Born in the heart of Latin America, it stands in testimony of a great originality and intellectual independence. A product of well-defined historical and social circumstances, it did not achieve a radical transformation of the university, but it did make significant steps in that direction. Its greatest concern was the formal organization of university government rather than that of academic programs. Not all of the Córdoban proposals were positive. Some might even be called counterproductive to the academic and scientific betterment of the universities, as, for example, the issue of open attendance. Yet insistence on autonomy, student participation, and university extension into the outlying community were, without doubt, positive achievements of the reform movement. Whatever the criticisms of the movement—and many are valid—it cannot be denied that, from a historical perspective, it represents a point of departure for the great process of reform that occurred within the Latin American university.

One of the last regions to benefit from the Latin American movement for university reform was Central America, largely because of political and social circumstances that inhibited development during the early years of the twentieth century. Although the Córdoban ideas found quick acceptance among Central American intellectuals and university communities, they were not incorporated in a legal context until the second quarter of the century. In El Salvador the University Statute of 1933 recognized for the first time the right of students to send delegates to the university council, and autonomy and the other Córdoban proposals were not legally sanctioned until 1951. In Guatemala a plan for university reform with clear Córdoban affiliations was passed into law in 1945. This legislation confirmed the autonomy of the university, proclaimed the previous year by a revolutionary junta; allowed for student and graduate participation in the governing bodies of the university, calling for a one-third representation from each class; established the election of university authorities by representative bodies of the university community; included university extension and cultural diffusion among the primary goals of the university; and provided for the selection of professors by merit, via competition.

In Costa Rica the University of Santo Tomas, abolished in 1888, was reestablished in 1940 as the University of Costa Rica. Its founding principles incorporated most proposals of the Córdoban reform: autonomy, election of rector and secretary

general by a university assembly, student participation in the university council, organization of student welfare, and priority for cultural extension. In Honduras the proposals of Córdoba found legal sanction in the law of 1957, which introduced a representative system of governance, giving the student body 50 percent representation in all governing bodies of the university. In Nicaragua it was the students themselves who took the initiative in 1944 and, with great decision and organization, transformed the university along the lines of the Córdoba manifesto. In 1953 these students issued a proposal clearly inspired by the Córdoban ideals. Although rejected by a congress controlled by the dictator Somoza García, it served as a base for the preparation of a text that became law in 1958, granting administrative, instructional, and economic autonomy to the university. The constitution of 1946 granted autonomy to the University of Panama and recognized the right of students to send representatives to the various governing bodies of the university.

In September 1948 the universities of the region held the *Primer congreso universitario centroamericano* (First University Congress of Central America) in San Salvador, El Salvador. This convention approved a document entitled *Fines y principios de la universidad contemporánea y en especial de las universidades centroamericanas* (Goals of the Contemporary Universities of Central America)—a paper strongly influenced by Córdoban ideals. It emphasized the need to overcome dependence on professionalism and called for reinstatement of the university as a unified body, uprooting of the universities' professionalist tendencies, and placing greater emphasis on the cultural development of the future graduate. These ideas constituted the leitmotiv of all academic reforms that took place in Central American universities during the 1960s.

The voices that arose in protest against the dangers of an excessively professionalized system of higher education were echoed among many Central American educators. The academic framework constructed on the model of the nineteenth century French university, which favored this professional tendency over a more general university structure, became an obstacle blocking the way to recuperation of the unified university and the maintenance of a balance between general studies and extreme specialization.

The ideas of the Spanish philosopher José Ortega y Gasset about the purpose of the university and his fervent belief in the need to train professionals with an understanding of the overall culture influenced many Central Americans who could not agree about the duties of the university. The movement toward general education—which reached its peak in the United States in the 1930s under Robert M. Hutchins, president of the University of Chicago—also contributed to the thesis that it was necessary to include general studies in the university curriculum.

The maturation of the ideas expounded by the First University Congress of Central America in 1948 started at the University of Costa Rica. Beginning in 1946, the educators of Costa Rica, dissatisfied with the current system, began a series of attempts to transform their university, which they saw as a conglomerate of isolated schools. The long debate over what a university ought to be culminated in 1957 with the advent of new reforms. The goals of reform were to unify the university and to place personal, cultural, and social development ahead of professional pursuits. To fulfill these goals meant to abandon the Napoleonic organizaiton of the nineteenth century and to introduce general education as the overriding function of the university. The first goal was accomplished through the creation of a faculty of arts and sciences, acting as the central faculty of the university on which the other, more fundamental departments, would depend; the second was achieved by making general studies obligatory for all entering students.

The founding of a faculty of arts and sciences, accompanied by the departmentalization of the basic disciplines, signified the recuperation of the old unified concept of the university. Departmentalization allowed for the cultivation of fundamental disciplines, independent of their immediate professional application. General studies constituted, in turn, the thirst for academic reform and facilitated the renovation of university study through the development of new teaching methods. All these attempted reforms were accompanied by revision of course offerings in any given subject, elaboration of new texts, introduction of a system of credits, creation of orientation services and student welfare, and greater esteem for cultural and artistic activities.

In 1961 the *Consejo superior universitario centroamericano* (CSUCA: Central American Higher University Council), inspired by the Costa Rican experience, included in its plan for the integration of higher education in Central America a recommendation that all national universities of the area undergo reform and introduce general education courses into their curricula. Document 3 of this plan promoted the idea of instituting general studies in the curriculum, defined the philosophy and goals of a general studies program, provided a plan for its initiation, and recommended the departmentalization of most academic disciplines (Consejo superior, 1963). The introduction of general studies was responsible for undermining the emphasis on professionalism, another desired objective. The general studies program also inspired new alternatives in academic organization; for example, the creation of a central faculty of arts and sciences, university centers of general studies, and departmentalization of instruction. The freeing of the basic disciplines from the tutelage of the professional faculties allowed for individual development of these disciplines. Thus, the sciences came to enjoy the same academic position previously reserved for the professions. For all its positive achievements in the field of academic reform, the movement toward modernization that began in the 1960s had its limitations. It was influenced in its early stages by the push for development *(concepciones desarrollistas)* then in vogue and encouraged by such organizations as the Program for Economic Integration in Central America; the Economic Commission for Latin America; and the ill-fated Alliance for Progress, initiated in the United States during the administration of President John F. Kennedy. The plan for regional integration included an agreement by which the said plan would represent the best way to establish professional centers in order to achieve full development of human potential necessary to the economic growth and integration of the region.

Advent of Private Universities

Various factors led to the creation of private universities in Central America during the 1960s: (1) the obvious need to amplify educational opportunities in the region; (2) the desire of certain influential sectors (the ruling classes) to complete their educational activities with a period of directed study; (3) the growing lack of confidence (by these same ruling classes) in the national university, mainly because its gradual politicization of students and sharpening of their social conscience would ultimately lead to a questioning of the status quo; and (4) the shift in attitude of Central American society, in which incipient industrialization and a growing middle class was creating new educational necessities. Moreover, the unfolding of the Central American Common Market and its attempts to stimulate industrialization through the importation of goods produced an increased demand for technically qualified personnel. Private universities were an answer to this need. The advent of private universities during the 1960s was continental in nature: one third of the total number of higher educational institutions operating in Latin America in 1975 were founded during this period.

The creation of these private universities provoked a negative response from the national universities, which until 1960 had been the only educational institutions in the region. One of the reasons for this reaction was the contradiction seen between the national universities' attempts to avoid unnecessary duplication in course offerings and the appearance of these new universities that were in fact doing just that.

Universidad centroamericana in Managua, Nicaragua, the first private university to appear in the region, opened in 1960. The following year the Jesuits founded another university in Guatemala City, *Universidad Rafael Landívar,* and in 1965 they opened the *Universidad centroamericana José Simeón Cañas* in El Salvador. In the same year the *Universidad Santa María la Antigua* was created in Panama as a project of the Panamanian Conference of Bishops. In 1966 two more private universities were established in Guatemala: *Universidad Mariano Gálvez* (by the initiative of various Protestant groups) and *Universidad del Valle* (under the auspices of the American College of Guatemala). The three private universities of Guatamala were created in accordance with the constitution of 1956, which allowed for their supervision by the University of San Carlos, the only state higher education institution. This situation changed with the constitution of 1965 and the Law for Private Universities, passed on January 27, 1966, which transferred supervisory powers to the Council on Private Higher Education (composed of the minister of education, two representatives from the University of San Carlos, two representatives from the private institutions, and two nonuniversity representatives elected by the National Association of Professional People). In 1972 a fourth private university was created in Guatemala: *Universidad Francisco Marroquín.* All of the aforementioned schools, plus the Polytechnic Institute of Nicaragua (founded in 1967) and the College of St. John (founded in 1964) in Belize, formed part of the *Federación de universidades privadas de América central y Panamá* (FUPAC: Federation of

Private Universities of Central America and Panama), whose headquarters are in Guatemala City.

Nonuniversity Higher Education

In Central America there are institutions of higher education (public and private) that form no part of the university system. In Guatemala the National School of Nursing, the School of Social Services, the Guatemalan Institute of Social Security, and the School of Dietetics and Nutrition are operated under the auspices of the Institute of Nutrition of Central America and Panama (INCAP). El Salvador's Teacher's College and School of Social Work are dependent on the minister of public education. The Panamerican School of Agriculture was established in 1941 in Zamorano, Honduras, under an agreement between the Honduran government and the United Fruit Company. In Nicaragua nonuniversity institutions include the National School of Agriculture and Animal Husbandry; the National School of Nursing, under the minister of public health; two private institutions dedicated to the advanced study of business finance, the School of Public Accounting and the Center for Higher Education; and the Central American Institute of Business Administration, which receives advisory assistance from Harvard University in the United States. In Costa Rica the School of Nursing is affiliated with the national university and several teacher's colleges; the Interamerican Institute of Agriculture was established by the Organization of American States; and the Central American Institute of Public Administration, under the auspices of the regional governments and with the aid of the United Nations, offers courses in public administration.

Regional Integration

Any overview of higher education in Central America would not be complete without including the efforts of the Central American University Confederation, a regional organization under CSUCA. It

was created in September 1948 by agreement of the First Congress of the Central American University at a meeting in San Salvador, El Salvador. CSUCA, a pioneer in the field of regional interuniversity cooperation, was the first Central American organization to promote regional integration, antedating the governmental attempts at economic integration that arose during the end of the 1950s under the sponsorship of the Economic Commission for Latin America. Since 1959 CSUCA has kept an administrative base at the University of Costa Rica in San José. Its permanent organization was outlined by the Second University Congress of Central America held in San Salvador, El Salvador, in 1968.

The principal program instituted by CSUCA is the Plan for the Regional Integration of Higher Education in Central America, approved in 1961 (Consejo superior, 1963). This plan calls for the academic reform of member universities and the creation of regional schools or faculties for the service of Central America as well as regional research facilities. Execution of the CSUCA plan has opened the way for rapid modernization of the national universities of Central America, signaling a new epoch in their historical development.

One of the unique characteristics of higher education in Central America is that of regional integration, encouraged by the programs and actions of CSUCA. In accordance with the Plan for the Regional Integration of Higher Education in Central America, several schools and institutes have been created to serve the educational needs (including graduate studies) of the entire region. The following regional centers are fully integrated into the overall system of higher education in Central America: (1) The Regional School for Sanitary Engineering offers a graduate degree in sanitary engineering that requires approximately four semesters of study. Its program stems from the faculty of engineering of the University of San Carlos in Guatemala, with assistance from the World Health Organization through the Office of Panamerican Health. Since 1965 it has trained over 100 Central American professionals. (2) The Regional Faculty of Veterinary Medicine and Animal Husbandry at the University of San Carlos offers the degree of veterinary doctor and zoologist after twelve semesters of study. More than 150 professionals have graduated from this school. (3) Created in 1970 as a dependent of the University of Costa Rica, the Regional School of Geology receives aid from such international organizations as UNESCO, United Nations Development Programme, and the Organization of American States. A degree in geology takes about ten semesters. (4) The Regional Faculty of Microbiology in the University of Costa Rica awards a degree after a six-year course of study. (5) The Central American School of Sociology was created in 1973 as a dependent of both the University of Costa Rica and the Program for Social Sciences of CSUCA. A degree in sociology is awarded on completion of four semesters of study. A previous university degree is required. (6) The Institute of Union Organization at the National University of Nicaragua offers courses in labor negotiations to union leaders lacking an academic degree. (7) The Central American Institute of Comparative Law, under the law school of the National University of Honduras, conducts research into the legal ramifications of economic integration and publishes a semiannual bulletin. (8) The Central American Institute of Historical Research is on the Managua campus of the *Universidad centroamericana,* Nicaragua. (9) The Central American Program for Social Sciences, created in 1970 to improve the teaching and research of the social sciences in the universities of the region, is based in the office of the secretary general of CSUCA. It publishes the quarterly *Estudios sociales centroamericanos;* sponsors conventions, courses, and seminars; and conducts regional investigations into such areas, as the economic and social development of Central America from independence to the crisis of 1930, rural society in Central

America, and rural development and demographic movements in Central America. (10) The Central American Program for Medical Education, under the auspices of the Central American Association of Medical Schools, is a subsidiary of CSUCA. Its objectives are the development of better curricula for the study of medicine, the strengthening of the teacher-student relationship, and the coordination of social and pedagogic practices required to prepare doctors to deal with the social reality of Central America. Its headquarters are also in the office of the secretary general of CSUCA. (11) The Central American University Press is the first regional publishing house organized in Central America. Created in 1969 by the national universities of the area, it has contributed greatly to the cultural integration of the region. It operates out of the University of Costa Rica, under the auspices of CSUCA. A nonprofit and self-sustaining organization, it publishes scientific, literary, and artistic works of value to Central American cultural development, as well as university texts. (12) The Central American Institute of Educational Planning, Administration, and Supervision, located in Panama, was created under the joint auspices of the Panamanian government and UNESCO. (13) The Federation of Private Universities of Central America and Panama sponsors programs at affiliated private universities. Representative areas of investigation are cultural and economic integration, development of tourism, education in rural societies, and marketing of food products.

Expansion of Higher Education

One of the outstanding characteristics of higher education in Central America is its extraordinary growth and diversification since the 1960s. When the first congress met in 1948, there was only one national university in each country; the combined student population was barely more than 6000; the teaching staff included no more than 600 professors, a majority of these working on an hourly basis; and the number of graduates in the entire region did not exceed 350 per year. Possible degrees were of the most traditional types: law, medicine, pharmacology, civil engineering, and the humanities. Eleven years later, the first census of the Central American universities (excluding the University of Panama), conducted in 1959 by CSUCA, revealed that the student population had doubled, reaching a total enrollment of 12,327 at the five national universities. By 1966 the fourth census (*Cuarto censo de población*, 1968) indicated that the number of students had doubled once again, to 23,949. In the same year, 2802 students attended the newly instituted private universities of Guatemala, Nicaragua, and El Salvador. The sum total of all university students in the region had reached 26,751. According to this fourth census, 2121 professors taught in the national universities of Central America. Of these, 23 percent were full time, 21 percent were part time, and 56 percent were on an hourly basis. The greatest concentration of full-time professors was in medicine and in the sciences. The census also demonstrated that a majority of university students pursued the fields of economics, education, law, civil engineering, medicine, and pharmacology. In 1967, after the University of Panama was included in the census, the total enrollment at the national universities rose to 36,273. In 1971, excluding Panama, the number of students in public and private institutions of higher learning passed the 60,000 mark, with the national universities accounting for 86.7 percent of the total university population.

Between 1960 and 1972, the student enrollment at all national universities of the region quadrupled, growing at an annual rate far greater than the Latin American average of 9.5 percent. Between 1973 and 1975, the enrollment growth in traditional fields had leveled off, registering greater increases in the areas of economics, business administration, engineering, architecture, science, and agronomy. The number of professional fields also increased considerably, resulting in new professional, scientific, and technological careers. By 1975 the number of full- and half-time professors equaled or surpassed those on an hourly basis who, only a decade earlier, were in the majority. Between 1961 and 1968, productivity in terms of trained professionals nearly quadrupled in some universities of the region. The number is still low, however, relative to the total number of enrolled students. The most important reasons for the accelerated growth of university enrollment were a demographic shift resulting from urbanization throughout Central America, the growth of the middle class and its average income, and the increasingly popular assumption that higher education leads to a better socioeconomic status. The fact that the population of Central American countries is predominantly young also contributes to the explanation for the rapid rise in enrollment, even though the number of university students represents a very small percentage of the student-age population (18 to 25 years of age). The largest percentage of university students come from the upper, middle, and lower-middle classes. The percentage of those from the working and rural classes is still very small.

The increase in student population has not been accompanied by a proportionate increase in university income. There exists, instead, a great disparity between the growing responsibilities of the university and its resources, resulting in a severe economic crisis and an inevitable drop in the quality of education.

University Planning

In an attempt to foresee and realize their continued development, all Central American universities have introduced a system of careful planning. Many offices of university planning, responsible for all aspects of physical, administrative, and academic growth, have sprung up in the region since the mid 1960s. Their establishment was encouraged by CSUCA in accordance with an ambitious regional study of human resources aimed at the elaboration of a specific plan for the further development of higher education. The plan attempts to deal with the problem of university expansion and the construction of new campuses—a need keenly felt by all universities of the region.

Several national universities (Guatemala, El Salvador, Nicaragua, and Honduras) have adopted five- to seven-year plans for university expansion that have been frustrated by a serious lack of funds. Designed to alleviate the problem of providing for an ever-increasing student population in spite of an insufficient budget, the plans have led to three important conclusions: (1) the need to decentralize the developing universities, thus avoiding the formation of excessively large and powerful seats of power and allowing for the establishment of university centers at several locations within the country; (2) the need for coordination of labor among the various universities, thus avoiding a duplication of effort; and (3) the importance of a regional perspective so unique to Central America.

The decentralization of the national universities of Central America has resulted in the formation of a more effective university system, benefiting the entire region. The University of Guatemala, for example, has two branches: San Carlos in Guatemala City, with an enrollment of 17,000, and the University Center of Quezeltanango, with enrollment of about 1000; university extensions also exist in the departments of Suchitepéquez and San Marcos. The University of El Salvador has university centers in the cities of Santa Ana and San Miguel. Since 1970 the University of Honduras has had a regional center in San Pedro Sula and another in La Ceiba. The University of Nicaragua is the most decentralized of Central America, boasting two important centers: León, seat of the rector, and Managua. By 1975 the campus at León was offering eleven professional degrees. Managua offered sixteen general studies degrees and nine

fields of specialization. The University of Nicaragua also controls a regional university center in Jinotepe and plans to open others in the cities of Estelí, and Puerto Cabezas. The University of Costa Rica, whose total enrollment in 1975 was 25,852, divides its student population among four centers: the central university, with 22,375 students; the regional center at San Ramón, 2340; the regional center at Turrialba, 499; and the regional center at Guanacaste, 628. The University of Panama is also divided into various regional centers, distributed among the major cities of the country.

Regional cooperation and planning is a unique characteristic of Central American higher education. The degree of democratization and modernization achieved by the national universities during the past half century—while still far short of the desired level—points to eventual realization of the goals proclaimed at the 1968 meeting of the Second University Congress—a free, autonomous, unified university system.

Bibliography

Administración universitaria—Análisis crítico de una estructura. II Reunión de administradores—Managua 1972. Guatemala City: Secretaría general, Federación de universidades privadas de América central (FUPAC), 1972.

Aguirre Beltran, G. "Estructura y función de la universidad latinoamericana." *Educación,* 1960, *18,* 36–55.

Aguirre Beltran, G. *La universidad latinoamericana.* Jalapa, Mexico: Biblioteca de la Facultad de filosofía y letras, Universidad veracruzana, 1961.

Consejo superior universitario centroamericano (CSUCA). *Plan para la integración regional de la educación superior centroamericana.* San José, Costa Rica: Secretaría permanente del CSUCA—Ciudad universitaria Rodrigo Facio, 1963.

Consejo superior universitario centroamericano (CSUCA). *Los estudios generales en Centroamérica.* San José: Secretaría permanente del CSUCA—Departamento de publicaciones de la Universidad de Costa Rica, 1964.

Consejo superior universitario centroamericano

(CSUCA). *Confederación universitaria centro-americana 1948–1973.* San José: Departamento de publicaciones de la Universidad de Costa Rica, 1973.

Cuarto censo de población universitaria centroamericana, 1966. San José, Costa Rica: CSUCA, 1968.

Educación rural en Centroamérica. II Conferencia FUPAC. Guatemala City: Secretaría general, Federación de universidades privadas de América central (FUPAC), 1973.

Educación superior en Centroamérica. Estadísticas 1961–1968. San José, Costa Rica: CSUCA, 1969.

Elementos de concientización en los currículos universitarios. II Reunión de académicos de FUPAC. Guatemala City: Secretaría general, Federación de universidades privadas de América central (FUPAC), 1975.

Facio R. *La federación de Centroamérica, sus antecedentes, su vida y su disolución.* San José, Costa Rica: Escuela superior de administración pública América central (ESPAC), 1965.

Galdames, L. *La universidad autónoma.* San José, Costa Rica: Editorial Borraxé Hermanos, 1935.

Herrarte, A. *La unión de Centroamérica (tragedia y esperanza).* (2nd ed.) Guatemala City: Centro editorial del Ministerio de educación pública, 1964.

Lara Lopez, G. *Análisis de la educación universitaria centroamericana.* (3 vols.) San José, Costa Rica: Secretaría permanente del Consejo superior universitario centroamericano, 1968.

Lascaris, C. *Historia de las ideas en Centro América.* San José, Costa Rica: Editorial universitaria centroamericana (EDUCA), 1970.

Mata Gavidia, J. *Fundación de la universidad en Guatemala, 1548–1688.* Guatemala City: Imprenta universitaria de la Universidad de San Carlos, 1954.

Mitchell, H. W. *CSUCA: A Regional Strategy for Higher Education in Central America.* Occasional Publication 7. Lawrence: University of Kansas, Center of Latin American Studies, n.d.

Molina Chocano, G. *Integración centroamericana y dominación internacional.* San José, Costa Rica: Editorial universitaria centroamericana (EDUCA), 1974.

Monteforte Toledo, M. *Centro América, subdesarrollo y dependencia.* (2 vols.) Mexico City: Universidad nacional autónoma de México, 1972.

Ortez Colindres, E. *Integración política de Centroamérica.* San José, Costa Rica: Editorial universitaria centroamericana (EDUCA), 1975.

Pedagogía de la nueva universidad—Seminarios FUPAC 3. Guatemala City, Guatemala: Secretaría general, Federación de universidades privadas de América central (FUPAC), 1975.

Ramírez Mercado, S. "Veinte años de integración regional." *Revista de la Universidad de El Salvador,* 1969, *3.*

Ribeiro, D. *La universidad latinoamericana.* Santiago: Editorial universitaria, 1971.

Soto Blanco, O. *La educación en Centroamérica.* San Salvador, El Salvador: Organization of American States, 1968.

Torres Rivas, E. *Interpretación del desarrollo social centroamericano.* San José, Costa Rica: Editorial universitaria centroamericana (EDUCA), 1971.

Torres Rivas, E., and others. *Centroamérica hoy.* Mexico City: Siglo XXI editores, 1975.

Tünnermann, C. "Integración universitaria centroamericana." *Universidades,* 1961, *5,* 38–40.

Tünnermann, C. "Cooperación regional al nivel universitario." In *Los problemas y la estrategia del planeamiento de la educación—La experiencia latinoamericana.* Paris: UNESCO International Institute of Educational Planning, 1965.

Tünnermann, C. *La universidad: Búsqueda permanente.* León: Editorial universitaria de la Universidad nacional autónoma de Nicaragua, 1971.

Waggoner, G., and Waggoner, B. A. *Education in Central America.* Lawrence: University of Kansas Press, 1971.

CARLOS TÜNNERMANN BERNHEIM

See also: Costa Rica, Republic of; El Salvador, Republic of; Guatemala, Republic of; Honduras, Republic of; Nicaragua, Republic of; Panama, Republic of.

CENTRAL AMERICAN UNIVERSITY CONFEDERATION
(Confederación universitaria centroamericano)

The *Confederación universitaria centroamericano* (Central American University Confederation) and its operational authority, the *Consejo superior universitario centroamericano* (CSUCA: Central American Higher University Council), were founded when the First Central American University Congress met in September 1948 in San Salvador, El Salvador. Members of the confederation include national universities in Guatemala, Honduras, Costa Rica, Nicaragua, and El Salvador. The confederation guarantees all member institutions academic, administrative, and economic autonomy.

CSUCA meets every two years to define general policy and approve regional programs. The administrative committee, composed of rectors and student union presidents of member universities, meets three times a year to organize and coordinate the confederation's activities. The secretariat, established in 1959, is responsible for the creation or modification of regional institutions; planning for integration of professional training; development of pre-professional programs in basic disciplines; stimulation and establishment of postgraduate programs; and establishment of a regional commission to assist regional integration of higher education in Central America. The secretariat analyzes study programs, sponsors seminars and meetings of university faculties for discussion of higher educational and basic programs, provides documentary services, and arranges for exchanges of academic staff and students among CSUCA member institutions.

By 1966 CSUCA had established institutes in statistics, comparative law, penal law, educational development, and social and economic research. The Central American Press was approved and funded in February 1969.

Publications include *Jornada,* monthly information sheet; *Repertoria,* quarterly journal; and reports of CSUCA meetings.

Ciudad universitaria Rodrigo Facio
San José, Costa Rica

CENTRAL BUREAU FOR EDUCATIONAL VISITS AND EXCHANGES (LONDON)

See Exchange, International: Student Employment Abroad, Student Exchange Programs.

CENTRAL ORGANIZATION OF SWEDISH PROFESSIONAL WORKERS
(Sveriges akademikers centralorganisation/Statstjänstemännens riksförbund)

The *Sveriges akademikers centralorganisation/Statstjänstemännens riksförbund* (SACO/SR: Central Organization of Swedish Professional Workers), a confederation of twenty-seven professional associations, aims to improve standards of working conditions for its members and to safeguard the economic and social interests of its groups. SACO/SR members have a university or college education or occupy senior positions normally filled by graduates, often shifting from one sector of employment to another—private, public, or self-employment. SACO/SR associations have approximately 150,000 members; most of them are in the public sector, but the number in the private sector is increasing. SACO/SR has an advisory body that looks after common interests of independent professionals—lawyers, architects, consulting engineers, doctors, and dentists. Students' interests are the concern of the Swedish National Union of Students, but many SACO/SR associations have special sections in which they enroll undergraduates. These student members are apprentices in the trade union sense but are given considerable independence within the organization because of the importance that SACO/SR and its affiliates attach to education.

An individual member of SACO/SR normally belongs to a local chapter which looks after union interests by representing its members on work councils (joint labor-management organs) and maintaining direct contacts with company management. Questions of interest to all members are dealt with by central authorities within the associations. The majority of SACO/SR affiliates have a grand council as their highest decision-making body, with delegates appointed by local chapters or sections. The grand council convenes yearly or every other year to elect a board, determine a budget, and draft policies for future work. The board is responsible for administering day-to-day activities of SACO/SR.

The highest decision-making body of the central organization is the general assembly, which meets yearly to examine the annual report and financial accounts, draft future policies, determine the budget, and elect the executive board. The eighty seats in the general assembly are apportioned among the affiliated associations according to their membership, each association sending at least one delegate. Between meetings of the general assembly, the governing body is the fifteen-member executive board headed by a chairman and two vice-chairmen. Meeting once a month, the executive board is assisted by seven advisory councils, whose representatives are appointed by the associations and whose decisions are implemented by the secretariat. A conference, made up of all association chairmen, has an advisory function.

Virtually all SACO/SR's revenues come from membership fees. Individual membership fees are high, but students pay a lower fee than fully employed members. The associations pay SACO/SR a set fee for each of their full subscription members. More than half of the organization's expenditures are accounted for by salaries and other secretariat costs. The secretariat has a staff of forty-five and departments of research and policymaking, collective bargaining, and organization and information.

The secretariat's research and policymaking department conducts extensive research programs. Some studies are undertaken at the organization's own initiative, and many of them result in proposals to authorities. Other studies help the organization formulate stands on negotiations, pending legislation, and administrative matters.

SACO/SR is often authorized to appoint experts to official committees investigating problems in labor market policy, education, and taxation; and its representatives serve on boards such as the National Labor Market Board and the National Board of Education. SACO/SR negotiates on salary questions and employment conditions of a general nature. The separate associations deal with matters that exclusively concern their membership, and SACO/SR coordinates their actions. The collective bargaining duties are gradually being taken over by the central organization's bargaining delegation. The council attempts to give professionals a fair share of the high standard of living by advocating appropriate changes in economic policy and the tax system.

With the appearance of new professions and forms of education, new groups become part of SACO/SR, and the organization and its member associations are restructured or merge into larger units. To coordinate this work, SACO/SR maintains a department of organization and information. This department also runs an educational program for members. To provide training in unionism for officials and executives of the organization, SACO/SR arranges conferences, which also serve to give information on its activities to student union leaders, journalists, and other outside groups.

SACO/SR was the first organization in the world to bring professional associations together and give a unionist bias to their activities. It was instrumental in helping to set up similar organizations in other Nordic countries and is interested in enlarging the scope of Nordic cooperation and in improving relations with organizations of professional workers in other countries.

The principal vehicle of information for SACO/SR members is *SACO-tidningen*, which is issued ten times a year. The affiliated associations publish their own house organs. SACO/SR also issues up-to-date reports on work in the organization as well as pamphlets and brochures of interest to members and nonmembers.

Valhallavägen 16
Box 5992
114 89 Stockholm, Sweden

CENTRE FOR LEARNING AND DEVELOPMENT, Canada

The Centre for Learning and Development was founded at McGill University, Montreal, Quebec, in 1969 as a research unit in higher education, although it also conducts research in primary and secondary education. Topics of higher education research, focusing on local and national problems, include the following: administration, especially academic policies; university students and faculty; educational technology; curricula and instruction; methodology of research in higher education; and reform in higher education. In particular, the center is interested in individualization of instruction and formative evaluation of instructional systems.

In addition to research activities, the center offers services and support to faculty in matters of course design, development, and evaluation. It serves as a resource center, providing literature, workshops, and individual and group consultation. The professional members of the staff, holding joint appointments with the faculty of education, teach courses and supervise the work of a number of graduate students.

The center is funded by the university and the government and is administered by the university's Office of Educational Development. Its staff includes five research professionals, six research assistants and/or graduate students, a part-time technician, one administrative assistant, and three secretaries. The center has a small research library and a computer station connected to the McGill Computer Centre.

The center publishes Learning and Development, a monthly newsletter containing articles and bibliographies on learning and teaching. The center's other publica-

tions include a number of bibliographies, monographs, and special papers on a variety of educational issues.

McGill University
P.O. Box 6070
Montreal, Quebec, Canada H3C 3G1

CENTRE FOR THE ECONOMICS OF EDUCATION, England

The Centre for the Economics of Education was established in April 1974 as the successor to the Higher Education Research Unit, set up in 1964 in the economics department of the London School of Economics and Political Science (LSE). The center conducts research in the economics of higher education, although higher education is no longer its exclusive research focus. Major fields of work include the following: the effect of state education on the distribution of income; the effect of social security programs and taxation on working hours, unemployment, and the labor force participation of women; the causes of urban unemployment in poor countries; and labor markets for teachers. Courses offered by the center include a workshop and research seminar on the economics of education, lecture courses on the economics of education and human capital, and lecture courses on economic models of educational planning.

The center receives grants from the Social Science Research Council, the Overseas Development Administration, and a charitable trust. Its library of material on the economics of education and educational planning is open to scholars from inside and outside the school.

Publications of the Higher Education Research Unit, available from the center, include Statistics of the Occupational and Educational Structure of the Labour Force in 53 Countries, issued in collaboration with the Organisation for Economic Co-operation and Development in 1969; the LSE Studies on Education Series; and other books and articles. The publications lists of the unit and the center are available from the center on request.

London School of Economics and
Political Science
Houghton Street
London WC2A 2AE, England

CENTRE FOR THE STUDY OF HIGHER EDUCATION, Australia

The Centre for the Study of Higher Education was founded in 1968 at the University of Melbourne, Parkville, Australia, as an academic department designed to conduct research on teaching methods. The center consolidated and extended the work that had previously been the responsibility of the university's Audio Visual Section, established in 1948; the Education Research Office, founded in 1958; and the University Teaching Office, founded in 1961. The center investigates teaching problems in various university departments and also conducts systematic studies on local, national, regional, and international issues in higher education.

Specific research projects have included the production of video programs for the departments of medicine, dental science, music, and engineering; design of survey techniques for conducting student evaluations of units, subjects, or courses; development of a methodology for evaluating course innovations; collection and analysis of student data to explore such problems as student workloads, causes and consequences of unplanned pregnancy among unmarried students, and students' lack of writing skills; and development of techniques for computer-aided instruction in university courses. Other areas of research in higher education at the center include the following: administration, including governance and academic policies; economics of higher education; manpower in higher education; educational planning; university faculty; history of higher education; and reform in higher education.

In addition to research activities, the center conducts postgraduate courses, offers courses and occasional seminars for academic staff, and provides consultation services to other Australian universities and colleges of advanced education.

The center is supported by university funds, foundation grants, publication sales, and contractual research and consulting services. The staff includes ten research professionals, three research assistants and/or graduate students, fifteen technicians, three paid consultants, two administrative personnel, and four secretarial and clerical personnel.

In August 1974 the center opened an experimental television and film studio. The center also has a computer, microfiche equipment, a student feedback system, and a motorized television studio. Staff members have access to the University of Melbourne library and its branches.

The center publishes *Educational Technology,* three times a year.

University of Melbourne
Parkville, Victoria, Australia 3052

CENTRE OF ADVANCED STUDY IN EDUCATION, India

The Centre of Advanced Study in Education began conducting research in higher education in 1974, under the Teacher Development Programme of the University Grants Commission of India. A teaching and research unit at the Maharaja Sayajirao University of Baroda, the center also conducts research in primary, secondary, adult, and vocational education. Higher education research at the center focuses on local, national, regional, and international problems in the following areas: administration, especially governance and academic policies; university students and faculty; educational technology; history of higher education; curricula and instruction; methodology of research in higher education; and reform in higher education.

In addition to research activities, the center evaluates curricula; conducts postgraduate courses in higher education; trains university teachers, administrators, and researchers; and develops evaluation tools such as tests and measurements. It also organizes conferences and seminars, including a seminar on higher education for university teachers.

Funded by the government and the university, the center has a staff of two research professionals and two to fifteen research assistants and/or graduate students. The staff has access to a library and microfiche equipment.

The center has published the *Review of Research in the M.S. University (1949-1972)*.

Maharaja Sayajirao
University of Baroda
Maharaja Sayajirao
Lokmanya Tilak Road
Baroda 390002, Gujarat, India

CEREMONIES

Ceremonial occasions are common to academic institutions throughout the world. They range from simple ceremonies and exercises to complex programs based on local customs and traditions that are centuries old. Such ceremonies may range in duration from a few hours to as much as an entire day or even a week. Many of the ceremonies conducted today have their origins in the pageantry of the churches and religious organizations that sponsored early academic institutions. Ceremonies that are commonly practiced by most present-day colleges and universities include convocations, both annual (to memorialize particular events) and special (to recognize achievements of individuals and confer honors upon individuals); groundbreaking ceremonies; dedications of areas and new buildings; inaugurations of new officers; baccalaureate (religious) services; and commencements.

Convocations

Some convocations are traditional annual events, and others take place only on special occasions. Convocations may be formal and ritualistic or informal and unstructured events.

Opening convocations. Most colleges and universities hold exercises to celebrate the opening of an academic year and to welcome new students and staff. Depending on local tradition, these may involve an academic procession, with university officials and other participants in full academic dress. Customarily, the chief executive officer (president, chairman, or rector) gives an address and acquaints the new students with the history and role of the college or university. At large institutions, convocations involving the entire student body are being replaced by small, individual college or school convocations.

Founders Day convocations. Founders Day celebrates the date of the founding of a college or university, the date of its initial charter, the original date of opening, or the first day of classes. It usually involves a formal academic convocation, with a procession of trustees, public officials, administrators, faculty, staff, and invited guests in full academic dress. The audience is usually formed of the student body, families of administrators and faculty, and guests. This occasion calls for appropriate music and an address by either an official of the institution or a guest speaker. Honorary degrees may be conferred upon eminent guests. At some institutions the Founders Day convocation is used to give special recognition to alumni and community leaders who have distinguished themselves by service to the institution, the community, or both. Persons so honored are usually presented with citations, certificates, or, on occasion, special medallions, as evidence of their election as fellows or cofounders of the institution.

Honors convocations. Honors convocations are designed to give recognition to outstanding scholars. Selected undergraduate and graduate students, for example, may be awarded certificates and prizes signaling outstanding scholastic achievements. In the United States such occasions may announce the names of students elected to membership in scholastic honor societies such as Phi Kappa Phi, Phi Beta Kappa, Tau Beta Phi, or Kappa Delta Phi. On this occasion, also, alumni whose achievements are outstanding in scholarship or the professions may be elected to scholastic honor societies. A printed program of the event usually lists the names of all honors recipients and sometimes includes the names of those still enrolled in the college who have received similar honors previously.

Groundbreakings

Colleges and universities often hold informal exercises commemorating the breaking of ground for a new building. The ceremonies are held at the site of the building, where a spade is used to symbolically break ground for the beginning of construction. Participants customarily include the donor of the building, if such exists, officers of the college or university, the board of trustees, representatives of the architects and contractors, and public officials if the institution is supported by tax monies. The ceremonies usually include a prayer or blessing of the site, appropriate remarks concerning the new edifice, and photographs of the actual shoveling of earth for both the press and the archival history of the institution. On occasion, small replicas of the spade used to break ground are presented to the participants.

Dedications

Dedication exercises take place when a campus area, room, or building is named in honor or in memory of a person or persons. People honored or memorialized at a dedication are usually individuals of special achievement, those who have given long service to the college or university, or those who have made financial donations to cover the cost of the facility or contributed a so-called naming gift—one that does not cover the entire cost of the facility but is the largest and most significant of all the gifts received to develop it. Dedication ceremonies may involve only the unveiling of a plaque inscribed with the names of those being honored, in which case the event will be informal and only a limited list of guests invited at the request of the honoree, the donor, or the immediate family. More elaborate ceremonies consist of a dedication, a luncheon or dinner for an extensive list of guests, a formal convocation in academic dress, and an address by either a guest speaker or university official describing the facilities being dedicated and their significance. When a building is dedicated as the headquarters of a field of study or to house the faculty and staff of a particular discipline, it is not uncommon to use the occasion to bring together distinguished scholars and scientists to present papers on their subjects.

Following the convocation, the naming plaque and other recognition plaques are unveiled. If the name of the facility, such as "John Smith Hall," is carved in stone or concrete above or adjacent to the entrance, this carving too is unveiled with a singular ceremony and reading of the carving. On occasion, attention is focused on a "cartouche," which may be carved above or adjacent to the entrance of the building. The features of a cartouche may symbolize the purpose of the building and its areas, or it may be a reproduction of a family coat-of-arms. Cartouches are multicolored and large enough to be visible and legible from a distance.

Printed dedication programs vary in format, but they are usually prepared as souvenirs of the event. More elaborate programs include pictures of the facility dedicated, pictures and biographical sketches of individuals whose names are memorialized or honored in the building or area, and descriptions of the facility and its intended uses. If naming plaques or other plaques regarding the facility are unveiled, reproductions of them may also be included in the program. It is also appropriate to include the seal of the college or university and photographs of the chairman of the board, the chief executive officer, and the dean or director of the school to be housed in the building.

Inaugurations

Traditionally, colleges and universities have ceremonies to install new chief executives. Such ceremonies may be "family affairs" involving only the governing boards, administrators, faculty, staff, and students of the institution, and, of course, the immediate family of the new executive. In the United States, however, inaugurations involve the participation of sister institutions. Representatives are invited from academic institutions in the immediate vicinity and from a select group of other national and international institutions. In addition, representatives from academic organizations, professional societies, and honor societies, as well as local public officials, participate in the ceremony. All the guests join the academic procession, along with trustees, administrators, and faculty of the institution. At large institutions such a procession may consist of several hundred people and may be very colorful because of the wide range of academic costumes. When everyone is seated, the new executive traditionally receives greetings from the governing board, representatives of the faculty, sister institutions, and the student body, as well as appropriate government officials. The chairman of the board of trustees usually reads a statement setting forth the responsibilities and duties of the office and the trust vested in him. Symbolically, the inauguree is handed a copy of the charter or bylaws of the institution and its keys. Frequently he is given a symbolic lavaliere to wear at all ceremonial occasions. Following the academic recessional, there is usually a reception for the new chief executive. A banquet may precede the inauguration ceremonies or follow the reception.

Baccalaureate Services

Baccalaureate services have been traditional in colleges and universities for centuries. These are religious services for the graduating class held either on the Sunday preceding commencement exercises or, when commencement is held on Sunday, in the morning prior to the exercises. Baccalaureate services are usually held in a church or chapel, and the speaker delivers a sermon. University officials and members of the graduating class wear academic dress.

Commencements

Commencement or graduation exercises are common to academic institutions. For the oldest and largest institutions, they are the epitome of pageantry and tradition. Commencement is carefully planned and executed because, more than any other ceremony, it involves the entire academic community—alumni, public officials, students, families and friends of graduates, and friends of the institution. For the graduating class commencement is a time when long and arduous study is rewarded by the conferring of degrees. For the institution it is a time to renew the traditions of scholarship with a public display. Commencement practices are colorful, with the participants wearing academic gowns, hoods, and tasseled mortarboards. The colors of the hoods and tassels represent the field of study in which the wearer has obtained a degree; the lining of the hood is the color of the university that conferred the degree. The many colors worn by the governing boards, executive officers, and faculty are thus symbolic of the wide variety of knowledge and institutional background represented, the traditions of scholarship, and the sisterhood of all institutions of higher learning. The commencement marshal and the chief executive officer may have academic regalia especially designed to signify their offices.

Commencement exercises may be held in an auditorium or at an appropriate outdoor site. In either event the pageantry and protocol are identical. The academic procession at a medium- or large-sized university is typically led by the commencement marshal, who calls the participants to order and announces their order of march and who has the prerogative to carry the institution's mace to the platform reserved for officials, dignitaries, and guests. The mace, a symbol of the authority of the institution to confer degrees upon deserving candidates, had its origin in the club or weapon carried in medieval times by guards, persons of high authority, or officials of government. Its design and appearance typically resemble a metal torch or cross, decorated by carvings including the college or university seal.

Following the marshal are the bearers of appropriate flags, banners, and emblems, who are usually referred to as the color guard and whose flags include the national and state emblems and that of the institution itself. Next, the marshals of the graduating class carry the flags of the respective colleges and schools, each flag having its own distinctive color, seal, and symbols. These flags are placed either on or in front of the platform.

The degree candidates follow, grouped according to college or graduate school and in order of the hierarchy of their degrees. Each grouping has its own marshal, carrying a special baton, who leads the graduates to their appropriate places. Faculty marshals then lead the faculty, arranged by rank or seniority of service. When all have been conducted to their appropriate places, the so-called platform party—trustees, administrative and faculty representatives, state and municipal officers, and honored guests—march as a group in appropriate order to the platform, which is decorated by colorful bunting, flags, flowers, and possibly a backdrop depicting the official seal of the institution. The degree-granting ceremony is then opened by the singing of the national anthem or a hymn, followed by the introduction of the commencement speakers. Addresses may be given by a representative of the graduating class, an invited guest (usually an honorary degree recipient), the chief executive officer, or a faculty leader. In the United States the practice of having guest speakers is disappearing in large institutions, in deference to the length of commencement exercises. In such instances only the chief executive makes a brief address. After such speeches, degree candidates are presented by the deans or directors of their schools and colleges.

The act of conferring degrees may be accomplished by addressing each group of graduates separately or all together. The chief executive states that "by virtue of authority vested in me by the commonwealth, [state, or nation] and the board of trustees of this institution, I hereby confer upon you the degree of . . ., with all the rights, privileges, and prerogatives thereunto pertaining." The candidates may then be instructed to change the tassels on their mortarboards from the right to the left side, an act symbolic of receiving the degree. Depending on the size of the graduating class, they may receive a token diploma for the entire group with individual diplomas presented at a later ceremony presided over by the dean or director of each school or college. The giving of the diploma is merely evidence that the degree has been conferred.

In some commencements all candidates wear their hoods, symbolic of degrees to be received, prior to the actual conferring. In other commencements candidates are hooded when the degree is conferred by coming to the platform where institutional officials place the hoods over the shoulders of one or more candidates at a time. It is quite common for recipients of doctoral and honorary degrees to have a special hooding ceremony. Honorary degrees are awarded to distinguished laymen and academics to recognize their special achievements and contributions to humanity and may be conferred prior to the awarding of all other degrees or just prior to the conclusion of the exercises. The commencement program concludes with a recessional and the academic procession in reverse.

Bibliography

Gunn, M. K. *A Guide to Academic Protocol.* New York: Columbia University Press, 1969.

Hall, L. H. "Commencement: Sacred Tradition or Irrelevant Vestige." *Community and Junior College Journal,* June 1973, *43,* 20–21.

Leeman, T. A. *The Rites of Passage in a Student Culture.* New York: Columbia University Press, 1972.

Miller, L. *Encyclopedia of Etiquette.* New York: Crown Publishers, 1967.

"New Style Graduation." *Life,* June 9, 1972, pp. 95–98.

Shattuck, G. E., and Kirkpatrick, P. B. "Commencement." *Encyclopedia of Higher Education.* New York: Crowell Collier, 1971.

Sheard, K. *Academic Heraldry in America.* Marquette: Northern Michigan College Press, 1962.

Spurr, S. H. *Academic Degree Structures: Innovative Approaches.* New York: McGraw-Hill, 1970.

Touraine, A. *The Academic System in American Society.* New York: McGraw-Hill, 1973.

Vanderbilt, A. *Amy Vanderbilt's New Complete Book of Etiquette, The Guide to Gracious Living.* Garden City, New York: Doubleday, 1958.

CHARLES M. DEVLIN

See also: Academic Dress and Insignia.

CERN: EUROPEAN CENTER FOR NUCLEAR RESEARCH
See Science Policies: Highly Industrialized Nations: Western Europe.

CERTIFICATES
See Degrees, Diplomas, and Certificates.

CHAD, REPUBLIC OF

Population: 3,363,000 (estimate). Student enrollment in primary school: 198,000 (1973); secondary school: 12,500 (1973); higher education–university: 600; higher education–nonuniversity: approximately 200. Language of instruction: French. Academic calendar: October to June, two semesters. [Figures are for 1974 unless otherwise noted. Source: Ministry of Education: Statistiques scolaires 1973–74.]

Prior to independence in 1960, Chad had no institutions of higher education. In the 1960s some institutions offering programs of a postsecondary nature were established: a school of public administration, a school of public works, and an insti-

tute of animal husbandry and veterinary medicine. The first true institution of higher education, the University of Chad, was founded in 1971.

Chad became a part of the French colonial empire in Africa after military conquests during the nineteenth century had allowed the French to advance inland from the Atlantic coast. By the first decade of the twentieth century, the area of Chad was conquered; and by 1910 France had established the federation of French Equatorial Africa, which consisted of three colonies: Gabon; Middle Congo (now the People's Republic of the Congo); and Chad/Ubangi-Shari, the latter now named the Central African Republic. In 1920 a reorganization separated Chad into a fourth colony.

The first educational decree to establish a formal educational system in Chad was passed by the French government on April 4, 1911, and was followed by further decrees in 1925. Educational development in the nation, however, was slow. By 1930 the entire system of education consisted of ten primary schools and three postprimary institutions.

No significant educational growth took place in Chad until 1956 and the passage of the *loi cadre,* the enabling act, which granted self-determination to the African colonies of France. In 1957 the first Ministry of National Education was established in Chad and charged with the responsibility to develop the nation's educational system. Increased educational efforts by the ministry almost tripled primary school enrollments between the school years 1955–56 and 1958–59, from 4.4 to 11 percent of the school-age population. Enrollments continued to increase after independence. By 1961–62 the primary school enrollments had grown to 20 percent of the age group. Secondary enrollments grew correspondingly, from 328 students in 1956–57 to some 1700 in 1961–62 (*La République du Tchad,* 1963).

In 1964 the newly independent Chad signed a bilateral educational agreement with France, which established close cooperation between the two nations. The agreement provided for substantial French assistance to Chad's educational system in the form of teaching staff and capital improvements. The French aid has mainly benefited secondary and higher education. Most of the nation's primary school teachers are nationals, while at the lower secondary level some 45 percent of the teachers are foreigners. Most of these are French, as are some 80 percent of the teachers in the higher secondary schools (*lycées*) and in the institutions of higher education.

The University of Chad (in N'Djaména), which was created to supply the manpower needed for national development, has concentrated much of its efforts on teacher training. In 1974–75 the university enrolled approximately 600 students, mainly in teacher training programs. It is hoped that this will alleviate the dependence on expatriate staff in education.

In the latter part of the 1970s the direction of educational efforts, as well as the educational level—primary, secondary, technical, or higher education—that will be accorded the greatest economic resources, will have to await political changes under way as a result of the *coup d'état* of April 13, 1975, which overthrew the nation's first president Ngarta Tombalbaye.

National Educational Policy

In accordance with the ordinance establishing the university, the function of all institutions of higher education and research in Chad is to create cadres in multidisciplinary study. These cadres are expected to serve the social, economic, cultural, and human development of Chad and Africa; undertake research at a level conducive to creating economic and social change; and promote regional and international cooperation.

Legal Basis of Educational System

Chad's educational system is strongly influenced by two educational agreements with France, one in 1960 and one in 1964, which established the mode of cooperation, the standards, and the extent of French

educational assistance. In addition, Ordinance 29/PR of December 27, 1971, created the University of Chad. It was augmented by Decree 71/PR/ENC of March 6, 1972, which was modified by Decree 108/PR-ENC of April 29, 1972, containing the statutes of the university. The statutes determine the administrative structure of the university and set guidelines for academic freedom. A decree of May 20, 1963, established the National School of Administration. The school was further organized by Decree 265/PR/SGG of December 19, 1974 and Decree 140/PR-SGG of April 29, 1974.

Types of Institutions

University education in Chad is available at the University of Chad, which offers instruction in four institutes: *Institut universitaire des sciences juridiques, économiques et de gestion* (University Institute of Law, Economics and Management), *Institut universitaire des lettres, langues vivantes et sciences humaines* (University Institute of Letters, Modern Languages and Human Sciences), *Institut universitaire des sciences* (University Institute of Sciences), and *Institut universitaire des techniques de l'élevage* (University Institute of Animal Husbandry).

Postsecondary education is available in two additional institutes offering training in administration, animal husbandry, and veterinary medicine. The *Ecole nationale d'administration* (ENA: National School of Administration), founded in 1963, offers education in three cycles—of three years, two years, and one year, respectively—leading to postsecondary diplomas. The *Institut d'élevage et de médecine vétérinaire des pays tropicaux* (Institute of Animal Husbandry and Veterinary Medicine for Tropical Nations), although specializing in research, also offers instruction and practical training for specialization as a veterinary doctor or technician.

Relationship with Secondary Education and Admission Requirements

As in most of the other francophone African countries, primary education in

Chad lasts six years. It leads to the *certificat d'études primaires élémentaires* (CEPE). Primary education is available in some 700 public and 50 private schools; most of the latter are missionary schools, which enroll about 9 percent of the total number of students.

In addition to the primary examination, students are required to take an entrance examination for secondary school. The program of secondary study is divided into a lower level of four years, leading to the *brevet d'études du premier cycle* (BEPC); and a higher cycle of three years, leading to the *baccalauréat* in one of four specialties (philosophy and literature, economics and social sciences, mathematics and physical sciences, or natural sciences), which determine the field of study in higher education.

Secondary education is offered in twenty *collèges d'enseignement général* (CEG), five of which are private, and in nine *lycées*, two of which offer technical education. The CEGs usually provide the first cycle of secondary school; *lycées* generally provide the upper cycle, although they may offer both cycles.

The *baccalauréat*, or equivalent qualification, is the entrance requirement to the university. Acceptance to the National School of Administration is by competitive examination for students in two categories: holders of the BEPC, with an age limit of twenty-three, and higher functionaries, with an age limit of twenty-five.

Administration and Control

The University of Chad is a public institution with internal financial autonomy. It is under the authority of the Ministry of National Education, Culture, Youth and Sports and, according to its statutes, is established to serve the needs of the state. The university is administered by a university council and by a rector, who is appointed by presidential decree on the recommendation of the minister of national education. Under Title Three of the statutes, the university council is broadly based, with representation from government, business, teaching staff, and students. Among members appointed by statute are the secretary general of national education, who is president of the council; the directors of secondary and higher education and the National Institute of Human Sciences; the presidents of the Chamber of Commerce and the Center for Development; two representatives of the national assembly and two representatives of the trade and employees' unions; the directors of the university institutes; and directors of other concerned ministries.

Among elected members are three representatives of the teaching staff from each university institute, one of whom is elected vice-president of the council, and three student representatives of each institute. The rector also participates in the council, and the secretary general of the university acts as secretary of the council. The council is convened by its president and meets at least twice a year. It adopts the budget of the university as presented by the rector, sets regulations and standards for remuneration of personnel, proposes programs of study, determines teaching methods and the selection of students, and establishes the internal rules of the university. Decisions on financing are subject to veto by the government. The rector handles the liaison between the university council and the National Council of Higher Education and Research, the planning body for higher education and research.

The university's four institutes are divided into departments. New departments can be created by the rector on recommendation by the councils of the institutes. Each institute is headed by a director, selected from among the teaching staff of the institute and appointed by the minister of education on the recommendation of the rector. The director is assisted by an educational council of the institute, composed of the director as president, an elected member of the teaching staff of each department, one or two representatives of teachers and researchers, one or two representatives of the administrative personnel, and one representative of students per section and year.

The National School of Administration is a public institution with internal financial autonomy. It is administered by a director, appointed by decree by the Council of Ministers. He is in charge of both administrative and academic supervision of the institution. The director is assisted by an administrative council of nine members, who are government functionaries such as the secretary general of national education, the director of planning and development, and the inspector general. The Institute of Animal Husbandry and Veterinary Medicine for Tropical Nations is similarly administered.

Programs and Degrees

During its first few years, the original three institutes of the university (*Institut des lettres, des langues et des sciences humaines; Institut des sciences exactes et appliquées; Institut des sciences juridiques, économiques et de gestion*) concentrated on training teachers, civil servants, and business personnel. The programs are now being diversified to include other fields of study. The fourth institute, *Institut universitaire des techniques de l'élevage,* established in 1974, was designed to provide needed manpower for the single important national industry, cattle breeding and agriculture.

The four institutes offer two cycles of higher education. The first consists of two-year diploma courses in (1) law and administrative studies, economics, and management; (2) mathematics, biology, chemistry, and physics; (3) geography, history, and modern languages; and (4) sciences (animal husbandry). The second cycle leads to the *licence,* the first degree, after three years of study in the institutes of law and letters. The Institute of Animal Husbandry awards the title of engineer.

Since the university has functioned only since 1972, postgraduate study has not yet been organized.

The National School of Administration offers education at three levels. The first cycle of three years leads to qualifications equivalent to the *baccalauréat;* the second cycle of two years is at the diploma level; and a third cycle leads to the *diplôme de l'ENA* (*troisième cycle*), which roughly corresponds to the first degree level at the university. In 1973–74 the school enrolled 112 students.

Financing

All revenues of the University of Chad originate from the government, which receives some 80 percent of needed funding from France. In 1974 the government of Chad supplied about one third of the capital expenditures for the university; two thirds, as well as all funds for laboratories and equipment, were received as technical assistance, mainly from France. The government of Chad also provided some 15 percent of recurrent expenditure, part of which consisted of grants for study at the university.

Student Financial Aid

Education in Chad is free; but, unlike the universities in most of the other francophone nations, the University of Chad does not provide dormitories, student cafeterias, and other services. All students, regardless of economic means, receive grants from the government. Scholarships are also granted by the European Economic Community and administered through the university.

Almost as many students study abroad as attend the University of Chad. They are mainly in fields of study not provided in Chad. According to the *Secrétariat national de la commission des bourses* (National Secretariat of the Commission on Grants), 470 Chadian students studied abroad in 1974 in thirteen different countries. The largest contingent, 67 students, studied medicine, primarily in France and the Soviet Union. In all, 208 Chadians studied in France, 64 in the Soviet Union, and large contingents of students were also in the neighboring nations of Cameroon, the Congo, Ivory Coast, and Senegal. In addition to medicine, the most popular fields of study were veterinary medicine and agricultural sciences.

Student Social Background and Access to Education

Some 86 percent of the population in Chad is rural (Cabot and Bouquet, 1974, p. 32) and, in the northern parts of the nation, nomadic. Most of the schools are located in the south. Student attendance at the primary level was estimated at some 23 percent of eligible students in 1972, and was higher in the more settled southern areas and lower in the sparsely populated north. Some 5 percent of primary school enrollees continue into secondary school, while about .3 percent of primary school enrollees enter the university (*Statistiques scolaires,* 1974).

Industrial development is low, with few employment opportunities for graduates. Furthermore, since the transportation network is poorly developed, with few roads accessible year-round, the students must live away from home—a factor often inhibiting school attendance, especially among women. Enrollments are also affected by cultural patterns, such as the early marriage age, particularly among the Muslim population. The Muslim population is estimated at some 50 percent of total population. Probably because of early marriages, female enrollment drops from some 30 percent to 10 percent of total enrollment between primary and secondary school. The university enrolled two female students in 1974–75.

Teaching Staff

Conditions for employment, promotion, and salaries of teaching staff are set by the government. The university council considers appointments and makes recommendations to the rector, who proposes faculty for appointment to the minister of national education. Professors of Chad nationality are civil servants and receive life appointments, while foreign staff are generally given contracts, in accordance with the agreement governing their employment.

The ranks of teaching staff are professor, *maître-assistant* (assistant lecturer), and assistant.

Promotion from assistant to *maître-assistant* usually requires three years of teaching experience and the *doctorat du troisième cycle.* To advance to full professor, a candidate is expected to attain a Ph.D. or *doctorat d'état.*

During the academic year 1973–74 the teaching staff at the university was multinational, consisting of three nationals of Chad, thirty-four from France, and eight from various nations such as Egypt, the Soviet Union, the United Kingdom, and the United States.

Research Activities

Research occupies an important position in national development planning. The university and the research institutions have been charged, according to the decree establishing the university, with "realizing research on a high level which can create social and economic change." Within the university the responsibility for planning research activities rests with the Council on Education and Research; most of the efforts of the young university have so far been directed at teaching activities.

The *Institut national tchadien pour les sciences humaines* (Chad National Institute for Humanities)—founded by Decree 003/EN of January 26, 1961, and reorganized under its present name in 1963, in accordance with Decree 113/PR of 24 June 1963—was created to "undertake all activities relating to research regarding the humanities." The institute has some full-time staff but also utilizes the part-time services of university personnel.

Other research organizations, such as the French *Office de la recherche scientifique et technique outre-mer* (ORSTOM), founded in 1943, the *Institut d'élevage et de médecine vétérinaire des pays tropicaux,* and the *Institut de recherches du coton et des textiles exotiques*

(IRCT: Institute of Cotton and Exotic Textile Research), also conduct research of importance to national development.

Current Problems and Trends

Educational problems in Chad, which is one of the poorest nations in Africa, are manifold. Total student enrollments at the primary level are some 23 percent of the age group. Although nearly 200,000 students attended primary school in 1973–74, only 12,000 were able to continue in secondary school; 15 percent of these were enrolled in the upper secondary schools.

The majority of teachers at the primary level are Chadian, and many have not received the necessary pedagogical training for their positions. Some 45 percent of the teachers in the *collèges d'enseignement général* and almost 80 percent of the teachers in the *lycées* and higher education institutions are foreigners. Dropout rates are high at the lower levels. Efforts have been made, with assistance from France and UNESCO, to create curricula more closely attuned to Chadian needs; however, the education is offered in a foreign tongue, French, and much of the time in the classroom is spent on language learning, to the detriment of other subjects. Preparation for the largely French examinations, therefore, is not sufficient; and failure rates are high.

International Cooperation

The University of Chad was founded with directives to "promote regional and international cooperation" and to concentrate its efforts on study suited not only to Chad but also to Africa. Cooperation with the other francophone countries has taken various forms. Chad participated in the *Fondation de l'enseignement supérieur en Afrique centrale* (FESAC: the Foundation of Higher Education in Central Africa), a cooperative educational center of the early 1960s; this center then led to the establishment of regional units of higher study, which were later converted into national institutions. Chad also participated in conferences of the ministers of national education of the African states, as well as in individual cooperation through the granting of scholarships to students to attend universities in neighboring countries. The teaching faculty, both in the *lycées* and the university, are multinational.

The University of Chad also maintains contacts with universities in France, the Federal Republic of Germany, the United States, Eastern European countries, and Japan, and has been a recipient of assistance from international agencies such as UNESCO and UNICEF.

[Information submitted by Jean Cabot, former Rector, University of Chad, N'Djaména.]

Bibliography

Cabot, J., and Bouquet, C. *Le Chad.* Paris: Hatier, 1974.
Gardinier, D. G. "Education in the States of Equatorial Africa. A Bibliographical Essay." *Africana Library Journal,* 1972, *3*(3), 7–20.
Gardinier, D. G. "Schooling in the States of Equatorial Africa." *Revue canadienne des études africaines/Canadian Journal of African Studies,* 1974, *8*(3), 517–538.
Labrousse, A. *La France et l'aide à l'éducation dans 14 états africains et Malgache.* Paris: International Institute of Educational Planning, 1971.
La République du Tchad. Fort-Lamy: Service d'information, October 1963.
Moumouni, A. *Education in Africa.* New York: Praeger, 1968.
Statistiques scolaires 1973–74. N'Djaména: Ministère de l'éducation nationale, de la culture, de la jeunesse et des sports, 1974.
Université du Tchad. Annuaire 1974–1975. N'Djaména: Université du Tchad, 1974.

See also: Africa, Sub-Saharan: Regional Analysis; Archives: Africa and Asia, National Archives of.

CHAIR FOR RESEARCH INTO HIGHER EDUCATION
(Lehrkanzel für Unterrichtswissenschaft-Hochschuldidaktik), Austria

The Chair for Research into Higher Education was established in 1971 at the University of Klagenfurt, in Austria, to conduct research in university education, especially the methods and organization of teaching and learning in higher education, and to provide counsel to Austrian organizations concerned with university problems. Research in higher education, maintaining a local, national, or international focus, is concerned with the following areas: administration, economics of higher education, manpower in higher education, educational planning, history of higher education, curricula and instruction, methodology of research in higher education, and reform in higher education.

In addition to research activities, the unit conducts undergraduate and postgraduate courses; trains university teachers, administrators, and researchers; and provides a documentation service. Funded and controlled by both the university and the government, the unit has a staff composed of three research professionals, ten graduate students, and one secretary. The unit's documentation center, containing material and papers published by higher education research units, includes a special collection of research papers published by Eastern European centers. Its specialized library in higher education contains books in various languages.

The unit publishes reports prepared for national and international conferences on higher education, lectures, and short bibliographies. The staff is preparing a handbook for research into higher education.

Universität Klagenfurt
Universitätsstrasse 67
A-9020 Klagenfurt, Austria

CHANCE TO LEARN, A
(Higher Education Report), United States

In its report *A Chance to Learn: An Action Agenda for Equal Opportunity in Higher Education* (New York: McGraw-Hill, March 1970), the Carnegie Commission on Higher Education endorses universal access to higher education in the United States, calling for the removal of all financial barriers

to higher education by 1976 and the elimination of all barriers of age, geographical location, ethnic identity, and low-quality early education by the year 2000.

To realize universal access, the commission recommends institutional diversity along with state and federal efforts to improve preprimary, primary, secondary school, and teacher training programs. Institutions of higher education should be actively involved in such efforts, working to end segregation and initiating programs that meet the needs of disadvantaged students. Educational opportunity centers that provide counseling and tutorial services, foundation years that include compensatory education, and vigorous recruitment are suggested as other ways of reducing barriers to higher education.

The commission recommends that a national commission within the United States Office of Education be established to direct overall planning and coordinate the nation's efforts to achieve universal access to higher education.

CHANGE, SOCIAL

The interrelationship between social change and higher education is reciprocal: social change transforms the structure and function of higher education, while higher education gives rise to social change.

Contemporary society is characterized fundamentally by its rapid and large-scale change. No social institution can be totally independent of change, since all the components of society are necessarily interdependent. However, major social institutions, once established, are unlikely to change, owing to a kind of inertia. Because of the long-standing tradition of academic freedom and autonomy, higher education is much less likely to be affected precipitously by social change than are other cultural institutions. Thus, higher education tends to lag behind society, reflecting change slowly rather than creating it.

However, as a nonprofit enterprise, education—especially state or public education—is necessarily dependent on public support. Because of the need for this support, higher education can be pressured into satisfying social demands and may conform too much to society's standards. At the same time, however, demands for social change are often inconsistent or in opposition to one another, making reasonable adjustment very difficult, especially for a large institution. The tension between autonomy and conformity will remain characteristic of the relationship between higher education and society.

History of the University

By observing the history of postsecondary institutions since the Arab-Islamic university mosques of the eighth century A.D. and the early universities in medieval Europe, we can understand the fundamental trends in the relationship between society and higher education. In medieval Europe, *universitas* meant a corporation or guild of students and teachers. With the establishment of a pan-European world created by Renaissance ideas, free cities, world commerce and the influence of the papacy, there emerged a universal demand for laws applicable in all Europe and for a universally accepted theology as the defense of the ecclesiastical orders. Scholarship came to have a real utility in society, and numbers of students gathered around world famous medieval scholars of law, such as Irnerius in Bologna, and of theology, such as Pierre Abelard in Paris. Universities grew from such relationships as Irnerius and Abelard were the key figures in the development of the universities of Bologna and Paris respectively. The university was originally a self-developing corporation of students and teachers without its own building. As noncitizens or as churchmen exempted from secular law, the scholars needed to create a legal entity to defend their rights against any attempts by the cities to dissolve their organization. Through the struggle between town and gown, the university succeeded in securing autonomy.

The curriculum of early institutions of higher education was intended for students of all nations. The degree offered, *licentia ubique docendi,* conferred the universal right to teach everywhere. Thus the university, as a social institution, transcended particular nations. On the other hand, its cosmopolitan and holy rights had to be authorized by the church.

Gradually churches, to defend orthodoxy against heretics and secular power, and to gain superiority over their rivals, came to establish their own universities. The universities of Toulouse and Naples, established in the early thirteenth century, and Prague and Vienna, founded in the fourteenth century, originated in this manner. In the sixteenth and seventeenth centuries, universities became more national in character and, through their rectors, exerted influence on society rather than being influenced by it. In those years, however, campus life degenerated so much and academic standards fell so low that universities could no longer keep up with scientific development nor with social change. Scientific research was carried out by other institutions, such as the *Académie française* in France and the Royal Academy in England.

By the early nineteenth century a new model for universities began to appear in Germany and France, supported by the emerging nation-state, by Protestantism, and by the effects of the Enlightenment. Research was its core function, philosophy instead of theology united the various sciences, and its autonomy was established by the state in order to ensure academic freedom.

The scientific achievement of German universities became a strong influence in the development of some American universities, such as Johns Hopkins University in Baltimore, Maryland (founded in 1876). However, the truly contemporary model of the university is primarily an American development. Contemporary universities are characterized by their orientation toward the mass of society rather than the elite. The expansion and diversity of higher education have their greatest expression in the liberal arts colleges, professional schools, teachers colleges, community colleges, graduate schools, and universities of the United States.

The contemporary university has developed in response to social change. Technological advance demands a larger educated population; bureaucracy and professionalism place high premiums on formal educational qualifications; the expansion of general education and the rise in economic standards increase the number of candidates for higher education. Contemporary universities are asked to be centers for research and for a wide variety of instruction, from general higher education and professional education to further education for the adult.

The University in Postindustrial Society

With the rapid development of knowledge, advanced nations are proceeding toward a postindustrial society in which not only tangible resources (such as material goods and money) but also more intangible resources (such as knowledge and science) are of vital importance. In response to the needs of individuals and organizations, knowledge and research industries and information technologies have been developed. Governments and businesses invest increasing amounts in such activities as research, planning, education, and public relations. Since it is the university that transmits the scientific knowledge necessary to these developments, it follows that there is a greater demand for higher education, and higher education has expanded accordingly.

Higher education has been greatly transformed by the increase in the university population and by the changes in what the university is being asked to do. The change is not merely quantitative but also qualitative. Science has become so advanced and differentiated that each university needs more professors in ever more diversified disciplines. Since the number of qualified teachers is limited, it is necessary to have

more students at each university. Increasing enrollments are especially likely in institutions committed not only to professional but also to general education or in countries where enrollment has expanded so rapidly that there has been no time to train a sufficient number of qualified teachers. Thus, most contemporary universities have reached unprecedented size in terms of professors, students, facilities, and finance. Three major developments have resulted: the development of a bureaucracy, an increasing impact of mass culture on the university, and an increasing dependence within the university on society.

The effects of bureaucracy. Universities, since they are huge organizations, are necessarily bureaucratized. Before knowledge became so specialized, professors of the same faculty could communicate more easily, and a climate of direct democracy existed in the university. The bureaucracy of the large contemporary university is characterized by formalism, red tape, differentiation of status and role, and a hierarchy of power. Such a bureaucracy is often at odds with education, which ideally is based on personal relations, and with research, which requires freedom. Thus, the necessary evil of bureaucracy may give rise to conflicts between departments and the university administration, between faculty and administration, and between teachers and students.

Increased enrollments and mass culture. As enrollment is expanded, the variety of motives, interests, values, and abilities of students also increases. When higher education was a privilege for the elite only, the university could cope with the limited variety of its students. Mass education, given as a right for all who wish to attend, or universal higher education, where attendance is mandatory, clearly creates great problems for the university. With such a broad variety of students, institutions of higher education have to be diversified; some are research-centered, others education-centered, sports-centered, and even recreation-centered.

Larger enrollments also bring more students who are dissatisfied with or badly adjusted to the university. And, while the knowledge that the university offers and seeks is more advanced, mass education can mean that the university must lower its standards in order to cope with the more limited abilities of a proportion of its students. Larger enrollments also bring mass culture into the campus environment. Students and, to a lesser extent, professors are no longer an actual or future social elite. The more students there are, the more representative a sample of the general population they become, and the greater the impact of mass culture on the university. Since mass culture is quite different from academic culture, the university is faced with a difficult choice; it must either adapt itself to mass culture in order to satisfy the students or find ways to continue to resist mass culture in order to maintain academic standards.

The social and economic status of students is also lower than it once was. When the university student was one of a small intellectual elite, he enjoyed high social status and prestige. In mass education students frequently come from less privileged economic backgrounds and are less financially secure than their working friends. Although the best positions are generally monopolized by university graduates, an increasing number of graduates are having to accept lower level jobs or face unemployment. Their social status is lowered when compared both with university students in the past and with other young workers in their society. These circumstances have produced an increase in the number of discontented students.

Dependence of the university on society. Money is needed for education and research; and, since students are a dependent population, the contemporary university is increasingly dependent on society for support. This dependency increases the pressure on the university to adjust itself to social demands and to serve society. Thus, some feel that the university is threatened by the loss of autonomy and freedom, if it refuses to conform to social demands. However, others feel freedom is lost if the university does conform. In addition, universities are increasingly vulnerable to criticism because they no longer hold a monopoly on higher education and higher learning. Research institutes and an education industry outside the campus are frequently engaged in education and research projects that are of greater importance than those being conducted within the university.

Diversification of Knowledge and Social Change

The development and diversification of knowledge, especially in the fields of science and technology, also influence the university's response to social change. Knowledge was once a system over which scholars could exert a general control. Philosophy, the science of sciences, once was proud of its status as the ground of all disciplines. Now knowledge is specialized and differentiated almost limitlessly. Scientists in the same discipline can no longer fully understand one another or be acquainted with all the achievements of their colleagues.

This development affects the traditional idea of the university. When there is only a handful of specialists in a particular field, the academic community can only be a nominal term. The greatest argument for academic autonomy and freedom has been that the assessment of an individual's ability and achievement can only be made by specialists in the same field, but as knowledge diversifies and there are fewer scholars in each specialty, this argument loses force. Some persons have predicted that scholarship will once again depend on personal communication and that the invisible university of extrainstitutional relations among scholars will be of more importance than the institutional university.

In addition to creating diversification, the development of knowledge helps to create interdisciplinary fields. Too much specialization can result in ignorance of the general context to which specific knowledge belongs. An awareness of this problem has led to the recognition of the need for joint research and to the discovery of new areas of study. International cooperation has also become more popular. Such international and interdisciplinary cooperation require not only intellectual contributions from specialized scientists but also management skills. To cooperate with colleagues from different fields and nations, to organize and lead a project, and to obtain support from a society formerly out of touch with the university, leading contemporary scientists must often become clever businessmen.

Diversification has also brought other pressures. Almost every area of science requires a vast number of researchers and huge sums of money for the development of facilities, the use of computers, and other related needs. To secure these funds, scientists must be able to publicize the importance and utility of their research and its achievement. Research that responds to social needs rather than to the logic of science is more likely to be appreciated and supported. Therefore, applied science, research on practical problems, and physical science are supported more often than basic research, the study of the classics, or of the humanities. This imbalance is particularly serious for the university, which is the most appropriate setting for basic research. The need for financial support from society thus limits the university's freedom to arrange its own priorities and creates a new academic hierarchy based on organizational skills.

Thus, the closer relationship between science and society, the differentiation of knowledge, and the transformation of science into big business are all responsible for the erosion of academic culture. In addition, professors and students have become increasingly political in many nations. It is widely recognized that radical students act as the advance guard for political movements and have a powerful effect on society, but such politicization is not confined

to students. When ideology is of major importance internally as well as internationally, it is natural that governments would wish to employ scholars with the ability to develop systematic theory. Such involvement of scholars, however, can create problems. Physical scientists, for example, invented the technology that has produced such social evils as pollution; consequently, the social and political responsibility of natural scientists is much in dispute. Social scientists, on the other hand, are by definition concerned with social and political issues; they cannot but be politically conscious. The political posture of scholars has shifted in many nations. When professors constituted an elite, they tended to defend the status quo; with the movement toward mass or even universal higher education, professors are more likely to be in sympathy with the counterculture.

The Impact of
Higher Education on Social Change

While a changing society has a profound effect on the function and structure of the university, institutions of higher education may also condition society. The university selects, trains, and allocates the manpower required by society and transmits and creates science and technology, thus promoting social change. In newly independent nations or postrevolutionary nations, the university plays a role in formulating the national ideology and in training national leaders and technocrats. But what is remarkable about the social function of higher education is the distortion it sometimes produces. The university can become a source of social tension when society at large is opposed to the university's function and when those within the university are critical of society. When, for example, a powerful and radical student movement places the university in the forefront of social and political change, such tension may be inevitable. When rapidly expanding higher education produces more graduates than the job market can accommodate, the number of jobless intellectuals can be a source of profound social anxiety. When higher education does not expand sufficiently to accept the growing number of candidates, the struggle for entrance into the universities also creates social strain.

Bibliography

Altbach, P. G. (Ed.) *The University's Response to Societal Demands.* New York: International Council for Educational Development, 1975.

Archer, M. S. (Ed.) *Students, Universities and Society: A Comparative Study of the Sociology of Higher Education in Europe, North America, U.S.S.R. and Japan.* London: Heinemann Educational Books, 1972.

Ashby, E. *Adapting Universities to a Technological Society.* San Francisco: Jossey-Bass, 1974.

Bereday, G. Z. F. *Universities for All: International Perspectives on Mass Higher Education.* San Francisco: Jossey-Bass, 1973.

Carnegie Commission on Higher Education. *Priorities for Action: Final Report of the Carnegie Commission on Higher Education.* New York: McGraw-Hill, 1973.

Carnegie Commission on Higher Education. *Toward a Learning Society: Alternative Channels to Life, Work, and Service.* New York: McGraw-Hill, 1973.

Hodgkinson, H. H. *Institutions in Transition.* Berkeley, California: Carnegie Commission on Higher Education, 1970.

Hofmann, W. *Universität, Ideologie, Gesellschaft.* Frankfurt am Main, Federal Republic of Germany: Suhrkamp-Verlag, 1968.

Jencks, C., and Riesman, D. *The Academic Revolution.* New York: Doubleday, 1960.

Kerr, C. *The Uses of the University.* Cambridge, Massachusetts: Harvard University Press, 1964.

Ladd, E. C., Jr., and Lipset, S. M. *The Divided Academy.* New York: McGraw-Hill, 1975.

Lawlor, J. (Ed.) *Higher Education: Patterns of Change in the 1970's.* London: Routledge and Kegan Paul, 1972.

Martin, W. B. *Conformity: Standards and Change in Higher Education.* San Francisco: Jossey-Bass, 1969.

Niblett, W. R., and Butts, R. F. (Eds.) *Universities Facing the Future.* London: Evans Brothers, 1972.

Schelsky, H. *Einsamkeit und Freiheit: Idee und Gestalt der deutschen Universität und ihrer Reformen.* Hamburg, Federal Republic of Germany: Rowohlt Taschenbuch Verlag, 1963.

Shimbori, M., and Kitamura, K. *Higher Education and the Student Problem in Japan.* Tokyo: University of Tokyo Press, 1972.

Stone, L. (Ed.) *The University in Society.* Vol. 1: *Oxford and Cambridge from the 14th to the Early 19th Century;* Vol. 2: *Europe, Scotland, and the United States from the 16th to the 20th Century.* Princeton, New Jersey: Princeton University Press, 1974.

Trow, M. *Problems in the Transition from Elite to Mass Higher Education.* Berkeley, California: Carnegie Commission on Higher Education, 1973.

MICHIYA SHIMBORI

See also: Philosophies of Higher Education, Historical and Contemporary; Trends in Higher Education.

CHARTER FLIGHTS
See Exchange, International: Travel Abroad.

CHARTERS—COLLEGIATE AUTHORITY
See Governance and Control of Higher Education: Charters.

CHEMICAL ENGINEERING
(Field of Study)

The chemical engineer develops, designs, constructs, and operates plants and processes which make chemical or physical changes in order to manufacture useful products. Educational programs in chemical engineering prepare the graduate to perform many functions in transplanting chemical laboratory developments to commercial plants, including process research and development, equipment and plant design, economic analysis, manufacturing, sales, and technical service. A knowledge of chemistry, almost as complete as that of the chemistry major, is essential to the chemical engineer. Also of importance is proficiency in mathematics, the engineering sciences, and computer methods. Some academic programs emphasize a particular field of application, such as petroleum, fertilizers, polymers, or wood pulp and paper.

The major branches of chemical engineering derive from the need to understand the nature and rate of chemical reaction, the physical and separation processes interacting with the reaction, and the control of the overall system. Branches associated with the reaction are reaction kinetics, reactor design, and thermodynamics. The important physical processing and separation branches are heat transfer, diffusional operations (gas absorption, adsorption, and ion exchange), multistage operations (contacting and separations, such as liquid-gas, liquid-solid, and liquid-liquid systems), size reduction and classification, and fluids and solids handling. The field of instrumentation and control systems constitutes the branch known as process control. Cutting across all of these branches are other subject areas such as materials of construction, cost analysis, and mechanical and plant design.

Wherever chemical change takes place, there is a role for the chemical engineer. The chemical and allied industries constitute the largest single group of employers of chemical engineers, although many chemical engineers are also employed by equipment manufacturers, consulting and engineering firms, educational institutions, and the government. Industries served include chemicals, petroleum, food, drugs, textiles, agriculture, nuclear energy, and plastics. Chemical engineering also provides preparation for advanced study in a number of special areas, including biochemical engineering, patent or corporate law, biomedical engineering, materials science, environmental engineering, and nuclear engineering. Related fields include safety, which requires an understanding of equipment and hazardous materials; purchasing, which requires technically trained persons to understand specifications; and technical writing, which requires an ability to present complex technical ideas in a clear, understandable, and interesting manner.

Chemical engineering is distinctly of United States origin, even though its early scientific background stemmed from Germany. The need for the profession was first expressed in the United Kingdom as early as 1880. The first book bearing the words *chemical engineering* (*A Handbook of Chemical Engineering,* by George E. Davis of the Manchester Technical School in England) appeared in 1901. Professor Davis saw the need to train students in principles common to many chemical processes, an idea that led to the concept of unit operations, wherein each step in a complex chemical process is studied and the steps are then integrated into the whole process. The unit operations include such topics as heat transfer, fluid flow, evaporation, distillation, liquid-liquid and liquid-solid extraction, crystallization, filtration, particle size separation, drying, grinding, and mixing.

The first recognized course of instruction in chemical engineering was offered at the Massachusetts Institute of Technology in 1888. In the intervening years the United States has continued to provide leadership in chemical engineering education. The elapsed time span can be divided roughly into four periods: the industrial chemistry period (1888–1923), the development of a distinctive engineering science (1923–1943), the era of engineering design (1943–1958), and the application of transport phenomena and systems analysis, which began in 1958. In this fourth period specialized instruction has been grouped under heat, mass, or momentum transfer and further subdivided according to individual unit operations. Mathematics for the undergraduate has advanced to include differential equations, matrices, Laplace transforms, and numerical analysis. Formal instruction in analog and digital computer applications has become common. Capstone courses to integrate prior instruction in the basic and engineering sciences emphasize process design, systems analysis and control, economics, and simulation. A trend toward greater flexibility is evident in the frequent appearance of elective options. There is also a move to include an enlarged experiential component through laboratory instruction, special projects, and cooperative programs with industry.

Recognition and growth of chemical engineering as a field of study and a profession followed formation of the American Institute of Chemical Engineers in 1908. The interdisciplinary character of chemical engineering is evident from the major divisions now active within the institute: food, pharmaceutics, and bioengineering; forest products; heat transfer and energy conversion; materials engineering and sciences; nuclear engineering; petroleum and petrochemical engineering; and environmental engineering. Comparable professional societies are active in many countries and have joined together under two federations, the European Federation of Chemical Engineering and the Inter-American Confederation of Chemical Engineering.

Established degree programs in chemical engineering exist in many countries and in nearly every case are patterned largely after those in the United States. The curricula follow the same progression of courses in the basic sciences, engineering sciences, and engineering specialty courses, and textbooks by American authors are used widely. In common is a broad, basic foundation in mathematics and the sciences. The upper-level courses vary from a strong engineering practice orientation (common in the United Kingdom) to an almost totally industrial chemistry emphasis (frequently encountered in Europe and Latin America). Programs in the Soviet Union and Eastern European countries began about 1950 and have gradually changed from chemical technology to well-balanced engineering curricula, often leading to the Master of Science as the first degree. Postgraduate study has kept pace and places much greater emphasis on research than on course work, as is true in most countries other than the United States. In countries where the baccalaureate is the first degree, the period of instruction varies from three to five years, depending upon the preparation of the entering student. Methods of instruction and evaluation also differ from the system of integrated lecture, recitation, problem solving, laboratory work, and examination in the United States and Canada. In many countries the lecture is the primary medium of instruction, and annual comprehensive examinations are used to measure achievement. The enrollment of women in chemical engineering is small, except in some Middle Eastern and Asian countries; in general, however, the enrollment of women is increasing. Undergraduate enrollment and degrees granted in chemical engineering are consistently in the range of 7 to 10 percent of the total for all fields of engineering.

GEORGE BURNET

Levels and Programs of Study

Programs in chemical engineering generally require as a minimum prerequisite a secondary education and lead to the following awards: certificate or diploma, Bachelor of Science or Engineering, Master of Science or Engineering, the doctorate, or their equivalents. Programs deal with the principles and practices of chemical engineering and consist of classroom and laboratory instruction and, on advanced levels, study, seminar or group discussion, and research in specialized areas of chemical engineering. Chemical engineering is largely concerned with the application of chemistry to industrial processes; the design, construction, and operation of plants that use or produce chemicals; and the development and production of a large variety of materials, such as synthetic fibers, drugs, and fertilizers.

Programs that lead to an award not equivalent to a first university degree deal with the principles and practices of chemical engineering technology. These programs generally emphasize the application of mathematics, physics, and chemistry to problems in the chemical process industries; the programs last two or three years, full time. Principal course content usually includes some of the following: mathematics, physics, basic electronics, analytical chemistry, organic chemistry, inorganic chemistry, industrial chemistry, engineering economics, chemical instrumentation, physical chemistry, X ray and radio chemistry, organic analysis, unit operations, and engineering materials.

Programs that lead to a first university degree deal with the principles and practices of chemical engineering. Principal course content usually includes basic courses in chemistry, such as inorganic chemistry, organic chemistry, and physical chemistry; specific courses in chemical engineering, such as transport phenomena, chemical thermodynamics, chemical process analysis, chemical process control, chemical unit design, chemical unit operation, and chemical plant design. These programs usually include some related courses in such engineering fields as civil, electrical, mechanical, and metallurgical engineering, as well as background courses in such fields as mathematics, computer science, physics, and biology.

Programs that lead to a postgraduate university degree deal with advanced studies in specialized areas of chemical engineering. Emphasis is placed on original research work as substantiated by the presentation and defense of a scholarly thesis or dissertation. Principal subject matter areas within which courses and research projects tend to fall include chemical engineering systems design, applied thermodynamics and chemical kinetics, fluidization phenomena, chemical reactor design, catalysis, polymer science, absorption and ion exchange, chemical unit operation, biochemical engineering, water pollution control, air pollution control, pulp and paper technology, corrosion and corrosion control, electrochemical engineering, and advanced process design. Subject areas within which background studies tend to fall include appropriate specialties from other engineering programs and appropriate specialties from related fields such as the natural sciences, the social sciences, mathematics, statistics, and computer science.

[This section was based on UNESCO's *International Standard Classification of Education (ISCED): Three Stage Classification System, 1974* (Paris: UNESCO, 1974).]

Major International and National Organizations

INTERNATIONAL

European Federation of Chemical Engineering
Fédération européenne du génie chimique
% DECHEMA, Theodor Heuss-Allee 25
6 Frankfurt/Main, Federal Republic of Germany

Inter-American Confederation of Chemical Engineering
345 East 47 Street
New York, New York 10017 USA

NATIONAL

Australia:
Institution of Engineers, Australia
Science House
157 Gloucester Street
Sydney, New South Wales 2000

Brazil:
Associação de engenharia química
Conjunto das químicas
Cidade universitária
Universidade de São Paulo
São Paulo

Canada:
Canadian Society for Chemical Engineers
151 Slater Street, Suite 906
Ottawa, Ontario, KIP 5H3

Chemical Institute of Canada
151 Slater Street, Suite 906
Ottawa, Ontario KIP 5H3

France:
Société de chimie industrielle
80 route de Saint-Cloud
92 Rueil-Malmaison

India:
Indian Institute of Chemical Engineers
Faja Subodh Mullick Road
P.B. 17001
Calcutta 32

Israel:
Israel Institute of Chemical Engineers
Technion City
Haifa

Italy:
Associazione italiana di ingegneria chimica
Piazzale Morandi, 2-20121
Milan

Japan:
> Society of Chemical Engineers
> Kyoritsu Building
> 6-19, 4-chome, Kohinata
> Bunkyo-ku, Tokyo

People's Republic of China:
> Chinese Society of Chemical Engineering
> Peking

South Africa:
> South African Institution of Chemical
> Engineers
> Kelvin House, P.O. Box 61019
> Marshalltown 2107
> Johannesburg

United Kingdom:
> Institution of Chemical Engineers
> 16 Belgrave Square
> London SW1 8PT, England

United States:
> American Institute of Chemical
> Engineers
> 345 East 47 Street
> New York, New York 10017

For a complete listing of European organizations see:

Anderson, I. G. (Ed.) *Directory of European Associations.* Detroit: Gale Research, 1971. Pp. 50–51.

Principal Information Sources

GENERAL

Guides to the literature include:

Bottle, R. T. *The Use of Chemical Literature.* (2nd ed.) Hamden, Connecticut: Shoe String Press, 1969. Includes some English-language sources on chemical engineering.
Bourton, K. *Chemical and Process Engineering Unit Operations: A Bibliographic Guide.* New York: Plenum, 1968. A guide to chemical engineering literature, including bibliographies, periodicals, abstracting and indexing services, and many reference works pertaining to specific aspects of chemical engineering.
Burman, C. R. *How to Find Out About Chemistry.* Oxford, England: Pergamon Press, 1966.
Chemical Engineering Library Book List. (5th ed.) New York: American Institute of Chemical Engineers, Chemical Engineering Educational Projects Committee, 1966. Covers general chemical engineering sources as well as sources on specialized aspects in the field.
Fundaburk, E. L. *Reference Materials and Periodicals in Economics: An International List in Six Volumes.* Vol. 4: *Four Major Manufacturing Industries–Automotive, Chemical, Iron and Steel,*

Petroleum and Gas. Metuchen, New Jersey: Scarecrow Press, 1972. Part 2, "Chemical Industry," includes references on chemical engineering.
Kobe, K. A. *Chemical Engineering Reports: How to Search the Literature and Prepare a Report.* (4th ed.) New York: Wiley-Interscience, 1957.
Woods, D. R. *Resources and Mechanics of Searching the Literature with Examples for the Chemical Engineer.* Hamilton, Ontario: McMaster University, 1970. Covers British and Canadian sources.
Yagello, V. E. *Guide to Literature on Chemical Engineering.* Washington, D. C.: American Society for Engineering Education, 1970. Includes guides to literature, bibliographies, dictionaries, abstracting services, and handbooks.
Yescombe, E. R. *Sources of Information on the Rubber, Plastics and Allied Industries.* Elmsford, New York: Pergamon Press, 1968.

General introductory works are:

Andersen, L. B., and Wenzel, L. A. *Introduction to Chemical Engineering.* New York: McGraw-Hill, 1961. An introduction to the profession of chemical engineering and the chemical industry.
Coulson, J. M., and Richardson, J. F. *Chemical Engineering.* (2nd ed., 3 vols.) Oxford, England: Pergamon Press, 1964–1971.
Nonhebel, G. *Chemical Engineering in Practice.* London: Wykeham, 1973. A general introduction to chemical engineering and technology geared to students embarking on careers in the field.
Piret, E. L. *Chemical Engineering Around the World.* New York: American Institute of Chemical Engineers, 1958. Includes international sources which discuss the historical development of chemical engineering in various countries.
Russell, T. F. *Introduction to Chemical Engineering Analyses.* New York: Wiley, 1972.

Sources dealing with chemical engineering education include:

Chemical Engineering Education. Gainesville, Florida: Chemical Engineering Division, American Society for Engineering Education, 1965–. A quarterly journal which provides articles on chemical engineering education throughout the world.
Chemical Engineering: A Guide to First Degree Courses in United Kingdom Universities and Colleges. Cambridge, England: Careers Research and Advisory Center, 1967. Offers a discussion of comparative programs in chemical engineering in the United Kingdom.

Mayer, M. W. *Industries Views of Current Chemical Engineering Education.* Madison, New Jersey: Esso Research and Engineering, 1963. A discussion of engineering education in the United States and its relationship to industry.

CURRENT BIBLIOGRAPHIES

Analytical Abstracts. Cambridge, England: Society for Analytical Chemistry, 1954–. Published monthly.

Chemical Abstracts. Easton, Pennsylvania: American Chemical Society, 1970–. Published weekly.

Chemischer Informationsdienst. Weinheim/Bergstrasse, Federal Republic of Germany: Verlag Chemie, 1973–. Supersedes *Chemisches Zentralblatt.*

"International Abstracts." In *Processing.* London: IPC Business Press, 1974–.

Referativnyĭ zhurnal. Khimicheskoe, neftepererabatyvayushchee i polimernoe mashinostroenie. Moscow: Akademiia nauk, SSSR, Institut nauchnoĭ informatsii, 1972–.

Referativnyĭ zhurnal. Khimii. Moscow: Akademiia nauk. SSR, Institut nauchnoĭ informatsii, 1953–.

Theoretical Chemical Engineering Abstracts. Liverpool, England: P.O. Box 146, 1964–.

Reports on current developments in chemical engineering are included in: *Advances in Chemical Engineering.* New York: Academic Press, 1956–.

PERIODICALS

The following chemical engineering journals are of international importance: *AIChE (American Institute of Chemical Engineers) Journal, Angewandte Chemie* (FRG), *British Chemical Engineering, Canadian Journal of Chemical Engineering, Chemical and Engineering News* (US), *Chemical and Petroleum Engineering* (US; translation of USSR publication *Khimicheskoe i neftyanoe mashinostroenie*), *The Chemical Engineer* (UK), *Chemical Engineering* (US), *Chemical Engineering Education* (US), *Chemical Engineering Journal: An International Journal of Research and Development* (Switzerland), *Chemical Engineering Progress* (US), *Chemical Engineering Science/Journal international de génie chimique* (UK), *Chemical Engineering World* (India), *Chemical Week* (US), *Chemie-Ingenieur-Technik* (FRG), *Chemische Technik* (GDR), *Chem Tech* (US), *Ingénieur chimiste* (Belgium), *Institution of Chemical Engineers: Transactions* (UK), *International Chemical Engineering* (US), *Journal of Applied Chemistry of the USSR, Journal of Chemical Engineering of Japan, Periodica polytechnica: Chemical Engineering* (Hungary).

For a complete listing of journals in chemical engineering see:

Ulrich's International Periodicals Directory. New York: Bowker, biennial.

Yagello, V. E. *Guide to Literature on Chemical Engineering.* Washington, D.C.: American Society for Engineering Education, 1970, pp. 20–22.

ENCYCLOPEDIAS, DICTIONARIES, HANDBOOKS

Clason, W. E. (Comp.) *Elsevier's Dictionary of Chemical Engineering in Six Languages: English/ American, French, Spanish, Italian, Dutch, German.* (2 vols.) Amsterdam: Elsevier, 1969.

Cremer, H. W. (Ed.) *Chemical Engineering Practice.* (12 vols.) London: Butterworth, 1956–1966.

Encyclopedia of Polymer Science and Technology: Plastics, Resins, Rubbers, Fibers. (16 vols.) New York: Wiley-Interscience, 1964–1972.

Fouchier, J., Billet, M., and Epstein, H. *Chemical Dictionary/Dictionnaire de chimie/Fachwörterbuch für Chemie.* (3rd ed.) Amsterdam: North University Press, 1970. Emphasis is on engineering.

International Encyclopedia of Chemical Science. New York: Van Nostrand, 1964.

Kirk-Othmer Encyclopedia of Chemical Technology. (2nd ed., 22 vols.) New York: Wiley-Interscience, 1963–1972. See also the Supplement.

Perry, R. H. *Chemical Engineers' Handbook.* (5th ed.) New York: McGraw-Hill, 1973.

Sobecka, Z., and Choinski, W. (Eds.) *Dictionary of Chemistry and Chemical Technology in Six Languages: English, German, Spanish, French, Polish and Russian.* Oxford, England: Pergamon Press, 1966.

Ullmanns Enzyklopädie der technischen Chemie. (4th ed.) Weinheim/Bergstrasse: Federal Republic of Germany: Verlag Chemie, 1972–. Eight volumes to date; to be completed in twenty-four volumes.

DIRECTORIES

American Chemical Society, Committee on Professional Training. *Directory of Graduate Research.* Washington, D.C.: American Chemical Society, 1953–. Published biennially. Includes faculties, publications, and doctoral dissertations in chemical engineering at United States universities.

Chemical Engineering Faculties 1974-1975. New York: American Institute of Chemical Engineers, 1975. Lists institutions in Australia, Belgium, Denmark, the Federal Republic of Germany, the United Kingdom, Ireland,

Israel, Japan, the United States, Canada, New Zealand, the Republic of China, and Switzerland.

Engineering College Research and Graduate Study. Washington, D.C.: American Society for Engineering Education, annual. Includes faculty, enrollments, degrees, fields of advanced study, and admission information for all fields of engineering at United States universities.

Peterson's Annual Guides to Graduate Study, 1976. Book 5: *Engineering and Applied Sciences.* Princeton, New Jersey: Peterson's Guides, 1975. See section on "Chemical Engineering Programs" for a listing of programs and universities in the United States.

For a listing of research centers and institutes in the field see:

Minerva, Forschungsinstitute. Berlin, Federal Republic of Germany: de Gruyter, 1972.

CHEMISTRY (Field of Study)

Chemical endeavors can be traced back almost to the beginning of recorded history. As practiced in ancient times by the Egyptians, Assyrians, Chinese, Hindus, Greeks, and Romans, chemical activities were represented by metallurgy, pottery, glass making, pharmacy, brewing, dyeing, and similar arts and crafts. The origin of the word *chemistry* is uncertain; it has been variously traced to *qemi,* the Egyptians' name for their country (Black Land), and to *chyma,* Greek for molten metal. In modern terms, chemistry can be broadly defined as the science dealing with the properties of substances, the relationship of these properties to composition and structure, and the transformations of substances into new substances. Originally an outgrowth of man's curiosity about the nature of materials and his desire to use them for his benefit and comfort, chemical activities have become the cornerstone of modern technology; and chemical concepts and approaches are widely used to achieve such goals as the development of drugs, structural materials, and fuels.

The four classical branches of chemistry, in order of their historical development, are (1) inorganic chemistry, concerned with the structure, properties, and reactions of the elements and of non-carbon-containing compounds; (2) organic chemistry, concerned with the structure, properties, and reactivity of carbon-containing compounds; (3) analytical chemistry, concerned with the development and utilization of techniques for the qualitative and quantitative determination of elements and compounds; and (4) physical chemistry, concerned with the nature of physical and chemical properties in terms of quantitative theoretical models. Since the 1950s the boundaries separating these branches of chemistry have become blurred, and new areas of activity use concepts and techniques from several or all of the classical branches. Examples of such areas are geochemistry (chemistry of the earth's crust), photochemistry (interaction of radiation with matter), medicinal chemistry (drug design), polymer chemistry (chemistry of very large molecules), nuclear chemistry (chemistry of radioactive elements), and clinical chemistry (analytical aspects of medical laboratory practice).

Chemistry bears a close relationship to other fields of science, particularly to biology, physics, and mathematics, and to the materials aspects of engineering. Biology—which deals with complex, naturally occurring structures—provides the impetus for much chemical activity. Efforts to understand biological functions and behavior in molecular terms have led to the development of the field of biochemistry, which links both biology and chemistry to medicine. Physics provides the framework for understanding the basic structure of matter. Chemical physics, a recent hybrid of the two fields, is concerned with the quantum and statistical concepts of chemical structure. Mathematics is, of course, the descriptive language used to formulate the quantitative and symbolic aspects of chemistry. Chemistry also plays an important role in materials science, which deals with properties of materials from the applications point of view, and in chemical engineering.

Chemistry began to emerge as a separate academic discipline around the beginning of the nineteenth century. Until that time, chemical concepts were taught in the European universities as part of natural philosophy or medicine. In fact, many of the early teachers held chairs in medicine and/or botany. During the eighteenth century, studies of combustion were made, and quantitative approaches were developed. In 1808, largely as a result of these earlier developments, John Dalton formulated the atomic theory of matter, which is considered the cornerstone of modern chemistry. In 1828 Friedrich Wöhler established the link between inorganic and organic chemistry, making possible impressive advances in organic chemistry in Germany. It was during this period that formal education in chemistry first began in Europe. The first doctoral degrees in the field were probably awarded in Germany. Until the early part of the twentieth century, many American professors of chemistry received their degrees and/or postgraduate education in Europe.

Chemistry is an intensely international field, and vigorous publication activity throughout the world fosters the free exchange of information and ideas. In recent years there has been an impressive worldwide growth in biochemical activities. The development of new experimental techniques—for example, magnetic spectroscopy, electron spectroscopy, Mössbauer spectroscopy, and laser excitation—has stimulated detailed investigations of biologically significant molecules and systems. There is also much interest in the chemical aspects of energy problems. Advances in research have inevitably led to greater sophistication in the teaching of chemistry, even at the most elementary level.

The importance of chemistry with respect to energy sources, food supplies, and environmental factors has generated broad interest in chemical phenomena. Some colleges and universities have introduced special chemical courses which focus on these topics. Many universities have

Ph.D. programs covering two or more very closely allied disciplines, such as chemistry and physics or chemistry and biology; and some offer loosely structured interdisciplinary doctoral programs that link diverse fields. Several United States universities offer new formal programs at the master's degree level in such broadly interdisciplinary areas as clinical chemistry, forensic chemistry, and environmental chemistry.

Because of its wide application in the activities of man, chemistry is recognized and taught in almost all countries. The pattern of instruction, used worldwide, reflects the structure of the discipline, although details of instruction may reflect national interests and views. The first degree (baccalaureate) in all countries usually provides core training in the basic branches of chemistry. Graduate training at the Ph.D. level may or may not require additional formal course work; on the other hand, Ph.D. training in all countries always requires a heavy commitment to research and a mastery of the field as demonstrated by appropriate examinations. Whether such mastery is obtained by formal course work or by self-study depends upon the individual university tradition.

As the science of chemistry has matured, theoretical models have been used more and more effectively for teaching and understanding chemistry. This worldwide trend has been criticized by some because it deemphasizes the important experimental foundations of chemistry. Again, differences among universities in the same country are frequently greater in this regard than are differences among countries.

In those developing countries where a strong chemical tradition does not exist, training patterns are usually taken from the United Kingdom, the Federal Republic of Germany, or the United States. In Eastern Europe the training is usually somewhat more classical, but the final professional standards are in the same general range as those of Western Europe.

KARL WEISS

Levels and Programs of Study

Programs in chemistry generally require as a minimum prerequisite a secondary education and lead to the following awards: certificate or diploma in chemical technology, Bachelor of Science degree, Master of Science degree, the doctorate, or their equivalents. Programs deal with the principles and practices of chemistry and consist of classroom and laboratory instruction and, on advanced levels, seminar sessions dealing with advanced topics in the field of chemistry.

Programs that lead to awards not equivalent to a first degree deal primarily with the practical application of chemistry. Principal course content usually includes some of the following: inorganic quantitative chemistry, inorganic quantitative analysis, the chemical bond, sample preparation, oil chemistry, inorganic quantitative chemistry, inorganic quantitative analysis, petroleum testing, organic chemistry (aliphatic compounds), organic chemistry (aromatic compounds), industrial organic chemistry, industrial inorganic chemistry, gas and water analysis, physical chemistry, and electrochemistry. Background courses often included are mathematics, mechanics, electronics photometry, general physics, computer programing, instrumental analysis, mineralogy, light, materials testing, biochemistry and glass blowing.

Programs that lead to a first university degree deal with fundamental principles of chemistry. At this level, the theoretical and general principles of the subjects studied are emphasized, although practical application is not ignored. Principal course content usually includes some of the following: principles and methods of chemistry, theories of chemistry, physical chemistry, analytical chemistry, chemistry of the elements, elementary and advanced inorganic chemistry, elementary and advanced organic chemistry, quantum chemistry, and industrial chemistry. Background courses often included are general biology, general physics, biochemistry, instrumental analysis, mathematics, humanities, social sciences, and languages.

Programs that lead to a postgraduate university degree deal with advanced topics in the field of chemistry. Emphasis is placed on original research work as substantiated by the presentation of a scholarly thesis or dissertation. Principal subject matter areas within which courses and research projects tend to fall include the following advanced courses related to chemistry: advanced analytical chemistry, crystal chemistry, X-ray crystallography, symmetry, metal chelates, electroanalytical chemistry, statistical thermodynamics, homogenous chemical kinetics, absorption and catalysis, chemical isotopes, chemistry of natural products, stereochemistry of carbon compounds, organic synthetic chemistry, chemical spectroscopy, molecular vibrations, molecular spectroscopy-diatomics, and quantum chemistry. Subject areas within which background studies tend to fall include appropriate specialties in physics, biology, geology, mathematics, statistical analysis, social sciences, and business management.

[This section was based on UNESCO's *International Standard Classification of Education (ISCED): Three Stage Classification System, 1974* (Paris: UNESCO, 1974).]

Major International and National Organizations

INTERNATIONAL

Federation of European Chemical
   Societies (FECS)
% Royal Institute of Chemistry
30 Russell Square
London WC1B 5DT, England
   The Committee on Chemical Education studies educational programs in European universities in order to provide comparative information for use in student placement internationally.

International Council of Scientific
   Unions (ICSU)
Conseil international des unions
   scientifiques (CIUS)
51 boulevard de Montmorency
75016 Paris, France

The Committee on the Teaching of Science encourages cooperation on all aspects of science teaching in the world.

International Institute of Physics and
  Chemistry
Université libre de Bruxelles
50 avenue Franklin Roosevelt
1050 Brussels, Belgium

International Union of Pure and Applied
  Chemistry (IUPAC)
Union internationale de chimie pure et
  appliquée (UICPA)
Bank Court Chambers
2-3 Pound Way, Cowley Centre
Oxford OX4 3YF, England
  Promotes international cooperation among chemists; the Committee on the Teaching of Chemistry is involved in chemical education; works on nomenclature rules and textbook selection and use; and serves as an information center for chemical education.

Organization of American States (OAS)
Organisation des états américains (OEA)
Galo Plaza, Pan American Union Building
Washington, D. C. 20006 USA
  Sponsors many chemical education programs in the Americas, including Latin American seminars of chemistry every two years. Representative are the fellowships in chemistry at the University of Buenos Aires and the multinational graduate program in chemistry at university centers in Argentina, Brazil, Chile, and Mexico.

United Nations Development Programme
  (UNDP)
United Nations
New York, New York 10017 USA
  Supports international cooperation in chemistry education through such projects as the Science Centre for the Advancement of Postgraduate Studies, established at the University of Alexandria, in Egypt, to train students to focus on local technical problems.

United Nations Educational, Scientific and
  Cultural Organization (UNESCO)
Division of Science Teaching
7 place de Fontenoy
75700 Paris, France
  Sponsors cooperative projects in nonindustrialized nations to develop science education at all levels. Conducts important publishing activities, sponsors meetings to disseminate and exchange information on chemical education, promotes research in chemical education, and provides advisory and consultative services to member states. The Bangkok pilot project for chemistry teaching in Asia (1965–1971) is one example of the type of work sponsored by UNESCO. In addition, UNESCO publishes *New Trends in Chemical Education* and *New Trends in the Use of Educational Technology in the Teaching of Chemistry.*

NATIONAL

Australia:
  Royal Australian Chemical Institute
  55 Collins Place
  Melbourne C1, Victoria

Austria:
  Verein österreichischer Chemiker
  Eschenbachgasse 9
  1010 Vienna

Belgium:
  Société chimique de Belgique
  Square Marie-Louise 49
  1040 Brussels

Canada:
  Chemical Institute of Canada
  Suite 906, 151 Slater Street
  Ottawa, Ontario K1P 5H3

Colombia:
  Sociedad colombiana de químicos e
    ingenieros químicos
  Carrera 6a
  14-42 Bogatá

Czechoslovakia:
  Ceskoslovenská spolecnost
    chemika
  Hradcanske námésti 12
  Prague 1

Denmark:
  Kemisk forening
  % H. C. Ørsted institutet
  Universitetsparken 5
  2100 Copenhagen

Federal Republic of Germany:
  Gesellschaft deutscher Chemiker
  Varrentrappstrasse 40-42
  6 Frankfurt/Main 90

Finland:
  Suomalaisten kemistien seura
  P Hesperiankatu 3B
  00260 Helsinki 26

France:
  Société chimique de France
  250 rue Saint Jacques
  Paris 5

Greece:
  Enosis ellinon chimikon
  Odos Kaningos 27
  Athens 147

Hungary:
  Magyar kémikusok egyesülete
  Anker Koz 1
  Budapest VI

India:
  Institution of Chemists
  Chemical Department, Medical College
  Calcutta 12

Israel:
  Israel Chemical Society
  P.O.B. 517
  Jerusalem

Italy:
  Società chimica italiana
  viale Luigi 48
  00198 Rome

Netherlands:
  Koninklijke Nederlandse chemische
    vereniging
  Burnierstraat 1
  The Hague

Norway:
  Norsk kjemisk selskap
  Rosenkrantz gate 7
  Oslo 1

People's Republic of China:
  Chung-kuo thia-hsiien-hui
  Tung-ssue Erh-t'iao Pei-k'ou No. 1
  Peking

Philippines:
  Philippine Council of Chemists
  P.O.B. 1202
  Manila

Poland:
  Polskie towarzystwo chemiczne
  ul. Freta 16
  00-227 Warsaw

Portugal:
  Sociedade portuguêsa de química e física
  Laboratório de química, faculdade de
    ciências
  Rua da Escola Politécnica
  Lisbon 2

Soviet Union:
  D.I. Mendeleyev All-Union Chemical
    Society
  Krivokolenny per 12
  Moscow

Spain:
  Asociación national de químicos de
    España
  Lagasca 83-1°
  Madrid 6

Sweden:
  Svenska kemistsamfundet
  Wenner-Gren Center
  Sveavägen 166
  113 46 Stockholm

Switzerland:
  Schweizerische chemische Gesellschaft
  Laboratorium für organische Chemie,
    ETH
  Universitätsstrasse 6
  8006 Zurich

Turkey:
  Türkiye kimya cemiyeti
  Halâskârgazi Caddesi 53
  Uzay Apt. D8, P.O.B. 829
  Harbiye, Istanbul

United Kingdom:
  Royal Institute of Chemistry
  30 Russell Square
  London WC1, England

  Chemical Society
  Burlington House, Piccadilly
  London WIV OBN, England

United States:
  American Chemical Society
  1155 Sixteenth Street NW
  Washington, D. C. 20036

  American Institute of Chemists
  60 East 42nd Street
  New York, New York 10017

Yugoslavia:
  Unija humijskin Pruštava Jugoslavije
  Karnedžweja 4
  1101 Belgrade

For more information on chemical societies see:

International Chemistry Directory. Reading, Massachusetts: W. A. Benjamin, 1969.

Chemical associations in many countries of the world are also listed in:

Guide to World Science. (2nd ed., 25 vols.) Guernsey, Channel Islands: Francis Hodgson, 1974–.

World Guide to Scientific Associations. New York: Bowker; Pullach/Munich, Federal Republic of Germany: Verlag Dokumentation, 1974.

Principal Information Sources

GENERAL

Guides to the literature of chemistry include:

Akademiia nauk, SSR, Bibliotika. *Bibliografiya Sovetskoĭ bibliografii po khimie i khimi-*

chiskoĭ tekhnologii, 1917–1965. Leningrad: Nauka, 1968. A bibliograpny of Soviet bibliographies on chemistry and chemistry technology.

Bottle, R. T. (Ed.) *The Use of Chemical Literature.* (2nd ed.) Hamden, Connecticut: Shoe String Press, 1969.

Burman, C. R. *How to Find Out About Chemistry.* (2nd ed.) Oxford, England: Pergamon Press, 1966. Includes a section on training and careers in chemistry.

Crane, E. J., Patterson, A. M., and Marr, E. G. *A Guide to the Literature of Chemistry.* (2nd ed.) New York: Wiley, 1957.

Mellon, M. G. *Chemical Publications: Their Nature and Use.* (4th ed.) New York: McGraw-Hill, 1965.

Nowack, A. *Fachliteratur des Chemikers: Einführung in ihre Systematik und Benutzung, mit einer Übersicht über wichtige Werke.* Berlin, Federal Republic of Germany: VEB Deutscher Verlag der Wissenschaften, 1962.

Of the large number of general works and texts dealing with chemistry, the following samples may be considered typical:

Busch, D. H., Shull, H., and Conley, R. T. *Chemistry.* Boston: Allyn & Bacon, 1973.

Geiser, G., and Delphin, G. *Chimie générale.* Paris: Dunod Editeur, 1973.

Kumli, K. F. *Introductory Chemistry: A Survey of General, Organic and Biological Chemistry.* Englewood Cliffs, New Jersey: Prentice-Hall, 1975.

Seese, W. *In Preparation for College Chemistry.* Englewood Cliffs, New Jersey: Prentice-Hall, 1974.

Some histories of chemistry are:

Asimov, I. *A Short History of Chemistry.* Garden City, New York: Doubleday, 1965.

Bäumler, E. *A Century of Chemistry.* Düsseldorf, Federal Republic of Germany: Econ Verlag GmbH, 1968.

Farber, E. *Evolution of Chemistry: A History of Its Ideals, Methods, and Materials.* (2nd ed.) New York: Ronald Press, 1969.

Garard, I. D. *Invitation to Chemistry.* Garden City, New York: Doubleday, 1969.

Inde, A. J. *The Development of Modern Chemistry.* New York: Harper & Row, 1964.

Partington, J. R. *A History of Chemistry.* (4 vols.) New York: St. Martin's Press, 1961–.

Weeks, M. E. *Discovery of the Elements.* (7th ed.) Easton, Pennsylvania: Chemical Education Publishing Co., 1968.

Comparative and international education developments are covered in the following:

Chisman, D. G. (Ed.) *University Chemical Education. Proceedings of the International Symposium on University Chemical Education, Frascati.* London: Butterworth, 1970.

Comber, L. C., and Keeves, J. P. *Science Education in Nineteen Countries.* Stockholm: Almqvist and Wiksell, 1973.

Lockard, J.D. *Ninth Report of the International Clearinghouse on Science and Mathematics Curricular Developments, University of Maryland, College Park.* College Park, Maryland: Science Teaching Center, 1974.

New Trends in Chemistry Teaching. Paris: UNESCO Press, 1975. Based on working papers prepared for discussion at the International Congress on the Improvement of Chemical Education held in Wroclaw, Poland, September 17–22, 1973. See especially G. Illuminati, "Promoting Improvements in Chemical Education at the National Level" (pp. 129–137), and R. W. Parry, "International Cooperation in the Improvement of Chemical Education" (pp. 138–147).

Primera conferencia interamericana sobre la enseñanza de la química, Buenos Aires, Argentina, 14–19 junio de 1965. Washington, D. C.: Departamento de asuntos cientificos, Unión panamericana, 1967.

"Report of the Snowmass Conference on Chemical Education." *Journal of Chemical Education,* 1971, *48,* 2.

Survey of Chemistry Teaching at University Level. IUPAC Committee on Teaching of Chemistry, and UNESCO. Oxford, England: International Union of Pure and Applied Chemistry, 1972. Summarizes problems and practices in university-level chemical education in twenty-two countries.

CURRENT BIBLIOGRAPHIES

Bulletin signalétique. Part 170: Chimie. Paris: Centre national de la recherche scientifique, 1940–. Published monthly.

Chembooks: New Books and Journals. Basel, Switzerland: Karger Libri, 1969–. Published annually.

Chemical Abstracts: Key to the World's Chemical Literature. Easton, Pennsylvania: American Chemical Society, 1907–. Published semimonthly. The most widely used abstracting service in English.

Chemischer Informationsdienst. Weinheim/Bergstrasse, Federal Republic of Germany: Verlag Chemie, 1973–. Supersedes *Chemisches Zentralblatt.*

Current Abstracts of Chemistry and Index Chemicus. Philadelphia: Institute for Scientific Information, 1970–. Published weekly.

Current Contents: Physical and Chemical Sciences. Philadelphia: Institute for Scientific Information, 1967–. Published weekly.

Referativnyĭ zhurnal. Khimii. Moscow: Akademiia nauk, SSSR, Institut nauchnoĭ informatsii, 1953–.

PERIODICALS

A selection of some of the more important chemical periodical literature includes *Académie des sciences. Comptes rendus hebdomadaires des séances. Part 2: Chemical Sciences* (France), *Acta Chemica Scandinavica* (Denmark), *Acta Chimica* (Hungary), *Akademiia nauk SSSR. Doklady* (Soviet Union), *Australian Journal of Chemistry, Bulletin of the Chemical Society of Japan, Canadian Journal of Chemistry, Chemicke listy* (FRG and Czechoslovakia), *Chemische Berichte* (FRG), *Dansk-Kemi* (Denmark), *Gazzetta chimica italiana, Helvetica Chimica Acta* (Switzerland), *Israel Journal of Chemistry, Journal of the American Chemical Society, Journal of the Chemical Society* (UK), *Journal of the Indian Chemical Society, Journal of Pure and Applied Chemistry* (UK), *Kemisk tidskrift* (Sweden), *Recueil des travaux chimiques des Pays-Bas* (Netherlands), *Roczniki chemii* (Poland), *Suomen kemistilehti* (Finland).

Periodicals concerned specifically with chemical education include *Education in Chemistry* (US), *International Newsletter on Chemical Education* (UK), and *Journal of Chemical Education* (US).

Lists of chemical periodicals may be found in:

The Chemical Abstracts Service Source Index (CASSI). Columbus, Ohio: Chemical Abstracts Service, 1975. With supplements; lists one thousand journals most frequently cited by *Chemical Abstracts.*

International Chemistry Directory. Reading, Massachusetts: W. A. Benjamin, 1969.

Mellon, M. G. *Chemical Publications: Their Nature and Use.* (4th ed.) New York: McGraw-Hill, 1965.

Ulrich's International Periodicals Directory. New York: Bowker, biennial.

ENCYCLOPEDIAS, DICTIONARIES, HANDBOOKS

Hampel, C. A. *The Encyclopedia of the Chemical Elements.* New York: Van Nostrand Reinhold, 1968.

Hampel, C. A. *The Encyclopedia of Chemistry.* (3rd ed.) New York: Van Nostrand Reinhold, 1973.

Handbook of Chemistry and Physics. (56th ed.) Cleveland, Ohio: Chemical Rubber Co., 1975.

Hawley, G. G. *The Condensed Chemical Dictionary.* (8th ed.) New York: Van Nostrand Reinhold, 1971.

International Encyclopedia of Chemical Science. New York: Van Nostrand, 1964. Includes a multilingual glossary of terms.

Lange's Handbook of Chemistry. (11th ed.) New York: McGraw-Hill, 1973.

Miall, L. M., and Sharp, D. W. A. *A New Dictionary of Chemistry.* (4th ed.) Essex, England: Longman, 1968.

The following is a selection of bilingual and polyglot dictionaries of chemistry:

Callaham, L. I. *Russian-English Chemical and Polytechnical Dictionary.* (2nd ed.) New York: Wiley, 1962.

De Vries, L. *Dictionary of Chemistry and Chemical Engineering.* Vol. 1: *German/English;* Vol. 2: *English/German.* New York: Academic Press, 1970.

Japan Ministry of Education. *Japanese Scientific Terms: Chemistry.* (Rev. ed.) Tokyo: Nankodo, 1964. English-Japanese, Japanese-English.

Patterson, A. M. *A French-English Dictionary for Chemistry.* (2nd ed.) New York: Wiley, 1954.

Sobecka, Z., and Choinski, W. (Eds.) *Dictionary of Chemistry and Chemical Technology in Six Languages: English, German, Spanish, French, Polish and Russian.* Oxford, England: Pergamon Press, 1966.

DIRECTORIES

American Chemical Society, Committee on Professional Training. *Directory of Graduate Research.* Washington, D.C.: American Chemical Society. 1953–. Published biennally.

American Universities and Colleges. (11th ed.) Washington, D.C.: American Council on Education, 1973.

Cass, J., and Birnbaum, M. *Comparative Guide to Programs in Biological Science and Chemistry.* New York: Harper & Row, 1972.

College Blue Book. (13th ed.) New York: CCM Information Corporation, 1969–70. Volume 8, *Professions, Careers and Accreditation,* includes an essay on chemistry as a career.

International Chemistry Directory. Reading, Massachusetts: W. A. Benjamin, 1969. Lists of academic departments and faculties with a geographical index of universities and colleges, and a faculty index.

World Guide to Universities. New York: Bowker, 1972.

A listing of undergraduate institutions in the United States whose chemistry departments are approved by the American Chemical Society's Committee on Professional Training is available from the Department of Educational Activities, American Chemical Society, 1155 Sixteenth Street NW, Washington, D.C., 20036.

RESEARCH CENTERS, INSTITUTES, INFORMATION CENTERS

For an international country-by-country listing of chemical research centers and institutes consult:

Minerva, Forschungsinstitute. Berlin, Federal Republic of Germany: de Gruyter, 1972.

Other directories to research institutes in chemistry include:

Directory of Research Institutions and Laboratories in Japan. Tokyo: Society for the Promotion of Science, 1964.
The Directory of Scientific Research Institutions in India. Delhi: Indian National Scientific Documentation Centre, 1969.
Hilton, R. *The Scientific Institutions of Latin America.* Stanford: California Institute of International Studies, 1970.
Scandinavian Research Guide: Directory of Research Institutions Within Technology and Physical Sciences. (3rd rev. ed.) Stockholm: Almqvist and Wiksell, 1971.
Scientific Research in British Universities and Colleges. London: H. M. Stationery Office, 1974.
Surveys and Research, Washington, D.C. *Directory of Selected Scientific Institutions in Mainland China.* Stanford, California: Hoover Institution Press, 1970.

See also: American Chemical Society.

CHESAPEAKE BAY CENTER FOR ENVIRONMENTAL STUDIES
See Smithsonian Institution.

CHICANOS
See Access of Minorities: Spanish-Speaking Peoples.

CHIEF EXECUTIVE OFFICERS
See General Administration, Organization for; Remuneration: Faculty, Staff, and Chief Executive Officers.

CHILE, REPUBLIC OF

Population: 10,405,000 (1974 estimate). Student enrollment in primary school: 2,314,000 (1973); secondary school: 445,000 (1973); higher education: 96,000 (1970). Language of instruction: Spanish. Academic calendar: March to December, two semesters.

The development of higher education in Chile illustrates the centrality of the university in national history, as well as the efforts of ruling groups to shape the university to their purpose. In twelve years, Chile has been jerked and jolted by a centrist technocratic government, by a populist president promising a new road to socialism, by a military junta governing under a state of siege. The university, once a leading voice in the political struggle to define a new social order, is now being organized to support a military regime that defines itself as at war with an internal enemy.

Because of its disadvantageous location and early poverty, Chile attracted few Spanish intellectuals during the colonial period (1541–1818). As a consequence, non-Spanish influence was strong—in education as well as politics and economics. Radical ideas from Europe, the North American colonies, and other colonies contributed to the loosening of the power of the church, reflected in the establishment in 1738 of the Royal University of San Felipe as a secular alternative to seminaries. A republican alternative, the *Instituto nacional,* was founded in 1813, shortly after the beginning of the independence struggle. In 1842 Andrés Bello, a Venezuelan, founded the University of Chile, which replaced both the institute and the Royal University of San Felipe. In the same period, Domingo Faustino Sarmiento, an Argentine, established the first Chilean normal school. A public institution for the training of secondary school teachers was not founded until 1889, when professors from Germany were imported to organize the curriculum and teach in the first pedagogical institute. Eventually this institute became the major part of the faculty of education of the University of Chile. Training of primary school teachers continued in secondary normal schools until the Education Reform of 1965, when universities began to offer programs for primary teachers.

The declining influence of the church in the University of Chile during the nineteenth century led to the creation of the Pontifical Catholic University of Chile in 1888, in Santiago, the capital. A second Catholic university was founded in 1928 in Valparaíso, the major port city. Both of these institutions were controlled by the Vatican and the local church hierarchy until 1968.

The University of Concepción (located in the third-largest city of Chile, three hundred miles to the south of Santiago) was modeled after universities in the United States. Built in 1919 with private funds, it was the first university in Chile to have a campus and dormitory facilities for students. It was also the first institution to break the pattern of providing all instruction through unrelated professional schools. The University of Concepción created a series of institutes (mathematics, languages, social science, biological sciences) that provided the equivalent of a general studies program for students prior to specialization in the profession.

Also privately financed, the Technical University Federico Santa María, founded in 1926 at Valparaíso, was designed to emulate technical schools in Germany. It began operation in 1931 with the provision that for the first ten years its technical teaching staff would be composed entirely of foreigners. Increasing concern for technical education also resulted in the establishment of the State Technical University at Santiago in 1947. It was created by combining several independent schools or faculties, one of which had been in existence since 1849.

The gradual expansion of higher education increased the importance of the university in Chilean society. One of the more benign indicators of this importance is the contribution of universities to national cultural life, in the form of concert orchestras, theater, and art. Chile's television network grew out of the university's experimentation with the medium, and

the University of Chile and the Catholic University of Chile control two of the three channels in Santiago.

More striking was the university's role in politics. Before 1968 students had no voice in the election of university administrations, and only at the University of Chile did professors elect the rector. But student federations were composed of factions representing national political parties, and campus elections for student federation president were hotly contested. The link between student politics and national politics was strong. Many leading political figures had their training as student politicians, and in each of three successive national presidential elections, 1958, 1964, and 1970, the party or the coalition winning the office was also that controlling the university student federation (Bonilla and Glazer, 1970).

Types of Institutions

With rapid changes in political participation, the university also began to change. The most serious sustained effort at educational reform in Chile had its origins in 1959, in efforts to modernize the University of Chile. A dynamic rector assisted by a technical staff sought capital development funds from international agencies and persuaded the government to increase its commitment to higher education. While also improving the quality of instruction, the university moved to provide educational opportunities for students traditionally denied higher education. In 1960 it opened its first regional college. By 1975 the eight universities of Chile had sixty-four different campuses, and some of the branch campuses offered full-length programs in an effort to relieve the strain on facilities in Santiago. Like community colleges in the United States, the regional colleges offer short-cycle programs lasting from eighteen months to three years and terminating in subprofessional degrees such as administrative technician, artistic designer, librarian, social service assistant. For other students the branch campuses offer the first two years of study prior to moving to the main campus of the university (Feliz, 1972).

The opening of the university to nontraditional students contributed to and was part of a process of "democratization" taking part in Chilean education and society in the 1960s. On the one hand, this process was reflected in the increased level of political activity in the country; on the other, it was seen in major reform efforts at all levels of education.

Relationship with Secondary Education

In 1964 the rector who had sparked the modernization of the University of Chile (1959) became the minister of education and directed the Educational Reform of 1965. As part of the reform, compulsory education was extended from six to eight years, and a major effort made to provide *educación básica* for all children. Secondary schools were modified to create two types. Students enrolled in the *liceo* follow a science or humanities track that prepares them for the university. Upon graduation they receive a secondary *licencia*. Students enrolled in professional/technical schools study vocational subjects and receive a technical secondary diploma. Students of both schools are now eligible for admission to the university, although professional/technical school graduates are expected to enroll in engineering or technical programs. Students are generally eighteen years of age on graduation from secondary school. The Ministry of Education and the universities also provide secondary education to adults who have interrupted their schooling. The *licencia* obtained through this program does not normally qualify a person to apply for admission to the university.

Admission Requirements

Prior to 1966 students seeking admission to a university were required to pass a *bachillerato* examination designed and administered by the university in question. Increasing dissatisfaction with the exami-

nation (consisting of general essays) and a scandal involving theft and sale of examination questions led to replacement of the *bachillerato* examination with a national Academic Achievement Test *(Prueba de aptitud académica:* PAA*)* based on multiple-choice items. Admission to the universities is now decided on the basis of a combination (varying from university to university) of grade point average in secondary school, scores on the PAA, and scores on tests of specific knowledge. Students can apply simultaneously to either the University of Chile, the two technical universities, the University of Concepción, the *Universidad austral,* the *Universidad del norte,* or the two Catholic universities. Applicants can list varying numbers of choices of faculties. Several of the universities set minimal scores on the PAA, varying according to the faculty that the student wishes to enter. The different faculties may also require different combinations of the scientific knowledge tests, which cover mathematics, art, social sciences, and natural sciences.

Administration and Control

The University Reform of 1968 began in 1966 with a demand from students at the Catholic University of Valparaíso that they, together with professors and staff, participate in the selection of administrators and the university rector. The movement spread quickly to the Catholic University in Santiago and then to the public and other private universities (Huneeus, 1973). The move to democratize participation in decision making broadened to include changes in the curricular structure of the university; opening of the university to nontraditional students; and increased involvement in national affairs through teaching, research, and consultative services.

The church-appointed rector in the Catholic universities was replaced by one elected by all the members of the university community. Similar structures were created at the level of faculty, institute, and school. The university council of the University of Chile was broadened to include—in addition to the rector, deans, and members appointed by the president of the republic—representatives from student, professorial, and staff groups. Similar governance structures were created in the other universities. Students and staff also participated, in varying degrees, in the selection of professors.

Programs and Degrees

The university reform resulted in a number of changes in curricular structure in Chilean universities. The traditional system of autonomous faculties, each with its own set of required courses and with no transfer between faculties, was modified in the direction of increased options for students. Institutes were created to provide courses, such as mathematics, previously taught in more than one faculty. Faculties were converted into schools, with departments replacing the classical *catedrático* system in which one professor controlled the content taught by assistants. Although some programs retained some required courses, elective courses and a credit hour system became available, thus necessitating the publication of a university course catalog and the development of a central student registration and services office and a university planning office.

Opportunities for course selection and cross-registration resulted in the creation of new degree programs. Although Chilean universities began as professional schools offering a few *carreras* (professional programs), by 1975 students were enrolled in approximately 250 different degree programs, some of them nonprofessional. These can be categorized according to the length of the study required. There are three-year programs, such as those for elementary school teachers and technical and administrative personnel for middle-level positions; four-year programs, such as those for medical service technicians and construction engineers; five-year professional programs for economists, geologists, psychologists, agronomists, odontologists,

and secondary school teachers. The traditional professions, such as law, architecture, and engineering, are taught in six-year programs. Medicine is a seven-year degree program. Graduate studies are offered in biology, chemistry, physics, education, and related subjects at both the University of Chile and the Catholic University of Chile. Graduate programs are modeled after the North American or German universities.

The reform also produced changes in instruction. Even traditional professional programs such as law and medicine went through a systematic exercise that required articulating performance objectives and evaluating courses. (Even though professional associations are theoretically responsible for the supervision of degree programs in their profession, in practice the university faculties have historically had considerable autonomy in curriculum and teaching, and there has thus been considerable variance in requirements.) Major efforts were put into the long-term task of upgrading teaching staff through seminars on instruction and evaluation, institutional publication, incentives for research, and opportunities for fieldwork. Programed instruction materials were developed in some disciplines, and use of videotape introduced in others. Available research suggests that by 1973 about one third of the courses given in the universities deviated in some significant way from the traditional lecture method, which required no outside reading (Avalos, Pavez, and McGinn, 1974).

Financing and Student Social Background and Access to Education

The opening of the university to sectors of the population that traditionally had not been included resulted in a rapid expansion of enrollments, increased public expenditure on higher education, and programs for nontraditional students. During the 1960–1969 period higher education enrollments expanded from 24,703 to 70,580, and doubled again by 1974. Between 1965 and 1969 enrollments in the six private universities declined from 37.3 to 34.3 percent of the total enrollment; at the same time, their share of public funds for higher education increased from 19.2 percent to 32.2 percent. More than 70 percent of the budget of the private universities was paid from public funds (Galdames and Auda, 1972).

Although by law access to higher education has traditionally been limited only by ability, in fact the university is unavailable to most of the Chilean population. Efforts of both the Educational Reform of 1965 and the University Reform of 1968 to democratize education resulted in enroll-ment increases of students from working-class and peasant families from 1 percent in 1960 to 5 percent in 1970, to an esti-mated 8 percent in 1973. Workers and peasants constitute at least 50 percent of the population in Chile (Barrera, 1974; Linzmayer and Pinto, 1973). Although women continue to enroll in the university in increasing numbers, approximately 65 percent of the student population is male.

Research in 1973 showed that the PAA used to screen applicants for admission to the university is related to the social-class origin of the student but that it is not a good predictor of grades in the university. Other studies have shown that criteria for admis-sion vary according to the region from which the student comes, the particular program selected, and the socioeconomic status of the student population in his or her secondary school (Barrera, 1974).

Recognizing the elitist character of higher education, universities sought to provide other educational opportunities. Approximately 70,000 adults are currently enrolled in nondegree courses offered by the various universities. The largest pro-gram, the *Departamento universitario obrero campesino,* was begun by the Catholic Uni-versity of Chile and now operates as a private nonprofit foundation. Originally intended for workers, it attracts many middle-class students.

Teaching Staff

Chilean university professors are more commonly identified by time commitment than by rank. Full-time professors tradi-tionally are chosen by a public competition among candidates. Publications, knowl-edge of subject, teaching ability, and formal education are compared. Professors ap-pointed through this procedure are pre-sumed to have the Chilean equivalent of tenure. Increases in salary have been gov-erned by a common schedule in which time in service is the principal factor.

Research Activities

The university reform movement af-fected the character of research sponsored by and carried out by the universities. Em-phasis on the role of the university in de-scribing and changing the national reality led to the creation of the National Com-mission on Scientific and Technological Research *(Comisión nacional de investigación científica y tecnológica:* CONICYT) that awards research grants to university pro-fessors from funds provided by the eight universities (about 2 percent of their bud-get). Until 1973 one could observe a dis-tinct shift in the kind of research problem pursued in Chilean universities, from prob-lems deriving from the interests of the international scientific community to which the professional belonged, to problems deriving from felt needs of Chile's society and economy (Schiefelbein and Kenrick, 1974).

Some research funds also reach Chilean universities through private foundations such as the Ford and Rockefeller Founda-tions of the United States and through foreign governments. Before 1973 the foundations financed multimillion-dollar collaboration projects between Chilean and North American universities. Basically, however, expenditures on research and development in Chile are low, amounting to between .1 and .4 percent of GNP, as compared to 3.2 percent for Israel and 3.4

percent for the United States (*El mercurio*, May 5, 1975, p. 1).

Current Problems and Trends

Chilean universities played critical roles in the events that culminated in the overturn of the constitutional government, the death of President Salvador Allende, and the seizure of power by the military in September 1973. University campuses were the scene of a number of demonstrations, manifestations, and occasional battles between rival groups of students and professors, and sometimes the police. The final stage of the reform of 1968 in the University of Chile was the creation of four separate divisions (or campuses) that were as much reflections of the balance of power among political parties represented by students and professions as reflections of academic logic. One of the campuses served as a stronghold from which supporters of the Allende government fought against the military units that seized control of the country (Sigmund, 1973–74).

One of the first acts of the military junta was to replace rectors with military officers. The structure of governance in the University of Chile was changed to create a higher university council, composed of the rector-delegate, the pro-rector and vice-rectors of the regional colleges (also military in most cases), and four administrative vice-rectors. All administrative staff are appointed by the rector-delegate, who must also approve the deans of the faculties (several of whom are military officers). Similar systems of governance are now in effect in the other seven universities. Decree 139, promulgated on November 21, 1973, gives rectors the right to eliminate at their discretion any officer or position in the university. The various university senates have been abolished, and there is no student or faculty participation in governance except through consultation.

The junta has stated that it considers the major tasks requiring attention in the universities to be the "eradication of polit-

ical infiltration and the reduction of public expenditures" (*El mercurio*, December 29, 1975; *Mensaje*, January 1976). The two objectives work together. The junta has been following a process of "purification" in the university and feels that the first task is nearly complete. It has been accomplished by reducing government support for higher education, 10 percent in 1974, 15 percent in 1975, and 10 percent in 1976 (*El mercurio*, December 22, 1975; January 18, 1976). Reductions in budgets have justified reductions in the number of professors and students. Firings of professors generally appear to be politically motivated, the first to go being Marxists and other active supporters of the Allende regime, then leaders in the centrist Christian Democratic Party, and then critical independents (*Ercilla*, March 17, 1976, p. 30). Between September 1973 and 1976, approximately five thousand students were dismissed from the universities. The total number of professors has been reduced about 30 percent (*El mercurio*, September 29, 1975).

While the junta defines its major problems in terms of "purification" and reduction of expenses, university professors may be more concerned about the loss to other countries of talented scientists trained in Chile. The Chilean "brain drain" was first noticed about twenty years ago but has increased since 1973, according to the military head of CONICYT. Approximately 8750 highly trained persons left Chile between October 1973 and May 1975. Estimates are that approximately one third of the mathematicians and physicists trained in Chile have left for other countries. In May 1975 the faculty of sciences of the University of Chile had sixty-six unfilled positions of a total of three hundred (*El mercurio*, May 9, 1975; October 13, 1975).

In an effort to rationalize the system of higher education in Chile, the junta has strengthened the Council of Rectors Chilean Universities to make it a national higher education planning board. Originally created by law in 1954, the Council of Rectors (composed, as its name suggests, of rectors of the eight universities) was intended only to join the universities together in the administration of a fund for construction and research. The minister of education has now been named head of the council; and the group's powers have been broadened to include review of the university budgets, the creation of new programs, the social service requirements of graduates, and general planning functions (*El mercurio,* September 29, 1975).

As a consequence, the distinction between public and private universities has blurred even further. Although the six private universities have for some time received most (for example, in the case of the Catholic University of Chile, more than 80 percent) of their income from the national government, there was little public control over their operations and degree programs. The Council of Rectors now makes decisions affecting internal operations of the universities, and has ordered the universities to reduce the number of degrees they offer and to close some of their branch campuses or consolidate them with other universities. The *Universidad del norte,* for example, has been given all the branch campuses previously operated in the north by other universities. Some changes involve curricular offerings. The Catholic University of Valparaíso plans to reduce its sixteen schools, seven institutes, and three centers to nine faculties, the same number as existed before the reform. The School of Juridical, Political and Social Sciences of the Catholic University in Santiago has returned to being a faculty of law. The faculty of law of the University of Chile has eliminated the credit system and elective courses and has reinstituted oral examinations.

The junta has shifted its financial policy for higher education away from the concept of "self-financing," announced shortly after it took power, to a policy in which the financial burden of higher education will be less onerous for the state (*El mercurio,* January 18, 1976). In addition to reductions in total budgets of the universities, student fees have been raised. For 1976 the undergraduate students at the University of Chile paid approximately US$130 for the year. The fees at the Catholic University and the University of Concepción were about US$170. In 1975 about half the students at the State Technical University could not pay tuition fees (*Ercilla,* March 17, 1976, p. 30). Chile's per capita GNP is about US$750, but official unemployment rates are about 18 percent and the inflation rate is over 200 percent per year.

Figures on the distribution of student financial aid are not available. In Chile the government is the almost exclusive source of aid (outside of families). For 1976 a sum of US$1,500,000 was budgeted for scholarships. This was approximately 2.8 percent of the total amount budgeted for higher education. Approximately US$1,200,000 was budgeted for research (*El mercurio,* January 18, 1976).

Restrictions in university autonomy have been accompanied by restrictions in academic freedom; thus, the university in this case reflects the influence of society. Since all political parties have been abolished and the congress dissolved, it is not surprising that the junta has also forbidden political activity on university campuses. The Association of Professionals and Technicians of the University of Chile (*Asociación de profesores y empleados de la Universidad de Chile:* APEUCH) and the Professional Association of Employees, Professors and Administrators of the Catholic University (*Sindicato profesional de empleados, profesores y administradores de la Universidad católica:* SPEPADUC) have been proscribed, as has the Student Federation of the University of Chile (*Federación estudiantil de la Universidad de Chile:* FECH) and constituent groups. The junta's attitude toward autonomy and academic freedom is conveyed in these lines from a television address given by the minister of education on February 13, 1976.

Because autonomy has a close connection with responsibility, it is naturally regulated by the values and objectives of university policy and at the same time the juridical rule of the country. It cannot, therefore, imply either personal or territorial sanctuary for the realization of actions incompatible with a society ruled by law, that would also be denied to the majority of the citizenry. Nor can it signify protection for political activity within the university confines, above all in the form of oral or written propaganda, relative to issues that are commonly understood as part of political debate and commitment. This limitation also applies to . . . teaching that exceeds natural limits of objective information and reasoned discussion of doctrines and points of view. [Author's translation.]

The minister ended his speech recommending that the universities be kept "tranquil" so that they could comply with their duty. Previous governments in Chile encouraged a free discussion of ideas and philosophies among all the citizenry and asked universities to contribute to and improve that debate. The present government sees such discussion as a source of distraction and confusion and seeks to build a university that will bring about a unitary nationalist perspective.

International Cooperation

Because of its reputation as an open society before the military coup, Chile was the home of several international institutions of postsecondary education, such as the Latin American Faculty of Social Sciences *(Facultad latinoamericana de ciencias sociales:* FLACSO), originally created by UNESCO but later autonomous, and the Latin American Institute for Social and Economic Planning *(Instituto latinoamericano de planificación económica y social:* ILPES), funded by the Organization of American States. Other inter-American and world agencies also frequently organized seminars, conferences, and short training programs in Chile. Between 1965 and 1975 international assistance other than development capital loans totaled US$95,000,000 from agencies such as the United Nations Development Programme, UNICEF, the World Food Program of the Food and Agriculture Organization, and the Organization of American States, and from nations such as Brazil, France, Israel, Japan, Spain, and Switzerland *(Ercilla,* February 1976). Prior to September 1971 both the Ford and the Rockefeller Foundations in the United States as well as the British Council promoted relationships between Chilean universities and those of their own countries and contributed to financing the expansion and improvement of the Chilean system of higher education. Chile belongs to the Andean Higher Education Committee and is a signatory of the Andrés Bello Pact, which commits the Andean nations to develop their educational systems so as to foster better relations among member countries. Chile is also an affiliate of the Royal Academy of Spain.

NOEL F. McGINN
ERNESTO TORO

Bibliography

Avalos, B., Pavez, J., and McGinn, N. "El impacto de la reforma de las universidades." In E. Schiefelbein and N. McGinn (Eds.), *Universidad contemporánea: Un intento de análisis empírico.* Santiago: Corporación de promoción universitaria, 1974. Pp. 144–180.

Barrera, M. "Trayectoria del movimiento de reforma universitaria en Chile." *Journal of Inter-American Studies,* October 10, 1968, *10,* 617–636.

Barrera, M. "Las universidades chilenas y la educación de los trabajadores." In E. Schiefelbein and N. McGinn (Eds.), *Universidad contemporánea: Un intento de análisis empírico.* Santiago: Corporación de promoción universitaria, 1974, pp. 121–143.

Bonilla, F., and Glazer, M. *Student Politics in Chile.* New York: Basic Books, 1970.

Feliz, G. C. *The Regional University Centers: Innovation in Chile.* Berkeley: Center for Research and Development in Higher Education, University of California, 1972.

Galdames G. J., and Auda J. H. *(Chile: Un país andino del Pacífico sur.* Santiago: Editorial universitaria, 1972.

Gill, C. *Education and Social Change in Chile.* Bulletin No. 7. Washington, D.C.: U.S. Department of Health, Education and Welfare, 1966.

Huneeus, C. *La reforma en la Universidad de*

Chile. Santiago: Corporación de promoción universitaria, 1973.

Linzmayer, T., and Pinto, A. M. *Características socioculturales del alumnado de la Universidad de Chile.* Santiago: Universidad de Chile, Oficina de planificación, 1973.

Schiefelbein, E., and Kenrick, C. "La investigación en la universidad." In E. Schiefelbein and N. McGinn (Eds.), *Universidad contemporánea: Un intento de análisis empírico.* Santiago: Corporación de promoción universitaria, 1974, pp. 181–200.

Sigmund, P. E. "Chilean Universities and the Coup." *Change,* Winter 1973–74, *10,* 18–22.

See also: Archives: Mediterranean, the Vatican, and Latin America, National Archives of; Cooperative Education and Off-Campus Experience: Cooperative Education Worldwide; Science Policies: Advanced Developing Countries: Andean Common Market Countries; South America: Regional Analysis.

CHINA, PEOPLE'S REPUBLIC OF

China (with an estimated population of almost 800,000,000 in 1974) has a long history of formal higher educational development, dating from the establishment of the Chinese Imperial College in 124 B.C. Confucian learning dominated the aims and goals of higher education up to the reign of the T'ung Chih emperor in 1862, when a series of reforms were instituted to align higher education to meet increasing internal and external pressures for social change and scientific and economic development. In practice this meant that a few selected technical colleges were established primarily to train military personnel. The establishment of the Republic of China in 1912 brought further changes in higher education. Western missionaries had founded several institutions of higher learning, and the Chinese government also responded to changing conditions by modernizing the organization and curriculum of Chinese universities. The most striking characteristic of modern Chinese higher education is the fact that it developed basically as a forced response to the demands put upon China by the West (and

Japan), and thus from the start the West and Western ideas played a disproportionate role in the development of post-1911 Chinese pedagogical theory and practice. An inordinate emphasis on training specialists with high-level skills resulted in a lack of middle-level technicians, who were precisely those necessary to begin the task of reforming and modernizing China. Few students engaged in studies related to agricultural development, and far too many were content with receiving a liberal arts education. Toward the end of the republican period China nevertheless possessed a significant corps of higher education faculty, scientists, and engineers, as well as an impressive physical plant. However, both human and material resources were considered inadequate and in need of reform and reorganization when the People's Republic of China was established in 1949.

From 1949 to 1953, as part of the general program of economic and social reconstruction, schools were reopened, rebuilt, and consolidated. An administrative structure was established to bring institutions of higher learning under Communist Party control—particularly in the cities, where the new government was least experienced. A Ministry of Education was formed in Peking with the responsibility of incorporating into the five-year plans educational needs and goals. Provincial, city, and county educational bureaus were also established or reformed, bringing education at all levels under a highly centralized system of control. Previously existing standard universities and colleges were reorganized to combine faculties and departments, thus separating polytechnic universities from the liberal arts or composite universities.

The Chinese government reorganized the colleges and universities and readjusted college departments five times during the period 1949–1960. Two reorganizations were aimed at colleges of science and engineering. Universities were dissected and the parts reformed to comprise more specialized university units. For example, the engineering college of Peking University and all departments of Yenching University's colleges of science and engineering were incorporated into Tsinghua University to make the latter a multidepartment technological school. At the same time, Tsinghua University's colleges of arts, science, and law, together with the three similar colleges of Yenching University, were incorporated into Peking University, which was to be made a composite university. This pattern of university and college reorganization occurred throughout China.

The third reorganization did not affect the universities nationwide but was confined to two administrative zones of North and East China. This movement was aimed at further consolidating the technical and scientific departments of those universities involved.

The fourth reorganization came in 1953 as a result of the Korean War. The first three reorganizations had expanded the educational institutions to an unmanageable number. The demands of the war necessitated a cutback. Therefore, in 1953 Hunan, Kuangsi, Kueichow, and Nanchang Universities were abolished; and Northeast Navigational School, Shanghai Navigational School, and Fukien Navigational School merged to become Dairen Navigational School. However, in the latter part of 1953, when the Korean War was brought to an 'end, many of the universities formerly closed were restored.

In the process of reorganization, foreign-run universities were expropriated and their organization and curricula accordingly transformed. In addition to the manipulating of previously established universities, the new government also established a number of political universities and universities for national minorities (for example, People's University of China and China National Minority School in Peking).

The fifth reorganization came in 1958 and was part of a broader movement, known as the Great Leap Forward. The Great Leap Forward affected many areas of Chinese life, especially higher education. During this period, emphasis was seriously put on the ideological and political implications of higher education.

A new type of college (called "red and expert") was established to recruit and train students from among the working class and peasantry in an attempt to break down traditional social-class barriers at this level of training. This entire educational program was summed up in the commune movement, which was to encompass all social and economic activities in Chinese society: "Our goal is to gradually and systematically organize our industry, agriculture, commerce, culture, education, and military [militia] into a great commune, making it the basic unit of our society" (Mao Tse-tung, 1969, p. 44). The commune concept as it related to education would have effectively shifted the delivery of educational services from the more conventional educational institutions to the broader segment of society.

Because of serious economic difficulties, this program was virtually abandoned, and a new higher educational policy emerged. The five-year period from 1960 to 1966 represented a retrenchment in one sense and a prelude to educational reform in another. Universities and colleges placed a renewed emphasis on entrance examinations, formal course examinations, and quality of student performance. Further centralization during this period increased controls both for local educational bureaus and the Ministry of Education in Peking. The net result was disaffection between educational authorities and the local communities, increased wastage as students dropped out rather than risk failure, and discontent between and among students and teachers. At the same time, serious political struggles were taking place within the Chinese government over a wide variety of issues, including educational policy. The Great Proletarian Cultural Revolution (GPCR), which gained momentum in the summer of 1966, changed virtually the entire social and economic program in

China. By 1968 the educational structure, and especially higher education, had been thoroughly restructured; gradually those institutions of higher education which had been closed during the GPCR were re-opened and began to implement a variety of reform measures. In addition, several new postsecondary learning structures emerged, representing an alternative higher educational network.

National Educational Policy

The basic tenets of China's educational goals and aims in the 1970s are contained in two official statements, which constitute the theoretical base for all educational decisions. The first is a statement by then chairman of the Chinese Communist Party (CCP), Mao Tse-tung (1968, p. 110): "Our educational policy must enable everyone who receives an education to develop morally, intellectually, and physically and become a well-educated worker with socialist consciousness." The second statement appears in the 1975 revised constitution of the People's Republic of China in the form of two articles: "Article 12: Culture, education, literature and art, physical education, health work, and scientific work must all serve proletarian politics, serve the workers, peasants, and soldiers, and be combined with productive labor. . . . Article 27: . . . citizens have the right to work and the right to education" (*Peking Review*, Jan. 24, 1975, pp. 15–17). In practice, Chinese institutions of higher education attempt to combine teaching, productive labor, and scientific research through the establishment of cooperative relationships with productive enterprises throughout China. The political orientation of higher education in China, as well as the emphasis on a specific social-class cluster (workers, peasants, and soldiers), has resulted in a program designed to train politically conscious skilled personnel who have been recruited from industrial workers and rural peasants and who will return to the areas of industry and agriculture upon completion of study. During the period from 1968

to 1975 the Chinese attempted to operationalize these goals and aims in all areas of higher education. It must be stressed that this is an ongoing process and that the current state of higher education in China is undergoing change.

Administration and Control

The administrative mechanism of higher education in China includes the management of the universities and colleges, the financing of higher education, curricular reform, and student-teacher relations. University and college administration in China is integrally linked with the actions and policy of the CCP. Two lines of decision making and command must be envisaged as running parallel: (1) government and university officials and (2) CCP committee members. A new Ministry of Education has been formed within the Chinese government's State Council. The Ministry of Education is linked directly with the CCP University Committees (CCPUC) on each campus. The CCPUC in turn is advised on administrative matters by a group called "three-in-one committees," composed of instructional faculty, student, and CCP representatives. Broad representation in university administration is thus achieved. Administration and management of the universities and colleges proceeds further into the university structure with a University Party Secretary (who often makes most of the day-to-day decisions), University Department Revolutionary Committees (concerned with the policy and activities of the various academic departments on campus), and various departmental CCP secretaries and educational reform groups. Universities and colleges are afforded basic autonomy in management within the broad guidelines articulated by the Chinese Communist Party and transmitted through the CCPUC. Placement of university and college graduates is also delegated to higher education institutions in consultation with local industrial concerns and according to the needs expressed in the overall state educational plan.

Financing

Higher educational institutions receive basic subsidies from the state and from local provincial and municipality levels. In addition, colleges and universities are encouraged to attempt to finance their own operations through a variety of productive activities. Often these institutions are exhorted to follow the principles of the "anti-Japanese military and political college" founded in Yenan in 1936: self-reliance; build it yourself; supply it yourself (food and materials). In short, financing is a mixture of state and local efforts.

Curricular and Instructional Reform

Curricular and instructional reform has been a major priority of Chinese educators since the GPCR. The process varies widely, depending on the nature of the individual institutions of higher learning. Many instructional materials were found to be unrelated to concrete conditions in China and are either being eliminated or rewritten. In general, Chinese educators are attempting to combine the theoretical core of instructional materials with practical conditions and problems in China. Many universities and colleges have established curriculum committees which—in consultation with faculty, students, and even community members (factory workers and technicians, and peasants and agrotechnicians)—constantly review and revise all teaching materials. As materials are rewritten, field studies are conducted to obtain latest findings, and international journals are consulted to assess the progress of other nations in the sciences and social sciences.

A similar reform procedure is currently underway in the area of instructional methodology. The general principle followed in China consists of combining teaching with scientific research and productive labor. In practice, students and instructors divide their courses of study between formal classroom instruction and a variety of field study opportunities. Some universities and colleges have established "teaching bases" in urban industrial enterprises and rural communes. As much as one third of all instruction is conducted at the "teaching base" site, where students participate in drawing up local production plans, engaging in scientific and social scientific experimentation, and attempting to solve practical problems. In spite of the emphasis on applied research and instruction, theoretical considerations have not been neglected. Each specific subject or topic determines to a large degree which side of the equation (theory-practice) is stressed in order to master the material.

Teaching strategy has been reformed to abolish the "injection" method and institute the "elicitation" method. Students are encouraged to study on their own as much as possible through reading and experimentation; instructional materials (such as reading materials and lecture notes) are distributed in advance; and the formal classroom is utilized almost solely for discussion. Outside consultation is sought on a regular basis from members of the working community (industrial workers and peasants) and technicians and professionals, who are invited to give occasional lectures and engage in class discussion.

Examination procedure has also been thoroughly reformed since 1968. Although there was an initial tendency to abolish examinations entirely (both entrance and course examinations), there has recently (1975) been a move to introduce several revised forms of student evaluation. Examination topics are often made public in advance, and students are to use whatever means necessary to prepare for and answer them. Marks are given for diagnostic reasons: for observing a change of attitude toward learning and method of study. The more creative and innovative the student's approach to solving the examination problem, the higher the mark. Marks are also a means of assessing faculty preparation and quality of instruction. Occasionally, examinations consist of a final paper or an experimental design, completed either jointly or individually. Entrance examinations are also diagnostic—to assess the student's preparation and possible need for tutoring. A "no-fail" policy is in operation, although students can be encouraged to transfer to a field of study for which they are better prepared.

Enrollment procedures and student-teacher relations also reflect post-GPCR reforms. Students may apply for admission to institutions of higher learning only after several years of practical experience in production or the armed forces and after they have been recommended by their work colleagues. Enrollment committees at each university or college have been instructed on priorities and state planning needs and conduct various screening activities. Current priorities include the need to recruit students from worker and peasant background, women, national minorities, and overseas Chinese. The average age of an entering college student is thirty. Teachers and students are to relate to each other as equals and comrades. The teacher is to be considered a guide and is encouraged to fraternize with the students and to know them personally. In addition, teachers and students combine activities as much as possible in research, teaching, and productive labor. A primary goal for teachers is to identify those students who exhibit high leadership and intellectual capabilities and utilize them to work with other students to upgrade standards and student performance. For their part, students are encouraged to conduct classes in conjunction with teachers and to challenge teachers and administrators concerning policy and leadership. It is felt that diverse views on teaching content and method, curriculum, examination policy, and administration will result in a dynamic approach to pedagogical theory and practice.

Types of Institutions

Standard universities. Standard universities and colleges in China comprise those institutions formally established by the imperial government (pre-1911), the nationalist government or missionaries (1911–1949), or

since the establishment of the People's Republic of China (1949–). They are funded by the state although encouraged to be somewhat self-sufficient. These institutions consist of several types, the most prominent being the composite universities (arts and sciences), polytechnical universities (technical and engineering sciences), and teacher education colleges.

The curriculum of the composite universities (for example, Peking University) includes language study, history, philosophy, political economy, international politics, law, and library science. Students are encouraged to "take society as the workshop," which means that as much as one third of the three-year course of study takes place in community settings and involves investigative research. Recent projects include a new annotated addition of the Confucian Analects (compiled by philosophy students), establishment of evening political economy classes for workers and peasants, fiction and nonfiction literary projects, and collaboration with faculty on writing journal articles and books related to social investigation. Emphasis is placed upon the ability of students to solve practical problems.

Polytechnical universities and colleges receive priority and are basic to China's scientific and technological development. The course of study has also been reduced to three years and covers a wide variety of technological and engineering fields (civil engineering, mechanical engineering, agricultural sciences, hydraulics, marine studies, chemical engineering, physics, electrical engineering, mathematics). Tuition, medical care, housing, and living expenses of students are provided by the state. The linking of theory with practice is stressed even more in the polytechnical universities through what is known as the "open-door" policy. In practice this means that students make links with productive enterprises and work on projects during their course of study. Often these projects are designed to fill a gap in China's current technological level (examples of projects are the designing of numerically controlled machine tools, crystal research, agrosciences such as pomiculture, and water conservancy). The courses of study in the polytechnical universities are directly related to national construction goals and aims as expressed in the state's economic plans.

Providing an adequate supply of trained teachers for China's expanding elementary and secondary schools has been of critical importance. Teacher training institutions exist at three levels: junior normal school, normal college, and higher normal institution. There is currently a move to merge the higher normal institution with the normal colleges. The course of study has been shortened to provide a two-year postsecondary training program for future students. Several courses have been dropped (educational psychology and teaching methods), to be replaced by practical work. From the first day of their training, students are expected to spend at least part of each day assisting a full-time teacher in the attached laboratory school or in one of the nearby community schools. The teacher education institutions also provide spare-time instruction, thus affording teachers in-service training.

The institutions described above constitute the core of standard higher education institutions in China. They are relatively few (approximately three hundred) in number (*Special Issue*, 1974, p. 153), and instruction and research are clearly applied. However, the Chinese are not ignoring graduate education and high-level research. There are over one hundred highly specialized research institutes in China (*Special Issue*, 1974, pp. 160–161). Graduate-level students and scientific personnel work jointly on various applied and theoretical problems. Many of the research institutes are directly under the Chinese Academy of Sciences, although provinces, municipalities, and autonomous regions also have established certain specific research institutes. Current research priorities include optics, electronics, nuclear physics, astron-

omy, semiconductors, oceanology, meteorology, crystal research, and laser and computer research. Several new institutes have recently been established, including the Hupeh Institute of Hydrobiology (aquaculture) and the Kunming Research Institute of Tropical Plants.

Alternative higher education network. The most important innovations in the field of higher education in China are the alternative higher education institutions, primarily the peasant and worker colleges. China's expanding agricultural and industrial base requires more skilled human resources than the relatively few standard universities and colleges can supply. For this reason, as well as for political reasons, there are now thousands of commune and factory colleges in China, charged primarily with the task of training agrotechnicians and industrial technicians.

The peasant and commune colleges are increasingly taking the lead in training agrotechnical personnel. In some provinces over 80 percent of all agrotechnicians are trained in peasant colleges (*Hsinhua*, 1975, pp. 16–17). The colleges are established by the county CCP committees, and cadre from the committees are members of the administrative revolutionary committees of each individual peasant college. Teaching and research efforts in the colleges are often in direct relation to the specific agricultural needs of each area. The teaching faculty is composed of a mixture of trained teachers, agrotechnicians, and veteran peasants. College graduates from the standard polytechnical institutes also engage in part-time teaching in the peasant colleges. The curriculum of the agricultural commune colleges varies widely and often includes as basic courses botany, plant physiology, and crop cultivation. Specialized courses are also offered in such areas as farm machinery maintenance and use, electricity, water conservancy, animal husbandry, veterinary science, and rural medicine. Courses of study range from six months to two or more years.

In the urban industrial centers, worker

colleges are increasingly supplying the major portion of China's technically skilled human resources. The colleges are established by factories, industrial companies or industrial bureaus, and municipal and district colleges. Courses of study range from one and a half to three years and are often geared toward specific industrial needs. Students are selected from among veteran workers and continue to draw their full wage while attending the college. The teaching faculty is composed of experienced workers, on-site technicians, and volunteers from nearby colleges and universities. Upon completion of studies the graduates return to production at a higher level of responsibility. The goal of this program is to expand the number of technicians in China's light and medium industries and to strengthen weak technical capabilities, thus promoting a more efficient transformation and transfer of technical skills.

Other postsecondary training efforts include hospital-run paramedical colleges, university- and college-run correspondence courses (in Chinese language, mathematics, physics, biology, and chemistry), handicrafts (silk, knitwear, textile methods, carpentry, masonry), in-service teacher training, and a variety of training courses in technical skills (electronics, mechanics, accounting, plant health).

Current Problems and Trends

The Chinese have restructured their higher educational system to relate directly to social, political, and economic developmental needs, as expressed locally and by the state planning documents. Expansion of higher educational opportunities is clearly a priority, as indicated by the emphasis on establishing a growing alternative higher educational network. Research has not been neglected, although it appears to be less emphasized than the applied training taking place in the standard universities and colleges and in the alternative institutions. If the Chinese are able to maintain the current pace of educational development, they will be able to

meet the growing human resource requirements of their expanding economy. Critical to the success of their program will be the continued cooperation of governmental and educational leaders in what is an innovative pedagogical enterprise.

JOHN N. HAWKINS

Bibliography

Biggerstaff, K. *The Earliest Modern Government Schools in China.* Ithaca, New York: Cornell University Press, 1961.

Changsha. Hong Kong News Agency, January 22, 1975, pp. 16–17.

Fraser, S. E. *Chinese Communist Education: Records of the First Decade.* Nashville, Tennessee: Vanderbilt University Press, 1965.

Fraser, S. E. *Education and Communism in China: An Anthology of Commentary and Documents.* London: Pall Mall Press, 1970.

Fraser, S. E., and Hsu, K. L. *Chinese Education: The Cultural Revolution and Its Aftermath: A Bibliographical Guide.* New York: International Arts and Science Press, 1972.

Hawkins, J. N. *Educational Theory in the People's Republic of China: The Report of Ch'ien Chun-ju.* Honolulu: University of Hawaii Press, 1971.

Hawkins, J. N. *Mao Tse-tung and Education: His Thoughts and Teachings.* Hamden, Connecticut: Shoe String Press, 1974.

Hinton, W. *The Hundred Day War: The Cultural Revolution at Tsinghua University.* New York: Monthly Review Press, 1974.

Mao Tse-tung. "Under the Red Flag of Mao Tse-tung." *Chinese Education,* 2 (3), 1958.

Mao Tse-tung. *Four Essays on Philosophy.* Peking: Foreign Languages Press, 1968.

Nee, V. *The Cultural Revolution at Peking University.* New York: Monthly Review Press, 1969.

Peake, C. H. *Nationalism and Education in Modern China.* New York: Columbia University Press, 1932.

Price, R. F. *Education in Communist China.* London: Routledge and Kegan Paul, 1970.

Special Issue for National Day. Hong Kong: Hsinhua News Agency, 1974, p. 153.

See also: Access of Minorities: Soviet Union, People's Republic of China, and Islamic Nations; Adult Education: Government Programs; Archives: Africa and Asia, National Archives of; Cooperative Education and Off-Campus Experience: Cooperative Education Worldwide; History of Higher Education; Illiteracy of Adults; Libraries: National Library of Peking; Library Administration Outside the United States; Northeast Asia; Regional Analysis; Philosophies of Higher Education, Historical and Contemporary; Religious Influences in Higher Education: Buddhism, Confucianism, Taoism; Science Policies: Advanced Developing Countries: China, People's Republic of; Women and Higher Education: Access of Women Students to Higher Education.

CHINA, PEOPLE'S REPUBLIC OF, SCIENCE POLICIES OF

See Science Policies: Advanced Developing Countries: People's Republic of China.

CHINA, REPUBLIC OF (TAIWAN)

Population: 16,223,102 (1975). Student enrollment in primary school: 2,364,961; junior and senior high schools: 1,505,993; higher education: 293,347. Language of instruction: Chinese and English. Academic calendar: August 1–July 31 or September 1–June 30, divided into two semesters. Percentage of national budget expended on all education: 6.3% (1976–77). [Except where noted, figures are for 1975–76. Source: Ministry of Education.]

The current system of higher education in Taiwan evolved from the structure existing on the Chinese mainland prior to 1949 rather than from the pattern left behind by the Japanese at the end of their fifty-year control of the island. Four major beliefs—Taoism, Catholicism, Buddhism, and Protestantism—have influenced the educational system. Confucian teachings, the essence of Chinese culture, have had the greatest impact, especially on curriculum and teaching methods. Considerable influence from the United States helped shape the present division of elementary, secondary, and tertiary education.

Rapid economic development has stimulated educational growth; and, since the implementation of the new basic nine-year education in 1968, higher education has expanded in rate and scope. The number of students in postsecondary education increased from 51,000 in 1964 to 293,000 in 1975. To ease the financial burden of such rapid expansion, the government has actively solicited support from the private sector. Private educational institutions at the senior secondary and the junior college levels have also increased in number. In addition, programs involving industry have been organized at various levels: in junior high schools, senior vocational high schools, and junior colleges.

According to estimates by the Manpower Development Plan adopted by the cabinet (Executive *Yuan*), vocational education will be accorded great emphasis throughout the 1970s. Seventy percent of all students will be channeled into vocational high schools by 1980. Higher technical education will expand accordingly.

National Educational Policy

The goal of education in Taiwan is to realize Sun Yat-sen's "Three Principles of the People." "In essence they are ethics, democracy, and science. In the spiritual sense, they are freedom, equality, and universal love. As guided by these principles, education in the Province of Taiwan aims at educating the people and reforming society" (*Education in Taiwan Province*, 1974, p. 3).

Legal Basis of Educational System

All laws, regulations, and policies concerning education in the republic are promulgated by the government in accordance with the constitution of 1947, which made special provision for education. Section 5, Chapter 13, "Education and Culture," Articles 158–167, has special relevance. It proclaims that all citizens shall have equal access to education and that students from poor families shall be given financial assistance. Article 162 establishes state supervision of all private and public educational institutions.

Types of Institutions

There are four types of higher education institutions, each with a special function. (1) The universities, which must consist of at least three colleges, provide general academic education in many subjects. (2) The colleges give training in specialized subjects, such as medicine or Chinese culture. (3) The junior colleges are divided into five-year junior colleges, which admit students from junior high school; and two- and three-year junior colleges, which accept students from senior high school and vocational high school. (4) The teacher training institutions are divided into five-year junior normal colleges, which prepare teachers for elementary school and admit students from junior high school; and normal colleges and normal universities, which admit graduates from senior and vocational high schools and train teachers for junior and senior high schools.

Private colleges may be established by individuals or organizations under the regulations of the Ministry of Education. Evening study programs, especially at junior colleges, usually requiring one more year of study than regular programs, are increasing rapidly.

In the 1975–76 school year there were 101 institutions of higher education in Taiwan Province, including 25 universities and colleges and 76 junior colleges. Of these, 11 institutions were administered by the central government; 22 were administered by the provincial government; and 68 were private institutions, mainly junior colleges.

Relationship with Secondary Education

The government offers nine years of compulsory education, divided into two stages: six years of public elementary school and three years of public junior high school. There are two types of upper secondary schools, both lasting three years: senior high school and vocational senior high school. Students not planning to enter tertiary education may receive vocational training through cooperative agreements with industry. Students in junior high schools and students in eight senior vocational schools are involved in such programs. The first three years of junior normal colleges (five-year program to train teachers for elementary school) and five-

year junior colleges are considered upper secondary education. The government actively encourages the establishment of private secondary schools, which are required to follow the same curriculum as public institutions.

The high schools generally award a senior high school graduation certificate, which qualifies the student for entry into higher education. Graduates are usually eighteen years old.

Admission Requirements

The number of students to be admitted to higher education institutions is determined annually by the Ministry of Education. Universities, colleges, and two- and three-year junior colleges admit graduates from senior high schools and senior vocational high schools who have successfully passed the competitive Joint Entrance Examination for Colleges and Universities or the Joint Entrance Examination for two- and three-year junior colleges, respectively. Applicants also have to pass a physical examination. Excellent students from senior vocational schools may be admitted to junior colleges without an entrance examination. To provide greater equality of opportunity, applicants who are discharged from the military, members of aboriginal tribes, children of diplomats in foreign service, and students from outlying rural areas are given preferential treatment.

Five-year junior colleges and junior normal colleges admit students possessing the Junior High School Graduation Certificate who have passed the mandatory entrance examination.

To be admitted to graduate study, a student must have a bachelor's degree and have passed the entrance examination. Doctoral programs admit students with a master's degree who have qualified in a special examination.

Administration and Control

According to Chapter 10 of the constitution, the central government shall have the power of legislation and administration of national education or delegate the power of administration to the provincial and city governments (*Education in the Republic of China,* 1972, p. 8). The educational system is administered on three levels—national, provincial, and county/municipal—but is centralized in the Ministry of Education. All national and private universities and colleges fall under the jurisdiction of the Ministry of Education. Within the ministry, two departments have specific responsibilities for higher education: the Department of Higher Education and the Department of Technological and Vocational Education. The minister takes overall charge, assisted by one political vice-minister and two administrative vice-ministers.

Under general supervision of the ministry, Taiwan Province has a Department of Education headed by a commissioner of education, who is responsible for education at all levels in the province, including colleges and junior colleges.

The chief executive of a public university or of a college is the president, who is appointed by the minister of education. The university president carries overall responsibility for academic and financial affairs; university development; and selection of academic administrators and teaching staff, subject to approval by the ministry. He is assisted by administrative deans (for studies, guidance, graduate school) and a university council. The deans are nominated by him and appointed by the Ministry of Education. The university council—which is composed of administrative deans, department chairmen, and representatives of professors—is concerned with budgets, college and departmental affairs, graduate studies, and internal university relations. Department chairmen are appointed by the president upon recommendation by the respective administrative dean. The council of studies, composed of deans and department chairmen, is in charge of curriculum. Each college and department has its own council.

Public junior colleges also are headed by a president, who is appointed by the Ministry of Education on recommendation of the respective provincial or municipal government. The administrative structure is simpler but similar to that of the universities. The president is assisted by an executive council and a college council.

A board of directors, with a membership of nine to fifteen, is the chief executive body at private universities, colleges, and junior colleges. According to government regulations, one third of the members of the board must have had previous experience in educational administration. The chairman of the board is elected by the members and may not be a foreigner. Foreign members may not exceed one third of the membership. The board appoints the president of the institution, subject to approval by the Ministry of Education. The internal administration is otherwise similar to that of the public institutions.

Programs and Degrees

Universities and colleges in the Republic of China have faculties offering courses in agriculture, architecture, humanities, natural and social sciences, commerce, engineering, law, mathematics, medicine, and veterinary science. These institutions follow the credit-hour system. The first degree, the bachelor's degree, is awarded after a minimum of four years of study. An additional year of practical training is required for teachers. Fields such as law, agriculture, and architecture require five years of study, and medical studies last seven years. The final examination is given by a committee appointed by the Ministry of Education and chaired by the president of the university; the committee is composed of professors, associate professors, and outstanding scholars. The examination may be supervised by a representative of the ministry. Most higher education institutions provide for practical training in industry, business, and the professions, especially during the last two years of study. To obtain a license for certain professions—such as accountant, lawyer, dentist, physician, pharmacist, and veterinarian—applicants have to take an additional examination sponsored by the Examination *Yuan.*

A master's degree is awarded after an additional two years of study at a research institute (graduate school); successful completion of a two-part (written and oral) examination given by a committee whose chairman is appointed by the Ministry of Education; and completion of a thesis, which must be approved by two nonuniversity members of the committee as well as by the Written Work Evaluation Council of the Ministry of Education. A doctoral candidate who has completed two years of successful study is required to pass a written and oral examination given by the ministry, and present and defend a dissertation to be awarded a doctoral degree.

Graduates from junior colleges are awarded a diploma upon successful completion of their study. Many public and private junior colleges offer cooperative education programs for their students in industry, business, and various other professions as part of the course requirement. Participants in short-term training programs are usually awarded a certificate.

Financing

All levels of government—national, provincial, and county/municipal—are required by law to set aside a certain percentage of their annual budgets for education and culture. All national universities and colleges as well as teacher education institutions are financed mainly by the central government, while provincial institutions of higher education are financed by the province. Students are charged a small tuition and some fees. Private institutions raise their funds through tuition and through contributions from industry and individuals, although some private institutions may receive additional government grants. The board of directors is responsible for budgets at the private institutions.

Student Financial Aid

All students at teacher education institutions are provided living allowances, books, and uniforms by the government. Most higher education institutions have some form of scholarship programs available for gifted students, while needy students may receive grants-in-aid under the auspices of private and public organizations. Graduate students are eligible for fellowships from the Ministry of Education, which also awards grants for study abroad.

Student Access to Education

The ratio of students to population in higher education has been increasing steadily—especially during the period 1963–1972, when students increased from .44 percent of the population to 1.64 percent. This phenomenon has occurred at each level of education; for instance, the attendance rate for nine years of education is 98.13 percent.

Women are well represented in the student body and are concentrated mainly in the humanities.

Students do not participate in decision making at the institutions of higher education. There are no formal national student organizations, although an organization such as the Chinese Youth Corps is quite active in student affairs. Every university also has a union of student associations, which is allowed to voice its recommendations on university policy.

Teaching Staff

Academic staff are appointed by the president of the institution after verification by the Ministry of Education. There are four ranks of teaching staff: professor, associate professor, instructor, and assistant. The requirements for appointment are as follows: A professor must have either three years of successful experience as an associate professor, with publishing background, or a doctoral degree and four years of experience in research. An associate professor should have either a doctoral degree with an outstanding dissertation, or have been a successful instructor for three years, or have a master's degree with four years of outstanding experience. An instructor must fulfill at least one of the following requirements: excellent results in his master's examination; more than four years of successful experience as an assistant; five years of experience as a secondary school teacher; or specialization in the Chinese classics. An assistant should have either a bachelor's degree or a diploma from a junior college with two or more years of experience in an academic institution.

The first teaching appointment is for one year, renewable for an additional year. The contract may then be renewed every two years until the age of sixty-three. Academic staff retire between sixty-five and seventy, depending on length of service.

The pay scale is standardized for each rank throughout the province.

Research Activities

Research is a very important aspect of higher education, since research institutes serve as graduate schools. According to the Tentative Regulation of Research Institutes, a research institute must be affiliated with a university, and its director should simultaneously serve as head of a department of the university. All well-administered public and private universities and colleges may establish research institutes after approval by the Ministry of Education.

An academic research allowance is paid by the Ministry of Education to university teachers engaged in research. The National Long-Term Science Development Program also provides special funds for researchers. Professors are given sabbatical leaves to undertake research after seven years of service.

Several universities are actively involved in joint research with national and international companies and organizations.

The Academia Sinica, the largest research organization in the nation, directs and promotes much of the research in Taiwan through its specialized research institutes. It is a government agency that, together with the Ministry of Education, has established the National Council for Science Development. The council sponsors research exchange abroad, awarding grants for research activities while encouraging foreign scientists to come to Taiwan by offering fellowships. Academia Sinica is involved in a number of joint research ventures with organizations abroad.

Current Problems and Trends

The rapid expansion of enrollments at the higher education level is making it difficult to provide enough facilities and competent staff. This problem has been compounded by the fact that a great number of scholars who had been studying abroad remained after their period of study, making the "brain drain" a problem in Taiwan. The government has tried to alleviate the shortage of staff by offering attractive contracts to overseas scholars.

To assist in financing the growth of the educational system, the government has encouraged the private sector to assume increased responsibility for higher education, although under government supervision. Most of the junior colleges are now in private hands.

The need for technicians in Taiwan's industrializing economy has resulted in a great stress on vocational and professional training in agriculture, commerce, engineering, maritime studies, and technical studies. The government has availed itself of loans from the World Bank to expand vocational education at all levels and has solicited the cooperation of local industry and professionals to arrange cooperative training programs for students at all levels, from junior high school to the university.

Current trends include an increased emphasis on research to determine manpower needs and educational expansion;

growth of cooperative education and short-cycle technical education on the high school and junior college levels and in technical institutions such as Ming-Chi Institute of Technology, Taishan; and support to graduate schools to strengthen research and advanced education. Teacher education is benefiting from new approaches such as in-service training and television courses; and foreign scholars are being encouraged to come to teach in the country, while graduate scholarships are offered to nationals for study abroad.

A unique aspect of education in Taiwan, which receives much emphasis, is mandatory military training, both on the secondary and collegiate levels. Tertiary-level students receive military training during semesters and at army bases during vacations.

International Cooperation

The Republic of China has shown great interest in international cooperation and has signed a number of cultural and educational agreements with various nations. The republic has set up educational and cultural advisory committees in the United States, Europe, and Asia to encourage cultural exchange programs. An international house designed to provide housing for foreign students attending institutions of higher education in the republic is being constructed. The Ministry of Education sponsors exchange programs whereby foreign educators are invited to Taiwan and nationals are provided scholarships for study abroad.

[Information received from the Department of Education.]

Bibliography

Chang, Shu-Yuan-Hsi Eh. "The Views and Contributions of Chinese Students and Intellectuals in the United States." *Dissertation Abstracts International*, December 1971, *32*, 3399-A.

Chen, J. A. "Higher Education in the Republic of China (Taiwan)." *Dissertation Abstracts International*, January 1971, *32*, 3714-A.

Education in Taiwan Province, Republic of China. Taiwan: Department of Education, 1974.

Education in the Republic of China. Taichung, Taiwan: Ministry of Education, 1972, 1975.

Fang, J. M. "Education and Economic Growth in Taiwan, 1952–65." *Industry of Free China*, December 1971, pp. 11–23.

To, Cho-Yee. "Education of the Aborigines in Taiwan: An Illustration of How Certain Traditional Beliefs of a Majority People Determine the Education of a Disadvantaged Minority." *Journal of Negro Education*, Summer 1972, *41*, 183–194.

See also: Academic Dress and Insignia; Archives: Africa and Asia, National Archives of; History of Higher Education; Philosophies of Higher Education, Historical and Contemporary; Religious Influences in Higher Education: Buddhism, Confucianism, Taoism.

CHINA YOUTH CORPS
See College Unions.

CHIROPODY
See Podiatry (field of study).

CHIROPRACTIC (Field of Study)

Chiropractic is a nondrug, nonsurgical healing arts profession dealing with the relationships of the structural and neurological aspects of the body in health and disease. Chiropractors believe that the integrity of the neurological system is an essential factor in the adaptability and responsiveness of physiological functions in the body. The title that chiropractors use varies by state; the most frequently used title is D.C. or Doctor of Chiropractic, but the term *chiropractic physician* is also recognized in some jurisdictions. A Doctor of Chiropractic is educated in the basic and clinical sciences; trained to diagnose, recommend, and program treatment procedures; and skilled in treating musculoskeletal disorders of the human body.

Because a contemporary chiropractor does not consider chiropractic a panacea for all diseases, he will consult and refer patients to other doctors—doctors of medicine (M.D.) or doctors of osteopathy

(D.O.)—if a condition requires treatment and care not within the scope of his practice. Most patients are treated in outpatient clinics, though private and hospital laboratories with registered technologists are often used to run analyses of body fluids. Modalities (electrogenic, thermogenic, mechanogenic, actinogenic, or cryogenic) are sometimes employed as an adjunctive means of therapy or diagnosis.

Among the fields closely related to chiropractic is osteopathic medicine, which has evolved from a similar theory and which has developed along similar paths. Like osteopathy, chiropractic theory first developed in the nineteenth century, and its pioneers were not generally accepted by practitioners of traditional medicine. The nineteenth-century founder of chiropractic, Daniel David Palmer, established chiropractic theory in 1895. Although some of his ideas have been modified, the profession still remains dedicated to his idea of the "natural healing process."

Like other professions, chiropractic sought to elevate its educational status early in its history. A Committee on Educational Status was organized by the National Chiropractic Association in 1935; in 1938 this committee merged with the Council on Chiropractic Examining Boards to become the Commission on Educational Standards, now known as the Council on Chiropractic Education (CCE). By 1939 the commission completed work on educational criteria for chiropractic colleges, and inspectors were sent to evaluate applicant institutions.

Chiropractic education has changed rapidly since 1974, when the CCE was recognized. The CCE's emphasis on educational quality has, in turn, had an immediate effect on state licensing boards. The Federation of Chiropractic Licensing Boards has recommended to the state boards that "all applicants for licensure who matriculate in a chiropractic college after October 1, 1975, must present evidence of having graduated from a chiropractic college having status with the Commission on Accreditation of the Council on Chiropractic Education." As of February 1976, thirty-eight states had adopted the federation's resolution, and five others were in the process of adopting it. In 1976 thirty-one states required attendance in approved postgraduate educational programs as a prerequisite to annual license renewal. The state of Colorado adopted the first such chiropractic statute in 1933.

There are thirteen chiropractic colleges in the United States. Those colleges which have CCE recognition have uniform requirements for admission, with an emphasis on chemistry, the biological sciences, English, and psychology; two years of pre-professional college work and four years of professional training are minimum educational requirements. As of February 1976 eight colleges had obtained status with the CCE:

Columbia Institute of Chiropractic (1919)
Glen Head, Box 167
New York, New York 11545

Logan College of Chiropractic (1935)
430 Schoettler Road, Box 100
Chesterfield, Missouri 63017

Los Angeles College of Chiropractic (1911)
920 East Broadway
Glendale, California 91205

National College of Chiropractic (1906)
200 East Roosevelt Road
Lombard, Illinois 60148

Northwestern College of Chiropractic (1941)
1834 South Mississippi Blvd.
St. Paul, Minnesota 55116

Palmer College of Chiropractic (1895)
1000 Brady Street
Davenport, Iowa 52803

Texas Chiropractic College (1908)
5912 Spenser Highway
Pasadena, Texas 77505

Western States Chiropractic College (1903)
2900 NE 132nd Avenue
Portland, Oregon 97230

The chiropractic colleges recognized by the CCE have encouraged research, which has developed two lines of procedure: research initiated in the colleges, financed through the Foundation for Chiropractic Education and Research (FCER); and research under the National Institute of Neurological and Communicative Disorders and Stroke (NINCDS) fellowship program.

Students from countries other than the United States are accepted for admission to the CCE-recognized colleges if they meet the same educational prerequisites as American students. Chiropractors who have matriculated at CCE-recognized colleges may obtain licensure in the Virgin Islands and Puerto Rico and within any United States jurisdiction. The CCE does not recognize chiropractic colleges from outside the United States, although representatives are invited to attend council meetings (as are nonaccredited colleges). Administrative representatives from nonaccredited institutions and from colleges in countries other than the United States have a voice but do not exercise a vote at the council meetings. Applicants to American colleges with CCE-accredited status must present a letter of approval from their national association to be considered for enrollment.

Requirements for licensure in countries outside the United States vary. In North America only one college, the Canadian Memorial Chiropractic College in Toronto, Ontario, exists beyond the borders of the United States. In Europe the Anglo-European College of Chiropractic is located in Bournemouth, England; and in the Southern Hemisphere there is the International College of Chiropractic in Melbourne, Australia.

Levels and Programs of Study

Programs of study in chiropractic lead to the Doctor of Chiropractic degree (D.C.). The curriculum is preceded by sixty hours of preprofessional work in areas specified by the CCE and at a level not less than a "C" average. The professional course of study is presented over a minimum period of eight semesters, or the equivalent, for a total of not less than 4200 hours.

Course content covers the basic sciences and includes such subjects as anatomy

(gross anatomy, osteology, myology, embryology, histology, and splanchnology with emphasis on neurology), physiology (including physiology of blood and lymph, circulation, respiration, excretion, digestion, metabolism, endocrines, special senses, and nervous system), chemistry (inorganic, organic, biochemistry, and nutrition), pathology, bacteriology, hygiene, sanitation and public health, diagnosis (physical, clinical, and laboratory), gynecology, obstetrics and pediatrics, X-ray (technique, interpretation, and radiation hazards), geriatrics, dermatology, syphilology, toxicology, psychology, and psychiatry. Chiropractic clinical competence is also emphasized in all programs of study.

RALPH D. STOAKS

Major International and National Organizations

INTERNATIONAL

European Chiropractors' Union
Zuchwilerstrasse 10
4500 Solothurn, Switzerland

International Chiropractors Association (ICA)
741 Brady Street
Davenport, Iowa 52808 USA

NATIONAL

A sampling of the national organizations in the field includes:

Australia:
    Australian Chiropractors' Association
    6 Pound Road
    Homsby, New South Wales

Belgium:
    Association des chiropraticiens belges
    5 rue de la Limite
    Brussels

Canada:
    Canadian Chiropractic Association
    1900 Bayview Avenue
    Toronto 17, Ontario

Denmark:
    Danish Chiropractors' Association
    Sdr. Boulevard 14
    Maribo

France:
    French Chiropractic Association
    29 rue Pastorelli
    Nice 06000

Hong Kong:
Hong Kong Chiropractors' Association
Room 1403, Tak Shing House
20 Des Voeux Road C.

Japan:
Japanese Chiropractic Association
5-9, 3-chome Kita-Aoyama
Minato-ku, Tokyo

New Zealand:
New Zealand Chiropractors Association
Box 2858
Wellington

Norway:
Norwegian Chiropractic Association
Bardagarden
Fredrikstad

South Africa:
Chiropractic Association of South Africa
29 Union Club Gebou Buildings
69 Joubert Street
2001 Johannesburg

Sweden.
Swedish Chiropractic Association
Karlbergsvägen 26
Stockholm

Switzerland:
Swiss Chiropractic Association
Rathausgasse 9
5000 Aarau

United Kingdom:
British Chiropractors Association
Mountpottinger House, The Mount
Belfast 5, Northern Ireland

United States:
American Chiropractic Association
3209 Ingersoll
Des Moines, Iowa 50312

Council on Chiropractic Education (CCE)
3209 Ingersoll
Des Moines, Iowa 50312

Foundation for Chiropractic Education
and Research
3209 Ingersoll
Des Moines, Iowa 50312

Principal Information Sources

GENERAL

Guides to the literature include:

Klein, L. *Chiropractic: An International Bibliography, 1879–1975.* Lombard, Illinois: National College of Chiropractic, forthcoming.

Overviews and standard texts include:

Basic Chiropractic Procedural Manual. Des Moines, Iowa: American Chiropractic Association, 1973.

Biedermann, F. *Grundsätzliches zur Chiropraktik vom ärztlichen Standpunkt aus.* (4th ed.) Heidelberg, Federal Republic of Germany: Haug, 1968.

Forster, A. L. *Principles and Practice of Spinal Adjustment for the Use of Students and Practitioners.* (2nd ed.) Chicago: The Author, 1920.

Harper, W. D. *Anything Can Cause Anything: A Correlation of Dr. Daniel David Palmer's Principles of Chiropractic.* (2nd ed.) Seabrook, Texas: The Author, 1966.

Homewood, A. E. *The Neurodynamics of the Vertebral Subluxation.* Toronto, Ontario: The Author, 1963.

Homewood, A. E. *The Chiropractor and the Law.* Toronto, Ontario: Chiropractic Publishers, 1965.

Illi, F. W. *The Vertebral Column, Life-Line of the Body.* Lombard, Illinois: National College of Chiropractic, 1975.

Janse, J. J. *Chiropractic Principles and Technic: For Use by Students and Practitioners.* Lombard, Illinois: National College of Chiropractic, 1947.

Laabs, W. *Atlas der Chiro-Gymnastik.* Ulm/Donau, Federal Republic of Germany: Haug, 1963.

Lake, T. T. *Treatment by Neuropathy and the Encyclopedia of Physical and Manipulative Therapeutics.* Philadelphia: The Author, 1946.

Levine, M. *The Structural Approach to Chiropractic.* New York: Comet, 1964.

Liekens, M. *Belgian Chiropractic Research Notes.* (8th ed.) Brussels: The Author, 1970.

Logan, H. B. *Textbook of Logan Basic Methods: From the Original Manuscript of Hugh B. Logan.* St. Louis, Missouri: The Author, 1950.

Palmer, B. J. *The Philosophy of Chiropractic.* (6th ed.) Davenport, Iowa: Palmer College of Chiropractic, 1920.

Peper, W. *Technik der Chiropraktik.* (6th rev. ed.) Ulm/Donau, Federal Republic of Germany: Haug, 1958.

Reinert, O. C. *Chiropractic Procedure and Practice.* (Rev. 3rd ed.) Florissant, Missouri: The Author, 1972.

Schwartz, H. S. *Mental Health and Chiropractic: A Multidisciplinary Approach.* New York: Sessions, 1973.

Verner, J. R. *The Science and Logic of Chiropractic.* (8th ed.) Brooklyn, New York: The Author, 1956.

Weiant, C. W. *The Case for Chiropractic in the Literature of Medicine.* New York: The Author, 1945.

Weiant, C. W., and Goldschmidt, S. *Medicine*

and Chiropractic. (5th ed.) Lombard, Illinois: National College of Chiropractic, 1975.

Zukschwerdt, L. *Wirbelgelenk und Bandscheibe: Ihre Beziehung zum Vertebragenen Schmerz. Zugleich eine Stellungnahme zur Chiropraktik und zur Frage der Begutachtung.* Stuttgart, Federal Republic of Germany: Hippokrates Verlag, 1960.

Special studies include:

Kuby, A. "The Chiropractic Patient." Unpublished thesis, University of Chicago, 1965.

Leis, G. L. "The Professionalization of Chiropractic." Unpublished doctoral dissertation, State University of New York at Buffalo, 1971.

Lin, P. L. "The Chiropractor, Chiropractic, and Process: A Study of the Sociology of an Occupation." Unpublished doctoral dissertation, University of Missouri, Columbia, 1972.

Wardwell, W. I. "Social Strain and Social Adjustment in the Marginal Role of the Chiropractor." Unpublished doctoral dissertation, Harvard University, Cambridge, Massachusetts, 1951. A classic in the field.

Wrestler, F. A. "The Development of Professional Identification Among Chiropractic Students." Unpublished doctoral dissertation, University of Maryland, College Park, 1972.

Sources dealing with education in the field include:

ACA Journal of Chiropractic. Des Moines, Iowa: American Chiropractic Association, 1964–. Includes regular features on chiropractic colleges and reports from the Council on Chiropractic Education.

La chiropraxie et l'ostéopathie: Rapport de Gerald Lacroix et Bertrand Marcotte. Quebec: Commission royale d'enquête sur la chiropraxie et l'ostéopathie, 1964.

Education Standards for Chiropractic Colleges. Des Moines, Iowa: Council on Chiropractic Education, 1976–.

Firman, G. J., and Goldstein, M. S. "The Future of Chiropractic: A Psychosocial View." *New England Journal of Medicine,* 1975, *293,* 639–642.

Firman, G. J., and Goldstein, M. S. "Letter: Chiropractic." *New England Journal of Medicine,* 1975, *294,* 346.

Hidde, O. L. "Accrediting Chiropractic Education." *ACA Journal of Chiropractic,* 1974, *11,* 12–13.

Independent Practitioners Under Medicare: A Report to the Congress. Washington, D.C.: U.S. Department of Health, Education and Welfare, 1969.

Mills, D. L. *Study of Chiropractors, Osteopaths and Naturopaths in Canada.* Ottawa, Ontario: Royal Commission on Health Services, 1966.

Official Directory of Chiropractic and Basic Science Examining Boards with Licensure and Practice Statistics. Long Beach, California: Federation of Chiropractic Licensing Boards, annual. Includes educational requirements for the United States and Canada, the standard basic curriculum, and a listing of chiropractic colleges.

Histories include:

Finlay, M. "Osteopathy and Chiropractic." *Manchester Medical Gazette,* 1971, *50,* 26–29.

Janse, J. J. "History of the Development of Chiropractic Concepts—Chiropractic Terminology." Paper presented at the National Institute of Neurological Diseases and Stroke, National Institutes of Health, Workshop on the Research Status of Spinal Manipulative Therapy, Bethesda, Maryland, February 1975.

Schiotz, E. H. "Manipulasjonsbehandling av columa under medisinsk-historick synsvinkel: Belyst ved primitiv-og folkemedisin, osteopatia og kiropraktikk. ("Manipulation Treatment of the Spinal Column from the Medical-Historical Viewpoint: Illustrated by Primitive and Folk Medicine, Osteopathy, and Chiropractic.") *Tidsskrift for den norske laegeforen,* 1958, *78,* 359–372 (April 14); 429–438 (May 1); 946–950 (Sept. 1); 1003–1021 (Oct. 15). This article has been translated into English by the National Institutes of Health (NIH Translation 75–22C).

CURRENT BIBLIOGRAPHIES

The Archives: An Anthology of Literature Relative to the Science of Chiropractic. Toronto, Ontario: Canadian Memorial College, 1976–.

Excerpta Medica. Section 19: *Rehabilitation and Physical Medicine.* Amsterdam: Excerpta Medica Foundation, 1958–.

Die Wirbelsäule in Forschung und Praxis. Stuttgart, Federal Republic of Germany: Hippokrates Verlag, 1957–.

PERIODICALS

ACA (American Chiropractic Association) Journal of Chiropractic, Archives of the California Chiropractic Association (US), *Canadian Chiropractic Association. Journal, Chiropractic Journal* (US), *Digest of Chiropractic Economics* (US), *European Chiropractic Union. Bulletin* (Belgium), *International Review of Chiropractic* (US), *JCC: The Journal of Clinical Chiropractic* (US), *Journal of the Australian Chiropractors' Association, Manuelle Medizin* (FRG), *Swiss Chiropractic Association. Annals.*

HANDBOOKS AND TERMINOLOGY

Basic Chiropractic Procedural Manual. Des Moines, Iowa: American Chiropractic Association, 1973.

"Chiropractic Current Procedural Terminology and Relative Value Study (With Common ICDA Numbers for Optional Use)." *ACA Journal of Chiropractic,* 1975, *12,* 1–8. Supplement, Nov. 1975.

DIRECTORIES

ACA Membership Directory, Des Moines, Iowa: American Chiropractic Association, annual.

European Chiropractors' Union Directory. Dijon, France: European Chiropractors' Union, annual. Includes names and addresses of individual and national members of the European Chiropractors' Union, national and state chiropractic associations in the United States, chiropractic colleges, and chiropractic periodicals.

ICA Membership Directory. Davenport, Iowa: International Chiropractics Association, annual.

Official Directory of Chiropractic and Basic Science Examining Boards with Licensure and Practice Statistics. Long Beach, California: Federation of Chiropractic Licensing Boards, annual.

[Bibliography prepared by Lawrence Klein.]

CHURCH COLLEGES

See Religious Influences in Higher Education: Protestantism.

CINEMATOGRAPHY

See Photography and Cinematography (field of study).

CITY AND REGIONAL PLANNING (Field of Study)

City and regional planning is concerned not only with the structure of the built environment but also with the social, economic, political, and technological forces that affect the everyday lives of men and women in residential, work, and recreational settings. For planners operating at the neighborhood, metropolitan, or national level, in the public or the private sector, the tasks are the same: to define goals, to formulate and implement programs and policies responsive to individual and group needs, and to allocate efficiently and equitably the economic and natural resources of various communities.

Unlike architects and civil engineers, city and regional planners work at a larger scale than a single building or an engineering project. Although some planners have been involved in the design and construction of entirely new cities and towns, most of the townscapes or cityscapes with which planners are concerned have evolved over hundreds of years. Thus, planners often must pinpoint particular environmental qualities that ought to be preserved or determine the consequences of alternative investment or development decisions.

The planner is often described as a "generalist with a specialty." Specialties are thought of in functional terms (housing, transportation, land use, health care) or in terms of the geographical levels at which decision making takes place (neighborhood planning, town planning, regional planning, planning for international development). Subspecialties within the planning field are also described in terms of the roles that planners are called upon to play: manager, designer, regulator, advocate, evaluator, futurist. In the United States, planners sometimes characterize themselves as either "physically oriented"—concerned with land use, public facilities, and development—or "socially oriented"—concerned with health, education, manpower, and other social service issues. This distinction, however, is beginning to fade.

Planning emerged from landscape architecture and civil engineering, and the field has broadened considerably in response to the growing realization that urbanization involves far more than the manipulation of land uses and buildings. Many graduate programs in city and regional planning in the mid 1970s, consequently, require their students to have backgrounds in social science, natural science, law and jurisprudence, mathematics, statistics, and computer science. Because of the interdisciplinary nature of planning, professionals in related fields, such as civil engineering, architecture, public administration, law, community organization, real estate development, and public policy analysis, often assist in the administration of municipal and regional planning efforts.

While it is possible to trace the origins of city planning in the United States to the earliest settlers, who were forced to structure their own communities, the 1893 Columbian Exposition in Chicago is most often cited as the beginning of planning in the United States. Other seminal influences in the planning profession include the efforts of muckrakers, housing reformers, and good-government advocates in the early 1900s; the development of urban sociology in Chicago in the 1920s and 1930s, which "served to document the conditions of urban living and shifted attention from the aesthetic of urban form to an analytical geography concerned with the social and economic landscape of the city" (Alonso, 1967, p. 581); the court's decision to uphold municipal zoning powers in response to the chaotic growth of crowded urban areas, especially in the East; and the rapid proliferation of automobiles, highways, and other transportation improvements that spread out the city and accelerated the process of land conversion.

The British version of city planning, called *town planning*, began in the mid 1960s. Before that time, the reconstruction of London after World War II had demonstrated that an architectural approach alone was inadequate. In 1947 the passage of the Town Planning Act introduced the idea that the use of land is important in planning—an idea that transformed planning thought and practice. The continental version of planning, sometimes referred to as *urbanism*, began with the reconstruction after World War I in 1919. The nature of planning gradually changed until, after World War II, the early emphasis on esthetics and the architectural and geometric approach were replaced by the idea of "urban functionalism," which stressed the achievement of the highest quality at the lowest building and maintenance cost. The application of scientific principles to planning for both urban and rural areas could result in the reduction of waste. Both the British town planning and the French urbanism are closer to the physical design tradition and further from the social sciences than United States city planning.

In the United States four important shifts in the thinking of urban and regional planners have occurred since the early 1960s. The first involved a rekindling of concern for urban poverty and other social problems. While the social sciences have been important in city and regional planning since the late 1920s, the "urban crisis" of the 1960s refocused the planning profession on the need to link social policy considerations to physical planning. The problems *in* cities took on importance equal to the problems *of* cities.

A second shift, related in part to the first, stemmed from criticisms of the federal urban renewal efforts in the 1960s. Attempts to level slums and blighted areas in central cities across the country came under sharp attack from within and outside the planning profession. Many critics charged that viable neighborhoods were being destroyed in the name of progress and business improvement. In recent years, the revitalization of declining urban neighborhoods has replaced their wholesale demolition.

Planners have also been criticized for planning *for*, but not *with*, community residents. This concern for citizen participation was largely stimulated by the federal government's emphasis on "maximum feasible participation" of community representatives in areas impacted by federal programs. Planning has come to be viewed in more political terms than ever before. The poor and the disadvantaged, distrustful of the plans drawn up by planners working directly for "city hall," now want their own "advocate planners" to prepare recommendations and proposals to serve their needs.

A fourth shift in planning practice in the United States involves the introduction of new computer-based modeling techniques. In spite of the complexity of urban and regional development processes, there is a growing belief that, with the aid of highly sophisticated computer software, the probable impact of alternative public policies and programs can be predicted. This effort to develop a more "scientific" approach to planning has long been an underlying theme in the profession, but advances in computer science have given it renewed importance.

In the United States the first degree in planning was offered at Harvard University in 1923; by 1945 nine other universities were offering degrees, and by 1975 more than 4500 students were enrolled in over seventy-five planning and related degree programs. Most of these degrees are offered at the graduate level, and more than twenty schools offer a Ph.D. in urban and regional planning. Undergraduate degrees in urban studies or urban life have been initiated, but these are not really professional degrees.

In Canada the first teaching program in physical planning was instituted in 1947 at McGill University in Montreal. During the early 1950s graduate programs were established at the Universities of British Columbia, Manitoba, and Toronto. By 1960 professional education was available in French at the University of Montreal. In 1975 there were more than 150 students enrolled in the six graduate schools of planning in Canada. The sixth is a new program at the University of Waterloo.

The education of planners in the United Kingdom is guided by the Royal Town Planning Institute in London, which governs and conducts examinations for candidates. In 1909 the institute recognized the department of civil design at the University of Liverpool, the first school to be so recognized. By 1958 there were twelve schools of planning in the United Kingdom. These schools offer two main types of courses: four- or five-year undergraduate courses

for entrants straight from school and three-year part-time or two-year full-time postgraduate courses for graduates in allied disciplines.

Although schools of architecture and, in some cases, departments of civil engineering offer courses in town planning as part of the curriculum in Scandinavian universities, there is only one advanced planning program—at the Nordic Institute for Town and Country Planning incorporated in 1968 in Stockholm. Candidates are drawn from the five Nordic countries and must have had some professional experience.

In the Federal Republic of Germany planners normally received their academic training in a related field covering some aspects of planning. In the late 1960s, however, full-time postgraduate courses were offered by the *Technische Hochschule* at Karlsruhe and the *Technische Universität München* in Munich. Programs are not yet available for training planners in the theoretical aspects of the field.

Until the late 1960s qualification to be a planner in France consisted of a diploma in architecture and a two-year course at the University of Paris Institute of Town Planning, which was first offered in 1915. Until 1969, when two other institutes of planning and development were formed at Grenoble and Aix-en-Provence, the institute in Paris had the only program devoted exclusively to the planning field.

In South America there are programs in planning in Argentina and Brazil. Since the 1950s, the faculty of architecture and town planning at Buenos Aires University has granted a degree in town planning to architects, engineers, and surveyors who complete a two- to three-year graduate course on a part-time basis. A two-year postgraduate course leading to the title of city planner has been established for architects and engineers in Pôrto Alegre, Belo Horizonte, and Rio de Janeiro.

Formal education in town and country planning was begun in India in 1956, with the establishment of an independent school for instruction in Delhi. At the same time, the department of architecture of the Indian Institute of Technology at Kharagpur (in West Bengal) started a course in urban and regional planning for graduates in architecture, engineering, and the social sciences. Three more institutions, in Madras, Poona, and Bombay, offer part-time courses in town and regional planning at the postgraduate level.

In Japan few schools offer urban planning, but there are university departments related to urban planning, including the urban engineering department at the University of Tokyo and the social engineering department established in 1967 at the Tokyo Institute of Technology.

In 1946 the first planning course was set up in South Africa in the department of architecture at the University of the Witwatersrand, Johannesburg, and in 1964 the first four-year undergraduate course in the country was established. There are also well-established postgraduate planning courses in the universities at Natal and Pretoria. Town planning as an independent academic study is well advanced in South Africa, but it emphasizes settlément policy rather than its esthetic or technical aspects.

There are facilities for training in town and country planning in each of the capital cities of the six states in Australia. The master's degree is offered at the University of Sydney, the University of Queensland, and the University of Adelaide. Diploma courses are available at Queensland Institute of Technology, South Australia Institute of Technology, Hobart Technical College, the University of Melbourne, and Western Australia Institute of Technology.

Urban planning education started in Romania at the beginning of the twentieth century at the *Institutul politehnic "Gh. Gheorghiu-Dej"* of Bucharest. After World War II, town planning education in Romania continued in the Institute of Architecture at Bucharest. In 1970 city planning departments were established at the polytechnic institutes of Cluj, Iaşi, and Timişoara. In the late 1950s five postgraduate courses were created in Poland in the major technical universities, and a postgraduate course for regional planners was established at the Central School for Planning and Statistics in Warsaw. In the Soviet Union specialists in planning and construction are trained at architectural and structural engineering institutes.

There are, of course, differences in emphasis in the educational programs in urban and regional planning throughout the world. The United States has moved the furthest from the strict physical orientation of town planning, but many other countries are also beginning to broaden their educational programs to include the social sciences in their planning curricula. Ironically, the countries with the strongest centralized governments and most elaborately managed economies have less commitment to the training of urban and regional planners, while the United States, with one of the least publicly "planned" or "controlled" economies, has a more extensive commitment to urban and regional planning than any other nation in the world.

[*Note:* **W. Alonso,** "Cities and City Planners," in H. Wentworth Eldredge (Ed.), *Taming Megalopolis* (Garden City, New York: Doubleday, 1967), vol. 2, pp. 581–596.]

LAWRENCE SUSSKIND

Levels and Programs of Study

Programs in urban planning generally require as a minimum prerequisite a secondary education and lead to the following awards: certificate or diploma, bachelor's degree (B.Arch., B.Sc.), master's degree (M.A., M.C.P., M.R.P., M.V.P., M.Sc.), the doctorate (Ph.D) or their equivalents. Programs deal with the principles and practices of city and regional planning and consist of classroom work, seminar or group discussion, and laboratory and practical demonstrations.

Programs that lead to an award not equivalent to a first university degree deal primarily with the technological and practical aspects of urban planning rather than with the underlying theoretical and scientific principles. Principal course content usually includes the following: the history of modern urban development, typical urban planning projects, social and institutional factors involved in physical urban planning, the role of urban transportation systems, construction of models using various materials, and the graphics of community development. Most programs of this kind also involve study of relevant specialties in sociology, economics, psychology, structural architecture, mathematics, civil engineering, and geography. Some programs also include statistics, computer programing, and systems design.

Programs that lead to a first university degree stress the theoretical and scientific principles of urban planning. These programs also include projects designed to develop an appreciation of city and regional planning techniques and of the practical problems involved. Principal course content usually includes the history of modern urban development, contemporary urban problems, urban planning projects, principles of urban planning, social and institutional determinants for physical urban planning, quantitative methods in urban planning, urban transportation systems in relation to community planning, regional planning and development, metropolitan area development, and problems and methods of urban redevelopment. Background courses often include processes and problems of social change, urban sociology, architecture, economics, political science, geography, psychology, natural sciences, mathematics, statistics, and computer science.

Programs that lead to a postgraduate university degree deal with advanced specialties in urban planning. Emphasis is placed on original research work as substantiated by the presentation and defense of a scholarly thesis or dissertation. Principal subject matter areas within which courses and research projects tend to fall include the history of city or regional planning, the history of modern urban development, principles of urban land use, principles and problems of urban planning, social and institutional determinants for physical urban planning, regional planning development, metropolitan area development, urban transportation and traffic movements in relation to community planning, urban renewal or redevelopment, community planning as a function of local, national, or provincial governments. Subject areas within which background studies tend to fall include relevant specialties from architecture programs; relevant specialties from engineering programs (particularly civil engineering); and relevant specialties from the fine and applied arts, social sciences, natural sciences, the humanities, law and jurisprudence, mathematics, statistics, and computer science.

[This section was based on UNESCO's *International Standard Classification of Education (ISCED)* (Paris: UNESCO, 1976).]

Major International and National Organizations

INTERNATIONAL

Commonwealth Association of Planners (CAP)
18 Northumberland Avenue
London WC2N 5BJ, England

Council of Europe
Committee on Co-operation in Municipal and
  Regional Matters
avenue de l'Europe
67006 Strasbourg, France

Eastern Regional Organization for Planning
  and Housing
Organisation régionale orientale pour
  l'habitation et l'urbanisme (EAROPH)
4-A Ring Road
Indraprastha Estate
New Delhi, India

Inter-American Planning Society
Sociedad interamericana de planificación
  (SIAP)
Carrera 16 No 39-82, Apartado Aéreo 21573
Bogotá, Colombia

International City Management Association
1140 Connecticut Avenue NW
Washington, D.C. 20036 USA

International Council for Building Research,
  Studies and Documentation (CIB)
Conseil international du bâtiment pour la
  recherche, l'étude et la documentation (CIB)
704 Weena, P.O. Box 299
Rotterdam, Netherlands

International Federation for Housing and
  Planning (IFHP)
Fédération internationale pour l'habitation,
  l'urbanisme, et l'aménagement des
  territoires (FIHUAT)
Wassenåarseweg 43
The Hague 2018, Netherlands

International Society of City and Regional
  Planners (ISOCARP)
Association internationale des urbanistes
Wassenaarseweg 43
The Hague 2018, Netherlands

International Union of Architects
Union internationale des architects (UIA)
1 rue d'Ulm 75005
Paris, France

Organization of American States
General Secretariat—Division of Urban
  Development
Department of Social Affairs
Washington, D.C. 20006 USA

Permanent and International Committee of
  Underground Town Planning and
  Construction (PICUTPC)
Comité permanent international des techniques
  et de l'urbanisme souterrains (CPITUS)
94 rue St. Lazare
75009 Paris, France

United Nations, Centre for Housing, Building
  and Planning
Department of Economic and Social Affairs
United Nations Secretariat
New York, New York 10017 USA

United Nations Economic and Social
  Commission for Asia and the Far East
  (ESCAP)
Sub-Committee on Housing, Building and
  Planning
Sala Santitham
Bangkok, Thailand

United Nations Economic Commission for
  Africa (ECA)
Commission économique des Nations unies
  pour l'Afrique (CEA)
Africa Hall, P.O. Box 3001
Addis Ababa, Ethiopia

United Nations Economic Commission for
  Europe (ECE)
Committee on Housing, Building and Planning

Palais des Nations
Geneva, Switzerland

United Nations Economic Commission for
  Latin America (ECLA)
Central American Sub-Committee on Housing,
  Building and Planning
Santiago, Chile

NATIONAL

Australia:
  Australian Planning Institute
  P.O. Box 292
  Canberra, A.C.T.

Austria:
  Österreichisches Institut für
    Raumplanung
  Franz-Josefs-Kai 27
  1011 Vienna

Belgium:
  Fédération belge pour l'urbanisme et
    l'habitation, le développement et
    l'aménagement du territoire
  rue Montoyer 61
  1040 Brussels

Brazil:
  Instituto de arquitetos do Brazil
  4° Andar
  Rua Bento Freitas 306
  São Paulo

Canada:
  Town Planning Institute of Canada
  Suite 30, 46 Elgin Street
  Ottawa, Ontario K1P 5K6

Chile:
  Sociedad chilena de planificación y
    desarrollo—PLANDES
  Monéda 973
  Santiago

Denmark:
  Foreningen af byplanloeggere
  Holbergsgade 23
  Copenhagen

Federal Republic of Germany:
  Deutscher Verband für Wohnungswesen,
    Städtebau und Raumplanung
  Wrangelstrasse 12
  5 Cologne—Mülheim 80

France:
  Société française des urbanistes
  52 rue Mathurin Régnier
  75015 Paris

Hungary:
  Hungarian Society of Urbanism
  Magyar urbanisztikai tarsasag
  Rakoczi ut 7
  Budapest VIII

Netherlands:
Bond van Nederlandse
stedebouwkundigen
Koninginneweg 10
Hilversum

Poland:
Towarzystwo urbanistów polskich
ul. Nowogrodzka 31
Warsaw

Sweden:
Föreningen för samhällsplanering
Storgatan 19, Box 5501
Stockholm

United Kingdom:
Royal Tour Planning Institute
26 Portland Place
London W1N 4BE, England

United States:
American Institute of Planners
1776 Massachusetts Avenue NW
Washington, D.C. 20036

City Management Association
1140 Connecticut Avenue NW
Washington, D.C. 20036

For additional national and international organizations see:

Directory of Building Research Information and Development Organizations. Rotterdam: International Council for Building Research, Studies and Documentation, 1971.
Directory of European Associations. Beckenham, Kent, England: CBD Research, 1971.
HUD International Information Sources Series: Urban Institutions Abroad. Washington, D.C.: U.S. Department of Housing and Urban Development, Office of International Affairs, 1974.
Whittick, A. (Ed.) *Encyclopedia of Urban Planning.* New York: McGraw-Hill, 1974.
Yearbook of International Organizations. Brussels: Union of International Associations, biennial.

Principal Information Sources

GENERAL

Guides to the literature of urban planning are:

Beck, G. M. K. *A Guide to Sources of Information in Planning.* London: Centre for Environmental Studies, 1973. Information Paper CES IP 12. British emphasis; includes major directories and reference books, sources of information on current research, indexes and abstracting services, and bibliographies.

Bestor, G. C. *City Planning Bibliography.* New York: American Society of Civil Engineers, 1972. Covers historical as well as current materials, and includes information on periodicals, organizations and associations, and bibliographical services; United States emphasis, but other countries are included.
Branch, M. C. *Comprehensive Urban Planning: A Selective Annotated Bibliography with Related Materials.* Beverly Hills, California: Sage Publications, 1970. Includes books and articles on city planning as well as other aspects of urban planning; includes countries other than the United States; lists planning agencies in the United States and Canada.
Bryfogle, R. C. *City in Print: A Bibliography.* Morristown, New Jersey: General Learning Press, 1974. Valuable for its listing of maps, audiovisual materials, simulation games, and multimedia kits; foreign-language works have been largely excluded, resulting in a North American and English emphasis; lists more than 1200 books.
Sable, M. H. *Latin American Urbanization: A Guide to the Literature, Organizations and Personnel.* Metuchen, New Jersey: Scarecrow Press, 1971. Extensive bibliographical listing of books and articles covering all aspects of urban affairs on Latin America. Lengthy listing of research centers and societies.
White, B. *Sourcebook of Planning Information.* London: Clive Bingley, 1971. Information sources discussed are primarily British; valuable discussion of different types of sources.
White, B. *The Literature and Study of Urban and Regional Planning.* London: Routledge and Kegan Paul, 1974. Presents sources of information about planning, primarily as it operates within the United Kingdom; intended for use by students; includes a subject bibliography on the various aspects of planning and a listing of periodicals.

Historical perspectives are offered by:

Beneuolo, L. *The Origins of Modern Town Planning.* Cambridge, Massachusetts: MIT Press, 1967.
Geitkind, E. A. *International History of City Development.* (8 vols.) New York: Macmillan, 1964–1972. Vol. 1: *Urban Development in Central Europe* (1964); Vol. 2: *Urban Development in the Alpine and Scandinavian Countries* (1965); Vol. 3: *Urban Development in Southern Europe: Spain and Portugal* (1967); Vol. 4: *Urban Development in Southern Europe: Italy and Greece* (1969); Vol. 5: *Urban Development in Western Europe: France and Belgium* (1970); Vol. 6: *Urban Development in Western Europe:*

The Netherlands and Great Britain (1971); Vol. 7: *Urban Development in East Central Europe: Poland, Czechoslovakia and Hungary* (1972); Vol. 8: *Urban Development in Eastern Europe: Bulgaria, Romania and the U.S.S.R.* (1972). Covers up to the mid nineteenth century.

Mumford, L. *The Culture of Cities.* New York: Harcourt, Brace Jovanovich, 1938. A classic.

Mumford, L. *The City in History: Its Origins, Its Transformations and Its Prospects.* New York: Harcourt, Brace Jovanovich, 1961. Covers the development of the city from historical times to the 1950s.

Schneider, W. *Babylon Is Everywhere—The City as Man's Fate.* New York: McGraw-Hill, 1963. Covers seven thousand years of urban development.

Sjoberg, G. *The Pre-Industrial City.* New York: Free Press, 1960. Provides worldwide perspective of the structure and growth of cities.

Toynbee, A. *Cities on the Move.* New York: Oxford University Press, 1970.

Education sources dealing with urban planning education internationally are:

Cockburn, C. *The Provision of Planning Education.* London: Centre for Environmental Studies, 1970. Describes planning education in Great Britain.

Education for Planning: The Development of Knowledge and Capability for Urban Governance. Report of a Working Group at the Centre for Environmental Studies, London. Oxford, England: Pergamon Press, 1973. A report on the trends in planning, and the provision of education for planners, in the United Kingdom.

Godschalk, D. R. *Planning in America: Learning from Turbulence.* Washington, D.C.: American Institute of Planners, 1974. Papers from a symposium on present planning education in the United States and changes needed to meet future demands on the planning profession.

"Reshaping Planning Education." *Journal of the American Institute of Planners,* July 1970, *36* (4), entire issue. A discussion of the problems of planning education in the United States and the steps which might be taken to improve it.

Rizvi, A. A. *City and Regional Planning Education: Response by Selected North American Institutions to the Needs of Underdeveloped Countries.* Vancouver: University of British Columbia, School of Community and Regional Planning, 1971.

A Survey of European Programs: Education for Urbanization in the Developing Countries. New York: Ford Foundation, 1972. A survey of European universities that offer planning programs for people from developing countries.

Whittick, A. (Ed.) *Encyclopedia of Urban Planning.* New York: McGraw-Hill, 1974. Included in the descriptions of planning in each country are sections on the education and training of planners and on planning as a professional practice.

Works that provide a broad introduction to the field include:

Altshuler, A. *The City Planning Process.* Ithaca, New York: Cornell University Press, 1965.

Daxiadis, K. A. *Ekistics: An Introduction to the Science of Human Settlements.* New York: Oxford University Press, 1968.

Eldredge, H. W. (Ed.) *Taming Megalopolis.* Vol. 1: *What Is and What Could Be;* Vol. 2: *How to Manage an Urbanized World.* Garden City, New York: Doubleday, 1967. A series of readings on a variety of aspects of urban planning in developed and developing countries.

Ewald, W. (Ed.) *Environment for Man.* Bloomington: Indiana University Press, 1967.

Friedmann, J. R. P., and Alonso, W. *Regional Policy: Readings in Theory and Applications.* Cambridge, Massachusetts: MIT Press, 1975. Covers the many aspects of city and regional planning. Originally published as *Regional Development and Planning.*

Friend, J. K., and Jessop, W. N. *Local Government and Strategic Choice.* Beverly Hills, California: Sage Publications, 1969.

Gans, H. *People and Plans.* New York: Basic Books, 1968.

Keeble, L. *Principles and Practice of Town and Country Planning.* (4th ed.) London: Estates Gazette, 1969. Standard text on British town planning, practice, and theory.

Kruckeberg, D. A., and Silvers, A. L. *Urban Planning Analysis.* New York: Wiley, 1964.

Meyerson, M., and Banfield, E. *Politics, Planning and the Public Interest.* New York: Free Press, 1955.

Rabinovitz, F. F. *City Politics and Planning.* Chicago: Aldine, 1970.

Reissman, L. *The Urban Process.* New York: Free Press, 1964.

Rivlin, A. *Systematic Thinking for Societal Action.* Washington, D.C.: Brookings Institution, 1971.

Rodwin, L. *Nations and Cities: A Comparison of Strategies for Urban Growth.* Boston: Houghton Mifflin, 1970. Compares regional and national planning practices of Venezuela, Turkey, Great Britain, France, and the United States.

Rodwin, L., and others. *Planning Urban Growth*

and Regional Development. Cambridge, Massachusetts: MIT Press, 1969.

Rothman, J. *Planning and Organizing for Social Change.* New York: Columbia University Press, 1974.

Scott, M. *American City Planning.* Washington, D.C.: American Institute of Planners, 1968.

CURRENT BIBLIOGRAPHIES

Bibliographical and abstracting services which provide useful current information in the field are:

Bibliographia IULA-IFHP; New Publications in the Library. The Hague: International Union of Local Authorities and International Federation for Housing and Planning, 1958–. Includes summaries of books, reports, and conferences; English- and non-English-language coverage.

Ekistic Index. Athens, Greece: Athens Center of Ekistics, 1968–. Indexes articles from more than sixty English- and non-English-language periodicals. Covers various aspects of planning, particularly urban and regional development.

Exchange Bibliographies. Monticello, Illinois: Council of Planning Librarians, 1958–. More than one thousand bibliographies covering all aspects of planning in developed and developing countries.

Geo Abstracts: F: Regional and Community Planning. Norwich, England: University of East Anglia, 1972–. Coverage of more than ninety English- and foreign-language periodicals.

International Bibliography of the Social Sciences— Sociology/Bibliographie internationale des sciences sociales—Sociologie. London: Tavistock, 1952–. Urban studies and related subjects are included in this international listing of articles from more than one thousand journals.

Library Bulletin. London: Department of the Environment, Library, 1972–. Semimonthly annotated listing of books, journal articles, reports, and conference proceedings received in the Department of the Environment's library; international coverage with emphasis on British publications.

Public Affairs Information Service Bulletin. New York: Public Affairs Information Service, 1915–. A major general index which includes urban studies and planning; lists English- and non-English-language publications.

Sage Urban Studies Abstracts. Beverly Hills, California: Sage Publications, 1973–. Abstracts of articles appearing in primarily United States journals.

Urban Affairs Abstracts. Washington, D.C.: National League of Cities/United States Conference of Mayors, 1971–. Abstracts of articles from about 175 English-language journals.

United States Department of Housing and Urban Development. *Housing and Planning References.* Washington, D.C.: U.S. Government Printing Office, 1948–. Includes journal articles, books, reports, conferences; United States orientation.

PERIODICALS

Australian Planning Institute Journal; Build International (Netherlands), *Ekistics* (Greece), *Environment and Planning* (UK), *Habitat* (Canada), *Journal of the American Institute of Planners, Journal of Development Planning* (United Nations), *Journal of the Town Planning Institute* (UK), *Plan* (Sweden), *Plan* (Switzerland), *Planning, the ASPO Magazine* (US), *Regional Studies* (UK), *Town and Country Planning* (UK), *Town Planning Review* (UK), *Urban Affairs Quarterly* (US), *Urbanistica* (Italy), *La vie urbaine* (France).

For a more complete listing of periodicals see:

Bestor, G. C., and Jones, H. R. *City Planning Bibliography.* New York: American Society of Civil Engineers, 1972. An international listing of periodicals appears on pp. 383–403.

Ulrich's International Periodicals Directory. New York: Bowker, biennial.

ENCYCLOPEDIAS, DICTIONARIES, HANDBOOKS

Akademie für Raumforschung und Landesplanung. *Handwörterbuch der Raumforschung.* Hanover, Federal Republic of Germany: Gebrüder Janecke Verlag, 1966. Encyclopedia of planning terms and practices; articles are primarily in German, with some in French or English.

Chapin, F. S. *Urban Land Use Planning.* (2nd ed.) Urbana: University of Illinois Press, 1965. Concentrates on techniques involved in land use.

Claire, W. H. *Handbook on Urban Planning.* New York: Van Nostrand Reinhold, 1973. Text on procedures and techniques of the various aspects of urban planning; United States bias.

Goodman, W. I. *Principles and Practice of Urban Planning.* (4th ed.) Washington, D.C.: International City Management Association, 1968. Thorough coverage of the many aspects of planning.

International Glossary of Technical Terms Used in Housing and Town Planning. (2nd ed.) Amsterdam: International Federation for

Housing and Town Planning, 1955. Terms are in English, French, German, Italian, and Spanish.

International Union of Architects. *Vocabulaire international des termes d'urbanisme et d'architecture/Internationales Wörterbuch für Städtebau und Architektur/International Vocabulary of Town Planning and Architecture.* Paris: Société de diffusion des techniques du bâtiment et des travaux publics, 1970.

Keeble, L. *Principles and Practice of Town Planning.* (4th ed.) London: Estates Gazette, 1969. Standard text on British town planning practice and theory.

McKeever, J. R. *The Community Builders Handbook.* Washington, D.C.: Urban Land Institute, 1968.

Whittick, A. (Ed.) *Encyclopedia of Urban Planning.* New York: McGraw-Hill, 1974. Lengthy articles on planning in countries throughout the world; includes biographical information as well as definitions of planning terms; comprehensive in scope.

DIRECTORIES

Architectural Schools in North America. Washington, D.C.: Association of Collegiate Schools of Architecture, biennial. Includes a listing of North American universities and colleges that offer degrees in city and regional planning.

Education for Planning: The Development of Knowledge and Capability for Urban Governance. Report of a Working Group at the Centre for Environmental Studies, London. Oxford, England: Pergamon Press, 1973. Lists United Kingdom institutions that offer courses and degrees in urban and regional planning.

International Handbook of Universities. Paris: International Association of Universities, 1959–. Published triennially.

A Survey of European Programs: Education for Urbanization in the Developing Countries. New York: Ford Foundation, 1972. Lists European universities that offer planning programs open to people from developing countries; includes descriptions and comments on the programs.

Susskind, L. (Ed.) *Guide to Graduate Education in Urban and Regional Planning.* East Lansing, Michigan: Association of Collegiate Schools of Planning, 1974. Comprehensive guide to United States and Canadian universities that offer degrees in urban and regional planning.

Whittick, A. (Ed.) *Encyclopedia of Urban Planning.* New York: McGraw-Hill, 1974. Lists educational institutions in countries throughout the world which offer education in urban

studies and planning or related fields.

The World of Learning. London: Europa, 1947–. Published annually. Lists universities, colleges, institutions, research centers, and learned societies throughout the world.

RESEARCH CENTERS, INSTITUTIONS, INFORMATION CENTERS

Economic Commission for Europe Secretariat. *Directory of National Bodies Concerned with Urban and Regional Research.* New York: United Nations, 1968. Dated but still very useful; includes descriptions of activities and publications programs.

HUD International Information Sources Series: Urban Institutions Abroad. Washington, D.C.: United States Department of Housing and Urban Development, Office of International Affairs, 1974. Lists names and addresses of institutions by country.

Organization of Urban and Regional Research in European Countries. London: Centre for Environmental Studies, 1969. Description of research organizations in twenty-two European countries; also includes international research organizations.

Research Centers Directory: A Guide to University-Related and Other Nonprofit Organizations. (5th ed.) Detroit: Gale Research, 1975. Extensive list of United States organizations; includes institutions engaged in research in urban and regional studies.

Sable, M. H. *Latin American Urbanization: A Guide to the Literature, Organizations and Personnel.* Metuchen, New Jersey: Scarecrow Press, 1971. Lists research centers and societies dealing with urban affairs in Latin America.

University Urban Research Centers. (2nd ed.) Washington, D.C.: Urban Institute, 1971. Includes brief descriptions of activities of urban research centers in United States universities.

"Urban Studies Research Centers." In *Urban Affairs Quarterly* (US). Annual list appearing in March issue; includes United States and foreign research centers.

Winston, E. V. A. *Directory of Urban Affairs Information and Research Centers.* Metuchen, New Jersey: Scarecrow Press, 1970. Brief descriptions of United States urban affairs research centers.

World Index of Social Science Institutions: Research, Advanced Training, Documentation and Professional Bodies. Paris: UNESCO, 1970. Lists more than 1500 institutions; updated regularly.

[Bibliography prepared by Ann Longfellow.]

CIVIL DISORDERS
(Higher Education Report), United States

Civil Disorders (Washington, D.C.: U.S. Government Printing Office, 1968)—the report of the National Advisory Commission on Civil Disorders, under the chairmanship of Otto Kerner—addresses the broad historical and social origins of the urban riots of the 1960s in the United States and discusses the role of higher education in solving the dilemma of the ghetto.

The commission discovered a wide participation of ghetto school dropouts in the urban riots of the 1960s. It found that these youths attend schools that are often staffed by teachers less experienced or less qualified than those in schools serving primarily white middle-class students. It heard testimony that only 8 percent of poor high school graduates, most of whom are black, enter college, whereas nationally over 50 percent of secondary school graduates pursue higher study.

Increased access to higher education for urban dwellers would, in the commission's view, improve the relevance of school education for disadvantaged youth. It recommends a national effort to train specialists to teach urban school students and thereby eliminate the short supply of qualified instructors. This effort should include expansion of the Teacher Corps Program established under the Higher Education Act of 1965. Additional teachers should be trained under the Education Professions Development Act of 1968, which provides grants and fellowships to attract qualified persons to the education fields, as well as funds for educational institutes, workshops, and agencies. Efforts should also be made to train teachers from urban areas at teacher training institutions. Also recommended are special, intensive in-service training programs, which place student teachers in the inner-city schools.

Specific measures recommended to increase opportunity for higher learning for the urban poor are the expansion of the Upward Bound program of the Office of Economic Opportunity and the creation of special one-year pretertiary schools to prepare the disadvantaged for college. In addition, the commission suggests that federal financial assistance for higher education for the poor be strengthened.

CIVIL ENGINEERING
(Field of Study)

Civil engineering, a term first used in the eighteenth century by the rebuilder of the Eddystone lighthouse, John Smeaton, is a broad professional field involving public works projects. Although *civil* is a modern term meant to differentiate public and private works from "military" engineering, the practice itself began with the pyramids and irrigation works in Egypt, the architectural monuments of Greece, and the highways and waterworks of Rome—substantial accomplishments in eras when engineering was an empirical art.

Modern civil engineering practice includes the design and construction of highways, airfields, railroads, and canals (transportation engineering); water supply, treatment, and distribution works, and wastewater collection, treatment, and disposal works (environmental engineering); hydraulic, irrigation, flood control, and drainage works (hydraulic engineering); docks, harbor facilities, jetties, buildings, bridges, and dams (structural engineering); and foundations and tunnels (soil mechanics and foundation engineering). The civil engineer is also involved in studies and reports, planning, supervision, and management.

The civil engineer must have a solid background in mathematics, physics, chemistry, mechanics, hydraulics, thermodynamics, and other specialized areas of science and technology. His profession is still largely as defined, in part, by the charter granted to the Institution of Civil Engineers at London in 1828: "the art of directing the great sources of power in nature for the use and convenience of man"; in many respects, however, it has evolved from art to science. Some areas that were originally part of civil engineering have developed into other specializations, such as mechanical, electrical, industrial, and chemical engineering.

Civil engineers are employed in private consulting practice, by governmental agencies from the town and municipal level through state and national levels, by corporations, by military services, by research and development firms, and by academic institutions. Each civil engineering project is one-of-a-kind, designed to fit a particular set of economic, environmental, and physical conditions.

Few written works on engineering survive from antiquity. Two exceptions are the ten-volume work on architecture *(De Architectura)* by Marcus Vitruvius Pollio, Roman architect and engineer (first century B.C.), and a volume on the water supply of Rome by Sextus Frontinus, commissioner of Rome's water supply system (first century A.D.). The first technical school to teach civil engineering in the modern era was an outgrowth of the *Corps des ponts et chaussées,* established to build a system of national highways in France in 1716. Jean Perronet, engineer to Louis XV, transformed the staff of that organization into a technical school in 1747; it was given official status in 1775 as the *Ecole des ponts et chaussées,* the first engineering school in the world. Perronet has since been referred to as the father of civil engineering. Early British engineers began their careers as tradesmen, masons, and builders: James Brindley (1716–1772), the canal builder; John Rennie (1761–1821), who built London Bridge; John Smeaton (1724–1792), who founded the Society of Civil Engineers (now the Smeatonian Society); and Thomas Telford (1757–1834), a road builder who became first president of the Institution of Civil Engineers, founded in 1818. They worked from empirical knowledge of engineering principles and set the stage for the beginnings of formal education in civil engineering.

In 1794 the *Ecole polytechnique* was founded in Paris; it served as the model for the United States Military Academy at West Point, New York, founded in 1802. Other early schools of engineering and applied science include the *Bauakademie* in Berlin, 1799; the Polytechnic Institute of Vienna, 1815; and King's College in London, where civil engineering was first taught in 1838. The first chair in civil engineering was founded by Queen Victoria in 1840 at the University of Glasgow. Rensselaer Polytechnic Institute (RPI), founded in 1824 in Troy, New York, offered the first formal civil engineering course in the United States. B. F. Greene, director of RPI, studied programs in engineering education in Europe and reorganized work at RPI. His report, *The True Idea of a Polytechnic Institute,* published in 1855, had great influence on engineering curricula.

Education in civil engineering is now available in most countries. Prior to 1870 the curriculum included mathematics (algebra, geometry, trigonometry, and calculus); one year each of physics, chemistry, astronomy, geology, and a foreign language; two years of surveying and English; and courses in mechanics, construction, hydraulics, and earth work. Since 1870 the curriculum has changed radically in depth and specialization, but not in concept. The program requires a foundation in the mathematical and physical sciences, usually for the first two years, followed by courses in structures, environmental sciences, transportation, soils, and fluid mechanics. Engineering programs in the United States require about 20 percent of the credits in the humanities. Courses are also required in economics and verbal communication. European, Soviet Union, and Latin American engineering programs stress mastery of foreign languages, a feature evident only in doctoral programs in the United States.

Changes in technology—for example, the computer, model studies, remote sensing capabilities, and the development of new materials—have had an impact on civil engineering study and practice. Specialization within the field is now almost a necessity, and graduate study has become a common requirement. Most engineers find that continuing education throughout the professional career is needed to keep abreast of a rapidly changing profession. These changes have brought about a tremendous growth in graduate programs and enrollment and a corresponding interest in part-time education at both graduate and undergraduate levels. Prior to 1890, only six United States colleges conferred advanced degrees in engineering, and only three earned doctorates had been conferred by 1896; yet by 1921 more than forty schools were offering graduate work. By the 1960s almost every engineering school had developed graduate programs.

Apprenticeship was part of the training of civil engineers in the nineteenth century. This philosophy carried over to the twentieth century in somewhat modified form; the British developed the "sandwich" plan, and the United States developed the "cooperative" plan, involving alternating periods of academic study and subprofessional employment. These plans provide practical experience prior to graduation and help to produce graduates better equipped to participate professionally immediately after the baccalaureate degree.

Professional registration or its equivalent is required in most countries. In the United States graduation from an accredited degree program, several years of professional experience, and successful performance in written examinations are required for professional registration. Many other countries provide certification only through a professional society. In the United Kingdom a university graduate with three years of supervised training must be examined by the Institution of Civil Engineers before becoming a "chartered civil engineer."

After establishment of the Society of Civil Engineers in Britain (1771) and the Institution of Civil Engineers (1818), other societies sprang up all over continental Europe and made possible additional educational opportunities for civil engineers through technical meetings and professional journals. In the United States the Engineers Council for Professional Development (ECPD) has assisted engineering schools throughout the world in developing professionally accepted engineering curricula.

The growing need for technicians has resulted in the initiation of many associate degree (two-year) programs at technical institutes and Bachelor of Engineering Technology (B.E.T.) degree programs at some universities; many such programs are offered part time. In civil engineering technology, programs are available in surveying, drafting, building construction, and architectural drawing. By the 1960s about six thousand degrees in engineering technology were granted annually by technical institutes in the United States.

Engineering education in the United Kingdom can be obtained either in a full-time program at an approved university or through part-time attendance at a technical college. The curriculum in each case is established by the Institution of Civil Engineers. In Canada entrance requirements are very high; correspondingly fewer engineers are graduated annually than in many other countries.

In continental Europe technical universities are often supported and controlled by government. Only one institution each in Denmark, the Netherlands, and Finland grants engineering degrees; there are two each in Sweden and Switzerland and five in Belgium. The Federal Republic of Germany, Italy, and France, however, have many engineering degree-granting colleges. In Italy a five-year program of study is common, and graduate work leading to a Doctor of Engineering is available. *Istituti professionali* provide education at the technology level, but most technicians are trained through apprenticeship. In France the title *ingénieur* is awarded at about 150 schools, which emphasize practical experience for engineering technicians. In general, European schools have developed a practical approach to engineering curricula; on-the-job training has become a vital part of most programs. Engineers assume management positions in government and industry; therefore, courses in the social sciences have become prerequisites for professional practice.

Latin American engineering training often uses visiting United States faculty or depends directly on United States engineering schools. Some countries regularly subsidize students at United States colleges, but more and more engineering schools are being founded in Latin America. About one of seven college students is enrolled in engineering, and the majority of these are civil engineering students. The *ingeniero* degree requires five to six years of study. Graduate study is in its infancy, however; the first Latin American graduate civil engineering program was introduced at the *Universidad autónoma del estado de México*, in Toluca, Mexico, in 1959.

Japanese civil engineering curricula are modeled on those of the United States, with four-year baccalaureate degrees followed by master's and doctor's degree programs. Emphasis on the mathematical and physical sciences, rather than on engineering courses, is evident in Japan. The social sciences and humanities, including foreign languages, are emphasized in the first two years of most Japanese engineering curricula.

In the Soviet Union the first professional degree requires five years at a technical institute; the "candidate" degree is roughly equivalent to the United States master's degree. Two years of basic mathematics, chemistry, physics, history, and foreign language are followed by three years of specialization in civil engineering courses, such as water and wastewater technology, construction management, mechanics, safety engineering, economics, and building design, with emphasis on design projects throughout. The degree usually requires defense of an individual design project of some magnitude. Acceptance requirements for graduate study are relatively

rigorous; successful performance for the doctoral degree hinges on publication of articles in technical journals related to the individual's research over a lengthy period.

In the People's Republic of China, practical work, even factory work, accompanies academic involvement for most engineering students. Since every citizen must be a productive laborer, college students spend at least two years in physical labor in a people's commune or equivalent time in the People's Liberation Army. Entry into higher education requires approval of party leadership, and only those with high potential are accepted. The present three-year baccalaureate curriculum emphasizes specialization early in the program. Because half the time is spent off campus on a construction site or on a research project, teaching is linked with projects. Students are directed toward specialization by the government, depending on critical needs.

ROBERT L. MESERVE

Levels and Programs of Study

Programs in civil engineering generally require as a minimum prerequisite a secondary education, with emphasis on science subjects, and lead to the following awards: certificate or diploma, Bachelor of Science or Engineering, Master of Science or Engineering, the doctorate, or their equivalents. Programs deal with the principles and practices of civil engineering and consist of classroom and laboratory instruction and, on advanced levels, study, seminar or group discussion, and research in specialized areas of civil engineering.

Programs that lead to an award not equivalent to a first university degree deal with the principles and practices of civil engineering technology and provide training for careers in the many phases of the design and construction of structural projects such as buildings, bridges, dams, and highways, and in the planning, construction, inspection, and maintenance of municipal services. Programs usually last two or three years, full time. Principal course content usually includes some of the following:

physics, chemistry, mathematics, applied mechanics, computer science, engineering graphics, electrical circuits, surveying, construction methods, strength of materials, theory of structures, design of structures, mechanics of fluids, highway technology, reinforced concrete, structural steel design, hydraulics, sanitary technology, contracts and specifications, hydrology, and foundations.

Programs that lead to a first university degree deal primarily with the principles and practices of civil engineering. Principal course content usually includes some of the following: strength of materials, structural engineering, hydraulic engineering, soil mechanics and foundations, highway engineering, concrete and reinforced concrete construction, and water supply and sewer construction. Background courses usually include mathematics, natural sciences such as physics and chemistry, basic engineering sciences such as thermodynamics and fluid mechanics, and land surveying and photogrammetry.

Programs that lead to a postgraduate university degree deal with advanced studies in specialized areas of civil engineering. Emphasis is placed on original research work as substantiated by the presentation and defense of a scholarly thesis or dissertation. Principal subject matter areas within which courses and research projects tend to fall include soil engineering, theoretical soil mechanics, hydraulic transients, sediment transport, hydraulics of open channels, advanced hydrology, analysis of engineering structures, strength of materials, structural dynamics, plate and shell structures, stability and vibration of structures, water quality analysis, sanitary engineering, municipal engineering, railway engineering, and highway engineering. Subject areas within which background studies tend to fall include appropriate specialties from other engineering programs and appropriate specialties from other related fields such as the natural sciences, the social sciences, mathematics, statistics, and computer science.

[This section was based on UNESCO's *International Standard Classification of Education (ISCED)* (Paris: UNESCO, 1976).]

Major International and National Organizations

INTERNATIONAL

Inter-American Association of Sanitary
   Engineering
Edificio Cediaz, Torre Este
Piso 12, Oficina E-125, avenida Casanova
Caracas, Venezuela

International Association for Bridge and
   Structural Engineering
Association internationale des ponts et
   charpentes
Ecole polytechnique fédérale
CH-8006 Zurich, Switzerland

International Association for Hydraulic
   Research
Association internationale de recherches
   hydrauliques
P.O. Box 177
Delft, Netherlands

International Commission on Irrigation and
   Drainage
48 Nyaya Marg, Chanakyapuri
New Delhi 110021, India

International Commission on Large Dams
Commission internationale des grands
   barrages
22 et 30 avenue de Wagram
95008 Paris, France

International Federation of Municipal
   Engineers
23 Shderoth Yelin
Beersheba, Israel

International Society of Soil Mechanics and
   Foundation Engineering
Institution of Civil Engineers
1-7 Great George Street
London SW1, England

NATIONAL

Canada:
   Engineering Institute of Canada
   2050 Mansfield Street
   Montreal 2, Quebec

Federal Republic of Germany:
   Verein deutscher Ingenieure
   Graf-Recke-Strasse 84
   4 Düsseldorf

France:
  Société des ingénieurs civils de France
  14 rue Blanche
  Paris IX
India:
  Institution of Civil Engineers, India
  8 Gokhale Rd.
  Calcutta
Japan:
  Japan Society of Civil Engineers
  Yotsuya 1-chome, Shinjuku-ku
  Tokyo
South Africa:
  South African Institution of Civil
    Engineers
  Box 1183
  Johannesburg
United States:
  American Concrete Institute
  P.O. Box 19150, Redford Station
  Detroit, Michigan 48219

  American Institute of Steel Construction
  1221 Avenue of the Americas
  New York, New York 10017

  American Society of Civil Engineers
    (ASCE)
  345 East 47th Street
  New York, New York 10017

Principal Information Sources

GENERAL

Guides to the literature of civil engineering include:

Bentley, H. B. *Building Construction: Information Sources.* Detroit: Gale Research, 1964.
Bestor, G. C., and Jones, H. R. *City Planning Bibliography: A Basic Bibliography of Sources and Trends.* (3rd ed.) New York: American Society of Civil Engineers, 1972.
Blaisdell, R. F. *Sources of Information in Transportation.* Evanston, Illinois: Northwestern University Press, 1964.
McDonald, R. *Guide to the Literature on Civil Engineering.* Washington, D.C.: American Society for Engineering Education, 1972. A guide to the various aspects of civil engineering, including guides to the literature, abstracting services, encyclopedias, dictionaries, and handbooks.
Moody, G. B. "Bonanza-Literature for Civil Engineers." *Civil Engineering,* January 1968, *38*(1), 46–47.
Petermann, H., Börner, W., and Kuhn, H. *Schrifttum über Bodenmechanik/Bibliography on Soil Mechanics.* (5 vols.) Bad Godesberg, Federal Republic of Germany: Kirschbaum

Verlag, 1951–1966. Continued in *Dokumentation Bodenmechanik und Grundbau.*
Smith, D. L. *How to Find Out in Architecture and Building.* Elmsford, New York: Pergamon Press, 1967.

The following works provide a general introduction to the field:

Hammond, R. *Modern Civil Engineering Practice.* London: Newnes, 1961.
Nash, L. K. *Civil Engineering.* (4th ed.) London: Hale, 1967.

Historical accounts of civil engineering are offered by:

History of Public Works in the United States, 1776–1976. Washington, D.C.: American Public Works Association, 1975.
Kirby, R. S., and Laurson, P. G. *The Early Years of Modern Civil Engineering.* New Haven, Connecticut: Yale University Press, 1932.
Straub, H. *A History of Civil Engineering: An Outline from Ancient to Modern Times.* (English translation by E. Rockwell.) Cambridge, Massachusetts: MIT Press, 1964.
Upton, N. *An Illustrated History of Civil Engineering.* London: Heinemann, 1975.

For a discussion of civil engineering education consult:

Civil Engineering Education. Washington, D.C.: American Society for Engineering Education, 1961. A study of United States civil engineering education sponsored jointly by the Cooper Union (New York), the American Society of Civil Engineers, and the American Society for Engineering Education.
Civil Engineering Education Related to Engineering Practice and to the Nation's Needs. (2 vols. in 3.) New York: American Society of Civil Engineers, 1974. Reports on civil engineering education in the United States from the ASCE conference on Civil Engineering Education, Ohio State University, Columbus, Ohio, February 28–March 2, 1974.
Professional Education in Public Works/Environmental Engineering and Administration: A Handbook for Establishing University Centers and Programs. Washington, D.C.: American Public Works Association, 1974.

A discussion of the various aspects of the civil engineering profession is offered by:

Hammond, R. *A Career in Civil Engineering.* London: Museum Press, 1966.
You Can Be a Civil Engineer, and Here's How to Start. New York: American Society of Civil Engineers, 1957.
Your Future in Civil Engineering. New York: American Society of Civil Engineers, 1963.

CURRENT BIBLIOGRAPHIES

There are many current bibliographies and abstracting journals for the various aspects of civil engineering. Some important abstracting and indexing services include:

Building Science Abstracts. London: H. M. Stationery Office, 1928–.

Bulletin signalétique. Section 890: *Industries Méchaniques. Génie civil. Transports.* Paris: Centre national de la recherche scientifique, 1961–.

Civil Engineering Hydraulics Abstracts. Bedford, England: BHRA Fluid Engineering, 1961–.

Engineering Index. New York: Engineering Index, Inc., 1884–.

Environment Abstracts. New York: Environment Information Center, 1971–. Covers all aspects of environmental literature; international in scope.

HRIS (Highway Research Information Service) *Abstracts.* Washington, D.C.: National Research Council, Highway Research Board, 1970–.

Pollution Abstracts. La Jolla, California: Oceanic Library and Information Center, 1970–.

Publications Abstracts. New York: American Society of Civil Engineers, 1961–.

Referativnyĭ zhurnal. 60: *Stroitel'nye i dorozhnye mashiny.* Moscow: Akademiia nauk, SSSR, Institut nauchnoĭ informatsii, 1964–. Monthly abstracts on building and road machinery.

Transportation Research Abstracts. Washington, D.C.: National Research Council, Highway Research Board, 1931–. International in scope.

Water Pollution Control Federation Journal: Annual Literature Review Issue (June). Washington D.C.: Water Pollution Control Federation, annual.

PERIODICALS

The following are important periodicals dealing with civil engineering: *American Society of Civil Engineers. Transactions and Proceedings, Bauingenieur* (FRG), *Bautechnik* (FRG), *Civil Engineering* (UK), *Civil Engineering* (US), *Civil Engineer in South Africa, Construction* (US), *Consulting Engineer* (UK), *Engineering Journal* (US), *Engineering News-Record* (US), *Environmental Science and Technology* (US), *Gidrotekhnicheskoe stroitel'stvo* (USSR), *Gidrotekhnika i meliotatsiya* (USSR), *Giornale del genio civil* (Italy), *Highway Engineer* (UK), *Ingénieur* (France), *Ingenieur-Archiv* (FRG), *Institution of Civil Engineers. Proceedings* (UK), *Inzynieria i budownictow* (Poland), *Journal of American Concrete Institute, Journal of Applied Mechanics* (US), *Journal of Hydraulic Research* (Netherlands), *Public Roads* (US), *Rakennustekniikka/Finnish Civil Engineering,*

Schweizerische Bauzeitung, Sciences et techniques (France), *Surveyor* (US), *Tiefbau* (FRG), *Travaux souterrains* (France), *Tunnels and Tunnelling* (UK), *Water and Wastes Engineering* (US).

For additional titles see:

Ulrich's International Periodicals Directory. New York: Bowker, biennial.

ENCYCLOPEDIAS, DICTIONARIES, HANDBOOKS

Abbett, R. W. (Ed.) *American Civil Engineering Practice.* (3 vols.) New York: Wiley, 1956.

Baker, R. F. (Ed.) *Handbook of Highway Engineering.* New York: Van Nostrand Reinhold, 1975.

Blake, L. S. (Ed.) *Civil Engineer's Reference Book.* (3rd ed.) London: Newnes-Butterworth, 1975. Includes bibliographies.

Gaylord, E. H., and Gaylord, C. W. (Eds.) *Structural Engineering Handbook.* New York: McGraw-Hill, 1968.

Glossary, Water and Wastewater Control Engineering. Prepared by Joint Editorial Board. Washington, D.C.: American Public Health Association, 1969.

Gros, E., and Singer, L. (Comps.) *Constructional Engineering Dictionary: Russian, English, French, German.* London: Scientific Information Consultants, 1965.

Hammond, R. *Dictionary of Civil Engineering.* New York: Philosophical Library, 1965.

Merritt, F. S. (Ed.) *Standard Handbook for Civil Engineers.* New York: McGraw-Hill, 1968.

Scott, J. S. *A Dictionary of Civil Engineering.* (2nd ed.) Baltimore: Penguin, 1965.

Urquhart, L. C. *Civil Engineering Handbook.* (4th ed.) New York: McGraw-Hill, 1959.

Van Mansum, C. J. *Elsevier's Dictionary of Building Construction in 4 Languages: English/American, French, Dutch, German.* New York: American Elsevier, 1959.

Visser, A. D. *Elsevier's Dictionary of Soil Mechanics in 4 Languages: English/American, French, Dutch and German.* New York: American Elsevier, 1965.

Vollmer, E. (Comp.) *Encyclopedia of Hydraulics, Soil and Foundation Engineering.* New York: American Elsevier, 1967.

Zilly, R. D. (Ed.) *Handbook of Environmental Civil Engineering.* New York: Van Nostrand Reinhold, 1975.

DIRECTORIES

Directory of Hydraulic Research Institutes and Laboratories. Delft, Netherlands: International Association for Hydraulic Research, 1971. A specialized directory to hydraulic research.

Engineering College Research and Graduate Study.

Washington, D.C.: American Society for Engineering Education, annual. Supplement to *Engineering Education;* lists colleges and universities in the United States, Canada, and Puerto Rico.

Moody, W. A., and Sholty, P. A. *Directory of Organizations Concerned with Environmental Research.* Fredonia, New York: Lake Erie Environmental Studies, State University College, 1970.

Peterson's Annual Guides to Graduate Study, 1976. Book 5: *Engineering and Applied Sciences.* Princeton, New Jersey: Peterson's Guides, 1975. See section on civil and environmental engineering programs for a directory to graduate study in the United States.

Petrik, M. *The Training of Sanitary Engineers: Schools and Programs in Europe and in the United States.* Geneva: World Health Organization, 1956.

CIVIL RIGHTS OF STUDENTS
See Courts and Higher Education.

CLASSICS (Field of Study)

Classics is the study of Greek and Roman civilization. In English, the term *classics* has generally replaced the older designation *classical philology,* or just *philology,* though the latter remains in other European languages (for example, in the French *philologie,* the German *Philologie,* and the Italian *filologia*). The word *classics* has ancient roots, however. It derives from Aulus Gellius, a second-century encyclopedist, who divided authors qualitatively into *classici* and *proletarii,* words originally designating the highest and lowest divisions of the Roman army. Today *classics* has more often a historical rather than a qualitative sense, so that anything pertaining to antiquity may be called *classical.*

The expansion of the term *classics* coincides with an expansion of the study itself. Until the eighteenth century, classics was mainly the study of the language and literature of Greece and Rome. Since that time, it has felt the influence of scientific and historical methods which extended classical scholarship to include every aspect of the Greco-Roman world and of its neighbors in the ancient Near East. This expansion has given classics an objective purpose in addition to its earlier subjective purpose. The humanists of the Renaissance advocated the study of classics because it provided models for the intellectual, aesthetic, and ethical development of its students. Its purpose was to establish values and make a student "civilized" in the highest sense of that word. One result of this view was the establishment of classics as the basis of education in the West. This is the "cultural" purpose of classical studies. The "scientific" purpose, on the other hand, is to accumulate scientific data about the ancient world. There is usually no conflict between these two viewpoints. In both, the purpose of classics is to provide an understanding of the ancient world, and to understand the ancient world is to understand the roots of Western culture.

The scientific development of classics has increased the divisions in the field. In 1785 F. A. Wolf divided classics into twenty-four categories. In 1973 Robert W. Carruba and George A. Borden needed thirty-nine categories for their list of classicists in the United States and Canada: ancient science, Byzantine studies, classical tradition, classics in translation, comparative literature, computers and classics, Greek archeology, Greek art, Greek civilization, Greek epigraphy, Greek history, Greek law, Greek literature, Greek paleography, Hebrew, humanities, language teaching, Latin epigraphy, Latin literature, Latin paleography, linguistics, medieval Latin, medieval studies, modern Greek, mythology, Neo-Latin, Near Eastern studies, New Testament patristics, papyrology, philosophy, Greek philosophy, Roman philosophy, religion, rhetoric, Roman archeology, Roman art, Roman civilization, and Roman history. The study of Greek and Roman history is further subdivided by period, and Greek and Roman literature is further subdivided by genre.

The fields most closely related to classics are the history of science, comparative literature, archeology, ancient history, medieval studies, Near Eastern studies, Biblical studies, philosophy, religion, and art. All of these disciplines overlap chronologically with classics. In a looser sense, however, all intellectual disciplines in Western culture are related to classics, since all its arts and sciences began, and most first flourished, in classical antiquity.

The history of classical studies falls into two parts: Greek studies and Latin studies. Greek studies began when the Greeks themselves began to preserve and study their own literature. Aristotle (384–322 B.C.) wrote a treatise on Greek tragedy and also is said to have revised a text of Homer's *Iliad* for his young pupil Alexander the Great. In the following two centuries the great libraries at Alexandria and Pergamum established canons of Greek classics from the earlier archaic and golden ages. One of the directors of the library at Pergamum, Crates of Mallos, encouraged the Romans to take up Greek studies. About 168 B.C., he went to Rome, broke his leg in a sewer, and remained at Rome lecturing on Greek literature. Eventually, Greek became part of Roman education and a basis for much of Latin literature.

The Greeks also stimulated the Romans to study their own authors. Latin studies had its first great scholar in Aelius Stilo (born c. 150 B.C), whose work on the Latin language and literature, especially Plautus, inspired two of his students, Varro and Cicero, to become ardent scholars themselves. Later, the Roman poets, such as Horace and Virgil, were incorporated into Roman education. Quintilian, who took charge of the first public school in Rome during the first century A.D., considered the study of Roman authors as necessary as the study of Greek for his students. Lucretius and Cicero had already brought Greek philosophy to Rome, while Catullus and Horace had naturalized the Greek lyric and Virgil had naturalized the Homeric epic. These Roman works are not mere borrowings but transformations of Greek thought by the Roman imagination.

After the merging of Greek and Latin studies at Rome, the dividing of the empire into East and West caused a sundering of the two disciplines, Latin being preserved mainly in the West and Greek mainly in the East.

By the end of the Middle Ages, after Byzantium had fallen to the Turks, the continuity of Greek culture would have been cut off but for the revival of learning in Italy. Italy not only revived the study of Greek but reunited the two halves of the classical tradition that had been severed a thousand years earlier. Petrarch (1304–1374) had taken an interest in Greek and had discovered some of Cicero's letters and his *Pro Archia*. A century later, Cosimo de Medici founded an academy in Florence for the study of Plato. At Rome, Nicholas V established the manuscript collection at the Vatican library, and the West produced its first modern Greek scholar in Politian (1454–1494). These scholars were aided by the printing presses, such as that of the Venetian Aldus Manutius (1450–1515), who made classical literature available on an unprecedented scale. The printing press also enabled the humanists, as they were called, to make classics the basis for education. From the fifteenth century on, classics was a prerequisite for the university and therefore a main study in the secondary schools. This concept of education spread throughout Europe and America over the next three centuries.

Though classics still continued to play its role in the creation of vernacular literature, it could not maintain its central role in education. The Renaissance had not only given a new impetus to classical studies; it had produced modern science. If the university wished to keep its control of higher education, it had to widen its curriculum. The question of widening the curriculum was debated as early as the eighteenth century in France and later in the other countries where humanism had become the basis for education: Germany, England, and the United States. Finally, early in the twentieth century Greek and Latin were dropped as requirements at the major universities. The universities have since become the home of the scientist and the historian as well as the humanist. One result of this expansion was the decrease in the study of classics in preparatory schools. In the United States the study of classics in the secondary schools has greatly declined. Until 1949 Latin was the most taught foreign language; then it yielded to Spanish, which in turn yielded to French. Greek had an even swifter decline after it was dropped as a university entrance requirement at the turn of the century.

Recently, new methods for teaching classical languages, especially Latin, have met with some success, even on the primary level. On the secondary and university levels, textbooks have been changed to let the student encounter real Latin and Greek, rather than editorial paraphrases, early in his course of study. Audiovisual, audiolingual, and linguistic approaches also have been tried. Perhaps these new approaches are responsible for the rise in the numbers, though not in the percentages, of those studying classics below the college level. In the university there has been an increase in the number of degrees taken on all levels in classics, especially in Greek studies, since World War II. The heaviest concentration of students and faculty is still in Greek and Roman literature, and there is also a growing number of classics courses being offered in translation.

Classics, therefore, remains a living discipline in the modern university. It is studied throughout North America and Europe as well as in Australia, South Africa, India, Japan, and elsewhere. In the United States and Canada there are over four hundred classics departments in colleges and universities. The purpose of these programs varies from providing general education to training specialists in classics. At Oxford the classical course *Literae Humaniores* ("Greats") remains the most prestigious curriculum in the university.

The courses of instruction in these programs are analogous. They usually involve for the baccalaureate a study of the grammar, morphology, and syntax of the Latin and Greek languages, followed by detailed reading in the literature of Greece and Rome. Sometimes courses in prose composition in Greek and Latin are required, as well as courses in German or other languages, paleography, linguistics, ancient history, and classical art. Advanced degrees concentrate on more extensive reading of classical texts and a greater command of the languages. They usually involve some work in Greek and Latin composition. These courses of study lead first to the M.A., or its equivalent, and then—with further concentration and more independent study, often including the writing of a dissertation—to a Ph.D., or its equivalent.

The modern student of classics may pursue these studies with advantages that earlier scholars did not possess. The invention of photocopying has enabled the classicist to examine manuscripts in his own study, aided by the results of over two thousand years of solid scholarship. Knowledge of the ancient world has also been extended by the study of classical art, ancient history, literary criticism, and especially archeology. Scientific methods such as air and underwater investigations, radar, radiography, chemical and neutron activation analysis, and X rays are widely used in archeology. Finally, a great impulse has been given to the study of economics, demography, and technology in the ancient world, especially the data of epigraphy and papyrology.

Classical scholarship has expanded geographically too. Contributions to classical scholarship come from every continent on the globe, though the heaviest concentration is in Western Europe and the United States. Those areas of the world where classical studies were born have become the sites of increasing archeological activity. Besides the work of the British, American, German, and French schools of archeology in Athens and Rome, excavations are being carried out by many countries that once formed part of the Greco-Roman world.

As a result, the modern classical scholar can know and appreciate more of the Greco-Roman world than at any time since, and perhaps even including, antiquity.

FRANCIS C. BLESSINGTON

Levels and Programs of Study

Programs in classics generally require as a minimum prerequisite a secondary education and lead to the following degrees: bachelor's, master's, the doctorate, or their equivalents. Programs deal with the grammar, syntax, and literature of languages no longer in current use (for example, Latin, Greek, Sanskrit or Pali) and the history and cultures of the people who used these languages. In many cases the study of two or three classical languages is carried on simultaneously. Programs consist of classroom sessions, guided reading, and group discussion. On advanced levels programs consist of study and seminar or group discussion, with emphasis on research work substantiated by the presentation of a scholarly thesis or dissertation. Principal course content for programs at the first university degree level usually includes grammar, morphology, and syntax of the language; translation and composition; literature of the language, with emphasis on its great writers and their works; interpretation of texts; historical development of the language; and sometimes courses in palaeography and archeology. Background courses usually include world literature, ancient history, natural sciences, and social and behavioral sciences. On the postgraduate university degree level, principal subject matter areas include specific periods in the literature, a particular writer or group of writers, structure and grammar of the language, history of the language, analysis of specific texts, and principles of literary criticism. Background studies usually include ancient history, comparative literature, linguistics, other foreign languages, philosophy, mathematics, natural sciences, and social and behavioral sciences.

[This section was based on UNESCO's *International Standard Classification of Education (ISCED): Three Stage Classification System, 1974* (Paris: UNESCO, 1974).]

Major International and National Organizations

INTERNATIONAL

Association internationale des études
  néo-latines
Université catholique de Louvain
Leopoldstraat 22
Louvain, Belgium

Association of Roman Ceramic Archaeologists
Rei Cretariae Romanae Fautores
Rijksmuseum G.M.
Kam
45 Nijmegen, Netherlands

Fernand de Visscher International Society for
  the Study of Rights in Antiquity
Société internationale Fernand de Visscher
  pour l'histoire des droits de l'antiquité
13 rue Maréchal-Galliéni
78000 Versailles, France

International Association for Byzantine Studies
Association internationale des études
  byzantines
rue Sissini 31
Athens 612, Greece

International Association for Classical
  Archaeology
Associazione internazionale di archeologia
  classica
49 Piazza San Marco
00186 Rome, Italy

International Association for Greek and Latin
  Epigraphy
Association internationale d'épigraphie
  grecque et latine
4 Springpool
University of Keele
Keele, Staffs. ST5 5BG, England

International Association for Patristic Studies
Association internationale d'études
  patristiques
Palais Universitaire
6700 Strasbourg, France

International Association of Papyrologists
Association internationale de papyrologues
Fondation égyptologique Reine Elisabeth
Musées royaux d'art et d'histoire
parc du Cinquantenaire 10
1040 Brussels, Belgium

International Association for the Study of
   Ancient Mosaics
Association internationale pour l'étude de la
   mosaïque antique
17 allée de Trévise
92230 Sceaux, France

International Federation of the Societies of
   Classical Studies
Fédération internationale des associations
   d'études classiques
11 avenue René Coty
75014 Paris, France
This is the most prominent international
organization, with forty-four national members
and fourteen international members, most of
which have been included in this international
listing.

International Organization for the Study of
   Ancient Languages by Teetollers
Organisation internationale pour l'étude des
   langages anciennes par ordinateur
110 boulevard de la Sauvenière
4000 Liège, Belgium

International Society for Classical Bibliography
Société internationale de bibliographie
   classique
Université de Paris-Sorbonne
1 rue Victor Cousin
75005 Paris, France

Standing International Committee for
   Mycenaean Studies
Comité international permanent des études
   mycéniennes
25 rue Gazan
75014 Paris, France

Unione internazionale degli istituti di
   archeologia, storia e storia dell'arte in Roma
Piazza dell'Orologio 4
Rome, Italy

NATIONAL

The International Federation of the Societies of Classical Studies maintains a complete
listing of national classical associations.

Principal Information Sources

GENERAL

Guides to the literature in the field are:

Hammond, N. G. L., and Scullard, H. H. (Eds.)
   The Oxford Classical Dictionary. (2nd ed.) Oxford, England: Clarendon Press, 1970. Includes short bibliographies at the end of
   each entry and a general bibliography at
   the end.
J. A. Nairn's *Classical Handlist.* (3rd ed.) Oxford,
   England: Blackwell, 1953.

McGuire, M. R. P. *Introduction to Classical Scholarship: A Syllabus and Bibliographical Guide.*
   (Rev. ed.) Washington, D.C.: Catholic University of America Press, 1961.

The following works trace the history of
scholarship in classics:

Pfeiffer, R. *History of Classical Scholarship from the
   Beginnings to the End of the Hellenistic Age.*
   Oxford, England: Clarendon Press, 1968.
Platnauer, M. (Ed.) *Fifty Years (and Twelve) of
   Classical Scholarship.* (2nd ed.) Oxford, En-
   gland: Blackwell, 1968. Provides a survey
   of recent work.
Reynolds, L. D., and Wilson, N. G. *Scribes and
   Scholars; A Guide to the Transmission of Greek
   and Latin Literature.* (2nd ed.) Oxford, En-
   gland: Clarendon Press, 1974.
Sandys, J. E. *A History of Classical Scholarship.*
   (3rd ed.) Cambridge, England: Cambridge
   University Press, 1921.

CURRENT BIBLIOGRAPHIES

*L'année philologique: Bibliographie critique et an-
   alytique de l'antiquité gréco-latine.* Paris: Société
   d'édition "Les Belles Lettres," 1928–. The
   annual index of international classical scholarship.
International Guide to Classical Studies. Darien,
   Connecticut: American Bibliographic Service, 1961–. Scholarship appearing in periodicals is indexed in this quarterly publication.
*Lustrum. Internationale Forschungsberichte aus dem
   Bereich des klassischen Altertums.* Göttingen,
   Federal Republic of Germany: Vandenhoeck
   and Ruprecht, 1956–.
Quarterly Check-List of Classical Studies. Darien,
   Connecticut: American Bibliographic Ser-
   vice, 1958–.

PERIODICALS

Some important journals in the field are
*American Journal of Archeology, American Jour-
nal of Philology, Classical Journal* (US), *Classical
Philology* (US), *Classical Quarterly* (UK), *Classical Review* (UK), *Classical World* (US), *Greece
and Rome* (UK), *Greek, Roman, and Byzantine
Studies* (US), *Harvard Studies in Classical Philology* (US), *Hermes* (FRG), *Journal of Hellenic
Studies* (UK), *Journal of Roman Studies* (UK),
Revue des études grecques (France), *Revue des
études latines* France), *Studi italiani di filologia
classica* (Italy), *Transactions of the American Philological Association, Yale Classical Studies* (US).

A comprehensive list of international classical journals will be found in:

*L'année philologique: Bibliographie critique et analy-
   tique de l'antiquité gréco-latine.* Paris: Société
   d'édition "Les Belles Lettres," 1928–.

ENCYCLOPEDIAS, DICTIONARIES, HANDBOOKS

Der kleine Pauly. Lexikon der Antike. Munich, Federal Republic of Germany: Alfred Druckenmüller, 1964–.

Enciclopedia classica. Turin: Società editrice internazionale, 1957–.

Enciclopedia dell'arte antica. (7 vols.) Rome: istituto della enciclopedia italiana, 1958–1966.

Hammond, N. G. L., and Scullard, H. H. (Eds.) *The Oxford Classical Dictionary.* (2nd ed.) Oxford, England: Clarendon Press, 1970.

Laurand, L., and Lauras, A. *Manuel des études grecques et latines.* (2 vols.) Paris: Picard, 1956. A handbook for the field.

Lexikon der alten Welt. Zurich, Switzerland; Stuttgart, Federal Republic of Germany: Artemis, 1965. A basic dictionary for the field.

Müller, I. von. *Handbuch der Altertumswissenschaft.* Nördlingen, Federal Republic of Germany: Beck, 1885–. The most comprehensive handbook.

Pauly, A. F. von. *Real-Enzyklopädie der klassischen Altertumswissenschaft.* Stuttgart, Federal Republic of Germany: Metzler, 1894–. The most comprehensive encyclopedia.

Reallexikon für Antike und Christentum. Stuttgart, Federal Republic of Germany: Hiersemann, 1950–. A basic dictionary for the field.

Sandys, J. E. *A Companion to Latin Studies.* (3rd ed.) Cambridge, England: Cambridge University Press, 1921.

Smith, W. *A Classical Dictionary of Greek and Roman Biography, Mythology, and Geography.* (Revised by G. E. Marindin.) London, England: Murray, 1894.

Whibley, L. *A Companion to Greek Studies.* (4th ed.) Cambridge, England: Cambridge University Press, 1931.

DIRECTORIES

Carruba, R. W., and Borden, G. A. (Eds.) *Directory of College and University Classicists in the United States and Canada.* University Park: Pennsylvania State University Press, 1973. Lists schools offering classical programs in the United States and Canada.

Study Abroad. Paris: UNESCO, 1974. Provides international information on classical programs.

[Bibliography prepared by Francis Blessington.]

CLUB OF ROME

The Club of Rome was established in 1968 for the purposes of exploring some of the long-term trends of society and informing political and other decision makers about these trends.

The club is an informal grouping of some eighty-five scientists, humanists, economists, and industrialists from many parts of the world. It includes individuals from the less developed as well as the industrialized parts of the world, from Marxist as well as capitalist countries. None of its members are in political office, although many of them are in close contact with the decision makers. It is inherently nonparty and nonpolitical in its attitudes but inevitably challenges features of the different ideologies.

The Club of Rome is in most senses the antithesis of an organization and all that organization entails. It has no president, no formal secretariat, no budget, and endeavors to remain free from all bureaucratic temptations. The principal purpose of the club is to act as a catalyst to promote research and thinking and to bring the club's ideas to the attention of those having the political authority to make policies.

The structural concepts of the Club of Rome were the result of conversations held in Paris in 1967 between the writer and Aurelio Peccei, an Italian industrialist. Many problems which seemed to be emerging spontaneously and separately in many countries, especially in the industrialized and prosperous societies, were particularly disturbing. Most of these problems were the result of certain characteristics of our societies, which can be summarized briefly as follows: the rapid rates of change—technological, social, economic, and political—which mark the present situation; the extraordinarily high levels of economic performance, and hence of material affluence, which the industrialized societies have achieved in recent years; the massive technological development, which is the main agent of society's present affluence; the development of worldwide systems of communications and rapid transportation; the increased disparities between rich and poor, both within and between countries; the rapid growth of world population without sufficient thought as to the consequences; and the alienation of individuals, who feel that they are controlled by a faceless bureaucracy and have no influence on decisions that affect them vitally. All of these elements add up to a turmoil of uncertainty which is likely to last for some years and from which a new type of society with new values is likely to emerge. In the meanwhile, the difficulties which arise from the trends described are being faced each day by governments, communities, and individuals. They constitute a cluster of interacting problems, described by the Club of Rome as *the world problematique:* an intermeshed tangle of difficulties with social, political, economic, technological, psychological, and other elements, within which discrete problems are difficult to isolate and impossible to solve without influencing many of the other nodes of the *problematique.*

In May 1968 a meeting was called of some twenty-five European intellectuals to discuss these contemporary problems. The meeting was held in Rome, at the Academia dei Lincei, the oldest scientific academy in the world. There was little initial agreement about the nature and causes of society's problems, but at the end of two days a few persons felt impelled to continue the discussions. In commemoration of the first meeting in that city, the new association was named the Club of Rome. There should be no confusion between the aims of the club and those of the Vatican, the Treaty of Rome, or even Imperial Rome.

For about eighteen months, meetings were held frequently, mainly in Geneva. During this time other people, including some from the United States, were drawn into the circle. Membership in the club gradually increased by cooption, but the members soon agreed that talking among themselves was not enough. Several members traveled extensively in connection with professional duties. These travels enabled them to talk to political, scientific, and industrial leaders about the club's views and objectives. Attention was concentrated on the cluster of problems termed *the world*

problematique. It was agreed early that the Club of Rome should have two functions: to make known to those in authority its views on the world's problems and the need to reassess policies and institutional arrangements, and to stimulate research on the real nature of the *problematique* and the interaction of problems within it.

The first public exposure of the club's ideas occurred at a seminar at Alpbach, Austria, after which the Austrian chancellor invited the members to Vienna for a discussion with other Austrian personalities. At the first plenary meeting of the club, held in 1970 at Bern, Switzerland, Jay Forrester of the Massachusetts Institute of Technology (MIT) described his method of systems dynamics. He presented the outline of a global model, which permitted identification of a number of the specific components of the *problematique,* and suggested a technique for analyzing the behavior and relationships of some of its most important material components. A few weeks later a symposium was arranged at MIT in Cambridge, Massachusetts, to enable some of the members of the club to assess more clearly the potential value of this method. A project group was set up at MIT, and the results of its work were summarized in a report presented to the Club of Rome in 1972 and published under the title *The Limits to Growth.* Nearly two million copies of this publication, now available in more than twenty language editions, have been sold.

The MIT study projected existing trends in world population growth, the food and agricultural requirements to sustain it, capital and industrial growth, and depletion of raw materials and pollution. The study then examined the interactions among these factors and concluded that a rapid slowing down of population growth, accompanied by a gradual slowing down of economic growth (expressed in material terms), would bring about a desirable steady state.

This first report to the Club of Rome gave rise to a bitter world controversy, because of the questions it raised: Can society continue unrestricted economic growth in the industrialized countries? Can the world support a rapid population increase with a decent standard of living? Can the gap between rich and poor nations be bridged if present attitudes continue? Many economists were hostile to the report and dismissed it as simplistic; but in some countries, such as the Netherlands and Japan, a number of prominent economists accepted the report's validity.

The Limits to Growth had many inadequacies. It was a pioneering effort in a new field of human inquiry and therefore could not be expected to yield all the answers (although some critics did expect just that). The report had the admitted limitations of a global approach in that the consequences of the continuation of present trends would not be the same in all parts of the world. In addition, the report discussed only a few of the more easily quantifiable variables and deliberately omitted social and political factors.

In spite of these shortcomings, the MIT report has had three extremely important effects: it has triggered worldwide debate; it has placed increased emphasis on the interactions between problem and policy areas, so that issues such as population policies, monetary affairs, and energy or environmental deterioration are not viewed independent of policy determination; and it has stimulated considerable new research into societal and global problems.

In some ten countries, national Club of Rome groups have formed spontaneously. Some, such as the club in Japan, have already attracted sufficient funding to allow them to begin serious studies of national and international problems. Similar efforts also are expected from groups in countries such as Australia, Canada, Finland, and Switzerland.

Since 1974 the club has sponsored much new research. At a meeting in Tokyo, progress reports on this research were presented, along with many reports on related investigations not directly under the club's patronage. Following a meeting of the Club of Rome in Rio de Janeiro, a group of Latin American scientists decided to undertake a world study from the point of view of the Third World. The club was able to persuade the International Development Institute of Canada to finance this enterprise, and a team of scientists from several Latin American countries started the work at the Bariloche Foundation in Argentina. A further project, headquartered in Amsterdam, concerns the infrastructural consequences of the next doubling of the world population, a process now expected to be completed by about the year 2000. The club also has assembled a group of "technological optimists" to examine the possibilities of research into the solution of basic problems of food and agriculture to feed a greatly increased population, problems of raw material availability, and problems relating to energy resources.

As of 1975 studies and discussions had been concerned primarily with material problems and the social and political aspects of these problems. The club is convinced, however, that present attitudes, policies, and institutions are inadequate to meet world problems. The hope of change toward a better and more open society and of a unified but richly diversified world depends on the evolution of the motivations and awareness of man, of an alliance between the rational and the intuitive. It is to this enlightenment that the Club of Rome is dedicated.

ALEXANDER KING

COLEMAN REPORT
See Equality of Educational Opportunity (Higher Education Report), United States.

COLLECTIVE BARGAINING AND NEGOTIATIONS (FACULTY)
See Faculty Unionism: The United States and Great Britain; Legal Status of Faculty Unionization in the United States.

COLLEGE AND UNIVERSITY PERSONNEL ASSOCIATION, United States

The College and University Personnel Association (CUPA) was founded in 1947 to assist educational institutions in developing improved personnel administration and to provide members with opportunities for exchanging information and ideas about college personnel practices.

CUPA has members in several countries; in the United States there are five regional chapters and a number of state and local affiliate chapters. Member institutions, numbering approximately eight hundred, appoint three representatives to the organization, including personnel directors, business officers, deans, affirmative action officers, and presidents. Associate membership is available to students, faculty members, or nonadministrative persons serving an institution of higher education. A nonprofit organization, CUPA is supported by membership dues, grants, and service contributions.

A headquarters office and a full-time staff in Washington, D.C., coordinate CUPA's activities. The executive director works with the board and officers in developing and implementing the purposes, plans, and programs of the association. The office also answers members' requests for information, advice, and technical assistance.

The association organizes conferences, seminars, and workshops in such areas as affirmative action, wage and salary administration, and college and university collective bargaining; it also conducts a national referral and placement service. CUPA holds an annual international conference, and the five regional chapters hold yearly conferences.

Publications of CUPA include the *Journal,* quarterly; and *Personnelite,* monthly newsletter. The association also publishes *Guidelines to Better Personnel Administration* and other monographs on personnel practices. *Administrative Compensation Survey,* published biannually, analyzes cash and noncash compensation programs of one thousand institutions. The CUPA's membership directory and handbook are updated yearly and mailed to each representative.

One Dupont Circle
Washington, D.C. 20036 USA

COLLEGE ENTRANCE EXAMINATION BOARD

The College Entrance Examination Board (CEEB) was chartered by the board of regents of the state of New York in 1957 as a nonprofit membership organization. A voluntary and nongovernmental association, the College Board has about two thousand four hundred member secondary schools, school systems, colleges, and universities in the United States. National headquarters are in New York City, with several regional offices throughout the country.

The College Board offers a wide range of tests and measurements, publications, and informational services in guidance and financial aid to students ranging from grade seven through the first two years of college. These activities are supported by membership dues, candidates' test fees, and grants from private foundations and state and federal agencies. The organization is governed by a twenty-five-member board of trustees and guided by a series of trustee and advisory committees and councils involving more than nine hundred educators. A professional staff is appointed by the board president. The annual membership meeting of the College Board is held each October.

The College Board provides local, regional, and national forums where school and college representatives meet to discuss issues and problems involved in providing access to higher education. Through publications and workshops, CEEB also offers extensive research and training activities for professional educators in counseling, admissions, and student financial aid. School and college representatives on the many advisory councils contribute to the planning and changing of curriculums and help to set trends in testing, admissions, placement, and guidance.

Although the College Board has changed dramatically since its founding in 1900, it is dedicated to its original purpose of improving and facilitating access to higher education. Several million students on school and college campuses in the United States and in many foreign countries receive help each year by one or more of the CEEB programs.

Historical Perspective

Established at the turn of the century by secondary school headmasters and college presidents from New England and the Middle Atlantic states, the College Board's early function was to develop a series of uniform college entrance examinations based on common syllabi. Such distinguished university presidents as Charles W. Eliot of Harvard and Nicholas Murray Butler of Columbia were leaders in the creation of the College Board.

The fourteen founding members—Barnard College, Bryn Mawr College, Columbia University, Cornell University, Johns Hopkins University, New York University, Rutgers College, Swarthmore College, Union College, University of Pennsylvania, Vassar College, Woman's College of Baltimore (Goucher College), Association of Colleges and Secondary Schools of the Middle States, and the National Education Association—had become concerned by the multiplicity of entrance examinations, conflicting requirements, and the general confusion in the process of transition from school to college, even though only 4 percent of the college-age population went on to college.

Within a dozen years of its founding, CEEB served approximately forty private colleges, located mainly on the Atlantic seaboard, and a few hundred private and public secondary schools—also mainly in the Northeast. This closely knit group, with common interests in the university entrance curriculum and in the development, grading, and assessment of standard examinations, lasted for several decades and had an important uplifting effect on secondary education in the period.

The use of College Board examinations in the first quarter century grew steadily from 973 to 19,000 candidates, but their effect on education was less in the Middle West and the West. In those areas systems of public higher education worked closely with secondary schools in the development of a parallel system of admission to college, a system that relied primarily on recognition and acceptance of high school records.

Research on the measurement of intelligence, begun during World War I, prompted the College Board to sponsor a number of studies that led Carl Brigham of Princeton University to develop a new test of scholastic aptitude. This test was first offered as an additional CEEB examination to some eight thousand candidates for admission to college in June 1926. The test was designed to provide an indication of a student's ability to do college work and to measure levels of development in basic verbal and mathematical skills. The Scholastic Aptitude Test (SAT), improved and changed in subsequent years, gained wide recognition as an important adjunct to subject matter examinations and as a supplement to high school grades. Studies through the years of relationships between SAT scores and college grades reveal a direct and substantial correlation between performance on this test and later academic performance.

The SAT provided a new format in testing, consisting of easily scored multiple-choice questions. After years of review and validation, the test came to be regarded as a national standard in its field. The new test enabled universities to broaden their search for able students from other areas and from public as well as private schools. It also helped identify potential recipients of national and regional scholarship awards. In the middle 1930s CEEB also developed multiple-choice tests in subject matter fields.

During World War II, the organization and its staff cooperated closely with government authorities in a number of mass testing programs, including the Army-Navy Qualifying Test, designed to help select and train personnel for the armed forces. Veteran enrollments in the postwar years forced the College Board into a period of adjustment and expansion. In 1948 CEEB (in cooperation with the Carnegie Foundation for the Advancement of Teaching and the American Council on Education) established the Educational Testing Service (ETS) in Princeton, New Jersey, as a separate organization designed to conduct test construction, administration, scoring, and research. While its basic purposes and services have expanded beyond admissions testing to include programs for elementary and secondary schools and for graduate and professional agencies, ETS continues to work closely with the College Board as a major contractor and partner.

In 1954 CEEB founded the College Scholarship Service to help coordinate student financial aid and to establish national principles of awarding aid on the basis of need. Also in 1954, the board inaugurated a ten-year series of colloquia on college admissions, involving educators throughout the country and resulting in the publication of a series of studies on problems of talent searching, admissions techniques and problems, and financing higher education.

In 1955 the College Board assumed responsibility for the Advanced Placement Program, until then an experimental concept being tried by a few schools and colleges. The program was founded on the principle that able and ambitious students in secondary schools could pursue college-level courses in their own school, be examined on their achievement, and receive credit or placement at college for this work.

Finally, in this period the College Board joined with groups such as the National Scholarship Service and Fund for Negro Students and the New York City Board of Education in experimental programs for early and intensive guidance and counseling for minority students. These efforts in New York paved the way for later and more extensive programs and studies in compensatory education, many under state and federal support. CEEB administers the Upper Division Scholarship Program and the Engineering Scholarship Program for Minority Community College Graduates, to aid the transfer of college students from two-year to four-year institutions.

In order to provide services relevant to the differing educational needs in different geographical regions of the country, the board established between 1959 and 1960 the first of several regional offices staffed with professional educators familiar with the special problems and issues of their regions. A separate office was created in Washington, D.C., to serve as a basic information source and to maintain regular relations with the executive and legislative branches of government and with education associations in Washington.

CEEB also developed and introduced other special programs, such as the Comparative Guidance and Placement Program, designed to aid two-year colleges in student assessment and placement; and the College-Level Examination Program, which offers a series of general and subject examinations to enable individuals to gain college credit on the strength of their informal learning.

Additional research and review of the needs of adult and nontraditional learners led CEEB to join with ETS in the appointment of a new Commission on Nontraditional Study in 1970 and to investigate and analyze the many developing programs of off-campus study through the cooperative support of an Office of New Degree Programs.

Membership

Institutions of higher education are eligible for permanent membership in the CEEB if they are members of the appropriate regional accrediting association and make regular and substantial use of one or more of the board's programs. Recognition is given, however, to the fundamental right of member institutions of various religious faiths to establish and maintain educational institutions exclusively or primarily for students of their own faith. Voting membership in the College Board is available to secondary schools authorized by the appropriate state agency to issue diplomas. State systems of education and local school systems may be members if they have enrollments of fifty thousand or more, from kindergarten through grade twelve.

Associations and organizations may also join CEEB if they have a comprehensive membership, sponsor programs that have significant impact on school-college relations, and are capable of supporting, through their own activities, programs that are clearly germane to the purposes of the board.

CEEB offers access services for high school students going on to college, entrance services for students entering college, college-level services of assessment and placement focusing on the first two undergraduate college years, financial services for individuals and institutions, and international services.

Access services. Deciding, a guidance curriculum with workbook materials and films, aids junior and senior high school students in learning about the decision-making process. Decisions and Outcomes is a related program for older high school students and adults facing educational and career decisions.

The Preliminary Scholastic Aptitude Test–National Merit Scholarship Qualifying Test (PSAT-NMSQT) aids secondary schools in the early guidance of high school students to plan for college and helps juniors who wish to be considered for scholarships awarded by the National Merit Scholarship Corporation. The PSAT-NMSQT provides an early measure of the verbal and mathematical abilities tested by the Scholastic Aptitude Test.

Entrance services. CEEB offers the Admissions Testing Program, which consists of the Scholastic Aptitude Test, achievement tests, and the Student Descriptive Questionnaire. Scores and information from these are sent to students and schools, and to colleges and scholarship agencies at the request of the student. The SAT is a three-hour objective test of verbal and mathematical abilities. Achievement tests are one hour in length and cover fourteen high school academic subjects, including six foreign languages. The Student Descriptive Questionnaire is completed at the time of registration for SAT or achievement tests and allows the student to describe educational objectives, extracurricular participation, and self-perceived skills.

The board has a Student Search Service, which helps colleges reach potential applicants with particular characteristics (such as intended field of study, place or residence, and test scores) who may not be aware of the unique offerings of a particular college or university. The information gathered, with permission of the student involved, is derived from the Admissions Testing Program or from PSAT-NMSQT. After receiving a college's specifications, the board supplies lists of names and addresses of students who have characteristics designated. Searches may be requested at three different times in the course of the academic year.

College-level services. Advance Placement is composed of a series of thirteen subject matter courses and examinations based on syllabi. More than a thousand colleges and universities now award credit or placement for AP work.

The College-Level Examination Program provides a program of more than thirty examinations that can be used to evaluate nontraditional college education. Two types of examinations are offered: general comprehensive tests of knowledge in five areas of liberal arts, and specific subject examinations in undergraduate college courses.

The Comparative Guidance and Placement Program (CGP) is designed to meet the special guidance and placement needs of two-year colleges and vocational-technical institutes. CGP encourages students to learn more about themselves and to correlate their interests and career aspirations with their abilities.

Financial aid services. The College Scholarship Service (CSS) has a membership assembly that operates as a forum with the board to consider policies and procedures for the economics of college attendance. CSS assists postsecondary institutions, state scholarship programs, and other organizations in the equitable distribution of student financial aid funds. By measuring a family's financial strength and analyzing its ability to contribute to college costs, CSS need-analysis services offer a standardized method of determining need that is based on a sound economic rationale. To aid colleges and agencies in the management of financial aid programs, the Institutional Summary Data Services was created by CSS to provide statistical information on student financial aid funds.

International services. The College Board maintains an office in San Juan, Puerto Rico, and has developed a variety of guidance, admissions, and placement services for students and institutions in the Commonwealth and in South America. A Spanish-language test, similar to SAT, has been developed in Puerto Rico. There are also achievement tests and a number of college-level examinations in Spanish to serve adults and nontraditional students as well as regular university students. The Puerto Rico office provides consultation services and training programs in admissions, and financial aid throughout Central and South America.

To aid colleges, universities, and government agencies in evaluating the English proficiency of students whose native language is not English, the Test of English as a Foreign Language was developed. CEEB administers the test in cooperation with ETS and the Graduate Record Examinations Board. The test, consisting of sections on listening and reading comprehension, English structure, vocabulary, and writing

abilities, is offered four times a year in test centers around the world and is also available for institutional testing in the United States.

The College Board is an active partner in the planning and conduct of international workshops, helping foreign educators counsel and advise students who plan to study in American colleges and universities. The board is a member of the National Liaison Committee of Foreign Student Admissions, which works with the Bureau of Educational and Cultural Affairs of the United States Department of State. Training workshops have been held in several areas of the world.

Research and Publications

CEEB sponsors a research program, in cooperation with ETS and a number of colleges and universities, devoted to the problems of student transition from school to college. The board also sponsors research and experimental programs (including special guidance centers, publications, and films) to increase access of minority students to postsecondary education.

The board publishes *College Board News,* newsletter; *College Board Review,* quarterly magazine; *College Handbook,* comprehensive guide to higher education in the United States; *New York Times Guide to Continuing Education in America,* directory for adult education; and books and booklets providing information to students, colleges, schools, and education agencies. The board has also developed four guidance films and circulates them on a free-loan basis.

888 Seventh Avenue
New York, New York 10019 USA

CHARLES M. HOLLOWAY

See also: Admissions: An International Perspective.

COLLEGE GRADUATES AND JOBS (Higher Education Report), United States

College Graduates and Jobs: Adjusting to a New Labor Market Situation (New York:

McGraw-Hill, April 1973), a report of the Carnegie Commission on Higher Education, examines the changing labor market in the United States and its effect on the college graduate of the 1970s. The following findings and recommendations are reported.

College graduates no longer hold a preferred place in the labor market. The United States Bureau of Labor Statistics estimates that 9,800,000 college-educated persons will enter the labor force during the 1970s and that the demand for college-educated workers will total only 9,600,000. Of these 9,600,000 workers, 3,300,000 will replace persons leaving the labor market, 3,300,000 will fill newly created positions, and 2,600,000 will fill positions that have been educationally upgraded and have not traditionally required a college-educated worker.

The health field is experiencing the most severe shortages of professional personnel. Business managers are also in demand, while opportunities for engineers tend to fluctuate with federal expenditures on research and development. Prospects for elementary and secondary school teachers and for college-level instructors are particularly dim. Consequently, increased emphasis should be placed on the development of teachers for the priority areas of special education, early childhood development, day care, and vocational education. Additional teachers are also needed for the inner-city schools.

Employment prospects for holders of the doctorate will probably become increasingly unfavorable during the 1970s. Therefore, the committee recommends strict limitations of the development of new Ph.D. programs and the continuous review of existing Ph.D. programs. It urges an expansion of Doctor of Arts degree programs, which lead mainly to college-level teaching positions.

With adequate information and reasonable options, students can and do make career choices responsive to labor market changes. Therefore, reliance on student choice is preferable to manpower planning, which restricts individual freedom and is inadequate in long-term forecasting. Institutions of higher education should adjust most programs in response to changing student choices and should provide adequate counseling services.

Employers should carefully review hiring policies and should avoid raising educational requirements in response to changes in the labor market for college graduates. Educational requirements should not be imposed by employers unless necessitated by job requirements.

The labor market is influenced by public policy in areas such as work hours and expenditures on teaching, health care, research, the arts, and graduate-level education. Constructive action in these areas and a policy of selective public involvement rather than public control are favored.

As a consequence of the changing labor market, the commission predicts that social tension will increase as some college graduates become frustrated with employment opportunities, as pressures for the redesign of jobs and work environments increase, and as wage differentials are readjusted. Moreover, society will become more meritocratic, alternative life styles will emerge, public subsidy of higher education will decrease, and the brain drain from abroad will be reduced and perhaps reversed. The most favorable potential consequences will be the increase in social justice through greater equal opportunity and the equalization of earned incomes. Citizens will develop more tolerant attitudes, and the human capacity to deal with social problems will be enlarged.

COLLEGE UNIONS

Except in Anglo-American and some Scandinavian universities, the term *student union* usually means a general government body or other student organization actively championing political and social causes. According to a statement of purpose adopted by the Association of College Unions–International, the student or college union in the United States is "the community center of the college, providing for the services, conveniences, and amenities the members of the college family need in their daily life on campus. . . . It is part of the educational program of the college" (*Proceedings of Association of College Unions,* 1956, p. 113). British, Canadian, and Australian union constitutions refer to a "common meeting ground."

One cannot make a simple distinction between unions concerned with buildings (and the services and social-cultural programs carried on within them) and those involved in general student government or political activism. Although this distinction is fairly clear in the United States, where political activity is not the function of unions but of separate student governments, many unions in other countries embrace both student government functions and building management.

To avoid identification of their union buildings with political unions of students or confusion with a labor union, a growing number of universities—particularly in the United States and Canada—have adopted the term *student center.* This is not an accurate term either, because such centers are designed for use also by faculty, alumni, and visitors, and the name neglects the union concept of an organization. The descriptive name recommended as most appropriate by the Association of College Unions–International is *college union.*

The term *union* was first associated with organizations which developed buildings for dining, recreation, and discussion. The first were organized in the early nineteenth century, long before labor unions were formed in England, and 130 years before the national unions of students (headquartered in the Netherlands) and the international union of students (Eastern Europe and the Soviet Union) were created after World War II.

The aim of this article is to report what provisions are made for the social, cultural, and recreational welfare of students through unions. Although some institutions supply extensive material, others do not respond at all, so that the information is incomplete. The union development is so varied and vast, with more than twenty-five hundred buildings in at least seventy countries, that only broad generalizations can be presented. Detailed accounts of individual unions and trends can be found in Butts (1967).

United Kingdom

The birthplace of the union was at Cambridge University in England in 1815, the original idea being to form a university-wide society to achieve a unity through debate and fellowship. The term *union* seemed natural because the new organization "united" the existing debating societies of the separate colleges.

The Cambridge and Oxford Unions still stand for excellence in debating, but to student members they represent much more. With the construction of their own quarters in the mid-nineteenth century, the idea of the union as a clubhouse emerged. The Cambridge Union now includes, besides a debate hall, a library with more than fifty thousand volumes, standard reference books, and copies of the *London Times* dating back to 1815; a lounge with tea service; a smoking room with television; a gramophone room with more than seven hundred records; a music room with a piano; a dining room, a cafeteria, and a liquor bar; and facilities for billiards, table tennis, and squash.

The Oxford Union has a debate hall seating 750, a reading room, two libraries containing more than fifty thousand books, a billiard room, a television-viewing center, a restaurant, and a cellar where dancing is held every night. The constitution now states that "the chief objects of the Society shall be the holding of debates and the maintenance of libraries, cellars, read-

ing, writing, dining, and billiard rooms"
(p. 72).

For a century and a half the Oxford and
Cambridge Unions continued as private
"gentlemen's" clubs, with the title to the
union property vested in the organizations'
unions own trustees and the buildings governed by elected undergraduates.

The two unions have become a symbol
of the traditional British twofold goal in
education: to promote civilized behavior
as well as learning and, by encouraging
independence of student thought and action, to infuse students with the idea that
they are responsible for the welfare of
their country.

The unions at the rapidly expanding
civic universities are also concerned with
debating, but from the outset they developed as general campus centers with a
broad recreational and cultural program
designed to bring students and teachers
together.

In many ways the larger unions at city
universities are a blend of the Oxbridge
(Oxford and Cambridge) and American
traditions, with two elements added: the
function of supervising and supporting
clubs and societies and of representing the
interests of the general student body to the
university administration and the public.
The University of London Union fosters
the activities of seventy clubs. It is at once
a social center, an athletic club, and a student voice. The costs of operations and
programs are financed through the university, which, as with all civic universities,
receives a union fee from the local education authorities for each student enrolled
and then turns these funds over to the
union governing body. Union membership is thus automatic rather than voluntary, as at Oxford and Cambridge.

In Scotland unions parallel Oxbridge
traditions. Scotland takes debating very
seriously, although the debate chamber
is converted for dancing every Saturday
night. Scottish unions are for men only,
except at Aberdeen; there are separate

unions for women, although plans have
been made at Edinburgh for a new union
that would serve both. Since graduates are
encouraged to be members at Edinburgh,
the union insists that it is not a "student"
union but a "university" union.

Virtually every university in Ireland and
Wales has a union, and facilities, purposes,
organization, and programs are much as
one finds them in England and Scotland.

In the British Isles, most buildings are
coming closer to the community center
type of union found in the United States,
with an increasing emphasis on cultural
facilities. The trend appears to be to combine men's and women's use of the same
building, or at least to admit women freely
as guests. By 1968 the Cambridge Union
had elected its first woman president, and
the Leicester Union had a woman president as well as a male president.

By and large, unions are controlled by
elected student councils, which combine
the functions of student government, union
board, and athletic association. All clubs
derive their recognition and often their
funds from the student council, except at
private clubs like the Oxford and Cambridge Unions. The council is also the general policymaking board. Except at unions
which have operated as private clubs, student union members have their fees paid
by the government. But this is changing.
Confronted by steeply rising costs and declining voluntary membership, the Oxford
Union has decided that it must open its
doors to all students, with their fees made
mandatory by the university, or close. The
largest part of union income, amounting to more than 90 percent in most cases,
comes from student fees paid for by the
government.

The British have long been persuaded
of the value of clubs and neighborhood
centers and of the importance to society
of the development of leadership that
comes from self-governing activity and the
useful employment of leisure time. The
union building and its student leadership

are thus a reflection of the national philosophy of education.

United States

The earliest unions in the United States were direct descendants of the Oxford and Cambridge Unions. The first was organized at Harvard University in 1832, but it was not until 1880 that the union embraced the idea of a general club. The name *Harvard Union* was revived in the hope that out of the debating society a large general society, like the unions at Cambridge and Oxford, would grow. A union building was constructed in 1901, its object being to promote comradeship among members of Harvard University.

American universities increasingly saw in British unions an element needed in American education. Charles Van Hise in his inaugural address as president of the University of Wisconsin in 1904 urged gifts for a union: "If the University of Wisconsin is to do for the sons of the state what Oxford and Cambridge are doing for the sons of England, not only in producing scholars but in making men, it must have a commons and a union." In 1909 Woodrow Wilson, president of Princeton University and later president of the United States, in an address delivered to the Harvard University chapter of Phi Beta Kappa on July 1, 1909, propounded a similar idea: "The real intellectual life of undergraduates, if there be any, manifests itself not in the classroom but in what they do and talk of and set before themselves as their favorite objects between classes. . . . If you wish to create a college, therefore, and are wise, you will seek to create a life. . . ." It was in this climate of ideas that the first unions developed in the United States as men's clubs where students could come together and talk among themselves, a place for comradeship.

In the 1920s unions turned into social centers for everyone and have, with few exceptions, been coeducational ever since. At this juncture, two circumstances launched

the massive union development of the last fifty years. First of all, college administrators had seen what the war recreation centers had meant to the servicemen away from home; its counterpart on the campus, a union, now loomed as an answer to the many problems of campus life. The question of how to get a building—namely, by asking donors to contribute to a living memorial to honor students who had served their country—also came out of the war. The memorial theme was joined to the felt need, and this fund-raising appeal gave a sudden impetus to the slowly maturing union movement on a wide front.

In the 1930s leaders saw the union as the campus counterpart of the community center elsewhere, with a positive educational and recreational mission. A salient development was bringing the arts into the mainstream of student life, the pioneering leaders recognizing that the union could bridge the gap between the classroom and leisure and enhance the quality of leisure.

Low-interest loans, made available through the federal college housing authority beginning in 1955, have made possible the construction of more than five hundred union buildings; by 1975 there were approximately two thousand unions, almost half at institutions with less than twenty-five hundred students.

Some unions, especially at the smaller colleges, emerged essentially as service centers, consisting of little beyond a snack bar, a bookstore, and a few meeting rooms, with few or no social-cultural program offerings. At the other end of the scale were comprehensive community centers embracing several types of dining rooms, music rooms, art galleries, craft shops, theaters, libraries, game rooms, dance and banquet halls, meeting rooms, adult conference facilities, hotel rooms, radio stations, bookstores, banks, post offices, barber shops, travel services, outing facilities, and a multitude of student organization offices.

In 1956 the members of the Association of College Unions undertook to consolidate their purpose by adopting the following statement (*Proceedings of Association of College Unions*, 1956, p. 113):

> The union is the community center of the college, for all members of the college family—students, faculty, alumni, and guests. It is not just a building. It is also an organization and program. Together they represent a well-considered plan for the community life of the college. . . .
>
> The union provides for the services and amenities the members of the college family need in their daily life on the campus and for getting to know and understand one another through informal association. . . .
>
> The union is part of the educational program . . . training students in social responsibility and for leadership . . . and providing a cultural, social, and recreational program aiming to make free time activity a cooperative factor with study in education. . . .
>
> The union serves as a unifying force in the life of the college.

Unions in the United States are characteristically nonpolitical in nature; operate usually independent of student government but under the close supervision of the university; are jointly governed by students and faculty; are campus community oriented, serving faculty, students, alumni, and visiting adult conference groups; and emphasize union-sponsored social-cultural programs such as art exhibitions, entertainment events, symposia, lectures, films, game tournaments, dances, concerts, outings, and the teaching of skills.

The most frequently adopted facilities (of a list of 132 types) are offices for student organizations (95 percent of all unions), billiards rooms (91 percent), meeting rooms (88 percent), snack bars (87 percent), table tennis facilities (79 percent), bookstores (75 percent), cafeterias (75 percent), dance and banquet halls (73 percent), television-viewing rooms (70 percent), music rooms (55 percent), and art display areas (54 percent). Increasing emphasis is being placed on cultural facilities such as music and reading rooms, art galleries, and theaters.

Most unions are self-sustaining financially, paying for costs of operation and often debt amortization from building earnings and fees paid by all students.

The widespread union development in the United States is due in large measure to the existence since 1914 of the nonpolitical Association of College Unions. The association has formulated common objectives among member unions, provided a mass of information to universities on how to develop a union, and persuaded the federal government to arrange low-interest loans for construction.

Canada

The earliest Canadian unions, McGill University in Montreal (1907) and Hart House at the University of Toronto (1911), perpetuated the Oxbridge tradition: emphasis on debate; rooms for book browsing, music, dining, billiards, and other facilities for men only; the title of warden for the chief staff officer (Hart House); and elected student officers who held vigorously to the concept of student autonomy, including the proposition that all union affairs and building management be under the sole control of students (McGill).

At Hart House the idea of a social-cultural center embracing the interests of the total university community came into being. It became a mecca for union planners from the United States, Britain, Australia, and Japan. Its facilities, including a theater, an art gallery, and a gymnasium, opened everyone's eyes to the ways of improving the quality of student life. By way of its unparalleled facilities, the strength of an important idea, and the influential leadership of the staff, Hart House has shaped the course of union development as much as any other single union. In 1967 a total of sixteen Canadian unions were in operation, with twenty more in the active planning stage.

The newer buildings are an admixture of British and United States influences. The planning groups have adopted facilities common to United States unions and lean toward the purposes expressed by the

Association of College Unions. But as in Britain, Canadian student governments largely leave programs of educational value to the vagaries of individual special-interest clubs.

Except at Hart House, the issue that seems to absorb Canadian student officers is who should manage and control the union. Student government leaders typically consider themselves to be in charge of everything outside the classroom, including the union, and they jealously maintain their independence of the university.

Australia, New Zealand

Every Australian university has a union, the University of Sydney having established its first in 1874. Some unions are firmly student controlled; others have a university-appointed warden as chief executive officer. Some are separate from student government; others are not. A few carry on their own programs of recreational and cultural activity; most leave it to the individual clubs. All unions are co-educational, and there is generally much greater emphasis on "university" union (vis-à-vis "student union") than in almost any other country, a reflection of the encouragement given to faculty and alumni to become members.

The Australian Universities Commission makes considerable grants for union construction, and students pay a membership fee to cover costs of operation. Food services are commonly operated at or below cost as a benefit to members.

The Australian and New Zealand unions have been much more interested in and knowledgeable of what is happening in the union field than unions in any other country. Sixteen of the twent unions are members of the Association of College Unions–International.

Nowhere among the unions of the Anglo-American nations is there greater similarity of purpose. The constitutional declarations are almost standard and are stated in almost identical language, the typical theme being "to create opportunities for the de-velopment of social intercourse between the students themselves, and between students, teachers, and graduates; and to provide premises which shall be a common meeting ground and social center for all" (*Bulletin of the Association of College Unions–International*, 1973, p. 8).

For decades the predominant concept has been that the union should be essentially a service organization, but this is changing, due in part to the programming emphasis and success seen by staff officers touring United States unions. At a student-staff conference in 1972 the student presidents resolved "that the union's role is not only to provide service facilities but also to make a real and significant contribution to the intellectual, cultural, and social life of the institution, with a view to the education of its members."

Scandinavia

Scandinavian unions are much more concerned with student welfare and economic needs than Anglo-American unions, mirroring the democratic socialism that characterizes their governments. Students of Norway and Sweden have organized national unions of students, but the major interest is to promote the welfare of students through "practical activities," and their national governments lend active support.

The union at the University of Oslo, Norway, has built what it refers to as a student town—complete with bookshop, supermarket, printing plant, post office, bank, gymnasium, hairdresser, shoe repair shop, tobacconist, perfumery, ski storage, cafeteria, and dormitory. It also has a nursery and kindergarten, a medical service, an insurance plan, and a travel office that employs twenty people. Every student, by law, is a member and pays a fee; the membership card is an open sesame throughout the city, allowing the student such benefits as free admission to museums, half prices at theaters, and one third off on bus fares. The University of Turku in Finland has also developed a similar student town.

In Stockholm, Sweden, all fourteen universities have unions. They all offer the same kinds of services, ranging from lectures and debates and the publication of a monthly magazine to theater performances, dances, and welfare services. By government charter, all unions must provide certain specified services.

The student council at the University of Copenhagen follows the Oslo union pattern. It does not engage in sponsoring student activities, feeling that this is the field of private student clubs, especially the *Studentforeningen,* which serves as a center for students of all Copenhagen universities.

Central and Southern Europe

Political-action student unions are everywhere in Europe, but union buildings are there also—especially in Central Europe, where they follow the Scandinavian service and welfare pattern. Services and facilities of the union type were brought about by the desperate emergencies left in the wake of World War I.

In 1919 a group of students at Dresden, Germany, almost penniless and facing food shortages and high prices, hit upon an idea that caused a revolution in student life in Central Europe in the 1920s. Organizing a Students Cooperative Economic Association, they secured a field kitchen and began to serve very cheap meals. Other student bodies followed by forming their own associations, and by 1924 they were united in one national organization called the *Deutsche Studentenwerk.* It became the largest student self-help organization in the world. Within seven years, aided by a subsidy from the social democratic government, it had established twenty-five buildings with the name *Studentenhaus.*

While some centers were modeled directly after American unions, they were brought into being primarily to minister to the material needs of students. Unfortunately, the program came too late to be effective as an antidote for Nazi influences. When the Nazis came into power, they abolished the new student organizations and took over the facilities as training centers for the Nazi Youth Corps. The union movement of course was revived after World War II.

The Scandinavian concept of a student town has spread also to Belgium, where the Student City flourishes at the University of Brussels. Here the complex of facilities includes a sports field and tennis courts, extensive parking, dormitories, a shopping center, student offices and meeting rooms, lecture room, and a snack bar and large restaurant.

In France there is the *Cité Universitaire* in Paris, a huge residence and dining complex used mainly by students from overseas. The University of Toulouse has a *Foyer des étudiants,* whose stated purpose is to provide "general culture."

The University of Athens in Greece has an activities center called the University Club, which was established by a philanthropic grant and in which the state furnishes free meals to poor students. The student union is the typically political group in Greece and, because of its opposition to the government, was shut down in 1963.

The union at the University of Ankara in Turkey is of the more authentic type: operation of a cafeteria, sponsorship of clubs and sports, and the aim of creating an atmosphere of belonging to the same institution regardless of department of study. In 1968, however, after the first major rebellion of students against government educational policies, police seized the national union offices and arrested the student leaders.

In Portugal unions are called associations. All are engaged primarily in political activity, although they managed to develop certain services for students before being banned by the government. No universities in Portugal or Spain answered inquiries concerning buildings for dining, social and cultural activities, and services.

All of Italy's forty universities have branches of a national student union, whose main objective is to give students a voice in university reform. There are recreation buildings in Florence and Rome, but union buildings are not generally a part of the Italian university scene.

Eastern Europe and the Soviet Union

Except for the University of Warsaw in Poland, whose building has some of the characteristics of Scandinavian unions, no university in the Soviet Union or Eastern Europe responded to inquiries concerning student centers. A building at the University of Zagreb, Yugoslavia, specializes mainly in providing inexpensive meals and rooms for meetings; and in Bulgaria there are student hostels with meeting rooms. In Moscow there are no unions in the social sense and few extracurricular activities, although most Soviet-bloc universities have active political unions.

Middle East

The American University of Beirut, Lebanon, has had a union since 1918, and the American pattern shows through clearly: bowling lanes, dance hall, lounge, auditorium, table tennis, post office, committee rooms, theatrical performances, and other culturally oriented activities.

The center at the Hebrew University in Jerusalem has a snack bar, music and reading rooms, and student offices, as in American unions; but it also reflects the influence of the Central European and Scandinavian unions in its sponsorship of self-help services such as a cooperative bookshop, medical care, housing, and employment.

The American concept continues at the University of Teheran in Iran, with students encouraged to meet each other and develop a sense of unity and engage in community service projects.

Africa

College union buildings exist in the Sudan, Rhodesia, Liberia, and South Africa. They copy the British unions fairly closely, but also borrow a little from the Scandinavian. The University of Cape Town student handbook could, with a few word changes, be a copy of British union handbooks, and its students' representative council sponsors a wide array of clubs and athletic activities. The council, as in Scandinavia, offers a medical service, discounts at local shops, tours, an employment service, and a baby-sitting service.

The one exception to the British style appears to be at the University of Dakar in Senegal, which has inherited the French tradition and calls its center the *Cité Universitaire,* as in Paris.

While the rest of Africa is sparsely populated with union buildings, politically oriented national unions of students have developed rapidly throughout the continent and have become a force in campus affairs and national life.

Latin America

Until recently, student centers or unions have been a blank spot on the maps of Central and South America, although political unions are everywhere, as in Africa. These unions have many welfare projects as part of their program, much in the vein of Scandinavian unions, but without benefit of a physical facility. They are primarily political, and their method is typically agitation, strikes, and violence.

A number of universities have made efforts, apart from student unions, to improve the welfare of students, including in some cases the establishment of physical facilities. "Departments of student welfare" were created to operate cafeterias, programs of financial aid, and discount bookstores; a separate department, usually termed the "department of cultural extension," was formed to organize social and cultural activities of the United States union type.

A promising breakthrough toward establishment of a comprehensive building facility and social-cultural program with students centrally involved occurred at the University of Puerto Rico in 1960. A large student center opened, with student committees under the guidance of recreation-minded staff members trained in the United States, initially sponsoring more than two hundred activities. But the promise was not to be realized, since the chancellor—fearing that radicals would take over and cause trouble—abolished the student committees and refused to permit student participation in governance. Committees were dissolved, the games area was converted to a bookstore, and the music, art, and social program was abandoned; funding for ordinary maintenance or even minimal programming was not provided.

A few new efforts to establish social and service centers have appeared recently in Latin America, notably at universities in Costa Rica, Colombia, and Peru.

South Asia

In India, where half of the more than sixty universities and nearly all of the two thousand colleges have unions or union organizations, one again encounters the British tradition. Prime examples are the unions at the University of Baroda, Banaras Hindu University, and the University of Bombay (called the Bombay University Clubhouse). The underlying situation, however, is troublesome and full of friction, as in Latin America. In 1966 the world press reported India's students, often led by union officers, were on a rampage from one end of the country to the other, threatening law and order. Riots, marches, and strikes occurred in nearly all sixteen states.

In Ceylon, the student union in 1965 called a strike to reinforce various demands. Police were called in, and students set fire to the vice-chancellor's house, demanding his resignation. Before the clash was over, more than two hundred police and students were injured, and the university closed indefinitely. This happened while the university, with the aid of the Asia Foundation and an American consultant on student service goals, was laying plans for the construction of a university center. The center finally opened in 1970 "to provide facilities to better meet the social and recreational needs of students."

Pakistan universities, also plagued by student strikes and demonstrations, were caught between a government ban on unions and the desire to do something positive about the conditions of student life. The traditional British union, turned political, was no longer a suitable vehicle. So the University of Dacca in East Pakistan (now Bangladesh) proceeded to plan a "teacher-student center." The government agreed to finance such a center, with assistance from abroad, and the building became a reality. The University of Punjab in West Pakistan has built a similar teacher-student center.

Southeast Asia

The University of Thammasat Union in Bangkok, Thailand, is impressively large, but is little more than a building for food and shelter. The overall student association, as in so many other instances, became involved in national politics, and the university changed solely to faculty control.

An example of what can happen even to the Anglo-American type of union caught in the middle of a struggle between students and their governments is illustrated by the story of the University of Rangoon in Burma. As the union became more actively partisan politically, its building became a center of meetings for leftist, disruptive elements. The government decided during one demonstration in 1962 to send in military units, which fired into the student throng and blew up the union building. The university had apparently foreseen the subversion of the original purposes. It had already started planning a new structure for student and faculty recreation and took pains to call it the University Recreation Center rather than a student union. The building is operated by the university administration exclusively.

The University of Malaya student handbook describes its union as "the pride of every student, the center of student recreation." But after the merger of Malaya with the neighboring British colonial territories in 1963, there was an awakening of student political consciousness. Student desires to form a strong simple "student unionism as a facet of Malaysian nationalism" culminated in the birth of the National Union of Malaysian Students in 1965. Earlier serenity gave way to militancy, however, and the Malaya union circulated to its fellow unions an appeal for solidarity in opposing the imposition of a dean of students, believing that it would curtail the fundamental rights of students.

No university in the Philippines has a union building, except on the two campuses of the University of the Philippines. On its Quezon City campus, the university built Vinzons Hall to foster an "active and vital student leadership and worthy activities," in memory of a former student who became a national hero in World War II. It is a large building, but hopes for its program and activities have yet to be realized. The hall is so beset by frustrations that it can do little for its own students, let alone set the pace for others. It has no governing board, no student committees, no recognized program, and only the most meager financial means of keeping house for the few rooms remaining under union jurisdiction. The newer Los Banos Union on the College of Agriculture campus in Laguna, opened in 1972, appears to offer greater promise, since its functions of providing a community center and an educational program are stressed strongly.

Northeast Asia

Since the 1950s union development has been more extensive in Japan than in any country other than the United States, a principal impetus being a year-long mission of a team of American specialists in student personnel services in 1951–52.

By 1958 Diffendorfer Memorial Hall had opened at International Christian University (ICU) in Tokyo with the purpose of serving as "a laboratory for practicing the ways of democracy and of brotherhood among students and faculty." There is a student-faculty council, which serves as an easy medium of communication between students and the administration, and the term *ICU Family* has come into general use. Western influence is evident everywhere.

Another pioneering development took place at Hokkaido University, where the Clark Memorial Student Center facilities are even more impressive than those at ICU. The university controls the building through a committee consisting of faculty members only.

A union that represents in one sense a successful adaptation of the American approach and in another a persistent problem unique to Japan is at Kwansei Gakuin University in Nishinomiya near Kyoto. It has an auditorium and carries on an extensive program of films, plays, concerts, festivals, and art exhibitions. It also has a full-time director, a joint student-faculty governing board, and student-faculty committees. But the dining area and store are managed by an employee-student cooperative, and two complete floors are devoted to private rooms for clubs.

These three pioneering universities and a few farsighted Japanese educators saw in the United States union idea one more possibility of moving toward democratic objectives and a new era of student-teacher cooperation. They persuaded the Ministry of Education to construct union buildings at government expense; private universities joined the movement and in seven years eighty-seven unions were built, and many more planned.

Once in operation, the new unions encountered enormous difficulties, occasioned by facility and funding deficiencies, lack of understanding of union purposes, and continuing active opposition from leftist student governments. The reasons for the faltering union movement are complex, but the main factors appear to be that funds were too limited to include game rooms, cultural facilities, and activity rooms; that the ministry made no financial provisions for the programs, so they could not be carried out; and that there is too much conflict over control.

The union in Japan is identified with

government authority, and the ministry originally laid down the condition that the dean of students was to be responsible for building maintenance. Students saw this as a defeat for their rights; and student leaders, usually leftist extremists, decided early that they must control the union. Therefore, when the first government union was built, at the University for Women at Ochanomizu, students boycotted it for a full year. Then followed boycotts at the University of Tokyo, Muroran University of Technology, and Doshisha University, Kyoto. The feud reached a climax in 1966 at Waseda University, Tokyo, where student demands to manage the new students' center touched off the largest-scale boycott and longest and most disastrous strike in the history of a Japanese university (fifteen months), during which the new union was never opened. In 1975 the boycotts and strikes were continuing at a number of universities.

In cosmopolitan Hong Kong, one finds both British- and American-style unions. The University of Hong Kong Union, founded in 1912, is one of the oldest in Asia and is thoroughly British. The building, paid for by the government, is dominated by a restaurant and student offices; other than a reading room and two billiard tables, there is no space for recreation or creative activity. The university gives only minor supervisory attention; it collects a union entrance fee from all students and turns the funds over to the union council to administer.

At the far opposite end of Hong Kong is the Benjamin Franklin Center of the Chinese University, which has the distinction of being the first building erected (1969) on the new university campus and of being the gift of Americans. It is described as a "university community center for the cultural, social, and recreational welfare of the university community," and is operated by a student-staff committee whose functions include the promotion of out-of-class activities.

China's long tradition of village neigh-borhood centers and programs for community welfare paved the way in Taiwan, as at Hong Kong's Chinese University, for acceptance of community centers at the colleges. It is no accident that the first Taiwan union is called Gregarious Hall. The government, faculty, and student support for the union has been such that in the 1960s thirty-seven of the forty-two colleges developed union organizations and twenty-two had constructed buildings.

At National Taiwan University, most recent and largest of the unions, the facilities approach the comprehensiveness of the larger unions in the United States: television room, auditorium, reading room, art workshop, art exhibition area, music rooms, cafeteria, soda fountain, faculty dining room, billiards and card room, student offices, six conference rooms, and bank.

At Tamkang College students staged benefit performances and paid individual fees to build and operate their union. All of their extensive and varied activities are managed by students. The entire approach—facilities, emphasis on program, student leadership, student-faculty cooperation—follows closely the pattern in the United States.

In Taiwan the unions owe their development largely to the influence and assistance of the China Youth Corps. The corps was established as a response to the threat of Communist subversion, but it is nongovernmental; it is an educational corporation operating under government charter, with funds received entirely from contributions, memberships, and hostels. The corps has assisted union development in every way, particularly by setting up a "college union service center," which is staffed by a director and three full-time assistants. Whatever the motives of the China Youth Corps, its leadership has produced thriving unions that are more successful than those in any other part of Asia.

Current Trends and Issues

While college unions remain widely diverse in facilities, organizational structure, and primary objectives, certain trends are identifiable:

1. An almost universal recognition that some sort of university provision for the out-of-class needs of students is highly desirable; growing evidence, and acknowledgment, that a great deal of valuable learning takes place outside the classroom.

2. The lessening of the need for the union as a place for dining, social interaction, and informal recreation; hence, a growing emphasis on union provisions for other services and programs, such as shops, the performing arts, films, group outings, and the teaching of skills—areas with which the living quarters of students do not compete.

3. In times of financial stress, progressively decreasing funding for cultural-recreational programs and facilities and at times the closing of recreational facilities or conversion to income-producing enterprises.

4. Continuing decline of union debate activity, with discussion of issues superseded by direct political action (except in the United States), accompanied by injury to or neglect of union buildings and student welfare services.

5. Continuing formidable obstacles to the attainment of the union goal of unifying the campus, intensified by the adversary posture of the extremist student leaders toward the faculty, the dispersal of facilities at the larger universities, an increasingly heterogeneous student population, and frequent neglect of the union potential on the part of faculty and administrators.

6. An increasing assumption of control over union management by administrators, especially when financial difficulties arise—often resulting in the dissolution of the union's self-governing and management structure.

7. An urgent need for trained union staff members; widespread efforts to improve preparation of staff members through conferences, the offering of academic degree programs, fieldwork fellowships, short courses, and the publication of numerous operating guidelines.

A number of problems remain in large measure unresolved. Who should manage union facilities? What priority should be accorded social-cultural programs? To whom should the union be accountable? Will university administrators give more than isolated recognition to the union as a valuable educational instrument, and therefore adequate funding of a social-cultural-recreational program?

Should unions be centers for students only, or should they include faculty and alumni? Will the universities of Latin America, Europe, Africa, and Asia be able to resolve the problems posed by politicization and/or demands for student autonomy? In turning over to union governing bodies funds collected as "entrance" fees, should the university impose restraints on how such funds are used? In larger universities, is it better to centralize or decentralize facilities? Is the restoration of a "community of teachers and students" possible?

Should separate quarters in a union be provided for the exclusive use of special-interest clubs, ethnic minorities, or faculty? What services should be extended to the surrounding community? In the event of demonstrations, strikes, or violence, what is the role of the union?

The overriding general issue is: Should the college union be primarily a service station, an instrument for political action, or an educational force?

PORTER BUTTS

Bibliography

Berry, C. (Ed.) *College Unions—Year Fifty.* Stanford, California: Association of College Unions–International, 1964.

Berry, C., Rion, W., and Butts, P. (Eds.) *The College Union at Work.* Monograph Series. Stanford, California: Association of College Unions–International, 1965–1974.

Bulletin of the Association of College Unions–International. Stanford, California: Association of College Unions–International, 1932–1976.

Butts, P. *The College Union Idea.* Stanford California: Association of College Unions–International, 1971.

Butts, P. *State of the College Union Around the World.* Stanford, California: Association of College Unions–International, 1967.

Butts, P. *Planning College Union Facilities for Multiple-Use.* Stanford, California: Association of College Unions–International, 1966.

Butts, P. *Planning and Operating College Union Buildings.* (7th ed.) Stanford, California: Association of College Unions–International, 1967.

Christensen, E. *Annotated Bibliography of the College Union.* Stanford, California: Association of College Unions–International, 1967.

"College Union Planning Aids." In *College and University Facilities Series.* Washington, D. C.: U.S. Office of Education, August, 1962.

Directory of Association of College Unions–International. Stanford, California: Association of College Unions–International, 1975.

Hollis, C. *The Oxford Union.* London: Evans Brothers, 1965.

Humphreys, E. *College Unions—A Handbook on Campus Community Centers.* Stanford, California: Association of College Unions–International, 1946.

Minahan, A. *The College Union and Preparation for Citizenship.* Stanford, California: Association of College Unions–International, 1957.

Montagnes, I. *An Uncommon Fellowship—The Story of Hart House.* Toronto, Ontario, Canada: University of Toronto Press, 1969.

Morrah, H. A. *The Oxford Union, 1823–1923.* London: Cassell & Company, 1923.

Noffke, F., and Butts, P. "College Unions—Programs and Services; Facilities and Administration." In A. S. Knowles (Editor-in-Chief), *Handbook of College and University Administration.* Vol. 2. New York: McGraw-Hill, 1970.

Pride, H. *The First Fifty Years—Iowa State Memorial Union.* Ames, Iowa: Iowa State University, 1972.

Proceedings of Association of College Unions–International. Stanford, California: Association of College Unions–International, 1915–1975.

Rules and Regulations of the Oxford Union Society. Oxford, England: University Press, 1915–75.

Standards for Professional Staff Preparation and Compensation in College Union Work. Stanford, California: Association of College Unions–International, 1974.

Wills, B. *Annotated Bibliography of the College Union.* Vol. 2. Stanford, California: Association of College Unions–International, 1974.

See also: Extracurricular Activities on Campus; Fraternities; Sport, Interuniversity; Students, Student Services, and Student Organizations.

COLLEGIALITY AND UNIONISM

See Due Process and Grievance Procedures; Faculty Unionism: The United States and Great Britain.

COLOMBIA, REPUBLIC OF

Population: 24,226,405. Student enrollment in primary school: 3,844,257; secondary school (academic, vocational, technical): 1,213,430; higher education: 186,635. Language of instruction: Spanish. Academic calendar: generally February to June, August to December. Percentage of national budget expended on all education: 17.9%; higher education: 4.5%. [Figures are for 1974. Source: Departamento administrativo nacional de estadística.]

The Spaniards arrived in the area which is today the Republic of Colombia at the end of the fifteenth century. It was included as part of their dominion until the country became independent in 1819. During the colonial period several centers of higher education were established, all with religious affiliations. In 1580, a papal bull approved the creation of the *Universidad de Santo Tomás,* which was modeled on the Old World universities such as Salamanca. In 1622 the Society of Jesus established the *Academia* or *Universidad Javeriana,* now the *Pontificia universidad Javeriana.* It was closed in 1767 due to the expulsion of the Jesuits from the country and reestablished as a university in 1931. The *Colegio mayor de Nuestra Señora del Rosario* was founded in 1653; and about half a century later, in 1715, the *Colegio mayor de San Buenaventura* was created. The major aims of these institutions were to spread the Christian religion through the teaching of theology and canonical law and to supervise the education of the upper classes in the arts, philosophy, law, and literature. These institutions exist today as private universities.

Secular universities, with new goals and influenced by the French system of higher education, appeared soon after independence. Among these universities, which reflected the liberal ideas of the times and which today comprise the state university system, were the *Universidad de Antioquia* (1822), the *Universidad nacional* (1826), and the *Universidad del Cauca* (1827).

Many institutions of higher education have been founded since World War II, most of them established by the private sector. The *Universidad la Gran Colombia* was established in 1951 to give people who are employed the opportunity to pursue a university education at night. The postwar period has also seen increased stress on the coordination of the various institutions of higher education in administrative as well as financial matters. To this end, the *Instituto colombiano para el fomento de la educación superior* (ICFES: Colombian Institute for the Promotion of Higher Education) was created to represent the national government in the academic, financial, and administrative areas of higher education. It originated in 1954 with the creation of the *Fondo universitario nacional* (FUN: National University Fund) by Decree 3686. The fund was joined to the *Asociación colombiana de universidades* (ASCUN: Colombian Association of Universities) by Decree 251 in 1958. The national government broadened the functions of ASCUN by Extraordinary Decree 3156 in 1968, and it assumed its present name of *Instituto colombiano para el fomento de la educación superior* (ICFES). This organization was responsible for closing more than a dozen pseudo-universities, which had begun to proliferate without any scientific or economic basis in the late 1960s.

Legal Basis of Educational System

The legal basis of higher education is found in the national constitution of the

Republic of Colombia. Articles 120 and 135 give the national government—in the person of the president or, by delegation, the Ministry of Education—the authority to regulate, advise, and supervise the teaching process at all educational levels, including higher education. In order to carry out these functions, ICFES was created by Extraordinary Decree 3156 in 1968.

Types of Institutions

In accordance with their administrative structure, ICFES has classified the universities into national universities, such as *Universidad nacional de Colombia, Universidad pedagógica nacional,* and *Universidad de Córdoba;* state regional universities, such as *Universidad de Antioquia, Universidad industrial de Santander,* and *Universidad del Valle;* private secular universities, such as *Universidad de Los Andes* and *Universidad de Medellín;* and private religious universities, such as *Pontificia universidad Javeriana* and *Universidad pontificia Bolivariana.* Nearly all universities in Colombia are academic institutions that prepare students for professional specialization. The responsibility for a liberal education has been assigned to the secondary schools.

In addition to the universities, there are also a number of state and private institutions, referred to as seminaries, institutes, military schools, and corporations, such as the *Seminario conciliar de Medellín* and *Escuala militar de cadetes.* There are also state and private technological institutes of higher education such as *Instituto tecnológico Pascual Bravo.*

Relationship with Secondary Education

Primary education in Colombia is offered by both public and private schools and is compulsory and free. It consists of one cycle of five years for students between the ages of seven and twelve.

Secondary education in Colombia encompasses grades 6 to 11 and is composed of two cycles: the first cycle lasts four years and consists of a general or basic studies curriculum; the second cycle lasts two years and offers a specialized curriculum. The two-cycle system offers flexibility in that a student can transfer from one school to another to take the second cycle, and thus can change his field of study.

The specialized programs offered are academic studies, teacher training, and technological study (commercial, industrial, vocational, and agricultural). The academic program mainly prepares students for entry to the university. Graduates receive the diploma *bachillerato*. The normal schools prepare teachers for the primary schools. Graduates receive the title *normalista*, which, in addition to qualifying them for teaching, allows them to enter a school of education at a university. If they prefer another field of study, graduates of the normal schools may take a special validating examination offered by the National Testing Service of ICFES. The technical programs prepare students either for work or for entry to higher education.

Admission Requirements

The minimum requirement for admission to a Colombian university is a secondary school diploma *(bachillerato)*. In addition, all public and private Colombian universities require an entrance examination. The content and the importance attached to the examinations vary from institution to institution. The *Servicio nacional de pruebas* (SNP: National Testing Service) administers the examinations not only for university entrance but also in order to validate the *bachillerato* and to grant scholarships to secondary school students. In 1975 SNP administered 80,000 examinations to students seeking entrance to institutions of higher education.

Some universities—for instance, the *Universidad de Antioquia,* the *Universidad del Valle,* the *Universidad industrial de Santander,* and the *Universidad de Los Andes*—do not utilize the entrance examinations administered by SNP and instead use tests given by the *Grupo unificado de admisiones universitarias* (GUAU: Unified Group of University Admissions). Other universities, such as the *Pontificia universidad Javeriana* and the *Universidad nacional de Colombia,* administer their own examinations.

The entrance examinations prepared by ICFES and administered through SNP are objective tests of aptitude and general knowledge. The results of these examinations are independently interpreted by each university, which makes its selection based on its quotas, the program of study the student wishes to enter, the student's secondary school record, and an interview.

Of the 132,303 graduates of the *bachillerato* program in 1974, only 52,386 were able to enter the first semester at the university *(Estadísticas universitarias,* 1975*)*.

Administration and Control

By delegation of the Ministry of National Education, ICFES is the controlling authority for all higher education, public as well as private. A decentralized institute, ICFES controls the establishment of new universities and supervises and evaluates new programs within existing universities.

The decision-making authority lies in the executive board *(junta directiva),* which is composed of a representative of the Colombian president, the minister of education, the director of the *Instituto colombiano de crédito educativo y estudios técnicos en el exterior* (ICETEX: Colombian Institute for Educational Credit and Technological Studies Abroad), two rectors representing the state and two representing the private universities, and the director of ICFES. The *Universidad nacional de Colombia,* however, is administered directly by the minister of education.

The universities of Colombia are autonomous bodies, governed by their own statutes, which are in conformance with the constitution and laws of the country. Each university has its own internal structure based on its needs and objectives. The governing bodies of the institutions may differ in title and makeup but not in their functions. Thus, the highest university authority is sometimes called the higher university council *(consejo superior universitario),* sometimes the academic body *(cuerpo académico)* or council *(conciliatura),* or plenary *(plenum);* however, their major functions are to pass and reform statutes; to establish, eliminate, or modify programs and teaching plans or university branches; and to organize or modify the structure, administration, and research activities of the branches (Perez, 1968).

At the administrative level are the academic or managing councils *(consejos académicos* or *consejos directivos),* composed of the rector, deans, and representatives from the teaching staff and student body. The councils are responsible for organizing the teaching staff and the statutes governing the faculty; implementing policies passed by the higher councils; and proposing changes or creating new programs in teaching and research to the higher university council.

The rector is the chief administrator and heads the higher university council. He is in charge of the budgetary matters of the institution. The deans are the heads of the faculties or schools of the university and preside over the faculty councils, carry out existing policy, and propose academic and administrative changes to the managing board.

Students and professors participate in both the councils and the boards. The extent of their participation differs from institution to institution.

Programs and Degrees

ICFES is responsible for academic standards, both for private and public institutions. Accreditation of a new program requires a series of visits by ICFES staff to the institution. During the first visit the institution presents details of its resources, the proposed program, and the need for it. If the program is accepted, authorization is granted to start it. After the program has its first graduates, the ICFES staff make further visits to evaluate how well the program has filled its objectives. Upon recommendation by ICFES, the Ministry of National Education gives approval for a title, which corresponds to the duration of study time. Two to three years are required for

the title of *perito* or *técnico* (expert or technician). Four years are required for the title *licenciado,* most commonly granted for teacher training for the secondary level but also for fields such as library science, social work, nursing, and communications. Professional titles such as economist, engineer, architect, agronomist, veterinarian, administrator, and lawyer require five to six years of study.

Since 1972 there has been a resurgence of postgraduate programs, principally in areas such as administration, economics, medicine, and pedagogy. Some of these programs lead to the master's degree; others are specialized study. There are no official norms regulating postgraduate study.

Technical education, generally lasting three years, can be undertaken at universities and, more commonly, at technological institutions. By Decree 1358 of 1974, the government has encouraged technological education and upgraded it to the level of higher education. The importance of technological education is evidenced by the fact that ICFES has a division for technological education. In 1976 thirty-two institutions enrolled 10,175 students in technological programs.

Financing

The national universities are supported entirely by the national government, while the state universities receive their financing partially from the state and partially from the national government. ICFES distributes the allocations for the state universities and, to ensure more effective use of the allocations, supervises their disbursement. The importance attached to education by the government is evidenced by the fact that, in 1974, 18 percent of the national budget was earmarked for education, 13 percent of the total for higher education. Tuition contributes an insignificant part of the income of the national and state universities.

The private universities are not fully subsidized by the government and rely primarily on income from tuition and contributions from the religious community and private enterprise.

Student Financial Aid

The Colombian government, through ICETEX, offers loans to gifted students who are of only limited economic means. ICETEX has served as a model for similar institutions in other Latin American countries. In 1975, 17,122 students were aided by ICETEX. Students are expected to repay their loans upon completion of their studies. Their repayment enables the institute to finance the education of other students. Another service offered by ICETEX is to channel scholarships offered by foreign governments to Colombians for postgraduate training abroad. In 1975, 750 professionals took advantage of this program to study abroad. Some institutions, both public and private, set aside funds for the professional development of their employees and children of employees. Such funds, which must be repaid, are also administered by ICETEX. The *centros de bienestar* at some of the universities (both public and private) assist the students by providing loan services, cafeterias, dormitories, and transportation. A few private banks offer loans to students for programs approved by the Ministry of National Education.

Student Social Background and Access to Education

Until the 1950s, with very few exceptions, only the middle and upper classes had access to higher education. Since 1960 the university has become more democratic, giving greater access to the lower classes—not only through the state universities, with the increasing of student quotas and expansion of various night school programs, but also by the creation of private universities, which are less elitist and have lower tuition costs. Thus, while in 1968 there were only 65,144 students in higher education, in 1975 there were 186,635

students, or an increase of 186 percent in seven years; of the total, 99,823 are in state universities and 86,812 are in private universities.

The participation of women in university academic life has also increased notably; in 1960, 4234 women attended classes, by 1970 there were 22,930 women enrolled.

Students have their own student councils with representation from each unit of the respective institution. Their meetings deal primarily with problems of an academic and political nature. The universities, through their *centros de bienestar* (students' services centers), give students an opportunity to participate in community projects and in sports and cultural activities.

Teaching Staff

Although the ranks of teaching staff at the institutions of higher education are not standardized, the most common are full professor, associate professor, assistant, and instructor. Almost all institutions have faculty statutes setting forth the requirements for promotion, social benefits, licensing, and salary. The requirements are not uniform among the institutions, but usually seniority, degrees, research, and publications are taken into consideration.

Most of the professors in the state universities are employed full time. Of the 6030 full-time professors in 1974, 4904 were in the public institutions, as against 1126 in the private institutions. On the other hand, 6237 of the 8825 part-time professors were employed in private institutions, as against 2588 in public institutions (*Estadísticas universitarias*, 1975).

Research Activities

Research in Colombian higher education is usually undertaken at the graduate levels. It is conducted as part of the professor's academic load and usually in connection with one of his graduate courses. Other research projects are carried out by a group of institutions connected to the universities solely for research purposes.

ICFES finances research projects in some Colombian universities, especially in the field of education. COLCIENCIAS finances research at the university level in the technical and scientific fields, in addition to coordinating research at the national level and distributing scientific information and research results. In order to obtain financing for research, universities are required to present proposals stating their objectives and costs; if these projects are in the national interest, the university obtains the necessary funding.

A few universities rely upon research departments within their faculties to carry out basic research, with a prime objective of preparing students for research at the graduate level.

Current Problems and Trends

Since 1965 the Colombian government has focused much attention on the problems posed by higher education and their solutions. ICFES was created to improve the university system in its academic and administrative aspects. The government and the institutions of higher education are encmuraging programs of short and medium duration. New state universities also are being opened in remote regions of the country. These teaching centers offer only training related to the needs of the region. A few universities have open university (*universidad a distancia*) programs, which bring programed higher education to areas where no educational centers exist.

Some institutions also offer teaching methodology courses to their faculty. Other schools offer programs to teachers at the primary and secondary levels that allow them to obtain their teaching qualifications and, at the same time, their licentiate degree.

The increase in university enrollment from 44,403 students in 1965 to 186,135 students in 1975 has imposed tremendous pressures on the higher education system; earlier, university entrance was limited to the upper classes. By offering night courses in programs that have traditionally been available only in the day, the national government intends to give the Colombian worker who has received his *bachillerato* the opportunity to take courses in the state universities.

ICFES and ASCUN have made a joint effort to set up commissions of professors and administrators representing the various fields of study, such as engineering, education, law, physics, mathematics, and architecture. The main objectives of these commissions have been to analyze the curricula and to propose revisions based on the present needs and demands of society. ICFES has also organized commissions representing the different universities; members of these commissions meet periodically and discuss matters relating to university administration.

International Cooperation

Many of the scholarships offered by foreign institutions and governments through ICETEX are for university faculty. Four hundred and fifty professors from thirty Colombian universities have already taken advantage of a program offered by the Latin American Scholarship Program of American Universities (LASPAU). UNESCO, through bilateral contracts, has focused attention on the Colombian universities, with an aim toward furthering education, improving university administration and planning, and giving impetus to teaching and research in the basic sciences. The Ford Foundation, the Fulbright Commission, the Agency for International Development (AID), and the Inter-American Development Bank (IDB) also have extended assistance to Colombian universities. Some universities have established direct contact with foreign institutions to obtain advice or financing for projects and research. During the 1970s Canada, France, the Federal Republic of Germany, the Netherlands, and the United Kingdom have channeled a large number of scholarships and other technical assistance to Colombia.

JAIRO CAICEDO C.

Bibliography

Boletín mensual de estadística. No. 284. Bogotá: Departamento administrativo nacional de estadística, March 1975.

La educación universitaria en Colombia. Introducción al análisis de sus conquistas, problemas y soluciones. Bogotá: Asociación colombiana de universidades Fondo universitario nacional, 1967.

Estadísticas universitarias 1974–1975. Bogotá: Instituto colombiano para el fomento de la educación superior (ICFES), Sección de estadística, 1975.

Instituto colombiano de crédito educativo y estudios técnicos en el exterior (ICETEX). *El crédito educativo en América latina.* Bogotá: Imprenta nacional, 1969.

Instituto colombiano para el fomento de la educación superior (ICFES). *La educación superior en Colombia: Documentos básicos para su planeamiento.* Bogotá: Imprenta nacional, 1970.

Pelczar, R. S. "University Reform in Latin America: The Case of Colombia." *Comparative Education Review,* June 1972, *16,* 230–250.

Perez, O. *Estructura y organización de la universidad colombiana.* Bogotá: Ediciones Paulinas, 1968.

Rama, G. W. *El sistema universitario en Colombia.* Bogotá: Dirección de divulgación cultural de la Universidad nacional, 1970.

Renner, R. *Education for a New Colombia.* Washington, D.C.: U.S. Government Printing Office, 1971.

See also: Archives: Mediterranean, the Vatican, and Latin America: National Archives of; Planning, Development and Coordination: Regional Planning; Science Policies: Advanced Developing Countries: Andean Common Market Countries; South America: Regional Analysis.

COLOMBIAN ASSOCIATION OF UNIVERSITIES
(Asociación colombiana de universidades)

In June 1958 the *Asociación colombiana de universidades* (Colombian Association of Universities) was created after a meeting of twenty-one university rectors in Bogotá in December 1957. The association integrates the official and private autonomous universities of Colombia. Its objectives are to safeguard university autonomy; preserve freedom of teaching and research; maintain high academic standards; promote patriotic conscience and responsibility, linking university progress to that of the nation; coordinate academic efforts; provide for the exchange of professors; establish ethical standards; work toward university economic solvency; and secure better living standards for professors and students. The association also encourages research; organizes seminars in science, letters, and the arts; and promotes communication between Colombian universities and foreign institutions.

An official institution in existence since 1954, the National University Fund, furnished the first administration and direction for the association. Early goals set by the fund were the inspection, evaluation, and licensing of the universities and upgrading of teaching standards. Collaborating with the association, the fund worked on the reform of the official university system. In 1968 the National University Fund was separated from the association and was given a new name, *Instituto colombiano para el fomento de la educación superior* (Colombian Institute for the Promotion of Higher Education). The association was then placed under the authority of the National Council of Rectors and its organ, the administrative committee. The association's executive director, appointed by the National Council of Rectors for two years, may be reappointed. The National Council of Rectors sets governing rules for the association and criteria for membership. Special nontaxable funds for the association are allocated by the government but controlled by the association.

One of the association's functions is to convene meetings such as the *Congreso nacional de universidades* (National Congress of Universities) for rectors, academic directors, professors, and students.

Apartado Aéreo No. 012300
Bogotá, D.E., Colombia

ULADISLAO GONZÁLEZ-ANDRADE

COLOMBIAN INSTITUTE FOR THE PROMOTION OF HIGHER EDUCATION
(Instituto colombiano para el fomento de la educación superior)

The Colombian Institute for the Promotion of Higher Education was founded by the Colombian government in December 1968 to replace the National University Fund, established in 1954. An auxiliary body of the national Ministry of Education, the institute conducts studies on higher education planning, in coordination with the ministry, the National Planning Department, and the Colombian Association of Universities, and makes recommendations to the national government concerning higher education development in Colombia. Higher education research focuses on the following topics: administration, financing, university students and faculty, educational technology, curricula and instruction, methodology of research in higher education, and reform in higher education.

The institute is divided into four offices and three divisions. The University Finance Office studies the economics of higher education, distributes the country's educational budget, and advises the higher education institutions on how to improve their financial positions. The University Development Office, staffed with economists, statisticians, and other professionals, studies higher education plans of Colombia in cooperation with the Ministries of Education and Labor, the National Planning Department, and the planning offices of the universities. The office also advises institutions of higher education on the elaboration and evaluation of their own development plans. The Public Relations Office provides information on the institute's activities and those of Colombian higher education in general. All legal advice required by the institute comes from the Legal Office.

The Tests and Professional Orientation Division prepares, administers, and evaluates examinations to be used in the selection, orientation, and classification of students by universities and other higher education institutions. For example, the division administers the National Testing Service, which includes aptitude tests and academic examinations that are given twice a year to university-bound students.

Technical assistance is offered to higher education institutions through the Special Services Division in collaboration with the Colombian Association of Universities and the *Instituto colombiano de crédito educativo y estudios técnicos en el exterior* (ICETEX: Colombian Institute for Educational Loans and Advanced Studies Abroad).

In addition, the institute sponsors meetings, research work, and special seminars on subjects related to higher education advancement and aids in training top-level educational personnel.

The policies and activities of the institute are determined by a board of directors, composed of four university rectors (elected by the entire body of university rectors in Colombia) and four representatives of the national government, including the minister of education, the director of ICETEX, and two representatives of the Colombian president. The board of directors studies and approves plans for technical, economic, and administrative assistance to the universities. Funded by the government, the institute has a staff of 265, including 98 executives and research professionals, 131 research assistants and technicians, and 36 secretarial and clerical personnel.

The institute publishes *Documentos de divulgación,* a series of documents on higher education.

Calle 17 #3-40
Bogotá, Colombia

COLOMBO PLAN FOR CO-OPERATIVE ECONOMIC DEVELOPMENT IN SOUTH AND SOUTHEAST ASIA

The Colombo Plan for Co-operative Economic Development in South and Southeast Asia, set up by the British Commonwealth in 1950, was founded to aid the economic development of South and Southeast Asia. The Colombo Plan region was extended in 1962 with the admission of the Republic of Korea. Iran was admitted in 1966 and Fiji in 1972. By 1975 the Colombo Plan region—composed of countries in West Asia, the Far East, and South Pacific—included twenty-seven national governments. The plan aims to develop these areas economically and socially through the cooperative endeavors of member countries. Almost from its inception, the plan began to lose its Commonwealth character, and by 1975 most of the members were not in the Commonwealth. Any country willing to subscribe to the aims of the Colombo Plan and accepted by member countries may seek membership.

The plan promotes economic development by offering member governments capital aid such as grants and loans for national development projects; commodities, including food grains, fertilizers, and consumer goods; and specialized machinery, farm and laboratory equipment, and transport vehicles. The plan also provides technical assistance through the services of experts and technicians, facilities for study abroad in advanced technology in various fields, and equipment for training and research and intraregional training.

Multilateral in approach but bilateral in operation, the plan takes cognizance of the problems in South and Southeast Asia as a whole while keeping regional requirements in view. Negotiations for assistance are made directly between a donor and receiving country. The aid-receiving countries are regional members, and the aid-giving nations are nonregional members. The main emphasis, however, is on the cooperative nature of the plan.

The plan is administered through the Colombo Plan Consultative Committee, Council for Technical Co-operation, and Colombo Plan Bureau. The Colombo Plan Consultative Committee, consisting of ministers representing member governments, is the highest deliberative body.

The committee surveys the development of the region, and assesses its needs; it then tries to determine how international cooperation can help fill the gaps in national resources and speed up the pace of development. Annual meetings are held in different member countries.

The Council for Technical Co-operation, comprised of the representatives of all Colombo Plan countries, reviews and coordinates technical assistance in the region. The council provides a forum for discussing problems and exchanging ideas on procedures, policies, and programs; makes suggestions for facilitating and promoting technical assistance; and implements recommendations of the Consultative Committee. Quarterly meetings are held in Colombo, Sri Lanka.

The International Bank for Reconstruction and Development, Asian Development Bank, and United Nations agencies maintain close liaison with the Colombo Plan Consultative Committee and are represented by observers at committee meetings. The United Nations Development Programme is regularly represented at council meetings.

The Colombo Plan Bureau is an international organization located in Colombo, Sri Lanka. Headed by a director, the bureau serves as a participating body at Consultative Committee meetings, records all technical assistance given to the council, develops a program of intraregional training, and disseminates information on the plan as a whole. The bureau publishes annual reports of the Consultative Committee and the Council for Technical Co-operation as well as *Colombo Plan Newsletter,* monthly.

12, Melbourne Avenue
P.O. Box 596
Colombo 4, Sri Lanka

COLONIAL POLICIES
AND PRACTICES

See Aid to Other Nations: Colonial Policies and Practices.

COMMENCEMENT SERVICE
See Ceremonies.

COMMERCE AND BUSINESS ADMINISTRATION (Field of Study)

Although the practice and processes of business administration are more or less culture-bound, its principles and functions are universal. Accordingly, there is a worldwide convergence of educational practices in commerce and business administration. Certain basic, interrelated trends are evident.

First, there is a continual upgrading of curricula. Accreditation standards have evolved to meet the contemporary needs of business, the professions, government, and graduate and professional schools. In the United States accreditation standards have been set since 1919, primarily by the American Assembly of Collegiate Schools of Business (AACSB), which is generally recognized as the sole accrediting agency for bachelor's and master's degree programs in business and administration. In 1976 the AACSB had a membership of 494 domestic educational institutions (of which 178 were accredited); 78 business, government, and professional institutions; and 32 international (non-American) educational institutions. In the United States the AACSB encompasses approximately 79 percent of the collegiate programs in business and 95.6 percent of all students pursuing degrees in business administration majors.

The curricula provide for a broad education and prepare students for leadership roles in business and society, both domestic and worldwide. Programs at the first university degree level usually concentrate their professional courses in the last two years of a four-year program, encouraging the student to acquire a foundation in the liberal arts and sciences. Early professional courses include principles of accounting, principles of economics, business law, statistics, and introduction to business. The second two years generally involve more specifically professional courses, including marketing, finance, accounting, quantitative methods, information systems, organizational theory and behavior, and general administrative policy determination. Efforts are also being made to broaden the clientele by instituting a variety of non-degree seminars and workshops of varying length for working managers. Such programs often adopt the Harvard University Graduate School of Business Administration's "case method," which calls for solutions to problems actually faced by real corporations.

Although schools of commerce and business administration generally developed at the beginning of the twentieth century, it was not until the mid 1950s that sophisticated, analytical tools, and methodology appeared in more than a few prestigious institutions. Quantitative tools of analysis have been refined by innovations in mathematics and statistics; digital computers have resulted from technological advances; and systems approaches reflect a broadening of perspectives. Furthermore, advances in one field have stimulated advances in others. Developments in finance, for example, have encouraged work in both mathematics and accounting; international business evolved out of a combination of international economics and foreign trade courses, the latter generally in the marketing field; public administration courses, slow to gain acceptance, have been methodologically stimulated by the adoption of business administration techniques and models, as well as by the application of economic theory; marketing courses have gained substantially from inputs from the behavioral sciences.

Generally, there has been a greater clarification of concepts and delineation of fields, aided by the distinction between macroanalysis and microanalysis. For example, such marketing terms as *distribution, merchandising,* and *selling* were once synonymous for the word *marketing* but are now descriptions of only a part of the marketing mix. Further clarification is necessary, to be sure. General management courses, for instance, still include such diverse subfields as production, operations analysis, and personnel and labor relations; even in these courses, however, the scope has been broadened to include nonindustrial organizations, and at present the trend is to link the physical and human aspects of organizations.

Although marketing as a discipline started in the 1920s, academic interest in the field focused more intensively during the 1950s and 1960s. Financing followed a similar maturation process. The first major in international business was introduced in 1956 at Columbia University, and professionalization of the field began in 1959 with the founding of what was to become the Academy of International Business; in 1968 the first comprehensive work in international business appeared. As a result of technological advances in the late 1950s, the occupation-oriented curricula of business and commerce technologies were first offered by universities. Even accounting, although one hundred years old in the United States, did not mature until after World War II, and the field is still pondering the complexities introduced with the international dimension.

As in accounting, finance has yet to develop mathematical models for international complexities, which call for increased flexibility of tools and techniques. The quantification of policy results in public administration is still far from refined. International business is still far from integrated in the other fields. Additionally, other problems must be resolved, such as the respective roles of university study and work experience, the balance between strictly professional and broader education, and the ever present though diminishing schism between theory and practice. In general, the more the subject area becomes refined, the greater the need for extensive training in technology as well as for a broader base in the behavioral sciences.

Interest has rapidly grown since 1960 in internationalizing the commerce and business administration curricula. It is still too early to predict that the international dimension will become fully integrated, but indications suggest a definite and continuing movement in that direction. The rapid growth of multinational firms, the creation of supranational organizations, the increased awareness of the interrelatedness of national economies, a departure from the nationalistic tendencies of the earlier part of the twentieth century—these are some of the major environmental developments that have stimulated the international dimension. Increasingly, the necessity of practical global strategies has fostered theoretical thinking along those lines.

Most of the pioneer work which has resulted in the refinement, sophistication, and rapid growth of the curricula has taken place in the United States, which has been more successful than any other major country in incorporating the commerce and business administration curriculum into its overall educational system. University-level training in the field abroad is evolving along American lines, although the response in the several subfields has not been uniform. International business as a course, for instance, was an innovation in the United States, and Western European and Japanese business schools have been slow to respond. Although the United Kingdom's financial picture was at one time more sophisticated in its global outlook, since the mid 1960s the United States has dominated the finance field, in part because the major money markets became American and because British graduate schools of business developed slowly. In Europe in general, the traditional university system has resisted recognizing management as a separate academic field. Although there are excellent special schools—for instance, the German *Handelsschulen* for accounting and finance and postgraduate institutes such as the *Institut pour l'étude des méthodes de direction de l'entreprise* (IMEDE) in Switzerland and the *Institut européen d'administration des affaires* (INSEAD) in France, which have developed along United States graduate school of business lines— these institutions have developed outside of the traditional universities.

In most of the developing countries, curricula tailored to local needs are at a relatively rudimentary stage. In a number of instances, schools of administration have been implanted through contractual arrangements with United States universities. Examples include the Asian Institute of Management (Philippines), the National Institute of Development Administration (Thailand), the *Instituto brasileiro de administração* of the *Fundação "Getúlio Vargas"* (Brazil), the *Escuela superior de administración de negocios* (ESAN), Peru, and the Indian Institutes of Management at Ahmadabad and Calcutta (India). Except for Eastern Europe, the Soviet Union, and the People's Republic of China, worldwide acceptance of the American business school model has been stimulated by the presence of American multinational firms, by foreign students being trained in the United States, and by the fact that many texts used overseas are adaptations from American studies.

While most university business administration programs provide a broad overview of general management with some in-depth exposure to accounting, marketing, or production, some schools focus on the industries and institutions in which the knowledge and skills are to be applied—for example, real estate and land use economics, hospital and health care administration, insurance and risk management, and hotel administration. In general, however, United States university faculties look with disfavor on the proliferation of applied "vocationally oriented" programs.

LAWRENCE E. MCKIBBIN

Levels and Programs of Study

Programs in commerce and business administration generally require as a minimum prerequisite a secondary education, though mature students with relevant work experience may be admitted with lower educational qualifications. For short programs and refresher courses, these admission requirements may be relaxed for individuals with less educational background who are well established in business management, public administration, or other business fields. Programs lead to the following awards: certificate or diploma, bachelor's degree (B.Com., B.S.B.A., B.S.), master's degree (M.Com., M.A., M.B.A.), the doctorate (Ph.D., D.B.A.), or their equivalents. The principal kinds of programs included are general programs dealing with business administration or management (including such specialties as personnel and labor relations, production and operations management, and business policy and strategy); programs in business and office technology (including secretarial science, information systems or. data processing, and office auxiliary services or business machines operation); and programs with a specialization in accounting, finance and investment, marketing, public administration, international business, or other specialty areas (for example, insurance, real estate, public utilities, or transportation). Background courses are chosen from the social and behavioral sciences, humanities, law and jurisprudence, selected natural sciences, engineering, mathematics, computer science, and statistics.

Programs that lead to awards not equivalent to a first university degree deal primarily with business practices, office procedures, record keeping and management, and business and institutional administration. These programs emphasize the practical, technological, and factual aspects of the subjects studied, spending relatively little time on historical, theoretical, and general aspects. Programs may be full time or part time, though many last less than a year and include retraining, refresher, and sandwich courses. Programs are usually conducted in institutions of technology, technical colleges, or community colleges. They are sponsored by a wide variety of agencies, including employers,

employers' associations, trade unions, co-operative societies, professional societies, and government departments and agencies.

Programs leading to a first university degree are concerned with the theory, analytical methods, and practices of business management; business methods; and public administration. These programs stress the theoretical and general principles of the subjects included without neglecting an understanding of the institutions involved and the analytical tools and methods of administration. Programs may be full time or part time, day or evening. At this level, however, most programs are full time; part-time programs are mainly refresher or retraining courses. Most programs are conducted by universities, colleges, or similar institutions, but some are provided by employers, trade unions, employers' associations, government departments, and institutions. Programs and courses are sometimes conducted by correspondence or through radio or television broadcasts. Executive development or management development programs for those already in management positions are becoming more common. Students attending these programs may have bachelor's, master's, or doctoral degrees. The main objective is to update practicing managers in the techniques of management. These programs are offered by business schools at colleges and universities; their curriculum is similar to that of M.B.A. programs.

Programs that lead to a postgraduate university degree are generally of two types or levels. The master's level programs are usually very broad in scope, particularly those leading to the M.B.A. These programs are usually full time, although part-time master's programs are fairly common. Programs leading to a Ph.D. or D.B.A. degree usually deal with a highly specialized aspect of business administration or related specializations. At this level, emphasis is given to the theoretical principles of the subjects, and original research work substantiated by a scholarly dissertation

is usually an important element.

[This section was based on UNESCO's *International Standard Classification of Education (ISCED)* (Paris: UNESCO, 1976).]

Major International and National Organizations

INTERNATIONAL

European Foundation for Management
  Development (EFMD)
51 rue de la Concorde
1050 Brussels, Belgium

International Association of Students of
  Economics and Commercial Sciences
avenue Legrand 45
B-1050 Brussels, Belgium

International Chamber of Commerce
Chambre de commerce internationale
38 Cours Albert 1er
74 Paris 8e, France

International Council for Scientific
  Management
Conseil international pour l'organisation
  scientifique (CIOS)
1-3 rue de Varembé
Geneva, Switzerland

International Federation of Business and
  Professional Women
Fédération internationale des femmes de
  carrières libérales et commerciales
54 Bloomsbury Street
London WC1B 3QU, England

International Management Association
avenue des Arts 4
B-1040 Brussels, Belgium

International Organization for Commerce
Organisation internationale du commerce
avenue Gribaumont 3
1150 Brussels, Belgium

International Society for Business Education
Société internationale pour l'enseignement
  commercial
1052 Le Mont sur Lausanne, Switzerland

Organisation for Economic Co-operation and
  Development (OECD)
2 rue André Pascal
Paris 16e, France

NATIONAL

A sampling of national organizations in the field includes:

Federal Republic of Germany:
  Rationalisierungs-Kuratorium der
    deutschen Wirtschaft (RKW)
  Gutleutstrasse 163, Postfach 9193
  D-6000 Frankfurt

France:
  Fondation nationale pour l'enseignement
    de la gestion des entreprises
  155 boulevard Haussmann
  Paris 75008, France

United Kingdom:
  British Institute of Management (BIM)
  Management House, Parker Street
  London WC2B, England

United States:
  American Assembly of Collegiate Schools
    of Business (AACSB)
  760 Office Parkway, Suite 50
  St. Louis, Missouri 63141

  American Management Association
  135 West 50th Street
  New York, New York 10020

  American Marketing Association
  222 South Riverside Plaza, Suite 606
  Chicago, Illinois 60606

  Conference Board
  845 Third Avenue
  New York, New York 10022

Additional international and national organizations may be found in the following directories:

Anderson, I. G. (Ed.) *Marketing and Management: A World Register of Organizations*. Bekenham, Kent, England: CBD Research, 1969.
Directory of European Associations. Part 1: *National Industrial, Trade and Professional Associations;* Part 2: *National Learned, and Scientific Societies*. Beckenham, Kent, England: CBD Research, 1971, 1975.
Encyclopedia of Associations. (9th ed.) Detroit: Gale Research, 1975. Lists organizations in the United States.
World Guide to Trade Associations. (2 vols.) New York: Bowker, 1973.
World Index of Social Science Institutions. Paris: UNESCO, 1970. With quarterly supplements.

Principal Information Sources

GENERAL

The field of commerce and business administration has numerous comprehensive guides to information sources; among them are:

A Basic Library of Management. London: British Institute of Management, 1974.

Business Books in Print. New York: Bowker, annual.
Coman, E. T. *Sources of Business Information*. (Rev. ed.) Berkeley: University of California Press, 1964.
Daniells, L. M. *Business Reference Sources*. Boston: Baker Library, 1971.
Daniells, L. M. *Business Information Sources*. Berkeley: University of California Press, 1976. The successor to Coman's book.
Frank, N. D. *Data Sources for Business and Market Analysis*. (2nd ed.) Metuchen, New Jersey: Scarecrow Press, 1969.
Harvard University Graduate School of Business Administration, Baker Library. *Core Collection: An Author and Subject Guide*. Boston: Baker Library, annual.
Johnson, H. W. *How to Use the Business Library, with Sources of Information*. (4th ed.) Cincinnati, Ohio: South-Western, 1972.
Maltby, A. *Economics and Commerce: The Sources of Information and Their Organization*. Hamden, Connecticut: Archon, 1968.
Vernon, K. D. C. *Use of Management and Business Literature*. London: Butterworth, 1975.
Wasserman, P. *Encyclopedia of Business Information Sources*. Detroit: Gale Research, 1970.
White, C. M. *Sources of Information in the Social Sciences*. (2nd ed.) Chicago: American Library Association, 1973.

Overviews and introductions to the field of business education include:

Agarwala, A. N. *Education for Business in a Developing Society*. East Lansing: Michigan State University, Graduate School of Business Administration, 1969.
Clark, J. J., and Opulente, B. J. (Eds.) *Toward a Philosophy of Business Education*. Jamaica, New York: St. Johns University Press, 1968.
Le Breton, P. P. *Dynamic World of Education for Business: Issues, Trends, Forecasts*. Cincinnati, Ohio: South-Western, 1969.
Nolan, C. A., and others. *Principles and Problems of Business Education*. (3rd ed.) Cincinnati, Ohio: South-Western, 1967.
Tonne, H. A. *Principles of Business Education*. (4th ed.) New York: McGraw-Hill, 1970.

Several works devoted to the history of management and business are:

Barker, T. C. *Business History*. London: Historical Association, 1960.
Bear, M. *A History of Business*. Ann Arbor: University of Michigan Press, 1963.
Heilbroner, R. *The Making of Economic Society*. (5th ed.) Englewood Cliffs, New Jersey: Prentice-Hall, 1975.
Larson, H. *Guide to Business History*. Cambridge,

Massachusetts: Harvard University Press, 1948.

Lovett, R. *American Economic and Business History. A Guide to Information Sources.* Detroit: Gale Research, 1971.

Merrill, H. (Ed.) *Classics in Management: Selections from the Historical Literature of Management.* New York: American Management Association, 1970.

Urwick, L. F., and Brech, E. F. L. *The Making of Scientific Management.* London: Pitman, 1945–1948.

Sources dealing with commerce and business education internationally include:

Farooque, O. *Commerce and Management Education in India and Abroad.* Aligarh, India: Aligarh Muslim University, 1970.

Gregoire, R. *The University Teaching of Social Sciences: Business Management.* Paris: UNESCO, 1966.

Internationalizing Management Education. Washington, D.C.: United States National Committee for UNESCO, 1973.

Kolde, E. J. *International Business Enterprise.* (2nd ed.) Englewood Cliffs, New Jersey: Prentice-Hall, 1973.

Mailick, S. (Ed.) *The Making of the Manager: A World View.* Garden City, New York: Doubleday, 1974.

McNulty, N. G. "European Management Education Comes of Age." *Conference Board Record,* December 1975, *12,* 38–43.

Methodological Aspects of Management Education in Developing Countries. Delft, Netherlands: International University Contact for Management Education, 1963.

Otteson, S. F. (Ed.) *Internationalizing the Traditional Business Curriculum in Accounting, Business Policy, Finance, Marketing.* Bloomington: Bureau of Business Research, Graduate School of Business, Indiana University, 1968.

Prasad, B. S. (Ed.) *Management in International Perspective.* New York: Appleton-Century-Crofts, 1967.

Rehder, R. R. (Ed.) *Latin American Management Development and Performance.* Reading, Massachusetts: Addison-Wesley, 1968.

Scott, J. D. *Educating Asian Students for Business Careers.* Ann Arbor: University of Michigan, Graduate School of Business Administration, 1966.

CURRENT BIBLIOGRAPHIES

Among the important abstracts and indexes are:

Anbar Management Services Joint Index. Wembley, England: Anbar, 1961–.

Business and Technology Sources. Cleveland, Ohio: Cleveland Public Library, 1930–.

Business Periodicals Index. New York; Wilson, 1958–. Published monthly.

Documentation économique. Paris: Presses universitaires de France, 1947–.

Economic Abstracts. The Hague: Library of the Economic Information Service, 1953–. Published semimonthly.

Harvard University Graduate School of Business Administration, Baker Library. *New Books in Business and Economics: Recent Additions to Baker Library.* Boston: Baker Library, 1960–.

Index of Economic Articles in Journals and Collective Volumes. Homewood, Illinois: Irwin, 1961–.

International Bibliography of Economics. Chicago: Aldine, 1960–. Published annually.

International Management Information. Stockholm: Fölags AB Information, 1970–.

Journal of Economic Literature. Nashville, Tennessee: American Economic Association, 1963–.

Management Abstracts. London: British Institute of Management, 1960–.

Management Index. Ottawa, Ontario: Keith Business Library, 1959–.

Management Review. New York: American Management Association, 1923–.

Public Affairs Information Service Bulletin. New York: Public Affairs Information Service, 1915–.

PERIODICALS

Among important journals in commerce and business are the following: *Business Education World* (US), *Business Horizons* (US), *Business Week* (US), *Columbia Journal of World Business* (US), *Conference Board Record* (US), *Dun's Review* (US), *Economist* (UK), *Fortune* (US), *Harvard Business Review* (US), *Industry Week* (US), *International Executive* (US), *International Management* (US), *International Review of Administrative Sciences* (Belgium), *Journal of Business* (US), *Journal of Business Education* (US), *Journal of Economics and Business* (US), *Journal of International Business Studies* (US), *Management International Review* (FRG), *Management Today* (UK), *Manager* (FRG), *Nation's Business* (US), *Le nouvel économiste* (France), *Sloan Management Review* (US), *Wharton Quarterly* (US).

For more complete listings of journals in the field see:

Harvard University Graduate School of Business Administration, Baker Library. *Current Periodical Publications in Baker Library.* Boston: Baker Library, annual.

Ledbetter, W., and Denton, L. W. *A Directory of American Business Periodicals.* Columbus, Ohio: Grid, 1974.

Ulrich's International Periodicals Directory. New York: Bowker, biennial.

ENCYCLOPEDIAS, DICTIONARIES, HANDBOOKS

Among the numerous encyclopedias, dictionaries, and handbooks in the field of commerce and business administration are:

Brown, S. M., and Doris, L. *Business Executive's Handbook.* (4th ed.) Englewood Cliffs, New Jersey: Prentice-Hall, 1953.

Hanson, J. L. *A Dictionary of Economics and Commerce.* London: Macdonald, 1974.

Heyel, C. *The Encyclopedia of Management.* (2nd ed.) New York: Van Nostrand Reinhold, 1973.

Lindemann, A. J. *Encyclopaedic Dictionary of Management and Manufacturing Terms.* (2nd ed.) Dubuque, Iowa: Kendall/Hunt, 1974.

Mager, N. H., and Mager, S. K. (Eds.) *The Office Encyclopedia.* Englewood Cliffs, New Jersey: Prentice-Hall, 1975.

Munniksma, F. *International Business Dictionary in Nine Languages.* Antwerp, Belgium: Kluwer Deventer, 1975.

Pitman's Business Man's Guide. (14th ed.) London: Pitman, 1968.

Servotte, J. *Commercial and Financial Dictionary in Four Languages: French, Dutch, English, German.* (4th ed.) New York: International Publications Service, 1972.

Standingford, O. *Newnes Encyclopedia of Business Management.* London: Newnes, 1967.

DIRECTORIES

Educational directories which include information on business, commerce, and management programs in various countries and regions are:

American Assembly of Collegiate Schools of Business. *Directory.* St. Louis, Missouri: American Assembly, annual.

American Universities and Colleges. Washington, D.C.: American Council on Education, 1928–. Published quadrennially.

British Institute of Management. *Management Education Yearbook: Higher Education.* Epping, Essex, England: Gower Press, 1975.

Commonwealth Universities Yearbook. London: Association of Commonwealth Universities, 1914–. Published annually.

Graduate Study in Management: A Guide for Prospective Students. Princeton, New Jersey: Graduate Business Admissions Council, annual.

International Handbook of Universities. Paris: International Association of Universities, 1959–. Published triennially.

McNulty, N. G. *Training Managers—The International Guide.* New York: Harper & Row, 1969.

Peterson's Annual Guides to Graduate Study, 1976. Book 2: *Humanities and Social Sciences.* Princeton, New Jersey: Peterson's Guides, 1975. A United States directory.

World Guide to Universities. New York: Bowker; Pullach/Munich, Federal Republic of Germany: Verlag Dokumentation, 1972.

The World of Learning. London: Europa, 1947–. Published annually. Lists universities, colleges, research institutes, and learned societies throughout the world.

RESEARCH CENTERS, INSTITUTES, INFORMATION CENTERS

A representative list of schools and institutes includes:

Belgium:
European Institute for Advanced Studies in Management
placc Stcphanic 20
B-1050 Brussels

Management Centre Europe
62 rue Royale
Brussels

Canada:
McGill University
P.O. Box 6070
Montreal 101, Quebec

France:
Center of Advanced Training in Business Management
Centre de perfectionnement dans l'administration des affaires
16 rue Chateaubriand
Paris 8e

European Institute of Business Administration (INSEAD)
boulevard de Constance
77300 Fontainebleau

Netherlands:
Nederlands Instituut voor Efficiency (NIVE)
18 Parkstraat
The Hague

Soviet Union:
Kiev Institute of National Economy
Brest-Litovsky prospekt 98/1
Kiev 57

Switzerland:
Centre d'études industrielles
4 chemin de Conches
Geneva, Switzerland

Institut pour l'étude des méthodes de
direction de l'entreprise (IMEDE)
23 chemin de Bellevue
CH-1007 Lausanne

United Kingdom:
London Graduate School of Business
Studies
Sussex Place, Regent's Park
London NW1, England

Manchester Business School
Booth St. West
Manchester M15 6PB, England

United States:
Harvard University
Graduate School of Business
Administration
Soldiers Field Road
Boston, Massachusetts 02138

Massachusetts Institute of Technology
Alfred P. Sloan School of Management
Cambridge, Massachusetts 02139

Stanford University
Graduate School of Business
Stanford, California 94305

University of Chicago
Graduate School of Business
Chicago, Illinois 60637

University of Pennsylvania
Wharton School of Finance and
Commerce
Philadelphia, Pennsylvania 19174

Additional centers and institutes may be
found in:

Minerva, Forschungsinstitute. Berlin, Federal
Republic of Germany: de Gruyter, 1972.
Research Centers Directory. (5th ed.) Detroit:
Gale Research, 1975. Updated by *New Re-
search Centers;* lists centers in the United
States only.
Vernon, K. D. C. *Use of Management and Business
Literature.* London: Butterworth, 1975.
The World of Learning. London: Europa, 1947–.
Published annually.

See also: Accountancy; Business and Office
Technologies; Finance; International Business;
Management Education; Marketing; Public
Administration.

COMMERCE TRAINING
See Business and Office Technologies (field
of study).

COMMITTEE FOR THE WORLD UNIVERSITY, United States

The Committee for the World University was organized in December 1959 to
promote the idea of a world university,
to develop an acceptable plan for such a
university, and to secure funds and take
such steps as might be necessary to establish such an institution. The committee was
incorporated in the state of New York in
1960. George Geng, a professor at Paine
College (Augusta, Georgia), prepared the
original proposal to form a committee. The
twenty-two-member committee is drawn
from distinguished educators, statesmen,
and other internationally oriented persons. Affairs of the committee are handled by a board of directors composed
of a president, vice-president, and secretary treasurer.

Most of the funding for the committee
has come from interested members and
friends and from grants from the J. M.
Kaplan Fund, the Schmerman Foundation,
and the SLR Foundation. No appeal for
funding has been made in the last decade
or so.

In the early 1960s the committee conducted three weekend-study conferences
to study the theoretical and practical aspects of the idea. Matta Akrawi, then the
UNESCO representative at the United Nations, acting as consultant to the committee, put together a comprehensive plan
derived from a preliminary proposal and
ideas that came out of the conferences.
The "Akrawi Paper," from that time on,
became a working paper for future discussions and planning.

Between 1961 and 1974, much groundwork was laid to convert the committee's
philosophy into ideas for action. World
conditions in 1974 were favorable to develop a world view, free of ethnocentrism
and chauvinistic nationalism. In fact, the
committee began to feel that such a growing attitude concerning the interdepen-
dency of the world had become the *sine
qua non* for peace in the world. In Septem-

ber of 1974 a two-day conference was held at Huntington, New York, where the original proposal was revised. The revision was accepted by the board of directors on June 1975 and accepted by the corporate membership in New York City, March 1976. Unique features of the accepted proposal included planning for globally oriented academic offerings, international living experiences, and participation by world-óriented scholars and leaders. The plan called for an interdisciplinary approach involving the humanities, education, social sciences, and applied sciences.

It is expected that the World University will offer undergraduate programs leading to a bachelor's degree and graduate programs leading to both master's and doctor's degrees. The committee hopes that headquarters for the new university can be established within fifty to one hundred miles of the United Nations, so that close working relationships can be established. Colleges and universities around the world will become working partners in the educational programs of the world university. Other unique features of the university will include a multinational board of trustees, administration, faculty, and students, and regional campuses and centers scattered all over the world.

Publications of the committee include *Educating Mankind for One World* (a summary report on the proposed World University), September 1963, and *A World University for World Education* (a report on the 1974 Planning Conference for the World University in America), March 1975.

1203 Glen Lake Blvd.

Pitman, New Jersey 08071 USA

COMMITTEE OF DIRECTORS OF POLYTECHNICS, United Kingdom

The Committee of Directors of Polytechnics (CDP), which was formally established in April 1970, has as its full members the directors of the thirty polytechnics formed in England and Wales since 1968.

There are also two observer members, one from Northern Ireland Polytechnic, the other representing a group of similar institutions in Scotland.

The objectives of CDP are to provide a forum for the discussion of matters of common interest to its members and to contribute to the evolution of policy on polytechnics. The committee represents the interest of polytechnics wherever necessary and maintains a constant dialog with the central government, local authorities, and other appropriate bodies. Consultations are held with teachers' organizations and students' unions. CDP is also represented in many national and international committees concerned with education.

CDP meets six times a year. Five standing committees cover areas of particular interest and may in turn be advised by specialist working parties. The executive function is performed by a Committee of Honorary Officers and Standing Committee Chairmen. A small permanent secretariat serves the committees, collects and publicizes data, and organizes a range of corporate activities. Throughout its activities, CDP has no authority to enforce its recommendations.

CDP publishes an annual *Handbook of Polytechnic Courses,* information leaflets, press releases, and corporate advertisements.

309 Regent Street

London W1R 8AL, England

COMMITTEE OF UNIVERSITY PRINCIPALS, South Africa

The Committee of University Principals (CUP) is a South African statutory committee consisting of the principals or rectors of the Universities of Cape Town, Stellenbosch, the Witwatersrand, Pretoria, Natal, the Orange Free State, Port Elizabeth; Potchefstroom University for Christian Higher Education; Rhodes University; Rand Afrikaans University; and nonresidential University of South Africa. Meeting twice a year, CUP is assisted by advisers, usually members of the senior administrative staff of the universities. A chairperson is appointed on a rotating basis for a period of two years.

CUP considers and makes recommendations to the minister of national education regarding matters of common interest to the universities or matters referred to the committee by the minister or the secretary for national education.

Following the recommendations in 1974 of the Commission of Enquiry into Universities, the committee reorganized, establishing a permanent secretariat with a full-time secretary, research officer, and other administrative staff. The committee has a number of specialized subcommittees that undertake investigations on such topics as financing, university planning, tertiary education, library services, computer services, and adult education. Chaired by principals, these committees advise CUP in the formulation of policy and in representations to the government. The secretariat, the administrative body of the committee, conducts research on various aspects of universities and acts as a bureau for the collection and dissemination of information on university affairs within South Africa. The committee is funded by members' contributions, calculated according to an agreed formula.

Momentum Building
83 Devenish Street
Sunnyside
Pretoria 0002, South Africa

COMMITTEE OF VICE-CHANCELLORS AND PRINCIPALS OF THE UNIVERSITIES OF THE UNITED KINGDOM

Founded in 1918, the Committee of Vice-Chancellors and Principals is primarily a consultative and advisory body. It provides a framework within which matters of common interest to universities may be defined and discussed. As a result of these discussions, a common or central arrangement for the resolution of particular problems may be explored, formulated, and adopted. Moreover, a university view on matters of policy can be defined and represented to the University Grants Committee, departments of government and other educational bodies, industry, and the public at large.

The committee, which is funded by annual contributions from universities, has nearly sixty members: the vice-chancellor or principal of each of the United Kingdom universities, together with additional representatives from the federal universities of London and Wales and from the universities of Oxford and Cambridge. The committee's chairman and vice-chairman are elected annually from among its members. The secretariat, composed of some twenty administrative and specialist officers headed by the secretary general, is located in offices adjacent to the Senate House of the University of London.

The full committee, which normally meets nine times a year to discuss an agenda centered on a small number of items of major or current significance, is supported by a General Purposes Committee and four standing committees, concerned primarily with the preparatory study of matters in the fields of finance and development, academic affairs, staff and student affairs, and international university affairs. There are also a number of specialist subcommittees. Arrangements have been made to provide regular consultation, both at vice-chancellor and officer level, with the University Grants Committee and the Association of University Teachers. Consultative meetings are also held with the National Union of Students, representatives of industry, head teachers, polytechnic directors, and those concerned with the problems of higher education. In addition, the committee occasionally holds conferences with members of academic staff in universities, in order to discuss specific issues of current interest.

The committee has been instrumental in

establishing the following university committees: the Standing Conference on University Entrance, which deals with matters of common concern to the universities in relation to university entrance; the Universities' Committee for Non-Teaching Staffs, which conducts central negotiations on pay for the technical staff employed by the universities and represents the universities in central negotiating machinery with the appropriate unions about the other aspects of the employment of nonacademic staff; and the University Authorities Panel, which represents the universities as employers in the negotiating machinery for academic staff salaries.

The committee issues reports of inquiries, statements of policy, and conference papers. Those currently in print are *An Enquiry into the Use of University Academic Staff Time* (1972), *Safety in Universities: Code of Practice. Part I General Principles* (1971), *Industry and the Universities—Aspects of Inter-Dependence* (1965), *Universities and the Future Pattern of Education* (1966), *Student Accommodation* (1971), *The Function of the University—Teaching and Research* (1972).

29 Tavistock Square
London WC1H 9EZ, England

B. H. TAYLOR

COMMITTEE OF VICE-CHANCELLORS OF NIGERIAN UNIVERSITIES

The Committee of Vice-Chancellors of Nigerian Universities was established in 1963 to promote cooperation and to discuss matters of material interest and common concern to Nigerian universities. Initially, the committee's meetings were held at the University of Ibadan. In 1966, through a $102,000 grant from the Carnegie Corporation of the United States, the committee set up its permanent secretariat (in Lagos), which is now maintained by subscriptions from member institutions.

The committee has no executive powers, but since it is recognized by the federal government, it assumes responsibility for expressing the views of the universities on issues of importance in which the government has an interest. It plays a significant role in coordinating the activities of the universities and works in close collaboration with the National Universities Commission, a statutory body which advises the federal government on the financial needs of universities and allocates the resources provided by the federal government to individual universities. Specifically, the committee coordinates personnel and establishes policies within the universities to ensure and maintain standards generally, including terms and conditions of service and staff appointments. It also investigates common university problems and tries to determine why Nigerian graduates sent abroad for training often decide not to return to Nigeria. Finally, it reports on university views concerning the all-important issue of creating new universities.

By convention, the committee does not become involved in discussions on matters affecting individual universities. It meets bimonthly and is advised by standing subcommittees and working parties set up as the need arises. Although the committee has not made much progress in establishing central bodies to assist the universities in finding solutions to problems such as admissions and central statistical records, it has sponsored studies and investigations in these areas, and plans are under way to establish appropriate central bodies.

No. 68 Randle Avenue
Suru-Lere
Lagos, Nigeria

I. OGBUE

COMMITTEE ON COLLEGE ENTRANCE OF THE EUROPEAN COUNCIL OF INTERNATIONAL SCHOOLS

The membership of the Committee on College Entrance of the European Council of International Schools (ECIS) consists of secondary school counselors from ECIS member schools in Europe and college admissions directors from United States colleges and universities. The committee, founded in 1971, fosters communication between European schools and United States institutions of higher education. The committee's primary activity has been the organization of an annual visit by college admissions officials to American and international schools in Europe. The visit coincides with the semiannual meeting of ECIS, held in Europe each year. In 1973 the meeting in Athens, Greece, was held jointly with the Near East–South Asia Association of Secondary Schools.

The committee sponsors workshops in the United States to talk about the college needs of overseas secondary school students with college admissions officials. Committee members also participate in programs of the National Association of College Admissions Counselors and the American Association of Collegiate Registrars and Admissions Officers to discuss the college-oriented problems and needs of these students.

The committee receives some fiscal support from ECIS. In the United States, however, the committee member's institution pays for the necessary transportation to committee meetings. Colleges and universities are encouraged to become associate members of ECIS. Member institutions are listed and described in the annual *ECIS Directory* and their representatives may participate in the annual tour of colleges.

49 Wrentham Road
Springfield, Massachusetts 01119 USA

COMMONWEALTH FUND
See Research: Role of Foundations in Academic Research.

COMMUNICATION, MASS
See Mass Communication (field of study).

COMMUNITY COLLEGES
See Short-Cycle Education.

COMMUNITY RELATIONS
See Town-Gown Relations.

COMORO ISLANDS

The Comoro Islands, a group of four large and a number of small islands, are located in the Mozambique Channel between the African coast and Mozambique. The islands declared independence in 1975, after having been a French colony, and later a French territory, since 1843. In 1973–74 the islands had a population of 294,000.

The school system follows the French model, and the language of instruction is French. In 1973–74 21,500 students attended 130 primary schools, and 2900 students were enrolled in one private secondary school and in the Moroni *lycée,* which has branches on the other three larger islands.

There is no higher education on the islands. Students go abroad for higher study, principally to France.

COMPARATIVE AND INTERNATIONAL EDUCATION SOCIETY

An international professional organization of educators and behavioral scientists founded in 1956, the Comparative and International Education Society (CIES) includes more than three thousand students, faculty, administrators, consultants, and scholars in educational institutions throughout the world. The society aims to promote and improve teaching, service, and research related to comparative and international education. To facilitate international exchange of professors, students, and documents, it cooperates actively with UNESCO, the Organisation for Economic

Co-operation and Development, the Organization of American States, and the World Bank, as well as with professors concerned with the comparative and international dimensions of their fields. Annual conference sessions are organized in conjunction with the American Association of Colleges for Teacher Education and the American Educational Studies Association. CIES has regional chapters in New York and in the midwestern, southeastern, and western sections of the United States.

The society's *Comparative Education Review* covers problems and developments in education with an international perspective. Published three times yearly, the publication contains book reviews, bibliographies, editorial introductions, and news notes. The society also publishes *Comparative and International Education Society Newsletter,* which informs members of national and regional conferences, professional concerns, business-meeting highlights, research and teaching activities, and publications in world education. The newsletter appears triannually.

> Secretariat
> Graduate School of Education
> University of California
> Los Angeles, California 90024 USA

COMPARATIVE EDUCATION CENTER, United States

Founded in 1958 with the support of the Ford Foundation, the Comparative Education Center at the University of Chicago undertakes cross-national and comparative studies in education at all levels and trains doctoral candidates in the application of sociology and economics to problems of educational development and planning. Focusing on problems of the developing countries, research in higher education has been conducted on the development of African universities and on former graduates of the University of the West Indies, with particular reference to occupational mobility and cost-benefit analysis. Other

research areas in higher education include the following: economics of higher education, manpower in higher education, educational planning, university students, and reform of higher education.

Receiving funds from foundations and the University of Chicago, the center's staff includes three research professionals, six research assistants, twenty-one graduate students, and one secretary. Paid consultants are used occasionally.

Staff members have access to the Joseph Regenstein Library of the University of Chicago, which has large holdings in education, and the university's computer facilities.

> University of Chicago, Judd Hall
> 5835 S. Kimbark
> Chicago, Illinois 60637 USA

COMPARATIVE EDUCATION CENTRE, Canada

The Comparative Education Centre *(Centre d'éducation comparée)* at the University of Ottawa, Ontario, was founded in 1954 to serve as a clearinghouse for information in the field of comparative and international education. A center for teaching and research, it offers a series of electives to graduate students in education, fosters interdisciplinary and interdepartmental studies, and tutors master's and doctoral students working on their dissertations. Any level of education, including higher education, and any area of interest in education may be considered for research. In addition to research and teaching activities, the center sponsors conferences, provides a documentation service, and coordinates bibliographical work.

Funded by the University of Ottawa, the center is staffed by three research professionals, three administrative personnel, and one secretary, aided by an interdepartmental and interuniversity advisory board of about fifteen professors. Staff members have access to university facilities and various Ottawa libraries, including the National Library and its computer services for accumulating current bibliographical materials. A specialized card catalog on comparative and international education is kept up to date by the center for researchers.

Faculty of Education
University of Ottawa
Ottawa, Ontario, Canada K1N 6N5

COMPARATIVE EDUCATION RESEARCH UNIT
(Arbeitsstelle für vergleichende Bildungsforschung), Federal Republic of Germany

Founded in 1972, the Comparative Education Research Unit at the University of the Ruhr, Bochum, Federal Republic of Germany, conducts research on the educational systems of socialist countries, including China, but with special reference to the Eastern European countries. Research in higher education includes studies of educational planning, history of higher education, curricula and instruction, and reform in higher education in the socialist systems. In a project for the Federal Ministry of Education, the unit studied educational developments in the German Democratic Republic and the Soviet Union and cooperation among Eastern European countries.

Funded by the government, the institute is located within the university's Institute of Education. The staff includes three research professionals, one research assistant, one secretary, and four part-time student aides. The library of the Institute of Education is available to the researchers.

The unit publishes *Bibliographische Mitteilungen,* an information bulletin containing short reviews of new publications dealing with all aspects of education in socialist countries. A special issue on China was published in 1975. Issued three times a year, the bulletin is available free of charge. The unit also has published *Die sowjetische Bildungspolitik 1958–1973,* edited by O. Anweiler, F. Kübart, and K. Meyer, which

contains documents on Soviet educational policies. The unit is preparing a handbook of basic data on education, including material on higher education, in the Soviet Union, the German Democratic Republic, Poland, and Czechoslovakia.

Institut für Pädagogik,
Ruhr-Universität
Postfach 2148
D-463 Bochum, Federal Republic
of Germany

COMPARATIVE HIGHER EDUCATION

Comparative higher education and international education are sometimes confused. Because these two subjects are closely linked, the following remarks of Fraser and Brickman (1968, p. 1) on the difference between comparative education and international education are useful: "The terms *international education* and *comparative education* are related but they are different in emphasis. International education connotes the various kinds of relationships—intellectual, cultural and educational—among individuals and groups from two or more nations. . . . International education refers to the various methods of international cooperation, understanding and exchange. . . . Comparative education is, on the other hand, the analysis of educational systems and problems in two or more national environments in terms of sociopolitical, economic, cultural, ideological and other contents. Judgments are arrived at not to determine which system, idea, or method is superior, but rather in order to understand the factors underlying similarities and differences in education in the various nations."

James A. Perkins, chairman of the International Council for Educational Development (ICED), in writing in January 1972 to various scholars for advice on an inventory of research centers and journals in comparative higher education that ICED was preparing, distinguished between national, international, and comparative international studies as follows: "National studies are those in which the data and analyses tend to be drawn exclusively from one culture or nation; *international* studies are those which include coverage of more than one nation but usually in separate country-by-country chapters, with a minimum of actual comparative treatment; *comparative international* studies are those which draw upon comparative data and offer extended comparative analyses." For purposes of this discussion, comparative higher education includes Perkins's international and comparative international categories.

The phrase *higher education* may have different meanings in the comparative context, and hence needs clarification. In the United States higher education normally refers to undergraduate, graduate, and professional programs that lead to academic degrees at colleges and universities. The word *postsecondary,* now frequently used in the United States, refers to all formal education after secondary school, including adult education, continuing or recurrent education, and even the educational programs of the proprietary institutions.

In the United Kingdom higher education is loosely distinguished from other education after secondary school (or after the compulsory attendance age at secondary school) on the basis of the level of studies offered. *Further education* is chiefly an administrative term, since some colleges of further education offer both advanced secondary-level studies and degree-level studies that are considered higher education. Now that the Open University in Britain offers degree programs to students without the usual university admissions requirements, higher education cannot be distinguished from other postsecondary education on the basis of admissions criteria.

Another term increasingly used to denote academic studies after the secondary school level is *tertiary education.* So far used mainly in Australia (which distinguishes between university and "advanced" tertiary

education), this term may be the most appropriate because postsecondary implies completion of secondary education, and now in some countries completion of secondary school is not required for admission to postsecondary education. In Sweden, for example, students can be admitted who are at least twenty-five years old and have been employed for four years.

A further alternative, which has a wider scope than tertiary and may fit better the trend toward alternating periods of work and study, is *postcompulsory* education. However, for the sake of simplicity and historical tradition, the word *higher* is used in this discussion of comparative higher education, and includes all postsecondary academic education.

Methodology

Assuming that a discipline involves a well-defined body of knowledge, a substantial literature, and a large number of scholars who share a rigorous methodology and are teaching and researching in the field, it would be premature to characterize comparative higher education as a discipline, since it does not yet meet these criteria. However, the time may not be far off when it will. If a subject must be represented as a separate department in a college or university before it can be considered an independent academic field, comparative higher education does not meet that criterion either. Furthermore, in that neither higher education nor comparative education, despite their remarkable growth since 1960, are fully recognized as academic disciplines, or at least may not be so recognized in most countries (the North American countries are the chief exception), it is hardly surprising that comparative higher education is more a nascent than an established discipline.

As already mentioned, comparative higher education as here defined includes research and studies relating to higher education in more than one country. This definition clearly excludes "mono-country" studies (research and scholarship on higher education in only one country), which are much more numerous than genuinely comparative studies. In this connection it is of interest that the journal *Comparative Education Review*, published in the United States since 1956, despite its title typically includes more articles dealing with aspects of education in a single country than comparative pieces. Noncomparative studies of higher education in other countries nevertheless contribute importantly to and are an essential foundation for comparative higher education studies. Apart from helping to inform policy decisions, to be discussed later, each of these types of studies aims to increase understanding of higher education in countries abroad—both as an end in itself and as a means of better understanding one's own system.

The second objective obviously is apt to be more effectively served by comparative studies that examine aspects of foreign higher education relevant to or in the context of one's own system. If a multicountry study involves such diverse higher education systems that useful comparisons can only be made at a level of extreme generality, a two-country or bilateral study, which can focus more systematically and comprehensively on shared problems or relationships between systems, is likely to be more useful. However, examining an aspect of the higher education system in a country in relation to only one other country neglects the larger contribution that studies of the systems in a number of countries can make. Whether a two-country or multicountry comparative study is more useful hinges in part on the degree to which the higher education system in one country shares common—or contrasting—traditions, structures, and trends with other countries. It also hinges on the comparative methodology followed.

Comparative studies can be categorized in several ways depending upon methodology. Most common are descriptive studies, which may juxtapose factual accounts of national higher education systems or deal with them seriatim. While such "accretive" studies produce useful information, they fall short of being really comparative. A second type of comparative study includes as part of such descriptive accounts a transnational or cross-cultural examination of the issues reviewed and thus is synthetic or simultaneous as well as seriatim. Only recently has a more genuinely comparative and analytical methodology begun to emerge. This methodology takes an issue- or problem-oriented approach, and attempts to define major categories for analysis applicable to all higher education systems despite their varying levels of development, typologies, and societal roots. An example would be Martin Trow's analysis of higher education systems under the rubrics of elite, mass, and universal.

The foregoing comments on methodology of comparative higher education suggest that a single methodology, even if elusive, is desirable. This suggestion is debatable. As Cerych and McGurn (1974a, p. 9) have observed, "It can be argued that comparative studies in higher education cannot and should not ever have a common methodology because the intervention of several disciplines, each of them with its own methodology, is needed. However it is precisely this interdisciplinary nature of comparative higher education which postulates the establishment of a solid conceptual framework within which the comparative methodologies of different social sciences could cross-fertilize each other and thus contribute to a better understanding of the phenomenon of higher education."

Research

The fact that comparative higher education research involves a range of disciplines is a significant feature of the field. In no way the monopoly of educationists, some of the most important comparative higher education research has been undertaken by sociologists, political scientists, and economists. Spurred by the rapid increases in funds devoted to higher education and by its expanding role in society since mid-century, specialists in public administration and public policy have turned their scholarly interests to comparative higher education.

Aims. As a consequence of or a parallel development to this expansion, an increasingly important aim of comparative higher education studies, referred to earlier, is to provide guidance to policymakers. No single country or higher education system can claim to have the answers to the many complex questions that higher education confronts. All can benefit from a greater awareness of higher education elsewhere and from knowledge of how other systems seek solutions to these questions. That governmental, intergovernmental, and international organizations concerned with the functions and costs of higher education have been instrumental in encouraging comparative higher education studies, or have themselves undertaken them, is a logical if not inevitable consequence of the burgeoning of higher education, especially after 1960.

It should be emphasized, however, that higher education strategies and instrumentalities developed in one country to deal with its particular problems are rarely exportable to others without significant adaptation. Seductive as the importation of foreign models might appear to embattled politicians, government bureaucrats, and academic decision makers, they should not expect that the approaches found effective in one country can be successful in another. Too many environmental variables are involved, such as different traditions and practices in organizational decision making, different societal values, and differences in the status and aims of higher education. In short, the experience of foreign education systems may be of limited relevance to one's own country because of the cultural bias that all higher education systems must have if they are to be responsive to their own society's needs.

Balancing this, however, is the fact that many problems faced by one higher education system may be common to others. Some problems are indeed universal, such as determining objectives, striking the appropriate balance between institutional autonomy and accountability, and adapting access policy to student demand and national needs for college and university graduates (if in fact these needs can be determined). Furthermore, just as the international interchange of students and scholars has characterized higher education since the development of medieval universities at Padua, Paris, and Oxford (and the comparative higher education specialist can facilitate such interchange because his understanding of the interface between systems enables him to advise on how students and scholars from one system can best be fitted into another), so has the exchange and reciprocal borrowing of ideas on the aims and functioning of higher education. For example, the British University Grants Committee served as the model for counterpart (although modified) organizations in various other countries. Comparative higher education studies can make an important contribution by documenting and analyzing how structures and strategies developed in one country have been or might be transplanted and adapted elsewhere.

The worldwide expansion of higher education in the latter half of the twentieth century has given a major impetus to comparative higher education studies as policymakers have groped for answers to practical problems, and the increased complexity and centrality of higher education to national policy have attracted more scholars to comparative higher education research.

Higher education enrollments worldwide increased from six million three hundred thousand students in 1950 to about twenty-six million in 1970. The proportion of students between twenty and twenty-five years old in higher education increased from about 3 percent in 1950 to around 11 percent in 1970. Based on the rate of increase in higher and secondary education enrollments in previous years, Dragoljub Najman, director of higher education at

UNESCO, estimated that higher education enrollments in 1980 may be fifty-four million, and one hundred fifteen million in 1990 (Najman, 1974). Obviously there are important regional differences in rates of enrollment. In 1970 the percentage of all persons enrolled in formal education who were in higher education varied from 1.2 percent in African nations to 14.4 percent in North America. Worldwide the percentage was 5.4 percent. Considering that higher education enrollments quadrupled during the 1950–1970 period and may well quadruple again 1970–1990, clearly higher education has become such a major force in society as to merit increasing study, including comparative study.

Government sponsors. Research on comparative higher education has received impetus not only from the sheer expansion of higher education worldwide but also from the expanded activity of international organizations in this field, including intergovernmental and private groups. Among the former, UNESCO has focused on teacher training, access, and the international equivalence of degrees and diplomas. UNESCO's International Institute for Educational Planning in Paris does some work on the planning of university development. Its European Center for Higher Education in Bucharest collects and diffuses information on postsecondary education in Eastern and Western Europe, and encourages international university cooperation and student and teacher exchanges. The Regional Center of Higher Education and Development, located in Singapore and set up with the assistance of UNESCO in 1970, plays a similar role in Southeast Asia, especially in fostering the contribution of higher education to national development.

The Organisation for Economic Cooperation and Development (OECD) has sponsored or itself undertaken important research on higher education structures and growth, the economics of education, short-cycle institutions, innovation, research policies, and higher education statistics in its twenty-three member countries. The OECD's Center for Research and Innovation in Education has been concerned with the use of computers in higher education. Also active in European higher education cooperation have been the Commission of the European Communities (CEC) and the Council of Europe's Council for Cultural Co-operation (CCC). The latter has encouraged cooperation on higher education curricular reform and on the equivalence of academic qualifications through its Special Project Mobility. An official mandate of one of the permanent CCC committees, the Committee for Higher Education and Research, is to promote research on higher education. The CEC encourages mobility and interchange in higher education; its Education Committee began work in 1974 on problems of equivalence in cooperation with the CCC. Since the establishment of the office of the Commissioner for Science, Research and Education, much more attention has been given by the European Communities to higher education problems.

Major world regions other than Western Europe do not have regional organizations that encourage higher education and cooperation to the same degree as do the OECD, the Council of Europe, and the European Communities in Western Europe, although the Organization of American States has undertaken studies pertinent to comparative higher education in Latin America. In general, comparative studies for major world regions other than Western Europe are, apart from the work of UNESCO, mainly generated by national governments, nongovernmental organizations, higher education institutions, and individual scholars. Moreover, with the possible exception of UNESCO, the intergovernmental organizations that do produce or sponsor comparative higher education research typically do so not as part of their official terms of reference but in connection with their programs to encourage international cooperation and exchange of information. Whether the United Nations University (chartered in 1973 and headquartered in Japan) or the European University Institute in Florence (founded in 1974) will contribute to the field of comparative higher education as a part or by-product of their other more central concerns remains to be seen.

At the national level a number of government-sponsored studies and reports have provided extremely useful data for comparative studies, although few, most notably the 1963 Robbins Report in Great Britain, have been comparative or cross-national. Somewhat comparable to the Robbins Committee was the Carnegie Commission on Higher Education in the United States. Funded privately by the Carnegie Corporation of New York, a philanthropic foundation, rather than by government, the commission undertook a major review of American higher education. Like the Robbins Committee, its focus was chiefly national; however, several of its more than one hundred publications were comparative—especially the volumes of Eric Ashby, Joseph Ben-David, and Alain Touraine, which analyzed the American situation in a comparative context. Researchers may have difficulty in learning about or gaining access to some government-sponsored studies on higher education; for example, a 1974 study by Raymond Barre and Jean-Louis Boursin on the articulation between secondary and higher education in seven countries, which was commissioned by the French Ministry of National Education, received little notice in the periodical literature of comparative higher education.

Private sponsors. Private international, regional, and national organizations have also contributed to comparative higher education research. Among private international organizations an increasingly important contributor is the International Council for Educational Development (ICED), headquartered in New York, one of whose major concerns is the design and management of higher education systems. ICED holds occasional seminars, bringing together scholars and higher education officials from a variety of countries to explore aspects of comparative higher education. Four of these seminars, held at the Aspen Institute for Humanistic Studies in the summers of 1973, 1974, 1975, and 1976 focused respectively on the crisis of higher education, the new missions of the university, the relationship between higher education and society, and access, systems, and employment. In addition to publishing a variety of occasional papers and a quarterly newsletter, the ICED has produced two important bibliographical studies on comparative higher education (Berdahl and Altomare, 1972; Altbach and Kelly, 1975). In early 1975 ICED took on a two-year study project on access to higher education in the Federal Republic of Germany and the United States, which includes some other countries as well. Another ICED project related to comparative higher education is its program on higher education for development, launched in 1974 with the sponsorship of twelve national and international donor agencies.

The International Association of Universities, another private international organization involved in comparative higher education, encourages cooperation and the exchange of information and ideas on higher education, primarily through its quarterly *Bulletin,* its *International Handbook of Universities,* and its triennial general conferences. The theme of the 1975 general conference, held in Moscow, was "Higher Education at the Approach of the Twenty-first Century." Also among private international organizations encouraging comparative higher education research, although its focus is mainly on other levels, is the World Council of Comparative Education Societies.

At the regional level, the European Cultural Foundation Institute of Education, launched in early 1975, is undertaking international, interdisciplinary, policy-oriented studies of postcompulsory education, with specific projects on the public service functions of higher education, nontraditional education, and education and employment. The institute grew, in part, out of the work of the European Cultural Foundation's Plan Europe 2000 education project, the focus of which was educating man for the twenty-first century. Other regional groups or organizations whose activities in cooperation and the exchange of information contribute to comparative higher education include the Association of African Universities, the Association of Southeast Asian Institutions of Higher Learning, the Confederation of the Universities of Central America, the Council on Higher Education in the American Republics, the Association of Caribbean Universities and Research Institutes, the Association of Commonwealth Universities, and various regional associations of university presidents, such as the Standing Conference of Rectors and Vice-Chancellors of European Universities, set up in 1964. Not to be overlooked also are regional or national professional organizations, such as the Comparative Higher Education Society in Europe, the Comparative and International Education Society in the United States, and the Society for Research into Higher Education in Great Britain, which includes some materials on comparative higher education in its *Research into Higher Education Abstracts* and *Register of Research into Higher Education.*

University sponsors. Among universities worldwide, relatively few engage in comparative higher education research. For example, although there are more than fifty centers for higher education research and teaching in the United States, only a handful—the State University of New York at Buffalo, Yale University (in sociology), the University of Chicago, the University of Wisconsin, Columbia University Teachers College, the University of California at Berkeley, to name some—are carrying out comparative studies. Elsewhere, research pertinent to comparative higher education is undertaken at Lancaster University and the University of London in Great Britain; the universities of Paris-Dauphine IX and Paris VII in France; the University of Toronto and Queen's University in On-

tario, Canada; the University of New England in Australia; and the University of Constance Center for Educational Research, the German Institute for Educational Research in Frankfurt, and the Max Planck Institute for Educational Research in the Federal Republic of Germany (the last two not attached to universities).

Literature. Although, as pointed out at the outset, genuinely comparative higher education studies constitute a small part of all comparative and/or international education research, a thoroughgoing review of even this literature is beyond the scope of this essay. Several bibliographical studies, however, are important. Robert Berdahl and George Altomare's *Comparative Higher Education: Sources of Information* (1972) provides an inventory of research centers, journals, newsletters, and scholars in comparative higher education. Philip G. Altbach's annotated bibliography, *Comparative Higher Education* (1973), is a comprehensive treatment of comparative as well as national studies; the more recent *Higher Education in Developing Nations* (Altbach and Kelly, 1975) focuses, as the title suggests, on the nonindustrialized world.

As pointed out earlier, much of the literature on comparative higher education appears in journals in fields other than education. However, several newsletters, journals, and the like, deserve mention as important sources of information and studies: the London Times *Higher Education Supplement; Minerva; Comparative Education; Comparative Education Review; Higher Education,* published in the Netherlands since 1972; and since early 1975 *Le monde de l'éducation.*

It is difficult to mention scholars in comparative higher education without running the danger of omitting some. Abraham Flexner pioneered in the field with his 1930 volume on American, English, and German universities (Flexner, 1968). A comparative study which had a tremendous impact in Germany in the late 1950s was Friedrich Edding's *International Trends in Expenditures for Schools and Universities*

(1958). The problem of importing foreign university models was impressively dealt with by Eric Ashby (1966). Another landmark study, Frank Bowles's two-volume work on access (1963), was jointly sponsored by UNESCO and the International Association of Universities. Christopher Driver, former writer for the *Manchester Guardian,* gave a vivid and highly readable account of higher education stresses and reforms in Italy, France, Britain, Germany, Japan, the United States, and other countries, with special attention to the impact of sharply increasing enrollments (1971). The ICED monograph by Cerych and McGurn (1974) on the relevance of comparative higher education studies deals briefly but effectively with this topic. Jack Embling's (1974) assessment of the relevance of the work of the Carnegie Commission on Higher Education to Western Europe tends to focus more on Great Britain than on the Continent, but offers useful insights.

Finally, although comparative higher education research may be uneven, incomplete, and elusive, its rapid growth since the early 1960s is impressive. It has tended to focus on situations of timely or situational importance—for example, student activism in the late 1960s, recurrent or lifelong learning in the early 1970s. The topics to which priority is likely to be accorded in the late 1970s and the 1980s will probably include systems coordination, access, cost effectiveness, lifelong learning, and the problem of achieving an appropriate balance between professional and liberal arts education. As such higher education problems increasingly become transnational and solutions to them become more urgent, the need for scholarly and policy-oriented research in comparative higher education is destined to increase. The statistical base for such expanded research has been developed, mainly through the work of UNESCO and OECD, and an identifiable and growing community of scholars and practitioners can be expected to respond to the enlarging needs of the field.

Bibliography

Altbach, P. G. *Comparative Higher Education.* Washington, D.C.: American Association for Higher Education, 1973. ERIC Higher Education Research Report No. 5.

Altbach, P. G., and Kelly, D. H. *Higher Education in Developing Nations: A Selected Bibliography, 1969–1974.* New York: Praeger (in cooperation with International Council for Educational Development), 1975.

Ashby, E. *Universities: British, Indian, African.* Cambridge, Massachusetts: Harvard University Press, 1966.

Ashby, E. *Any Person, Any Study: An Essay on Higher Education in the United States.* New York: McGraw-Hill, 1972.

Ben-David, J. *American Higher Education: Directions Old and New.* New York: McGraw-Hill, 1972.

Berdahl, R., and Altomare, G. *Comparative Higher Education: Sources of Information.* New York: International Council for Educational Development, 1972.

Bowles, F. *Access to Higher Education.* Paris: UNESCO (and International Association of Universities), 1963.

Cerych, L., and McGurn, G. *Comparative Higher Education: Relevance for Policy Making;* and *Comparative Higher Education: A United States View.* New York: International Council for Educational Development, 1974.

Comparative Education. Oxford, England: Carfax Publishing Company (three times per year).

Comparative Education Review. Madison, Wisconsin: School of Education, University of Wisconsin (three times per year).

Driver, C. *The Exploding University.* London: Hodder and Stoughton, 1971.

Edding, F. *International Trends in Expenditures for Schools and Universities.* Kiel, Federal Republic of Germany: Forschungsberichte des Instituts für Weltwirtschaft, 1958.

Embling, J. *A Fresh Look at Higher Education: European Implications of the Carnegie Commission Reports.* Amsterdam: Elsevier, 1974.

Flexner, A. *Universities: American, English, German.* New York: Oxford University Press, 1968.

Fraser, S. E., and Brickman, W. *A History of International and Comparative Education, Nineteenth Century Documents.* Glenview, Illinois: Scott, Foresman, 1968.

Higher Education. Amsterdam: Elsevier (quarterly).

Higher Education: Report of the Committee Appointed by the Prime Minister Under the Chairmanship of Lord Robbins, 1961–1963. Cmnd.

2154. London: H. M. Stationery Office, 1963.

International Association of Universities. *Bulletin.* Paris: IAV (quarterly).

International Association of Universities. *International Handbook of Universities.* (6th ed.) Paris: IAV, 1974.

Minerva, A Review of Science, Learning and Policy. London: International Association for Cultural Freedom (quarterly).

Le monde de l'éducation. Paris: Le Monde (monthly).

Najman, D. *L'enseignement supérieur, pour quoi faire?* Paris: Librairie Artheme Fayard, 1974.

Organisation for Economic Co-operation and Development. *Analytical Report.* Paris: OECD, 1971.

Organisation for Economic Co-operation and Development. *Development of Higher Education 1950–1967, Statistical Survey.* Paris: OECD, 1970.

Organisation for Economic Co-operation and Development. *Policies for Higher Education, General Report, Conference on Future Structures of Postsecondary Education.* Paris: OECD, 1974.

Organisation for Economic Co-operation and Development. *Short-Cycle Higher Education, A Search for Identity.* Paris: OECD, 1973.

Society for Research into Higher Education. *Register of Research into Higher Education.* London: SRHE (annual).

Society for Research into Higher Education. *Research into Higher Education Abstracts.* London: SRHE (quarterly).

The Times Higher Education Supplement. London (weekly).

Touraine, A. *The Academic System in American Society.* New York: McGraw-Hill, 1973.

UNESCO Statistical Yearbook. Paris (annual).

BARBARA B. BURN

See also: Internalization of Higher Education; Literature of Higher Education, Sources of and Access to; Periodicals, Higher Education; Publications, Higher Education.

COMPARATIVE LITERATURE
(Field of Study)

Comparative literature, as taught in Western countries, includes major authors and works chosen from the Western heritage, works following the cultural and literary development from ancient Greece and Rome westward across Europe, and sometimes extending to the New World. Thus, students of comparative literature trace genres, themes, and movements from antiquity to the present, keeping alive the study of Greek and Latin.

Even though Goethe, Madame de Staël, August Wilhelm von Schlegel, and Henry Hallam, followed later in the nineteenth century by Louis Betz and Joseph Texte and others, explored the possibilities of *comparatism,* the discipline was slow to be incorporated into university curricula. In the United States, Harvard University created a chair for A. R. Marsh in 1890–91. In France a chair was founded in Lyon in 1897, followed by chairs at the Sorbonne in 1910 and Strasbourg in 1918. At the turn of the century, Joel Elias Spingarn initiated courses in comparative literature in the English department at Columbia University, where a short-lived journal in the field was launched in 1903. Similar chairs were not created in the German universities until the late 1920s.

Because systematic government and foundation sponsorship of teaching foreign languages during World War II had given it a linguistic base, after the war comparative literature found a permanent place in the undergraduate and graduate curricula of American universities. In the United States Harvard started the revival in 1946. Other universities—the University of California at Berkeley, the University of North Carolina, Indiana University, Yale University, New York University, and the University of Oregon—quickly followed. In the spring of 1974 the American Council of Learned Societies made the American Comparative Literature Association (ACLA) one of its constituent societies.

Comparative literature also developed in many countries outside of the West—in Japan, the Republic of Korea, Algeria, India, and Taiwan. Countries outside the Greco-Roman heritage, however, tend to set their own geographical limits for this discipline; for example, the University of Tokyo started by emphasizing English influences upon Japanese literature. The same preoccupation with British literature and its affiliations with Indian writers is found in India. Some Indian scholars limit their comparison to works in Hindi, Bengali, Malaylam, and other native languages of the subcontinent. Egypt and other Arab countries have long specialized in influences of Arabic literature on that of Andalusia and southern France.

Perhaps the interest shown in comparative literature by Asian scholars in the 1970s will hasten the development of the complex discipline of World and East-West literature. World literature, first dreamed of by Goethe after reading Chinese poetry, implies an encompassing view of the literature of five continents. It would have to be taught by a team of specialists and limited to broad themes and forms applicable to disparate bodies of literature. For example, the generic forms of comedy and tragedy which the West inherited from Aristotle have little applicability to India, Japan, or Indonesia. The profusion of translations of works from all over the world into the major languages, indicated by the yearly *Index Translationum* published by UNESCO, is currently one of the few movements toward world literature.

The East-West study of literature presents similar obstacles to a lesser degree. The teaching of such courses by a team of two specialists, one from the West and one from the East, is virtually impossible. Although Western-trained comparatists are familiar with the 2000-year-old Western heritage, comparatists in Asia are unequipped to teach the great works of an Eastern heritage. Consequently, the East-West approach to literature is still distant.

Comparatists in the United States in the mid 1970s are actively pioneering in interrelating literature with art, music, psychology, law, and politics. The sixth International Comparative Literature Association (ICLA) Congress in Bordeaux (1970) emphasized the fruitful possibilities of relating literature and sociology. Nine universities or seminaries in the United States in 1976 offered courses on literature and theology,

but the interrelations with music and art dominated the field.

Adhering to the Western heritage, comparative literature departments offer a selection of courses representing five major categories: (1) movements/generations/periods; (2) themes/myths; (3) genres/forms; (4) interrelations with another discipline; (5) literary theory and criticism. These departments generally operate with a core of two or three full-time comparatists, borrowing other professors with language and research qualifications as teachers, oral examiners, or thesis readers. But the numbers of trained comparatists emerging from United States graduate schools each year may be sufficient to meet most departmental needs in the future.

The greatest danger the discipline faces is the linguistic isolation of the United States and the resultant decline in knowledge of foreign languages; the student of comparative literature needs two foreign languages for the master's degree and three for the doctorate, one of which may be an ancient language. The bachelor's program is offered less often than the graduate programs, which usually include four to six literatures.

The widespread development of comparative literature is indicated by the host cities of the ICLA congresses: Venice; Chapel Hill, North Carolina; Utrecht, Netherlands; Fribourg, Federal Republic of Germany; Belgrade, Bordeaux, Montreal, and Budapest. The Soviet Union has rather hesitantly supported comparative literature and world literature (as evidenced by the varying fortunes of the Gorki Institute of World Literature in Moscow).

ROBERT J. CLEMENTS

Levels and Programs of Study

Programs in comparative literature generally require as a minimum prerequisite a secondary-level education and lead to the following degrees: Bachelor of Arts (B.A.), master's, the doctorate, or their equivalents. Programs consist primarily of classroom sessions, seminar or group discussions, and research.

Programs that lead to a first university degree deal with the study of international literary and cultural relationships. Principal course content usually includes some of the following: the currency, reception, and influence of writers and their works in countries other than those of their origin; the transmission and evolution of international literary movements; the characteristics of and relationships between genres, themes, and motifs; folk literature and folklore; criticism; esthetics; intermediaries; and the relationships between literature and other disciplines. Background courses usually include history, the social and behavioral sciences, philosophy, religion and theology, and the natural sciences.

Programs that lead to a postgraduate university degree deal with the advanced study of international literary and cultural relations. Emphasis is given to research work as substantiated by the presentation of a scholarly thesis or dissertation. Principal subject matter areas into which courses and research projects tend to fall include the origin and evolution of international literary movements, folk literature and folklore, criticism, esthetics, intermediaries, epics and sagas, tragedy, comedy, modern drama, the contemporary novel, problems of comparative literature, the comparative method in literary studies, the forces in contemporary literature, and research techniques in comparative literature.

[This section was based on UNESCO's *International Standard Classification of Education (ISCED)* (Paris: UNESCO, 1976).]

Major International and National Organizations

INTERNATIONAL

International Comparative Literature
 Association (ICLA)
Association internationale de littérature
 comparée (AILC)
% Institut de littérature générale et compareé
17 rue de la Sorbonne
75005 Paris, France

Secretariat for the Americas is Frederick Garber, State University of New York, Binghamton, New York 13901 USA. Secretariat for other parts of the world is Douwe W. Fokkema, Institute of Comparative Literature, University of Utrecht, Utrecht, Netherlands.

International Federation for Modern
 Languages and Literatures
Fédération internationale des langues et
 littératures modernes
% Professor S. C. Aston
St. Catherine's College
Cambridge CB2 1RL, England

NATIONAL

Canada:
 Association canadienne de littérature
  comparée
 Department of Comparative Literature
 University of Alberta
 Edmonton, Alberta T6G 2E6

Federal Republic of Germany:
 Deutsche Gesellschaft für allgemeine und
  vergleichende Literaturwissenschaft
 University of Bonn
 Bonn

France:
 Société française de littérature comparée
 Institut de littérature comparée
 Université de Caen
 Caen

Japan:
 Nihon hikaku bungakkai
 Aoyama gakuin daigaku
 Shibuya-ku
 Tokyo

Netherlands:
 Nederlandse vereniging voor algemene
  literatuurwetenschap
 % Institute of Comparative Literature
 University of Utrecht
 Utrecht

Republic of China:
 Comparative Literature Association in
  the Republic of China
 Department of Foreign Languages and
  Literature
 National Taiwan University
 Taipei, Taiwan

Romania:
 Comitetul naţional pentru literatură
  comparată
 Str. Onesti 11
 Bucharest

United States:
    American Comparative Literature
    Association
    State University of New York
    Binghamton, New York 13901

Principal Information Sources

GENERAL

Guides to the literature include:

Baldensperger, F., and Friederich, W. P. *Bibliography of Comparative Literature.* Chapel Hill: University of North Carolina Press, 1950. Reissued in 1960 by Russell and Russell, New York.

Bibliographie de littérature comparée, 1949–1958. Paris: Boivin, 1958.

"Bibliography of Comparative Literature." In *Yearbook of Comparative Literature.* Bloomington: Indiana University Press, 1952–.

Friederich, W. P. *Outline of Comparative Literature from Dante Alighieri to Eugene O'Neill.* Chapel Hill: University of North Carolina Press, 1954.

Jost, F. *Introduction to Comparative Literature.* Indianapolis, Indiana: Bobbs-Merrill, 1974.

Literature: General and Comparative. Widener Library Shelflist No. 18. Cambridge, Massachusetts: Harvard University Library, 1968. Distributed by Harvard University Press.

McCormick, J. O. (Ed.) *Syllabus of Comparative Literature.* (2nd ed.) Metuchen, New Jersey: Scarecrow Press, 1972.

Introductions to the field include:

Ďurišin, D. *Vergleichende Literaturforschung.* Berlin, German Democratic Republic: Akademie-Verlag, 1972.

Fugen, H. N. (Ed.) *Vergleichende Literaturwissenschaft.* Düsseldorf, Federal Republic of Germany: Econ Verlagsgruppe, 1973.

Pichois, C., and Rousseau, A. M. *La littérature comparée.* Paris: Librairie Armand Colin, 1967.

Rudiger, H. (Ed.) *Komparatistik: Aufgaben und Methoden.* Stuttgart, Federal Republic of Germany: Verlag W. Kohlhammer, 1973.

Stallknecht, N. P., and Frenz, H. (Eds.) *Comparative Literature: Method and Perspective.* Carbondale: Southern Illinois University Press, 1961.

Weisstein, U. *Comparative Literature and Literary Theory.* Bloomington: Indiana University Press, 1973.

Comparative education sources include:

"Canadian Programmes in Comparative Literature." *Littérature comparée au Canada,* 1973, *5*(1), 12–29.

Chambers, L. H. "Comparative Literature Programs in the United States and Canada." *Yearbook of Comparative and General Literature,* 1971, *20,* 89–109.

Rudiger, H. "Comparative Literature in Germany." *Yearbook of Comparative and General Literature,* 1971, *20,* 15–20.

"Symposium on the Teaching of Comparative Literature." *Comparative Literature: Proceedings of the 2nd Congress of the ICLA,* 1959, *1,* 216–245. University of North Carolina Studies in Comparative Literature No. 23.

Yearbook of Comparative and General Literature. Bloomington: Indiana University Press, 1952–. *YCGL* provides best coverage of information on the study and teaching of comparative literature in individual countries; periodically surveys teaching programs and updates these revisions in its "News and Notes" column.

CURRENT BIBLIOGRAPHIES

"Comptes rendus critiques." In quarterly issues of the *Revue de littérature comparée.* Paris: Librairie Marcel Didier, 1921–.

Modern Language Association International Bibliography of Books and Articles on the Modern Languages and Literatures. New York: Modern Language Association of America, annual. See "General Literature and Related Topics," Part 3: "Literature, General and Comparative," in Volume 1.

PERIODICALS

Some of the best journals in the field are *Arcadia* (FRG), *Cahiers algériens de littérature comparée, Comparative Literature* (US), *Comparative Literature Studies* (US), *Forschungsprobleme der vergleichenden Literaturgeschichte* (FRG), *Hikaku bungaku/Journal of Comparative Literature* (Japan), *Jadavpur Journal of Comparative Studies* (India), *Komparatistische Studien (Beihefte zu Arcadia)* (FRG), *Littérature comparée au Canada, Neohelicon: Acta Comparationis Litterarum Universarum* (Hungary), *Poetica* (FRG), *Poétique* (France), *Revue de littérature comparée* (France), *Tamkang Review* (Republic of China), *Yearbook of Comparative and General Literature* (US).

There is no comprehensive directory of journals in the field of comparative literature. The "News and Notes" column in *YCGL* reviews and provides background information on new journal titles and records the vicissitudes of those already in existence. The list offered below, cited by Jost, is brief:

"Current Periodicals." In F. Jost, *Introduction to Comparative Literature.* Indianapolis, Indiana: Bobbs-Merrill, 1974, p. 306.

ENCYCLOPEDIAS, DICTIONARIES, HANDBOOKS

Dizionario letterario Bompiani delle opere e dei personaggi di tutti i tempi e di tutti le letterature. (5th ed., 9 vols.) Milan: Bompiani, 1947–1950. Supplement (2 vols.), 1964–1966.

Dizionario universale della letteratura contemporanea. (5 vols.) Milan: Mondadori, 1959–1963.

Epplesheimer, H. W. *Handbuch der Weltliteratur von den Anfängen bis zur Gegenwart.* (3rd rev. ed.) Frankfurt/Main, Federal Republic of Germany: Klostermann, 1960.

Escarpit, R. *Dictionnaire international des termes littéraires.* The Hague: Mouton, 1973–. Sponsored by the ICLA.

Kindlers Literaturlexikon. (7 vols.) Zurich: Kindler Verlag, 1965–1970.

Penguin Companion to Literature. (4 vols.) New York: McGraw-Hill, 1969–1971.

Smith, H. (Ed.) *Columbia Dictionary of Modern European Literature.* New York: Columbia University Press, 1947.

DIRECTORIES

General directories in which comparative literature is covered include:

Commonwealth Universities Yearbook. London: Association of Commonwealth Universities, 1914–. Published annually.

International Handbook of Universities. Paris: International Association of Universities, triennial.

World Guide to Universities. New York: Bowker, 1972.

The World of Learning. London: Europa, 1947–. Published annually.

RESEARCH CENTERS, INSTITUTES, INFORMATION CENTERS

Comparative Literature Office
Ballantine Hall 402
Indiana University
Bloomington, Indiana 47401 USA

A. M. Gorki Institute of World Literature
ul. Vorovskogo 25a
Moscow, Soviet Union

Institut de littérature comparée
University of Alberta
Edmonton, Alberta, Canada T6G 2E6

Institut de littérature générale et comparée
University of Paris
17 rue de la Sorbonne
75005 Paris, France

Instituut voor algemene literatuurwetenschap
Rijksuniversiteit Utrecht
Ramstraat 31
Utrecht, Netherlands

Technische Hochschule, Aachen
Institut für Komparatistik
Templergraben 55
51 Aachen, Federal Republic of Germany

Western Literature Research Institute
Tamkang College, Tamsui
Taiwan, Republic of China

There is no directory of research centers in the field of comparative literature. The names on the above list have been taken from recent issues of the *Yearbook of Comparative and General Literature* (Bloomington: Indiana University Press, 1952–), which acts as a clearinghouse for current information on research in the field.

See also: Literature.

COMPENSATION, ADMINISTRATORS
See Remuneration: Faculty, Staff, and Chief Executive Officers.

COMPENSATION POLICIES
See Remuneration: Faculty, Staff, and Chief Executive Officers.

COMPREHENSIVE UNIVERSITIES
See Innovation.

COMPUTER AUGMENTED
See Computers, Role of in Higher Education: Computers in Instruction.

COMPUTER MANAGED
See Computers, Role of in Higher Education: Computers in Instruction.

COMPUTER SCIENCE
(Field of Study)

Computer science deals with the construction and use of computer systems to increase the efficiency of technical activities of society. This field developed as a consequence of the applications of certain branches of mathematics to the calculation tasks in engineering. The specialist in computer science must deal both with abstractions (algorithms, information structures, and computation schemas), which require a background in fundamental mathematical principles, and with practical applications (devices to process data).

Computer science may be conveniently divided into three main categories: (1) abstract automata theory (the pure theory of computing); (2) computer science, which combines theory with a wide range of applications in business, education, industry, and research; and (3) design of computer systems—programing systems (software) and electronic equipment to support the systems (hardware).

Abstract automata theory may be defined as the mathematical investigation of the general questions raised in the study of both human and mechanical information-processing systems. Parts of this theory were developed in the 1930s, well before electronic digital computers were built. Engineering applications of automata theory are found in the theory of sequential machines, which deals with the macroscopic behavior of the discrete parameter information systems. Switching theory, which describes the microscopic details of the system's construction, and the theory of sequential machines offer a mathematical basis for applied computer science, particularly the building of computers.

Other divisions have evolved from the three basic branches of computer science. For example, the theory of computability forms the basis for the algorithms for effective mathematical operations. Nonnumerical methods have been developed to solve problems that cannot be solved by classical algebraic calculus. Other new branches of computer science have evolved to employ computers more intelligently. For example, artificial intelligence and heuristic programing solve problems of understanding and translating languages, proving theorems, making decisions in game theory (a part of operations research), and learning. Pattern recognition classifies sounds and

visual objects and processes information in this area.

Early developments in computing machines were contributed by Blaise Pascal, who invented the first digital calculator in 1642; Gottfried Wilhelm Leibniz, who invented a machine that performed the multiplication process in 1671; and Charles Babbage, who developed a mechanical "analytical engine" in the nineteenth century. However, the modern electronic computer started with ENIAC, used for ballistic calculations in 1946 at the University of Pennsylvania. ENIAC, whose memory and operations were performed by mercury relay tubes, was a considerable improvement on the electromechanical calculator Mark I, built at Harvard University in 1944. As computers developed in complexity, their link with automata became more apparent. Applications in the field of natural and programing languages led to the development of formal, self-contained languages.

The first programs of study in automata theory were offered in departments of mathematics to solve problems in algorithmic computation. At the same time, the need of software for computers led to training in compiling systems. The need for specialists in computer design introduced switching theory and sequential machines in departments of electrical and electronic engineering. In computer science–oriented degree programs in mathematics and electrical engineering, numerical methods for improving discrete and continuous parameter systems play an important role.

Although programs in computer science are diverse and designed to meet regional needs, they all require solid preparation in both fundamental mathematical principles and practice in the application of these principles to problems. Furthermore, the application of computer science to various fields has led to interdisciplinary programs such as data processing in management, economics, biology, medicine (neurophysiological data, diagnosis, electrocardiogram analysis), and bioengineering.

Courses in computer science are generally given in departments of mathematics and engineering. Although they overlap, the programs of computer science given in mathematics departments are more oriented toward automata, formal languages, compiling systems, and numerical methods. Among the subjects studied are numerical techniques in optimization, discrete-state systems, algorithms and computational complexity, theory of formal languages, context-free languages, computer operating systems, structures for data presentation, theoretical models in computer science, on-line computer systems, programing languages and systems, compiler construction, simulation and models, theory of queuing systems, graphs and network flows, heuristic programing and artificial intelligence, optimization methods for large-scale systems, and operations research. Computer science offered in engineering departments, on the other hand, is usually more oriented toward switching circuits, sequential machines, computer systems, and numerical optimization methods. Subjects commonly studied are electronic circuits, digital signal processing, logic design, digital computer organization, discrete systems and automata, computer-aided circuit design, computer systems design, computer memory and memory systems, communication of data in computer systems, and interactive computer terminals, as well as some of the subjects usually given in mathematics departments.

The wide adoption of computers in the 1960s resulted in a change in computer science education in the early 1970s, from emphasis on abstract automata theory to the applications of computer theory to business, industry, education, and research. The changes took place particularly in technologically developed regions and especially in the United States. The recommendations of the Association for Computing Machinery (ACM) and the Mathematics Association of America (MAA) have strongly affected virtually every computer science program and are cited frequently as stan-

dards for computer science programs. These guidelines provide for several alternative study options: (1) an option for hardware specialists, who concentrate on the design and fabrication of present and future computer systems; (2) an option for software specialists—such as compiler designers, system programers, and specialists in the management of information systems—who concentrate on the design of software to support the hardware; and (3) an option for application specialists, who concentrate on methodologies for using computer systems and related software packages to solve large-scale problems in engineering, business, management, medicine, and other computer involved disciplines.

Although the emphasis of computer science varies depending on local needs and levels of technology, computer science is becoming an increasingly important discipline in countries throughout the world. Almost all countries offer programs or courses in computer science. Programs for exchange students and meetings for computer science specialists at such professional international organizations as the International Federation for Information Processing and the International Federation of Operational Research Societies, and such national organizations as the Association for Computing Machinery (in New York) and the British Computer Society (in London), contribute to the development and internationalization of education in computer science.

MARIUS HĂNGĂNUT
IOAN ALFRED LETIA

Levels and Programs of Study

Programs in computer science generally require as a minimum prerequisite a secondary education and lead to the following awards: diploma or certificate, bachelor's degree (B.Sc., B.A.), master's degree (M.Sc., M.A.), the doctorate (Ph.D.), or their equivalents. Programs deal with the theory and practice of computer science and consist of classroom, seminar, and practice sessions and group discussion.

Programs leading to an award not equivalent to a first university degree focus on systems analysis, computer functioning, and new applications for computers; these programs emphasize the practical technological aspects of the subjects rather than the underlying theory. Principal course content usually includes general mathematics, calculus, and probability theory. Specialized courses tend to include the various computer languages, machine codes, program documentation, the structure and design of the principal kinds of computer hardware, systems analysis (including charting), computer applications (including systems of programing), information science, and program library organization. Usual background courses are natural science, social sciences, engineering, and computer-applied mathematics.

Programs that lead to a first university degree deal primarily with systems analysis, the theory and practice of computer functioning, and new applications of computers. Three or four years of study are normally required, with about one third of the program composed of courses in computer science. Principal course content usually includes general mathematics, calculus, differential equations, probability theory, and introductory analysis. Specialized courses are usually selected from the following, according to a student's specialty: the Egdon computer system, Fortran, advanced Algol, other languages, machine codes, on-line systems, program documentation, computer structures and hardware, computer systems and systems programs, batch-processing systems, multiaccess systems, queuing problems in computer science, simulation, data structures and their application, information storage and retrieval, computer programing in machine-oriented and user-oriented languages, design of computer systems and associated hardware and software, numerical methods, nonnumerical methods, numerical analysis, combinational theory, statistical programing, informational science, and library organization.

Programs that lead to a postgraduate university degree consist primarily of study, seminar or group discussion, and research in the theory and practice of computer science. Programs at this level tend to be highly specialized in subject content, and an important element is original research work resulting in the presentation and defense of a scholarly thesis or dissertation. Principal course content and areas of research usually include computing with symbolic expressions, topics in computer science, theory of switching, logic design and digital systems, models of thought processes, artificial intelligence research, the representation problem in artificial intelligence, numerical methods of optimization, advanced numerical analysis, compiler construction, graphic data processing, mathematical theory of computation, computer models for natural languages, analog computation, data processing in business problems, information and communication theory, and information organization and retrieval.

[This section was based on UNESCO's *International Standard Classification of Education (ISCED)* (Paris: UNESCO, 1976).]

Major International and National Organizations

INTERNATIONAL

Federation of Data Processing Associations
Fédération européenne des associations de
   mécanographes
% Arbeitsgemeinschaft für Datenverarbeitung
Feldmühlgasse 11
A-1130 Vienna, Austria

Five International Associations Coordinating
   Committee (FIACC)
% International Measurement Confederation
   (IMEKO)
P.O. Box 457
1371 Budapest, Hungary
   A coordinating committee for the following organizations: IFIP, IFAC, IFORS, IMEKO, and AICA.

International Association for Analog
   Computation
Association internationale pour le calcul
   analogique (AICA)
50 avenue Franklin D. Roosevelt
Brussels, Belgium

International Association for Cybernetics
Association internationale de cybernétique
Palais des Exposition
place A. Rijckmans
Namur, Belgium

Intergovernmental Bureau for Informatics
   (IBI)
P.O. Box 10253
23 viale Civiltà del Lavoro
00144 Rome, Italy
   The only international organization devoted
to informatics.

International Federation for Information
   Processing (IFIP)
3 rue du Marché
Geneva, Switzerland

International Federation of Automatic Control
   (IFAC)
Graf-Recke-Strasse 84
Postfach 1139
4 Düsseldorf, Federal Republic of Germany

International Federation of Operational
   Research Societies (IFORS)
% Operational Research Society
62 Cannon Street
London, England

International Mathematics Union
Collège de France
11 place Marcelin-Berthelot
75231 Paris, France

International Measurement Confederation
   (IMEKO)
P.O. Box 457
1371 Budapest, Hungary

Mathematics Programming Society
% International Statistical Institute
2 Oøstwinlaan
The Hague, Netherlands

World Organization of General Systems and
   Cybernetics (WOGSC)
Temporary Secretariat
% College of Technology
Blackburn BB2 1LH, Lancashire, England

   For a complete listing of international organizations in the field of computer science and
mathematics see:

Carter, C. *Guide to Reference Sources in the Com-
   puter Sciences.* New York: Macmillan, 1974.
The Europa Yearbook: A World Survey. London:
   Europa, annual.
Yearbook of International Organizations. Brussels:
   Union of International Associations, 1948–.
   Published biennially.

NATIONAL

Australia:
   Australian Computer Society
   Caulfield Institute of Technology
   900 Dandenong Road
   Caulfield East, Victoria 3145

Brazil:
   Sociedade brasileira de simulação
   School of Engineering of Itajubá
   P.O. Box 50
   Itajubá, Minas Gerais

Canada:
   Canadian Information Processing
      Society
   Association canadienne de l'informatique
   42 Mercer Street
   Toronto, Ontario

Denmark:
   Dansk selskap for operationanalyse
   Danmarks tekniske højskole
   2800 Lyngby

Federal Republic of Germany:
   ADL-Verband für
      Informationsverarbeitung e.V.
   Postfach 1030
   2 Hamburg

   Deutsche Gesellschaft für Kybernetik
   Strassemannallee 21
   Frankfurt/Main

France:
   Association française pour la
      cybernétique économique et
      technologie
   avenue de Pologne
   75775 Paris, France

Italy:
   Associazione italiana per il calcolo
      automatico
   % Rassegna elettronica
   via Crescenzio 9
   00193 Rome

Japan:
   Information Processing Society of Japan
   1–5 Shiba-Koen
   Minato-ku
   Tokyo

Netherlands:
Studiecentrum NOVI
Stadhouderskade 6
Amsterdam

Spain:
Asociación española de informática y
automática
Facultad de ciencias
Universidad complutense de Madrid
Ciudad universitaria
Madrid 3

United Kingdom:
British Computer Society
29 Portland Place
London, England

United States:
American Federation of Information
Processing Societies (AFIPS)
210 Summit Avenue
Montvale, New Jersey 07653

American Society for Cybernetics
1130 17th Street NW
Washington, D.C. 20036

American Society for Information
Science
1155 16th Street NW
Washington, D.C. 20036

Association for Computing Machinery
1133 Avenue of the Americas
New York, New York 10036

For names of additional national organizations consult:

Carter, C. *Guide to Reference Sources in the Computer Sciences.* New York: Macmillan, 1974.
Minerva, Wissenschaftliche Gesellschaften. Berlin, Federal Republic of Germany: de Gruyter, 1972.

Principal Information Sources

GENERAL

Among the guides to literature in the field of computer sciences are:

Carter, C. *Guide to Reference Sources in the Computer Sciences.* New York: Macmillan, 1974. A comprehensive guide; includes organizations throughout the world, research and information centers, bibliographies, encyclopedias, dictionaries, and directories.
International Computer Bibliography: A Guide to the Use, Application and Effect of Computers in Scientific, Commercial, Industrial and Social Environments. Manchester, England: National Computing Centre, in cooperation with Stichting het Nederlands studiecen-

trum voor administratieve automatisering, 1968.
Morrill, C., Jr. *Computers and Data Processing Information Sources: An Annotated Guide to the Literature, Associations and Institutions Concerned with Input, Throughput, and Output of Data.* Detroit: Gale Research, 1969.
Pemberton, J. *How to Find Out in Mathematics.* Oxford, England: Pergamon Press, 1963.
Pritchard, A. *A Guide to Computer Literature: An Introductory Survey of the Sources of Information.* (2nd ed.) London: Clive Bingley, 1972.
Youden, W. W. *Computer Literature: Bibliography 1946–1963.* Washington, D.C.: National Bureau of Standards, 1965.
Youden, W. W. *Computer Literature: Bibliography 1964–1967.* Washington, D.C.: U.S. Department of Commerce, National Bureau of Standards, 1968.

The following works provide an introduction to the field:

Cardenas, A. F. *Computer Science.* New York: Wiley-Interscience, 1972.
Davidson, C. H., and Koenig, E. C. *Computers: Introduction to Computers and Applied Computer Concept.* New York: Wiley, 1967.
Forsythe, A. I. *Computer Science: A First Course.* New York: Wiley, 1969.
Nagel, H. T., and others. *An Introduction to Computer Logic.* Englewood Cliffs, New Jersey: Prentice-Hall, 1975.
Perlis, A. J. *Introduction to Computer Science.* New York: Harper & Row, 1975.

Historical treatment of computers and programing languages is offered by:

Goldstine, H. H. *The Computer from Pascal to Von Neumann.* Princeton, New Jersey: Princeton University Press, 1976.
Sammet, J. E. *Programming Languages: History and Fundamentals.* Englewood Cliffs, New Jersey: Prentice-Hall, 1969.

For works dealing with education and computer science see:

Bushell, D. D., and Allen, D. W. *The Computer in American Education.* New York: Wiley, 1967. A discussion of the role of computers in United States education.
Computer Yearbook 1972. Detroit: Computer Yearbook Company, 1972. See pages 314–325, "Computer Education in Colleges and Universities," for a brief discussion of computer education in United States institutions.
Finerman, A. *University Education in the Computing Sciences.* New York: Academic Press, 1968. Offers a discussion of the university teaching of computer science.

Systems Analysis for Educational Planning: Selected Annotated Bibliography/Méthodes analytiques appliquées à la planification de l'enseignement: Bibliographie choisie et annotée. Paris: Organisation for Economic Co-operation and Development, 1969.

Van der Aa, H. J. Computers and Education: An International Bibliography on Computers and Education. New York: Science Associates/International, 1970.

Also see the Proceedings of the World Conference on Computer Education, held in Amsterdam, Netherlands (1970), and in Marseille, France (1975). New York: American Elsevier, 1970 and 1975.

CURRENT BIBLIOGRAPHIES

For sources of current information in the field of computer science consult the following bibliographic and abstracting services:

Bulletin signalétique. Section 1: Mathématiques. Paris: Centre national de la recherche scientifique, 1940–.

Computer Abstracts. London: Technical Information Company, 1957–. Outstanding in its field.

Computer and Control Abstracts Science Abstracts, Series C. London: Institution of Electrical Engineers; New York: Institute of Electronic and Electrical Engineers, 1966–.

Computer and Information Systems. Cambridge, Massachusetts: Cambridge Communication Group, 1962–.

Computing Reviews. New York: Association for Computer Machinery, 1961–.

Electrotechniek, Literatuuroverzicht. The Hague: Technisch documentatieen informatiecentrum voor de krijgsmacht, 1952–.

New Literature on Automation: International Classified Abstract Journal on a.d.p. Amsterdam: IFIP, Administrative Data Processing Group, 1961–.

Quarterly Bibliography of Computers & Data Processing. Phoenix, Arizona: Applied Computer Research, 1971–.

Referativnyĭ zhurnal. Nauchnaya i tekhnicheskaya informatsiya. Moscow: Akademii nauk, SSSR, Institut nauchnoĭ informatsii, 1963–.

Review journals contain important information on current events and recent developments in the computer field. The following two reviews of progress offer critical reviews and summaries of research annually:

Advances in Computers. New York: Academic Press, 1960–.

Annual Review in Automatic Programming. Oxford, England: Pergamon Press, 1960–.

PERIODICALS

Leading periodicals in the field of computer science are Acta Informatica (FRG), Akademiia nauk SSSR, Izvestiya: Tekhnicheskaya kibernatika (USSR), Angewandte Informatik (US, UK, FRG), Archiwum automatyki i telemechanki (Poland), Australian Computer Journal, Automatica si electronica (Romania), Automatisme (France), Automatika/Yugoslav Professional Journal for Automation, Automation and Remote Control/Avtomatikai telemekhanika (US), Avtomatyka/Soviet Automatic Control (US), Computer (US), Computer International (UK), Computer Journal (UK), Computers and Automation (US), Computers and Education (US, UK), Cybernetica (Belgium), Cybernétique et pédagogie cybernétique (France), I.B.I. Newsletter (Italy), I.B.M. Journal of Research and Development (US), I.B.M. Systems Journal (US), International Association for Analog Computation Proceedings: Modelling and Computer Simulation (Belgium), International Journal of Computer Mathematics (US), International Journal of Control (UK), Journal of Computer and Systems Sciences (US), Journal of Cybernetics (US), Journal of Educational Data Processing (US), Mathematical Sciences (US), Mathematics of Computation (US), Network: International Communication Library Automation (US), Numerische Mathematik (FRG), Operational Research Quarterly (UK), Operations Research (US), Simulation (US), Sistemi e automazione (Italy), Software: Practice and Experience (UK), Soviet Mathematics (US), Zeitschrift für Operations Research (FRG).

For guides to additional computer periodicals see:

Brown, P., and Stratton, G. B. World List of Scientific Periodicals Published in the Years 1900–1960. (3 vols.) Hamden, Connecticut: Shoestring Press, 1964.

Computer Group News. New York: Institute of Electrical and Electronics Engineering, 1967–.

Pritchard, A. A World List of Computer Periodicals. Manchester, England: National Computing Center, 1970.

ENCYCLOPEDIAS, DICTIONARIES, HANDBOOKS

The following are useful dictionaries and handbooks in the field:

Broadbent, D. T. (Ed.) Multilingual Dictionary of Automatic Control Terminology. Philadelphia: Instrument Society of America, 1967. Published for the International Federation of Automatic Control in English, French, German, Russian, Italian, and Spanish.

Burger, E. Four Language Technical Dictionary of Data Processing, Computers and Office Machines. Oxford, England: Pergamon Press; Berlin, Federal Republic of Germany: VEB Verlag Technik, 1970.

Clason, W. E. *Elsevier's Dictionary of Computers, Automatical Control, and Data Processing in Six Languages.* (2nd rev. ed.) Amsterdam: Elsevier, 1971. English/American, French, Spanish, Italian, Dutch, and German.

Huskey, H. D., and Korn, G. A. *Computer Handbook.* New York: McGraw-Hill, 1962.

Jourdain, P. D. *Condensed Computer Encyclopedia.* New York: McGraw-Hill, 1969. Provides definitions and concept explanations of computer techniques and operating procedures.

Klerer, M., and Korn, G. *Digital Computer User's Handbook.* New York: McGraw-Hill, 1967.

Murray, T. J. *Mathematical Machines.* (2 vols.) New York: Columbia University Press, 1969.

Seven Language Dictionary of Automation Control Computers and Measuring. Moscow: Fizmatgiz, 1963.

Sippl, C. J. *Computer Dictionary and Handbook.* (4th ed.) Indianapolis, Indiana: H. W. Sams, 1970.

Weik, M. H. *Standard Dictionary of Computers and Information Processing.* New York: Hayden, 1969.

DIRECTORIES

The major directory in the field covering computer services in seventy-two countries is *International Directory of Computer and Information System Services,* published for the Intergovernmental Bureau for Information Technology (London: Europa, biannual). This work includes details of services provided by educational and research institutions, commercial firms, training establishments, universities and colleges, and governmental agencies.

Other useful directories in the field include:

BCS Educational Yearbook. London: British Computer Society, annual. Includes programs and courses offered in computer sciences in the United Kingdom.

Commonwealth Universities Yearbook. London: Association of Commonwealth Universities, annual.

Computer Courses 1969–70. A Guide to Computer Education Facilities in the United Kingdom. Manchester, England: National Computing Center, 1969–70.

Directory of Educational Programs in Information Science. Washington, D.C.: Society for Information Science, 1971/72. Directory of graduate courses in the United States. A supplement was published in 1972/73.

Hsiao, T. C. *Directory of Computer Education and Research.* (2 vols.) Vol. 1: *Senior Colleges.*

Vol. 2: *Junior Colleges.* Washington, D.C.: Science and Technology Press, 1973. A United States directory.

Peterson's Annual Guides to Graduate Study, 1976. Book 5: *Engineering and Applied Sciences.* Princeton, New Jersey: Peterson's Guides, 1975. See section on "Computer and Information Science Professions."

Précis de l'enseignement informatique. Le Chesnay, France: Institut de recherche d'informatique et d'automatique (IRIA), 1972. Includes a listing of programs and courses offered in France, as well as admission requirements.

Survey of Computer Science Courses at Canadian Institutions. Toronto, Ontario: Canadian Information Processing Society, annual.

Van der Aa, H. J. *Computers and Education: An International Bibliography on Computers and Education.* New York: Science Associates/International, 1970.

World Guide to Universities. Pullach/Munich, Federal Republic of Germany: Verlag Dokumentation, 1972.

The World of Learning. London: Europa, 1947–. Published annually. Lists universities and colleges, learned societies, and research institutes throughout the world.

For additional directories to various aspects of the field, including education and training, see:

Carter, C. *Guide to Reference Sources in the Computer Sciences.* New York: Macmillan, 1974.

RESEARCH CENTERS, INSTITUTES, INFORMATION CENTERS

For a complete listing of the research centers and institutes in computer science throughout the world consult:

Carter, C. *Guide to Reference Sources in the Computer Sciences.* New York: Macmillan, 1974. See Section B, "Research and Information Centers."

Hsiao, T. C. *Directory of Computer Education and Research.* Washington, D.C.: Science and Technology Press, 1973. See pages 1315–1337 for computer research and service centers in the United States.

International Directory of Computer and Information System Services. London: Europa, 1969–, biennial. Lists organizations, governmental establishments, universities, and colleges in over seventy countries. Replaces *International Directory of Computation Laboratories.*

Minerva, Forschungsinstitute. Berlin, Federal Republic of Germany: de Gruyter, 1972. Lists research centers and institutes worldwide.

A major international research center is:

Intergovernmental Bureau for Informatics
P.O. Box 10253
23 viale Civiltà del Lavoro
00144 Rome, Italy

Formerly known as the International Computation Centre, the IBI works to develop informatics internationally. Its aims include the promotion of education in and through informatics and the promotion of research and study in the field.

See also: Business and Office Technologies (field of study).

COMPUTERS AND REGISTRAR
See Registrar.

COMPUTERS, ROLE OF IN HIGHER EDUCATION

1. COMPUTERS IN ADMINISTRATION

2. COMPUTERS IN INSTRUCTION

3. COMPUTERS IN RESEARCH

1. COMPUTERS IN ADMINISTRATION

Computer support of the administrative functions of institutions of higher education requires significant resources and talent. Administrators faced with problems such as student registration, maintenance of physical plant, fiscal accountability, and record keeping have increasingly looked to the computer not only to reduce the costs of performing these functions but also to improve services. But a computer does not automatically improve operations; its success in reducing costs or improving services is dependent on the creativity of the people responsible for the design of systems using the computer.

The uses of computers in the administration of higher education include accounting functions, such as budgeting, purchasing, billing and collection, and payroll check writing; maintenance of inventory, personnel, student, and alumni records; scheduling of classes, dormitory assign-

ments, car pools, and sporting and theater events; retaining data files for admissions, library circulation, course catalogs, reports to governmental agencies, and internal management reports; design and analysis of planning simulations and systems for preventive maintenance of facilities; and examination grading. Although these uses are varied, in each application the computer is used in a production mode in which the systems are designed to run on a predefined schedule without the personal involvement of those who designed or programed the computer. Computer systems must therefore be reliable and well documented. While creativity in design is important, the final system must also adhere to the computing standards defined for the organization if reliability and established production commitments are to be achieved. Skillful documentation and a design that is flexible enough to easily accommodate future changes are attributes directly proportional to the success of each administrative application involving the use of computers.

Historical Development

Administrative uses of the computer in colleges and universities have paralleled those in other industrial and governmental organizations that need to process large amounts of data. Use of automated equipment to assist clerical and bookkeeping functions began in the late 1940s with the use of machines to count, reproduce, and sort punched cards and print reports at rates of 150 lines per minute. Higher education institutions usually first acquired such support in their business or registration offices.

The first generation of commercial computers was acquired by colleges and universities during the 1950s. While primary usage of these early computers was for research applications, administrative staffs began to develop techniques for using computers to speed up the processing of clerical operations—to reduce the amount of manual work involved in counting, sorting, and reporting. Little impact was made on the procedures themselves. Students, faculty, and staff were still required to fill out multiple cards that were then sorted, counted, and distributed to various offices; data were simply distributed more efficiently.

Second-generation computers with capabilities for magnetic tape storage of data and high-speed printers became commercially available in the early 1960s. However, the actual impact on the design of administrative systems was minimal—students and faculty were required to fill out fewer forms, but data continued to be batch processed and sequential files were matched to prepare administrative reports. In fact, many types of tabulating procedures for administrative applications continued to be processed by computer throughout this period.

The third generation of computers, with capabilities for use of remote, on-line terminals, direct-access storage, time sharing, and sophisticated operating systems, appeared in the mid 1960s. These capabilities enabled administrative systems to support on-line data entry and retrieval and to develop information systems whereby data are collected only once, at the most logical place and time, and used to support multiple applications. These systems could be designed to fulfill the needs of the entire institution rather than only specific departments. Thus, the application of computers to student record keeping evolved from simple tabulation and recording of registration figures and grades in the 1950s into information systems that provide the data files, computations, and reports for admissions, registration scheduling, drops and adds, class rosters, grades, transcripts, classroom utilization, student aid, housing, testing and evaluation, and enrollment forecasting. Similarly, the check-writing application of early payroll operations has expanded into personnel information systems that contain biographical material, job descriptions, and appointment and benefits data.

The development of information systems has had significant impact on the manner in which administrative functions are performed. Computers are no longer viewed in the context of providing support for a specific administrative application but in terms of support for various processes with multiple applications. Out of this environment has emerged the data-base concept of systems development. A database system uses one master file to support the data needs of all applications. For example, previously, an institution's computer would create a new file of data each semester for registering students and a separate file for collecting and reporting grades. Using a data-base approach, a master file of student data is maintained that includes both registration and grade information for all semesters for which a student is enrolled. Each time a student registers, his scheduled courses are added to the data base; at the end of the semester the grades received are added; all reports are then generated by computer programs written to select the appropriate data from the data base, perform computations, and either print or display the data. Changes to the data base may be made using either remote on-line terminals or batch-processing techniques. The data-base approach has been made possible through the development of sophisticated computer software, called data-base management systems, that can file data and retrieve it when necessary and use devices that store large amounts of data economically and efficiently. The increase in the level of sophistication of computing hardware and software has required an equally increased level of sophistication in the operation and staffing of administrative computing departments.

Applications

The administrative use of the computer has tended to concentrate in five areas in colleges and universities—student records, personnel records, accounting, physical plant maintenance, and academic scheduling. In the United States an average of 50 to 55 percent of computing resources is expended for administrative purposes rather than for research or academic uses. This percentage differs greatly in other countries of the world, where the use of administrative computing by universities averages only 16 percent of the total available computing resources. Administrative computer application in the United States is concentrated in several areas of administrative computing support. Universities in other countries have placed their emphasis on single areas of support, such as development of strong student admissions and registration systems or strong payroll and personnel support. The *CAUSE Exchange Index* (1975) lists over 120 computer systems, developed for administrative use by colleges and universities, that are available for use by other institutions, as well as proceedings and papers in the area of administrative computing.

Student data files. In the area of student admissions and registration, computers are used to keep track of the applicants requesting admission to the university, to store information about them, and often to print out correspondence to be sent to them. Computers are also used to generate statistical data on the types of applicants versus projection targets. Once a student is admitted, his name is entered into the student data system, which maintains files on enrolled students and provides information for registration, fee payment, and grade processing. One of the major computer applications in this area is the scheduling of students into classes. Many large universities have computer scheduling routines and a computerized master schedule of classes to provide input data for the scheduler. Some systems are quite sophisticated—the student need only indicate what classes he wants and the computer routines will search the master schedule and provide the student with a nonconflicting class schedule; other scheduling routines search to see that the times the student has requested are available and then enroll the student into those classes.

The computerized student data system is also used to generate mailing lists, to compile background data on the types of students enrolled and their academic progress, to monitor library circulation, to schedule dormitory assignments or car pools, and to analyze data for institutional research studies. Many times computer scanning equipment and statistical packages are used to assist the faculty in grading examinations and to post grades to students' records. Once a student has graduated, his data file may be passed on to the alumni records system.

Computers are also used to maintain student financial records. More and more students are receiving financial assistance to attend universities, and computers are being utilized to match the student need profiles with various types of available funding. In addition, computers are utilized to indicate the amount of fees the student owes and to record students' payments so that services that are only administered to students who have paid their fees—processing of registration, posting of grades, health care services, library privileges—can be initiated. Various offices in the university can retrieve these records through the use of on-line systems.

Personnel data files. Many colleges and universities also use computers to collect and store data regarding faculty and staff. Early applications in this area included production of payroll checks, maintenance of accounts and records of employee benefits and deductions, and establishment of timekeeping systems for wage employees. More recently, institutions have created computerized employee data files comparable to the student systems described above, which are used, for example, to maintain statistical records on the types of applicants applying for positions (their qualifications, educational backgrounds, and employment histories), the types of employees hired (their terms of employment, accrued benefits, and payroll records), and the rate of turnover in various departments. These data provide key information for decision making throughout the university.

Accounting. Computers are also used to monitor budgets and expenditures and distribute monthly reports to each department about the status of its budget account. Colleges and universities usually operate on a combination of fund accounting for their academic operations, project accounting for research operations, and general accrual accounting for their auxiliary services. The accounting operations required are therefore complex.

Computers are also used to write purchase orders and then to maintain data regarding the status of the purchases for receiving, inventory, and payment purposes. Systems coordination between the accounting and budgeting areas is very important to ensure fiscal integrity and control, and computer-generated reports are often used for internal auditing.

Maintenance files. Computer data files identifying a university's or college's buildings and facilities and describing how rooms within these buildings are utilized are important to enable the university to have up-to-date information regarding availability of space. These data bases are used to monitor how efficiently classroom and nonclassroom facilities are being utilized and to schedule reassignment of space to support new programs when new facilities are not available.

Computer programs have also been written to provide data to support preventive maintenance programs for buildings and equipment, to maintain control over the use of telephone billing, and to maintain environmental control of physical facilities. This latter application is handled by minicomputer systems that continually monitor the temperatures and ventilation levels in buildings to minimize the use of heating and cooling systems.

Academic scheduling. Computerized records of academic programs may consist of descriptions of courses offered, requirements for enrollment, and resources needed to support the courses. These data are used to produce college catalogs, to evaluate requests for new courses in light of existing course offerings, and to review the demand for courses as demonstrated by past enrollments.

Library circulation systems are also supported extensively by computers. Computer systems are used to record book ordering and to provide information regarding the status of books. Some systems can even retrieve books from the library stacks, thus reducing the personnel costs of book transfers.

Management decision making. Computer systems have yet to become a significant tool in the management decision process. Computers are used to expedite the operations of institutions and to provide data to assist managers in decision making, but very little direct interaction and simulation have yet been done. One reason for this is historical: administrative computing in colleges and universities was originally introduced to help improve operational performance during the periods of great enrollment growth in the late 1950s and the 1960s. Most of the development emphasis was on processing increased numbers of students, staff, and facilities. Only in the 1970s have administrators begun to realize the potential of the computer to analyze alternatives for management decision making, and lack of definite directions for utilizing this potential is largely responsible for its neglect.

In many instances, administrators have begun to question whether the computing center is really supporting the proper areas of the university, but little has yet been done to control how this important resource is utilized. Emphasis grew in the 1970s toward gaining control of the administrative computing resource and directing it toward priorities set by university management. Many institutions throughout the world have done specific planning studies to determine the overall needs for computing services and to define the management priorities for allocating them. These priorities are then given to the director of the computer center to implement as available resources permit. This procedure represents a significant improvement in universities' approach to the allocation of the computing resource for overall management of colleges and universities. Having set priorities, administrators can better evaluate actual performance and better determine the degree to which administrative computing is meeting the needs of the institution.

System Development

As colleges and universities have placed more emphasis on the use of computer applications to assist their administrative functions, administrators have increasingly realized that careful planning in the development of these systems is necessary to ensure their success. The historical approach of generally defining the institution's needs and then turning the project over to an applications programing group to do the work is no longer acceptable. Administrators now want to know whether the system they are acquiring is the most efficient available and want to be able to compare the costs of alternative systems.

Increasing cost awareness has also influenced the procedures by which administrative systems are developed. The project development cycle has become a business-like process in which all parties involved collaborate to define, design, develop, and install the system. The formal goal of a development cycle is to ensure that each system project is a joint effort, each member of the project team taking responsibility for those functions for which he or she is most qualified.

The development cycle proceeds as follows. Once a request for data-processing support has been made, project analysis is conducted to define the actual need and to establish a proposed solution. In addition, a cost-benefit analysis is conducted. The results of the project analysis and the cost-benefit estimates are presented in an overview document, which must be accepted by both the user and the computer center before any further work on the project proceeds. This built-in checkpoint requires an early management decision regarding the availability of resources to support the project prior to the commitment to further system analysis. The next step is to define the technical requirements of the proposed solution—the types of data required by the system, the final data-base design, the equipment necessary to support the system—and to make more definite cost estimates. Again, all parties must agree that the requirements, as set forth in the requirements document, will meet the user's needs, and that needed funding and computer support are available to warrant further work on the project. Once these commitments have been made, a detailed system design is produced; this design is the plan for writing the specific computer programs to satisfy the system requirements and to establish a schedule for implementation. This activity completes the system analysis phase. The next step is to begin actual programing to develop the system, pending final agreement by the user and the computer center that the design is accurate and complete and that funds are available for development, installation, and operation of the proposed system.

This shared-responsibility approach to system development ensures that all involved—system designer and potential user alike—understand the exact status of each project and can resolve problems that may be delaying its completion. Further, the project development cycle ensures that development efforts are subject to continuing management review and approval. The necessity of advance funding commitments, detailed cost estimates, and cost-benefit justification enable management to know the actual cost of the system before it is developed and ensure that funding will be provided for the system's operation. Thus, the project development cycle not only provides for the planned development of a desired system but also ensures the most effective use of the computer center's resources to meet university priority needs.

Bibliography

Albrecht, L. K. *Organization and Management of Information Processing Systems.* New York: Macmillan, 1973.

CAUSE Exchange Index. Boulder, Colorado: College and University Systems Exchange, 1975.

Computers in Higher Education. Edmonton, Alberta: Ministry of Education, 1974.

Head, R. V. *Manager's Guide to Management Information Systems.* Englewood Cliffs, New Jersey: Prentice-Hall, 1972.

Hussain, K. M. *Development of Information Systems for Education.* Englewood Cliffs, New Jersey: Prentice-Hall, 1973.

Interuniversity Communications Council. *Defining the Future.* Princeton, New Jersey: Interuniversity Communications Council, 1975.

Kanter, J. *Management-Oriented Management Information Systems.* Englewood Cliffs, New Jersey: Prentice-Hall, 1972.

Krauss, L. I. *Computer-Based Management Information Systems.* New York: American Management Association, 1970.

Lundell, E. D., Jr., and Bridle, E. J. *Computer Use—An Executive's Guide.* Boston: Allyn & Bacon, 1973.

Mann, R. L. "A Study of the Development of Computer Based Management Information Systems in Institutions of Higher Education." Unpublished doctoral dissertation, University of Illinois, Urbana, 1972.

Mann, R. L. (Ed.) *An Overview of Two Recent Surveys of Administrative Computer Operations in Higher Education.* Boulder, Colorado: Western Interstate Commission for Higher Education, 1975.

Mosmann, C. *Academic Computers in Service: Effective Uses for Higher Education.* San Francisco: Jossey-Bass, 1973.

Ohio Board of Regents. *Computer Services.* Columbus: Ohio Board of Regents, 1973.

WELDON E. IHRIG

2. COMPUTERS IN INSTRUCTION

Computers have been generally available since the early 1950s and were introduced into the university curriculum at that time. Students and faculty originally used the computer as an aid in solving problems in various scientific disciplines; many of these activities evolved into the field now called computer science (often also called computing or information science).

Advances and improvements in computer technology since the early 1960s have made possible the widespread use of computers in instruction. Computers can now be used to present instructional material to students and to monitor each student's progress. By performing these functions with the computer, the teacher is freed to devote time to the more creative aspects of education and to tailor educational programs to each student's ability. Computers also augment the learning process in other ways: they may be used to do more realistic calculations in quantitative courses, and, with access to large amounts of data, they can help to quantify descriptive subjects. By using computers to simulate models of reality, it is possible to explore situations that could not be duplicated in the laboratory or classroom, because of cost, safety, or time constraints. More and more students are being exposed to the computer in their academic programs, and in the 1980s computer technology will become an increasingly important part of the instructional process. A concise description of computers and computer technology related to education is presented in a 1973 study (Armsey and Dahl, 1973, pp. 58–67).

Computer uses in education may be divided into three categories: administration, instruction, and research. The emphasis here is on instructional use. Educational applications of computers at the secondary and postsecondary level often overlap, so there is no attempt to distinguish between them in this article.

The instructional use of computers may be divided into four areas: computer-assisted instruction or learning, computer-managed instruction, computer-augmented learning (including simulation, gaming, and problem solving), and computer education.

Computer-Assisted Instruction

In computer-assisted instruction or learning (CAI or CAL), a terminal connected to a computer is used to present the student with instructional material; the student's response to questions is also conveyed to the computer through the terminal. This device, which responds to the computer or student on command, usually resembles a typewriter or a keyboard with a video screen. Normally, textual material or graphics (such as graphs or simple pictures) are presented to the student on this device. The terminal may also include such items as a slide projector, videotape recorder, or an audio playback unit; this additional equipment allows the computer to present both still and moving pictures and to communicate by voice. The computer is given a set of instructions, called a program, to control the terminal and to present material to the student. A teacher writing such tutorial computer programs would use such computer languages as COURSEWRITER or TUTOR (Armsey and Dahl, 1973, p. 62).

Material from many different areas of study may be presented on the terminal. For example, a computer-assisted instruction program could be developed to teach skills in arithmetic, higher mathematics, or the conjugation of French verbs. It could also be used for learning specific geographical or historical facts, for occupational training, and for many other purposes. An instructional program might also be prepared to present the student with a problem in one of several disciplines, such as mathematics, physics, or history. In this situation, the student must do some analysis or discuss possible solutions.

Several postsecondary institutions are using computer-assisted instruction in their daily teaching activities both to teach remedial programs and to assist students in developing new skills. Ohio State University in Columbus, Ohio; Orange Coast Community College in Costa Mesa, California; and Seneca College in Toronto, Ontario, all use such computer-assisted instruction systems. In the industrial sector, the International Business Machines Corporation (IBM) has used computer-assisted instruction in the area of field engineering to teach its employees about the hardware and software currently available.

Modes of computer-assisted instruction. These examples indicate that computer-assisted instruction may be classified into two modes: the drill-and-practice mode and the tutorial mode. In the drill-and-practice mode, the student is presented with material and is then asked specific questions to which he is expected to reply with specific answers; the responses can then be easily analyzed by a computer program. In the tutorial mode, the student is presented with a problem or a situation and must either discuss a solution or present an analysis. Responses to this mode may span a wide range; this makes it very difficult to program the computer to analyze such responses and react accordingly, since an adequate understanding of the semantics of natural language has not yet been developed. Careful structuring of the material may make drill-and-practice sessions appear more tutorial in nature. Present computer-assisted instruction systems are most useful in academic subjects and occupational training when the material can be presented in drill-and-practice mode.

There are a number of systems that have been developed for computer-assisted instruction, but it is quite difficult to purchase all the hardware (the computers) and software (all programing packages developed for the computer) and difficult to establish a specific system without the assistance of highly skilled personnel. The cost of the hardware for such a system is decreasing significantly with advances in computer technology, but the cost of software, the prepared programs, is high and not decreasing to any degree. Furthermore, the preparation of programs is a lengthy process; it often takes one hundred hours to produce one hour of instruction.

Research in computer-assisted instruction. Research in computer-assisted instruction has been conducted since 1965, and a few of the projects have been well documented.

The reports of research have been mainly descriptive, covering the equipment and programing methods used, and much creative work remains to be done in this area. Since there is little knowledge about the learning process, most work in computer-assisted instruction in the near future will probably be experimental in nature. The inherent record-keeping ability of the computer will make this empirical research extremely valuable, since, with controlled experiments, some learning models may be able to be inferred from an analysis of the experimental data.

Computer-assisted instruction can often be used to augment limited manpower in teaching certain skills, thus freeing the teacher to perform more creative and communication-dependent tasks. A number of educational institutions and companies have adopted some form of computer-assisted instruction for this purpose; a number of experiments are also being conducted, using actual classroom situations.

Three comprehensive research programs in computer-assisted instruction are the PLATO project at the University of Illinois, the Institute for Mathematical Studies at Stanford University, and the TICCIT project of the MITRE Corporation. A number of other projects are described in various articles and studies (Morton, 1967–1976; Armsey and Dahl, 1973; Baker, 1971).

Computer-Managed Instruction

Computer-managed instruction is a computer-based system that is used to assist the teacher in managing the instruction of one or more students and in pinpointing any instructional problems. Ideally, such a system provides the means by which a teacher presents each student with an optimum set of educational experiences.

The functions provided by a computer-managed instruction system occur in stages. Before a certain unit of instruction is started, the students are given a pretest, which is marked on the computer and then analyzed to determine each student's status with respect to the unit of instruction about to begin. Based on the results of the pretest, the pupil is assigned to specific learning tasks. These tasks can consist of a number of educational experiences, including desk work, group activities, reading, tutoring other students, or the use of a computer-assisted instruction system. During the study of a unit of instruction, further tests may be given to assess the student's progress toward the educational objectives contained within that unit. After the unit of instruction is complete, the students are tested again, and the results are analyzed to determine the level of understanding and either to prescribe remedial work or to choose the next unit of instruction. In addition, the teacher receives a report measuring the performance of the class against expected results for that unit of study and comparing each student with his peer group. The tests must be presented in such a way that explicit answers are required, so that the tests can be readily machine-marked and analyzed. Obviously, multiple-choice questions are suited to this model.

In summary, computer-managed instruction can be described as providing four functions to assist the teacher: test scoring before, after, and during a unit of instruction; diagnosis of the student's level of comprehension; prescription of the next unit of instruction and its form; and reporting of the performance of the student group and of individual students in that group. A number of computer-managed instruction systems are being tested and developed (Baker, 1971).

Computer-managed instruction systems may be implemented at low cost, since the computer is essential only for grading and reporting. The actual instruction can be carried out by many different methods, including conventional techniques. As yet, there has been no clear description of the way in which the teacher can use the reports to manage the classroom. Individual educational programs obviously depend on how well one can diagnose the student's progress and the effectiveness of the resulting prescriptions; research has to be done in this area to determine the utility of various diagnostic procedures.

Computer-Augmented Learning

The computer can be an effective aid in the learning process in those modes where it can be classified as a unique tool, such as problem solving, simulation, and games, and inquiry into and manipulation of large quantities of data. These areas could be collectively termed *computer-augmented learning.*

Simulation and games. The learning process can often be reinforced by allowing the student to play games, and computers are quite well suited to game playing. For example, computers can be programed to simulate the throwing of dice or the movement of a counter, and they can also act as opponents in games. Computers can also be programed to adapt quickly as a student's skills develop. Because of their flexibility and ability to simulate many situations, computers have been programed to play many games, which have often been used in teaching situations; these games range from such simple ones as tic-tac-toe to an acceptable version of chess.

The technique of simulation has also been used to teach people various skills, and computers have been used to simulate many situations. Business games have been programed that allow the students to study the operation of a business organization by actively participating in the management of a fictitious company in a fictitious marketplace. The computer simulates a model of the relevant economy and allows the students to see the effects of their "business" decisions on the growth of their companies. This scheme allows the students to explore safely the ideas inherent in running a business, and it also allows them to shorten the time during which their decisions are implemented.

Scientific experiments can also be simulated on a computer. In the PLATO system, there is a simulation of a biological experiment in which the students are asked to breed fruit flies and to study the resulting mutations; such an experiment, if conducted in a laboratory, takes a significant amount of time and requires the student to develop certain manual skills. The computer simulation significantly decreases the time for the experiment, makes it possible to conduct more experiments, and replaces an expensive laboratory.

A computer simulation thus has the potential to allow the safe exploration of ideas, decrease the time needed for an experiment, increase the number of experiments, make some new learning experiences possible, and perhaps replace expensive facilities. (For information on the use of computers in games and simulation, see Tomasso, 1974; Lambert and Dally, 1974; Morton, 1967–1976; Scheepmaker and Zinn, 1970.)

Problem solving. A computer can perform arithmetic rapidly and accurately, making it a valuable aid in many academic courses. A student may program the computer to solve a problem by numerical techniques or to tabulate or use statistical methods to reduce data for presentation in a more comprehensible format. For example, a student could plot or tabulate the growth of an animal population based on mathematical models of population dynamics or tabulate or reduce certain demographic data in a geography course.

Such applications are still the most common uses of the computer in education; students either learn to program the computer or use prepackaged programs for these calculations. In the latter case, students need to learn little more about the computer than the format for the data that are to be processed. When students prepare their own programs, they have to develop a basic understanding of computers and a working knowledge of at least one programing language. Many postsecondary educational institutions conduct classes in elementary programing, using languages such as BASIC, FORTRAN,

ALGOL, and APL, so that the students enrolled may make use of the computer.

In order to teach students programing, a certain environment is desirable. Programs written by students usually have a short lifetime and are rarely used to produce more than four or five separate calculations. Since the programs are so short-lived, it is important that the period between conception and actual operation of the program be minimized. Specifically, the software and hardware available should be able to detect common errors and diagnose them so that the student may make corrections quickly and put the program into production. Both time-sharing systems (users of the computer submit jobs at a point remote from the central computer site) and batch-processing systems (users of the computer submit jobs at the central computer site) have been developed to alleviate this problem. This approach to problem solving with computers is exemplified by the WATFIV, WATBOL, and PL/C software systems (Cress, Dirksen, and Graham, 1970; Cooper and others, 1973; Conway and Gries, 1973).

Because of their speed and their data storage capabilities, computers can store large amounts of data on various subject areas, and the data can then be used for educational purposes. Masses of historical, demographic, or geographical data can be accessed and used to test various hypotheses. For example, a computer system at the University of Iowa has utilized nineteenth-century data about several Iowa counties to quantify nineteenth-century American frontier history (Winkler, 1975). These developments in data bases for education in various subjects will introduce students to quantitative methods in courses that were previously considered descriptive or qualitative and will also allow quantitative courses to have access to "realistic" data.

Computer Education

Computers are becoming an important component of our culture, and various types of computer experts are needed to maintain and develop new and existing computer systems. Various curricula have been established at both secondary and postsecondary levels of education to provide the education required by these experts (Amarel, 1971; Austing and Engel, 1973; Couger, 1973; Ontario Ministry of Education, 1966, 1970a, 1970b, 1972).

Because the significant influence of computers on society will no doubt increase, it is generally agreed that an educated person should be made aware of the power and limitations of the computer. An informed population will be necessary for appropriate control and development of the computerized society. Courses in computer awareness are designed for this need (Lambert and Dally, 1974; Tomasso, 1974; Morton, 1967–1976; Scheepmaker and Zinn, 1970).

Bibliography

Amarel, S. "Computer Science: A Conceptual Framework for Curriculum Planning." *Communications of the Association for Computing Machinery,* 1971, *14*(6), 391–401.

Armsey, J. W., and Dahl, N. C. *An Inquiry into the Uses of Instructional Technology.* New York: Ford Foundation, 1973.

Atchison, W. F. "Recommendations for Academic Programs in Computer Science." *Communications of the Association for Computing Machinery,* 1968, *11*(3), 151–197.

Austing, R. H., and Engel, G. L. "A Computer Science Course Program for Small Colleges." *Communications of the Association for Computing Machinery,* 1973, *16*(3), 139–147.

Baker, F. B. "Computer-Based Instructional Management Systems: A First Look." *Review of Educational Research,* 1971, *41*(1), 51–70.

Bonnette, D. T. (Ed.) *SIGCSE Bulletin.* New York: Special Interest Group on Computer Science Education of the Association for Computing Machinery, 1969–1976.

Caffrey, J., and Mossman, C. J. *Computers on Campus.* Washington, D.C.: American Council on Education, 1967.

Conway, R., and Gries, D. *An Introduction to Programming.* Boston: Winthrop, 1973.

Cooper, R. H., and others. *File Processing with COBOL/WATBOL.* Waterloo, Ontario: WATFAC, 1973.

Couger, J. D. (Ed.) "Curriculum Recommendations for Undergraduate Programs in Information Systems." *Communications of the Association for Computing Machinery*, 1973, *16*(12), 727–749.

Cress, P. H., Dirksen, P. H., and Graham, J. W. *FORTRAN IV with WATFOR and WATFIV.* Englewood Cliffs, New Jersey: Prentice-Hall, 1970.

Lambert, P., and Dally, C. W. *Computer Education.* London: Computer Education Group of the British Computer Society, 1974.

LeCarme, O., and Lewis, R. *Second`World Conference on Computers in Education.* Amsterdam: International Federation for Information Processing, North Holland Publishing Company, 1975.

Morton, A. K. (Ed.) *SIGCUE Bulletin.* New York: Special Interest Group on Computer Uses in Education of the Association for Computing Machinery, 1967–1976.

Ontario Ministry of Education. *Data Processing.* Toronto, Ontario: Ontario Ministry, 1966.

Ontario Ministry of Education. *Computer Science.* Toronto, Ontario: Ontario Ministry, 1970a.

Ontario Ministry of Education. *Elements of Computer Technology.* Toronto, Ontario: Ontario Ministry, 1970b.

Ontario Ministry of Education. *Informatics.* Toronto, Ontario: Ontario Ministry, 1972.

Pierce, J. R. *Computers in Higher Education.* Washington, D.C.: U.S. Government Printing Office, 1967.

Rosser, J. B. *Digital Computer Needs in Universities and Colleges.* Publication 1233. Washington, D.C.: National Research Council, 1966.

Scheepmaker, B., and Zinn, K. L. *World Conference on Computer Education.* Amsterdam: International Federation for Information Processing, North Holland Publishing Company, 1970.

Tomasso, C. *International World of Computer Education.* Edinburgh: International Centre for Computing in Secondary Education of the Organisation for Economic Co-operation and Development, 1974.

Winkler, K. J. "Using Computers to Teach History." *Chronicle of Higher Education,* April 1975, *10,* 3.

DONALD D. COWAN

3. COMPUTERS IN RESEARCH

It is difficult and perhaps presumptuous to describe in a short article the uses of computers in research. It is an accepted truism that the application of computers is now pervasive throughout the United States; indeed, any researcher in a field with quantifiable or systematic aspects must employ computers, directly or indirectly, to remain current. It is tempting to find analogies that dramatize in a more familiar way the extent of the unconscious acceptance and dependence on these amazingly versatile machines. Such attempts inevitably fail to capture the unique controllability attributes of digital machines. However, the very consideration of such an analogy causes one to appreciate the extent to which computers have been employed. For example, electric motors, devices to convert electrical energy to mechanical energy, range from shavers to large accelerators, and an average person is affected by their performance in hundreds of unobserved ways each day. When computing was limited to large central machines, this comparison would have been entirely inappropriate, but now, with digital voice communication, hand calculators, digital watches, digitally controlled fuel injection, and point of sale transaction recording, the pervasiveness of the devices has become more similar. Although the motor example includes greater variation in function than one might at first anticipate, the basic function of a computer to execute some class of algorithms completely dominates the comparison in terms of variety of function. The class of algorithms may be a single, fixed algorithm such as an elevator controller, a digital signal transformer, or a laboratory sample analyser; or the class may be broad, including data processing and equation solution in the case of general-purpose machines. The broad but slightly more specialized prescription of a machine suitable for the solution of systems of partial differential equations is a category of great interest in research.

Three General Uses

These observations suggest a rough three-way categorization of the roles of computers in research.

Facilitation of analysis. In the first category the use of computers has not affected the way in which research is carried out. The same sorts of measurements and analyses are done as in the precomputer period, but, with the aid of the digital machines, much more work, or more accurate work, can be accomplished. Examples of this use are laboratory automation in the collection and reduction of data, connection of computers to analog measurement devices to obviate the human variability, and processing of data by routine statistical methods. This is not to say that applications of this sort have not had a profound effect. Quantitative and organizational improvements have indeed produced marked qualitative changes in research. For example, in the biological and medical areas, as theories become more developed, the opportunities for computer modeling increase. The deoxyribonucleic acid (DNA) mechanism for the transmission of genetic information is an illustration. Once the underlying theory was established, computers could then be used extensively and profitably to explore the many molecular combination possibilities.

Physical modeling. Any categorization of computer use will have fuzzy boundaries, and the DNA computation borders on the second grouping. In the physical sciences there is often a sufficiently explanatory, mathematically formulated theory to predict, in principle, the behavior of complex physical systems. This fact has accounted for most of the time spent in research computation. Goldstine and von Neumann recognized this potential in 1946: "Indeed, to a great extent experimentation in fluid dynamics is carried out under conditions where the underlying physical principles are not in doubt, when the quantities to be observed are completely determined by known equations. The purpose of the experiment is not to verify a theory but to replace a computation from an unquestioned theory by direct measurements. Thus wind tunnels are, for example, used at present . . . in large part as computing devices . . . to integrate the partial dif-

ferential equations of fluid dynamics" ([1946] 1963, p. 4).

In essence, when the theory is known and formulated, an experiment can be regarded as an analog computer computation, where the physical variables are the real-world counterparts. This interpretation may seem twisted, but it is often viewed this way when electrical voltages are analogously represented as electrical voltages in circuit analysis. Although the concept of substituting computation for experimentation is simple, the practical difficulties in computation can be enormous, and the comparative cost of the two approaches may still favor experiment. However, as computers become less expensive, faster, larger, and more varied in construction, the trend is toward the computation. It was interesting to observe, over a period of some years, the disappearance of an industrial engine model laboratory as the computational techniques for predicting the performance of hypothetical engine designs improved.

In this replacement of experimentation the partial differential equations that generally describe the physical phenomena must be integrated numerically. Alternately, the phenomena can be simulated at a microscopic level, where the physical laws are applied on a particle-by-particle basis. Either approach is very demanding in terms of the complexity of the numerical formulation and the enormous number of elementary computer operations required to produce a solution. Although the replacement of wind tunnels was foreseen in 1946, the project seems capable of realization only now, when the numerical formulation has reached a very sophisticated level and, more important, high-performance machines have been developed.

In this second category, it is clear that computers have had a much more fundamental effect on the way research is done. Problems can be solved that do not yield to an analytic solution as opposed to a numerical solution, and experimenting by computer has greatly accelerated the pace of research. Conventional experimentation has not vanished, but, typically, preliminary computations reduce the range of necessary experiments to the point where the information yield from an experiment is optimized. One natural side effect of this approach is that numerical formulation and implementation have become major research considerations in these areas. A second effect is that continuing pressure for more effective computation leads to investigations into computer technology and performance, only secondarily connected to the underlying physical problems.

Computer science. The transition to intrinsic research in computers and algorithms begins to define the third category. Interestingly, this work, which is often described under the headings of computer science and computer engineering, does not consume as much computing time or facilities as the second category of physical modeling. The interest in this area of research arises not only from the problems of physical simulation but also from a rapidly improving digital technology and the rapidly increasing complexity of computer systems in all fields of application. It has been stated that technology drives computing research, but, in fact, the relation is reflexive. The nearly universal applicability of computers has motivated, for profit if nothing else, a remarkable technology that continues to revolutionize research.

The relationship between research applicability and demand has been widely recognized. Brooks states, for example, "Computer techniques so alter the character of research and the scope of the problems that can be successfully attacked in many fields that competitive pressures are likely to spread the demand for this new capability (for teaching as well as research) much faster than has been the case with other types of more specialized instrumentation" (1968, pp. 72–73).

Research on computers and programs as such does not constitute a major portion of the totality of research. The goals are difficult to characterize succinctly, but one description—the quantification and management of complexity—comes close to including the various research interests that have arisen from computing experience.

In his testimony before the United States House of Representatives, Creutz saw such research as a unifying force: "There are many reasons why scientists nowadays are required to analyze extremely complicated systems ranging from ecologies to very hot dense plasmas and from economic 'models' to hemoglobin molecules. In every such case computers are crucial, and in many areas we are confident that advances in computer science will lead straight to other scientific advances. It is even true that, properly used, computers can contribute to the improvement of computer science. The study of processes that can be carried out by computers has led to new ways to look at information and to organize knowledge about the world (in ways different from the traditional mathematical approaches), and this is why computer science has now emerged as a major program of study and research at most of the nation's colleges and universities" (1976).

Examples of Computer Use

As illustrations of these three categories of the research use of computers, several detailed examples follow.

Analytic examples. The computer implementation of well-established laboratory procedures are often listed under the heading of digital instrumentation or automation; some of the procedures in chemical research are good examples (see Secrest, 1970, pp. 433–462). Data collection and reduction from gas chromatography columns is a case where there is no control aspect but simply a very effective measurement and recording function. An automated mass spectrometer is similar, except that here the memory and logical capabilities of the computer can be used to suggest the identification of the compound being measured. The instrument ionizes the molecules, and the ions of different masses are separated by varying techniques. The masses of the separated components are recorded digitally, and the computer then identifies the molecule to the extent possible. Beyond this, a program can, by a combining procedure, produce a list of compounds or mixtures of compounds that could have produced the measured distribution of masses.

A more sophisticated procedure that relates to a very demanding computation problem is the automated generation of measurements for subsequent crystallographic analysis. If a substance has a crystalline structure, then an incident X-ray beam is refracted in a regular way, depending on the molecular structure of the substance. The resultant pattern can be seen on an X-ray-sensitive film as a symmetric pattern of spots of differing intensity. When a sample has been exposed from the various crystal orientations, the intensity and relative spot position can be used as input to a multidimensional Fourier analysis program to deduce the molecular structure. (This latter calculation is extremely time consuming and for relatively complex molecules requires hours on the largest computers.) However, the actual measurement of position and intensity can be made by using digitized radiation sensors as computer inputs and automatically controlling the position of the sample. In essence, after being given some initial positioning information, the computer positions the sensor to find the radiation peaks and predicts, from anticipated symmetry, the position of other peaks. Moreover, the computer has a two-angle control over the position of the sample so that movement to other crystal orientations can also be done automatically.

These kinds of computer use have had a profound effect on chemical research. Clearly the same kinds of developments have occurred in other areas of physical research where complex, experiment-controlled positioning is required in the collection of data. Computer control of wind tunnel model positioning is another example. A related application—the analysis of the results of an experiment as opposed to the data collection itself—is the computer processing of bubble chamber films. Subatomic events from high energy particle experiments are recorded on film from their original appearance in a bubble chamber. The problem is to identify geometrical patterns, among the noise and insignificant lines, that indicate interesting particle interactions. Computers have been employed to search photographs for such patterns and produce digital input for large, sophisticated programs that test the patterns for their possible physical significance.

Modeling examples. The statement of Goldstine and von Neumann about the use of experiments as substitutes for computation is the basis for much of the computer work in the second category. When the current underlying physical theory models well the phenomena of interest, numerical formulation and solution of the appropriate partial differential equations becomes a major research goal. This formulation and computer solution is research *per se,* which was not pursued before the advent of big computing machines. However, experimentation has not vanished; as the frontiers of research are extended, it becomes clear that the underlying theory is not always adequately descriptive, and there is a three-way interplay among theory modification, numerical formulation, and experiment. Certainly in plasma research, an area of great significance due to fusion research, theoretical models do not yet adequately describe observed results. But the cost of experiments is such that an enormous amount of computer simulation is justifiable to narrow the range for experimentation.

Weather prediction provides an interesting example of a computation based on the partial differential equations of fluid dynamics, which describe the complex interaction of the elements that produce the continually changing global weather patterns (Kasahara, 1970, pp. 517–594). Obviously, such computation is motivated not by the replacement of experiment but by the desire to accurately predict the weather well in advance. In the basic formulation there are seven equations that describe the atmospheric system. The independent variables are the three space coordinates and time. The dependent variables, whose values must be derived by solving these differential and algebraic equations simultaneously, are the three spatial velocities, pressure, entropy, density, and temperature. The continuous derivatives are replaced by gridlike discrete approximations in the computer formulation, and the numerical values of the dependent variables are computed for each physical grid point for each point in time. There are a number of subtle difficulties with such a numerical solution. One difficulty, an instability or magnification of the small errors to the discrete approximation of the physical system, can be avoided by keeping the ratio of the product of the speed of sound and the time interval to the spatial interval less than unity. The import of this constraint is that for reasonable vertical space steps of, say, three kilometers, the time step must be ten seconds. Considering the global grid and the desire to predict well in advance, the computation becomes too large for the largest machines. There are alternative formulations that alleviate this problem, but the necessary time and space interval relationship continues to force the problem into the category of the very large.

Computer science examples. Predictably, much of the research in the third category—that is, computational procedures (or algorithms) as objects of study—does not require a large amount of computer use. Much of this work is removed by one level of abstraction and attempts, by analytic deductive methods, to characterize and devise algorithms. It should be apparent that the notion of an algorithm or procedure is very general. Included under this broad category are such diverse developments as register transfers in computer circuitry to the previously mentioned solution techniques for large systems of equations. Given this wide spectrum, the general research goal is to specify algorithms in identified subareas that are optimal by some criteria, such as time required, space required, or amount of circuitry. However, many practical problems are so complex that optimality cannot be proved, and it then becomes important to demonstrate the effectiveness of the methods under study. Such demonstrations do involve the use of computers in a research context. Human problem solving often involves the development of ingenious "tricks"—that is, transformations or manipulations which do indeed result in an efficient solution but cannot be guaranteed to work in every instance of a problem or necessarily produce the best solution. These heuristic approaches are of great interest in the development of computer methods for problem solving. A well-known example is the traveling salesman problem: finding the least costly path connecting a number of cities. For problems of practical size, the problem can consume a large amount of computing time, but the use of some well-devised heuristics can greatly improve the rate of solution.

An application of the heuristic approach to a possibly more familiar problem domain is analytic integration. The computer program receives as input the characters of a mathematical expression and produces as output the characters that are the indefinite integral of the input formula. The analogous problem of formal differentiation is much simpler because the rules for differentiation can be applied in a known sequence that will produce the result. Integration, as every student in a first calculus course knows, involves the recognition of integrable patterns and the substitutions and transformations that produce such patterns. Clearly, since some functions are not integrable in closed form, there can be no fixed procedure that will produce the indefinite integral for an arbitrary input function.

Perhaps the best-known program of this type is SAINT—Symbolic Automatic Integrator (Slagle, 1963). By heuristic methods of recognizing standard forms, making substitutions in attempts to produce standard and partition the problem, and remembering a number of derived intermediate forms for later continuation, the program was able to perform at the level of a very good calculus student. It required an average two minutes of computer time to solve each of fifty-two problems taken from calculus final examinations. It failed to solve two problems.

Such research problems require considerable computer use to develop and demonstrate their utility, but it is still small compared with the time required for the solution of physical systems problems. Once such a program is completed and is demonstrably effective, it passes from the realm of computing research to possibly the first category of research use. Someone whose research involves repeated complex integrations will then use the program to accelerate the work. The SAINT program was an early effort, and it is not clear that it would be sufficiently useful to make this transition. Nonetheless, it does illustrate the use of computers in research on the development of heuristic algorithms.

A more recent development in programs to manipulate mathematical formulas exhibits also the computer use required for algorithm development, but the subsequent application to a variety of research problems is clearer. Specifically, the program manipulates expressions that are partially truncated Fourier series in several angles and partially truncated analytical series in several variables. Such mathematical forms arise in the study of nonlinear oscillations. The case that motivated André Déprit of the Boeing Aircraft Corporation was the need to find expressions which described the moon's orbit with the accuracy of current laser measurements. A fascinating aspect of this problem is that

such a manipulation was done manually in the mid nineteenth century, through phenomenal effort and with truly remarkable results. Charles Delaunay (French mathematician and astronomer, 1816–1872) spent thirty years at the task and produced three formulas. One such formula, for longitude, is a string of characters extending over 182 pages. The appearance of computers permitted the numeric integration necessary to determine the orbit but did not, until recently, improve upon Delaunay's closed-form formulation. His work was verified by a formula manipulation program (incredibly there was only one small error) but could not be appreciably extended. The manipulation of such complex series, called Poisson series, was itself formulated as a mathematical problem, and a special program for manipulation was devised by Déprit. It depended heavily on compact, list-structured data organizations to be able to manage the enormous number of symbols. In 1969 the program was applied to the moon orbit problem. The earlier results were again verified and the formulation greatly extended. Terms up to order 19 were produced, whereas the early manual work had produced terms of order 7. The basic literal version of the resultant series was about fourteen million characters. The derived Fourier series has no more than eight hundred terms, and the predictive capability of the evaluated formulas is equal to that of the laser orbit measurements now made.

This accomplishment illustrates two aspects of the use of computers in computer research. The work, in this case the development of an efficient program to correctly manipulate the expressions, was done in close conjunction with another discipline, in this case mathematics. Once such a program is completed, its subsequent use in research will be listed under the subject area in which it is found to be applicable. Once developed, an algorithm passes rapidly from a research topic to a research tool. These observations tend to reinforce the widely held belief that research in computing is a pervasive interdisciplinary activity.

Funding

In addition to the usual problem of separating research from development, the fraction of research and development funding that supports computer installations and the development of programs apparently is not known. Even if it were known, it would be necessary to separate out that portion which was not used for research—for example, administrative data processing. However, it is possible to make some gross estimates of research support for the third category at universities and colleges. This category involves people and projects concerned with computers as such and not simply as a means to some other specific research goal. As discussed earlier, such computer-oriented work does arise from demanding problems that require bigger, faster machines or more effective algorithms, but the effort along these lines becomes abstracted and separated from the originating problems.

In 1973, of the 132,692 doctoral scientists and engineers employed in educational institutions, 1506 (approximately 1.1 percent) were identified as computer specialists (National Science Foundation, 1975). With regard to research and development expenditures, $4,700,000,000 of the national total of $38,100,000,000 went to universities and colleges (National Science Foundation, 1976). On the simplistic assumption that this support was distributed in proportion to the number of professionals at the institutions, 1.1 percent, or approximately $50,000,000, would be devoted to computer science and engineering research. This figure seems compatible with estimates of the total of federal agency support.

The uses of computers in research are myriad—and growing. The inherent logical and computational power of computers makes them invaluable for the collection and organization of complex experimental data and for the refinement of experimental work by increasingly realistic simulation. Their potential has produced new research directed to the improvement of these already prodigious capabilities. This research is paced by continuing achievement in computer technology, and the impact on research procedures will, no doubt, continue to grow.

Bibliography

Brooks, H. "The Future Growth of Academic Research." In H. Orlans (Ed.), *Science Policy and the University.* Washington, D.C.: Brookings Institution, 1968.

Creutz, E. National Science Foundation Statement to the House Subcommittee on Science, Research, and Technology. February 4, 1976.

Goldstine, H. H., and von Neumann, J. "On the Principles of Large Scale Computing Machines." (Originally published 1946). In *John von Neumann, Collected Works.* Vol. 5. Elmsford, New York: Pergamon Press, 1963.

Kasahara, A. "Computer Simulations of the Global Circulations of the Earth's Atmosphere." In S. Fernbach and A. Taub (Eds.), *Computers and Their Role in the Physical Sciences.* New York: Gordon and Breach, 1970.

National Science Foundation. *Characteristics of Doctoral Scientists and Engineers in the United States 1973.* National Science Foundation Publication NSF 75–312. Washington, D.C.: National Science Foundation, 1975.

National Science Foundation. *National Patterns of R&D Resources, Funds and Manpower in the United States 1953–76.* National Science Foundation Publication NSF 76–310. Washington, D.C.: National Science Foundation, 1976.

Secrest, D. "On Line Uses of Computers in Chemistry." In S. Fernbach and A. Taub (Eds.), *Computers and Their Role in the Physical Sciences.* New York: Gordon and Breach, 1970.

Slagle, J. R. "A Heuristic Program That Solves Symbolic Integration Problems in Freshman Calculus." *Journal for the Association of Computing Machinery,* 1963, *10*(4).

BRUCE W. ARDEN

CONCURRENT COOPERATIVE EDUCATION

See Cooperative Education and Off-Campus Experience: Cooperative Education in the United States.

CONFERENCE BOARD, United States

The Conference Board, founded in 1916, is an independent nonprofit institution for business and economic research. Its purpose is to promote broader understanding of business and the economy and of the society that shapes the business system. The board is a fact-finding agency; it takes no positions on public policy issues, nor does it act as a consulting organization.

One third of the board's financial resources comes from conference receipts, specially financed research projects, sales of publications, and investments. The remaining two thirds comes from voluntary subscriptions of the more than four thousand member organizations—mainly business corporations, financial institutions, and service organizations—that the board calls associates. In addition, the board has several hundred noncorporate members (including labor unions, colleges and universities, trade associations, government agencies, and libraries) that have an interest in business and the economy.

A full-time president and chief executive officer directs the Conference Board's staff of 250 at the New York headquarters. The president of the Conference Board of Canada heads sixty staff members in Ottawa. Several hundred executives are elected members of the corporation. In the United States members of the corporation elect thirty trustees, who function as a board of directors and select a chairperson and vice-chairperson. The Conference Board in Canada receives guidance from a thirty-member Canadian council.

The Conference Board studies domestic and international business management practices, economic trends, and public affairs issues and publishes the results. Almost two hundred conferences, seminars, and briefings—where associates exchange ideas with leaders in business, labor, government, and education—are conducted annually. A library that contains one of the largest business collections in the United States is maintained in New York.

The board releases its research findings to the public; opens board conferences for coverage by the public information media; and encourages reporters, editors, and broadcasters to consult the board for needed information. Authors and scholars are granted access to board data for use in their writings, and policymakers are invited to consider pertinent research findings. Within the limits of the board's financial resources, research publications are provided for teacher training programs and classroom use.

Publications devoted to research on business management practices include *Top Executive Compensation, Corporate Retirement Policy and Practices, Corporate Directorship Practices, Membership and Committees of the Board, Managing Product Recalls,* and *Evolving Corporate Policy and Organization for East-West Trade.* Research that concentrates on outside forces that influence or are likely to influence corporations has resulted in the following publications: *Inflation in the United States: Causes and Consequences, Environmental Policy and Impact Analysis,* and *The Federal Budget: Its Impact on the Economy.* The Conference Board *Record,* a general business magazine, has a readership of 150,000.

845 Third Avenue
New York, New York 10022 USA

CONFERENCE CENTERS IN GREAT BRITAIN
See University Conference Centers in Great Britain.

CONFERENCE CENTERS IN THE UNITED STATES
See University Conference Centers in the United States.

CONFERENCE OF DANISH RECTORS (Rektorkollegiet)

The Conference of Danish Rectors was set up by the Danish Ministry in July 1967 to facilitate and further cooperation among institutions of higher education in Denmark. The conference consists of eighteen Danish rectors who consider questions of common interest to the institutions of higher education and award special grants to the universities.

The secretariat of the conference, integrated with the Danish Ministry of Education in 1975, also serves the Committee of Administrators, a body established by the Ministry of Education in April 1969. Composed of the permanent administrators of the institutions for higher education, the committee studies the problems of university administration. Both the conference and the committee work closely with the Ministry of Education, the Ministry of Cultural Affairs, and departmental bodies under these ministries concerned with higher education.

Vester Voldgade 117
1552 Copenhagen V, Denmark

CONFERENCE OF FRENCH RECTORS
(Conférence des recteurs français)

Established after World War II, the *Conférence des recteurs français* (Conference of French Rectors) provides an opportunity for an exchange of views among French rectors. In each of the academies (educational regions which usually correspond to the national administrative regions) the rector, working under the minister of education, directs primary and secondary education. In addition, serving as chancellor, he acts as a link between the universities in his academy and the secretary of state to the universities and between the universities and other levels of education. Chosen among university professors, the rector is named by decree of the president of the republic after consultation with the ministers.

In its efforts to provide a permanent exchange of views among those responsible for the French educational system, the conference attaches particular importance to international relations—contributing, for example, to the founding and development of the *Association des universités partiellement ou entièrement de langue française* (Association of Partially or Wholly French-Language Universities) and is a member of the organization.

The conference, meeting monthly at its seat in Paris, is directed by an elected bureau composed of a president, a vice-president, and a secretary-treasurer. Government funds and membership dues finance the conference.

6 rue de la Toussaint
67081 Strasbourg, France
MAURIUS-FRANÇOIS GUYARD

CONFERENCE OF RECTORS AND PRINCIPALS OF QUEBEC UNIVERSITIES
(Conférence des recteurs et des principaux des universités du Québec), Canada

The Conference of Rectors and Principals of Quebec Universities, a voluntary consortium of six universities, analyzes the direction and development of higher education in Quebec. Regarding the university as a place of free intellectual activity, the conference opposes all forms of ideological intolerance and political interference and affirms the responsibilities and prerogatives of universities regarding admissions policies, hiring and status of personnel, choice and quality of programs, and distribution and use of available resources. By interpreting its role to public and private organizations, the conference encourages a climate of mutual confidence among the Quebec universities, government, and society.

Through close cooperation with the higher education division of the Department of Education, the conference seeks to avoid duplication of effort. Meeting frequently with government officials in such areas as financing and university accountability, salaries and cost-of-living adjustments, and academic and physical planning, the conference also evaluates the quality of proposed programs for the government.

Furthermore, acting as a body of inter-institutional coordination and cooperation and as an organization for study and analysis, the conference promotes collaboration between institutions and an optimal use of resources; preserves the collective autonomy of universities through the promotion of common policies; and carries out analysis and planning on subjects submitted by the universities.

Services of the conference include a permanent interlibrary loan system, and collective negotiations for both teaching and nonteaching personnel. The conference is engaged in defining the limits within which each university may negotiate, so that a settlement at one university will not set a precedent for bargaining elsewhere. In addition, certain items are negotiated at a common table.

A board of directors and an executive committee plan conference activities. The conference has standing committees on academic affairs, financial and administrative affairs, and research. There are also special committees on libraries, pedagogical methods, student services, registrars, finance, and physical planning. The conference has a permanent secretariat of approximately twenty persons and is financed primarily through members' dues.

6600 chemin de la Côte des Neiges
Montreal, Quebec, Canada

CONFERENCE OF RECTORS OF BELGIAN UNIVERSITIES
(Conférence des recteurs des universités belges)

The Conference of Rectors of Belgian Universities was officially incorporated as a nonprofit association in November 1973. The rectors' conference seeks to coordinate university activities. It also studies all problems concerning higher education and scientific research and, acting as a spokesman for Belgian universities, debates and defines their point of view at the national and international levels.

The board of the association includes rectors of the *Rijksuniversiteit te Gent* (State University of Ghent), *Université de l'état à Liège* (State University at Liège), *Université catholique de Louvain/Katholieke universiteit te Leuven* (Catholic University of Louvain), *Université libre de Bruxelles/Vrije universiteit Brussel* (Brussels Free University), *Université de l'état à Mons* (State University at Mons), and *Universitaire instelling Antwerpen* (University Institution, Antwerp).

rue d'Egmont 5
1050 Brussels, Belgium

CONFERENCE OF RECTORS OF SWISS UNIVERSITIES
(Schweizerische Hochschulrektorenkonferenz/ Conférence des recteurs des universités suisses)

The *Schweizerische Hochschulrektorenkonferenz/Conférence des recteurs des universités suisses* (Conference of Rectors of Swiss Universities), grouping ten rectors of higher education institutions in Switzerland, serves as a consultative body for Swiss universities. Meeting three times a year, the rectors examine common problems that demand mutual agreement among the universities. A president is elected among the rectors for a three-year term, which is renewable. Since 1948 the conference has sent a permanent delegate to the *Office central universitaire suisse* (Central Office of the Swiss Universities) in Zurich. The office, serving as a secretariat for the conference, is financed by dues of member universities and by federal government grants.

Gloriastrasse 59
8044 Zurich, Switzerland

CONFERENCE OF RECTORS OF TURKISH UNIVERSITIES
(Türk üniversite rektörleri konferansi)

The *Türk üniversite rektörleri konferansi* (TÜRK: Conference of Rectors of Turkish Universities) is composed of the presidents of all Turkish universities, who are automatically members, and vice-presidents and former presidents of universities, upon their application and election by the conference.

The executive body of the Conference of Rectors includes a president; three vice-presidents; a treasurer; and a secretary general, who is appointed for a period of five years. Committees are as follows: executive committee, university presidents committee (the executive committee plus the university presidents), and the general assembly (the university presidents committee and other elected members from among former presidents and current vice-presidents). The presidents committee and the executive committee rotate their meetings six times a year at different universities; the general assembly meets annually at the headquarters in Ankara. The president of TÜRK is elected by the general assembly for a three-year renewable period.

Through the conference, university presidents exchange their views and make recommendations; however, since each university in Turkey has its own charter and is autonomous, the recommendations are not binding. TÜRK appoints representatives to international organizations and also recommends candidates to the government to represent Turkish higher education in the Council of Higher Education and Research in the Council of Europe.

Atatürk Bulvari 223/5
Kavaklidere
Ankara, Turkey

CONFERENCE OF RECTORS OF UNIVERSITIES AND COLLEGES IN NORWAY

The Conference of Rectors of Universities and Colleges in Norway is an association comprised of the rectors and directors of the Norwegian universities (the universities at Oslo, Bergen, Trondheim, and Tromsø) and the rectors of Norwegian colleges at university level (the Norwegian School of Economics and Business Administration, Bergen; the Norwegian Advanced Teachers' College, Trondheim; the Veterinary College of Norway, Oslo; and the Agricultural College

of Norway, Vollebekk). The conference is held at the university or college of the rector or director who has been elected as host chairman for one year and, if re-elected, for one further year.

At meetings, members discuss matters of common interest and elect representatives to European and other organizations. A representative of the Ministry of Education (director of division) and a similar representative of the Ministry of Agriculture have regularly been invited to take part in the discussions.

Secretary General
University of Oslo
Blindern
Oslo 3, Norway

OLAV M. TROVIK

CONFERENCE OF THE SCANDINAVIAN RECTORS

The Conference of the Scandinavian Rectors was formed in Copenhagen in 1948 at a meeting called by the rector of the University of Copenhagen and attended by the rectors of Norwegian, Swedish, Danish, and Finnish universities. The conference offers an opportunity for the rectors to discuss common problems and ways of achieving cooperation among the universities of Scandinavia. The Scandinavian rectors rotate in hosting the meetings every two years.

University of Uppsala
Uppsala, Sweden

CONFERENCE OF UNIVERSITY PRESIDENTS
(Conférence des présidents d'universités), France

The *Conférence des présidents d'universités* (Conference of University Presidents) groups the presidents of universities and other independent scientific and cultural public institutions. It acts as a consulting body for the Ministry of Education and provides an opportunity for members to discuss common goals and problems. The conference is governed by the minister of education as conference president; three vice-presidents; and a permanent commission composed of sixteen members: the three vice-presidents, six presidents of work commissions, and seven other elected members. The permanent commission meets twice a month and permanently represents the conference. The three vice-presidents, the presidents of the commissions, and other members of the permanent commission are elected each year. The first vice-president presides over the conference.

The six work commissions are pedagogy and permanent training, research, social questions and the life of the student, financial problems and personnel, relations with other institutions, and rules and legislation. The commissions send delegates to the full conference to report on their conclusions.

The conference studies problems that concern universities and similar institutions and presents to the minister of education suggestions and projects related to its questions. When the conference is called upon to give advice on questions submitted to it by the minister, the minister convenes a meeting, chaired by him or by his representative. The conference may act immediately upon the issue or may form a committee to discuss the question. The meetings of the conference, attended by the full membership, are not open to the public. In addition to the full committee, the conference may form special commissions to debate certain issues. When these questions concern the National Council of Higher Education and Research, the conference directs its advice to that body.

12 rue de l'Ecole de Médecine
Paris (VIe), France

CONFUCIANISM
See Religious Influences in Higher Education: Confucianism.

CONGO, PEOPLE'S REPUBLIC OF THE

Population: 1,300,000 (1974 census). Student enrollment in primary school: 277,384 (1972–73); secondary and technical schools: 54,132 (1972–73); higher education: 1436 (1972–73). Language of instruction: French. Academic calendar: October–June/July. Percentage of national budget expended on higher education: 2.1% (1975).

During the last decades of the nineteenth century, France occupied the lands that today form the Congo. Between 1910 and 1960 it administered the Congo as a territory of the federation of French Equatorial Africa, which also included Gabon, the Central African Republic (then called Ubangi-Shari), and Chad. By decrees in 1911 and 1925, France started to apply in French Equatorial Africa educational policies previously developed in French West Africa. The French followed the same general policies in all of their African territories (the eight territories of French West Africa, the four territories of French Equatorial Africa, and Cameroon and Togo) and thus endowed them with similar institutions. While the fourteen countries achieved independence as individual republics, they retained many ties with one another and with France.

Roman Catholic missionaries from France established the first primary schools in the Congo in the 1880s. After the separation of church and state in France in 1905, the colonial government opened a few public schools but continued to grant small subsidies to the mission schools. The government required all schools to follow an official curriculum that devoted a majority of its program to the study of the French language and culture. It limited the use of indigenous African languages to religious instruction.

During the colonial period, educational opportunities were accessible to only a small portion of the population. In March 1934, out of a total population of 770,000, the Congo had only 6571 pupils in the six primary grades (2411 in public, 3407 in Roman Catholic, and 753 in Swedish Evangelical Protestant schools). Most of the pupils were enrolled in the first three grades. An advanced primary school, which opened later in 1934 at Brazzaville to train administrative employees, could find only ten eligible students from the entire federation who were interested in attending. The few graduates of the primary schools became auxiliaries in the colonial administration, the missions, and European commercial firms.

After World War II, France made greater efforts to promote the advancement of its African territories while retaining them within a French framework. It instituted a policy of assimilation that reproduced the metropolitan curriculum in Africa. The diplomas granted by the secondary schools organized in the Congo during and after the war were identical to those given in France. These diplomas gave access to public employment and entrance to French educational institutions. From the late 1940s the French government granted scholarships to Congolese for study in France, both in higher education and in secondary and technical programs not available in Equatorial Africa or Cameroon. During the 1957–58 school year, just after the granting of limited self-government, 87 Congolese were studying in French universities, 49 of them on government scholarship. At that time the Congo had 79,000 pupils at the primary level and 2000 at the secondary and technical levels.

When independence came in French Equatorial Africa, an insufficient number of Africans had been educated to staff top- and middle-level positions in the government and civil service. Therefore, in 1959 at Brazzaville, France organized courses in higher education to upgrade the level of existing civil servants within the four states and quickly to train others. Within five years these needs were largely satisfied. Thereafter, Gabon, the Central African Republic, and Chad preferred to prepare as many of their future *fonctionnaires* (functionaries) as possible on their own soil and to send them to France for periods of in-service training. The Congo, with French assistance, then organized its own *Ecole nationale d'administration* (ENA: National School of Administration).

In order to provide university educa-

tion in Equatorial Africa, the four states and France in 1961 established the *Fondation de l'enseignement supérieur en Afrique Centrale* (FESAC: Foundation for Higher Education in Central Africa). Special institutes of the FESAC were distributed among the other Equatorial states: animal husbandry at N'djaména, Chad; agronomy at M'baiki, Central African Republic; and a polytechnic at Libreville, Gabon. The *Centre de l'enseignement supérieur de Brazzaville* (CESB: Center of Higher Education in Brazzaville) provided two- and three-year programs in law and economic sciences, letters and social sciences, physical sciences, and mathematics. Future secondary school teachers took courses there and their professional programs at the *Ecole normale supérieure de l'Afrique centrale* (ENSAC: Higher Normal School of Central Africa), which was organized at Brazzaville in 1962 with the aid of UNESCO and the French government.

France provided nearly all of the funding for the FESAC, as well as most of its personnel, and between 1959 and 1969 spent 17,886,000 FF (US $4,000,000). It helped to select the academic administrators, who in turn supervised programs that were closely patterned after those in French universities. France continued to help graduates from the four states attend French institutions for programs not available in Equatorial Africa. During 1971–72, 463 Congolese held scholarships in France, and about the same number of students were studying there at their own expense.

In the late 1960s French efforts to maintain interstate universities foundered both in former French West Africa and French Equatorial Africa, as did the idea of patterning the programs closely upon those in French institutions. Each country wanted its own university, with programs better adapted to national needs. Many states wished to keep their students at home, for study abroad had led to many maladjustments and the failure of a good many to return. In French Equatorial Africa, the Marxist-Leninist tendencies of the Congo governments of Alphonse

Massamba-Debat (1963–1968) and Marien Ngouabi (1968–) and the political turbulence in Brazzaville made the governments of the other three states hesitant about sending many students there. On several occasions classes were disrupted or the university closed as a result of demonstrations linked at least as much to Congolese politics as to educational issues. In April 1971 representatives of the four states voted to dissolve FESAC.

During 1971–72, the last year of FESAC's operation, CESB had 1169 students, over 90 percent of whom were Congolese, 351 of the total enrolled in the two-year preuniversity law program for the *capacité en droit*. In university programs proper, law and economic sciences had 356 students, letters and social sciences 307, and physical sciences and mathematics 155. ENSAC enrolled 314 students (*Statistiques scolaires*, 1973).

During the 1960s the Congo acquired a system of higher education based upon that of France and operated with French aid. Under French auspices it cooperated with other francophone states in Africanizing portions of the university curriculum. At the same time, it was unable to deal with the deeply rooted problems that had arisen from the rapid expansion of a largely unadapted French system of education, especially at the primary and secondary levels.

Types of Institutions

A government order of April 12, 1971, created the *Université de Brazzaville*, which was further organized by presidential decree Number 74–121 of March 18, 1974. CESB was divided into three faculties: law and economic sciences, letters and social sciences, and sciences. ENSAC became the *Institut pédagogique des sciences de l'éducation* (IPSE: Pedagogical Institute of the Science of Education). In June 1975 the *Ecole polytechnique* for four hundred students, constructed by the People's Republic of Korea to train *techniciens supérieurs* (higher technicians), was completed. Attached to

it will be an *Ecole normale supérieure d'enseignement technique* (ENSET: Higher Normal School of Technical Education) to educate secondary teachers of technical subjects. An *Institut des sciences de la santé* (Institute of Health Sciences) opened in September 1975. In cooperation with the World Health Organization, it trains physicians, dentists, pharmacists, and various middle-level health personnel (*Marchés tropicaux*, July 18, 1975, p. 2122).

Relationship with Secondary Education and Admission Requirements

The Congolese educational system as a whole resembles the French. Primary education has six grades, one more than in France, to enable the children to spend their first year adjusting to instruction in French. Until August 1965 the Congo supported the private schools of the Christian churches, mainly by funding the salaries and housing of their African teachers and up to 50 percent of the cost of new classrooms. During 1964–65 the Christian schools were educating 93,352 of the 171,528 primary and 2488 of the 12,515 secondary pupils. On August 12, 1965, at the urging of the *Jeunesse du mouvement national de la révolution* (the youth branch of the official party at the time), the National Assembly established a single public system that was secular and did not allow even optional religious instruction. A decree of April 12, 1966, nationalized the buildings of the private schools, exempting only the seminaries.

The law establishing a single system also made education free and obligatory from ages six to sixteen. To implement this goal, a decree of March 1, 1967, established a single *moyen cycle* for grades 7 to 10, leading to a new diploma, the *brevet d'études moyennes générales* (BEMG). Some holders of the BEMG continue their education in the *lycées*, whose programs (grades 11 to 13) lead to the *baccalauréat* diploma. Holders of the *baccalauréat* are eligible for the university, whereas BEMG holders may enroll in programs to become primary teachers, middle-level civil servants, nurses, medical-social assistants, and various kinds of technicians.

Admission to the university is open to all holders of the *baccalauréat*. Other institutions, such as the ENA, generally have entrance examinations or admission procedures because of prerequisites and often a limited number of places.

Administration and Control

The university is organized along the lines of the French system of higher education as reformed under the law of November 12, 1968. The university is administered by a rector appointed by the *Conseil supérieur de l'université*, which since 1974 is composed of top officials of the government and the single legal party (*Parti congolais du travail*). Levy Makany, a former minister of national education who holds a French doctorate, *doctorat d'état,* became the first rector. The faculty are civil servants and have the same rights and responsibilities as French academics, but within limits to be determined by the *Parti congolais du travail.* Because the PCT is committed to the promotion of scientific socialism in Marxist-Leninist terms, education at all levels is expected to contribute toward the realization of a socialist society. To these ends, the youth and student affiliates of the PCT undertake orientation and study programs among the university students.

The former Ministry of National Education was divided into two ministries after the adoption of a new constitution in 1973. One ministry has responsibility for primary and secondary education and the other for technical and higher education and scientific research. The new constitution institutionalized the role of the PCT in decision making within the central government of this unitary state. Educational policies and appointments are discussed in the Council of State (*Conseil d'état*), which includes the top leaders of the party and the National Assembly, and in the Council of Ministers. Both councils are involved in selecting the members of the Higher Council of the

University (*Conseil supérieur de l'université*), which includes representatives from the party's youth group, the *Union de la jeunesse socialiste congolaise* (UJSC), and its affiliated student union, the *Union générale des élèves congolais* (UGEC). After being suspended in the wake of political disorders in the university and secondary schools of Brazzaville in January and February 1974, the UGEC was reconstituted in early 1975 within the framework of the UJSC but is no longer autonomous.

Programs and Degrees

The *Université de Brazzaville* and other institutions offer general programs in law and economic sciences, letters and social sciences, and physical sciences and mathematics, as well as professional programs in national administration, secondary teaching, and technology. Graduates of these programs go to France for advanced studies.

By a decision of the ministers of education of the francophone states in 1972, diplomas granted by their institutions and by those in France, Belgium, and Canada are valid in all fourteen countries. Congolese diplomas are considered to be equivalent to French. Thus, the diplomas granted by the *Université de Brazzaville* permit entrance to advanced programs in francophone Africa and in France.

Financing

French aid to higher education, under a new cooperation agreement of January 1, 1974, included 96 million francs CFA (US $400,000) for the period January to September 1974 and 141 million francs CFA (US $630,000) for the 1974–75 academic year. In addition to these credits for operations, which include funds for some of the Congolese staff, France gave an undisclosed amount for construction of classrooms, a dormitory, and a student restaurant. These facilities are urgently needed in view of overcrowding of the present accommodations. But during 1974 the budgetary situation was improving. Additional revenues, mainly from oil, allowed the original 1974 budget to be raised and earlier budgetary deficits to be paid off.

Student Financial Aid

As at the primary and secondary levels, education in the university is free. Until 1974 all students in higher education received scholarships that covered room and board, books, some clothing, and allowances for the long vacation. They were given free medical care, allowances for dependents, and annual travel expenses to the school if they were nonresidents. In 1972 scholarships for students at home and abroad were taking 5 percent of the national budget. In the wake of the 1974 troubles at the university, the policies on scholarships are being reviewed.

Student Social Background and Access to Education

The Congo achieved nearly universal primary education in the early 1960s. To equalize opportunities at the secondary level, the government has provided some scholarships to cover the room and board of students who must live away from home. Several secondary schools have boarding facilities. Since the mid 1960s the government has sought to build schools in all sections of the country. It has given special attention to the North, which was considered disadvantaged.

Since World War II, the government has taken steps to promote the education of women, with a real degree of success. During 1971–72 there were 117,166 girls and 144,945 boys in the primary schools (total: 262,111); 11,187 girls and 21,688 boys in grades seven to ten (total: 32,875); 567 girls and 3988 boys in the *lycées* (total: 4555); and 1550 girls and 2536 boys in technical programs (total: 4086) at the primary and secondary levels combined. During 1971–72 there were 89 women among the 1169 students at the CESB, and 74 women had scholarships in French higher education institutions.

Until recently the Congo lacked the funds and staff to provide all primary and secondary graduates with further education. Most of the 152 members of religious orders teaching in the private secondary schools at the time of nationalization departed and never were replaced by staff of equal competence.

Political activism among university and even *lycée* students has a long tradition in France. The transfer of this tradition into Africa has taken place during a period of conflict within the Congo over the very nature of the state and society. The Ngouabi regime, in particular, has sought to enlist the university and its students in constructing a new society based on the principles of scientific socialism. In the process, it has further politicized the students and sharpened the differences between supporters of its goals and those who desire a socialist regime on the Chinese and Cuban models or liberal democracy. A small number of students have been drawn into the various unsuccessful plots that have plagued the stability of the regime. Thus, the history of higher education in the Congo has involved student demonstrations and strikes in which educational, cultural, social, and political issues have been mixed together in often confusing fashion. Instruction has often been interrupted and institutions closed on several occasions. In January 1974 UGEC spokesmen criticized the government for its alleged failure to institute an educational system that considered the welfare of the masses; official replies denounced the students as petty bourgeois individualists and anarchists. In the wake of demonstrations proceeding from these incidents, 20 out of the 111 students and pupils arrested were enrolled in the army for political and civic education. President Ngouabi subsequently announced that they would be released to resume their studies.

Current Problems and Trends

Articles by young militants of the UJSC and the UGEC in the party newspaper, *Etumba*, during 1975 reflect a concern to adapt the educational system to present needs or to construct an entirely new system. Many obstacles make the achievement of these goals difficult. Starting in 1957 the Congo's leaders felt strong popular pressures to expand educational opportunities. While recognizing the necessity for reform, they possessed neither the funds nor the staff to undertake the desired changes. In these circumstances, rapid expansion of enrollments occurred without the training of many new teachers or the construction of adequate facilities. The quality of instruction has suffered and there has been a high rate of attrition. Most of the minority who finish their programs are prepared only for public employment or unemployment.

A national colloquium in December 1970—sponsored by the PCT and attended by educators, party and government leaders, and observers from socialist countries— formulated principles for a new School of the People; and these principles have served as the basis for most subsequent discussions.

But changes so far have been modest. The primary and secondary levels include the changes made in the teaching of French and mathematics by all fourteen francophone states (excluding Guinea but including Madagascar) jointly with French assistance. The programs include new Africa-centered courses in history, geography, and literature (emphasizing black writers such as Léopold Senghor, Aimé Césaire, and Frantz Fanon). But they have undergone little adaptation that is particular to the Congo. Moreover, the language of instruction is still French, despite the problems that this policy entails for the majority of children, especially in the early grades. The *Institut pédagogique,* in cooperation with the university's professors of Bantu linguistics, is presently studying indigenous languages in order to examine the possibilities for teaching elementary classes in the vernacular.

The programs in higher education for the moment remain almost identical to those adopted in France in implementation of the law of November 12, 1968. They also contain the modifications made in the late 1960s by the fourteen francophone states. Thus, the history and geography courses have much material on Africa and the Third World. Literature students read the works of black francophone writers, including Congolese writers like Jean Malonga and Tchicaya U'Tamsi. The letters faculty has a sequence in Bantu linguistics.

By sending hundreds of students to the Soviet Union and Romania, and by utilizing professors from socialist countries, the Ngouabi government is strengthening the Marxist elements within the educated classes. But at the same time it is probably accentuating the divisions among the Marxist segments, and between Marxists and non-Marxists, that have contributed to governmental instability since the mid 1960s. In the long run, this educational pluralism may enrich the country, but for the moment it is likely to make more difficult the achievement of the strong consensus that is necessary to plan and implement educational reforms. The improving financial situation, which may give the Congo the means for educating all of its young people to the highest level of their abilities in the near future, increases the urgency for changes at all levels of the system.

International Cooperation

Given the orientation of the regime, the government has sought and obtained the assistance of socialist nations in developing its educational system, especially on the secondary and higher levels, and in increasing educational opportunities. During 1974–75, under the agreement of December 1964 with the Soviet Union, eight hundred Congolese were studying in Soviet technical and higher institutions, including two hundred who attended for the first time. Of the thirty-three Congolese physicians who graduated from overseas institutions in 1973, twenty-five were educated in the Soviet Union. During 1974–75 over two hundred Soviet professors were teaching in Congolese secondary and higher institutions (*Etumba,* July 26–Aug. 2, 1975, p. 358).

Under a protocol of 1972, during 1974–75 around four hundred Congolese were studying agriculture, forestry, mining, and industrial technology in specialized and higher institutions in Romania; Romanian technicians in these fields were working in the Congo, in part to supervise the practical training of the graduates (*Etumba,* Aug. 30–Sept. 6, 1975, p. 363). During 1975 there were only nine professors, most of them in health fields, among the 423 technical personnel provided by the People's Republic of China. Of the 132 permanent faculty positions at the University of Brazzaville during 1974, ninety-six were provided by foreign technical assistance, sixty-six were from France, and the rest were mostly from the Soviet Union and the German Democratic Republic.

DAVID E. GARDINIER

Educational Association

Fédération nationale des syndicats des enseignants congolais
B.P. 2285
Brazzaville
People's Republic of the Congo

Bibliography

Gardinier, D. E. "Education in the States of Equatorial Africa: A Bibliographical Essay." *Africana Library Journal,* 1972, *3,* 7–20.
Gardinier, D. E. "Schooling in the States of Equatorial Africa." *Revue canadienne des études africaines/Canadian Journal of African Studies,* 1974, *8,* 517–538.
Gauze, R. *The Politics of Congo-Brazzaville.* Translation, editing, and supplement by Virginia Thompson and Richard Adloff. Stanford, California: Hoover Institution Press, 1973.
L'Hénoret, M. *Précis de morale professionnelle à l'usage des enseignants de la République Populaire du Congo.* Paris: François Maspéro, 1970.
Labrousse, A. *La France et l'aide à l'éducation dans 14 états africains et malgache.* Paris: International Institute for Educational Planning, April 1971.
Lucas, G. "Formal Education in the Congo-Brazzaville: A Study of Educational Policy and Practice." Unpublished doctoral dissertation, Stanford University, Stanford, California, 1965.
"Orientation Law on Higher Education." *Western European Education,* 1974, *6,* 82–102. (Text of the French law No. 68–978 of Nov. 12, 1968, in translation.)
Statistiques scolaires, 1971–72. Brazzaville: Ministère de l'éducation nationale, 1973.
Tchichaya, J.-G. *La réforme de l'enseignement primaire en République Populaire du Congo: Une approche qualitative par les aspects pédagogiques de la formation des élèves et des maîtres.* Paris: International Institute of Educational Planning, 1971.

See also: Africa, Sub-Saharan: Regional Analysis; Archives: Africa and Asia, National Archives of.

CONSERVATION STUDIES
See Museum Studies (field of study).

CONSORTIA IN THE UNITED STATES

Consortia represent only one form of interinstitutional cooperation among the colleges and universities of the United States. Consortia, as distinguished from other interinstitutional arrangements, are characterized as multipurpose voluntary organizations composed of three or more member institutions that cooperate in a variety of academic programs; consortia are professionally administered and require annual contributions by member institutions.

All forms of interinstitutional cooperation have shown dramatic growth in the last decade. In the mid 1960s, for example, there were approximately one thousand formal institutional linkages in the United States, primarily among graduate schools; by 1975 approximately ten thousand cooperative arrangements provided linkages among the more than three thousand American institutions of higher education. Consortia have shown a similar pattern; by far the greatest growth has occurred since 1965. Between 1925 and 1965 nineteen consortia were established: four had been created by 1948, five more by 1958, and an additional ten by 1965. In the next five years, from 1965 to 1970, thirty-two new consortia came into being. As of 1975 more than one half of the 106 multipurpose consortia in United States higher education had been organized in the preceding five years.

Such growth in interinstitutional cooperation seemed, to some observers, to be a symptom of the beginning of a new era in the organization of higher education in the United States. The old pattern of institutional separatism appeared to be undergoing change, primarily because of the pressure of virtually unlimited needs on limited institutional resources. In the decade from 1965 to 1975, almost every college and university in the United States, public and private, came to face the fact that its costs were rising faster than its income. In addition, the expansion of knowledge, with which higher education was expected to deal, was so great and exponential that cooperative relationships seemed necessary if instruction was to be adequate in quality and variety. The growth of multipurpose consortia of institutions of higher education reflected a growing belief that the welfare of the whole educational enterprise required the cooperative association of diverse institutions, based either on location or on special areas of interest. But neither of the two principal doctrines that informed the consortium movement was fully realized by 1975. The first of these doctrines was that, through cooperation, the academic programs available to students could be substantially enriched and diversified. This doctrine, as of 1975, has been realized only on a modest scale even among the best of the multipurpose consortia. In academic matters faculties of institutions in consortia have proved to be as conservative in protecting vested institutional interests as faculties elsewhere. Certainly, no one in the voluntary multipurpose consortium movement could be faulted for excessive zeal in promoting the cooperative interinstitutional planning of academic programs. Instead, in 1975, institutional territoriality tended still to prevail; many in the movement

appeared to be more willing to accept redundancy, if necessary, than planned academic complementarity.

The second doctrine, that cooperation would mean economic gain, proved to be even more a matter of shadow rather than substance, despite the fact that the doctrine of economy seemed to many to have self-evident validity. Certainly, a strong factor in the growth of multipurpose consortia was the notion that survival and viability for institutions in a time of limited or declining resources might be found through group affiliation. In discussing avenues to effective use of resources in colleges and universities, the Carnegie Commission on Higher Education asserted that "significant economies can be achieved through consortium agreements and other forms of interinstitutional cooperation." Largely on the basis of economic arguments, the commission recommended "the development and strengthening of consortia in higher education" and urged "increased cooperation and sharing of facilities by public and private institutions . . . in all states" (Carnegie Commission on Higher Education, 1972, pp. 127–128).

There is enough evidence in the experience of consortia to suggest that interinstitutional cooperation might permit financial economies, or, at least, a wiser and more effective use of resources than individual institutions could conduct alone. At the same time, the Carnegie Commission noted that "a good many of the consortia are paper arrangements with little significance in practice," and that there is "serious resistance in colleges and universities to any departure from the traditional goal of independent development of the resources of each institution" (Carnegie Commission on Higher Education, 1972, p. 128). And, in fact, as late as 1975, few serious joint decisions were being made within multipurpose consortia about avoiding redundancy in new physical plant development or about achieving cooperative economies in purchasing, admissions, or the use of educational technology. A number of institutional presidents spoke in favor of cooperation, but their substantive commitment was not usually as strong as their words; further, it was clear that whatever their commitment, it tended to outrun that of their faculties and trustees.

Historical Development of the Consortium Movement

The multipurpose consortium movement grew slowly in the three decades after the mid 1920s. The Claremont Colleges in Southern California are considered by most observers to have begun the movement in the United States. In 1925 James A. Blaisdell, then president of Pomona College, created a plan reminiscent of Oxford by establishing a small group of colleges around Pomona that shared a library and other facilities. The first product of this cluster was the Claremont Graduate School, followed over the next several decades by Scripps College, Claremont Men's College, Harvey Mudd College, and Pitzer College.

In 1929, four years after the founding of the Claremont Colleges, the Atlanta University Center was created in Georgia by agreement among Atlanta University, Morehouse, and Spelman Colleges. Later, Clark College, the Interdenominational Theological Center, and Morris Brown College entered into working arrangements with the center, and in 1964 they finally joined under a new charter.

The multipurpose consortium movement developed at a slow pace for some years after these beginnings in Claremont and Atlanta. A pickup in momentum began in the early 1960s, as United States colleges and universities began to feel the full impact of the greatest enrollment rise in the history of American higher education, coupled with economic inflation and the knowledge explosion.

By 1962, the momentum for multipurpose consortia was sufficiently strong, and the awareness of common consortial problems sufficiently great, for a conference on college and university interinstitutional cooperation to be held. The conference,

which took place at Princeton, New Jersey, was sponsored by one consortium, the College Center of the Finger Lakes (CCFL), and was supported by the Ford Foundation, the Corning Glass Works Foundation, and Arthur A. Houghton, Jr. The Princeton conference brought together staff leaders of existing consortia with other educators and foundation representatives. In many ways it was a milestone, marking the beginning of serious professional dialogue about the consortium movement in the United States. The Princeton discussions, summarized in published proceedings, set forth thirty-two areas of possible cooperation. These areas covered the range of collaborative considerations that would eventually come before most institutions of higher education (Wittich, 1962).

In 1965 the United States Congress endorsed interinstitutional cooperation as a means for improving higher education in the nation. Title III of the Higher Education Act of 1965 provided support for "cooperative arrangements" among "developing institutions." Colleges judged to be "struggling for survival" and "isolated from the main currents of academic life" could qualify to receive Title III funds for cooperative efforts to improve their position; a substantial number of consortia came into being under the direct stimulus of Title III.

By 1975 this national intervention had, in several cases, been supplemented at the state level. New York, Illinois, and Connecticut, for example, enacted legislation to encourage interinstitutional cooperation. In New York the Bundy Committee (a Governor's Select Committee on Aid to Private Higher Education) urged state appropriation of a million dollars annually to stimulate cooperation among colleges and universities. By the time the College Center of the Finger Lakes sponsored a second major conference in 1969, the number of multipurpose consortia had doubled. The 1969 conference reflected the rapid growth of the movement through a preoccupation with organizational concerns;

the 1969 conferees were principally occupied with questions of organizational
structure, intraconsortium relationships,
the role of the executive director, cooperative program development, and ways to finance interinstitutional cooperation (Burnett, 1970).

The consortium movement arose out of
a complex of factors characteristic of American higher education in the 1960s and the
1970s. The day of the wholly autonomous
institution was coming to an end. The approach of a postindustrial society presented
higher education with complex social and
educational demands and financial constraints, which made it increasingly difficult for institutions to be wholly separate.
For a large number of private institutions in
the United States, including such hitherto
invulnerable giants as Columbia University
and the University of Pennsylvania, the
institutional question of the 1970s was becoming that of economic survival. The
Higher Education Act of 1972, which authorized some nineteen billion dollars of
federal support for colleges and universities (if adequately financed by legislative
appropriations), appeared to signal a turning point in federal aid to higher education. But it was not likely that the public,
through government or gift, would provide
progressively more massive subsidies to
allow each institution to remain in isolation, trying alone to offer education of high
quality in all disciplines. It seems increasingly clear that, no matter how austere
and efficient internal institutional management could be made, nor how friendly the
federal government might be to their
cause, few, if any, United States colleges
and universities will be able to stand wholly
alone much longer.

Current Trends

A new era in the organization of United
States higher education appeared likely,
in the mid 1970s, to bring with it more
joint planning and collaboration among
institutions in the future. Some educators
thought the issue could be simplified to

the question of whether such collaboration
would be involuntary, coordinated by state
and national government, or voluntary, by
joint agreement of public and private institutions. In fact, however, both more
government coordination and more interinstitutional cooperation appear likely. As
the twentieth century continues, increasing dependence on governmental support—even by the richest institutions—is
likely to bring with it a new kind of accountability, and, with that, more coordination
from outside. A realistic question about
multipurpose consortia in the mid 1970s
has been whether voluntary cooperation
will be able to take hold and work well
enough to lessen some of the thrust toward
externally directed coordination.

Ideally, if cooperation adequate to academic and economic needs could be established voluntarily, higher education in
the United States during the closing years
of the twentieth century might follow a pattern of interinstitutional self-government
rather than one designed by the requirements of federal and state accountability. Under voluntary cooperation, decisions about complementary educational
missions, faculty development and support, and costly installations could be made
by those more directly involved, acting
through self-governing groups of institutions. But it is not clear whether voluntary multipurpose consortia will be able
to achieve genuine and significant cooperation, adequate to the needs and conditions
of higher education.

An impressive list of consortia activities had been compiled by the middle of
the 1970s: administrative and business
services, joint business operations, training to improve management, collective
public and private purchasing, free or
carefully costed interinstitutional student
enrollment, joint computer facilities, telephone networking, fuel oil savings, and
lower insurance rates. In addition, enrollment and admissions activities included
the single application method of the Associated Colleges of the Midwest, joint

student recruitment of the United Independent Colleges of Art, and other cooperative approaches to the student market. And, in joint academic programs, several instances of true cooperative academic planning occurred, such as the combined field of study approach developed by the Worcester Consortium for Higher Education, the joint programs of the New Orleans Consortium, a few collective decisions to phase out redundant graduate and undergraduate offerings, consortium-enlarged choices of courses for concentration, the use of television instruction in the institutions of the Texas Association for Graduate Education and Research (TAGER), and jointly sponsored field study opportunities. Cooperative activities in some multipurpose consortia also included certain library operations, student services, community services, and faculty utilization and development.

At the same time, careful assessment makes clear that this inventory of activities is still thin: activities of all the consortia as a whole are more impressive than those of any single consortium. Perhaps the most candid observation about such arrangements in the United States was that of one consortium director who said that "consortia cooperate on the easy things." Genuinely hard decisions about planned academic complementarity among institutions and planned capital outlay are hard to find.

One study of the multipurpose consortium movement came to five related conclusions in 1974. First, the need for maximum effective voluntary cooperation by groups of colleges and universities appears critical. Second, the multipurpose consortium movement is not adequately meeting this need. Third, the principal direct impediment to effective interinstitutional cooperation is the traditional commitment of colleges and universities to institutional autonomy. Fourth, institutional autonomy ought to be modified, not killed; and, for most institutions, voluntary cooperation might be the only means by which modified institutional autonomy can sur-

vive at all. Fifth, the achievement of an adequately effective consortium movement in the United States depends on intelligent outside intervention and support. This final conclusion was reached because it was considered unlikely that institutional heads—or their faculties or trustees—would take sufficient initiative in modifying institutional autonomy to secure cooperation on basic decisions of program and operation (Patterson, 1974).

Bibliography

Burnett, H. J. *Interinstitutional Cooperation in Higher Education.* Corning, New York: College Center of the Finger Lakes, 1970.
Carnegie Commission on Higher Education. *The More Effective Use of Resources: An Imperative for Higher Education.* New York: McGraw-Hill, 1972.
Patterson, F. *Colleges in Consort: Institutional Cooperation Through Consortia.* San Francisco: Jossey-Bass, 1974.
Patterson, L. D. *Bibliography on Interinstitutional Cooperation with Special Emphasis on Voluntary Academic Consortia in Higher Education.* Kansas City, Missouri: Kansas City Regional Council for Higher Education, 1971.
Patterson, L. D. *1975 Consortium Directory.* Washington, D.C.: American Association for Higher Education, 1975.
Wittich, J. J. (Ed.) *College and University Interinstitutional Cooperation.* Corning, New York: College Center of the Finger Lakes, 1962.

FRANKLIN PATTERSON

See also: Interinstitutional Cooperation.

CONSTRUCTION

See Building and Construction Administration; Business Management of Higher Education: Facilities, Physical Plant.

CONSTRUCTION AND BUILDING TECHNOLOGY (Field of Study)

Construction and building technology is the study of the systematic utilization of natural and man-made materials in the building of socially functional structures. The construction technologist uses physics, mathematics, and a knowledge of materials to design and construct buildings for industrial, business, and residential use, as well as systems for transportation, sewage, and water supply.

Construction technology is composed of two general categories: construction design and construction methodology. Construction design involves the design and preparation of working drawings of a structure in advance of building it. Construction designers must have a sound knowledge of mathematics, physics, and materials. Those engaged in construction methodology, on the other hand, are concerned primarily with the actual building of the designed structure and must have a sound background in construction techniques, proper utilization of materials, available equipment, cost effectiveness, and project-scheduling techniques. Clear distinctions between the two general categories are not easily specified, since they are dependent on each other and must constantly interrelate while a construction project is under way. Both categories also have common divisions of specialty, including surveying, hydraulics, structural design, sanitary (environmental) design, and transportation.

Because of the diversity of engineering disciplines, most institutions of higher education involved in construction and building technology must offer a wide range of specialized programs in the main subject divisions and in related topics. The majority of those divisions generally fall under the auspices of civil engineering departments at most institutes and colleges; but exposure to related fields, such as architecture, mechanical engineering, and electrical engineering, is recommended. Because of the expansion of specialized divisions and their related fields and the concomitant academic development of construction and building technology, the education of students within these disciplines has become generally homogeneous and international.

Historically, the availability of materials, as well as technological and scientific expertise, has determined the size and archi-

tectural forms of buildings. Ubiquitous forests were the raw material for construction in northern Europe. The Tigris and Euphrates Valley civilizations were dependent on the clay with which the inhabitants produced sun-dried brick. Stone was not introduced as building material until later. Egyptian and Greek architecture was dependent on the expert use of stone. The Egyptians were also expert stonemasons by the third millennium. It was the Roman Empire, however, which was to assimilate all of the lessons and advances in construction technology and create a systematic, comprehensive, expansive urban empire. The Romans built new cities in far-flung provinces, rebuilt ancient centers, and connected all areas to promote commercial prosperity and provide for urban growth and well-being. Aqueducts in southern France or Spain, public baths in England, temples in Armenia or Israel, circuses, apartment houses at Ostia, roads and more roads (complete with hotels for travelers) were built with efficiency and attention to detail. The Romans effectively combined inexpensive materials with the scientific principle of the arch. They developed concrete, a mixture of volcanic earth and lime that was water and fire resistant. Their contribution to construction technology and public works was solid and represented the interests of the highest levels of government. After Rome's decline, urban planning in Europe did not reach a comparable level until the nineteenth century.

Europe experienced dynamic changes between the mid eighteenth and early nineteenth centuries, because of a dramatic increase and shift in population, expansion of commercial activity, development of improved methods of food production, political and social transformation, and rapid industrialization. Mass production required mass building construction methods, since new factories, offices, and urban dwellings had to be built quickly. During the eighteenth century the architect-artist gradually became differentiated from the builder-engineer. Plaster, mortar, and concrete construction methods were developed, and wrought iron was used to strengthen timber and masonry. A significant advancement in building technology came with the substitution of cast iron for masonry and supporting columns in bridges. Later, steel replaced cast iron in buildings and bridges, and, by the early twentieth century, steel and concrete became the prime ingredients in all major construction projects. Steel, which had been the spine of the transportation system, became the multipurpose structural element for the skyscraper. Only with the creation and expansion of the bicycle and then the automobile industry was there a shift in emphasis to highway construction; until then, road construction had been the concern of local authorities. National and international road systems —to equal the railroad systems of Europe and Asia—were not given priority in Europe, Asia, or North America until after World War II.

The postwar years opened an era of planned construction, when men and materials were fully utilized. Safety standards and quality control assumed major significance. Plans and specifications were prepared before completion of the work, and materials and their availability were considered thoroughly. The methodology and scheduling of construction became important factors in feasibility studies. The most important factor in any construction project, however, has been and remains its economic viability. Rising material costs will require the development of newer, less expensive materials, as well as the more efficient use of existing resources.

The use of the computer has resulted in extensive preliminary analysis and design in all phases of construction planning and scheduling. Individual countries continue to depend on methods based on assessment of their needs; but—as a result of international communication systems among industrialized societies, industry publications, and international symposia—new techniques are adopted rapidly throughout the world. New systems and

methods of construction will have to be developed to provide shelter and transportation for an expanding and increasingly urban population.

New cities are being planned or are in the process of construction in the developing nations of Asia, South America, and Africa, as well as in the more industrialized nations of France, the United Kingdom, and the Soviet Union. An efficient mass transit system has been the key to Japanese urbanization, and similar efforts will be required globally if this increasingly urban environment is to be viable in an era of high energy costs. Industrial facilities, irrigation and hydroelectric projects, sewage and water distribution systems are either in the planning stages or in construction. India, Egypt, and China are concerned with irrigation and hydroelectric power because they must increase food production to feed their expanding populations and to provide the energy resources necessary for industrial development and a mass consumption society. What was once accomplished in one hundred years will have to be completed in ten, and construction technology will have to address itself to complex problems and demands. It will have to become more scientific in its approach to problem solving. The increased utilization of a systems approach to construction technology is evidence of this trend. It is also likely that construction and building technology will become even more homogeneous internationally and that higher education will increasingly reflect a uniformity of technique and method. Construction design generally must depend on those college disciplines commonly associated with civil engineering and related programs, although these programs often also service the construction methodology field.

College programs in construction and civil engineering grant degrees ranging from an associate level to a doctoral level. Construction curricula generally offer very few degrees beyond the bachelor's, thus restricting graduates at this level to the methodology segment of construction. The advanced degree levels, commonly associated with civil engineering programs, provide qualified personnel in the design segment of construction, with the lower degree levels also serving the methodology segment.

In the future, fewer distinctions will be made between construction and civil engineering programs, and more emphasis will be placed on project systems curricula. The degree level, however, will generally reflect the segment of the construction industry being served. Methodology will be served by associate and bachelor's degree programs, and design will depend primarily on the master's or advanced degree levels for personnel.

HENRY POYDAR

Levels and Programs of Study

Programs in construction and building technology generally require as a prerequisite a secondary education, although mature students with relevant work experience may be admitted with lower qualifications, especially into programs designed to upgrade the performance of those already employed. Programs consist primarily of classroom, laboratory, and workshop study and practice and deal with the design, materials, and methodology of building and construction.

The usual award for programs in construction and building technology of one year or more, typically given in technological or similar institutes, is a certificate, diploma, or associate degree issued by the institution or by the examining board of a professional or technical organization. For short courses, many of which are sponsored by employers or employers' associations, a certificate of satisfactory completion is usually given. Programs in construction engineering may lead to the following degrees: bachelor's (B.Sc., B.Eng.), master's (M.Sc.), the doctorate (Ph.D.), or their equivalents. In most instances, advanced degrees are awarded by a department of civil engineering.

Principal course content for construction and building technology and construction engineering programs usually includes some of the following: construction methods and equipment; heavy and highway construction; construction administration, planning, and scheduling; cost engineering; soil mechanics; surveying and mapping; static mechanics; safety engineering; mechanical systems; construction operation analysis; structural design; foundations and concrete structures; behavior of materials; and strength of materials. Background and related courses may include economics, business administration and management, natural and social sciences, mathematics, and architecture.

[This section was based on UNESCO's *International Standard Classification of Education (ISCED): Three Stage Classification System, 1974* (Paris, UNESCO, 1974).]

Major International and National Organizations

INTERNATIONAL

Bouwcentrum
Weena 700
Rotterdam, Netherlands
An independent, private foundation which acts as an international development institute for building. Possesses a library on building literature and sponsors courses on building and construction.

International Association of Crafts and Small
  and Medium-Sized Enterprises (IACME)
98 rue de Saint-Jean
CH-12211 Geneva 11, Switzerland

International Council for Building Research
  Studies and Documentation
Conseil international du bâtiment pour l'étude,
  la recherche et la documentation (CIB)
Weena 704, P.O. Box 299
Rotterdam, Netherlands
Encourages and facilitates cooperation in building research, studies, and documentation internationally. National organizations in fifty countries are members.

International Federation for Housing and
  Planning
Wassenaarseweg 43
The Hague, Netherlands
Promotes the practice and study of housing and of regional, town, and city planning throughout the world.

International Union of Building Centres
Union internationale des centres du bâtiment
　(UICB)
26 Store Street
London WC1E 7BT, England

Trade Unions International of Workers of
　the Building, Wood and Building Materials
　Industries
Box 10281
Helsinki, Finland

World Federation of Building and
　Woodworkers Unions
22 Krome Nieuwe Gracht
Utrecht, Netherlands

NATIONAL

Australia:
　Building Workers' Industrial Union of
　　Australia
　Trades Hall, Goulborn Street
　Sydney, New South Wales 2000

Austria:
　Gewerkschaft der Bau-und Holzarbeiter
　Ebendorferstrasse 7
　A-1082 Vienna

Belgium:
　Confédération nationale de la
　　construction
　13 rue des Poissoniers
　Brussels

Federal Republic of Germany:
　Hauptverband der deutschen
　　Bauindustrie e.V.
　Friedrich-Ebert-Anlage 38
　D-6000 Frankfurt/Main

Ireland:
　Irish Building Societies Association
　98 St. Stephen's Green South
　Dublin 2

Japan:
　Associated General Constructors of
　　Japan
　Tokyo kensetsu kaikan 5-1
　Hatchobori 2-chome
　Chuo-ku, Tokyo 104

Mexico:
　Centro regional de construcciones
　　escolares para América Latina
　Apartado Postal 41-518
　Mexico 10, D.F.

South Africa:
　Building Industries Federation of
　　South Africa
　P.O. Box 11359
　Johannesburg

Soviet Union:
　Building and Building Materials
　　Industry Workers' Union
　Leninsky prospekt 42
　Moscow

Spain:
　Agrupación nacional sindical de
　　constructores promotores de
　　edificios urbanos (ACPE)
　Paseo del Prado 18-20
　Madrid 14

United Kingdom:
　Amalgamated Union of Building Trade
　　Workers
　The Builders', Crescent Lane
　London SW 4, England

United States:
　Associated Schools of Construction
　P.O. Box 12374
　Oklahoma City, Oklahoma 73112

　National Association of Building
　　Manufacturers (NABM)
　1619 Massachusetts Avenue NW
　Washington, D.C. 20036

Principal Information Sources

GENERAL

Guides to literature in the field include:

Bentley, H. B. *Building Construction Information Sources.* Management Information Guide No. 2. Detroit: Gale Research, 1964. Although mainly a guide to the literature, includes details of organizations.

Smith, D. L. *How to Find Out in Architecture and Building: A Guide to Sources of Information.* Elmsford, New York: Pergamon Press, 1967.

Guides to technological and career education are:

Heywood, J. *Bibliography of British Technological Education and Training.* London: Hutchinson, 1971.

Lederer, M. *The Guide to Career Education.* New York: Quadrangle Books, 1974. A comprehensive United States guide to postsecondary education; includes career descriptions and methods of career selection, as well as organizations and associations involved with technical and vocational education.

Among the numerous introductory works in this field are:

Benson, B. *Critical Path Methods in Building Construction.* Englewood Cliffs, New Jersey: Prentice-Hall, 1970.

Bush, V. G. *Construction Management.* Reston, Virginia: Reston Publishing, 1973.

Collier, K. *Fundamentals of Construction and Estimating Cost Accounting.* Englewood Cliffs, New Jersey: Prentice-Hall, 1974.

Day, D. A. *Construction Equipment Guide.* New York: Wiley, 1973.

Douglas, J. *Construction Equipment Policy.* New York: McGraw-Hill, 1975.

Halperin, D. A. *Construction Funding.* New York: Wiley, 1974.

Oppenheimer, S. P. *Directing Construction for Profit.* New York: McGraw-Hill, 1971.

Testa, C. *The Industrialization of Building.* New York: Van Nostrand Reinhold, 1972.

Histories of building are:

Bowyer, J. *History of Building.* New York: Beekman, 1973.

Condit, C. W. *American Building: Materials and Techniques from the Beginning of the Colonial Settlements to the Present.* Chicago: University of Chicago Press, 1968.

CURRENT BIBLIOGRAPHIES

Current abstracting and indexing services in the field are:

Applied Science and Technology Index (formerly *Industrial Arts Index*). New York: Wilson, 1913–. Published monthly, with quarterly and annual cumulations.

Building Research Station, Department of the Environment. *Building Science Abstracts.* London: H. M. Stationery Office, 1925–. Published monthly. About two thousand abstracts, in four main subject groups: "Materials," "Engineering," "Construction," and "Design and Environment."

CIRF Abstracts: Ideas Drawn from the Current Writings on Vocational Training for Workers, Supervisors and Technicians. Geneva: Centre international d'information et de recherche sur la formation professionnelle (CIRF), 1961–.

Civil Engineering. New York: American Society of Civil Engineers, 1930–. Published weekly; contains current bibliographies.

Engineering Index. New York: Engineering Index, Inc., 1884–. The most comprehensive collection of abstracts on worldwide developments in all areas of engineering and related disciplines.

Technical Education Abstracts, from British Sources. London: National Federation for Educational Research in England and Wales, Information Service, 1961–. Published quarterly. About five hundred abstracts for those concerned with scientific, technical, and further education, including education and

training for industry and commerce at all levels. About fifty journals are scanned.

PERIODICALS

Some of the many useful journals in the field are *Asian Building and Construction* (Hong Kong), *Bouw* (Netherlands), *Building Progress* (New Zealand), *Building Research and Practice* (UK), *Building Science* (US), *Building Technology and Management* (UK), *Canadian Building Digest, Cement Technology* (UK), *Concrete Construction* (US), *Construcción mexicana, Engineering and Construction World* (US), *Industrialization Forum* (US), *Industrialisierung des Bauens/Industrialization of Building/Industrialisation du bâtiment* (FRG), *Informes de la construcción* (Spain), *Przeglad budowlany* (Poland).

For additional journals see:

Ulrich's International Periodicals Directory. New York: Bowker, biennial.

ENCYCLOPEDIAS, DICTIONARIES, HANDBOOKS

Cagnacci Schwicker, A. *International Dictionary of Building Construction.* Milan: Techno-Print International, in association with McGraw-Hill and Dunod-Paris, 1972. In English, French, German, and Italian.

The Construction Industry Handbook. (2nd ed.) Boston: Cahners, 1973.

McGraw-Hill Encyclopedia of Science and Technology. New York: McGraw-Hill, 1971. With annual supplements.

Merritt, F. *Building Construction Handbook.* (3rd ed.) New York: McGraw-Hill, 1975.

United States Department of Labor, Bureau of Labor Statistics. *Occupational Outlook Handbook.* Washington, D.C.: U.S. Government Printing Office, 1957–. With quarterly supplements. Includes bibliographies, charts, current United States occupational trends, and perspectives.

United States Department of Labor, Manpower Administration. *Dictionary of Occupational Titles.* Vol. 1: *Definition of Titles;* Vol. 2: *Occupational Classifications.* (3rd ed.) Washington, D.C.: U.S. Government Printing Office, 1965. A supplement was published in 1966.

Urquhart, L. C. *Civil Engineering Handbook.* (4th ed.) New York: McGraw-Hill, 1959.

DIRECTORIES

Construction Education Directory. (2nd ed.) Washington, D.C.: Associated General Contractors Education and Research Foundation, 1974. Lists eighty-three schools in the United States, with construction curricula in three general categories: colleges and universities offering undergraduate and/or graduate programs specifically in construction, colleges and universities offering basic programs in engineering or architecture with elective courses in construction, and institutions offering two-year programs in construction technologies. Each listing includes the name of the program, the sponsoring unit, length of the program, degree offered, objective, and the courses offered. The directory also includes education and training requirements for construction industry positions and educational goals and recommended curricula for the construction industry.

Dent, H. C. *The Yearbook of Technical Education and Careers in Industry.* London: Black, 1957–. A directory to technical careers and vocational study in the United Kingdom.

Gleazer, E. J. *American Junior Colleges.* (8th ed.) Washington, D. C.: American Council on Education, 1971.

Russell, M. M. *Occupational Education.* (2nd ed.) New York: Macmillan, 1973. A United States directory.

Technician Education Yearbook. Ann Arbor, Michigan: Prakken, 1963–, annual. Each annual volume deals with a pertinent subject in vocational education. Also contains a listing of institutions in the United States offering 118 technologies.

RESEARCH CENTERS, INSTITUTES,
INFORMATION CENTERS

International Council for Building Research Studies and Documentation
Conseil international du bâtiment pour l'étude, la recherche et la documentation (CIB)
Weena 704, P.O. Box 299
Rotterdam, Netherlands

International Union of Testing and Research Laboratories for Materials and Structures
Réunion internationale des laboratoires d'essais et de recherches sur les matériaux et les constructions (RILEM)
12 rue Brancion
75737 Paris, France
Conducts research on the properties of construction materials; sponsors colloquia and symposia; exchanges scientific publications.

Other organizations may be found in:

1971 Directory of Building Research Information and Development Organizations. Rotterdam: CIB, 1971. Data on institutes in Europe, non-European CIB member institutes, and international organizations.

[Bibliography prepared by Lynn Robinson.]

CONSULTANTS, USE OF

The need for the continuing improvement of business and financial practices and principles presents every college or university with a major challenge. Computer operations, labor relations, security measures, insurance, and student housing are but a few examples of specialized areas in which problems arise that cannot always be solved by personnel or resources within the university. Of necessity, therefore, college administrators are turning with increasing frequency to outside consultants for assistance. The Association of Consulting Management Engineers (ACME), the leading trade association of consulting firms in the United States, defines consulting as follows (1974a, p. 3): "the service performed for a fee by independent and objective professional men or a group of consultants organized as a firm or similar entity who help managers analyze management and operating problems associated with the goals, objectives, policies, strategies, administration, organization, and the principal functional or operating areas of the various institutions of society; who recommend practical solutions to these problems; and help to implement them when necessary. This professional service is concerned with the improvement of the managerial, operating, and economic performance of these institutions."

In general, consultancy may be divided into two broad classifications: top consultancy and operational consultancy. Top consultancy includes (1) overall organization, in which a client organization is restructured with a definition of the responsibilities of each department and key personnel; and (2) long-term planning, which means assistance in the setting of long-term objectives and of the means to meet these objectives. Operational consultancy includes those areas of consultancy that affect a specific aspect of the administrative functions and operations of an organization, such as human resources, organization and methods, or budgetary systems.

Excluded from the given definition of consultancy are technical advice, market research, and executive search, although all three overlap with consulting, inasmuch as their practitioners often call themselves consultants and take on consulting assignments.

Some of the specific areas in which an institution might seek assistance from a consultant are: administration involving information systems, organization, and planning; auxiliary enterprises, such as bookstores, housing, and food service; communications, such as mail and telephone service; construction, including design and financing; finance, consisting of accounting, auditing, budgeting, payroll, and reporting; financial aid administration; government relations (sponsored projects); institutional research; insurance; investment, consisting of endowment, fund raising, fund management, gifts and bequests, short-term; personnel, including collective bargaining, compensation, fringe benefits, labor relations, and wage and salary administration; physical plant, such as maintenance, operations, parking, and utilities; purchasing; real estate; and security (National Association of College and University Business Officers, n.d.).

Role of the Consultant

Knowing when and how to seek the services of a consultant is important, especially for the smaller institution. Over the past several decades, the role of the consultant has become solidly established among business, governmental, and nonprofit institutions. ACME estimates that there are about 3500 consulting firms in North America, plus about seventy-five public accounting firms, that derive a significant portion of their total revenue from consulting services. All told, consulting firms and individuals generate gross billings of about two and a half billion dollars annually. Many smaller businesses and institutions assume that consulting help is too expensive for them, a luxury only large institutions and big government can afford. This is not necessarily so. Consulting fees vary

widely, depending on the scope and complexity of the consulting project. Although exceptions may abound, it is generally true that a smaller company will require less time for the consultant to become familiar with the various ins and outs of the organization in order to get at the root of the problem and thus propose a suggested course of action.

The consultant is, in no small measure, a change agent vis-à-vis the organization. Whereas most organizations may possess the knowledge to cure many of their problems, the crux lies in the implementation of that knowledge. The consultant urges and persuades the client, and, when necessary, helps him toward a sound course of action.

Lippitt (1959, p. 5) cautions that consulting is not a panacea for the ills of an institution. He writes: "1. The consultation relationship is a voluntary relationship between 2. a professional helper (consultant) and a help-needing system (client) 3. in which the consultant is attempting to give help to the client in the solving of some current or potential problem, 4. and the relationship is perceived as temporary by both parties. 5. Also, the consultant is an 'outsider,' i.e., is not part of any hierarchical power system in which the client is located."

The art of counsel transcends the knowledge and skills the consultant possesses.

This art includes at least four distinct aspects: fidelity and its associated responsibilities, understanding, persuasion, and education. The consultant is a fiduciary; that is, he stands at one end of a particular type of confidential relationship. He must think through what he owes his client in terms of responsibility, of candor, of ability and willingness to turn down an assignment which either exceeds his competence or, even more important, does not appear to him to be what the client really needs or should do. Fidelity to his client is his duty, including vigorous persuasion toward a sound course of action. In exercising this responsibility, the consultant must create a mutual understanding of the problem and persuade client executives to put his recommendations into effect so they will get lasting results. Finally, he has responsibility for the improvement and education of the client's employees.

These four aspects constitute the essence of

the client-consultant relationship. In addition to these factors, three other ingredients play important parts in this relationship. They are proper communication, mutual cooperation, and confidence in each other. The professional practices employed by the consultant in the conduct of client engagements represent the technical part of this relationship (ACME, 1974, p. 3).

There are four main reasons behind the successful use of management consultants. First, they bring specific skills and experience to complement those available within the user organization. Second, they provide concentrated effort toward specific objectives within a clear time frame. The progress of the work can be measured against the realization of the objectives. Third, they are practiced in using the project approach to solving a problem—that is, they call on various skills, including those of the client, and combine them. The project management is itself a specific skill. Finally, they act as change agents more effectively than many internal teams or individuals. Their objectivity in itself is a reason to respect their recommendations.

The ability of consultants to encourage change in no way lessens the authority of the administrators for whom they are working. An administrator does not resign his authority when he hires a consultant. Rather, he must retain his authority while looking to the consultant for advice. The final decisions must be those of the administrator. A successful consulting study, based on a healthy administrator-consultant relationship, not only helps the client as an organization but also advances the responsible administrator as an individual.

When a large organization has an internal consulting group, the use of the consultants tends to increase, but with correspondingly greater emphasis on the external consultants providing the skills and experience not available in-house.

Selecting a Consultant

The potential user of consultants has at his disposal a variety of sources listing consulting services. Chief among these are the following: Association of Consulting Management Engineers, Inc., 347 Madison Avenue (Suite 2010), New York, New York 10017, telephone (212) 686-7338; Institute of Management Consultants, Inc., 347 Madison Avenue (Suite 1810), New York, New York 10017, telephone (212) 686-7795; The Consultant Registry, National Association of College and University Business Officers, One Dupont Circle (Suite 510), Washington, D. C. 20036, telephone (202) 296-2346. The most common method for selecting a consultant is reliance on the personal recommendations of business acquaintances. However, this method usually produces no more than a list of names; the real selection is made after meeting the consultant. There are two approaches that are often used during this process; either many consultants are requested to make a presentation of their services and are then asked to prepare a full proposal, or one consultant is invited to offer services from the beginning. Neither extreme is satisfactory, the former wasting both the user's and the consultant's time, the latter reducing the chances that one has selected the best consultant for the job. (The current practice in Europe is heavily in favor of inviting only one consultant to offer his services.)

An alternative is to meet consultants at a preselection stage, without asking them to prepare a proposal. These meetings can be related to a possible study, or, if the use of consultants is great enough, the meetings can serve as future reference, so that when a need for a consultant arises, the administrator is aware of the services available.

The nearer the administrator comes to making a final selection, the more emphasis should be given to the qualifications of the personnel in the consulting firms under review and particularly to those persons responsible for the project. In most large consulting firms, it is common practice for a director to accept overall responsibility for a project, while delegating the day-to-day work to a senior consultant, the project leader. The potential user must, of course, have confidence in the director, but it is necessary to look beyond the director to the project leader who will be spending a great deal of time on the study. The director will be following matters from a distance and will probably devote no more than 10 percent of his time to a given study.

During the selection stage, the potential user should involve those parts of his organization that are to be the subject of the study. This procedure can avoid a common source of failure in consulting projects, which occurs at the selection stage, with senior management selecting a consultant and defining his work and only then delegating the study to the persons directly involved. Consultants imposed from above are often resented by medium and lower ranks of administration, who, perhaps unwittingly, can sabotage a project by poor collaboration.

In the case of organizations that have internal consulting groups, it is an excellent idea to formalize all links with external consultants through the internal group. However, this should not prevent administrators and their subordinates who are the subjects of the study from being present at preliminary discussions with the consultant groups.

Nature of Consultancy Work

Normally, the consultant's first step is to conduct a brief preliminary survey, the main purpose of which is to establish appropriate terms of reference. Its aims and content should include: (1) identification and clear definition of the problem and agreement with the client on these matters; (2) assessment of the likely implications, consequences, and benefits of an assignment and whether, after considering all the circumstances, consultancy should be recommended; (3) setting limits to the scope of the study, which are appropriate to the problem as defined; (4) discussion of the preliminary survey findings with the client; (5) mutual understanding of the objectives of any proposed consulting work and of the

possible benefits; (6) indication of the main stages of the proposed assignment and their sequence; (7) prescribing the preparations for the proposed assignment, such as participation of the client's management and staff, consultant contact at the senior management level, notification to the client's management and staff, and formation of a steering committee; and (8) preparation and presentation of a proposal letter, incorporating the survey findings and resulting proposals, for consideration by the client. An estimate of time and fee should be included in this letter.

The preliminary survey usually involves no fee or obligation to the client. However, in other cases, special arrangements may have to be made, depending on the particular circumstances, such as combining the survey with a trip to the area for another reason. Reputable consultants make every effort to keep the cost of preliminary surveys to a minimum.

If the prospective client accepts the consultant's proposals, appropriately qualified staff are then assigned to carry out the investigation and installation work involved. The client should expect the use of appropriate scientific and statistical techniques in support of all work.

The consulting manager carrying out the preliminary survey normally supervises any subsequent assignment. During the project, meetings with the client's administration should be arranged at suitable intervals for the purposes of planning and carrying out the assignment, for providing an indication of the direction in which the proposals and methods are developing, and for seeking approval for, and the participation of, the client's administration in specified courses of action.

Oral presentations of findings and recommendations and written reports should be presented to the client, as needed. Follow-up arrangements should be made after any installation work to ensure satisfactory systems maintenance and development.

The consultant should agree to an assignment only if he is satisfied that the prospective client will achieve a substantial return from his investment in the consultant's services. Furthermore, each assignment should be so structured as to maximize that return. This approach has, in the past, led to the establishment of some unusually close, long-term counseling relationships between clients and consultants. Familiarity with a client's administrative priorities, organizational style, and working methods has frequently enabled consultants to improve the cost-effectiveness of their work on successive assignments, quickly achieving results from each new project with a minimal disruption of the client organization. These arrangements, however, should be noncontractual. Each study should be negotiated independently, and the results to be achieved should be specified in advance.

Clients should be critical of a consultant's work; in addition, consultants should seek the client's active involvement. On many consulting studies, key client personnel may even participate as full-time team members, particularly if they have specialized skills that can usefully complement those of the consultant. This involvement can have other benefits as well. By multiplying the efforts of the consultant, it can gain the client a higher return from his investment; on pilot projects to be repeated elsewhere in the organization, it can provide a valuable training opportunity; and it can increase the probability of swift and effective implementation because the client's team members are likely to develop a personal commitment to the project.

Methods of operation. Consultants usually undertake their assignment in one of two ways. They may do their work more or less in isolation and present a report at the end of their study, or they may serve as an *animateur* (moving spirit) to decision-making teams made up of client personnel—a practice known as process consulting.

While both methods have their place, it is usually more effective to combine report preparation with the responsibility of making clear recommendations, using the control mechanism of a strong client-consultant interaction. There is no one best method for this interaction, but the following observations may be useful in defining, a priori, the mechanism for a given project: (1) there should be one person from the client organization with whom the consultancy firm has a client relationship; (2) the role of working liaison is frequently best assigned to another individual from the client organization, probably someone from the department or departments affected by the project; (3) it may be advisable to release one or more client staff members to the consultancy project team; such staff would collaborate with the consultants as team members and not as client representatives; (4) for very ambitious projects, the project team might report progress to a steering committee composed of directors from both the client organization and the consulting firm (this does not preclude the need for a final, clearly defined client).

Most users of consultants see themselves as hiring outsiders with specific skills for work on a well-defined problem. Sometimes the problem is not well-defined, however, and the consulting study involves further preliminary investigation, which usually implies placing a greater trust in the consultants and permitting them more freedom in their work. Under these circumstances, the user should not assume that he has fully defined the problem; rather, he should encourage originality from the consultants. This mode of consultancy involves a higher risk on the part of the user; it can, however, lead to much higher returns.

Importance of progress reports. No matter what the mode of consultancy, clients should insist on progress reports that indicate not only the effort spent but also the results achieved. Preliminary conclusions can often serve as a guide to the way consultants are thinking and can indicate the direction in which the study is proceeding. However, a careful compromise has to be found between ideal and practical solutions—that is, whether or not the suggestions can be implemented. There may be a case for having consultants prepare recommendations that they feel are ideal and then confronting the political constraints so as to move from the ideal to the realistic. Moving directly to the realistic runs the severe risk of the consultants only producing mediocre recommendations, which reflect the opinion of the client organization's administrators.

Implementation. Measuring results achieved implies that the project's objectives, priorities, and timetable have been well defined. In ambitious projects there is a distinction between results achieved in the sense of implemented recommendations and those that are a step toward overall study completion. The second type of result may be of value only in the context of the completed study, for it has no value per se. Both types of intermediate results can be achieved, but the distinction between them must be recognized.

The success of a study depends on the implementation of the results, and many studies have failed at that stage. In fact, implementation is just as important as creativity in a consulting study; both are essential and both deserve resource allocation. There is a strong case for the client's staff playing a dominant role in the implementation, especially if the staff will be working with the new system. However, the consultant's role should continue, even if at a reduced level. As a minimum, regular meetings—for example, once a month—or specific checkpoints should be agreed on in advance so that the implementation team is not left alone.

Implementation, like selection, problem definition, working relationships, and progress reports, should be seen as part of the total process of maximizing the effectiveness of using consultants.

Contribution of the Consultant

Serious financial and organizational problems beset today's college and university administrators. Inflation, overexpansion, shrinking enrollments, and inadequate resources are just a few of the difficulties threatening the existence of many institutions of higher education. The administrators of these institutions have become painfully aware of the necessity to become more efficient in their day-to-day operations, while simultaneously attempting to placate the incessant stream of demands made on an already strained set of resources. It is to this scenario that the educational consultant can effectively bring to bear his skills and make an important contribution.

The Association of Consulting Management Engineers (1974a) has provided two important guides for clients and consultants. The first, a list of requirements for the effective use of consultants, describes six important considerations: definition of the problem, careful selection of the consultant, agreement on mutual obligations, supervision, and support of the consultant's work, implementation of recommendations, and measurement of results (pp. 6–9). The second, a set of standards of professional conduct and practice, gives a code of conduct that covers the areas of professional attitude, responsibilities to the client, proper arrangements with the client, and client fees, as well as a set of professional practices designed to promote the highest quality performance (pp. 75–80).

Appendix One: Requirements for Effective Use of Consultants

The principal requirements for the effective use of consultants, as suggested by ACME (1974a, pp. 6–9), are as follows:

1. *Careful definition of the problem.* Complete definition of a problem is generally achieved only after the consultant has been retained and has gathered and studied the facts necessary to isolate the real problem and its underlying causes. However, management should have thought through its situation with sufficient thoroughness to arrive at its own definition of the problem, including estimates of the potential values to be achieved by solving it, and the desir-

ability of tackling the job at all. Vague feelings of discontent or unrest do not constitute adequate reasons for retaining a consultant. There should be specific reasons for considering the use of outside assistance in any situation. Consultants can waste time and money in defining and planning the project if management is not prepared at the outset to tell them as accurately as possible what it thinks the problem is. This should include a full discussion of its understanding of the problem and background, the conditions for its solution, the end results which should be achieved by the solution, and any limitations within which it must be solved.

Furthermore, an understanding of management's intent in deciding to place an assignment with a management consultant can have a strong bearing on the way a consultant will proceed in the assignment. If there are differences in view that the consultant is expected to resolve or reconcile, the assignment may have a different focus than it would if all parties have an uncommitted point of view. If the principal desire is to find a new approach to the resolution of a problem, the consultant will naturally emphasize the innovative and interpretive aspects as contrasted with fact-gathering. If the problem is one that has already been tackled but no solution found, this fact also can provide a focus for the consultant's approach. All these expressions of intent can be meaningful to the consultant in designing his approach, and to the client in terms of yield for the dollars spent.

2. *Careful selection of the consultant.* When management is considering the use of consulting services, it should deal directly with the professional staff of the consultant. The professional salesman has little or no place in the selling of professional services. He can only function as a middleman. But when you talk to members of the professional staff of the consultant who are qualified to understand your problem and to tell you how they might be helpful in terms of their ability and experience, you can be certain that what you are considering will be of real value.

Furthermore, it is important for management to give close attention to the task of selecting the consultant who will best meet its particular needs. The best assurance of satisfaction with results is to give the matter of choosing a consultant the time and effort it deserves. A consultant should not be retained unless management is convinced of his objectivity and integrity, and unless careful investigation demonstrates he is well qualified to meet the requirements of the project in terms of competence, organization, and resources.

When selecting a consultant, some clients look primarily at fees. This practice can be misleading for a number of reasons. It is important to study each proposal in terms of its understanding of the problem, proposed approach to its solution, probable benefits to be attained, cost, and the particular experience and ability of each consultant in relation to the project. The final selection should be based on a careful weighing of all these factors. In consultant services, like any other professional service, the important factor is the result. A good job is well worth the cost; a poor one is a loss, no matter how attractive the price tag may have seemed.

3. *Agreement with consultant on mutual obligations.* A consulting engagement is always a joint undertaking. The amount of active client participation will vary with each situation, and is likely to be greater in certain kinds of projects than in others. But client participation and involvement to an appropriate degree are required for the success of any consulting engagement. The client should remember that the work is being done because he wants it done and has authorized it. If he cannot devote the time and effort required to insure successful completion of the project, he should not undertake it at all.

It is general practice for management to share responsibility with the consultant for definition of the purpose and scope, general time and cost of the study. Follow-through from this point on is equally important. Findings and conclusions developed during a study have practical application only to the extent that management reviews them, understands them, challenges them, and accepts those that are practical, timely, and suited to its individual requirements. During the study, it is wise to have periodic meetings to explore progress, to evaluate the thinking of the consultant, and to make certain that the anticipated results of the study appear reasonable and attainable.

4. *Proper supervision and support of the consultant's work.* It is important to set a clear and firm course and maintain an active interest in progress made during the engagement. Consulting engagements are not "ivory tower" in nature. Successful results, more often than not, stem from mutual stimulation and thinking. In most cases, it is desirable to ask for interim progress reports. These serve two sound purposes if they are kept within bounds. They keep management fully in the picture, able to move with the consultant's recommendations at once. And they help to crystallize and organize the consultant's own thinking and conclusions as he proceeds.

Moreover, on almost any engagement, the consultant contends with the disadvantages of being an outsider, an expert hired to tell men of experience how to do their work more effectively. He represents change, disturbance of accepted routine, probably criticism. Some resentment is inevitable. If management wants results, it must take definite measures to smooth the way. These measures include support at the top level; a single, strong liaison point through which the consultant can obtain necessary assistance; and advance indoctrination of personnel concerning the purpose of the work being done, its relationship to their job assignments, and the importance of cooperation. This thorough briefing of company personnel can do much to prevent the development of morale problems caused by the tendency of some employees to feel their relationship

to the company may be jeopardized by the consultant's recommendations.

5. *Implementation of recommendations.* At the conclusion of the engagement, it is usual for the consultant to submit a report which includes his conclusions and recommendations. Read this carefully, review it with the consultant, and be sure you understand it. Once recommendations have been accepted, they should be installed. The whole purpose of most assignments is action; unless that follows the report, the effort is barren. Implementation of the recommendations often requires a further educational period for your organization.

Determine with the consultant whether your personnel are capable of implementing the recommendations or whether you need his help. Though consultants sometimes have no reason to be involved in extensive implementation of their recommendations, they still don't like to feel they are dropping their reports down a bottomless well. A client can use a consultant to best advantage by involving him at least in preliminary plans for implementing his recommendations. Such implementation planning is especially useful when his recommendations call for coordinated action by several groups within the company.

The normal inertia within any medium-size or large organization fosters a practice of file and forget. A useful means of overcoming this is for management to require a report from its personnel on each engagement 30 days after completion. This report should state the progress being made in installing or implementing the recommendations. At suitable intervals (e.g., three, six, and nine months), additional reports should be made to cover further progress and state any problems being encountered.

Finally, it is often desirable to ask the consultant to make a post-installation review of the recommended improvements or changes after they have been in operation for a period of between three to six months, or a year. Such reviews not only safeguard the company's investment of time and money originally spent in developing and installing the recommendations, but also allow the consultant to correct any misunderstandings, make any necessary modifications, and incorporate any new methods, techniques, or ideas.

6. *Measure the results.* When an engagement is completed, management should measure its choice of the consultant and its own part in making the project a success, as well as the performance of its own personnel. There may well be dollars-and-cents savings immediately evident; or the improvements effected may not pay off until sometime later and then only as one of many contributions to the company's success. But tangible or intangible, short-run or long-run, there should be definite indication of a "job well done." Here are some of the plus signs to look for:

- The engagement was carried out with a minimum of disruption in the organization.
- The cost and time estimates were realistic.
- The recommendations were realistic and practical and were able to be implemented promptly and economically.
- Management received a stimulus to its own thinking.
- The company is willing to employ the same consultant again.

If your problem has been diagnosed properly, if you have selected your consultant carefully, if you have worked as a team in solving your problem, and if you carry out his recommendations, you will profit by using a consultant. But it is well to remember that a consultant cannot finally solve your problem. He can only suggest the practical solution and urge you to take action. He cannot run your business. Only you can do that.

Appendix Two: Standards of Professional Conduct and Practice

ACME (1974a, pp. 75–80) has adopted the following code of conduct for its member firms to uphold. This can serve the potential client both in the selection and use of a consultant.

PURPOSES OF STANDARDS OF PROFESSIONAL CONDUCT

These Standards of Professional Conduct and Practice signify voluntary assumption by members of the obligation of self-discipline above and beyond the requirements of the law. Their purpose is to let the public know that members intend to maintain a high level of ethics and public service, and to declare that—in return for the faith that the public places in them—the members accept the obligation to conduct their practice in a way that will be beneficial to the public. They give clients a basis for confidence that members will serve them in accordance with professional standards of competence, objectivity, and integrity.

They express in general terms the standards of professional conduct expected of management consulting firms in their relationships with prospective clients, clients, colleagues, members of allied professions, and the public. The Code of Professional Responsibility, unlike the Professional Practices, is mandatory in character. It serves as a basis for disciplinary action when the conduct of a member firm falls below the required standards as stated in the Code of Professional Responsibility. The Professional Practices are largely aspirational in character and represent objectives and standards of good practice to which members of the Association subscribe.

The Association enforces the Code of Professional Responsibility by receiving and investigating all complaints of violations and by taking disciplinary action against any member who is found to be guilty of code violation.

THE PROFESSIONAL ATTITUDE

The reliance of managers of private and public institutions on the advice of management consultants imposes on the profession an obligation to maintain high standards of integrity and competence. To this end, members of the Association have basic responsibilities to place the interests of clients and prospective clients ahead of their own, maintain independence of thought and action, hold the affairs of their clients in strict confidence, strive continually to improve their professional skills, observe and advance professional standards of management consulting, uphold the honor and dignity of the profession, and maintain high standards of personal conduct.

These Standards have evolved out of the experience of members since the Association was incorporated in 1933. In recognition of the public interest and their obligation to the profession, members and the consultants on their staffs have agreed to comply with the following articles of professional responsibility.

1. *Basic Client Responsibilities.* 1.1 We will at all times place the interests of clients ahead of our own and serve them with integrity, competence, and independence.

We will assume an independent position with the client, making certain that our advice to clients is based on impartial consideration of all pertinent facts and responsible opinions.

1.2 We will guard as confidential all information concerning the affairs of clients that we gather during the course of professional engagements; and we will not take personal, financial, or other advantage of material or inside information coming to our attention as a result of our professional relationship with clients; nor will we provide the basis on which others might take such advantage. Observance of the ethical obligation of the management consulting firm to hold inviolate the confidence of its clients not only facilitates the full development of facts essential to effective solution of the problem but also encourages clients to seek needed help on sensitive problems.

1.3 We will serve two or more competing clients on sensitive problems only with their knowledge.

1.4 We will inform clients of any relationships, circumstances, or interests that might influence our judgment or the objectivity of our services.

2. *Client Arrangements.* 2.1 We will present our qualifications for serving a client solely in terms of our competence, experience, and standing, and we will not guarantee any specific result, such as amount of cost reduction or profit increase.

2.2 We will accept only those engagements we are qualified to undertake and which we believe will provide real benefits to clients. We will assign personnel qualified by knowledge, experience, and character to give effective service in analyzing and solving the particular problem or problems involved. We will carry out each engagement under the direction of a principal of the firm who is responsible for its successful completion.

2.3 We will not accept an engagement of such limited scope that we cannot serve the client effectively.

2.4 We will, before accepting an engagement, confer with the client or prospective client in sufficient detail and gather sufficient facts to gain an adequate understanding of the problem, the scope of study needed to solve it, and the possible benefits that may accrue to the client. The preliminary exploration will be conducted confidentially on terms and conditions agreed upon by the member and the prospective client. Extended preliminary or problem-defining surveys for prospective clients will be made only on a fully compensated fee basis.

2.5 We will, except for those cases where special client relationships make it unnecessary, make certain that the client receives a written proposal that outlines the objectives, scope, and, where possible, the estimated fee or fee basis for the proposed service or engagement. We will discuss with the client any important changes in the nature, scope, timing or other aspects of the engagement and obtain the client's agreement to such changes before taking action on them—and unless the circumstances make it unnecessary, we will confirm these changes in writing.

2.6 We will perform each engagement on an individualized basis and develop recommendations designed specifically to meet the particular requirements of the client situation. Our objective in each client engagement is to develop solutions that are realistic and practical and that can be implemented promptly and economically. Our professional staffs are prepared to assist, to whatever extent desired, with the implementation of approved recommendations.

2.7 We will not serve a client under terms or conditions that might impair our objectivity, independence, or integrity; and we will reserve the right to withdraw if conditions beyond our control develop to interfere with the successful conduct of the engagement.

2.8 We will acquaint client personnel with the principles, methods, and techniques applied, so that the improvements suggested or installed may be properly managed and continued after completion of the engagement.

2.9 We will maintain continuity of understanding and knowledge of clients' problems and the work that has been done to solve them by maintaining appropriate files of reports submitted to clients. These are protected against unauthorized access and supported by files of working papers, consultants' log-books, and similar recorded data.

2.10 We will not accept an engagement for a client while another management consulting firm is serving that client unless we are assured, and can satisfy ourselves, that there will be no conflict between the two engagements. We will not endeavor to displace another management consulting firm or individual consultant once we have knowledge that the client has made a commitment to the other consultant.

2.11 We will review the work of another management consulting firm or individual consultant for the same client, only with the knowledge of such consultant, and such consultant's work which is subject to review has been finished or terminated. However, even though the other consultant's work has been finished or ter-

minated, it is a matter of common courtesy to let the consulting firm or individual know that his work is being reviewed.

3. *Client Fees.* 3.1 We will charge reasonable fees which are commensurate with the nature of services performed and the responsibility assumed. An excessive charge abuses the professional relationship and discourages the public from utilizing the services of management consultants. On the other hand, adequate compensation is necessary in order to enable the management consulting firm to serve clients effectively and to preserve the integrity and independence of the profession. Determination of the reasonableness of a fee requires consideration of many factors, including the nature of the services performed; the time required; the consulting firm's experience, ability, and reputation; the degree of responsibility assumed; and the benefits that accrue to the client. Wherever feasible, we will agree with the client in advance on the fee or fee basis.

3.2 We will not render or offer professional services for which the fees are contingent on reduction in costs, increases in profits, or any other specific result.

3.3 We will neither accept nor pay fees or commissions to others for client referrals, or enter into any arrangement for franchising our practice to others. Nor will we accept fees, commissions, or other valuable considerations from individuals or organizations whose equipment, supplies, or services we might recommend in the course of our service to clients.

PROFESSIONAL PRACTICES

In order to promote highest quality of performance in the practice of management consulting, ACME has developed the following standards of good practice for the guidance of the profession. Member firms subscribe to these practices because they make for equitable and satisfactory client relationships and contribute to success in management consulting.

1. We will strive continually to advance and protect the standards of the manage-

ment consulting profession. We will strive continually to improve our knowledge, skills, and techniques, and will make available to our clients the benefits of our professional attainments.

2. We recognize our responsibilities to the public interest and to our profession to contribute to the development and understanding of better ways to manage the various formal institutions in our society. By reason of education, experience, and broad contact with management problems in a variety of institutions, management consultants are especially qualified to recognize opportunities for improving managerial and operating processes; and they have an obligation to share their knowledge with managers and their colleagues in the profession.

3. We recognize our responsibility to the profession to share with our colleagues the methods and techniques we utilize in serving clients. But we will not knowingly, without their permission, use proprietary data, procedures, materials, or techniques that other management consultants have developed but not released for public use.

4. We will not make offers of employment to consultants on the staffs of other consulting firms without first informing them. We will not engage in wholesale or mass recruiting of consultants from other consulting firms. If we are approached by consultants of other consulting firms regarding employment in our firm or in that of a client, we will handle each situation in a way that will be fair to the consultant and his firm.

5. We will not make offers of employment to employees of clients. If we are approached by employees of clients regarding employment in our firm or in that of another client, we will make certain that we have our clients' consent before entering into any negotiations with employees.

6. We will continually evaluate the quality of the work done by our staff to insure, insofar as is possible, that all of our engagements are conducted in a competent manner.

7. We will endeavor to provide opportunity for the professional development of those men who enter the profession, by assisting them to acquire a full understanding of the functions, duties, and responsibilities of management consultants, and to keep up with significant advances in their areas of practice.

8. We will administer the internal and external affairs of our firm in the best interests of the profession at all times.

9. We will not advertise our services in self-laudatory language or in any other manner derogatory to the dignity of the profession.

10. We will respect the professional reputation and practice of other management consultants. This does not remove the moral obligation to expose unethical conduct of fellow members of the profession to the proper authorities.

11. We will strive to broaden public understanding and enhance public regard and confidence in the management consulting profession, so that management consultants can perform their proper function in society effectively. We will conduct ourselves so as to reflect credit on the profession and to inspire the confidence, respect, and trust of clients and the public. In the course of our practice, we will strive to maintain a wholly professional attitude toward those we serve. toward those who assist us in our practice, toward our fellow consultants, toward members of other professions, and the practitioners of allied arts and sciences.

Adopted February 1, 1972

Bibliography

Association of Consulting Management Engineers. *Directory of Membership and Services, 1974–1975.* New York: ACME, 1974a.

Association of Consulting Management Engineers. *How to Get the Best Results from Management Consultants.* New York: ACME, 1974b.

Brown, W. R. "Help from the Management Consultant." *Educational Executives Overview,* November 1962, *3,* 36–37.

Cocking, W. D. "Role of the Educational Consultant." *School Executive,* 1956, *75*(7), 7.

Duerr, C. "The Art of Using Outside Helpers." *International Management,* April 1971, *26,* 51.

Egerton, H. C., and Bacon, J. *Consultants: Selection, Use and Appraisal.* New York: The National Industrial Conference Board, 1970.

Golightly, H. O. "How to Select and Effectively Use a Management Consultant." *International Management,* November 1964, *19,* 47–48.

Gottfried, I. S. "Selecting a Consultant." *Journal of Data Management,* October 1969, *7,* 32–35.

"Is There a Consultant in Your Budget?" *College Management,* November 1968, *3,* 16–22.

Kintzer, F. C., and Chase, S. M. "The Consultant as a Change Agent." *Junior College Journal,* April 1969, *39,* 54–60.

Lippitt, R. "Dimensions of a Consultant's Job." *Journal of Social Issues,* 1959, *15*(2), 5–12.

Lippitt, R., Watson, J., and Westley, B. *The Dynamics of Planned Change.* New York: Harcourt Brace Jovanovich, 1958.

Menefee, S. "When Junior Colleges Need Help." *American Education,* December 1968–January 1969, *5,* 23–25.

Messing, R. F. "What Consultants Expect of Their Clients." *Management Review,* May 1970, *59,* 11–15.

Mial, A. C. "What Is a Consultant?" *Public Relations Journal,* November 1959, *15,* 37–45.

National Association of College and University Business Officers. *The Consultant Registry.* Washington, D.C.: NACUBO, n.d.

Tilles, S. "Ideas for a Better Consultant-Client Relationship." *Business Horizons,* Summer 1963, *6,* 31–34.

Vonderheide, A. C. "The Use of Consulting Services by Private Colleges and Universities." Unpublished doctoral dissertation, Catholic University of America, 1970.

Webster, E. "What to Do Before the Consultant Comes." *Management Review,* June 1969, *58,* 14–20.

Weil, R. I. "How to Select a Management Consultant." *Administrative Management,* November 1966, *27,* 59–60.

Wittreich, W. "How to Buy/Sell Professional Services." *Harvard Business Review,* March–April 1966, *44,* 127–134.

BRANCH K. STERNAL

CONSULTATION AND REMUNERATION

See Remuneration: Faculty, Staff, and Chief Executive Officers.

CONSUMERISM

See Legal Aspects of Higher Education.

CONTINUING EDUCATION, CENTERS FOR

See University Conference Centers in Great Britain; University Conference Centers in the United States.

CONTINUITY AND DISCONTINUITY (Higher Education Report), United States

Continuity and Discontinuity: Higher Education and the Schools (New York: McGraw-Hill, August 1973), a report of the Carnegie Commission on Higher Education, examines the historical relations between schools and colleges in the United States and suggests that a new phase in their relationships is emerging. The following findings and recommendations are reported.

As the nation approaches universal access to education, there are serious challenges to the existing system, a system that imposes artificial patterns upon the continuity of student learning. Closer school-college ties must develop in many areas, including college admissions, curricular and structural revision, and effective resource allocation.

The history of school-college relations can be divided into four phases. During the first phase (1870–1910), schools and colleges searched for a coordinated system; each offered a narrow academic program to a small minority of youth. While the schools prepared students for college, colleges prepared teachers for the rapidly growing secondary schools. From 1910 to 1940, the schools responded to the industrial growth in the United States. School enrollments skyrocketed, and schools mainly prepared students for life, rather than for college. The third phase (1940–1970) saw the development of mass higher education, largely as a result of World War II veterans flooding the campuses under the G.I. Bill. School-college relations were in a transitional period as schools remained oriented toward their own programs while an increasing number of students began to seek a college education.

In the fourth or current phase (1970–2000) there is a movement toward universal access to higher education. In response to this movement, the admissions process should be reformed; fixed requirements and rigid testing policies should be reconsidered, coherent information and counseling services developed, applications standardized, and experimentation encouraged.

The commission advocates priority attention to improving the nation's schools, where failures in the provision of basic education and vocational training are accompanied by symptoms of deep malaise. States should undertake massive reviews of the roles and objectives of the schools, and new approaches and programs should be developed. Teacher education should include programs aimed at the specific problems of different kinds of schools, and clinically oriented programs should be attempted.

Educational structures also need reform, particularly at the interface of school and college, where curriculum overlap and learning discontinuity are critical. Proposals include reducing the thirteen-year school system to twelve years and establishing three-year bachelor's degree programs, accelerated courses, and middle colleges which would span the last two years of high school and the first two years of college. Although there is little incentive for college and school staff to work together, colleges are still able to provide vital assistance to the schools in the areas of teacher education, research and evaluation, and production of teaching materials, textbooks, and software for technology.

Relations between schools and colleges are complicated by traditional barriers and prejudices. But learning is a continuous process, and closer articulation between schools and colleges is necessary to reduce harmful discontinuities in the areas of college admissions, curricular planning, guidance and career counseling, and the extent of career and vocational programs. Closer continuities between schools and colleges are needed to provide equal opportunity for all students, to accommodate the growth of nontraditional study and more flexible curricula, and to make maximum use of limited financial resources.

CONTRACTS, CONSTRUCTION
See Building and Construction Administration.

CONTROL OF HIGHER EDUCATION
See Governance and Control of Higher Education.

COOKERY (Field of Study)

Cookery is the art and science of the total preparation of foods for the table by heating or chilling them until they are changed in flavor, tenderness, appearance, and/or chemical composition. Although the precise origin of the art of cooking is not known, cookery is part of the history of civilization. Primitive people learned to make fire about 500,000 years ago by striking a spark from stones, but even before this discovery, prehistorics made their meat less tough and more palatable by cooking it over burning wood taken from fires that had started naturally. As civilization progressed, cooking evolved from a simple to an elaborate process.

Heat-proof pots for boiling water were invented about 6000 B.C. Broiling was first done by placing food on a stick and turning it over hot coals. Later this stick was made of an iron rod called a spit, which was put over the fire. When manmade fire was moved indoors, earth and stone fireplaces were built, and iron utensils were used. Fireplaces made of building bricks contained built-in ovens, and food was preserved by smoking and by cooling it in a stream. Baking, boiling, roasting, broiling, frying, and stewing were practiced by the ancient Egyptians, Jews, Assyrians, and Babylonians. The Romans cooked over charcoal on grills or on stone hearths. Boiling and broiling, furthermore, were common in the Middle Ages. Closed stoves of brick or porcelain tile were used in Northern Europe at the end of the Middle Ages; and in colonial North America nearly every home had its own oven.

Cooking became increasingly efficient with the arrival of gas and electric ranges; refrigerators; portable cooking appliances; modern metal, glass, and enamel cooking utensils; tested recipes; equipment of standard sizes; improved methods of transportation; cold storage; fast freezing; canning; and modern methods of dehydration.

The field of the culinary arts now represents one of the largest enterprises in the world. In the United States food service is the second-largest industry, next to defense; and its dollar volume is equal to the entire gross national product of France. One out of every four meals in the United States is consumed away from home. The food service hospitality industry includes three major categories of establishments: public feeding operations, from *haute cuisine* restaurants to outdoor hot-dog stands; institutional feeding, found in hospitals, schools, the military, and similar operations; and industrial feeding, from employee cafeterias to executive dining rooms.

Prior to the nineteenth century there was no widely developed food service industry, and the larger and better kitchens were primarily under the auspices of the nobility. During the mid 1700s in Paris restaurants as we know them really began, and with them grew the demand for professionals in food preparation, particularly in Europe. Originally, restaurateurs were licensed to sell restoratives or soups of all sorts. They also sold eggs, macaroni, boiled capons, and fruit preserves and compotes. One or several of the original restaurateurs began setting meals out on tables and encouraging the public to come and leisurely enjoy a dinner rather than take out a piece of dinner. The notion

quickly became popular, and restaurants began to appear, especially in public amusement gardens and assembly halls.

The concept of a public place devoted exclusively to eating spread rapidly throughout Europe and to the United States. In the mid eighteenth century there were already roadside taverns and inns in the United States, patterned after the taverns and inns in England. But by the end of the eighteenth century, *émigrés* from the French Revolution of 1789 were bringing to the United States a taste for French food and the notion that a restaurant could be a place separate from overnight lodging or a pub. In 1790 Samuel Fraunces set up an inn in New York City, probably the first restaurant in the United States, which served the finest French food. By the 1820s Sans Souci and Niblos Garden, also a French restaurant, had become the most fashionable eating establishments in New York. Between 1800 and 1830 the public, appreciating food for its own sake, treated restaurants as places to go for an evening's amusement. From 1830 to 1860 food took second place to the theater as a form of amusement. Then, gradually the restaurant again took first place. Delmonico's in New York City became popular at this time and served as a model for hotel restaurants in hotels in the larger cities across the United States. The Delmonico tradition began to influence American commercial cooking.

When restaurants began, there was no formal system of training; and the apprenticeship system, common to most occupations, was in use. The would-be cook simply learned by doing. This system of training held sway in the United States until recently, and it is still the most important training system in Europe.

Noting the severe shortage of European-trained chefs in the United States after World War II, and the apprenticeship system's inability to supply this demand, many professionals recognized the need for more efficient methods of training qualified personnel. Formal vocational education, which was developing rapidly in other trades, was the logical solution.

Technical advances too have outstripped the old system's ability to keep pace. The culinary arts have become so complex that formal education is more and more necessary. Recent advances in sanitation, cooking techniques, food chemistry, equipment technology, and energy production and conservation are making increasing demands on the professional chef. Furthermore, the modern executive chef is as much a businessman as he is a cook. He must be familiar with the elements of costing and budgeting as well as with the government regulations on everything from labor management to taxation and hygiene. The failure to train for management has been a significant weakness in the apprentice system.

With the growth of the food service industry has come an increased demand for skilled workers. In 1970 there were 2,231,590 people classified as food service workers in the United States. In 1980 the need for food service workers will be 2,780,900, an increase of 24.6 percent.

In 1970 there were 77,028 students enrolled in United States secondary and postsecondary schools that offered food service programs. In 1975 there were 128,081 students enrolled in food service schools, as a result of the increase, since 1965, in vocational education and in junior colleges.

In addition to formal vocational education, United States schools and industry share students and information. For example, large hotel and restaurant corporations which have their own training programs are increasingly hiring those with higher education in vocationally oriented subjects. The schools, with their increasingly sophisticated training methods and variety of instructional media, are becoming major storehouses of information available to the food service industry.

JAMES M. BERRINI
BARBARA L. FERET-SCHUMAN

Levels and Programs of Study

Programs in cookery generally require as a minimum educational prerequisite a secondary education, although mature students with relevant work experience may sometimes be admitted with lower qualifications, especially into programs designed to upgrade the performance of those already employed. The usual award for programs of one year or more, often given in technological or similar institutes, is a certificate or diploma. In shorter programs, which are often of the in-service or retraining type, a certificate of satisfactory completion may be given. In addition, four-year programs which lead to a first university degree (bachelor's degree or equivalent) may sometimes be offered in colleges or universities.

Programs deal with the principles and practices of quality cooking, such as that appropriate for hotel dining rooms and restaurants. In addition, these programs usually include instruction in food technology and kitchen management. Principal course content usually includes such subjects as the qualities of various food materials; techniques of food buying; storage characteristics of various food materials; principles of recipe formulation; preparation and use of condiments and special sauces; food preparation; methods of cooking; preparation of special dishes such as salads, entrées, and desserts; and methods of serving food. In many programs general courses are included as an aid in the development and understanding of the special vocational subjects. Some examples of these general courses are chemistry, physics, mathematics, psychology, principles of staff supervision, hygiene, the establishment and maintenance of filing systems, and other various record-keeping procedures.

[This section was based on UNESCO's *International Standard Classification of Education (ISCED)* (Paris: UNESCO, 1976).]

Major International and National Organizations

INTERNATIONAL

International Chefs Association
121 West 45th Street
New York, New York 10036 USA

NATIONAL

Canada:
  Canadian Federation of Chefs de Cuisine
  13507 109th Street
  Edmonton, Alberta

United States:
  American Culinary Federation
  202 South State Street
  Chicago, Illinois 60604

  Chefs de Cuisine Association of America
  Paramount Hotel
  235 West 46th Street
  New York, New York 10017

  Council on Hotel, Restaurant, and
    Institutional Education
  1522 "K" Street
  Washington, D.C. 20005

  Culinary Institute of America
  Albany Post Road
  Hyde Park, New York 12538

  National Restaurant Association
  1 IBM Plaza
  Chicago, Illinois 60611

Principal Information Sources

GENERAL

Guides to the literature in the field include:

Bitting, K. *Gastronomic Bibliography.* Ann Arbor, Michigan: Gryphon Books, 1971. Originally published in 1939. Descriptions of 6000 books on cooking and gastronomy.

Bootle, V., and Nailon, P. *A Bibliography of Hotel and Catering Operation.* London: New University Education, 1970. Four main sections, including Food Science and Technology, Food Preparation, Hotel and Catering Operations, and a section listing directories and periodicals. Includes 5000 entries, some of which are briefly annotated.

Simon, A. L. (Ed.) *Bibliotheca Gastronomica: A Catalogue of Books and Documents on Gastronomy.* London: Wine and Food Society, 1953.

Small Business Administration. *Restaurants and Catering.* Washington, D.C.: U.S. Government Printing Office, 1968.

Vicaire, G. *Bibliographie gastronomique.* Paris: Chez P. Rouquette, 1890. Authoritative bibliography of historically important works on cooking and gastronomy.

Introductory works and historical perspectives include:

Beeuwkes, A. M., and others. *Essays on the History of Nutrition and Dietetics.* Chicago: American Dietetics Association, 1967. See Part 2: History of Food and Cookbooks.

Clair, C. *Kitchen and Table: A Bedside History of Eating in the Western World.* New York: Abelard-Schuman, 1965.

Culinary Institute of America. *Introduction to Professional Food Service.* Boston: Cahners Books, 1968.

Folsom, L. *The Professional Chef.* (4th ed.) Boston: Cahners Books, 1973.

Gee, A. C. *Hotel and Institutional Cooking.* London: Barrie and Rockcliff, 1969.

Hale, W. H. (Ed.) *The Horizon Cookbook and Illustrated History of Eating and Drinking Throughout the Ages.* New York: American Heritage, 1968.

Jones, E. *American Food: The Gastronomic Story.* New York: Dutton, 1975.

Klein, C. *The Professional Chef: His Training, Duties and Rewards.* New York: Helios, 1967. Includes information on history, current trends, duties, and educational preparation.

Klinger, H. *Die Hotel- und Restaurations-Küche.* Giessen, Federal Republic of Germany: Pfanncher, 1972.

Lallemand, R. *Le livre de l'apprenti cuisinier.* Paris: Jacques Lanore, 1972.

Langseth-Christensen, L., and Smith, C. S. *The Complete Kitchen Guide: The Cook's Indispensable Book.* New York: Grosset & Dunlap, 1968.

Lundberg, D. E., and Kotschevar, L. H. *Understanding Cooking.* (Rev. ed.) Amherst: University of Massachusetts Press, 1967.

Norman, B. *Tales of the Table.* Englewood Cliffs, New Jersey: Prentice-Hall, 1972.

Page, E. B. *The Master Chefs: A History of Haute Cuisine.* New York: St. Martin's, 1971.

Ray, M., and Ray, L. *Exploring Professional Cooking.* Peoria, Illinois: Bennett, 1976.

Terrell, M. E. *Professional Food Preparation.* New York: Wiley, 1971. Designed as a textbook for beginning study of large-quantity cooking.

Wason, E. *Cooks, Gluttons and Gourmets: A History of Cooking.* Garden City, New York: Doubleday, 1962. Includes extensive bibliography on cooking history.

Works dealing with career opportunities in the field include:

Lattin, G. W. *Careers in Hotels and Restaurants.* New York: Walck, 1967.

Rosenthal, J. *Opportunities in Food Preparation and Service: The Professional Chef.* New York: Vocational Guidance Manuals, 1969.

Westbrook, J. *Your Future in Restaurants and Food Service.* New York: Arco, 1971.

CURRENT BIBLIOGRAPHIES

Current sources of information are provided by:

Cornell Hotel and Restaurant Administration Quarterly. Ithaca, New York: Cornell University, 1960–. See August issue for research and bibliographical index.

Educational Materials Center Catalog. Chicago: National Restaurant Association, annual.

Education Index. New York: Wilson, 1929–. See "Restaurants—Employees training."

The New York Times Index. New York Times, Inc., 1851–. See "Cooking."

Public Affairs and Information Service. New York: Public Affairs and Information Service, 1914–. See "Restaurants."

Readers' Guide to Periodical Literature. New York: Wilson, 1900–. See "Cookery, Study and teaching"; "Restaurants."

United States Department of Agriculture, National Agricultural Library. *Catalogue, Food and Nutrition Information and Educational Materials Center.* Washington, D.C.: U.S. Government Printing Office, 1973–.

PERIODICALS

Some of the many periodicals in the field of cookery include *American Chef, Canadian Food Journal, Caterers' Association Bulletin* (UK), *Catering Quarterly* (UK), *Chef Magazine* (US), *Commercial Kitchen* (US), *Comple* (Sweden), *Cornell Hotel and Restaurant Administration Quarterly* (US), *Cuisine collective* (France), *Culinary Review* (US), *Food and Cookery Review* (UK), *Food Science Training and Management Education Report* (US), *Gastronomie* (FRG), *Gastronomie: l'art culinaire* (France), *Gourmet* (US), *Institutions Magazine* (US), *International Food and Cooking Review* (UK), *Volume Feeding Management* (US).

For additional titles see:

Ulrich's International Periodicals Directory. New York: Bowker, biennial.

ENCYCLOPEDIAS, DICTIONARIES, HANDBOOKS

Conil, J. *Haute Cuisine.* London: Faber & Faber, 1953.

Desola, R., and Desola, D. *A Dictionary of Cooking.* London: Constable, 1971. Multilingual dictionary containing about 8000 terms for culinary ingredients, methods, and utensils.

Escoffier, G. H. *A Guide to Modern Cookery* (2nd ed.) London: Batsford, 1962. Includes information on employment and chefs' societies.

Fitzgibbon, T. *The Food of the Western World.* New York: Quadrangle Books, 1976.

Hering, R. *Hering's Dictionary of Classical and Modern Cookery.* Giessen, Federal Republic of Germany: Pfanneberg, 1972.

Montagne, P. *Larousse gastronomique: The Encyclopedia of Food, Wine and Cookery.* London: Hamlyn, 1961.

Neiger, E. *Gastronomisches Wörterbuch zur Übersetzung und Erklärung der Speisekarten in vier Sprachen.* Munich, Federal Republic of Germany: Carl Gerber, 1971. Approximately 20,000 terms.

Reitz, C. A. *A Guide to the Selection, Combination and Cooking of Food.* (2 vols.) Westport, Connecticut: AVI Publishing, 1961–1965. A detailed manual discussing food preparation.

Saulnier, L. *Le répertoire de la cuisine.* Westminster, Maryland: Christian Classics, 1961.

Senn, C. H. *Dictionary of Foods and Culinary Encyclopedia.* London: Ward Lock, 1962.

Shannon, E. *American Dictionary of Culinary Terms: A Comprehensive Guide to the Vocabulary of the Kitchen.* New York: Barnes & Noble, 1962.

Simon, A. L. *Guide to Good Food and Wines: A Concise Encyclopedia of Gastronomy. Complete and Unabridged.* London: Collins, 1956.

Simon, A. L., and Howe, K. *A Dictionary of Gastronomy.* (Rev. ed.) London: Nelson, 1970.

Smith, H. *The Master Dictionary of Food and Cooking.* London: Practical Press, 1950. English definitions of French, German, Italian, Latin, and Russian cooking terms.

Waldo, M. *Dictionary of International Food and Cookery Terms.* New York: Macmillan, 1967.

DIRECTORIES

Directories of educational institutions in cooking and restaurant trades are:

Directory of Educational and Training Courses for the Food Service Industry. Toronto, Ontario: Canadian Restaurant Association, 1966. Lists English-language and French-language courses in Canada.

Russell, M. M. (Ed.) *Occupational Education.* (2nd ed.) New York: Macmillan, 1973. See "Food Preparation and Service"; Food Service and Management"; "Cooking, Commercial"; "Hotel and Restaurant Cooking."

U.S. and International Directory of Hotel Restaurant Institutional Schools on the High School, Post Secondary, Community College and University Levels. Washington, D.C.: Council on Hotel, Restaurant and Institutional Education, 1976.

The following directory includes special collections and information sources in the field:

Ash, L. *Subject Collections: A Guide to Special Book Collections and Subject Emphases as Reported by University, College, Public and Special Libraries and Museums in the United States and Canada.* (5th ed.) New York: Bowker, 1975. See "Cookery" and "Gastronomy."

[Bibliography prepared by Nancy Cottrill.]

COOPERATIVE COLLEGE REGISTRY, United States

The Cooperative College Registry (CCR) is a nonprofit organization founded in 1963 and incorporated in 1970. Membership is open to all institutions of higher education throughout the world and numbers 320. The purpose of the registry is to assist colleges and universities in finding qualified faculty and administrators at all levels. Functioning as a referral agent, the registry—through correspondence with departments, through continuous contact with graduate school placement offices, and through professional journals—locates candidates who have academic qualifications for teaching or administrative positions in higher education. Special recruitment efforts are made to assist in affirmative action compliance.

The registry maintains an active file, renewed each year, of senior-level candidates seeking top teaching and administrative positions and of young scholars seeking beginning-level appointments. A master's degree in a teaching field is the minimum requirement for registration. Experience in lieu of advanced degrees is sometimes acceptable for nonacademic administrative positions.

CCR also maintains a confidential roster of senior-level careerists in higher education. This file serves as a source of confidential leads for senior positions and is also used to seek specialists for short-term or ongoing projects. There is no implication of active job seeking on the part of those who register in this permanent resource file, and no fee is required.

Information concerning vacancies listed with CCR is not published or revealed to candidates. CCR, however, urges deans and department heads to adopt a policy of open listing of vacancies, not only with CCR but through other appropriate channels, to avoid the use of the personal network system which obstructs equal opportunity employment. The CCR's files are available to authorized personnel at all times at the organization's Washington office and during the annual meeting of the Association of American Colleges (in January) and the American Association for Higher Education (in March). Candidates' fees and membership dues help defray the referral costs.

The organization publishes an annual handbook of information on further recruitment sources.

One Dupont Circle
Washington, D.C. 20036 USA

COOPERATIVE EDUCATION AND OFF-CAMPUS EXPERIENCE

1. ORGANIZATION AND ADMINISTRATION OF PROGRAMS

2. COOPERATIVE EDUCATION IN THE UNITED STATES

3. EXPERIENTIAL EDUCATION IN THE UNITED STATES

4. SANDWICH PLAN IN THE COMMONWEALTH NATIONS

5. COOPERATIVE EDUCATION WORLDWIDE

1. ORGANIZATION AND ADMINISTRATION OF PROGRAMS

Cooperative education programs have enjoyed, since the 1960s, a tremendous expansion that is part of the growing recognition of the value of experiential education. Many institutions have broadened existing programs, and many others have decided to introduce cooperative education.

Early Development Stage of Cooperative Programs

Since adoption of a cooperative education program requires dramatic changes within the structure of a college or university, an administration contemplating the introduction of such a program should be totally committed to it as educationally viable. By its very nature cooperative education can provide financial assistance to students, improve relations with the community, allow for fuller utilization of facilities, assist in job placement after graduation, and attract new students to the institution. These secondary benefits, however, should not be confused with the primary objective of enriching the educational experience of students through the combination of off-campus work and on-campus study. If, at some time, one of these goals emerges as the prime objective of the program, the program will lose its credibility as a strategy of education and disenchant both the population it seeks to serve and other members of the institutional community.

Because of its history and traditions, each institution is unique, and each serves a distinctive student population. An institution's special features should be emphasized when initiating a program of cooperative education. Indeed, one of the greatest administrative advantages of such a program is its flexibility of management, as programs can be adapted to meet most needs.

Wherever a cooperative program is to be successfully installed and operated, there should be either teaching faculty or administrators who advocate the philosophy of cooperative education and are strongly convinced that this educational plan will best serve the students in achieving their educational goals, reaching their career objectives, and increasing their self-development. These individuals often become leaders

in the investigation and development of the cooperative education program. To proceed beyond the initial stage, the administration and faculty alike must believe in cooperative education and must collaborate in making it work. Without open-mindedness among a majority of the faculty and administrators, the program will not advance beyond the exploratory stage. This open-mindedness involves a willingness to consider the possibility of major changes in the academic calendar, the mechanics of operation, and the curricula.

It is essential that the president or chief administrative officer of an institution be involved in the early development of a program; without his commitment the program's potential for becoming an integral part of the institution is greatly diminished. This commitment must be announced publicly through press releases and campus news media. Philosophic commitment must then be translated into a financial commitment sufficiently large to support a professional staff to implement the program. The chief executive should also use his influence to ensure the cooperative education office a central location on campus and a director responsible to an academic vice-president or dean. By its very prominence on the campus and association with the academic side of the institution, the cooperative education program will avoid any suggestion of not being an educational program.

Planning and Implementation

It is customary for the college or university to establish a planning committee of administration, faculty, and student representatives, with input sometimes solicited as well from employers during the planning stages. This planning committee is responsible for proposing preliminary policy decisions, developing curriculum changes, planning the transition period, and setting target dates for the accomplishment of these objectives.

Preliminary policy decisions. Many decisions must be made before a cooperative education program can become operational. The first issue to be resolved is the determination of the program's principal educational objective. If, for example, it is decided that the program will emphasize career development, then the cooperative work assignments and the educational program must be carefully correlated. However, if the objective is more for the student's personal and social development, the work assignments will be structured to stress growth in these areas.

It must also be decided if the cooperative program will be mandatory or optional. If optional, it may also be selective, in which case only students with high academic standing are allowed to participate. The subject areas in which cooperative education will be offered must be selected as well. Some institutions choose to limit cooperative education to the professional areas such as engineering and business, while others elect to make it available also in the humanities and the sciences. Determining the size of the program is essential when considering the financial impact the program will have on the institution.

Calendar design. Another basic issue requiring early resolution is the design of the academic calendar. One of the great strengths of cooperative education is its operational flexibility. The basic concept of integrating work experience with an educational curriculum can be applied in a variety of different ways. The calendar and schedule also can be designed to fit the needs of the particular institution, the students to be served, and the surrounding community of employers.

One of the most common calendars found in four-year institutions is the *alternating* system—an alternation between study and work of a dual student body. In this system the work assignments are almost always paid and career-related. Students who participate in the program are divided into two equal groups: while one attends classes, the other goes off campus on cooperative work assignment. At periodic

intervals, the groups change places. The time period generally varies from either thirteen weeks (when the institution's calendar is divided into quarters) or sixteen weeks (when the calendar is divided into semesters). This alternating schedule is particularly popular with employers because it ensures year-round coverage of the job assignment. On campus the course sequences must be set to allow for a logical progression toward a degree; this scheduling may entail a frequent repetition of core courses. As the design of the alternating plan in all cases envisions the year-round operation of the educational plant, the conventional summer vacation common in academic calendars is eliminated. Moreover, the alternating plan does complicate certain areas of administration. The assignment of student housing, for instance, becomes more difficult with the periodic changes in off-campus and on-campus living requirements. Student activities and athletic programs are directly affected by this calendar as well, for almost all student clubs and organizations must be duplicated, with a set of officers and activities in each division of the student body. For some athletic teams, the competitive season covers both school and work periods, so in these cases the potential team members have to be placed on job assignments near the institution to allow attendance at practice sessions as well as participation in the games.

Since the institution operates on a year-round basis, the faculty must be hired on a longer than normal contract year. Salary adjustments will have to be made, and it may become necessary to hire extra faculty for courses not covered by the regular faculty.

In the early 1970s, primarily as a result of the rapid development of cooperative education at many community colleges throughout the United States, the *parallel* system of cooperative education emerged. In this type of calendar, each student alternates during each working day between half a day in class and half a day at work.

Therefore, the work period and the study period are parallel with one another. Although this system limits the placement of students to within commuting distance of the school, it does have the advantage of eliminating many of the administrative problems associated with the alternating pattern. In the parallel system, jobs are almost always career-related, paid positions, as the main objective of this type of program is career development. It is not uncommon for a student to remain with the same employer throughout the program.

The *field experience* program is not as common as either the alternating or the parallel system. On this type of calendar the students all leave the campus at one time, and the institution closes completely. As the program often occurs during January, the program is sometimes referred to as the "January" or "Jan Plan." It is also called the 4-1-4 plan, because students attend class for four months, leave on their field experience for one month, and then return to the campus for four more months. The main objective is to create opportunities for students to experience career and personal development. It is difficult with the field experience program to find jobs that are both paid and directly related to a student's career goals or major field of interest, and one of the limitations of this calendar design is that it does not guarantee students financial assistance. Also, because of the short work period, an employer is not able to make an accurate assessment of the student's abilities or potential as a full-time employee after graduation. The problems of housing, athletic scheduling, and faculty contracts are not nearly so great with a field experience program as they are with the alternating system. The program, however, is successful in finding jobs because the work period falls during the Christmas season, enabling students to do seasonal work, particularly in the retail trade areas.

Extended-day plan. A relatively recent innovation is the extended-day plan, which has gained popularity as continuing and adult education programs have proliferated. Students work full time during the day and attend class in the evening, with the full-time work considered a cooperative education work experience only after it receives faculty approval. Generally, extended-day programs attract an older student population seeking upward mobility and further self-development.

Staffing requirements. The status of the cooperative education staff is very important. The program can be operated by teaching faculty on a part-load basis or by a central staff devoting full time to the coordination. It must also be determined whether the coordinators—the professionals who place and counsel the students—will be eligible for faculty rank. Similar decisions must be made as to the administrative rank of the program's director, the person to whom he will report must be identified, and his (and the coordinators') committee assignments must be stipulated.

Experience has shown that a centralized staff of faculty coordinators is most effective in reducing variations in the employment market. Student employment can be held at an optimum level because of the coordinators' unique knowledge of various companies; their relationships with personnel directors, department managers, and owners of businesses; and their ability to maintain a balanced program under diverse economic conditions.

In seeking talented and qualified coordinators, a basic question arises—whether, in selecting the candidates, to stress familiarity with the institution; experience—academic or professional—in those areas in which cooperative education will be offered; or prior experience in cooperative education. In establishing a new cooperative program, the most common pattern has been to appoint coordinators from within the institution who are already familiar with the channels of authority and communication and are likely to have the acceptance and respect of faculty colleagues. If no one is available from the current staff, institutions frequently have turned to alumni, the advantage again being familiarity with the institution and its goals.

If a mandatory cooperative program in a number of disciplines is instituted, it is highly advantageous to hire coordinators who have experience in these particular areas. Not only will the coordinators relate better to the students and teaching faculty, but they will also be able to develop a better rapport with the employers.

Fortunately, with the tremendous growth of cooperative education since the 1960s, there are a substantial number of highly qualified directors and coordinators of cooperative education in the United States. Each of them would offer a dimension of expertise and knowledge to the development of a new cooperative program not present in the backgrounds of other candidates. In addition, consulting assistance is available in the United States from federally-funded training centers. Conferences and specialized workshops are also scheduled throughout the year to assist both new and experienced coordinators.

Rules and regulations. The planning committee must also resolve several policy matters regarding the conduct of the program. Such issues include: the procedures to be followed when students fail their work assignments, the types of reports to be filed by employers on student job performance, and the types of reports to be filed by students regarding the job and the employer.

Fiscal Policies

The implementation of a cooperative education program entails operating expenses that include not only direct costs of the department but also other teaching and administrative expense. However, by admitting a larger entering class, an institution can replace students who are off campus on their work assignments. Some institutions charge the students a fee for off-campus experience. The size of the fee can be calculated, at least partially, to offset the program cost. Many public institutions,

by charging a fee or by granting academic credit for the off-campus experience, are able to consider cooperative students as actively enrolled and thus can qualify for state funds that otherwise would not be available. Since 1970 the United States Office of Education has provided at least partial support of the costs of developing a cooperative education program.

A financial advantage of cooperative education programs is the simplification of financial management due to the periodic flow of cash income, a pattern of income quite different from that found in a conventionally operated institution. Another benefit is the goodwill of employers, which often leads to new sources of funding.

Establishment of programs in cooperative education does not, of course, entail only financial advantages. Among the immediate expenses of implementing a new program to be considered on budgetary planning are salary and fringe benefits for a director and secretary; office expenses, including supplies, telephone, postage, and publications; and a travel account to cover the cost of the director's attending training workshops and inviting consultants to visit the campus.

A sizable mandatory cooperative program based on alternating periods generally creates a favorable financial situation for several reasons. The dual student body allows for more efficient use of both physical facilities and faculty; at the same time, many services, such as the library, admissions office, and student activities, do not have to be expanded in proportion to the larger student body. The year-round use of institutional facilities provides an additional financial benefit, particularly when the institution also offers extensive adult and continuing education programs.

Generally, it takes seven years for a four-year institution to convert fully to a mandatory five-year cooperative program. This period allows students not in cooperative education time to complete their degrees before coop becomes mandatory and the admission each year of a freshman class sufficiently large to provide optimum use of the facilities at all times. Of course, the transition period will require some necessary increases in tuition, fees, faculty compensation, and other operational allotments. Not until the fourth year of conversion will income exceed expenditures, with the financial advantage coming from the additional tuition income.

Conversion to an optional or selective program, by contrast, may actually increase the cost of operation without a matching increase in income. In such programs it is extremely difficult to predict the number of students who will participate; it is therefore impossible to admit a number of freshmen equal to the number of students off campus, or to schedule sequential courses accommodating all students with any degree of accuracy or economy. At community colleges, where the attrition rate is unpredictable, there may be a financially unfavorable imbalance in the faculty/student ratio.

Publicity

Once preliminary planning is completed and the staff is hired, the program must be publicized both on and off campus through such means as the institution's catalog, articles in newspapers, and brochures directed to students and employers. The student brochure should include action pictures depicting cooperative students on work assignments, with a brief and easily understood description of the program, while the employer brochure should omit pictures but include a short and informative description of how cooperative education can be cost-beneficial to an employer. It is equally important that information on the institution's cooperative program be distributed to high school counselors and principals, who can then pass the information to their students.

As soon as the publications are ready, the coordinating staff should begin the process of job development. Some of this task may be done by mail, but the most consistently successful means of finding co-operative assignments is through personal visits to prospective employers. One effective means of job development on a large scale is through presentations to groups whose memberships consist largely of representatives from the business community.

The decision to initiate a cooperative education program on a college or university campus requires an accurate assessment of the characteristics of the institution, its students, faculty, and employing community. Cooperative education strives to broaden a student's educational experience by presenting opportunities for linking practical work assignments with academic study. The accomplishment of this educational objective takes patient and exact planning.

Bibliography

Collins, S. B. "Types of Programs." In A. S. Knowles and others, *Handbook of Cooperative Education.* San Francisco: Jossey-Bass, 1971, pp. 29–36.

Cross, K. P. *The Integration of Learning and Earning: Cooperative Education and Nontraditional Study.* Washington, D.C.: American Association for Higher Education, 1973.

Knowles, A. S. "Cooperative Education and Financing Higher Education." Unpublished paper prepared for the Committee on Economic Development on Management and Financing of Colleges and the Task Force on Alternate Sources of College Funding, Northeastern University, Boston, Massachusetts, 1973.

Knowles, A. S., and Associates. *Handbook of Cooperative Education.* San Francisco: Jossey-Bass, 1971.

Wilson, J. W. *Cooperative Education and Degree Credit.* Boston: Northeastern University Cooperative Education Research Center, 1972.

Wilson, J. W., and others. *Implementation of Cooperative Education Programs.* Boston: Northeastern University Cooperative Education Research Center, 1975.

Wooldridge, R. L. "Cooperative Education." In A. S. Knowles (Ed.), *Handbook of College and University Administration.* Vol. 2: *Academic.* New York: McGraw-Hill, 1970, pp. 2-223–2-233.

ROY L. WOOLDRIDGE

JANICE C. FIRESTEIN

2. COOPERATIVE EDUCATION IN THE UNITED STATES

Cooperative education is an educational plan or method which integrates productive work experience into a student's regular program of study. The college or university sponsoring the cooperative program assumes responsibility for this integration of work and study by coordinating individualized instruction and student counseling with job placement, student-employer liaison, and assessment of learning. The plan entails a cooperative and often collaborative relationship between institution and employer.

The First Phase of Development

Herman Schneider, an engineering professor and dean at the University of Cincinnati in Ohio, was the first American to conceive of formally linking university-level study with practical work experience. Schneider grew up in a coal mining town of Pennsylvania and worked in the fields prior to and during his college years at Lehigh University in Bethlehem, Pennsylvania. While an engineering student, he was prodded by his employer to find connections between his studies and his practical engineering experience. Schneider noted that, on graduation, the majority of engineering students at Lehigh were employed at the neighboring steel mill, and he wondered if such experience might not be made available to students prior to graduation. He perceived that university-based classroom and laboratory experiences alone were not adequate for the education of an engineer; moreover, he observed, most students sought part-time work while attending college (Park, 1943). These experiences and observations were the immediate basis for Schneider's scheme to incorporate practical and productive work experience into the educational program. In 1906 he initiated the first cooperative education program in the United States.

However, the foundation for cooperative education was fundamentally embedded in educational thought and philosophy at the beginning of the twentieth century. During the 1800s United States higher education changed from a system providing general education for a limited constituency to a system which, while continuing its own tradition, strongly supported education for able youth from a broader social base in order to prepare them for participation in an increasingly industrial society. Institutions had adopted an educational-social philosophy, called "functional utility" (Harris, 1969), which asserts that institutions of higher learning have the responsibility of entering into the affairs of the society of which they are a part—they should be responsive to the educational needs of their society and must search for knowledge which can be used by that society. Development of professional, career-directed curricula; extension programs; research programs; and faculty consultation with industry are results of this philosophy. Schneider's idea of cooperative education was conceived within the context of these basic changes in the character of higher education. Even the name he chose for his scheme—cooperative education—reflects the interaction between an institution of higher education and the world around it.

There is an implicit pedagogical assumption in cooperative education that had been largely absent from educational thought before the plan was evolved—that important learning can occur outside the classroom and away from direct contact with teaching faculty. Skepticism about the validity of such off-campus learning as a component of education was important in the slowness with which cooperative education was adopted by United States colleges and universities. A second program was initiated by Northeastern University in Boston, Massachusetts, in 1909, and, by 1920, only ten programs had been implemented. By 1930 the number of programs had risen to sixteen and by 1945 to twenty-one. After World War II, partly to accommodate large numbers of returning veterans and partly because veterans demonstrated the educational value of practical experience, a relatively large expansion took place. In 1954 a United States government publication, *Cooperative Education in the United States,* reported forty-three programs, thirty-five in baccalaureate degree institutions and eight in community colleges and technical institutes (Armsby, 1954).

Early leaders in cooperative education. During the early years of cooperative education, a number of institutions made significant contributions. The University of Cincinnati (in Cincinnati, Ohio) initiated not only the first cooperative education program, but also the first nonengineering program; in 1919 the institution expanded its program to include participation by what is now its college of business administration. Antioch College (in Yellow Springs, Ohio) demonstrated that the concept of cooperative education could become an integral part of the liberal arts by instituting a mandatory program for all students in 1921. The Rochester Institute of Technology (then Rochester Atheneum and Mechanics Institute) established a cooperative education program in 1912, demonstrating the value and applicability of cooperative education in nonbaccalaureate degree institutions (Rochester Institute of Technology is now a senior and graduate-level institution). Northeastern University established a policy that all existing and envisioned programs of study would be designed on the cooperative plan. Indeed, Northeastern pioneered cooperative education in a number of fields, including education, pharmacy, nursing and other health services, actuarial science, criminal justice, and law.

Resolution of early problems. By 1961 seventy-one, or approximately 3 percent, of the nation's postsecondary institutions had cooperative education programs (Collins, 1968). Although the first fifty-five years of cooperative education were not characterized by great expansion, they did constitute a time of development, of experiencing and solving problems, and of gaining acceptance. Strong relationships were established with business and industry through the efforts of program cordinators responsible for developing and maintaining work assignments. Obviously, without employer support there could be no cooperative education; yet it has never been an easy task to persuade an employer to hire a cooperative student for the first time. Generally, once an employer accepts a cooperative student, it is the student himself who convinces the employer to continue participation. Today, virtually all large corporations and thousands of medium-sized and small employers participate in cooperative education. Strong and broad-based support by business and industry is principally due to the dedication and pioneering efforts of the early cooperative education staffs.

One of the most serious problems faced by cooperative education in its earlier stages was the rise of strong labor unions and passage of the National Recovery Act of 1935, which made the strike a legal bargaining strategy. Unions were concerned about students taking jobs away from full-time workers, and students not joining appropriate unions. Each institution had to establish functional relationships with the unions operating where its students had cooperative work assignments. In time, when employers demonstrated that union workers were not losing jobs to students, and when union leaders realized the potential for developing positive attitudes toward unions among future management, most of the difficulties disappeared. Today, conflict between cooperative education and labor unions is minimal.

Although economic recessions in the United States in 1914, 1921, 1958, 1972, and 1975 caused disruptions, particularly among those cooperative programs that required participation by all students, efforts by coordinators lessened the potential impact of employer cutbacks. The real test, of course, came during the great depression of the 1930s. Programs suffered severe hardship and unemployment among students reached as much as 50 percent (White, 1933; Burns, 1934). Nonetheless, only one program terminated. The important lesson learned during that period was not to rely on a few employers but to spread students among as many employers as possible. Cooperative education also survived two world wars. During World War II, thirteen institutions suspended their programs because most cooperative programs then required an additional year for graduation, and the War Department requested institutions to accelerate education as much as possible. Most programs were resumed immediately after the war. The conclusion from all these early struggles has been that cooperative education is, by its very nature, sensitive to events in society; but though it may be disrupted and tested, it can survive those events.

The Second Phase

National Commission for Cooperative Education. The second and current phase of cooperative education in the United States began in 1957, with a conference called "Cooperative Education and the Impending Educational Crisis," sponsored by the Thomas Alva Edison Foundation and attended by representatives of over eighty colleges and universities and nearly one hundred employers. The purpose of the conference was to examine existing models of cooperative education in order to use physical plants more effectively and thus to provide one solution to the space problem posed by the anticipated surge in enrollment as the "war babies" reached college age. The conference participants were enthusiastic about the potential of cooperative education but agreed that substantial expansion of programs had to be based upon a systematic assessment of needs and resources. As a direct result of this conference, a committee of three was formed to draft a proposal for a national study. This initial committee became the nucleus of a twelve-person study committee, which selected a research staff and on July 1,

1958, began the first national evaluation of cooperative education.

The research was concluded in eighteen months, and the report, *Work-Study College Programs,* was published in 1961 (Wilson and Lyons, 1961). The findings made clear the benefits of cooperative education to students, institutions, and employers. In light of the report, the National Commission for Cooperative Education, a nonprofit agency, composed of leading educators, industrialists, and businessmen, was created in 1962 to acquaint colleges and universities with cooperative education and to provide assistance in initiating a program. The work of the commission was largely responsible for doubling the number of programs within five years. By providing congressional testimony, the commission contributed greatly to the passage of federal legislation which, since 1970, has resulted in over $50 million in grants from the Bureau of Postsecondary Education in the United States Office of Education for the planning, implementation, and expansion of cooperative education.

Other developments. Concurrently with the work of the national commission, a group of program directors, envisioning that cooperative education should expand not only in number of programs but in diversity as well, established a national forum for the exchange of ideas—a professional society called the Cooperative Education Association (CEA). Prior to the formation of the CEA, the only such association was the Cooperative Education Division (CED) of the American Society for Engineering Education. Though the CED served, and continues to serve, the needs of cooperative education in engineering, it could not meet the diversifying interests of a rapidly growing field. The charter meeting of the CEA was attended by 114 people (Miller, 1964); the 1976 roster lists 1100 members.

In 1965 the Ford Foundation gave a grant to Northeastern University to provide training and consulting services to a number of institutions establishing cooperative education programs. The grant resulted in the foundation of the Northeastern Center for Cooperative Education. This center, and others which developed later, provides training programs for institutional personnel considering and operating cooperative programs. In 1967 the Ford Foundation gave Northeastern a second grant, which the university matched, to establish the first endowed chair in cooperative education. The basic intent of the professorship was to develop and publish empirical research about various aspects of cooperative education and to contribute to its educational rationalization. In honor of its retiring president, the university's board of trustees in 1975 named this chair the Asa S. Knowles Professor of Cooperative Education. The expanded research efforts of the professorship in turn led to the creation of Northeastern University's Cooperative Education Research Center.

Expansion and Diversity

Throughout the first fifty-five years of its existence, cooperative education in the United States was, for all practical purposes, a uniform, unvarying, and single-minded scheme of education in the more than seventy institutions with such programs. Basically, the cooperative plan was offered in professional and technical fields, first in engineering and later in business administration; the principal objective was to further the students' career development; student participation was a requirement for graduation; a calendar of alternating periods of full-time study and full-time work was followed; student work assignments were discipline-related and of increasing levels of responsibility, with the same employer successively; students were compensated for their work by the employer; either no academic credit was given for work assignments successfully completed, or credit was awarded in addition to that normally required for graduation.

Following the 1961 report and the formation of the National Commission for Cooperative Education, and particularly after the United States Office of Education began in 1970 to give grants, the programs began to grow dramatically. By the spring of 1976 there were 1030 known programs in United States colleges and universities, with an estimated two hundred thousand students participating (Brown and Wilson, 1976). As new programs were established, institutions applied and adapted cooperative education to their special needs and circumstances. Consequently, while the essential concepts continue much the same, program implementation has become increasingly diverse.

During the early years of cooperative education, programs were, with few exceptions, found in four-year, baccalaureate degree–granting institutions. During the period of rapid expansion large numbers of two-year junior and community colleges developed programs as well. This development is explained in part by the large increase in the number of community colleges. As of 1976, 46 percent of all cooperative education programs in the United States were found in junior and community colleges (Brown and Wilson, 1976). There is also an increasing number of cooperative education programs for students in graduate study. In 1971 there were twenty cooperative programs for graduate students (Borman, 1971); by 1976 this number had increased to ninety operational programs and an additional forty-seven being planned (Brown and Wilson, 1976). Indications are that this trend will continue and will increasingly include doctoral programs.

Diversity in cooperative fields of study. The most dramatic example of increased diversity is found in the curriculum fields in which cooperative education is available. As noted, cooperative education was begun in engineering education and did not move to business administration until 1919 and to liberal arts until 1921. And although

Northeastern University from time to time pioneered in new curriculum areas, a substantial expansion in fields of study did not take place until after 1961. By the mid 1970s, cooperative education was offered in 165 different fields of study (Collins, 1975). Table 1 indicates the number of programs reporting participation in fourteen curriculum categories. Although programs in business-related curricula are still those most often provided by both junior and senior colleges, there are now fewer programs in engineering and preengineering than in the social and behavioral sciences.

Program classification. In a study of program implementation, the staff of Northeastern's Cooperative Education Research Center concluded that the most useful basis for classification is the mode of program operation (Wilson and others, 1975). Three principal modes were identified: *alternating,* in which a class of students is divided into two groups, which alternate between periods (usually semesters or quarters) of full-time study and full-time work; *field,* in which participating students leave the campus for a specified period no more than once in a given year; and *parallel* or *concurrent,* in which participating students attend classes full or part time during one segment of the day and work part time during the other segment.

A fourth possible mode is called *extended-day,* in which students are employed full time and attend classes part time, usually in the evening. Coordination between work and study is generally achieved by means of a seminar, course, or project at the college designed to integrate the work experience with classroom study. The principal question as to whether the extended-day approach qualifies as a mode of cooperative education centers around the relevance of student work assignments. One of the principal tenets of cooperative education has been that the institution assumes primary responsibility for securing work assignments matching student needs and interests. Extended-day programs are typically followed by full-time employees pursuing further education. Nonetheless, the extended-day is an interesting and functional mix of work and study. Table 2 shows the distribution of these types of operating modes among 1976 programs.

Policies of student participation. The 1976 data show that 40 percent of all programs make cooperative education available to students in all fields; only 9 percent offer it in only a single field. In 37 percent of the programs cooperative education is wholly optional; in 31 percent participation is voluntary, but students must have grades higher than average in order to qualify. Ten percent of the programs require students to participate in all curricula that have cooperative education. An additional 20 percent operate mandatory cooperative education in one or more fields and some form of optional program in other fields.

Despite substantial variation, many programs have similar characteristics. For

Table 1. Number of Programs Offering Cooperative Education in Various Curriculum Fields

Field	Junior College	Senior College	Total
Agriculture	136	65	201
Applied arts and crafts	82	72	154
Architecture	71	49	120
Business	354	367	721
Computer science	123	134	257
Education	170	207	377
Engineering, preengineering	122	181	303
Health professions	185	158	343
Humanities, fine arts	129	210	339
Physical science, mathematics	98	250	348
Secretarial science	271	100	371
Social and behavioral sciences	195	277	472
Technologies	238	131	369
Vocational arts	113	47	160

Source: Cooperative Education Research Center.

Table 2. Classification of Cooperative Education in Each Major Program

Classification	Percent of Junior College Programs	Percent of Senior College Programs	Percent of All Programs
Alternating	14	46	31
Field	3	7	5
Parallel	22	7	14
Extended-day	2	1	1
Alternating and field[a]	3	7	5
Alternating and parallel[a]	16	13	14
Parallel and extended-day[a]	20	3	11
Other combinations[a]	20	16	19

[a]These programs conduct simultaneously two or more of the principal types of program.

Source: The annual census of cooperative programs at the Cooperative Education Research Center.

example, 87 percent of all cooperative programs assert that their single most important objective is career development; 7 percent rank this objective as second most important. In addition, 90 percent of the programs seek discipline-related cooperative work assignments. In 89 percent most cooperative students have paid positions.

Innovations

Academic credit. An increasing number of institutions are granting degree credit to students for participation in cooperative education. In fact, while the number of programs grew from 127 to 1030 (an eight-fold expansion) between 1969 and 1976, the number of programs granting degree credit increased from 23 to 776 (a thirty-four-fold expansion). Table 3 illustrates this trend from 1969 through 1976.

Institutions have been motivated to award credit for economic reasons and because of increased institutionalization of alternative approaches to education. Specific economic reasons include the oppor-

tunity to charge tuition for credits awarded, and thus defray program costs; the opportunity to attract additional students to the institution by means of this unique approach to earning degree credits; the opportunity, among public institutions, to meet the credit-earning definition of *student* and thus receive government funds for students on work assignment; and the opportunity to incorporate work terms into the academic calendar without increasing the total time required for the degree. Credit is also granted out of a desire to institutionalize the cooperative program; that is, the program is legitimized by offering the same reward for work accomplishment that traditional academic study receives. Credit helps to equate the cooperative program with other innovative off-campus programs and helps to guarantee that cooperative education will, through formal academic policy, be incorporated into the very structure of the institution.

Nevertheless, there continues to be substantial faculty concern and often outright resistance to degree credit for cooperative education. First, faculty take seriously their historic and traditional responsibility of certifying student progress toward the degree; they regard the giving of credit by persons or groups not directly a part of the teaching faculty as actual or potential debasement of academic standards. This

Table 3. Percentage of Cooperative Education Programs Awarding Academic Credit

Year	Estimated Percentage of Programs Awarding Nonadditive Credit[a]
1969	18
1970	25
1971	35
1972	46
1973	58
1974	65
1975	73
1976	73

[a]The term *nonadditive* refers to credit that takes the place of credits normally earned through formal courses or independent study.

Source: Cooperative Education Research Center.

opposition has often been resolved either by faculty working with cooperative education coordinators in granting credit, or by faculty monitoring the credit-granting practices of coordinators who have been delegated specific responsibility. Second, faculty have been concerned that if substantial numbers of students were to receive credit for cooperative work experience, the number of on-campus courses required would be reduced and faculty positions would be jeopardized. There is no evidence that such fears have been realized, but the concern persists. Third, some faculty are concerned about the means of evaluating student work experience. For the most part, evaluation has focused on student reports and employer appraisals. However, there is a growing effort, particularly in community colleges, to assess student achievement of specified learning objectives as a basis for granting credit. This trend is viewed by many as the only way in which faculty resistance may be fully overcome and the only conceptual justification for granting degree credit to students who participate in cooperative education.

The consortium. The essential characteristic of a consortium is the collaborative interaction of two or more institutions developing programs of cooperative education. As of 1976 the thirty-four cooperative education consortia in the United States involved 182 institutions. Among these thirty-four, three types are distinguishable. In the first type, which was the earliest to emerge, institutions knowing nothing about cooperative education but seeking to plan and implement programs band together to assist one another, to discuss problems and propose actions, and to share consultants. The second type is essentially a loose cluster of institutions with cooperative education ranging from young, developing efforts to well-established programs. This type of consortium involves many institutions and is generally organized on a statewide basis, with periodic meetings

to discuss common issues, to hear guest speakers, and to conduct training programs. In the third type of consortium a person, institution, or agency knowledgeable in cooperative education provides leadership and counsel to developing programs. The lead person or organization may act as fiscal agent for consortium members or serve as resident consultant and mentor, as is most often the case when grant monies support program development. Members are encouraged to develop their own programs within three to five years to the point where they no longer need the guidance of the lead person or organization and so can leave the consortium.

Institute for Off-Campus Experience and Cooperative Education. The purpose of this institute, created as an affiliate of Northeastern University in 1972, is to provide, at institutions which do not themselves operate cooperative programs, the functions of counseling students and finding them relevant work assignments. In 1975 membership in the institute was held by eleven colleges, largely, but not exclusively, New England liberal arts colleges. Each college pays a membership fee, at which time an institute liaison person (coordinator) is assigned to counsel students about work opportunities and to find appropriate jobs. If a job placement is made, an additional fee is charged to the student. It is a goal of the institute that, through the combination of member and placement fees, it will eventually become self-sufficient.

Job banks. One effort of the various collaborative arrangements has been the creation of job banks. The Institute for Off-Campus Experience and Cooperative Education, for example, has a staff of full-time professional personnel, called *job developers,* who, knowing the needs of students, develop relevant jobs. This job bank, as of 1976, consists of a detailed list of possible positions for students; computerization of the list is under way. A computerized job bank is already in operation at the Borough of Manhattan Community College in New York City, and a number of consortia have developed job banks for the use of members.

Assessment for the Future

As manpower needs evolve and shift in the years to come and as new curricula are developed in response to these needs, there will be new applications of cooperative education programs. Moreover, cooperative education will figure strongly in the commitment to lifelong career education in the United States. Already, through extended-day and alternating programs, older students seeking career changes are participating in cooperative education.

It is difficult to predict whether cooperative education will continue to expand at the same rate over the next several years as it has recently. Its growth will depend largely on the extent of federal financial support in the future. However, there are indications that the late 1970s will constitute a period of assessment for cooperative education in the United States. The federal government let a substantial contract in 1975 to examine the economic implications of cooperative education for students, institutions, and employers. Professional and regional accrediting bodies have begun to ask institutions to document both immediate and long-term outcomes for students participating in cooperative education. Within the cooperative education community itself, questions concerning the effectiveness of the diverse programs have been raised and will surely lead to systematic appraisal. It is essential that these assessment efforts focus attention on the relationship of program design to educational outcomes and on program innovation and diversity.

Bibliography

Armsby, H. *Cooperative Education in the United States.* Bulletin No. 11. Washington, D.C.: Office of Education, Department of Health, Education and Welfare, 1954.

Borman, A. K. "Graduate Programs." In A. S. Knowles and others, *Handbook of Cooperative Education.* San Francisco: Jossey-Bass, 1971.

Brown, S. J., and Wilson, J. W. "Survey of Cooperative Education, 1976." *Journal of Cooperative Education,* 1976, *13*(1), 57–65.

Burns, G. W. "Effect of the Present Economic Dislocation on Our Cooperative Programs." *Journal of Engineering Education,* 1934, *24*, 557–561.

Collins, S. B. *The Philosophy and Operation of Cooperative Education: A Directory of Participating Colleges in the United States and Canada.* Philadelphia: Cooperative Education Association, 1968.

Collins, S. B. *Cooperative Education: Its Philosophy and Operation in Participating Colleges in the United States and Canada.* Philadelphia: Cooperative Education Association, 1975.

Harris, M. R. *Five Counter-Revolutionaries in Higher Education.* Corvallis: Oregon State University Press, 1969.

Knowles, A. S., and Associates. *Handbook of Cooperative Education.* San Francisco: Jossey-Bass, 1971.

Miller, G. H. "Charter Meeting—Detroit." *Journal of Cooperative Education,* 1964, *1*(1), 5–9.

Park, G. W. *Ambassador to Industry—The Idea and Life of Herman Schneider.* Indianapolis, Indiana: Bobbs-Merrill, 1943.

White, W. C. "The Cooperative Plan in the Depression." *School and Society,* 1933, *37*(942), 65–67.

Wilson, J. W., and Lyons, E. H. *Work-Study College Programs: Appraisal and Report of the Study of Cooperative Education.* New York: Harper & Row, 1961.

Wilson, J. W., and others. *Implementation of Cooperative Education Programs.* Boston: Northeastern University Cooperative Education Research Center, 1975.

JAMES W. WILSON

3. EXPERIENTIAL EDUCATION IN THE UNITED STATES

The term *experiential education* describes off-campus activities undertaken by college or university students as partial fulfillment of requirements for certificates and degrees. Off-campus experiential practices in higher education in the United States through the 1960s were largely limited to two major areas: (1) cooperative education—a process that formally integrates the student's academic study with work experience related to his field of study with cooperating employer organizations; and (2) internships or practicums—programs that involve students in career-oriented work experience as a degree requirement in selected fields, such as medicine or teaching. The cooperative education program instituted at Antioch College in Yellow Springs, Ohio, however, stresses work experience both within and outside the major field of study to best prepare the student for a total role in society as well as for a specific career.

The whole philosophy of experiential education was reexamined in the 1960s as part of that decade's general questioning and challenging of relevancy in higher education. Students desired greater opportunities to apply theory to practice and to learn in the real world outside the classroom in a manner responsive to their needs and interests. Both cooperative education and internship programs had relied on the work experience as the only community resource for learning. But off-campus resources—such as travel abroad, living-learning experiences in diverse cultural environments, historical journeys, and other experiences—could, with careful planning, also be helpful in preparing students for life in a society of ever increasing complexity.

Similarly, experiential education needed not only to offer a broader range of off-campus experiences but also to reach a greater student clientele. Internships were designed only for a select group of students, while cooperative programs best served students in specialized fields, such as business, science, or engineering. Indeed, some universities—such as the Drexel Institute of Technology (in Philadelphia), the University of Detroit (in Michigan), and the University of Houston (in Texas)—offer outstanding specialized cooperative programs. And a few institutions—most notably Antioch College (in Yellow Springs, Ohio), Northeastern University (in Boston), Wilberforce University (in Wilberforce, Ohio), and LaGuardia Community College (in New York City)—

served through their excellent cooperative programs the needs of students in all major fields of study, in the liberal arts as well as in vocational programs. But the need was obvious for equally comprehensive programs at other institutions to reach a broader spectrum of students. From the recognition of these needs came the impetus for change in the 1970s—change directed not so much at altering established and workable patterns as at developing those patterns onto new horizons reaching many more students.

A New Approach to Experiential Education

Experiential education in the 1970s has encouraged students to be creative in identifying, planning, and implementing educational experiences unique to their own needs. With the creation of so many new options, students in experiential programs no longer need be confined by the artificial barriers of the campus.

Closely related to this opportunity for creativity has been the students' increased responsibility for managing at least a part of their own education. The traditional classroom experience is managed by the instructor, the off-campus experience by the student. Higher education in the United States, stepping back from a generations-old philosophy that universities should, as one of their roles, serve *in loco parentis* (in the place of the students' absent parents), has come to realize that success is often more likely if students are treated as adults and given the opportunity to function on their own. As part of this realization, experiential education programs of the 1970s have come to permit, if not urge, students to involve themselves with a greater part of society through off-campus experiences that they implement entirely on their own and for which they often earn full academic credit.

The new approach to experiential education also serves the needs of those students not necessarily career oriented as well as those who are career oriented but desire an education broader than mere occupational training. Travel in Europe, for example, may, for less vocationally oriented students—such as liberal arts majors—be a far more significant off-campus experience than job training in an office. On the other hand, such travel for students with strong vocational objectives—such as business majors—offers an educational experience clearly inaccessible in a traditional business curriculum.

The other very important opportunity created by innovative experiential programs concerns offering students, at difficult points in their academic career, an educational alternative to "dropping out," to leaving their studies altogether. Dropping out can unfortunately be a stigma in American society. Students leave the classroom for many reasons: financial problems, loss of motivation, fatigue, need for an environmental change, discouragement with their academic progress, or the perceived absence of relevance in their education. Rather than dropping out, however, troubled or dissatisfied students now can sometimes find workable alternatives in off-campus programs. Experiential projects can help students avoid an indefinite interruption in their education and offer them a meaningful educational change from the classroom.

Expansion of Experiential Education

The innovations in experiential education are as varied as the programs themselves. In some institutions existing programs have been expanded, while in others entirely new projects have been introduced. It is therefore useful to review the major forms of experiential education.

Cooperative education. Cooperative education is by definition productive off-campus work closely related to the student's major field of study. It is a major form of experiential education that underwent a dramatic metamorphosis in the 1970s. In 1961 seventy-one schools offered cooperative education; by 1976, 1030 institutions reported cooperative education programs on their campuses. No longer limited to

engineering and business, cooperative programs began to be offered in liberal arts, science, criminal justice, nursing, education, and law. Some of this growth can be attributed to the rise of the public community college systems in the United States. In addition, many faculty members who had been distraught and confused by the campus upheavals of the 1960s found cooperative education a realistic vehicle for making education more relevant. Student pressure was an essential factor in the growth of cooperative education for students sought more practical application of their studies as they faced a depressed economy no longer able to guarantee a satisfying career to all university graduates.

Cooperative education is based on alternating periods of work and study. These periods may vary from half a day (as in the parallel system, where the student works half a day and studies the other half) to a full year, but the most common approach is to alternate quarters or semesters. A few institutions have made cooperative education an integral part of all their curricula—the student body is divided in half, with one group off on work assignment while the other half is on campus studying. At the designated dates, the students change places. Because this pattern offers the employer full-time job coverage, it is a financially sound program.

Students may or may not receive academic credit for the cooperative experience. At some institutions the off-campus experience is linked with related seminars that may occur either concurrently with the work assignment (as at LaGuardia Community College) or after the work assignment is completed (Crusoe, 1975). At other institutions where academic credit is offered, contracts are drawn up by the student, faculty coordinator, and employer establishing goals and criteria for evaluating the student's success in meeting these goals. It should also be noted that cooperative programs, unlike some other experiential education programs, have the advantage of not requiring extensive supervisory time. Students are not observers but paid employees who must meet the same standards set for regular full-time employees.

Internships. The new approach to experiential education in the 1970s is typified by the innovations in internship practices. Traditionally only available to, and required for, students in particular professional programs, internships have been expanded to enable students to work— either on a salaried or a volunteer basis—in local, state, or federal programs. Through public service internship placements, a history major may now work on a legislator's staff, a biology major in a mayor's office, or a psychology major in an environmental agency. This expansion has made internships available to students who might have otherwise eagerly sought out and profited from internships but could not because of restrictive requirements. There are several benefits of these new internship programs, as the literature shows: young people begin to understand government better; professionals who have worked in government for years have access to new concepts and ideas; government and youth begin to find better ways to interact, reducing considerably the alienation that many felt in the past; and college students graduate better prepared to play a responsible role in society. These changes have encouraged many states to establish offices to coordinate placements and to bring education and government together in implementing statewide internship programs.

A specialized type of internship is service learning, in which students work, usually as volunteers, with social agencies or organizations to provide much needed services to that segment of society often plagued by severely limited financial resources. All those involved gain from service-learning programs—the recipients of the students' social services; the agencies providing the services; the participating educational institutions, which are able to provide a new dimension to the education process not possible in the classroom; and of course the students themselves.

International student experiences. International student experiences have also taken on new dimensions in the 1970s. In the past, international programs tended to be entirely classroom centered. The students either enrolled in courses in foreign institutions and transferred credit hours back to their universities or attended classes abroad sponsored by a United States university for academic credit in the home institution. But through innovations in the 1970s, students may now go abroad to achieve preplanned educational objectives for academic credit through practical experience, interaction in a foreign environment, and research—all without stepping inside a classroom. For example, in some programs students live for six months on an Israeli kibbutz. They gain intense cross-cultural· experiences; study the kibbutz system of operation; learn to speak Hebrew; and become familiar with kibbutz education, art, and family life—all through preplanned and faculty-sponsored experiential projects for which they receive academic credit.

Independent study. Another major form of experiential education, and one that encompasses a wide range of programs, is independent study. Creative and talented students may, for example, plan and implement their own, unique off-campus experiences. In one program of independent study, a student majoring in Russian sought an off-campus experience that would enrich her knowledge of the language and culture of the Soviet people. Unable to afford a trip to the Soviet Union, the student instead spent three months in a Russian convent in Spring Valley, New York, living with Russians, speaking only Russian, and engaging in the Russians' dietary, religious, and cultural practices. This project was indeed a unique off-campus educational experience, particularly since every member of the convent was Czarist Russian, the youngest seventy-two years old at the time of the project. Another student spent three months following the travels of an early explorer-diplomat in Guatemala. Other students have designed such projects as a study of alternative life-styles in the United States and Canada by living for three to six months in a number of communes. Through these self-designed programs, students gain experience, understanding, and expertise that are vital to their overall education but inaccessible through traditional classroom study.

Another type of self-directed program is independent research or study projects. Instead of taking required course work, a student, with guidance from a faculty adviser, defines a particular problem to be researched and prepares a plan of investigation. This study would probably entail an extensive reading list, some laboratory or field work, and either a paper presenting the student's conclusions based on the research or a final examination. This type of independent study is usually made available to the particularly capable students who are able to organize their time effectively without being required to attend class.

Cross-cultural programs are another innovative and an increasingly popular form of experiential education that allow students to experience cultural environments very different from their own. In Florida, for example, Urban Survival Project sends Floridians into urban centers in the United States for a combined cross-cultural, environmental, and volunteer work experience. In contrast is Outward Bound, a program that emphasizes rural survival. Related to Outward Bound, but with a different thrust, are special rural-oriented projects, particularly in the Appalachian area of the United States, that are usually self-designed efforts with a strong cross-cultural emphasis.

Special emphasis programs are a type of off-campus project that entail interaction in an area of particular interest to the student. The student seeking specialized training in art, for example, may design

a project at the Penland School in North Carolina or the Peters Valley Craftsmen in New Jersey. The Sea Semester program in Massachusetts offers the interested student experience at sea, and the Washington Center for Learning Alternatives in Washington, D.C., emphasizes exposure to the federal government.

University Year for Action. The University Year for Action (UYA) is a federally funded program that deserves special consideration. Utilizing the strengths of VISTA and the Peace Corps and recognizing the interest of higher education in expanded experiential programs, the UYA program was developed in the early 1970s as another unique approach to off-campus learning. Since the program's inception, grants have been awarded to higher education institutions to establish year-long social action field experiences that combine the concepts of cooperative education and internships. Under the UYA provisions, students working on a "paid" volunteer basis earn a full year's academic credit during the year off campus. UYA provides some funds to support the program's administrative costs, but the bulk of the funding is used to "pay" the volunteers a stipend sufficient to cover minimal living expenses, with a certain amount held back until the end of the year to use as "seed" money when the student returns to the classroom.

Contract learning. Contract learning is an important aspect of the growing field of experiential education and one that emphasizes an individualized approach to learning. In a contract-learning system, students meet with a faculty member to determine their long-range objectives and draw up a formal contract outlining a program that will meet these objectives. The contract consists of a description of the activity to be undertaken, the length of time required to complete the activity, the criteria for evaluation, and the amount of credit that will be awarded on successful completion of the activity (Avakian, 1974). The student has a variety of alternatives from which to choose in order to fulfill the learning contract: formal course work; a correspondence course utilizing study guides offered on tapes, cassettes, television, radio, or in the newspapers; research conducted either independently or under the guidance of a tutor; an internship either in the public or private sectors; or travel in the United States or abroad.

The method of evaluating the activity very often is determined by the activity itself. If the student's contract requires formal course work, then completion of the course with a passing grade fulfills the terms of the contract. Another contract may require the completion of a bibliography, in which case submission of the completed bibliography would terminate the contract.

Contract learning may be costly, however, because it requires a one-to-one interchange between student and faculty. To alleviate this problem, Lupton (1976) developed the project syllabus method, in which standardized syllabuses (contracts) are prepared in various topical areas and later easily adapted to suit individual student projects. This method keeps the faculty-student communication time manageable without reducing the flexibility essential to creating unique student experiences off campus.

An excellent example of an institution where contract learning is being utilized fully is Empire State College, a component of the State University of New York system. Empire State is a nonresidential college with regional learning centers throughout the state. All the academic work at the college is based solely on learning contracts, with progress toward a degree measured in terms of contract months. One contract month is determined to equal four weeks of full-time study or eight weeks of half-time study and is equivalent to four semester hours, six quarter hours, or one course in a four-course system.

Collaborative programs. A number of institutions are finding that by joining together in collaborative programs, they can offer experiential programs to more students

more efficiently. One notable effort in collaborative education is the University Without Walls (UWW), an association of institutions of higher education that was conceived by the Union for Experimenting Colleges and Universities (although not all UWW institutions are members of the union). Its programs are based on three basic convictions: students should be involved in developing their own programs of study; students too often are not prepared for self-directed study and are not able to conceptualize their own educational goals; and a mixing of individuals from all ages is advantageous to the educational process. The UWW thus seeks to provide alternative education for undergraduate students of all ages. A student and faculty adviser determine the educational objectives the student must achieve to graduate and then plan a program to meet these objectives. The program might include a combination of internship, independent study, travel, course work, or programed learning, with the length of study depending on the length of time it takes the student to achieve the predetermined objectives. This time may vary, from one year to twenty. Each UWW institution remains autonomous but receives guidance from the union.

The College Venture Program, another important new collaborative endeavor, was developed by the Institute for Off-Campus Experience and Cooperative Education at Northeastern University. It is an association of a number of liberal arts colleges and universities in the New England region of the United States. In the early 1970s, many institutions, particularly the liberal arts colleges, recognized that their curricula were not meeting the changing needs of their student population. They also understood that instituting an effective large-scale program to meet these needs would be a very expensive investment. As an alternative, the New England schools turned to Northeastern University, an institution with over seventy years of experience in developing off-campus experiential programs. Northeastern established the College Venture Program to provide off-campus experiences for the students from member colleges. As the program now operates, the Venture staff undertakes job development and provides career education and counseling for the students of the member institutions. The administration of each program is the responsibility of each participating college, as are the evaluation of each student's experience and the awarding of credit. The off-campus experiences themselves fall into various categories of experiential education as either paid or nonpaid placements in the United States or abroad. For example, an English major may be placed with a newspaper or publishing company; a biology major may work on a research expedition sponsored by the Oceanographic Institute in Woods Hole, Massachusetts; a history major may work on an archeological dig in England; and a business major may work as a bank teller in Paris. Students who are unsure of their career goals may find themselves pitching hay on a Kansas farm or waiting tables in a San Francisco diner.

Assessing Educational Outcomes

Academic credit is often granted for successful completion of these new programs in experiential education. The amount of credit can vary, ranging from twelve to fifteen credit hours per term for the traditional internship to an average three to four credit hours per term for cooperative work experience. It is in the contract method that the most attention is given to educational objectives rather than academic credit expectations because the student must define expectations with one or more instructors, develop a conceptual base for achievement of educational goals, and devise a system for assessing this achievement. Although no definitive study has yet been made, the practice seems to be that students on contracts develop an academic "package of credit" much as they would during a regular term on campus; that is, just as students enroll in a number of courses to acquire an average of fifteen credit hours per term, so contracts specify a series of accomplishments in several areas to provide a "package" of academic credit to be earned in the term off campus. The credit package may involve the experiential project as well as other activities with more scholarly content. The exact amount of credit is determined by student interests, faculty concurrence, and the amount of time the student wishes to devote to intellectual pursuits while off campus.

Grading systems in experiential education have incorporated both the traditional letter grading system in the United States as well as the newer satisfactory/unsatisfactory (S/U) or pass/fail method. Proponents of the S/U system believe that with the lack of the regular contact common to the traditional classroom, the lack of a supervised and prescribed program, and the lack of a common vehicle such as examinations for measuring progress, satisfactory or unsatisfactory is as precise and definitive an assessment as can be made of an off-campus experience. Others argue that with in-depth, written papers or alternative measures that meet specified objectives, a precise, letter-grade evaluation is possible. Consequently, there is no accepted standard pattern for grading off-campus experiences. Systems and methods are being tried, and a standard may one day be adopted.

The methods used to figure experiential credits into total degree requirements are also varied, but the following four systems generally encompass the practices accepted in the mid 1970s for awarding credit in experiential education: parallel system, additive system, regular academic credit system, and no-credit system.

The parallel system requires academic as well as experiential education credits, with the two credit tracks maintained separately on the student's official record. In this system there is neither particular relevance between the two types of credit nor any attempt made to equate experiential credits with academic credits in the traditional sense.

In the additive system, off-campus experiences receive regular academic credit, but the number of credits earned are added to the total number of credit hours required for a degree. For example, if 120 semester hours of credit are ordinarily required for a degree in sociology and a sociology major participates in an experiential program providing twelve semester hours of credit, the student would be required to earn a total of 132 credits for the degree. The experiential credits earned, however, are not identical to normal classroom credit nor do they count directly toward meeting regular degree requirements.

The regular academic credit system, unlike the parallel or additive approaches, merges experiential and traditional classroom education. Simply stated, the system grants experience off campus exactly the same type of credit awarded for classroom accomplishments. Both kinds of learning are judged equally, and no distinction is made between experiential and classroom credits.

Finally, those programs in which the off-campus experience receives no type of credit recognition at all deserve mentioning because inherent benefits are sometimes involved. For instance, in the United States veterans benefits are linked to the number of hours for which a veteran is enrolled. An exception is cooperative education, because a student formally registered for cooperative education on a no-credit basis may receive partial veterans benefits for the time off-campus. In addition, many colleges and universities that do not award credits for cooperative work experience do nevertheless enter the experience on the student's record, thus providing a more impressive transcript that will be beneficial to the student when seeking permanent employment after graduation.

It should be noted that the trend toward crediting off-campus learning experiences, as evidenced in these varied systems and

approaches, is by no means without some constraints. One of the favorite arguments of traditional educators who oppose any form of credit for activity outside the classroom is that granting such credit will cost the institution its accreditation. Accreditation is indeed vital for the survival of a college or university in the United States, and in years past the awarding of credit for any activity outside the classroom would have been dangerous, if not fatal. But that mood, too, is changing. Some accrediting commissions (always important in setting acceptable trends and suggesting constraints) are advocating credit for experiential education. The Western Association of Schools and Colleges and the Southern Association of Colleges and Schools have adopted "enabling" policies that within a certain logical framework permit accreditation for off-campus experiences. These policies do not encourage license to award credit without substantiation or careful accountability, but they also do not prohibit the thoughtful granting of credit for experiential projects. This change in attitude is significant and will become even more so as the future of crediting practices in experiential education is shaped.

Organizations Promoting Experiential Education in the United States

The tremendous expansion in experiential education in the United States has led to the establishment of a number of new national organizations to meet the needs of the growing programs. Providing a forum for the exchange of ideas and approaches vital to the life of a profession, these organizations are as follows: (1) the National Center for Public Service Internships (Washington, D.C.), an organization engaged in developing internships with public agencies and providing program and agency information on internship placements; (2) the National Center for Voluntary Action (Washington, D.C.), an agency that works with campus groups and community organizations in promoting service-learning opportunities for students; (3) the National Student Volunteer Program of Action (Washington, D.C.), an organization that encourages service-learning among college students, provides free program consulting services to colleges and universities, and publishes *Synergist,* a periodical publication on service learning; (4) the Association of Voluntary Action Scholars (Washington, D.C.) and the American Association of Voluntary Services Coordinators (Chicago, Illinois), two associations that are partially involved in the promotion of service-learning experiences for college students; (5) the Association for Innovation in Higher Education (St. Petersburg, Florida), an organization that promotes experiential, midwinter terms for colleges using the four-one-four system (in which the fall and spring semesters are separated by a four- to six-week midwinter term, generally reserved for self-directed study or field experience); (6) the Society for Field Experience Education, a nonspecialized organization that serves the general needs of those engaged in all kinds of experiential education programs; and (7) the Cooperative Education Association, an organization promoting cooperative education, linking employers and educators in furthering work opportunities for students, and publishing the *Journal of Cooperative Education,* a periodical publication of scholarly papers on various topics of interest in experiential education.

In addition to these bodies, two national organizations are engaged in research and impact studies of experiential education: the Cooperative Assessment of Experiential Learning (CAEL) project, originally sponsored by the Education Testing Service, and the Experiential Education Project, sponsored by the National Institute of Social Sciences (NISS). The CAEL project emphasizes the development of assessment techniques for experiential learning gained through normal life processes prior to formal higher education. The NISS project, on the other hand, focuses on assessing the impact of experiential education on traditional college students and developing means by which experiential education can be made available to students in universities where programs do not exist.

The Future of Experiential Education

Experiential education is still as a whole viewed as a nontraditional part of higher education. Although many colleges and universities in the United States have developed strong experiential education programs, many educators consider the experiential movement to be in its infancy. In addition, some opposition to experiential programs remains among the many educators who wish to maintain the long-standing policy that academic credit can be earned only through traditional classroom methods. However, the strong support from many faculty members and the demonstrated successes of experiential education are helping to overcome resistance.

It is likely that by the 1980s experiential education programs will have become a traditional part of the education process and will be available to most students in most colleges and universities in the United States. The expansion from specialized to comprehensive programs serving a wide student clientele should solidify student interest and faculty support, and the CAEL and NISS studies, with their supporting data, should further illustrate the significant and viable role experiential programs have to play in higher education. It is hoped that although experiential education is considered nontraditional today, it will become a traditional part of higher education in the future.

Bibliography

Avakian, A. N. "Writing a Learning Contract." In D. W. Vermilye (Ed.), *Lifelong Learners— A New Clientele for Higher Education: Current Issues in Higher Education 1974.* San Francisco: Jossey-Bass, 1974.

Carnegie Commission on Higher Education. *Less Time, More Options: Education Beyond the High School.* New York: McGraw-Hill, 1971.

Crusoe, J. A. "Academic Credit—A Case at

Hand." *Journal of Cooperative Education,* 1975, *2*(2), 17–22.

Dressel, P. L., and Thompson, M. M. *Independent Study: A New Interpretation of Concepts.* San Francisco: Jossey-Bass, 1973.

Duley, J. (Ed.) *Implementing Field Experience Education.* San Francisco: Jossey-Bass, 1974.

Gould, S. B., and Cross, K. P. (Eds.) *Explorations in Non-Traditional Study.* San Francisco: Jossey-Bass, 1972.

Keeton, M. T., and Associates. *Experiential Learning: Rationale, Characteristics, and Assessment.* San Francisco: Jossey-Bass, 1976.

Knowles, A. S., and Associates. *Handbook of Cooperative Education.* San Francisco: Jossey-Bass, 1971.

Lupton, D. K. "The Project-Syllabus Method in Experiential Education." *Alternative Higher Education,* 1976, *1*(1).

Lupton, D. K. (Ed.) *The Student in Society.* Totowa, New Jersey: Littlefield, Adams, 1969.

Meyer, P. *Awarding College Credit for Non-College Learning: A Guide to Current Practices.* San Francisco: Jossey-Bass, 1975.

Meyer, P., and Petry, S. L. *Off-Campus Education: An Inquiry.* Atlanta, Georgia: Southern Regional Education Board, 1972.

Newman, F., and others. *Report on Higher Education.* Washington, D.C.: U.S. Government Printing Office, 1971.

Ritterbush, P. C. (Ed.) *Let the Entire Community Become Our University.* Washington, D.C.: Acropolis Books, 1972.

Sexton, R. F., and Ungerer, R. A. *Rationales for Experiential Education.* Washington, D.C.: American Association for Higher Education, 1975.

Trivett, D. A. *Academic Credit for Prior Off-Campus Learning.* Washington, D.C.: American Association for Higher Education, 1975.

Vermilye, D. W. (Ed.) *Lifelong Learners—A New Clientele for Higher Education: Current Issues in Higher Education 1974.* San Francisco: Jossey-Bass, 1974.

Wilson, J. W. "Cooperative Education and Degree Credit." *Journal of Cooperative Education,* 1973, *9*(2), 28–38.

D. KEITH LUPTON

[The writer acknowledges with gratitude the services of Janice Firestein for assisting in the preparation of this article.]

4. SANDWICH PLAN IN THE COMMONWEALTH NATIONS

Sandwich courses, like the cooperative plan of education in the United States, seek a meaningful integration of classroom and work experience, thereby increasing the value to the student of the total educational process. In addition, such courses acknowledge the responsibility of the teaching institution for the total educational process and for the integration of the complementary experiences. The differences that occur among the individual Commonwealth nations, and between the sandwich plan and American cooperative education, are not differences of concept but differences in the strategy by which the goals are achieved. In many cases, they have arisen because of the different social environments in which the courses were originally mounted and in which they currently operate.

The sandwich method of training and the term *sandwich system* are reported to have originated at the University of Glasgow, Scotland, where this method has "characterized the engineering school . . . since it was set up in 1840" (Small, 1958). It was not until 1903 that the sandwich idea of integrated periods of classroom and work experience appeared in England with the establishment of sandwich courses at Sunderland Technical College, now Sunderland Polytechnic (Wrangham, 1956). Real growth in the sandwich plan for Great Britain as a whole did not occur until the late 1950s, but since that time there has been a substantial increase in the number of courses offered in this way. The establishment of sandwich programs in Australia and in India occurred in the 1960s and seems to have stemmed from the late British growth. The only other Commonwealth country with any real involvement in sandwich courses is Canada, which, by contrast, has derived its sandwich courses from the American cooperative plan of education.

Development of the Sandwich Plan

Teaching institutions offering sandwich courses seek to integrate the complementary aspects of classroom and work experience following the same philosophy, but not necessarily with the same detailed method of implementation, as in American cooperative programs. A typical description of this approach is given in the statement of the Council for National Academic Awards (CNAA): "Sandwich courses . . . consist of periods of study in college combined with one or more stages of practical training in industry, commerce or professional work. The training programs are carefully designed by the college and the firm in collaboration to ensure that the training is related to the college course" (1973).

In Great Britain wide-scale application of the sandwich plan to first degree programs occurred in 1956. At that time, the National Advisory Council for Education for Industry and Commerce strongly recommended the introduction of sandwich courses as a means of increasing the supply of engineers and technologists of a high standard. The National Advisory Council's recommendation was subsequently adopted as government policy in its *White Paper of Technical Education* of February 1956. Related developments included the creation of the National Council for Technological Awards (NCTA), the introduction of the diploma in technology at honors degree level, and the designation of a number of colleges of advanced technology. By 1959 the NCTA had approved sixty-six sandwich courses for the diploma in technology, covering a wide range of engineering and applied science disciplines (Venables, 1959, p. 18). In addition, there were at this time a number of other professional and subprofessional programs of the sandwich type.

The growing strength of the sandwich course and of the college of advanced technology was recognized, in 1963, in the report to parliament by the Committee on Higher Education. This report recommended that the colleges of advanced technology become technological universities, and that the NCTA be replaced by a Council for National Academic Awards, with the power to award degrees. The disciplines formerly catered for by the NCTA were to be extended beyond the fields of science and technology and into additional areas, such as business, humanities, and the social sciences (Committee on Higher Education, 1963). In 1975, among the British universities, only the nine technological universities, which developed from the colleges of advanced technology, were heavily involved in sandwich courses. However, the CNAA has a similarly heavy involvement through its degrees awarded for programs in a number of polytechnics and other colleges.

The number of students undertaking professional programs through sandwich courses grew rapidly between 1959 and 1974, an indication of the ready acceptance of the sandwich plan. At the beginning of the period, just over two thousand students were undertaking the diploma in technology, with a smaller number following Bachelor of Science degree courses (Venables, 1959, p. 18). In 1974 the enrollment for sandwich courses in the technological universities was over thirteen thousand according to a study by Brunel University (in Uxbridge, Middlesex); a further twenty thousand students were enrolled through the CNAA (Council for National Academic Awards, 1974, p. 21). In addition, in 1972, some thirteen thousand students were following subprofessional sandwich training through higher national diploma courses (Joint Working Party on Sandwich Courses, 1975).

In Australia higher education is handled by two groups of institutions, the universities and the colleges of advanced education, both fully financed from Australian government funds. The universities, supported through the Universities Commission, have not become involved in sandwich courses. The colleges of advanced education, supported through the Commission on Advanced Education (CAE), have only recently, and only in a few institutions, begun to develop them actively.

Knowledge of the strength of British and American programs and the documented success of Australian programs are leading to new activity (Davie and Russell, 1974). Colleges of advanced education that are already offering some sandwich courses are acting to expand the range of such courses, while other colleges are considering the introduction of sandwich courses either for new programs or to supplement or replace existing full-time programs. Australian employers with experience of students and graduates from sandwich courses have shown a preference for such employees, and a recent survey has suggested that many employers would welcome greater availability of sandwich courses covering a wide range of disciplines. All of the Australian programs lead to professional qualifications with, in 1974, a total of twenty-two courses throughout the country offered in the sandwich format. (These figures are obtained from an ongoing research project being conducted by R. S. Davie, W. Stern, K. J. Doyle, and J. K. Russell.) Many additional courses are currently under consideration.

In India the development of the sandwich course in engineering has taken place over the last decade and is now accepted as a desirable format for both professional and subprofessional education in a number of engineering colleges. L. S. Chandrakant (n.d., Appendix III) former education adviser to the government of India, lists seventeen such institutions at degree level and a further forty-three at junior level. In 1975 there appeared to be no development of sandwich courses in fields other than engineering, while even in this field the development is recent and slight compared to the total university population.

In Canada development has not derived from the British sandwich course, as in Australia and India, but has stemmed from a knowledge of American cooperative education. The Canadian sandwich plan began in 1956 with the establishment of Waterloo College (now the University of Waterloo) as a cooperative engineering institution (Wright, 1963). An initial enrollment of some seventy engineering students, strongly supported by employers in the Ontario region, has grown to over five thousand students in health, science, and architecture, as well as engineering, with support

drawn from employers covering a wide geographical region. In addition, a further five senior institutions and eight junior colleges are now embarked on sandwich-type courses (Cooperative Education Research Center, 1975).

Thick and Thin Sandwich Courses

The incorporation of work and academic experience requires sandwich courses to be of longer duration than their full-time equivalents. In British courses this usually amounts to an additional year over a conventional three-year program, while in some Australian courses the increase may be as small as one semester in eight. Attendance arrangements fall into two basic patterns, known as thick and thin sandwich courses, for each of which there are a number of individual variations. In the British technological universities alone, there are six thick sandwich patterns and a further twenty-four thin patterns. In the thick sandwich course, one full year of work experience is included in the total program; this year may occur as early as the beginning of the second year but more commonly occurs after two years of academic study. Thin sandwich courses include a number of periods of work experience, usually of six months' duration, spread throughout the total program. The work periods range from as few as two to as many as five, with the first work period placed from as early as the beginning of the course to as late as the middle of the second year.

In Britain, of the approximately 440 individual courses listed by the technological universities and the CNAA, just over half follow the thin pattern. This pattern is particularly common in engineering, is about equally favored in the sciences, and is somewhat less common in business, arts, and social sciences. In a study made by the University of Bradford, 52 percent of the employers responding favored the thin sandwich, while 32 percent preferred the thick and 16 percent had no preference (Musgrove and others, 1970). Employers saw the thin sandwich as giving a better balance between work and study and as a better means of keeping employers and students in touch. In surveys made by Davie and others, respondents from a group of British engineering and scientific concerns and from a group of Australian employers with experience in both systems also showed a decided preference for the thin pattern. Academic staff and students showed an overwhelming satisfaction with the system under which they operated, whichever this might be.

Advocates of thick sandwich courses argue that they automatically arrange for employers to have the continuous services of students, as a student returning to college may be replaced by one undertaking his work experience. Many of the early thin sandwich courses attempted to obtain this same benefit to employers, along with benefits to the college in terms of utilization of facilities, through the use of alternating groups, similar to those used in many American cooperative programs. Such courses, known as end-on sandwich courses, have now become comparatively rare, except in Canada, where alternation on a trimester basis is general (Barber, 1971). Elsewhere, the advantages of employment continuity and facility utilization are apparently of insufficient weight to overcome the disadvantage of increased administrative complexity.

Student Programs in Sandwich Plans

The sandwich plan allows for two types of students: those enrolled by the college and then placed by the college in employment for each work period, and those sponsored by an employer and subsequently enrolled by the college. The former students are referred to as college or university based, while the latter are referred to as works or industry based. Industry-based students are found only in Britain and Australia and even in these countries are becoming less common. The creation of the industry-based student probably arose from the early and active interest

of employers, a unique feature of the development of the British sandwich plan. In many cases, employers demonstrated their involvement both through direct participation in the planning and operation of programs and in the sponsoring of their own staff as industry-based sandwich students. Industry-based students were in the majority in the early years of the sandwich plan; Jahoda (1963, p. 7) reported that "the overwhelming majority of engineering students are industry based (in March 1962 about 80 percent); among diploma in technology students in applied sciences the proportion is much smaller (48 percent), but still considerable." These proportions have now changed considerably; the majority of the students are college based, with the proportion in that group increasing. For example, at Brunel University the proportion of university-based students increased from 55 percent in 1970–71 to 76 percent in 1973–74 (Brunel University, 1974). Industry-based students are more common in engineering than in other courses, and while employers do not sponsor their own staff to the same extent as they did ten years ago, they frequently transfer college-based students into industry-based positions. In addition, they are very interested in the students' total experience, seeking to ensure that the work experience is relevant to the academic experience and actively maintaining contact with the industry-based students while they are attending college.

The placement of college-based students and the amount of free choice for employers and students vary among different institutions in various countries. Attempts to match student and employer are common, with each student being interviewed by two or three prospective employers and each employer having the opportunity to interview a number of students. This concept of free choice is particularly strong in Canada, where the "cooperative programs give students free choice of job assignments and also give employers free choice of students" (Barber, 1971). Employer job descriptions, student histories, multiple interviews, and a final matching by computer form a complete systematized approach to placement that appears to work well and is credited by Barber "for much of the acceptance of the cooperative programs by employers."

Coordination of academic and work experience. The need for coordination of academic and work experience is a recognized feature of the sandwich plan and one that is generally accepted by the Commonwealth universities and colleges. With the exception of Canadian institutions, which use coordinators of the American type, the care of the student, in either academic or work experience, is part of the responsibility of the teaching staff. The student frequently receives guidance, while in industry, from a member of the college teaching staff who can relate the two sets of experiences in a meaningful way. However, a survey taken at four British universities suggests that, while almost all agree that there is a clear interest by the academic staff in the total educational experience of the student, attempts by the staff to relate their teaching to the work experience of the students are not always successful from the students' point of view. The involvement of the lecturer in both aspects of the student's experience is, nonetheless, beneficial, both from the academic standpoint and for the maintenance of contact between the academic staff and industry. All of these benefits are, however, achieved at a cost. In Britain the additional time required for the sandwich course by comparison with the full-time course (with the maintenance of the same staff/student ratios in the two types of courses) leads to an additional teaching cost of approximately 20 percent. Similarly, in Australia the CAE (Australian Commission on Advanced Education, 1972, p. 96) notes the cost of the contact with the student at work and estimates that it necessitates one additional member of the teaching staff for every sixty students at work.

The much less expensive system of using nonteaching coordinators to handle the work experience is predominant in Canadian universities, which follow the American practice, but is virtually unknown in other Commonwealth countries. Although this system is economical and leads to efficiency of placement, Commonwealth institutions have preferred the advantage of teacher involvement in the whole of the educational program in order to avoid the possibility of a dichotomy in the students' minds between the two experiences.

A few British universities see the efficiency of placement and the consistency of university relations with industry that result from the use of coordinators as of sufficient merit to warrant the use of the central placement and industrial counseling service. However, they also maintain the traditional belief in the value of arranging liaison through the teaching staff. Thus, the new services act in conjunction with the old: the coordinators concentrate on the administrative tasks of maintaining centralized employer records and arranging placement, while the monitoring of progress and the counseling of individual students remain in the hands of the teaching staff. The centralized service thus adds a small, but inescapable, further cost. No effort has yet been made to reduce costs by a reduction in the involvement of the teaching staff, even though the introduction of the central service would appear to warrant such a reduction.

In all of the Commonwealth nations offering sandwich courses, this form of education was first introduced in engineering, from which it was extended to science; the bulk of enrollments is still in the engineering and scientific fields. Only in Great Britain has there been any substantial extension into the humanities and social sciences; in those fields, and including business, there are now over 7000 first degree students from a total of 33,000 (Joint Working Party on Sandwich Courses, 1975). It is believed that the future growth of sandwich education will occur mainly in these nonscientific areas.

Numbers of students. The number of students undertaking degree work through sandwich courses in proportion to the total population of degree students varies markedly among the Commonwealth nations. In Britain there is a total of just over 33,000 students (11.5 percent) out of a total university and polytechnic population of 285,000. At the other extreme, the number of sandwich students in the universitiès and colleges of advanced education in Australia is less than .5 percent, while in India a similarly small proportion is involved. For both Britain and Australia, the bulk of sandwich students are in the nonuniversity sector and obtain their degrees through external bodies, the polytechnics and colleges being authorized to offer courses accredited outside the individual institution. By contrast, the ten thousand Canadian students are all enrolled at universities, with those at the University of Waterloo comprising over 60 percent of the total. As a proportion of the total university population, Canadian sandwich students comprise 1.8 percent. Sandwich courses are also available to students undertaking work at the subprofessional level in Britain, Canada, and India. However, it is only in Britain that substantial numbers (twelve thousand in 1972) are involved (Joint Working Party on Sandwich Courses, 1975).

Compensation during sandwich courses. While the sandwich plan in Great Britain appears to have evolved almost equally from the initiatives of industry and education, in the other countries it has been largely fostered through the efforts of individual educational institutions that have gradually involved industry in the planning and operation of courses. The assessment of student work performance by employers, the increased knowledge by employers of educational facilities, and the greater involvement by academic staff in industry provide tangible evidence of the partnership. Employers have also accepted a basic premise of the sandwich plan by providing adequate salaries for

students during the work periods. In many cases, salaries are related to the student's standing in the course.

The provision of a salary during the study period, normal for the true industry-based student, is no longer common. Many British employers now provide a small allowance to assist the student without reducing the normal student grant made by the local education authority to each student, whether full time or sandwich, during the study period. Australian students also receive government support during the academic period through the Tertiary Education Assistance Scheme. However, as student earnings outside of normal vacation times may reduce the level of assistance, employer support during the study period is rare. In other countries, financial benefit to the student is limited to the increase in earning capacity above that of the full-time student, who is generally restricted to vacation employment.

Developments in the Sandwich Plan

In both Great Britain and Australia, there is evidence that a greater number of the academically less able were initially enrolled in sandwich courses than in full-time courses. There is also evidence, in Australia, that academic performance improved following work experience (Davie and Russell, 1974). Such an improvement is consistent with the results of American investigations into the performance of cooperative students. Because of such factors and because employers have the opportunity to assess the talents of individual students during work periods, sandwich students generally find it easier to obtain jobs on graduation than do their full-time counterparts. This situation may improve further as the current trend of more able students entering sandwich courses continues. The Joint Working Party on Sandwich Courses (1975) states: "In the opinion of employers, the calibre of sandwich course graduates has much improved in recent years, probably because a growing number of students now opt for a sandwich education in its own right rather than considering it as second best to a full-time degree course." At institutions where both sandwich and full-time options exist, there appears to be a growing trend for students to favor the sandwich course, despite its additional length and despite the lack, in the award, of any special recognition of the additional training provided through the sandwich course.

With the exception of Great Britain, the percentage of students undertaking sandwich courses is comparatively low. Given the apparent growth in interest in this form of education in the other countries, sandwich courses outside Great Britain will probably assume greater importance in both numbers and diversification beyond the traditional fields of engineering and science. In Great Britain it has been suggested that the number of sandwich students in the universities may have reached a plateau; further growth, however, is expected in the polytechnics.

Experiments in both Commonwealth and American practices are now leading to a convergence and narrowing of differences. While some Commonwealth institutions are experimenting with coordination by using nonteaching staff to strengthen the traditional system (which relies solely on teachers to coordinate), some American universities are trying to obtain greater involvement of teaching staff in this work. In the Commonwealth, there is a decreasing dependence on the provision of works-based positions, without appreciable decrease in the interest of employers in the total education of their students. By comparison, American employers appear to be taking more interest in the total experience of the students and to be approaching the level of involvement of British employers.

In all countries, there is a steady growth of government interest and support for cooperative education. With a growing realization of the universality and advantages of the concept, cooperative and sandwich programs have outgrown their early application to engineering and science studies and are appearing increasingly in other areas of higher education. There is a corresponding increase in the interchange of ideas among countries using the sandwich plans. Such discussion reveals that similarities far outweigh differences and that the technical and social advantages of integrated education are recognized by academic staff, students, and employers in many countries.

Bibliography

Australian Commission on Advanced Education. *Third Report on Advanced Education.* Canberra: Australian Government Publishing Service, 1972.

Barber, A. S. "Cooperative Education in Canada." In A. S. Knowles and Associates (Eds.), *Handbook of Cooperative Education.* San Francisco: Jossey-Bass, 1971.

Brunel University. *1973–1974 Student Numbers: Technological Universities.* Uxbridge, England: Brunel University, Institute of Industrial Training, 1974.

Chandrakant, L. S. *Innovations in Technical Education—Sandwich Courses.* New Delhi: Government of India, n.d.

Committee on Higher Education. *Higher Education Report of the Committee Appointed by the Prime Minister Under the Chairmanship of Lord Robbins, 1961–63.* London: H. M. Stationery Office, 1963.

Cooperative Education Research Center. *Undergraduate Programs of Cooperative Education in the United States & Canada.* Boston: Northeastern University, 1975.

Council for National Academic Awards. *Introduction to Degree Courses, 1974.* London: Council for National Academic Awards, 1973.

Council for National Academic Awards. *Annual Report for 1972–1973.* London: Council for National Academic Awards, 1974.

Davie, R. S., and Russell, J. K. "Attitudes and Abilities of Cooperative Students." *Australian Journal of Education,* 1974, *18*(2), 160–171.

Grant, J. "Sandwich Plan in England." In A. S. Knowles and Associates (Eds.), *Handbook of Cooperative Education.* San Francisco: Jossey-Bass, 1971.

Hanson, C. "The Philosophy of a British Undergraduate Cooperative Programme in Chemical Engineering." *Journal of Cooperative Education,* 1970, *6*(2), 30–38.

Jahoda, M. *The Education of Technologists.* London: Tavistock, 1963.

Joint Working Party on Sandwich Courses. *The Future Development of Sandwich Courses.* London: Confederation of British Industry, 1975.

Moore, J. P., and Urry, S. A. "Engineering Sandwich Courses in British Technological Universities." *Engineering Education,* 1971, *61*(7), 813–815.

Musgrove, F., and others. *Sandwich Course Studies.* Bradford, England: University of Bradford, 1970.

Small, J. "First Sandwich." *Technology,* 1958, *2*(8), 238.

Venables, P. F. R. *Sandwich Courses.* London: Max Parish, 1959.

Wrangham, D. A. "Sandwich Courses. Part 1: In Sunderland." *Proceedings of the Institution of Mechanical Engineers,* 1956, *170*(15), 455–458.

Wright, D. T. "The First Five Years of the Co-operative Engineering Programme at the University of Waterloo." *Transactions of the Engineering Institute of Canada,* 1963, *6*, D1.

ROBERT S. DAVIE

5. COOPERATIVE EDUCATION WORLDWIDE

In all parts of the world, an emerging social awareness within colleges and universities is accompanied by an urgent concern for educational reform. The Netherlands Ministry of Education voiced such concern in a recent publication: "The modernization of higher education is not specifically a Dutch problem. People everywhere are looking for new ideas. It is important that the Netherlands does not remain behind in these developments and that the growth of a new structure fits in with models which have already been established in other countries" (Goote, 1973–74, p. 27).

The universal search for models for making education more relevant and for breaking down the inflexibility in existing patterns of higher education often results in the discovery that cooperative education and similar systems of education can aid necessary reform. Cooperative education, the educational methodology that combines theory and practice in a planned relationship, is being seriously studied and increasingly accepted as a viable means of developing manpower across virtually the entire spectrum of technical and professional careers. Although the growth of cooperative education programs on an international scale cannot be reported in exact numbers, a 1975 survey indicates that it is quite extensive (Mosbacker, 1975a).

Problems in Research on Cooperative Education

In attempting to research the growth of cooperative education programs around the world, one difficulty encountered is the problem of defining cooperative education so as to include all of the basic variations of the concept. Since cooperative education works best when the program is adapted to the needs of the students, the institution, and the society, there is great variation in the structure of programs. In the United States and in some other nations, cooperative education means that type of education in which the student is exposed to periods of both academic study and employment in business, industry, and government; in which the two phases of learning relate to one another in a planned manner; and in which the university or college takes responsibility for the total educational program. The line of demarcation between this form of cooperative education and other types of programs that combine theory and practice is sometimes very hazy. In the United States and in some other nations, for example, neither the internship programs for doctors and nurses nor practice teaching for teachers is usually included as cooperative education programs.

Another difficulty in researching the growth of cooperative education outside of the United States is the confusion that surrounds the word *cooperative*. Cooperative education was the name chosen by Herman Schneider, who first launched this system of education in the United States at the University of Cincinnati (Ohio) in 1906 to emphasize the cooperation required between education and business. In other countries, however, it is often confused with "cooperatives," associations established for advantageous group buying and selling.

Because of this verbal confusion, there have been attempts to find a more descriptive and less confusing name to embody the philosophy of such educational programs. Many find *sandwich course* equally unacceptable because it is felt to be too narrow and *work-study* too suggestive of a vocational or financial-need connotation. In a recent Swedish publication *(Kombinationsutbildning, 1975–76),* the term *kombinationsutbildning* (combined education) is used: a French booklet (de l'Ain, 1974) uses *l'enseignement en alternance* (alternating instruction, or cooperative education); and a Netherlands brochure (Goote, 1973–74 p. 34) refers to "participation education."

The classification *higher education* also presents difficulties, since the structure of educational levels varies a great deal throughout the world. In addition, the line of demarcation between upper secondary school and higher education in any one country is subject to constant reappraisal and change and therefore cannot be finally determined.

Growth and Development of Cooperative Education Worldwide

A recent study of the growth and development of cooperative education and similar programs outside of the United States revealed that thirty-one countries are offering some form of cooperative education in their institutions of higher learning (Mosbacker, 1975b). Follow-up inquiries and other sources have indicated that there are such programs or somewhat similar programs in twenty-four additional countries, bringing the total of nations with operational programs or with programs currently being implemented to fifty-five. The nations are Albania, Algeria, Australia, Austria, Belgium, Brazil, Cameroon, Canada, Chile, People's Republic of China, Colombia, Czechoslovakia, Cuba, Egypt, Ethiopia, Fiji, France, Federal Republic of Germany, Ghana, Great Britain, Greece, Guatemala, Guinea, Guyana, Hong Kong, Hungary, India, Iran, Iraq, Ireland, Israel, Ivory Coast, Democratic People's Republic of Korea, Republic of Korea, Lesotho, Malaysia, Mauritius, Mexico, Netherlands, Nigeria, Norway, Paraguay, Philippines, Romania, Saudi Arabia, Senegal, Sierra Leone, South Africa, Sweden, Turkey, Union of Soviet Socialist Republics, Venezuela, Yemen Arab Republic, Yugoslavia, and Zambia.

Additionally, a number of nations have indicated that they are now considering such programs. A large Spanish foundation, *Fundación universidad de empresas,* recently allocated funding for the establishment of a model organization at the University of Madrid to assist in developing closer ties between Spanish universities and Spanish industries. The director of the foundation and two professors from the University of Madrid visited the United States to learn more about cooperative education; as a result, the foundation is currently conducting a survey to determine the feasibility of such a program in Spain (Mosbacker, 1975b, pp. 54–55).

In Costa Rica the Ministry of Education has prepared a National Educational Development Plan calling for comprehensive reform of the educational system to make it responsive to economic development needs; it is expected that cooperative education will be seriously considered as one reform (Mosbacker, 1975b, p. 51). In Burma a movement to make university training utilitarian by creating a close relationship with industry is being fostered by university professors who serve on the executive boards of various industries and head joint research projects. It is hoped that the next step will be to include a period of practical training in all fields of study.

Similar movements are found elsewhere in Asia and Europe. In Pakistan, under the National Development Volunteers Program, educational institutions and industrial concerns are planning to cooperate in providing on-the-job training. In Singapore the administrator of Ngee Ann Technical College has recently proposed to a large industrial corporation in Singapore that a joint training program be established for students of the college. In Denmark, too, there is evidence of a growing interest in cooperative education. In a June 1974 article, K. Helveg Petersen, Denmark's former minister of education, emphasized that society and all industry and business functions should be incorporated in the student's education, not only as an introduction but as a necessary part of the general education (Mosbacker, 1975b, p. 52).

The cooperative education concept was launched in the United States and England shortly after 1900. During the fifty years immediately following its inception, however, its growth in the United States, England, and elsewhere was very slow. A marked increase in cooperative education and similar programs began in Europe and other areas in the 1960s, while in the United States the greatest increase occurred in the 1970s (Mosbacker, 1975b, p. 64), sparked by the availability of government funds for the establishment of such programs in both public and private institutions of higher education.

Organization and Objectives of Cooperative Education Programs

In the United States approximately 70 percent of the colleges and universities offering cooperative education and similar programs are publicly supported institutions; elsewhere in the world 81.4 percent are publicly supported, and an additional 10.8 percent are supported by a combination of public and private funds (Mosbacker, 1975a, p. 18). In many nations there is evidence of quite direct government involvement in decisions and provisions relative to cooperative education.

At the outset, most programs outside of the United States were industry based. The employer carried out a recruitment campaign and selected students for development in the organization under the guidance of a company official. However, since the late 1960s the balance of the new intake of students has shifted, so that ap-

proximately 59 percent of the programs outside of the United States are now college based (Mosbacker, 1975a, p. 20).

There is a marked similarity in the major objective of the programs. In all parts of the world outside of the United States, "career development" is cited as the principal objective by 89 percent of the colleges and universities responding to a recent survey. "Personal and cultural growth" is mentioned as the prime objective by 6 percent of the institutions, with "improved community relations," "attraction of more students to the college or university," and "financial assistance provided through earnings" ranked in descending order (Mosbacker, 1975a, p. 21).

In several countries discussed in this article, information was drawn from material compiled by the *International Encyclopedia of Higher Education*. These countries include Burma, Pakistan, Singapore, Ireland, Senegal, Iran, and Turkey. Although there is also a separate essay on sandwich plan courses in Commonwealth nations, data from those nations are included in this essay in order to give as complete a picture as possible of the development of cooperative education.

Schedules of programs. Approximately 89 percent of the programs offered in institutions around the world are from three to five years in length, with 52.6 percent of four years' duration. For 7.4 percent of the programs, the number of years required to graduate ranges from five and a half to seven years. There is no uniformity in the length or the frequency of the individual education and industry blocks; a spread of two weeks to one year in length and of one to six in number was reported. However, in almost all cooperative education programs around the world some academic study is required prior to the student's initial work period (Mosbacker, 1975a, p. 21).

Great variation in the scheduling of practice periods exists between institutions and even to some degree within institutions. Of the institutions outside of the

United States, 45.6 percent report that the basic scheduling plan for their programs is the alternation of periods of full-time school with periods of full-time work (Mosbacker, 1975a, p. 20). Interesting schedule adaptations to fit the seasonal fluctuations of some career fields are evident. For example, at Georgian College (in Barrie, Ontario, Canada) all marine navigation majors work each year from July 1 to January 1, because it is during that six-month period that beneficial experience is available to them on Great Lakes vessels. For similar reasons all resort and hotel administration majors work each year from late May to mid October and again from mid December to mid February, the periods when Canadian resorts and hotels are busiest.

Payment of students. The percentage of programs in which all students are paid a salary during their practice periods is similar all over the world; 78.4 percent of those outside of the United States and approximately 76 percent in the United States work in paid positions. Only 8 percent of the students elsewhere in the world are working on a totally voluntary basis. Data supplied on the types of employers outside the United States indicate that, of the 6,510 employers reported, 75.1 percent are in the business and industry segment of the economy and 18.9 percent are government employers (Mosbacker 1975a, p. 24).

Most cooperative education programs in the United States are optional, with only 11 percent of the programs requiring students to participate when cooperative education is offered in their disciplines. Elsewhere, an almost inverse ratio of mandatory programs to optional programs seems to exist, with 70.5 percent of the programs reported as being mandatory (Wilson and Brown, 1975).

Fields of study in cooperative education. Technical training has high priority in most nations around the world, particularly in terms of national development in Third World nations. It is not surprising, therefore, to find that a large percentage of the institutions offering cooperative education or similar programs have made them available first, and in many cases exclusively, to students majoring in engineering and technology. However, there is an increase in the number of students participating in such programs in the fields of business, architecture, the humanities, social sciences, health, and other nontechnical disciplines. In 1975, 52.2 percent were enrolled in engineering programs, 6.2 percent in technology programs, 14.2 percent in physical science and mathematics programs, 8.1 percent in business programs, 4.7 percent in architectural programs, 3.7 percent in the social and behavioral sciences, 3.1 percent in the health professions, 2.3 percent in the vocational arts, 1.5 percent in the humanities and fine arts, .5 percent in applied arts and crafts, .2 percent in agriculture, .2 percent in secretarial studies, and 3.1 percent in other disciplines, including hotel studies, maritime studies, leisure studies, and environmental studies. A comparison of the number of students participating in cooperative education in a discipline and the total number of students in the discipline in each institution reporting reveals that in the architectural program 75.2 percent of the students enrolled in the discipline were participating, in health programs 66.0 percent, in engineering programs 64.3 percent, in the humanities 48.7 percent, in the social and behavioral sciences 41.3 percent, and in the business program 36.8 percent (Mosbacker, 1975a, p. 24).

Academic credit for cooperative education. Since there is no system of academic credit in some countries of the world, the following data are based only on reports from the institutions that do award academic credit. Of the colleges and universities in countries other than the United States, 30.4 percent indicated that they award credit for participation in cooperative education programs but that the credit is in addition to that normally required for graduation; 17.4 percent responded that they award credit and that the credit given takes the place of credits otherwise earned through college (on-campus) courses. In 13 percent of the institutions credit is not given, but academic departments permit the students to complete papers or other projects based on their work experience and grant credit for them (Mosbacker, 1975a).

Cooperative Education in Canada and Europe

The development of cooperative education in Canada and Europe has moved rapidly since the 1960s. Programs are to be found in most countries, and the number of disciplines inaugurating cooperative programs is also increasing.

Canada. At the vanguard of the cooperative education movement in Canada is the University of Waterloo, where the first Canadian cooperative education programs were launched. However, the movement spread rapidly to other Canadian colleges and universities, with 71.4 percent of the institutions initiating their programs in the 1970s. This rapid growth has been achieved with government approval but without government financial assistance. A survey prepared by Gordon Lancaster (1974, 1975), chairman of cooperative education at Fanshawe College in London, Ontario, indicates that 56.8 percent of the student placements made by fourteen Canadian colleges and universities during 1974–75 were in engineering and technical studies; 22.1 percent were in mathematics and computer science; 5.7 percent in kinesiology and recreation; 5.5 percent in business; and 4.8 percent in architecture. The data also indicated that Canadian employers are receptive to the cooperative education concept and that in a number of majors more students could be accommodated than normally participate in cooperative education programs. According to the survey, approximately ten thousand students had been placed on job assignments during the 1974–75 academic year. In four disciplines, the schools were a total of thirty-one job assignments short, but for all other disciplines offered there was a surplus of 652 job openings for which no students were available. In September 1975 several of the colleges and universities expanded or initiated programs. Among the programs introduced in 1975 were surveying technology, food and science technology, chemistry technology, electrical technology, industrial design, interior design, urban design, graphic design, landscape design, applied economics, applied geography, and applied statistics.

European attitudes toward practical work experience in education. Although the cooperative education concept was introduced almost simultaneously on both sides of the Atlantic Ocean, most of the growth and development in Europe was concentrated, until recently, in Great Britain. In the past, the importance of relevant experience in the educational program was evidenced only in the admission requirements of many colleges and universities in Europe; the candidate for enrollment was required to complete practical work experience, usually of at least one year's duration and usually in the major to be studied, as a prerequisite for entrance. There are indications that this requirement is being altered in some institutions where students must either gain practical experience prior to admission as in the past or meet the requirement by doing practical work during their course of study. In most instances, no formal structure exists, as yet, for fulfillment of this latter requirement. However, in colleges and universities in a number of countries of Europe, greatly increased resources of time and money are being put into planning for labor-market orientation. Although there is evidence that increasing interest in cooperative education and similar programs is developing, the adoption of this educational methodology on the continent is still limited.

France. In September 1973 a national colloquy on *l'enseignement alterné* (alternating instruction or cooperative education) was held in Rennes, France. As a result of the conference, some directors of placement offices, assisted by the French government, began immediately to develop plans for introducing cooperative education at their institutions (de l'Ain, Bernard, Collet, and Delors, 1975). For example, the University of Rennes is planning to start a cooperative education program involving its business school and some selected firms.

In connection with the colloquy at Rennes, a survey was undertaken in France to determine whether students would like to have a "concrete experience of work" and whether such programs would be possible (de l'Ain, 1974). The employers interviewed had some reservations about the difficulties they might encounter, but many indicated an interest in having young people in their organizations on a program alternating work periods and study periods. The professors of business and technical subjects were very favorable to the program, but those in literature and science rejected the idea. A total of 620 students majoring in business, law, literature, human sciences, and technology were included in the survey. Sixty-six percent felt that training periods are indispensable in their education programs and that the work periods should be compulsory. As to the number and length of the work periods, the students felt that there should be at least two training periods, each of two months or more in length, and that the work should be scheduled in the second and third years of their college program.

An institution at the vanguard of cooperative education in France is the *Institut de préparation à l'administration et à la gestion des entreprises* (Institute for Preparation in Administration and Management of Enterprises) in Paris. The institute was founded in 1965 and placed its first cooperative education students on work assignments in 1972 (de l'Ain, Bernard, Collet, and Delors, 1975, p. 17). The three-year program provides for four "coop" work periods: the first in a factory; the second, a sales training period; the third, a research project for a French company; and the final period, a work quarter in the United States.

Netherlands. A program in international business studies, providing an opportunity for study and practical training to fit the students for senior posts in the Netherlands and abroad, is offered at the *Stichting nijenrode instituut voor bedrijfskunde* (Netherlands School of Business). *Stichting nijenrode* is a university-level institution that was founded by some leading educators and businessmen from about fifty business and industrial companies in the Netherlands. In the founding plans, emphasis was placed on the importance of practical experience; consequently, the students at the institute spend six to eight weeks on work assignments relative to their career interests (David, 1968).

Throughout the Netherlands there are compulsory practice periods in many educational programs, often totaling one academic year of work in one or more companies. This requirement applies to senior and higher vocational education, to the universities of technology, and to the universities of agriculture (Goote, 1973–74). For example, at the *Technische hogeschool Twente* (Twente University of Technology) in Enschede, at least fifteen weeks of practical work (usually performed in three work periods) are required for the baccalaureate examination (*University Studies in the Netherlands: The Engineering Studies,* 1974–75). At the graduate level, every doctoral candidate must complete a period of at least four months of practical training (*University Studies in the Netherlands: The Gamma Studies,* 1974–75). Within all faculties at the Technological University of Delft, there is a system of compulsory practical work in industry of one to five months during the five-year curriculum of the engineering discipline. The practical work is evaluated for credit and students cannot receive their final engineering degrees without acceptable work periods in industry.

Belgium. After completing a thorough feasibility study regarding the possible introduction of cooperative education or a similar plan, the *Université libre de Bruxelles* (Free University of Brussels) in Belgium has recently taken two steps toward cooperative education: the organizing of a program for a certificate in environment and human ecology and a more ambitious program leading to graduation in civil engineering in building. In addition, extramural periods or periods of professional practice are scheduled in many other university disciplines, but the university does not take the responsibility for managing such periods. Each student is responsible for obtaining work in his professional field and for making all necessary arrangements for the required field term.

A somewhat negative experience was reported by K. Van Goethem, director of the academic planning department at the *Universitaire instelling Antwerpen* in Antwerp, where some experiments in cooperative education were tried during the 1974–75 academic year. The administrators of the university found the organization of acceptable training for cooperative education students very difficult to accomplish because of lack of enthusiasm on the part of industry, government, and other institutions, and on the part of most of the academicians (personal communication, January 9, 1976). Nevertheless, there is some evidence of successful attempts to introduce cooperative education at the university. In 1975 students in the mathematics department spent approximately one month in a business environment studying problems in applied mathematics, and the department evaluated the experiment in a positive way. It is anticipated that in the future such work will be accepted for credit. In addition, in the department of political and social sciences, the students are being given an opportunity to include practice periods in their studies. If the student's practice program is accepted by the professor of the relevant course, the student may be granted credit for his work experience in his academic program.

Sweden. In Sweden, at the institutes of technology and the schools of journalism, two years of academic study may be combined with work experience outside the institutions for those planning careers in secretarial work, public administration, tourism, or banking. In the schools of journalism in Stockholm and Göteborg, the training consists of a one-year basic course, followed by four months' experience on career-related jobs and a further academic term of more advanced study. To obtain an engineering degree in the Swedish universities, it is necessary to have four months of practical experience in addition to completing a four-year academic course ("The Swedish Educational System," 1972; Swedish Ministry of Education and Cultural Affairs, 1973). During 1975 it also became possible to take shorter *kombinationsutbildning* (combined education) courses at the universities in preparation for careers in personnel and educational administration, accounting, administrative systems, recreational leadership, transport administration, and data processing *(Kombinationsutbildning,* 1975–76). The concept of recurrent education is also being explored in Sweden for training workers in a parallel program of study and work. Under this proposal, the workers will alternate periods of study with periods of work, achieving progressively higher educational levels.

Norway. A program being offered in local economics at Norway's regional colleges can also be classified as cooperative education. The objective of the colleges is to break down the inflexibility in existing patterns of higher education in Norway and thereby achieve a changed relationship to society. These colleges are offering training geared toward future careers in industries predominant in the local economy, such as tourism, fisheries, and oil ("The Regional College," 1973).

Republic of Ireland. In the Republic of Ireland, a carefully structured plan for cooperative education is under development with the cooperation of Irish employers, federations, professional societies, and government agencies. There are two schedules: some programs in technical colleges and in the National Institute for

Higher Education are full time, with the work requirement satisfied during summer vacations; others are on an alternating basis, with periods of theory alternating with periods of work throughout the student's program. Courses are offered in such fields as architecture, engineering, surveying, nutrition, business, and the health sciences. The National Council for Technological Education is striving to develop a functional cooperative education plan that will help to raise the economic, cultural, and technological status of the Republic of Ireland in Europe.

Cooperative Education in Eastern Europe

The cooperative education concept seems also to have been applied rather extensively in Eastern European countries. Historically, when the Soviets were launching their first five-year plan, striving toward economic self-sufficiency with its necessary emphasis on large-scale agriculture, manufacturing, and various phases of production and transportation, they were faced with an urgent need to devise an educational program to meet their massive training problem. In 1929 Soviet university professors visited the University of Cincinnati to study the cooperative education concept. After the visits, it was reported that it was expected that cooperative education would be introduced immediately in seventy-five or more colleges in the Soviet Union, involving initially some 40,000 students. Less than one year later, another visiting Soviet professor reported that approximately 65,000 engineering students had been put on the cooperative basis for alternating study and work and that there were also 15,000 cooperative students of agriculture and considerable numbers in forestry and medicine (Park, 1943, pp. 250–255).

It has not been possible to obtain complete and accurate data on the contemporary status of cooperative education in institutions of higher education in the Soviet Union, although there are many indications that the concept is still being widely applied. For example, an article describing the Patrice Lumumba People's Friendship University in Moscow states that students of this university, like regular Soviet students, receive some production practice or on-the-job training in industrial plants or on farms. In the Patrice Lumumba Friendship University curriculum, there are fifteen weeks of such training, compared with twenty-eight weeks in the regular Soviet engineering curriculum.

More than 210 industrial units, experimental farms, research institutions, hospitals, and museums, situated in thirty-five cities, towns, and other population centers in nine union republics of the country provide facilities for training for undergraduates of all the main Lumumba University faculties. On-the-job and field practice is seen as of prime importance for training competent personnel in the Soviet Union (Rosen, 1973, p. 5).

Gerald de l'Ain reports that in 1973 a national education act was voted by the legislature of the Union of Soviet Socialist Republics stating that "practical learning is a constituting part of education." To complete graduation requirements, students must train in their major field of study for at least twenty-one months, divided into two or three training periods (de l'Ain, 1974, pp. 101–103).

In other Eastern European countries, there seem to be similar work requirements for higher education programs. Young people graduating from general vocational schools in Albania, for example, must go through a probation period of one year or more in production work before being eligible to pursue higher education studies. The structure of the school year for university students is seven months of studies, two months of production work, one month of military training, and two months of vacation (*Education for All,* 1973).

In all of the programs in the less developed Eastern European countries, the initial emphasis has been on the creation of technical skills in both vocational and engineering fields. In the past, students were frequently assigned to identical jobs and for the same length of time without regard to their particular specialization. However, measures are being adopted that are aimed at eliminating the shortcomings inherent in the uniform application of practice work. For example, in Romania, the first- and second-year students engage in "initiation into the profession" work periods, each assignment lasting four weeks. This requirement may be fulfilled either by working one day a week or by working the full period toward the end of the academic year. The third- and fourth-year students engage in "specialization practice" work periods, taking four weeks at the end of the academic year. Third-year students concentrate on technology and equipment and fourth-year students on production processes. The final type of practice work is the "practice connected with the elaboration of diploma projects," which lasts three to four months (Braham, 1972, pp. 72–75). In the Hungarian People's Republic, students enrolled in a technical university must work a minimum of thirty weeks in their respective field during the first, fourth, and fifth years of study.

Internships for doctors and nurses have long been established in most parts of the world; the cooperative education concept is also being applied to the education of other workers in the health field. An institute of tropical medicine in Belgium, *Instituut voor tropische geneeskunde Prins Leopold* (Prince Leopold Institute for Tropical Medicine), is attempting to implement a two-year course of epidemiology and control of diseases on a cooperative basis, in spite of such difficulties as the high cost of transporting the students to tropical and developing countries and internal problems at the institute. There is a similar course in France, in which students are sent abroad to Senegal for field training during their months of education in tropical medicine. In a new health education program in Iran, students are alternating periods of study with periods of work under supervision in rural areas (personal communication from P. L. Gigage, coordinator of teaching, *Instituut voor tropische geneeskunde,* January 2, 1976). In Turkey, as part of the program of the faculty of pharmacy at Istanbul University, students participate in one semester of practical training in hospital pharmacies and one semester of training in retail pharmacies. At the school of physical therapy and rehabilitation in Hacettepe University in Ankara, Turkey, health and science majors are required to work for one month at the end of the second year and one month at the end of the third year in the department of physical medicine and rehabilitation at the university's teaching hospital.

Cooperative Education in Africa, the Middle East, and Latin America

Many developing nations are recognizing that higher education in their countries has been a privilege enjoyed by a small minority, that it has tended to be too theoretical and too remote, and that the use of foreign teaching materials has accentuated the alienation of the young people from their environment. Concern over this situation in education is leading education administrators in colleges and universities in the Third World to introduce the cooperative education concept.

Africa. At the University of Mauritius in Réduit degree and diploma courses in the schools of agriculture and industrial technology, particularly in sugar technology, require work experience. In these two schools, mandatory work experience can consist of as much as one third of a student's course time plus additional time on the job during vacations.

The Higher National School of Agronomy in Abidjan, Ivory Coast, requires two months of practical training between the first and second year. Its National School of Administration has a two-year course leading to the certificate and a three-year course leading to a diploma, both incorporating periods of practical work experience in the Ivory Coast and abroad.

In Nigeria the National Universities

Commission recently decreed that 70 percent of the total student enrollment in Nigerian universities should be in science and technology. In accordance with this policy, the Institute of Applied Science and Technology at the University of Ibadan was established as an interdisciplinary, interfaculty enterprise to facilitate greater integration between academic studies and the industrial and social needs of Nigeria and to generate technology for Nigeria's industrial and technological advancement. The cooperative education programs in petroleum, agriculture, forestry, wood engineering, and food technology extend over four years and include ten terms of study and five terms of related employment.

In Sierra Leone it is anticipated that cooperative education will be put on a sounder basis as the government becomes increasingly involved in trade and industry. Cooperative education can help to meet the need for new programs and new emphases within the university and the need to diversify and establish new industries. For example, for the newly established cattle industry, students majoring in agriculture will combine work and study periods on a firm, planned, and meaningful basis.

The faculty of science at the University of Ghana (Accra) now requires its students to work in industry on jobs related to their field of study. The funding for this type of program comes partly from the government and partly from industry.

In the Republic of Senegal the two-year program in the *Institut universitaire de technologie* (University Institute of Technology) combines periods of theoretical instruction at the institute with two-month periods of practical work in enterprises in Dakar. As in the programs in the United States and elsewhere, it has been found that in addition to giving value of a "strict educational character, these practical professional training periods are advantageously establishing contacts between future employers and future employees" (University of Dakar, 1970–71, pp. 659–660).

At the University of South Africa, in Pretoria, some of the degree and diploma programs offered on a cooperative educational basis include the public service law examination, Bachelor of Law (for intending advocates of the Supreme Court), Bachelor of Accounting Science, certificate in the theory of accountancy; and master's degrees in business leadership. In addition, since 1975 the department of psychology requires two periods (of two weeks each) of practical training in each year of the academic program (personal communication from H. T. Gous, director of the Búreau for University Research, January 13, 1976).

At the University of Durban-Westville, in Durban, South Africa, there has been steady growth in the engineering department, where a work-study program is operating. The university feels strongly that the good results already achieved justify the extra effort that is required to run the program (personal communication from H. Reddy, registrar, January 21, 1976). Also in Durban, the University of Natal requires the candidate for the Bachelor of Architecture degree to spend twelve months with a registered architect. The candidate for the Bachelor of Science in quantity surveying degree must include with his studies a period of approved practical experience, normally one year in length (personal communication from G. Blake, registrar, January 13, 1976).

Rand Afrikaans University in Johannesburg, South Africa, does not offer cooperative education in the full sense of the word but does offer some courses in which there is an element of cooperative education. All students majoring in engineering must work for a two-month period in a firm or institution engaged in the branch of engineering they are studying; the placements are arranged by the departments of engineering involved. In transport economics, the students are employed by the Administration of the South African Railways and Harbors, moving in rotation to different divisions of the Railway Administration.

It is anticipated that, in the future, students in communications will be required to work under the supervision of the university during part of their college years in journalism, radio, television, or another branch of communications. Also being considered is a requirement of practical experience strongly related to, and integrated with, theoretical studies in the undergraduate course in business administration (Mosbacker, 1975b, pp. 58–59; personal communication from J. R. Pauw, January 30, 1976).

The Middle East. In Iran the National Iranian Oil Company (NIOC) School of Accountancy and Finance (Tehran), an independent school of higher education, trains accountants for all government and private organizations. The school provides a five-year program in which students are required to undergo practical training in the accounts department of a governmental or private organization during their entire period of academic study.

In Saudi Arabia the University of Petroleum and Minerals (Dhahran) offers five-year work-study programs in engineering, science, data processing, and industrial management. The students are required to work in industry either in Saudi Arabia or abroad for a total of twenty-eight weeks. Successful completion of the work assignments, with a satisfactory rating and an acceptable written report, carries nine semester hours academic credit; the grade contributes full weight to the student's cumulative grade point average (Cooperative Program Regulation Committee, 1975; personal communication with A. A. Ai-Akkad, director of cooperative programs and alumni, University of Petroleum and Minerals, Dhahran, Saudi Arabia, June 1975).

At the Technical University of Istanbul, Turkey, students in architecture and civil engineering are required to complete a minimum of twenty-four weeks of practical training; twenty-six weeks are required of those in electrical and mechanical engineering. Students majoring in chemistry work two months in a chemical institute or chemical plant in the diploma program.

Latin America. In Brazil cooperative education has been introduced on a sound basis in three of the country's leading universities: *Universidade federal de São Carlos* (Federal University of San Carlos), *Universidade federal de Santa Catarina* (Federal University of Saint Catherine), and *Universidade federal da Paraíba* (Federal University of Paraíba) (Mosbacker, 1975b, p. 61). The programs are exclusively in the engineering disciplines, with approximately seven hundred students on paid assignments with fifty-six business employers. All of the programs are college based, five years in length, with the practical experience a requirement for graduation (Mosbacker, 1975a, pp. 14–15).

In Chile all students at the *Universidad técnica "Federico Santa Maria"* (Technical University "Federico Santa Maria," Valparaíso) and at the *Universidad austral de Chile* (Southern University of Chile, Valdivia) and 80 percent of those at the *Universidad católica de Chile* (Catholic University of Chile, Santiago) are required to complete work periods to qualify for graduation in agriculture, architecture, business, engineering, health professions, physical sciences and mathematics, technologies, and vocational arts (information from questionnaires sent in preparation for Mosbacker, 1975a).

A report on the expanding technical education program in Venezuela points out that in order for the educational centers to produce experts with the right kind of practical training, a need exists for much closer links with industry than is usually the case in Latin America (Ardagh, 1974). As one step toward solving the problem, a number of universities in Venezuela are turning to cooperative education and similar programs. At the center specializing in petrochemicals, biochemicals, and food technology at the *Universidad de Oriente* (University of Oriente, Cumaná), the confidence of the local industries is being gained in part through the performance of the students who are employed by the industries during their sandwich course work assignments. A new polytechnic for engineers and technicians in the steel town of Ciudad Guayana, working closely with the local factories, has elaborate sandwich courses for its students. A cooperative education program is being implemented at the *Instituto pedagogía de Barquisimeto* (Pedagogical Institute of Barquisimeto) in the fields of agriculture, mechanics, business education, and electricity. At *Universidad Simón Bolívar* in Caracas, a cooperative education program for engineers was introduced in July 1972; practice periods are scheduled during two long vacations and one trimester, in lieu of academic study, in the fourth year (Mosbacker, 1975b, p. 53).

In Cuba the Castro government planned to include practical training in its educational programs in order to bring about a "smaller investment in laboratories, better utilization of industrial installations, more solid theoretical and practical training, higher technical level in industrial centers, and the training of worker-technician-engineer teams as the base of the skilled labor force needed in Cuban industry" (Read, 1969). Cooperative education is the general rule in the three Cuban universities at Santa Clara, Santiago de Cuba, and Havana. There is daily alternation between work and study that continues throughout the student's entire university program (de l'Ain, 1974, pp. 95–98).

Cooperative Education in Asia

When the heavy industries and chemical industries, key industries in the Republic of Korea, began to show rapid progress in the 1970s, the government decided to introduce cooperative education on a nationwide basis. In 1973 an industry-education promotion law was revised to require schools to offer cooperative education programs to all students and to require industries to provide the facilities for relevant work experience. Students in agriculture, technical, marine, and fisheries colleges are em-

ployed for two four-month periods, two six-month periods, and one six- to twelve-month period of practical training selected by their college and supervised by professors assigned to particular industries. If a college encounters difficulty in securing the cooperation of industry, ministries in the central government assume the role of mediation on the request of the college (Mosbacker, 1975b, pp. 60–61).

In the Democratic People's Republic of Korea in 1959, work experience became mandatory in all school programs classified as "junior middle" schools or higher. Each college or technical school was required by law to assemble a factory for training purposes as well as for productive purposes. A "mother factory" was established in several major colleges to furnish small colleges and technical schools with the necessary equipment and facilities.

During the Cultural Revolution in the People's Republic of China, the curriculum in the university programs was redesigned, making practical work experience a prerequisite to university entrance as well as a major part of the curriculum. The students, regardless of their major, are expected to work up to four months a year. As in other parts of the world, relevant assignments have been easier to obtain in science and engineering than in the liberal arts. While the students in science and engineering are provided work experience related to their disciplines in Chinese industries, the liberal arts students, concentrating mostly on political theory, go out into society three months each year and work in such places as factories, shops, newspapers, or the docks (Ferriman, 1974).

At the University of the Philippines (Quezon City), a form of cooperative education exists within specific academic units. Internship training of students from the college of public administration is undertaken in some government offices, and a consortium has been established by De La Salle College (Manila), Ateneo de Manila University (Quezon City), and the University of the Philippines for degree programs in mathematics and the physical sciences (Mosbacker, 1975b, p. 60).

At the Derrick Technical Institute in Fiji, two types of cooperative education programs are offered to students in business, engineering, maritime studies, hotel and catering studies, the physical sciences, and mathematics. The first type consists of sandwich courses, in which students alternate full-time periods of academic study with periods of paid full-time employment; the second type consists of day-release courses, an industry-based program through which young people are released from work one or two days a week to attend full-time classes for relevant studies (Mosbacker, 1975b, p. 60).

It is reported that cooperative education is being offered in India in seventeen engineering college degree programs and in forty-three polytechnics in diploma courses. The programs are usually labeled sandwich courses after the British custom; many involve the alternation of periods of full-time academic study with several periods of full-time employment. For example, at the Murugappa Chettiar Memorial Polytechnic in Madras, which started its sandwich course program five years ago, the twelve months of field training are arranged in three phases of three months, three months, and six months (personal communication from G. Rama Rao, principal, December 31, 1975). At the C.I.T. Sandwich Polytechnic in Coimbatore, after twelve months of academic study, the students work for six months, return to the campus for six months, work for six months, and complete their academic studies in the remaining twelve months (personal communication from K. Palaniswami, superintendent, December 31, 1975).

The latest development affecting cooperative education in India is the Apprentice Act of 1974, which includes candidates enrolled in sandwich courses. Under this act, most of the major industries are obliged to take a certain number of student trainees in engineering, give them one year of training, and pay them stipends as designated

in the act. Of the total stipends paid by an employer, 50 percent is reimbursed from government funds. As a result of this act, the institutions of higher education in India have available to them a much wider spectrum of establishments in which to place their students for suitable training.

G. Rama Rao, principal of the Murugappa Chettiar Memorial Polytechnic, has cited some definite advantages of the cooperative system of education in India. It is his observation that cooperative students have a better understanding of the course content and of its applications and that they develop a "bold attitude" and a spirit of inquiry in meeting people and discussing problems. They also seek clarification from faculty and from library books for problems they encounter. (The idea of referring to books beyond textbooks is practically absent in the case of regular students, whose study is generally examination-oriented.) According to Rama Rao, sandwich course candidates have developed a problem-solving attitude in addition to obtaining all the knowledge necessary to face the examination.

He also notes that the percentage of sandwich course candidates from the institution passing the final (external) examination has been very high (90 to 100 percent) and that most candidates have secured first-class degrees. In addition, there is a great demand by employers for sandwich course candidates.

Finally, Rama Rao points out that the stipend that is paid while on industrial placement or field training attracts some candidates who could not otherwise go through the course because of financial difficulties. Thus, students from poorer sections of Indian society have also been drawn or inducted into the course (personal communication from G. Rama Rao, December 31, 1975).

Other Forms and Benefits of Cooperative Education

Several interesting developments in the attempt to meet the pressing needs of developing nations could be called offshoots of the educational philosophy of cooperative education. In Brazil's *"Projeto rondo"* thousands of university seniors participate in training and work programs in Brazil's wastelands and rain forests. The students both learn firsthand the immense economic and social problems besetting their country and provide much-needed professional manpower to overcome these problems. In addition to *Projeto rondo,* which covers all of Brazil, several universities have organized programs, called *Centro rural universitario de treinamento agro comunitaria* (CRUTAC: Rural University Center of Agricultural Community Training), in local areas to provide similar experiences for their students (Haussman, 1973).

Concerned by the alienation of educated young people from their social, economic, and cultural environment, Haile Selassie University (now Addis Ababa University) in Ethiopia launched the Ethiopian University Service, a program that requires every university student to spend one academic year in the provinces doing rural service in his or her field of training to qualify for a degree or diploma. The first group, of 129 students, was assigned to the provinces in 1964. During the ten-year period from 1964 to 1974, 3759 students participated successfully in the program.

In France a program that attempts to relate theory and practice is related to the cooperative education concept. Legislation on technology and continuing education adopted by the French National Assembly grants workers time off to attend government-approved programs of continuing education (the "worker's sabbatical"). The employees continue to receive a salary during their time off for classes, paid partly by the government and partly by the worker's employer, and they continue to build up vacation, seniority, and fringe benefits (Wanner, 1973, pp. 1–24).

In Austria the parliament has recently adopted legislation for the creation of a *Verwaltungsakademie* (Administrative Academy) designed to offer career education to government employees. It will provide civil servants already employed by federal agencies with the opportunity to continue their education.

Cooperative education and similar programs can be found in operation in all parts of the world. As educational leaders everywhere are faced with the formidable task of preparing young people to live successfully in societies characterized by very rapid change, it is increasingly being recognized that education has to be more than an inculcation of theoretical knowledge and teaching skills, that theory and practice should go together, and that practice will illuminate learning.

Bibliography

Ardagh, J. "Training Rides High on Crest of Oil Wave." *Times (London) Higher Education Supplement,* September 13, 1974, p. 11.

Braham, R. L. *Education in Romania: A Decade of Change.* Washington, D.C.: U.S. Government Printing Office, 1972.

David, H. *"Gedo nulli* (I Yield for No One)." *Circuit Magazine,* Netherlands Emigration Board, 1968, *24,* 18–21.

de l'Ain, B. G. *L'enseignement supérieur en alternance.* Paris: La documentation française, Association d'étude pour l'expansion de la recherche scientifique, 1974.

de l'Ain, B. G., Bernard, M. Y., Collet, O., and Delors, J. *Enseignement alterné et formation à la gestion.* Paris: Fondation nationale pour l'enseignement de la gestion, 1975.

Education for All. Tiranë, Albania: Naim Frasheri, 1973.

Ferriman, A. "Leaping Forward by Choosing the Hardest Way." *Times (London) Higher Education Supplement,* March 29, 1974, p. 11.

Goote, M. (Ed.) *The Kingdom of the Netherlands: Education and Science.* The Hague: Netherlands Ministry of Education and Science, 1973–74.

Haussman, F. "Projeto Rondo: Brazil's Domestic Peace Corps." *Saturday Review/World,* 1973, *1*(3), 50–51.

Kombinationsutbildning. Stockholm: Office of the Chancellor of the Swedish Universities, 1975–76.

Lancaster, G. M. "The Status of Cooperative Education in Canada." Paper presented at the annual conference of the Canadian Association for Cooperative Education, University of Waterloo, Ontario, September 1974.

Lancaster, G. M. *The Current Status of Cooperative Education in Canada.* London, Ontario: Fanshawe College, 1975.

Mosbacker, W. B. *Growth and Development of Cooperative Education in Countries Outside of the United States.* Cincinnati, Ohio: University of Cincinnati, 1975a.

Mosbacker, W. B. "Growth and Development of Cooperative Education Outside of the United States." *Journal of Cooperative Education,* 1975b, *12,* 49–65.

Park, C. W. *Ambassador to Industry.* Indianapolis, Indiana: Bobbs-Merrill, 1943.

Read, G. H. "New Politics for Cuban Education." *School and Society,* 1969, *97*(2318), 290–292.

"The Regional College." In *Norway Information.* Oslo: Royal Norwegian Ministry of Foreign Affairs, 1973.

Rosen, S. M. *The Development of People's Friendship University in Moscow.* Publication (OE) 72-132. Washington, D.C.: U.S. Department of Health, Education and Welfare, 1973.

"The Swedish Educational System." In *Fact Sheets on Sweden.* Stockholm: Swedish Institute, 1972.

Swedish Ministry of Education and Cultural Affairs. *Higher Education in Sweden: A Survey.* Stockholm: Swedish Ministry, 1973.

University of Dakar. *Annuaire de l'Université de Dakar.* Dakar, Senegal: University of Dakar, 1970–71.

University Studies in the Netherlands: The Engineering Studies. The Hague: Netherlands University Foundation for International Cooperation, 1974–75.

University Studies in the Netherlands: The Gamma Studies. The Hague: Netherlands University Foundation for International Cooperation, 1974–75.

Wanner, R. *A French Approach to Career Education.* Washington, D.C.: U.S. Government Printing Office, 1973.

Wilson, J. W., and Brown, S. J. "Survey of Cooperative Education 1975." *Journal of Cooperative Education,* 1975, *12,* 33–43.

WANDA B. MOSBACKER

COOPERATIVE EXTENSION
See Independent Study.

COOPER-HEWITT MUSEUM OF DECORATIVE ARTS AND DESIGN
See Smithsonian Institution.

COORDINATING COMMITTEE FOR INTERNATIONAL VOLUNTARY SERVICE
(Comité de coordination du service volontaire international)

The Coordinating Committee for International Voluntary Service (CCIVS), an international, nongovernmental organization, was founded by twenty affiliated organizations attending the First Conference of Organizers of International Voluntary Workcamps convened by UNESCO in 1948. Initially concerned with short-term voluntary service, by the early 1960s the committee was sending skilled volunteers from industrialized countries to work for one or two years in developing countries. CCIVS has 122 affiliated organizations, including some 50 national and 18 international organizations with branches in more than one hundred countries. About one third of the affiliates are located in developing countries. Of the 122 affiliates, 86 are member organizations with the right to vote in committee conferences. The remaining affiliates are corresponding organizations that may utilize all committee services and participate in committee meetings but have no vote. Both categories of affiliates make annual financial contributions to CCIVS.

Every two years a general conference is convened to decide the committee's general program and budget. The general conference elects an executive committee, composed of twenty-four organizations elected to assure regional, political, and program representation. Meeting at least twice a year, the executive committee elects its own officers and appoints the director of the secretariat. The secretariat, headed by a director and deputy director, assures the day-to-day administration and execution of the committee's program.

The CCIVS Latin America Regional Centre for Voluntary Service, based in Santiago, Chile, is supported by the committee's affiliates in that region. Every two years, the center has an assembly meeting to adopt a program and budget and elect officers. The center collects and publishes information concerning volunteer activities in Latin America and organizes leadership training sessions and seminars.

CCIVS gathers and disseminates ideas and information on existing voluntary service programs and answers over six thousand requests every year from individuals and organizations interested in voluntary service. It aids voluntary service organizations through regional seminars for leadership training, services, and fund raising for special projects. The secretariat serves as a clearinghouse to match requests for volunteers with available candidates throughout the world, particularly in conjunction with the United Nations Volunteers Program.

The secretariat provides a directory of organizations involved in international service; the directory also gives information about the aims and functions of these agencies. Research papers, reports, and books on voluntary service are also made available to interested individuals or organizations.

CCIVS publishes a monthly bulletin giving news about the activities of volunteer organizations and publishes *Volunteer World,* a quarterly review.

1 rue Miollis
Paris XV, France

COORDINATION COMMITTEE OF FACULTY ORGANIZATIONS IN THE INSTITUTES OF HIGHER LEARNING IN ISRAEL

The Coordination Committee of Faculty Organizations in the Institutes of Higher Learning in Israel represents faculty associations in the following institutions: Hebrew University of Jerusalem; Technion—Israel Institute of Technology, Haifa; Weizmann Institute, Rehovot; Tel Aviv University; Bar-Ilan University, Ramat Gan; Haifa University; Ben-Gurion University, Beersheba.

Each institution has its own faculty association, which represents the institution in negotiations over pay and working con-

ditions. The larger universities have two such associations, one representing the junior faculty and the other representing the senior. Each of these associations is elected by a general meeting or by secret ballot, according to its statutes. The faculty associations' activities include providing for insurance services at reduced rates, acquiring and selling products at wholesale prices, giving children's parties on holidays, and welcoming new faculty members and visitors.

Technion—Israel Institute of
   Technology
Haifa, Israel

S. BRANDES

COPYRIGHTS

Copyright is, simply put, the legal right to prohibit the copying of original literary, artistic, or musical works. It is the right of the author or his successors in interest. In many foreign languages the term for copyright is "the right of the author"; for example, *le droit d'auteur* in French and *das Urheberrecht* in German. The act prohibited is copying and certain other uses that have been assimilated to copying by statute or court decision. For material to qualify for copyright protection, it must be original; that is, the author must have created it without copying from another source. Thus, the entire system pivots on copying: one is entitled to a copyright only by producing a work without copying, and one infringes a copyright only by copying.

Development of British and American Copyright Law

Although the basic notion of copyright was apparently known in early English common law, and although there were statutes in some countries that seem to embody some of its principles, copyright law as such is one of the children of Gutenberg in that it grew out of the conditions resulting from the invention and development of modern printing. While printing in the sixteenth and seventeenth centuries was under royal control, the eighteenth century saw in England the enactment of a law called the Statute of Anne, which provided that, beginning in 1710, "the author of any book or books...shall have the sole liberty of printing and reprinting such book or books" for a period of fourteen years measured from the date of first publication, with the right of renewal on the expiration of the first term by the author, if then living, for another period of fourteen years. Though the Statute of Anne by its own terms applied only to Great Britain, it and the leading court decisions interpreting it were well known in America. During the period of the Articles of Confederation all the thirteen states except Delaware enacted protective statutes, each different in some details from the others, but all largely modeled on the Statute of Anne.

When the Constitution of the United States was drawn up and adopted, it contained in Article I, Section 8, the provision that "Congress shall have Power... To promote the Progress of Science and useful Arts, by securing for limited Times to Authors and Inventors the exclusive Right to their respective Writings and Discoveries." This provision has remained the constitutional basis for federal copyright statutes and patent laws. In 1790 the Second Session of the First Congress enacted the first United States copyright act, which secured protection to the authors of "any map, chart, book or books" under the conditions of the act, again along the same general lines as the Statute of Anne and, like it, designated as "an act for the encouragement of learning." While there have been more than fifty amendments over the years, there have been only three general revisions of the copyright statute: (1) in 1831, when new classes of copyrightable material, including musical compositions, were added, and the first term of protection was increased from fourteen to twenty-eight years, with the renewal term remaining fourteen years; (2) in 1870, when the

law was generally recast and copyright deposit and registration were centralized for the first time in the Library of Congress rather than remaining with the United States district courts; and (3) in 1909, when the present copyright law was enacted.

The present law. The copyright law (Title 17 of the United States Code), which is the act of 1909 as amended, establishes what is essentially a dual system. From the time a work is created until it is published or copyrighted under the provisions of the statute, it is protected by the common law of the states against copying, publication, or use without the consent of the author or his successors. So works that remain unpublished and uncopyrighted are protected without limitation in time and without any formalities whatever.

When a work that has been enjoying the common-law protection is published, that protection terminates and one of two things happens. If the copyright-notice provisions of the law are complied with, statutory copyright is secured by that act; but if the work is published without the copyright notice as required by the law, the right to obtain a copyright is irretrievably lost. As to works published with notice, the law also calls for the copyright owner to make registration by sending to the Copyright Office, Library of Congress, Washington, D.C. 20559, promptly after publication, two copies of the best edition of the work, an application for registration, and the required fee. Statutory copyright may also be secured for certain unpublished materials.

Publication in the copyright sense is generally regarded as the public distribution of copies of the work. The copyright notice is the legend consisting, in the case of a book, of the word *Copyright,* the abbreviation *Copr.,* or the letter *C* enclosed within a circle, accompanied by the name of the copyright owner, and the year date of first publication—for example, © by John Doe 1975. This notice is to be placed on the title page of the book or on the page immediately following. Statutory requirements as to the form and position of the notice vary with the kind of material. Sound recordings call for a special kind of notice consisting of the symbol Ⓟ (the letter *P* in a circle together with the name of the copyright owner of the sound recording and the year date of its first publication. The statute and detailed instructions based thereon, should therefore be consulted before a work is reproduced in copies and published.

Another important condition of United States copyright protection in the case of certain books, periodicals, and separate lithographs and photoengravings, particularly those by authors who are United States citizens or domiciliaries, is that these materials must be first published using copies manufactured in the United States. This provision, called the "manufacturing clause," also restricts as a condition of copyright the importation into the United States of foreign-manufactured copies of the English-language books and periodicals to which it extends. However, it does permit an interim copyright for these works and the importation of 1500 copies, upon the fulfillment of certain conditions specified in the statute.

Statutory copyright may also be secured for certain unpublished materials by making registration in the Copyright Office.

The law provides that the works for which copyright may be secured include books, periodicals, lectures and similar works prepared for oral delivery, dramas, musical compositions, maps, works of art, reproductions of works of art, drawings and sculptural works of a scientific or technical character, photographs, prints and pictorial illustrations, prints and labels for articles of merchandise, motion pictures, and sound recordings. The law accords to the copyright owner the exclusive right to "print, reprint, publish, copy, and vend the copyrighted work" and grants him the exclusive right to make adaptations, such as translations, dramatizations, arrangements, and other new versions. Moreover, it provides, subject to various limitations,

the right to make a sound recording of the work and to perform the work in public. These limitations include the "compulsory licensing" provision, which allows recordings to be made by third persons, upon payment of a royalty specified in the statute, without the consent of the copyright owner of the musical composition, provided that the owner has authorized an initial recording. For musical compositions and nondramatic literary works, only the right of public information *for profit* is granted by the statute.

The duration of copyright under the statute is twenty-eight years. In the case of a work originally copyrighted in unpublished form, this period begins on the date of registration; for published works it begins on the date of first publication. In either case a second period of copyright may be secured if a renewal claim is registered in the Copyright Office in the name of the author or other category of claimant specified in the statute, during the last year of the original twenty-eight-year term. If no renewal registration is made, United States copyright protection for the work ceases and cannot be revived. The period of renewal copyright is also twenty-eight years, making a total of fifty-six years. But by a series of special acts of Congress the period of protection for renewed copyrights has been extended, so that works copyrighted as early as September 19, 1906, can still be under protection if they were renewed. It is important to note, however, that the time limits for renewal registration are strict and remain unchanged.

New law effective January 1, 1978. The foregoing information, which pertains to the United States, is still copyright law in this country. A new law, to become effective on January 1, 1978, was enacted by the United States Congress in 1976. This represents the first major revision of the copyright law of the United States Code in over fifty years. It is the result of over twenty years of consideration by the Congress and organizations representing the interests of authors, and of users of copyrighted works.

The new act provides for a single national system of protection. For example, as to most works created after the new law takes effect, the term of protection shall be the life of the author plus fifty years after his death. However, for works already under statutory protection when the new law enters into force, the period of protection remains twenty-eight years, with a renewal term of forty-seven years; thus although the renewal requirement will not apply to new works, it will remain necessary to make renewal registration for works which are in their first term of statutory protection when the new act takes effect, if such works are to be protected beyond the twenty-eight-year first term.

The five fundamental and exclusive rights granted to copyright holders by the revised copyright bill are those of reproduction, adaptation, publication, performance, and display. Of interest to educators and librarians is the delineation of the concept of *fair use* (or *fair dealing,* as it is known in other English-speaking countries), which is not mentioned in earlier United States copyright statutes; the new law sets forth certain factors to be considered in determining whether a particular use is "fair use." In addition, the new act exempts certain libraries and archives from liability in reproducing and providing copies under certain specified circumstances.

In addition to the above provisions, the revised copyright law extends protection to two new areas of use—jukebox and cable television use of copyrighted works. Also, the clause requiring that certain works be manufactured in the United States to be eligible for United States copyright protection is to be eliminated entirely on July 1, 1982.

The Copyright Office. The primary functions of the Copyright Office, which is a department of the Library of Congress, are to register claims to copyright, to record assignments of copyrights, to publish a *Catalog of Copyright Entries,* and to maintain as a public record the Copyright Card Catalog and the various documents filed there. In addition the office provides to members of the public search reports based on its records at an hourly fee established by law. Application forms, circulars, and other general information on copyright are supplied free on request. Although the office is located in Crystal Mall, 1921 Jefferson Davis Highway, Arlington, Virginia, its mailing address is Copyright Office, Library of Congress, Washington, D.C. 20559. In 1975 it registered more than 400,000 claims to copyright in all categories combined (including 28,000 renewals), recorded over 8000 assignments, and provided search reports on over 100,000 titles.

Limitations on Scope of Copyright Protection

Nothing in copyright law provides any limitation or brake on creative spontaneity because, as mentioned, a work created independently and without taking material by another cannot be a copyright infringement. Moreover, it is an established principle of the law that ideas are not copyrightable apart from their expression in particular works. Therefore, an idea taken from a work without using the expression in that work is not considered a copyright infringement. Although mere paraphrasing takes more than the idea and may infringe, expressing entirely in one's own way ideas taken from other sources is not a copyright infringement. Similarly, taking a particular fact from another's work and embodying it in one's own manner of expression is not prohibited by the copyright law.

Names, titles, slogans, other short phrases, and material in the public domain are not as such copyrightable, since the courts have held that the copyright law does not concern itself with writings containing only a minimal amount of original expression. Similarly, utilitarian features are not copyrightable, since copyright concerns itself solely with the nonfunctional aspects of a work. This is not to say that these things are incapable of any form of protection. Names, titles, emblems, and the like, may be protected as trademarks, or under the principles of unfair competition, or by special statutory enactments; unpublished facts and ideas may be protected as trade secrets; and the functional features of a work may be protected by the patent law. But they are not within the scope of copyright protection.

Perhaps the most far-reaching practical problem in copyright involves the principle of "fair use." In effect, fair use is the rule of reason applied in copyright infringement actions, and it means that not every use in contravention of the statute is actionable. Thus, for example, the copying by one scholar of a single sentence from a three-volume work by another scholar would probably be a fair use, but his copying an entire volume would almost certainly not be. In dealing with what is "fair" or "reasonable," the question is where to draw the line; no adequate rule of thumb can be devised, since each case must depend upon its own circumstances. In fact, fair use is not referred to in the present United States copyright statute; the statute speaks of the rights of the copyright owner, and it has been the judges in deciding cases who have enunciated and applied the principle of fair use. In what seems to be the first American case raising the question, Justice Joseph Story in *Folsom* v. *Marsh* (1841) 9 Fed.Cas. 342, No. 4901 (C.C.D. Mass. 1841), formulated in the following words a list of the factors to be considered, which has been generally used in coping with this issue: "In short, we must in deciding questions of this sort, look to the nature and objects of the selections made, the quantity and value of the materials used, and the degree in which the use may prejudice the sale, or diminish the profits, or supersede the objects, of the original work." Probably the largest area where problems of fair use arise today is that of photocopying. In the narrow context the problem is usually whether in a particular instance the photocopying supersedes the actual or potential market of the copyright owner for his work. In the broad context the question is the extent to which all the photocopying of copyrighted works affects the market for those works and the attainment of the ends that the Congress seeks to promote through the copyright law. Among the elements that lend special difficulty to the overall problem are the claims of imperative need by science in general and the life sciences in particular, and the aspirations of educators who feel they must use copies of materials on current events to take advantage of the "teachable moment."

International Aspects of Copyright

There is in law no such thing as a world copyright. Rather, there are as many copyrights in a particular work as there are countries which recognize rights in that work. Thus, for a work by an American there may be, in addition to the American copyright, a Canadian copyright, a United Kingdom copyright, a French copyright, and so forth. Since the copyright laws of the different countries vary considerably from one another, the principle upon which most international agreements on copyright are founded is "national treatment"—the concept that a country will protect foreign works in the same way that it protects its own works.

One means of international cooperation on copyright is through bilateral agreements. Under legislation passed in 1891, for example, the United States began formulating bilateral copyright agreements with foreign nations in accordance with the principle of national treatment, with the result that in 1977 the United States had bilateral relations with thirty-seven foreign countries, as evidenced by treaties and presidential proclamations.

Another means of instituting copyright relations is through multilateral treaties. These conventions are generally based on national treatment and also contain provisions for certain basic requirements to which the laws of a country must conform in order for it to be eligible for membership. The United States is a member of two such conventions of significance: the Buenos Aires Convention (BAC) and the Universal Copyright Convention (UCC).

The BAC, which the United States ratified in 1911, forms a basis for copyright relations between seventeen Central and South American nations and the United States. It specifies that the authors of any signatory state shall enjoy "the rights that the respective laws accord" in all the other signatory countries to their own works, without the necessity of complying with any formality, "provided always there shall appear in the work a statement that indicates the reservation of the property right." As a result of this provision many works bear such words as "All Rights Reserved" or *Todos los derechos reservados,* although these words are not required by the United States copyright statute and their use is not considered a substitute for United States copyright notice or for renewal registration, both of which are prescribed by the United States law.

The United States adhered to the original version of the UCC in 1955 and to the revised version in 1974. This important convention, of which there are more than sixty-five major member states, provides that the works of nationals of any member state and works first published in a member state shall enjoy national treatment. Furthermore, any member state that requires under its domestic law compliance with formalities such as deposit, original registration, notice, notarial certificates, payment of fees, or manufacture or publication in that state "shall regard these requirements as satisfied with respect to all works protected in accordance with this Convention and first published outside its territory and the author of which is not one of its nationals, if from the time of its first publication all the copies of the work published with the authority of the author or other copyright proprietor bear the symbol © accompanied by the name of the copyright proprietor and the year of first publication placed in such manner and location as to give reasonable notice of claim of copyright." Although the UCC reduces the number of formalities among the member states, it is not considered to remove such requirements as that of renewal registration under the United States law. The recently revised version of the UCC enumerates certain basic rights of authors and provides within the framework of the constitution special exceptions for the benefit of developing countries, permitting them to institute procedures for the compulsory licensing, under certain conditions, of translations and reproductions of works for educational purposes.

Through one or more of these means, the United States has copyright relations with more than half of the nations of the world, including virtually all the major producers of intellectual materials. In addition, in 1974 the United States became party to the Convention for the Protection of Producers of Phonograms Against Unauthorized Duplication of Their Phonograms, which combats the widespread unauthorized duplication of phonograph records, tapes, and similar aural fixations of sounds by providing that each contracting state shall protect producers who are nationals of other contracting states against the reproduction, for distribution to the public, of their works without their consent. This convention provides that if, as a condition of protecting the producers of phonograms, a contracting state requires formalities, these shall be considered to be fulfilled by the use of the symbol ℗, accompanied by the year date of first publication and the name of the producer or his successors in interest.

Notice should also be taken of the Bern Convention for the Protection of Library and Artistic Works, and revisions thereof, to which the United States is not a party; under this convention (whose framers were inspired by the proposition that copyright is not so much a grant to the author in the public interest as a recognition of one of the natural rights of man) protection applies to works by authors who are nationals of one of the member countries and to works first published in a member country, and the "enjoyment and the exercise of these rights shall not be subject to any formality." Also of general international significance as a long-range goal is Article 27 of the Universal Declaration of Human Rights, adopted in 1948 by the General Assembly of the United Nations, which states: "Everyone has the right to the protection of the moral and material interests resulting from any scientific, literary or artistic production of which he is the author."

The Future

If present trends continue, it seems clear that the demands of education, especially in the developing countries; increases in literacy and in world population; and the market created, particularly in the developed countries, by the amusement industries, which seems to grow in proportion to the increase in leisure time, all offer fertile ground for the expanding production of copyrightable materials. Concurrently, the hastening pace of modern life and the ready availability of machines for the capturing and multiplication of copyrighted works appear to call for new modes of remuneration for authors. It remains to be seen whether legal mechanisms can be successfully devised within the traditional concepts of copyright law to accommodate both society and authors.

Bibliography

Bogsch, A. L. *The Law of Copyright Under the Universal Convention.* (3rd ed. rev.) Leiden, Netherlands: A. W. Sijthoff; New York: Bowker, 1968.

Copyright Laws and Treaties of the World. (2 vols.) Paris: UNESCO; Washington, D.C.: Bureau of National Affairs, 1956. Kept up to date by annual supplements.

Drone, E. S. *A Treatise on the Law of Poverty in Intellectual Productions in Great Britain and the United States.* Boston: Little, Brown, 1879.

Latmon, E. (Ed.) *Howell's Copyright Law.* (4th ed. rev.) Washington, D.C.: Bureau of National Affairs, 1962.

Lindey, A. *Entertainment, Publishing, and the Arts: Agreements and the Law.* New York: Clark Boardman, 1963–. (Looseleaf.)

Nimmer, M. B. *Nimmer on Copyright.* Albany, New York: M. Bender, 1963–. (Looseleaf.)

Weil, A. W. *The American Copyright Law.* Chicago: Callaghan, 1917.

Winkler, K. J. "A Sweeping Revision of the Copyright Laws." *Chronicle of Higher Education,* 1976, *14*(6), 1, 12.

WALDO H. MOORE

See also: Legal Aspects of Higher Education.

CÓRDOBA MANIFESTO, THE (Higher Education Report), Argentina

In 1918 Argentine students at the National University of Córdoba presented their demands for university reform in the Córdoba Manifesto *(Manifesto of Argentine Youth of Córdoba to the Free Men of South America).* The students denounced the existing university regime because, they felt, it reflected a decadent society. They opposed dogmatic and authoritarian structures that, they felt, isolated the university from science and other modern thought and prohibited effective student participation. The university, in their view, should be more concerned with national problems and a force for Latin American unity.

The manifesto is concerned primarily with the reorganization of the university government. It proposes university autonomy in all its political, instructional, administrative, and economic aspects. Also recommended are the free election of all principal university authorities by the university community; the participation of professors, students, and graduates in all governing bodies; competitive selection of professors and a limited tenure of chairs; instructional freedom; open attendance; and gratuity of instruction.

The manifesto also calls for an academic reorganization of the university. It proposes the creation of new faculties and the modernization of teaching methods, the democratization of university admissions, financial assistance for students, and the extension of the university into the outlying community.

CORPORATE SUPPORT OF HIGHER EDUCATION
See Development, College and University.

CORRECTIONAL INSTITUTIONS
See Prisoners, Postsecondary Education Programs for.

CORRESPONDENCE EDUCATION
See Independent Study.

CORRESPONDENCE STUDY
See Independent Study.

COST ANALYSIS
See Financial Affairs: Cost Analysis.

COST OF LIVING AND REMUNERATION
See Remuneration: Faculty, Staff and Chief Executive Officers.

COSTA RICA, REPUBLIC OF

Population: 1,921,000 (1974). Student enrollment in primary school: 378,175; secondary school (academic, vocational, technical): 135,879; higher education: 32,807. Language of instruction: Spanish. Academic calendar: March to December. Percentage of gross national product (GNP) expended on all education: 5.52% (1974); higher education: .93% (1974). [Except where otherwise indicated, figures are for 1975. Sources: Ministry of Education, Department of Statistics; Banco central de Costa Rica, for GNP percentages.]

Costa Rica, a Spanish colony from conquest in 1530 to 1821, and a member state of the Central American Federation from 1824 to 1838, lacked a cohesive university system during the colonial period and the early years of the republic. On April 24, 1814, the first institution of higher education was established by the municipal government of San José (the capital was then at Cartago) and dedicated to Saint Thomas. In 1823 San José was named the capital. Although the school continued to be managed by the municipal government for almost a year, on December 10, 1824, it was adopted by the national government and awarded a percentage of the state's assets. The official decree of May 3, 1843, established the university; its various governing statutes were adopted on September 1 of the same year. University study was divided into two programs: one, of a preparatory nature, offered courses in Castilian, Latin, arithmetic, geometry, geography, and philosophy; the second was dedicated to the advanced study of theology, jurisprudence, and medicine. The formal dedication of the university took place on March 10, 1844. Its first rector was the priest Don Juan de los Santos Madriz. Prior to the founding of the university, all young Costa Ricans who desired higher education had to enroll either at the University of León in Nicaragua or at the University of San Carlos in Guatemala.

The University of Santo Tomás was created to fulfill a great cultural need. Although its achievements were not always deeply rooted—perhaps because of the colonial influences still apparent in its organization and teachings—it played an important role in the education of the leaders who were to guide the development of Costa Rican democracy during the last forty years of the nineteenth century. These men encouraged passage of laws that would improve the structure of the university and keep it abreast of the social and scientific advancements of the age.

In spite of attempts to preserve the University of Santo Tomás, an institution in which many talented young people found an environment receptive to the development of democratic ideals, by 1887 it had been reduced to nothing more than a School of Law, and in 1888 it was closed by the government of Bernardo Soto. The teaching of law, however, was never interrupted, and this faculty educated men of great civic stature and patriotic spirit.

On July 29, 1890, under the government of Don José Joaquín Rodríguez, the Constitutional Congress overrode the above decree and reestablished the university, but it did not actually start to function. Thus, Costa Rica was without a university for the last twelve years of the nineteenth century and for almost half of the twentieth century. The one higher education institution available was the School of Law, an academic center that gave Costa Rica outstanding jurisconsults for more than a hundred years (*Reforma académica*, 1957).

It was not until August 26, 1940, that the Constitutional Congress passed a law (Law 362) creating the *Universidad de Costa Rica* (University of Costa Rica). Thirty years later, on June 10, 1971, a new law (Law 4777) established the *Instituto tecnológico de Costa Rica* (Technological Institute of Costa Rica). The *Universidad nacional* (National University) was created on February 23, 1973 (Law 5182).

Legal Basis of Educational System

Title VII, Education and Culture, of the constitution of Costa Rica establishes the autonomy of its three institutions of higher learning (Articles 84-88). This document allows for the independent development of all university functions, the unrestricted exercise of all rights and obligations, and administrative autonomy. The state agrees to subsidize the university by allocating the necessary annual grants and contributing to university maintenance no less than 10 percent of the total budget of the Ministry of Public Education. Academic freedom is established as a fundamental right of university education. Each institution of higher education, in accordance with the constitution, draws up its own statutes, regulations, and programs. These must be published, however, in the official newspaper, *La gaceta.*

Types of Institutions

Two types of higher education are now offered in Costa Rica: university and tech-

nological education. The Higher Council of Education is studying the possibilities of authorizing the introduction of a post-secondary education system comparable to that offered by junior colleges in the United States. The system would provide short and complete career training. Its structure would be similar to that now existing for private institutions.

In late 1975, by Decree 5622-E, an executive decision of the government of Costa Rica authorized the founding of the *Universidad autónoma de Centroamérica* (Autonomous University of Central America), a new private center of higher education. According to the decree, the minister of public education or his representative shall form part of the governing bodies of this university and shall direct its policies with both a voice and a vote. This will be the first institution of its kind anywhere in the country.

Relationship with Secondary Education

No real articulation has been established between secondary education (*enseñanza media*) and higher education. However, the Higher Council of Education, an official body in charge of primary and secondary education, has a university representative. This is an attempt, perhaps, to establish some communication between the various levels of education.

The constitution of 1869 made primary education both free and compulsory. Secondary education has been free only since the constitution of 1949. Children between the ages of seven and fourteen must attend school. Legal action is taken against parents who do not allow their children to attend. Generally, a student finishes secondary school at the age of seventeen, after five years of study. Some programs, however, require six years.

Secondary education is offered in two cycles: a three-year general program for all students and a two- or three-year diversified cycle. The programs are academic or vocational (agricultural, commercial, or industrial study) and lead to the title *bachiller* with a mention of the student's field of study. The title *bachiller* is required for entry to the university.

Admission Requirements

Because of the continually increasing number of candidates for admission, the institutions of higher education have had to establish admission examinations (*examen de admisión*). Every applicant must take this examination, and answers are scored in relation to minimum standards of proficiency required for university entrance. Results are published at least one month prior to registration. These examinations are based on aptitude and intellectual capacity rather than on specific academic knowledge. After the posting of results, those admitted must take a battery of aptitude tests, designed to aid them in selecting a professional career. Students are not, however, required to follow the advice of their academic adviser. In addition to these admission examinations, each institution of higher education requires the completion of the secondary school (*enseñanza media*).

Administration and Control

The constitution of Costa Rica includes several articles protecting the autonomy of higher education. The state, however, retains some control by placing the minister of public education, or his representative, on the various governing councils of the university. The controller general of the republic also has some power under the law. The institutions of higher education have internal autonomy: they control their own structure and administration, elect their own governing authorities, and exercise all rights and obligations granted them by the constitution. Academic freedom (*libertad de cátedra*) is a fundamental right.

Internal administration of each higher education institution is under the direction of a university council. This council is composed of professors, administrators, and students (approximately 25 percent of the total number of seats), as well as one representative from the graduate schools.

In some of these bodies, the minister of national planning also has voice and vote. The council is presided over by one of its own members, chosen by secret ballot. Decisions are made by an absolute majority. In some cases a two-thirds majority is required. The rector is a member of the council with a voice but not a vote. The council also has committees that study subjects under discussion.

The rector is assisted by an advisory council (*consejo de rectoría*), comprised of the vice-rectors and student delegates. It has some decision-making power but is mainly responsible for advising the rector. At the lower end of the university hierarchy are the faculties; each has a faculty council, with some student representation. The council is presided over by a dean. The schools (*escuelas*) and chairs (*cátedras*) utilize the same elective system, selecting officers from among their own members. Their decisions and depositions are made within the proper academic and administrative channels. They depend, however, upon the university council for recognition of their authority. Thus, the hierarchical structure of the university leads from the university council to the individual chair.

The administrative bodies are well defined within the system of higher education. Specific regulations determine their radius of action. The rector exercises the greatest authority, which diminishes accordingly through vice-rector, dean, director, faculty head, coordinator, and, finally, professor.

Programs and Degrees

The institutions of higher education offer the diploma *bachillerato* and the titles *licenciado* and *ingeniero* (engineer). Possibly in the next few years a master's degree will be substituted for these last two. The highest degree is *doctor académico* (the doctorate), but it is not yet offered in many fields. In some fields the doctorate is awarded on a professional but not on an academic level. There are also short programs that offer diplomas.

All study is divided into a system of credits: one credit equals one fifty-minute academic session per week during an eighteen-week semester for courses of a theoretical nature. A half credit is awarded in practical courses. The short programs generally require a minimum of sixty-four credits (four semesters of eighteen weeks); the *bachillerato* requires 128 credits (eight semesters); the *licenciatura* and *ingeniería* require no less than 160 credits (ten semesters).

Financing and Student Financial Aid

The constitution allocates an annual grant of at least 10 percent of the budget of the Ministry of Public Education for the maintenance of higher education. In addition, the government has passed several laws which distribute certain taxes for university use. Contributions from the private sector are very rare. Even the Committee for University Development has not been able to effect a substantial increase in aid to higher education.

In an attempt to distribute the payment of registration fees more fairly, students are classified according to their economic status. Certification from the registrar and from the payroll offices of both government and private business, as well as a socioeconomic study of the family, establishes the student's ability to pay. This economic apportionment plays an important role. Once a student has been assigned a given economic status, he must remain in good academic standing. If his work degenerates or his economic status changes, the amount of aid will be decreased or, in some cases, terminated. Under the established system, most students receive some form of aid. Only the most affluent, approximately 10-15 percent of the total student population, pay the full cost.

A work-study program, in which the student earns his tuition, does not exist. Only in a few isolated cases does the student repay the assistance given him.

In 1974 one of the state banks (*Banco anglo costarricense*) established the *Fondo nacional de préstamos para educación* (FONAPE:

National Fund for Loans to Education). In its first year of operation, 156 requests were negotiated. This fund makes loans to students, which they begin to repay only upon graduation. The system will, without doubt, allow more students to continue their education. Because it is a system of loans, rather than grants, the yield is very high.

Student Social Background and Access to Education

It is calculated that 90 percent of the student body are middle class and from rural areas. Applications for admission have increased at an alarming rate, especially considering the limitation of funds, teaching staff, and facilities. In 1975, 13,500 students applied for admission, and only 8000 were accepted. Serious problems confront a society when young people are allowed into the job market with a high school diploma and no specific professional training. In an attempt to relieve this situation, secondary schools are offering preparation in industrial, commercial, and service-related fields. Many young people, however, aspire to greater academic success and feel frustrated when they are refused admission to an institution of higher education. Full recognition has not yet been given to the social and financial success that can accompany careers of a technical nature. This is beginning to change, however, as necessity creates a more practical attitude.

Overall enrollment figures show that a larger percentage of men than women attend university-level institutions. The fields of agriculture, law, economics, engineering, medicine, and chemistry attract more males than females; women dominate the fields of fine arts, education, and social work. Under the constitution, any form of discrimination is prohibited on all levels of the Costa Rican educational system.

Students have organized associations, federations, a system of student government, and cultural and sporting events. The lack of interest in the selection of student officers is notorious. This apathy results in the control of student activities by a small, well-disciplined minority.

Teaching Staff

The teaching profession is regulated in every detail by titles, categories, promotions, salaries, vacations, and competitions. The academic staff comprises five ranks. At the lowest level is the instructor, generally a student who has completed all required course work but has not yet been awarded a degree. At the next level is the full instructor, who must hold a degree. At the professorial level there is the assistant professor (*profesor adjunto*), the associate professor (*profesor asociado*), and the full professor (*catedrático*). Promotion from one step to the next is based on merit, which is evaluated in terms of degrees, independent study, publications, length of service, and other standards of proficiency. To become a full professor, at least fifteen years' teaching experience is required.

Academic freedom (*libertad de cátedra*) is a constitutionally guaranteed right (Article 87). Once hired into the profession, a professor can be dismissed only for behavior directly prejudicial to his ability to teach.

Research Activities

Although higher education institutions have established programs of research, they must depend heavily upon contributions from international organizations, foundations, and government alliances. In the mid 1970s a decision was made that all outside aid must be given without the imposition of any rules or regulations, and agreements are contracted accordingly. Research activities in general are seriously hampered by the difficulty in obtaining funds; however, some progress has been made in practical, applied research.

In 1973 the *Consejo nacional de investigación científica y tecnológica* (CONICIT: National Technological Research) was created. This council, which directs all national matters dealing with research and has proven to be very effective, is a state-run organization.

Current Problems and Trends

A developing country such as Costa Rica, where malnutrition and parasitism are deeply rooted, faces many problems: a constantly growing national and student population and a lack of funds, facilities, and professors. Such obstacles seriously hinder the vigorous development of the educational system. Because of a shortage of funds, thousands of students who hold the title of *bachiller* have been refused entry to higher education. The country is attempting to diversify its system of secondary education, offering technical training to young men and women in the hope that some will pursue careers that do not require university attendance. A postsecondary education system, offering courses similar to those offered by junior colleges in the United States, is also being designed. This would offer a new alternative to students and should alleviate some of the pressure now felt by institutions of higher learning. In the development of teaching methods and programs, every attempt is made to modernize. Economic pressures, however, have limited the development of many plans.

In the late 1950s a reform initiated at the University of Costa Rica (the only university at the time) required every student to begin his university program with no less than two semesters of study in general education. This program was designed to give the student an overall understanding of his culture and to cultivate the classical ideals of the well-educated mind. The reform has had very positive results and has produced significant change in the structure of university study. During the same period, a system of departmentalization was introduced, and the results have also been very satisfactory.

In the field of methodology—and this is true at all three institutions of higher education—every attempt is made to progress with the times. Most notably, student participation is emphasized, and the professor's role as lecturer is deemphasized. This method is believed to strengthen the student's interest and awareness of the problems of the modern world. There are also special preparatory courses and individual tutorials, both regulated by a separate set of rules. In 1975 the quarter system (the division of the academic year into four semesters) was introduced for the first time into several departments of the University of Costa Rica. It is still too early to evaluate the results, but it seems that many positive achievements have been realized. Under this system, the student studies for three of the four quarters instead of the standard two semesters.

An increasing flexibility in academic and administrative organization has prompted growth of interdisciplinary programs. Departmentalization avoids the duplication of courses and, with good coordination, results in an expansion of academic opportunities.

Relationship with Industry

Higher education offers several different industrial programs: industrial chemistry, engineering, and agronomy. The Technological Institute of Costa Rica has a very close relationship with the nation's industry, and its programs and degrees depend heavily on industrial expansion. Most of the practical experience required by the institute's programs is gained in the factories and laboratories of the private sector. Some businesses offer scholarships for advanced technological study, especially for the shorter degree programs. In the few years since its founding (1971), the institute has developed strong ties with the business community.

International Cooperation

The educational institutions of Costa Rica have established joint programs with similar institutions throughout the world. They have, for example, student and faculty exchange programs and joint research proj-

ects. The national universities of Central America have created a confederation, *Confederación universitaria centroamericana* (Central American University Confederation), which maintains a headquarters in San José, Costa Rica. This organization has sponsored many important programs and has received donations from the Ford and Rockefeller Foundations of the United States and the Friedrich Ebert Foundation of Germany. Several governments have also donated materials, scholarships, and grants for student travel.

The Central American Bank of Integration (*Banco centroamericano de integración*) has made loans to many university programs. Similar loans are made by the Interamerican Bank of Development (*Banco interamericano de desarrollo*).

CARLOS A. CAAMAÑO

Bibliography

Actuales estructuras académicas de la educación costarricense. San José: Oficinas de planeamiento de la educación, 1971.

Caamaño, C. A. *Centros universitarios regionales.* San José: Universidad de Costa Rica, 1972.

Caamaño, C. A. *Gobierno y administración universitaria.* San José: Universidad de Costa Rica, 1972.

Caamaño, C. A. *Centro universitario regional de Turrialba: Primeros pasos.* San José: Universidad de Costa Rica, 1975.

Gutiérrez, C. *Un modelo de simulación para planificación universitaria.* San José: Universidad de Costa Rica, Oficina de planificación universitaria, 1972.

Indicadores educativos, 1970–1980. San José: Ministerio de educación pública, Dirección general de desarrollo educativo, 1974.

Karsen, S. *Desenvolvimiento educacional de Costa Rica con la asistencia técnica de la UNESCO, 1951–1954.* San José: Ministerio de educación pública, 1954.

Molima Guzmán, G. *La educación en Costa Rica: Sus problemas y deficiencias.* San José: Editorial Fernández Arce, 1973.

Obregón, L. R. *Los rectores de la Universidad de Santo Tomás de Costa Rica.* San José: Talleres gráficos de trejos hermanos, 1955.

Pérez, H. *Educación y desarrollo: Reto a la sociedad costarricense.* San José: Editorial Costa Rica, 1971.

Reforma académica. Sección cuadernos universitarios No. 4. San José: Universidad de Costa Rica, 1957.

Torres, P. O. *Un estudio de utilización. Los profesionales en servicio social y el mercado de trabajo.* San José: Universidad de Costa Rica, Departamento de publicaciones, 1972.

See also: Adult Education: Adult Education in Developing Countries; Archives: Mediterranean, the Vatican, and Latin America, National Archives of; Central America: Regional Analysis.

COSTS AND POTENTIAL ECONOMIES—UNIVERSITY OF BRADFORD

See Organisation for Economic Co-operation and Development.

COUNCIL FOR ADVANCEMENT AND SUPPORT OF EDUCATION, United States

The Council for Advancement and Support of Education (CASE), a nonprofit organization, was created in 1974 through the merger of the American Alumni Council and the American College Public Relations Association. Assuming the functions of the parent organizations, CASE strives to serve education through six programs: alumni administration, educational fund raising, government relations, institutional relations, publications, and executive management. More than 1800 colleges, universities, two-year colleges, and independent schools, represented by 6700 individuals, are members of CASE.

The council is governed by a twenty-eight-member board of trustees, a nine-person executive committee, and an executive officer. Representatives from eight geographical districts and the six CASE programs serve on the board; other trustees include members-at-large and persons from outside education.

Membership is open to universities, colleges, junior and community colleges, and independent schools in the United States, Canada, Mexico, and overseas. To qualify, United States institutions of higher edu-

cation must be tax-exempt and must be listed in the current *Higher Education Directory* published by the United States Office of Education. Individual campuses or units of colleges and universities hold separate membership if they are located outside the immediate area of the main institution.

Membership dues, based on institutional enrollment, entitle each school, college, or university to a stated number of member representatives, each having equal voting rights. One individual on each campus serves as a liaison between the institution and the national office. Independent alumni associations and university-related foundations may hold separate membership, with their fees determined by the enrollment of the parent organizations. Other categories of affiliation with CASE include educational associates, open to nonprofit-education-related organizations; and subscribers, available to commercial enterprises with activities that complement those of CASE.

Each year CASE holds fifteen to twenty conferences. Topics include corporate and foundation support, the annual fund, small-college development, student recruitment, management, direct mail solicitation, alumni travel programs, CASE-Newsweek Conference on Communications, alumni programs, university-related foundations, and government affairs. Each summer CASE offers week-long institutes in alumni administration, educational fund raising, and communications. These programs feature sequential courses of study, small classes, and experienced faculty members. The CASE annual assembly brings together member representatives from the United States, Canada, Mexico, and abroad. The council's eight geographical districts hold annual conferences.

Through Creative Communications, CASE offers art and photography for use by educational institutions. Original art is commissioned and made available in a form ready for reproduction. Also available is a Creative Communications Idea

Package, which contains newsletters, monographs, and other materials on design and printing production.

The council's extensive recognition program honors superior work in the six CASE programs. Awards identify outstanding professionals and programs that can be emulated on other campuses.

The council monitors federal legislation and regulations, and reports to concerned members via regular publications and special "alerts." One of the seventeen educational associations that make up the Washington Higher Education Secretariat, CASE helps to coordinate activities and responses of the city's educational community. The CASE members on the American Council on Education's committee on taxation speak for the special concerns of educational fund raisers.

The council gathers current data on salaries of personnel in the area of institutional advancement and on the organizational structure of campus advancement offices. Special attention is given to the status of women working in college advancement areas.

The renewal of a special project grant from the United States Department of State has allowed the council to continue a special program for institutions with large numbers of international alumni. Special programs are offered for two-year colleges, independent schools, and independent alumni associations.

The council publishes a monthly magazine, *Case Currents,* as well as books, flyers, and monographs. A monthly *Placement Letter* assists institutions seeking professionals in the area of college advancement. The *Survey of Voluntary Support,* published annually in conjunction with the Council for Financial Aid to Education and the National Association of Independent Schools, reports all nongovernment income received by educational institutions. The council also publishes the *Federal Affairs Handbook,* an outline of aid-to-education programs of the federal government; *Guide to the Administration of Charitable Remainder Trusts;*

Matching Gift Details; and the Matching Gift Leaflet Series. The *CASE Membership Directory* is published annually.
One Dupont Circle
Washington, D.C. 20036 USA

COUNCIL FOR FINANCIAL AID TO EDUCATION, United States

The Council for Financial Aid to Education (CFAE) is a nonprofit service organization that encourages voluntary financial support of higher education, especially by the corporate community. The CFAE was founded in 1952 by five corporation board chairmen: Irving S. Olds, of United States Steel; Alfred P. Sloan, Jr., of General Motors; Frank W. Abrams, of Exxon; Walter P. Paepcke, of the Container Corporation; and Henning W. Prentis, of Armstrong Cork. Originally funded by Carnegie Corporation of New York, Ford Foundation, Rockefeller Foundation, and Alfred P. Sloan Foundation, CFAE now draws its support from more than three hundred United States corporations. Thirty-one business leaders and college or university presidents comprise the board of directors.

Staff members call personally upon hundreds of business leaders every year to explain the financial needs of higher education. CFAE offers counseling services to corporate administrators who want to improve or develop aid-to-education programs. The organization does not solicit or disburse funds for higher education but aims to bring the opportunities and responsibility for voluntary financial support of higher education to the attention of leaders in business, industry, labor, civic and service organizations, and the public.

In cooperation with the Advertising Council, CFAE sponsors the nationwide public service advertising campaign "Give to the college of your choice. Now." The campaign has elicited as much as twenty-five million dollars in free time and space from the media in one year.

CFAE publishes an annual report on voluntary support of colleges and universities, a biennial report on corporate support of higher education, and special studies in educational philanthropy. The organization also issues informational publications and materials designed to help broaden the base of educational support.

680 Fifth Avenue
New York, New York 10019 USA

COUNCIL FOR INTERINSTITUTIONAL LEADERSHIP, United States

The Council for Interinstitutional Leadership became an independent organization in July 1975, after five years of sponsorship by the Kansas City Regional Council and three by the American Association for Higher Education. In October 1975 the council held its first cooperative program seminar in Washington, D.C. The council aims to assist in developing cooperative strategies and programs designed to strengthen postsecondary education; to conduct and encourage research and evaluation in the field of interinstitutional relations; to articulate the philosophy of the voluntary consortium in postsecondary education; and to find ways to make both the philosophy and the practice widely known. Furthermore, the council intends to maintain a service and resource center for the consortia; to play an active role in broadening the numbers and kinds of cooperative agencies; to assist in the continuing education of persons for consortium work; and to represent consortia in appropriate places.

An academic consortium may become a member and send representatives to the council if it is a voluntary formal organization of two or more institutions, has at least one full-time professional person on the staff, requires an annual contribution or other tangible evidence of long-term commitment of its member institutions, and pays annual council dues. Associate membership is open to representatives of any group subscribing to the purposes of the council, and individual membership is open to persons who are in sympathy with the council's aims. Neither associate nor individual members are entitled to vote or hold office, but they may participate in business meetings.

The council's board consists of six executive directors of consortia plus the executive director and two other persons selected by the board. The executive director of the council, appointed by the board, serves as an ex officio member and is entitled to vote. Board meetings are three times a year, and members are elected at the fall meeting. The board manages the business affairs of the council, decides on the spring and fall council meetings, recommends the members' dues, and appoints task forces to carry out the council's work.

Council officers—consisting of a president, a vice-president, and a secretary-treasurer—constitute the executive committee, which conducts routine business subject to review by the board. The executive director is ordinarily present at these meetings but does not vote.

8606 Jones Mill Road
Washington, D.C. 20015 USA

COUNCIL FOR INTERNATIONAL EXCHANGE OF SCHOLARS, United States

The Council for International Exchange of Scholars (CIES) is a nongovernmental organization for international exchanges in the field of higher education. Under contract with the United States Department of State, CIES cooperates in the administration of the Mutual Educational Exchange Program (Fulbright-Hays Act) for scholars interested in lecturing, consultation, and research at the university level.

CIES (until late 1973 the Committee on International Exchange of Persons) was established in 1947 by the Conference Board of Associated Research Councils

(American Council on Education, American Council of Learned Societies, National Research Council, and Social Science Research Council). Since its inception, CIES has participated in the exchange of some 13,000 American and 14,000 foreign scholars.

CIES is composed of thirteen members— a chairperson and three representatives from each of the sponsoring research councils—appointed for overlapping three-year terms. The full council meets twice a year, and a five-member executive group meets when necessary. Subcommittees include planning, operations, and the underrepresented.

Members of CIES also serve on six area advisory committees, each corresponding to one of the Department of State's geographical divisions. Serving with them are a number of committee associates with particular area and discipline competence. The area committees are responsible for nominating panels of American scholars for individual countries, and for reviewing applications of foreign scholars. In the initial review of applications from American scholars, CIES depends upon subject matter screening committees in nearly fifty disciplines or specializations. Screening committee members and area committee associates are approved by the appropriate sponsoring council. Faculty Fulbright advisers at over a thousand American colleges and universities arrange publicity and furnish information on the program.

CIES reviews more than 2500 applications annually from Americans for openings in programs planned abroad by binational educational foundations and commissions in some forty-five countries, and by the United States embassies in approximately forty-five others. About one thousand nominations are made each year for more than five hundred awards. Approximately 75 percent of the awards are for lecturing and 25 percent for research. All Fulbright-Hays grantees are selected by the Board of Foreign Scholarships, whose members are appointed by the president of the United

States to oversee the program and provide policy guidance.

Foreign scholars apply in their own countries to the binational commission or the United States embassy, which makes nominations to the Board of Foreign Scholarships. Over five hundred awards are granted annually, about 75 percent for travel only, with stipends provided generally by host institutions, foreign governments, the United States government, and private foundations. The remainder are for travel and maintenance. The council organizes conferences to broaden scholars' acquaintance with American social and political institutions and, in particular, higher education in the United States. In Los Angeles, Chicago, Boston, and New York, where there are large numbers of visiting Fulbright-Hays scholars, CIES has appointed coordinators to assist scholars and provide opportunities for them to participate in the cultural and intellectual life of the community.

CIES has developed a register of American scholars interested in appointments abroad. The register, which contains about 15,000 entries, is computerized and lists each scholar's age, sex, number of dependents, highest academic degree, fields of specialization, affiliation, language competency, and preferred countries or areas. The register is updated regularly.

2101 Constitution Avenue NW
Washington, D.C. 20418 USA

ROY A. WHITEKER

COUNCIL FOR NATIONAL ACADEMIC AWARDS, United Kingdom

The Council for National Academic Awards (CNAA) was founded in 1964 by Royal Charter to replace the former National Council for Technological Awards. It has the authority to award degrees and other academic distinctions to students who satisfactorily complete courses approved by the council in further education institutions which do not have the power to award their own degrees. In September 1974 CNAA merged with the National Council for Diplomas in Art and Design (NCDAD) and now awards degrees in this field as well as in many others. By the terms of its charter the council's degrees have to be, and are, comparable in standard to those awarded by universities in the United Kingdom. They are held as such by professional institutes, employers, and universities for the purposes of professional membership, employment, and entry to higher degrees, provided they are obtained at the appropriate level. In many instances the professional bodies recognize the courses as being of a standard sufficient to afford the graduates exemption from the relevant professional examinations.

The council considers proposals for courses, in full detail, through a range of committees, subject boards, and panels. The members of these groups are drawn from every type of educational institution—from the universities, polytechnics, colleges of education, and other institutions of higher education—and from industry and the professions. The plans submitted by the colleges contain the following information: a statement on the aims and structure of the course, the proposed curriculum and syllabi, intended methods of assessment, and the resources available to conduct the course. When the plan has been considered, a visit to the college by members of the subject board usually takes place; the impressions gained during this visit help the board decide the outcome of the college's application. The council is concerned not only with the course submission but with the general college environment and the quality of the total educational experience the institution can offer the student. To ensure that standards are maintained, the council reviews all courses every five or six years.

More than one hundred institutions are offering some 900 courses validated by CNAA, and more than 62,000 students are registered in these courses. The institutions involved are mainly the polytechnics,

but also colleges of art, colleges of education, colleges of technology, the services' colleges, and various others geographically dispersed throughout the United Kingdom.

The range of courses validated by the CNAA broadens continually. Courses now approved cover the sciences, construction, architecture and planning, engineering, arts and humanities, business studies, social studies, education, and art and design. Nearly all the courses lead to the award of B.A., B.Ed., or B.Sc.—unclassified or with the appropriate honors classification. The council also awards degrees of M.A. and M.Sc., diplomas for completion of postgraduate courses of study, and the research degrees of M.Phil. and Ph.D.

The contents of the courses are individual to the colleges offering them, as are university courses, but the emphasis of a CNAA degree course often differs from that of its university equivalent. Practical competence is highly valued, as is the amount of teaching and guidance given to the students. Project work forms an important part of a course, especially in courses involving design and other science courses. The courses are offered on a full-time, sandwich, or part-time basis. The courses can be in single subjects, or they can be multidisciplinary or interdisciplinary. A number of colleges now offer modular courses, in which the student chooses his own program of studies from a wide range of possible subject combinations.

The council encourages the colleges, wherever appropriate, to suit their courses to the needs of industry, commerce, and the professions. This approach adds the extra dimension of industrial or business practice to a course. There are, of course, subject areas where this experience is not relevant, such as the arts; but even so, efforts are made to ensure that courses have satisfactory career outlets.

Sandwich courses—courses combining academic study with practical training in the relevant industry, profession, or service—usually last for four years and lead to a CNAA degree. They include at least one year of practical training; a training period of forty-eight weeks is regarded as the minimum, but many courses include about sixty weeks of training. The practical training undertaken during a course must be directly related to the student's chosen profession. There is no single pattern for interleaving the periods of academic study and practical training, and the council has accepted a number of solutions proffered by the colleges. In one pattern, called a "thick" sandwich course, two years (October–July) of academic study are followed by a calendar year of practical training and a final year of academic study. A second pattern provides a maximum amount of interleaving of academic study and training, usually on the basis of alternate periods of approximately six months. This pattern has some disadvantages for students because three training periods are required. A variant which is increasingly common is to arrange for two training periods instead of three, making one considerably longer than six months. These patterns are described as "thin" sandwich courses.

Part-time courses are designed mainly with the mature applicant in mind. The period of study is related to the qualifications of the entrant—often an appropriate Higher National Certificate or Higher National Diploma (HNC/D), teacher's certificate, or professional qualification. Part-time study usually involves a combination of daytime and evening attendance at college but is sometimes completed on an "evening-only" basis.

The Diploma of Higher Education (DIPHE) is a new award to be conferred on students who successfully complete a two-year course of study on a full-time basis. The diploma course, equivalent in standard and often similar in content to that of the first two years of a degree course, will normally be designed to facilitate transfer to a suitable degree program with two years' credit. The diploma should also be viewed as a terminal qualification in its own right, thus giving diplomates the

choice of further study on a degree program, further study leading to a professional qualification, or employment with an acceptable qualification. Entry requirements for such courses are basically the same as those for a degree program, with additional flexibility to allow entry for students with evidence of appropriate attainment in such fields as art, drama, music, and physical education.

The council is also empowered to award a certificate to students completing approved courses of study at subdegree level. The certificate may serve as a qualification in its own right; mark the completion of a stage in a degree course (for instance, a part-time B.Ed. course for nongraduate serving teachers); or give a first-year exemption in an approved degree course. Most of the certificate courses approved by the council are in the field of education, leading to a Certificate in Education. There is only one other approved certificate course, in arts, social science, or social studies. Entry requirements for certificate courses are a minimum of five passes (at grade C or above) in the General Certificate of Education (GCE), ordinary level, or equivalent; but colleges may require additional qualifications. Provision is made for the admission of mature students with other qualifications or even, in some cases, no formal educational qualifications.

The usual entry requirements for CNAA first degree courses are two subjects at advanced level and three others at ordinary level in the GCE examinations or three subjects at advanced level and one other at ordinary level. In accordance with the new GCE regulations, ordinary-level passes must be at grade C or above. The Certificate of Secondary Education (CSE) passes at a sufficiently high standard will be accepted in lieu of ordinary-level passes. Ordinary National Certificate and Ordinary National Diploma (ONC/D) passes at a good standard, at least credit + level, in directly appropriate subjects which will be specified by the college, are also acceptable.

For colleges in Scotland the normal entry requirements are passes in the Scottish Certificate of Education (SCE) in five subjects (three at H grade) or four subjects at H grade or an appropriate ONC/D at a "good" standard. Specific requirements for a particular subject are stated in terms of GCE passes. These should be interpreted as SCE passes for the colleges in Scotland offering courses in that subject area. In all instances, specific entry requirements should be confirmed with the college concerned. Certain qualifications, such as Higher National Diplomas and Certificates and a Teacher's Certificate/Certificate in Education, may afford exemption from the first year of a degree course.

The requirements for courses in art and design are slightly different. Applicants should normally have completed a full-time foundation course in art and design of not less than one year, though colleges may make exceptions to this general rule.

Students accepted on CNAA degree, diploma, and certificate courses are normally eligible for mandatory awards from local educational authorities on the same basis as students admitted to university courses.

344-354 Gray's Inn Road
London WC1X 8BP, England

COUNCIL FOR THE ADVANCEMENT OF SMALL COLLEGES, United States

The Council for the Advancement of Small Colleges (CASC), founded in 1956 with fifty-two charter members, seeks to improve the educational programs and administrative processes of small, private, independent, four-year colleges of liberal arts and sciences. Membership in 1974 numbered ninety. CASC maintains liaison with other educational associations, both national and regional, cooperating in programs and publications with several of them. It also maintains contact with the United States Office of Education and other federal agencies.

Membership in CASC is open to non-profit, private, independent, four-year colleges of liberal arts and sciences in the United States. A college applying for membership must be a recognized candidate for accreditation with its regional accrediting association; or it must be listed, or present evidence of eligibility for listing, in the *Education Directory, Higher Education* of the United States Office of Education. In addition, the college must have been in operation for a minimum of three years and must have no more than two thousand full-time students.

CASC is governed by a sixteen-member board of directors, each of whom is president of a member college. The Commission on Academic Affairs is made up of deans of member colleges, with a member of the CASC board as liaison. An executive director and staff direct CASC activities from the council's headquarters in Washington, D.C.

The council's programs are planned on the basis of the needs of member colleges. Service to member colleges is of primary concern. The emphasis of the programs is on the development of leadership capabilities and management skills for the personnel of small colleges, particularly the college president and administrative team. The priorities of the board of directors include faculty development, team training, small-college research projects, training in institutional planning and research, a management program for administrative teams, and career education model development.

Summer institutes have been funded by grants from the United States Office of Education, major corporations and foundations, and the general budget of CASC. Regional and smaller institutes and seminars, held following the summer institutes, develop specific summer institute themes.

Other CASC projects include a pilot study in institutional long-range planning, cost-analysis program, institutional research and planning, management seminars, proposal writing, and workshops on educational change and innovation. The association also holds annual workshops designed to assist neophyte deans in their orientation to their complex responsibilities.

Newsletters and bulletins are prepared for member colleges and the higher education community. Publications of CASC include *The Trustee, Development: A Team Approach, The Small College: A Bibliographic Handbook* (with Education Resources Information Center), *Long-Range Planning Case Studies* (with National Association of College and University Business Officers), *Cost Analysis in Liberal Education, Alternative Futures, Academic Alternatives,* and *Student Development.*

One Dupont Circle
Washington, D.C. 20036 USA

COUNCIL OF EUROPE
(Conseil de l'Europe)

Founded in 1949, the Council of Europe aims to achieve a greater unity among its members for the purpose of safeguarding and realizing their ideals and principles, which are their common heritage, and facilitating their economic and social progress. Membership in the council is open to all European countries that wish to become members but is subject to certain conditions in respect to democratic forms of government. The following eighteen countries make up the council: Austria, Belgium, Cyprus, Denmark, France, the Federal Republic of Germany, Greece, Iceland, Ireland, Italy, Luxembourg, Malta, the Netherlands, Norway, Sweden, Switzerland, Turkey, and the United Kingdom.

The two component parts of the Council of Europe are the Committee of Ministers, which is the intergovernmental body, and the Consultative Assembly, which is the parliamentary body. The administrative machinery for both is provided by the secretariat.

The permanent headquarters of the Council of Europe is in Strasbourg, France.

"Europe House" contains the offices of the secretariat and the meeting rooms of the Consultative Assembly, the Committee of Ministers, and their committees.

Each member state contributes to the council's budget in accordance with the size of its population. A draft budget is prepared each year by the secretary general and approved by the Committee of Ministers. According to the statute, the official languages of the Council of Europe are French and English. Italian and German are recognized as working languages in the Consultative Assembly and its committees.

The Council for Cultural Cooperation, founded in 1962, draws up proposals for the cultural policy of the Council of Europe and allocates the funds of the cultural fund, which finances the cultural program of this council. One of the permanent committees assisting the council is the Committee on Higher Education and Research, established in 1960. It has a membership of twenty-one countries, members of the Council of Europe or signatories of the European Cultural Convention. Each country is represented by an academic member, usually a rector or vice-chancellor of a university, and one senior civil servant designated by the government. The committee promotes cooperation among European countries in the sphere of higher education and research; transmits to governments and intergovernmental organizations opinions and recommendations on problems in this field; fosters relations among European universities and institutes of higher education and research; assembles information, undertakes appropriate studies, and issues such publications as may appear desirable; and maintains contacts with international organizations concerned with higher education and research. The council supports research seminars and cooperation among European research libraries.

The activities of the committee deal with problems of tertiary education, staff structure and status, admission to higher education, equivalences and mobility participation of students and staff, curriculum reform and development, and new media and methods.

F-67006 Strasbourg, France

COUNCIL OF GRADUATE SCHOOLS IN THE UNITED STATES

Established in 1961, the Council of Graduate Schools (CGS) in the United States supports the improvement of graduate education in the United States. The 318 public and private member institutions of the council award 99 percent of all research doctorates and 85 percent of all master's degrees earned annually in the United States.

CGS maintains a consultation service that aids in establishing new programs, appraising established programs, examining resources for future development, and reviewing organizational and administrative structure. To encourage legislation that would improve graduate education, the council provides information on graduate school needs to United States congressional committees and government agencies.

In collaboration with the Graduate Record Examinations Board, CGS conducts an annual survey of graduate schools to gather information on graduate enrollment, assistantships and fellowships, degree productivity, and disciplines. CGS also sponsors an annual summer workshop for new graduate deans.

The council maintains an advisory committee to the Institute of International Education. Through membership on the national liaison committee, CGS helps to coordinate the academic activities of foreign students in United States universities. The council also participates in overseas workshops on the admission of foreign students to the United States and serves in an advisory capacity to foreign governments seeking to strengthen and expand their own graduate programs.

The council is financed primarily by dues of member institutions. Special projects, however, are supported by grants from foundations and governmental agencies.

Graduate Programs and Admissions Manual, updated annually by the Graduate Record Examinations Board and CGS, is distributed on a worldwide basis. The manual contains information about graduate institutions—including information on institutional size, academic calendar, financial aid deadlines, departmental size, graduate programs, and department specialties. The council also publishes a newsletter, a membership directory of institutional deans, proceedings of annual meetings, and periodic reports and studies relating to graduate education. In addition, brief statements describing quality programs of graduate education are distributed.

One Dupont Circle
Washington, D.C. 20036 USA

COUNCIL OF MINISTERS OF EDUCATION
(Conseil des ministres de l'éducation), Canada

The Council of Ministers of Education *(Counseil des ministres de l'éducation)* was founded in September 1967, replacing the Standing Committee of Ministers of Education. It is composed of the ministers responsible for education in each of the ten provinces and meets three times a year. It was formed to provide a means for the fullest possible cooperation among provincial Canadian governments in areas of mutual interest and concern in education. Provision was also made for consultation with other educational organizations to promote the development of education in Canada.

The council, an interprovincial educational agency, enables the ministers of education in Canadian provinces to consult on matters of common interest. Each provincial department of education is autonomous within the council. No recommendations or decisions of the council are binding on provincial ministers with respect to their jurisdictions. The council, however, is the only educational organization whose membership represents the constitutional authorities responsible for policymaking in the field of education. Concerned with all aspects of education, the council attempts to deal with the interests of all Canadians and seeks to aid members through the work of its committees, task forces, and work groups.

The council's executive committee is responsible for the management of the council's business during its one-year term of office. Composed of a chairperson, a vice-chairperson, and three other members, the executive committee members represent the five principal regions of Canada. The executive committee meets prior to each council meeting to review the agenda and make recommendations to the council.

The advisory committee of deputy ministers of education is composed of members from all provinces, under the leadership of the deputy minister from the province represented by the council chairperson. The advisory committee, meeting at least thirty days prior to each full council meeting, prepares the agenda and documentation for each meeting.

A secretariat in Toronto, incorporated under the laws of Ontario, includes a secretary general, an associate, an assistant, eight professionals, eight stenographers, two translators, and a bookkeeper. All council meetings and activities are funded by grants from the provincial departments of education on a per capita basis.

Council committees consist of senior officials from each department of education representing all provinces. All committees operate on the basis of a one-year mandate, renewed as necessary. Council task forces deal with specific projects within a clearly defined time limit. Members of work groups are generally appointed on the basis of regional representation.

The Post-Secondary Education Committee was established in 1968 to study problems of mutual concern in postsecondary education, such as testing, student assis-

tance, and financing. The committee subsequently became involved in federal and provincial financial support of postsecondary education and undertook the study of interprovincial implementation of the Fiscal Arrangements Act (FAA). The study resulted in the Peitchinis Report, *Financing Post-Secondary Education in Canada*. After the completion of the Peitchinis Report, follow-up studies on various aspects of FAA were made by specific task forces, operating at both the interprovincial and the provincial-federal levels. The committee was then disbanded.

In April 1971 an agreement was reached by the Department of the Secretary of State and the Council of Ministers of Education to implement the Summer Language Bursary Program on a regular basis. The program is administered by the Bursary Committee and funded by the Department of the Secretary of State.

First meeting in September 1969, the Curriculum Committee was set up for the exchange of information in the curriculum field. An investigation on Canadian studies resulted in the publication in 1971 of *Canadian Studies in Canadian Schools*. In September 1973, at the recommendation of the Curriculum Committee, the council established a metric task force, a task force on the teaching of English or French as a second language, and a task force on equivalency assessment for transferred students and the granting of school credit for out-of-school experiences. The Curriculum Committee meets three times a year to carry out its various functions.

In January 1974 a federal-provincial working group was appointed to reevaluate the question of student aid. In April 1974, at a meeting held with the council chairperson and vice-chairperson and the minister of state for science and technology, the council established a federal-provincial task force to study federal involvement in university research.

The Interprovincial Second-Language Monitor Program Committee first met in September 1973 as a three-year pilot project to promote the learning and use of Canada's official languages. The Media Programming Committee was established to coordinate the programing of the Canadian School Broadcasts. The committee consists of two sections—one for French and one for English programing.

At the request of the Organisation for Economic Co-operation and Development (OECD), the council and the federal government agreed to undertake a review of educational policies in Canada. The purposes of the review were to acquaint others with educational developments in Canada and to assist the Canadian education authorities in planning more effectively for the future. The OECD Review Coordinating Committee was established in September 1973 to take on the responsibility for the overall management of this project. The committee is composed of four provincial delegates, representing the Western provinces, Ontario, Quebec, and the Atlantic provinces. Two federal delegates, representing the Department of External Affairs and the Department of the Secretary of State, also participated in the activities of this group. In addition, each region appointed a regional director to be responsible for the production of that region's report.

The Statistics Committee was established in September 1971 to coordinate the exchange of statistical information on education among the provinces, in cooperation with Statistics of Canada. The committee also organizes future statistical studies.

The council maintains close contact with the Department of the Secretary of State and a number of federal agencies, such as the Canadian Broadcasting Corporation, National Film Board, and Canadian Radio-Television Commission. The Department of External Affairs consults with the council on all matters pertaining to Canada's international commitments in the field of education. The department relies upon the cooperation and advice of the council in selection of official delegates to represent Canada at international educational conferences, selection of topics for discussion at these conferences, and preparation of working papers and reports for Canada. Through the department, the council serves as the official channel between the departments of education and such international organizations as UNESCO, International Bureau of Education, International Institute for Educational Planning, Organisation for Economic Co-operation and Development, Centre for Educational Research and Innovation, and Commonwealth Secretariat.

The council sends observers to meetings of the International Council for Educational Media and the European Broadcasting Union. In addition, the council has played a major role in the selection and preparation of the Canadian education delegations to the Soviet Union and has been responsible for coordinating visits of Soviet education delegations to Canada. The council also maintains close contact with *Association canadienne d'éducation de langue française* (Canadian French-Language Education Association), Association of Universities and Colleges of Canada, Canadian Education Association of Universities and Colleges of Canada, Canadian Education Association, Canadian School Trustees' Association, Canadian Teachers' Federation, and *Fédération des commissions scolaires du Québec* (Federation of School Commissions of Quebec).

Council publications include *Canadian Studies in Canadian Schools* (September 1971); *Metric Style Guide* (June 1975); *Financing Post-Secondary Education in Canada* (September 1971); *Review of Educational Policies in Canada,* six volumes in French and English (September 1975); *Seminar on Transmission Technology for Education* (December 1972); and *Study Papers to Assist in the Foundation of a Policy Position on Manpower Training* (May 1972). The council has also published annual reports for 1972–73, 1973–74, and 1974–75.

252 Bloor West
Suite S-500
Toronto, Ontario, Canada M5S 1V5

COUNCIL OF
ONTARIO UNIVERSITIES, Canada

The Council of Ontario Universities, formerly the Committee of Presidents of Universities of Ontario, was established in 1962 to promote cooperation among the provincially assisted universities of Ontario and to work for the improvement of higher education in Ontario. In the original committee, members were the presidents of the provincially assisted universities. Following the reorganization in 1970, the council was composed of executive heads and academic colleagues elected by the senior academic body of each provincially assisted university in Ontario with power to grant degrees in more than one field. The council meets monthly during the academic year to consider matters of concern to the Ontario universities. Numerous specialized subcommittees offer advice to the council.

Major council activities include studies of operating and capital financing, development of graduate studies in the province, and coordination of admissions. The council encourages cooperation among libraries, including development of computer-based union catalogs and cataloging support systems and computer resource sharing. The council supports an active research program on a range of subjects relevant to the council's objectives.

An executive director heads a staff of forty full-time members in Toronto. Sixteen of these members are in charge of the Ontario Universities' Application Centre.

130 St. George Street
Toronto, Ontario, Canada M5S 2T4

Universities. Further council objectives—to serve higher education institutions through research and services—were defined in 1964 following the adoption of a new law. Each of the following universities is represented on the council by its rector: *Universidad de Chile*, Santiago; *Universidad católica de Chile*, Santiago; *Universidad de Concepción*, Concepción; *Universidad católica de Valparaíso*, Valparaíso; *Universidad técnica Federico Santa María*, Valparaíso; *Universidad técnica del estado*, Santiago; *Universidad austral de Chile*, Valdivia; and *Universidad del norte*, Antofagasta.

Four departments and ten commissions operate under the direct administration of the general secretary. These units conduct technical studies, assemble statistical data on higher education, publish information and studies, design teaching and research policies, and identify and interpret new and emerging problems and needs of higher education in the country.

The council prepares proposals and advises Chilean universities in accordance with its own independently defined educational objectives. At the same time, it safeguards and strengthens the academic work, legal protection, and international relations of universities. Improvement in the organization and administration of Chilean universities is further accomplished through consultations with individuals, institutions, regional and national organizations, and public or private agencies related to the nation's development.

Moneda 673, 8 piso
Casilla 14798
Santiago, Chile

JAIME SANTIBAÑEZ GUARELLO

COUNCIL OF RECTORS OF
CHILEAN UNIVERSITIES
(Consejo de rectores de
universidades chilenas)

The *Consejo de rectores de universidades chilenas* (Council of Rectors of Chilean Universities) was founded by law in 1954 to provide coordination among the Chilean

COUNCIL OF RECTORS OF THE
BRAZILIAN UNIVERSITIES
(Conselho de reitores das universidades
brasileiras)

The Council of Rectors of Brazilian Universities, founded in 1966, studies problems of university development; coordinates the activities of member universities; and promotes interuniversity cooperation in science, recreation, and academic exchange. Membership includes seventy full members (rectors of Brazilian universities), seven associate members (heads of federations and higher education institutions composed of more than three faculties or schools), and twenty-three cooperative members (former rectors).

The council is directed by a president, an executive director, an executive board composed of three members, and a finance committee. All are elected annually from among the full members. The board, meeting six times a year, makes recommendations to the biannual plenary meeting of the council and is responsible for carrying out decisions of the council. A permanent secretariat implements the plans and projects of the council.

Quadra 704, Bloco A, Casa 9
70000 Brasilia, Distrito Federal, Brazil

COUNCIL OF UNIVERSITIES, QUEBEC
(Conseil des universités, Québec), Canada

The Council of Universities, Quebec was established in December 1968 to advise the Quebec minister of education on the needs of higher education and university research and make recommendations to meet such needs. The minister consults the council on higher education development plans, annual university budgets, and division of funds among the institutions of higher education. Composed of seventeen members, the council includes a president, nine persons from the university community, four persons representing business and labor, the president of the University Research Commission, and two government officers. The Council of Universities is assisted by program, finance, and planning committees. Meeting at least six times a year, the council makes an annual report before June 30 to the minister of education.

On its own initiative, the council has published works on a model of higher education applicable to Quebec. The council

is making studies of university planning and research. The council also studies the principles of continuing education on the level of higher education, training of university teachers, and unionization in the university community.

2700 boulevard Laurier (8e)
Sainte Foy, Quebec 10, Canada

COUNCIL ON EVALUATION OF FOREIGN STUDENT CREDENTIALS, United States

Founded in 1956, the Council on Evaluation of Foreign Student Credentials reviews studies of the educational systems of countries that send students to the United States and makes recommendations for the evaluation of foreign student credentials. The council is composed of representatives of eight United States organizations in higher education, including the American Association of Collegiate Registrars and Admissions Officers, American Association of Community and Junior Colleges, Association of American Colleges, Association of Graduate Schools, Institute of International Education, National Association for Foreign Student Affairs, College Entrance Examinations Board, and Council of Graduate Schools.

Observer organizations include the American Council on Education, University of the State of New York, Agency for International Development and Bureau of Educational and Cultural Affairs in the United States Department of State, and United States Office of Education.

The council makes recommendations to the American Association of Collegiate Registrars and Admissions Officers concerning the World Education Series, studies of various educational systems and guides to the academic placement of foreign students in educational institutions in the United States.

Admissions Office
1220 S.A.B.
University of Michigan
Ann Arbor, Michigan 48104 USA

COUNCIL ON INTERNATIONAL
EDUCATIONAL EXCHANGE,
United States

The Council on International Educational Exchange (CIEE) is a private, nonprofit organization with a membership of 176 North American colleges, universities, secondary schools, educational organizations, and youth-serving agencies that sponsor educational exchange programs. The council correlates, stimulates, and furthers the activities of organizations engaged in international student travel; broadens the experience of individuals participating in international exchange programs; and aids the achievement of peaceful interchange among people and nations.

The council, first known as the Council on Student Travel, was founded in 1947 by a small group of organizations trying to reestablish student exchange and facilitate transatlantic transportation after World War II. From its founding until 1969, the council was well known for its chartered student ships traveling between America and Europe. As an increasing number of academic institutions joined the council and the interests of the members gradually spread beyond Europe to other continents, the council became more directly involved in sponsoring and administering educational exchange programs. In 1967 the council changed its name to the Council on International Educational Exchange to reflect more accurately its expanded activities.

A board of directors is elected by the membership and meets three times during the year. Representatives of the entire membership are convened once a year. The council finances its operations through membership dues, administrative fees for services to members and other organizations, and grants and contributions.

The council arranges overseas transportation for university groups, provides orientation programs for program participants, and makes travel and program arrangements at the foreign destination. The council also sponsors regional, national, and international workshops and conferences, bringing together educators and program administrators to exchange ideas and discuss mutual problems of educational exchange. Committees of representatives from council member organizations study particular areas of concern, including academic programs abroad, secondary school programs, and programs in the United States for foreign visitors.

The council has been active in the administration of educational exchange programs sponsored by consortia of colleges and universities or by the council itself in cooperation with other organizations. The council's Cooperative Study Centers in Rennes, France, and Seville, Spain, enable prospective teachers and other undergraduates to study language and civilization for a semester. Forty universities cooperate in sponsoring the program. A program in Paris offers a one-year course in film theory and history for students at the advanced undergraduate and graduate levels. In cooperation with eighteen United States universities. CIEE conducts an intensive program in Russian-language study in the Soviet Union. Both an eight-week summer program and a spring or fall semester program are offered at Leningrad State University. In cooperation with the National Association of Secondary School Principals, the council administers a service enabling American secondary schools to exchange groups of students and teachers with schools in England, the Federal Republic of Germany, France, and Japan. Another service offered by CIEE enables United States students to obtain summer jobs in the United Kingdom, and a similar service permits students from the United Kingdom, Ireland, France, Denmark, Australia, and New Zealand to work and travel in the United States.

Summer study and travel programs in the United States are administered by CIEE for Japanese students, Japanese secondary school teachers of English, and young Japanese bankers. CIEE administers two summer study and travel programs in Japan: a program for American educators (sponsored by the National Association of Secondary School Principals) and an introduction to Japanese culture for members of the Japan Society of New York. Living with families is an important feature of these programs.

Each year the council receives letters and phone calls from more than 80,000 students, teachers, parents, and advisers inquiring about various aspects of work, study, and travel in the United States and abroad. One department of the council provides information to answer these questions and offers a number of services that help students save money on travel throughout the world. During 1973–74, CIEE issued 110,000 International Student Identity Cards entitling the holder to discounts and reductions on transportation, accommodations, and entertainment in Europe and elsewhere. Throughout the year the CIEE staff arranges overseas transportation by ship and air at the lowest possible fares for students and teachers, both individually and in groups. The council also books eligible students on intra-European charter flights operated by member organizations of the Student Air Travel Association. The council's student travel services are available through 275 campus offices authorized by CIEE.

The New York staff directs the worldwide activities of the council, while the Paris and Tokyo offices perform similar services in Europe and East Asia. A regional affiliate of CIEE, Student Services West in San Jose, California, provides student travel services on the West Coast. In addition, the council has established cooperative relationships with educational travel and exchange organizations in many countries of the world.

The council publishes a *Guide to Institutional Self-Study and Evaluation of Educational Programs Abroad.* CIEE also distributes *Student Hostels and Restaurants; Touring Students,* directory of low-cost student tours offered within individual countries abroad;

and student guides to various cities, issued by the CIEE or local student travel bureaus. In conjunction with Frommer-Pasmantier Publishing Corporation, CIEE publishes two paperbacks: *Whole World Handbook: A Student Guide to Work, Study and Travel Abroad,* information by geographical area on more than a thousand United States–sponsored study programs; and *Where to Stay: USA,* state-by-state listing of low-cost accommodations and travel information. The thirty-two-page *Student Travel Catalog* describes CIEE's student travel service and publications. A complete list of publications is available on request.

777 United Nations Plaza
New York, New York 10017 USA

MARGARET E. SHERMAN

COUNCILS, ACADEMIC

See Governance and Control of Higher Education.

COUNSELOR EDUCATION
(Field of Study)

Counselor education, a professional field within the disciplines of education and psychology, has been developed almost exclusively in the United States, where counselors are trained to provide individual or group help in a wide variety of settings (schools, colleges and universities, mental health agencies, rehabilitation agencies, employment service agencies) to a broad spectrum of clientele. Because the earliest developments of this field were in the guidance and vocational counseling services in the schools, programs of counselor education have remained based largely within education. As an international field, counselor education is still oriented mainly toward vocational counseling.

As the field has expanded, there has been an increased emphasis on its psychological basis: the psychology of normal growth and development, the psychology of personality, vocational psychology, educational or learning psychology, and psychological testing. Counselor education can be differentiated from the education given in related "helping service" fields by its emphasis on normal growth and development instead of the medical psychology models of pathology, which are emphasized in social work, psychiatry, and clinical psychology. There is, however, considerable interface between counselors trained in counselor education programs and professionals in social work, medicine, and clinical psychology.

In addition to having its roots in education and psychology, counselor education draws on certain aspects of sociology, economics, philosophy, and history. Some of the better-known professional variants of the field of counseling are vocational counseling, guidance or school counseling, psychological or psychotherapeutic counseling, and rehabilitation counseling. Vocational counseling provides help in career decision making and draws on vocational psychology or theories about how such choices are made over the life span. Guidance or school counseling provides helping services in elementary and secondary schools to improve the educational experience for pupils. This field draws on educational psychology, educational sociology, learning theory approaches to behavior, and vocational counseling. Psychological or psychotherapeutic counseling—which combines vocational with psychological counseling in universities, hospitals, and industries—emphasizes individual, marital, family, or therapeutic group counseling for behavioral, emotional, social, or personality problems. This branch of counseling most closely interfaces with psychiatry and social work but draws more on behavioral, developmental, and personality psychology than on medical, social work, or psychiatric models. Rehabilitation counseling provides therapeutic, vocational, consultative, and related services to physically, mentally, emotionally, and socially handicapped persons, most of whom are legally defined and entitled to legislatively mandated services,

chief of which are vocational and job placement services. This field draws on medical knowledge of physical handicaps, job task analysis information, and psychological training for various handicaps.

Counselor education in universities began in the United States in the late 1920s and early 1930s with the offering of a few guidance courses, but full degree programs at the master's degree level did not emerge until the late 1930s. John M. Brewer of Harvard University wrote one of the earliest textbooks in guidance, which was published in 1935. Programs in counseling psychology were first formalized in 1951 and grew rapidly until the late 1960s, largely as a result of massive funding by the United States government to increase the supply of school, college, and rehabilitation counselors. Internationally, formal training programs for counselors came much later in other countries than it did in the United States, and their growth has tended to be slow and limited.

Because the field of counseling is largely an American development, trends in the field tend to reflect the American experience, or, in Latin American countries, the somewhat different French developments. A recent trend in counselor education, competency-based program development, emphasizes the specific competencies that counselors in different settings must have in order to be effective with clients. Training programs are beginning to be based on the development of instructional modules designed to help the student develop necessary competencies. Such programs move away from theoretical courses as the basis for the degree and toward the evaluation of performance following more individualized learning modules. Another trend in counselor education involves a concern for the effect of organizational environments on learning and mental health. Information about the role of counselors in bringing about improved organizational environments is therefore being included in many counselor education programs. There is also a trend toward preparing paraprofessionals in counselor education at the undergraduate level. Some of these paraprofessional programs lead to a bachelor's degree and may also lead to more advanced training. Finally, as part of its long-established training practice, counselor education has pioneered the use of videotape and audiotape equipment to study the counseling process in detail and to aid in the learning experience. The use of this equipment provides rapid feedback on counselor performance and client response.

Counselor education outside the United States is focused mainly on vocational counseling and oriented toward service in the schools or the employment service. University-level counselors in the United Kingdom and France more often stress psychological counseling. In the United Kingdom there are small but well-developed counselor education programs at the graduate (diploma) level, at the Universities of Keele, Reading, and Exeter. Several hundred counselors are employed; with possible changes in the external examination system, the need for counselors may increase. The Department of Employment has trained vocational counselors since the 1930s. In France, which has had a long-established university program to prepare vocational counselors, a centralized bureau sets standards for the examination and licensure of vocational counselors. In France, as well as the United Kingdom, postgraduate courses of one or two years lead to a specialty diploma.

Switzerland, the Netherlands, and Sweden have active counseling services and training programs, but counselor education programs in some other European countries are in the embryonic stage. Counseling services are available at most of the major universities, and there are school, employment, and rehabilitation counselors in some of the larger cities. Growth of counseling services is likely to occur as more and more middle-class and working-class youth raise their level of education and as there is an increase in the complexity of choices available for life and work.

Counseling services may be found in a number of Latin American countries, with the most well developed in Puerto Rico, Venezuela, Brazil, Chile, Costa Rica, Panama, and Guatemala. Most of the other Latin American countries, which have strong ties with Europe, are less influenced by American forms of education; consequently, the development of their counselor education programs has followed the French pattern or, for economic reasons, has been very slow.

India and Japan have some relatively well-established programs of counseling and counselor education. Japan has had a vocational guidance association since 1927, but its counseling services and training programs developed after World War II. There has been an All-India Vocational and Educational Guidance Association since the 1950s, but formal training for guidance counselors in India has come about largely since the late 1950s, assisted by the Fulbright program of visiting scholars from the United States and the subsidization of Indian trainees in American universities. In some respects, these countries have gone further than any others, except the United States and France, in developing counseling services and counselor preparation.

Counseling as a profession and counselor education as a field of higher education are culturally conditioned. The field emerged in the United States from a peculiar combination of circumstances: immigration from many different countries and emphasis on individualism, freedom, concern for others, and choosing for oneself. The individual and his welfare have been placed above all other considerations in the development of the philosophy of training. Where these same conditions do not exist in the same way, the development of counseling services and of counselor education varies considerably. On the other hand, industrial and economic development and the growth of technology bring change and complexity to individual life in any country. Counseling for individual decision making on important life questions has been the cornerstone of counseling services and counselor education from the beginning. With appropriate sensitivity to the important cultural differences that exist from country to country, development of the counseling profession is likely in many countries other than the United States.

DAVID R. COOK

Training of Guidance Personnel in Eastern European Countries

The training of guidance personnel in Eastern European countries differs markedly from American counselor education. United States guidance theory emphasizes the uniqueness of the individual and his needs, while Marxist guidance is primarily committed to its classless society, which provides norms to which an individual must adjust. Shortly after the October Revolution in 1917, Lenin spelled out some basic principles of Soviet educational policy: free education for the masses, primacy of ideological factors in the curriculum, emphasis on socialist character formation, and use of the dialectic method in all educational work. Ever since, Soviet education has focused on the attitudinal and value-related development of youth to a degree unmatched in nonsocialist countries.

Guidance work in other Eastern European countries dates back to the 1920s. One of the pioneering efforts resulted in the establishment of the Institute of Work in Prague, which was to serve as a clearinghouse for ideas on work morale, job safety, and vocational guidance. Somewhat later, a government advisory board was created to promote the mental health movement among Czechoslovak educators. Parallel efforts were initiated in Poland and Hungary, but World War II and the subsequent Soviet takeover brought all such activities to a standstill.

In the initial stages, Soviet guidance work was carried out by teachers who had little training in behavioral sciences—an arrangement which, in terms of Lenin's guide-

lines, was considered appropriate, since it safeguarded the unity of curriculum and ideological character formation. During this period, cadres of educational psychologists known as "pedologists" were active in the school system. They served as consultants in planning educational experiences suitable to various groups of children, offered in-service training for teachers, did diagnostic work, and conducted systematic research in child psychology. The professional preparation of pedologists was sketchy—involving a loose mixture of basic education courses, social sciences, psychology. Yet, in spite of this rudimentary training, the work of pedologists was generally successful and received recognition at the highest level of party and government. The 1928 Congress on Pedology was addressed by Lenin's widow, who endorsed the role of applied psychology in Soviet education.

However, the influence of pedology on the school system and the relative independence it enjoyed were resented by ideological purists among the educators. Sporadic criticism of pedology emerged in the early 1930s, and in 1936 the Central Committee of the Soviet Communist Party issued a decree against "pedological perversions," which resulted in the suppression of pedology as a legitimate profession. For the next twenty years, specialized psychological services in schools and factories, and even the term *mental health*, were considered suspect in Marxist society. The only professional activities retaining their legitimacy were comprehensive prophylactic care and treatment of illness.

Not until the mid 1950s did a gradual rehabilitation of applied psychological services begin. Yet the fate of pedology was not forgotten by Soviet psychologists and educators. To counteract any lingering suspicions of disloyalty, members of the profession stated in their literature that ideological guidance is the highest priority in education. In the late 1950s much of the professional literature published in Soviet countries was political—interspersed with remarks about the effectiveness of psychology for socialist character formation. Since then, Soviet guidance has acquired a higher degree of professionalism. Though remnants of the ideological rhetoric have survived in the official statements of central administrators and middle-management personnel, the preoccupation with orthodoxy has virtually vanished from the profession as a whole.

The exclusively collectivist concept of personality has been modified, and the satisfaction of individual needs has been given more attention. Guidance methodology is shifting away from peer pressure applied in the collective, toward a more humanistic operational model. The stereotype of an authoritarian guidance educator is being gradually replaced by a professionally trained counselor whose role is perceived as supportive.

At present, three distinct professional groups are involved in guidance work of Eastern European countries: counseling psychologists, school psychologists, and vocational guidance workers. Counseling psychologists staff guidance clinics in central locations and closely cooperate with schools in their districts. They are available for consultations, diagnostic work, and counseling of students. Staff members of these clinics are generally well trained, with an education roughly equivalent to a master's degree or doctorate. Training is at the university level and includes developmental and social psychology, personality assessment, abnormal psychology, counseling processes, internship, and research methodology. Emphasis is placed on the dialectic process in linking behavioral theory and practice. This new model of psychological guidance is defined as a professional effort to help individuals—from childhood through adult life and retirement—overcome developmental problems and adjust to changing social situations while making effective use of opportunities available in Marxist society. School psychologists work in the educational system itself. Their training, which is less rigorous, consists of courses in education,

diagnostic and remedial psychology, and social sciences. Although this professional group is still understaffed, it will likely play a major role on the expanded guidance team in Eastern European schools in the future. Vocational guidance workers are usually teachers in upper grades, with various educational backgrounds, who either volunteered for the guidance job or were asked to assume such a responsibility. Some have virtually no training in vocational guidance; others have graduated from a pedagogic institute, where they received basic counselor training—including some courses in economics and applied psychology and practical experiences in vocational counseling.

Since the mid 1960s, various pilot projects in training vocational guidance personnel have been initiated in Eastern European countries. Some teachers colleges have been offering guidance curricula designed specifically for the economic needs and the job market of a particular region. Vocational guidance is closely interdependent with the five-year projections of economic planning, which require periodical adjustments in the guidance sector.

VICTOR DRAPELA

Levels and Programs of Study

Programs in counseling and guidance generally require as a minimum prerequisite a secondary education and lead to the following awards: certificate or diploma, bachelor's degree, master's degree (M.A., M.S.), the doctorate, or their equivalents. Programs are concerned with the principles and practices of educational and vocational counseling. Programs consist primarily of classroom sessions, group discussions, lectures, practical work in and observation of counseling procedures, and, on advanced levels, seminars, independent and directed study and research, and fieldwork.

Programs that lead to awards not equivalent to a first university degree are generally full-time and require at least one year's study. Short programs, often part time, are provided in the form of refresher and sandwich courses designed to upgrade the qualifications of those already employed (for example, teachers, social workers, or personnel and placement officers). Principal course content usually includes child and adolescent development, learning and motivation, vocational development, human relations and communication, information utilization and decision making, and interviewing and modification. Emphasis is usually placed on the techniques of devising and using tests.

Programs that lead to a first university degree are usually full time and require a minimum of one year's study. Supervised practical work may take one quarter to one third of the total time. Principal course content usually includes child and adolescent development, learning and motivation, social and organizational behavior, cognitive processes, human traits (intelligence, aptitudes, interests, and personality), vocational development, human relations and communication, utilization of information, decision making, experimental methods, interviewing, and behavior modification. Emphasis is placed on the techniques of constructing and applying tests.

Programs that lead to a postgraduate university degree are usually full time and last from two to three years. Students acquire a comprehensive knowledge of the broad area of counseling. Emphasis is placed on practical work in counseling procedures. An essential part of the programs is the preparation of a thesis or dissertation. Principal subject areas within which study and research projects tend to fall include counseling theory; effective employment placement; job analysis and occupational analysis; learning motivation; human traits; interviewing methodology; and the construction, application, and scoring of aptitude tests. Background study in such subjects as psychology, education, science, humanities, social sciences, and statistics is usually included.

[This section was based on UNESCO's

International Standard Classification of Education (ISCED) (Paris: UNESCO, 1976).]

Major International and National Organizations

INTERNATIONAL

Asian Regional Association on Vocational and Educational Guidance (ARAVEG)
1-1 Kanda Hitotsubashi, Chyiodaku
Tokyo, Japan

International Association for Applied Psychology (IAAP)
University of California
Irvine, California 92664 USA

International Association for Educational and Vocational Guidance (IAEVG)
Association internationale d'orientation scolaire et professionnelle (AIOSP)
257 route d'Arlon
Strassen, Luxembourg
    Members include governments, public and private institutions, national associations, and individual correspondents in forty-one countries; organization maintains a documentation center.

International Association for Educational and Vocational Information
Association internationale d'information scolaire universitaire et professionnelle (AIISUP)
20 rue de l'Estrapade
75005 Paris, France

International Labour Organisation (ILO)
Human Resources Department, Vocational Training Branch
1211 Geneva 22, Switzerland

International Round Table for the Advancement of Counseling (IRTAC)
Table ronde internationale pour le développement de l'orientation
64 West Ham Lane
London E15 4PT, England

Scandinavian Vocational Guidance Federation
Arbetsmarknadsstyrelsen
10220 Stockholm 12, Sweden

NATIONAL

Belgium:
    Association nationale d'orientation professionnelle (ANOP)
    28, rue Estiévenart
    7270 Dour

Centrale voor studie- en
beroepsorientering (CSBO)
M. Lemonnierlaan 129
1000 Brussels

Fédération des centres p.m.s. et
d'orientation libres
296 avenue de Tervueren
1150 Brussels

Canada:
Canadian Guidance and Counselling
Association
Corporation of Vocational Guidance
Counsellors of Quebec
1895 avenue de LaSalle
Montreal, Quebec PQ H1V 2K4

Federal Republic of Germany:
Deutscher Verband für
Berufsberatung (DVB)
Platz der Deutschen Einheit 1
6200 Wiesbaden

France:
Association des conseillers d'orientation
de France (ACOF)
Rectorat
1 rue Navier
51 Reims

Société médicale d'orientation
professionnelle
78 avenue de Suffren
75015 Paris

Israel:
Association for Vocational Guidance
in Israel
4 Rabbi Benjamin Street
Jerusalem

Italy:
Unione italiana per l'orientamento
professionale (UIOP)
via Vancini 3
40134 Bologna

Japan:
Japan Vocational Guidance Association
1-1 Kanda Hitotsubashi, Chiyodaku
Tokyo

Mexico:
Sociedad de estudios profesionales
Tepexpam No. 22, bulevar del
Niño Jesús
Mexico 21, D. F.

Netherlands:
Federatie van samenwerkende
organisaties van
beroepskeuzeadviseurs
Torenstraat 36
The Hague

Republic of Korea:
Korean Association for Educational and
Vocational Guidance
P.O. Box 5498
Seoul

Spain:
Sociedad española de psicología
San Julio 11
Madrid 2

Switzerland:
Schweizerischer Verband für
Berufsberatung
Eidmattstrasse 51
8032 Zurich

Yugoslavia:
Yugoslav Federation of Vocational
Guidance
Savez udruzenja za profesionalnu
orijentaciju
Savezni biro za poslove zaposljavanja
ul. Zmasj Jovina 21
Belgrade

United Kingdom:
Institute of Careers Officers
37a High Street
Stourbridge, Worcester DY8 ITA,
England

United States:
American Personnel and Guidance
Association (APGA)
1607 New Hampshire Avenue NW
Washington, D.C. 20009

National Vocational Guidance
Association (NVGA)
1607 New Hampshire Avenue NW
Washington, D.C. 20009

For additional international and national
organizations contact:

International Association for Educational and
Vocational Guidance
257 route d'Arlon
Strassen, Luxembourg

Principal Information Sources

GENERAL

Guides to the literature include:

Educational Documentation and Information. Bulletin of the International Bureau of Education: Educational Guidance, 1971, *180*, entire issue. Prepared by the International Association for Educational and Vocational Guidance; contains a bibliography on educational guidance.

Educational Documentation and Information. Bulletin of the International Bureau of Education: Vocational Guidance, 1971, *181,* entire issue. Prepared by the International Association for Educational and Vocational Guidance; contains a bibliography on vocational guidance.

Okruhlicova, L. *Bibliography of Literature on Educational and Vocational Guidance and Counselling, 1965–1969.* Bratislava, Czechoslovakia: Comenius University, 1970.

Selected References on Guidance and Counseling. Washington, D.C.: Professional Information Services of the American Personnel and Guidance Association, January 16, 1975.

Introductions and overviews to the field include:

Feingold, N. S. *A Counselor's Handbook: Readings in Counseling, Student Aid and Rehabilitation.* Cranston, Rhode Island: Carroll Press, 1972.

Gilmore, S. K. *The Counselor-in-Training.* New York: Appleton-Century-Crofts, 1973.

Herr, E. L. (Ed.) *Vocational Guidance and Human Development.* Boston: Houghton Mifflin, 1974. Discusses nature of the field.

Hughes, P. *Guidance and Counseling in Schools.* Oxford, England, and Elmsford, New York: Pergamon Press, 1971.

Seligman, M. (Comp. and Ed.) *Counselor Education and Supervision: Readings in Theory, Practice and Research.* Springfield, Illinois: Thomas, 1972.

Wrenn, C. G. *The World of the Contemporary Counselor.* Boston: Houghton Mifflin, 1973.

Sources on guidance internationally, including education and training, are:

CAPS Capsule, 1969, *3* (1), entire issue. Entitled International Guidance Issue.

Drapela, V. J. "Comparative Guidance Through International Study." *Personnel and Guidance Journal,* 1975, *53* (6), 438–445.

Dupont, J. B. "Thoughts on the Training of Counsellors." *Bulletin of the International Association for Educational and Vocational Guidance,* July 1974, *27,* 2–8.

Esen, A. "A View of Guidance from Africa." *Personnel and Guidance Journal,* June 1972, *50*(10), 792–798.

Espin, O. M., and Renner, R. R. "Counseling: A New Priority in Latin America." *Personnel and Guidance Journal,* 1972, *50,* 792–798.

Fletcher, F. M., and Riddle, C. W. "The Guidance Movement in India." *Personnel and Guidance Journal,* 1962, *40* (9), 807–810.

Goldman, L. (Ed.) "Guidance U.S.A.: Views from Abroad." *Personnel and Guidance Journal,* 1974, *53* (1), 40–56.

Heller, K. (Ed.) *Handbuch der Bildungsberatung.* (3 vols.) Stuttgart: Klett Verlag, 1975.

Hughes, P. *The Training of Counsellors.* Working document for the conference at the UNESCO Institute for Education, Hamburg, June 21–25, 1971, on the theme "The Future of Vocational Guidance in the Federal Republic of Germany."

Mitchell, M. H. "Guidance Activities in Selected Foreign Countries." *School Counselor,* 1967, *14* (5), 323–327.

Pal, S. K. *Guidance in Many Lands.* Allahabad, India: Central Book Depot, 1968.

Penny, J. F. "Vocational Guidance in Europe and the United States." *Vocational Guidance Quarterly,* 1968, *16* (4), 287–291.

Proceedings: Fifth World Congress of the International Association for Educational and Vocational Guidance. Quebec: Université Laval, 1973.

Reuchlin, M. *Pupil Guidance.* Strasbourg, France: Council of Europe, 1964.

Reuchlin, M., and Bacquet, R. *La formation des personnels de l'orientation scolaire et professionnelle.* Paris: UNESCO, 1970.

Vaughn, T. D. *Education and Vocational Guidance Today.* London: Routledge and Kegan Paul, 1970. Focuses largely on counseling and guidance in the United Kingdom.

Vaughn, T. D. *Education and the Aims of Counseling.* Oxford, England: Blackwell, 1975. A description of counseling in the United Kingdom and, in general, on the continent.

CURRENT BIBLIOGRAPHIES

CIRF Abstracts. Geneva: International Labour Organisation, 1962–.

Counselor's Information Service. Washington, D.C.: B'nai B'rith Career and Counseling Services, 1970–. Quarterly annotated bibliography of current literature on educational and vocational guidance.

Education Index. New York: Wilson, 1929–.

Guidance Exchange. Bronx, New York: S. Slaver, 1960–. Annual digest of current recommended guidance literature.

Psychological Abstracts. Washington, D.C.: American Psychological Association, 1927–.

Resources in Education (RIE). Washington, D.C.: Educational Resources Information Center (ERIC), 1968–. Abstracts and indexes recently completed research.

PERIODICALS

A sampling of the important journals in the field includes *Berufsberatung und Berufsbildung/Orientation et formation professionnelles* (Switzerland), *British Journal of Counseling and Guidance,* *Bulletin de l'Association internationale de psychologie appliquée* (Belgium), *Bulletin de l'Institut national d'étude du travail et d'orientation professionnelle* (France), *Bulletin de psychologie* (France), *Canadian Counsellor/Conseiller canadien, CAPS Capsule* (US), *Counseling and Values* (US), *Counseling Psychologist* (US), *Counselor Education and Supervision* (US), *Elementary School Guidance and Counseling* (US), *Focus on Guidance* (US), *Guidepost* (US), *International Association for Educational and Vocational Guidance. Bulletin* (Luxembourg), *Journal of College Student Personnel* (US), *Journal of Counseling Psychology* (US), *Journal of Employment Counseling* (US), *Journal of Vocational and Educational Guidance* (India), *Journal of Vocational Behavior* (US), *Measurement and Evaluation in Guidance* (US), *National Vocational Guidance Association Newsletter* (US), *Orientation professionnelle/Vocational Guidance* (Canada), *Personnel and Guidance Journal* (US), *Rehabilitation Counseling Bulletin* (US), *Review of Educational Research* (US), *School Counselor* (US), *Technical and Vocational Education in Canada, Vocational Guidance Quarterly* (US).

For a more complete listing of journals dealing with counseling issues consult:

Current Index to Journals in Education (CIJE). New York: Macmillan Information Division, 1969–. Published monthly.

DICTIONARIES, ENCYCLOPEDIAS, HANDBOOKS

Counselor's Handbook. Washington, D.C.: U.S. Employment Service, 1967. Handbook for vocational guidance counselors; lists requirements for some careers and professional qualifications; includes descriptions of techniques for tests and interviews.

Dictionary of Vocational Guidance. Belgrade: Savezni biro za poslove zaposljavanja, 1970. A comparative dictionary of terms in Serbo-Croatian, French, English, German, and Italian.

Farwell, G. T., Gamsky, N. R., and Mathieu-Coughlan, P. (Eds.) *The Counselor's Handbook*. New York: Intext Educational Publishers, 1974.

Hopke, W. E. (Ed.) *Dictionary of Personnel and Guidance Terms*. Chicago: Ferguson, 1968.

Hopke, W. E. (Ed.) *The Encyclopedia of Careers and Vocational Guidance*. (2 vols.) Garden City, New York: Doubleday, 1972.

United States Bureau of Labor Statistics. *Occupational Outlook Handbook*. Washington, D.C.: U.S. Government Printing Office, biennial.

DIRECTORIES

Directory of Counseling Services. Washington, D.C.: International Association of Counseling Services (APGA Affiliate), 1973–. Provides a listing of accredited counseling services in the private sector, universities and colleges, and community and junior colleges in the United States.

Hollis, J. W, and Wantz, R. A. *Counselor Education Directory 1974*. Muncie, Indiana: Accelerated Development, 1974. Includes personnel and programs of over 95 percent of the institutions in the United States and its territories that offer undergraduate and graduate counselor education.

RESEARCH CENTERS, INSTITUTES, INFORMATION CENTERS

The following organizations provide important research or information facilities for the field:

Educational Research Information Center (ERIC)
Counseling and Personnel Services
University of Michigan
Ann Arbor, Michigan 48104 USA
A specialized information center, part of a national system sponsored by the United States Office of Education; indexes and abstracts publications on counseling and personnel.

European Economic Community (EEC)
200 rue de la Loi
1040 Brussels, Belgium

Institut national d'étude du travail et d'orientation professionnelle (INETOP)
75 Paris, Seine, France

Institut national d'orientation professionnelle
41 rue Gay-Lussac
Paris 6e, France

International Association for Educational and Vocational Guidance
257 route d'Arlon
Strassen, Luxembourg

International Bureau of Education (IBE)
Palais Wilson
1211 Geneva 14, Switzerland

International Labour Organisation
1211 Geneva 22, Switzerland

National Institute for Career Education and Counseling
Bateman Street
Cambridge, England

Organisation for Economic Co-operation and Development
Centre for Educational Research and Innovation (CERI)
2 rue André Pascal
75772 Paris, France

UNESCO
place de Fontenoy
75007 Paris, France

United States Bureau of Labor Statistics
United States Department of Labor
441 G Street NW
Washington, D.C. 20212 USA

**COURSE AND DEGREE
REQUIREMENTS**
See Registrar.

COURTS AND HIGHER EDUCATION

The distinguished French-Canadian legal scholar, Yves Ouellette (1970), has written: "Sans doute, parce que l'Université est antérieure à l'Etat moderne, qu'elle bénéficie d'une longue tradition d'autonomie administrative et intellectuelle, qu'elle a ses coutumes et souvent ses propres mécanismes d'arbitrage de ses disputes, les juges ont toujours manifesté la plus grande réticence à intervenir dans l'exercice de ses fonctions académiques et à renverser ses décisions."

In countries with a strong tradition of university autonomy, the charter of higher education institutions often includes provisions for resolving internal disputes by a tribunal existing as an organ of internal governance of the institution, rather than by the civil courts. In countries where a considerable degree of control is conventionally exercised by a national ministry of education or some smaller bureaucracy, the tendency is to settle conflicts in so-called administrative courts that are only quasi-judicial bodies within the administrative branch itself and not independent judicial tribunals outside the administrative structure.

Interactions between the civil courts and universities and colleges have undoubtedly been more numerous and more influential in the United States than in any other country. Not a great many national governments have an independent judiciary functioning as a distinctly separate and coordi-

nate branch and exercising the power of judicial review over legislative and administrative acts at the federal and lower levels, under which the courts may declare these acts void if a complainant successfully contends in appropriate cases that the acts are in violation of the federal or state constitutions.

Thus, court decisions affecting universities and colleges seem everywhere to be fewer than in the United States, and almost no discrete, book-length surveys or analyses of the judge-made law of higher education appear to have been published for other countries. This essay therefore deals only with a few countries, chiefly in the Western world, but including India and the Philippines, where the requisite records are relatively accessible.

Great Britain

In Britain the tradition of centuries is that a university is an independent corporation, having its own charter from the crown and its own apparatus for the resolution of internal conflicts. An element in this structure is the visitor (a person of high status representing the crown and acting, when necessary, as a final tribunal of appeal, whose decisions are final—a forum of last resort, so to speak). In the late twentieth century, however, the older prerogatives of the visitor fell into decline; in some instances no visitor was appointed, and in others the civil courts consented to hear an appeal from a decision of a visitor. A similar state of affairs seems to prevail in Canada and the English-speaking Commonwealth countries. Should the atrophy of this traditional function of the visitor continue, interactions between the universities and the civil courts will undoubtedly increase.

Yet the number of judgments reported (in toto for the whole field of law, not merely a small branch such as higher education law) is relatively small. Says Karlen (1963): "Not all decisions are published— far from it. Only about 25 per cent of those rendered by the Court of Appeal appear in the officially sanctioned *Weekly Law Reports.* About 70 per cent of those rendered by the House of Lords and the Privy Council appear, and about 10 per cent of those rendered by the Court of Criminal Appeal. The main body of case law from all the courts of England, including other appellate and trial courts as well, grows at the rate of only three volumes a year. This is the standard output of both the *Weekly Law Reports* and the . . . *All England Reports* (which contain in general identically the same cases)."

Universities and other institutions of higher learning. A decision of 1951 declared that a small college in Wales (not one of the four colleges composing the University of Wales, but one older than any of them) could not be classified as a university. The college, St. David's College, resisted association with the University College of Wales at Aberystwyth but in 1960 assented to a sponsorship scheme with the University College of South Wales and Monmouthshire, Cardiff, and subsequently received financial assistance from the University Grants Committee (*St. David's College, Lampeter* v. *Ministry of Education,* 1 A. E. R. 559, 1951).

Approximately half the students in higher education in Britain are in institutions other than the universities. By 1975 the status of the thirty polytechnics was, in many respects, equivalent to that of the universities. While these colleges are generously subsidized by the Ministry of Education and Science, portions of their financial support are supplied by local authorities. Institutions such as the colleges of education also draw their support partly or wholly from local sources. Thus, some litigation regarding these institutions is recorded and reported only locally. In 1974 and 1975 the numerous colleges of education underwent drastic reorganization (double and triple mergers, absorption by polytechnics, and, in some instances, outright abolition), in part due to national economic stress.

Decisions involving university personnel.

Only rarely, as compared with the United States, do cases involving the behavior, rights, and obligations of students or of faculty members reach the civil courts. The occasional affinity of male teachers for female students seems, however, not to be confined within any national boundaries; it has sometimes been found in staid England as well as on the opposite side of the world. For example, in 1922 an assistant in the chemistry department at University College, London—who had been found to have taken an 18-year-old female student into a dark lecture hall, where he put his arm around her, squeezed her, and kissed her—was confronted by the provost of the college and asked to resign immediately. This he refused, not considering the matter serious enough to justify such a penalty; but when the provost wrote to him, requesting that he hand in his keys and leave in the evening, he did so. He then sued for salary due for the remainder of the term or, in alternative, as damages for wrongful dismissal. His claim was dismissed on appeal (*Jones* v. *University of London,* K. B., reported in the *Times* of London, March 21 and 22, 1922). It might be hazarded that, if such a case were to occur today, with the offender allowed a formal hearing before an impartial academic body, the process might result in a lesser penalty, in view of advancing civil liberties and life styles.

English courts appear to be more reluctant than American courts to accept jurisdiction in matters of faculty employment. When fifty members of the University of London signed a petition requisitioning a special meeting of convocation to discuss the refusal of one of the schools of the university to reemploy one of its teachers, the chairman of convocation refused, on the ground that the issue belonged to the particular school and not to the university. The fifty members then asked a civil court for a writ of mandamus to compel the chairman to call the meeting. The writ was refused for lack of jurisdiction, the judges saying that the issue was a domestic one, to be decided within the university organization, in which the authority of last resort in such matters was the visitor *(R. v. Dunsheath, ex parte Meredith,* 1 K. B. 127, 1951).

In the 1966 case of *Rex* v. *Aston University Senate,* the civil courts accepted jurisdiction without deferring to the historic but disappearing prerogative of a visitor. (In fact, no visitor had been appointed; in such an instance, some courts insist that the crown is automatically the visitor, while other courts reject that doctrine.)

In a 1972 suit by a college principal against a member of his local education authority for libel and slander, Lord Denning, Master of the Rolls, forthrightly proclaimed the law of that subject: "If the defendant honestly believed his statement to be true, he is not to be held malicious merely because such belief was not based on any reasonable ground; or because he was hasty, credulous, or foolish in jumping to a conclusion or irrational, indiscreet, pig-headed or obstinate in his belief" *(Horrocks* v. *Lowe,* 3 A. E. R. 1095, 1972).

In Britain, as in the United States, the judge-made law becomes somewhat more humane as it contemplates university and professor as employer and employee, modifying in some respects the older and harsher common law of master and servant. A 1972 decision of an English court held that a university lecturer, who had been dismissed because he had done no research, could claim his compensation for the remainder of his term; he had been dropped "unfairly" or "unjustly in all the circumstances" because he had not been warned that such a result might follow and given opportunity to improve his performance.

The *London Times Higher Education Supplement* of May 2, 1975, reported a case in the Court of Appeal in which the British Broadcasting Corporation (BBC) dropped a program assistant who was under a term contract, in which he agreed not to claim any compensation if dismissed before the terminal date. The BBC could not escape,

thought the court. because a fixed-term contract is one that cannot be unfixed by notice by either party. Thus, universities that have employed lecturers with a similar escape clause in their contracts are likely to find these clauses ineffective. The Court of Appeal made it clear, however, that the decision did not affect either party's right to terminate the agreement summarily if the other party committed a gross breach of contract.

In matters of academic concern—such as examinations and the conferring of degrees and diplomas, as distinguished from disciplinary actions against students or staff members—neither English nor American courts are inclined to interfere with the discretion of the university authorities. When a candidate failed in the examination for the degree of bachelor of laws at the University of London, he alleged that the examiners were negligent in marking his papers and claimed damages for negligence as well as a writ of mandamus to compel them to award him the grade justified. The court said: "The High Court does not act as a court of appeal from university examiners. . . . The action is wholly misconceived, and the decision of the judge to . . . dismiss the action was clearly right" *(Thorne* v. *London University,* 2 Q. B. 237, 1966). The same result had been reached in an essentially similar case approximately a century earlier *(Thomson* v. *London University,* 33 L. J. Ch. 625, 1864).

There are books that list and discuss, in an organized fashion, hundreds of British decisions dealing with primary and secondary schools, with an occasional reference to higher education (Barrell, 1970, 1975; Taylor and Saunders, 1971), but few discuss decisions dealing with higher education alone. There are, however, book-length works on the modern governance of British universities and their relationships with the state (Moodie and Eustace, 1974; Berdahl, 1959) and some useful articles in legal periodicals (Bridge, 1970; Wade, 1969).

Canada

The British North America Act of 1867 assigned responsibility for education to the provincial governments, as distinct from the dominion government, and the bulk of subsequent lawmaking relative to higher education has accordingly been done by the respective provincial parliaments, with comparatively sparse input by the courts of the dominion parliament. In Canada, where criminal law is federal legislation, there is no trace of the notion that a university campus is a sanctuary for students who commit crimes, such as once had some support in certain Latin countries. The concept of no sanctuary also prevails in the United States, where the bulk of criminal law originates in state legislatures and courts, although there is also federal criminal jurisdiction in specified fields. In the sphere of tort law, Canada is ahead of the United States, for the doctrine of sovereign immunity from tort liability on the part of a provincial university has entirely disappeared; although it has long been in decline in the United States, sovereign immunity survives to some extent in several states.

On the issue of exempting real property of educational institutions from taxation, Canadian and American statutes and judicial interpretations appear similar. An example is afforded by a recent court decision holding that land and buildings in actual use for educational purposes (including residence halls for students, the president's house, and student union buildings) would not be taxed, even if the use were no more than temporary. Only lands held idle for future development were deemed taxable (*Governors of Acadia University* v. *Town of Wolfville*, S. C. N. S., March 25, 1971).

For scholarly sketches of the basic constitutional relationships of the levels of government in Canada and of the place of higher education in the complex, useful sources are cited in Benoist (1956–1957), Corry (1966), and Ouellette (1970).

Human rights law in Canada—touching on the rights of university students, faculties, and staffs—is developing much the same as in the United States, but its source is chiefly in provincial legislatures, in contrast to its American derivation from the Bills of Rights in the federal and respective state constitutions. There are differences in terminology, but these are of little real consequence; for example, the phrase *due process of law* in the Fifth Amendment and in the Fourteenth Amendment to the United States Constitution, which embodies essentially the idea of fairness, is not used in Canada. Instead, the phrase is *natural justice,* and it derives, not from a written constitution, but from a succession of Great Writs, running as far into English history as the signing of the Magna Carta in 1215.

The basic concept of fairness is the same in Britain, the Commonwealth countries, and the United States. The United States, however, appears to be perhaps a decade ahead in modern extensions and applications of civil rights principles to students and teachers in institutions of higher education.

Civil rights of students. In Ontario, in 1968, the McRuer Commission's inquiry into civil rights included in its recommendations a capitulation of "Minimum Rules of Procedure for All Tribunals" exercising judicial or administrative powers where fair procedure is required. The essentials enumerated embrace (1) notice of hearing; (2) notice of the case to be met; (3) adjournment (postponement); (4) power to issue subpoenas; (5) hearings in public, with specified exceptions; (6) enforcement of orders; (7) oaths; and (8) right to counsel. These prescriptions are similar but not identical to the prescriptions usually insisted on by federal and state courts in the United States. Two differences stand out. The first is that academic-administrative tribunals in United States universities do not possess the power of subpoena—they can only invite witnesses to attend or to provide affidavits in lieu of attendance. The comparable body at the University of Toronto—a seven-member tribunal bearing the name of *caput*—is empowered by the law of Ontario to compel the attendance not only of witnesses from the academic community but also of other citizens having no connection with it; a refusal to obey a subpoena can be punished by a citation for contempt, though only after application for approval of this penalty in each instance to the high court of the province of Ontario. The second difference is that, in Ontario, somewhat greater stress is laid on the right of an accused student to be represented by legal counsel than is generally the case in the United States.

It would be a mistake to assume that all these matters are solidly settled in either country. For example, in July 1974, the University of Ontario's caput suspended for three and four years, respectively, two graduate students who were members of Students for a Democratic Society, an activist organization, because they participated in disrupting lectures by a visiting professor from the University of Pittsburgh, causing him to leave the podium without finishing his series. The students' alleged reason for their action was that the professor's writings and speeches were well-known to be "flagrantly racist," since he claimed to have discovered evidence that race is an important factor in determining mental capacity—a notion the students thought so obviously wrong and divisive that it ought not to be tolerated on a university campus. Caput took the view that freedom of speech and expression is a value of much higher rank and must supersede any asserted right to suppress expression thought by some persons to be obviously erroneous. In the United States similar issues are generally resolved in favor of full freedom of expression.

As another example, in Canada an editorial in the *Toronto Globe and Mail* of July 15, 1974, severely criticized the Ontario legislature for having authorized the university tribunal, in an act of 1971, to compel the attendance of witnesses from outside the academic community, as it did in the case just recited. The editor pointed out that this feature of the act was contrary to the recommendations of the McRuer Commission, saying trenchantly, "These are powers that should belong only to the courts." The *Globe and Mail* did not speak to the issues of free speech or racism.

Civil rights of professors. Progress in judicial application of fairness in disputes between faculty members and their respective universities is indicated in an early 1975 unanimous decision of the Supreme Court of the Dominion of Canada at Ottawa. An associate professor of Slavic languages at the University of Alberta had been provided by the university with a confidential form, on which he was requested to write his judgments and recommendations as to whether a faculty colleague named thereon should be granted or denied tenure. Responding to the request, he wrote some highly derogatory statements, with the understanding that they would be held confidential.

Later, the associate professor was dismissed from the faculty, after a hearing on four charges of professional misconduct and misbehavior. One of the four charges was that the confidential communication, which had in fact been circulated, had been written in bad faith and with malice. The paper itself was admitted in evidence at the hearing. A three-member arbitration board, set up by the university, rejected the other three charges as trivial but upheld the professor's dismissal on the ground of alleged lack of good faith in his unflattering appraisal of the colleague whom he had been asked to judge. The determination was sustained on appeal to the Alberta Court of Appeals.

With the help of the University of Alberta Staff Association and the Canadian Association of University Teachers, the associate professor appealed to the Supreme Court of Canada. There the unanimous decision was that the tenure form, originally understood to be confidential and so stamped, could not properly be admitted as evidence before the arbitration board in the first place, and therefore no charges could be based on it. Hence, the professor's dismissal was unlawful, and all legal costs in the case were assessed against the university (*Slavutych* v. *University of Alberta,* Supreme Court of Canada, January 31, 1975).

Several other judgments touching on civil rights of university personnel have been made by Canadian courts. In one case the Nova Scotia court accepted jurisdiction and reviewed the dismissal of a university employee after it had been approved by the visitor, thus eroding the traditional function of that dignitary; another case, at Laval University, centered on a futile charge of "failure to educate"; and in a third, at Western Ontario University, the court spoke of the type of hearing to which a tenured professor is entitled when efforts are made to terminate his tenure (*Chamberlain* v. *University of Western Ontario,* 44 C. L. R. 453, 1973).

Australia

Like the Dominion of Canada and the United States of America, the Commonwealth of Australia is a federal union of states. Although the bases of federalism are different in each of these countries, higher education in all three is much more a function and responsibility of the component states than of the federal government. On that point an Australian high court decision declared that education is not an "industry" within the meaning of the Commonwealth Conciliation and Arbitration Act, and that university faculty members or other employees are not therefore federally registered and are not permitted to bring litigated controversies with the universities directly into federal courts (*States of Victoria and Tasmania* v. *Commonwealth,* Australian High Court, 1929).

Of a contrary tendency (but perhaps to be discounted somewhat because it was made in wartime) is a decision in New South Wales upholding the power of the commonwealth to impose quotas on admissions to the universities—thus excluding some qualified male applicants, who, as a consequence, became eligible for military service—over the claim for exemption of the plaintiff, a student (*R.* v. *University of Sydney,* 67 C. L. R. 95, 17 A. L. J. 103, A. H. C., 1943). This judgment is reported to have lent support to the idea of the then newly established Universities Commission, from which has subsequently developed a considerable federal educational bureaucracy.

In the realm of the relationships between universities and their faculties and staffs, a case arising at the University of Tasmania concerning the dismissal of a faculty member is relevant. The faculty member was accused of scandalous misconduct with a female student. The case terminated in a decision by the commonwealth high court (*Orr* v. *University of Tasmania,* 100 C. L. R. 526, 1957) that the legal relation between the university and its faculty and staff members is that of master and servant at common law, and hence the accused faculty member had no recourse. This conservative decision became a cause célèbre in the world of the Antipodes, and at least two books were subsequently published about it (Council of the University of Tasmania, 1958; Eddy, 1961).

A more recent judgment, regarding another facet of the relationship between educational institutions and their students, rejected the long-held doctrine of delegation of parental authority and responsibility to teachers (in the United States commonly called *in loco parentis*) and held that school authorities (including state education departments) could be liable for negligent conduct by teachers (*Ramsay* v. *Larsen,* 111 C. L. R. 16, 1964). In American higher education institutions, where practically all students are over eighteen years of age, *in loco parentis* is dead, but not in lower schools, whose pupils are largely below that age. As to the institutional liability for negligence (tort), a strong tendency toward abolition of the earlier doctrine of immunity has been in motion since the early 1950s in the United States, but it has not yet been spread to all fifty states.

Other Australian decisions include one of 1973, which held that a student who had graduated in arts and then entered law school was qualified to be elected to the council of the University of Adelaide, under the terms of an act of the state of South Australia of 1971, which conferred eligibility on any student who had been an undergraduate for at least two terms prior to election *(Graeme-Evans* v. *University of Adelaide,* 6 S. A. S. R. 302, 1973). Another, involving the New South Wales University of Technology, declared: "The Legislature intended the university to be a body substantially independent of the Crown in the exercise of its powers and functions" (Re *Crown Employees, University of Technology,* A. R., N. S. W. 1088, 1955); ten years later a judgment of the nature and character of the University of Sydney as a public institution reached similar conclusions regarding its autonomy *(Ex parte Forster;* re *University of Sydney,* S. R., N. S. W. 723, 1963). (Compare Michigan, Minnesota, and California decisions discussed below and in Chambers, 1964, 1967.) "University Discipline" (1970) discusses natural justice in disciplinary dealings with students in Australia. (Compare the discussions of natural justice in Canada, above, and due process of law in the United States, below.)

The matter of a student-elected fellow of the senate of the University of Sydney, who believed he was denied access to numerous types of university records and documents essential to the proper execution of his duties as a senator, reached the Supreme Court of New South Wales in 1974. The plaintiff sought a declaration of his rights and a mandatory order to the university. During the pendency of the suit, it transpired that the university had devised and adopted a method of transmitting to the plaintiff all the official documents he desired, in a manner entirely satisfactory to him. Hence, there being no point in pursuing the proceedings further, the complaint was dismissed as moot,

but Justice Holland delivered a lengthy opinion justifying his decision not to order costs against either party *(Joseph* v. *University of Sydney,* S. Ct. of N. S. W., Eq. Div., No. 23 of 1974).

An earlier decision of the same court upheld a resolution of the university senate authorizing the faculties to require a student to show cause why he should be allowed to repeat a year or course in which he had failed more than once and to exclude such student if he failed to show good cause. The applicant in this case had been excluded from the annual examinations in 1961 because of failure to complete required essays. In 1962 he repeated the course (in the faculty of economics), attended the examinations, and failed. He was then excluded from repeating the course, and his exclusion was confirmed by the senate. His petition for mandamus to command the university to enroll him in the course was denied by the court, in an opinion that discussed the scope and intendment of the University Act of 1900 and the bylaws of the university and that concluded that the university had power to preclude or defer the attendance of a student whose performance had been unsatisfactory *(Ex parte Forster:* re *University of Sydney,* S. R., N. S. W. 723; 80 W. N. 1047, N. S. W. R. 1000, 1964).

Late in 1975 an uncertainty arose concerning the rights of authors and publishers under copyright law as against libraries that permit the use of copying machines for purposes of instruction and research. In 1973 a syndicate of many of Australia's leading authors, under the name of Copyright Agency, Ltd., pursued the matter by demanding a specified fee for each copy of their works, and an author sued the University of New South Wales for breach of copyright. The Supreme Court of New South Wales decided against the university in 1974, and both parties appealed to the commonwealth high court, which, according to a report by John Kirkaldy in the *Times* (London) *Higher Education Supplement* of October 17, 1975, handed down an indecisive opinion that left librarians, students, and professors in doubt as to what they could lawfully do. Temporarily confused, the university was said to have removed from the library shelves all books by the syndicate authors and to have ordered that, before any student or staff member could use the photocopying machines, he must produce identification and sign a register assuming sole risk of any possible violation of the copyright act. (A similar case in the United States, which reached the Supreme Court, is discussed below.)

New Zealand

As in Britain and the other English-speaking Commonwealth countries, litigation involving universities has been comparatively sparse in New Zealand. Cases that have reached the civil courts have involved such issues as public land reserves made available for the endowment of Canterbury University, siting of a second university for the Auckland area, dismissal of a professor during World War I at the Victoria University of Wellington, and dispute over the use of government funds to pay salaries of "Presbyterian chairs" at the University of Otago (reputed to be the only litigation touching religion). All New Zealand universities are public, created by the national parliament in a manner analogous to the American state universities, which are established either by state constitutions or by state legislatures.

One recent case bears considerable resemblance to the Canadian case of *Slavutych* v. *University of Alberta*. In the New Zealand case, the plaintiff had given the University of Auckland names of sources from which confidential information about him could be obtained. Later, he sought to compel the university to produce these confidential documents as evidence in court. Judge Turner refused, pointing out that the parties had agreed before the suit that these documents would not be other than confidential, and that they had been brought into existence on the "solemn understand-

ing of both of them that the plaintiff would not be allowed to see the documents." Therefore, the plaintiff could not demand that they be exhibited (*Bell* v. *University of Auckland,* N. Z. L. R. 1029, 1969).

Another issue, in a 1975 decision, is related to the power of local zoning authorities to regulate the design of university buildings. Victoria University of Wellington erected a ten-story tower named the *von Zedlitz* building. The Wellington city council, asserting its jurisdiction as a local zoning authority, ordered the height reduced by twenty feet or by two stories. The case went to the New Zealand Supreme Court and was decided in favor of the university, on the ground that the crown is not subject to local regulations of that type. The structure was erected on land owned by the crown and financed with money provided by the crown. Both the New Zealand government and the University Grants Committee supported the university's argument (reported by Brian Priestley, in the *Times* (London) *Higher Education Supplement* of April 18, 1975, and May 23, 1975). Legal controversies of this nature, though at first sight seemingly somewhat petty, occasionally plague universities in many parts of the world.

Federal Republic of Germany

Two prominent issues of higher education that have reached the courts in the Federal Republic of Germany involve the principle of *numerus clausus* (closed number) and loyalty requirements for university personnel.

Numerus clausus. The federal constitution guarantees all holders of the secondary school certificate of graduation *(Abitur)* university admission in fields of study as a basic constitutional right. From 1960 to 1973, the number of persons qualifying for university admission increased threefold. There was some expansion of university facilities, but nowhere near enough to accommodate all applicants. The result was that the universities tended to adopt a *numerus clausus* rule, excluding many applicants, which amounts to a rationing of higher education. This rule seems to have been made policy of the state of Bavaria in 1972, as well as of Hamburg (a city-state), and was sustained by the highest state court.

In restricting admissions Bavaria gave preference to residents of the state and excluded many nonresidents, which was considered revolutionary, since place of residence had never had any bearing on admissions to German universities. Immediately, the Bavarian policy was contested in a case before the federal Constitutional Court. That tribunal cited the constitutional guarantee of admissions, declaring that the only basis on which a qualified applicant could be excluded from any university was lack of facilities.

Stretching its powers beyond the judicial realm, the court also directed that a national office for the assignment of study places be established to handle admission of students in all fields where applicants outnumber the available study places and suggested that the eleven states *(Länder)* composing the Federal Republic should act jointly in this matter. (Financing of the universities is almost wholly by the states.) The state ministers of education promptly devised an interstate agreement, which was ratified by the legislatures of all the states; by the summer of 1973 the *Zentralstelle für die Vergabe von Studienplätzen* (central point for assigning study places) was controlling admissions to approximately a dozen of the most crowded fields in all the universities (Carbone, 1974–1975).

Under this form of control, each application must carry the applicant's first, second, and third choices of university and field of study. The result may be that he will be offered admission to his third-choice university, in his third-choice field of study. Thus, he may study art history in a university he does not want to attend, when his aim is to study medicine. He has other alternatives, however. He may wait one or several semesters and try again, or he may go to his second-choice university and study in a second-choice field closely related to his first choice (for example, biochemistry instead of medicine).

Some Germans predict that, within a few years, all fields will be controlled. This is only a short step from the manpower management doctrine prophetically set forth in George Orwell's nightmarish novel *1984,* under which exact quotas are centrally established for studies leading to every profession and occupation. Others correctly contend that such a scheme would be clearly unconstitutional. While the ramifications are of great importance to the concept of higher education, they cannot be further pursued in this discourse, which is limited to court decisions; however, it should be remarked in passing that the German existentialist philosopher, Karl Jaspers, once stated that every selection is an injustice.

The issue of *numerus clausus*—the rationing of higher education by some manner of limiting enrollments—exists in every country of the world. It is, in part, elitism versus egalitarianism, and the latter is the wave of the future. Legally, the ultimate defense of a university against applicants is "insufficient facilities" (the common expression in Western Europe is "lack of places"), and the provision of additional places is a very important question of public policy.

In a report prepared for the Committee for Higher Education and Research on behalf of the *Westdeutsche Rektorenkonferenz* (West German Rectors' Conference), Karpen (1973) has written: "The effects of *numerus clausus* are obvious. Expectations cannot be fulfilled and entitlements cannot be given effect; there are long waiting periods before higher education begins; studies are protracted (especially by the covert 'internal' *numerus clausus* system); difficulties arise for foreign students." In 1974 he prepared, for the federal cabinet, a detailed analysis of criteria used in the admissions process for all universities in the eleven states of the federal republic, with recommendations for revision (Karpen, 1975).

Loyalty requirements for university personnel. All university employees hold public posts and are in what is called *civil service.* Thus, the appointment and retention of professors and other university staff is within the meaning of a federal administrative order—the "extremists' decree"—issued jointly in January 1972 by the chancellor of the republic and the prime ministers of the eleven federated states. The essence of the decree is that if an applicant for a public post belongs to an organization having anticonstitutional aims, this raises doubts of fitness that normally justify rejection. But the federal constitution guarantees freedom of opinion, freedom in learning and the arts, and the individual right to freely choose one's occupation. As early as 1961 the Constitutional Court proclaimed that only it, and no other body, could lawfully proclaim the unconstitutionality of any political organization.

Conflict between the constitution and the decree is apparently unavoidable. Professors in several universities have signed protests against the application of the decree in different states, in alleged instances of injustice. In July 1975 the federal Constitutional Court decided a case arising in Schleswig-Holstein, in a somewhat ambivalent judgment which declares that an applicant's membership in an extremist party or group *may be* a factor in determining suitability for a public post, but that it is only one among several factors. The opinion stresses that each case must be considered individually; it also uses words designed to discourage overemphasizing loyalty investigations and warns that such practices could be held to violate the federal constitution (reported in G. Kloss in the *Times* (London) *Higher Education Supplement* of August 22, 1975). The concerned judges and professors would no doubt be interested in the judicial history of this subject in the United States, where, after years of litigation, negative disclaimer oaths of loyalty have been discredited and invalidated as unconstitutional. There is generally no objection to a different oath—one that is simply a positive affirmation of allegiance to the state and the nation, and no more.

France

Under French law and custom, the affairs of universities have always been grist for quasi-judicial administrative courts *(tribunaux administratifs)*—of which there is a symmetrical hierarchy in the centralized unitary national government—when not locally adjudicated within the structure of each university itself. At the apex of the pyramid is the Council of State *(Conseil d'état).* The council has not had the power of judicial review as known in the United States, but in 1958 a constitutional council of nine judges was set up to oversee elections and constitutional amendments in cases where there is reason to believe that a new law violates individual civil liberties. If persuaded that civil liberties were infringed, the council could declare such law null and void, but such action could be taken only at the request of the president of the republic, the premier, the president of the senate, or the president of the national assembly. Thus, even the constitutional council was, in a way, subsidiary or subordinate to the executive and legislative branches.

The constitution of the Fifth Republic of France was amended October 21, 1974, by a joint session of both chambers of the national legislature, in the first constitutional assembly in eleven years. This amendment empowers the council to void any law it adjudges to infringe civil liberties, thus broadening its power in that respect and moving it further toward the status of the United States Supreme Court. It also authorizes any group of sixty or more members of either legislative chamber to initiate an action before the council *(New York Times,* October 22, 1974).

The significance of the amendment is

not easy to estimate. The premier was reported as saying it would strengthen civil liberties and give opposition parties a better chance to fulfill their missions, but some leftist deputies declared it to be of little consequence. The sweeping changes made in the system of French universities since 1965 have apparently been largely the work of the administrative and legislative branches rather than an independent judiciary and, therefore, are not a subject of court decisions. No comprehensive book-length treatise on the courts and higher education in France exists. Recently published illustrative items in the copious but fragmented periodical literature of the subject are Chevallier (1971b) and Toulemonde (1971b). Chevallier (1971a) and Toulemonde (1971a) are more general works on the law of higher education. Some current reports appear in *Le Monde de l'éducation,* published by the well-known newspaper *Le Monde,* and in the periodical journal *Revue de l'enseignement supérieure.*

India

India has a national supreme court in a relatively independent position, with jurisdiction to scrutinize the compatibility between state laws and the national constitution. An example of a judgment in such a case involves the succession in the vice-chancellorship of Osmania University in the state of Andhra Pradesh in 1966. At that time D. S. Reddi was serving in his third year as vice-chancellor under the 1959 Osmania University Act (a statute of the state of Andhra Pradesh), which provided for a term of six years. The act was amended in 1966, reducing the term to three years and empowering the chancellor to appoint a new vice-chancellor within ninety days of the effective date of the act. Under this authority a new vice-chancellor was promptly appointed, and the Andhra Pradesh high court dismissed Dr. Reddi's petition to be allowed to serve out the term for which he had been appointed. He appealed this decision, and the Supreme Court of India enjoined the newly ap-

pointed successor from assuming his duties, holding that the 1966 amendment violated Article 14 of the constitution of India. Although the amendment fixed a three-year term, it was silent on the question of terminating the tenure of a vice-chancellor who was incumbent at the time it was enacted. The Supreme Court pointed out that the Osmania University Act (both original and as amended) provided that a vice-chancellor can be removed only for misbehavior or incapacity and after due inquiry by a former judge appointed for that purpose by the chancellor. Both points had been ignored in the case of Dr. Reddi. The case is commented on in the newspaper, *Hindu,* December 12, 1966, and recounted in the autumn 1967 issue of *Minerva.*

Rights of religious communities. An illustration of a litigated issue in Indian higher education is provided by the case of *Basha* v. *Union of India,* decided by the Supreme Court of India in 1968 *(All India Reports* 1968 Supreme Court 662, V 55 C 134). The Aligarh Muslim University was founded by a statute of the Indian government of 1920. This act provided that the university should be "open to all persons of either sex and of whatever race, creed, or class," that instruction in the Muslim religion be compulsory for all Muslim students, and that members of the university court (governing body) be appointed by the British governor-general in council, under a mandate in the act that all appointees to this body must be Muslims.

The statute of 1920 was amended in 1951 (after Indian independence) to delete compulsory religious instruction and the requirement that all appointees to the governing body be Muslims. This was in harmony with the new Indian constitution, which stipulated that no person attending any educational institution recognized by, and receiving financial aid from, the government be required to take any religious instruction against his will. The amendment went unchallenged until a second amendment was made in 1965, whereupon the constitutionality of both amendments was contested in court. The second amendment reduced the university court to advisory status, changed its composition, and transferred many of its powers to a smaller, internal executive council. It also terminated the service of all members of each of these bodies as of May 20, 1965, creating a hiatus until they could be reconstituted. During the interval, all authority resided in the office of the visitor (which office had succeeded to the powers of the rector, who was ex officio the governor-general until 1951).

The contention of Azeez Basha and other plaintiffs in this case was that the amendments of 1951 and 1965 to the statute of 1920 were in violation of Article 30 (1) of the Indian constitution, which states: "All minorities, whether based on religion or language, shall have the right to establish and administer educational institutions of their choice." The contention was denied by Chief Justice Wanchoo and his colleagues, who reasoned that, although the Muslim community might be said to have established the predecessor school, known as Muhammadan Anglo-Oriental College, at Aligarh in 1873, the Muslim community had advocated and assented to the enactment of the Aligarh Muslim University Act of 1920, under which the university corporation succeeded to all the powers and property of the former college. So it must be said that Aligarh Muslim University was established by the government of India and not by the Muslim minority.

Language of instruction in Indian universities. India is not only a land of several religions but also of many languages. Under British colonial rule, the language of instruction in the universities was English. This had the advantage of fostering a single language, understood by all educated Indians, but also the disadvantage of discouraging the perpetuation of the local languages and cultures. Since India's independence, the issue has been frequently disputed, with some of the separate states arguing for the use of their state or regional languages as the media of instruction in their own universities.

Under the constitution the power to specify the language of instruction for the primary and secondary schools belongs to the separate states; but for the universities and other institutions of higher education, it belongs to the national government. Thus, when Gujarat University at Ahmedabad adopted the rule that "Gujarati or Hindi shall be the language of instruction and examination," the Supreme Court declared that it was beyond the powers of the university to make any regional language the exclusive medium *(State of Gujarat* v. *Srikrishna,* A. I. R. 1963 S. C. 703; *Chitralekha* v. *State of Mysore,* A. I. R. 1964 S. C. 1823).

Powers of the national and state governments. As in any federal system, the division of authority between the central national government and the component states is neither precise to the smallest detail nor rigid and unchanging. In general, the central government has exclusive jurisdiction over a growing list of "institutions of national importance" (at first, those named, in a pertinent annex to the constitution, were Banaras Hindu University, Aligarh Muslim University, and Delhi University, but the annex also included an expansion clause—"and any other institution declared by Parliament by law to be an institution of national importance"—and the list has been greatly expanded).

It is within the domain of the concurrent powers that many judicial decisions have been necessary, to define the respective spheres of the national and state governments. The key to federal authority is a clause of the constitution that charges the republic with power to provide for "coordination and determination of standards in institutions for higher education or research and scientific and technical institutions." The trend of decisions since the early 1950s has been toward making this authorization somewhat broader and more efficacious, but expressly not in derogation of the much-prized internal autonomy of universities. Detailed scholarly reviews of the decisions have been published by the Indian Law Institute at New Delhi (Sharma, Raizada, and Bhagwan, 1969; and Nayak, 1972, 1973).

The Supreme Court of India has held that it is permissible for a state or a university to charge discriminatory fees to students who are not residents within the state. (The constitution prohibits discrimination on the basis of place of birth, caste, sex, or religion.) Place of birth and place of residence are often not the same. As to the latter, the court said: "Classification [on the basis of residence] is quite a legitimate and lawful objective for a state to encourage education within its borders" (*Joshi* v. *State of Madyha Bharat*, A. I. R. 1955, S. C. 340).

The courts, notably the High Court of the State of Kerala, have approved the classification of applicants residing in the same state on the basis of geographical or historical reasons related to the backwardness of their home districts—allotting proportionally larger numbers of places to educationally deficient districts (*Thomas* v. *State of Kerala,* A. I. R. 1958, Kerala 33). Thus, the comparatively disadvantaged district of Malabar, which had just come into the state of Kerala, was given places in the state educational institutions on the basis of a ratio of eight to five. The same high court later held it unconstitutional to allocate places on a district basis if assignment was not based on demographic data or other scientific or reasonable grounds. Thus, a statewide scheme that was not based on the literacy census report or on any other historical or geographical reason was judicially struck down (*Mathew* v. *State of Kerala,* A. I. R. 1964, Kerala 39).

Some form of rationing of higher education goes on in every nation in the world. A thoughtful remark of Judge B. N. Banerjee, of the high court at Calcutta, is apropos: "Scratch the green rind of a sapling repeatedly or wantonly twist it in the soil, and a scarred or crooked oak will tell of the act for years to come. So it is with the youngster: treat him unsympathetically or shut to his face all the doors of educational institutions, and an uneducated or a half-educated youth may live a useless life to proclaim what men wantonly did by refusing to him all opportunities for college education." India has the third largest number of students in higher education of any nation, but its total population is more than twice that of any other nation except the People's Republic of China.

Republic of the Philippines

Since the mid 1920s, a substantial—and increasing—number of institutions of higher education in the Philippines have been proprietary, profit-seeking private enterprises. There are also some of the nonprofit, charitable sort, of which the prototype is the old and respected University of Santo Tomas in Manila. Then there are the public institutions of higher education, with the University of the Philippines in Quezon City standing at the apex. Distinction among these three types is essential to a comprehension of court decisions.

Private proprietary universities and colleges. Statutory regulation of private colleges began early in the twentieth century. The legislative acts were amended at intervals. Since the early 1950s, the main thrust of the law has been that no private school or college can be opened or operated without a license from the Secretary of Public Instruction in the National Department of Education. Inspection of all such colleges and schools is a mandatory duty of this government agency.

In 1955 an original action in the Philippine Supreme Court was brought by the Philippine Association of Colleges and Universities, asking that this legislation be declared unconstitutional. The suit failed because there was no allegation that a complainant had actually suffered any damage or detriment. Because a mere hypothetical threat is not sufficient to invoke judicial intervention in such a matter, no justiciable issue was presented. Besides, the court reasoned that inspection and regulation of private schools is a part of the inherent police power of the state in the public interest, but it was mindful that if the state's actions went beyond the limits of reasonable regulation and amounted to complete control of private schools, it might become an unconstitutional invasion of the rights of persons who prefer such schools or choose to operate them as a means of livelihood *(Philippine Association of Colleges and Universities* v. *Secretary of Education,* P. R. Vol. 97, pp. 806–821, October 1955).

Academic and other university personnel. Fair employment practices legislation *is* applicable to proprietary universities, as illustrated in a decision wherein an order of the Court of Industrial Relations against Far Eastern University was affirmed by the Supreme Court. A full-time instructor in the Tagalog language claimed that he was dropped because of his activities in promoting a faculty labor union at the university. The Court of Industrial Relations ruled that the circumstances of his separation did indeed constitute unfair labor practices and ordered him reinstated with back pay, though he had since taken a low-paying clerical job in the central bank and also a part-time assignment as teacher of accounting at Philippine College of Commerce. The rationale was that his combined pay for these concurrent employments was much less than his former compensation as a full-time teacher of Tagalog and could by no means be called the equivalent of his employment at Far Eastern University, because the later positions did not offer the prospect of a career for a specialist in language, being low-ranking, dead-end jobs in a field for which his education had not prepared him *(Far Eastern University* v. *Aguirre and Philippine Association of College and University Professors,* S. C. R. A. Vol. 5, pp. 1082–1088, August 1962).

In a litigated controversy between University of Santo Tomas and its own local Employees' and Laborers' Association, which charged unfair labor practices, the university asked that the determination by a judge of the Court of Industrial Relations be set aside by the Philippine Supreme Court. The petition was granted on the grounds that University of Santo Tomas "is not a corporation created for profit, but an educational institution and therefore not an industrial or business organization," and that the entire body of industrial relations legislation is intended to apply only to employers and employees "in industry or occupations pursued for profit and gain." Pointing out that this conclusion had been reiterated in many earlier decisions involving various nonprofit charitable organizations, the court declared that the Court of Industrial Relations had no jurisdiction over the University of Santo Tomas. This view prevailed over the opposing contention that "the criterion in determining jurisdiction in any unfair labor practice case in any enterprise be it industrial or nonindustrial is the existence of the employer-employee relationship" *(University of Santo Tomas* v. *Employees' and Laborers' Association,* P. R. Vol. 106, pp. 439–444, October 1959).

The University of the Philippines, unquestionably a public institution of higher education, chartered in 1870, is not within the coverage of the fair employment practices legislation. It enjoys the same legal standing as described for the private, nonprofit University of Santo Tomas. Thus, when three female employees working in the south dormitory of the university compound in Diliman, Quezon City, were dropped at the expiration of their temporary short-term contracts on the recommendation of the matron in charge of the dormitory, they complained that this was in retaliation to their demands for better working conditions, and thus constituted an unfair labor practice. The Court of Industrial Relations asserted jurisdiction, but on appeal to the Philippine Supreme Court, the high tribunal denied that assertion, accepted original jurisdiction, and dismissed the complaint as not supported by the evidence and not presenting a cause of action *(University of the Philippines* v. *Court of Industrial Relations,* P. R. Vol. 107, pp. 848–852, April 1960).

Some other decisions involving personnel of the University of the Philippines have nothing to do with labor relations legislation. For example, the Supreme Court has held in two cases that the resolution of the Board of Regents of the University of the Philippines in 1959—stipulating that the terms of all deans of colleges and directors of schools or institutes of the university (in their administrative, not their professorial, capacity) should terminate on the completion of five years in that administrative capacity unless recommended for renewal—could not apply to deans or directors who had been given their appointments in the unclassified civil service prior to the effective date of the resolution, and such personnel were therefore protected by the statutes and rules governing the civil service. Hence, the application of the resolution to that particular class of individuals would be unconstitutional (*Tapales* v. *University of the Philippines,* S. C. R. A. Vol. 7, 1963; *Mitra* v. *Subido,* Vol. 21, 1967).

More recently it was decided that, under existing statutes of the Republic of the Philippines, there was no authority for the Board of Regents of the University of the Philippines to extend the period of service of a professor beyond the compulsory retirement age of sixty-five. The decision came after an aggrieved professor had already served an additional year; the court ruled that in this case the professor was entitled to the agreed salary for that year because it could be construed as being, not an *ultra vires* extension, but a special contract for services indispensable to the university due to circumstances existing at that time (*Jamias* v. *Auditor General,* S. C. R. A. Vol. 30, pp. 5–22, 1969).

Freedom of the student press. A case arising at the Philippine Normal College in Negros Oriental turned out to involve the rights of both students and a teacher. The president of the school became concerned that some articles in the two monthly news

organs of the college were discourteous if not vulgar in tone (referring in an uncomplimentary way to "old maids" on the faculty) and would lower the popular image of the institution. Accordingly, he asked the director of publications (a faculty member) to exercise more care in guiding the students in the preparation of articles and editorials and suggested that perhaps she would be willing to have the page proofs monitored by his personal assistant.

Within a few weeks the president also requested that the director call a meeting of a newly reconstituted board of management for these publications "to restudy the policies affecting editorial and reportorial practices and business management." Much agitated by these written requests and believing they were in violation of specified sections of the constitution of the republic, the director instituted a suit in the Court of First Instance in Manila, asking that the memoranda be annulled on the grounds that they "abridge the fundamental liberties of thought, speech, and press, deny the Philippine Normal College the right to enjoy academic freedom, and relieve it from the duty to develop moral character, personal discipline, and civic conscience, and to teach the duties of citizenship to the students." The director also alleged that the president was bent on removing her as director of publications and shifting her to a full-time teaching assignment and asked for a preliminary injunction to restrain these actions pending determination of the merits of her complaint.

The complaint was dismissed, and this conclusion was affirmed by the Supreme Court, reasoning that the memoranda did not in themselves invade the constitutional freedoms, and that the acts of the president were within the lawful scope of his duties in maintaining the morale and discipline of the institution. The court seemed happy, however, to note that the president had quickly withdrawn his request that the publications be monitored by his assistant and hence refrained expressly from deciding the issue of constitutionality in that particular matter *(Laxamana* v. *Borlaza,* S. C. R. A. Vol. 47, pp. 29–45, 1972).

United States

In English colonial America all colleges were private. The concept of a state university was unthought of, and, for a century and a half (until about 1930), more than a majority of all college students were in private institutions. This is thought to have been mainly a result of the historic decision of the United States Supreme Court in 1819—that the royal charter of Dartmouth College in New Hampshire subsisted as a contract between the state and the college after the revolution, and that any change in its terms, without the consent of the trustees of the college, would violate the clause of the United States Constitution that forbids any state to "enact any law impairing the obligation of a contract." Hence, the state of New Hampshire could not alter the charter or make Dartmouth a state institution *(Trustees of Dartmouth College* v. *Woodward,* 4 Wheat. 518, 4 L.Ed. 629, 1819).

The decision had great initial impact and stimulated the founding of private colleges in the new states, but its effect was greatly reduced during the 1850s, when most of the state constitutions were amended to prohibit the granting of any charters without reserving to the state the right to amend or repeal. In 1862 congressional enactment of the Morrill Act (offering large grants of public lands to any state that would establish or designate a new type of college that "without excluding other classical and scientific subjects" would teach agricultural and mechanical arts) set the stage for the ultimate development of a nationwide chain of sixty-nine land-grant universities, most of which have become large cosmopolitan institutions.

Thus, from 1930 to 1950 the national total of students was about half in the private sector and half in the public sector; enrollments in both sectors grew rapidly, but by 1975 slightly more than three fourths of all students were in public universities and colleges.

Some nine hundred decisions of state and federal courts affecting higher education were collected, classified, indexed, and discussed in the first volume of the eight-volume series by Elliott and Chambers (1936). Subsequent volumes in the same series carry the story through 1973, bringing the aggregate to some twenty-five hundred decisions (Chambers, 1941, 1946, 1952, 1964, 1967, 1972, 1973). Meanwhile, Blackwell (1961) published a small volume on college law; Alexander and Solomon (1972) published a one-volume treatise on college and university law, involving perhaps one thousand cases; and Brubacher (1971) published a summary dealing with some seventy-five landmark decisions.

Rights and obligations of students. The Fourteenth Amendment to the United States Constitution forbids any state to "deprive any person of the equal protection of the laws" (Schwartz, 1970). As early as the 1930s federal courts began to interpret this amendment to prohibit state colleges and universities from discriminating in admission of students on grounds of race or color *(Missouri ex rel. Gaines* v. *Canada,* 59 S. Ct. 232, 83 L.Ed. 207, 1938). Thus began a line of decisions advancing this principle in higher education distinct from, and earlier than, the historic federal Supreme Court judgments of 1954 and 1955, which made desegregation of public elementary and secondary schools the law of the land. The higher education decisions continue, and, having largely settled the right of individual applicants of minority races not to be discriminated against, have taken the form of declarations that any state having dual racially segregated systems of higher education institutions has an affirmative obligation to dismantle and reorganize such systems and institutions, so that eventually there will be no public universities or colleges in which members of a minority race predominate heavily or any in which the majority race is present to an extent greatly disproportionate with its relative numbers *(Sanders v. Ellington,* 288 F. Supp. 937, 1968; *Lee v. Macon County,* 317 F. Supp. 103, 1970).

Confronted with intractable problems such as this, the federal courts have lost much of their historic reluctance, based on traditional solicitude for state sovereignty, to issue to the states injunctions or other orders. This is a major trend of the times. Administrative pressures are also applied by such agencies as the civil rights divisions of the Department of Justice and the Department of Health, Education and Welfare, but controverted issues of compliance tend to find their way into the tribunals of the independent federal judiciary.

The swift pace of expansion of the public colleges and universities after 1950 led to a novel recognition that another clause of the Fourteenth Amendment—providing that "no state shall deprive any person of life, liberty, or property without *due process of law"*—should be applied fully to students. Hence, students accused of university disciplinary infractions were held to be entitled to a formal academic-administrative hearing, with some but not all the procedural protections customary in courts of law, before being subjected to serious penalties, such as expulsion or suspension *(Dixon v. Alabama,* 294 F. 2d 1150, 1961; see also Seavey, 1967; Van Alstyne, 1968). Since about 1960 there has been an understanding that students are also entitled to the First Amendment's guarantees of freedom of speech, expression, petition, and association, and the Fourth Amendment's protection against unreasonable searches and seizures *(Edwards v. South Carolina,* 372 U. S. 229, 1963; *Cox v. Louisiana,* 379 U. S. 559, 1965; *Saunders v. Virginia Polytechnic Institute,* 417 F. 2d 1127, 1969).

The Twenty-sixth Amendment, adopted in 1972, established the right to vote in federal, state, and local elections for persons of either sex aged eighteen or older; the fifty states immediately began enacting one-by-one provisions making eighteen the age of majority for all, or nearly all,

purposes, including an end to parental obligation for financial support and other protections and limitations of minority age. Abandoning the relationship of *in loco parentis* between college and student and lowering the age of majority imply that eventually virtually all college students will be legally independent adults (Young, 1973, pp. 38–41).

One result may be the termination or reduction of the widely spreading bureaucratic practice of requiring complicated computations of parents' assets, incomes, and other family conditions as prerequisite to the granting of federally funded or state-funded student aids. Another result has already come about: a decision of the United States Supreme Court invalidating an unreasonable, but very generally applied, rule of state universities and colleges regarding the classification of students as nonresidents of the state for the purposes of charging them much higher tuition fees than in-state students. Permissible is a rule that, having newly come into the state for the purpose of attending a public institution of higher learning, the student must be classified as nonresident during a waiting period (usually one year); but unconstitutional is the remainder of the customary rule, to the effect that the student will not be reclassified as long as he continues uninterrupted attendance on a year-to-year basis. The court has now declared that nonresidence is a rebuttable presumption that the student may refute by declaring his intent to reside permanently in the state and by offering satisfactory supporting evidence, and that the student is entitled to be heard on the issue as soon as the statutory waiting period has expired *(Vlandis v. Kline,* 93 S. Ct. 2222, 1973).

Rights of faculty and staff members. The civil rights guaranteed in the First Amendment and in the Fourteenth Amendment are also being recognized as having full application to faculty and staff members. Since the 1960s more than one federal court has implied that neither students nor faculty members shed their civil rights at the campus gate. Three examples of the newer view are relevant.

First, state statutory prescriptions requiring special disclaimer loyalty oaths of all university teachers, which have been enacted in waves, following the reactionary periods during and after national participation in wars, have been declared unconstitutional infringements of free speech so many times by the highest federal and state courts that the whole idea may be said to be dead *(Keyishian* v. *Board of Regents* (New York), 385 U. S. 589, 1967).

Second, the new alertness of the federal courts may be seen in the current, firmly established doctrine that if a teacher—whether or not employed for a short term or under a contract of indeterminate duration (tenured)—is able to allege plausibly that he was dropped or discharged in retaliation for exercise of a constitutional right (free speech, peaceable assembly, petition, or association), the case will be heard in a federal court (under 42 U. S. Code section 1983, a part of the Civil Rights Act of 1871), and it will be heard without prior exhaustion of administrative remedies or of remedies in state courts. Many federal and state decisions establish this.

Finally, a different case, that of an aggrieved teacher who claims entitlement to a written statement of reasons for being fired, followed by an administrative hearing (even though neither the statutes of the state nor his contract provide for these, and even though the contract is for a short term and stipulates the date of its termination) was left in a somewhat ambiguous condition by decisions of the Supreme Court in two companion cases decided June 29, 1972 *(Regents of Wisconsin State Colleges* v. *Roth; Perry* v. *Sindermann,* 40 U. S. Law Week 5079; 5087). Five of the justices concurred in an opinion that, in the case of *Regents of Wisconsin State Colleges* v. *Roth* (first heard in a United States district court in Wisconsin), the plaintiff professor should have no recourse on this issue, because the governing board of the university had made no charges against him to damage his reputation, and he had in fact quickly obtained similar employment in a state university in another state. The opinion carefully noted, however, that the decision would have been different under a different set of facts, and no sweeping uniform, unqualified rule to apply to all cases was intended. Roth's plea, based on his right of free-speech as distinguished from his plea on due process, had simply been stayed by the United States district court, and he could resume it in that forum. In due course, on that issue, he was awarded a modest sum in damages against the university that had fired him, as well as small punitive damages against three administrative officers of that university (reported in Oshkosh, Wisconsin *Advance-Titan,* November 15, 1973).

In the case of *Perry* v. *Sindermann* (first heard in a United States district court in Texas), a summary judgment of the district court dismissing the case had been remanded by the Fifth Circuit United States Court of Appeals, and the majority opinion of the Supreme Court affirmed the remand for trial of the facts, because it embodied too many unresolved complexities to be a proper subject of summary dismissal. Before the trial could be held, however, the defendant college negotiated with Sindermann for a settlement out of court, paid him $48,000 for attorneys' fees and back salary, and offered him reinstatement, which he refused. Thus, the controversy ended.

In neither of the foregoing companion cases did the Supreme Court achieve a final decision, a general doctrine, or a unanimous judgment. One justice did not participate, and three (known as liberal or progressive in their tendencies) dissented vehemently and eloquently, believing that both decisions should have been unqualifiedly in favor of the plaintiff professors.

With respect to university students,

members of the faculties and staffs, and administrators, the turnaround in the stance of the federal courts since about 1960 is hardly less than a revolution of great consequence. A former justice of the Supreme Court, Abe Fortas, has said: "It is a revolution based on the principle of human rights . . . central to all its phases is the Court's rediscovery of the human values which our Constitution states" (reported in the *New York Times*, November 26, 1972).

Copyright law. One lesser matter of federal jurisdiction is that of copyright law as applied to the use of copying machines by libraries to reproduce small parts of copyrighted books and journals, solely for the convenience of students and teachers in improving instruction or research and not for any commercial purpose. A commercial publisher who sued the National Library of Medicine for infringement of copyrights was rebuffed by the United States Court of Claims (487 F. 2d 1345, November 27, 1973), and the appeal to the Supreme Court resulted in a tie vote, so the decision of the lower court stands *(Williams and Wilkins* v. *United States,* 43 *U. S. Law Week* 4314, February 25, 1975). There is little doubt that ways will be found to permit as lawful fair use the reasonable use of modern copying technology solely to enhance the processes of learning; but if reproductions are intended for sale, profit, or any commercial purpose, the practice will continue to be unlawful infringement of the rights of authors or publishers of copyrighted works.

University autonomy. There have also been many court decisions in the fifty states regarding the corporate entity, property, and financial affairs of universities and colleges and their relations with state government. These are, in considerable part, regulated by state constitutions and statutes, and no sharp changes in judicial interpretations have occurred. The principle of a high degree of institutional autonomy (freedom from interference by other state agencies) has been maintained for the prin-

cipal state universities in Michigan, Minnesota, California, and half a dozen other states. The story of the historic decisions is sketched in Elliott and Chambers (1936), and the story of the more recent decisions is given in subsequent volumes of the Chambers (1941–1973) series.

The new constitution of the state of Michigan, effective in 1963, extended the principle of university autonomy to all the state universities and colleges then in existence and such others as may be established in the future; and the supreme court of Michigan, in a notable decision of October 29, 1975, reaffirmed that each of the separate governing boards (one for each institution) has exclusive power to determine the program of the institution and to make internal allocations of funds received from all sources (including legislative appropriations made in lump sum). This decision culminated a long series of similar decisions extending over somewhat more than a century. Thus, the salutary doctrine that state universities should possess a sphere of discretion within which they are constitutionally independent of all other agencies of state government is continued.

Major Global Issues

Perusal of the opinions of the judges in different countries reveals that the questions brought for decision bear a considerable similarity in all parts of the world. A few great issues, of tremendous consequence to the future of civilization, emerge from what at times may seem to be a welter of petty local controversies, in which judgments are sometimes influenced by procedural technicalities as well as by principles of justice.

Without doubt, the paramount issue the world over is that of access to higher education. The problem is obviously of different dimensions in each country, depending in part on its current stage of economic development, but in no nation has universal higher education (more than half the relevant population in postsecondary institutions) been achieved, nor is it likely to be accomplished before the year 2000. The elitism versus egalitarianism question ultimately poses no dilemma, for both ideals can and will be served in different types of institutions and programs.

Another great issue, to some extent overlapping the first, is that of human rights or entitlements. No state in the world has yet unequivocally guaranteed to all persons the right to pursue studies of benefit to themselves and to the nation as far as their ambitions and capabilities permit, surmounting all discriminations growing out of economic hardship or financial handicap or based on race, sex, age, religion, ethnic or national origin, ideology, or any form of arbitrary exclusion. Progress is taking place, but slowly, and at diverse rates in different countries.

A third issue of profound importance is that of the autonomy of universities. In the age of technology, there is everywhere a pernicious tendency for institutions of higher learning to be regarded as branches of a national or statewide bureaucracy, having no more distinctive character than the local post office. Fortunately, an increasing number of persons in many parts of the world recognize that this concept is repugnant to the essential idea of the free search for truth in an open society, and that care must be taken to continue the entity and individual élan of universities everywhere.

Bibliography

Alexander, K., and Solomon, E. S. *College and University Law.* Charlottesville, Virginia: Michie Company, 1972.

Barrell, G. R. *Legal Cases for Teachers.* New York: Barnes and Noble, 1970.

Barrell, G. R. *Teachers and the Law.* (4th ed.) London: Methuen, 1975.

Benoist, B. "La constitution canadienne, la diffusion, et les universités." *Thémis,* 1956–1957, *7,* 93–100.

Berdahl, R. O. *British Universities and the State.* Berkeley: University of California Press, 1959.

Blackwell, T. E. *College Law: A Guide for Administrators.* Washington, D.C.: American Council on Education, 1961.

Bridge, J. W. "Keeping Peace in the Univer-

sities: The Role of the Visitor." *Law Quarterly Review,* 1970, *86*(344), 531–551.

Brubacher, J. S. *The Courts and Higher Education.* San Francisco: Jossey-Bass, 1971.

Carbone, R. F. *West German Universities—The Problem of Too Many Students.* College Park: University of Maryland Comparative Education Center, 1974–1975.

Chambers, M. M. *Colleges and the Courts, 1936–40.* New York: Carnegie Foundation for the Advancement of Teaching, 1941.

Chambers, M. M. *Colleges and the Courts, 1941–45.* New York: Carnegie Foundation for the Advancement of Teaching, 1946.

Chambers, M. M. *Colleges and the Courts, 1946–50.* New York: Columbia University Press, 1952.

Chambers, M. M. *Colleges and the Courts Since 1950.* Danville, Illinois: Interstate, 1964.

Chambers, M. M. *Colleges and the Courts, 1962–66.* Danville, Illinois: Interstate, 1967.

Chambers, M. M. *Colleges and the Courts: The Developing Law of the Student and the College.* Danville, Illinois: Interstate, 1972.

Chambers, M. M. *Colleges and the Courts: Faculty and Staff Before the Bench.* Danville, Illinois: Interstate, 1973.

Chevallier, J. *L'Enseignement supérieur.* Paris: Presses universitaires de France, 1971a.

Chevallier, J. "La Réforme de la loi d'orientation de l'enseignement supérieur." *Revue de droit social,* 1971b, 513 ff.

Corry, J. "Higher Education in Dominion-Provincial Relations." *University Affairs,* 1966, *8*(2), 3.

Council of the University of Tasmania. *The Dismissal of S. S. Orr.* Hobart: University of Tasmania, 1958.

Eddy, W. H. C. *Orr.* Brisbane, Queensland: Jacaranda Press, 1961.

Elliott, E. C., and Chambers, M. M. *Colleges and the Courts: Judicial Decisions Regarding Institutions of Higher Education in the United States.* New York: Carnegie Foundation for the Advancement of Teaching, 1936.

Karlen, E. *Appellate Courts in the United States and England.* New York: New York University Press, 1963.

Karpen, U. *Admission to Higher Education and "Numerus Clausus."* Strasbourg, France: Council of Europe, 1973.

Karpen, U. *Revision and Evaluation of University Admission Criteria—Some Comparative Observations on the German and American University Systems.* Cologne, Federal Republic of Germany: University of Cologne, 1975.

Moodie, G. C., and Eustace, R. *Power and Authority in British Universities.* London: George Allen and Unwin, 1974.

Nayak, R. K. "Education: The Centre-State Relationship." *Journal of the Indian Law Institute,* 1972, *14*(4), 562–582, and 1973, *15*(3). 171–414.

Ouellette, Y. "Le Contrôle judiciare sur l'université." *Canadian Bar Review,* 1970, *48,* 631–650.

Schwartz, B. (Ed.) *The Fourteenth Amendment.* New York: New York University Press, 1970.

Seavey, W. A. "Dismissal of Students: 'Due Process.'" *Harvard Law Review,* 1967, *70*(8), 1406–1410.

Sharma, G. S., Raizada, S. R. K., and Bhagwan, S. V. *Judicial Review and Education: A Study in Trends.* New Delhi, India: National Council of Educational Research and Training, 1969.

Taylor, G., and Saunders, J. B. *The New Law of Education.* (7th ed.) London: Butterworth, 1971.

Toulemonde. "Les Libertés et franchises universitaires en France." Unpublished thesis, University of Lille, Lille, France, 1971a.

Toulemonde. "Abstract." *Revue des droits de l'homme,* 1971b, *1,* 5.

"University Discipline: A New Province for Natural Justice?" *University of Queensland Law Journal,* 1970, *7,* 85–108.

Van Alstyne, W. W. "The Student as University Resident." *Denver Law Journal,* 1968, *45*(4), 582–613.

Wade, H. W. R. "Judicial Control of Universities." *Law Quarterly Review,* 1969, *85*(40), 469–472.

Young, D. P. "Lowering the Age of Majority: Some Possible Ramifications." In *Higher Education: The Law and Institutional Response.* Athens: University of Georgia, Institute of Higher Education, 1973.

M. M. CHAMBERS

See also: Legal Aspects of Higher Education.

CRAFTS (Field of Study)

The original meaning of the word *craft* is strength—strength allied to skill; but *craft* has gradually come to denote technical mastery over a particular medium, as in "the craft of poetry" or "woodcraft." The concept of crafts contains many false assumptions, however. First of all, the term *crafts* is preferable to *handicrafts,* since the term *hand* in *handicrafts* has led to the false assumption that crafts can be made only by hand. If this were so, only basketry would qualify as a craft. Another false notion—inherited from John Ruskin and the Arts and Crafts movement—is that anything handmade is "good" or "beautiful." Unfortunately, thousands of ugly and inadequate handmade objects are circulating the world. Nonetheless, crafts can be distinguished from articles which are mere manufacture. The craftsman has a skill and sensitivity denied to man-as-machine, a skill closely connected with the hands that guide and control tools, either sophisticated or simple. The craftsman creates with a strong sense of design and tradition and with high personal standards.

There are four broad categories of craftsmen: (1) producers of traditional or folk arts and nonfunctional objects such as wall hangings; (2) producers of utilitarian objects such as pots; (3) producers of articles such as jigs and tools, together with assemblers and adjusters, such as carpenters; and (4) service and repair craftsmen, such as watchmakers. Only the first two categories are discussed here, because the latter two fall more properly into engineering and similar technical and vocational education programs.

Although crafts have a long history, they are a relatively recent academic discipline. Historically, they were handed down from father to son and from mother to daughter. Family groups became guilds; and in time these guilds admitted outside apprentices, who pledged themselves to seven years of study in return for more or less guaranteed work as a journeyman or master. Relying on the brotherhood of the guild, they could journey from place to place and be reasonably sure of work. But as times grew harder, favoritism or bribery in admission to apprenticeships created a demand for training outside the guilds. The apprenticeship system became a means of exploiting cheap labor until finally the guilds broke up. Some became trade unions; others disappeared as their work was supplanted by machines; and some, such as the anachronistic livery companies of London, remained. Many crafts died out completely, some were carried on by a few eccentrics; and some were maintained by the demands of the rich, who found in them a distinction, individuality, and prestige denied to the mass-produced object. This same desire for distinction and individuality was in large part behind the renaissance of crafts.

The demand for leisure-time activities, both during and at the end of the working life, particularly in the developed countries, is another reason for the upsurge of craft activities. Large numbers of people are enrolling in evening classes, adult education classes, and similar educational programs to study pottery, weaving, and metalworking as a hobby. Although teachers and tools are often limited, especially in rural areas, basic pottery techniques can be taught, as well as simple kiln techniques. Similarly, various off-loom weaving techniques and the use of various types of looms can be taught. There is also a growing interest in associated techniques—spinning, for example. Added to these courses are traditional techniques that have become popular: tie and dye, batik, and macramé.

There are, of course, other uses and values for crafts beyond their value as leisure activity. For example, crafts have been widely employed for therapeutic purposes for the physically and mentally handicapped. Their value in rehabilitation is the same as their value to the person who pursues a craft in his leisure time: the profound degree of job satisfaction that they give. Unlike the frustrations of learning to play the piano or guitar, many of the basic skills, such as coiling a pot, are acquired in a very short time and give a high degree of satisfaction from the very first attempt.

Crafts cannot exist in a vacuum; there are several important related fields. Courses in design, the use of tools, restoration techniques, and business methods are particularly necessary in the educational programs of the full-time craftsman. Design in all aspects, theoretical and historical, is a vital aspect of crafts. The craftsman must understand industrial design; and many craftsmen, especially in Europe, do experimental work for industry. The craftsman also must understand tools, not just the hand-controlled variety but also the most sophisticated. As countries become concerned with preserving their cultural heritage, authentic restoration becomes highly valued. Therefore, the craftsman must be familiar with and able to practice historical techniques. Finally, the craftsman must understand business methods and procedures; indeed, many craftsmen around the world are suffering economically because they do not understand simple bookkeeping and accounting.

The demand for the finest crafts exceeds the supply in almost every country in the world. Therefore, one of the major problems facing the educational system is to produce craftsmen capable of fulfilling that demand without simultaneously neglecting the leisure-time practitioner. Although universities and colleges in the developed countries have taught crafts in a serious way since the 1950s, nations in Africa, Latin America, and parts of Asia have little organization and schooling in crafts as understood and practiced in the West.

Internationalism in crafts is promoted through such organizations as the World Crafts Council (WCC), founded in 1964 by an international group of craftsmen and educators. The major international crafts organization, the WCC seeks to advance the craftsman's welfare and the world. In 1976 it was affiliated with over eighty crafts organizations. Exhibits such as the First World Crafts Exhibition (which was presented in Toronto in 1974 and included crafts from more than fifty countries), competitions, publications, and exchanges of teachers and students have all contributed to internationalism in crafts.

PETER WEINRICH

Levels and Programs of Study

Programs in crafts are designed to develop skill in crafts for professional, cultural, or recreational purposes, and consist

of lectures, group discussion, and studio
practice sessions. Students normally devote
themselves to one aspect of crafts, such as
pottery, weaving, jewelry, or woodcarving.
Programs generally do not lead to an award
equivalent to a first university degree. A
certificate of competence may be awarded
upon completion of the program, either
by the institution itself or by a public authority. Programs usually are given on a
full- or part-time basis in a college of art
for the equivalent of one to three years
of full-time study. The chief aim of the
program is the development of creative-
ness and skill in the chosen field of study,
but related prescribed courses may be included in such things as centrifugal casting,
common hand and machine tools, kilns,
soldering torches, color, and history of art.

[This section was based on UNESCO's
*International Standard Classification of Edu-
cation (ISCED)* (Paris: UNESCO, 1976).]

Major International and National Organizations

INTERNATIONAL

Council of Nordic Master-Craftsmen
Conseil des artisans pour les pays du nord
Norske handverks og industribedrifters
  forbund
Rosenkrantzgaten 71V
Oslo 1, Norway

International Association for Crafts and the
  Teaching of Art
Association internationale des métiers et
  enseignement d'art (AIMEA)
avenue J. G. Van Goolen 32
1150 Brussels, Belgium

World Crafts Council (WCC)
29 West 53rd Street
New York, New York 10019 USA
  The major organization, with over eighty
national organization members.

NATIONAL

A sampling of national organizations for the
field includes:

Australia:
  Crafts Council of Australia
  27 King Street
  Sydney, New South Wales 2000

Canada:
  Canadian Crafts Council
  46 Elgin Street, Suite 16
  Ottawa, Ontario K1P 5K6

Czechoslovakia:
  Czechoslovak Committee for WCC
  Obchodná ul. 62
  892 11 Bratislava

Denmark:
  Danish Society of Arts and Crafts and
    Industrial Design
  Sankt Annae Plads 10B
  1250 Copenhagen K

Finland:
  ORNAMO, Association of Finnish
    Designers
  Unioninkatu 30
  00100 Helsinki 10

India:
  Crafts Council of India
  20 Canning Lane
  New Delhi 11001

Iran:
  Iranian Handicrafts Organization
  296 North Villa Avenue
  Tehran

Israel:
  Israel Designer-Craftsmen's Association
  P.O. Box 26421
  Tel Aviv

Mexico:
  Comité mexicano para artesanías y
    artes populares
  Apartado 1856
  Mexico, 1, D.F.

Netherlands:
  C. O. S. A.
  Oude Delft 145
  Delft

Poland:
  Cepelia
  ul. Rutkowskiego 8
  Warsaw 1

Sweden:
  Svenska slöjdföreningen
  7 Nybrogatan, P.O. 7047
  S-103 82 Stockholm 7

United Kingdom:
  British Crafts Centre
  43 Earlham Street
  London WC2H 9LD, England

  Crafts Advisory Committee
  12 Waterloo Place
  London SW1Y 4AU, England

United States:
    American Crafts Council
    44 West 53rd Street
    New York, New York 10019

For a more complete listing of crafts organizations see:

Paz, O., and World Crafts Council. *In Praise of Hands: Contemporary Crafts of the World.* New York: New York Graphic Society and World Crafts Council, 1974.

World Crafts Directory. New York: World Crafts Council, 1975.

Principal Information Sources

GENERAL

Guides to the literature include:

American Crafts Council. *Contemporary Crafts Market Place.* New York: Bowker, 1975. Includes bibliographies on various craft media.

Bibliothèque Forney. *Catalogue matières: Arts-décoratifs, beaux-arts métiers, techniques.* Paris: Société des amis de le Bibliothèque Forney, 1970–1974.

Chamberlin, M. W. *Guide to Art Reference Books.* Chicago: American Library Association, 1959.

Chicorel, M. (Ed.) *Chicorel Index to Craft Books.* Vol. 13: *Needlework-Crochet to Tie-Dye;* Vol. 13A: *Ceramics, Glass;* Vol. 13B: *Metalwork;* Vol. 13C: *Woodwork, Leathercraft, Model and Toymaking;* Vol. 13D: *Crafts for Education, Recreation and Therapy.* New York: Chicorel Library, 1974. This volume set is part of the Chicorel Index Series; contains subject bibliographies.

Ehresmann, D. *Fine Arts: A Bibliographic Guide.* Littleton, Colorado: Libraries Unlimited, 1975.

Specialized Bibliographies Available in Clay, Enamel, Glass, Wood, Metal, Fiber. New York: American Crafts Council, 1975.

Weinrich, P. H. "Selected Bibliography." In O. Paz and World Crafts Council, *In Praise of Hands: Contemporary Crafts of the World.* New York: New York Graphic Society and World Crafts Council, 1974. Includes a bibliography of works on crafts, classified by world region and medium.

Weinrich, P. H. "A Bibliographic Guide to Books on Ceramics." *Guide bibliographique des ouvrages sur la céramique."* Ottawa: Canadien Crafts Council, 1976. 288 pages listing more than 3500 titles.

The following is a small sampling of overviews and introductions to various aspects of crafts:

Adams, J., and Stieri, E. *The Complete Woodworking Handbook.* New York: Arco, 1960.

Birrell, V. L. *The Textile Arts. A Handbook of Fabric Structure and Design Processes: Ancient and Modern Weaving, Braiding, Printing, and Other Textile Techniques.* New York: Harper & Row, 1959.

Black, M. E. *New Key to Weaving.* New York: Macmillan, 1961.

Burton, J. *Glass: Philosophy and Method: Hand-blown, Sculptured, Color.* Philadelphia: Chilton, 1967.

Collingwood, P. *Techniques of Rug Weaving.* New York: Watson-Guptill, 1969.

Fournier, R. *Illustrated Dictionary of Practical Pottery.* New York: Van Nostrand Reinhold, 1973.

Hamer, E. *The Potter's Dictionary of Materials and Techniques.* London: Pitman; New York: Watson-Guptill, 1975.

Harwell, R. M., and Harwell, A. J. (Eds.) *Crafts for Today: Ceramics, Glasscrafting, Leather Working, Candle Making and Other Popular Crafts.* Littleton, Colorado: Libraries Unlimited, 1974.

Nelson, G. C. *Ceramics: A Potter's Handbook.* New York: Holt, Rinehart and Winston, 1971.

Nordness, L. *Objects, U.S.A.* New York: Viking Press, 1970.

Robertson, S. M. *Craft and Contemporary Culture.* London: Harrap, 1961.

The following provide information on education in crafts:

Counts, C. *Encouraging American Craftsmen.* Washington, D.C.: National Endowment for the Arts, n.d.

Coyne, J., and Herbert, T. *By Hand: A Guide to Schools and a Career in Crafts.* New York: Dutton, 1974.

Craft Guidelines. Washington, D.C.: National Endowment for the Arts, 1975. Explores craft programs.

Craft Horizons. New York: American Crafts Council, 1941–. Special issues of this journal discuss crafts internationally.

Crafts. London: Crafts Advisory Committee, 1973–.

Directory of Craft Courses. New York: American Crafts Council, annual. Directory of courses in universities, colleges, workshops, museums, and art centers in the United States.

Holden, D. *Art Career Guide.* New York: Watson-Guptill, 1973.

Patch, M. M. "Guide to World Crafts." In R. Slivka, *The Crafts of the Modern World.* New York: Horizon Press and World Crafts Council, 1968.

World Crafts Directory. New York: World Crafts Council, 1975. Lists schools, museums, organizations, craft-producing centers in four sections: Africa, Asia, Europe, and the Americas.

The following provide a historical treatment of crafts:

Batchelder, E. A. *Design in Theory and Practice.* New York: Macmillan, 1925.
The Craftsman in America. Washington, D.C.: National Geographic Society, Special Publications Division, 1975.
Jenkins, J. G. *Traditional Country Craftsmen.* London: Routledge and Kegan Paul, 1965.
Osborne, H. (Ed.) *Oxford Companion to the Decorative Arts.* New York: Oxford University Press, 1975.
Pye, D. *The Nature and Art of Workmanship.* Cambridge, England: Cambridge University Press, 1968.

CURRENT BIBLIOGRAPHIES

Art/Kunst: International Bibliography of Art Books. Basel, Switzerland: Helbing and Lichtenhahn, 1973–.
Art Bibliographies Current Titles. Santa Barbara, California: ABC-Clio, 1972–.
Art Bibliographies Modern. Santa Barbara, California: ABC-Clio, 1973–.
Art Index. New York: Wilson, 1933–.

PERIODICALS

A sampling of journals, newsletters, and catalogues for the field includes *American Ceramic Society. Journal, Art and Craft in Education* (UK), *Ceramic Review* (UK), *Ceramics Monthly* (US), *Craft Dimensions Artisanales* (Canada), *Craft Education* (UK), *Craft Horizons* (US), *Crafts* (UK), *The Craftsman's Gallery* (US), *Cras, Tidsskrift for kunst & kultur* (Denmark), *Design* (US), *Deutsches Handwerksblatt* (FRG), *Glass Art Magazine* (US), *Handweaver and Craftsman* (US), *Heimatwerk* (Switzerland), *International Biennial of Tapestry* (Switzerland), *New Zealand Pottery and Ceramics Research Association Technical Report, Quarterly Journal of the Guilds of Weavers, Spinners, and Dyers* (UK), *Shuttle, Spindle and Dye-Pot* (US), *Stained Glass* (US), *Studio Potter* (US), *Textile Museum Journal* (US), *World Crafts Council Bulletin* (US).

For additional journal listings consult:

Art Institute of Chicago, Ryerson Library. *Index to Art Periodicals.* Boston: Hall, 1962.
Ulrich's International Periodicals Directory. New York: Bowker, biennial.

ENCYCLOPEDIAS, DICTIONARIES, HANDBOOKS

Boger, L. A., and Batterson, H. *The Dictionary of Antiques and the Decorative Arts: A Book of Reference for Glass, Furniture, Ceramics, Silver, Periods, Styles and Technical Terms.* New York: Scribner's, 1957.
The Craftsman's Art. London: Crafts Advisory Committee, 1973.
Diderot, D. *A Diderot Pictorial Encyclopedia of Trades and Industry: Manufacturing and the Technical Arts in Plates Selected from "L'encyclopédie, ou Dictionnaire raissonné des sciences, des arts et des métiers."* New York: Dover, 1959.
Di Valentin, M., and Di Valentin, L. *Practical Encyclopedia of Crafts.* New York: Sterling, 1971.
Ickis, M., and Esh, R. *The Book of Arts and Crafts.* New York: Dover, 1973.
Karlen, T. *Basic Craft Techniques.* New York: Drake, 1973.
Slivka, R. *The Crafts of the Modern World.* New York: Horizon Press and World Crafts Council, 1968. Includes glossary of craft terms in English, French, German, and Spanish.
Whitaker, I. *Crafts and Craftsmen.* Dubuque, Iowa: W. C. Brown, 1967.

DIRECTORIES

American Crafts Council. *Contemporary Crafts Market Place.* New York: Bowker, 1975.
American Crafts Guide. San Jose, California: Gousha, 1973.
American Federation of Arts. *American Art Directory.* New York: Bowker, 1974.
Crafts Directory. Marietta, Ohio: Marietta College, 1975.
Cultural Directory: Guide to Federal Funds and Services for Cultural Activities. New York: Associated Councils of the Arts, 1975.
Cummings, P. (Ed.) *Fine Arts Market Place.* New York: Bowker, biennial.
International Directory of Arts. Berlin, Federal Republic of Germany: Art Address Verlag Müller GMBH, 1952/53–. Published biennially.
World Crafts Directory. New York: World Crafts Council, 1975. Includes information on ninety-three countries; lists schools, museums, organizations, and government agencies involved with crafts.

RESEARCH CENTERS, INSTITUTES, INFORMATION CENTERS

The following are important research centers for the field:

American Crafts Council Library
44 West 53rd Street
New York, New York 10019 USA

British Crafts Centre
43 Earlham Street
London WC2H 9LD, England

Ontario Crafts Council, Craft Resource Center
346 Dunbar Street West
Toronto, Ontario, Canada

The following sources provide information on museums, research and information centers and special collections for the field:

American Federation of Arts. *American Art Directory.* New York: Bowker, 1974.
Chicorel, M. (Ed.) *Chicorel Index to Craft Books.* Vols. 13, 13A, 13B, 13C, 13D. New York: Chicorel Library, 1974. Provides listings of museums and special collections.
International Directory of Arts. Berlin, Federal Republic of Germany: Verlag Müller GMBH, 1952/53–. Published biennially.
World Crafts Directory. New York: World Crafts Council, 1975.

[Bibliography prepared by Nancy S. Allen.]

See also: Trade, Craft, and Industrial Programs.

CRAUSAZ REPORT

See Diversification of Tertiary Education (Higher Education Report), Multinational.

CREDIT, ASSESSMENT OF LEARNING FOR POSTSECONDARY EDUCATION

Academic credentials awarded by institutions of higher education have a significant impact on the economic, occupational, and social status of the individual. Required for many professional- and technical-level occupations, academic credentials also have generally provided passageway to broader opportunities for higher paying and more responsible jobs and to increased social stature for the recipient.

Occupational and social deference to those who hold academic credentials is based on general assumptions borne out by experience regarding their attributes as a collective group: their ability to communicate effectively, to analyze and evaluate concepts and ideas, to participate intelligently and responsibly as members of a democratic society, to learn rapidly and to adapt to new situations, and—increasingly as the society and economy grow

more complex and technological—to be proficient in an occupational specialty.

Given the social use of educational credentials, it is important that the degrees, diplomas, and certificates awarded by institutions of higher education provide a high level of assurance about the competencies and learning of the recipient. And, because of the impact on the individual, it is important for institutions of higher education to be effective not only in granting credentials based on their own instruction but also in evaluating equivalent competency and learning attained outside their sponsorship. This importance grows as educational and public policy encourages use of alternatives to the traditional classroom.

The credentialing role of colleges and universities is, thus, an important function. The institution's faculty, administration, and board of control share responsibility for establishing policies, practices, procedures, and standards for awarding credentials. Each institution, within the limits of commonly accepted practices, determines how learning, knowledge, and competencies are evaluated, what credit is placed on the student's record, and what types of credit may be applied toward the degree or other educational credential it grants.

In turn, institutional policies, practices, and procedures attain legitimacy for third-party utilization (employers; certification, registration, and licensure agencies; other educational institutions; and students) through their value in the marketplace and accreditation by nongovernmental institutional and specialized accrediting agencies.

Evaluation of student achievement is the sine qua non of credentialing, for credentials have meaning and social utility only if they distinguish among types and levels of competency and learning. In the classroom, the instructor who teaches also evaluates and makes judgments about student achievement in a variety of ways: instructor-prepared and instructor-graded examinations; observation of class participation; and class projects, papers, and reports. The instructor certifies that the student has met the objectives of the course and at what level, in most institutions, by assigning a grade on a four-point scale.

In addition to credentialing the learning outcomes of its own instruction, the higher education community is generally also creating institutional policies and practices that permit the credentialing of learning that occurs outside the walls or sponsorship of the campus (Commission on Non-Traditional Study, 1973). Such policies and practices have recently become more pervasive, but they are hardly a new experience for higher education in the United States. Formalized procedures have existed since 1945, when the American Council on Education (ACE) developed its Commission on Accreditation of Service Experiences (CASE) to help institutions award credit to veterans for competency and learning attained while serving in the armed forces, and to assist active-duty service personnel and veterans in earning a high school diploma or its equivalent by passing a battery of examinations.

These practices have grown and evolved to meet new needs and emphases in higher education, until in January 1974 CASE was expanded into the Office on Educational Credit. For a variety of reasons, not all American colleges and universities award credit for learning gained outside the sponsorship of academic institutions, but many now do so if the credit meets three general considerations: (1) the competency or learning meets acceptable levels of student achievement; (2) the competency or learning being credited is generally equivalent to the learning outcomes resulting from courses in the college or university curriculum; and (3) the credit is appropriately applicable toward the student's program of study or requirements for an academic credential.

Currently, there are three basic ways that students can obtain credit toward academic credentials (in addition to studying in the traditional classroom setting and

being tested and graded by course instructors): (1) national credit-by-examination programs; (2) credit recommendations provided by the American Council on Education for noncollegiate-sponsored instruction and for occupational assessment programs; and (3) individualized assessment procedures, usually a central responsibility of teaching faculty, at individual colleges and universities.

National Testing Programs

The General Educational Development Testing Program (GED), which is now operated by the American Council on Education to measure high school–equivalent knowledge, included college-level tests as well between 1945 and 1961, when they were replaced by the Comprehensive College Test. In addition, subject standardized tests and correspondence course examinations were administered by the United States Armed Forces Institute (USAFI) from 1944 until its disestablishment in 1974. These programs were the forerunners of large national credit-by-examination programs, intended to serve postsecondary-age adults.

In 1967 the College Entrance Examination Board developed the College-Level Examination Program (CLEP) from the Comprehensive College Test. CLEP includes in its inventory five general examinations in English composition, humanities, mathematics, natural sciences, and social sciences and history, and forty-four subject matter examinations. During 1975 approximately 100,000 candidates took CLEP examinations.

The College Proficiency Examination Program (CPEP) of the University of the State of New York, established in 1960 and now administered nationally outside New York by the American College Testing Program, offers twenty-five examinations in the arts and sciences, education, and nursing. Between 1963 and 1975, more than 80,000 credits were granted by colleges and universities in New York and elsewhere on the basis of these tests.

In addition to CLEP and CPEP, many of the USAFI examinations have been administered since 1974 by a new Department of Defense agency, the Defense Activity for Non-Traditional Education Support (DANTES). The American Council on Education currently recommends that seventy-four of the DANTES tests be accepted for college-level credit.

To take the CLEP, CPEP, or DANTES exams, the candidate need not be a matriculated student at a college or university. He receives a test score report that can be presented to the college or university where he later decides to enroll. A large number of institutions will award credit on the basis of the test score report, providing the credit can be applied toward requirements for a degree. CLEP, for example, lists more than 1800 colleges and universities that make use of its examinations.

While CLEP, CPEP, and DANTES examinations are directed primarily toward postsecondary-age adults, another national testing program, the Advanced Placement (AP) Examinations of the College Entrance Examination Board and the Educational Testing Service (ETS), serves the secondary school graduate about to enter a college or university. By presenting acceptable scores on the AP examinations, a high school student graduating in June can enter a large number of colleges and universities the following September with sophomore (second-year) standing. Participating institutions cover a broad range, including many of the nation's most prestigious colleges and universities. During 1975 more than 85,000 candidates took the AP examinations.

Credit by examination is so important to higher education that in 1976 the Commission on Educational Credit of the American Council on Education, the policymaking and advisory board for its Office on Educational Credit, decided to extend its function of making recommendations to colleges and universities for awarding credit on the basis of CLEP and DANTES examinations to other national examination programs. The expanded function will include the evaluation of examinations by subject matter experts and psychometricians. Under the program, ACE will validate and publish information and make recommendations to assist institutions in developing their own credit-by-examination policies.

ACE Credit Recommendations

After World War II, the American Council on Education, at the request of institutions and the regional accrediting associations, began to evaluate formal military training to establish its credit equivalency to college and university curricula. Under this program, professors who taught similar subject matter content on their campuses worked as teams to review formal military courses and reach consensus about their value in meeting requirements for academic credentials awarded by colleges and universities. Five editions of a *Guide to the Evaluation of Educational Experiences in the Armed Services* have been published, the most recent in 1976. On the basis of these credit recommendations formulated by civilian professors, millions of veterans and active-duty service personnel have been awarded credit by colleges and universities for formal military training. The establishment of credit equivalency recommendations for military education is an important part of the educational inducements offered members of the all-volunteer armed services, many of whom combine military service with study at civilian colleges and universities.

On the basis of surveys in 1975 and 1976, the American Council on Education estimates that approximately 2000 colleges and universities make use of the military credit equivalency recommendations in awarding credit for formal military courses. In responding to a 1975 questionnaire, 227 institutions indicated that their records showed or they estimated that they awarded 290,391 semester hours of credit over a twelve-month period (Sullivan and Suritz, 1975), which is roughly equivalent to

12,000 full-time students for one academic year.

The credit recommendations for military education prompted the Commission on Non-Traditional Study, in its 1973 report, *Diversity by Design,* to recommend that the ACE program be adapted to formal courses offered by other noncollegiate sponsors, such as business, industry, government agencies, occupational and professional associations, and labor unions, for their own employees or members. The New York Board of Regents began a pilot effort to review courses of noncollegiate sponsors in 1973 and combined with ACE in 1974 in a joint project to develop a national system for making such credit recommendations. The first national edition of *A Guide to Educational Programs in Noncollegiate Organizations,* containing credit recommendations for more than 600 courses of 38 sponsors, was published by the University of the State of New York and ACE in April 1976 and distributed nationwide. The Consortium of the California State University and Colleges entered the project as a collaborating organization in June 1976 in the first major extension of the program.

This Program on Noncollegiate Sponsored Instruction is too new to provide extensive documentation of the acceptance of the credit recommendations, but it is estimated that more than 500,000 persons enroll each year in the courses recommended thus far for credit. The program is similar to the program that establishes credit recommendations for military education. Teams of college and university professors review the courses of noncollegiate sponsors and establish credit recommendations. The resulting recommendations will be published regularly and the courses reviewed periodically to determine if substantive changes have occurred that require new reviews.

It has long been recognized that a great deal of learning occurs outside formal educational programs of either educational institutions or noncollegiate sponsors.

People learn on the job, through independent reading and study, and through interaction with their peers. Much of what is learned is equivalent to the educational outcomes achieved through study in formal educational programs. Recognizing this fact, the ACE Commission on Educational Credit authorized the development of a program to base credit equivalency recommendations on occupational assessment programs. During 1974–75 a feasibility study was conducted of the army's enlisted military occupational specialty (MOS) classification system. It was determined that (1) the MOS system provides a codification of learning and competencies that can be equated with the intended outcomes of college and university courses, (2) the assessment procedures used by the army to measure a soldier's learning and competencies before assigning him an MOS met psychometric considerations, and (3) the system provided adequate documentation of personnel records.

On the basis of the feasibility study, the commission authorized the establishment of an ongoing program. As of 1976, credit recommendations had been established for more than four hundred military occupational specialties. The program is being expanded to officer occupational specialties, and a similar effort is under way to establish credit recommendations for the navy's enlisted classification system. ACE is now interested in determining whether the system can be adapted to civilian occupational certification and registration procedures that have characteristics similar to the military personnel classification systems.

As with the formal courses reviews of military and noncollegiate sponsors, the occupational assessment programs rely extensively on professional judgment. Psychometricians evaluate the assessment procedures, and professors from colleges and universities translate the learning and competencies codified by a particular definition into a credit recommendation. Results of the credit recommendations are published and updated regularly by ACE's Office on Educational Credit.

Individualized Assessment Procedures

In addition to national testing programs and the ACE credit recommendations, a great deal of competencies and learning equivalent to those attained through study in the institutional classroom goes unvalidated. Until recently, examinations prepared by academic departments of institutions were the main approach to assessing unvalidated learning. With the growing interest in experiential learning and nontraditional study during the early 1970s, however, attention was directed to new and more effective means for assessing unvalidated learning. Techniques such as portfolio assessment and a variety of individualized measures began to be used by faculty and assessment experts at colleges and universities for noninstitutionally sponsored learning.

In 1974 this growing interest spawned the Cooperative Assessment of Experiential Learning (CAEL) project, a research and development effort involving the Educational Testing Service and an assembly of some two hundred institutions of higher education and other educational organizations. The purpose of CAEL is to advance understanding and practice in the assessment of experiential learning (Keeton and Associates, 1976, p. XVI).

Role of the Faculty

Each of the four general approaches to awarding credit for postsecondary education outcomes in the United States relies extensively on the use of expert judgment. Faculty members from recognized colleges and universities form the core of the professionals who develop national credit-by-examination programs. Faculty teams establish the ACE credit recommendations, and faculty members assess student achievement in the traditional classroom. Members of the faculty also constitute the core of professionals who conduct individualized assessment procedures at institutions.

The results of these faculty endeavors, in turn, are applied toward a student's program of study or requirements for a degree, likewise established largely by faculty and under policies and procedures that are the main responsibility of faculty. While the procedures and techniques vary, faculty participation and control is paramount in awarding credit for postsecondary learning.

Bibliography

American Council on Education. *Guide to the Evaluation of Educational Experiences in the Armed Services.* Washington, D.C.: ACE, 1976.

American Council on Education and the State University of New York. *A Guide to Educational Programs in Noncollegiate Organizations.* Washington, D.C.: ACE; Albany: State University of New York, 1976.

Commission on Non-Traditional Study. *Diversity by Design.* San Francisco: Jossey-Bass, 1973.

Keeton, M., and Associates. *Experiential Learning: Rationale, Characteristics, and Assessment.* San Francisco: Jossey-Bass, 1976.

Sullivan, E. J., and Suritz, P. W. "Credit-Granting Policies and Practices Relating to Formal Military Courses in Postsecondary Education." *College and University,* 1975, *50* (Summer), 311–315.

JERRY W. MILLER

CREDIT FOR COOPERATIVE EDUCATION AND OFF-CAMPUS EXPERIENCE
See Cooperative Education and Off-Campus Experience.

CREDIT SYSTEMS
See Curriculum and Instruction.

CREDIT UNION, COLLEGE AND UNIVERSITY

A credit union is an independent, nonprofit, cooperative financial association. It is organized by and for persons with a common bond—a common employer, for example—who pool their savings as deposits in the credit union to earn a high level of interest and make low-cost loans to each other.

The World Council of Credit Unions reports that, as of 1974, approximately fifty thousand organized credit unions existed throughout the world. These ranged in size from the credit union of a nationwide trade union in the United States with over two hundred thousand members and many millions of dollars in assets to a local village credit union in Thailand with thirty-nine members and total assets of $700.

Origins and History

The credit union idea began in a small German community in the mid nineteenth century. Friedrich Raiffeisen, the mayor of Heddesdorf, was profoundly moved by the suffering caused by the hard winter of 1846–1847. He sought to alleviate the burden imposed on local farmers by oppressive money lenders who charged high interest on loans and foreclosed quickly on property if payments were not prompt. Raiffeisen organized several welfare and consumer societies which evolved into credit cooperatives, the forerunners of modern credit unions. Their members were rural workers who initially used funds contributed by wealthy local citizens and later used common funds to grant loans to each other. Applicants were admitted to the societies if they were judged to be of good character by their neighbors and had tangible assets, such as land, livestock, or equipment.

Development of Credit Unions in the United States

Greatly influenced by Raiffeisen, Edward A. Filene, a prosperous Boston businessman, played a leading role in the development of credit unions in the United States both through his financial support and his organizational efforts. He traveled extensively throughout the world and was particularly affected by the poverty he witnessed on a tour of the Indian subcontinent in 1907. A well-read man of the world, Filene was aware of agricultural cooperative banks modeled after those started by Raiffeisen in Germany. He soon came into contact with Alphonse Desjardins. Desjardins had been in the vanguard of credit union development and legislation in Canada and was instrumental in organizing the first credit union in the United States at Manchester, New Hampshire in 1909. Filene helped spread the credit union idea throughout the United States; he was later joined by Roy F. Bergengren, who became the first managing director of the Credit Union National Association.

Bank failures during the depression of the 1930s prompted workers to look into the possibility of alternative ways to save and borrow money, and they found the unique personal services of credit unions particularly well suited to their needs during those hard times. Credit unions spread rapidly as a result. Presently, the United States has nearly twenty-three thousand credit unions with more than thirty-one million members. Close to three hundred institutions of higher education alone have affiliated credit unions. Despite their relatively recent entrance into the market, credit unions are among America's most successful financial institutions, with assets in excess of $39 billion.

Philosophy of Credit Unions

Credit unions around the world remain essentially self-help, nonprofit institutions dealing primarily in consumer loans and individual share savings accounts. They are democratically run by members, who are the owners and operators. The leaders of each union are chosen by the membership and, with certain exceptions (the treasurer/manager, for example), serve without financial remuneration. Credit unions promote thrift by offering prudent financial guidance to members and by participating actively in consumer affairs.

The common-bond concept is the foundation on which credit unions are built. The common bond of employment among members in a college or university credit union, for example, allows the union to grant loans on the basis of its members' character as well as their credit standing. Since members of a credit union usually know and depend on each other, it is less likely that a loan will not be repaid, for the debtor who fails to pay may be cheating a fellow worker or associate.

Interest on loans is the main source of income for credit unions, which are exclusively nonprofit organizations. While their rates vary, they commonly charge 1.0 percent interest per month (12 percent annually) on the unpaid balance. Because of their high level of member cooperation, they have continued to offer lower interest rates than commercial lending institutions.

Credit unions determine how much income they have received on loans at least once each year. After money for operating expenses and requisite reserve funds is deducted, the balance is distributed to members in the form of dividends. In 1974, for example, 40 percent of all credit unions returned dividends of 6 percent or better.

Almost without exception the family of a member who borrows from a credit union is not responsible for repaying the loan if the borrower becomes disabled or dies. The unpaid balance is paid by means of loan protection insurance, a standard feature with most credit unions. Furthermore, a member's savings are usually insured against death and disability up to specified limits.

College and University Credit Unions

The credit unions of institutions of higher education throughout the world are similar in form and function. Where differences exist they are attributable primarily to size and local legal regulations. In the United States, Canada, and Australia, university credit unions vary in size from fewer than a hundred members to well over a thousand. University credit unions in developing nations such as Lesotho, Kenya, Uganda, the Republic of Korea, and the Philippines have fewer members, not only because of the relative smallness of their institutions but also because most faculty members in those countries find that their needs are adequately met by community credit unions.

Member needs in industrialized nations vary somewhat from those in developing nations, where teachers and professors are less well paid and often rely on credit union loans as alternate sources of income. Members in industrial countries often take out loans for their personal needs; for unexpected expenses from sickness, unemployment, or sudden deaths in the family; and for professional expenses such as research projects, equipment, travel, and further education. Set up primarily to serve institutional faculty and staff, higher education credit unions sometimes allow students and other members of the community to join. Experience has proven that this practice is worthwhile, since their delinquency rate (the incidence of unpaid or neglected debts) is surprisingly low.

Despite these variations, the similarities of higher education credit unions around the world are far more striking than their differences. These credit unions are unique in their response to the particular needs of their membership. For example, many of them provide a service known as a "twelve-month salary stretcher," whereby faculty members set aside a certain amount of their salary in a special account during the months they receive compensation and then use these savings for income during months when classes are not in session.

World Council of Credit Unions

The World Council of Credit Unions is the international organization that encourages and assists credit union development around the world. The World Council began operating under its present name and structure on January 1, 1971. Formerly sponsored and organized by the Credit Union National Association, the World Council is composed of national or regional confederations of credit unions in Africa,

Asia, Canada, Latin America, the Caribbean, and the United States and individual unions elsewhere around the globe.

The World Council provides technical services designed to expand and improve credit unions worldwide. To do this it coordinates the technical and financial assistance programs of the international credit union movement, offers guidance for improving credit union legislation, sends and receives educational information to and from member federations and confederations, and carries on public relations at the international level. Although it links its member confederations, federations, and leagues, it takes care to ensure their autonomy.

The World Council's confederations promote credit unions among workers in rural and urban areas, who find that the financial and technical assistance available from other agencies is inadequate to meet their needs. Among confederations served by the World Council are the Africa Cooperative Savings and Credit Association, with eighteen affiliates and representation in all of Africa's linguistic and geographical areas; the Asian Confederation of Credit Unions, with eleven affiliates in Southeast Asia, Taiwan, Japan, the East Indies, and Hong Kong; the Australian Federation of Credit Union Leagues, serving eight federations across the continent; the World Council of Credit Unions and Credit Union National Association, serving fifty-one leagues and twenty-three thousand credit unions; the National Association of Canadian Credit Unions in North America's pioneer credit union country, with leagues in nine provinces serving more than four thousand credit unions, including one for residents of the Yukon Territory; the Caribbean Confederation of Credit Unions, which works toward the establishment of a full-time community credit union in each of the major cities of the associated states in the Eastern Caribbean and with thirteen federations serving almost five hundred credit unions spread throughout the islands; and the *Confederación latinoamericana*

de cooperativas de ahorro y crédito, which administers much-needed credit to low-income people in South and Central America through sixteen federations and more than two thousand credit unions serving a membership of one million.

Structure of a Credit Union

Membership. Members are the lifeblood of every credit union, and the most effective credit unions encourage members to participate actively in their services. The leadership of a credit union is chosen by the members to serve voluntarily, so every member has a voice in how the credit union is run. No member is allowed more than one vote on a given issue, no matter how many shares he owns. It is through such procedures that credit unions can lay claim to exemplifying democracy in action.

To become a credit union member, one must have a common bond with the present membership and must purchase at least one share in the credit union. The shares, which provide the funds for operating the credit union, are obtained by making a deposit which may be as small as one dollar per share. Like bank savings deposits, credit union deposits belong to the members and they yield annual dividends very much as a bank savings account yields interest.

Leadership. The members of a credit union meet annually to elect a board of directors from among the membership. The board sets policies, approves membership applications, and sets interest and dividend rates. The members and the board elect a president, vice-president, and secretary to serve the credit union.

The key person in a credit union is the treasurer, who is an elected, salaried officer. Remuneration is necessary for this officer, since the treasurer's tasks may require full-time attention. In many credit unions the treasurer is also the manager, the resident financial expert responsible for maintaining ledgers and passbooks and for reporting monthly to the board of directors on financial operations.

Committees. The credit union committee structure is also important to union operations. Three committees are standard in well-run credit unions: (1) a credit committee, which meets on a regular basis to review loan applications (although this task is delegated in some unions to loan officers); (2) a supervisory committee, which audits the books and monitors the operation of the credit union, reporting its observations periodically to the membership and the board of directors; and (3) an education committee, which seeks to communicate with the present and potential membership on the services offered by the credit union and coordinates most advertising and promotional efforts. Committee members, like officers, donate their services as volunteers.

Sponsor. The responsibility of the sponsor of a credit union is very limited. Many universities merely authorize the use of their name to their credit unions for identification purposes. Others may lend office space, materials, and personnel to a fledgling union. A new credit union should become independent of the sponsor at the earliest possible time, but, once established, the credit union should maintain a healthy relationship with the sponsor through free-flowing communication at all times.

Establishing a Credit Union

In the United States those interested in the formation of a credit union should consult with the Credit Union National Association (CUNA). This association, formed in 1934 by credit union leagues (statewide service associations for credit unions) of the continental United States, now serves leagues in the fifty states and the District of Columbia. CUNA will provide informational material about credit unions and the development of a charter of organization and will help establish contacts with the league, groups, and individuals in local areas. Outside the United States this assistance is provided by the World Council of Credit Unions at the same address.

A committee of about twenty people

should be established to form a credit union. This organizing group must apply for a charter from either the state or the federal government. Federally chartered credit unions are supervised by the National Credit Union Administration (NCUA). State-chartered credit unions are supervised by various state agencies according to individual state law. All federal credit unions are required to insure deposits in member accounts up to $40,000 through the NCUA. The NCUA insurance program is also available to state-chartered unions. Each of the two types of charter has distinct advantages and disadvantages, which vary from situation to situation. State credit union leagues can be of assistance in making this choice. The relationship of the sponsor to the state or federal government should be considered, particularly in the s'ate-owned university systems. The World Council can assist groups outside the United States in the particulars of governmental acceptance in the country in which the credit union will operate.

The group organizing the credit union elects the officers and enlists community support and membership. The board of directors arranges for a surety bond, which is required to cover all personnel who handle funds. As soon as funds allow, the credit union should retain a qualified full-time professional treasurer/manager.

The experience of the teachers' credit unions in the United States—almost two thousand as of 1973—has shown that three steps aid the successful establishment of such a union. First, the charter should be broad enough to include all members of the university community, including faculty; administrators; students; and clerical, custodial, and service employees. Second, the credit union should offer a wide range of services, to all members of the university community beyond loans and share savings, including payroll deductions, twelve-month salary stretchers, student loans guaranteed by government or private agencies, and consumer information services that are important in establishing the thrift reputation of the credit union. Third, the credit union should initiate a data-processing system as soon as feasible. Taking this step early can yield savings and efficiency in the operations of the credit union.

The Credit Union Family

Credit unions are served by a network of related and affiliated organizations in addition to CUNA and the World Council.

The ICU Services Corporation provides special financial programs and services for credit unions, such as government securities investments, credit union interlending, money orders, travelers checks, share drafts, plastic cards, and tax-sheltered retirement savings programs.

The National Association of Federal Credit Unions works to advance the legislative interests of federally chartered credit unions in the United States.

CUNADATA Corporation, a data-processing system designed, owned, and controlled by the credit union movement, serves countries throughout the world and is expected eventually to provide a link in an international communications chain enabling credit unions to participate more effectively in the electronic transfer of funds.

Credit Union National Association Supply Corporation is engaged in the development and marketing of a comprehensive range of promotional, operational, and educational materials for credit unions and organizations of credit unions.

CUNA (part of the CUNA Mutual Group) Mutual Insurance Society is a life insurance company that provides share, life, and loan protection wholly oriented to the objectives of the credit union movement. All income, less operating expenses and legal reserves, is returned to policyholders in the form of dividends.

The CUNIS Insurance Group, a stock company, is the property, casualty, and fidelity insurance arm of the credit union movement, with ownership vested in members, leagues, credit unions, chapters, and CUNA Mutual.

The Credit Union Executives Society is an international professional organization which provides services and programs for credit union managers and their key assistants.

Future of the Credit Union Movement

Since 1950 the worldwide credit union membership has grown from sixteen million to over fifty-one million. It is expected that this growth is just the beginning of an explosion in credit union development that will help people around the world provide for their own and their families' financial needs.

In the future credit unions will be very much involved in the cashless, checkless society that has been forecast by monetary experts. A great deal of research is being done on the emerging electronic funds transfer systems which are expected to revolutionize the manner in which financial transactions are made by the 1980s. Credit unions in the United States are already experimenting with pilot electronic funds transfer programs intended to maximize services to their members. However, while keeping pace with this evolving technology credit unions remain committed to their traditional role of providing personal services that promote the financial well-being of individual members and their families.

Addresses of Credit Union Confederations

Africa Cooperative Savings and Credit Association
Post Office Box 43278
Nairobi, Kenya

Asian Confederation of Credit Unions
% National Credit Union Federation of Korea
Suhdaemoon, Box 8
Seoul, Republic of Korea

Australian Federation of Credit Union Leagues
Post Office Box 28
Homebush, New South Wales 2140

Caribbean Confederation of Credit Unions
155 Tragarete Road
Port-of-Spain, Trinidad

Confederación latinoamericana de
    cooperativas de ahorro y crédito
Apartado 6664
Panama 5, Republic of Panama

National Association of Canadian
    Credit Unions
Box 800, Station U
Toronto, Ontario, Canada M8Z 5R2

World Council of Credit Unions and
    Credit Union National Association
Post Office Box 431
Madison, Wisconsin 53701 USA

Bibliography

Credit Union National Association. *Using Credit Wisely.* Madison, Wisconsin: CUNA Supply Corporation, 1966.
Credit Union National Association. *A Teacher's Guide to Credit Unions.* Madison, Wisconsin: CUNA Supply Corporation, 1967.
Dublin, J. *Credit Unions: Theory and Practice.* Detroit: Wayne State University Press, 1966.
International Credit Union Yearbook. Waterloo, Wisconsin: Credit Union National Association, 1975.
Prindle, J. (Ed.) *It's Not Just Money.* Madison, Wisconsin: Credit Union National Association, 1967.

EDWARD G. WOLFMAN

CRIMINOLOGY (Field of Study)

Criminology, which has only recently become an integrated science, has been defined by different authors in a variety of ways: as the science that deals with all aspects of the perpetration of crime and the fight against crime (Seelig, 1956); as the scientific study of crime as a social-political phenomenon (Sutherland and Cressey, 1966); and, finally, as the complete study of crime and the criminal, the former being regarded not as a juridical abstraction but as a human act—a natural and social fact (Carroll and Pinatel, 1956). The scope of the criminological field varies with the concept of different authors. Reckless (1967) suggests ten areas of activity that seem to encompass all elements of criminology:

1. The reporting of law violations, clearance by arrest, criminal identification, and the improvement of measures to record crime, arrest criminals, and identify violators.

2. A comparative study of criminal law and judicial systems in various countries as related to economic, political, and social systems, with appropriate attention to transitions in developing countries and to the system of traditional sanctions in tribal societies.

3. Specification of demographic characteristics of juvenile and adult offenders at points in the legal process where it is possible to record such things as age, birth, ethnic group, marital status, occupation, educational level, place of criminal offense, and place of residence. Such registration of population characteristics enables specialists to pinpoint high-risk areas.

4. Formulation, testing, and verification of hypotheses or theories which attempt to explain crime and delinquency in general or any particular pattern of offense or criminal activity in particular.

5. Identification and description of basic components of the behaviors which are legally defined as criminal and delinquent in various countries of the world, leading to classifications approximating the kinds that natural scientists have made.

6. The study of recidivism and habitual criminals and the identification of first offenders, recidivists, and hard-core offenders, including offenders with character disorders and mental disturbances.

7. The study and control of problems of deviancy—such as abnormal sex offenses, prostitution, suicide, narcotic drug addiction, chronic alcoholism, addictive gambling, begging, and vagrancy—which have a close connection with crime.

8. The study and implementation of law enforcement and the operation of special laws, such as the laws regarding habitual offenders and abnormal sex offenders.

9. The study of the effectiveness of measures for treatment and rehabilitation of offenders by penal and correctional institutions, probation, and after-care service (parole), including the study of

impact of detention while awaiting trial or disposition.

10. Evaluation and operation of programs for the prevention of delinquency and crime.

Criminology includes four basic disciplines: psychopathology and psychiatry, criminal sociology, criminal geography or ecology, and criminal statistics. Psychopathology and psychiatry undertake the biological, neurological, psychological, and pathological investigations necessary to study the delinquent; the aspects of man's personality as a biological and psychosocial being are the main concerns. Criminal sociology is concerned with the social characteristics of the delinquent (for example, age, sex, social class, ethnic origin) and the typology of acts and delinquent personalities in relation to such things as age, social background, economic status, and politics; the social reasons motivating the offense and the forming of the criminal personality through association with criminal subcultures or countercultures; and the genesis of mechanisms of social control—the development of regulating devices for normal and deviant behavior, including the legal devices. Criminal geography or ecology records the regional variations in crime in relation to the environment. Finally, criminal statistics keeps a record of crimes, criminals, and victims and tries to establish the dark number (the difference between crimes actually committed and those officially known). It also keeps data on the operation of the justice system (police, courts, and prisons).

The body of theoretical and empirical knowledge in criminology is enriched by the findings of a number of other disciplines. Criminalistics is the sum of the procedures used to establish the material evidence in connection with an infraction. Penology includes the implementation of sanctions, research on the influence of imprisonment on the individual, and the study of the role of detention in rehabilitation. Criminal law comprises the written legislation of a country concerning acts of violation, sanctions, and the means for social defense. Criminal law is a norm which society establishes and imposes for its own protection. Forensic psychiatry includes all psychiatric knowledge applicable to judicial procedure. It particularly deals with the psychopathological elements which can solve questions of criminal responsibility and the need for internment. Forensic medicine, operating within the framework of criminal and civil law, affords important specialized medical services. It furnishes some of the means used by criminalists, for example, to determine the origin of wounds on victims and the type of instrument used to commit a crime. Another of its services is the performance of autopsies. Forensic chemistry has a function in judicial procedure; it investigates cases of poisoning, the adulteration of foodstuffs and their safety, and performs chemical analyses to find and identify material clues. Forensic psychology studies the behavior in court of the judge, the witnesses, and the accused. Finally, prophylaxis or criminal policy deals with the problems of crime prevention and the treatment of delinquents within the general framework of a given social policy.

Several schools of thought have contributed to criminological concepts and research. These schools also reflect the great chapters in the history of scientific, social, and philosophical thought. The classical school, for example, began in the late eighteenth century with works by Beccaria and Howard. In the wake of the Encyclopedists, Cesare Beccaria published his treatise *Dei delitti e delle pene* (1764) and John Howard his work on the state of prisons in England and Wales (1777). These two writers outlined a theory of the causes of crime and demanded a criminal policy inspired by enlightened and humane laws; their books mark the beginnings of criminology. Beccaria and his disciples were interested in humanitarian principles and stressed penal reform, but it is with Cesare Lombroso and the Italian positivist school that criminology passed from a speculative phase to a scientific one.

In 1876 Lombroso put forward the hypothesis of atavism to explain criminal behavior. His disciples, Enrico Ferri (1929) and Raffaele Garofalo (1885), came to the conclusion that criminals should not have to expiate their crime but should be neutralized, without moral judgment, in order to protect society. Thus, the Italian positivist school gave birth to the social defense movement, a movement whose definition of crime stresses the idea of social danger rather than moral responsibility.

The German and Austrian criminological school was founded by Franz von Liszt and Hans Gross and was continued by E. Seelig and P. Grassberger. According to this school, the criminal cannot be separated from his act, nor can he be studied in isolation from his behavior. The Austrian school attached great importance to circumstantial or external factors.

The Anglo-American school is represented by Charles Buckman Goring (1916), who criticized the methodology of Lombroso; by Cyril Burt, who studied the psychiatric characteristics of delinquents; and by the pioneering works of the Chicago school of sociologists in the United States. In addition, Clifford Shaw, Henry McKay, Ernest W. Burgess, Thorsten Sellin, Edwin Sutherland, Walter Reckless, and Karl Menninger (in the United States) and Leon Radzinowicz, Hermann Mannheim, Max Grünhut, and Hans J. Eysenck (in Great Britain) may be considered pioneers of the criminological theory that developed between 1930 and 1960. These researchers show close links with sociology in the United States and with law in Great Britain. Menninger, a psychiatrist, and Eysenck, a psychologist, however, are concerned with the contribution of psychiatry and psychology to the field of criminology.

Criminology in the Scandinavian countries was dominated by the work of Olof Kinberg (1935) between 1930 and 1960; during the same period, Stephan Hurwitz in Denmark and Johannes Andenaes in Norway exercised a considerable influence.

Kinberg, a psychiatrist, conceived of criminology as an exact science closely related to biology; Hurwitz and Andenaes had sociological and juridic concepts directed toward penal reform. In Holland, during the period 1930 to 1960, outstanding names in the field were those of W. H. Nagel and F. Van Bemmelen.

The French and Belgian sociological school was based on the work of the cartographical or geographical school. Such members of the school as Adolphe Quételet and André de Guérry devoted special attention to the distribution of criminality in certain areas, both geographical and social. An infraction was considered to be related to certain social conditions. Other leaders of this school include Gabriel Tarde, whose theory is a synthesis of psychology and sociology; Tarde considered social environment and imitation the most important factors in the etiology of criminal behavior. Emile Durkheim, who saw crime as a normal social phenomenon, stressed the idea of anomie to explain the specifically social causes of delinquency. L. Vervaek and E. De Greeff, both attached to the anthropological service of the Belgian penitentiaries, also made important contributions to criminology.

Beginning in 1950, in North America and Europe, a more integrated concept of criminology emerged—both in research and, especially after 1960, in the field of teaching. Although the contribution of medicine was more marked in Europe, and that of the social sciences in North America, there was an increasing trend toward multidisciplinary integration. The works of Giacomo Canepa and Franco Ferracuti in Italy; of Günther Kaiser, A. Mergen, and H. Göppinger in Germany; of Jean Pinatel in France; of Inkeri Antilla, Nils Christie, and K. O. Christiansen in Scandinavia; and Koudriavtsev in the Soviet Union are of particular significance in the field of criminology. T. C. N. Gibbens, Nigel Walker, J. E. Hall Williams, D. McClintock, Roger Hood, and Stanley T. Cohen in the United Kingdom; W. Buikhuisen and L. H. C.

Hulsman in the Netherlands; and C. G. Debuyst in Belgium—all stimulated important work, both in teaching and research. Important figures who had a great influence in the field in the United States, where by far the most work has been produced, include Marvin Wolfgang, Lloyd Ohlin, Norval Morris, A. H. Becker, and Gerhard O. W. Mueller.

Training in criminology is offered in Europe within the framework of the faculties of medicine and law as a special course, accessible to doctors and jurists as well as to social workers and specialists in the social sciences. In France these studies are part of the curriculum in criminal law and forensic medicine; in Belgium the schools of criminology are attached to the faculties of law; in Italy criminology falls within the realm of criminal anthropology and is attached to the faculties of medicine; in Germany and Spain the study of criminology is included in criminal law or criminology but within the law faculties. In the Scandinavian countries and the Netherlands, institutes of criminology are attached to law faculties. In the United Kingdom courses are given at Cambridge University, in an autonomous institute, and in many other universities within the framework of the social science and law schools.

All of these courses in criminology were instituted between 1930 and 1960. However, they cannot be considered sufficient university training for accreditation as a criminologist. Essentially, this training is supplementary to the basic training obtained in another discipline (Radzinowicz, 1961).

The trend in criminological education in Europe in the mid 1970s is toward the constitution of multidisciplinary research centers in both the universities and government services. Such centers include the *Max-Planck-Institut für ausländisches und internationales Strafrecht—Forschungsgruppe Kriminologie* in the Federal Republic of Germany, the research center of the Home Office in London, the research services of the *Chancellerie* in Paris, and the research

center attached to the office of the public prosecutor in Moscow.

In North America the teaching of criminology, which from 1930 to 1960 was confined to departments of sociology and social service schools, has been established in schools, special departments, or institutes of criminology or criminal justice. These establishments assure a multidisciplinary training at both the undergraduate and postgraduate levels, and their programs lead to professional standing. In Canada, Simon Fraser University in Burnaby, British Columbia, and the universities of Montreal, Toronto, and Ottawa all offer criminology programs (Szabo, 1964).

The number of universities in the United States offering a diploma in criminal justice and conferring the title of Associate of Arts went from over 40 in 1960 to 664 in 1975. This diploma is designed for practitioners and technicians working in the field of justice administration. In 1975, according to an estimate of the Law Enforcement Assistance Administration, 740 university diplomas (Associate of Arts) were issued, 423 Bachelor of Arts degrees, 164 Master of Arts degrees, and 21 doctorates (Ph.D.), for a total of 1348 (Lejins, 1975). Some of the universities offering these degrees are the University of Pennsylvania, State University of New York at Albany, University of Florida, Ohio State University, University of Illinois at Chicago, University of Maryland, Rutgers University, and John Jay College of New York University.

Outside of Europe and North America, criminology is taught in institutes modeled on those of continental Europe. These centers of research and training give specialized postgraduate courses. In Asia, for example, the Institute for Penal Studies and Criminology of the University of Tehran; the Tata Institute of Social Sciences in Bombay; the institutes of criminology at Tel Aviv University, the Hebrew University of Jerusalem; and *Istanbül universitesi* all offer programs. In Africa, there is the National Centre of Social and Criminological Research in Cairo, which is an autonomous institution; and south of the Sahara, the *Université d'Abidjan* in the Ivory Coast. In Latin America there are several such institutes, including those at the *Universidad nacional autónoma de México;* the *Universidad central de Venezuela* in Caracas; the *Universidad central del Ecuador* in Quito; and the *Universidad del Zulia* in Maracaibo, Venezuela. There is also an institute at the *Universidad de Chile* in Santiago and at the *Museo social argentino* in Buenos Aires. In the socialist countries, with the exception of Poland, criminological research is done in institutes under the jurisdiction of the office of the public prosecutor. There is no teaching of criminology outside the courses given in the faculty of criminal law.

Apart from the conferences held by the United Nations, and those of nongovernmental bodies such as the International Society of Criminology, the International Association of Penal Law, and the International Society for Social Defense, only the courses of the International Society of Criminology can be considered programs of an international nature. The activities of the Social Defense Section of the Arab League, of the Council of Europe, of the socialist countries of Eastern Europe, and of the Scandinavian Research Council of Criminology constitute the major criminological activities at the regional level.

Beginning in 1969 the International Society of Criminology organized teaching and international and interdisciplinary research by creating international centers in important areas of criminological activity: the International Centre for Comparative Criminology, attached to the University of Montreal, Canada; the International Center of Biological and Medico-Forensic Criminology, attached to the faculty of medicine of the *Universidade de São Paulo,* Brazil; and the International Centre of Clinical Criminology, attached to the faculty of medicine of the *Università degli studi di Genova,* Italy. The United Nations, in turn, created the United Nations Social Defense Research Institute (UNSDRI) in Rome, as well as regional institutes designed for the training of personnel in the field of criminal justice in Japan, Egypt, and Costa Rica.

[*Notes:* **C. Beccaria,** *Des délits et des peines* (Paris: Bastien, 1773). **C. Burt,** *The Young Delinquent* (London: University of London Press, 1925). **D. Carroll** and **J. Pinatel,** *Rapport général sur l'enseignement de la criminologie et des sciences sociales dans l'enseignement supérieur* (Paris: UNESCO, 1956). **E. De Greeff,** *Introduction à la criminologie* (Brussels: Van des Plas, 1946). **E. Durkheim,** "Deux lois de l'évolution pénale," *L'année sociologique,* 1899–1900, *4,* 65–95. **H. Ellenberger** and **M. Dongier,** "Conceptions actuelles de la criminogénèse," in *Encyclopédie médico-chirurgicale: Psychiatrie,* Fascicle No. 37760, A30-12 (Paris: Julien Prelat, 1958). **H. Ellenberger** and **D. Szabo,** "L'approche multidisciplinaire des problèmes de la criminologie," *Informations sur les sciences sociales,* 1967, *6*(5), 95–114. **H. J. Eysenck,** *Crime and Personality* (London: Routledge and Kegan Paul, 1964). **E. Ferri,** *Sociologia criminale,* 2 vols., 5th rev. ed. (Turin, Italy: Unione tipografico, 1929–1930). **R. Garofalo,** *La criminologie* (Paris: Alcan, 1888). **H. Göppinger,** *Kriminologie* (Munich, Federal Republic of Germany: C. H. Beck'sche, 1971). **C. Goring,** *The English Convict* (London: H. M. Stationery Office, 1913). **A. M. Guérry,** *Essais sur la statistique morale de la France* (Paris: Crochard, 1833). **O. Kinberg,** *Basic Principles of Criminology* (Copenhagen: Levin & Munksgaard, 1935). **P. Lejins,** "La justice pénale (1970–1975)" (presented at the Fifth Congress of the United Nations, Geneva, 1975). **C. Lombroso,** *L'uomo delinquente* (Milan, Italy: n.p., 1876). **R. J. McLean,** ed., *Education for Crime Prevention and Control* (Springfield, Illinois: Thomas, 1975). **K. Menninger,** *Man Against Himself* (New York: Harcourt Brace Jovanovich, 1938). **A. Quételet,** *Recherches sur le penchant au crime aux différents âges,* 2nd ed. (Brussels: Hayez, 1833). **L. Radzinowicz,** *In Search of Criminology* (London: Heinemann, 1961). **W. Reckless,** *The Crime*

Problem, 4th ed. (New York: Appleton-Century-Crofts, 1967). **E. Seelig,** *Traité de criminologie* (Paris: Presses universitaires de France, 1956). **T. Sellin,** *Culture Conflict and Crime* (New York: Social Science Research Council, 1938). **E. H. Sutherland** and **D. R. Cressey,** *Principes de criminologie* (Paris: Cujas, 1966). **D. Szabo,** "The Teaching of Criminology in Universities: A Contribution to the Sociology of Innovation," *International Review of Criminal Policy,* 1964, *22,* 17–28. **D. Szabo,** *Criminologie,* abridged ed. (Montreal, Quebec: Les presses de l'Université de Montréal, 1970). **G. Tarde,** *Les lois de l'imitation,* 2nd ed. (Paris: Alcan, 1890). **M. F. Wolfgang** and **F. Ferracuti,** *The Subculture of Violence: Towards an Integrated Theory in Criminology* (London: Tavistock, 1967).]

DENIS SZABO

Levels and Programs of Study

Programs in criminology generally require as a minimum prerequisite a secondary education and lead to the following degrees: bachelor's (B.A. or B.Sc.), master's (M.A. or M.Sc.), the doctorate, or their equivalents. Programs deal with the principles and practices of criminology and consist of classroom sessions and seminars and, for advanced degrees, emphasis on original research work substantiated by the presentation of a scholarly thesis or dissertation. Principal course content for work leading to a first university degree usually includes introduction to criminology, principles of criminal investigation, psychopathology and psychodynamics of crime, components of normal and abnormal personality, methods of personality measurement and clinical diagnosis, social origin and characteristics of crime, sociology of legal and correctional institutes, history of crime and its treatment, scientific methodology, law enforcement policies and social structure, criminal law in action, and fieldwork in criminology. Background studies include courses in economics, history, the social and behavioral sciences, and law and jurisprudence. At the postgrad-

uate degree level, principal subject matter areas into which courses and research projects tend to fall include the history of crime and its treatment, organized crime and the professional criminal, constitutional and procedural problems in law enforcement, the prison community, the alcoholic and the narcotic addict, sexual offenders and character disorders, white-collar crime, nonconformist cultures, forensic toxicology, juvenile delinquency and its prevention and control, law and discretion in criminal sentencing, group psychotherapy in correctional institutions, the prevention and control of crime in metropolitan areas, and practical work and research techniques in criminology. Background studies include courses in history, economics, the social and behavioral sciences, mathematics, natural sciences, and statistics.

[This section was based on UNESCO's *International Standard Classification of Education (ISCED)* (Paris: UNESCO, 1976).]

Major International and National Organizations

INTERNATIONAL

International Association of Penal Law
Association internationale de droit pénal
    (AIDP)
Faculté de droit de Paris
12 place du Panthéon
75005 Paris, France

International Criminal Police Organization
    (Interpol)
26 rue Armengaud
92210 Saint-Cloud, France

International Penal and Penitentiary
    Foundation (IPPF)
Fondation internationale pénale et
    pénitentiaire (FIPP)
Prison Administration
Koninginnegracht 19
The Hague, Netherlands

International Society for Social Defense
28 rue Saint-Guillaume
75007 Paris, France

International Society of Criminology
Société internationale de criminologie
4 rue de Mondovi
75001 Paris, France
    The major international association in the

field, with 180 corporate and 1020 individual, associate, and student members in seventy-nine countries.

United Nations
Crime Prevention and Criminal Justice Section
New York, New York 10017 USA

NATIONAL

Canada:
Canadian Criminology and Corrections
Association
55 Parkdale
Ottawa 3, Ontario

Federal Republic of Germany:
Deutsche kriminologische Gesellschaft
e.V.
Postfach 16720
6 Frankfurt/Main

France:
Association française de criminologie
Centre français de criminologie
12 avenue Rockefeller
69 Lyon (8e)

United Kingdom:
British Society of Criminology
Institute for the Study and Treatment
of Delinquency
8 Bourdon Street
London W1, England

United States:
American Correctional Association
4321 Hartwick Road, Suite L208
College Park, Maryland 20740

American Society of Criminology
Department of Sociology and
Anthropology
Bates College
Lewiston, Maine 04240

National Council on Crime and
Delinquency
Continental Plaza
411 Hackensack Avenue
Hackensack, New Jersey 07601

Sources for additional national organizations in criminology include:

World Index of Social Science Institutions. Paris: UNESCO, 1970.
The World of Learning. London: Europa, 1947–. Published annually.

Principal Information Sources

GENERAL

Among general guides to the literature of criminology are:

Pinatel, J. "Select Bibliography." *International Social Science Journal,* 1966, *18,* 224–246. Lists publications of international scope published between 1950 and 1964.
Selected Documentation of Criminology. Paris: UNESCO, 1961. A comparative international bibliographical guide to documentation on criminology.
Sellin, T., and Savitz, L. D. *A Bibliographic Manual for the Student of Criminology.* Hackensack, New Jersey: National Council on Crime and Delinquency, 1965. A major listing of bibliographies specifically relating to criminology; includes an annotated list of general reference works.
Wolfgang, M. E., Figlio, R. M., and Thornberry, T. P. *Criminology Index.* (2 vols.) New York: American Elsevier, 1975.
Wright, M. *Use of Criminology Literature.* Hamden, Connecticut: Shoestring Press, 1974.

Works on comparative education in the field of criminology include:

Szabo, D. "The Teaching of Criminology in Universities: A Contribution to the Sociology of Innovation." *International Review of Criminal Policy,* 1964, *22,* 17–28.
The University Teaching of Social Sciences: Criminology. Paris: UNESCO, 1956. An international study on the teaching of criminology, consisting of reports prepared by Denis Carroll and others on behalf of the International Society of Criminology.

The annual international lecture courses on criminology published since 1952 by the International Society of Criminology (various publications and titles) are also important publications, as are the proceedings of the criminology congresses of the same organization.

Introductory books in the field of general criminology include:

Ancel, M. *Social Defence.* New York: Schocken Books, 1966.
Göppinger, H. *Kriminologie.* (2nd ed.) Munich, Federal Republic of Germany: C. H. Beck'sche Verlagsbuchhandlung, 1973.
Hood, R., and Sparks, R. *Key Issues in Criminology.* New York: McGraw-Hill, 1970.
Lopez-Rey, M. *Crime: An Analytical Appraisal.* New York: Praeger, 1970.
Pinatel, J. *Criminologie.* (3rd ed.) Paris: Dalloz, 1975.
Radzinowicz, L. *In Search of Criminology.* London: Heinemann, 1961.
Reckless. W. C. *American Criminology: New Directions.* New York: Appleton-Century-Crofts, 1973.
Sutherland, E. H., and Cressey, D. R. *Crimi-*

nology. (9th ed.) Philadelphia: Lippincott, 1974.

A history of important persons in the field is:

Mannheim, H. *Pioneers in Criminology.* London: Stevens, 1960.

CURRENT BIBLIOGRAPHIES

Abstracts on Criminology and Penology. Deventer, Netherlands: Kluwer B. V., 1961–. Formerly *Excerpta Criminologica,* this international abstracting service covers the etiology of crime and juvenile delinquency, the control and treatment of offenders, criminal procedure, and the administration of justice.

Crime and Delinquency Literature. Hackensack, New Jersey: National Council on Crime and Delinquency, 1970–. American oriented and selective, but useful for current awareness.

International Bibliography on Crime and Delinquency. New York: National Research and Information Center on Crime and Delinquency, 1963–. Each issue features a special bibliography on a particular country or a specific topic.

International Review of Criminal Policy. New York: United Nations, 1952–, A semiannual publication which frequently, but irregularly, contains extensive bibliographies in criminology.

International Annals of Criminology. Paris: Société internationale de criminologie, 1962–. A semiannual publication.

PERIODICALS

Periodicals of international importance in the field of criminology include *Acta Criminologica* (Canada), *Australian and New Zealand Journal of Criminology, British Journal of Criminology, Canadian Journal of Criminology and Corrections, Criminology* (US), *International Annals of Criminology* (France), *International Criminal Police Review* (France), *International Journal of Criminology and Penology* (US), *International Journal of Offender Therapy and Comparative Criminology* (UK), *International Review of Criminal Policy* (Switzerland), *Issues in Criminology* (US), *Journal of Criminal Justice* (US), *Journal of Criminal Law, Criminology, and Police Science* (US), *Journal of Research in Crime and Delinquency* (US), *Kriminalistik und forensische Wissenschaften* (GDR), *National Review of Criminal Sciences* (Egypt), *Nederlands tijdschrift voor criminologie, Nordiska kriminalistföreningarnas årsbok* (Sweden), *Revue de droit pénal et de criminologie* (Belgium), *Revue de science criminelle et de droit pénal comparé* (France), *Revue internationale de criminologie et de police technique* (Switzerland), *Revue internationale de droit pénal* (France).

A current country-by-country list of periodicals can be found in:

Abstracts on Criminology and Penology. Deventer, Netherlands: Kluwer B. V., 1961–.

ENCYCLOPEDIAS, DICTIONARIES, HANDBOOKS

Adler, J. A. (Ed.) *Elsevier's Dictionary of Criminal Science in Eight Languages.* Amsterdam: Elsevier, 1960. English/American terms with translations in French, Italian, Spanish, Portuguese, Dutch, Swedish, and German.

Branham, S., and Kutash, S. B. *Encyclopedia of Criminology.* New York: Philosophical Library, 1949.

Glaser, D. *Handbook of Criminology.* Chicago: Rand McNally, 1973.

Kaiser, C.; and others. *Kleine kriminologisches Wörterbuch.* Freiburg, Federal Republic of Germany: Herder, 1974.

Scott, H. R. (Ed.) *The Concise Encyclopedia of Crime and Criminals.* London: Deutsch, 1961. A comprehensive set of articles on crime and criminals of the modern world.

Yamarellos, E., and Kellens, C. *Le crime et la criminologie.* (2 vols.) Paris: Marabout université (No. 196–197), 1970. A dictionary.

DIRECTORIES

American Correctional Association. *Directory of Correctional Institutions and Agencies of the United States of America, and Canada.* Washington, D.C.: American Correctional Association, annual. Includes juvenile and adult correctional institutions, parole authorities, and short-term institutions.

International Prisoners' Aid Association. *International Directory of Prisoners' Aid Agencies.* Milwaukee: International Prisoners' Aid Association, 1968. International guide listing voluntary organizations in many countries.

Kobetz, R. W. *Law Enforcement and Criminal Justice Education Directory 1975–76.* Gaithersburg, Maryland: International Association of Chiefs of Police, 1975. A listing of degree programs in law enforcement and criminal justice offered in colleges and universities in the United States and Canada.

United States Department of Justice, Law Enforcement Assistance Administration. *Criminal Justice Agencies.* Washington, D.C.: U.S. Government Printing Office, 1975. Lists 57,575 criminal justice agencies, including enforcement, courts, prosecution and legal services, defender, correctional, probation, and parole agencies at the state and local government levels.

RESEARCH CENTERS, INSTITUTES,
INFORMATION CENTERS

The following are important research and
teaching institutes and centers in criminology
and social defense:

All Union Institute for the Study of the Causes
of Crime and the Elaboration of Preventive
Measures
2nd Zvenigorodskaya, 15
Moscow D-22, Soviet Union

Center for Knowledge in Criminal Justice
Planning
38 East 85th Street
New York, New York 10028 USA

Center for Criminal Justice
Law School
Harvard University
Cambridge, Massachusetts 02138 USA

Center for Studies in Criminal Justice
University of Chicago Law School
1111 East 60th Street
Chicago, Illinois 60637 USA

Center for Studies in Criminology and
Criminal Law
3718 Locust Street
University of Pennsylvania
Philadelphia, Pennsylvania 19104 USA

Center for the Study of Crime and
Delinquency
1314 Kinnear Road
Columbus, Ohio 43212 USA

Center for the Study of Crime, Delinquency
and Corrections
Southern Illinois University
Carbondale, Illinois 60637 USA

Center for the Study of Law and Society
2224 Piedmont Avenue
University of California
Berkeley, California 94708 USA

Centre of Criminology
University of Toronto
John P. Robarts Research Library
130 St. Georges Street
Toronto, Ontario, Canada M5S 1A5

Centro internazionale di criminologia clinica
Facoltà de medecina
Università di Genova
via de Toni 12
16132 Genoa, Italy

Centro de investigaciones criminológicas
Facultad de derecho
Universidad del Zulia
Ciudad universitaria
Maracaibo, Venezuela

College of Criminal Justice
Northeastern University
Boston, Massachusetts 02115 USA

Correctional Planning and Development
Department of Youth Authority
714 P Street
Sacramento, California 95814 USA

Department of Criminology
Florida State University
Bellamy Building
Tallahassee, Florida 32306 USA

Department of Criminology
Simon Fraser University
Burnaby, British Columbia, Canada

Department of Criminology
University of Ottawa
556-562 King Edward
Ottawa, Ontario, Canada K1N 6N5

Home Office Research Unit
Romney House
Marsham Street
London SW1P 3DY, England

Institut de criminologie
Faculté de droit
Université d'Abidjan
B.P. 20901
Abidjan, Ivory Coast

Institute of Criminological and Criminalistic
Research
Gracanika 18
Belgrade, Yugoslavia

Institute of Criminal Justice and Criminology
University of Maryland
College Park, Maryland 20742 USA

Institut für Kriminologie
Universität Tübingen
Corrensstrasse 34,
D-7400 Tübingen, Federal Republic of
Germany

Instytut profilaktyki spolecznej resocjalizacji
Université de Varsovie
ul. Podchorazych 20
Warsaw, Poland

International Centre for Comparative
Criminology
University of Montreal
C.P. 6128
Montreal 101, Quebec, Canada

John Jay College of Criminal Justice
City University of New York
315 Park Avenue South
New York, New York 10010 USA

Law Enforcement Assistance Administration
  (LEAA)
National Institute of Law Enforcement and
  Criminal Justice
U.S. Department of Justice
Washington, D.C. 20530 USA

Max-Planck-Institut für ausländisches und
  internationales Strafrecht-
  Forschungsgruppe Kriminologie
Günterstalstrasse 72
7800 Freiburg, Federal Republic of Germany

National Centre for Social and Criminological
  Research
Awkaf City, Gezirah P.O.
Cairo, Egypt

Research Division
Ministry of Solicitor General
340 Laurier West
Ottawa, Ontario, Canada K1A OP8

Scandinavian Research Council of Criminology
  (SRCC)
Pengerkatu 30 E
Helsinki 50, Finland

School of Criminal Justice
Rutgers University
18 Bishop Place
New Brunswick, New Jersey 08903 USA

School of Criminology
University of California
101 Haviland Hall
Berkeley, California 94720 USA

School of Criminology
University of Montreal
C.P. 6128
Montreal 101, Quebec, Canada

United Nations Social Defence Research
  Institute (UNSDRI)
via Giulia 52
Rome 00186, Italy

The many important centers in the United
States are listed in:

*Criminological Research Institutes in the United
  States and Canada.* Hackensack, New Jersey:
  National Council on Crime and Delin-
  quency, 1969.

For a listing of institutions—observation
and treatment centers, research, teaching, and
documentation centers—in twenty-five countries (mainly in Europe and the Americas)
which specialize in the study of criminal phenomena and their prevention, see the following, compiled by the International Society of
Criminology:

Selected Documentation of Criminology. Paris:
  UNESCO, 1961.

CROP SCIENCE
(Field of Study)

Crop science is the branch of agriculture that treats the principles and practices of crop culture, production, and improvement, as well as management and
utilization of crops grown on a field scale.
Crop science is an integral part of *agronomy*,
a term derived from two Greek words,
agros (field) and *nomos* (to manage). Originating largely from the basic sciences of
botany, chemistry, and physics, crop science deals with the leading world field
crops: wheat, rice, soybeans, corn, barley,
oats, sorghum, rye, cotton, and potatoes.
These, and other minor field crops, are
often grouped into cereal or grain crops,
legumes (for seed, forage, root, fiber, tuber,
sugar, drugs, and oil), and rubber crops.

There are seven main branches or divisions of crop science. (1) Crop breeding,
genetics, and cytology covers the development of natural populations and their manipulation by man; recent advances in biochemical, population, and developmental
genetics; discoveries associated with composition and nature of pest resistance on
the development of superior varieties; and
the role of new breeding systems in meeting projected world food needs. (2) Crop
physiology and metabolism is the study of
biochemical and biophysical processes at
the cellular, tissue, and organismic levels
and their impact on adaptation, productivity, and quality of crop plants. (3) Crop
ecology, production, and management involves the changing environmental requirements of crop plants and their physiological bases; the effects of climate, soil, and
cultural practices upon the environment;
and adaption and competition within and
among interacting genotypes. (4) Seed production and technology concerns the development, structure, morphology, and physiological characteristics on germination,
dormancy, and longevity; the influence of
environment on seed quality; environmental and economic factors affecting the use
of vegetative material in propagation; and
legal aspects and regulations governing

seeds and vegetative propagules in commerce. (5) Crop quality, storage, and utilization considers the effects of the environment, management practices, growth stage, harvest treatment, storage, and utilization on crop quality. (6) Crop protection is concerned with genetic, biological, chemical, and physical control systems which improve crop yield and quality. (7) Turfgrass has to do with the culture, management, and improvement of grasses for lawns, golf courses and greens, cemeteries, and airfields.

Crop science depends on a large number of basic sciences for its promotion and foundation. The very fact that crop plants are composed of chemical constituents leads to the direct relation of crop science to chemistry and biochemistry. Genetics, the study of genes and gene function, is fundamental to the crop scientist whose responsibility is field crop plant improvement. Taxonomy classifies the more than 22,000 species of grasses and legumes—the mainstay families of plants extremely important in crop science. The performance of different crop plants in different environments also leads to close relationships with ecology. The study of crop production hazards, such as insects, diseases, and weeds, leads directly to entomology, plant pathology, and weed science. Since the causal organisms of plant diseases include bacteria, fungi, viruses, and nematodes, bacteriology, mycology, virology, and nematology are involved in the understanding of the growth habits, life cycles, and methods of control of these organisms. The study of physics or biophysics and plant physiology, involving the effects of heat, light, and sound on plant growth and reproduction, is also important to crop science. Plan nutrition and food science help answer problems related to the food needs of plants and human beings. Since soils are the substrate in which crops grow, soil science and earth sciences, including geology, also are important to crop science. Irrigation and drainage directly relate to hydrology and the atmospheric sciences in general. Finally, since considerable

human food comes from animal products produced through the grazing or feeding of crop plants, animal, dairy, and poultry sciences are indirectly involved with crop science.

Crop science may be said to have begun with the establishment of the first experiment station by J. B. Boussingault in Alsace in 1834, although many empirical tests long before that time had established facts about crops. The research work of John Bennet Lawes (1814–1900) and Joseph Henry Gilbert (1817–1901) in a private laboratory at Rothamsted, England—a laboratory which became world famous as the Rothamsted Agricultural Experiment Station—provided the catalyst for crop science, and the field has been a recognized branch of agricultural science since about 1900. The Crop Science Society of America, an integral part of the American Society of Agronomy, organized in 1908, was known first as the Crops Section in 1925. The society received its new name—and a more independent status—in 1955. In 1976 the section names were redesignated as the following divisions: crop breeding, genetics, and cytology; crop physiology and metabolism; crop ecology, production, and management; seed production and technology; turfgrass; and crop quality and utilization. More than 3500 crop scientists from around the world are members of the Crop Science Society of America, which holds regular annual meetings to discuss new research findings in the various crop science divisions. Research papers are published in the society's three journals: bimonthly in *Crop Science* and/or *Agronomy Journal*; and more recently the *Journal of Environmental Quality*, initiated to publish papers, especially in the general area of the effects of environmental pollutants on crop growth.

Formal courses in universities and agricultural colleges were initiated about 1915 in the United States and somewhat earlier in Western Europe. Nearly all agricultural universities require a plant science course (quite often crop science rather than horticulture or forest science) in their basic program for agricultural Bachelor of Science degrees. Crop science, agronomy, and crop protection majors usually must take a basic crop science course in partial requirement for the baccalaureate degree in agriculture.

Since about 1925 there have been many changes in crop science, both nationally and internationally. The current emphasis is on food production and energy sources. Because famine and threats of famine are a part of modern life, especially in Africa and India but in many other countries of the world as well, food production is a primary objective of crop scientists nationally and internationally. The World Food Conference in Rome, the National Academy of Sciences, and the National Science Foundation have undertaken a reappraisal of the world food, population, and nutrition situation. Crop scientists are discovering new technologies to provide for higher food productions needed in countries throughout the world. The International Rice Research Institute in the Philippines, established in 1960, has been instrumental in developing rice strains with very broad adaptation as a result of reduction of sensitivity to photoperiod and temperature. The International Maize and Wheat Improvement Center in Mexico, established in 1966, has been responsible for substantial increases in wheat yields by the use of dwarf adn semidwarf varieties of wheat. Other international organizations working to increase world food production are the International Institute of Tropical Agriculture in Nigeria, the International Center for Tropical Agriculture in Colombia, the International Potato Center in Peru, and the International Crops Research Institute for the Semi-Arid Tropics in India. There are intensive research efforts under way at international centers for rice, wheat (spring, winter, durum), maize, sorghum, and pearl millet; potatoes; cassava; field beans; cowpeas; chickpeas; pigeonpeas; mung beans; and cropping systems.

In consultation with the United Nations

Development Programme (UNDP) and the Food and Agriculture Organization (FAO), the World Bank formed the Consultative Group for International Agricultural Research, a consortium of foundations, national and international assistance agencies, and international banks. Among other projects, the Consultative Group has established a new agricultural research institute for the Middle East and a Board of Plant Genetic Resources, which is concerned with the systematic collection, evaluation, preservation, and exchange of germ plasm of the basic food crops. Interdisciplinary team approaches to crop science research are also being augmented nationally and internationally. For example, efforts to increase agricultural output have spawned new associations of crop scientists and financiers; crop, biological, and physical scientists; and crop scientists with economists, businessmen, governments, and industry.

Until about 1955, most crop science research and postsecondary education was in temperate regions of the world. Much greater emphasis is being placed on the development of tropical agriculture and/or global crop science. In addition, international crop science has produced new crop science training programs, which give students overseas experience in crop science. Graduate students not only participate in resident and travel studies abroad but also carry out crop science research projects abroad. More important, such students return to their nativve country to help put into practice the knowledge they have gained. In recent years American colleges of agriculture have developed courses and research relevant to India, Indonesia, Nepal, Chile, Brazil, and Nigeria, so that graduate student trainees can return to their respective countries to conduct new crop science research programs in their home country. Specialized United States nondegree training of students from Asia, Africa, and South America has contributed to the development of these students as leaders in their native countries.

In addition to undergraduate and graduate student exchange among various countries, there has been considerable faculty exchange of crop scientists and other specialists, researchers, teachers, extension teams, and administrators. On the whole, however, the educational institutions have been among the weakest links in world crop science because they have not been involved seriously in crop science development in the region or regions they serve. University-trained crop scientists often lack the skills required for intensive crop management. However, steps are being taken to exchange crop scientists who are experienced in farming; and nations are beginning to train crop scientists at several educational levels at their own institutions.

A. W. BURGER

Levels and Programs of Study

Programs in crop science generally re quire as a minimum prerequisite a secondary education and lead to the following awards: certificate or diploma, bachelor's degree (B.Sc.), master's degree (MmSc.), the doctorate (Ph.D.), or their equivalents. Programs deal with the principles and practices of crop science (crop husbandry) and consist of classroom, laboratory, and field instruction.

Programs that lead to an award not equivalent to a first university degree deal primarily with the technological aspects of cro science, although theory is not ignored. Principal course content usually includes some of the following: field crop production, forage crops, grain crops, cropping systems, pest control, weed control, soil science, and soil preparation. Background courses usually include marketing, entomology, chemistry, botany, plant pathology, and farm management.

Programs that lead to a first university degree deal with the principles and practices of crop science. Principal course content usually includes some of the following: principles of crop husbandry, soil preparation, soil chemistry, seed technology, fertilizer technology, agronomy, pest

and weed control, and harvesting and preservation of crops. Background courses usually include botany, plant physiology, microbiology, chemistry, farm management, marketing or agricultural products, and statistical analysis.

Programs that lead to a postgraduate university degree consist primarily of study and research dealing with advanced specialties in the field of crop science. Emphasis is given to original research work as substantiated by the presentation of a scholarly thesis or dissertation. Principal subject matter areas within which courses and research projects tend to fall include plant genetics, plant breeding, soil fertility, soil chemistry, soil genesis and classification, soil physics, soil biochemistry, soil microbiology, seed technology, pest and weed control, production of crops, and control of crop environment. Subject areas within which background studies tend to fall include specialties in botany, biochemistry, biophysics, microbiology, seed biology, mathematics, and statistical analysis.

[This section was based on UNESCO's *International Standard Classification of Education (ISCED)* (Paris: UNESCO, 1976).]

Major International and National Organizations

INTERNATIONAL

Among the many important international and regional organizations dealing with crop science are:

Caribbean Food Crops Society
Río Piedras, Puerto Rico

Commonwealth Bureau of Pastures and
    Field Crops
Hurley, Maidenhead
Berkshire, England

East-West Center
East-West Food Institute
1777 East-West Road
Honolulu, Hawaii 96822 USA

European Association for Research on
    Plant Breeding (EURARPIA)
P.O. Box 128
Wageningen, Netherlands

Food and Agriculture Organization of the
United Nations
Organisation des Nations unies pour
l'alimentation et l'agriculture
via delle Terme di Caracalla
00100 Rome, Italy

Inter-American Committee for
Crop Protection
Comité inter-americano de protección
agrícola (CCIPA)
avenida Pueyrredon 1959, 13 piso "A"
Buenos Aires, Argentina

International Center for Tropical Agriculture
Centro internacional de agricultura
tropical (CIAT)
Apartado Aéreo 67-13
Cali, Colombia

International Institute of Tropical
Agriculture (IITA)
P. M. B. 5320
Ibadan, Nigeria

International Maize and Wheat
Improvement Center
Centro internacional de mejoramiento de
maiz y trigo (CIMMYT)
Mexico D. F., Mexico

International Soybean Program (INTSOY)
113 Mumford Hall
University of Illinois
Urbana, Illinois 61801 USA

NATIONAL

Japan:
Nippon sakumotsu gakkai
% University of Tokyo
Tokyo
United States:
Crop Science Society of America
677 South Segoe Road
Madison, Wisconsin 53711
Major United States organization in the
field; international membership.

A comprehensive listing of national organizations throughout the world may be obtained from:

International Soybean Program
University of Illinois
Urbana, Illinois 61801 USA

For additional international and national
organizations see:

The World of Learning. London: Europa, 1947–.
Published annually. Lists learned societies
in countries throughout the world.
Yearbook of International Organizations. Brussels: Union of International Associations,
biennial.

Principal Information Sources

GENERAL

Guides to the literature include:

Blanchard, J. R., and Ostvold, H. *Literature of
Agricultural Research.* Berkeley: University of
California Press, 1958. Somewhat dated but
a classic guide to reference materials.
Bush, E. A. R. *Agriculture: A Bibliographic Guide.*
(2 vols.) London: Macdonald, 1974. Includes
references to field crops, crop protection,
and special crops.
Commonwealth Bureau of Pastures and Field
Crops. *Crop Physiology Abstracts.* Farnham
Royal, Bucks, England: Commonwealth Agricultural Bureaux, n.d.
*Selected List of American Agricultural Books in
Print and Current Periodicals.* Beltsvillw, Maryland: National Agricultural Library, 1975.
An extensive listing of books on various
aspects of agriculture and related subjects
published by United States publishers.

Introductory works include:

Burger, A. W. *Laboratory Studies in Field Crop
Science.* (2nd ed.) Champaign, Illinois: Stipes,
1967.
Chapman, S. R., and Carter, L. P. *Crop Protection: Principles and Practice.* San Francisco:
W. H. Freeman, 1976.
Delroit, R. J., and Ahlgren, H. L. *Crop Production Principles and Practices.* (4th ed.) Englewood Cliffs, New Jersey: Prentice-Hall, 1974.
Dungan, G. H., and Ross, W. A. *Growing Field
Crops.* New York: McGraw-Hill, 1957.
Evenson, R. E., and Kisler, Y. *Agricultural Research and Productivity.* New Haven, Connecticut: Yale University Press, 1975.
Foundations for Modern Crop Science. Madison,
Wisconsin: Crop Science Society of America
and American Society of Agronomy, 1975–
1977. A series of seven books: *Crops and
Man,* J. R. Harlan; *Propagation of Crops,*
J. C. DeLouche; *Crop Breeding,* D. R. Wood;
Physiological Bases for Crop Growth and Development, M. B. Tesar; *Ecological Bases foor
Crop Growth and Development,* W. L. Colville;
Crop Protection, W. B. Ennis, Jr.; *Crop Quality,
Storage and Utilization,* C. S. Hoveland.
Fream, W. *Fream's Elements of Agriculture: A
Textbook Prepared Under the Authority of the
Royal Agricultural Society of England.* (14th
ed.) London: Murray, 1962. Includes sections on crop diseases and crop cultivation.
Hughes, H. D., and Metcalfe, D. S. *Crop Production.* (3rd ed.) New York: Macmillan,
1972.
Janick, J. *Plant Science: An Introduction to World
Crops.* (2nd ed.) San Francisco: W. H. Free-

man, 1974. A survey of the technological, scientific, and economic aspects of world crops and their production.

Kipps, M. *Production of Field Crops.* (6th ed.) New York: McGraw-Hill, 1970.

Lockhart, J. A. R. *Introduction to Crop Husbandry.* (3rd ed.) Oxford, England; Elmsford, New York: Pergamon Press, 1975.

Martin, J. H., and others. *Principles of Field Crop Production.* New York: Macmillan, 1976.

Milthorpe, F. L., and Moorby, J. *An Introduction to Crop Physiology.* Cambridge, England: Cambridge University Press, 1974.

Pearson, L. C. *Principles of Agronomy.* New York: Van Nostrand Reinhold, 1967.

Schutt, P. *Weltwirtschaftspflanzen; Herkunft, Anbauverhältnisse, Biologie, und Verwendung der wichtigsten landwirtschaftlichen Nutzpflanzen.* Berlin, Federal Republic of Germany: P. Paney, 1972.

CURRENT BIBLIOGRAPHIES

Bibliographie der Pflanzenschutzliteratur. Berlin-Dahlem: Biologische Bundesanstalt für Land- und Forstwirtschaft, 1921–. Bibliography of plant protection.

Bibliography of Agriculture. Scottsdale, Arizona: Oryx Press, 1975–. Monthly index to literature on agriculture and related sciences; includes crop science sources. Covers monthly periodical articles, special current reports, and proceedings.

Commonwealth Bureau of Pastures and Field Crops. *Herbage Abstracts: Compiled from World Literature on Grassland and Forage Crops.* Farnham Royal, Bucks, England: Commonwealth Agricultural Bureaux, 1931–. Includes world literature from sixty countries.

Commonwealth Bureau of Pastures and Field Crops. *Field Crop Abstracts: Monthly Abstract Journal on World Annual Cereal, Legume, Root, Oilseed and Fiber Crops.* Farnham Royal, Bucks, England: Commonwealth Agricultural Bureaux, 1948–. Covers world literature.

Commonwealth Bureau of Plant Breeding and Genetics. *Plant Breeding Abstracts.* Farnham Royal, Bucks, England: Commonwealth Agricultural Bureaux, 1930–.

Refereratiunyĭ zhurnal. 55: Rastenievodstvo. Moscow: Akademiia nauk, SSSR, Institut nauchnoĭ informatsii, 1964–.

PERIODICALS

Some of the important journals in crop science include *Agronomia lusitana* (Portugal), *Agronomía tropical* (Venezuela), *Agronomy Journal* (US), *Canadian Journal of Plant Science, Crops and Soils* (US), *Crop Science* (US), *Estudos agronómicos* (Portugal), *Journal of Agronomic Education* (US), *Journal of Environmental Quality*

(US), *Journal of Plantation Crops* (India), *NACTA Journal* (US), *Pesticidal Science* (UK), *Proceedings of the Crop Science Society of Japan/Nippon sakumotsu gakkai kiji, Tso wu hsüeh pao* (People's Republic of China), *Vegetable Crop Management* (US), *Weed Science* (US), *World Crops* (UK).

For additional titles see:

List of Serials Currently Received by the Food and Agriculture Organization of the United Nations. Library. Rome: Food and Agriculture Organization, 1973.

Ulrich's International Periodicals Directory. New York: Bowker, biennial.

ENCYCLOPEDIAS, DICTIONARIES, HANDBOOKS

Harrison, S. G. *The Oxford Book of Food Plants.* London: Oxford University Press, 1969. Illustrated.

Kallos, T., with Bregonje, J. G. (Comps.) *Six Language Grain Dictionary.* Rotterdam: Eurimpex, S.A., 1968. English, with French, German, Dutch, Italian, and Spanish equivalents.

Kratochvil, V., and Urbanova, S. *Agricultural Dictionary in Eight Languages/Nyole yelvu mezogazdasagi szotar: Russian, Bulgarian, Czech, Polish, Hungarian, Roumanian, German, English.* (2 vols.) New York: International Publications Service, 1970.

A Multilingual Glossary of Common Plant Names. 1: Field Crops, Grasses and Vegetables. Wageningen, Netherlands: International Seed Testing Association, 1968. Latin-based with forty-one languages.

Rice Terminology. Rome: Food and Agriculture Organization, 1974. In English, French, and Spanish.

DIRECTORIES

American Colleges and Universities. Washington, D.C.: American Council on Education, 1928–. Published quadrennially.

Commonwealth Universities Yearbook. London: Association of Commonwealth Universities, 1914–. Published annually.

Hall, T. H. R. *World Crops International Directory and Handbook.* London: Leonard Hill, 1967. An international directory that includes listings of organizations and research centers throughout the world, principal journals on tropical agriculture, agricultural tables, manufacturers, and machinery.

International Handbook of Universities. Paris: International Association of Universities, 1959–. Published triennially.

The World of Learning. London: Europa, 1947–. Published annually.

World Guide to Universities. New York: Bowker, 1971.

RESEARCH CENTERS, INSTITUTES,
INFORMATION CENTERS

Boalch, D. H. *World Directory of Agricultural
Libraries and Documentation Centers.* Oxford,
England: International Association of Agri-
cultural Librarians and Documentationalists
(IAALD), 1960. Records nearly two thou-
sand libraries in over one hundred countries.
Out of print; a new revised edition is being
planned.

*Directory of Institutes, Universities and Other Or-
ganizations Where Research on Agriculture, Animal Husbandry, Forestry and Fisheries Is in
Progress.* Karachi, Pakistan: Agricultural Research Council, 1966. Directory to agricultural research in Pakistan.

*Estaciones experimentales agrícolas de América lat-
ina.* Washington, D.C.: Inter-American Development Bank, 1971.

Index of Agricultural Research Institutes of Europe.
Rome: Food and Agriculture Organization,
1963. A guide to agricultural research institutes in Europe.

National Agricultural Library. *Directory of Information Resources in Agriculture and Biology.*
Washington, D.C.: U.S. Government Printing Office, 1971. A United States directory
to agricultural information sources, designed
primarily for agricultural researchers and
teachers.

Paylore, P. *Arid-Lands Research Institutions: A
World Directory.* Tucson, Arizona: University
of Arizona Press, 1967.

*Roster of Scientists for the Major Food Crops of
the Developing World.* Washington, D.C.: Office of Agriculture, Technical Assistance
Bureau, Agency for International Development, 1975. Includes an institutions directory of significant research institutes.

Among the many important research centers in the field are:

Centre for Overseas Pest Research (COPR)
College House, Wrights Lane
London W8 5SJ, England

International Crops Research Institute for the
Semi-Arid Tropics (CRISAT)
Institut international de recherche sur la
culture des zones tropicales semi-arides
1-11-256 Begumpet
Hyderabad 500016, Andhra Pradesh, India

International Potato Center
Centro internacional de la papa (CIP)
Apartado 5969
Lima, Peru

International Rice Research Institute
(Communications Center)
P.O. Box 1300
M. C. C. Makati, Rizal, Philippines D-708

Royal Tropical Institute
63 Mauritskade
Amsterdam, Netherlands

Southeast Asian Regional Center for Graduate
Study and Research in Agriculture
(SEARCA)
Los Baños, Philippines

CROWTHER REPORT

*See 15 to 18: A Report of the Central Advisory
Council for Education* (Higher Education
Report), England.

CUBA, REPUBLIC OF

*Population: 8,860,000 (official estimate,
1972). Student enrollment in primary school:
1,925,700 (1975–76); intermediate school:
613,800 (not including special schools, handicapped education); higher secondary: 389,400;
professional technical education: 105,500; university: 76,900. Language of instruction:
Spanish. Academic calendar: September–June.
Percentage of national budget expended on
education: approximately 20% (1973).* [Source:
Center for Cuban Study, New York, New
York.]

The history of Cuban higher education
falls into three rather distinct periods:
(1) the colonial period, from the founding
of the University of Havana in 1728 to the
end of Spanish rule in 1898; (2) the republican period, from independence in 1898
to the Castro revolution of 1959; and (3)
the period of revolutionary socialist reconstruction since 1959.

Following the secularization of the University of Havana in 1842, the institution
became a stronghold of *criollo* (nationalist)
interests. On November 27, 1871, Spanish
authorities tried and executed eight medical students and imprisoned thirty-four
others for anti-Spanish subversive activities.
This punitive act increased anti-Spanish
sentiment at the university and placed the
university at the forefront of the independence movement led by the young student
José Martí.

With independence from Spain in 1898,
two periods of United States military occupation (1899–1902 and 1906–1909), and
American economic domination, the Uni-

versity of Havana became increasingly divorced from the social and economic needs of the country. The disciplines of law and medicine dominated: the first as a road to a political career; the second, as a means to high social status. With the university reform movement of 1923, the students once again took up political activism, this time addressed to the need for a modern university directed toward national development. Influenced by the Córdoba reform movement and the Mexican and Russian revolutions, this movement also opposed United States supervision of Cuban affairs and instead proposed a vague romantic nationalism. With the leadership of Julio Mella, a student, a part of the reform movement sought for the first time to transcend the university's walls and make the cause of university reform "another battle of the class struggle" (Mella, 1960, p. 19).

From 1927 to 1933 university students used urban violence to oppose President Gerardo Machado's repressive rule and continuation of the humiliating Platt Amendment, which permitted direct United States intervention in Cuban affairs. Machado closed the university from 1930 to 1933 while students fought for termination of the Platt Amendment and Cuba's monetary and financial dependence on the United States, and for land reform, the eventual nationalization of the sugar and mining industries, and for the creation of an autonomous university removed from political interference. With Machado's overthrow, Ramón Grau, a professor and student leader, eventually became president in 1933 to lead a government that was for labor and against foreign investment. Although Grau led the way to the granting of autonomy to the University of Havana, the students soon withdrew their support from him as military participation in his government increased. On January 14, 1934, Army Chief Fulgencio Batista forced President Grau to resign and within five days received United States government recognition. Previously the United States had refused to recognize Grau's government.

From 1934 to Fidel Castro's triumph in 1959, with a hiatus during World War II, the Cuban student movement became increasingly radicalized and politicized. The powerful Federation of University Students (*Federación de estudiantes universitarios:* FEU) called for social justice and attacked widespread corruption in government and immorality in public life, especially in the violent and materialistic years after World War II. At the same time, *bonches* (gangs of armed students) and others used the university's autonomy to carry out political warfare, assassination, and gangsterism. The university council rejected police entrance into the campus, while acknowledging its own total inability to repress the *bonches*.

During this turbulent period in the late 1940s and early 1950s, Fidel Castro studied law at the University of Havana and became actively involved in student politics. Castro generally shared the goals of the student movement: economic independence, political liberty, social justice, and an end to corruption. Without national leaders, the university students assumed leadership of the anti-Batista struggle. The University of Havana was closed from 1956 to 1959, and in 1956 the leaders of the FEU attempted to assassinate Batista at the presidential palace while Castro began rural guerrilla warfare in the mountains of Oriente province.

Although the University of Havana retained its dominant position during the period of quasi-independence, from 1898 to 1959, a number of lesser universities came into being during the 1940s and 1950s. Most important among these was Villanova University, founded by Catholic Augustinian monks in 1940. Wealthier families who could afford the tuition favored this stable and disciplined institution over the highly politicized public universities. The University of Havana opened branch campuses at Santiago de Cuba (1947), Las Villas (1959), Camagüey (1953), and Pinar del Río (1954). A number of small private universities, commercial ventures seeking to capitalize on the closing of the University of Havana, flourished briefly during the late 1950s.

Upon taking power in 1959, Castro proclaimed the state and the university to be identical. The university reopened in 1959, and the students, with government support, formed the University Reform Commission to purge pro-Batista students, professors, and staff and to plan a new curriculum and university structure. On December 31, 1960, university autonomy ended with the government's creation of the Higher Council of Universities—headed by the minister of education and composed of government representatives, faculty members, and students—to run the state universities operating at Havana, Las Villas, and Oriente. In January 1962 Juan Marinello, president of the Cuban Communist Party, became rector of the university and dedicated its efforts "to the complete service of the revolution" (Marinello, 1960). Also in 1962 the Union of Young Communists (*Unión de jovenes comunistas:* UJC) organized the University Bureau, which was responsible for political indoctrination. And in the same year, on the anniversary of Mella's death, the Higher Council of Universities presented a comprehensive university reform plan, which continues to serve as the foundation of Cuban higher education.

Legal Basis of Educational System

Following two years of conflict between the revolutionary government and the still-powerful democratic elements in the universities, the university reform of 1962 had profound effects on Cuban higher education. The reform eventually eliminated university autonomy, terminated or nationalized all private universities, and concentrated instruction in the national universities at Havana, Las Villas, and Oriente. In 1975 the University of Havana's regional center at Camagüey became Cuba's fourth university. Renamed Ignacio Agramonte University, the institution enrolls over 3200 students in twelve undergraduate career programs, mainly in rural development.

In 1964 the Higher Council of Universi-

ties was replaced by a National Council of Universities, responsible to the minister of education. Similarly, the university council, composed of the representatives of the faculties at each university, was replaced by a new university advisory board, including deans, representatives from the Union of Young Communists and the Federation of Students Board, and other members. University faculties became departmentalized, and the departments were organized in a manner similar to the advisory board. Faculty tenure was abolished, and the rectors were made government appointees, subject to dismissal by the minister of education.

In addition to basic structural changes, the reform clearly spelled out the government's expectation that the university would contribute to the creation of a socialist society. The university, a citadel of revolt during the colonial and republican periods, would now be integrated into the revolution. This strategy, called *universalización*, attempted to break down the high walls isolating the universities from society. Workers and farmers would attend special programs on university campuses, while professional work teams of students and faculty (*equipos*) carried their special skills out to fields and factories.

The reform also called for emphasis on ideological instruction in Marxism-Leninism and a shift in priority from theoretical to practical studies, with heavy emphasis on work-study programs. In contrast to prerevolutionary university studies—which, for the most part, gave a broad education in the humanities and professions—it urged that university programs should seek to prepare specialists of high quality in technical fields.

Types of Institutions

Cuban higher education programs are, to a considerable extent, concentrated in the four national universities. Of these, the University of Havana enrolls some 70 percent of all students at the university level. Other higher education programs are offered at the separate Institute of Economics, the Andrés González Higher School of Fishing, and the several military academies that prepare officers for the Cuban armed forces.

A preparatory program for workers and farmers in the *Facultad preparatoria obrero campesino* (worker-farmer faculty) has been created to link adult education and the universities. Workers eighteen through forty-five years of age who complete the three-year adult education program (a program at the upper secondary level) are then entitled to enter the faculties of science, agriculture, or technology, or an institute of education at any of the four national universities. Enrollment in this program increased from eighty-five students in 1959–60 to over 20,000 in 1973. Classes are offered at factories and in local schools after working hours. However, absenteeism, the lack of qualified faculty, and the lack of organization have limited the program's effectiveness.

Relationship with Secondary Education

School attendance is required through the sixth grade. Upon completion of elementary school, students are urged to continue their formal education up to age seventeen. Plans are currently underway to require all youth to remain in the educational system up to the thirteenth grade or twenty-one years of age, whichever comes first, and to incorporate military service and productive labor requirements into the compulsory educational program.

Secondary education programs are divided into two levels. The lower level includes the four-year basic secondary school, the three-year lower secondary technical school, and a five-year training school for elementary school teachers. Upper secondary schools are the three-year preuniversity institutes that prepare graduates for entrance into university faculties. Also, four-year programs at the upper secondary level are offered at technological institutes, language institutes, technical institutes of economics, and advanced schools of physical education. In addition, the institutes of education at each university offer five-year

combined programs at the upper secondary and postsecondary levels to prepare secondary school teachers. Graduates from the language institutes may apply for entrance to a university faculty of humanities, whereas graduates of the technical institutes of economics may seek entrance into a university faculty of economics. Although the technical institutes specialize in the preparation of middle-level specialists in engineering and agricultural fields, graduates may under certain conditions apply for entrance into an appropriate university faculty or program.

The secondary school-leaving age depends on the program followed and ranges between nineteen and twenty years of age. The basic secondary school-leaving certificate is the preuniversity diploma, or the *bachillerato*. Other upper secondary programs that qualify students to apply for university admission offer appropriate certificates of achievement in their specialized fields.

Admission Requirements

Before the revolution Cuban universities served the small commercial and social elite through professional preparation and the certification of their superior status. The university continues to enjoy great prestige, but it also serves a new political elite seeking fundamental change in socioeconomic structures and individual behavior. Prior to 1959 university admission depended primarily on socioeconomic class. Since 1959, however, admission requirements have increasingly been based on outstanding academic achievement at the secondary level; a "correct" revolutionary attitude, as evidenced by the student's voluntary work and participation in communist youth organizations; and, frequently, the support of a mass organization. Thus, the universities remain highly selective institutions.

Applicants must also pass a rigorous entrance examination and an extended personal interview. Once accepted, the students are periodically evaluated as to ideological orientation, academic achievement, and contribution to preprofessional or extramural development programs in their field of study. Students receive free education, room and board, books, and supplies.

Administration and Control

As dependencies of the Ministry of Education, Cuban universities have since 1971 been represented by a vice-minister of higher education, or *educación superior*. As an integral part of the state, higher education is under the direct control of the ministry, which determines policy and sees that universities contribute to national plans and expectations for education. The vice-minister of higher education works directly through the National Council of Universities, composed of faculty and student representatives, to make all major administrative and academic decisions. The council works closely with the rectors, who, as government appointees, hold full responsibility for the operation of each university and for the implementation of ministry plans and directives. Each rector is assisted by three vice-rectors, in charge of instructional affairs, scientific studies, and administration.

The reform of 1962 also produced sweeping changes in the internal organization of higher education. With the elimination of faculty chairs, or *cátedra por asignatura*, professors of similar disciplines have been organized into departments. Several departments, in turn, comprise a school, and a merging of schools makes a faculty, or *facultad*. The *facultad* mainly carries out administrative tasks; the school, through faculty and student committees, directs and evaluates the academic performance of students and faculty in each school. The *facultades* are directed by a governing council, or *junta de gobernación*, composed of a presiding dean of the faculty, three professors, and two student representatives.

The reform also reinstituted the policy of *co-gobierno*, or joint university governance by professors and students. General student participation in university affairs has, nevertheless, greatly decreased since 1962; however, government-supported students involved in the decision-making pro-

cesses have made significant contributions to the implementation of reforms seeking to modernize and upgrade the universities.

The senior faculty have lost much of their administrative power and many of their special privileges. Along with the elimination of university chairs, the reform has also ended faculty tenure. Faculty members are now appointed on the basis of teaching performance and ideologically correct behavior, with contracts ranging from one to three years.

In the early years of the revolution, a vast exodus of Cuban professionals took place; and the universities lost a large number of their most able professors (287 of some 300 medical professors, for example). The ensuing gap has been partially filled by upperclassmen, recent graduates, and visiting professors from abroad. However, the shortage of high-level teaching personnel in Cuban universities remains a serious problem, especially with the recent attempts to improve the quality of graduates while simultaneously admitting more of the rapidly growing number of upper secondary school graduates.

Programs and Degrees

Academic programs offered by Cuban universities are located in the Institute of Economics at the University of Havana and in the six *facultades* (faculties) found in all four national universities. These are as follows, with corresponding representative departments which may be found only at Havana: the faculty of humanities and social sciences (literature, history, law, political science, and economics); the faculty of life and physical sciences (physics, mathematics, chemistry, biology, geography, psychology, geology, and pharmacology); the faculty of engineering and technology (civil, electrical, mechanical, chemical, industrial, mining, geological, geophysical, and architectural engineering); the faculty of medical sciences (medicine and dentistry); the faculty of agricultural sciences (agronomy, veterinary study, animal husbandry); the worker-farmer faculty; and the Teacher Training Institute.

With a strong government priority to integrate higher education into the ongoing process of revolutionary reconstruction and development, enrollments in technology, engineering, medicine, and the natural and agricultural sciences jumped from a total of 35.1 percent in 1959 to 75.9 percent at the three universities operating in 1970.

The university school year is divided into two semesters of some eighty days each, and a minimum attendance of 80 percent overall is required for promotion. Although formal examinations have been deemphasized, individual students are periodically evaluated by their peers and the faculty. Efforts have been made to shorten the curricula leading to the *licenciado* or *doctor* degrees granted university graduates. By 1966, for example, duration of study in the medical faculty had been reduced from seven to four years; in the school of dentistry, from five to three years; and in agronomic engineering, from five to two years.

Financing

Since 1962, with the nearly total elimination of the private sector in higher education (two Catholic seminaries preparing about one hundred priests continue to operate with church support), the state has monopolized the financing of higher education. By 1970 total financial contributions to all educational programs totaled over 20 percent of governmental expenditures, and higher education received far and away the greatest expenditure per pupil (14.9 times more than at the secondary and over 30 times the amount at the primary level). These great inequalities have been considerably narrowed as a result of the crash program to build one thousand residential junior high schools in the countryside.

Most financial resources for Ministry of Education programs, including higher education, come to the ministry from the central government's Central Planning Board, or *Junta de planificación.* Capital investment requests for higher education, made within the context of the ministry's plans for development, are submitted to the board for consideration within the context of the overall national plan.

During the 1960s the budget for higher education showed only a gradual increase as enrollments first declined and again reached their prerevolutionary level in 1966. Although current data are not available, rapid enrollment increases in higher education in the mid 1970s have called for sharply increased financial allocations. How the universities will cope with the wave of preuniversity institute graduates that will arrive in the late 1970s poses a serious problem. Given the heavy commitment to higher education, increased resource demands will quite likely be met by having students spend more time in productive labor, with less time spent on campus and with increased requirements for public service after graduation. At the same time, this attempt to universalize the university will also require increased financial contributions, both direct and indirect, from other government ministries, from the mass organizations, and from the students themselves through their nonsalaried labor contributions.

Student Financial Aid

Since 1962 all educational expenses have been borne by the Cuban government. In addition, some 232,000 students have received state scholarships for residential study away from home. Of the 43,234 students enrolled in higher education in 1972–73, some 18,642 held full scholarships that paid for their studies, their room and board, and similar other expenses, and provided a small cash stipend as well. In exchange, students are expected to study in fields that the government has selected for them, to view their education as social development capital rather than private investment capital, to contribute voluntary productive labor on a university farm or in a factory for one weekend a month and one month in the summer, and to become integrated into the revolution through the combination of study and work with small *equipos* (teams of students and faculty working closely together in the countryside on some project deemed important for educational, economic, or political reasons). *Equipos*, for example, have worked on road building, built fertilizer factories, organized "people's courts" in rural areas, provided medical and dental services, run a newspaper, analyzed soils, and developed computer centers. Students are also expected to participate in some paramilitary organization, such as the national militia; and increasing numbers of university graduates have been recruited into the armed forces, where the demand for technical skills far outstrips the supply. All new graduates are also required to spend two years, usually in a rural area, in public service work related to their field of study.

Student Social Background and Access to Education

With the expansion and universalization of higher education, three groups grossly underrepresented in prerevolutionary higher education have vastly increased their participation. These are rural and working-class youth, blacks, and women. The provision of full scholarship and the worker-farmer faculty have been useful devices for bringing students from these groups into the universities and reinforcing their dedication to the work of the revolution. Moreover, with the provision of subsidized university study and the exodus of many middle-class professionals and technicians, intellectually able and ideologically dedicated youth from working-class homes now have unusual opportunities for upward social mobility via university studies, political activism, and going "where the revolution needs them."

University students are represented by the Federation of University Students (*Federación de estudiantes universitarios:* FEU), an organization that has been deeply involved in revolutionary struggle since its founding in 1923 by Julio Mella. The FEU was the only organization in Cuba to call for violent opposition to the Batista dictatorship, which ended with Castro's tri-

umph in 1959. In 1967 the government fused the FEU with the Union of Young Communists (*Unión de jovenes comunistas:* UJC), an elite group representing 30 percent of all university students, to create the University Bureau of the UJC-FEU. The secretary of the UJC is at the same time president of the FEU. The UJC is also active in maintaining study discipline and ideological conformity among all university students, especially among those on government scholarships. Before 1965 the UJC strictly limited membership to students of proven communist militancy. Recent efforts to increase membership, despite the obvious advantages for career advancement, have met with resistance and scant success. Despite its coercive aspects, the UJC does offer university students their sole legitimate organization for political activity and a direct channel through which they can communicate their concerns and complaints to the party.

Teaching Staff

Although faculty are still ranked by titles (*profesores, profesores auxiliares,* and *instructores*), status differences between professors, students, and staff in higher education have been vastly reduced since the prerevolutionary period. Professors and UJC-FEU student representatives jointly plan curriculum, evaluate each other's goals and accomplishments, consult on promotions, and jointly collaborate in the administrative policy and practice of *co-gobierno* (cogovernance). During weekend and summer periods of voluntary productive labor, expected as an obligation of all who are "integrated into the revolution," senior administrators, faculty, and students, along with staff and plant-maintenance people, eat and sleep in the men's and women's barracks and work from 7 A.M. to 5 P.M. in the university farm fields without distinctions or special privileges.

Since the reform of 1962 eliminated faculty tenure, professors are hired on the basis of annual contracts, which can be terminated at any time. Professors are expected to teach in strict conformity to the revolutionary ideology; that is, they must demonstrate their subject's contribution to revolutionary goals for socioeconomic development and the creation of a new, socialist man. Those unable to meet these expectations are dropped from the university. The remaining professors receive great social prestige and many of the special rewards reserved for the ruling group. Meanwhile, the teacher shortage in higher education continues, as do efforts to fill the deficit with recent graduates and visiting professors from Europe, Latin America, and South America.

To meet requirements for contract renewal, faculty members usually are required to take periodic courses in Marxism-Leninism, in teaching methods, and in subject knowledge. These in-service training courses are offered during the summer months at all universities and related institutions. Faculty members receive full salaries while attending these courses, which also qualify them for promotion and salary increases.

Faculty members are relatively well paid. However, since the highest wage paid in Cuba (for a brain surgeon) is only about ten times higher than the lowest (for a sweeper), the differential for senior professors is about eight to ten times that of field workers. All salaries (professional and staff salaries) in higher education are determined by the Ministry of Education according to a fixed salary schedule. All who work in higher education are employees of the ministry and, from the rectors and deans down, are responsible to the minister and subject to his direction as the government's representative. Thus, the concept of academic freedom as it is often espoused and more rarely practiced in some Western countries does not exist. In fact, the concept is officially rejected as a middle-class sham and incompatible with the revolutionary role of Cuban universities today.

Research Activities

Cuban universities have traditionally shared the Latin American university's emphasis on preparing professionals. There was, accordingly, a scant tradition of research when the 1962 reorientation took place. And just as the United States attempted to develop research capabilities in Latin American universities through Alliance for Progress programs and foundation assistance, so the Soviet Union, with support from the German Democratic Republic and other socialist countries, sought to develop research capabilities in Cuban higher education and in the National Academy of Sciences. Most research studies are the responsibility of the National Center of Scientific Research and the National Academy of Sciences. All research in Cuba is thus directed and funded by the government as a state monopoly. Most research studies address practical problems in the areas of technological development, tropical agriculture, and tropical medicine. Some basic research is also carried out, usually in collaboration with Soviet academics and scientific institutes.

With the press toward pragmatism and specialization in the universities, graduates who have been taught research skills are expected to apply them to the task of rural development and production. The Ministry of Education claims that the universities do not produce researchers; instead, they produce knowledgeable, practical people who can run factories and provide basic health services. University professors, for example, are promoted by student-faculty committees on the basis of their teaching ability and "revolutionary" commitment rather than their research contributions.

Current Problems and Trends

Perhaps the major problem in Cuban higher education is the attempted creation of a revolutionary socialist consciousness in all students. This effort to form the so-called new man takes place in educational programs at all levels. It is, however, most difficult with older students, with their greater independence of thought and action. In 1971 the discrepancy between goals for ideological formation in education and actual student behavior had become so great that the government convened the

First National Congress of Education and Culture to address the problem. As a result, discipline and regimentation were increased, individual choice in the selection of a field of training was diminished, and time spent outside the university in work teams and rural extension facilities was increased.

This attempt to orient and discipline a new generation of Cuban youth who know the revolutionary struggle of the 1950s only as history and mythology has, in turn, contributed to the chronic problem of low academic achievement and inadequate skills development. Combining study with productive labor may or may not produce the new man. What is certain, however, is that such efforts will seriously reduce time available for learning the special behaviors that go with being an engineer or a physician or a chemist. In China, this same problem is viewed as the dilemma between being "red" (ideologically correct) and being "expert" (technically proficient). If the Cuban revolution continues to move toward institutionalization, we may well see a corresponding shift of educational priority toward technical competence, as in the Soviet Union. This incipient trend will also quite likely gather strength from the continuing highly selective nature of Cuban higher education and the movement of university graduates into the new ruling elite, composed of the overlapping Communist Party leaders, the top military, and the emerging technician group.

Castro has been able to place the ideological returns of higher education over the economic returns in large measure because of massive Soviet economic contributions to the Cuban economy. Future priorities for higher education must accordingly take into account Cuba's relations with the dominant world powers. As a small, underdeveloped country, Cuba is attempting to create a more egalitarian society and to implant the requisite values of social conscience to support such a vast undertaking. The undeniable problems in higher education and in society at large following from this utopian effort do not discredit or detract from the effort. That Cuba has made many admirable changes in its educational system is as apparent as are the many difficult problems arising from these efforts toward social and behavioral change.

Relationship with Industry

Relations between higher education and industry are increasingly close. *Equipos* (work teams of university students and professors) contribute to the planning and construction of industrial facilities and to the increased efficiency of industrial processes and worker training; and university graduates frequently devote their two years of public service to work in industry, especially the sugar industry. Since all Cuban industry is in the public sector, the flow of university personnel and skills into the productive process is relatively uncomplicated. In addition, managers and technicians from industry teach courses in higher education.

In the worker-farmer program, workers from industry study on campus and participate in student affairs and university governance. Also, university faculty in the program teach classes at the factories and in rural settings as well.

In these joint programs and exchanges, universities have become closely linked with industrial development and manpower training. Here again the Soviet model, although much adapted, has been put into operation.

International Cooperation

Relatively large numbers of Cuban students study abroad on full scholarships. During 1963–64 some 2183 students (about 9 percent of the enrollment in Cuban universities) studied in twelve socialist countries and Mexico. By 1968–69 the total had dropped to 1085; and the number of host countries, all socialist, dropped to six, with the Soviet Union and the German Democratic Republic predominating. This pattern of diminishing study abroad concentrated in a few countries continues. In 1975, for example, five hundred Cubans studied in the Soviet Union at the undergraduate and graduate levels. Study programs are closely integrated with Soviet technical assistance projects in Cuba, with particular emphasis on courses in tropical agriculture and tropical medicine. Of the more than 1500 Cubans who completed studies in the Soviet Union between 1961 and 1974, over 85 percent studied engineering and other technical subjects, while some 13 percent studied in pedagogical institutes. In 1974 Cuban students in the Soviet Union achieved an average grade level of 4.20, while that of all Soviet students was 3.87.

A large number of Soviet academics teach in Cuba's four universities and cooperate on curriculum development projects as well as research projects in the fields of biochemistry and organic chemistry, virology, physiology, histology, and mining (such as the utilization of Cuba's rich nickel resources).

Direct cooperative arrangements between universities and the academies of science in both countries proliferated in the 1970s, with special agreements signed between the universities of Moscow and Havana, Leningrad and Oriente, and Kiev and Las Villas.

Numerous foreign academics from a variety of nonsocialist countries teach special postgraduate courses offered at the university, especially during the summer months. In 1970–71, for example, fifty-six courses in medicine, the sciences, and developmental technology were taught in Spanish, English, or French by professors from Western Europe and the United States.

In addition to substantial assistance from the socialist nations and sympathetic academics, Cuban higher education also benefits from well-established UNESCO and UNICEF programs in support of teaching, development, and health.

ROLLAND G. PAULSTON

Educational Association

Federación de estudiantes universitarios (FEU) (Federation of University Students) University of Havana, Havana, Cuba

Bibliography

Acuerdos de la comisión mixta de reforma universitaria. Havana: Universidad de Habana, 1959.

Aja, P. V. "Crises at the University of Havana." *Science and Freedom,* March 1961, *18,* 7–15.

Bunn, H. *The Universities of Cuba, the Dominican Republic, and Haiti.* Washington, D.C.: Pan American Union, 1946.

Butler, W. "The Undergraduate Education of Physicians in Cuba." *Journal of Medical Education,* 1973, *48* (9), 846–858.

Caberera, L. R. "La formación de profesionales en las universidades cubanas." *El siglo veinte* (Mexico), March 1966, *64,* 28–38.

Castro, F. "The Mission of the Universities Is Not Just to Train Technicians, but Revolutionary Technicians." *Granma Weekly Review,* December 18, 1966, pp. 6–12.

Castro, F. "The Large-Scale Application of Study and Work in All Three of Our Universities Is Undoubtedly a Historic Step." *Granma Weekly Review,* December 17, 1972, pp. 9–10.

Compendio estadístico de Cuba, 1970. Havana: Junta central de planificación, Dirección central de estadística, 1971.

"Cooperation Between Cuba and the USSR." *Bulletin,* International Association of Universities, 1974, *22* (3), 190.

Estadísticas de la educación: Curso 1965–66. Havana: Ministerio de educación, 1967.

Hartmann, H. "Die Universitätsreform in Kuba." *Deutsche Universitätszeitung,* June 1963, *18,* 24–29.

Hernández Pardo, H. "The Universalization of Higher Learning." *Granma Weekly Review,* December 3, 1972, p. 4.

Hochschild, A. "Student Power in Action." *Trans-Action,* 1969, *6* (6), 16–21.

Implementation of the Reform of Cuban Higher Education. Havana: Cuban National Commission for UNESCO, 1963.

Levin, L., Lind, A., Löfstedt, J.-I., and Torbiörnsson, L. *U-Bildning. Skola och Samhälle i Kina, Kuba, Tanzania och Vietnam.* Stockholm: Rabén & Sjögren, 1970.

Magid, L. J. "Cuba's Student Workers." *Change,* 1973, *5* (3), 22–23.

Marinello, J. *Revolución y universidad.* Havana: Gobierno provincial revolucionario de la Habana, 1960.

Mella, J. A. "Los estudiantes y la lucha social."

In *Ensayos revolucionarios*. Havana: Editora popular de Cuba y del Caribe, 1960.

Mensaje educacional al pueblo de Cuba: Discursos de Osvaldo Dórticos T. y Armando Hart D. Havana: Ministerio de educación, 1960.

Mesa-Lago, C. *Cuba in the 1970s: Pragmatism and Institutionalization.* Albuquerque: University of New Mexico Press, 1974.

Organization of the Educational Movement. Report to the 34th International Education Conference. Geneva: International Office of Education, 1973.

Packland, R. L. *Education in Cuba, Puerto Rico, and the Philippines: Report of the Commissioner of Education, 1897–98.* Washington, D.C.: U.S. Government Printing Office, 1899.

Paulston, R. G. "Education." In C. Mesa-Lago (Ed.), *Revolutionary Change in Cuba.* Pittsburgh: University of Pittsburgh Press, 1971, pp. 375–398.

Paulston, R. G. *Cambio social y educacional en Cuba.* Buenos Aires: Paidos, 1975a.

Paulston, R. G. *The Educational System of Cuba.* Washington, D.C.: U.S. Government Printing Office, 1975b.

Portuondo, J. A. *Tres temas de la reforma universitaria.* Santiago: Universidad de Oriente, Departamento de extensión y relaciones culturales, 1959.

Primer congreso nacional de educación y cultura. Havana: Instituto cubano del libro, 1971.

The Principle of the Combination of Study and Work in Cuban Higher Education. Report of Cuban Delegation to the Ninth Conference of Higher Education in Socialist Countries. Havana: Ministry of Education, 1974.

Ramos, E. *La Universidad de Oriente y la industria azucarera.* Santiago: Universidad de Oriente, 1951.

La reforma de la enseñanza superior en Cuba. Havana: Consejo superior de universidades, 1962.

Rego, O. F. "Plan de organización para las tres universidades." *Vida universitaria,* February 1966, *186,* 22–29.

Report of Cuba to UNESCO, 1972–73. Havana: Cuban Book Institute, 1973.

Rodríguez, C. R. "La reforma universitaria." *Cuba socialista,* 1962, *2* (6), 22–44.

Sorin, M., and Gavilondo, L. "Acerca del rendimiento académico en una escuela universitaria." *Etnología y folklore,* July–December 1966, *2,* 12–19.

Suchlicki, J. *University Students and Revolution in Cuba, 1920–1968.* Coral Gables, Florida: University of Miami Press, 1969.

"Una sola reforma para las 3 universidades oficiales." *Revolución,* April 6, 1960, *1,* 6.

Universidad de la Habana al consejo ejecutivo y a la asamblea general de la Unión de universidades de América Latina. Havana: Universidad de Habana, 1964.

Varona y Pera, E. J. *Las reformas en la enseñanza superior.* Havana: El Figaro, 1900.

See also: Archives: Mediterranean, the Vatican, and Latin America, National Archives of; Caribbean: Regional Analysis; Cooperative Education and Off-Campus Experience: Cooperative Education Worldwide; Illiteracy of Adults.

CUBANS
See Access of Minorities: Spanish-Speaking Peoples.

CURRICULUM AND INSTRUCTION

No processes are more central to postsecondary education than curriculum and instruction, for they are the primary and direct inculcators of knowledge in students. Curriculum refers to the systematic, rational structures under which the learning processes of students are organized. These structures establish the priorities for, and the sequences in which, students experience different elements of learning. They provide an overall conceptual framework whereby the learning process is ordered. Curriculum is thus, in the broadest sense, a technique or technology for the rational ordering of human thought for the purpose of transmitting knowledge to others. Instruction refers to the mechanisms whereby the elements of curriculum are directly transmitted or are made available to students.

Administration includes the overall management of curriculum and instructional procedures, the provision and allocation of resources so that curriculum and instruction can be carried out, the day-to-day operational control of curricular and instructional procedures, and the evaluation of curricular and instructional outcomes.

The policies and practices followed in the administration of curriculum and instruction vary among nations. This article discusses the topic in general perspective, with emphasis on the philosophy, procedures, and practices followed by educators in the United States. The following sections will present a general picture of the activities, forms, and procedures whereby curriculum and instruction are planned, developed, managed, and evaluated.

Administrative Roles Related to. Curriculum and Instruction

Because curriculum and instruction are central to the operation of postsecondary education, administrators at all levels are involved in their organization. Of course, some forms of involvement are more direct than others; but everyone from president to maintenance person has a responsibility for curriculum and instruction. Generally, academic administrators provide the resources and the support services by which curriculum and instruction can be developed and implemented, and they supervise the evaluation of outcomes.

Direct administrative responsibility. The president or chancellor of an institution has a major overall responsibility of selecting the administrators who manage curriculum and instruction, and also of bearing final responsibility for the recruitment, promotion, and tenure of professors, who are the central agents of curriculum and instruction. Depending on the size of the institution, the president may be directly involved in decisions about faculty appointments and promotions or may establish general evaluation and maintenance policies for those involved with curriculum and instruction.

The administrative officer most directly in charge of curriculum and instruction is the chief academic officer, often called the academic vice-president or provost. This officer has overall responsibility for developing the curriculum and for recommending the appointment of individual faculty members and administrative officers. The vice-president or provost is also responsible for the establishment of administrative policies in all educational areas.

Deans, division heads, and directors of colleges are responsible for the allocation of curricular and instructional resources among their several departments, and they thereby control the management of curricular and instructional processes through those who directly carry them out. When the faculties are organized primarily according to disciplines, the dean's activities are oriented toward the management of faculty personnel and the supervision of the academic advising and support services. An administrative officer at the level of dean or division head may also have responsibility for the quality of the curriculum and instructional processes. In this role, the administrator reviews the curricular and instructional practices of the several departments and evaluates them in terms of the academic policies of the institution. Often it is the dean who is responsible for curriculum evaluation within a division. If and when practices diverge from curricular and instructional policy, the dean consults department chairpersons.

The department chairperson. The role of department chairperson is central to the administration of curriculum and instruction and can take two forms. If the chairperson is operating in a traditional context, that is, as "first among equals" with departmental colleagues, and if decisions are made collegially, the chairperson's role is that of curriculum planner and educational leader. In such a role the department chairperson consults faculty and students about appropriate curricular and instructional programs and uses the support services of the institution to secure the necessary resources to implement the program. The bulk of the chairperson's efforts are oriented to curricular and instructional development activities. In institutions where the department chairperson is more of a direct administrator and supervisor to the faculty (a scheme more common in community colleges than in large universities), the chairperson may serve as evaluator of both curriculum and instruction. In this role the chairperson gathers information on the successes and failures of the instructional and curricular processes. This information is passed back to the faculty to stimulate curriculum improvement and on to the dean of the division for overall curriculum improvement. The department chairperson under both schemes is responsible for the management of the academic calendar, the maintenance of student records, the review of problem cases, and the supervision of required academic procedures. Thus, the department chairperson may monitor faculty office hours, attendance of faculty at their classes, faculty classroom effectiveness, and the progress of students.

Faculty responsibility. The most direct day-to-day responsibility for the implementation of curriculum and instruction is borne by the individual faculty member. Faculty serve as carriers of the processes of learning via instructional techniques within the overall systematic plan of a departmental or division-wide curriculum. The individual faculty member chooses instructional techniques and applies them to the instructional situation which that member has devised and controls. The faculty member then evaluates student performance and determines the nature and extent of student achievement. The faculty member may also serve a direct role as an adviser to students, helping to resolve problems of learning style and suggesting new methods by which the instructional procedures can be more effective in individual cases. Faculty members, working in departmental groups, evaluate and develop curricular procedures and plan individual programs for students. Faculty members serve on interdepartmental committees that recommend policy changes to department chairpersons, division heads, and chief administrative officers.

Under newly developing curricular forms and instructional systems, the role of a faculty member is shifting somewhat from that of the traditional purveyor of information and transmitter of knowledge to that of manager of the learning situation.

As student needs become more diverse, and as more becomes known about matching instructional procedures to the needs of students, the role of a faculty member is gradually changing to that of the cooperative provider of resources and feedback to students.

Student responsibility. Students' roles in instruction and curriculum are also changing. Traditionally, students were seen as novices who entered the institution to learn and to be taught and who typically functioned as rather passive recipients of knowledge. Students were viewed as clients availing themselves of an expert's knowledge and in doing so were responsible for listening to and abiding by the expert's judgment. As more diverse students have sought higher education, however, students are more appropriately being viewed as consumers of education. In the roles of consumers, students have much greater freedom and involvement in choosing instructional techniques and curricular forms. Students also are more deeply involved in evaluating their own performances and in evaluating the instructional processes. It seems likely that the roles of students will continue to become more central to education and that faculty and student roles will become more cooperative in the use of instructional procedures and curriculum planning.

Staff and support functions. Throughout the administrative structure, particularly in larger institutions, there are administrators who provide staff support for curriculum and instruction. These administrators include deans of instruction, who act as staff members to faculty committees and academic vice-presidents during curriculum review, teacher evaluation, and faculty development projects. In most cases such administrators have no direct administrative authority or responsibility but instead gather information for analyses. They then make their recommendations to the administrative officers and to faculty members and students.

Often, large institutions provide a separate academic advisement office to assist students in their choice of a field of study. Advisers provide counseling and advice about courses, instructional procedures, and the resources of the institution.

Offices of computer services are increasingly acting as adjuncts to the instructional and curricular arm of the university by providing learning opportunities for students engaged in research and by providing for the development of computer-assisted and computer-aided instructional techniques.

The library is an academic support service that serves as an instructional resource center. Its traditional role of providing print materials for use in curriculum instruction and research is being widened to include new techniques of audiovisual and programed learning. Other instructional support services include instructional systems analysis, programed learning centers, instructional television centers, learning laboratories, multimedia libraries, and educational networks. These services are all the results of the adaptation of technological developments to the purposes of curriculum and instruction. Normally, such services are administered by experts, who act as resource staff to the faculty and the administration.

Administration of Curricular Processes

One major task of those charged with administering curriculum and instruction is choosing, from a broad array of curricular possibilities, those processes most appropriate to their faculty, students, and institution. In evaluating the worth and effectiveness of different curricular forms, an administrator must consider curricular philosophy, the types of students to be served, and the available faculty.

Trends in curriculum: administration. Administering the curriculum demands consideration of a host of diverse elements that must be integrated under a series of seemingly conflicting interests of faculty, students, and society. Four major problems, which those responsible for curriculum must resolve, arise from these diverse interests: (1) Should the curriculum emphasize mastery of a discipline-based content, organized according to faculty expertise, or should it emphasize total, personal, effective development of the student? (2) Should the curriculum be organized to focus on practical problems, or should it emphasize abstractions and seek to inculcate ideas, theories, and an orientation to conceptual analysis? (3) Should the curriculum be rigidly prescribed according to the faculty perception of the best ways to turn students into ideal scholars, or should it be kept flexible and adaptive to individual needs and interests? (4) Should the curriculum seek maximum coherence and unity in the learning process or emphasize a deeper study of discrete elements, allowing students to find their own integration through the interaction with intellectual diversity?

Faced with these alternatives, the curriculum planner (whether dean, department chairperson, or individual faculty member) must develop an appropriate mix of liberal and vocational education. A liberal education means an exposure to a cultural heritage, an opportunity to develop conceptual and communication skills, and the attainment of value commitments. Vocational preparation means a specific exposure to skills and concepts that will serve short- and long-range goals of practical contribution to society and to students' own livelihoods. The planner must also give due consideration to the breadth of a curriculum, or the extent to which students are engaged with essential facts, concepts, and values of all major areas of knowledge. Of no less importance is the depth of a curriculum, or the extent to which students are brought to develop the skills, knowledge, and modes of inquiry sufficient to attain mastery of a given content area. Curriculum administration also implies that students' experiences be organized for continuity, so that notions introduced early in the sequence continue to be used during subsequent experiences.

Curricula should be organized for integration so that students are encouraged to detect relationships among all their curricular experiences.

Trends in curriculum: course requirements. A study undertaken in the United States in 1969 for the American Council on Education led to a number of descriptive conclusions about the kinds of curricular formations that are available to administrators (Dressel and DeLisle, 1969). The study focused on undergraduates and dealt with the degree requirements normally placed on students. Basic and general education were found to make up about 37 percent of the degree requirements and consisted of roughly 17 percent humanities, 10 percent social sciences, and 10 percent natural sciences. The study revealed that decreases have taken place in the formal requirements for English composition, literature and speech, and foreign languages, due to the number of students able to meet the requirements through proficiency testing rather than course completion. Philosophy and religion course requirements have been reduced as well and are more frequently options available in a distribution requirement.

There has been a trend away from rigid requirements through the elimination or reduction of courses and their absorption into other courses. Distribution requirements, for example, call for a certain number of courses in given knowledge domains rather than specifying exact courses. Many requirements have been made optional to meet individual needs more readily. A greater emphasis on breadth is recognized by most colleges as essential to the early college experience. When students reach their third and fourth years, required courses occur primarily as part of a departmental, interdepartmental, or interdisciplinary major.

Throughout the undergraduate program, requirements do allow for some individual choice, often as options within a set of distribution requirements. These options range from a choice between two alternate courses to a choice of three or four courses from among as many as fifteen or more possibilities. Often alternatives to specific requirements are permitted in such areas as mathematics, foreign language, and English composition. In such cases students are allowed to waive some courses and choose others on the basis of previous study, tested competence, or interest.

Individualization is introduced by students' choices of major fields of concentration and their choice of electives. There are two types of electives usually available to students: directed electives that students can select from a list of specific courses related to their major fields of study and subject to approval by an adviser, and electives that are genuinely optional. Often there are elective courses available in fields other than the students' majors. Students can take these courses on a pass/fail basis, which encourages them to broaden their undergraduate curricular experience. Most institutions do not direct or recommend the elective choices of students in the arts and sciences programs.

In traditional curricular approaches there are often special individualizing and integrating experiences available to students. One such possibility is advanced placement, whereby students are allowed to waive specific undergraduate requirements on the basis of examinations. Many institutions offer honors programs, which may be composed of special sections of required courses or constitute an entirely separate general program fashioned to meet the needs of advanced students. Honors programs make extensive use of seminars, tutorials, and specialized research opportunities.

Independent study, another vehicle for broadening students' experiences, is a learning activity motivated largely by students' personal desires to learn; its reward lies in its intrinsic values. Independent study designates a significant undertaking in lieu of class activities and utilizes the services of teachers and other professional personnel primarily as resources for the learner. Usually students propose a study, investigation, survey, research, or creative project to an appropriate sponsor and then carry it out under his own general supervision. Sometimes the project is undertaken jointly by two or more students.

Special seminars, designed for first-year students provide small-group experience and encourage increased student participation from the beginning of the college years. Seminars also make some of the more advanced and well-known research professors in the institution available to the students.

Some institutions, aware of the educational value of study-abroad programs, sponsor their own programs in foreign cultures or enter into an association with other institutions for this purpose. Often a wide variety of programs is offered, some of which do not require fluency in a foreign language.

Finally, there are programs that seek to expand students' educational experience beyond the classroom. These include residence hall programs, living-learning environments, work-study programs, community service, off-campus extension, and cooperative programs.

Experimental approaches to curricular processes. In addition to the traditional curricular pattern, a number of comprehensive curricula have been developed. These comprehensive patterns involve more than requirements in common; they are also based on a program rationale that emerges from the many specifics of the program and are based on a well-expressed educational philosophy. Each requirement and feature is seen as a meaningful part of a total pattern, expressed by its educational goals and the acceptance by faculty and students of a set of principles and assumptions about the nature and organization of learning experiences. On the basis of these considerations, Dressel and DeLisle have specified ten different comprehensive curriculum patterns: (1) traditional pattern, (2) hourglass curriculum, (3) planned

interruptions in general education through the undergraduate years, (4) cooperative education plan, (5) the interim term and the coordinate curriculum, (6) general education as a major concentration, (7) divisional interdisciplinary or interdivisional major emphasis, (8) the experimental college program, (9) program planning according to key concepts, and (10) individual program planning (1969, pp. 45–73).

Academic calendars. The planning of curricular forms and instructional techniques is affected by the structure of the academic calendar. Most prevalent is the semester system, currently being used by about 80 percent of the higher education institutions in the United States. This system consists of two regular terms of fifteen weeks of classes, extending from mid or late September to early June. In addition, there is usually a summer session, which normally takes place outside the regular academic pattern and caters to a different clientele through a varied and limited array of course offerings. One weakness of such a fixed calendar system is that the Christmas holidays occur in the middle of the first semester, which causes a dysfunctional break.

Another academic calendar is the quarter system, which is composed of three regular twelve-week terms per year and constitutes a school year of about thirty-seven to thirty-eight weeks. The fourth quarter of such a program is most often a summer session. The quarter system avoids the major weakness of the semester system by ending a term just before Christmas, but it does not usually allow enough time for the preparation of extensive term papers, extensive reading, and the maturing processes of students. A major administrative disadvantage seems to be that the quarter system requires more time for the operational procedures of registration, scheduling of classes, examinations, grading, and record keeping.

On the other hand, the quarter system permits a readier evaluation of student progress and more frequent student counseling. It also allows greater flexibility in planning of programs of study. The quarter system is well adapted to cooperative education programs, which fully utilize the fourth quarter. Some critics contend that the quarter terms are too short and act to the detriment of contemplation; colleges sometimes attempt to overcome this problem by allowing students to take only three rather than four courses a term.

Another academic calendar variation currently being tried is called the 4-1-4 plan. Under this plan there is a first term, usually two weeks shorter than the traditional semester term, during which students take four courses. This is followed by the Christmas vacation and then a short term in January, during which students are allowed to take one course of an experimental or independent study nature. From February to June a normal term is held, but students are again restricted to four courses. The advantages of the 4-1-4 program are the wide variety of activities that can be undertaken in the interim term; the fact that the calendar takes advantage of the natural break at the Christmas vacation period; and the informality of the interim period, which allows students and faculty to experiment.

A fourth alternative calendar form is the trimester system, which is a year-round system composed of three fifteen-week terms. This system was devised to allow for greater use of the university's facilities, to cope with larger numbers of students, and to allow students to accelerate their education. One major deterrent to its acceptance has been the unwillingness of students to attend college during the summer; until such attitudes change, it is unlikely that the trimester plan will be widely used.

Administration of Instructional Procedures

Traditionally, the individual faculty member has played the most dynamic and direct role in the choice and implementation of instructional techniques.

Traditional approaches to instruction. Typically, instructional techniques have been limited to a relative few that have characterized university instruction for many years. Principal among these techniques is the lecture system, in which professors, as experts in content areas, transmit an organized version of the knowledge in their fields to students. Students take notes and then supplement those notes with their own readings in preparation for examinations. This method has been, and remains, the primary mode of instruction in institutions of higher education. In the hands of a competent lecturer, the technique can be highly effective, condensing enormous amounts of material into highly organized, stimulating, and relevant patterns.

Another traditional form of instruction is the seminar, a method commonly used at the graduate level. During seminars students gather with a professor, develop ideas, make presentations to the group, and conduct group discussions of ideas.

Current developments in instructional methodology. As knowledge about the learning process has grown, the traditional lectures and seminars are no longer viewed as the only effective instructional methods. Studies have shown that three major developments are changing the traditional approach to instruction: individualization, modularization, and use of instructional media.

Individualized instruction is instruction adapted to individual needs in a more specific way than curriculum flexibility. Individualized instruction has certain characteristic features, including: (1) the elimination of arbitrary time units for subject matter coverage, such as semester hours, allowing students the opportunity to work at their actual levels of accomplishment and to move ahead as they master the appropriate prerequisites for advancement; (2) well-defined and well-structured curricular objectives for each subject area; (3) well-developed procedures for assessing student readiness, needs, and accomplishments in terms of the objectives; (4) instructional materials designed to provide a variety of paths for achieving any given objective; (5) individual lesson plans or prescriptions for each student, which designate learning tasks the student is to undertake, suggested materials and techniques of instruction, and the standard of performance expected as an outcome; and (6) strategies for information feedback, designed to provide students, teachers, and curriculum coordinators with opportunities for continual evaluation and assessment.

Closely allied to individualization is the process of modularization, in which highly complex subject areas are broken into segments that involve less than a full semester's work. Modules can be chosen to fit the interests and needs of the students and are designed on a foundation of thorough knowledge of the particular content area and the teaching/learning situation. These modules are usually created by a design team composed of a content expert in the discipline, a college instructor, and a student. All team members are involved from the outset in the design of the module, for each has experience of central importance. The module builds on the notion that learning must be based upon previous learning and must serve to develop the student's knowledge and interests. It also is based on the fact that learning occurs in a variety of ways, all of which should be brought to bear upon an educational situation.

Frequently the materials for a module consist of a student booklet and a teacher handbook on the chosen topic; together, these are adequate for the proposed instruction. The primary task of the module design team is to prepare the manuscripts for these two components. The contents of the student booklet include the textual material for the student, a set of meaningful learning activities, a set of optional learning activities, and a set of annotated references chosen with the student in mind. The teacher handbook contains an overview of the content and goal of the module, the principles which the module is to illustrate, and a set of objectives stated in a form that permits student progress and

competence to be measured as learning advances. In addition, the teacher handbook contains background material, suggestions for advanced planning, suggested instructional strategies, and sources of laboratory and demonstration materials.

A third development of importance for instruction is the use of instructional media, which offer the educational administrator a powerful source of new methods that, in many cases, may be better suited to student needs than the traditional methods. The new methods of acquiring, assembling, analyzing, and disseminating the almost overwhelming flood of facts and ideas emanating from all sources as a result of the information explosion are highly critical to the instructional process.

Instructors currently are as much managers of learning as they are transmitters of knowledge, and they must be able to design learning plans for diverse students by using both print and nonprint media. As a result of individualization, modularization, and new media, instructors now serve the learner as diagnosticians, investigators, evaluators, and counselors.

With the advent of the cassette tape recorder, audiotaping offers a highly convenient way of transmitting lectures. Electronic video recording enables the teacher to bring prerecorded demonstrations into the classroom. Another device, called a dial access information retrieval system (DAIR), is an electronic system for managing the distribution of stored audio and visual materials. Students can obtain a program simply by dialing an assigned three-digit number. Since there is no limitation on where information can be sent, receiving stations can be located anywhere on campus.

Two other forms of media available for instruction are computer-aided and computer-assisted instruction. Computer-assisted instruction involves the presentation of materials by the computer to the student in a logical sequence that is controlled by a prior program; the student is the passive responder to the system.

Programed materials are organized in advance, and the student is allowed very little choice. Computer-aided instruction, on the other hand, involves the student's direct use and programing of the computer to solve problems given by a teacher or by the computer itself. Computer-aided instructional procedures require more sophistication and more initiative on the part of the student, but they are a powerful means of generating learning.

Evaluation of Curriculum and Instruction

An important task in the administration of curriculum and instruction involves the process of evaluation, which can be defined broadly as the gathering, analyzing, maintaining, and feeding back of information to all participants. Academic administrators and directors of support services gather and maintain records on the contexts of instruction, available resources, and instructional outputs and outcomes, which then form the basis for the planning and modification of development. The major forms of evaluation, as they pertain to the administration of curriculum and instruction, include the evaluation of the instructional context, the evaluation of instruction itself, and the evaluation of student outcomes.

The instructional context: curriculum. Curriculum evaluation must include an evaluation of cost, efficiency, and effectiveness.

Curricular cost can be evaluated as a function of a series of interrelated variables over which faculty and administrators have control. By altering any one of these variables, faculty or administration can change the cost of instruction within an institution. A comprehensive formula has been devised that relates this series of variables: (1) Number of students (N) times semester student load in credit hours (L) equals total student credit hours. (2) Average class size (C) times average semester credit hours taught by teachers (F) equals average student credit hours taught by each teacher. (3) Total semester student credit hours divided by average credit hours taught by teachers equals the number of teachers. (4) Number of teachers times average academic year salary of teacher (S) equals total teacher salary. (5) Total year's expenditures less teachers' salaries equals overhead on teachers' salaries. (6) Overhead expressed as a relative of salary equals overhead divided by salaries (O) (here overhead stands for all costs other than salaries). (7) Thus: $(NL/CF)S(1 + O) =$ cost of instruction (Harris, 1962, p. 519). It is important to recognize that the effective administration of curriculum requires the information that is listed in these seven steps. Decisions are made to increase or decrease various factors, and these decisions are usually made not only on the basis of fiscal considerations but also in terms of the overall purposes of the college.

Curricular efficiency refers to the extent to which an institution can achieve greater productivity without increasing costs; this is usually expressed as a ratio between the variables of input and output. Outputs are defined solely in terms of quantifiable factors; efficiency is defined as maximum output for a given input or minimum input for a given output. Normally, in the analysis of curricular efficiency the term *cost* is substituted for the broader term *input*. Output, which is a difficult and debatable term in the definition of efficiency, includes quantitative measurements of that which the institution produces.

Curricular effectiveness refers to the extent to which the institution achieves its goals, meets the needs of its students, and fulfills the social goals which it is contributing. Both efficiency and effectiveness must be considered if a full evaluation of curriculum is to be undertaken.

The instructional context: the institution. The evaluation of the learning environment refers to evaluating the conditions, circumstances, and influences that indirectly affect the processes of instruction. These include the social, psychological, and physical components of institutions, such as campus traditions; rules; acceptable standards of behavior; the grounds and architecture;

and the value orientations of the organizational structure. The following eight characteristics have been selected for describing and evaluating the instructional environment: (1) selectivity (the number of students who apply for admission divided by the number admitted); (2) size (total full-time enrollment); (3) realistic orientation (the percentage of degrees in agriculture or several other applied fields; (4) scientific orientation (percentage of degrees in natural science); (5) social orientation (percentage of degrees in education, nursing, social work, and social science); (6) conventional orientation (percentage of degrees in accounting, business economics, library science); (7) enterprising orientation (percentage of degrees in advertising, business, history, political science, prelaw, journalism, international relations, and foreign service); (8) artistic orientation (percentage of degrees in fine arts, language, music, and speech). On the basis of these variables, it is possible to distinguish among different kinds of institutions (Astin and Holland, 1961).

Other characteristics that influence the instructional environment include college image, personal characteristics of students, and the atmosphere of the institution, as defined on the basis of the College and University Environment Scales (CUES) (Pace, 1969). The CUES describe an institution's practicality orientation, community orientation, awareness orientation, propriety, and scholarship.

Another ETS scale, the Institutional Functioning Inventory (IFI), describes an institution's values and commitments in the following terms: (1) intellectual, esthetic, and extracurricular values; (2) academic and personal freedom; (3) human diversity; (4) improvement of society and the solving of social problems; (5) undergraduate learning; (6) democratic governance; (7) meeting local needs and educational manpower; (8) self-study and planning; (9) advancing knowledge, research, and scholarship; (10) innovation (commitment to innovate and to explore); and (11) insti-

tutional spirit (sense of shared purposes and high morale). The IFI is an attempt to allow institutions to assess their priorities among various outcome and process goals; it can be seen as contributing to an understanding of the role of instruction in the total operation of an institution.

Instructional processes. The evaluation of instruction is practically synonymous with the evaluation of faculty in the minds of students, faculty, and administrators. Such a process is fraught with so many political pitfalls that the administrator must be extremely cautious both in carrying out the evaluations of faculty performance and in expressing those results to interested parties.

There are three common purposes for the evaluation of instruction: (1) improving instruction by providing feedback to faculty members and curriculum planners regarding the techniques of instruction that seem to be improving student performance and student morale; (2) contributing information on faculty performance for purposes of promotion, tenure, and merit pay decisions; and (3) providing information to students.

The most common form of instructional evaluation makes use of questionnaires to be filled out by students; despite the many drawbacks of this technique, it is consistently used. There are now numerous attempts to make this evaluation process more sensitive to differences in courses and faculty approaches, more sophisticated, and more likely to provide adequate feedback to faculty members for the improvement of their instructional methods.

Instructional outcomes. Assessing student performance is a task typically carried out by faculty members, with administrative support in maintaining student records. Professors evaluate students according to criteria they establish themselves or to standards established by a department, an institution, or a discipline. There are three general approaches to the evaluation of student outcomes.

"Critique" is a process whereby the professor reacts directly to the student in unique terms, designed to help the student improve. Verbal and nonverbal reactions to a student's statements in class, written comments on student papers, and open-ended evaluation of examinations are all examples of formative evaluation. The primary purpose of evaluation is to provide feedback to the student as an aid to learning; its major advantage lies in the detailed, personal, and direct conveyance of information to the student.

"Norm-based evaluation" is a process through which a student's performance is compared to the performance of others who have experienced the same instructional processes for the same time period. This process is often referred to as evaluating "on-the-curve," because an individual's standing is determined by statistics that assume a bell-shaped distribution of ability in a given class. Given the traditional practices of fixed-length college terms, common instructional experiences, and instructor-designed tests, such norm-based evaluation probably provides the fairest description of the majority of students; it manifests a real, but usually unstated, function of student selection.

"Criteria-based evaluation" is a process whereby a student's performance is compared to a fixed standard of quality. The judgment made about a student's achievement can be in quantitative terms or in terms that indicate whether or not an adequate standard of performance was reached. This form of evaluation is most consistent with individualized or modularized instruction in a competence-based or objective-based curriculum.

Both norm- and criteria-based evaluations are examples of summative evaluation in that their primary purpose is to report to both the student and others a summary of performance at the completion of an instructional event rather than to serve as an ongoing process.

Administrative uses of evaluations of student performance include reporting them to academic advisers and recording them on the student's permanent record. This reporting and recording process takes various forms, collectively known as credit systems.

Credit Systems

As higher education curricula became more diversified and as students began engaging in different forms and combinations of instructional experiences, a unit was sought that would equate student progress over various programs. This administrative device was designed as a measure of the contribution of a given instructional experience (usually a course) to the completion of degree requirements.

Credit-hour systems. In the United States most colleges and universities grant a degree upon the successful completion of 120 to 128 credits. Each undergraduate course provides a number of credits toward the degree requirement. A combination of credits and hours yields the more common unit of academic progress, the credit hour. Traditionally, a three–credit hour course requires three fifty-minute classroom lectures per week plus six hours of study over ten weeks in the quarter system or fifteen weeks in the semester system. Credits for laboratory work, fieldwork, and internships usually require far more hours of work than do course credits.

Despite the fact that credit hours have very little relation to course difficulty, course substance, or course requirements, they play an enormously important role in the administration of instruction. Among other uses, they form a basis for prescribing degree requirements, for allocating time to different programs, for setting up student schedules, and for designating course prerequisites. In addition, credits weighted by grades have been used as the basis of academic rewards and punishments, as a means of allocating faculty workloads, and as the basis for granting or refusing accreditation to programs and institutions.

Despite their widespread use as measures of effort, achievement, or exposure, credits have certain weaknesses. They imply time but indicate achievement (two factors that are often not equivalent); they do not necessarily imply learning. They are of little value at the graduate level and are not useful for describing nontraditional instructional forms.

Alternative credit systems. These weaknesses have led to the development of alternative systems for measuring the progress of students. Under the "credit calculated in contract months" system, developed by Empire State College of the State University of New York, a student and a mentor work out a contract regarding the purposes, activities, and leases for evaluation of a student's work. This contract describes the rights and responsibilities of both student and mentor for a designated period of time within a student's degree program. Academic credit is expressed in terms of contract months, with the length of each contract being determined by the student's degree plan. A contract month is considered four weeks of work at a rate of thirty-six to forty hours per week. Students are given advanced placement, also calculated in terms of months, for prior credit and experience. Once this prior learning is assessed and an individual's standing is established, the remainder of the degree program is fulfilled through the learning contracts.

The "continuing education unit" (CEU) represents a new, and as yet relatively untested, method of measuring the contribution to a student's degree program made by highly diverse activities and experiences that cannot readily be equated with course credits. Students earn CEUs for job-related and leisure-time activities that have educational value and that can legitimately, if unconventionally, be taken to contribute to a coherent degree program. As degree programs rely more and more on evidences of competence, the CEU, as an indicator of competence-producing experiences, may well become more prominent.

Under the "credit-by-examination" system, a student is awarded credit by demonstrating proficiency on a standardized examination. The credits are calculated in terms of hours, so they may be equated with traditional credits, but they are not attained by spending specific amounts of time in prescribed instructional experiences. No attention is paid to the source of the skill or knowledge a student demonstrates but only to adequate test performance. The College-Level Examination Program (CLEP) is the best known of the credit-by-examination programs; it is used by many colleges and universities to provide advanced academic standing for students and contributes heavily to the calculation of credits toward the Regents External Degree program in New York State as well as other external programs.

Grading Systems

Grades are symbols given by instructors to indicate an individual degree of accomplishment in an instructional experience. Unlike credits, which measure the time and level of exposure of the instructional experience, grades reflect the instructor's judgment of quality of performance and mastery of content. In the administration of instruction, grades serve to distinguish students in terms of their performance; to inform them of their relationship to some fixed or variable standard of achievement; and, ideally, to motivate them toward increased proficiency and accomplishment. Even though the information they provide is not extensive, grades have an obvious value administratively in that they are not difficult to process and are easily retrieved and reported.

Typical grading systems include numerical procedures based upon artibrarily chosen intervals such as 0–100. Letter-grading systems are also commonplace, with A, B, C, D, and F grading occurring most frequently. Letter grades are typically associated with numbers (A = 4, B = 3, C = 2, D = 1, F = O), so that grade point averages can be calculated. These numerical equivalents of letter grades are used in conjunction with credit hours to calculate quality point averages (QPA), which are the basis for such academic awards as scholarships. The QPA can also be the basis for academic sanctions such as probation, under which students are warned about low achievement and are given a specified period in which to raise their QPA above a certain minimum.

Weaknesses of grading systems. Grades are highly condensed expressions of very complex judgments, and the bases on which they are made cannot usually be specified. Particular grades may reflect an instructor's subjective judgment of students' interest, performances on tests, written papers, oral participation in a class, or some complex combination of all these criteria. In addition, grades often generate anxiety that is disruptive to learning. Grades may unfairly penalize students who wish only to sample a domain rather than plumb its depths and may become ends in themselves rather than feedback indicators to enhance instruction. Grades have a seductive appeal to many administrators, parents, and employers, who sometimes give more evaluative significance to grades than their nature deserves. The importance of grading as a selection device for academic and social rewards tends to increase the likelihood of cheating, especially in large classes and mass test-taking situations. From an administrative standpoint, the monitoring practices needed to hold such cheating to a minimum are expensive and diminish the quality of the academic atmosphere.

Improving grading practices. The use of grades as indicators can be improved by careful recognition of their limitations and by a concerted effort to establish and maintain consistent grading practices and standards. The information potential of grades can be enhanced by a series of symbols that serve different administrative purposes. Such symbols might represent a grade for the student independent of the rest of the class; a grade comparing the student with other class members; a grade comparing the student with others at the same educational level; or a grade indicat-

ing the student's final status in the course.

Other grading systems have been introduced that have the advantage of recording a student's status without trying to make potentially misleading fine distinctions. Pass/fail (or satisfactory/unsatisfactory) grading consists of two distinct options that record whether or not a student has achieved a requisite level of performance. Such grades are commonplace for publicly sponsored examinations of professional competence, such as bar examinations in law and board examinations in medicine,

Pass/no credit (or satisfactory/incomplete) grading offers the added advantage of eliminating the stigma associated with the failure to achieve an established level of proficiency. It implies that failure to achieve is a temporary phenomenon and withholds potentially negative judgments to allow for added and diversified effort.

Under systems such as pass/no credit (and, to a lesser extent, pass/fail), students are at liberty to pursue new areas of interest for which their preparation may be minimal. They can enroll freely in courses without anxiety about competition from other students or excessive pressure from instructors. Instructors also benefit by not being required to develop distinctions among students that may be invalid.

Despite their advantages, the alternatives to traditional grading are not widely practiced. Where they are used they are heavily restricted in regard to the number and level of courses to which they apply. Concern that pass/fail or pass/no credit grading will lead to lower standards has resulted in limiting the practice to juniors and seniors only, to courses outside a student's major field, to a certain absolute number of pass/fail credits, or to only certain elective courses. These limits on the use of a system that both students and instructors find conducive to real learning have a cogent rationale in the recognition that grades serve the social function of providing classificatory evaluative information about students to graduate schools, professional schools, and employers. Until education's social function of certification is handled by some agency other than the college or university, the traditional methods of grading will remain.

Administrative Decisions for the Future

What relative emphasis in the design of curricula and in the application of instructional techniques shall be given to self-initiated, responsible learning as opposed to more directed manipulative procedures? On the one hand, the very term *instruction* implies that the responsibility for learning rests with the agents of the institution; on the other hand, new curricula and instructional procedures increasingly emphasize the unique characteristics, needs, and abilities of individuals. Yet to be realized is clear understanding of the subtle, fine, but ever so profound distinction between behaviorist-based manipulative interpretations of terms like *individualization* and the humanistic interpretations that emphasize personal freedom and responsibility.

Who shall control the curriculum and the techniques of instruction? New research in learning and teaching, the development of instructional media, and the growth in importance of techniques such as systems analysis, as well as fiscal exigency and consequent demands for accountability, have led to the development of new concepts in administration of curriculum and instruction that may be inimical to traditional procedures and values. These new concepts imply that traditional faculty responsibility for curriculum and instruction should be shifted to those whose expertise is the process of instruction itself. The major question seems to be whether faculty, trained to be expert in a given content domain, can adequately administer processes of curriculum and instruction that have grown increasingly complex with the passage of time.

It is in resolving such current issues as well as in addressing the perennial questions of general versus specialized curricula and efficiency versus effectiveness in eval-uation that the administration of instruction and curriculum will find its greatest challenge.

Bibliography

Astin, A., and Holland, J. L. "The Environmental Assessment Technique: A Way to Measure College Environment." *Journal of Educational Psychology,* 1961, *52,* 308–317.

Dressel, P. *College and University Curriculum.* (2nd ed.) Berkeley, California: McCutchan, 1971.

Dressel, P. *Handbook of Academic Evaluation.* San Francisco: Jossey-Bass, 1976.

Dressel, P., and DeLisle, F. *Undergraduate Curriculum Trends.* Washington, D.C.: American Council on Education, 1969.

Educational Testing Service. *Institutional Goals Inventory.* Princeton, New Jersey: Educational Testing Service, 1972.

Harris, S. *Higher Education: Resources and Finance.* New York: McGraw-Hill, 1962.

Knowles, A. S. (Ed.) *Handbook of College and University Administration.* New York: McGraw-Hill, 1970.

Pace, C. R. *College and University Environment Scales.* Princeton, New Jersey: Educational Testing Service, 1969.

J. BRUCE FRANCIS

See also: Calendars, Academic; Cooperative Education and Off-Campus Experience; Educational Resources; Evaluation; Examinations and Tests; Exchange International: Study Abroad; Independent Study; Innovation; Instruction, Individualized; Internationalization of Higher Education; Reform, University.

CYPRUS, REPUBLIC OF

Greek Cypriot Education *Student enrollment in primary school: 56,649; secondary school (public, private, technical, vocational): 46,907; higher education: 611 in Cyprus, 12,400 abroad. Language of instruction: Greek.* [*Figures are for 1974–75. Source:* Department for Higher and Secondary Education, Ministry of Education, Nicosia.]

Turkish Cypriot Education *Student enrollment in primary school: 18,036; secondary education (general, vocational, technical): 9956; higher education: 45 in Cyprus (Turkish Teachers Training College), 3350 abroad. Language of instruction: Turkish.* [*Figures are for 1975–76. Source:* Ministry of Education, Turkish Federated State of Cyprus.]

Cyprus, an island in the eastern Mediterranean, lies about sixty miles south of Turkey. The island's population, estimated at 639,000 in 1975, is divided into two main ethnic groups, Greek and Turkish, and about 4 percent other groups. Greek Cypriots (about 78 percent of the population) are descended from the island's earliest inhabitants and subsequent invaders, particularly the Ionians from Greece. The Turkish Cypriots (about 18 percent of the population) are descended from the Ottoman Turks, who ruled the island from 1571 until the start of British occupation in 1878. In 1960 Cyprus achieved independence from Great Britain after five years of armed struggle.

Since independence the Greek Cypriots have demanded union with Greece, but the Turkish Cypriots have favored either partition or union with Turkey. In 1974 open warfare erupted between the two factions, which prompted intervention by troops from Turkey. Since the Turkish intervention, the two communities have lived in separate regions. On February 13, 1975, the Turkish Cypriots proclaimed the Turkish Federated State of Cyprus in the northern 40 percent of the island held by Turkish forces.

Greek Cypriot Education

The Greek Cypriot educational system is administered by the Ministry of Education in Nicosia. Primary education extends six years and is free and compulsory for the six to fourteen age group. Most secondary programs are six years in length and are divided into two three-year cycles. General secondary education is provided by the *gymnasion* on the lower secondary level and the *lykeion* on the upper secondary level. The *lykeion* is divided into three sections: classics, science, and economics. Six-year secondary programs are also offered at technical schools and by the agricultural *gymnasion*. On completion of the *lykeion,* the upper secondary programs at the technical schools, or the agricultural *gymnasion,*

students who successfully pass a final examination are awarded the *apolyterion* (leaving certificate) required for higher study at home or abroad.

Higher education is provided by the Pedagogical Academy of Cyprus, which prepares primary school teachers; the Cyprus Forestry College, affiliated to the Ministry of Agriculture; and the Higher Technical Institute, operated by the Ministry of Labor. The majority of secondary school graduates, however, pursue higher studies abroad. During the 1974–75 academic year some 12,400 Greek Cypriots studied abroad; of these, some 7200 were in Greece and 2900 in the United Kingdom.

Studies abroad are financed mainly by the families, although some loan schemes are available for students in financial need. A small number of students study abroad on Cypriot or foreign government scholarships. The financing for a number of students abroad was disrupted by the 1974 war.

[Assistance provided by C. E. Hadjistephanou, Head of the Department for Higher and Secondary Education, Ministry of Education, Nicosia.]

Turkish Cypriot Education

The Turkish Cypriot educational system is administered by the Ministry of Education of the Turkish Federated State of Cyprus. Basic education, which is free and compulsory for the six to fifteen age group, is provided by a six-year primary school and a three-year *orta okul,* or middle school. Secondary education, which is free but not compulsory, is available in general, vocational, and technical schools. The secondary program extends three years beyond basic education and leads to the State *Lycée* Finishing Diploma, a prerequisite for higher study abroad.

Parallel to the formal educational system is the adult education system, which is administered by various ministries and provides training for students beyond the compulsory school age. During the 1975–76 academic year 1456 students were receiving adult education in home economics and cottage industry, hotel and catering, and nursing and midwifery.

Postsecondary education is offered by the Turkish Teachers Training College, which prepares primary school teachers and also provides in-service training for teachers, and by two specialized institutions: the Theological School administered by the *mufti's* office (religious head of the Muslim community) and the Police Training Center operated by the director general of the police force. Most of the Turkish Cypriot secondary school graduates abroad study in Turkey. In the 1975–76 academic year about 3000 Turkish Cypriots were enrolled in universities and other higher education institutions in Turkey; of these, some 1750 were offered scholarships or financial aid by the Turkish Federated State of Cyprus. A further 350 students studied abroad in the United Kingdom, the United States, and Western European countries.

[Information provided by M. A. Raif, Under-Secretary, Ministry of Education, Turkish Federated State of Cyprus.]

CZECHOSLOVAK SOCIALIST REPUBLIC

Population: 14,738,377 (1974). Student enrollment in basic school (grades 1-9): 3,027,616 (1973–74); secondary school (grammar, vocational, apprentice): 757,210 (1973–74); higher education: 140,905 (1974–75). Language of instruction: Czech or Slovak. Academic calendar: October to September or October to June, two semesters. [Source of enrollment statistics: Thirty Years of Socialist School in the Czechoslovak Socialist Republic, 1975.]

The modern Czechoslovak state was created at the end of World War I, following the collapse of the Austro-Hungarian Empire. By this time the former Austrian-controlled lands of Bohemia and Moravia possessed an educational system that included Charles University in Prague (1348), the oldest university in Central Europe;

the Czech University of Technology in Prague, established in 1707 as the first school of engineering in Central Europe; and the University of Technology in Brno, established in 1899 as one of the first technical schools of university standing in Central Europe. However, in Slovakia, the area formerly controlled by Hungary, education had been neglected, and educational facilities at all levels lagged behind those in Bohemia and Moravia.

After World War I, the government of the newly established Czechoslovak Republic expanded the existing university system; however, expansion was confined mainly to the traditional centers of industry and culture, and most of the population had little access to higher education. In 1919, Comenius University, the first and most prestigious Slovak university, was established in Bratislava. For nearly twenty years it remained the only higher education institution serving the Slovak population. In 1937 the first Slovak University of Technology was established at Košice; it was moved to Martin and finally to its present location in Bratislava in 1939.

Further educational expansion was precluded by the outbreak of World War II and the German occupation of the Czechoslovak Republic. In November of 1939 all higher education institutions in Bohemia and Moravia were closed for the duration of the war, while the universities in Slovakia were forced to operate according to fascist ideology. The end of World War II marked the beginning of a new stage in the development of education in the republic, under the influence of the Soviet Union. Renewed emphasis was placed on higher education, and university studies were adapted to the economic and cultural needs of the state. The number of universities and technical colleges increased during this period, and new specialized schools and faculties were added. A significant portion of the expansion effort was undertaken in Slovakia, where by 1970 more than a dozen universities and colleges existed.

National Educational Policy

In Czechoslovakia education is viewed as the basis for the continual development of socialist society. The stated role of the schools is to educate the youth and the working people with a scientific outlook to function as socially useful citizens of the republic. To this end, the right of every citizen to education is ensured by a unified school system and by unified educational establishments.

The task of the universities in the Czechoslovak socialist society is to provide third-level education and advanced training for professional workers, to develop scientific or artistic activities and educate new scientific workers or workers in the field of art, and to be the centers for the cultural and educational development of the people.

Legal Basis of Educational System

Every citizen is guaranteed the right to education by Article 24 of the constitution of the Czechoslovak Socialist Republic. The educational system is regulated by School Act 186 of December 15, 1960, which sets forth the structure and purpose of the schools. The major legislation concerning higher education is Universities Act 19 of 1966 and its amendment, Act 163 of 1969, which outline the position, organization, and management of the universities. The details concerning the control, organization, and activities of individual universities are set forth in university and faculty statutes.

Types of Institutions

A general university education is offered at Comenius University, Bratislava; Jan E. Purkyně University, Brno; Charles University, Prague; Palacký University, Olomouc; and Pavel Josef Šafařík University, Košice. These universities offer programs in fields such as law, medicine, natural sciences, pharmacy, mathematics, and physics as well as philosophy, culture, journalism, and pedagogy.

Technical higher education is available at five universities of technology and at thirteen colleges and schools, which are divided into the following areas of study: economics, agriculture, veterinary medicine, technology, chemical technology, forestry and wood technology, mining and metallurgy, mechanical and electrical engineering, mechanical and textile engineering, and transport engineering. Higher education in the fields of art and music is offered in three academies of music and dramatic arts, an academy of fine arts, a college of fine arts, and a college of applied arts (*Thirty Years,* 1975, Vol. 3).

Teachers for the basic nine-year schools are trained at seven independent pedagogical faculties, while secondary school teachers receive their degrees at the faculties of arts, natural sciences, mathematics, and physics or at the faculty of sport and physical training at the university. The universities of technology and the schools of economics and agriculture train teachers for secondary vocational schools and apprentice schools. Other higher education institutions include a military university; a higher school of political science, run by the Central Committee of the Communist Party of Czechoslovakia; and a higher police school. In addition, outside the unified educational system the state operates seven theological faculties, which prepare priests for the main churches in the country (*Thirty Years,* 1975, Vol. 3).

Adult education has been a vital part of the Czechoslovak higher education system since 1954, when degree courses for employed persons were first introduced in the universities. Any student may pursue higher education on a full-time or part-time basis and qualify for the same degrees. In 1973 the state reactivated a program, which had operated for a short time after 1948, enabling gifted young workers and farmers to take a one-year intensive course in order to gain their secondary school-leaving certificate. The one-year course also serves as preparatory training for university study.

During the 1974–75 academic year 43.6

percent of the total number of students at institutions of higher education were enrolled in the universities; 36 percent in universities of technology; 9.3 percent at schools of economics; 9.7 percent at colleges of agriculture; and 1.4 percent in courses in the fine arts (*Thirty Years,* 1975, Vol. 3).

Relationship with Secondary Education

Higher education is based on a nine-year compulsory basic school followed by a four-year secondary program of general, technical, or apprenticeship training. Most children up to six years of age receive preschool education in day nurseries, nursery schools, and kindergartens before entering the basic school.

After completing basic school, students enter one of several secondary school programs, which lead to higher education or to employment. Complete secondary general education leading to a school-leaving certificate is provided at the *gymnasia* (secondary grammar schools) and in secondary boarding schools for working people. The general secondary program prepares students for university study and for selected medium-level positions in the national economy. Complete secondary vocational education, also leading to a school-leaving certificate, is provided at secondary vocational schools. After attaining the school-leaving certificate, students in this program serve as middle-level personnel or further their education at the university.

During the 1973–74 academic year a four-year apprenticeship secondary program leading to the school-leaving certificate was introduced. This program prepares students for positions in the exacting trades or for university study.

The two remaining types of secondary education lead to employment. Vocational schools provide two- to three-year programs, which train personnel for lower-level positions in the national economy. A two- to four-year apprenticeship program preparing personnel for the skilled trades is also available (*Thirty Years,* 1975, Vol. 2).

Admission Requirements

Only students who possess a school-leaving certificate may be admitted to a third-level institution. The number of students admitted to a faculty and to a course is governed by the institution's production plan. Students must apply within a certain period and are required to have a recommendation from the secondary school they attend. A commission at the university or college admits a student on the basis of an interview, the secondary school's recommendation, and an employer's assessment (if the student is working). The commission also tests the candidate's academic ability on the basis of his secondary school syllabus. Preference is given to candidates who have worked a year after completing secondary school.

University graduates who wish to undertake postgraduate work are required to take an entrance examination and must meet the requirements set for workers of scientific research institutions.

Administration and Control

Under the Universities Act of 1966, the minister of education of the Czech Socialist Republic (CSR) and the minister of education of the Slovak Socialist Republic (SSR) control all aspects of higher education in Czechoslovakia. Each minister is advised on major university matters by a permanent committee, the Czech or the Slovak Committee for Universities and Higher Education Institutions. Committee members include rectors of universities and higher schools and other experts appointed by the ministers of education. Representatives of the Socialist Union of Youth and the Revolutionary Trade Union Movement also attend committee meetings.

Education is a major concern of the two legislative bodies of the republic (the Czech and the Slovak National Councils) and the Federal Assembly, which regularly assesses the state and development of educational work through special commissions and committees (*Thirty Years,* 1975, Vol. 3).

The higher education institutions are headed by rectors, appointed by the president of the republic on the recommendation of the chief governing board of the institution, the academic board. The rector, as the chief administrative officer, is responsible to the minister of education. Rectors are assisted by pro-rectors in research and instructional matters and by a questor in financial and administrative matters.

Most third-level institutions are divided into faculties, which may be further divided into separate departments. Each faculty is headed by a dean, who is responsible to the rector. Deans and their assistants, pro-deans, are elected by the academic board and officially appointed by the minister of education. Rectors, pro-rectors, deans, and pro-deans all serve for a term of three years.

Students in Czechoslovak institutions of higher learning are represented by the Socialist Union of Youth (*Socialisticky svaz mládeže: SSM*). SSM cooperates with the Ministry of Education, the committees for universities and higher education institutions, university bodies, and social organizations in solving the problems of university students and in determining the role of students in the management of the universities.

Programs and Degrees

The majority of students enrolled at the higher education level are involved in full-time degree programs consisting of normal day-time courses, evening courses, correspondence or external courses, or a combination of these types. The average length of higher education programs leading to the first degree is four to six years. Students take the state final examination upon completion of their undergraduate studies, after which they are awarded their first diplomas or degrees.

The following titles are awarded for the first degree course: graduates in medicine receive the title of Doctor of Medicine (MUDr.), and graduates in veterinary science receive the title of Doctor of Veteri-

nary Science (MVDr.); students graduating from the universities of technology, schools of economics, or colleges of agriculture, with the exception of graduates of veterinary medicine, use the title of Engineer or Engineer Architect; graduates in painting, sculpture, or architecture from schools of fine arts are awarded the title of Academic Painter, Academic Sculptor, or Academic Architect. University graduates, with the exception of those in medical science and the schools of fine arts, who pass the state examination in a given branch of study at the honors level are awarded the title of Doctor of Law (JUDr.), Doctor of Natural Sciences (RNDr.), or Doctor of Philosophy (PhDr.). Graduates from all higher education institutions who hold a teaching diploma and who teach in a secondary school may use the professional title of Secondary School Professor (*Thirty Years*, 1975, Vol. 3).

A major function of the universities is the training of scientific workers. Selected professors and associate professors educate scientific workers "in the form of regular postgraduate candidate studies, external postgraduate candidate studies, and by means of a scientific preparation during the accomplishment of normal work duties" (*Educational System*, 1974, p. 45). The requirements for postgraduate study include a first university degree and original scientific or research activity. Scientific degrees are awarded on two levels: Candidate of Sciences (*candidatus scientiarum*: CSc.) and Doctor of Sciences (*doctor scientiarum*: Dr.Sc.). Candidates of Science are required to prepare and publicly defend a thesis as well as sit for the candidate's examination. The scientific degree of Doctor of Sciences requires "exceptionally high scientific qualifications verified by a public defense of a doctorate thesis" (*Educational System*, 1974, p. 45). Scientific degrees are also awarded by the Czechoslovak Academy of Sciences.

A recent development in the universities is postgraduate study, designed to improve the qualifications of specialists with university-level education by providing opportunities for greater specialization or instruction in recent scientific and technological developments in a given field. Postgraduate study takes the form of in-service training or full-time course work. Since 1967 teachers at basic and secondary schools have been required to take postgraduate courses involving some two hundred hours of tutorials and summer school sessions designed to acquaint teachers with new facts in their field of qualification. At the end of the program, they are required to present a written dissertation and pass an oral examination. Teachers are entitled to a pay increase upon the completion of such in-service postgraduate courses (*Thirty Years,* 1975, Vol. 3).

Financing and Student Financial Aid

Higher education institutions in Czechoslovakia are financed by the state. All costs are included in the state budget. No tuition or examination fees have been charged since 1945. In addition, students are provided with scholarships, low-interest loans, grants for practical work, inexpensive accommodation in halls of residence, inexpensive food in student canteens, reductions on public transportation, and free medical care.

Students in financial need may obtain special grants for a ten-month period, based on the parents' income. In certain cases, the dean of faculty may award a special grant. The amount of these grants is increased for women students with children; married students, particularly those with children; students over the age of twenty-six; and married women students whose husbands are in military service (*Thirty Years,* 1975, Vol. 3).

Scholarships based on academic excellence are awarded beginning with the second year of study and are renewed annually if the student maintains above-average marks. Special scholarships are provided by businesses, regional and national committees, state administrative bodies, and ministries. These scholarships are generally given to students on a competitive

basis during their last two years of study. In return, students must work in a position chosen for them for at least five years upon completion of their studies.

For students in financial need the state also grants loans which are repayable two years after graduation (one year in the case of female students, who do not serve in the military).

Student Social Background and Access to Education

The educational system of the Czechoslovak Socialist Republic is based on the philosophy of John Amos Comenius, the seventeenth-century educational reformer and last bishop of the Moravian church. Comenius introduced the concept of universal education, which was adopted in Czechoslovak lands as early as 1869, when school attendance was first made compulsory. Since World War II equal access to education has been assured with the abolishment of all tuition fees, the initiation of an extensive adult education program, and the introduction of a generous scholarship program. These policies have brought about a change in the family background of students enrolled in university institutions. During the 1974–75 academic year 55.7 percent of students enrolled in university studies were from the families of workers and farmers. The changing status of women in the Czechoslovak society is reflected in the rise in enrollment of women in university studies: from 17.3 percent in 1937 to 40.8 percent in 1974–75 (*Thirty Years,* 1975, Vol. 3).

Teaching Staff

The main category of university-level teachers includes professors, associate professors, and assistant professors. There are also special assistants, lecturers, assistants, special instructors, and external teachers. University institutions also have scientific, technical, special, and assistant workers on their research staffs.

University professors and associate professors are appointed by the president of the republic on the recommendation of the government, and assistant professors are appointed by the ministers of education (*Educational System,* 1974).

Research Activities

Research is an integral part of all higher education institutions in Czechoslovakia. The major part of the research effort in the universities is devoted to state and ministry task projects, which, in 1973, represented 85 percent of the total hours spent on research at all university-level schools in the republic. A substantial amount of research is also conducted outside the universities by organizations such as the Czechoslovak Academy of Sciences, the Slovak Academy of Sciences, and ministerial research institutes. Close cooperation exists between the universities and the institutes. Experts from these institutes often work as external university staff, and, in turn, many university staff are members of the academies and their institutes and councils (*Thirty Years,* 1975, Vol. 3).

Current Problems and Trends

The educational system in Czechoslovakia is continually under review in an effort to keep pace with the development of the socialist society and with recent scientific and technological changes. At the university level, plans call for a rationalization and modernization of the teaching process, with an emphasis on active methods of learning. Changes are planned in the organization of university studies to effect a "compact presentation of scientific and technical information by means of generalization, the introduction of wider, more comprehensive courses, better programmes, textbooks, teaching aids, reduction of duplication and repetition of study material in various subjects, a rational division of time between classes on theory and hours of practical work" (*Thirty Years,* 1975, Vol. 3, p. 23).

In the area of teacher training, greater care is being given to the selection of candidates, and further emphasis is being placed on in-service training. University research centers are assuming a greater role in the state plan for the development of science and technology in an effort to meet the needs of society.

International Cooperation

Czechoslovakia pursues an active policy of international cooperation in the area of education. Close cooperation exists among the ministries responsible for higher education in the socialist countries, with regular meetings held to discuss educational developments, cooperation, and coordination. Individual Czechoslovak universities have also established arrangements for cooperation with universities in the Soviet Union and other socialist countries.

Czechoslovakia has numerous cultural agreements with nonsocialist states and is an active member of UNESCO. It also provides aid for educational institutions in developing countries by sending experts to those countries to teach at local higher education institutions and by accepting students from those countries in Czechoslovak universities. Students from more than seventy developing countries in Asia, Africa, and Latin America are represented in Czechoslovak universities. Certain preparatory facilities are available for these students, including Czech- or Slovak-language courses.

Graduate courses for foreign students are also offered by Czech and Slovak universities. Seventy-four university centers provide 220 specializations at the graduate level. An increasing number of Czechoslovak students on scholarship are enrolled in degree programs in universities in the Soviet Union, the German Democratic Republic, Poland, Bulgaria, Hungary, Yugoslavia, and other countries (*Thirty Years,* 1975, Vol. 3).

[Materials supplied by the Embassy of the Czechoslovak Socialist Republic, Washington, D.C.]

Educational Associations

Socialisticky svaz mládeže ČSSR (SSM)
(Socialist Union of Youth of the
  Czechoslovak Republic)
1 Nové Mesto
nám. M. Gorkého 24
Prague 1, Czechoslovakia

Czechoslovak Trade Union of Educational
  and Scientific Workers
nám. M. Gorkého 23
Prague 1, Czechoslovakia

Commission of Scientific Workers
nám. M. Gorkého 23
Prague 1, Czechoslovakia

Bibliography

Apanasewicz, N. *Education in Czechoslovakia.*
  Washington, D.C.: U. S. Department of
  Health, Education and Welfare, Office of
  Education, 1963.
Baláž, O. *Učiteľ a spoločnosť.* Bratislava: Sloven-
  ské pedagogické nakladateľstvo, 1973.
Country Education Profiles: Czechoslovakia. Gen-
  eva: UNESCO, International Bureau of
  Education, May 1973.
Educational System in the CSSR. Prague: Institute
  of Educational Information, Ministry of
  Education of CSR, 1974.
Golan, G. *The Czechoslovak Reform Movement.*
  Cambridge, England: Cambridge Univer-
  sity Press, 1971.
Krejci, J. *Social Change and Stratification in
  Postwar Czechoslovakia.* New York: Columbia
  University Press, 1972.
Kujal, B. "Research into New Educational
  Methods of Czechoslovakia." *Prospects,* 1975,
  5(1), 105–110.
Marek, M. *Cultural Policy in Czechoslovakia.* Paris:
  UNESCO, 1970.
Šiler, J. *Technical and Agricultural Universi-
  ties in Czechoslovakia.* Prague: State Pedagogi-
  cal Publishing House, 1974.
*Thirty Years of Socialist School in the Czechoslovak
  Socialist Republic, 1945–1975.* Vol. 1: *Ele-
  mentary Schools;* Vol. 2: *Secondary Schools;*
  Vol. 3: *Universities.* Prague: State Pedagogi-
  cal Publishing House, 1975.
Tymowski, J., and Januszkiewicz, F. *Postsecond-
  ary Education of Persons Already Gainfully Em-
  ployed in European Socialist Countries.* Warsaw: Study Undertaken for UNESCO, 1975.
  (Mimeographed.)
Universities in CSSR. Prague: Ministry of Edu-
  cation of CSR and Ministry of Education of
  SSR, 1972.

See also: Academic Dress and Insignia; Eastern
European Socialist Countries: Regional Analy-
sis; Library Administration Outside the United
States: Science Policies: Industrialized Planned
Economies: Eastern European Socialist
Countries.